LAWYER'S DESK BOOK

TENTH EDITION

Prentice Hall Editorial Staff

Revised by David Minars

PRENTICE HALL
Englewood Cliffs, New Jersey 07632

Prentice-Hall International (UK) Limited, *London*
Prentice-Hall of Australia Pty. Limited, *Sydney*
Prentice-Hall Canada, Inc., *Toronto*
Prentice-Hall Hispanoamericana, S.A., *Mexico*
Prentice-Hall of India Private Limited, *New Delhi*
Prentice-Hall of Japan, Inc., *Tokyo*
Simon & Schuster Asia Pte. Ltd., *Singapore*
Editora Prentice-Hall do Brasil, Ltda., *Rio de Janeiro*

© 1995 *by*
PRENTICE HALL, Inc.
Englewood Cliffs, NJ 07632

This publication is designed to provide accurate and authoritative information in
regard to the subject matter covered. It is sold with the understanding that the
publisher is not engaged in rendering legal, accounting, or other professional service.
If legal advice or other expert assistance is required, the services of a competent
professional person should be sought.

—*From a Declaration of Principles jointly adopted by a Committee of
the American Bar Association and a Committee of Publishers and Associations.*

10   9   8   7   6   5   4   3   2   1

Library of Congress Cataloging-in-Publication Data

Lawyer's desk book / Prentice Hall editorial staff ; revised by David
Minars. — 10th ed.
    p.   cm.
Includes bibliographical references and index.
ISBN 0–13–206749–8
    1. Law—United States.   2. Practice of law—United States.
I. Minars, David. II. Prentice Hall, Inc.
KF386.L39   1995
349.73—dc20
[347.3]

95–13736
CIP

ISBN 0-13-206749-8

PRENTICE HALL
PH Direct
Englewood Cliffs, New Jersey 07632
A Simon & Schuster Company

Printed in the United States of America

INTRODUCTION

The law doesn't stand still, and the well-informed lawyer needs current references easily available. That's the idea behind this Tenth Edition of the *Lawyer's Desk Book,* which has been updated to reflect statutory and case-law changes.

The *Desk Book* will also give you a view of the new universe you must operate in after the enactment of the Tax Code of 1993 and the less cataclysmic, but still meaningful, changes wrought by the Revenue Acts of 1986 and 1987.

Look for future editions of the *Desk Book;* Prentice-Hall will keep this valuable reference and practice tool current so it will always be a handy source of information and practice tips.

PUBLISHER'S FOREWORD

The publication of the Tenth Edition of the *Lawyer's Desk Book* represents a land-mark of which we are very proud. Since its initial publication in 1965, the *Desk Book* has become the legal practitioner's "Bible." First prepared by William C. Casey, with the support of Prentice Hall's Institute for Business Planning Research and Editorial Staff, the seven editions that followed have sold well over 130,000 copies. Dana Shilling revised the Ninth Edition and prepared subsequent Supplements. Now updated and expanded to cover a number of new areas of legal practice, the Tenth Edition has been prepared by the Prentice Hall Editorial Staff with significant contributions by David Minars, a practicing attorney, prominent author, and legal researcher. The Appendix section was revised and updated by Steven Fine. It is our hope that *Lawyer's Desk Book* will continue to serve the profession for many years to come.

TABLE OF CONTENTS

APPENDICES

AGENTS, PRINCIPALS, AND INDEPENDENT CONTRACTORS

[¶101] The distinctions between an agent and an independent contractor can influence the liabilities of the principal, powers of the parties, tax-withholding consequences, workers' compensation, and ability to seek relief under national labor relations laws. Parties will not necessarily be able to establish the nature of their relationship merely by a recital of their agreement. While this recital may be binding as between principal and agent/independent contractor, it may not bind third parties.

[¶102]   Who Is a Principal?

As a general rule, one who has contractual capacity himself may be a principal and enter into a contract through an agent.

There are four ways in which an agent-principal relationship may be created:

(1) Principal may appoint an agent to act for him.

(2) Principal may tell a third party that an agent has authority to act.

(3) Principal may authorize an agent to act, and may subsequently become liable for additional actions by the agent. This apparent agency power protects third parties who come in contact with principal's agent.

(4) Principal may subsequently ratify the actions of someone who was not previously authorized to act on principal's behalf.

Ratification may be done expressly or may be indicated by the principal's conduct; e.g., by accepting benefits of agent's acts, by failing to disaffirm, or possibly by suing on the underlying transaction.

The agency relationship may be created by the act of the parties or by operation of law. For example, some statutes may presumptively create an agency relationship; e.g., someone driving a car within the state is said to designate the Secretary of State as his agent for purposes of accepting service of process in the event he is involved in an auto accident while driving in the state.

A minor who cannot bind herself absolutely in contract can void a contract made by her agent. However the following special situations will cause the minor-principal to be held liable.

❐ *A Contract for Necessities:* An infant can appoint an agent to contract for "necessaries."

❐ *A Contract Made by a Minor in the Entertainment Industry:* Some jurisdictions will hold a minor principal liable where the contract is guaranteed against disaffirmance due to prior court approval, or if prior judicial approval has not been obtained, the contested provision was standard in the industry, was reasonable, and there was no claim for fraud or misrepresentation.

A principal may not cite the infancy of its agent as a reason for avoiding a contract made by that agent.

1

[¶103]   ESTABLISHING THE AGENT-PRINCIPAL RELATIONSHIP

Any person can act as an agent provided he is not incompetent. Restatement of Agency 2d §21, Comment a, even permits an adjudicated incompetent who retains volition to serve as agent unless the contract was for necessities or some other contract the infant could not avoid if he were the principal and contracted himself.

The principal/agent relationship is a fiduciary relationship.

[¶104]   COMPARISON OF AGENT AND INDEPENDENT CONTRACTOR

An independent contractor is a highly skilled individual who is hired to do particular work for a stated sum. He or she is engaged in a distinct business and is not subject to outside supervision or control. The independent contractor uses his or her own equipment and tools, may work at his or her own place of business, and sets his or her own hours. Independent contractors include building contractors, truck drivers who own their own equipment and hire out on an ad hoc basis, collection agencies, physicians, lawyers, and plumbers.

On the other hand, an agent, or employee, is subject to the control and supervision of the person who employs him. These individuals work for a salary, hourly wage, or receive "piecework" rates. These individuals continuously work for the same employer over a long period of time with regular hours, within a specific area of employment, or over a fixed route. The employer usually supplies the tools and equipment. Thus, truck drivers who drive company trucks on a regular basis over a particular route are usually employees.

[¶105]   ABILITY TO BIND PRINCIPAL

Agents may bind a principal when the agency relationship is disclosed. However, the ability to bind the principal will be governed by the nature of the agency and the authority that has been expressly vested in the agent. If an agent has been expressly denied particular authority, but the principal has made it appear that the agent has the authority, or has placed the agent in a position when it would be customary for the agent to have such authority, the principal will be estopped from denying the agent's authority. However, if the agent acts beyond his authority and the doctrine of apparent authority is not applicable, the third party dealing with the agent generally will not have a cause of action against the principal. In some jurisdictions, the third party will have a cause of action against the agent for breach of the agency's implied warranty of authority. The principal is also liable for acts performed by the agent and later ratified by the principal.

❏ ***Undisclosed Principal:*** When an authorized agent acts for an undisclosed principal (identity and existence unknown to the contracting third party), usually both agent and principal are liable.

[¶106] IMPLIED AUTHORITY OF AGENT

An agent generally has whatever authority is necessary to carry out the purpose of the agency—subject to extension or limitation of the agreement between the parties.

Implied authority refers to power that an agent *reasonably* believes he has. An agent may also assume implied authority if he knows that agents in a similar position usually have such authority, or if the principal has previously sanctioned though not expressly authorized similar conduct.

[¶107] AGENT'S ABILITY TO DELEGATE

A principal may authorize an agent to delegate some or all of the agent's authority. But no sub-agent can have greater authority than that originally delegated from principal to agent. Absent express or implied authority from the principal, an agent cannot delegate. If the agent is the principal's employee, his right to delegate to or employ sub-agents may be implied due to the nature of the employment. For example, if an employee is hired to manage a business, he will generally be deemed to have broad authority to bind his principal and will be authorized to hire sub-agents or employees for the principal.

When the agent is hired "for personal or confidential" reasons, delegation may not be allowed unless specifically authorized by the principal.

In the case of an authorized delegation, the principal will be bound by the sub-agent's acts and will be liable for the sub-agent's torts to the same extent as he would be for actions by the agent. If the delegation is authorized, and the agent has used due diligence and care in selecting a sub-agent, then the sub-agent is considered an agent of the principal, and the principal must recover directly from the sub-agent for negligence or misconduct.

If the delegation is unauthorized, the agent is liable for any actions of the sub-agent.

[¶108] AUTHORITY TO PURCHASE AND SELL

The agent's authority to make purchases of personal property will depend on the nature of the position in which the principal has placed the agent. If the agent is a manager of a retail shop, it will appear that he has the authority to purchase goods so long as it is customary for an agent in his position to have the authority to make such purchases. If an agent has the authority to make purchases, he will generally have the implied authority to set the price. An agent is deemed to have authority to pay for the goods she is authorized to purchase. She may do this either out of the principal's funds or on credit if such funds are unavailable. An agent with authority to purchase is also deemed to have authority to accept delivery of the goods.

As a corollary, an agent authorized by a principal to sell goods may have certain implied powers. They include general warranties respecting quality and quantity; for real property the agent may also grant the customary covenants.

[¶109]   AGENT'S DUTY OF LOYALTY

An agent has an absolute duty of loyalty to his principal unless this absolute duty has been altered by the agreement between the agent and principal. Generally, absent a specific agreement to the contrary, an employee will be required to devote his full time to the principal's business—and not compete with the principal. When the contract calls for full-time employment, the employee will be permitted to use some time for the conduct of his personal affairs without breaching the employment contract.

An agent must obey the principal's directions unless they are unreasonable, or be liable for losses resulting from disobedience.

An agent paid by a principal must conform to a standard of due care and the skills for which the agent was hired. The standard of care for the gratuitous agent is far more lenient and less exacting.

If the agent breaches his duty to the principal, the principal may pursue the following course of action:

(1) Sue the agent for contract breach or for tortious conduct.

(2) Sue to recover "secret profits" made by the agent due to his relationship with principal.

(3) Sue for an accounting to have dollars returned to principal.

[¶110]   UNDISCLOSED PRINCIPAL

Often an agent will have the authority to enter into a transaction but will not disclose the identity of his principal. If the agent indicates that he is representing a principal and fails to identify the principal, or if he conceals the fact that he is representing a principal, the agent remains liable on the contract. However, if the agent indicates he is representing a principal and also discloses the identity of the principal, he will not be liable on the contract. The undisclosed principal is liable to the third party if his identity or existence is discovered.

[¶111]   LIABILITY PROBLEMS

If the representative is an employee, the principal will have vicarious liability for the employee's torts—and other wrongs arising out of the employment. A principal may be relieved of liability for his employee's torts when the torts occur outside of the scope of the employment. The employer is generally not liable for the torts of an independent contractor or the employees of the independent contractor. However, if the employer maintains control of the work or interferes with the independent contractor's performance of the work, the employer will then be responsible for any tortious injuries that occur as a result of his interference or control over the work. An exception may also be made to the rule if the work performed is inherently dangerous.

The employee's liability will generally be concurrent with that of his employer. In many situations the employer will be entitled to indemnification from the employee, if the employer was required to answer for the employee's torts.

When the employer *knows* he has selected an incompetent to perform the task, the employer may be liable for the employee's or the contractor's negligence.

An employer is usually not liable for *intentional* torts committed by an employee, since an intentional tort is, by definition, outside the scope of employment. But in some circumstances, an employer could be liable, such as when an intentional tort is committed incidentally within the scope of employment. A common example is that of a bouncer inflicting injury on a rowdy bar patron, since it is the bouncer's job to remove rowdy persons from the premises.

[¶112]   SPECIAL PROBLEMS REGARDING SALES AGENTS

Special rules are applicable to sales agents. The greatest flexibility in setting up a transaction in advance generally surrounds the treatment of sales agents or other sales people. A sales agent will generally have the authority to do whatever is necessary to make the sale. This is true without regard to what specific category he may fit into (independent contractor, employee, etc.). A commercial traveler who has been given a catalog, and possibly samples, will generally be authorized only to solicit orders for acceptance by his home office. A salesman who has been entrusted with the goods will generally have the apparent authority to accept the money and deliver the goods. When the sales agent is a merchant dealing in the type of goods involved, he will have the authority to sell any goods that have been entrusted to his possession. Section 2-403(2) of the Uniform Commercial Code provides that any entrusted possession of goods to a merchant who deals in goods of that kind gives him power to transfer all rights of the person entrusting him with possession to a buyer in the ordinary course of business. Assuming this entrusting rule applies, the buyer cuts off the entruster's claim to the goods.

As a general rule, an agent who is authorized to sell is authorized to sell only for cash unless he is specifically authorized to sell on credit. Payment may also be based on past practices between the parties or based on custom or usage.

An agent may have the express authority to give a warranty. Absent express authority, the agent will have implied authority to warrant the goods if it would be normal for an agent in his position to have such authority. The agent will also have the authority to bind his principal to a warranty that would, in the absence of an express warranty, be implied. Thus the agent would have the authority under the Uniform Commercial Code to bind his principal to the warranty of merchantability and the warranty of fitness for purpose. Similarly, when a sales agent makes a sale by sample, there is a warranty that the bulk of the goods will conform to the sample. Agents have no implied authority to *negate* warranties.

In some states an agent will require express authority of his principal to sell real property. In some states, this express authority must be in a writing sufficient to satisfy the requirements of the statute of frauds. Further, authority to *sell* real property does not necessarily include authority to *convey* it; a separate authorization may be required.

[¶113]   WITHHOLDING PROBLEMS

Wages paid to an "employee" are subject to income tax withholding. The Treasury Regulations provide that the employer-employee relationship generally exists when the person for whom services are performed has the right to control and direct the individual who performs the services, not only as to the result to be accomplished by the work but also as to the details and means by which that result is accomplished. It is not necessary that the employer actually direct or control the manner in which the services are performed to bring the employee within the definition for withholding tax purposes; it is enough that the employer has the right to do so. As is the case in state law, the right to discharge is also an important factor indicating that the person possessing that right is an employer [see Reg. §31.3401(c)-1].

The following list illustrates situations when tax withholding is or is not required to be made.

➤ **Partnerships:** If the employer-employee relation in fact exists, then employees of the partnership are subject to withholding.

➤ **Managers, officers, directors:** No distinction is made between classes or grades of employees. Generally, a corporate officer is an employee, but a director, as such, is not. Withholding, therefore, is required on officers' salaries, but not on directors' fees.

➤ **Minors/students:** Minors are treated the same as other employees. For example, tax is withheld from wages of a student working during vacation, even if he will not earn enough to pay income tax (unless he files a proper certificate to claim exempt status).

➤ **Substitutes** who are properly working in place of regular employees are considered employees for purposes of withholding. However, if a person is engaged without the company's knowledge or consent, he is not an employee for withholding purposes.

➤ **Medical equivalent of a W-2:** Under a new tax law, Form H-2 must be filed each year by employers who provide medical benefits for even one employee. The first health forms are due with 1994 W-2 forms. The new forms must show the name and Social Security number of each employee receiving medical coverage and each covered dependent, the effective dates of coverage, type of coverage, and plan number.

[¶113.1]   Self-Employed Persons and Independent Contractors

Individuals who are, in fact, partners, independent contractors, or sole pro-prietors of a business are not subject to withholding on their drawings or earnings [Reg. §31.3401(c)-1]. For example, auctioneers, contractors and subcontractors, dentists, doctors, free-lance professional models, lawyers, public stenographers, veterinarians, and others who follow an independent trade, business, or profes-sion, in which they offer their services to the public, are not employees.

In addition, the tax law classifies licensed real estate agents and direct sell-ers as self-employed persons [IRC §3508]. Two conditions must be satisfied: (1) substantially all of their income for services as real estate agents or direct sellers must be directly related to sales or other output; (2) their services are performed under a written contract that calls for them not to be treated as employees for tax purposes. A special formula is provided to compute the employer's liability if he makes a mistake in his classification [IRC §3509].

[¶113.2]   Tips Subject to Withholding and Reporting Requirements

(1) Tips subject to withholding. Tips (cash or charge) of $20 or more a month received by an employee during one employment and reported to the employer are wages subject to withholding. The employer withholds only if the tax can be collected from the employee's wages after social security taxes have been deducted. The employee can voluntarily furnish funds if the regular pay can-not cover withholding. Tips are considered paid when the employee reports them to the employer. The employee must report them by the 10th of the month after the month they were received. Unreported tips are considered paid when received [IRC §3401(a)(16)].

(2) Tips subject to reporting requirements. Large food and beverage establishments must report annually the gross and charge sales receipts (except carryout sales and mandatory 10% or more service charge sales), the total amount of tips on charge receipts, employees' reported tip income, and mandatory service charges of less than 10% [IRC §6053(c)(1)]. If reported tip income is less than 8% of the gross receipts, the employer must make an allocation of the difference among the tipped employees. If average tips are under 8% of gross sales, either the employer or a majority of the employees can petition the IRS under Section 6053(c) to have the allocation reduced to the appropriate amount between 2% and 8%. Also, the employer must furnish a statement to each employee during January of the year following the year for which the statement is made. Failure to do so is subject to penalty.

"Large food and beverage establishments" are those that provide food or bev-erage for which tipping is customary and which normally employ 10 or more employees on a business day [IRC §6053(c)(4)]. "Fast-food" restaurants are gener-ally excepted.

— FOR FURTHER REFERENCE —

Bulloch, Steven N. "Fraud Liability Under Agency Principles: A New Approach," 27 *William & Mary L. Rev.* 301 (Winter '86).

Earnest, G. Lane, "Agency by Surprise: The Disclosure Dilemma in Real Estate," 15 *Colo. Law.* 1185 (July '86).

Fiore, Nicholas J., "IRS Clarifies Tax Status of Independent Contractors," 18 *Tax Adviser* 200 (March '87).

Hyland, Clement L. & Laura A. Quigley, "Determination of Employee Status: Right to Control and Economic Reality—Is There a Difference?" 61 *Fla. B.J.* 43 (January '87).

Miller, Geoffrey P., "Some Agency Problems in Settlement," 16 *J. Legal Studies* 189 (January '87).

Rasmussen, Richard, "Labor Law: Are Creative Artists Independent Contractors or Employees?" 6 *Loyola Entertainment Law J.* 199 (Annual 1986).

ANTITRUST PROBLEMS: PRICES AND UNFAIR COMPETITION

[¶201] Businesses cannot operate effectively without a knowledge of the restrictions placed on them by the federal antitrust laws, particularly in the area of pricing arrangements and market agreements. Antitrust law reflects the legislative judgment that competition will produce not only lower prices but also better goods and services. The following paragraphs highlight some of the areas of common concern to most business operations.

During the Reagan administration, it was widely perceived that federal regulators saw antitrust as a low priority, because they believed that large businesses (including businesses formed by merger or acquisition) could achieve significant economies of scale that would be beneficial both to the business community and to consumers. There are some indications that the Bush administration saw more danger in concentration, leading to a more interventionist view of antitrust enforcement, which is likely to be continued under President Clinton.

Some very large acquisitions have been completed or negotiated without challenge from the Clinton administration: for instance, Tele-Communications Inc.'s acquisition by Bell Atlantic Corp. and AT&T's purchase of McCaw Cellular Communications Co. A 1994 speech by Anne Bingaman, Assistant U.S. Attorney General for Antitrust, hinted at some toleration for transactions with potential antitrust problems if they also foster innovation or speed the delivery of innovative products to the market; in 1993, the Department of Justice settled an antitrust action with an agreement that allows certain institutions of higher education to exchange financial-aid information.

In *California v. ARC America Corp.*[1] the Supreme Court held that state antitrust laws that allow indirect purchasers to recover all overcharges resulting from illegal price fixing that were passed along to direct purchasers are enforceable and are not preempted by federal antitrust laws. This is very useful for antitrust plaintiffs, because Clayton Act Section 4 treble damages are available only to direct purchasers, not indirect purchasers harmed by price fixing.

In a similarly named case, *California v. American Stores,*[2] the High Court held that, in appropriate cases, divestiture is a permissible remedy under Clayton Act Section 16 (as a form of injunctive relief). The case was remanded for a determination of the appropriateness of the remedy in the particular case.

Prior to this case, it was decided that the All Writs Act gives a federal District Court the power to issue a preliminary injunction against a planned merger to preserve jurisdiction under the Antitrust Procedures and Penalties Act.[3] There was some authority that a preliminary injunction can be granted to rescind a consummated acquisition given a showing that the FTC is likely to prevail on a Clayton Act Section 7 claim that the merger will have the effect of lessening competition and creating monopoly in the relevant market.[4]

Congressional attitudes toward antitrust can be discerned from the Antitrust Amendments Act of 1990 (P.L. 101-588). This Act increases the potential antitrust fines that can be assessed to a maximum of $350,000 against an individual, $10 million against a corporation, and permits the government, as plaintiff, to seek treble damages. The bill relaxes the Clayton Act Section 8 prohibition of interlocking directorates (and repeals the special interlock rules for common carriers under Clayton Act Section 10), providing a safe harbor for interlocks that do not pose a threat to competition. However, interlocks among officers, not just directors, have been brought within the coverage of the Clayton Act.

Of current national concern is health care reform. Hospitals, doctors, and other providers need to work together for the benefit of the community. This means that the government will have to adopt antitrust policies that allow providers to eliminate excess capacity and duplication of equipment and services. Hospitals in various states have sought and won relief by agreeing to let the state actively supervise certain of their collaborative activities for the consumer's protection.

[¶201.1]   Antitrust Aspects of Mergers

In 1988, the FTC announced proposed changes in its pre-merger notice rules.[5] The proposal calls for easing the reporting requirements when less than 10% of a corporation's stock is acquired, on the theory that such minority acquisitions are not anticompetitive in nature and therefore do not violate the antitrust laws.

In 1992, the Department of Justice and Federal Trade Commission adopted unified guidelines for the analysis of horizontal mergers replacing those of the FTC's 1982 Statement Concerning Horizontal Mergers and the DOJ's 1984 Merger Guidelines. The 1992 Guidelines contain an overview of horizontal merger issues: definition of the relevant market; entry analysis; efficiencies; competitive effects; and the implications of the merger of a failing firm. In 1993, the National Association of Attorneys General adopted its own horizontal merger guidelines for the use of state regulators. These guidelines call for a four-step analysis. First, the product and geographic market must be defined. The level of concentration in the market before and after the merger must be compared. Other relevant factors, such as ease of entry, must be considered. The fourth step is to analyze whether a failing-company defense is available.[6]

In 1992, the FTC adopted a program of helping the states investigate the Clayton Act Section 7 effects of proposed mergers. Under this program, if and when merging parties agree to waive confidentiality, the FTC will provide certain documents and data to the states, thus expediting the merger process.[7]

In 1991, the Supreme Court ruled[8] that the Interstate Commerce Commission is empowered by the Interstate Commerce Act, 49 U.S.C. Sec. 11301, to exempt railways from antitrust as well as labor laws, if this is necessary to carry out an approved consolidation of railways. Also note that under *FTC v. University Health Center,*[9] Clayton Act Section 7 governs the acquisition of one non-profit hospital's assets by another non-profit hospital. In 1993, joint guidelines on health care antitrust policy were issued by the Department of Justice and the FTC. The statements deal with hospital mergers and joint ventures; the provision of non-price information by doctors to purchasers of health care services; joint purchasing agreements among health care providers; and network joint ventures among doctors who share substantial financial risks.[10] Health care antitrust issues will become far more important in the mid-1990s, because most proposals for health care reform rely on increasing use of networks to provide lower-cost health care; if health care providers are subjected to antitrust liability for sharing information and purchasing, then these cost-cutting measures will not be feasible.

The existence and effect of monopoly power is an emerging issue that may become the most significant antitrust issue of the 1990s. The Third Circuit required[11] threatened or actual monopoly (not mere proof of competitive advantage in the relevant market) to prove a Sherman Act Sec. 2 "monopoly leveraging" claim. But the Seventh Circuit didn't even find it necessary to reach the question of market power when it decided that the National Basketball Association violated Sherman Act 1 by refusing to let its teams broadcast more than twenty games a season on cable television.[12] The court treated the NBA's action as an output restriction that provided no benefits to consumers, and thus obviously failed to satisfy the rule of reason whether market power was present or absent. A later sports antitrust case[13] limits the baseball antitrust exemption to the reserve clause; club owners can still be guilty of restraint of trade if they conspire to prevent the sale and relocation of a baseball team.

[¶201.2] Antitrust Standing

One of the most significant issues in antitrust is the question of standing. It has been held that standing is available under the Clayton Act for a target company seeking an injunction against a hostile takeover (because the antitrust injury would be the target's loss of the ability to compete independently in the relevant market).[14] A competitor who claims that the contemplated merger will produce an entrant with sufficient market power to eliminate competition also has standing under the Clayton Act.[15] But a shareholder of a target company failed to state an antitrust claim by alleging that two bidders for the target conspired to lower the price of the acquisition: buying stock in a single company is not "trade or commerce" as defined by Section 1 of the Sherman Act.[16]

Under *American Stores,* above, a private litigant's standing to seek divestiture depends on a threatened loss or damage to its interests. Furthermore, a would-be litigant can be barred by "unclean hands."

The Supreme Court has dealt with antitrust standing in other cases. *Atlantic Richfield Co. v. U.S. Petroleum Co.*[17] holds that a company alleging that its competitor has engaged in a vertical conspiracy to fix maximum prices has standing only if it can prove predatory pricing; there is no injury to the plaintiff if the fixed price is non-predatory, and hence no standing.

In *Kansas et al. v. Utilicorp United Inc.*[18] the Supreme Court tackles the question of who has standing under Clayton Act Section 4 when a supplier is guilty of antitrust violations by overcharging a public utility for gas overcharges that are passed along to customers. The Supreme Court's answer is that only the utility, not the customers, has suffered antitrust injury and thus only the utility has standing to sue.

[¶201.3]   Antitrust Penalties

The Seventh Circuit has ruled[19] that defendants convicted of price fixing and mail fraud should have been sentenced under the federal sentencing guidelines for antitrust offenses, not the tougher guidelines for fraud and deceit offenses; the fraud in this case was perpetrated in furtherance of price fixing and was not a separate offense.

A corporation pleaded *nolo contendere* to one Sherman Act count, and settled 60 Clayton Act Sec. 4 treble-damage claims. Internal Revenue Code Sec. 162(g) holds that two-thirds of Clayton Act damages are disallowed as tax deductions if the taxpayer is convicted of or even pleads guilty to a criminal antitrust violation. A 1993 Tax Court case[20] holds that the determining factor is the degree of connection between the Clayton and Sherman Act violations. The IRS and defendant either must agree on an allocation, or reopen the record to supply evidence on the connection and thus the scope of the potential tax deduction.

[¶202]   MONOPOLIZATION

Monopoly power is the power to control prices or exclude competition in the relevant market. Section 2 of the Sherman Act reads:

"Every person who shall monopolize, or attempt to monopolize, or combine or conspire with any other person or persons, to monopolize any part of the trade or commerce among the several States, or with foreign nations, shall be deemed guilty of a felony, and, on conviction thereof, shall be punished by fine not exceeding one million dollars if a corporation, or, if any other person, one hundred thousand dollars, or by imprisonment not exceeding three years, or by both said punishments, in the discretion of the court."

To come within the §2 prohibition of monopolization, a single firm must (1) possess monopoly power in the relevant market, and (2) have acted purposefully or deliberately.

The Supreme Court has set out a simple two-part test for proof of attempted monopolization in violation of Sherman Act Section 2: specific intent to monopolize, and a dangerous probability of reaching monopoly power in the relevant market.[21]

The Seventh Circuit held that a defendant was entitled to summary judgment on a Sherman Act Section 2 monopolization claim, where the plaintiff admitted that the defendant, who was allegedly guilty of predatory pricing, could not control the supply of groceries in the relevant market sufficiently to raise prices.[22]

In 1993, other issues of pricing were addressed. Continental Airlines sued American Airlines, charging that American's fare cuts and reductions in the number of different fares for a particular route were done to identify and punish competitors who failed to follow American's lead. However, a Texas jury found that the defendant lacked specific intent to monopolize, and thus was not liable.[23] New York City passed a law forbidding car rental companies to vary their charges based on where the renter lives. The Second Circuit permitted a Sherman Act Section 1 challenge to the statute, finding it to be a "hybrid" restraint that controls one aspect of pricing and thus risks anticompetitive effect.[24]

In attempt-to-monopolize Sherman Act cases in which the defendant moves for summary judgment, the Eleventh Circuit takes the position that the test of predatory pricing includes the defendant's intent, and no inference of predatory intent can be drawn if the cost charged is above the defendant's average total cost.[25] However, the Seventh Circuit rejects this definition.[26]

The Sixth Circuit decided that a "split agreement" among movie theaters, under which they agreed not to compete in licensing films from distributors, is not a per se Sherman Act violation (or an unlawful group boycott). Instead, the rule of reason must be applied to determine whether there is a real effect on competition.[27]

The Ninth Circuit reached a similar conclusion in another case dealing with movie theaters.[28] A movie theater operator bought out all competing local theaters except one (which was basically a revival house; the others were first-run theaters). The Ninth Circuit did not find monopolization (even though the defendant controlled 75% of local movie receipts, even 98% at one point) absent entry barriers (the defendant did not prevent others from purchasing movie theaters) or the ability to control prices.

Movie studios' suit against a hotel, charging that the hotel violated studio copyrights by renting videodisks to its guests, generated a counterclaim by the hotel defendant. The counterclaim charged that the studios brought suit to cloak their acts of monopolization and conspiracy to restrain trade. In May, 1993, the Supreme Court held that the plaintiffs were entitled to Noerr-Pennington immunity, which applies unless litigation is brought with no possible chance of success. According to the Supreme Court, the studios' suit was a plausible attempt to enforce rights in an unsettled area of law, and thus immunity is available.[29]

Although the plaintiffs alleged that Blue Cross/Blue Shield of Rhode Island engaged in boycotts, coercion, and intimidation, the First Circuit held that the insurer's response to competition by lowering of costs, improvement of coverage, and lower rates to employers who offer only Blue Cross coverage was immune from antitrust scrutiny.[30] First of all, the conduct complained of fell within the McCarran-Ferguson Act exemption of the "business of insurance" from antitrust coverage. Second, a vigorous effort by suppliers to cut their costs and achieve a higher market share was held to be the kind of pro-consumer response that the antitrust laws are designed to provoke.

McCarran-Ferguson immunity was not forfeited even if domestic insurers did, as alleged, conspire with foreign reinsurers to keep foreign coverage off the market unless domestic companies changed their CGL policies. Even if the conspiracy existed, the Supreme Court has held that the companies were still engaging in the "business of insurance" and thus entitled to antitrust immunity.[31]

An ophthalmologist who lost his hospital staff privileges was deemed by the Supreme Court to have stated a Sherman Act Section 1 claim against the hospital and other doctors. The hospital policy called for the presence of a second surgeon at certain eye operations. Plaintiff Dr. Pinhas called this requirement unnecessarily costly since Medicare will not reimburse the second surgeon; the hospital said it was necessary to maintain quality. The Supreme Court held that, if proved, a conspiracy to boycott a single doctor can have the effect of reducing the availability of medical services in the relevant geographic market, generating enough impact on interstate commerce to implicate the Sherman Act.[32]

Joint ventures are embraced within the reach of Sherman Act Section 1, so Visa USA violated Section 1 by adopting a bylaw that kept Sears (and other would-be issuers) from joining the Visa joint venture and issuing Visa credit cards. Visa had market power; the exclusion of Sears harmed competition; the harm outweighed any beneficial effects of the exclusion; and Sears suffered antitrust injury, all adding up to liability for the defendant.[33]

[¶203]   THE RELEVANT MARKET

The share of the product and geographical markets that any company has presently captured is the principal determinant of monopoly power. When looking to the product market, those items that consumers can reasonably use interchangeably must be taken into account.

[¶204]   PURPOSEFUL ACT

Conduct that is used to attain or maintain a monopolistic position (e.g., predatory or coercive conduct) is in violation of the law. The fact that a company did not have a specific intent to monopolize is not relevant.

An "innocently acquired monopoly"—i.e., one gained through superior skill, a lawfully obtained patent, or thrust upon a company by other factors—does not violate §2. However, the later predatory use of such innocently acquired power will violate §2.

[¶205]   ATTEMPT TO MONOPOLIZE

The attempt to monopolize is also prohibited by §2 of the Sherman Act. Even if the monopolization attempt fails, a company's conduct that creates a dangerous probability of success is proscribed.

[¶206]   HORIZONTAL RESTRAINTS

Section 1 of the Sherman Act provides that "every contract, combination in the form of trust or otherwise, or conspiracy, in restraint of trade or commerce among the several States, or with foreign nations, is hereby declared to be illegal. Every person who shall make any contract or engage in any combination or conspiracy hereby declared . . . to be illegal shall be deemed guilty of a felony, and, on conviction thereof, shall be punished by fine not exceeding 1,000,000 dollars, if a corporation, or if any other person, 100,000 dollars or by imprisonment not exceeding three years, or both said punishments, in the discretion of the court."

Price-fixing, division of markets among competitors, tying arrangements, and group boycotts are all examples of per se violations of §1. The following paragraphs discuss this proscribed conduct.

[¶207] PRICE-FIXING

Setting a minimum price is illegal, as is fixing maximum resale prices. Even if competitors are free to sell below the maximum, the fact that a maximum price exists is sufficient to artificially stabilize prices. Agreements to limit production are illegal and agreements among buyers setting the price they will offer is also a per se violation. State laws imposing retail price maintenance on liquor sales are illegal—like other forms of retail-price maintenance, such laws are a per se violation. The laws were intended to protect small retailers, not to promote temperance, so they are not insulated by the Twenty-First Amendment's grant of power over liquor sales to the states.

[¶208] INTERSELLER PRICE VERIFICATION

Interseller exchanges of price data do not invariably have anticompetitive effects and are not, therefore, per se violations of the Sherman Act. However, such exchanges of price data will be subject to close scrutiny under Sherman Act criteria. A violation of the Act occurs when interseller price verification is employed to produce anticompetitive effects.

This does not mean that the price cannot be lowered to meet the competition. If there is a *good faith belief* that a price concession is being offered by a competitor, the price may be lowered as per §2(a) of the Robinson-Patman Act. Good faith belief can be established by showing that:

❏ Evidence was received of a competitor's lower price from other complaining customers;

❏ Threats of cancellation of sales were made, if the discount price was not met; or

❏ The competitor's discount price could be corroborated from available market data.

In other words, if the need to match the competition's price is shown to be within the business's interest, and that a diligent attempt has been made to independently verify the existence of a price discount, no violation of §1 of the Sherman Act will be found.

[¶209]   DIVISION OF MARKETS

An agreement among businesses that perform similar services or that deal in similar products to divide the available product market among them is illegal per se, and there is no justification or defense, since the agreement operates to give each participant a monopoly with respect to his market share.

[¶210]   REFUSALS TO DEAL

When a group of competitors agrees not to deal with a certain party, or to deal only on certain terms, that amounts to a §1 combination in restraint of trade. To the extent that an industry attempts self-regulation in this area, courts have found a §1 violation to exist.

However, if several companies all feel that it is in their best economic interests not to deal with a particular party, and each can show that its decision was *independently* arrived at, this probably will not constitute a concerted refusal to deal. But remember, it must be verifiable that the refusal to deal was *unilateral* as opposed to conspiratorial conduct. The best safeguard is to make certain that there is sufficient evidence to document the position taken. The following checklist offers some helpful suggestions:

❏ Retain all correspondence and memoranda concerning customer accounts, particularly where bills are outstanding.

❏ If a customer's order is refused, state the reasons in a letter to the customer, and/or in an interoffice memorandum for the files.

❏ If contemplating a change in the terms of a contract with a customer, in response to rumors circulating in the industry, confer with corporate counsel to make certain that the business is not engaging in conscious parallelism or a group boycott.

[¶211]   CONSCIOUS PARALLELISM

Even in the absence of an actual agreement among companies, substantially identical conduct among competitors may violate §1 of the Sherman Act. The proof of parallel behavior does not in itself establish a §1 conspiracy—it would depend upon whether the businessperson can show his independent decision to act. Such "independence" might be evidenced by minutes of corporate meetings, economic factors, and lack of discussion with other competitors.

[¶212]   DATA DISSEMINATION

Frequently, competitors will exchange information through their trade association regarding prices, costs, production, and inventories. The exchange of price information is inherently suspect as a §1 violation. Such discussion should be avoided, particularly where:

(1) There is an exchange of information on current or future prices;

(2) The business is part of a concentrated or oligopolistic market structure, since such disclosure might discourage price variation to the point of stabilizing and preserving each company's market share;

(3) The members of the trade association deal with the same parties.

If the businessperson and his competitors do participate in a trade organization, advise him that all participants should limit such discussions to past performance, and that this information should be distributed to all members of the industry—regardless of membership in the trade association. If the trade association meetings should begin to stray into "forbidden" conversations, it may be necessary to resign as a member to avoid antitrust problems.

[¶213]   LOBBYING ACTIVITIES

Lobbying activities are not illegal, even if undertaken for anticompetitive purposes. However, the attempt to monopolize a market by instituting state and federal proceedings to the point of harassing competitors or interfering with their right to access would violate §1.

[¶214]   VERTICAL RESTRAINT AGREEMENTS BETWEEN SELLER AND BUYER

An indirect attempt to achieve price maintenance by contractually setting the price (minimum *or* maximum) at which customers can resell products is a per se violation of §1 of the Sherman Act. Furthermore, if there are attempts to induce customers to adhere to suggested retail prices by the use of any system of suspensions and reinstatements of retailers who have not adhered to the suggested price, this too constitutes unlawful resale price maintenance. Once goods are sold to the buyer, price restrictions can no longer be imposed.

Although vertical price restrictions are a per se violation of §1 of the Sherman Act, this is not the case with *nonprice vertical restrictions* (i.e., a location restriction). The Supreme Court has held that the imposition of nonprice vertical restrictions would be governed by the "rule of reason." In order to withstand an allegation that a nonprice vertical restraint violates §1 of the Sherman Act, the manufacturer imposing the restraint must be able to show that:

(1) Sufficient *interbrand* competition exists to provide a significant check on the exploitation of the manufacturer's intrabrand market power; or

(2) The potential benefits of vertical restraints in promoting interbrand competition are particularly strong where the manufacturer imposing the restraints is seeking to enter a new market or to expand a small market share; or

(3) The manufacturer has used the least restrictive means to enhance its ability to compete. In January 1985 the Department of Justice issued guidelines on

nonprice vertical restraints, including a statement that the vertical practices of firms with a market share of less than 10% will not be challenged, because such small firms do not pose a challenge to competition. The Guidelines focus on interbrand rather than intrabrand competition.

Vertical restraints are deemed illegal automatically only when there is evidence of explicit retail price-fixing, not when there is mere evidence of a price effect.

Dual distribution (the commercial practice of selling both to dealers and to the ultimate consumer) is treated as a vertical restraint—i.e., subject to the rule of reason and other rules.

However, in 1985 the National Association of Attorneys General adopted tough vertical restraints guidelines; since attorneys general are the primary enforcers of state antitrust laws, planners should consult these guidelines as well.

[¶215]   TYING ARRANGEMENTS

Section 3 of the Clayton Act prohibits "tying arrangements" that "may substantially lessen competition or tend to create a monopoly in any line of commerce." Note that §3 applies only to goods or commodities.

Tying arrangements that involve intangible services (e.g., loan of copyright license) or real property are dealt with by §1 of the Sherman Act.

A tying arrangement is usually illegal per se if its effect is to substantially lessen competition or tend to create a monopoly in any line of commerce. For example, if your client enjoys a monopolistic position with respect to the "tying product," or if there is simply great demand for the "tying product," the tacking on of a "tied product" would tend to create a monopoly in the tied product as well, or would substantially lessen competition.

[¶216]   PATENTS AND THE ANTITRUST LAWS

A patent is a legal monopoly granted pursuant to statutory authority. Therefore, a valid patent can be a defense to a §2 Sherman Act monopolization charge. A patent is granted only for the discovery of any new and useful process, provided such invention is not obvious to a person having only ordinary skills in the particular art (see ¶2201 et seq.). The granting of a patent gives the inventor the right to exclude others from making, selling, or using the invention for a period of time (see ¶2201).

A patent holder may assign or license his patent rights.

A patentee cannot extend his lawful patent monopoly by engaging in an unlawful tying arrangement. A royalty agreement or contract extending beyond the expiration date of a patent is unlawful per se.

Sometimes competitors can enter into a joint venture to perform research or produce new technology. If this is inspired by efficiency rather than anticompetitive motives, the joint venture is likely to survive antitrust scrutiny even if a merger of the two firms would not.

[¶217] PATENT ACCUMULATION

It is not illegal per se to include in a patent license a covenant requiring the licensee to assign to the licensor any improvement patents developed by the licensee.

[¶218] PRICE-RESTRICTED LICENSES

Abusive licensing and cross-licensing can operate as restraints of trade, with anticompetitive effects. Owners of two patents may not cross-license and fix prices to be charged by themselves and their licensees for their respective products, nor may they divide up territories or agree to boycott others.

[¶219] USE-RESTRICTED LICENSES

A patentee can properly limit a license to one or more uses, and grant such rights exclusively or nonexclusively. A patentee may restrict his licensee to any territory he wishes.

--- **ENDNOTES** ---

1. 488 U.S. 814 (Sup.Ct. 4/18/89).
2. 110 S.Ct. 1 (Sup.Ct. 4/30/90).
3. U.S. v. BNS, Inc. 848 F.2d 945 (9th Cir. 5/27/88).
4. FTC v. Illinois Cereal Mills Inc., 691 F.Supp. 1131 (N.D. Ill. 7/18/88).
5. See 60 LW 2617.
6. Norfolk & Western Railway v. Train Dispatchers, ##89-1027, 1028, 111 S.Ct. 335 (Sup.Ct. 3/19/91).
7. 60 LW 2761.
8. See Norfolk & Western, supra.
9. 938 F. 2d 1206 (11th Cir. 7/26/91).
10. 62 LW 2182 (9/15/93).
11. Fineman v. Armstrong World Industries Inc., 980 F.2d 171 (3d Cir. 10/28/92), cert. denied 113 S.Ct. 1285.

12. Chicago Professional Sports Limited Partnership v. NBA, 961 F.2d 667 (7th Cir. 4/14/92).

13. Piazza v. Major League Baseball, 62 LW 2081 (E.D. Pa. 8/4/93).

14. Consolidated Gold Fields PLC v. Minorco SA, 871 F.2d 252 (2d Cir. 3/22/89).

15. R.C. Bigelow, Inc. v. Unilever, Inc., 867 F.2d 102 (2d Cir. 1/17/89).

16. Finnegan v. Campeau Corp., 722 F.Supp. 1114 (SDNY 10/18/89).

17. 110 S.Ct. 1884 (Sup.Ct. 5/14/90), remand 972 F.2d 1070 (9th Cir. 8/12/92).

18. 110 S.Ct. 2807 (Sup.Ct. 6/21/90).

19. U.S. v. Rubin, 62 LW 2046 (7th Cir. 6/30/93).

20. McDermott Inc., 101 T.C. #10 (7/29/93).

21. Spectrum Sports Inc. v. McQuillan, #91-10, 113 S.Ct. 884 (Sup.Ct. 1/25/93).

22. Indiana Grocery Inc. v. Super Valu Stores Inc., 864 F.2d 1409 (7th Cir. 1/6/89).

23. Continental Airlines Inc. v. American Airlines, 805 F.Supp. 1392 (S.D.Tex. 8/10/93).

24. Hertz Corp. v. New York, 62 LW 2150 (2d Cir. 8/2/93).

25. McGahee v. Northern Propane Gas Co., 858 F.2d 1487 (11th Cir. 10/27/88).

26. AA Poultry Farms Inc. v. Rose Acre Farms Inc. 881 F.2d 1396 (7th Cir. 8/4/89).

27. Balmoral Cinema Inc. v. Allied Artists, 885 F. 2d 1313 (6th Cir. 9/13/89).

28. U.S. v. Syufy Enterprises, 903 F.2d 659 (9th Cir. 5/9/90).

29. Professional Real Estate Investors Inc. v. Columbia Pictures Industries Inc., #91-1043, 113 S.Ct. 1920 (Sup.Ct. 5/3/93).

30. Ocean Physicians Health Plan Inc. v. Blue Cross/Blue Shield of RI, 883 F.2d 1101 cert. den. 110 S.Ct. 1473 (1st. Cir. 8/21/89).

31. Hartford Fire Insurance Co. v. California, ##91-1111, -1128, 113 S.Ct. 2891 (Sup.Ct. 6/28/93).

32. Summit Health Ltd. v. Pinhas, #89-1679, 111 S.Ct. 1842 (5/28/91). On effect on commerce, see Brown v. Our Lady of Lourdes Med. Ctr., 767 F.Supp. 618 (D.N.J. 7/15/91); Loitman v. Antani, 1991 Westlaw 117209 (N.D. Ill. 1991).

33. SCFL ILC Inc. v. Visa USA Inc., 819 F.Supp. 956 (D.Utah 4/1/93).

— FOR FURTHER REFERENCE —

Baker, Donald I. and Mark R. Stabile, "Arbitration and Antitrust Claims," 48 *Business Lawyer* 395 (February '93).

Besanko, David and Daniel F. Spielber, "Contested Mergers and Equilibrium Antitrust Policy," 9 J. *Law, Economics & Organization* 1 (April '93).

Blakley, Alan F., "Antitrust Issues for Lawyers Representing Small Business," 54 *Montana L. Rev.* 227 (Summer '93).

Callman, Rudolf, *Unfair Competition Trademarks and Monopolies* (4th ed.) (Callaghan & Co., looseleaf, 6 volumes).

Cass, Ronald E., "Price Discrimination and Predation Analysis in Antitrust and International Trade," 61 *U. of Cincinnati L. Rev.* 877 (Winter '93).

Chu, Michael Paul, "An Antitrust Solution to the New Wave of Predatory Patent Infringement Litigation," 33 *William and Mary L. Rev.* 1341 (Summer '92).

Durie, Darolyn J. and Mark A. Lemley, "The Antitrust Liability of Labor Unions for Anticompetitive Litigation," 80 *California L. Rev.* 757 (May '92).

Fenton, Kathryn M., "Antitrust Implications of Joint Efforts by Third Party Payors to Reduce Costs and Improve the Quality of Health Care," 61 *Antitrust L.J.* 17 (Summer '92).

Gesell, Laurence E. and Martin T. Farris, "Antitrust Irrelevance in Air Transportation and the Redefining of Price Discrimination," 57 *J. of Air Law & Commerce* 173 (Fall '91).

Gifford, Daniel J., "Rethinking the Relationship Between Antidumping and Antitrust Laws," 6 *American U. J. of Int'l Law & Policy* 277 (Spring '91).

Ginsburg, Douglas H., "Nonprice Competition," 38 *Antitrust Bulletin* 113 (Spring '93).

Grimes, Warren S., "The Seven Myths of Vertical Price Fixing," 21 *Southwestern U.L. Rev.* 1285 (Fall '92).

Hovenkamp, Herbert, "Mergers and Buyers," 77 *Virginia L. Rev.* 1369 (October '91).

Iannicone, Adolph C. and Linda Volonino, "Marginal Cost and Relevant Market Determination in Information Technology Antitrust Cases," 18 *Rutgers Computer & Technology L.J.* 681 (Winter '92).

Krauss, Lynn D., "Antitrust Issues and Pitfalls in Distribution Relationships," 72 *Mich.Bar J.* 539 (June '93).

Lazaroff, Daniel E., "Rule 11 and Federal Antitrust Litigation," 67 *Tulane L. Rev.* 1033 (March '93).

Mantell, Edmund H., "Potential Antitrust Obstacles to a Merger and the Role of the Economist," 97 *Commercial L.J.* 123 (Spring '92).

Maxwell, Philip K. and Tim Labadie, "Deceptive Trade Practices and Antitrust," 46 *SMU L. Rev.* 1325 (Spring '93).

Melendez, Julia M., "The McCarran-Ferguson Act: Has It Outlived Its Intent?" 42 *Federation of Insurance and Corporate Counsel Q.* 283 (Spring '92).

Ordover, Janusz A. and Jonathan B. Baker, "Entry Analysis Under the 1992 Horizontal Merger Guidelines," 61 *Antitrust L.J.* 139 (Summer '92).

Pitofsky, Robert, "Merger Analysis in the '90s: The Guidelines and Beyond," 61 *Antitrust L.J.* 147 (Summer '92).

Ray, Harry B., "Practicing Preventive Law in the Antitrust Area," 29 *Tenn. Bar J.* 30 (May-June '93).

Richmond, Douglas R., "Antitrust and Higher Education," 61 *UMKC L. Rev.* 417 (Spring '93).

Rock, Edward B., "Corporate Law Through an Antitrust Lens," 92 *Columbia L. Rev.* 497 (April '92).

Steuer, Richard M., "Functional Discounts After Texaco v. Hasbrouck, 59 *Fordham L. Rev.* 791 (April '91).

Stewart, David O., "Raising the Stakes: Resisting the Upward Transformation of Antitrust and Fraud Charges," 20 *Am. J. Crim. Law* 207 (Winter '93).

Von Kalinowski, Julian O., *Antitrust Laws and Trade Regulation* (Matthew Bender; 17 volumes; looseleaf).

APPEALS

[¶301] After the rendition of a verdict, it's possible that both sides will be dissatisfied with the court's judgment, and both an appeal and a cross-appeal will be filed.

However, this step cannot be taken lightly: appellate practice is extremely formal, and one of the appellate attorney's major tasks is to find out which appellate rules apply (for instance, federal appeals are governed by the Federal Rules of Appellate Practice, but each Circuit and District—and sometimes smaller units within the Circuit and District—have their own, idiosyncratic rules about matters such as notice, timing, and the physical appearance of briefs and other appellate documents)—and follow them in every particular.

A simple but important technicality is to make sure that you are admitted to the appropriate appellate bar before you submit a brief or appear to argue the case. (If you are not admitted, and time is too short to arrange your permanent or pro haec vice admission, you will need co-counsel who have the appropriate admission.)

There are both advantages and disadvantages to handling the appeal of a case you handled at the trial level. You will be familiar with the case, its facts, your legal theories, and the trial record (one of the most vital elements in the success of the appeal). However, the client will probably be angry at you, believing that the lack of success at trial level was at least partly your fault. If you enter a case at the appellate stage, you will be able to highlight the mistakes made by the earlier lawyer. However, it will probably be too late to introduce entirely new legal theories.

[¶302] COMMENCING AN APPEAL

Although there are differences among federal courts, and among the states, the general rule is that an appeal is taken by serving and/or filing a notice of appeal (or a document given a different title by local practice, but serving the same purpose) with the trial court. Sometimes an assignment of errors or bill of exceptions will be required. If your client is a losing defendant, it may be necessary to post an appeal bond—perhaps even in an amount equal to several times the amount of the judgment.

In federal practice, relief pending appeal (e.g., a stay or injunction) must be sought from the trial court; seeking such relief from the Court of Appeals requires either a showing that you have already sought the relief from the District Court, or that it would be useless to do so.

Depending on the circumstances of the case and the jurisdiction, it may be necessary to obtain leave to appeal as a preliminary step. Check local practice: sometimes leave to appeal is granted by the court whose decision is being reviewed; sometimes it is granted by the court that will review the lower court's decision.

Because so much of the appeal concerns the record in the lower court, be sure you understand local practice vis-a-vis the record. It's particularly important to find out how much of the record must be filed with the appeal. If you have the right to decide how much and what to reproduce, do not leave out crucial items or abbreviate items in a way that creates a misleading impression (something your opponent or the appeals court is likely to detect)—but don't fall into the opposite trap of including too much. Even if expense is no object, the appellate court will be annoyed at having to wade through excessive and irrelevant material.

It may be necessary to have the record certified by the clerk of the trial court (which can be a lengthy process); perhaps the transcript will have to be certified. Either the certification process must be begun shortly after you take on the appeal, or you may need an extension of your time to appeal. Make sure you know the whereabouts of the trial exhibits, and whether or not they must be duplicated and filed with the appeal.

A pro se litigant's filing of a timely brief that contains all the necessary information can also operate as the Notice of Appeal required by the Federal Rules of Appellate Procedure 3.[1]

When parties settle a suit on appeal, they can get the federal appeals court to vacate its prior judgment or opinion in appropriate cases (such as instances in which the controversy really has become moot), but the court does not have to vacate the prior decision; the Tenth Circuit has ruled that, because the public paid for the trial of the suit, the public is entitled to be informed of the opinion and its possible precedential value.[2]

[¶302.1] Timing of Appeals

Local practice determines how much time is given to appeal, and also the starting point for computing time to appeal. It may run from the time the lower court's order is entered, from the time the order is served, or from the service of the order with notice of entry. It's usually good practice to file the notice of appeal as soon as possible; it's easier to get the time to perfect the appeal extended than to get an extension for the original filing.

Sometimes the notice of appeal must be served before filing; if this is a requirement, local practice determines whether the clerk of the court, or the appellant, handles this duty. The place of filing varies with local custom; so does the need for, and amount of, an appeals bond. Sometimes attorneys who wish oral argument on the appeal must file a pre-argument statement justifying this desire.

Docketing an appeal usually requires that the record below be filed by a certain time; it may also be necessary to pay a fee.

It's good strategy for the winner in the lower court to check with the clerk's office just before the time to appeal expires, and on the last day; that way, a notice of cross-appeal can be prepared if necessary, and filed to protect the right of cross-appeal.

[¶302.2]   Interlocutory and Immediate Appeals

The general rule is that a final order is a prerequisite to an appeal. However, under certain circumstances, interlocutory appeals will be permitted. In federal practice, there are only four types of interlocutory appeals as of right: injunctions; receiverships; admiralty cases in which the final decree can be appealed; certain civil actions for patent infringement. All other interlocutory appeals are discretionary.

State practice varies on interlocutory appeal. Some states allow interlocutory appeals of right at least to the first level of appellate review; others make interlocutory appeals discretionary.

Experts suggest that these are arguments that can induce courts to accept discretionary appeals:

➤ serious injustice perpetrated by the lower court—especially if you can show the immediacy of the need for correction.

➤ the lower court's opinion contributes to conflicts or lack of clarity in the rule of law.

➤ the lower court's opinion states a new—and incorrect—rule of law. (This argument is dangerous in jurisdictions that permit courts to "depublish" their decisions; if the opinion is withdrawn, this may help the cause of legal scholarship in the abstract, but won't help your client.)

➤ make the case so interesting that the judges can't turn it down—perhaps by tying it to an issue that the appeals court has already shown interest in pursuing.

The Supreme Court has ruled that under Federal Rules of Appellate Procedure 4(a)(2), a notice of appeal can be filed from a nonfinal decision announced by a court if the decision would be appealable if entered immediately. Such a notice of appeal will be effective with respect to the subsequently entered final judgment. The High Court's rationale is that this situation presents no risk of surprise to the non-appealing party.[3] A later Supreme Court opinion[4] permits a state, or an entity that is an arm of the state, to get an immediate appeal from a District Court judgment that denies an Eleventh Amendment assertion of *immunity* from being sued.

In a related development, Section 1291 of the Judicial Code confines appeals as a right to those from "final decisions of the district courts." 28 U.S.C. §1291. Thus the refusal to enforce a settlement agreement claimed to shelter a party from suit altogether is not immediately appealable.[5]

An interlocutory order by one court, enjoining a party from pursuing a related action in a different court, is not an "injunction" appealable under 28 U.S.C. Sec. 1292(a)(1), according to the Third Circuit; the order neither grants nor denies the substantive relief sought in the underlying action.[6]

The Circuit Courts have power under 28 U.S.C. Sec. 158(d) to review final orders of District Courts or bankruptcy appellate panels; but their power does not extend to review of District Court orders that were entered on appeal of inter-locutory orders of bankruptcy courts.[7] When a federal judge hears a bankruptcy case in the Court of Appeals, that judge's interlocutory orders are appealable; the Supreme Court has found that there is no evidence that Congress wished to prevent this type of interlocutory review.[8]

Where the sole issue to be resolved is the arbitrability of a dispute, and money damages are not sought, a District Court order compelling arbitration is a final order as defined by 9 U.S.C. Sec. 16(a)(3). Because such an order is final, it is appealable. However, if the issue of arbitrability were only one component of a broader dispute, the order relating to arbitrability would be interlocutory and hence not appealable.[9]

Where the order to arbitrate a claim is issued by a District Court that is hearing a case for other relief, the District Court arbitration order is a non-appealable interlocutory order; the Seventh Circuit has held[10] that the order does not constitute a "final decision with respect to an arbitration" that would be appealable pursuant to the Federal Arbitration Act.

[¶302.3]   Intermediate Appellate Courts

In the federal system, the District Courts are the trial courts, with appeal to the Circuit Courts of Appeal and the possibility of appeal or certiorari to the Supreme Court.

Thirty-six states have two or more levels above the trial court. (Alaska has an intermediate appeals court for criminal, but not civil, matters.) Fourteen jurisdictions have only one appellate court: Delaware, the District of Columbia, Maine, Mississippi, Montana, Nebraska, Nevada, New Hampshire, North Dakota, Rhode Island, South Carolina, South Dakota, Utah, and Wyoming.

[¶303]   SCOPE OF APPELLATE REVIEW

When you handle a case at the trial level, you must always consider the possibility of review, and frame the complaint to raise all potentially appealable issues (especially Constitutional issues)—unless you've discussed the matter with a client who doesn't want to appeal if the case is lost at the trial level. It's important to object and take exceptions where necessary to preserve potential issues for review (although, as a matter of trial strategy, it may be necessary to give way on a few points to avoid angering the trial judge so much that he or she will rule against your client out of sheer annoyance).

This is necessary because generally only issues raised at trial can be raised on appeal. (The issue of the trial court's jurisdiction can be raised at any time.) It's possible that a court will review an error raised for the first time on appeal if it's fundamental to the case.

On appeal of a jury verdict, the appellate court views the evidence in the light most favorable to the winner—including all reasonable inferences that arise from a favorable review of the evidence. Damages approved by the trial court will stand unless they are so excessive that they suggest passion or prejudice. Nor will the appeals court substitute its judgment for that of the trial court: the appeals court's job is to look for errors committed, not to render the judgment it would have rendered if it had tried the case initially.

New issues can be raised on appeal if they literally could not have been raised below: for instance, new facts (such as a change in the status of the parties—an injured plaintiff dies of his injuries; a partnership is severed) or new legal issues (a precedent relied on by the lower court is reversed). As a strategic matter, it may be best to raise such matters by motion in the appellate court; that way, you won't take up precious space in your appellate brief discussing issues that the appellate court won't even consider.

[¶304] THE APPELLATE BRIEF

The appellate brief is a potent tool in convincing the appeals court of the merits of your client's case. If the appeals court has a summary calendar, or if you waive oral argument, it will be your *only* tool. It may be possible to sneak a hastily written or thinly argued trial brief past an overworked trial court. Although appeals courts are certainly busy, the level of legal scholarship among judges and clerks is so high, you won't be able to get away with anything less than clear, concise arguments backed by a thorough knowledge of the trial record and impeccable legal research. The mission of the appellant's brief is to demonstrate beyond doubt that reversible error was committed below. Just as all roads lead to Rome, all arguments in the appellant's brief should return to this theme.

Concise arguments are very important; nothing annoys an appeals court more than a lawyer who has ten pages worth of things to say, but continues writing for fifty pages because that's the maximum permitted length for a brief; or one who fills pages with string citations of cases with a dubious relevance to the case (or none at all).

For state courts, the most influential courts (and thus the most persuasive authority to cite) are probably that panel; the Supreme Court of your state; other panels of the court before which your appeal is pending; other appellate courts in your jurisdiction—in that order. Cases from the federal circuit courts, respected appeals courts in other states, and federal district courts are less persuasive.

Given the generally higher level of judicial (and adversarial) skill at the appellate level, it is often important to anticipate arguments that will be raised by the opponent, and to deal with them in the brief. It's unwise to hope that they will be ignored or forgotten. It's also unwise to trust that no one will notice that a point is raised without legal support; that a cited case has been withdrawn, overruled, or reversed; or that unmentioned statutes or regulations are germane to the issue at hand. Because more than a year can elapse between the initiation of an appeal and the writing of the brief, make sure that cases cited below are still valid precedents, and monitor interim developments in the law.

Although it saves time to use the statement of facts from the trial brief, be sure to write your own statement of facts. It can be a powerful tool for convincing the appeals court of the justice of your arguments. The extra time is well spent! (The appellee's statement of facts in a reply brief can also be used to discreetly correct the appellant's stated view of the case.)

Organize your brief into points and subpoints; the titles assigned to the various sections can also be persuasive. Experts differ on whether a good brief arrays a large number of arguments (showing that your client's position is unassailable) or concentrates on one, two, or three really strong points instead of wasting valuable space (and lawyering time) on weak or questionable points.

How should the appellant's brief be organized? If the issues are factually interrelated, chronological order is suggested so that points need not be repeated. If the issues are factually interdependent, they should be discussed in order of strength. Experts disagree on whether you should lead with your strongest issue (in case the clerk or judge stops reading part-way through) or start with your weakest issue, and build to a triumphant climax.

The task of the appellee is easier. First of all, the appellee (unless the party is also a cross-appellant) merely wants the lower court's judgment to be left alone; the appellee isn't asking for anything new to be done. Then, the appellee can poke holes in the appellant's argument, challenging the validity of the citations, or making policy arguments to rebut the appellant's arguments.

Depending on the rules of the appellate court, it may be possible for the appellant to file a rebuttal brief, either of right or by permission. Occasionally, a commentator will suggest leaving an especially devastating argument for the rebuttal brief; but this practice will backfire if the appeals court refuses to deal with theories that could have been, but were not, raised in the original appellate brief.

[¶305] APPELLATE ARGUMENT

Again, local practice will decide whether all appeals get oral argument; whether you must request oral argument in advance; whether the time for oral argument is fixed, or variable. The perennially busy appeals courts feel more kindly toward attorneys who request short arguments instead of long ones (and those who waive oral argument and submit on the papers when oral argument is not really required). It can create hostility if you demand oral argument after your opponent has waived oral argument.

However, many attorneys feel that appellate argument is the culmination of all legal practice. An effective oral argument requires superb preparation and familiarity with every portion of the record and the applicable precedents (and the ability to find materials as soon as required, without wasting time groping). The attorney must anticipate the judges' questions, and be ready to answer (and to "ride with" unanticipated questions). Although the lawyer must have every nuance of the case at his or her fingertips, the argument must appear spontaneous. An easy way to make a bad impression is simply to read out a prepared speech—or, worse, to read from the brief. The court will wonder why its time is being wasted.

Experienced appellate attorneys have many ways to prepare their arguments. Some of them write out what they expect to say, and rehearse their delivery in front of a mirror. An even more effective rehearsal technique is to ask a fellow attorney to play the part of an appellate judge, and to interrupt the speech with questions. Other appellate attorneys prefer to keep their notes informal: a series of index cards, with an important point on each card. That way, the points can be rearranged as necessary to respond to the rhythm dictated by the judge's questions.

Finally, if you win on appeal, be sure you understand how to enforce your judgment (and move for attorneys' fees, in appropriate instances)!

— Endnotes —

1. Smith v. Barry, #90-7477, 112 S.Ct. 678 (Sup.Ct. 1/14/92).

2. Oklahoma Radio Associates v. FDIC, 62 LW 2173 (10th Cir. 9/2/93).

3. FirsTier Mortgage Co. v. Investors Mortgage Ins. Co. #89-1063, 111 S.Ct. 648 (1/15/91).

4. Puerto Rico Aquaduct & Sewer Authority v. Metcalf & Eddy, Inc. #91-1010, 113 S.Ct. 684 (Sup.Ct. 1/12/93).

5. Digital Equipment Corp. v. Desktop Direct, Inc. No. 93-405 (Sup.Ct. 6/6/94).

6. Hershey Foods Corp. v. Hershey Creamery Co., 945 F.2d 1272 (3d Cir. 10/31/91).

7. Germain v. Connecticut Nat'l Bank, 926 F.2d 191 (2d Cir. 2/15/91).

8. Connecticut National Bank v. Germain, #90-1791, 112 S.Ct. 1146 (Sup.Ct. 3/9/92).

9. Stedor Enterprises Ltd. v. Armtex Inc., 947 F.2d 727 (4th Cir. 10/18/91).

10. Perera v. Siegel Trading Co., 951 F.2d 780 (7th Cir. 1/3/92).

— For Further Reference —

Bowen, Veronica L., "Finality-appealability: Trying to Clarify Prejudgment Appeals," 59 *Defense Counsel J.* 50 (January '92).

Bruff, Harold H., "Coordinating Judicial Review in Administrative Law," 39 *U.C.L.A. L. Rev.* 1993 (June '92).

FitzGerald, Kerry P., "Criminal Procedure: Pretrial, Trial and Appeal," 4S *Southwestern L.J.* 1593 (Spring '92).

Hall, W. Wendell, "Revisiting Standards of Review in Civil Appeals," 24 *St. Mary's L.J.* 1045 (Spring '93).

Hofer, Ronald R., "Standards of Review—Looking Beyond the Labels," 74 *Marquette L. Rev.* 231 (Winter '91).

Krull, Charles R., "Eliminating Appeals from Guilty Pleas, " 29 *Arizona Attorney* 34 (October '92).

Liapakis, Pamela Anagnos, "Appellate Advocacy," 10 *Trial Diplomacy J.* 27 (Fall '87).

Lowenstein, Harold, "Frivolous Appeals, Not Frivolously Granted: A Practical Analysis," 60 *U. M. K. C. Law Rev.* 492 (Spring '92).

Markey, Howard T., "The Federal Circuit and Congressional Intent," 41 *American U. L. Rev.* 577 (Spring '92).

Mihaila, Marcelle E., "Achieving Success on Appeal," 12 *California Lawyer* 49 (June '92).

Nosacka, Mark Daniel, "Bendectin, Birth Defects, and Brock: A Study in Appellate Review," 13 *J. of Products Liability* 231 (Summer '91).

ARBITRATION

[¶401] Commercial arbitration is often an attractive alternative to litigation: it's more economical, speedier, offers more privacy, and is more effective. Naturally, these benefits are qualified by the individual situation—in some cases the parties may end up in court litigating the right to arbitrate the underlying dispute.

Arbitration has a preferred status in the law. If parties have agreed in advance to arbitrate, courts are loath to involve the judicial process. Ordinarily, except for the factors mentioned in ¶414 (vacating arbitration award), unless the arbitrator has exceeded the specific authority granted by the parties, the award will not be upset or overturned or even modified by the courts, no matter how outrageous it may appear on its face. Arbitration is also frequently invoked under labor-management collective bargaining agreements and construction contracts.

Since most states have statutes governing arbitration, check local law. Arbitration under the auspices of the court system may be *required* for small claims in order to cope with court congestion.

Every year, more and more people want the courts to hear their disputes; yet the court system is not increasing in size as fast as the volume of cases, and much of the courts' time is taken up with drug and other criminal cases. One solution to this impasse is to increase the number and scope of situations in which arbitration can be used, or will be required. Arbitration does not cut costs to the legal system but does save the disputants a significant amount of attorneys' fees.[1]

In a sign of the times, more law firms are seeking arbitration for internal disputes. Fearful of big judgments in discrimination and sexual harassment cases, law firms are starting to require partners and staff to agree to arbitrate such disputes rather than go to court.[2]

[¶401.1] Securities Arbitration

For over thirty years, it was assumed that a pre-dispute agreement to arbitrate claims under Section 12 (2) of the Securities Act of 1933 was void under Section 14 of the Act.[3] In 1989, however, the Supreme Court ruled[4] that such pre-dispute agreements are valid and enforceable. When read in conjunction with the 1987 *McMahon* decision,[5] which requires enforcement of a brokerage-agreement arbitration clause, and makes arbitration the sole avenue of remedy for Section 10(b) claims asserted by brokerage customers who have signed such an agreement, this case makes it clear that there is a Supreme Court policy in favor of securities arbitration. Where investor claims are subject to an arbitration agreement with the broker, the state securities commissioner does not have the power to carry out the state-law remedy of rescission.[6]

This pro-arbitration policy has had a practical effect. The American Arbitration Association (AAA), which hears securities cases, adopted its first set of separate securities arbitration rules (although the rules are quite similar to the familiar commercial arbitration rules): the rules were amended effective January 1, 1989 to shorten the time for responses from 14 to 10 days; increase the amount in controversy required for a three-arbitrator panel to $25,000 (formerly $20,000); and provide that a panel will not consist only of arbitrators from the securities industry unless the disputants ask for an all-industry panel.[7] Although these rules say that the arbitration award "shall include a statement regarding the disposition of any statutory claims," this requirement is not a mandate that the arbitrator must offer an explanation; thus, the absence of an explanation is not tantamount to imperfect execution of the arbitrators' duties or a manifest disregard for law that would justify a partial vacation of the award.[8]

It can be inferred that, although the courts favor the use of arbitration in securities disputes, this is a somewhat consumer-oriented preference. At least one state (Massachusetts) requires investors to be given a free choice of whether or not to sign an arbitration clause in a brokerage agreement; the arbitration clause cannot be included on a "take it or leave it" contract of adhesion basis.

In several recent cases, brokerage firms have been unable to compel arbitration: for instance, if the explicit language of the brokerage contract gives an aggrieved customer the right to sue,[9] or "unambiguously creates a substantive securities claim exception" to the arbitration clause.[10] This is true even if the contract language was drafted before *McMahon,* or in compliance with the SEC's former Rule 15c-2, which mandated the existence of a litigation alternative. (An object lesson to brokerage firms to revise their standard forms to keep up with developments in the law.)

The various stock exchanges and other self-regulating organizations (SROs) have their own arbitration procedures. It has been held that a customer can compel a broker to use the National Association of Securities Dealers (NASD)'s arbitration procedure even if there is no arbitration clause in the brokerage agreement, because the customer is an intended third party beneficiary of the NASD rules.[11] Once a customer signs a pre-dispute agreement calling for arbitration by the New York Stock Exchange, he has waived application of the NASD arbitration procedure.[12]

A bank can compel a New York Stock Exchange–member firm to arbitrate a dispute involving American Depository Receipts (ADRs), even though the bank seeking arbitration is not an NYSE member, and even though the disputed transactions were not processed by the NYSE.[13]

The so-called Amex window is a provision of the American Stock Exchange which permits customers to arbitrate securities disputes before the AAA. However, where the customer's brokerage agreement specifies arbitration only by the NASD or the exchange itself, the text of the agreement prevails over the "Amex window".[14] Customers who want AAA arbitration must demand it when negotiating the contract.

In *Flink v. Carlson,*[15] the customer initiated arbitration against the brokerage house; the brokerage house had a third-party claim against the broker. The customer's agreement with the brokerage and the brokerage's employment agreement with the broker named different arbitral bodies. The Eighth Circuit held that the brokerage firm would not be able to compel arbitration of its claim against the broker in the customer's forum, because the forum of arbitration (as well as the arbitration/litigation distinction) is a contractual matter.

A brokerage firm is not compelled to arbitrate investor claims of material misrepresentation in trades conducted by the brokerage's predecessor firm.[16]

Brokerage firms will find it more difficult to delay or prevent customers from arbitrating limited-partnership disputes and other claims, as a result of a 1994 decision. In a decision favorable to investors, a New York trial court judge found that New York courts don't have jurisdiction to dismiss claims that certain out-of-state customers (in this case investors in soured limited partnerships) sought to have arbitrated in their home states.[17]

[¶401.2] Labor Arbitration

Although it sounds like a securities case, *Shearson Lehman/ American Express v. Bird*[18] is in fact a labor case. The Second Circuit held that a pre-dispute agreement to arbitrate pension fund claims cannot be enforced as to claims of substantive violations of ERISA. However, the Supreme Court vacated the Second Circuit's judgment and remanded the case to the Second Circuit. On remand[19] the Second Circuit held that an agreement to arbitrate statutory ERISA claims is enforceable. In this analysis, agreement to arbitrate doesn't entail surrender of possibly meritorious claims; it only changes the forum in which they are to be resolved. The Eighth Circuit has held that judicial remedies under state anti-discrimination laws are not preempted by the federal Arbitration Act.[20]

Where the standard securities registration form is signed as a condition of employment, arbitration can be compelled of a broker's claims under the Employee Polygraph Protection Act.[21] It has, however, been ruled[22] that NASD rules do not require arbitration of disputes between NASD member-dealers and their employees, although arbitration of such disputes is required under New York Stock Exchange rules.

It's up to the federal District Court to decide if a dispute about layoffs is arbitrable even if it is claimed that the District Court's decision would also dispose of the merits of the case. The Ninth Circuit has ruled[23] that the District Court should follow the procedure set out in Justice Brennan's concurring opinion in *AT&T v. Communications Workers*.[24] Under this procedure, the first step is to determine if the contract, on its face, brings the right to transfer work to another location within the ambit of the contract's management rights clause. If this is not facially apparent, the District Court must determine if "the most forceful evidence" exists that the transfer of work was a management right before the contract was signed. Matters that were pre-contract management rights are not arbitrable.

The Supreme Court ruled in 1991 that an employer has no obligation to submit a union grievance to binding arbitration if the grievance arose after the contract expired, if the grievance is not related to a vested contractual right.[25]

However, in *United Steelworkers of America v. ASARCO Inc.*[26] the employer and union were unable to agree on a policy about workplace drug and alcohol testing during the negotiations for the collective bargaining agreement. The upshot was that the employer withdrew its proposal for workplace testing. However, three months after the contract was signed, the employer unilaterally imposed a testing program, and refused to address the grievances based on the testing. Nor would the employer submit these grievances to arbitration. In the judgment of the Fifth Circuit, union claims with respect to the testing program were arbitrable, because the claims are the equivalent of a union contention that the employer has violated the collective bargaining agreement's obligation that the employer make reasonable provision for workplace safety and health. To the Fifth Circuit, the unilateral imposition of the testing program was unreasonable, and thus violative of the collective bargaining agreement.

The Eleventh Circuit vacated[27] the decision of an arbitrator who held that employees who honored a picket line of a union other than their own were entitled to notice before their employer hired permanent replacements. The decision was voidable because it did not "draw its essence" from the literal terms of the collective bargaining agreement: arbitrators do not have broad powers to dispense industrial justice or grant due process outside the ordinary arbitration process.

A provision in a collective bargaining agreement that requires the union to pursue a grievance within 15 days of the employer's answer (or the grievance will not be arbitrable) operates as a condition precedent to arbitration. Therefore, it is up to the court, not the arbitrator, to decide whether a union that missed the 15-day deadline can still get arbitration of the grievance.[28]

An employer can be enjoined from implementing a drug testing program for employees until its contractual right to impose the program unilaterally has been arbitrated; in this case, the Tenth Circuit held that the union is likely to succeed on the merits.[29]

Once the case has gone to arbitration, the arbitrator's award can only be overturned by a court if there has been a violation of a well-defined, dominant, explicit public policy of the state.[30]

The Second and Sixth Circuits use the same standard: the arbitrator's award can be set aside if a reasonable person would have to conclude that the arbitrator was partial to a party.[31] This standard falls somewhere between "appearance of bias" and "proof of actual bias." The statute of limitations for actions to vacate an arbitration award under Section 301 of the Labor-Management Relations Act is three months.[32] The LMRA Section 301 statute of limitations for a suit to compel arbitration is six months. The period runs from a party's express rejection of a request for arbitration, and cannot be triggered by mere constructive notice to the other side that a party will not cooperate with the arbitration process. Thus, if there is no express rejection, the statute of limitations cannot start to run, and a union lawsuit cannot be untimely if the employer failed to deliver an express rejection of the arbitration request.[33]

The Fourth Circuit, unlike the Third,[34] held that an arbitration clause dealing with age discrimination claims can be a valid and enforceable part of an employment agreement. The Supreme Court resolved the issue in favor of enforcement of compulsory arbitration clauses in the Age Discrimination in Employment Act (ADEA) context.[35]

The arbitration clause in the U-4 Form (the Uniform Application for Securities Registration Transfer) commonly signed by persons working in the securities industry is enforceable with respect to claims of race and sex discrimination even if the employee would prefer to litigate the claims in state court.[36] As New York's highest court ruled in 1993, the policy favoring arbitration outweighs the policy of expanding the remedies available to persons perceiving themselves as victims of discrimination.

A 1993 Illinois case holds that an arbitration clause in a law firm's employment contract is broad enough to require the arbitration of a former partner's claim for termination compensation, and also of claims asserted by the firm that the ex-partner committed a breach of duty by taking firm clients with him after his departure.[37]

[¶401.3]   Federal Taxation

In 1990, the Tax Court adopted a new Rule 124 permitting parties to a Tax Court case to use voluntary binding arbitration to resolve any disputed issues of fact.

[¶402]   APPRAISEMENT

Arbitration must be distinguished from appraisement. Although these two terms are frequently used interchangeably, they are separate concepts. An arbitration agreement will involve the resolution of an entire dispute, an award will be made, and judgment will be entered. An appraisal will involve only a determination of actual value and/or the amount of loss, with the court retaining jurisdiction over the remaining issues.

[¶403]   COURT-APPOINTED REFEREE

Arbitration must also be distinguished from the use of a court-appointed referee. Whereas arbitration is extra-judicial in the sense that the parties will agree among themselves to submit a dispute to arbitration and be bound by the arbitrator's decision, a referee has no final authority—his findings are turned over to the court, which may follow his advice or disregard it.

[¶404]   HOW TO PROVIDE FOR ARBITRATION

An agreement to arbitrate future disputes does not constitute a submission, but only a basis for a motion to compel arbitration. The American Arbitration

Association (AAA) recommends that a standard arbitration clause be inserted in all commercial contracts:

"Any controversy or claim arising out of or relating to this contract, or the breach thereof, shall be settled by arbitration in accordance with the Rules of the American Arbitration Association, and judgment upon the award rendered by the Arbitrator(s) may be entered in any Court having jurisdiction thereof."

The AAA also recommends a form that may be used for submitting *existing* disputes to arbitration:

"We, the undersigned parties, hereby agree to submit to arbitration under the Commercial Arbitration Rules of the American Arbitration Association the following controversy: (cite briefly). We further agree that the above controversy be submitted to (one) (three) Arbitrators selected from the panels of Arbitrators of the American Arbitration Association. We further agree that we will faithfully observe this agreement and the Rules and that we will abide by and perform any award rendered by the Arbitrator(s) and that a judgment of the Court having jurisdiction may be entered upon the award."

Parties to an agreement to arbitrate may amend the agreement, as they would amend any other part of a contract. An invalid arbitration agreement is usually severable from the main body of the contract.

It is within the court's jurisdiction to decide whether a specific issue is included in an agreement to arbitrate. An intent to arbitrate all issues stemming from the principal agreement is usually given full effect by the courts.

The agreement to arbitrate is a contractual obligation. Therefore, the parties must have capacity to contract and consideration must be furnished (the consideration requirement is usually satisfied by the parties' agreement to abide by the arbitrator's award).

[¶405]   ARBITRABLE ISSUES

Parties may provide for arbitration even if there is no corresponding cause of action for court suit available.

In order to arbitrate, there must be a controversy—a question of fact—between or among the parties. Arbitration is usually unavailable when a party clearly violates the unambiguous terms of the contract.

Arbitration is generally available for the following (however, check local law for variations):

(1) Party rights in real property or personalty;

(2) Probate matters and decedents' estates. (However, since probate proceedings are *in rem,* some states may not allow arbitration.)

(3) Tort nuisances.

Claims based on underlying *illegal* contracts are *not* arbitrable. There are also categories of issues that government has reserved to the exclusive jurisdiction of the courts and which, therefore, are not arbitrable—divorce (state law) and antitrust violations (federal law) are examples of such issues. However, issues of spousal or child support are probably arbitrable.

The Supreme Court also dealt with arbitration outside the securities context, in *Volt Information Sciences Inc.v.Trustees of Stanford University*.[38] The clause at issue was part of a construction contract which had both an arbitration clause and a choice of law clause stating that the contract would be interpreted according to the laws of the place in which the construction project was located. That, in turn, invoked a California statute that stays arbitration until related litigation has been resolved.

The Supreme Court held that the state law is not preempted by the Federal Arbitration Act; instead, the federal act merely permits parties who do want to arbitrate to enforce the eventual arbitration decree. In the case at bar, one party demonstrated its unwillingness to arbitrate by commencing litigation, so the Federal Arbitration Act was not in the picture.

Later, the Fourth Circuit held that another state statute—Virginia's ban on binding arbitration clauses in automobile dealership contracts—is preempted by the FAA and is hence invalid even if construction of the statute is limited to non-negotiable clauses.[39] According to the Seventh Circuit, the rule that courts (not arbitrators) determine the arbitrability of a dispute takes precedence over the rule preventing courts from addressing the merits of the underlying dispute.[40]

An arbitration clause in a stock purchase agreement between business owners is not enforceable under the FAA where there is no involvement of interstate commerce, and local law (in this case, the law of Alabama) does not provide for the enforcement of pre-dispute arbitration agreements.[41]

A Colorado statute requiring arbitration of all civil suits for damages less than $50,000 has been upheld as against claims that it denied access to the courts, violated the Sixth Amendment right to a jury trial, and denied equal protection.[42]

If a contract between two companies, arrived at to keep them from raiding one another's employees, calls for arbitration of a claim "believed to constitute a breach or violation" of the contract, a claim of fraud in the inducement of the agreement itself is arbitrable.[43]

It is for a court, and not an arbitrator, to resolve the threshold issue of whether a signatory to an arbitration agreement initially had the authority to create a valid contract.[44]

A bankruptcy trustee is bound by an arbitration clause in a contract signed by the debtor to the same extent as the debtor would be. However, the trustee's claims under Section 544(b) of the Bankruptcy Act are not arbitrable, because they do not derive from the debtor, and the trustee is not bound by the debtor's actions for Section 544(b) purposes.[45]

Where the arbitration clause itself is silent, and state law permits, a federal court has power to consolidate two arbitration proceedings; nothing in the Federal Arbitration Act forbids consolidation.[46] However, the Second Circuit decided in 1993 that arbitration proceedings arising under separate arbitration agreements cannot be consolidated by a federal District Court over the objection of a party, even if the various proceedings do share common questions of law and fact.[47]

[¶406]   WHO MAY ARBITRATE

Since arbitration is part of the underlying contractual obligation, contract law also governs the capacity of the parties to enter into an arbitration agreement.

General contract law usually regulates the ability of an infant to make an arbitration agreement. Fiduciaries may also submit the dispute to arbitration, if allowed under state statute. Usually, court approval is required for executors and trustees to engage in arbitration in their representative capacity.

In general, an agent cannot bind his principal to submit to arbitration unless such authority is express or implicit in their agency relationship. The fact that an agent is authorized to accept payment or settle an account may not be taken to imply an ability to submit the dispute to arbitration.

An attorney generally has the implied authority to submit his client's case for arbitration, but law may vary, so check the applicable state statute first.

Partners may not usually bind their partnership by a submission, although an individual partner may bind himself. However, if all the partners agree to arbitrate a future issue, then one partner may, at a later date, submit an issue to arbitration.

Corporations may submit disputes to arbitration, and such submission is made by the appropriate officer or board member.

[¶407]   ENFORCEMENT OF ARBITRATION AGREEMENTS

Many state statutes provide machinery for the enforcement of arbitration agreements on a summary basis.

The Uniform Arbitration Act and the Federal Arbitration Act (9 U.S.C. 1 *et seq.*) provide for summary remedy in case one of the parties refuses to arbitrate or denies the existence of a valid arbitration agreement.

If the agreement is revocable, the courts will generally refuse to specifically decree performance of agreements to arbitrate because the parties have a right to revoke. See *Red Cross Line v. Atlantic Fruit Co.*, 264 US 109(1924).

If the arbitration agreement is irrevocable, the statutes in many states provide for a proceeding to enforce the arbitration clause, in which case it will be treated as an action for specific performance. Under the Federal Arbitration Act a proceeding for enforcement of an arbitration agreement is treated as an action for specific performance.

Usually, a party to an arbitration agreement may not revoke it, but certain events may constitute revocation: e.g., bankruptcy, lunacy, or the destruction of the subject matter. Check local law.

Although the death of a party will revoke an agreement to arbitrate, the parties may expressly state that death prior to the rendering of an award will not revoke the agreement. After a party's death, his legal representatives may ratify the submission by continuation of arbitration and acceptance of the award. Revocability by death may be dealt with by state statute; therefore, consult local law.

Assignees of a contract containing an arbitration clause that is irrevocable and enforceable may have the agreement to arbitrate enforced against them as if they were the original party to the agreement. Similarly, an assignee may also enforce the arbitration agreement as against the other original party to the contract.

[¶408] RATIFICATION OF ARBITRATION AGREEMENT

If a party appears at an arbitration hearing without objecting to any terms of the agreement, he or she is deemed to have ratified the agreement in its entirety and may not object to particulars later on.

[¶409] WAIVER OF ARBITRATION RIGHTS

If a party to an arbitration agreement sues in court, that party may be deemed to have waived his right to arbitration. If the other party in his court pleadings fails to raise his right to enforce the arbitration agreement, then he, too, is deemed to have waived that right. However, a defendant may assert his right to arbitration as a defense and move for a stay of the court proceedings. A party can waive a contractual right to arbitration by unreasonable delay in enforcing the right.

[¶410] QUALIFICATIONS OF THE ARBITRATOR

Any competent, disinterested person can be an arbitrator irrespective of legal status. However, in some cases, the parties will want to designate an attorney or someone familiar with the applicable legal principles. If the arbitrator is biased or interested in the transaction or dispute, he may be removed. An arbitrator will not necessarily be disqualified although he has previously served as counsel to one of the parties in different litigation, is friendly with one of the parties, or has previously served as an arbitrator in similar cases. Trade associations frequently employ a panel of arbitrators to settle disputes between their members.

[¶411] SELECTING THE ARBITRATOR

When a contract calls for settlement of disputes by arbitration, the arbitrator will be determined either prior to the dispute or subsequent to the dispute. When a particular arbitrator is appointed prior to the time the dispute arises, the parties should appoint an alternate in the event the original arbitrator is unable to serve. The parties may also provide that the arbitrator is to be determined in accordance with the rules prescribed by the American Arbitration Association. Under those rules the American Arbitration Association will send each party a copy of a list of proposed arbitrators, technically qualified to resolve the controversies involved. In preparing this list, the Association is guided by the nature of the dispute.

Each party has seven (7) days from the time of mailing to cross off any objectionable arbitrators from the list and to number the remaining arbitrators according to preference.

The Association will appoint an arbitrator who is acceptable to both parties. If no arbitrator is acceptable to both parties, a new list will be provided. If the parties are unable to select an arbitrator mutually acceptable, the Association will administratively appoint an arbitrator, but the appointed arbitrator will not be one of those crossed off previously by the parties.

An alternative method for selecting arbitrators is to provide that each party to the controversy will appoint an arbitrator and the arbitrators will appoint a third arbitrator. If the arbitrators are unable to agree upon a third arbitrator, the court may be called upon to do so. Section 3 of the Uniform Act specifies court appointment if the contract provision for appointment can't be followed, or if the arbitrator so chosen can't or won't serve.

[¶412]   ARBITRATION PROCEDURE

The Commercial Arbitration Rules of the American Arbitration Association as amended may be obtained by request to 140 West 51st Street, New York, N.Y. 10020, or from any regional AAA office. (See the Appendix for locations of regional offices.)

[¶413]   ENFORCEMENT OF THE ARBITRATION AWARD

An arbitration award is not self-executing. However, either party is entitled to bring an action on the award and have it enforced as a contract. The Federal Arbitration Act provides for confirmation of an arbitration award within one year. However, the parties will not be precluded from maintaining an action on the award after the one-year statute of limitations for the summary remedy of confirmation has elapsed.

The Uniform Arbitration Act (§11) also provides for the confirmation of an award unless grounds are urged for vacating, or modifying, or correcting the award. In addition, the Uniform Act provides for the entry of the award as a judgment enforceable as any other judgment (see Uniform Arbitration Act §§14 and 15).

Once an award is reduced to judgment in one state, it is entitled to full faith and credit in other states. Other states cannot question the judgment unless it could be questioned in the state rendering it.

[¶414]   VACATING ARBITRATION AWARD

The Uniform Arbitration Act provides that a court may vacate an arbitration award under the following circumstances:

(1) There was evidence of corruption, fraud, or other unlawful behavior in the procurement of the award;

(2) A party's rights were prejudiced in that the arbitrator was partial to the other side, although the arbitrator was agreed on as a neutral party;

(3) The arbitrator exceeded his powers;

(4) The arbitrator refused to hear all relevant evidence, or to accord a party a reasonable delay or postponement based upon compelling reasons;

(5) A party objected to the arbitration proceeding on the ground that no arbitration agreement existed, and the hearing was conducted over the party's objections. (Also see 9 U.S.C. §10(a)–(d) as to vacation of an arbitration award.)

In addition, the Uniform Act provides that a party seeking to have an award vacated must make such a request to the court within 90 days of the award, except that a party may request vacation of the award under (1) above within 90 days after discovery of the fraud, or 90 days after such corruption should have been known. But once a party has accepted benefits under an arbitration award, it waives the right to demand appellate review of the award.

— **ENDNOTES** —

1. See Hayes, Arthur S. and Ann Hagedorn, "Arbitration in Commercial Cases Found to Save Money, not Time," *Wall St. J.* 9/5/90 p.B10.

2. Law item, "More Firms Seek Arbitration for Internal Disputes," *Wall St. J.* 9/26/94 p. B18.

3. Wilko v. Swann, 346 U.S. 427 (1953).

4. Rodriguez y Quijas v. Shearson/American Express, 109 S.Ct. 1917 (5/15/89).

5. Olde Discount Corp. v. Tupman, 62 LW 2090 (3d Cir. 7/30/93).

6. See the *New York Law Journal* 3/9/89 p. 3.

7. Ketchum v. Prudential-Bache Securities Inc., 710 F.Supp. 300 (D. Kan. 3/30/89).

8. Ballay v. Legg Mason Wood Walker Inc., 878 F.2d 729 (3d Cir. 6/29/89); Amodio v. Blinder Robinson & Co., 715 F.Supp. 32 (D. Conn. 6/23/89).

9. Standard v. Financial Clearing & Services Corp., 58 LW 2148 (SDNY 8/10/89).

10. Scobee Combs Funeral Home Inc. v. E.F. Hutton, 711 F.Supp. 605 (S.D. Fla. 3/2/89).

11. Roney & Co. v. Goren, 875 F.2d 1218 (6th Cir. 5/26/89).

12. In re Nomura Securities Int'l Inc. v. Citibank, 62 LW 2064 (N.Y.App. 7/9/93).

13. Merrill Lynch Pierce Fenner & Smith v. Georgiadis, 903 F.2d 109 (2d Cir. 5/7/90); Luckie v. Smith Barney, Harris Upham & Co., 62 LW 2168 (11th Cir. 8/26/93). Also see Paine Webber Inc. v. Rutherford, 903 F.2d 106 (2d Cir. 5/7/90) holding that the Amex window operates as a forum selection clause requiring that AAA arbitration be conducted in New York City.

14. 856 F.2d 44 (8th Cir. 8/24/88).

15. Wheat, First Securities Inc. v. Green, 62 LW 2032 (11th Cir. 6/21/93).

16. In re Merrill Lynch et al. v. Barnum, Supreme Court of New York, No. 100599/94.

17. 871 F.2d 292 (2d Cir. 1989), vacated #89-231; remanded to the Second Circuit.

18. 59 LW 2441 (2d Cir. 1/17/91).

19. Swenson v. Management Recruiters Int'l, 858 F.2d 1304 (8th Cir. 10/5/88); 872 F.2d 264 (4/12/89). Also see Pritzker v. Merrill Lynch, 62 LW 2258 (3d Cir. 10/15/93). [FAA §2 makes ERISA claims involving cash management accounts opened by pension plan trustees subject to arbitration.]

20. Saari v. Smith Barney, Harris Upham & Co., 968 F.2d 877 (9th Cir. 6/29/92), cert. denied 113 S.Ct. 494.

21. Farrand v. Lutheran Brotherhood, 61 LW 2688 (7th Cir. 5/3/93).

22. Teamsters Local 287 v. Frito-Lay Inc., 849 F.2d 1210 (9th Cir. 6/16/88).

23. 475 U.S. 643 (1986).

24. Litton Financial Printing Division v. NLRB, #90-285, 111 S.Ct. 2215 (Sup.Ct. 6/13/91).

25. 970 F.2d 1448 (5th Cir. 9/8/92).

26. Harry Hoffman Printing Inc. v. Graphic Communications Int'l Union, 950 F.2d 95 (2d Cir. 11/27/91).

27. General Drivers Local 89 v. Moog Louisville Warehouse, 852 F.2d 871 (6th Cir. 7/27/88).

28. Oil Workers Local v. Amoco, 886 F.2d 1200 (10th Cir. 9/15/89), cert. denied 110 S.Ct. 2205.

29. Stead Motors v. Automotive Machinists Lodge #1173, 58 LW 2252 (9th Cir. 10/6/89): here, the arbitrator's order of reinstatement for an auto mechanic who was fired for improperly affixing lug bolts was held not to embody such a violation. Compare this to Stroehmann Bakeries Inc. v. Teamsters, 969 F.2d 1436 (3d Cir. 6/29/92), cert. denied 113 S.Ct. 660, where the arbitrator's award reinstating an employee accused of sexual harassment could not be confirmed, because public policy against sexual harassment requires that there be a full-scale inquiry into the facts and the credibility of witnesses before an alleged harasser can be reinstated.

30. Morelite Construction Corp. v. Carpenters, 748 F.2d 79 (2d Cir. 1984); Apperson v. Fleet Carr. Corp., 879 F.2d 1344 (6th Cir. 7/13/89).

31. Occidental Chemical Corp. v. Chemical Workers, 853 F.2d 1310 (6th Cir. 8/1/88).

32. Local Joint Executive Board v. Exber Inc., 62 LW 2753 (9th Cir. 5/28/93).

33. Cf. Gilmer v. Interstate/Johnson Lane Corp., 895 F.2d 195 (4th Cir. 2/6/90) with Nicholson v. CPC Inc., 877 F.2d 221 (3d Cir. 6/2/89).

34. Gilmer v. Interstate/Johnson Lane Corp., #90-18, 111 S.Ct. 1647 (Sup.Ct. 5/13/91). Also see Dancu v. Coopers & Lybrand, 925 F.2d 1136 (E.D. Pa. 12/3/91) applying the Federal Arbitration Act to an executive's ADEA claim under a partnership agreement containing an arbitration clause. In this analysis, the FAA excludes workers in the transport industry only, not everyone subject to a written contract.

35. Fletcher v. Kidder, Peabody & Co., 62 LW 2051 (N.Y.App. 7/9/93).

36. Nagle v. Nadelhoffer *et.al.,* 62 LW 2078 (Ill.App. 5/5/93).

37. 489 U.S. 468 (Sup.Ct. 3/3/89).

38. Saturn Distrib. Corp. v. Williams, 717 F.Supp. 1147 (4th Cir. 6/6/90).

39. Independent Lift Truck Builders v. Hyster Co., 62 LW 2152 (7th Cir. 8/17/93).

40. Ex Parte Jones, 62 LW 2100 (Ala.Sup. 7/26/93).

41. Firelock Inc. v. District Court, 58 LW 2074 (Colo. Sup. 7/24/89).

42. Peoples Security Life Ins. v. Monumental Life Ins., 867 F.2d 809 (4th Cir. 2/10/89).

43. Three Valleys Municipal Water Dist. v. E. F. Hutton & Co., 259 LW 2544 (9th Cir. 2/5/91).

44. Hays & Co. v. Merrill Lynch, 885 F.2d 1149 (3d Cir. 9/15/89)

45. New England Energy Inc. v. Keystone Shipping Co., 855 F.2d 1 (1st Cir. 8/24/88).

46. United Kingdom v. Boeing Co., 62 LW 2017 (2d Cir. 6/29/93).

— **FOR FURTHER REFERENCE** —

Baker, Donald I. and Mark R. Stabile, "Arbitration of Antitrust Claims," 48 *Business Lawyer* 395 (February '93).

Biega, Marshall A., "Amendments to Procedure Act Encourage Agencies to Use ADR," *Nat.L.J.* 3/4/91 p. 22.

Breslin, Philip H. and Perry A. Zirkel, "Arbitrator Impartiality and the Burden of Proof," 44 *Labor Law J.* 381 (June '93).

Brown, Harold, "The Case Against Contractual Arbitration Covenants," 11 *Franchise L.J.* 112 (Spring '92).

Buckstein, Mark A., "American Arbitration Association's Large, Complex Case Dispute Resolution Program, " *Arbitration J.* 17 (March '93).

Cox, Gail Diane, "Arbitrating What Lawyers Bill," *Nat.L.J.* 4/8/91 p. 1.

Dienett, John F. and Jerome D. Pinn, "State Efforts to Limit Arbitration," 11 *Franchise L.J.* 104 (Spring '92).

Fisher, Paul, "Tips to Attorneys and Mediators: How to Successfully Mediate a Case," 46 *Arbitration J.* 59 (September '91).

Fitzgibbons, Susan A., "Sexual Harassment and Labor Arbitration," 20 *Georgia J. of Int'l & Comp. Law* 71 (Spring '90).

Fuchsberg, Abraham, "The Arbitrariness of Arbitrators: Anything Goes," 22 *Trial Lawyers Q.* 8 (Summer '92).

Gordon, Paul, "Submitting Fair Value to Final Offer Arbitration," 63 *U. of Colo. L. Rev.* 751 (Summer '92).

Hochman, Stephen A., "A Bar Association-Sponsored Forum for Arbitration Is Needed," *NYLJ* 10/22/92 p. 1.

Hunter, Keith W. and Jim Hoenig, "Dispute Resolution and Avoidance Techniques in the Construction Industry," 47 *Arbitration J.* 16 (September '92).

Kauffman, Nancy, "Expedited Arbitration and Other Innovations in Alternative Dispute Resolution," 43 *Labor Law J.* 382 (June '92).

Lobel, Ira B., "Addressing Environmental Disputes With Labor Mediation Skills," 47 *Arbitration J.* 48 (September '92).

Morris, Frank C. Jr., "Arbitration After Gilmer," 38 *The Practical Lawyer* 71 (June '92).

News item, "Brokers Cleared of Charges of Fraud in Arbitration," *Wall St.J.* 10/14/93 p. B12.

Petersen, Donald J., "Trends in Arbitrating Falsification of Employment Application Forms," 47 *Arbitration J.* 31 (September '92).

Spielfogel, Evan J., "New Trends in the Arbitration of Employment Disputes," 48 *Arbitration J.* 6 (March '93).

Tien, Wendy S., "Compulsory Arbitration of ADA Claims: Disabling the Disabled," 77 *Minn.L. Rev.* 1443 (June '93).

Ward, David M., "The Scope of Binding Arbitration Agreements in Contracts for Medical Services," 8 *Oh.State J. on Dispute Resolution* 361 (Spring '93).

Ware, John P., "Consolidating Arbitrations in the Federal Courts," 8 *Oh.State J. on Dispute Resolution* 457 (Spring '93).

Williams, Andrea D., "American Arbitration Association's Sexual Harassment Claims Resolution Process," 22 *Colorado Lawyer* 1217 (June '93).

Wilner, Gabriel M., ed. *Domke on Commercial Arbitration* (Callaghan & Co; looseleaf).

ATTORNEYS' FEES

[¶501] Theoretically the "American rule," as distinguished from the "English rule," is that each litigant pays his, her, or its own legal fees. However, the rule is very far from absolute. A common contract provision obligates the breachor to pay the attorneys' fees encountered when the victim of a breach of contract sues. Furthermore, a number of statutes provide explicitly for the payment of attorneys' fees by tortfeasors and other violators of statute.

Currently courts pronounce frequently on attorneys' fee awards. Issues ruled on were the applicability of Equal Access to Justice Act (EAJA) awards; who is a "prevailing party"; attorneys' fees in Social Security cases; and proportionality of attorneys' fees to damage awards. In decisions guaranteed to be unpopular, the Supreme Court also held[1] that the 21 USC Section 853 provision for forfeiture of profits of drug dealing does not contain an exemption for money intended for the payment of legal fees, so that pre-conviction forfeiture (leaving the defendant bereft of funds to pay a lawyer) is permissible on probable cause to believe that the assets are forfeitable.

Furthermore, attorneys are subject to the Internal Revenue Code Section 6050 mandate to report the names of anyone making a cash payment over $10,000.[2] In this analysis, lawyers are practicing a trade or business that is subject to the cash reporting requirement. The reporting requirement does not impair the Sixth Amendment right to counsel because clients are still permitted to retain counsel of their choice. The reporting requirement can be avoided by paying in some form other than cash.

Apropos of non-cash payments, an ethics opinion takes the position that fees paid by credit card do not constitute client funds if they are either a retainer or an advance on services. Therefore, such fees do not have to be placed in a client-protection escrow account unless the retainer agreement so requires.[3]

A New York court has ruled that attorneys cannot charge fees that are totally non-refundable: the attorney has an ethical obligation to return unearned fees, and the client has the right to discharge the attorney before the full amount of the retainer has been earned.[4]

In these parlous times, you may be glad to discover that, if state law makes the attorney's charging lien relate back to the beginning of representation, and if the attorney-client relationship commences more than 90 days before a bankruptcy filing, the lawyer becomes a secured creditor as of the beginning of representation, and therefore satisfying the charging lien within 90 days of the filing does not constitute a voidable preference.[5]

[¶501.1] Exceptions to the American Rule

In *Alyeska Pipeline Service Co. v. Wilderness Society*, 421 US. 240 (1975), the Supreme Court has upheld the American rule as the normal one in civil litigation. However, this case recognizes three exceptions to the rule even where there is no applicable statute calling for payment of attorneys' fees by the unsuccessful party:

➤ Where a party willfully violates a court order, the other party is entitled to reimbursement of fees to enforce the order: *Toledo Scale Co. v. Computing Scale Co.,* 261 U.S. 399 (1923).

➤ A losing party who acted in bad faith, vexatiously, wantonly, or with an intention to oppress can be taxed with attorneys' fees: *Vaughan v. Atkinson,* 369 U.S. 527 (1962).

➤ A winning party is entitled to attorneys' fees for securing a common trust fund for others; e.g., by securities or antitrust litigation (*Sprague v. Ticonic National Bank,* 307 U.S. 161 (1939); this principle has been extended to those who preserve a common fund that confers benefits on a class: *Mills v. Electric Auto-Life Co.,* 396 U.S. 375 (1970).

The Supreme Court has held[6] that unsuccessful intervenors in Civil Rights Act cases are not responsible for their opponents' attorneys' fees unless the intervention was frivolous, unreasonable, or undertaken without foundation. Under Section 11(e) of the Securities Act, an attorney's fee award can be assessed against a "party litigant" who burdens the court system with a frivolous claim. However, fees cannot be assessed against the litigant's attorney because the attorney is not a "party" (although, as discussed below, the attorney may be subject to Rule 11 sanctions). The Securities Act Section 11(e) fee provision is treated as a "cost," and parties, not their attorneys, are responsible for the payment of costs.[7]

In 1993, several courts tackled the question of whether attorneys' fees are "necessary costs of response" that are recoverable under a private CERCLA (Superfund) suit. The Eastern District of Virginia and Western District of Michigan ruled that such fees are recoverable response costs. The Ninth Circuit said they are not. The Tenth Circuit said that fees for litigating the private cost recovery suit are not recoverable as response costs, but attorneys' fees outside the litigation context (for designing removal actions; preparing and supervising the approved work plan) are response costs. The Supreme Court granted certiorari, reviewed these cases, and in 1994 ruled that CERCLA §107 does not provide for the award of private litigants' attorneys' fees associated with bringing a cost recovery action. The fees for prosecuting the action are not recoverable "necessary costs of response" under §107 because the "enforcement activities" do not encompass a private party's action to recover cleanup costs from other potentially responsible parties.[8]

[¶502]   FEDERAL STATUTES RE ATTORNEYS' FEES

Approximately 100 federal statutes specify payment of attorneys' fees. They include:

➤ Federal Contested Election Act, 2 U.S.C. Sec. 396.

➤ Freedom of Information Act, 5 U.S.C. Sec. 552(a)(4)(E).

➤ Privacy Act, 5 U.S.C. Sec. 552a(g)(3)(B).

➤ Bankruptcy Act, 11 U.S.C. Sec. 104(a).

➤ Clayton Antitrust Act, 15 U.S.C. Sec. 15.

➤ Federal Trade Commission Act, 15 U.S.C. Sec. 72.

➤ Securities Act of 1933, 15 U.S.C. Sec. 77k(e); of 1934, 15 U.S.C. Sec. 78i(e), 78r(a).

➤ Fair Credit Billing Act, 15 U.S.C. Sec. 1640(a).

➤ Fair Credit Reporting Act, 15 U.S.C. Sec. 1681(n).

➤ Magnuson-Moss Warranty Act, 15 U.S.C. Sec. 2310(d)(2).

➤ Federal Tort Claims Act, 28 U.S.C. Sec. 2678.

➤ ERISA, 29 U.S.C. Sec. 1132(g).

➤ Labor-Management Reporting & Disclosure Act, 29 U.S.C. Sec. 431(c), 501(b).

➤ Age Discrimination in Employment Act, 29 U.S.C. 626(b).

➤ Fair Housing Act, 42 U.S.C. Sec. 3612(c).

➤ Safe Drinking Water Act, 42 U.S.C. Sec. 300j-8(d).

➤ Clean Air Act, 42 U.S.C. Sec. 1857h-2.

➤ Title VII of the Civil Rights Act of 1964, 42 U.S.C. Sec. 2000e-5(k).

The award of fees in civil rights and civil liberties actions is covered by the Civil Rights Attorneys' Fee Awards Act, 42 U.S.C. Sec. 1988—and an award is virtually automatic to prevailing plaintiffs. The Equal Access to Justice Act, 28 U.S.C. Sec. 2412, provides fee awards to private parties who prevail in civil actions when they sue or are sued by the federal government, in a case in which the government's position was not substantially justified.

[¶503] DEFINITION OF PREVAILING PARTIES

The simplest case of a prevailing party is a plaintiff who is successful on every count of the complaint. However, it is not necessary to meet this test to qualify as a "prevailing party." To prevail, one must win concrete substantive rights, not merely succeed on procedural issues such as the reversal of a directed verdict (*Hanrahan v. Hampton,* 446 U.S. 754 (1980)). A party who achieves objectives through a consent decree has prevailed (*Maher v. Gagne,* 100 S.Ct. 2560 (1980)). In Title VII cases, time spent in administrative and state court proceedings is compensable, under *New York Gaslight Club, Inc. v. Carey,* 447 U.S. 54 (1980). Appellate attorneys' fees are compensable (*Perkins v. Standard Oil Co., of California,* 399 U.S. 222 (1970)).

Under some circumstances, a prevailing *defendant* will be entitled to attorneys' fees. However, it is unlikely that the defendant will be awarded fees unless the plaintiff's action was frivolous or groundless (*Christiansburg Garment Co. v. EEOC,* 434 U.S. 412 (1978)); those who think themselves aggrieved must be encouraged to use the legal process, not penalized—unless they are using the process for harassment rather than in a legitimate quest for a solution to a dispute.

[¶504] COMPUTATION OF FEES

The usual method of setting attorneys' fees recoverable under such statutes is the "lodestar method." The "lodestar," or guiding factor, is the number of hours the attorney spent on the matter (or the number of hours that reasonably should have been spent if the attorney took too leisurely an approach) multiplied by a reasonable billing rate, and adjusted for "quality factors." That is, an attorney who sacrifices many opportunities in order to strive to make new law is entitled, when he or she succeeds, to a larger fee than an attorney who carries out routine litigation that is only part of a busy practice.

Johnson v. Georgia Highway Express, Inc., 488 F.2d 714 (5th Cir. 1974), a Title VII case, outlines 12 factors determining the size of a fee award:

➤ Time and labor involved.

➤ Novelty and difficulty of questions presented.

➤ The skill needed to perform the legal services properly.

➤ The degree to which other legal work was precluded.

➤ The attorneys' customary fee.

➤ Whether the agreement with the client calls for a fixed or contingent fee.

➤ Time limitations on the case.

➤ The amount involved in the case, and the results obtained.

➤ The attorneys' experience, reputation, and ability.

➤ The undesirability of the case—if the attorney had to take on the entire local power structure, or associate with undesirable clients, the award should be higher.

➤ The nature and length of the attorneys' professional relationship with the client.

➤ The awards granted in other similar cases.

However, novel fee arrangements are slow to take root in U.S. Bankruptcy cases. While lawyers in other areas are agreeing to alternatives such as contingency fees, fixed fees, fee caps and task-based billing, none of this gets applied in the bankruptcy area. The reason seems to be a combination of tradition and lawyers' self-interest. The U.S. Bankruptcy Code and accumulated case law point toward hours worked as the standard for payment of legal fees, going so far as to establish a "lodestar" calculated by multiplying hourly rates by hours worked. The court, which must approve all legal fees, reviews the lodestar to determine if fees meet the statutory requirement that they be "reasonable, necessary and beneficial to the estate." Judges can lower fees if they choose. And if the estate ultimately has adequate funds, and lawyers are paid, the law permits judges to enhance fees. Some attorneys refer to this as a reverse contingency fee. Once the attorney has succeeded, he or she asks for more.[9]

[¶505] DEDUCTIBILITY OF LEGAL FEES

As a general rule, legal fees are deductible if they are ordinary and necessary business expenses (IRC §162) but not if incurred in connection with the acquisition of a capital asset such as goodwill. In the case of individuals, a deduction is also allowed for those legal expenses paid or incurred for the production, collection, maintenance, or conservation of income, as well as for the management, conservation, or maintenance of property held for the production of income. Also, deductions made in connection with the determination, collection, or refund of any tax (nonbusiness expenses) are permitted (IRC §212). Expenses incurred in defending or perfecting title to property are capital expenditures (Reg. §1.263(a)-2(c)). Thus, expenses that are incident to ownership are deductible while those designed to acquire, defend, or perfect ownership are nondeductible.

[¶506] DEDUCTIBILITY OF SPECIFIC TYPES OF LEGAL FEES

Certain specific legal fees may be deductible, as outlined in the paragraphs below:

➤ Payments for the resolution of National Labor Relations Board problems are considered ordinary and necessary business expenses. Accordingly, legal and accounting fees for this purpose are deductible.

➤ Bankruptcy claims, as ordinary and necessary business expenses, are deductible.

➤ Except to the extent that legal services relate to the imposition of a fine or penalty under federal antitrust legislation, expenses involved in the defense of federal or state antitrust actions are generally deductible.

➤ To the extent that a corporation employs an attorney for day-to-day consultation, the cost of his advice is an ordinary and necessary expense of doing business—even if the services performed relate to the acquisition of capital assets. As long as an employer-employee relationship exists, the salary is deductible.

➤ Legal fees incurred for tax planning in the overall estate plan are deductible under §212(3) (see *Merians*, 60 TC 187, 1973, *acq.* CB 1973-2, 2). The costs of review of estate plans submitted by another law firm are fully deductible (*Nancy R. Bagley*, 8 TC 130, 1947). To the extent that legal fees are directly connected with the management and conservation of the taxpayer's income-producing properties, a portion of the attorneys' fees incurred for preparation of a will is deductible under IRC §212(2),(3).

➤ Expenses involved in opposing a suspension of a professional license or disbarment from practicing in a profession may be deductible (compare *Buder*, TC Memo 1963—73; *Tellier*, 383 US 687, 1966).

➤ If a taxpayer's trade or business is directly affected or involved, the legal expenses of defending a libel or slander action may be deductible. The key question in this area is whether the claim arose out of the taxpayer's business activity or his personal life. If the claim's nature and origin is personal rather than business, the expense is nondeductible (see *McDonald*, CA-2, 8/8/78, *rev'g* TC Memo 1977-202; *Lloyd*, CA-7, 55 F.2d 842, 1932).

➤ When a taxpayer appears before specific legislative bodies or committees in connection with specific legislation in which the taxpayer has a direct interest, §162(e) of the Internal Revenue Code authorizes deductibility of his expenses. The same applies if an attorney appears on behalf of the taxpayer (*Johnson*, TC Memo 1962-299).

➤ Costs of prosecution of patent infringement suits are deductible, as are attorneys' fees needed to perfect a patent application (see Reg. §1.174-2). Expenses allocated to defend a patent title are not deductible.

➤ If the taxpayer expends money in order to obtain a tax ruling, it's deductible under IRC §212.

➤ Under certain circumstances, legal fees incurred in the defense of a criminal charge may be deductible. The expense is deductible only if the claim against the taxpayer arises in connection with his business or a profit-seeking activity. Legal fees are not deductible as a business expense merely because a failure to incur the expense might result in the taxpayer losing his trade or business (*Messina*, Ct. Cl., 6/20/73). Similarly, the effect that the litigation may have on the taxpayer's income-producing property is not determinative. If the legal fees are otherwise deductible as a business expense, the outcome of the criminal suit will not affect the taxpayer's deduction. In *Tellier* (383 US 687, 1966), the Supreme Court held that it does not violate public policy to permit a taxpayer to deduct the expense of an unsuccessful defense to a criminal charge when the illegal activity arose in connection with the taxpayer's business.

➤ If a spouse's divorce claim stems entirely from the marital relationship and not from any income-producing activity, expenses of another taxpayer to resist the claim may not be deemed "business" expenses and therefore are not deductible. However, fees incurred to *collect* alimony are gain-seeking expenses and hence deductible. The portion of fees identified as stemming from tax advice is deductible, but only if paid by the spouse receiving the advice—not if paid by the other spouse.

— ENDNOTES —

1. U.S. v. Monsanto, 491 U.S. 600 (6/22/89) and Caplin and Drysdale v. U.S., 491 U.S. 617 (6/22/89).

2. U.S. v. Goldberger & Dubin P.C., 935 F.2d 501 (2d Cir. 6/7/91).

3. New York County Lawyers' Association ethics opinion #690. See *N.Y.L.J.* 2/3/92 p. 4.

4. In re Cooperman, 187 A.D.2d 56, 591 N.Y.S.2d 855 (A.D.1/15/93).

5. Grant v. Kaufman, 922 F.2d 742 (11th Cir. 1/2/91).

6. Independent Ass'n of Flight Attendants v. Zipes, 491 U.S. 754 (6/22/89).

7. Healey v. Chelsea Resources Ltd., 947 F.2d 611 (2d Cir. 10/18/91).

8. Key Tronic Corp. v. U.S. et al. No. 93-376 (Sup.Ct. 6/6/94). Attorneys' fees are response costs: Chesapeake & Potomac Tel. Co. of Virginia v. Peck Iron & Metal Co., 61 LW 2473 (E.D.Va. 2/3/93); Hastings Building Products Inc. v. National Aluminum Corp., 815 F.Supp. 228 (W.D. Mich. 3/4/93). Fees are not response costs: Stanton Road Associates v. Lohrey Enterprises, 984 F.2d 1015 (9th Cir. 1/28/93). Litigation/non-litigation distinction: FMC Corp. v. Aero Industries Inc., 62 LW 2079 (10th Cir. 7/9/93).

9. News item, "Lawyers and Clients: Novel Fee Arrangements Are Slow to Take Root In U.S. Bankruptcy Cases," *Wall St.J.* 7/12/94 p. B8.

— FOR FURTHER REFERENCE —

Bocchieri, Breton August, "Obtaining Attorney Fees in Intellectual Property Cases," 32 *Idea* 211 (Spring '93).

Brickman, Lester, "Setting the Fee When the Client Discharges a Contingent Fee Attorney," 41 *Emory L.J.* 367 (Spring '92).

Brickman, Lester and Jonathan Klein, "The Use of Advance Fee Attorney Retainer Agreements in Bankruptcy," 43 *South Carolina L. Rev.* 1037 (Summer '92).

Dooher, Patrick G., "Recovering Attorneys' Fees and Other Costs Incurred in Tax Controversies: Recent Developments," 33 *Tax Management Memorandum* 197 (June 29, '92).

Duffey, William S. Jr. and Phyllis B. Sumner, "Attorneys' Fees in Business Disputes: Who Really Bears the Burden?" 29 *Ga.State Bar J.* 216 (May '93).

Edwards, Allyson L., "Attorneys and Real Estate Commissions," 16 *J. of the Legal Profession* 283 (Annual 1991).

Freeling, Kenneth A., "Recovery of Attorneys' Fees in CERCLA Private-Party Cost Recovery Actions," 25 *Env. Law Reporter* 10477 (August '93).

Haig, Robert L. and Steven P. Caley, "What's a Fair Bill for Winning a Big Case?" 16 *Trial Diplomacy J.* 143 (July-August '93).

Knopf, Christopher D., "Breaking New Ground: Recovery of Transaction Costs in Private CERCLA Cost-Recovery Actions," 28 *Willamette L. Rev.* 495 (Summer '92).

Kunstler, William M. and James Holzhauer, "The Unquiet Death of Contingency Fees," 13 *California Lawyer* 31 (July '93).

Lowery, Daniel L., "Prevailing Party Status for Civil Rights Plaintiffs," 61 *U. of Cincinnati L. Rev.* 1441 (Spring '93).

Mezey, Susan Gluck and Susan M. Olson, "Fee Shifting and Public Policy," 77 *Judicature* 13 (July-August '93).

Morrison, Gregory S., "Fee-Setting Alternatives," 46 *Washington State Bar News* 46 (May '92).

Raby, William L., "Can Personal Injury Lawyers Pay the Expenses of Litigation?" 59 *Tax Notes* 1659 (June 21, '93).

Silver, Charles, "Updating the Lodestar: Toward a New Fee Award Procedure," 70 *Texas L. Rev.* 865 (March '92).

Smith, Bradley L., "Three Attorney Fee-Shifting Rules and Contingency Fees: Their Impact on Settlement Incentives," 90 *Michigan L. Rev.* 2154 (June '92).

ATTORNEYS' RULES OF PROFESSIONAL CONDUCT

[¶601] An attorney is responsible for more than just advising clients on how to handle business and personal affairs. The lawyer's conduct must also conform to the legal ethics of the profession vis-a-vis present clients, former clients, potential clients, and the judicial system itself.

After years of study and debate, the American Bar Association adopted the *Model Rules of Professional Conduct,* replacing the former *Model Code of Professional Responsibility.* This Chapter excerpts a number of the new Rules of Conduct which deal with areas of particular concern and conflict for attorneys.

Attorneys should be aware that since 1983, about half the states have adopted their own codes of conduct for attorneys, based on—but in some cases diverging sharply from—the Model Rules.

In June, 1994, the Supreme Court ruled in a Florida case which challenged a state rule forbidding attorneys who are also CPAs or certified financial planners (CFPs) to identify themselves as such on their letterheads, business cards, and in advertisements. It ruled that the plaintiff's use of the CPA or CFP designation qualifies as "commercial speech." Thus the state may ban such speech *only* if it is false, deceptive, or misleading.[1]

[¶601.1] Sanctions Under FRCP 11

A real constraint on attorneys practicing in federal court comes from courts' willingness (indeed, eagerness) to impose sanctions under Federal Rules of Civil Procedure 11 for the filing of frivolous, inaccurate, or other improper motions and other paperwork. Even the filing of a factually and legally meritorious pleading or motion can lead to sanctions if the attorney's purpose was improper (for instance, serving as a delaying tactic).[2] A District Court has inherent power to impose sanctions on other types of bad-faith conduct other than signing pleadings, such as attempts to harass an opponent into submission, or fraudulent attempts to deprive a court of jurisdiction.[3]

Indeed, lawyers (and clients) can be sanctioned by a federal judge even if it later proves true that the judge lacked subject-matter jurisdiction over the case.[4] However, the Second Circuit has held that the decision to impose sanctions belongs to the court and the parties to the litigation; non-parties generally lack standing to demand sanctions, even if they charge that their reputations were damaged by the inclusion of false matter in a pleading.[5]

Sanctions can be imposed only if the document in question (e.g., an allegedly frivolous motion to intervene) was actually filed in federal court; sanctions are unavailable if the document was merely alluded to orally.[6]

The lawyer must place an actual manual signature on a paper to justify sanctions based on improper signing: a typed signature is not sufficient.[7] However, substitute counsel escaped sanctions in *Bakker v. Grutman.*[8] The only motions she signed were motions to delay discovery-papers necessary for her to determine if the suit was justified. Because she did not sign any papers lacking factual and legal support, she was not subject to sanctions. Indeed, even voluntary dismissal of an improper or frivolous action will not rule out the imposition of sanctions, although the irked judge is not permitted to award attorneys' fees incurred on the appeal.[9] But the Fourth Circuit said Rule 11 does not mandate withdrawal of a paper that subsequently proves to have been groundless.[10] Nevertheless, the attorney has a duty to make sure that later filings are supported and not groundless. This case also finds it improper for an attorney knowingly to make time-barred claims, then wait until the affirmative defense is stated before withdrawing the claims.

Even a single frivolous claim in an otherwise meritorious pleading can give rise to sanctions.[11] Although the Rule 11 sanctions are federal, the Sixth Circuit takes the position that an attorney has a continuing duty to review (and, if necessary, modify or even withdraw) complaints including a baseless complaint filed in state court, then removed to federal court. Therefore, sanctions were ordered.[12] Sanctions are appropriate where an attorney fails to mention cases directly on point that contradict the client's position; the attorney is not permitted to relax in the assumption that the opposing counsel will find and cite the problematic cases.[13]

But the appropriate remedy is contempt of court, not sanctions, where the attorney deliberately engages in conduct leading to a mistrial; the Illinois Court of Appeals took the position that giving the eventual winner in the case a cause of action against the loser merely triggers off another round of litigation.[14] An attorney who warned the client-affiant to consider statements carefully cannot be sanctioned for preparing an affidavit that included statements that had not previously been discussed with the client; the lawyer did not know that the statements were false.[15] Nor is an attorney subject to sanctions for introducing a study that the expert witness believed supported the client's position without disclosing that the authors of the study did not approve of the particular use of their research by the expert witness.[16]

In 1989, the Supreme Court resolved another contentious sanction issue: whether the sanction is imposed on the law firm on whose behalf the motion or pleading is signed, or only on the attorney actually signing the document. To the discomfiture and anxiety of many attorneys, the Supreme Court held[17] that the sanction falls on the attorney as an individual. The court imposing the sanctions has discretion to order that the attorney pay them personally, without insurance coverage or indemnification, on the theory that the Rule was enacted to deter attorney misconduct, and that the deterrent effect will be lacking if the attorney does not suffer personal financial injury as a result of a violation.[18]

Clients are seldom sanctioned, unless their conduct constitutes actual bad faith; attorneys can be sanctioned if their conduct fails to satisfy a test of objective reasonableness.[19] If the sanctions are levied against the attorney only, the federal court cannot hear an appeal brought in the name of the client only, because the lawyer is the real party in interest.[20] Note, however, that in a later case[21] the Ninth Circuit applied the same objective standard of reasonable factual inquiry to clients as to attorneys, whether or not the client has actual knowledge of wrongful conduct.

Sanctions are not limited to the trial court level: *Mays v. Chicago Sun-Times*[22] imposed a $1,000 sanction for untrue assertions of fact made in a Court of Appeals brief. Much larger sanctions have been imposed: $36,000 in the case of *Ortho Pharmaceutical Corp. v. Sona Distributors,* for instance,[23] which permits an immediate appeal of a pre-trial sanction, without the need to wait for the determination of the merits of the underlying case. In setting the amount of the sanction, the District Court is directed to consider both the attorney's ability to pay and mitigating factors (such as discipline applied by the organized bar, or unfavorable press attention attracted by the maladroit attorney).[24] Furthermore, the opposing party has a duty to mitigate its damages attributable to frivolous motions (for instance, by moving to dismiss); failure to do so will lead to denial of even a meritorious motion for sanctions.[25]

The Eleventh Circuit upheld sanctions in excess of $1 million against both plaintiff and the plaintiff's public interest law firm, finding that they should have known their claim of victimization as part of South American political intrigue was baseless. Therefore, they either should have refrained from bringing the suit or should have withdrawn it as the lack of justification became clear. The court did not believe that the firm's public interest nature insulated it from sanctions.[26]

Even larger sanctions have been imposed for discovery abuse in asbestos litigation. The corporate defendant was ordered to pay $2.36 million to the plaintiffs and $160,000 to their attorney. One defense law firm was sanctioned $50,000, another $250,000.[27]

In 1992, a New York law firm was ordered to pay a contempt fine of $4 million for holding back files required by the trustee of a bankrupt investment firm that was implicated in fraud on investors.[28]

The order imposing sanctions does not become final and appealable until the amount of the sanction has been set. If the government is entitled to recover attorneys' fees from a defendant whose dilatory and sanctionable tactics prolonged the litigation, market rates (not Equal Access to Justice Act rates) set the attorneys' fee award.[29] The standard of review for the District Court's order of sanctions is a deferential one: the reviewing court determines whether or not there has been an abuse of discretion, and does not undertake de novo review of the matter.

[¶602]   CLIENT-LAWYER RELATIONSHIP

Rule 1.1—Competence

A lawyer shall provide competent representation to a client. Competent representation requires the legal knowledge, skill, thoroughness, and preparation reasonably necessary for the representation.

Rule 1.2—Scope of Representation

(a) A lawyer shall abide by a client's decisions concerning the objectives of representation subject to paragraphs (c), (d), and (e) and shall consult with the client as to the means by which they are to be pursued. A lawyer shall abide by a client's decision whether to accept an offer of settlement of a matter. In a criminal case, the lawyer shall abide by the client's decision, after consultation with the lawyer, as to a plea to be entered, whether to waive jury trial and whether the client will testify.

(b) A lawyer's representation of a client, including representation by appointment, does not constitute an endorsement of the client's political, economic, social, or moral views or activities.

(c) A lawyer may limit the objectives of the representation if the client consents after consultation.

(d) A lawyer shall not counsel a client to engage, or assist a client, in conduct that the lawyer knows is criminal or fraudulent, but a lawyer may discuss the legal consequences of any proposed course with a client and may counsel or assist a client to make a good faith effort to determine the validity, scope, meaning, or application of the law.

When a lawyer knows that a client expects assistance not permitted by the Rules of Professional Conduct or other law, the lawyer shall consult with the client regarding the relevant limitations on the lawyer's conduct.

Rule 1.3—Diligence

A lawyer shall act with reasonable diligence and promptness in representing a client.

Rule 1.4—Communication

(a) A lawyer shall keep a client reasonably informed about the status of a matter and promptly comply with reasonable requests for information.

(b) A lawyer shall explain a matter to the extent reasonably necessary to permit the client to make informed decisions regarding the representation.

Rule 1.5—Fees

(a) A lawyer's fee shall be reasonable.

The factors to be considered in determining the reasonableness of a fee include the following:

(1) The time and labor required, the novelty and difficulty of the questions involved, and the skills requisite to perform the legal service properly;

(2) the likelihood, if apparent to the client, that the acceptance of the particular employment will preclude other employment by the lawyer;

(3) the fee customarily charged in the locality for similar legal services;

(4) The amount involved and the results obtained;

(5) the time limitations imposed by the client or by circumstances;

(6) the nature and length of the professional relationship with the client;

(7) the experience, reputation, and ability of the lawyer or lawyers performing the services; and

(8) whether the fee is fixed or contingent.

(b) When the lawyer has not regularly represented the client, the basis or rate of the fee shall be communicated to the client, preferably in writing, before or within a reasonable time after commencing the representation.

(c) A fee may be contingent on the outcome of the matter for which the service is rendered, except in a matter in which a contingent fee is prohibited by paragraph (d) or other law. A contingent fee agreement shall be in writing and shall state the method by which the fee is to be determined: the percentage or percentages that shall accrue to the lawyer in the event of settlement, trial or appeal, litigation; other expenses to be deducted from the recovery, and whether such expenses are to be deducted before or after the contingent fee is calculated. Upon conclusion of a contingent fee matter, the lawyer shall provide the client with a written statement about the outcome of the matter and, if there is a recovery, showing the remittance to the client and the method of its determination.

(d) A lawyer shall not enter into an arrangement for, charge, or collect:

(1) any fee in a domestic relations matter, the payment or amount of which is contingent upon the securing of a divorce or upon the amount of alimony or support, or property settlement in lieu thereof; or

(2) a contingent fee for representing a defendant in a criminal case.

(e) A division of a fee between lawyers who are not in the same firm may be made only if:

(1) the division is in proportion to the services performed by each lawyer or, by written agreement with the client, each lawyer assumes joint responsibility for the representation;

(2) the client is advised of and does not object to the participation of all the lawyers involved; and

(3) the total fee is reasonable.

Rule 1.6—Confidentiality of Information

(a) A lawyer shall not reveal information relating to representation of a client unless the client consents after consultation, except for disclosures that are impliedly authorized in order to carry out the representation, and except as stated in paragraph (b).

(b) A lawyer may reveal such information to the extent the lawyer reasonably believes necessary:

(1) to prevent the client from committing a criminal act that the lawyer believes is likely to result in imminent death or substantial bodily harm; or

(2) to establish a claim or defense on behalf of the lawyer in a controversy between the lawyer and the client, to establish a defense to a criminal charge or civil claim against the lawyer based upon conduct in which the client was involved, or to respond to allegations in any proceeding concerning the lawyer's representation of the client.

Rule 1.7—Conflict of Interest: General Rule

(a) A lawyer shall not represent a client if the representation of that client will be directly adverse to another client; unless:

(1) the lawyer reasonably believes the representation will not adversely affect the relationship with the other client; and

(2) each client consents after consultation.

(b) A lawyer shall not represent a client if the representation of that client may be materially limited by the lawyer's responsibilities to another client or to a third person, or by the lawyer's own interests, unless:

(1) the lawyer reasonably believes the representation will not be adversely affected; and

(2) the client consents after consultation.

When representation of multiple clients in a single matter is undertaken, the consultation shall include explanation of the implications of the common representation and the advantages and risks involved.

Rule 1.8—Conflict of Interest: Prohibited Transactions

(a) A lawyer shall not enter into a business transaction with a client or knowingly acquire an ownership, possessory, security, or other pecuniary interest adverse to a client unless:

(1) the transaction and terms on which the lawyer acquires the interest are fair and reasonable to the client and are fully disclosed and transmitted in writing to the client in a manner which can be reasonably understood by the client;

(2) the client is given a reasonable opportunity to seek the advice of independent counsel in the transaction; and

(3) the client consents in writing.

(b) A lawyer shall not use information relating to representation of a client to the disadvantage of the client unless the client consents after consultation, except as permitted or required by Rule 1.6 or Rule 3.3.

(c) A lawyer shall not prepare an instrument giving the lawyer or a person related to the lawyer as parent, child, sibling, or spouse any substantial gift from a client, including a testamentary gift, except where the client is related to the donee.

(d) Prior to the conclusion of representation of a client, a lawyer shall not make or negotiate an agreement giving the lawyer literary or media rights to a portrayal or account based in substantial part on information relating to the representation.

(e) A lawyer shall not provide financial assistance to a client in connection with pending or contemplated litigation, except that:

(1) a lawyer may advance court costs and expenses of litigation, the repayment of which may be contingent on the outcome of the matter; and

(2) a lawyer representing an indigent client may pay court costs and expenses of litigation on behalf of the client.

(f) A lawyer shall not accept compensation for representing a client from one other than the client unless:

(1) the client consents after consultation;

(2) there is no interference with the lawyer's independence of professional judgment or with the client-lawyer relationship; and

(3) information relating to representation of a client is protected as required by Rule 1.6.

(g) A lawyer who represents two or more clients shall not participate in making an aggregate settlement of the claims of or against the clients, or in a criminal case an aggregated agreement as to guilty or *nolo contendere* pleas, unless each client consents after consultation, including disclosure of the existence and nature of all the claims or pleas involved and of the participation of each person in the settlement.

(h) A lawyer shall not make an agreement prospectively limiting the lawyer's liability to a client for malpractice unless permitted by law and the client is independently represented in making the agreement. Furthermore, a lawyer shall not settle a claim for such liability with an unrepresented client or former client without first advising that person in writing that independent representation is appropriate in such connection.

(i) A lawyer related to another lawyer as parent, child, sibling, or spouse shall not represent a client in a representation directly adverse to a person who the lawyer knows is represented by the family member except upon consent by the client after consultation regarding the relationship.

(j) A lawyer shall not acquire a proprietary interest in the cause of action or subject matter of litigation the lawyer is conducting for a client, except that the lawyer may:

(1) acquire a lien granted by law to secure the lawyer's fee or expenses; and

(2) contract with a client for a reasonable contingent fee in a civil case.

Rule 1.9—Conflict of Interest: Former Client

A lawyer who has formerly represented a client in a matter shall not thereafter:

(a) represent another person in the same or a substantially related matter in which the person's interests are materially adverse to the interests of the former client unless the former client consents after consultation; or

(b) use information relating to the representation to the disadvantage of the former client except as Rule 1.6 or Rule 3.3 would permit with respect to a client or when the information has become generally known.

Rule 1.13—Organization as Client

(a) A lawyer employed or retained by an organization represents the organization acting through its duly authorized constituents.

(b) If a lawyer for an organization knows that an officer, employee, or other person associated with the organization is engaged in action, intends to act or refuses to act in a matter related to the representation that is a violation of a legal obligation to the organization, or a violation of law which reasonably might be imputed to the organization, and is likely to result in substantial injury to the organization, the lawyer shall proceed as is reasonably necessary in the best interest of the organization. In determining how to proceed, the lawyer shall give due consideration to the seriousness of the violation and its consequences, the scope and nature of the lawyer's representation, the responsibility in the organization and the apparent motivation of the person involved, the policies of the organization concerning such matters, and any other relevant considerations. Any measures taken shall be designed to minimize disruption of the organization and the risk of revealing information relating to the representation to persons outside the organization. Such measures may include among others:

(1) asking reconsideration of the matter;

(2) advising that a separate legal opinion on the matter be sought for presentation to appropriate authority in the organization; and

(3) referring the matter to higher authority in the organization, including, if warranted by the seriousness of the matter, referral to the highest authority that can act on behalf of the organization as determined by applicable law.

(c) If, despite the lawyer's efforts in accordance with paragraph (b), the highest authority that can act on behalf of the organization insists upon action, or a refusal to act, that is clearly a violation of law and is likely to result in substantial injury to the organization, the lawyer may resign in accordance with Rule 1.16.

(d) In dealing with an organization's directors, officers, employees, members, shareholders, or other constituents, a lawyer shall explain the identity of the client when it is apparent that the organization's interests are adverse to those of the constituents with whom the lawyer is dealing.

(e) A lawyer representing an organization may also represent any of its directors, officers, employees, members, shareholders, or other constituents, subject to the provisions of Rule 1.7. If the organization's consent to the dual representation is required by Rule 1.7, the consent shall be given by an appropriate official of the organization other than the individual who is to be represented, or by the shareholders.

Rule 1.16—Declining or Terminating Representation

(a) Except as stated in paragraph (c), a lawyer shall not represent a client or, where representation has commenced, shall withdraw from the representation of a client if:

(1) the representation will result in violation of the rules of professional conduct or other law;

(2) the lawyer's physical or mental condition materially impairs the lawyer's ability to represent the client; or

(3) the lawyer is discharged.

(b) Except as stated in paragraph (c), a lawyer may withdraw from representing a client if withdrawal can be accomplished without material adverse effect on the interests of the client, or if:

(1) the client persists in a course of action involving the lawyer's services that the lawyer reasonably believes is criminal or fraudulent;

(2) the client has used the lawyer's services to perpetrate a crime or fraud;

(3) a client insists upon pursuing an objective that the lawyer considers repugnant or imprudent;

(4) the client fails substantially to fulfill an obligation to the lawyer regarding the lawyer's services and has been given reasonable warning that the lawyer will withdraw unless the obligation is fulfilled;

(5) the representation will result in an unreasonable financial burden on the lawyer or has been rendered unreasonably difficult by the client; or

(6) other good cause for withdrawal exists.

(c) When ordered to do so by a tribunal, a lawyer shall continue representation notwithstanding good cause for terminating the representation.

(d) Upon termination of representation, a lawyer shall take steps to the extent reasonably practicable to protect a client's interests, such as giving reasonable notice to the client, allowing time for employment of other counsel, surrendering papers and property to which the client is entitled, and refunding any advance payment of fee that has not been earned. The lawyer may retain papers relating to the client to the extent permitted by other law.

[¶603] COUNSELOR

Rule 2.1—Advisor

In representing a client, a lawyer shall exercise independent professional judgment and render candid advice. In rendering advice, a lawyer may refer not only to law but to other considerations such as moral, economic, social, and political factors, that may be relevant to the client's situation.

Rule 2.3—Evaluation for Use by Third Persons

(a) A lawyer may undertake an evaluation of a matter affecting a client for the use of someone other than the client if:

(1) the lawyer reasonably believes that making the evaluation is compatible with other aspects of the lawyer's relationship with the client; and

(2) the client consents after consultation.

(b) Except as disclosure is required in connection with a report of an evaluation, information relating to the evaluation is otherwise protected by Rule 1.6.

[¶604] ADVOCATE

Rule 3.1—Meritorious Claims and Contentions

A lawyer shall not bring or defend a proceeding, or assert or controvert an issue therein, unless there is a basis for doing so that is not frivolous, which includes good faith argument for an extension, modification, or reversal of existing law. A lawyer for the defendant in a criminal proceeding, or the respondent in a proceeding that could result in incarceration, may nevertheless so defend the proceeding as to require that every element of the case be established.

Rule 3.3—Candor Toward the Tribunal

(a) A lawyer shall not knowingly:

    (1) make a false statement of material fact or law to a tribunal;

    (2) fail to disclose a material fact to a tribunal when disclosure is necessary to avoid assisting a criminal or fraudulent act by the client;

    (3) fail to disclose to the tribunal legal authority in the controlling jurisdiction known to the lawyer to be directly adverse to the position of the client and not disclosed by opposing counsel; or

    (4) offer evidence that the lawyer knows to be false. If a lawyer has offered material evidence and comes to know of its falsity, the lawyer shall take reasonable remedial measures.

(b) The duties stated in paragraph (a) continue to the conclusion of the proceeding, and apply even if compliance requires disclosure of information otherwise protected by Rule 1.6.

(c) A lawyer may refuse to offer evidence that the lawyer reasonably believes is false.

(d) In an *ex parte* proceeding, a lawyer shall inform the tribunal of all material facts known to the lawyer which will enable the tribunal to make an informed decision, whether or not the facts are adverse.

Rule 3.7—Lawyer as Witness

(a) A lawyer shall not act as advocate at a trial in which the lawyer is likely to be a necessary witness except where:

    (1) the testimony relates to an uncontested issue;

    (2) the testimony relates to the nature and value of legal services rendered in the case; or

    (3) disqualification of the lawyer would work substantial hardship on the client.

(b) A lawyer may act as advocate in a trial in which another lawyer in the lawyer's firm is likely to be called as a witness unless precluded from doing so by Rule 1.7 or Rule 1.9.

[¶605]   TRANSACTIONS WITH PERSONS OTHER THAN CLIENTS

Rule 4.1—Truthfulness in Statements to Others

In the course of representing a client a lawyer shall not knowingly:

(a) make a false statement of material fact or law to a third person; or

(b) fail to disclose a material fact to a third person when disclosure is necessary to avoid assisting a criminal or fraudulent act by a client, unless disclosure is prohibited by Rule 1.6.

Rule 4.2—Communication with Person Represented by Counsel

In representing a client, a lawyer shall not communicate about the subject of the representation with a party the lawyer knows to be represented by another lawyer in the matter, unless he or she has the consent of the other lawyer or is authorized by law to do so.

Rule 4.3—Dealing with Unrepresented Person

In dealing on behalf of a client with a person who is not represented by counsel, a lawyer shall not state or imply that the lawyer is disinterested. When the lawyer knows or reasonably should know that the unrepresented person misunderstands the lawyer's role in the matter, he or she shall make reasonable efforts to correct the misunderstanding.

[¶606]   LAW FIRMS AND ASSOCIATIONS

Rule 5.1—Responsibilities of a Partner or Supervisory Lawyer

(a) A partner in a law firm shall make reasonable efforts to ensure that the firm has in effect measures giving reasonable assurance that all lawyers in the firm conform to the *Rules of Professional Conduct.*

(b) A lawyer having direct supervisory authority over another lawyer shall make reasonable efforts to ensure that the other lawyer conforms to the *Rules of Professional Conduct.*

(c) A lawyer shall be responsible for another lawyer's violation of the *Rules of Professional Conduct* if:

(1) the lawyer orders or, with knowledge of the specific conduct, ratifies the conduct involved; or

(2) the lawyer is a partner in the law firm in which the other lawyer practices, or has direct supervisory authority over the other lawyer, and knows of the conduct at a time when its consequences can be avoided or mitigated but fails to take reasonable remedial action.

Rule 5.4—Professional Independence of a Lawyer

(a) A lawyer or law firm shall not share legal fees with a nonlawyer, except that:

(1) an agreement by a lawyer with the lawyer's firm, partner, or associate may provide for the payment of money, over a reasonable period of time after the lawyer's death, to the lawyer's estate or to one or more specified persons;

(2) a lawyer who undertakes to complete unfinished legal business of a deceased lawyer may pay to the estate of the deceased lawyer that proportion of the total compensation which fairly represents the services rendered by the deceased lawyer; and

(3) a lawyer or law firm may include nonlawyer employees in a compensation or retirement plan, even though the plan is based in whole or in part on a profit-sharing arrangement.

(b) a lawyer shall not form a partnership with a nonlawyer if any of the activities of the partnership consist of the practice of law.

(c) A lawyer shall not permit a person who recommends, employs, or pays the lawyer to render legal services for another to direct or regulate the lawyer's professional judgment in rendering such legal services.

(d) A lawyer shall not practice with or in the form of a professional corporation or association authorized to practice law for profit, if:

    (1) a nonlawyer owns any interest therein, except that a fiduciary representative of the estate of a lawyer may hold the stock or interest of the lawyer for a reasonable time during administration;

    (2) a nonlawyer is a corporate director or officer thereof; or

    (3) a nonlawyer has the right to direct or control the professional judgment of a lawyer.

A law firm's agreement with a withdrawing partner cannot include an outright, complete ban on competing with the firm; but it is permissible to make the withdrawing partner give back his or her withdrawal benefits under the contract if he or she competes with the firm. The California Supreme Court has upheld such a provision as long as the restriction is reasonable as to amount and geographic scope.[30] An Oregon attorney was suspended from practice for four months for secretly signing firm clients to personal retainers while he was still working for the law firm, instead of disclosing his projected departure to clients and informing them of their options to remain as clients of the firm or become his clients.[31] An arbitration clause in a law firm's employment contract was broad enough to subject an ex-partner's claims for termination compensation to arbitration. The firm's claims against the ex-partner, including a claim of breach of duty by taking clients with him when he left, were also arbitrable.[32] A law firm was not entitled to malpractice coverage under its "claims made" policy because it failed to inform its insurer of a pending FDIC suit against the firm because of newly hired partners' actions at the firm where they used to work.[33]

[¶607]   INFORMATION ABOUT LEGAL SERVICES

Rule 7.1—Communications Concerning a Lawyer's Services

A lawyer shall not make a false or misleading communication about himself or herself or the services provided. A communication is false or misleading if it:

(a) contains a material misrepresentation of fact or law, or omits a fact necessary to make the statement considered as a whole not materially misleading;

(b) is likely to create an unjustified expectation about results the lawyer can achieve, or states or implies that the lawyer can achieve results by means that violate the *Rules of Professional Conduct* or other law; or

(c) compares the lawyer's services with other lawyers' services, unless the comparison can be factually substantiated.

Rule 7.2—Advertising

(a) Subject to the requirements of Rule 7.1, a lawyer may advertise services through public media, such as a telephone directory, legal directory, newspaper or other periodical, outdoor, radio or television, or through written communication not involving solicitation as defined in Rule 7.3.

(b) A copy or recording of an advertisement or written communication shall be kept for two years after its last dissemination along with a record of when and where it was used.

(c) A lawyer shall not give anything of value to a person for recommending the lawyer's services, except that a lawyer may pay the reasonable cost of advertising or written communication permitted by this rule and may pay the usual charges of a not-for-profit lawyer referral service or other legal service organization.

(d) Any communication made pursuant to this rule shall include the name of at least one lawyer responsible for its content.

Rule 7.3—Direct Contact with Prospective Clients

A lawyer may not solicit professional employment from a prospective client with whom the lawyer has no family or prior professional relationship, by mail, in-person or otherwise, when a significant motive for the lawyer's doing so is the lawyer's pecuniary gain. The term "solicit" includes contact in-person, by telephone or telegraph, by letter or other writing, or by other communication directed to a specific recipient, but does not include letters addressed or advertising circulars distributed generally to persons not known to need legal services of the kind provided by the lawyer in a particular matter, but who are so situated that they might in general find such services useful.

Rule 7.4—Communication of Fields of Practice

A lawyer may communicate the fact that he or she does or does not practice in particular fields of law, but shall not state or imply any specialty except as follows:

(a) a lawyer admitted to engage in patent practice before the United States Patent and Trademark Office may use the designation "Patent Attorney" or a substantially similar designation;

(b) a lawyer engaged in Admiralty practice may use the designation "Admiralty," "Proctor in Admiralty," or a substantially similar designation; and

(c) (provisions on designation of specialization of the particular state).

— ENDNOTES —

1. Ibanez v. Florida, #93-639, (Sup.Ct. 6/13/94).

2. Aetna Life Ins. v. Alla Medical Services Inc., 855 F.2d 1470 (9th Cir. 9/2/88).

3. Chambers v. NASCO Inc., #90-256, 111 S. Ct. 2123 (Sup.Ct. 6/6/91).

4. Soules v. Kauaians for Nukolii Campaign Committee, 849 F.2d 1176 (9th Cir. 6/14/88).

5. Willy v. Coastal Corp., #90-1150, 112 S.Ct. 1076 (Sup.Ct. 3/3/92), rehearing denied 112 S.Ct. 2001.

6. New York News Inc. v. Kheel, 972 F.2d 482 (2d Cir. 8/11/92).

7. Giebelhaus v. Spindrift Yachts, 938 F.2d 962 (9th Cir. 7/10/91).

8. 942 F.2d 236 (4th Cir. 7/29/91).

9. Cooter & Gell v. Hartmarx Corp., 110 S.Ct. 2447 (Sup.Ct. 6/11/90).

10. Brubaker v. Richmond, 943 F.2d 1363 (4th Cir. 8/8/91).

11. Cross & Cross Properties Ltd. v. Everett Allied Co., 886 F.2d 497 (2d Cir. 9/21/89); accord Townsend v. Holman Consulting Corp. 881 F.2d 788 (9th Cir. 9/6/90).

12. Herron v. Jupiter Transp. Co., 858 F.2d 332 (6th Cir. 10/3/88).

13. Jorgenson v. Volusia County, 846 F.2d 1350 (11th Cir. 6/14/88).

14. Kilpatrick v. First Church of the Nazarene, 57 LW 2626 (Ill.App. 3/23/89).

15. Resolution Trust Co. v. Bright, 62 LW 2310 (5th Cir. 11/9/93).

16. Coffey v. Healthtrust Inc., 62 LW 2115 (10th Cir. 8/3/93).

17. Pavelic & LeFlore v. Marvel Entertainment Group, #88-791 (493 U.S. 120, 12/5/89). Earlier, Borowski v. DePuy Inc., 876 F.2d 1339 (7th Cir. 6/17/88) held that sanctions caused by an attorney's poor judgment (i.e., drafting a complaint containing clearly unavailable causes of action) fall on the attorney, whereas Callaway v. Marvel Entertainment Group, 854 F.2d 1452 (2d Cir. 8/12/88) states that sanctions are usually imposed at the firm level, both because the firm represents all its clients, and because putting pressure on the firm encourages the firm to avoid (and prevent) abusive litigation.

18. Derechin v. State University of New York, 963 F.2d 513 (2d Cir. 4/28/92).

19. Callaway, supra.

20. DeLuca v. LILCO, 862 F.2d 427 (2d Cir. 12/2/88); Collier v. Marshall, Dennehey, Warner, Coleman & Goggin, 977 F.2d 93 (3d Cir. 10/13/92).

21. Business Guides Inc. v. Chromatic Communications Enterps. Inc., 892 F. 2d 802 (9th Cir. 12/21/89), aff'd #89-1500 111 S.Ct. 922, (Sup.Ct. 2/26/91).

22. 856 F.2d 134 (7th Cir. 1/4/89).

23. 847 F.2d 1512 (11th Cir. 6/27/88).

24. Deering v. Union County Board of Freeholders, 57 LW 2181 (3d Cir. 9/14/88).

25. Brooks v. Allison Division of GM, 874 F.2d 489 (7th Cir. 5/18/89).

26. Avirgan v. Hull, 932 F.2d 1572 (11th Cir. 6/18/91).

27. See Gary Taylor, "$3 Million in Discovery Abuse," *Nat.L.J.* 2/4/91, about Heathman v. Owens-Corning Fiberglass Corp., #87-C-1934, Searls v. Owens-Corning Fiberglass Corp., #88-C-0615 (23d Dist., Texas).

28. In re Stockbridge Funding Corp., 153 BR 654 (Bank.-S.D.N.Y. 1992); see *Wall Street Journal* 10/19/92 p. B6.

29. Napier v. 30 or More Unidentified Federal Agents, 855 F.2d 1080 (3d Cir. 8/31/88).

30. Howard v. Babcock, 62 LW 2373 (Cal.Sup. 12/6/93).

31. In re Smith, 315 Ore. 260, 843 P.2d 449 (Ore.Sup. 12/31/92).

32. Nagle v. Nadelhoffer et.al., 62 LW 2078 (Ill.App. 5/5/93).

33. National Union Fire Insurance Co. of Pittsburgh v. Baker & McKenzie, 62 LW 2078 (7th Cir. 6/22/93).

— **FOR FURTHER REFERENCE** —

Aitken, Lee J.W., "'Chinese Walls' and Conflicts of Interest," 18 *Monash U. L. Rev.* 91 (March '93).

Bridge, Elizabeth A., "Professional Responsibility and the First Amendment," 57 *Mo.L. Rev.* 699 (Spring '92).

Brill, Steven, "Toward a Code of 'Business' Ethics for Law Firms," 13 *American Lawyer* 3 (October '91).

Burlin, Johannes P., "Lawyer Certification and Model Rule 7.4: Why We Should Permit Advertising of Specialty Certifications," 5 *Georgetown J. of Legal Ethics* 939 (Spring '92).

Cox, Gail Diane, "Arbitrating What Lawyers Bill," *Nat.L.J.* 4/8/91 p. 1.

Fafan, Kathryn P. and Patricia L. Elwood, "Discovery Sanctions and the New Supreme Court Guidelines," 55 *Texas Bar J.* 804 (September '92).

Feagan, Cynthia B., "Issues of Waiver in Multiple-Party Litigation: The Attorney-Client Privilege and the Work Product Doctrine," 61 *UMKC L. Rev.* 757 (Summer '93).

Fischer, James M., "Why Can't Lawyers Split Fees?" 6 *Georgetown J. of Legal Ethics* 1 (Summer '92).

Foss, S. Sheldon, "The Attorney's Dilemma Under Model Rules 1.2 and 1.6: Clients Who Do Not Return Children in Custody Cases," 17 *J. of the Legal Profession* 231 (Annual '92).

Garwin, Arthur, "Parent Trap: Corporate Mergers and Acquisitions Can Create Conflicts of Interest," 79 *ABA J.* 116 (September '93).

Goding, James B., "Lawyer-Client Confidentiality: What Should Counsel Tell the Court?" 23 *Trial* 59 (August '87).

Jones, Gwyneth, "Nonlawyers in the Discipline Process," 49 *Bench and Bar of Minn.* 11 (July '92).

Jorgenson, Linda Mabus and Pamela K. Sutherland, "Fiduciary Theory Applied to Personal Dealings: Attorney-Client Sexual Conduct," 45 *Ark.L. Rev.* 459 (Summer '92).

McElheny, James W., "Staying Out of Jail: Keeping Your License and Staying Out of Trouble," 79 *ABA J.* 98 (September '93).

Meltzer, Peter E., "Whom Do You Trust? Everything You Never Wanted to Know About Ethics, Conflicts and Privileges in the Bankruptcy Process," 97 *Commercial L.J.* 149 (Summer '92).

Nelson, Ann M., "Fifty Ways to Leave Your Client," 66 *Wisconsin Lawyer* 35 (June '93).

Nies, Helen Wilson, "Rambo Lawyering: The Need for Civility in Civil Litigation," 32 *Idea* 1 (Summer '91).

O'Connell, John M., "Keeping Sex Out of the Attorney-Client Relationship: A Proposed Rule," 92 *Columbia L. Rev.* 887 (May '92).

O'Leary, Kimberly E., "Creating Partnership: Using Feminist Techniques to Enhance the Attorney-Client Relationship," 16 *Legal Studies Forum* 207 (Spring '92).

Owen, Amy, "May a Lawyer Agree with the Client that the Lawyer Must Approve All Settlements?" 12 *Review of Litigation* 665 (Summer '93).

Shoop, Julie Gannon, "To Speak or Not to Speak: Lawyers Test Limits of Their Speech Rights," 29 *Trial* 12 (September '93).

Simon, William H., "The Ethics of Criminal Defense," 29 *Trial* 68 (September '93).

Siegel, David, "Lawyer, Protect Thyself: Recent Trends in Professional Liabilities and Duties of Attorneys," 27 *Beverly Hills Bar Ass'n J.* 67 (Spring '93).

Slovut, Brian J., "Eliminating Conflict at the Termination of the Attorney-Client Relationship: A Proposed Standard Governing Property Rights in the Client's File," 76 *Minnesota L. Rev.* 1483 (June '92).

Steinberg, Marc I., "Securities Malpractice Exposure: Client Representation Certain Problematic Solutions," 20 *Securities Regulation L.J.* 199 (Summer '92).

Swanson, Richard P., "Guilt by Partnership: How Malpractice Coverage Vanishes," 39 *Practicing Lawyer* 15 (July '93).

BANKRUPTCY

[¶701] The Bankruptcy Reform Act of 1978 became effective October 1, 1979. Although the Bankruptcy Act of 1898 was repealed, the provisions of the new Code do not affect cases commenced under that Act. Those cases will proceed, with respect to both substantive and procedural matters, in the same fashion as though the new Code were not in effect.

A complete revision of the Rules of Bankruptcy and Official Forms became effective in 1983, with amendments in 1984, 1986, and 1990. In 1994, the Senate approved a further comprehensive overhaul of the nation's bankruptcy law, the first major overhaul in 11 years. The new rules, if they become law, will make it easier for individuals to repay their debts on installments plans and harder for big corporate debtors to avoid their creditors. The current limit for Chapter 13 cases (Adjustment of Debts of an Individual with Regular Income) is $100,000 for fixed unsecured debts, and fixed secured debts of less than $350,000. The alternative is Chapter 7, which forces an individual to liquidate assets immediately. The proposed bill allows individuals with up to $1 million in debts to file for bankruptcy under Chapter 13. The bill also sets a much easier legal test for prosecutors to meet in court in trying to show that various maneuvers were fraudulent. At the present time, bankruptcy fraud is punishable with a fine of up to $5,000 and up to five years in prison.[1]

The bill also makes it much harder for individuals to avoid alimony and child support payments by filing for bankruptcy.

The current Code is composed of Chapters 1, 3, 5, 7, 9, 11, 12, and 13. The operative chapters of the Code are Chapter 7, Liquidation; Chapter 9, Adjustments of Debts of a Municipality; Chapter 11, Reorganization; Chapter 12, Adjustment of Debts of a Family Farmer with Regular Annual Income; and Chapter 13, Adjustments of Debts of an Individual with Regular Income. Chapter 1, General Provisions; Chapter 3, Case Administration; and Chapter 5, Creditors, the Debtor, and the Estate, apply no matter which chapter a case is filed under with certain exceptions for Chapter 9, and where certain provisions are applicable only under a particular chapter. Additionally, Chapters 7 and 11 have special sub-chapters relating to the unique problems of stock and commodity brokers and railroad reorganizations.

The bankruptcy courts have been busy, and the District Courts and Courts of Appeals have been busy interpreting the provisions of the Bankruptcy Act and its amendments. In fact, "business" was so good in the bankruptcy courts that P.L. 102-361 (8/26/92) created an additional 25 permanent and 10 temporary bankruptcy judgeships.

Until recently, the Supreme Court seldom decided bankruptcy cases; by 1994, there were at least a handful of bankruptcy cases in each term. An early exception (which perhaps was taken on more as a tax than as a bankruptcy case) permits a state to impose sales and use taxes on bankruptcy liquidation sales.[2]

Another case dealt with the interface between bankruptcy and tax law:[3] a case in which the debtor owed both "trust fund" federal taxes (those for which a business owner can be held personally liable) and non-trust-fund taxes. The reorganization plan called for payment of all federal taxes, in installments allocated first to the trust fund taxes. The effect of the statute was to relieve the business owners of liability more quickly than if the allocation had been done differently, and to subject the IRS to the risk of non-payment if the reorganized company ran out of money before all tax payments had been made. The First Circuit held that the court has the power to order an allocation under its own discretion—even in violation of IRS policy of allocating "involuntary" payments in the manner that is most beneficial to the IRS. The Supreme Court affirmed.

A recent statute, P.L. 100-334 requires companies that have filed Chapter 11 petitions to continue paying retiree benefits provided under life, health, or disability insurance policies. The benefits may be modified during pendency of the petition if representatives of the retirees agree to the modification. If the company and the representatives cannot reach an agreement, the bankruptcy judge has power to order benefit modifications.

However, the Act does not require a debtor to continue making retiree health benefit payments if the terms of the plan in effect at the time of the bankruptcy filing shift responsibility for the payments from the employer to the union.[4]

[¶702]   THE NEW BANKRUPTCY COURTS

The Code created a Bankruptcy Court in each judicial district of the United States. They are courts of record, and are known as the United States Bankruptcy Courts for the districts. Bankruptcy judges serve as adjuncts of the Federal District Court.

The Bankruptcy Court is in continuous session on all business days of the year. For the convenience of all parties, court may be held at any place within the territory served. Each Bankruptcy Court may establish (by local rule or order) a schedule of court sessions which will take place at locations other than the court's headquarters.

With respect to any action, suit, or proceeding, the Code gives judicial power to a single Bankruptcy Judge. He may exercise the power, except as otherwise provided by law, rule, or order of the District Court. The judge may preside alone, and may hold a regular or special session of court at the same time that other sessions are being held by other bankruptcy judges of the same district.

In 1982, the United States Supreme Court, in *Marathon Pipeline Co. v. The Northern Pipeline Company*, 102 S. Ct. 2858, struck down the provisions of the Bankruptcy Code which gave bankruptcy judges the power to consider and rule on issues that weren't directly part of the bankruptcy proceeding. Amendments to the Code in 1984 addressed this situation.

The 1984 Act contains a definition of what a bankruptcy judge can properly do, defined as all cases arising under the Bankruptcy Code and all "core" proceedings. The Act lists a category of cases not to be construed as core proceedings. Non-core cases may not be heard to final judgment by a bankruptcy judge, unless with the consent of all of the parties. In those non-core cases where the parties insist, the District Court shall try the case to judgment. A personal injury or wrongful death tort claim against a pending or future bankrupt estate is to be tried in a Federal District Court with a jury.

[¶703] INVOLUNTARY BANKRUPTCY

The only basis for an involuntary case is the inability of the debtor to meet his debts. An involuntary case may be commenced only under Chapter 7, Liquidation, or Chapter 11, Reorganization. An involuntary petition cannot be filed against a farmer or a non-commercial corporation such as a church, school, or charitable organization or foundation.

Section 303 provides that if there are fewer than 12 holders of claims, excluding any employee or insider and any transferee of a transfer that is voidable, one or more of such holders that hold in the aggregate at least $5,000 of such claims may file an involuntary petition.

If there are 12 or more holders of claims against the debtor that are not contingent as to liability or the subject of a bona fide dispute or an indenture trustee representing such a holder, then three or more entities holding an aggregate of at least $5,000 more than the value of any lien on property securing the creditors' claims may file an involuntary petition.

If the debtor is a partnership, an involuntary petition may be filed by fewer than all of the general partners in such partnership.

The appointment of a custodian not under the Code of any property of the debtor within 120 days before the date of the filing of a petition for relief under the Bankruptcy Code is an irrebuttable presumption that the debtor is unable to pay its debts as they mature, and the Bankruptcy Court shall order relief against the debtor.

Caution: If the Bankruptcy Court dismisses a petition for involuntary bankruptcy other than on consent of all petitioners and the debtor, the Court may grant judgment against the petitioners and in favor of the debtor for costs, reasonable attorney's fee, and any damages caused by the taking of the debtor's property by a trustee. If the petition was filed in bad faith, the Court may grant judgment against the petitioners for any damages caused by such filing, including such items as loss of business during and after the case and punitive damages.

[¶704] VOLUNTARY BANKRUPTCY

The commencement of a voluntary case constitutes an order for relief under the appropriate operative chapter.

The filing of a petition for relief operates as a stay of all proceedings against the debtor whether or not before a governmental tribunal. The automatic stay is one of the fundamental debtor protections provided by the bankruptcy laws. It gives the debtor a breathing spell from his creditors by stopping all collection efforts, all harassment, and all foreclosure actions. The automatic stay also provides creditor protection. Without it, those who acted first would obtain payment of the claims in preference to and to the detriment of other creditors. A creditor can be held in contempt if the stay is violated, and an individual injured by any willful violation of the stay shall recover actual damages including costs and attorneys' fees, and in the appropriate circumstances, punitive damages.

[¶704.1]   Operation of the Automatic Stay

Actions filed during the automatic stay are not absolutely void, but they are voidable, and will be voided except in limited equitable circumstances.[5] The automatic stay under Section 362 of the Bankruptcy Code applies only to the debtor, not guarantors of the debtor's notes.[6] A government CERCLA ("Superfund" environmental) suit to recover response costs at a hazardous waste site is not subject to the automatic stay.[7] A tax sale is not treated as a "transfer of property of the estate" (and therefore a bona fide purchaser at a tax sale does not get a Section 549 lien). A tax sale and tax deed violating the automatic stay are void even if neither the county mandating the sale nor the purchaser knew at the time of sale that a bankruptcy petition had been filed.[8]

The IRS and the bankruptcy trustee can enter into a settlement that resolves a Chapter 11 debtor's tax liability, and the court can approve the settlement (even if the debtor objects to the settlement terms) even though the issue is pending before the Tax Court and even though the automatic stay has been lifted. This follows from the Fourth Circuit's conclusion that the bankruptcy court and Tax Court have concurrent jurisdiction, even after the stay has been lifted.[9]

[¶705]   PROCEDURAL STEPS IN BANKRUPTCY PROCEEDINGS

A voluntary case is commenced by filing a petition conforming substantially to Official Form No. 1 under the particular operative chapter of the Code under which the debtor wishes to proceed—either Chapter 7, 9, 11, 12, or 13. If the petitioner is an individual whose debts are primarily consumer debts and such petitioner is represented by an attorney, that attorney shall file a declaration or affidavit informing the petitioner that he or she may proceed under Chapter 7 or 13 of the Code, and explaining the relief available under each chapter. If the debtor is married, a single case may be commenced by filing with the Bankruptcy Court a single petition by the debtor or spouse.

The petition is filed at the Bankruptcy Court for the judicial district in the United States which is the debtor's domicile, residence, principal place of business, or in which the debtor's principal assets are located for the 180 days immediately preceding commencement of the case, or for a longer portion of such 180-day period than in any other district.

In addition to filing the petition, the debtor must also file a Schedule of Assets and Liabilities, a Schedule of Current Income and Current Expenditures, a

Statement of Financial Affairs, and a Statement of Executory Contracts, prepared as prescribed by Official Forms No. 6 and either No. 7 or No. 8, whichever is appropriate, unless the Court orders otherwise. The debtor in a Chapter 13 individual's debt adjustment case shall file with the Court a Chapter 13 statement conforming to Official Form No. 10 and, if the debtor is engaged in business, a Statement of Financial Affairs prepared as prescribed by Official Form No. 8 with the petition or within 15 days thereafter. An extension of time for the filing of the schedules and statements may be granted only on motion for cause shown and on notice to any committee, trustee, examiner, or other parties that the Court may direct. A voluntary petition will, nevertheless, be accepted by the clerk if accompanied by a list of all the debtor's creditors and their addresses. Many Bankruptcy Courts have adopted a local rule requiring that a separate mailing matrix containing the name and address of the debtor, the attorney of record, and all creditors and parties who must be notified of the proceedings be filed with the petition. In those districts adopting such a rule, the master list or matrix becomes the official mailing list. In a Chapter 9 or Chapter 11 case a debtor shall file with the petition a list containing the names, addresses, and claims of the creditors that hold the 20 largest unsecured claims, excluding insiders, as prescribed by Official Form No. 9. An original and one copy in a Chapter 7 Liquidation and Chapter 13 Adjustment of Debts of an Individual with Regular Income case shall be filed, but additional copies may be required by local rule. In Chapter 9, Adjustment of Debts of a Municipality, and Chapter 11, Reorganization, an original and five copies shall be filed, but additional copies may be required by local rule.

Within 30 days after the date of the filing of a petition under Chapter 7 or on or before the date of the meeting of creditors, whichever is earlier, or within such additional time as the Court, for cause, within such period fixes, the debtor shall file with the clerk a statement of his intention with respect to the retention or surrender of property securing a consumer debt, and if applicable, specifying that such property is claimed as exempt, that the debtor intends to redeem such property, or that the debtor intends to reaffirm debts secured by such property.

Within 45 days after the filing of such a notice of intent, or within such additional time as the Court, for cause, within such 45-day period fixes, the debtor shall perform his intention with respect to such property.

Within a reasonable time after the order for relief, the Court must call a meeting of creditors. Usually, the interim trustee presides at the meeting of the creditors—the Bankruptcy Judge is not permitted to do so. The debtor cannot be compelled to testify unless he receives use immunity against criminal prosecution. However, a debtor who is given immunity and still refuses to testify will be denied a discharge. The meeting operates like a deposition. Electronic sound-recording equipment is used by the clerk of the Bankruptcy Court to record the meeting.

Conversion of a bankruptcy case from Chapter 11 to Chapter 7 does not constitute a "filing of petition" that gives rise to a second automatic stay.[10] But as long as the filing is done in good faith, a debtor whose original Chapter 11 plan has failed can file a new Chapter 11 plan rather than converting the plan to Chapter 7.[11] Chapter 7 liquidation has been denied, however, to an individual debtor who had income that would permit payment of a substantial portion of the debts under a 60-month Chapter 13 plan.[12] There is an implicit requirement that voluntary petitions be filed in good faith; but to dismiss such a petition, the court must find both "objective futility" (that the reorganization plan could not have been completed as scheduled) and subjective bad faith in the filing.[13]

If a Chapter 13 plan is converted to Chapter 7, property in the Chapter 13 estate goes into the Chapter 7 estate unaltered, and the Chapter 7 "separate acquisition" deadline is not applied. Therefore, after-acquired property cannot be kept out of the Chapter 7 estate even if it would not have been included if the debtor had filed a Chapter 7 petition in the first place.[14] Where a Chapter 11 debtor makes a second Chapter 11 filing, the IRS' priority claim for FICA and withholding trust fund taxes retains its priority status.[15]

Despite the lack of explicit statutory authority, a bankruptcy court does have the power to consolidate the estates of a bankrupt partnership and its bankrupt general partners if and when this would be fair to all creditors.[16] Angry creditors who claim to be aggrieved by a business owner's diversion of corporate funds from a bankrupt corporation do not have standing to bring a RICO suit against the owner. If the alleged diversion did take place, the corporation is the real victim, and creditors cannot "jump the line" by using RICO to bypass the bankruptcy action.[17] A bankruptcy court cannot punish a debtor for tardiness in reorganization by ordering him or her not to file any more bankruptcy petitions for a period of three years.[18]

[¶706] BANKRUPTCY FILING FEES

28 U.S.C. §1930 requires the following fees to be paid to the clerk by the parties commencing a case:

1. For a case commenced under Chapter 7 or 13 . . . . $90;
2. For a case commenced under Chapter 9. . . . . $300;
3. For a case commenced under Chapter 11. . . . . $500;

$1,000 if the case concerns a railroad. There is a quarterly fee until the plan is confirmed or the case converted to another Chapter or dismissed; the fee is assessed on a sliding scale from $150 to $3,000, depending on the disbursements.

4. For a case commenced under Chapter 12. . . . . $200.

An individual commencing a voluntary case or a joint case may pay his filing fees in installments if the debtor signs an application stating that he is unable to pay except in that way. The number of installments cannot exceed four, and the final installment is payable no later than 120 days after filing the petition. If cause is shown, the Court may extend the time of any installment, provided the last installment is paid no later than 180 days after filing the petition. The filing fee must be paid in full before the debtor may pay an attorney for services in connection with the case.

[¶707] PROPERTY OF THE ESTATE

The bankruptcy estate is comprised of all the debtor's legal or equitable interests in property, wherever located as of the commencement date. The scope of this section of the Code is broad; it includes all kinds of tangible and intangible property, causes of action, and all other forms of property, including tax refunds and accrued vacation pay—even exempt property. After the property comes into the estate, the debtor is permitted to exempt it. The Court has jurisdiction to determine what property may be exempted and what remains as property of the estate. Schedules B-1, B-2, and B-3 of Official Form 6, "Schedule B—Statement of All Property of Bankrupt" filed with the petition requesting relief itemizes the property making up the debtor's estate. Schedule B-4 itemizes the property claimed by the debtor as exempt.

If state law defines a 401(k) plan as a spendthrift trust, plan assets do not become part of the bankruptcy estate, because ERISA does not preempt state law on this point; hence, the 401(k) assets are excluded from the estate by "applicable nonbankruptcy law" (11 USC Section 541(c)(2)).[19]

If both spouses are obligated on a debt, personal property held by the entireties constitutes part of the bankruptcy estate even if only one spouse is bankrupt.[20]

Property acquired after a Chapter 13 filing (e.g., post-petition earnings), but before conversion of the plan to Chapter 7 becomes part of the Chapter 7 estate.[21] A post-filing inheritance was held to enter the bankruptcy estate,[22] but the automatic stay prevents a pre-petition tax lien from attaching to, or being perfected against, the post-filing inheritance.

[¶708] EXEMPTIONS

The exemption section of the Code permits an individual debtor to take out of the estate any property which is necessary for a fresh start and for the support of the debtor and dependents. Corporations and partnerships are not, of course, entitled to exclude property from the estate.

Property may be exempted even if it is subject to a lien, but only the unencumbered portion is to be counted in computing the "value" of the property for the purposes of exemption.

Where the debtor continues to reside in a house that is a potential homestead, the trustee is not permitted to charge the debtor rent until the imputed rental value of the accommodations exceeds the dollar value of the homestead exemption.[23]

The Code permits an individual debtor a choice between exemption systems. The debtor may choose the Federal exemptions, or he may choose the exemptions to which he is entitled under other Federal law and the law of the state of his domicile. The debtor cannot pick and choose between the Federal and the State exemptions, however, but must pick either. The Code permits the states to "opt-out" of the Federal exemptions list and requires debtors to follow those exemptions permitted under state law. At least 32 states have forbidden debtors from excepting property pursuant to the Federal list. You must, therefore, check your state statutes to see whether this option still exists in your state.

Where the debtor's choice of exemption, Federal or State, was improvident and should be changed, the Code contemplates that the debtor may, under certain circumstances, be able to switch from the Federal list to the State list and vice versa.

In a case where a husband and wife have filed a joint petition, they may claim separate exemption rights. They may take two Bankruptcy Code exemptions or they may both claim the State exemptions. The Code no longer permits stacking of exemptions. The 1984 Act also places a limit on the amount of personal and household items which can be exempted.

[¶709]   ATTORNEYS' FEES

The new Bankruptcy Code has a significant breakthrough with regard to attorneys' fees. In determining these amounts, the Court is to base its determination on the nature, the extent, and value of such services, the time spent on such services and the cost of comparable services in other areas of legal practice.

A provision has also been added to the Code allowing reimbursement of necessary expenses and compensation of para-professionals employed by attorneys. The drafters of the Code believed that much of the routine work could be handled by an attorney's assistant at a much lower cost to the estate. The provision insures that the estate, not the attorney, will bear the costs, thus benefiting both the estate and the attorneys involved.

An attorney representing a debtor, whether or not such an attorney applies for compensation, must file a statement of the compensation paid or agreed to be paid, including the particulars of any sharing or agreement to share by the attorney.

For a fee to be recoverable from the debtor's estate, the attorney's services must benefit the estate, not merely the debtor.[24]

[¶709.1]   Other Fees

In order to motivate potential lenders to provide financing after filing of a bankruptcy petition, the Ninth Circuit has permitted a debtor to pay an "enhancement fee" to a post-petition lender, despite the lack of specific authorization for such fees under Bankruptcy Code §364.[25] The Southern District of New York has allowed a Chapter 11 company to agree to pay a reasonable "breakup fee" in connection with its reorganization. The fee was payable if the debtor sold certain of its assets to anyone except a particular bidder, or if the debtor failed to adopt the reorganization plan proposed by the bidder. This case[26] applies the business judgment rule (standard in analysis of corporate transactions) to the bankruptcy context, and permits the breakup fee as long as it doesn't hamper bidding for the company, and as long as there is no self-dealing involved.

[¶710] THE TRUSTEE'S AVOIDING POWER

In addition to the law of preferences and fraudulent transfers, the trustee's power includes Section 544, the "strong-arm clause." Section 544(a) places the trustee in the position of a hypothetical judicial lien creditor whose interests vest in all the bankrupt's property at the commencement of the case. Commencement is defined as the date the petition is filed. In addition, the trustee will have the rights and powers of actual creditors and of a "bona fide purchaser of real property from the debtor."

Consequently, the trustee is placed ahead of all unsecured creditors and secured creditors who have not perfected their interests at the date of the filing of the petition, thus facilitating the prime bankruptcy policy of equal distribution among creditors of the debtor. Any debtor that receives a larger payment than others of his class is required to give up part of it so that all may share equally.

Section 545 permits the trustee to avoid the fixing of certain statutory liens. Liens that first become effective on the bankruptcy or insolvency of the debtor are voidable by the trustee. Liens that are not perfected or enforceable at the commencement of the case against a bona fide purchaser are voidable. Statutory liens are disguised priorities, enacted by the states to favor a particular class of creditors at the expense of general unsecured creditors in bankruptcy. A lien for rent or of distress for rent is voidable, whether the lien is a statutory or common law lien of distress for rent. The trustee may void a transfer of a lien under this section even if the lien has been enforced by sale before the commencement of the case. A mechanic's lien, for example, although created by statute, may not be voided.

The rights and powers of a trustee as a lien creditor are, however, subject to the limitation that if a transferee is able to perfect under Section 546(b) and that perfection relates back to an earlier date, then in spite of the filing of the bankruptcy petition, the trustee would not be able to defeat the lien, because the lien would be perfected and enforceable against a bona fide purchaser that purchased the property on the date of the filing of the petition.

A bankruptcy trustee cannot avoid the funds paid to corporate shareholders for their stock pursuant to a leveraged buyout (LBO) by claiming that such sums constitute a Bankruptcy Code Sec. 546(e) "settlement payment" "by or to a stockbroker, financial institution, or securities clearing agency."[27]

A corporate debtor's ESOP (Employee Stock Ownership Plan), for which employees have sacrificed payment of some wages in cash, has been defined[28] as an integral element in their compensation, not a mere contract for the employer to sell and the employees to buy the employer corporation's stock. Therefore, the trustee cannot define the ESOP arrangement as an "executory contract" and reject it.

Under 11 USC Section 1113, either a trustee or a debtor-in-possession can reject collective bargaining agreements if rejection is "necessary" to permit the reorganization. The Tenth Circuit has defined a necessary rejection as one which is made in good faith, and is more than potentially helpful, but need not be absolutely essential to the reorganization.[29]

[¶711]   Fraudulent Conveyances

Fraudulent transfers or obligations may be voided if made with actual intent to hinder, delay, or defraud a past or future creditor. Transfers made for less than a reasonably equivalent consideration are also vulnerable if the debtor was or thereby became insolvent, was engaged in a business with unreasonably small capital, or intentionally incurred debts knowing that he would be unable to repay them.

The trustee of a partnership debtor may void any transfer of partnership property to a partner of the debtor if the debtor was or thereby became insolvent.

If this is the transferee's only liability to the trustee and if he takes for value and in good faith, then he is granted a lien on the property transferred, or other similar protection.

Where the NLRB does not appear in a corporate employer's Chapter 7 case to challenge an allegedly fraudulent transfer of corporate assets to the sole share-holder, it cannot later attack the transfer in an attempt to impose personal liability for back pay on the sole shareholder.[30]

If a target company in an LBO receives economic benefits, even indirect ones, from the transaction, the LBO will not be construed to be a fraudulent conveyance as defined by Bankruptcy Code Sec. 548.[31]

Where a company filed for bankruptcy 18 months after a leveraged buyout (LBO), the trustee attempted to recover $12 million by claiming that the transaction was a fraudulent conveyance, but the attempt failed. The court took the position that the bankruptcy resulted from poor sales, not a lack of capital attributable to the LBO.[32] Where the debtor failed to pay taxes as well as other obligations, the trustee cannot use a fraudulent conveyance argument to set aside the tax sale of the property at least without challenging the underlying tax forfeiture.[33]

[¶712]   Avoidance of Preferences

A bankruptcy trustee may avoid preferences for creditors through the use of Section 547 of the Code. The preference section is a substantial modification of the Old Act [Section 60], bringing it into closer conformity with the UCC.

A preference is a transfer that enables a creditor to receive a greater percentage of his claim than he would have received had the transfer not been made and had he been a participant in the distribution of the assets of the bankrupt estate. The aim of avoiding preferences is twofold: (a) to discourage creditors from racing to the courthouse to dismember the debtor during his slide into bankruptcy, and (b) to assure equitable treatment for like-situated creditors.

A trustee may establish that a voidable preference has been made by proving each of the following factors:

(1) That a transfer of the debtor's property to or for the benefit of a creditor has been made. "Transfer" includes any method of disposition of any interest in property. Generally, the transfer of a security interest in property occurs at perfection, not creation.

(2) For or on account of an antecedent debt owed by the debtor.

(3) During the time the debtor was insolvent.

(4) And, on, or within 90 days before, the commencement of the proceeding. Section 547(f) creates a rebuttable presumption that a debtor was insolvent during the 90-day period prior to the commencement of the case.

Note: Installment payments within the 90-day period on a partially secured consumer debt are preferential insofar as the payments are applied to the unsecured portion of the debt.

Special insider rule: If the creditor is an "insider," the crucial time is extended to the period within one year of bankruptcy. If the debtor is an individual, an "insider" is defined as a partner, relative, relative of a partner, or a corporation in which the debtor is a director, officer, or "person in control." If the debtor is a corporation or partnership, an "insider" includes a director, officer, person in control, partner, or a relative of any persons who fall into these categories.

(5) As a result of the transfer the creditor received more than he would receive under a Chapter 7 liquidation, if the transfer had not been made, considering relative distribution between classes as well as within the creditor's class.

The 90-day period for computing preferential transfers runs backward from the date the petition is filed, not forward from the date of the transfer. The Third Circuit selected this method of calculation[34] so that there would be only a single period, not several periods calculated if several allegedly preferential transfers were made.

Bankruptcy Code Section 548(a)(2)(A) lets the debtor set aside as fraudulent any transfer of property that yields less than a "reasonably equivalent value" for the property. The Seventh Circuit permits this to be done with respect to the foreclosure sale of the debtor's home. Although the Bankruptcy Court said that the price yielded by a regularly conducted, non-collusive foreclosure sale is presumed to be reasonably equivalent, the Seventh Circuit denied the applicability of any presumption: instead, the facts of each case must be analyzed, and factors other than a simple comparison of price to fair market value may be invoked.[35]

Several recent cases explore the bankruptcy status of tax payments and tax liens. The government lost in *U.S. v. Daniel*,[36] which holds that a governmental seizure (enforcing a tax lien) made more than 45 days after the due date of the taxes is an avoidable preferential transfer unless the seized funds can be traced to unpaid taxes. But note the later *Isom* case.[37] Although Section 6325(a)(1) requires the release of a tax lien when an assessed liability is either satisfied or legally unenforceable, *Isom* holds that a property lien imposed on an underlying tax debt that has been discharged in bankruptcy is not to be considered legally unenforceable.

Looking at the same problem from another angle, *Begier v. IRS*[38] involves a taxpayer's pre-petition transfer of non-segregated funds from its general operating account for the purpose of paying withholding taxes. The transfer was held not to be a preferential transfer; the Third Circuit's position (although the D.C. Circuit disagrees),[39] like the IRS, is that money to pay withholding taxes is in effect held in trust for the IRS even if there is no separate account dedicated to tax funds.

Under Bankruptcy Code Section 547(c)(2)(C), it is not a preference to pay a creditor according to ordinary business terms. The Seventh Circuit does not require a single, uniform set of business terms; non-preferential payments can be made under practices that fall within a range of terms usual in the creditor's industry.[40]

[¶713]   EXCEPTIONS TO AVOIDANCE

The Code contains numerous exceptions to the trustee's power to avoid transfers. Section 547 provides that the trustee cannot avoid the following transfers:

(1) A transfer of property that is intended to be, and substantially is, contemporaneous with an extension of new credit. *Note:* Although a check is a credit transaction, if it is presented in the normal course of affairs (generally, 30 days) the transfer will be deemed "substantially contemporaneous."

(2) The payment of a debt that is within the ordinary course of business affairs (or financial affairs if the debtor is a consumer) between the debtor and creditor, and made according to ordinary business terms.

(3) A transfer that secures a loan to enable the debtor to acquire collateral, if it is perfected within 10 days after the security interest attaches (i.e., a purchase money security interest under UCC Section 9-107).

(4) A preferential transfer to a creditor who thereafter extends new unsecured credit (i.e., the amount of the new credit reduces the amount of the preferential transfer that the trustee can avoid).

(5) A transfer of inventory or receivables in which the creditor has a perfected security interest, unless it improves that creditor's position (at the expense of unsecured creditors) at the time the petition of bankruptcy is filed over his position as of 90 days (one year for insiders) before bankruptcy.

[¶714]   RIGHTS OF SECURED CREDITORS

A stay may be lifted if the debtor does not have an equity interest in the property and it is not needed for reorganization. A failure to provide adequate protection also constitutes cause for lifting of the stay. Section 361 offers three nonexclusive means of providing adequate protection:

(1) Requiring the trustee to make a cash payment or periodic cash payments, resulting in a reduction of the entity's interest in the property;

(2) Providing an additional or replacement lien;

(3) Granting other relief that will result in the realization of the indubitable equivalent of the affected entity's interest in the property.

A request for relief from stay is made by motion under Bankruptcy Rule 9014. If the Court does not rule within 30 days from a request for relief from the stay, the stay is automatically terminated with respect to the property in question. In order to accommodate more complex cases, the Code permits the Court to make a preliminary ruling after a preliminary hearing. After such a hearing, the Court may continue the stay only if there is a reasonable likelihood that the party opposing relief from the stay will prevail at the final hearing. No hearing on a motion to lift the stay will be held unless the debtor makes a timely request for such a hearing.

Due process requires that secured creditors must be given notice and the right to a hearing whenever confirmation of a Chapter 13 plan reduces a secured claim.[41]

A Chapter 12 (family farm bankruptcy) plan is permitted to convert a five-year to a 30-year mortgage; the conversion does not constitute a "taking" under the Fifth Amendment, because the creditor can be expected to get the value of its allowed secured claim (albeit slowly).[42]

In a Chapter 13 plan, where the home mortgage note did not provide for interest on arrears, an oversecured creditor is nevertheless entitled to both pre- and post-confirmation interest on arrears that are paid off under the Chapter 13 plan. The arrears are "provided for" by the plan, so Bankruptcy Code Section 1325(a)(5)(B)(ii) permits the creditor to receive interest.[43]

The interest rate payable to a secured creditor who is subject to "cramdown" under a Chapter 13 plan is the rate the lender would charge for a similar loan, not the prime rate the creditor itself pays for its own borrowing.[44]

[¶715] MAKING CLAIMS AGAINST A BANKRUPT

A proof of claim is a written statement setting forth a creditor's claim. Creditors are allowed to file a proof of claim, but are not required to do so. In a Chapter 7 or Chapter 13 case, unsecured creditors must file a proof of claim for their claim to be allowed. In a Chapter 11 reorganization case the schedule of liabilities constitutes prima facie evidence of the validity and amount of claims of creditors, unless they are scheduled as disputed, contingent, or unliquidated, or not scheduled at all.

A proof of claim for wages, salary, or commissions must conform to Official Form No. 20 or No. 21; any other proof of claim must conform to Official Form No. 19. The originals or duplicates of documents supporting a claim, or an interest in property of the debtor securing the claim, must be filed with the proof of claim. Evidence of a perfected security interest in property of the debtor must also be filed, if a security interest is claimed.

To be allowed, the proof of claim in a Chapter 7 or Chapter 13 case must be filed within 90 days after the first date set for the creditors' meeting. In Chapter 11 cases, the court fixes the time within which proofs of claim or interest may be filed.

[¶716]   HOW CLAIMS ARE PROVED

All proofs of claim are permitted to be filed, whether based on contract or tort, whether liquidated or unliquidated, and regardless of whether such claims can be liquidated in a reasonable time.

A creditor or indenture trustee may file a proof of claim. If a creditor does not file a timely proof of claim, a co-debtor, surety, or guarantor may file a proof of such a claim. The proof of claim must be filed within 30 days after the expiration of the original period for the filing of claims.

In liquidation and individual repayment plan cases, the trustee or debtor may file a proof of claim if the creditor does not file on or before the first day set for the meeting of creditors.

Under Bankruptcy Rule 9006(b)(1), a proof of claim can be filed late if neglect is "excusable." In 1992, the Supreme Court ruled[45] that an equitable balancing of factors must take place. Factors to be considered include the length of the delay; the effect both on the debtor and on judicial economy; the reason for the delay; and if outside creditors control the delay or could not speed up the process. Thus, a 20-day delay was held permissible, especially since the notice of the creditor's meeting did not disclose the bar date conspicuously.

Bankruptcy Code Section 502(e)(1)(B) requires the bankruptcy court to disallow contingent claims. The First Circuit decided in 1993 that contingent CERCLA claims are included in this category: Congress should have provided legislative guidance if it intended contingent CERCLA claims to be allowed in bankruptcy.[46]

[¶717]   ALLOWANCE OF CLAIMS

A claim or interest, proof of which is filed pursuant to Section 501, is deemed allowed, unless a party in interest (including a creditor of a partner in a partnership that is a debtor in a case under Chapter 7 of the Code) objects in writing.

If an objection to a claim is made, the court, after notice and a hearing, shall determine the amount of such claim as of the date of the petition.

[¶718]   ATTACK ON UNDERLYING DEBT

If a trustee can disprove the validity of a debt, he can defeat the secured creditor—no matter what the validity of the security interest. Debts may not necessarily be legally enforceable, even though there is a security interest that is otherwise valid and enforceable.

If, for example, a debt is barred by the statute of limitations, it may be unenforceable though the security interest remains valid. In this regard, it is important to note that the trustee is heir to "any defense available to the debtor as against any entity." Such defenses can be construed to include statutes of fraud, usury, unconscionability, consideration, or other personal defenses.

The trustee may also elect to attack the amount of an actual debt on the grounds that it is inflated, thereby reducing the indebtedness. Claims for unmatured interest also stop as of the date of filing.

The Code separates an under-secured creditor's claim into two parts. He has a secured claim to the extent of the value of his collateral as of the date of his valuation hearing, and an unsecured claim for the balance of his claim. A creditor with an over-secured claim is entitled to any reasonable fees, costs, or charges provided by the agreement under which the claim arose. Claims for interest may, however, be limited to the legal rate of interest.

Under certain circumstances, mutual debts owing by the creditor to the debtor and by the debtor to the creditor which arose before the commencement of the case can be set off.

[¶719]   HOW ASSETS OF THE BANKRUPT ARE DISTRIBUTED: PRIORITIES OF CLAIMS

Six distinctive classes of unsecured claims entitled to priority are set up. (See *Secured Transactions* for the priority of secured interests.) The order of payment to the priority classes (requiring satisfaction of each category before the next category may be satisfied) is:

(1) Administrative costs. Note:fees for referees' salaries are no longer included in this category, but attorneys' fees are.

(2) In an involuntary case, unsecured claims arising in the ordinary course of the debtor's business or financial affairs after the commencement of the case, but before the appointment of a trustee or the order of relief (whichever is earlier).

(3) Unsecured claims for wages, salaries, or commissions earned within 90 days before the date of filing the petition or cessation of the debtor's business (whichever is earlier), with a maximum claim of $2,000 per individual.

(4) Unsecured claims for contributions to employee benefit plans arising from services rendered within 180 days before the filing of the petition or cessation of business (whichever is earlier). The claim cannot exceed the number of employees, multiplied by $2,000, minus any monies paid for wage claims (see (3) above).

(5) Unsecured claims of $900 per individual for monies deposited in connection with the purchase, lease, or rental of property, or the purchase of services for the personal, family, or household use of such individuals, that were not delivered or provided.

(6) Unsecured tax claims of governmental units:

(a) Income or gross receipts tax provided tax return due (including extension) within three years prior to filing petition.

(b) Property tax last payable without penalty within one year prior to filing petition.

(c) Withholding taxes.

(d) Employment tax on wages, etc., due within three years prior to the filing of the petition.

(e) Excise tax due within three years prior to the filing of the petition.

(f) Customs duty on merchandise imported within one year prior to the filing of the petition.

(g) Penalties related to a type of claim above to be used as compensation for actual pecuniary loss.

A bankruptcy trustee is considered the fiduciary of a trust. Thus, the Supreme Court has permitted the IRS to look to the trustee rather than the debtor for filing of returns and payment of whatever federal taxes are owed on sale of the debtor's property.[47] However, the Ninth Circuit permits a bankruptcy court to order the IRS to allocate payment of taxes under a Chapter 11 plan first to the trust fund taxes, with the result that the personal liability of the corporate officer who is the responsible person can be discharged.[48]

Where the federal government fails to appeal the order confirming a reorganization plan placing a tax lien subordinate to secured creditors' interests, and also fails to seek revocation or even modification of the plan when the proceedings were dismissed, the government will not be entitled to relitigate the priorities assigned under the plan.[49]

Under Bankruptcy Code Section 507(a)(3), third priority is given to vacation pay "earned" within 90 days of bankruptcy; "earned" is in quotation marks because it must be determined when vacation pay is considered to be earned. In re Northwest Engineering Co.[50] states that the pay is earned continuously as the employees work, even if the company's obligation to pay the wages does not vest until later.[51]

Pension Benefit Guarantee Corporation claims for pension plan underfunding (with respect to work performed before the petition was filed) are deemed to be pre-petition claims, but they neither preserve the estate nor have the status of a tax, and therefore are not entitled to administrative priority.[52]

In contrast, the Internal Revenue Code Sec. 4971(a) pension excise tax imposed on failure to meet the minimum funding obligation is an excise tax entitled to priority; it is not a tax penalty. The excise tax cannot be equitably subordinated to other claims unless it can be demonstrated that the government behaved in some inequitable fashion.[53]

The same is true of the 10% excise tax imposed by Internal Revenue Code Sec. 4980 on the reversion of funds to the employer when a qualified plan is terminated, and therefore the IRS has an unsecured priority claim on the excise tax in a Chapter 11 case.[54]

A Chapter 13 plan can permissibly create a separate class for arrears of child support assigned by an ex-wife to the county support collection agency, even though the effect is that the county gets paid in full whereas other unsecured creditors get only eight cents on the dollar.[55]

[¶ 720] DISCHARGE OF THE DEBTOR FROM HIS DEBTS

Discharge of a debtor's debts is the single most important feature of any bankruptcy proceeding. A debtor is entitled to discharge as a matter of right, unless proper objections are made and sustained. For everyone but a corporation, adjudication operates as an automatic application for discharge. A corporation may not obtain a discharge under Chapter 7 of the Act.

An individual, whether a wage-earner or self-employed, may, as an alternative, seek discharge under Chapter 13 of the Code, which provides for a flexible plan of repayment of or composition with creditors in lieu of straight liquidation.

The Chapter 13 discharge includes all debts except alimony, maintenance or support, and certain long-term obligations specifically provided for under the plan. Also excepted are post-petition consumer debts arising after the commencement of the case for property or services necessary for the debtor's performance under the plan (if prior approval by the trustee was obtained or practicable). The plan also must provide for full payment of all claims entitled to priority, so that as a practical matter all tax or wage claims must be paid or the case cannot be closed, and the debtor cannot receive a discharge.

The debtor is entitled to a "fresh start"; it has been held that it is a violation of Section 366 of the Bankruptcy Code for a utility company to discriminate by requiring bankruptcy debtors (but not new customers in general) to pay a deposit to restore service that was shut off before the bankruptcy petition for nonpayment of bills.[56]

In *Bush v. Taylor,*[57] a divorcing wife was awarded half of her husband's pension benefits; he later filed under Chapter 7. The Eighth Circuit held that she had received a property settlement rather than alimony or maintenance, and that the obligation to remit part of pension payments to be received in the future is a dischargeable debt. Maintenance and child support, however, are not dischargeable. Two recent Tenth Circuit cases explore the issues, holding that whether a debt is in the nature of maintenance, and thus not dischargeable, depends on both the intent of the ex-spouses and the substance of the obligation to pay maintenance.[58] A court-ordered obligation to pay attorneys' fees in a custody case is in the nature of support (because custody actions are deemed to be for the benefit and support of the minor children), and thus not dischargeable.[59]

When a Chapter 11 debtor converts the petition to Chapter 7, a creditor bound by the Chapter 11 confirmation order can only contest the dischargeability of certain debts: those arising between the dates of confirmation and conversion.[60] A malpractice judgment against an attorney who is a Chapter 7 debtor is dischargeable; the debt does not arise out of fiduciary misconduct.[61] Future response costs under CERCLA, for which the debtor is potentially liable, are dischargeable claims but only to the extent that they were "fairly contemplated" by the parties when the Chapter 11 filing was made.[62]

On a showing of reasonable cause, a bankruptcy court can waive penalties imposed by the IRS for failure to file or pay taxes, but the court lacks the power to reduce the penalty; it's an all-or-nothing decision.[63]

[¶721]   EXCEPTIONS TO DISCHARGE

Here is a checklist of what a bankruptcy discharge under Chapter 7 of the Code does not relieve by way of obligation:

❏ Taxes—generally, federal, state, or local, owing within three years preceding bankruptcy;

❏ Liability for obtaining money, property, services, or an extension, renewal, or refinance of credit by false pretenses or representations. Consumer debts aggregating more than $500 for "luxury goods or services" within 40 days before the order for relief, or cash advances aggregating more than $1,000 that are extensions of consumer credit under an open-end credit plan within 20 days before the order for relief;

❏ Liability for willful and malicious injuries to the person or property of another;

❏ Alimony, maintenance, and child support payments;

❏ Debts not scheduled;

❏ Liability for fraud while acting as a fiduciary; larceny or embezzlement by the bankrupt.

❏ Fines, penalties, or forfeitures payable to and for the benefit of a governmental unit.

❏ Governmental or nonprofit institution of higher education, education loans, unless such loans first become due more than five years before the date of the filing of the petition, or if nondischarge of the loan would impose an undue hardship on the debtor and the debtor's dependents.

❏ Debts arising from a judgment or consent decree entered in a court of record against the debtor for liability incurred by the debtor because of his or her operation of a motor vehicle while legally intoxicated under the laws or regulations of any jurisdiction within the United States or its territories.

❏ Claims from a prior bankruptcy.

Debts that may be excepted from discharge for false pretenses or representations, embezzlement, or larceny, or willful and malicious injury require a creditor who is owed the debt to initiate proceedings in the Bankruptcy Court. He or she must file a complaint under Section 523(c) of the Code to obtain a determination of the dischargeability of the debt within 90 days following the first date set for the meeting of creditors. The Bankruptcy Court has exclusive jurisdiction to determine dischargeability of these debts. For all other debts, the Bankruptcy Court and any appropriate non-bankruptcy forum will continue to have concurrent jurisdiction to determine dischargeability.

If an individual debtor not represented by an attorney wishes to reaffirm a debt, the Court holds a hearing to approve such agreement within 30 days after the entry of an order granting or denying a discharge and on at least ten days notice to the debtor and trustee, if one is appointed. Application by the debtor for approval of reaffirmation agreement shall be filed before or at the discharge hearing. Prior court approval is not required if the debtor has been represented by an attorney, but the reaffirmation agreement must be filed with the court accompanied by a declaration or an affidavit of the attorney stating that the agreement represents a fully informed and voluntary agreement by the debtor. The reaffirmation agreement must contain a clear and conspicuous statement advising the debtor that the agreement may be rescinded at any time prior to discharge or within 60 days after the agreement is filed with the court. Nothing prevents a debtor from voluntarily repaying any debt.

In the case of *Pennsylvania v. Davenport* [64] the Supreme Court agreed that obligations to make restitution for criminal acts fit within the definition of "debts" which can be discharged under Chapter 13. A civil assault judgment (in the case at bar, for deliberate shooting) has been held to be dischargeable under Chapter 13 but not under Chapter 7.[65] The court's rationale is that the requirement for a Chapter 13 discharge is good-faith filing of a reorganization plan, not good conduct in any general sense.

In contrast, punitive damages awarded under a state court's finding of fraud are not dischargeable: Bankruptcy Code Section 523(a)(2)(a) says that there can be no discharge of a debt for money or property obtained by fraud.[66]

Post-petition interest and penalties on an unpaid tax debt that is not itself discharged cannot be discharged under Chapter 7.[67] Where the debtor failed to file a gift tax return, the gift tax liability is not dischargeable under Bankruptcy Code Section 523 even though the IRS filed a notice of claim with respect to income tax but not gift tax. According to the Tenth Circuit, the IRS did not waive the right to collect the gift tax, precisely because the gift tax liability is non-dischargeable. Although the IRS could not participate in the debtor's reorganization, it could collect the gift tax liability outside the bankruptcy system.[68]

A debtor that fails to assert a lender liability claim against its creditor during the bankruptcy proceeding will find that *res judicata* bars the bringing of a subsequent tort suit. The Second Circuit has held[69] that if the bankruptcy court deemed such claims to have any validity, the asset disposition and/or payment schedule would have been structured accordingly.

The non-student co-maker of a guaranteed student loan is subject to the same limitations on dischargeability under Bankruptcy Code Section 523(a)(8) as the student.[70]

[¶722]   GROUNDS FOR OBJECTING TO OR DENYING DISCHARGE

The following ten statutory provisions require that the debtor be denied a discharge. The debtor:

(1) Is not an individual.

(2) Within one year prior to, or after, the filing of the petition, transferred, destroyed, or concealed, or permitted to be transferred, destroyed, or concealed, any of his property with the intent to hinder, delay, or defraud creditors.

(3) Failed to keep or preserve adequate books, or accounts, or financial records from which the debtor's financial condition or business transactions might be ascertained.

(4) Knowingly and fraudulently made a false oath or claim, offered or received a bribe, or withheld information in connection with the case.

(5) Failed to explain satisfactorily any losses of assets or deficiency of assets to meet his liabilities.

(6) Refused to obey any lawful order or to answer any material questions in the course of the proceedings after being granted immunity from self-incrimination.

(7) Within one year prior to the filing of the petition, committed any of the above acts in connection with another case or during this case concerning an insider.

(8) Within the past six years received a discharge in bankruptcy under Chapter 7 or 11 of the Code or under the Bankruptcy Act.

(9) Within the past six years received a discharge under Chapter 13 of the Code or Chapter XIII of prior law, unless payments under the plan totalled 100 percent of such claims or payments totalled at least 70 percent of such claims under a plan proposed in good faith and determined to have been performed according to the debtor's best effort.

(10) After the order for relief, submits a written waiver of discharge and the Court approves.

The issuance of false financial statements to obtain credit, which was grounds for denial of discharge under the old law, will only prevent discharge for that particular debt rather than bar a discharge for all debts.

— **ENDNOTES** —

1. 18 USC. §152.

2. California State Board of Equalization v. Sierra Summit Inc., #88-681, 490 U.S. 844 (6/12/89).

3. IRS v. Energy Resources Co., 871 F.2d 223 (1st Cir. 3/31/89), aff'd 495 U.S. 545 (Sup.Ct. 5/29/90). Where a bankrupt officer of a bankrupt corporation was a "responsible person" for payment of payroll taxes, but the corporation eventually satisfied the payroll tax liability, the corporate payments cannot be credited against the officer's personal liability in Chapter 11—only in a bankruptcy reorganization: U.S. v. Pepperman, 976 F.2d 123 (3d Cir. 9/3/92).

4. LTV Steel Co. v. UMW (In re Chateaugay Corp.), 945 F.2d 1205 (2d Cir. 9/17/91).

5. Easley v. Pettibone Michigan Corp., 990 F.2d 905 (6th Cir. 4/8/93).

6. Credit Alliance Corp. v. Williams, 851 F.2d 119 (4th Cir. 7/5/88).

7. U.S. v. Nicolet Inc., 857 F.2d 202 (9/16/88).

8. Phoenix Bond & Indemnity Co. v. Shamblin, 878 F.2d 324 (9th Cir. 6/30/89).

9. U.S. v. Wilson, 974 F.2d 514 (4th Cir. 9/3/92), cert. denied 113 S.Ct. 1352.

10. British Aviation Ins. Co. v. Menut, 873 F.2d 264 (11th Cir. 5/17/89).

11. Fruehauf Corp. v. Jartran Inc., 886 F.2d 859 (7th Cir. 9/29/89).

12. In re Walton, 866 F.2d 981 (8th Cir. 1/19/89).

13. Carolin Corp. v. Miller, 58 LW 2214 (4th Cir. 9/28/89).

14. In re Lynbrook, 60 LW 2421 (7th Cir. 12/18/91).

15. In re Official Committee of Unsecured Creditors of White Farm Equipment Co., 943 F.2d 752 (7th Cir. 9/17/91).

16. FDIC v. Colonial Realty Co., 966 F.2d 57 (2d Cir. 6/1/92).

17. Wooten v. Loshbough, 951 F.2d 768 (7th Cir. 12/26/91).

18. Frieouf v. U.S., 938 F.2d 1099 (10th Cir. 7/10/91).

19. In re Kincaid, 917 F.2d 1162 (9th Cir. 10/25/90); Schlein v. Mills, 62 LW 2358 (11th Cir. 12/2/93). For other ERISA plans excluded from the estate, see FDIC v. Felts (In re Dyke), 943 F.2d 1435 (5th Cir. 10/15/91); Forbes v. Holiday Corp. Savings & Retirement Plan, 924 F.2d 597 (6th Cir. 1/14/91). There was a split among the circuits. Checkett v. Vickers, 954 F.2d 1426 (8th Cir. 1/24/92) and Reed v. Drummond, 951 F.2d 1046 (9th Cir. 12/11/91), vacated #92-26, 61 LW 3277 refused to treat ERISA as "applicable non-bankruptcy law" that would justify exclusion of the pension plan from the bankruptcy estate. But the split was resolved by Patterson v. Shumate, #91-913, 112 S.Ct. 1662 (Sup.Ct. 6/15/92), characterizing the ERISA anti-alienation rule as applicable non-bankruptcy law. Patterson does not settle the question of the status of non-corporate plans such as IRAs and Keoghs. In re Lane, 1993 Bankr. LEXIS 103 (E.D.N.Y. 1993) says that Patterson does not apply where the business owner and spouse are the sole participants in the pension plan.

20. Garner v. Strauss, 60 LW 2479 (8th Cir. 12/26/91).

21. Calder v. Job, 973 F.2d 862 (10th Cir. 8/25/92).

22. U.S. v. Fuller, 134 BR 945 (Bank-9th Cir. 1/6/92).

23. In re Szekely, 936 F.2d 897 (7th Cir. 7/2/91).

24. In re Reed, 890 F.2d 104 (8th Cir. 11/27/89).

25. Resolution Trust Corp. v. Unofficial Unsecured Creditors Committee of Defender Drug Stores, 61 LW 2222 (Bank-9th Cir. 10/2/92).

26. Official Committee of Subordinated Bondholders v. Integrated Resources Inc., 147 BR 650 (S.D.N.Y. 10/28/92).

27. Kaiser Steel Corp. v. Pearl Brewing Co., 952 F.2d 1230 (10th Cir. 12/30/91).

28. In re Crippin, 877 F.2d 594 (7th Cir. 6/19/89).

29. Sheet Metal Workers, Local 9 v. Mile Hi Metal Systems Inc., 899 F.2d 887 (10th Cir. 3/20/90).

30. NLRB v. Martin Arsham Sewing Co., 873 F.2d 884, 882 F.2d 216 (6th Cir. 4/21/89).

31. Mellon Bank, N.A. v. Metro Communications Inc., 945 F.2d 635 (3d Cir. 9/25/91) See Alan B. Miller, "LBOs, Fraudulent Transfers Revised," *Nat.L.J.* 1/20/91 p.20.

32. James Moody v. Security Pacific Business Credit Inc., 858 F.2d 137 (3d Cir. 8/7/92), cert. denied 109 S.Ct. 1529, 489 U.S. 1078.

33. Weinman v. Simons, 971 F.2d 577 (10th Cir. 7/28/92).

34. Nelson Co. v. Counsel for the Official Committee of Unsecured Creditors, 959 F.2d 1260 (3d Cir. 3/26/92).

35. Bundles v. Baker, 856 F.2d 815 (7th Cir. 8/25/88).

36. 887 F.2d 981 (9th Cir. 10/23/89).

37. Isom v. Comm'r, 901 F.2d 744 (9th Cir. 4/13/90).

38. 878 F.2d 762 (3d Cir. 6/30/89).

39. Drabkin v. Dist. of Columbia, 824 F.2d 1102 (D.C. Cir. 1987).

40. In re Tolona Pizza Products Corp., 62 LW 2136 (7th Cir. 8/19/93).

41. Fireman's Fund Mortgage Corp. v. Hobdy, 130 B.R. 318 (9th Cir. Bank. 8/23/91).

42. Travelers Ins. Co. v. Bullington, 878 F.2d 354 (11th Cir. 7/21/89). Nor is it a "taking" under the Fifth Amendment for a Chapter 12 plan to adjust the secured claims of the seller of a farm from the $124,000 unpaid balance to the $75,000 fair market value of the farm: Congress can constitutionally provide debt relief in ways that are inconvenient to creditors: Dahlke v. Doering, 94 BR 569 (D. Minn. 1/10/89).

43. Rake v. Wade, #92-621, 113 S.Ct. 2187 (Sup.Ct. 6/7/93).

44. General Motors Acceptance Corp. v. Jones, 62 LW 2065 (3d Cir. 7/20/93).

45. Pioneer Investment Services Co. v. Brunwick Associates Limited Partnership, #91-1693, 113 S.Ct. 1489 (Sup.Ct. 3/24/92).

46. Juniper Development Group v. Kahn, 62 LW 2678 (1st Cir. 5/4/93).

47. Holywell v. Smith, #90-1361,-1384, 112 S.Ct. 1201 (Sup.Ct.4/21/92).

48. IRS v. Creditors' Committee (In re Deer Park Inc.), 62 LW 2375 (9th Cir. 12/6/93).

49. U.S. v. Standard State Bank, 91 BR 874 (W.D. Mo. 9/30/88).

50. 863 F.2d 1313 (7th Cir. 12/7/88).

51. Employers Insurance of Wausau v. Plaid Painters Inc., 62 LW 2312 (9th Cir. 11/1/93).

52. LTV Corp. v. PBGC (In re Chateaugay Corp.), 130 BR 1751 (S.D.N.Y. 9/13/91).

53. U.S. v. Mansfield Tire & Rubber Co., 942 F.2d 1055 (6th Cir. 8/28/91).

54. U.S. v. Unsecured Creditors' Committee of C-T of Virginia, Inc., 977 F.2d 137 (4th Cir. 10/2/92).

55. Mickelson v. Leser, 939 F.2d 669 (8th Cir. 8/1/91).

56. Whittaker v. Philadelphia Electric Co., 92 BR 110 (E.D. Pa. 10/5/88).

57. 893 F.2d 962 (8th Cir. 1/11/90).

58. In re Sampson, 62 LW 2062 (10th Cir. 6/21/93).

59. Jones v. Jones, 62 LW 2370 (10th Cir. 11/16/93).

60. Bank of Louisiana v. Pavlovich, 952 F.2d 114 (5th Cir. 1/30/92).

61. In re Stokes, 142 BR 908 (Bank-N.D. Cal. 7/23/92).

62. In re National Gypsum Co., 139 BR 397 (N.D. Tex. 2/12/92); California Dep't of Health Services v. Jensen, 61 LW 2782 (9th Cir. 6/15/93). But Torwico Electronics Inc. v. New Jersey Department of Environmental Protection, 62 LW 2281 (3d Cir. 10/25/93) holds that state efforts to get a bankrupt company to clean up a hazardous waste site do not constitute a "claim," much less a claim that can be discharged in bankruptcy.

63. U.S. v. Sanford, 979 F.2d 1511 (11th Cir. 12/29/92).

64. #89-156, 110 S.Ct. 2126 (Sup.Ct. 5/29/90); below, Pennsylvania Department of Public Welfare v. Johnson-Allen, 871 F.2d 421 (3d Cir. 3/28/89).

65. Handeen v. LeMaire, 898 F.2d 1346 (8th Cir. 3/26/90).

66. St. Laurent v. Ambrose, 61 LW 2734 (11th Cir. 5/20/93).

67. Hanna v. U.S., 872 F.2d 829 (8th Cir. 4/21/89).

68. J. Grynberg, 93-1 USTC ¶60,129 (10th Cir. 2/17/93).

69. Sure-Snap Corp. v. State Street Bank & Trust, 948 F.2d 869 (2d Cir. 11/7/91).

70. In re Pelkowski, 990 F.2d 737 (3d Cir. 3/24/93).

— FOR FURTHER REFERENCE

Altman, Edward I., "Evaluating the Chapter 11 Bankruptcy-Reorganization Process," 1993 *Columbia Business L. Rev.* 1 (Winter '93).

Brickman, Lester and Jonathan Klein, "The Use of Advance Fee Attorney Retainer Agreements in Bankruptcy," 43 *South Carolina L. Rev.* 1037 (Summer '92).

Cadigan, Michael J., "Environmental Liability: Bankruptcy and Insurance Issues," 22 *Environmental Law* 1279 (Spring '92).

Friedrich, Craig W., "Tax Consequences Taken into Account in Determining Whether to Allow Bankruptcy Trustee to Abandon Property," 20 *J. of Real Estate Taxation* 94 (Fall '92).

Furay, Catherine J., "Dischargeability of Taxes in Bankruptcy," 66 *Wisconsin Lawyer* 14 (June '93).

Herbert, Michael J., "Consumer Chapter 11 Proceedings After *Toibb v. Radloff*" 45 *Consumer Finance L. Quarterly Rep.* 370 (Fall '91).

Herzog, Asa S. and Lawrence P. King, eds., *Collier Bankruptcy Practice Guide* (8 volumes; Matthew Bender; looseleaf).

Johnson, Alex M. Jr., "Critiqueing the Foreclosure Process," 79 *Virginia L. Rev.* 959 (August '93).

Kaye, Luisa, "The Case Against Class Proofs of Claim in Bankruptcy," 66 *NYU L. Rev.* 897 (June '91).

Klingenberg, Erik D., "Strip Down of Home Mortgages: Undressing 11 USC 1322(b)(2)," 66 *St. John's L. Rev.* 443 (Spring '92).

Kutz, Kristy, "Who Is Going to Pay: CERCLA v. Bankruptcy," 31 *Washburn LJ.* 573 (Spring '92).

Litton, T. Richard Jr., "The Proper Treatment of ERISA Qualified Pension Plans in Bankruptcy: A Tax Perspective," 11 *Virginia Tax Rev.* 195 (Summer '91).

Luper, Frederick M. and Kenneth M. Richards, "Valuation of Property Issues in Bankruptcy," 98 *Commercial LJ.* 35 (Spring '93).

McGuinness, K.G. and L.M. Goldman, "Courts Decide on Lenders' Right to Attack Reorganization Plan," *Nat.LJ.* 4/22/91 p. 20.

Meltzer, Peter E., "Whom Do You Trust? Everything You Never Wanted to Know About Ethics, Conflicts and Privileges in the Bankruptcy Process," 97 *Commercial LJ.* 149 (Summer '92).

North, Christopher Colt, "Filing Mechanic's Liens After the Debtor's Bankruptcy Petition Not So Fast!" 18 *Virginia Bar Ass'n J.* 21 (Summer '92).

Ong, Tomson T., "The Effects of Bankruptcy Petitions on Civil Asset Forfeiture Actions," 19 *Western State U.L. Rev.* 493 (Spring '92).

Polednak, Donald T., "Is the Secured Creditor Really Secure?" 31 *Washington LJ.* 344 (Winter '92).

Reilly, Robert F., "Understanding Bankruptcy Appraisals," 38 *Practical Lawyer* 33 (July '92).

Rocen, Donald T., "Federal Tax Procedures in Bankruptcy Proceedings," 51 *Inst. on Federal Taxation* 24-1 (Annual '93).

Shelley, Scott Christopher, "Bankruptcy: Assignment of Rents," 23 *Seton Hall L. Rev.* 1257 (Summer '93).

Stabile, Susan J., "Protecting Retiree Medical Benefits in Bankruptcy," 14 *Cardozo L. Rev.* 1911 (May '93).

Stevenson, John G. Jr., "Discovery Under the Federal Rules of Bankruptcy Procedure," 9 *Bankruptcy Developments J.* 643 (Spring '93).

Sullivan, Shawn F., "Discharge of CERCLA Liability in Bankruptcy," 17 *Harvard Environmental L. Rev.* 445 (Summer '93).

BROKERAGE

[¶801] A broker's right to his commission will depend on the contract with his principal, for whom he is acting as agent. The arrangement can vary from an open listing (in which the principal is free to hire other brokers) to an exclusive agency (no other broker can bring about the sale) or an exclusive right to sell (broker earns his commission when the property is sold even if the principal sells it himself).

[¶802]   WHEN IS THE COMMISSION EARNED?

Unless some additional condition is provided in the contract between the parties, a broker is entitled to his commission when he can show the following:

(1) His services were performed during the time of the agency as specified in the contract.

(2) The broker produced a buyer who was ready, willing, and able to buy. "Ready" means that the buyer will execute a contract of sale. "Willingness" is the voluntary act of the purchaser without any compulsion or coercion. If the broker has brought the parties together and they make a different contract than the one that the broker was employed to make, the broker will nevertheless be entitled to his commission. "Able" means that the buyer will be able to get up the necessary funds to close the deal within the time required. He must have the money to meet the cash payment and be able financially to meet later installments.

(3) There was a meeting of the minds between the parties. This basic tenet of the contract doctrine provides that a binding contract exists between parties when all the material terms of the agreement between them exist.

(4) The broker was the procuring cause. The broker must be able to show that his efforts were the primary and direct cause of the consummation of the transaction. If the broker had an exclusive right to sell, procuring cause would not enter into the brokerage situation and he would be entitled to his commission regardless of how the sale took place. Or in the case of an exclusive agency, the broker gets his commission even if the principal hired another broker who actually sold the property, since here the owner broke a contract he made to sell only through this broker. To establish that he was the procuring cause the broker can show that: he advertised the property; he introduced the parties; he was the first to call the purchaser's attention to the property; he was continuously engaged in the transaction by correspondence or conversations.

If several brokers were involved, if there was a disagreement between the parties after the first broker brought them together, and later a second broker came in and got the parties to agree, the second broker is the procuring cause. However, the first broker is a procuring cause if he brought about a substantial agreement and the second broker worked out details.

(5) The deal was consummated. This will be important if the broker's right to a commission has been conditioned upon the consummation of the transaction.

Here, again, if the deal goes through the broker is entitled to his commission even if the parties have changed the terms from those that were originally given to the broker. Or, if the deal does not go through because of default (in bad faith) on the part of the owner, the broker is entitled to his commission. In an exclusive agency or an open listing, when the broker's right to a commission has not been conditioned on the final conclusion of the transaction, the broker will get his commission even if the purchaser fails to carry out the deal after having made a valid contract.

[¶802.1]   Brokers Serving Conflicting Interests

A broker acts in a *fiduciary* capacity and cannot serve two masters with conflicting interests. For example, the broker may act for both buyer and seller to the point of bringing them together. However, if the broker is hired by the one to negotiate the purchase, and by others to negotiate the sale, the broker cannot properly discharge his or her duties of loyalty and good faith toward both by procuring the highest price for the seller and the lowest price for the buyer. Thus a broker in such a position cannot have a claim against either the buyer or seller for services rendered.

— **FOR FURTHER REFERENCE** —

Deason, Marshall, "An Outline of Real Estate Broker Liability," 61 *Florida B.J.* 39 (February '87).

Frew, James R. and G. Donald Jud, "Who Pays the Real Estate Broker's Commission?" 10 *Research in Law and Economics* 177 (Annual '87).

Goldstein, Bernard H., "Broker's Tort Liability: Some Observations," 1 *Probate and Property* 7 (September–October '87).

Karam, Gregory L. and Suzanne W., "Back to Basics: Entitlement of Ohio Real Estate Brokers to Selling Agent Commissions," 59 *Ohio State Bar Ass'n Rep't* 1804 (11/24/86).

Levin, Murray S., "Overstating the Value of Property to Induce a Listing," 34 *U. of Kansas L. Rev.* 757 (Summer '86).

Neri, Joan M., "State Contracts—Commissions," 16 *Seton Hall L. Rev.* 889 (Summer-Fall '86).

Thurm, Gil, "Reporting Real Estate Transactions," 15 *J. of Real Estate Taxation* 98 (Fall '87).

Wachter, Susan M., "Residential Real Estate Brokerage, Rate Uniformity, and Moral Hazard," 10 *Research in Law and Economics* 189 (Annual '87).

BUSINESS ORGANIZATION

[¶ 901] Tax costs, liability exposure, and the practical convenience of various forms of business are the points that most clients raise when they consider setting up a business organization. Different types of ventures require different organizational means: the sole proprietorship, the general and limited partnership, the limited partnership, and the corporate form are all possibilities. Even within the corporate structure, many different kinds of operating procedures are possible. The following paragraphs offer summaries of various aspects of business organization.

A new and risky business or one in which losses are sustained to build capital value should be operated in unincorporated form or partnership form so that any losses may be applied against income and offset with tax savings. A form of incorporated partnership, known as an "S Corporation," may also be utilized.[1] S status avoids the corporate income tax at the corporate level and corporate operating losses can be claimed by the shareholders. For a detailed discussion of the tax consequences of Subchapter S incorporation, see ¶4208 et seq.

[¶ 902] THE CORPORATION

There are many definitions of what a corporation is. Some call it an "artificial entity," enjoying certain legal functions, rights and duties. Being an artificial or fictitious person, it can only act through its directors, who are elected by the shareholders.

[¶ 902.1 Advantages of a Corporation

A corporation may be formed for a wide variety of purposes, both profit or non-profit. Shareholders have limited liability in most cases. This limited liability is not absolute and a corporate shareholder can still be liable for the full price of his corporate stock if the stock was purchased at a discount. Shareholders are also liable in most states for unpaid wages.

Example: According to Section 630 of the New York Business Corporation Law, the ten largest shareholders will be jointly and severally liable for all debts, wages, and salaries owed for services performed for the corporation.

Ownership of corporate stock may be transferred freely by sale or by gift. The corporation has perpetual existence that remains unaffected by the death of any director, officer, or shareholder. The corporation, as a legal person, can sue and be sued, make contracts, hold both real and personal property, and issue stock. A corporation also has flexibility in choosing the securities (stocks, notes, or bonds) it may issue in raising capital. Finally, a corporation can elect the advantages of being an S corporation and the use of Section 1244 stock. Code Section 1244 was enacted in an attempt to attract financing for small businesses. Under this section, an individual is allowed to deduct, as ordinary loss, a loss on the sale or exchange of certain stock owned in a "small business." This provision allows individuals to deduct up to $50,000 annually (if filing as a single taxpayer) or $100,000 (for those people filing joint).

If the corporation prospers, its owners are generally permitted to transfer interests, in the form of the corporation's stock, to their children. Such transfers cannot be done directly in a sole proprietorship and only with the consent of all the partners if a partnership.

[¶902.2]   Disadvantages of a Corporation

There are several disadvantages inherent in the formation of a corporation. The limited liability of a shareholder might limit the amount of credit that the corporation might be able to obtain. If the corporation has few shareholders, the majority shareholders have the ability to make decisions that may not be in the best interest of the minority shareholders. If the corporation is publicly traded, voting rights might prove insignificant due to the widespread ownership. Management of a corporation is in the hands of the directors and therefore separate from the shareholders who are the true owners of the corporation. A corporation is subject to the laws of any state in which it does business. In addition a corporation is not protected by the Fifth Amendment's guarantee against self incrimination. This privilege is deemed purely a personal one available only to individuals. Corporations are subject to greater governmental control than other forms of doing business. Finally, corporate shareholders are subject to double taxation, one at the corporate level (as high as 35%) and the other at the individual level. As stated in ¶901, double taxation can be avoided by the election of S corporation status.

[¶903]   PROFESSIONAL CORPORATIONS

Members of the professions (i.e., those entities engaged in the practice of law, medicine, or accountancy) have found themselves confronted with a substantial tax liability because of their status as either sole proprietorships or partnerships. By forming a *professional corporation* and incorporating their practice, professionals and their employees become eligible to participate in employee fringe benefit and pension and profit-sharing plans. The corporate contributions to these plans are tax deductible, and the income generated by these retirement plans is tax-free (sometimes called *sheltered income*) until distributed to its employees-participants. Every state has enacted corporate legislation allowing professionals to incorporate their practices.

Creation of the corporation does not exempt the professional shareholder from personal liability caused by his or her own negligence, but it will prevent other practitioners who are shareholders from being held jointly liable for the negligence of employees unless they participated in the wrongdoing.

[¶904] LIMITED LIABILITY COMPANIES

When forming or reorganizing a company or venture, the choice of what form of organization to use has expanded in recent years to include limited liability companies (LLCs). An LLC has the advantages of a partnership's flow-through tax treatment, a corporation's limited liability, and an owner's control of management.

States that have enacted LLC statutes include Arizona, Colorado, Delaware, Florida, Illinois, Iowa, Kansas, Louisiana, Maryland, Minnesota, Nevada, New York, Oklahoma, Rhode Island, Texas, Utah, Virginia, West Virginia, and Wyoming. Four others have enacted foreign LLC recognition statutes; they only recognize LLCs formed in other states but do not permit them for in-state businesses. Virtually all other states are currently considering LLC statutes.

[¶904.1] Requirements

An LLC resembles a partnership, but it is a legal entity distinct from its members. A business wishing to exist in the form of an LLC must meet the partnership requirements of the Internal Revenue Code,[2] as well as file documents (e.g., Articles of Organization) with its respective state and meet the state's requirements for organization. LLC statutes presently vary from state to state, but a uniform LLC statute is now being drafted by a committee of the National Conference of Commissioners on Uniform State Laws as a model for adoption by all states.

[¶904.2] Advantages

The LLC form of organization may be more desirable than other business forms for various reasons, such as:

(a) Limited liability—members of LLCs are not liable for the organization's debts, obligations, or liabilities; they are generally liable only to the extent of their capital contribution to the LLC.

(b) Tax purposes—LLCs are taxed as partnerships, rather than as corporations. This means, among other things, a single level of Federal income tax and much greater tax flexibility.

(c) Management flexibility—unlike S corporations, there are no limitations on the number and type of owners, and unlike limited partnerships, all members may manage the corporation without losing liability protection

[¶904.3] Disadvantages

LLCs presently do have risks and disadvantages, however. For example:

(a) states may not recognize the limited liability feature of an LLC formed in another state, so members may still have personal liability.

(b) LLCs are new types of entities, so there is very little (if any) general or tax case law.

(c) all states do not recognize the LLC form of organization, which may be troublesome for a multi-state operation.

(d) LLC statutes can be rather restrictive regarding, for example, the ability to transfer one's interest.

[¶905]   SPLITTING INCOME

A family partnership may be the best way of splitting both income and capital values to children and other members of the family. However, the impact of the "kiddie tax" must be considered if transfers are made to family members younger than 14.

To reduce the tax savings that result from shifting income from parents to children, the net unearned income (commonly called investment income) of minor children who have not reached the age of 14 by the close of the taxable year, will be taxed at the parents' tax rate.[3]

[¶906]   PARTNERSHIP VS. CORPORATION

The choice isn't limited to either incorporating or remaining a proprietorship. For instance, there is the alternative of operating as a partnership. Following is a comparison between the two forms—corporation and partnership—with respect to the factors that will be most important. The checklist covers first general considerations, then tax considerations.

[¶906.1]   General (Nontax) Considerations

Partnership	Corporation
Life	
For the term specified in the partnership agreement; death of a partner may dissolve it earlier.	Continues until dissolved by law (unless statute limits the time).
Entity	
Has no separate entity from the partners.	Has entity separate from its stockholders. Can sue and be sued, hold and deal in property.

Liability

General partners are individually liable for all partnership obligations; limited partners usually liable only up to the amount of their capital contributions.

Stockholder has no individual liability; only his capital contribution is involved (exception: some state laws subject bank stockholders to double liability)—shareholders may be liable if the "corporate veil" is pierced.

Changing Ownership

Change in interests may create a new partnership. Arrangements necessary to end liability of ex-members.

Stock can ordinarily be sold or otherwise transferred at will.

Raising Capital

Only by loan, by new membership, or contributions of present members, or by remaking the firm.

By sale of new stock or bonds or other securities.

Making Policy

Unanimous agreement of partners usually required; involves problems of personality.

Authority centered in board of directors, acting by majority agreement.

Credit

Depends on standing of individual partners; partnership interests usually can't be pledged.

As separate entity, has credit possibility apart from stockholders; in close corporation, stock is available as collateral.

Management

By partners; they are responsible (except silent partners).

Stockholders not responsible; managers are employed.

Flexibility

Partners have leeway in their actions except to the extent limited by the partnership agreement (occasionally by law).

Limited to the powers (express and implied) in its charter from the state; may be subjected to judicial consideration.

[¶906.2]   Tax Considerations

Partnership   **Corporation**

Income Tax

Partners taxed on proportionate shares of partnership income whether or not distributed. Partnership return is merely an information return.

Income taxed to corporation; stockholders taxed only on dividends distributed to them.

Accumulation

Partners taxed on accumulated as well as distributed earnings.	Stockholders not taxed on accumulations. However, penalty tax applies if purpose is to avoid tax and accumulation exceeds certain amount.

Capital Gains and Losses

Partners taxed on their proportionate shares of gain and loss. They apply the limitations just as if they had only individual gains and losses.	Uses the alternative computation.

Exempt Interest

Partners not taxed on exempt interest received from the firm.	Exempt interest distributed by a corporation would be fully taxable income to the stockholders.

Charitable Contributions

The partners add their proportionate shares of the partnership's contributions to their own personal contributions in computing their incomes.	Corporations take their own deduction for charitable contributions; but maximum deduction is a fraction of an individual taxpayer's maximum deduction.

Pension Planning

Partners can be beneficiaries of a Keogh plan.	Officer and employee stockholders can be beneficiaries of a pension plan.

Social Security

Partners don't pay Social Security tax on compensation from the firm, but must pay self-employment tax.	Compensation to officer and employee stockholders is subject to Social Security tax.

Death Benefits

Up to $5,000 of a lump-sum distribution to partner's beneficiaries is tax-free.	Benefits up to $5,000 can be received tax free by stockholder-employee's beneficiaries.

State Taxes

In most states, partnerships not subject to state income and purchase taxes.	Corporations subject to these taxes, although deductibility on federal return lessens cost.

[¶907]   THE USE OF MULTIPLE CORPORATIONS

It might be possible to divide a business into several corporations and realize substantial tax savings, if it were not for IRC Sections 1561–1563. The potential tax breaks are prevented by the special rules that apply to corporations that are members of a "controlled group." A controlled group is treated as a single taxpayer for the purpose of selecting tax brackets—that is, each corporation does not have the privilege of paying the lowest corporate rate on part of its income. Only one $250,000 accumulated earnings credit and one $40,000 Alternative Minimum Tax exemption is allowed for the entire controlled group. (Absent agreement, each group member gets an equal—not a proportional—share of these items.) It doesn't matter if there is a bona fide business purpose for operating an enterprise as two or more corporations. Likewise, it doesn't matter if the multiple corporations are used to operate multiple businesses. If common ownership of the multiple corporations makes them component members of a controlled group, they are subject to the rules. A controlled group of corporations can always elect to file a consolidated return that, roughly speaking, disregards intercompany income and expenses in order to tax the members of the group solely on income generated by the group's transactions with outsiders.

Of course, there may be valid nontax reasons for using multiple corporations.

— ENDNOTES —

1. IRC §1361.
2. Subchapter K.
3. IRC §1(g).

— FOR FURTHER REFERENCE —

Beebe-Snell, Cheryl, "Dealing the Right Business Card," 3 *Compleat Lawyer* 6 (Winter '86).

Bloom, Gilbert D., "Buying and Selling Corporations After Tax Reform," 14 *J. of Corporate Taxation* 167 (Summer '87).

Blumberg, Philip I., "Limited Liability and Corporate Groups," 11 *J. of Corporation Law* 573 (Summer '86).

Claus, Gary R., "Revised Section 195 Still Leaves Many Issues Unresolved," 17 *Tax Adviser* 440 (July '86).

Dienelt, John F. and H. Brett Lowell, "Don't Give Away the Store (Franchise or Business Opportunity)," 1 *Compleat Lawyer* 28 (Summer '84).

Fellows, James A., "S Corporations and Losses Under Section 1244: A Critical Note," 65 *Taxes* 228 (April '87).

Schwartz, Sidney and Sidney Meyer, "Tax Aspects of Investment Decisions Changed by TRA '86," 65 *J. of Taxation* 420 (December '86).

Shaffer, Andrew B. and Brian D., "A Practical Checklist for Buying or Selling a Small Business in Colorado," 15 *Colorado Lawyer* 2171 (December '86).

Shaw, Richard A., "Tax Deliberations on the Disposition of Corporate Real Property," 38 *Major Tax Planning* 19 (Annual '86).

Yates, Robert, "A Tax Law Checklist for Business Clients," 72 *ABA J.* 84 (10/1/86).

CHECKLIST FOR DRAFTING A CONTRACT

[¶1001] The following checklist should be consulted whenever a contract is contemplated or drafted.

❏ What restrictions are necessary to keep the other party from adding an unwanted term or condition?

❏ Will all prior communications be merged into the written agreement?

❏ Will the possibility of future oral modifications be excluded?

❏ What future acts may be deemed to constitute a waiver of a contractual right?

❏ If the other party's representations are being relied on, they should be stated as an express warranty, rather than as a mere "whereas" recital. If it is merely a recital, fraud must be proved in order to get relief if the facts are different; if the misrepresentation is innocent, the contract may be voided if it's set up as a warranty.

❏ Does the party who signs the agreement have the necessary authority?

❏ If one side's obligation is dependent on the other party doing something, make the condition express and explicit. Otherwise there may be a claim for damages in the event the other party fails to perform.

❏ Stipulate whether or not representations are to survive the transaction.

❏ If something is sold "as is," expressly exclude any implied representations. State that the assignment is without recourse if there are to be warranties of title.

❏ Provide for duration and right to terminate. If it appears that the parties are likely to continue on in a business relationship beyond the express term, consider providing for automatic renewals for a year or some other appropriate period of time, always preserving the right to terminate on appropriate notice.

❏ Spell out exactly what constitutes performance (use quantities, descriptions, time, drawings, specifications, acceptance tests, etc.). Specify who is responsible for taking all steps necessary for getting permits and meeting all other necessary requirements of performance.

❏ Insert a time-of-the-essence clause, with a provision for cancellation of the contract, if the other party fails in timely performance.

❏ Guard against liability from unforeseeable contingencies by inserting a force majeure clause.

❏ In the absence of a contrary provision, delivery and payment are concurrent provisions. If the intention is otherwise, express provision is needed. If payment is to be made in installments, consider acceleration and prepayment provisions.

❏ If collateral security is to be furnished, see ¶3401 et seq.

❏ If the other party's performance is to be guaranteed or a party is to be indemnified or held harmless, see ¶3401 and 3801.

❏ If the sale or use of an item might infringe on a third party's patent, have a patent indemnity clause.

❏ If a deposit is made, consider getting that accepted as liquidated damages. If liquidated damages are provided for, make sure they are not so heavy as to be held to be a penalty.

❏ Protect against inadvertent default by providing for notice and a subsequent time period within which any default may be cured. Provide whether notice becomes effective upon mailing or upon receipt and whether it has to be given by registered or certified mail.

❏ If the governing law can be specified, this will avoid perplexing conflict of laws problems.

❏ Provide explicitly whether the contract is to be assignable or not, and whether or not the original party is released from liability upon assignment. Consider providing that the assignment is not effective until the assignee assumes the assignor's obligations in writing.

❏ Use special care in drafting conditions. If one party is excused from performance on the happening of a condition, say so clearly. If the condition is concurrent, as, for example, delivery of merchandise on payment of the price, make this clear. If the condition is subsequent, as where the agreement is continued until either party exercises his option to cancel it, make it clear that only on compliance with the termination procedure may the agreement be canceled. If the condition is precedent, as where one party must complete his part of the agreement before the other party is obligated to render his performance, make it clear that substantial or full completion is necessary before the other party is obligated to act. The use of conditions will also determine whether the parties intend the agreement to be entire or severable. Provide for concurrent or conditional performance, if it is not desirable to have the agreement divided into separate, self-contained units each independent of the next unit and standing alone as a separately enforceable agreement.

❏ Whenever money or goods have to be advanced before completion of the other party's performance, find out whether protection against insolvency is needed. If it is, have money placed in escrow and see that either title to or a lien on property is retained.

❏ Is a provision to be included stating that each party has made his own investigation and has not relied on any statement or preliminary representation made by the other?

❏ If arbitration is to be used, see ¶401 et seq.

❏ It is always safest to specify the consideration that makes the contract binding, even though in some states the law makes a written instrument of agreement binding without consideration. If consideration is necessary it will make later proof easier if it is specified.

❏ In preliminary negotiations, avoid the risk that oral and letter negotiations may create an agreement; make it clear that there is no agreement until a final document is signed.

❏ If a party is to have the right to cancel the agreement if it is breached by the other party, it is advisable to include a clause to that effect. Otherwise, it may be necessary to establish that the breach is serious enough to defeat the purpose of the contract in order to be relieved of its obligations.

❐ Exclude the authority of any salesperson or agent of one of the parties to change the conditions of sale and shipment specified in the agreement.

❐ Are the parties to have any right to inspect the books and records of another party?

❐ Specify who is to carry risk of property loss during contract period. What insurance is to be carried? By whom?

❐ Consider the inclusion of a liquidated damages clause—making sure to specify that the amount of damages so provided is not intended as a penalty.

❐ If concurrent performance is a condition, say so. If complete and exact performance is a condition, say so. If a party is to be relieved of a performance upon the happening of some event, say so. If exact performance is required, expressly exclude the doctrine of substantial performance.

❐ Should a provision be included requiring any change and modification of the contract to be in writing and signed by both parties?

❐ Is the illegality of any provision to invalidate the contract as a whole?

❐ An all-purpose modification clause should spell out the "how" of changing the agreement, especially when there is maximum daily contact on all levels between both parties. This will protect against unauthorized amendments agreed upon by subordinates without the party's approval. Limit modifications to formal contacts between the highest levels, or name the authorized personnel.

❐ If the agreement leaves certain items (price, delivery dates, etc.) to be revised later, as conditions change, make sure an "escape," an arbitration, liquidated damage, or cancellation clause is included.

❐ Is an escape clause necessary? Usually, escape clauses are two-way streets—each party has the same option to end the agreement. But the one-way escape clause is not uncommon and serves usefully to end an agreement when the other party has defaulted or has breached or when some basic consideration (obtaining favorable tax rulings, zoning clearance, export license, steel quota, franchise renewal, etc.) has backfired. A good escape clause should fix a period and method of notice, leaving no doubt about items that have accrued prior to the termination date.

COMMERCIAL PAPER

[¶1101] Checks, certificates of deposit, notes, drafts, and all forms of negotiable instruments except money, documents of title, or investment securities are governed by Article 3 of the Uniform Commercial Code (Commercial Paper). Provisions of Article 3 of the UCC are also subject to the provisions of the Articles on bank deposits and collections (Article 4) and secured transactions (Article 9). Both Articles 3 and 4 are in effect in each of the 50 states and the District of Columbia.

[¶1102] THE IMPORTANCE OF NEGOTIABILITY

"Substitutes for currency" is the best definition of negotiable instruments. Essentially, negotiable instruments are contracts to pay money—but, unlike money, negotiable instruments are characterized by the following two additional features: (1) intangible transferable rights in the instrument and (2) the fact that a "good faith" transferee's rights can be greater than those that were held by the transferor prior to negotiation.

[¶1103] TYPES OF COMMERCIAL PAPER

The following are the types of promises that, if in writing, will form negotiable instruments (UCC §3-104(2)):
(a) A draft (bill of exchange), if it is an order to pay;
(b) A check, if it is a draft drawn on a bank and made payable on demand;
(c) A certificate of deposit, if it is an acknowledgment by a bank of receipt of money with the promise that the money will be repaid;
(d) A note, if it is a promise that money will be repaid other than a certificate of deposit.

It is important to recognize that the terms "draft," "check," "certificate of deposit," and "note" may also refer to instruments that are not negotiable—the qualification following each of those terms is what makes them negotiable instruments.

[¶1104] PROMISSORY NOTES AND BILLS OF EXCHANGE

A promissory note is a written promise to pay a certain sum at a future time or on demand. Installment notes, mortgage notes, and collateral notes are some examples of promissory notes. Even if a note is not for a definite sum (e.g., for a specified amount plus interest), it may nonetheless be a promissory note because a certain sum is defined as being either a stated or determinable amount. Bills of exchange—a check or draft instrument—differ from promissory notes because the maker or drawer orders a drawee (bank) or acceptor to pay. In a promissory note, the issuer promises to pay.

Simple time and demand notes with interest, judgment notes, secured notes, installment notes, and other varied forms of notes are found in the *IBP Forms of Business Agreements and Resolutions.*

[¶1105] HOW TO MAKE A NOTE NEGOTIABLE

In order to make a promissory note negotiable, UCC §3-104(1) sets forth the following requirements. The note must be:

- ❑ A writing,
- ❑ Signed by the maker or drawer,
- ❑ Containing an unconditional promise (or order) to pay a sum certain in money,
- ❑ Containing no other promise (order, obligation, or power),
- ❑ Payable on demand or at a definite time,
- ❑ Payable to order or to bearer.

[¶1106] MAKING A PROMISE UNCONDITIONAL

Conditional promises are sufficient to defeat negotiability of an instrument. UCC §3-105 provides a number of instances when certain qualifications that may appear to make a promise conditional do not do so. In the chart below, several different types of provisions, commonly found in commercial paper, are listed. Each relates to certain "qualifications" that might affect conditionality; the UCC has legislatively stated that in the examples below there is no effect directly or indirectly on negotiability.

Type of Provision in Note	Rule Under UCC
Statement in note that it was given in exchange for an executory promise (i.e., one still to be carried out).	Not conditional; note is negotiable.
Promise to pay is expressly conditioned on carrying out executory promise.	Conditional; not negotiable.
Informational references—e.g., nature of the consideration given for the note; the transaction that gave rise to the note; the promise to pay matures in *accordance with or as per* some transaction.	Not conditional; references to a separate agreement or that notes arise out of the agreement, and references to letter of credit under which the notes are drawn, do not create conditions or affect negotiability.

Statement that the note is *subject to* or *governed by* another instrument.	Conditional; not negotiable.
Recital of the security given in so-called title security notes.	Not conditional; negotiable.
Statement that note is to be paid only from a particular fund.	Conditional; not negotiable.
Same as above, but note is issued by a government, government agency, or government unit; or note is issued by a partnership, unincorporated association, trust, or estate payable out of the entire assets of the issuer.	Not conditional; negotiable.

[¶1107] PROMISE TO PAY A SUM CERTAIN IN MONEY

In order for the amount of the note to qualify as a sum certain, the holder must be able to determine from the instrument itself the amount that is payable. Computations are permissible—such as a requirement for interest at a specified percentage rate. However, wording such as "current interest rates" render the instrument nonnegotiable because the computation cannot be made from the instrument itself (UCC §3-106).

Where the language of the contract provides that the holder *may* pay taxes, assessments, and insurance if the obligor fails to do so, and then recover what is paid from the obligor, the instrument is nonnegotiable because of the uncertainty as to the sum actually owed.

If a note provides for interest at a particular percentage, the phrase "or at maximum legal rates" has been held to be an expressed provision to pay a definitely ascertainable maximum legal rate and no more, therefore making it negotiable.

[¶1108] ADDITIONS TO A SUM CERTAIN

Following is a checklist of what may be included in addition to a fixed monetary sum that will not render an instrument nonnegotiable (UCC §3-106).

❑ Payments to be made with stated interest and stated installments.

❑ Payments to be made with stated different rates of interest before or after default of a specific date.

❑ Payment to be reduced by a stated discount for early payment.

❑ Additional payment required if paid after maturity.

❑ Payment to be with exchange or less exchange, whether at a fixed rate or at current rate.

❑ Provision for acceleration of payment (UCC §3-109).

❐ Provision for payment with costs of collection or attorneys' fees or both upon default (UCC §3-106). But consult local law as to validity and enforceability of this type of provision. Even in states where these provisions are unenforceable, the note's negotiability isn't otherwise affected, whether the provision is for a percentage or a fixed amount. In any event, only reasonable fees will be allowed (UCC §3-106(e)).

❐ Provision for payment in foreign currency (UCC §3-107). The UCC provides that *unless otherwise agreed,* an instrument payable in foreign currency "may be satisfied by payment of that number of dollars which the stated foreign currency will purchase at the buying sight rate for that currency on the day on which the instrument is payable, if payable on demand, on the day of demand."

[¶1109] ADDITIONS TO SUM CERTAIN AFFECTING NEGOTIABILITY

Provisions permitting interest to be computed at the "current rate" render an instrument nonnegotiable since the sum payable is not certain. Provision to pay taxes levied on commercial paper would also render the instrument nonnegotiable according to judicial decisions (the UCC itself is silent).

[¶1110] WHEN THE NOTE IS PAYABLE

In order for an instrument to be negotiable it must either be payable at a specified time or on demand. To the extent that a note provides for payment at or before a specified date, it is considered payable at a definite time.

[¶1111] DEMAND INSTRUMENTS

Demand instruments are payable at sight or on presentation (UCC §3-108). Use of the phrase "payable on demand" or "on demand promises to pay" removes any ambiguity. The holder of the note has the option to call for payment at any time. The maker retains the option to pay anytime before the holder demands payment.

[¶1112] PAYABLE AT A FIXED TIME

The time of payment is definite only if it can be determined from the face of the instrument (UCC §3-109). Promissory notes payable at a fixed period of time after the death of the maker are not considered negotiable. For example, an instrument payable "one year after the death of Uncle John Mahoney" is not payable at a definite time even if Mahoney is already dead when the instrument is issued. However, a postdated check payable at the death of the drawer or at the stated date is an enforceable negotiable instrument.

[¶1113] ACCELERATION CLAUSES

An acceleration clause does not alter the effect of payment at a definite time. If the holder of a note feels insecure about payment, and an acceleration clause permits a calling in for payment at whim, the note is nonetheless negotiable (UCC §3-109(1)(c)).

[¶1114] WORDS OF NEGOTIABILITY

In order to render an instrument negotiable, words of negotiability (payable to order or bearer) must be used. A note payable to order is payable to (1) either the order, or (2) assigns of a named person, or (3) to him, or (4) to his order. Both order and bearer instruments are negotiable—although there is a significant difference between the two that dictates the use of order instruments in most situations. If a bearer instrument is either lost or stolen and winds up in the hands of a bona fide purchaser for value, the instrument is good and cannot be defeated in an action for payment. Order paper, on the other hand, is protected against theft even through fraudulent endorsement by the payee (UCC §3-110 and §3-111).

If a note meets the basic requirement of order paper, it may be payable to the maker, a payee not the maker, or two or more payees together or in the alternative. If payable to two or more payees, give thought to whether they're to be joint tenants with a right of survivorship or simply tenants in common, and use clear enough language to accomplish the intention of the client (UCC §3-116).

The UCC provides that an order instrument may be payable to an estate, trust, or fund (§3-110), in which case it is payable to the representative or to his successor. The UCC also provides that an order instrument may be payable (1) to an office or an officer by his title, in which case it is payable to the principal, but the incumbent or his successors may act as the holder, or (2) to a partnership or unincorporated association, in which case it is payable to the partnership or association and may be transferred by any person authorized by it. UCC §3-117 further provides that an instrument made payable to a named person with the addition of words describing him as an agent, officer, or fiduciary is payable to the principal.

It's clear that a note will be considered bearer paper if it's payable to: (1) bearer; (2) a named person or bearer; or (3) cash or the order of cash. Occasionally a note will be issued payable to "order of bearer." This usually happens when a printed form of order note is used and the word "bearer" is filled in where the name of the payee is intended to go. In such case some authorities had taken the view that this is an order note. The UCC, however, rejects this view and makes it a bearer instrument (UCC §3-111).

Where checks bore a restrictive notation stating that the instrument would be dishonored unless a particular contract was awarded, the instrument made as a bid deposit could not be considered as either a draft, check, or demand note within the meaning of the requirement that a bid deposit be made payable on demand. This and any other limitation upon payability to order or bearer should be sufficient to negate negotiability.

[¶1115] ADDITIONAL AND OMITTED TERMS THAT DO NOT AFFECT NEGOTIABILITY

Following is a checklist of terms that may be added or omitted without affecting an instrument's negotiability (UCC §3-112).

❏ Statement of consideration is omitted.

❏ Place where the instrument is drawn or payable is omitted.

❏ Statement that collateral has been given to secure obligations either under the instrument or otherwise is included.

❏ Statement that, in case of default, the holder may realize on or otherwise dispose of collateral is included.

❏ Promise or power to maintain or protect collateral, or to give additional collateral, is included.

❏ Term authorizing confession of judgment, if the instrument is not paid when due, is included.

❏ Term purporting to waive the benefit of any law intended to protect the obligor is included.

❏ Term in a draft providing that the payee's indorsing or cashing the draft acknowledges full satisfaction of an obligation of the drawer is included.

❏ Statement in a draft drawn in a set of parts (to the effect that the order is effective only if no other part has been honored) is included.

[¶1116] PROVISIONS TO INCLUDE OR AVOID IN A NEGOTIABLE INSTRUMENT

Interest Rates—Usury: It is permissible to include a provision for interest at a particular rate, or at maximum legal rates. Use of this type of provision does not render the note usurious: the note remains negotiable, even though it contains an express provision to pay a definitely ascertainable maximum legal rate, and not more.

Also see: "State Guide to Interest Rates" in the Appendix.

Sale of Collateral: A provision can be incorporated in a note that will authorize sale of collateral by the holder of the note, without destroying negotiability of the note. Such a provision might be desirable if the maker of the note doesn't have an especially good credit rating—and so is required to give collateral that may be sold pursuant to the authority in the provision. Under the UCC it may be made operative upon any default, including default in the payment of interest (§3-112(b)). The UCC also permits a clause containing a promise or a power to maintain or protect collateral, or to give additional collateral, whether on demand or on some other condition, which will not affect negotiability. See also UCC §9-504.

Confession of Judgment: A confession of judgment is authorized by the UCC only if the instrument is not paid when due (§3-112). If the clause allows judgment to be confessed prior to the default, the instrument is nonnegotiable.

Notes Payable at a Bank: A draft drawn on a bank payable when it falls due out of any funds of the maker or acceptor available for payment may or may not be considered an order or an authorization for the bank to pay it. UCC §3-121 permits the various jurisdictions to elect either of these choices. Alternative A states that a note payable at a bank is equivalent to a draft drawn on the bank; Alternative B says that the note or acceptance is not an order or an authorization to pay—merely a designation of a location where payment will be made.

Alternative "A" has been adopted in Alaska, Connecticut, Delaware, District of Columbia, Hawaii, Kentucky, Maine, Massachusetts, Missouri, Nevada, New Hampshire, New Jersey, New York, North Dakota, Ohio, Pennsylvania, Rhode Island, Texas, Vermont, Virgin Islands, West Virginia, and Wyoming.

Alternative "B" has been adopted in Alabama, Arizona, Arkansas, California, Colorado, Florida, Georgia, Idaho, Illinois, Indiana, Iowa, Kansas, Louisiana, Maryland, Michigan, Minnesota, Mississippi, Montana, Nebraska, New Mexico, North Carolina, Oklahoma, Oregon, South Carolina, South Dakota, Tennessee, Utah, Virginia, Washington, and Wisconsin. Both California and Virginia have adopted additional modifications to Alternative "B."

Waiver of Benefit of Any Law: A provision under which the obligor waives the benefit of any law intended for his benefit will not destroy negotiability under the UCC, although it might be invalid under local law. A waiver of the benefits of the statutes of limitations, for example, is invalid under the law of many states. On the other hand, a waiver of presentment and notice of dishonor is universally recognized as valid, and is included in most notes as a matter of course (UCC §3-511).

[¶1117] TRADE ACCEPTANCES AND BANK ACCEPTANCES

Trade acceptances are drafts drawn on the purchaser of goods and accepted by him (which the purchaser promises to pay upon presentation). If, instead of the draft being drawn on the purchaser, it is drawn on the purchaser's bank, which has agreed with the purchaser to accept on his behalf, then such acceptance is a bank acceptance (UCC §3-410).

Here's how a bank acceptance might be used in foreign commerce: Let's say a person in San Francisco wants to sell $5,000 worth of widgets to a merchant in Yokohama, Japan, with whom he's never done business and whom he doesn't know. The Japanese merchant might make arrangements with his bank in Yokohama to accept drafts drawn on it up to the amount of $5,000 on presentation of specified documents (bill of lading, insurance papers, etc.). The bank on presentation of the draft and documents will accept as agreed on and the seller will have a piece of paper, assuming that the Yokohama bank is sound and well known, that will be readily convertible into cash. A trade acceptance in that situation would obviously not be so readily convertible.

[¶1118] DISCOUNTING TRADE ACCEPTANCES

If a draft is payable at sight or on demand, any Federal Reserve Bank may purchase or discount the draft if it arose in connection with a domestic shipment or foreign shipment of nonperishable, readily marketable goods.

There are four basic requirements for this:

❐ The acceptance must bear on its face the statement that it arises out of the purchase and sale of goods.

❐ The acceptance must be a clear, definite order to pay without any qualifying conditions.

❐ The acceptance must be written across the face of the draft.

❐ The draft must be conspicuously labeled "Trade Acceptance."

The Code provides that an otherwise unconditional promise or order does not become conditional merely because the nature of the underlying transaction is stated on the face of the instrument (UCC §3-105(b)). Therefore, this phrase should be included on an acceptance:

"The transaction which gives rise to this instrument is the purchase of goods by the acceptor from the drawer."

Any variance from this form may involve the risk of having the instrument declared nonnegotiable. For example, the addition of words such as "per invoice of" or "as per contract" has been held to affect negotiability. A title retention clause has also been held to render it nonnegotiable. However, the UCC contains provisions in §3-105 that may alter the result of these decisions and permit references such as those quoted above and to retention of title.

In any case, the following clauses may be inserted without affecting negotiability:

❐ Waiver of exemption and attorneys' fees.

❐ Provision for costs of collection.

❐ Provision for payment of interest after maturity.

[¶1119] CHECKLIST FOR TRADE ACCEPTANCES

Here are the major additional points that must be kept in mind in dealing with trade acceptances. Because these rules aren't limited only to trade and bank acceptances but apply to all drafts, they are discussed below under a separate heading at §1120.

❐ A trade acceptance should never be used if you wouldn't grant an open account credit.

❐ A trade acceptance shouldn't be used to cover a past due account.

❐ If the seller indorses an acceptance, he guarantees that it will be met at maturity. The seller must, therefore, be sure that the paper is good.

❐ An acceptance form authorizing a discount if paid before a certain date may render the instrument nonnegotiable according to some authorities. Make this arrangement outside the draft; e.g., 2%, 10 days, net 30, would give the purchaser the option of discounting in 10 days.

❐ Make sure that the acceptance form matches the terms of the sale.

❐ If a trade acceptance is made payable at a bank, as a general rule, it will be treated as a check drawn on a bank.

❐ The acceptor of a trade acceptance has the same right to stop payment as the maker of a check would have.

❐ If the drawer of a trade acceptance would otherwise have a mechanic's lien for the goods, he won't as a general rule lose his lien merely by taking the trade acceptance. However, watch out if the time of payment of the trade acceptance runs beyond the time for enforcing the mechanic's lien. Some courts have held that this amounts to waiver of the lien.

[¶1120] UCC RULES AS TO TRADE ACCEPTANCE

A drawee isn't liable on a draft or check until he assents in writing to the order of the drawer. This assent is called acceptance in the case of a draft and certification in the case of a check.

Under the UCC, acceptance may be simply by signature. It is perfectly clear that the acceptance must be written on the draft (§3-410). The drawee's failure to accept before the close of business the day after presentment does not operate as a constructive acceptance (UCC §3-506). It should be noted that the UCC's rejection of the doctrine of constructive acceptance in case of refusal of the drawee to accept or return the draft doesn't mean that the drawee can't be held liable for conversion or breach of a contractual obligation. On the contrary, UCC §3-419 recognizes the possibility of liability for conversion and UCC §3-409 recognizes the possibility of contractual liability.

The UCC provides that if the holder of an instrument assents to an acceptance varying the terms of the draft, each drawer and indorser who does not affirmatively assent to the variance is discharged (§3-412(3)).

The UCC contemplates that the drawee named in the bill is the person to be looked to in the first instance for acceptance, but states that you may designate another person to whom resort may be had in case of dishonor by the named drawee. This secondary party is known as a "referee in case of need." The usual form followed is to write below the drawee's name: "In case of need apply to John Doe." This will give the holder the option to resort to the person secondarily named. He may, however, ignore this and treat the instrument as dishonored if the drawee refuses to accept (UCC §4-503).

[¶1121] CERTIFICATION OF CHECKS

Certification of checks is acceptance (UCC §3-411(1)). Usually, a certification discharges the drawer and all prior endorsers, but a certification requested by the drawer continues liability for that party. Unless otherwise agreed, a bank is not required to certify a check (UCC §3-411(2)).

The statutory effect of a certification is to render the bank directly liable on the instrument when it is properly endorsed. A drawer has no power to stop payment on a check following certification whether the certification was made at the request of the holder or the drawer. However, if a bank voluntarily chooses to dishonor a certified check—which it might do for a good customer—the holder will have a valid cause of action against the bank. There have been some lower court rumblings with respect to a stop-payment order on a bank check; however, the consensus is that even though businesspeople treat bank checks like cash, it is not proper for a bank check to discharge a buyer from the underlying obligation under UCC §3-802.

Under the UCC, a certification must be in writing and signed by the drawee (§3-410 and §3-411).

The UCC says certification must be on the check itself. The UCC rejects all forms of extrinsic acceptances or certifications.

Even if the drawer's signature is forged, the certifying bank will be liable to a holder in due course—on the theory that it knows the drawer's signature and, by certifying, warrants its genuineness.

Under UCC §3-413, the certification relates to the check as it is at the time of certification and not as it was originally. So even though the amount of the check has been increased or the name of the payee changed, the bank will be fully liable—provided that the bank's form of certification doesn't undertake to pay the check only as originally drawn. In the past, many banks had adopted this form of limited certification.

[¶1122] POSTDATING AND ANTEDATING CHECKS

Negotiability of a check is not necessarily affected by the fact that it is postdated, provided the bank handling the check acts in good faith and in accordance with the obligations to use ordinary care in handling customer funds. However, the purchaser of a postdated instrument who knows at the time of the purchase that the instrument is postdated may be precluded from asserting a holder-in-due-course defense. If a check is antedated or postdated, and it is payable either on demand or after a fixed time, the stated date controls (UCC §§3-114, 3-304, 3-305).

[¶1123] STOPPING PAYMENTS ON CHECKS

The UCC permits orders for stop payment on a check that has been issued. Payments made in violation of an effective stop order are improper and the bank is liable for damages suffered (although the customer has the burden of proving the amount of loss) (§4-403(3)). Payment may be stopped any time before acceptance, certification, or actual payment. Both oral and written stop payment orders are recognized. An oral order is good for only two weeks (14 days), while a written one is valid for six months unless renewed in writing (UCC §4-403(2)). It is useful to remember that checks are considered stale after 30 days, and thus a written stop payment order rarely must be renewed. This section of the UCC is in effect in 50 states, the District of Columbia, and the Virgin Islands. Minor variations of this section are made by the states so local law should be consulted.

[¶1124] BAD CHECK LAWS

An individual who makes or issues or negotiates a check knowing that it will bounce violates the "bad check laws," which are individual to each state. Generally, the offense is a misdemeanor (although it may be a felony, depending upon the amount involved). At common law, a bank was permitted to recover the amount of an overdraft that was paid against a customer's account. This is given full credence in UCC §4-401(1), which permits a bank to charge the customer whenever the customer writes a check that is in other respects properly payable from his account, even if payment creates an overdraft. In this instance, the customer remains liable and the check is good. The bank usually imposes a service charge or treats it as a loan. The basic requirement is that the bank act in good faith in making payment to a holder.

Intent to defraud may generally be proved by the mere issuance of the check and its subsequent dishonor for lack of funds. The presumption is, of course, rebuttable.

[¶1125] HOW AN INSTRUMENT IS NEGOTIATED

You can negotiate an instrument either by delivery or by indorsement and delivery. If it's "bearer" paper, delivery will be enough. For "order" paper, it will take indorsement plus delivery.

Set forth below in checklist form are the matters to be considered in making or dealing with indorsements:

❐ **Who Must Make:** An indorsement must be made by the holder or someone authorized by the holder (UCC §3-403).

❐ **Where Made:** Usually on the instrument and on the back side. The use of an allonge (a writing attached to the instrument) is acceptable only when necessary; for example, if the instrument is covered with indorsements and there's no more room (UCC §3-202).

❐ **Ambiguous Signature:** Unless the instrument clearly indicates a signature is made in some other capacity, it will be considered an indorsement (UCC §3-402).

❐ **Two or More Indorsees:** Indorsement in favor of two or more indorsees; e.g., "Pay A and B," will be effective negotiation. Indorsees will normally take as tenants in common, rather than joint tenants. Spell out the desired result in order to make sure (UCC §3-116).

❑ *Partial Assignments:* An indorsement that purports to transfer less than the entire instrument or the unpaid balance under it is a partial assignment and will be ineffective as a negotiation. Examples of partial assignments: "Pay A one-half"; "Pay A two-thirds and B one-third." (UCC §3-206).

❑ *Words Accompanying Indorsement:* Words of assignment, condition, waiver, limitation or disclaimer of liability or guaranty will not, under UCC §3-202(4), prevent an indorsement from being effective as a transfer of the indorser's interest, but they may affect the rights and liabilities of the indorser, the indorsee, or subsequent holders.

❑ *Misspelling or Wrong Name:* Under the UCC, if an instrument is payable to someone under a misspelled name or a name other than his own, he may indorse in either name or both and a person paying value for the instrument can require indorsement in both (§3-203). As a transferee, you would insist on both names.

❑ *Maiden Name of Married Woman:* If the paper uses the maiden name of a woman and she tries to negotiate by her married name, have her use both names in her indorsement.

❑ *Rights if Order Paper Transferred Without Indorsement:* In such case the transferee gets whatever rights his transferor had, and if the transferee paid value, he can insist on indorsement, but he gets status of holder in due course only from the time of indorsement and not from the time of transfer (UCC §3-201).

❑ *Blank, Special, Qualified, Restrictive, or Conditional Indorsements:* These are the various types of indorsements that may be used. Set out at ¶1126 is a table listing these various types of indorsements giving specimen forms of each type, and showing their meanings and effect.

❑ *Effect of Indorsement:* An unrestricted, unqualified, and unconditional indorsement passes title to the paper and makes the indorser secondarily liable to subsequent holders—that is, the indorser impliedly contracts to pay if the party primarily liable, the maker, drawer, or acceptor, fails to pay (UCC §3-414).

[¶1126] TABLE OF INDORSEMENTS—THEIR MEANING AND EFFECT

Type and Wording	Meaning and Effect Under the UCC
Blank:	
(1) Kay Johnson	Specifies no indorsee of person to whom paper payable; payable to bearer and negotiable by delivery until specially indorsed (§3-204(2)).
(2) Pay to bearer Kay Johnson	Blank indorsement may be converted into special indorsement by holder (§3-204(3)).

Special:

(1) Pay to John Jones or order Kay Johnson (2) Pay to order of John Jones Kay Johnson	Specifies person to whom or to whose order instrument is payable and may be negotiated only by special indorsee's indorsement (§3-204(1)).

Qualified:

(1) Without recourse Kay Johnson	Code doesn't use term, but §3-414 makes clear that ordinary contract of indorser can be disclaimed or qualified.

Restrictive:

(1) Pay to order of First National Bank for Deposit Kay Johnson	Makes bank agent of deposit for collection and credit to depositor's account. Any transferee other than intermediary bank must act consistently with purpose of collection. Does not prevent further negotiation. See §§3-205, 3-206.
(2) For collection Jane Silver	Makes indorsee agent of indorser for collection. Comments in re paragraph (1) above apply. Relatively rare.
(3) Pay any bank all prior indorsements guaranteed Second National Bank	Indicates purpose of deposit or collection. Except for intermediary bank must act consistently with purpose. Does not prevent further negotiation. See §4-205, §4-206. "Prior indorsements guaranteed" is implied (§4-207(3)).
(4) Pay any bank, banker, or trust company Third National Bank	Common form used by banks but not expressly mentioned in UCC. See comments re paragraph (3) above.
(5) Pay to John Jones only Jane Silver	Same as unrestricted indorsement. Further transfer or negotiation not prevented. See §§3-205, 3-206. Same is true of any other indorsements purporting to bar further transfer.
(6) Pay to John Jones as trustee for Jack Smith Kay Johnson	Rule is the same as for restrictive indorsements for deposit or collection, except here the duty to act consistently with indorsement is limited to first taker. See §3-206(4).
(7) Pay John Jones as agent for Jack Smith Joe Rose	See comments re (6).
(8) Pay John Jones for Jack Smith Jim Kelly	See comments re (6).

Conditional:

(1) Pay the within sum if and only if the SS Roe arrives in N.Y. by Sept. 30, 1981. John Doe.	Rarely used. Treated as restrictive indorsement. Payor *must* disregard condition. Collecting bank not affected by. Other indorsees must see application of proceeds and to extent they do become holders in due course and further negotiation not prevented (§3-205, §3-206).

[¶1127] CHANGING BEARER PAPER TO ORDER PAPER (AND VICE VERSA)

The last indorsement on order paper controls the next negotiation. If the last indorsement is in blank, the order paper is bearer paper negotiable by mere delivery. If, however, the indorsement is special, it is order paper that may be negotiated only pursuant to the special indorsement. Bearer paper that is specially indorsed becomes payable to the order of the special indorsee and may be further negotiated only by that individual's indorsement (UCC §3-204). A blank indorsement may be converted into a special indorsement by writing over the indorsee's signature the words "payable to the order of (specified person)." This protects against the possibility of loss or theft of paper and acquisition by a bona fide purchaser.

[¶1128] PRESENTMENT, NOTICE OF DISHONOR, AND PROTEST

In order to charge parties who are secondarily liable with liability if the primary party fails to pay an instrument, presentment is required. Presentment is a demand for payment or acceptance on the part of the maker, drawee, acceptor, or other payor by or on behalf of the holder.

Notice of dishonor is an indication of an item that a primarily liable party has refused to pay or accept.

In order to make an indorser liable, presentment and notice of dishonor are both necessary (UCC §3-501).

Several states (e.g., Hawaii, Idaho, Maryland, North Carolina, Washington) have adopted additional provisions in Part 5 of Article 3 in their versions of the UCC, providing additional damages against the writer of a dishonored check.

[¶1129] RIGHTS OF A HOLDER IN DUE COURSE

The single most important feature of any negotiable instrument is that a holder in due course takes the instrument free of any claims or defenses that would be available against another holder—for example, an assignment of a claim. In order to qualify as a holder in due course, a holder must have:

☐ taken the instrument for value;

☐ taken the instrument in good faith;

☐ taken the instrument without notice that it is overdue;

☐ taken the instrument without notice that it has been dishonored;

☐ taken the instrument without any knowledge of any defense or claim against it (UCC §3-302).

Purchases of limited interests in a negotiable instrument may qualify for holder-in-due-course treatment to the extent of the interest purchased (UCC §3-302(4)).

The Federal Trade Commission has acted to preserve certain consumer claims and defenses against negotiable instruments that they have executed that are subsequently sold or assigned to an individual who would otherwise be able to raise a holder-in-due-course defense against the consumer. The FTC Trade Regulation Rule concerning preservation of consumer claims and defenses became effective in 1976 (16 CFR Part 433). In adopting the rule, the FTC determined that it was an unfair and deceptive practice in trade for the seller in the course of financing or arranging the financing of a purchase of consumer goods or services to employ any procedure that rendered the consumer's duty to pay independent of the seller's duty to fulfill his obligations. The rule specifically requires the insertion of a clause in the consumer credit contract to permit the consumer to raise against the creditor any claim or defense that he could raise against the seller under applicable law.

The clause must be in 10-point boldface type, and must contain the following: "Notice: Any holder of this consumer credit contract is subject to all claims and defenses which the debtor could assert against the seller of goods or services obtained pursuant hereto or with the proceeds hereof. Recovery hereunder shall not exceed amounts paid by the debtor hereunder." The same provision must be included in purchase-money loan agreements; the FTC rule defines a purchase-money loan as a cash advance, on which a finance charge is imposed, made to facilitate the purchase of goods or services from a seller who arranges credit or is affiliated with the lender. (See ¶1133–1135 for further discussion of seller-lender affiliation.) A consumer does not have the right to withhold payment unilaterally under the rule. Both the manner and procedure by which any buyer may assert a claim or defense are governed by the terms of applicable state law and contractual obligations.

[¶1130] REAL DEFENSES AGAINST A HOLDER IN DUE COURSE

Although personal defenses may not be asserted against a holder in due course, "real" defenses may be successfully asserted against him. Failure of consideration, mistake, and breach of warranty are considered personal defenses and, consequently, not assertable against a holder in due course. Forgery and fraud in the execution, however, are real defenses that may be raised. Infancy is a real defense to the extent that it would be a defense against a simple contract (an infant may assert the defense against a holder in due course, even though the effect of infancy would be to make the instrument voidable, not void) (UCC §3-305(2)(a)). Misrepresentation to induce a party to sign an instrument (fraud in the inducement) is also a real defense (UCC §3-305(2)(c)). Discharge and bankruptcy or insolvency proceedings are also good against a holder in due course.

[¶1131] RIGHTS AND LIABILITIES OF A HOLDER NOT IN DUE COURSE

Holders of a negotiable instrument who have not taken in due course take subject to the following:
- ❒ All valid claims against it on the part of any person;
- ❒ All defenses of any party available in a simple contract action;
- ❒ The defense of no consideration;
- ❒ The defense of nonperformance of any condition precedent;
- ❒ The defense of improper delivery or improper payment inconsistent with the terms of a restrictive indorsement.

[¶1132] DISCHARGE OF UNDERLYING OBLIGATION

If a bank is either the drawer, maker, or acceptor of an instrument that is taken for the settlement of an underlying obligation, the obligation is *discharged* and there is no recourse against the underlying obligor (UCC §3-802). Where the instrument has been drawn, made, or accepted by other than a bank, the underlying obligation is *suspended* until such time as it is dishonored. Upon dishonor, an action may then be maintained on either the instrument or the obligation. Taking in good faith a check that is not postdated does not in and of itself extend the time on the original obligation so as to discharge a surety.

[¶1133] AFFILIATED COMPANIES AND THE HOLDER IN DUE COURSE

If a seller is affiliated with the creditor by common control, contract, or business arrangement, the FTC rules require that the seller use the notice found in ¶1129 in a consumer loan contract. Common control is defined as when a creditor and seller are "functionally part of the same business entity," or if the affiliation has been created by contract or business arrangement. The arrangement may be oral or in writing. Commercial checking accounts are not affiliations between banks and customers within the meaning of the rule, nor is a commercial credit agreement between a seller and credit institution that has no relationship to the consumer sales activities or the financing. The FTC has further stated that the mere fact that a creditor issues a joint proceeds check to the seller and the buyer (which is common in a purchase of an automobile, for example) does not necessarily constitute a business arrangement or contract if the seller and lender must confer in order to perfect the security agreement under applicable law.

[¶1134] REFERRALS AND THE HOLDER-IN-DUE-COURSE RULE

Sellers are prohibited from accepting proceeds of purchase-money loans under any credit contract unless the required notice is given when the seller "refers consumers to the creditor." The FTC has stated this provision is intended to deal with those situations in which a seller cooperates with a lender to steer consumers towards that credit source on a continuing basis. This differs from affiliation, and requires that seller and creditor be engaged in a cooperative or concerted conduct to channel or direct a consumer to a particular lender. The fact that a seller may suggest credit sources to his customers does not invoke the rule.

When a seller and lender work together to arrange financing for the customers of a seller, the notice must be incorporated into the loan contract. The FTC states that the conduct must occur on a continuing basis—that occasional referrals not a part of the ordinary business routine of the seller are insufficient to trigger the rule. The FTC emphasizes that the fact that no money changes hands between the seller and the lender for these services is not important. That the seller and the lender are cooperatively engaged in an effort that is mutually beneficial to their separate business interests is considered sufficient.

[¶1135] EXAMPLES OF THE HOLDER-IN-DUE-COURSE RULE

(1) The creditor makes an agreement with a seller to maintain loan application forms in the seller's office. When a buyer requests financing, the seller assists the buyer in filling out the forms. This relationship constitutes an *affiliation,* and notice must be included in the consumer credit contract.

(2) Seller regularly sends customers to a particular creditor, who in turn agrees to provide favorable financing arrangements for the seller's inventory, or directly or indirectly provides some other consideration. Seller and lender are *affiliated,* and notice must be included in the consumer credit contract.

(3) Seller routinely suggests that customers in need of credit go to a particular source of financing. Although the creditor is aware that seller is referring some of his customers, creditor provides no tacit or explicit *quid pro quo.* Notice is not required.

(4) Buyer asks seller for credit sources and the seller provides a list of lenders in the area and information on the general availability of credit merely as an accommodation to his customers. Seller does not contact the creditor to arrange credit nor is there any affiliation with the creditors. Notice is not required.

(5) Seller has an existing referral or affiliation contractual relationship with the creditor. A buyer, on his own, goes to that very creditor to obtain a loan to purchase an item from the seller. The notice must be included.

— FOR FURTHER REFERENCE —

Bailey, Henry J., *Brady on Bank Checks* (6th ed.) (Warren, Gorham & Lamont 1987, 1988 supplement).

Clark, Barkley, *The Law of Bank Deposits, Collections, and Credit Cards* (Rev.ed.) (Warren, Gorham & Lamont 1981, 1988 supplement).

Dow, Steven B., "Determining Bank Status in Article Four Check Collections," 49 *U. of Pittsburgh L. Rev.* 43 (Fall '87).

Glidden, William B., "Bank Sales of Commercial Paper," 42 *Business Lawyer* 1 (November '86).

Koon, Richard M., "Solving Everyday Check Problems on Checking and NOW Accounts," 49 *Legal Bulletin* 185 (July '83).

Leary, Fairfax Jr., "Letter of Credit Drafting Considerations," 11 *ALI/ABA Course Materials J.* 89 (December '86).

Lucie, Stephanie A., "Check Kiting: The Inadequacy of the Uniform Commercial Code," 1986 *Duke L.J.* 728 (September '86).

Miller, Fred H. and Robert G. Ballen, "Commercial Paper, Bank Deposits and Collections and Commercial Electronic Funds Transfers," 41 *Business Lawyer* 1399 (August '86).

[¶1201] Compensation includes salary and bonuses and so-called "fringe benefits" which are an essential ingredient in attracting key personnel. Fringe benefits include such arrangements as qualified pension and profit-sharing plans, employee stock ownership plans, cash or deferred arrangement plans, incentive stock option plans, cafeteria-type plans, death benefits, "golden parachute packages," and group insurance. With a maximum tax rate of 39.6 percent for individuals, high-income taxpayers can lower their tax bill by participating in one or more deferred arrangements.

[¶1202] PENSION AND PROFIT-SHARING PLANS

Pension and profit-sharing plans are two of the most attractive methods of compensation. A pension plan is a deferred compensation arrangement that provides for systematic payments of definitely determinable retirement benefits to employees who meet the requirements set forth in the plan. Benefits are based on such factors as years of service and employee compensation, and employer contributions under a qualified pension plan must not depend on profits.

There are two basic types of qualified pension plans, *defined benefit plans and defined contribution plans*. A defined benefit plan includes a formula that defines the benefits employees are to receive.[1] Under a defined contribution pension plan (or money purchase plan), a separate account must be maintained for each participant. Benefits are based solely on (1) the amount contributed and (2) income from the fund that accrues to the participant's account.[2] In essence, the plan defines the amount the employer is required to contribute based on either a flat dollar amount, an amount based on a special formula, or an amount equal to a certain percentage of compensation. Consequently, actuarial calculations are not required to determine the employer's annual contribution. When an employee retires, his or her pension will depend on the value of his or her account.

A *profit-sharing plan* is a deferred compensation arrangement established and maintained by an employer to provide for employee participation in the company's profits. Contributions are paid from the employer's current or accumulated profits to a trustee and are commingled in a single trust fund. Thus, an employer does not have to have a profit for the current year to make a contribution, meaning that the contribution can be from prior or accumulated profits. In a *stock bonus plan,* an employer establishes and maintains the plan in order to contribute shares of its stock. The contributions need not be dependent on the employer's profits. A stock bonus plan is subject to the same statutory requirements as a profit-sharing plan for purposes of allocating and distributing the stock among the employees.

When a pension or profit-sharing plan qualifies under IRS rules, the company gets a tax deduction for its contributions. In addition, the contributions earn a tax-free return. The employee is not taxed until monies are withdrawn from the fund. Further, in the case of a profit-sharing plan, the worker's account may increase as a result of the reallocation of the "non-vested" units forfeited by employees who have left the job.

These are some of the tax advantages of pension and profit-sharing plans that qualify under IRC §401:

❏ The corporation can deduct contributions to the plan.

❏ Earnings on funds held by the plan are allowed to appreciate tax-free.

❏ Lump-sum distributions on retirement, death, or other termination may be taxed under a favorable income-averaging formula. Distributions attributable to pre-1974 contributions may be taxed at capital gain rates. (Lump-sum preferences are greatly limited by the '86 Code.)

❏ Distributions paid out over a long period get special annuity tax treatment.

❏ Up to $5,000 of death benefits provided by an employer can be received income tax-free by the employee's beneficiary.

❏ Distributions can be taxed at a lower rate if the employee receives them at a time (retirement) when he is in a lower tax bracket.

❏ Employees can also use the plan as a tax-sheltered savings account if the plan permits voluntary contributions.

Comparison Between Profit-Sharing and Pension Plans

Profit Sharing	**Pension**
(1) Annual contributions for any single participant (plus forfeitures and employee contributions exceeding 6% of his compensation) cannot exceed the lesser of $30,000 or 25% of his compensation. Tax-deductible contributions cannot exceed 15% of total compensation of all participants.	(1) As a general rule, in defined-benefit plans, annual benefits payable for any participant may not exceed the smaller of (1) $118,800 (in 1994), indexed annually, or (2) 100% of the participant's average earnings in the three highest paid consecutive years of employment. Benefits must be actuarially adjusted for early or late retirement, and may be adjusted based on the cost of living.
(2) Employer's contributions are made from profit, usually profit before taxes, and vary in amount depending upon size of profit and contribution formula of plan.	(2) Employer's contributions are not related to profits, but are amounts actuarially necessary to provide the planned benefits. Contributions are affected by each employee's age and length of past service (except for money purchase plan).
(3) It provides a share of company profits as additional compensation, usually payable in whole or in part at retirement.	(3) It provides income after retirement not based on company profits.

(4) Company profits contributed in any year to plan are usually allocated among accounts of employees in ratio to annual compensation, with age and years of service ignored under most plans.

(4) Company contributions for an employee are usually the actuarial installments necessary to provide the planned benefits, thus based generally on compensation, age, and years of past service.

(5) Cash disbursements from employer's account can be made at prescribed occasions during employment, in addition to retirement, death, disability, layoff, discharge, or resignation.

(5) Benefits are usually payable only at retirement, death, disability, discharge, or resignation.

(6) Benefits usually distributable in lump but other methods available, too.

(6) Benefits usually distributable in installments, beginning at retirement age.

(7) Benefits at retirement, death, disability, layoff, and sometimes discharge or resignation, are the amount in the employee's account.

(7) Benefits at retirement, death, disability, discharge, or resignation are fixed by the plan's benefit scale.

(8) Severance benefits at discharge or resignation are usually in cash.

(8) Severance benefits at discharge or resignation are more often than not in form of retirement income deferred to normal retirement age.

(9) Vesting of employee's rights is usually at faster rate than under pension plan.

(9) Rate of vesting is usually slower than under profit-sharing plan.

(10) Plan termination insurance is not required.

(10) Defined benefit plans will have to be insured with the Pension Benefit Guaranty Corporation (PBGC).

Pension benefits taken as property under a divorce judgment can be considered in assessing the employee-spouse's ability to pay alimony.[3] At first it was held that the pension benefits of an employee whose fraudulent conduct caused a pension plan to suffer more than a million dollars' worth of losses can be reduced to satisfy the judgment but the employee's innocent spouse's 50% share of the benefits cannot be reduced,[4] but the Court of Appeals reversed.

In 1993, the New York Court of Appeals decided that ex-spouses are entitled to a percentage of the worker ex-spouse's early retirement incentives, measured according to the percentage of the incentive that was earned during the marriage, as long as this percentage enhances pension benefits already divided under the decree (i.e., if the worker had 20 years' experience with the company, 15 of which were during the marriage, $3/4$ of the incentive will be deemed divisible).[5] In contrast, a 1993 Pennsylvania decision[6] does not permit salary increases, incentive awards, or years of service after marital separation to be used to determine the ex-spouse's share; in this reading, the non-worker ex-spouse's share of retirement benefits depends on the employee's earnings at the time of separation. The non-employee spouse can share post-separation increases in benefits unless they are attributable to post-separation service, incentives, or salary enhancements.

Plans can be required to make payments to a retiree's ex-spouse, pursuant to a Qualified Domestic Relations Order (QDRO).

[¶1203] QUALIFICATION REQUIREMENTS

In order for a plan to be *qualified* and receive favorable tax treatment, a plan must meet the following requirements:

❐ *Exclusive Benefit Requirement:* A pension, profit-sharing, or stock bonus plan must be created by the employer for the exclusive benefit of the employees or their beneficiaries.

❐ *It Must Be Nondiscriminatory:* The plan must not discriminate in favor of highly compensated employees.[7] A plan that provides for contributions to be paid into the plan based on a flat 5 percent of each employee's salary is not considered discriminatory.

❐ *Participation Requirements:* The plan must provide, at a minimum, that all employees who are 21 years of age or over are eligible for coverage after completing one year of service. A year of service is generally defined as 1,000 hours of service performed within a period of 12 consecutive months.

❐ *Vesting Requirements:* An employee's right to accrued benefits from his or her own contributions must be nonforfeitable from the date of his or her contribution. These vesting requirements protect a worker who has either changed jobs or is fired from losing his or her employer contributions.

❐ *Distribution Rules:* There are minimum distribution rules for all qualified defined benefit and defined contribution plans, Individual Retirement Accounts (IRAs) (see below) and certain types of annuity plans. Once age 70 $1/2$ is reached, minimum annual distributions must be made over the life of the participant and a designated beneficiary.

[¶1204] CASH OR DEFERRED ARRANGEMENT PLANS

A cash or deferred arrangement plan, sometimes referred to as a §401(k) plan, allows participants to elect either to receive up to $9,240 (in 1994)[8] in cash (taxed currently) or to have a contribution made on their behalf to a profit-sharing or stock bonus plan. Any pretax amount elected by the employee as a plan contribution is not included in gross income and is 100 percent vested. Employer contributions are tax deferred, as are earnings on contributions in the plan.

A popular technique for obtaining greater security in deferred compensation arrangements is the "rabbi" trust, named as such because the first IRS ruling that permitted the arrangement applied to a rabbi.[9] Under a rabbi trust, funds for the employee's benefit can be placed in trust and the employee's control of the funds is subject to substantial limitations. The employee will not be in constructive receipt of the funds, just because the trust has been set up, provided: (1) the company remains the owner of the funds, all deductions and income are reported on the company's tax return, and (2) the trust assets are available to the employer's general creditors, in the event of insolvency or bankruptcy of the employer. Thus the trust's assets are treated as if they were regular company assets in the event of insolvency or bankruptcy.

[¶1205] INDIVIDUAL RETIREMENT ACCOUNTS (IRAs)

Employees who are not covered by a qualified plan may wish to establish individual retirement accounts to which a deductible contribution of up to $2,000 (or $2,250 for a spousal IRA) can be made annually. The contribution is further limited by the amount of compensation (i.e. salaries, alimony, etc.) earned for the year.

If the employee or employee's spouse is covered by an employer-sponsored retirement plan, the IRA deductions phase-out is based on the following statutory levels of adjusted gross income:

Filing status	Phase-out begins	Phase-out ends
Single or head of household	$25,000	$35,000
Married, filing jointly	40,000	50,000
Married, filing separately	-0-	10,000

An IRA deduction cannot go below $200 if adjusted gross income has not reached the above phase-out levels.

Example: Louis Patten, a single individual who is covered by an employer-sponsored retirement plan, has adjusted gross income of $34,600 for 1994. Using the phase-out formula, his IRA deduction would be only $80 ($2,000 − [($34,600 − $25,000)/$10,000 × $2,000]). However, because of the special provision regarding the floor for deductions, Louis may deduct $200 for an IRA contribution.

An IRA contribution can be made for a tax year at any time up to the filing deadline for that year's return (not including extensions).[10] A taxpayer can make a contribution to an IRA, or to a spousal IRA, for a year at any time during the year or by the due date of the return for that year, not including extensions. For most taxpayers, the due date is April 15.

[¶1206] SIMPLIFIED EMPLOYEE PENSIONS (SEPs)

An employer may contribute to an IRA covering an employee in an amount equal to the lesser of $30,000 or 15 percent of the employee's earned income.[11] Known as simplified employee pension (SEP) plans, these plans are subject to many of the same restrictions applicable to qualified plans such as age, period-of-service requirements, and top-heavy rules.

[¶1207] DEFERRED PAY CONTRACTS

With a maximum individual tax rate of 39.6 percent, many taxpayers attempt to reduce their tax burden by entering into deferred compensation arrangements. The company can accumulate funds to be paid out at a later period (usually in the post-retirement years), which minimizes the individual's income tax liability. An employee who takes a deferred compensation arrangement is not taxed on the amounts until they're actually or constructively received. The company is not entitled to any deduction for monies owed until payment is actually made.[12]

For tax years beginning on or after January 1, 1994, a publicly held corporation will not be able to deduct certain compensation in excess of $1 million per tax year paid to either the chief operating officer or to the four highest compensated officers whose total compensation is required to be reported to shareholders under the Securities Exchange Act of 1934. A publicly held corporation is any corporation issuing any class of securities required to be registered under Section 12 of the Securities Exchange Act of 1934.[13]

[¶1208] EMPLOYEE STOCK OWNERSHIP PLANS

An Employee Stock Ownership Plan (ESOP) is a qualified retirement plan—either a stock bonus plan or a combined stock bonus and money-purchase pension plan. An ESOP must be designed to invest primarily in employer securities (common or preferred that are easily converted into common). The employer's contribution can be either cash or securities. Like other qualified retirement plans, an ESOP is tax-sheltered: the employees pay no tax on their accounts until they later withdraw them at retirement. And the payouts receive the same favorable tax treatment as do payouts from other retirement plans.

❏ **Quicker vesting:** Usually, retirement plan contributions are not fully vested right away. But with an ESOP, each participant has a nonforfeitable right to any employer security once it is allocated to his account. (On the other hand, no security may be distributed until seven years after the month the security is allocated. *Exception:* Distributions made when an employee separates from service, dies, or becomes disabled.)

❏ **Control in the company:** An ESOP lets employees get a piece of the action. *Reason:* The stock they receive must have voting and dividend rights. (Exception: Profit-sharing plans can deny this voting right for securities acquired after 1979.) For closely held stock, the employee must have the right to vote on issues requiring more than a majority of the outstanding shares voted—i.e., mergers, acquisitions, etc.

❏ **Flexible payouts:** The ESOP may elect to make distributions in cash, in employer securities, or a combination of both. A company can prohibit a demand for securities if (1) the company's charter restricts its securities to employees or a qualified retirement plan and (2) the participants have a right to receive cash. If the company is closely held, the stock probably won't have a ready market.

Solution: The tax law provides the employee with a guaranteed market. Any participant who receives a distribution of closely held stock must be given a put option on the stock. The option gives the employee the right to require the employer to repurchase the stock at its fair market value.

[¶1209] INCENTIVE STOCK OPTONS

An incentive stock option (ISO) is available for options granted after 1975 and exercised after 1980. Incentive stock options qualify for three special tax breaks.

(1) No taxable income when the option is received.

(2) The "bargain element" or "spread"—that is, the difference between fair market value at exercise and the actual exercise price—is not taxable but is a tax preference for purposes of the alternative minimum tax.

(3) Profit on the sale of stock is treated as capital gain if the stock is held at least one year after the option is exercised and the stock acquired, and at least two years after the option is granted or within one year after acquiring the stock.[14]

[¶1210] NONQUALIFIED STOCK OPTIONS (NQSO)

A nonqualified stock option (NQSO) does not satisfy the statutory requirements for being an ISO. Thus, if the NQSO has a readily ascertainable fair market value, such as the option being traded on a nationally known or recognized exchange, the value of the option must be included in the employee's income at the date of grant. Thereafter, the employer is subject to capital gain or loss when he or she disposes of the stock. The basis for reporting any gain or loss is what the employee paid for the stock plus any amount reported as ordinary income.[15]

Example: On June 1, 1993, Pamela was granted a NQSO to purchase 1,000 shares of her employer's stock at $5 per share. On this date, the option was selling for $3 on a recognized stock exchange. For 1993, Pamela must report $3,000 (1,000 shares x $3 value of option) as ordinary income. She exercised her option on December 5, 1994 and sold the stock for $10 per share. For 1994, Pamela must report long-term capital gain of $2,000 calculated as follows:

Selling price of stock $10 × 1,000 shares	$10,000
Less: Cost of stock: $8 ($5 + Option $3) × 1,000 shares	8,000
Long-term capital gain	**$ 2,000**

[¶1211] GOLDEN PARACHUTE CONTRACTS

A corporation that enters into a contract with an employee whereby it agrees to pay that individual an amount in excess of the employee's usual compensation in the event that control or ownership of the corporation changes or the employee is terminated *is barred from taking a deduction for an "excess parachute payment"* made to a "disqualified individual." The disqualified individual is subject to an excise tax of 20% of the excess parachute payment in addition to the income tax due.[16] A disqualified individual is an employee who performs personal services for any corporation and who is an officer, shareholder, highly compensated person, or personal service corporation.[17]

The base amount is the individual's annualized includible compensation for a base period, consisting of the most recent five tax years ending before the date on which the ownership or control of the corporation changed, or the portion of this period during which the individual was an employee of the corporation.[18]

Example: Jason, an executive, receives a golden parachute payment of $400,000 from his corporate employer. His average compensation for his most recent five years is $220,000. The corporation is barred from taking a deduction of $180,000 ($400,00–$220,000) as an "excess parachute payment." Jason's excise tax is $36,000 ($180,000 × 20%) which must be paid in addition to his regular personal income tax liability.

Golden parachute payments do not include payments from qualified pension, profit-sharing, stock option, or simplified employee pension plans (SEPs).

[¶1212] KEY-PERSON INSURANCE

In this type of arrangement, the employer takes out an insurance policy on the life of a valuable employee. The employer pays the premiums and collects the proceeds of the policy. The employer can use the proceeds, for example, to pay death benefits to the employee's family for a period of time as a continuation of the employee's salary after death, or can buy the deceased employee's stock in the company at his or her death.

The employer gets a tax deduction when benefits are paid—not when the premiums are paid on the insurance. When the premiums are paid all the employer is doing is building up an asset, the life insurance policy. But when the benefits of the policy are paid over to the beneficiary of the deceased employee, the employer is paying compensation and is therefore entitled to a deduction.

[¶1213] DEATH BENEFITS

Up to $5,000 can be paid to the family of a deceased employee income tax-free (IRC §101(b)). If an employee's family receives benefits from two or more employers, the excludable amount is still limited to only $5,000. The rule applies to distributions under a qualified plan, but does not apply to amounts to which the employee had a nonforfeitable right. However, death benefits that the employer was not obligated to offer, but were provided as a matter of policy, are taxable income to the surviving spouse. *Sweeney,* TC Memo 1987-550.

[¶1214] SPLIT-DOLLAR INSURANCE PLANS

Under a typical arrangement, the employee pays that part of the premium on an ordinary life insurance policy that is attributable to life insurance protection; the employer pays the balance that is attributable to the annual increase in cash surrender value. The cash surrender value is owned by the employer. At the employee's death, the employer receives an amount equal to the cash surrender value; the employee's beneficiary receives what's left of the proceeds. The advantage of such an arrangement is that after the first few years, the employee is able to obtain high insurance protection at a very low cost, since the employer is, in effect, paying for part of this protection through earnings on funds that belong to the employer. The "economic benefit" received by the employee under this plan is taxable (*Rev. Rul. 64-238,* CB 1964-2, 11; *Rev. Rul. 66-110,* CB 1966-1, 12, amplified by *Rev. Rul. 67-154,* CB 1967-1, 11).

The rates used to compute the cost of split-dollar must be standard rates, not preferred rates (e.g., rates for nonsmokers), even if the employee in question qualifies for the preferential rates: Letter Ruling 8547006.

[¶1215] GROUP TERM LIFE INSURANCE

This provides pure insurance protection for the insured for a specified period of time, usually on a year-to-year basis. It has no paid up or cash surrender value. An employer can provide an employee with up to $50,000 of this type of insurance tax-free, provided it is "group term" as defined in IRS Regulations under IRC §79. This is the only type of life insurance coverage that an employer can provide for an employee tax-free. All other forms of life insurance protection are taxable to the employee. Imputed income from excessive group term life coverage is taxable to the employee and subject to Social Security taxes. Furthermore, if the plan discriminates in favor of key employees, the key employee must recognize gross income in the amount of the actual cost of the insurance or the cost calculated by using the uniform premium tables, whichever is higher.

[¶1216] GROUP HEALTH INSURANCE

This is another very valuable fringe benefit. It provides for the reimbursement of medical and hospitalization expenses incurred by an employee and his family. Premiums are tax deductible by the employer and not taxable to the employee—even if the plan provides for the protection of the employee's family. Some employers extend their plan to include reimbursement of major medical expenses. This coverage supplements the basic plan and provides some shelter to the employee in the event of a serious or prolonged illness.

[¶1217] MEDICAL EXPENSE REIMBURSEMENT PLANS

Corporations may provide reimbursement for medical expenses incurred by employees under a medical expense reimbursement plan (see IRC §105(b) and §106). However, a company's uninsured medical reimbursement plan cannot discriminate in favor of key execs (the five highest-paid officers, more-than-10% shareholders, and the highest paid 25% of all employees). The plan must meet broad coverage requirements similar to those for qualified pension plans. In general, 70% of the employees must be plan members. And the plan may not provide greater benefits for key execs than for the rank and file. For example, a plan can't pay benefits in proportion to compensation.

➤ If the plan discriminates, a key exec pays tax on some or all of the benefits he or she receives from the plan. (*Note:* Benefits paid to ordinary employees are always tax-free.)

➤ If the plan provides a benefit to a key exec that's not available to other employees, the entire benefit is taxable to the key exec. And that's true even though the terms of the plan meet the tax law's coverage requirements.

➤ If the plan fails the new nondiscrimination test on its face, the key exec is taxed on a portion of his reimbursement. His reimbursement (other than the amount representing benefits not available across-the-board) is multiplied by a fraction—the numerator is the total amount paid to key execs; the denominator is the total amount paid to all employees. The result is the amount of his reimbursement that's taxable.

[¶1218] CAFETERIA PLANS

A "cafeteria plan," also referred to as flexible spending accounts, is a written plan in which all participants are employees (though all employees need not be participants) and in which participants can choose between cash and various nontaxable benefits such as group term and medical insurance. The major advantage of taking fringe benefits in lieu of a cash payment is the fact that employees do not have to use after-tax income to obtain the product or service. Employees will generally recognize taxable income only to the extent that they actually select taxable benefits.

The plan cannot discriminate in favor of highly compensated individuals or their dependents or spouses.[19] However, if a cafeteria plan is discriminatory, highly compensated individuals must recognize income to the extent that they *could have* selected taxable benefits.

A plan is considered discriminatory if it favors highly compensated individuals with respect to participation. For this purpose, the term "highly compensated individuals" is defined to mean those who are "officers, 5% shareholders, highly compensated employees," or spouses of persons in those three classes.

Whatever their actual terms, collectively bargained plans are deemed nondiscriminatory. Class plans are treated as nondiscriminatory if:

➤ IRS approves the plan's classification requirements;

➤ No more than three years of service is required for eligibility to participate; and

➤ An employee can participate at the beginning of the first plan year after he or she meets the participation requirements.

[¶1219] FAMILY AND MEDICAL LEAVE ACT OF 1993

The Family and Medical Leave Act (FMLA), P.L. 103-5, 29 U.S.C. Section 2612(a)(1) et.seq., was signed into law as one of the first official acts of the Clinton administration, effective on August 5, 1993. The FMLA preempts state family-leave laws unless they are more protective of employees than the federal enactment.

Under the FMLA, covered employers must provide access to up to 12 weeks' unpaid leave per year (calendar, fiscal, or employee's own leave year) for the employee's own illness; the illness of a close family member; or the birth or adoption of a child. Covered employers are those with 50 or more employees in each day of 20 or more workweeks in a year in which an employee seeks to take leave.

When an employee returns from leave, the employer is obligated to reinstate the worker in the old job, or to provide another job with equivalent duties, pension rights, and benefits. FMLA leave is not permitted to result in the loss of any benefit accrued before the leave, but further benefits do not accrue while the employee is on leave. The highest-paid 10% of the employees at a workplace can be denied reinstatement if such reinstatement would harm the employer economically, and the employee was notified that reinstatement would not be available.

Employers are forbidden to interfere with employees' right to FMLA leave, or to retaliate against an employee for filing a charge of FMLA violations. There is a private right of action against the employer for damages or equitable relief; the Department of Labor can also bring FMLA enforcement suits. The measure of damages is the compensation (including benefits) lost because of the denial of FMLA leave, or the actual amount of costs encountered by the employee only because of the denial of leave. The maximum damages equals twice the 12 weeks' leave period compensation, plus interest. The statute of limitations is two years from the last event constituting an FMLA violation, three years if the violation was willful.

— ENDNOTES —

1. IRC §414(j).

2. IRC §414(j).

3. Lang v. Lang, 425 NW2d 800 (Mich.App. 6/20/88).

4. Brock v. Lindemann, 689 F.Supp. 678, (N.D. Tex. 7/25/88) rev'd 853 F.2d 1307 (5th Cir).

5. Olivo v. Olivo, 62 LW 2347 (N.Y.App. 11/11/93).

6. Berrington v. Berrington, 62 LW 2346 (Pa.Super. 11/12/93).

7. IRC §§401(a)(4) and (5).

8. This amount is indexed annually.

9. PLR 8113107.

10. IRC §219 (f)(3).

11. IRC §408(j).

12. *Rev. Rul. 60-31,* CB 1960-1, 1.

13. IRC §162(m).

14. IRC §422(a)(1).

15. IRC Reg. §§1.421-6(c), (d), (e) and (f); Reg. §1.83-7.

16. IRC §4999.

17. Code Sec. 280G(c).

18. IRC §§280G(b) and (d).

19. IRC §125.

— FOR FURTHER REFERENCE —

Allman, Phillip H. and David R. Baker, "Three Economic Issues in Pension Valuation," 16 *Family Advocate* 12 (Summer '93).

Baker, Pamela, "Executive Compensation in Mergers and Acquisitions," 39 *Practical Lawyer* 75 (June '93) and 45 (July '93).

Bowers, Jennifer J., "Employer Stock Rabbi Trusts," 24 *Tax Adviser* 494 (August '93).

Dwyer, Thomas J., "Take Shelter: Enjoying the Benefits of Pension and Profit-Sharing Plans," 79 *ABA J.* 104 (September '93).

Fenton, Kathryn M., "Antitrust Implications of Joint Efforts by Third Party Payors to Reduce Costs and Improve the Quality of Health Care," 61 *Antitrust L.J.* 17 (Summer '92).

Hoffman, Susan Katz, "Discrimination Litigation Relating to Employee Benefits," 43 *Labor Law J.* 362 (June '92).

Keppelman, Nancy, "Keeping Plans Qualified: Some Practical Solutions to the Minimum Participation Rules," 19 *Michigan Tax Lawyer* 11 (April-June '93).

Kidder, James L., "Avoiding 401(k) Traps," 176 *J. of Accountancy* 42 (September '93).

Lindgren, Christian L. and Michael J. Langan, "DOL Clarifies Cafeteria Plan Audit and Trust Requirements," 5 *Benefits L.J.* 427 (Autumn '92).

Lustig, D. Carl III, "Recovery of Lost Wages by Illegal Workers," 22 *Trial Lawyers Q.* 40 (Summer '92).

Munnell, Alicia H., "Are Pensions Worth the Cost?" 44 *Nat'l Tax J.* 393 (September '91).

Rose, Michael D., "Pension Plans: Why Antenuptial Agreements Cannot Relinquish Survivor Benefits," 43 *Florida L. Rev.* 723 (September '91).

Schultz, Paul T. and Russell E. Hall, "Tax Court Provides New Guidance on Partial Plan Terminations," 19 *Employee Relations L.J.* 285 (Autumn '93).

Seelig, Steven A., "Qualified Plan Distributions in Corporate Acquisitions and Mergers," 18 *J. of Pension Planning and Compliance* 53 (Summer '92).

Semo, Joseph, "Salary Reduction SEPs Can Be a Low-Cost Employee Benefit," 21 *Taxation for Lawyers* 92 (September-October '92).

Serota, Susan B., "Counseling the Client on ERISA Notification Requirements," 18 *ALI-ABA Course Materials J.* 7 (August '93).

Simmons, John G., "What You Should Know About Section 475(b) Deferred Compensation Plans," 6 *The Practical Tax Lawyer* 31 (Summer '92).

Stabile, Susan J., "Protecting Retiree Medical Benefits in Bankruptcy," 14 *Cardozo L. Rev.* 1911 (May '93).

Stanley, Jane Kheel, "The Definition of a Fiduciary Under ERISA," 27 *Real Property, Probate and Trust J.* 467 (Fall '92).

Supovitz, Marcy L., "The Age-Weighted Profit Sharing Plan," 6 *Probate and Property* 48 (September-October '92).

Walker, David M. and Theresa M. Vogler, "Common Problems With Form 5500 Filings and Employee Benefit Plan Audits," 22 *The Tax Adviser* 722 (November '91).

Walker, Deborah and Sally Olson, "Maximizing the Benefits of Deferred Compensation Plans Funded Through Secular Trusts," 77 *J. of Taxation* 90 (August '92).

Welber, Nancy H. and Nancy Keppelman, "Retirement Plan Distributions Revisited," 72 *Michigan Bar J.* 696 (July '93).

Whitehorn, Matthew I., "Qualified Plans for Service Partnerships, Professional Corporations," 19 *Estate Planning* 208 (July-August 1992).

Zwick, Gary A., "Property Transfers to Qualified Plans," 24 *Tax Adviser* 507 (August '93).

COMPUTER LAW

[¶1301] Widespread adoption of the computer has revolutionized the world of law in many ways. Computerized legal research gives attorneys access to a plethora of current information. (In December, 1989, the U.S. Supreme Court announced a new policy of making its opinions available on-line virtually simultaneous with the announcement of the opinions.) Computers in the law office make it possible for the attorney to keep track of evidence used in litigation, to communicate quickly with colleagues and adversaries, and to generate documents quickly and accurately.

Moreover, the computer itself has generated an entire body of law, dealing with questions such as intellectual property and the problems inherent in designing computer systems and software.

[¶1302] PROBLEMS OF SYSTEM AND SOFTWARE DESIGN

Many companies enter into a contract for design of custom software, or for the purchase and installation of hardware and software suitable for the corporation's particular needs. Negotiating such contracts is a difficult task; so is coping with an existing agreement that has developed problems. In the computer world, the common contract phrase "time is of the essence" is meaningless, and a project that comes in only 20% over budget is deemed to be a triumph of economy. A fair estimate is that 80% of the work on a project occurs after the hardware and software are installed; and the purchaser must do much of this work.

Reputable computer consulting firms tend to be staffed by optimists, who have great faith in the ability of computers to solve business problems and in their own ability to solve computer problems. But many projects, entered into in good faith, founder because the problems prove more difficult than anticipated, or because the personnel involved are overcommitted to other projects. (Moreover, it's a proverb in the computer business that "adding manpower to a late software project makes it later.") Not all consulting firms are reputable; some may accept a hefty retainer and make constant demands for more money for projects they knew perfectly well could not be achieved on schedule (if they could be achieved at all).

Part of the problem is that few professional managers or business owners really understand computers, and what is or isn't possible; and few computer consultants really understand the needs of businesses. The problem of "creeping elegance" arises when everyone involved in the project thinks of a way to make the software just a little bit better; on the customer's side, the counterpart is refusing to accept the project without these improvements.

When problems arise, neither side really wants to terminate the contract. The buyer probably can't find anyone to pick up the project (and even if someone did, there would be inevitable delays because he or she would have to study the buyer's needs and what has already been done on the project). The seller probably can't find anyone who wants to buy a half-finished software project that pertains to someone else's needs. This is not to say that there may not be a great deal of ill-will, or even protracted preparations for litigation (or actual litigation) before the problems are ironed out.

Bearing in mind that some degree of conflict is inevitable, here are some guidelines for drafting comparatively conflict-free computer contracts:

➤ Try to get the specifications for product functions reduced to writing; verbal specifications are easy to confuse.

➤ At the outset, get a determination that the buyer's needs can realistically be met.

➤ Get an agreement as to when the project will be considered "finished," and when it will be considered "successful."

➤ Who tests the product, using what criteria? How many bugs of what kind are considered acceptable, and when is either party considered to be in breach of contract?

➤ When "change orders" are issued, based on improved technology or the buyer's changed expectations, who pays for the changes (or adds time to the schedule)?

➤ What problems will be considered "bugs" rather than changes in requirements?

➤ What are the remedies of buyer and seller for perceived unreasonable conduct on the part of the other party?

[¶1303] SOFTWARE LICENSING

The developers of software license the use of the software under various circumstances. The software could be created specially for an end user, with the licensing provisions contained in a development and marketing agreement. Or, the software could be licensed in connection with a support agreement, under which the creators agree to fix bugs, revise and upgrade the software, and enhance it as the buyer's needs and technical developments make necessary. If the developer intends the software to be sold to a wider public, rather than to a single custom buyer, the license may be part of a marketing and publishing agreement; here, the drafter's main tasks involve setting out clear and fair clauses for royalty computations and for setting out the publisher's or distributor's obligations to the end user. Finally, if the software is sold to the public, the package will probably include a "shrinkwrap license," an end-user license that is part of the packaging, and spells out the user's rights to copy and adapt the software.

The provisions of the Uniform Commercial Code may have to be consulted, because the UCC definition of "goods" includes anything that is movable at the time of sale—a category that naturally includes computer software.[1]

Under the Software Rental Amendments Act of 1990 (Title VIII of H.R. 5316, the Judicial Improvements Act of 1990), the scope of the "first sale" doctrine has been limited to permit the copyright proprietor of a computer program to forbid commercial rental or leasing of the program. However, the proprietor does not have this right in the case of rentals or licenses where both parties are non-profit educational institutions; where the program is a video game; or for software embodied in a device such as a calculator where the device does not permit software copying during normal operation.

According to a 1993 Eighth Circuit decision, a copyright holder has the right to bring a state-law, breach of contract claim for letting a third party use a licensed computer program. Because the issues involved go beyond copyright issues, the state-law case is not federally preempted.[2]

Typical drafting problems in creating a license include:

> Giving specifications for the software, explaining what it does and how.

> Setting a delivery schedule, with provisions for delays and delivery of only part of the software licensed and contracted for.

> Specifying who is entitled to test the software, and what must be done to fix perceived "bugs."

> Warranty provisions; assumption or disclaimers of liability. For instance, what if an end user claims that the software scrambled its inventory records, causing direct and consequential losses of $58,296? Must the designer, distributor, or both pay any part of those losses?

> Setting out the scope of the license: is it exclusive, or can others use the same software?

> If a licensee creates derivative software or improves on the original, to whom does the adapted software belong?

> If the license deals with marketing and distribution, what efforts must the "publisher" make to promote and distribute the software?

> Does any part of the software or documentation consist of a trademark or trade secrets?

The agreement should also clarify the ownership of other software developed by the personnel involved in the project. For example, *Simplified Information Systems, Inc. v. Cannon*[3] holds that software developed by the president of a corporation formed to market software for doctors' offices, in his spare time at home, still constituted a "work for hire" (and thus the copyright belonged to the corporation). This result was reached because the development was in the scope of his employment, and there was no agreement to the contrary.

[¶1303.1] Software Licenses and Bankruptcy

For bankruptcy cases commenced after 10/18/88, the Intellectual Property Bankruptcy Protection Act[4] deals with all kinds of licenses of intellectual property (except trademarks). To summarize the statute, any license that is not rejected by the trustee can continue to be used after bankruptcy. The trustee has the option of rejecting the license on behalf of the bankrupt licensor; if the trustee does so, the licensee can either consider the license terminated and claim damages, or keep the licensed material, continue to pay royalties, and waive any claim for setoff. If the license is rejected, neither the trustee nor the bankruptcy estate has an obligation to provide maintenance or upgrades of the licensed property.

[¶1304] COMPUTERS AND COPYRIGHT ISSUES

Our copyright law was originally drafted to protect authors and publishers against unauthorized printing of books; later accommodations (more or less successful) had to be made to deal with problems such as musical compositions and movies. The wide spread of photocopying technology has created severe (perhaps insoluble) problems for publishers.

However, the computer offers even more difficult conceptual problems to the copyright law (and the law of intellectual property in general). Distribution of copyrighted material on computer is perhaps as big a threat as widespread photocopying.[5]

It takes only a few minutes (or even seconds) to copy even a highly elaborate and expensive computer program and, in fact, the only way a computer can make use of software is to "copy" the software into its memory. Computer networking gives many users access to a single program. The most common method of distributing programs is on floppy disks; yet most users have hard disks, and therefore must transcribe the program to the hard disk in order to use it. Loading copyrighted software into RAM (Random Access Memory) is a copyright infringement because it creates a tangible, fixed copy.[6]

The "archival copying" provision of the Copyright Act, Section 117, permits the owner of a program to copy and adapt it "as an essential step of using it with a machine" but this formulation creates at least as many problems as it clarifies.

Furthermore, one of the most basic principles of copyright law is that no one can copyright an idea (even a profound and original idea) or a system for doing something (such as a method of bookkeeping), but copyright protection of expression is possible (even if the expression is trivial, or if the copyright claimant has added only a very limited quantum of originality to public domain or previously copyrighted materials). That brings up difficult questions of what precisely is being protected in a copyright of a computer program or portions of a program, and what form the copyright application and deposit must take.

It's clear that some degree of copyright protection for software is available: the Software Amendments of 1980[7] added a definition of "computer program" (a set of instructions used in a computer to bring about a desired result) to Section 101 of the Copyright Act. Application or operating system programs can be registered on Form TX as literary works, and only one registration can be made per work: that is, the screen displays can't be registered as audiovisual works, with separate registration of the instructions as literary works. However, if the predominant authorship in the work is audiovisual, the single registration can be made on Form PA, audiovisual works. Under the Copyright Office's Docket #86-4,[8] digital or digitized typefaces are not eligible for copyright, although the computer programs that generate the fonts are copyrightable.

In 1993, a software company was ordered to recall thousands of copies of a screen saver program containing cartoons spoofing another copyrighted screen saver program. The parody defense was not accepted; the program was redesigned featuring flying toasters distinct in appearance from the flying toasters in the infringed copyrighted program.[9]

For works published after March 1, 1989, under the Berne Convention Implementation Act (see ¶2601 et seq., Intellectual Property) affixation of a copyright notice is optional. Affixation remains a good idea, because it prevents infringement damages from being reduced based on a defense of "innocent infringement." For works published between 1/1/78 and 3/1/89, 17 USC Section 405 provides that, if more than a few copies of a work are published without the copyright notice, the owner must register the work within five years of the publication date in order to retain the copyright; and a reasonable effort must be made to add the copyright notice to all copies distributed after the omission of the notice has been discovered.

The method for affixing copyright notice to machine-readable copies is set out in 37 CFR 201.20, which permits the following:

➤ Notice in machine-readable form, appearing with or near the title or at the end of a printout

➤ Displayed on the terminal at sign-on

➤ Maintained continuously on the terminal display

➤ A durable printed notice, affixed to the box, reel, cartridge, or cassette the software comes in

The copyright symbol can be contained within a hexagon rather than a circle, if this is easier for the display to handle; but infrequent, random appearances of the notice that appear only when the reset button is pressed do not constitute reasonable copyright notice.[10]

These questions become especially difficult in the context of custom software, because there is a temptation for the buyer to alter the program a little, and then claim proprietorship (and perhaps try to sell it to another user). Programmers can usually eliminate this threat by writing the program in "source code" (using a high-level computer language and/or a more basic assembly language), including comments and instructions to the computer. However, the customer gets only the "machine language," i.e., just the instructions for the computer, not the comments. The buyer can't retrieve the comments just by "taking apart" the machine language. (If you represent the buyer, negotiate for at least some disclosure of the source code; if you represent the seller, either resist this or demand that the source code, and changes to the source code, be placed in escrow either permanently or until the buyer has fully performed.) Also note that *Hudson v. Good Rush Messenger Service Inc.*[11] holds that when a person is hired to furnish "programs," he or she must furnish the object code, which the buyer can then copyright; the source code continues to belong to the programmer.

It is common for software to be developed that represents a significant advance over earlier software: perhaps it combines more tasks, is easier to use, faster, or has other significant advantages. It is equally common for the software to be emulated in competing software that takes advantage of the new break-throughs and makes minor modifications. Developers of the imitative software come as close as they can to the "look and feel" of the more expensive software, in order to appeal to users of the earlier software, or to those who feel comfort-able with a close approach to a market leader. Often, virtually identical end results (at least from the user's point of view) can be achieved even though the comput-er programs themselves are quite dissimilar.

"Reverse engineering" is a common technical practice: that is, once a prod-uct comes on the market, other engineers or designers buy the product and take it apart to see how it works, then devise their own version. Under *Brooktree Corp. v. Advanced Micro Devices, Inc.,*[12] an accused infringer who can document reverse engineering is entitled to a more permissive standard: infringement occurs only if the two programs are "substantially identical," not "substantially similar." Reverse engineering is no defense to a claim of patent infringement (because a patent can be infringed by a person who develops the same device independently; inventors are presumed to be on notice of all patents). However, in the computer context, the patent process is lengthy, expensive, and problematical, because a patent requires both novelty and non-obviousness in the light of prior inventions. This is a much more stringent test than the small amount of originality required to justify the grant of a copyright.

A computer can be used to infringe the copyright on a printed book: see *Williams v. Arndt,*[13] holding that a "translation" from English into BASIC, convert-ing a manual for commodities trading into a program, infringed the copyright on the printed manual.

Apple, the company that popularized the personal computer, was a party to two of the pioneering computer copyright cases. *Apple, Inc. v. Franklin Computer Corp.,*[14] holds that both source and object code can be copyrighted. (In fact, the object code is a "decryption" of the source code, so they are considered part of a single work and therefore copyrighting the source code protects the object code as well.[15] (According to a later case,[16] where a copyright infringement defendant admits to copying the object code, the plaintiff is not obliged to produce its own source code for the court.) *Apple v. Franklin* also holds that a computer's operat-ing system program is entitled to copyright protection (even if it implements a sys-tem of calculations that is otherwise ineligible for copyright); and embodying a program in read-only memory (ROM) does not deprive the owner of the right to copyright protection.

Another Apple case, *Apple Computer, Inc. v. Formula International Inc.,*[17] limits protection for operating system programs to those in which the idea can be expressed in various ways. (That is, if there is only one way an operating system can be devised, the first deviser will not be entitled to a copyright.) *Apple v. Formula* also holds that the expression of the operating system need not be communicated to the user: there is no requirement of an "audience" for copyright protection of programs. Yet another Apple case[18] rejected Apple's infringement claims, finding that the Graphical User Interface (GUI; the appearance of the program as seen by the user) of certain Microsoft products either did not infringe Apple copyrights, or was permissible under a 1985 licensing agreement between the two companies. Apple tried, but failed, to protect its use of menu bars, mini-screens in window form, and mouse-manipulated displays as a copyrightable "desktop metaphor."

A three-step analysis was adopted by the Second Circuit[19] in a case in which a computer company rewrote a program's codes after discovering that the program included codes stolen from a competitor. This was done even though the literal elements of the program were not substantially similar to those of the stolen program. The original copyright owner sought protection for the non-literal elements such as general flow charts, macros, and parameter lists. The three steps are:

➤ Isolate the level of abstraction in the structure of the allegedly copied program.

➤ See if the structural components at each level were included as "ideas" or required by considerations of efficiency, whether they were required by factors outside the program, or whether they were non-protectable elements that form part of the public domain.

➤ Identify the remaining "golden nugget" of core-protectable expression. Once that is done, the question becomes whether there has been any copying of the golden nugget, and how important the copied portion is to the entire program.

It has been held that the "SSO" (structure, sequence, and organization) of a program are copyrightable.[20] In the case cited, the two programs were not even written in the same programming language. To reach its decision, the court compared the file structures, screen outputs, and structures of five of the sub-routines (modules) in each program. However, just as there is a "scene a faire" (obligatory scene) defense to alleged infringement of copyright in a literary work, copyright protection will not be granted to file structures if only a limited number of file structures can be used for a task. A preliminary injunction was denied in *Telemarketing Resources v.Symantec Corp.*[21] Although the "look and feel" of display screens on the original and alleged infringing program were similar, the similarity was not strong enough to justify the grant of preliminary injunction.

Each program had 211 keystroke commands; only 25 of the commands were identical, and of those, 14 commands were industry standards.

According to *SAS Institute, Inc. v. S&H Computer Systems,*[22] unauthorized "conversion" of a program to make it run on another computer system is a copyright infringement (because the copyright holder controls the right to make derivative works), and also infringes on the software license, which prohibited the buyer from modifying the program or using it on hardware other than that contemplated in the license. Similarly, *Telerate Systems,Inc. v. Caro,*[23] grants a preliminary injunction against a defendant whose software program let database subscribers save money by disconnecting their dedicated terminals and using an ordinary PC to access the information; it was held that it was likely that this violated the license mandating the use of the special-purpose terminal.

It's possible to obtain copyright protection for the overall structure of a program, including its audiovisual displays,[24] since menu screens have aesthetic appeal and demonstrated stylistic creativity. Furthermore, the court permitted the plaintiff to prevail by showing access to and direct copying of the screen displays, with no need to prove access to the source code or object code of the original program. This case was extended by *Pearl Systems, Inc. v. Competition Electronics*[25] which permits copyrighting of separate subroutines; infringement of a program's "total concept and feel" was found.

In 1991, the Eastern District of Pennsylvania held that IBM 3090 microcode is a single original work functioning only as a whole, even though several tapes are required to store it.[26]

Copyright issues involving computers are also discussed at ¶2646.

[¶1304.1] Video Games and Copyright

The most significant thing about video games and the key to their marketability is precisely the "look and feel" of the game's display screens, and the way the user accesses and plays the game. Furthermore, unlike software used in business, computer games are unlikely to be adapted by their users.

An early case involving video games, *Atari, Inc. v. JS&A Group, Inc.*[27] grants a preliminary injunction against the manufacturer of a device for copying the Programmable Read Only Memory (PROM) chips used in Atari video games. The Northern District drew an explicit analogy between the copying device and the videocassette recorder: unlike the VCR, which has a "time shifting" function that does not infringe on copyright, the chip copying device had no substantial noninfringing use. Purchasers of the Atari games were not entitled to make "archival copies" (Copyright Act Section 117) because ROM chips don't fade or lose power over time, so no back-up copy is necessary.

Midway Manufacturing v. Strohon[28] similarly holds that an "enhancement" kit sold to speed up play of a copyrighted video game is an infringement of the game's copyright, even though the enhancement kit does not infringe the audiovisual display of the game. *Midway* makes two important points: that the audiovisual displays and underlying program for a video game are separately protectable; and that copyright protection extends to object code stored in the chip.[29]

In contrast, the 1992 *Galoob* case[30] holds that the "Game Genie," a device enhancing the operation of another manufacturer's video game, but not altering the underlying copyrighted game, makes permissible fair use of the copyrighted game's screen display. Nor is the Game Genie a derivative work of the computer game, because the Game Genie's alteration of the game is not permanent and does not physically incorporate the allegedly infringed game.

In *Kramer Manufacturing Co. v. Andrews*[31] the plaintiff held the copyright only in the audiovisuals of the game; someone else held the copyright on the underlying program. However, the Fourth Circuit held that either element (program or audiovisual) can be the subject of an infringement; and that the audiovisual elements are fixed in the program, which is a copy of the audiovisual elements: therefore, the plaintiff's copyright protects the program as well.

The "scene a faire" doctrine extends to video games: that is, if there is an obligatory scene, theme, motif, or expression (such as the theme of a quest, or a display showing one element shooting, chasing, or engulfing another), the later expression will not be held to infringe an earlier expression of the same common or unavoidable themes.[32]

The Ninth Circuit decided[33] that reverse engineering of a computer game does involve intermediate copying, but is not an infringement; the court said that a contrary ruling would give the copyright holder a monopoly over functional elements of a video game that are not otherwise qualified for copyright protection.

In 1992, the D.C. Circuit decided, at long last, that the Copyright Office should have granted Atari Corp. a copyright in its early video game, Breakout.[34] The Copyright Office claimed (and the trial judge agreed) that Breakout's elements of "simple geometric shapes and coloring" are not entitled to copyright protection; but the D.C. Circuit ruled that only a modest degree of creativity entitles an original work to a copyright.

[¶1305] Developments Relating to Commercial On-Line Services

Commercial on-line services are troubled by a recent government paper on copyrights in cyberspace. Thus, a White House committee in July, 1994, produced a draft report for updating the law on intellectual property.

Current law needs updating to deal with new technologies that weren't imaginable when the law was created. But CompuServe Inc., America Online Inc. and other commercial on-line services feel that their legal problems were overlooked. The on-line companies fear they will be held liable for copyright infringements by mischievous subscribers. Commercial services, such as America Online, are basically collections of such bulletin boards, through which users exchange information.

The attorneys working on the on-line services' response to the White House report argue that infringers themselves should be liable for copyright violations. They also argue that the liability of on-line services begins only when they are alerted to infringements.[35]

[¶1306] Protection for Chips

Title III of P.L. 98-620, the Semiconductor Chip Protection Act of 1984, enacted as 17 USC Section 901-914, permits copyright protection for the owners of "mask work" fixed in semiconductor chips (i.e., the design used to wire computer chips for a particular purpose). The owner has the exclusive rights to use optical, electronic, and other means to reproduce the mask work and import or distribute the chips that use the mask work. However, reverse engineering used to create other mask works, or for "fair use" purposes such as teaching, analysis, or evaluation, does not constitute an infringement.

Under the Semiconductor International Protection Extension Act of 1991, P.L. 102-64, 17 U.S.C. Section 914(e) is amended to give the Secretary of Commerce an additional four years' authority to grant interim protection to the semiconductor chip designs of the nationals of other countries that make good-faith efforts and reasonable progress toward the protection of U.S. chip designs in their countries.

Under the Copyright Remedy Clarifications Act, P.L. 101-533, notwithstanding the Eleventh Amendment, states, state instrumentalities, and their employees can be held liable if they commit copyright or mask work infringement.

— ENDNOTES —

1. Advent Systems Ltd. v. Unisys Corp., 925 F.2d 670 (3d Cir. 2/14/91).

2. National Car Rental System Inc. v. Computer Associates International Inc., 991 F.2d 426 (8th Cir. 4/6/93).

3. 89 BR 538 (W.D. Pa. 1988).

4. P.L. 100-506.

5. See Junda Woo, "Electronic Copying May Bring Lawsuits," *WSJ* 10/6/93 p. B12, describing a settlement under which software company Atlas Telecom paid $100,000 to Phillips Business Information Inc. after admitting it had distributed Phillips' newsletters via computer.

6. MAI Systems Corp. v. Peak Computer Inc., 991 F.2d 511 (9th Cir. 4/7/93).

7. P.L. 96-517.

8. FR 38110 (9/27/88).

9. See William M. Bulkeley, "Flying Toasters Singe a Software Maker Over Its Copyright," *WSJ* 10/1/93 p. B5A and news items, *WSJ* 10/11/93 p. D6 and *NYT* 10/16/93 p.40.

10. Videotronics Inc. v. Bend Electronics, 586 F.Supp. 478 (D. Nev. 1984).

11. CCH Copyright Law Decisions §26,089 (S.D.N.Y. 1987).

12. 705 F.Supp. 491.

13. 626 F.Supp. 571 (D. Mass. 1985).

14. 714 F.2d 1240 (3d Cir. 1983), cert.dism. 464 U.S. 1033.

15. GCA Corp. v. Chance, 217 USPQ 718 (N.D. Cal. 1982).

16. Data General Corp. v. Grumman Systems Support Corp., 803 F.Supp. 487 (D.Mass. 10/9/92).

17. 725 F.2d 521 (9th Cir. 1984).

18. Apple Computer Inc. v. Microsoft Corp., 779 F.Supp. 133 (N.D.Cal. 8/7/92).

19. Computer Associates Inc. v. Altai Inc., 893 F.2d 26 (2d Cir. 6/22/92). Later, part of Computer Associates' trade secrets claim against Altai was reinstated,

the Second Circuit deciding that these claims had been improvidently dismissed: 982 F.2d 693. See *National Law J.* 1/11/93 p.19.

20. Whelan Associates Inc. v. Jaslow Dental Laboratory, Inc., 797 F.2d 1222 (3d Cir. 1986), cert.den. 479 U.S. 1031.

21. N.D. Cal. #C-88-20352-RPA (8/9/88).

22. 605 F.Supp. 816 (M.D. Tenn. 1985).

23. 689 F.Supp. 221 (S.D.N.Y. 1988).

24. Broderbund Software Inc. v. Unison World, Inc., 648 F.Supp. 1127 (N.D. Cal. 1986). Also see Lotus Development Corp. v. Borland Int'l Inc., 788 F.Supp. 78 (D.Mass. 7/31/92), where the extent of copying of non-functional, expressive elements in menu commands and menu command structures rendered the Borland Quattro spreadsheet an infringement on Lotus' 1-2-3 spreadsheet.

25. 8 USPQ 2d 1520 (S.D. Fla. 1988).

26. Allen-Myland Inc. v. IBM, 770 F.Supp. 1014 (E.D. Pa. 8/1/91).

27. 597 F.Supp. 5 (N.D. Ill. 1983).

28. 564 F.Supp. 741 (N.D. Ill. 1983).

29. On copyright protection of chips, also see news item, "Intel Advances Its Copyright Cases," *NYT* 12/30/93 p. D3.

30. Lewis Galoob Toys Inc. v. Nintendo of America Inc., 964 F.2d 965 (9th Cir. 5/21/92), cert. denied 113 S.Ct. 1582.

31. 783 F.2d 421 (4th Cir. 1986).

32. Frybarger v. IBM, 812 F.2d 525 (9th Cir. 1987); Data East USA, Inc. v. Epyx Inc., 862 F.2d 204 (9th Cir. 1988).

33. Sega Enterprises Ltd. v. Accolade Inc., 977 F.2d 1510 (9th Cir. 10/20/92). A preliminary injunction was granted in April but lifted in August. Also see Atari Games Corp. v. Nintendo of America Inc., 975 F.2d 832 (Fed.Cir. 9/10/92), to the point that intermediate copying for reverse engineering purposes can be fair use if the copying is not greater in extent than that required to understand the unprotected element of the program.

34. See Paul M. Barrett, "Atari Corp. Wins Key Legal Victory in Copyright Case," *Wall Street J.* 11/23/92 p.B2.

35. News Item, "Government Paper on Copyrights in Cyberspace Vexes Some Firms," *Wall Street J.* 9/2/94 p. B3.

— **For Further Reference** —

Brenner, Susan W., "Computers and Common Law: Precedent as Information," 35 *Res Gestae* 550 (June '92).

Cutrera, Terri A., "Computer Networks, Libel and the First Amendment," 11 *Computer Law J.* 555 (December '92).

Ellis, David R., "Computer System Malfunction Remedies," 65 *Florida Bar J.* 86 (October '91).

Glenn, Martin and Dale M. Cendali, "Lotus Case Highlights Copyright Issues and High-Tech Problems," *Nat'l Law J.* 11/1/93 p. S17.

Hamilton, Gary W. and Jeffrey C. Hood, "The Shrink-Wrap License: Is It Really Necessary?" 10 *Computer Lawyer* 16 (August '93).

Ignatin, Gary R., "Let the Hackers Hack: Allowing the Reverse Engineering of Copyright Computer Programs to Achieve Compatibility," 140 *U. of Pennsylvania L. Rev.* 1999 (May '92).

Jackson, Jonathan C., "Legal Aspects of Computer Art," 19 *Rutgers Computer & Technology L.J.* 495 (Winter '93).

Kashi, Joseph L. and Thomas Boedeker, "Great Lines from Technical Support," 3 *Law Office Computing* 10 (June-July '93).

Kerrigan, William J., "Books on Disk: Technology that Really Makes Lawyering Easier," 80 *Illinois Bar J.* 469 (September '92).

Korn, Gary Clifford and Alan H. Blankenheimer, "First Amendment Issues Involved in Legislation on Software Licensing," *Nat.L.J.* 11/2/92 p. 32.

Losey, Ralph C., "Legal Protection of Computer Databases," 65 *Florida Bar J.* 80 (October '91).

Lyman, Susan C., "Civil Remedies for Victims of Computer Viruses," 21 *Southwestern U.L. Rev.* 1169 (1992).

Menard, Vicki S., "Admission of Computer Generated Visual Evidence: Should There be Clear Standards?" 6 *Software L.J.* 325 (April '93).

Neuner, Robert, "Trade Secret Protection for Computer Software," *N.Y.L.J.* 2/3/92 p. 3.

Paray, Paul E., "Freedom of Contract Under the UCC: The Ability of Software Vendors to Exclude Recovery of Consequential Damages," 25 *Uniform Commercial Code L.J.* 133 (Fall '92).

Samuelson, Pamela, "Computer Programs, User Interfaces, and Section 102(b) of the Copyright Act of 1976," 55 *Law and Contemporary Problems* 311 (Spring '92).

Sandholm, Carl A., "High Technology Jurisprudence: In Defense of 'Look and Feel' Approaches to Copyright Protection," 8 *Santa Clara Computer & High-Tech L.J.* 209 (May '92).

Sprague, Robert D., "Developing Theories of Legal Liability for Inaccurate Computer Information," 24 *Law-Technology* 1 (Spring '91).

Stedronski, H. James, "Prepare Your Own Trial Database," 3 *Law Office Computing* 64 (June-July '93).

Stern, Richard H., "Copyright Infringement by Add-On Software," 24 *Intellectual Property L. Rev.* 429 (1992 annual).

Tunick, David C., "Legal Advice for a Company Hiring Computer Programmers From Another Company," 19 *Rutgers Computer & Technology L.J.* 405 (Winter '93).

Verdesco, Joseph T. Jr., "Copyrighting the User Interface: Too Much Protection?" 45 *Southwestern L.J.* 1047 (Fall '91).

Vietzke, Lance L., "Design Patents for Icons: What Is the Article of Manufacture?" 10 *Computer Lawyer* 1 (June '93).

CONDOMINIUMS AND COOPERATIVES

[¶1401] Traditional property concepts include fee-simple ownership of property (e.g., a house, or the infamous Blackacre) and leaseholds (e.g., renting a farm, a house, or an apartment within a multiple dwelling). However, modern economic realities make it necessary to supplement these concepts with other ways to develop, hold, and own residential and commercial property.

Two of the most popular new concepts are the condominium and the cooperative. (The so-called "condop" is a hybrid combining features of both.) Because community planning is involved, cities frequently have detailed regulations in addition to those imposed by the state. Therefore, practitioners should be aware of the advantages and disadvantages of each form under local regulation when they represent a real estate developer constructing a project in condominium form; a landlord contemplating conversion of a rental building to condominium or coop form; one or more tenants involved in the conversion process; or disgruntled unit owners engaged in litigation.

In 1982, the National Conference of Commissioners on Uniform State Laws adopted the Uniform Common Interest Ownership Act governing various types of "common interest communities," defined as "real estate with respect to which a person, by virtue of his ownership of a unit, is obligated to pay for real estate taxes, insurance premiums, maintenance, or improvement of other real estate described in a declaration."

Although federal condominium and coop regulation is limited (other than in terms of income taxes), 15 U.S.C. Section 3601 et seq., The Condominium and Cooperative Conversion Protection and Abuse Relief Act of 1980 operates to control abuses in the use of long-term (over three-year) self-dealing contracts between project developers and unit owners or owners' associations, entered into at a time when the developer still controlled the project. Aggrieved unit owners can avoid the contract under conditions specified in the statute.

[¶1402] DISTINCTIONS BETWEEN CONDOMINIUMS AND COOPERATIVES

In a condominium, the unit owners each own their units (usually apartments in a multiple dwelling; sometimes townhouses in a development) in fee simple. They are tenants in common as to the common areas, which include the roof, corridors, and elevators, and which can also include amenities such as laundry rooms, health clubs, even golf courses.

However, in a cooperative, title to the real estate itself is held by the cooperative (usually organized as a corporation; more rarely as a trust; even more rarely, the cooperators own the real estate as tenants in common or joint tenants). The cooperators receive shares of stock in the condominium corporation, plus a proprietary lease giving them the right to occupy a unit.

Thus, the ownership of a condominium unit is much more like ownership of a house than coop ownership is. A condo owner can sell it to whomever he pleases; coop boards have the right to approve those to whom a cooperator's shares will be sold. To discourage speculation, coops sometimes institute a "flip tax" on resales, obligating cooperators who sell their apartments within a certain period of time of purchase, to remit part of their profits to the coop board. Although both condominiums and coops are managed by an association elected by unit-dwellers, the voting in a condominium is usually proportional to the size or value of the unit; the usual rule in a coop is "one apartment, one vote."

Each condominium unit owner must finance his or her own unit separately (but banks are quite willing to issue mortgages to qualified buyers of condominium units). The building in which the coop is located can be (and often is) mortgaged, with debt service making up part of the monthly maintenance charge each cooperator pays. (There is also a monthly maintenance charge for condominium units, but it's much smaller because it relates only to the common areas of the project.) This factor can make a coop conversion more attractive than a condominium conversion to a landlord who owns a building with a large mortgage: the mortgage must be "cleared" as part of a condo conversion, but can be left in place when the conversion is made to coop operation. It can also make coop ownership much less attractive to potential buyers, who risk foreclosure if other cooperators stop paying their maintenance.

Each owner of a condo unit pays property tax on that unit separately (probably as one component of a mortgage payment); property taxes on a coop building are, once again, an element of the monthly maintenance charge.

There are also differences in the federal income tax implications of each form. A condominium unit owner (but not a cooperator) is entitled to a deduction for the uninsured portion of a casualty loss to the unit (as long as the loss exceeds the appropriate "floor amount"). Condo unit owners, like single-family homeowners, are entitled to a federal income tax deduction for mortgage interest and real estate taxes. A taxpayer who is age 55 or over may elect to exclude a gain of up to $125,000 from the sale of a principal residence, which includes a condominium.[1]

Cooperators are entitled to a similar deduction, based on their share of these items for the building, but the deduction is unavailable if the coop derives more than 20% of its income from sources other than payments from cooperators (e.g., if substantial income is derived from renting stores or professional offices on the ground floor of the building).

Although coops are quite common in New York State (especially New York City) and are found in some other cities (e.g., San Francisco, Chicago, Washington, D.C.), the condominium form is by far the more popular method of handling ownership of units in a building or development. Their use has also become more widespread as the general costs of owning real estate have increased.

Although each method has its advantages and disadvantages, the practitioner handling a development or conversion should be certain to select the right method the first time. IRS Letter Ruling 8812049 interprets the Tax Code of 1986 to require that, when a coop changes ownership form to condominium operation, a liquidation has taken place—and tax is due on appreciation in value of the assets distributed to the owners of the new condo units.

[¶1403] CREATION OF A CONDOMINIUM

A developer can construct a building with the intention of selling its units as condominium units, or build a development of townhouses to be operated in condominium form; or, a landlord can convert a rental building to the condominium form of ownership.

To create a condominium, the owner or developer must draft and record a declaration describing the physical lay-out of the building and units and its intended condominium arrangement; a map of the project; Articles of Incorporation; and bylaws for the owners' association (containing the covenants, conditions, and restrictions on the project; sometimes the owners' association is given an option or right of first refusal if an owner wants to sell his unit). As the units are purchased, deeds are executed to the purchasers, and the management of the common areas is vested in the owners' association.

Because the sale of condominium units is somewhat similar to the sale of stock (and, in fact, the sale of a coop is a sale of stock), about half the states impose security-like regulation on the sale of coops and condos. It may be necessary to submit the offering plan to the state or city Attorney General for review, to prepare a preliminary prospectus ("Red Herring") and have it approved, and to furnish potential buyers with a copy of the final prospectus before the sale. It may be worthwhile to prepare a prospectus even if the state does not require it; if the condominium complex is in a resort area, it may be suitable for timesharing or purchase by outsiders interested in beach or skiing facilities, and the prospectus makes it possible to advertise the units in states with a prospectus requirement. The state or city may retain the power to institute a moratorium on conversions altogether, where the rental vacancy rate is low.

If the project is a conversion, it may be necessary to get an agreement by a certain percentage of the tenants that they will buy their apartments (e.g., 15%) before the conversion can be approved by the regulatory authorities. Customarily, one price ("insider's price") is set for tenants who agree to buy their apartments within a certain period (e.g., 90 days); a higher, "outsider's price" is charged to others, who buy apartments that were vacant at the time of the conversion or that are emptied when non-purchasing tenants move away or die.

State and local law must be consulted as to whether a landlord has the right to evict non-purchasing tenants. Tenants may have the option of remaining and paying rent after the conversion; or, the landlord may be able to sell occupied apartments to investors who are interested in collecting the rent and eventually moving into or selling the apartment. Even if eviction of non-purchasing tenants is permitted under other circumstances, there may be a special provision protecting low-income, senior-citizen, or disabled tenants from eviction, or compelling the landlord to provide them with extensive notice of the conversion or with relocation assistance.

Tenants need not be passive spectators of the conversion process. They can hire an attorney to monitor the process and make sure that no violations of state law occur. They can band together and sign "no-buy" pledges, preventing the landlord from converting the building at all, or requiring him to offer better terms (e.g., a lower insider's price; more repairs prior to the conversion; a larger reserve fund to be turned over to the owners' association once the conversion takes place).

A condominium can also be commercial, retail, or a hybrid, containing both residential and other types of units. In response to urban crowding, there are even parking condominiums (buyers get a parking space instead of an apartment) and "dockominiums" for boats.

[¶1403.1] Steps in a Typical Conversion

Although the fact situation or local conditions or regulation can alter this schedule, a typical condominium conversion will involve these steps:

➤ The landlord's (or other sponsor's) attorney drafts an offering plan that satisfies applicable local disclosure requirements.

➤ An engineer inspects the building and drafts the "Sponsor's Statement of Building Condition." The conditions so disclosed will do a lot to determine the level of the sponsor's reserve fund.

➤ The real estate brokerage firm selected as selling agent consults on the price to be asked for each apartment.

➤ An accountant draws up a certified financial statement giving several (three to five years') actual operating expenses.

➤ The sponsor draws up a schedule indicating the number of rooms in each apartment; each unit's percentage share of interest in the common elements; how expenses of the common elements will be allocated (usually either proportionate to the interest in the common elements, or as agreed to in the Declaration or bylaws); the monthly maintenance for each unit; the inside and outside price for the unit; and an estimate of the tax deductions available to the purchaser in the first year after the closing.

➤ The sponsor's attorney drafts documentation and closing papers, including an opinion as to the income tax position of the buyers; a list of the tenants buying and those not buying; contracts with the rental and managing agents; and the initial bylaws and house rules. (Later, the owners' association can amend the bylaws and rules.)

➤ If the Attorney General's or other regulator's approval is required, the sponsor sends the preliminary offering plan to the regulator, and makes any changes required so that it can be accepted for filing. The preliminary plan is submitted to the tenants.

➤ Usually, there is a time period (e.g., 90 days) during which tenants have the exclusive right to acquire apartments. Before or during this period, the tenants set up a committee and usually hire their own attorney and engineer to review the physical condition of the building and the legal condition of the offering plan. A no-buy pledge may be solicited during this time.

➤ As soon as the required number of tenants agree to buy their apartments, the sponsor files an amendment with the Attorney General declaring the plan effective; the closing of title is scheduled, usually within 30 days. If no approval is required, the sponsor can schedule the closing as soon as the requisite number of tenants agree to buy. If there is no requirement as to number of tenants purchasing before a plan can become effective, the sponsor can schedule the closing at its convenience.

[¶1404] CREATION OF A COOPERATIVE

The process of creating a cooperative is quite similar to that of creating a condominium. However, the documents involved are slightly different. To begin with, a not-for-profit corporation or other entity is formed to take title to the building and the land on which it is located. The task of the attorney includes drafting proprietary leases rather than deeds for the individual units, in addition to a charter (or Articles of Incorporation) and bylaws setting rules that cooperators must follow. A common bylaw provision gives the coop corporation a lien on a cooperator's shares if maintenance on the apartment is not paid.

The number of shares of stock allocated to each apartment must be set; usually, this is determined by the value of the apartment. Note that shares of stock in a cooperative are personal property, not real estate. A cooperator who needs financing to buy the shares must get a personal loan, not a mortgage (which may involve higher rates). Also note that, in planning the estate of a cooperator, the shares of stock must be treated as personal property; they will not pass under a general provision devising the cooperator's real property.

— ENDNOTE —

1. IRC §121.

— FOR FURTHER REFERENCE —

ALI/ABA Condominium, Planned Unit Development and Conversion Documents (3d. edition, 1985).

Burr, Clinton, "Counseling the Timeshare Buyer," 50 *Texas B.J.* 712 (July '87).

Czachor, Bruce, "Cooperative and Condominium Conversions in New York," 31 *New York Law School L. Rev.* 763 (Fall '86).

Hyatt, Wayne S. and Anne P. Stubblefield, "Community Association Board Should Minimize Potential Liability," 1 *Probate and Property* 25 (May—June '87).

Kaster, Lewis R., "Co-Op Units Must Have Housekeeping Facilities," 67 *J. of Taxation* 122 (August '87).

Lambert, Thomas F., Jr., "Premises Liability: Condo Association," 29 *ATLA Law Reporter* 390 (November '86).

Lemons, Janet R., "Condominium Use Restrictions," 38 *Baylor L. Rev.* 1003 (Fall '86).

Lippman, William Jay, *Condominium and coop Closings* (Practising Law Institute, 1987).

Marshall, Richard D., "Statutorily Protected Tenants Vis-a-Vis the Free Market," 16 *Real Estate L.J.* 265 (Winter '88).

Miller, Joel E., "What Is a Condop?" 3 *Tax Management Real Estate J.* 182 (August '87).

Payne, John M., "The Condominium as Landlord—Determining Tort Liability," 15 *Real Estate L.J.* 365 (Spring '87).

Rohan, Patrick J. and Melvin A. Reskin, *Condominium Law and Practice* (8 volumes) (Matthew Bender, 1987 with 1988 Supplement).

CORPORATE DIRECTORS' AND OFFICERS' DUTIES AND LIABILITIES

[¶1501] Directors, officers, and even controlling shareholders of a corporation stand in a fiduciary relationship to the corporation. Each must carry out his or her management responsibilities in good faith. Their powers, whether derived from charter or statute or both, may be exercised only for the benefit of the corporation.

[¶1502] DIRECTORS' DUTIES

Directors of a corporation have many duties beyond merely sitting on a board and occasionally approving decisions of management. These are explored below.

[¶1503] DUTY TO ATTEND DIRECTORS' MEETINGS

If poor health or other factors necessitate missing meetings on a regular basis, a director should resign rather than incur the risk of liability for board decisions to which he or she was not a party. If an occasional meeting is missed, there are ways in which a director can become familiar with what transpired by conferring with fellow directors and examining the minutes and corporate records. If specific issues will be on the agenda, the director can make his or her views known via a written instrument, particularly in the case of a minority view.

[¶1504] EXAMINATION OF FINANCIAL STATEMENTS

A director is supposed to spot the chief executive who may be treating the business as personal property; e.g., misapplying funds in good or bad faith for personal benefit. It's the director's job to supervise the acts of officers. He or she should get financial reports directly from the responsible financial officer, not secondhand. A director should know the terms of underlying corporate obligations, as well as the provisions of the company's charter and bylaws. If management is pursuing improper policies and practices, a director cannot avoid responsibility on grounds of ignorance.

[¶1505] LIABILITY UNDER THE INTERNAL REVENUE CODE

Under the Internal Revenue Code, any officer or director who willfully fails to collect or pay over any tax, shall, in addition to all other penalties, be liable to a penalty equal to the total amount of the tax evaded, or not collected, or not accounted for and paid over.[1]

[¶1506] INSPECTION OF BOOKS AND RECORDS

As a corollary to the obligations as a corporate fiduciary and as part of management duties, a director enjoys the right and has an obligation to inspect the corporate books and records. The right of inspection exists only for as long as the director remains in office. However, some courts have allowed former directors the right of inspection of records relating to the years during which they served, in order to protect their own liability interests. A few states consider the right of inspection a "qualified" right in that it ceases if it can be shown that the director seeks inspection for reasons adverse to the corporate interest.

[¶1507] DUTY OF CARE

Because directors are responsible for the management of the corporation, they must ultimately be called to account for any corporate losses. While it is clear that a director who perpetrates a fraud, derives a personal benefit at the expense of the corporation, or is found to have engaged in wanton acts of omission or commission is liable for the resultant losses, a more important issue is the standard of care to which a director is to be held for acts that may later appear to have been imprudent, wasteful, or negligent.

The Supreme Court has noted that directors of banks and other financial institutions are legally bound to use that degree of care "which ordinarily prudent and diligent men would exercise under similar circumstances." This standard has been adopted for directors of business corporations as well. Pennsylvania's Business Corporation Law §408 requires that "directors act in good faith and exercise such care as the 'ordinarily prudent man' would exercise under similar circumstances."

New York imposes a similar standard of care upon its directors. Section 717 of the New York Business Corporation Law states that "directors and officers shall discharge the duties of their respective positions in good faith and with that degree of diligence, care, and skill which ordinarily prudent men would exercise under similar circumstances in like positions." The general rule, in force in Delaware, requires directors to exercise "diligence and reasonable judgment honestly and in good faith."

[¶1508] DUTY OF LOYALTY

A director's duty of loyalty to the corporation encompasses many types of activities. The duty of loyalty is frequently used to invalidate a contract between the corporation and the director, to recover profits made by a director from trans-actions with the corporation, to prevent directors from competing with the corpo-ration, and to prevent a director from taking personal advantage of a transaction based upon his or her position in the corporation—usually referred to as the doc-trine of corporate opportunity.

A director who makes a profit by taking advantage of a business opportu-nity for which the corporation should have had "first call" is liable to the corpo-ration for those profits. However, not every business opportunity need first be offered to the company. If the opportunity is not essential to the corporation, nor one in which it has an interest or the expectancy of an interest, the director may then treat such an opportunity as personal. A director may also take advantage of a corporate opportunity if the corporation is legally and financially unable to do so, or if the corporation has turned down the opportunity in a good faith exer-cise of its business judgment. However, a director may not, after resigning as a director, take advantage of a corporate opportunity that came about during his or her directorship.

With the increase in the number of corporations having common directors, a frequent issue is the validity of transactions between corporations with inter-locking directorates. The liberal trend in this area is to uphold the validity of such contracts, unless the contract is unfair, unreasonable, or fraudulent. Usually, direc-tors seeking to uphold the contract have the burden of overcoming the presump-tion against the contract's validity. In many states, it makes no difference if the number of common directors constitutes a majority of the board, so long as the contract is fair. For jurisdictions with a more conservative approach, the contract may be voidable at the option of either corporation, without regard to the fairness or reasonableness of the transaction.

Section 8 of the Clayton Act (15 USC §19) prohibits interlocking directorates on the boards of competitor corporations if either company has capital and sur-plus in excess of $1,000,000. This is to prevent the possibility of agreements not to compete, which would be in violation of the federal antitrust laws. Section 8 does not apply to banks or railroads.

Directors can't play favorites among the stockholders. They can't favor one group of stockholders within the same general class, nor can they favor one class of stockholders over another, except as the stock itself calls for higher preferences or rights of one class of stock over another.

It's expected that an outside director will have other business interests—these may even be competitive. There's no harm so long as information gained from the relationship with the corporation is not used to its disadvantage. An outside direc-tor who goes too far must expect, if a stockholder prevails in a derivative suit, to account to the corporation for profits derived from the competing business.

Chances are that the employment contract specifically prohibits competi-tion—unless certain exceptions are expressly enumerated. An officer or other employee is required to use her full working time and best efforts on behalf of the corporation. Failure to do so is a breach, even if the other activity is not competi-tion. She is then accountable to the corporation for profits from the other venture.

[¶1509]　OUTSIDE DIRECTORS

An invitation to join a board of directors as an outside director may prompt visions of power, prestige, and influence. Prior to acceptance of this responsibility, a nominee should consult the following checklist:

☐ *Articles of Incorporation and Bylaws:* A careful reading should give some insight as to the purpose of the corporation and its day-to-day operation. These documents also spell out the duties of a director and indicate what provisions the corporation has made with regard to director liability.

☐ *Present Financial and Legal Status of the Corporation:* Review past filings with the Securities and Exchange Commission, inquire as to how the directors are kept apprised of all current financial information, and check as to whether the corporation is facing any pending litigation. Remember, whatever a director doesn't know about the corporation *can* hurt him.

☐ *Any Conflicts of Interest?* Carefully review the position in the business community to determine if there is even the slightest appearance of a conflict, regardless of whether one actually exists. (*Note:* No matter how neutral a director knows he or she can be, the shareholders, other directors, and general public will not grant benefit of the doubt.)

☐ *Time Commitment:* Will there be enough time to attend all board meetings, as well as to investigate matters that will be discussed? Frequent absence and lack of preparation can come back to haunt one should future problems develop. Remember, a director is answerable for the actions of the board as a whole despite absence from the meeting or if there is no record of opposition to the contested action.

☐ *Compensation:* Since monetary compensation is usually low, find out whether there will be some additional expenses to assume in order to carry out the duties as a director. Even if there are, the challenge, prestige, and opportunity associated with the position may make it worthwhile anyway.

☐ *Insurance Liability:* Even though an individual may ultimately be adjudged innocent, the costs involved in defending a legal suit can be prohibitive. Find out whether the corporation will absorb legal costs, as well as indemnification for any damages or settlements that might have to be paid.

☐ *Composition and Operation of the Board:* Finally, how is the board divided between inside and outside directors? Do any of the other directors have real or potential conflicts of interest? Are the actions of the whole board merely a reflection of the opinions of the inside directors or control group, or do board meetings provide the basis for thorough discussion prior to a vote? What is the relationship between the board and the officers of the corporation?

[¶1510]　CONSEQUENCES OF NEGLECT—SHAREHOLDER DERIVATIVE SUIT

In a shareholder's derivative suit, a shareholder "steps into the shoes" of the corporation to seek relief for wrongs committed against the corporate entity. Since it is unlikely that a corporation would sue its own directors for violations of the duties of loyalty and care, or that a majority shareholder would want to change the status quo, the derivative suit enables a minority shareholder to advance the corporation's claims against its directors or third parties. Following is a list of improper actions that could give rise to a derivative suit:

(1) Improper loans to shareholders.

(2) Continual absence from directors' meetings permitting improper acts to be done by others.

(3) Improper expenditures of corporate funds in proxy contests.

(4) Improvident investment of corporate funds.

(5) Improvident expansion of corporate activities into new fields resulting in losses.

(6) Failure to discover and prevent antitrust violations.

(7) Recovery of treble damages for damages caused to the corporation by violation of antitrust laws.

(8) Failure to take action against directors who make short-term profits in violation of §16(b) of the Securities Exchange Act.

(9) Use of corporate funds to purchase shares of corporation to combat takeover bid by outside interests—or, more likely, failure to take steps to protect the corporation and its shareholders from takeover.

(10) Improper payment of a dividend.

(11) Issuance of stock without obtaining valid consideration.

(12) Failure to obtain competitive bids where required by prudent business practice.

(13) Wasting corporate assets.

(14) Forgiving an improper loan made by a prior board to an officer.

(15) Diverting the proceeds of a public offering to pay debts other than those authorized to be paid from such proceeds.

(16) Embezzlement by an employee that could have been prevented by careful supervision.

[¶1511] DIRECTORS' DEFENSES TO DERIVATIVE SUIT

Since a plaintiff-shareholder is required to make a demand upon the directors prior to the commencement of the derivative suit, defendants may raise the "business judgment" rule as a defense. Such a defense is predicated on the theory that upon review of plaintiff's allegations, the directors may conclude that the complaint lacks merit. However, business judgment is not a defense if the directors have breached their duties of loyalty and due care to the corporation—for instance, where self-dealing has occurred.

[¶1512] DUTIES AND LIABILITIES UNDER THE FEDERAL SECURITIES LAWS

Liabilities under the Securities Act of 1933 and the Securities Exchange Act of 1934 mandate care on the part of corporate officers, directors, and other insiders. Heavy judgments as a result of derivative suits, criminal penalties, and large fines await those who do not diligently meet the laws' requirements. Listed below are some of the areas in which caution is required.

[¶1513] LIABILITY UNDER THE SECURITIES ACT OF 1933

Most commonly used in the prosecution of a securities law violation is the 1933 Act. Corporate insiders should avoid conduct that might be construed as:

❐ Fraud in connection with the offer or sale of a security [15 USC §77q(a)].

❐ Sale of unregistered stock [15 USC §77(e)].

❐ Promotion or "touting" of a security without disclosing that a promoter has a financial interest [15 USC §77q(b)].

❐ Filing a false or misleading registration statement [15 USC §77x].

❐ Manipulation of the over-the-counter market [15 USC §77q(a)].

The SEC takes the position that public policy forbids a corporation to indemnify its directors and officers against violations of the 1933 Act (although it is not opposed to corporations buying D&O liability insurance).

[¶1514] LIABILITY UNDER THE SECURITIES EXCHANGE ACT OF 1934

❐ Filing a false annual report or false periodic reports [15 USC §78l].

❐ Filing false proxy materials [15 USC §78n, ff(a)].

❐ Unlawful short sales of listed securities [15 USC §78j(a)].

❐ Manipulation of securities listed on over-the-counter or national exchanges [15 USC §78l].

❐ Failure to file insider ownership reports [15 USC §78p(a)].

The major areas of concern for directors and officers are discussed in detail in the following paragraphs.

[¶1515] RULE 10b-5

Section 10(b) of the 1934 Act and Rule 10b-5 prohibit the use of any manipulative or deceptive devices in connection with the purchase or sale of securities. The Rule protects both defrauded buyers and sellers. Rule 10b-5 imposes a liability for the use of "inside" information or the disclosure of such information in the trading of securities. Not only are corporate officers, directors, and majority security holders potentially liable under this Rule, but any person having access to or receiving information also is liable for any trading based on nonpublic information. Those persons to whom the material information is transmitted are known as "tippees."

[¶1516] DISCLOSURE UNDER RULE 10b-5

Rule 10b-5 makes it unlawful to mislead a buyer or seller by omitting a material fact in connection with the purchase or sale of a security. Any information known to an insider that would tend to influence the investment decision of a buyer or seller is probably a "material" fact necessitating disclosure. Here are some illustrations of material facts calling for disclosure under the Rule:

(1) The improved or worsening financial condition of the firm.

(2) A dividend cut.

(3) A contract for the sale of corporate assets.

(4) A contemplated liquidation of a subsidiary for the purpose of capturing inventory appreciation of the subsidiary.

(5) A new ore discovery.

(6) The fraudulent trading in company's stock by a third party (broker-dealer).

(7) Promissory notes in a financial statement used in connection with an exchange offer.

(8) Dividend increase.

(9) Possible corporate merger.

(10) New discoveries relating to products or processes.

[¶1517] WHEN MUST DISCLOSURE UNDER RULE 10b-5 BE MADE?

Basically, Rule 10b-5 is aimed at insiders taking advantage of their position to make a profit on the purchase or sale of securities. Thus, when "inside" information becomes public knowledge, insiders should be able to trade without disclosing, since the public will already have access to the same information.

Courts have struggled with the problem of determining when information becomes public knowledge. There is dictum in the *Texas Gulf Sulphur* (CA-2, 401 F.2d 833, 1968) case to suggest that insiders should refrain from trading for a "reasonable waiting period" when the news is of the sort that is not readily translatable into investment action, thus giving it an opportunity to filter down and be evaluated by the investing public.

[¶1518] WHEN DOES RULE 10b-5 APPLY?

Rule 10b-5 applies whether or not the firm has securities registered under the 1933 or 1934 Acts. It applies whether the purchase or sale takes place on a securities exchange, in the over-the-counter market, or privately.

Securities Covered: Rule 10b-5 covers transactions in any form of securities, encompassing (but not limited to) any note, bond, certificate of interest, or participation in any profit-sharing agreement, preorganization certificate or subscription contract, agreement to form a corporation, or joint venture agreement expressly providing for the distribution of shares of stock in a corporation thereafter to be formed.

Interstate Transactions: The Rule applies only when the requisites of federal jurisdiction are present—use of the mails, any means or instrumentality of interstate commerce, or stock exchange facilities. Even for wholly intrastate transactions, at least one-half the states have adopted the Uniform Securities Act §101, which has the same provisions as the Rule.

[¶1518.1] The Use of Computer Simulation of Stock Trading to Estimate Aggregate Damages Under Rule 10b-5

The parties in Rule 10b-5 securities class actions have begun to use computer simulation of stock trading to estimate aggregate damages. Although these models often generate damage estimates amounting to hundreds of millions of dollars, they have never been publicly tested against actual class claims. Estimated damages using computer simulation in Rule 10b-5 cases have been tested against the actual claims data from two cases. In both cases, the computer-based damages overpredicted the actual damages awarded.[2]

[¶1519] RELEASE OF INFORMATION DURING REGISTRATION

Insiders must also be acquainted with the special rules affecting the release of information when a company is involved in the process of registration. It is well established that during such period neither the company nor its representatives should instigate publicity for the purpose of facilitating the sale of securities in a proposed offering. In addition, any publication of information by a company that is in registration other than by means of a statutory prospectus should be limited to factual information and should not include such things as predictions, projections, forecasts, or opinions with respect to value.

If information should be released, the SEC has indicated how to handle the problem (SEC Act of 1933, Release No. 5180): "In the event a company publicly releases material information concerning new corporate developments during the period that a registration statement is pending, the registration statement should be amended at or prior to the time the information is released. If this is not done and such information is publicly released through inadvertency, the pending registration statement should be promptly amended to reflect such information."

[¶1520] SECTION 16(b)—SHORT-SWING PROFITS RECAPTURE

Section 16(b) applies only to profits made in the trading of equity securities that are basically stocks, as distinguished from debt securities such as bonds or debentures. But it takes in more than stocks. It includes any security that is convertible, with or without additional payment or other consideration, into stock or any security that carries a warrant or right to subscribe or to purchase stock. It also includes any warrant or right to subscribe or to purchase stock; in other words, the warrant or right itself separated from or apart from any other security. It can also include any security that the SEC treats as an equity security under its rules and regulations, but so far the SEC hasn't acted under this authorization.

If any of the equity securities of a firm are registered under the Securities Exchange Act, it will be subject to the short-swing profits recapture provision, §16(b), even though the profits are made in unregistered securities.

[¶1521] BENEFICIAL OWNERSHIP

There are at least a couple of gray areas on the matter of 10% stockholders. Section 16(b) itself says it is not "to be construed to cover any transaction where such beneficial owner was not such both at the time of purchase and sale, or the sale and purchase of the security involved."

Prior to 1976, there was considerable debate over the language of part of §16(b), particularly the "at the time of" sale provision. A federal Court of Appeals decision indicated that the shareholder who became a 10% stock owner just after or just before a sale was liable. In the landmark case of *Foremost-McKesson, Inc. v. Provident Securities Co.* (423 US 232, 1976), this part of the controversy was put to rest. A unanimous Supreme Court stated that the question presented was whether a person purchasing securities that put his holdings above the 10% level is a beneficial owner "at the time of the purchase" so that he must account for profits realized on a sale of the securities within six months. The point is now settled as to the meaning of that particular phrase in §16(b).

There is no authoritative decision on the question of whether to count the transaction by which the stockholder ceases to be a ten percenter; however, one of the outstanding authorities in the field, Professor Louis Loss, has expressed the opinion that such a transaction must be counted. Again, to play it safe, it will be best to count the unloading transaction. In certain situations, a shareholder might want to consider a gift of a portion of the stock as a means of divesting himself of 10% status. There might be situations in which such a technique could be valuable even on a dollar-and-cents basis. Of course, a gift won't help unless it's completely bona fide and with no strings attached. In any case, great care and advice of specialized counsel are called for before trying this.

The duties and liabilities of §16 cannot be escaped by an insider's having securities registered in someone else's name. Section 16 is aimed at direct or indirect beneficial ownership, not so-called legal ownership.

[¶1522] PURCHASE OR SALE

The short-swing profits recapture section applies to the following types of securities transactions:

(1) Contracts to buy or sell;

(2) Stock options, warrants, or subscription rights granted to an officer or director as compensation for services (although they may be exempt if granted under an option plan);

(3) Acquisitions of stock pursuant to the exercise of an option, warrant, or subscription right.

[¶1523] TIMING OF SHORT SWINGS

Section 16(b) defines the short-swing period as "any period of less than six months." It's been decided that this means that the last day of the period is the second day before the date in the sixth month that corresponds numerically with the day of the month in which the first transaction took place. For example, if you buy or sell on February 1, 1995, the last day of the period would be July 30, 1995. This means you could sell or buy on July 31, 1995, or any time later and be home free as far as §16(b) is concerned. In the case of an ordinary purchase or sale, the transaction takes place when there is a firm commitment to buy or sell. In other cases, the transaction takes place when the right of the parties is fixed. An option, for example, dates from the time it is irrevocably granted. The fact that a sale agreement gives the buyer a right to rescind within a fixed period of time doesn't mean that the sale isn't counted until the time for rescission has run.

[¶1524] MEASUREMENT AND RECOVERY OF SHORT-SWING PROFITS

The measure of damages in an action brought under §16(b) is the profit realized on any purchase or sale or any sale and purchase within six months without any right of set-off, or the adoption of any rule of "first-in-first-out" or other minimizing of recovery. "The only rule," it has been said on good authority, "whereby all possible profits can be surely recovered is that of the lowest price in, highest price out—within six months."

Exchanges: If a purchase and sale involve an exchange of stock for assets and not a direct payment in money, the determination of profit realized will turn on the value of the assets exchanged for the stock.

Commissions and Transfer Taxes: The purchase or sale prices for the purpose of computing profit are determined after the deduction of commissions and transfer taxes.

Dividends: Dividends received are added to the profits; dividends not received are deducted.

A suit to recover short-swing profits can be brought by the corporation or any security holder if the corporation fails or refuses to do so within 60 days of request. The federal district courts have exclusive jurisdiction of these suits.

Statute of Limitations: The suit must be brought within two years from the time the profits are realized, but failure to file a Form 4 reporting the transaction prevents the time period from running. The period will run from the time Form 4 is filed.

Counsel Fees: Counsel is entitled to a generous percentage of the profits recovered as a fee. A fee may also be earned by serving a request on the corporation to institute suit where the corporation does so and recovers.

[¶1525] SUMMARY AND COMPARISON OF §16(b) AND RULE 10b-5

The following chart summarizes the different coverage, application, and liabilities under the Rules:

Risks and Pitfalls Under §16(b) and Rule 10b-5

	§16(b)	*Rule 10b-5*
Transactions covered	Short-swing purchase *and* sale or sale *and* purchase	Purchase *or* sale
Subject matter of transaction	Equity security, registered or not	Any security, registered or not
Must firm have other registered securities?	Yes, equity securities	No
Who is subject to liability?	Officers, directors, and 10% stockholders	Officers, directors, and controlling stockholders, plus corporation, and persons with "inside" information
Is misrepresentation, omission, or scheme necessary to impose liability?	No	Yes
Exempt transactions?	Yes, a variety of exemptions exist	No
Is direct dealing with party necessary?	No	No
Who has right of action?	Corporation; shareholder derivative action is also available	Person buying from or selling to insider or SEC
Remedies available?	Action for damages	Action for damages, rescission, disciplinary proceedings, criminal proceedings
Measure of damages?	Lowest price in, highest out, or vice versa, during short-swing period	Compensatory

[¶1526] INDEMNIFICATION AND INSURANCE PROTECTION FOR CORPORATE OFFICERS AND DIRECTORS

Generally speaking, legal liabilities incurred by corporate directors, officers, and employees as a result of their on-the-job conduct that results in a lawsuit may, under certain circumstances, be subject to indemnification by the corporation. Usually, an initial distinction must be made between a civil or criminal action instituted against a corporate director, officer, or employee by reason of conduct within the scope of employment that has injured another party, and those actions undertaken that are alleged to have injured the corporation itself. Standards for indemnification in each of these cases will vary. In fact, in the latter case, the corporation may end up suing the errant officer or director.

Roots for all indemnification are either statute, portions of the corporate Articles of Incorporation, bylaw provisions, private agreement (such as an employment contract), a resolution of the board of directors, a vote of the shareholders, or, in some states for a successful defendant only, in a common law (nonstatutory) right to reimbursement.

An unsuccessful defendant to an action, absent corporate provisions or statutory requirements to the contrary, usually has no right to indemnification.

A list of the corporate indemnification statutes may be found in the Appendix at the back of this volume.

[¶1527] CORPORATE INDEMNIFICATION PURSUANT TO STATUTE

To give a better idea of the factors and exacting requirements of sample indemnification statutes, those of two of the most popular states, New York and Delaware, are examined briefly below.

(1) State Law: State law is the decisive factor in determining whether there's a right or privilege of indemnification ("right" when indemnification is mandatory; "privilege" when it's discretionary). The Delaware Corporation Laws make indemnification permissible except when the corporate official is "successful on the merits or otherwise." If wholly successful, indemnification becomes mandatory. (See (4) below.) The statutory provision is nonexclusive, which means that the corporation can by proper corporate action provide indemnification in cases when not permitted or required by statute.

If the statutory scheme is nonexclusive or there is no applicable statute, then, of course, theoretically, the officer or director can look to common law principles to secure indemnification. But the common law is rather a slender reed to lean on, being based on an agency theory and generally requiring a showing of some benefit to the corporation to support indemnification.

(2) Who's Covered? The Delaware law covers past and present officers, directors, employees, or agents, or any person serving in such capacity for another corporation at the request of the corporation. The New York statute limits coverage to officers and directors. However, others may be indemnified on an agency theory.

(3) Type of Case: The right to or extent of indemnification permitted or required may vary, depending on whether the litigation, threatened or brought, is a derivative action, that is, one brought on behalf of the corporation by a stockholder—or is an action, civil or criminal, brought against the corporate officials by third parties, i.e., nonshareholders.

In the Delaware law, for example, any threatened, pending, or completed derivative action or suit is covered; but the New York statute doesn't cover threatened derivative actions. As to third-party matters, the Delaware law covers not only threatened, pending, or completed actions, suits, or proceedings, civil or criminal, but specifically covers administrative and investigative proceedings.

(4) Success: If the defense is successful on the merits or otherwise (for example, failure to bring suit within the time permitted), both the Delaware and New York statutes require indemnification. Nevertheless, the courts have taken the view that they may still disallow indemnification when they think it inequitable.

(5) Settlement: Delaware permits indemnification for the amount paid in settlement if ordered by the court or if, within the corporation, there's a proper determination that the official or executive acted in accordance with the applicable standard (see below). In New York, the rule is the same in third-party suits; but in suits brought on behalf of the corporation, there can be no indemnity for a settlement as such, although expenses may be allowed if approved by the court.

(6) No-Contest Plea: Both Delaware and New York provide that a no-contest plea or *nolo contendere* plea does not give rise to a presumption of a breach of standards.

(7) Failure: Delaware permits indemnity, even though there's a finding of a breach of duty in a derivative action, for such "expenses" as the court deems proper. In both Delaware and New York in third-party actions, indemnification is possible, despite finding of breach of duty, if the individual charged acted in accordance with a certain standard set up in the indemnification law.

(8) Standard of Conduct: In Delaware, the corporation may generally indemnify if the official or executive "acted in good faith and in a manner he reasonably believed to be in or not opposed to the best interest of the corporation," with the added proviso that if in a derivative action he or she is "adjudged to be liable for negligence or misconduct in the performance of duty," indemnification can only be for negligence for such "expenses" as the court deems proper. In criminal actions, it must also be shown that the person"had no reasonable cause to believe his conduct was unlawful." In New York, in a derivative action, there can be no indemnification if a person is adjudged to have breached a statutory duty as an officer or director. In third-party actions, New York follows the Delaware provision except that it omits reference to cases in which the defendant believed that any actions were "not opposed" to the best interests of the corporation. In criminal actions, New York follows Delaware.

(9) How Satisfaction of Standard Is Determined: The court has power to determine whether or not the required standard has been met and, if so, to award indemnification. But beyond this, the determination may be made by a majority vote of a quorum of disinterested directors, independent legal counsel, or the shareholders.

(10) Advancement of Expenses: In Delaware, the board of directors may make advance payment of expenses on receipt of an undertaking to repay. In New York, the board may do the same but it must first find that the applicable standard has been met.

(11) Reimbursement for Costs in Suit: The successful defendant can usually recover "costs," but costs don't normally include attorney's fees in the absence of a statute so providing. Security-for-expenses statutes may give successful individual defendants some protection in derivative suits.

[¶1528] USE OF INSURANCE POLICIES FOR CORPORATE OFFICERS AND DIRECTORS

The only real alternative to or way of filling in the gaps left by indemnification is insurance. There are two basic types of insurance to cover the risks involved:

(1) Insurance that reimburses the company for the payments it makes on behalf of directors, officers, and others; and

(2) Insurance protecting the individuals involved by reason of their corporate associations.

Basic Legal Limitations of Insurance: At the outset, there is the policy of the common law against permitting a person to insure one's self against the consequences of intentional wrongdoing. The same consideration would likely apply to acts of extreme negligence.

Also, with insurance, as with indemnification, while state law and policy considerations generally determine what liabilities may be insured against, the policy considerations reflected in federal securities laws may override state law.

The Power of the Company to Buy Insurance: Look to state law and the corporate charter and bylaws to determine the power of the company to buy insurance.

The Delaware statute, which follows the Model Business Corporation Law in force in a number of states, gives the corporation broad power to purchase insurance against any liability asserted against a director, officer, employee, or agent in such capacity, "whether or not the corporation would have the power to indemnify him against such liability" under a particular section of the Delaware law.

What Policies Cover and What They Exclude: Policies generally cover any amount the corporation is required to pay to a director, officer, or any other covered person, as indemnity for claims(s) made against such person during the policy period. Amounts may be paid for damages, judgments, settlements, costs, charges, or expenses incurred in connection with the defense of any action, suit, or proceeding alleging a "wrongful act," to which the covered person is a party.

"Wrongful act" is defined as "any breach of duty, neglect, error, misstatement, misleading statement, omission, or other act done or wrongfully attempted" by individual insureds alleged by any claimant or any matter claimed against them solely by reason of their being officers or directors.

The current trend is to exclude acts undertaken for personal profit (e.g., "short-swing" activities), pollution, and the effect of takeover battles. Some insurers also take the position that they do not have a duty to defend or to advance money for litigation costs (especially if the sued director or officer can choose his own counsel) only to reimburse for judgments or settlements actually obtained.

The policy excludes fines or penalties imposed by law and any matter that may be deemed legally uninsurable under judicial precedents, administrative determinations, or unilateral determinations by the underwriters.

Amount Payable: Generally, and subject to possible variations among companies, the company policy will pay 95% of the indemnity paid or payable over $20,000, subject, of course, to the overall policy limit.

Ten million dollars is usually adequate. It's hard to get more than $15,000,000.

The deductible amount applies only once to interrelated acts by more than one insured. The policy limit is for each policy year.

[¶1529] STATE REGULATION OF SECURITIES: BLUE SKY LAWS

The state's right to regulate securities is specifically referred to in §18 of the Securities Act of 1933.

Although several states have adopted the Uniform Securities Act, it is still necessary for the attorney of a corporation planning a public offering to check the "Blue Sky" laws for the jurisdictions in which its securities are going to be sold and to comply with each state's registration requirements.

Most people tend to associate federal regulation with securities transactions. That is a mistake if a corporation is contemplating an offering, since compliance with the federal laws does not automatically give the issuer a right to sell its shares in a particular state. In addition, the fact that a particular offering is exempted from registration under federal law does not necessarily mean that it will be exempt from registration under state law. A classic example is the intrastate offering—even though exempt from federal registration, securities offered within the state where the issuer is located will have to be registered with that state.

Despite the variance among the states, there are certain features common to almost all state Blue Sky statutes:

(1) Prevention of fraud;

(2) Registration of securities;

(3) Registration and/or licensing of securities dealers and salespersons;

(4) Requirement, under most Blue Sky laws, to make periodic reports to the Blue Sky law administrator;

(5) Civil liability provision enabling anyone who purchased a security that was sold in violation of the law, or by means of an untrue or omitted material fact in registration or prospectus, the right to recover the purchase price paid, plus interest and costs (usually including attorney's fees);

(6) Criminal liability provision, subjecting an issuer who willfully violates the state law to a fine and/or imprisonment;

(7) Usual requirement for a nonresident issuer to appoint the Blue Sky law administrator (or Secretary of State) as agent to receive process in connection with civil suits arising out of issuer's efforts within that state.

Most Blue Sky laws also exempt certain types of securities from registration, such as:

(1) Securities that are listed on a national or regional stock exchange (needless to say, this will be the most important exemption for many companies);

(2) Securities of nonprofit organizations;

(3) Obligations of federal, state, or local governments;

(4) Securities of national and state banks or savings and loan associations; and

(5) Short-term commercial paper (less than a nine-month maturity period).

— ENDNOTES —

1. IRC §§6671(b), 6672.

2. Cone, Kenneth R. and Laurence James E. "How Accurate Are Estimates of Aggregate Damages in Securities Fraud Cases," 2 *Business Lawyer* 505 (Feb. 1994).

— FOR FURTHER REFERENCE —

Baysinger, Barry D. and Henry N. Butler, "Corporate Governance and the Board of Directors," 1 *J. of Law, Economics, and Organization* 101 (Spring '85).

Burgman, Dierdre A. and Paul N. Cox, "Corporate Directors, Corporate Realities and the Deliberative Process," 11 *J. of Corporation Law* 311 (Spring '86).

Fishman, James J., "Standards of Conduct for Directors of Nonprofit Corporations," 7 *Pace L. Rev.* 389 (Winter '87).

Fredrick, Thomas W., "Indemnification and Liability of Corporate Directors and Officers," 43 *J. of the Missouri Bar* 287 (July–August 1987).

Grassi, Sebastian V. Jr., "Changes in Corporate Director Liability," 66 *Michigan Bar J.* 538 (June '87).

Hanks, James J. Jr., "State Legislative Responses to the Director Liability Crisis," 20 *Review of Securities and Commodities Regulation* 23 (2/11/87).

Hayes, Deborah K., "Corporate Director Conflicts of Interest," 53 *Tennessee L. Rev.* 799 (Summer '86).

Kane, Thomas P., "Corporate Directors at Risk Whatever They Do," 16 *Brief* 22 (Spring '87).

Meyer, Pearl, "The Rise of the Outside Director as Equity Owner," 10 *Directors and Boards* 41 (Spring '86).

Schwab, Douglas M. and Daniel E. Titelbaum, "Indemnifying and Insuring Officers and Directors," 7 *California Lawyer* 46 (March '87).

CORPORATE FORMATION AND OPERATION

[¶1601] Once the decision has been made to incorporate, it is important that orderly procedures be followed. Some of the main considerations when forming a corporation appear below.

(1) Determine the basic business objectives of the principals.

(2) Develop the concept of a corporate form, capital structure, financing arrangements, and supplementary agreements that fit these objectives.

(3) Check the organizational plan in light of tax considerations and make the necessary modifications.

(4) Make the fundamental decisions prerequisite to drafting corporate papers, where to incorporate, how many shares and what kind (par or no par, preferences or not), preemptive rights, any organizational controls, and put them in the charter or separate agreement, etc.

(5) Draft the corporation charter, bylaws, stock certificates, and organizational minutes.

(6) Make the filings, pay the taxes, and take the other procedural steps necessary to bring the corporation into being.

(7) Hold the organizational meeting, have directors accept subscriptions, accept transfers of property, etc.

(8) Determine how corporate control will be established and maintained.

[¶1602] CHECKLIST OF PROCEDURAL STEPS IN CORPORATE FORMATION

Listed below is a comprehensive checklist of steps for corporate organization. Note that not all of them are required in every jurisdiction.

☐ Select *state of incorporation.*

☐ Select *corporate name;* check availability and reserve.

☐ Complete and execute *pre-incorporation agreement.*

☐ Draft and file *articles of incorporation.*

☐ Determine whether corporation is going to elect S corporation status.

☐ Pay filing fees and organization tax.

☐ File with federal government for *employer identification number.*

☐ File for *workers' compensation and unemployment compensation* insurance in appropriate jurisdictions.

☐ Hold organizational meeting.

☐ Select corporation's *accounting system* and select calendar or fiscal year (if tax law permits).

☐ Obtain *corporate seal,* stock register, minute book, and issue securities.

☐ Get subscriptions for stock.

☐ *Designate agent* for service of process and file any other required papers.

☐ *File* in local county or city, as required by law.

☐ *Draft bylaws.*

❏ Elect first *permanent board of directors* to handle other organizational steps.

❏ *Hold organizational meeting* of permanent board; establish officers' salaries, and prepare Form W-4 for withholding.

❏ *Establish corporate bank account(s)* and designate those persons authorized to transact corporation's business.

❏ Obtain *insurance* on property and key employees.

❏ Obtain any *special licenses* needed for corporate operation.

❏ Pay applicable taxes for stock issuance.

❏ Look into *employee benefit plans;* determine desirability of pension and/or profit-sharing plan.

[¶1603] SELECTING THE STATE OF INCORPORATION

While the state of principal business activity is usually the state of incorporation there are other factors that may influence the choice of a particular state. Prior to selecting a state for incorporation, review its corporation laws, keeping these factors in mind:

❏ ***Corporate Name and Purpose:*** Some states place restrictions on the use of a corporate name. Most modern corporation laws permit broad purposes.

❏ ***Capitalization Requirements:*** Some states require a minimum amount of paid-in capital prior to commencement of business. Some states will not allow the issuance of no-par shares; other states do not permit par value shares of less than $1.

❏ ***Shareholders' Meetings:*** Some states permit shareholders to meet outside the state of incorporation; this option may be an important factor in choosing a state of incorporation.

❏ ***Cumulative Voting:*** Some states require cumulative voting.

❏ ***Voting Rights and Control:*** The percentage of the vote required for certain corporate acts varies from state to state. While many states require only a majority vote for corporate action, some states have supermajority or two-thirds requirements. In addition, some states prohibit the issuance of nonvoting stock. If such restrictions exist, it is not possible to create nonvoting preferred or nonvoting class A stock, and other methods of corporate control must be devised.

❏ ***Restrictions on Corporate Indebtedness:*** Some states may place restrictions on the corporate power to borrow money or pledge corporate assets. In many instances, such limitations can be overcome by a shareholder vote.

❏ ***Restrictions on Stock Redemptions:*** Most states prohibit redemption if it causes corporate insolvency. Other states impose limitations preventing redemption if capital stock would be diminished to an amount less than the corporate indebtedness.

❏ ***Incorporators:*** Some states require as many as three incorporators, while others have reduced their requirement to one.

❏ ***Preemptive Rights:*** Most states provide that a corporation's shareholders shall have preemptive rights unless specifically denied them by the certificate of incorporation.

❏ *Appraisal Rights:* In the event of a merger or consolidation, how are the shares of minority shareholders to be appraised?

❏ *Shareholder Liability:* What liability do shareholders have for corporate acts? Some states hold shareholders liable for back wages due to employees in the event of corporate insolvency.

❏ *Directors' Liability:* There may be differences among states as to liability of directors for improper declaration of dividends, or for acts or omissions that result in loss to the corporation. These differences may involve the scope of liability or the measure of damages.

❏ *Provisions for Indemnity:* Some state corporation laws set forth comprehensive guidelines regarding corporate indemnification of directors, officers, agents, etc., for alleged misconduct.

❏ *Dividends:* Are there restrictions as to the sources from which dividends may be paid?

❏ *Tender Offers:* Does the state of incorporation regulate tender offers for corporations incorporated there or doing business within the state?

❏ *Antitakeover Laws:* A number of states regulate attempts to take over domestic corporations—if the corporation is a potential takeover target, such protection can be extremely helpful.

[¶1604] TAX FACTORS IN SELECTING STATE OF INCORPORATION

The difference in costs of incorporating and operating in the various states may be important in determining the state of incorporation.

❏ *Property Tax:* Because property tax is generally levied by the state in which the property is physically located, the property tax is generally not a factor in choosing a state of incorporation, although it may be relevant in determining whether or not a corporation wants to locate its business in a particular state.

❏ *Intangibles:* When it appears that there may be an attempt by both jurisdictions to tax intangibles, it may be to your client's advantage to incorporate initially in the state where the principal business office is to be maintained.

❏ *Income Taxes:* The income tax may include income from in-state property, in-state or out-of-state business or resources.

❏ *Capital Stock Tax:* Some states impose a tax on the market value of the capital stock.

❏ *Franchise Taxes:* Some states impose an annual franchise tax on domestic (in-state) corporations and qualified foreign (out-of-state) corporations. The base is the proportion of issued capital or capital and surplus represented by property located and business transacted within the state.

[¶1605] SELECTION OF THE CORPORATE NAME

The selection, clearance, reservation, or registration of the corporate name in the state of incorporation and in states where business is to be carried on involves not merely legal but also advertising and public relations considerations. While it is easy enough to legally change a name to meet changing needs and styles, the initial selection should be made with a view to permanence so that goodwill attached to the name will not be lost later on, and also to avoid the future expenses of reprinting stationery, packaging, and advertising materials.

The following factors should affect the decision:

(1) In some states, a name can be selected that is similar to one used by an existing corporation, provided the existing corporation consents. Some states permit the use of similar names by related corporations. In any event, before picking a name, check to see whether it is available, usually with the Secretary of State. Another way is to go through telephone directories, trade directories, trademark records, and county clerks' files.

(2) Check local law when deciding to use a name that does not include the words, "Corporation," "Inc.," or "Ltd."

(3) Some states also bar or regulate the use of words denoting fraternal, benevolent, or other nonprofit organizations, or labor or union, official, or professional connections.

(4) In addition, a corporation cannot be given a name that suggests the corporation will be engaged in a business that it cannot lawfully follow, or that it is to be a form of public agency, or that it will be affiliated with an organization with which it is, in fact, not affiliated.

(5) The use of a living person's name without his consent may amount to a violation of his right to privacy and is expressly forbidden by some statutes.

(6) While in most states there is no requirement that a corporation's name be in the English language, check local law to make sure a particular jurisdiction does not expressly require the use of English letters or characters.

(7) Statutes in some states regulate the use by corporations of fictitious names or trade names, so check local law.

(8) The Securities and Exchange Commission is apprehensive regarding the inclination of corporate issuers to include "glamour" terms such as "nuclear," "space," "missile," or "electronics" as part of their corporate names when they are not actually engaged in a business normally associated with those words, or are engaged in such a business to a very limited extent. In view of this practice, the SEC Division of Corporate Finance has released a guide relating to the misleading character of corporate names.

(9) Finally, in selecting a name, bear in mind the cost of reproducing the name on signs, corporate property, etc.

[¶1606] TAX CONSIDERATIONS IN CORPORATE FORMATION

Under Reg. §301.7701-2(a)(1), an organization will be taxed as a corporation if its characteristics (i.e., continuity, limited liability, free transferability of interests) are more like those of a corporation than those of a noncorporate organization.

The checklist below indicates the major tax considerations in the formation of a corporation.

(1) Tax-Free Incorporation: No gain or loss is recognized when property is transferred to a corporation solely in exchange for stock or securities if the transferors are in "control" of the corporation immediately after the transfer (IRC §351). "Control" is defined as ownership of at least 80% of the voting power of all voting stock and at least 80% of all other classes of stock (IRC §368(c)).

If money or other property (boot) is received by the transferors in addition to stock and securities, gain (but not loss) is recognized, but only to the extent of the money or other property (IRC §351(b)). In most incorporations, the assumption of a liability by the corporation is not treated as money received by the transferor (IRC §357). However, there are two exceptions:

(a) When the transferor's principal purpose in having the corporation assume his or her liability or acquire property subject to a liability is to avoid tax on the exchange or is not a bona fide business purpose (IRC §357(b)).

(b) When the liabilities assumed by the new corporation exceed the bases of the assets transferred to it (IRC §357(c)). Note that liabilities of a cash-basis transferor are not counted in determining if liabilities exceed basis, if payment of the liability would be deductible or constitute a payment to a retiring partner or deceased partner's successor in interest of his distributive share or guaranteed payment.

(2) Disproportionate Stock Interests: Giving an edge to a promoter or a member of the family may result in taxable compensation to the promoter. There may be a taxable gift by a party who contributes more to the corporation than he receives in order to benefit a member of his family.

(3) Step-Up in Basis of Transferred Property: If the property being transferred to the corporation has increased in value and if it is desirable to pay a capital gain tax to step up its basis in order to get higher depreciation allowances or for other purposes, it may be desirable to make the incorporation a taxable transaction. Unfortunately, a tax-free incorporation under §351 is not elective. If the requirements discussed above are met, IRC §351 applies automatically. Outside a bona fide sale of assets or the receipt of boot, avoiding §351 usually amounts to avoiding the 80% control requirement.

Keep in mind that various recapture provisions may apply to a taxable transaction to convert capital gain into ordinary income. These same provisions operate when the receipt of boot in an otherwise tax-free incorporation causes recognition of gain. The recapture provisions normally encountered are:

(a) If the transferred asset is depreciable, all gain is ordinary income if the transferor and his or her spouse own 80% of the corporation (IRC §1239).

(b) Prior depreciation deductions for personalty are recaptured as ordinary income (IRC §1245).

(c) Prior depreciation deductions in excess of straight line for realty are recaptured as ordinary income (IRC §1250).

(d) Prior investment credit may also be recaptured (IRC §47(a)).

(4) Transfer of Liabilities: If encumbered property is transferred to the corporation and it assumes the debt, the excess of the liabilities assumed, plus liabilities to which the property is subject, will be taxed to the transferors to the extent that the liabilities exceed the cost or other tax basis of the property (IRC §357(c); see (1) above).

(5) Leasing Instead of Transferring Property: There may be tax savings in leasing property to the corporation and having it pay deductible rent, while the lessor deducts depreciation, rather than transferring the property to the corporation.

(6) Avoiding Tax to Promoters: Consider saving the promoters from having stock received by them taxed as compensation by having them buy cheap stock prior to the full financing of the corporation or by having them transfer patents, plans, or models in exchange for stock in the incorporation transaction. The earlier the promoters acquire their stock the safer they are.

(7) Use of Debt Plus Equity: Ideally, insiders would prefer to have outside investors merely lend the corporation money on an unsecured basis. Practically, though, the cost of such loans would be prohibitive. However, a corporation may still be able to issue unsecured debt instruments (debentures or promissory notes) to outside investors. A commonly used method enables the investor to purchase both common stock (equity) and unsecured debt instruments. In this way, insiders are giving up some of their control in exchange for unsecured loans to the corporation at reasonable rates. The outside investors have some degree of say in the management by which they can protect their unsecured investment.

(8) Thin Capitalization: There are also significant tax advantages to be realized from the issuance of debt instruments to insiders in addition to stock ("thin capitalization"):

(a) It permits tax-free withdrawal of cash from the successful corporation in order to repay the shareholder loans, and shareholders have no tax liabilities on the loan repayments;

(b) It provides the corporation with additional deductions, thus lowering its tax liabilities, since interest paid on the debt instruments is deductible;

(c) It avoids the accumulated earnings penalty tax;

(d) If the corporation fails, then, in an insolvency proceeding, the insiders are creditors of the corporation as well as shareholders, and as creditors may receive a partial repayment on their loan, whereas as shareholders they would receive nothing.

There are some risks involved in thin capitalization, namely, that the debt instrument will be deemed an equity investment (stock). If that occurs, the "interest" paid on the instrument will be deemed a nondeductible dividend. In addition, the repayments of principal will be treated as a dividend to the investor rather than a tax-free return of capital. In order to avoid this problem, here are steps to insure that the loans will be treated as debt instruments:

(a) Debt-to-equity ratio should be between 2:1 and 3:1;

(b) Debt instrument should on its face bear interest and unconditionally obligate the corporation to pay both interest and principal at designated times;

(c) Debt must be treated as such on the corporate books;

(d) No subordination of the shareholders' debts to those of the corporation's general creditors;

(e) A stated maturity date, not too far off in the future. A happy medium of about 10 years should be set with provisions for repayment.

(9) Making Debt Obligations Stand Up: Make sure the debt obligations obtained from the corporation constitute genuine debt—i.e., have a real and definite maturity date, call for interest payments at a fixed rate, give the holders a security status over stockholders. Making stockholder debts subordinate to regular corporate creditors is frequently necessary but it increases the risk that the debt will be considered equity. (See *Wetterau Grocer Co.,* CA-8, 179 F.2d 158, 1950; *Gooding Amusement Co.,* CA-6, 236 F.2d 159, 1956. See IRC §385 and regulations thereunder.)

(10) Using Preferred Stock: Consider creating preferred stock as part of the original capitalization. Subsequent creation of preferred stock after the corporation has earnings and profits may result in the preferred stock becoming IRC §306 stock so that gain on its sale is taxed as ordinary income.

(11) Assuring Ordinary Loss Deductions if Business Goes Bad: Qualifying common or preferred stock under IRC §1244 assures that any loss on the investment will be deductible against ordinary income to the extent of $50,000 a year or $100,000 on a joint return. This rule applies whether the loss was incurred on sale of the stock or on its becoming worthless. It can only be used by the original purchaser of the stock. The following requirements must be met:

❏ The corporation must be a small business corporation; that is, only the first $1,000,000 of stock issued qualifies under §1244.

❏ Section 1244 stock must be issued in exchange for money or other property. Stock issued for service does not qualify. Also, stock of any corporation does not qualify as property for purposes of §1244.

❏ If, during the five-year period prior to the shareholder's loss, or the period of corporate existence, if less, the corporation derived 50% or more of its gross receipts from royalties, rent, dividends, interest, annuities, and sales or exchanges of stock or securities, the stock will not qualify as §1244 stock.

(12) Avoid the Collapsible Corporation Trap: Don't overlook the collapsible corporation rules. These provisions convert the capital gains available on liquidations and the sale of corporate stock into ordinary income. If part of the gain is attributable to appreciated corporate property that has been held for less than three years, these rules may apply (IRC §341). However, if the corporation has realized at least two-thirds of the income from collapsible assets, collapsible status may be avoided.

There are some other steps that can be taken to avoid "collapsibility" in order to get capital gain treatment.

❏ *Stock Ownership Not High Enough:* The rules do not apply if after commencement of construction by the corporation of the collapsible property you do not own more than 5% of the value of the corporation's stock. This defense by itself should exempt most shareholders of widely held corporations.

❏ *Right Timing:* The rules do not apply if gain is realized by the shareholder after the expiration of three years following the completion of construction of the property.

Note: While routine repairs would not constitute "construction" for purposes of IRC §341, substantial improvements would prolong completion of the activity and thus the running of the three-year waiting period.

❏ *Sale of Assets:* If the corporation is thought to be collapsible, it may be best to have the corporation sell its assets and then liquidate. If the corporation is in fact collapsible, the corporation will presumably pay a capital gain tax on the sale, and the stockholders will have to pay a capital gain tax on the liquidation of the amount that's left.

❑ *Tax-Free Reorganization:* The adverse results of a collapsible situation can also be avoided by a tax-free reorganization, since the collapsible rules do not extend to transactions in which there is no recognized gain. However, post-1986, structuring a transaction as a tax-free reorganization is far more difficult.

❑ *Multiple Entities:* When the intention is to develop more than one property, it may be advantageous to incorporate each property separately. In this way, the favorable three-year rule can be applied on an individual basis. What's more, if an unfavorable determination is made with regard to one property, it will not affect other properties.

(13) Deducting Organization Expenses: IRC §248 permits a corporation to treat organization expenditures as "deferred expenses," and to write them off as tax deductions. The length of the "writeoff" period may be selected by the corporation provided it is not less than sixty months; and it starts when the corporation begins business. (Absent such election, the expenses must be capitalized.)

(14) Employee-Stockholder Benefits: Employee-stockholders of the corporation may secure the benefits of a pension or profit-sharing trust. And the corporation's contributions (within certain limitations) are deductible by the corporation. See IRC §401—404, 1379. In addition other fringe benefits, such as group term insurance (up to $50,000 coverage), reimbursement of medical expenses, etc., are also available. See IRC §79, 104—106.

(15) Avoiding Personal Holding Company Penalties: A corporation in which five or fewer individuals own more than half the stock during the last half of the taxable year may be a personal holding company if 60% or more of its income comes from dividends, royalties, interest, and rents. Rents equal to at least 50% of adjusted ordinary gross income are not personal holding company income if other personal holding company income does not exceed 10% of ordinary gross income. A personal holding company is subject to a 39.6% penalty tax on undistributed income (IRC §541—543).

(16) Accumulation of Surplus: A corporation may accumulate up to $250,000 before it becomes liable for the accumulated earnings penalty tax ($150,000, in the case of personal-service corporations). After that, there is an additional tax liability ($27 1/2$% on the first $100,000 of accumulated taxable income and $38 1/2$% on the balance of that income) if there are unreasonable surplus accumulations. However, a corporation may retain earnings for such business purposes as the redemption of stock to pay death taxes (IRC §537). If there is an excess accumulation, the penalty tax can be avoided by showing "reasonably anticipated needs of the business" as the purpose of the accumulation (IRC §537). It is not necessary to show that earnings and profits must be reinvested in the busi-

ness immediately; it is enough to show that future needs (not vague or uncertain) of the business will require that these earnings and profits be plowed back.

[¶1606.1] Tax Considerations: The Subchapter S Corporation

For an overview of the tax features of Subchapter S corporations, see below.

[¶1607] The Capital Structure

The basic elements that may be used to build a capital structure that will reflect the economic interests of the various business participants are earnings, assets, and voting or management power. These various elements are considered separately in the following paragraphs.

[¶1608] Earnings

One investor or class of investors may be given a preference in or disproportionate share of earnings by using preferred stock or by using two classes of stock. The use of preferred stock is perhaps the most common way of giving one class of investors a priority in earnings. If the investors are in a position to demand a share in earnings in addition to their preferred dividend, this may be done either (1) by making the preferred participating as to further dividends or (2) by giving them common in addition to their preferred. The first route presents problems, however, if the preferred is to be callable as it normally should be, because then it should also be made convertible if the holders are to share in the growth of the company (as they bargained for), and if it's convertible for an extended period there will be serious problems in working out fair conversion rates. Hence, the second route is apt to be favored.

When the situation calls for one class of investor to receive a disproportionate share of earnings, as distinguished from priority in the earnings, a two-class stock set-up will usually be called for. For example, a two-class stock arrangement might be used if investor A is willing to put in $55,000 and is willing to settle for 45% of the earnings provided he is given 55% of the voting control of the business and B is willing to put in $45,000 provided he gets 55% of the earnings and is willing to wield only 45% of the vote.

If two classes of stock are used, care must be exercised to make sure they are properly labeled. When the two classes share dividends on a percentage basis, for example, it might be incorrect to designate the class getting the larger percentage as "common." Differentiate by calling it Class A. The other class could be designated common.

[¶1609] ASSETS

Some investors may demand priority or preferential participation in the distribution of assets on premature liquidation. For example, suppose one group of investors makes two-thirds of the cash or tangible investment for one-third of the shares, and the so-called talent gets two-thirds of the shares for only one-third of the tangible investment, and let's say the respective investments are $100,000 and $50,000. If the corporation were to liquidate at a time when the assets were worth $150,000, the "talent" would come out with $50,000 more than they invested, this at the expense of the "money" investors. The "money" investors would come out even only if liquidation occurred at a time when the asset value had doubled. Two classes of shares bearing different participation rights in the distribution of assets, as distinguished from a preference in distribution, might be used to assure an equitable result. Thus, Class A might be given $2 for every $1 to be distributed to Class B until the original investments were repaid, with provision for equal distribution of assets thereafter.

[¶1610] VOTING

The use of securities with different voting rights also affects the distribution of voting power.

Minority investors may want representation on the board of directors. One way of assuring such representation is by establishing two or more classes of shares and providing for the election of a certain number of directors or a certain percentage of the total number of directors by each class. The latter will, of course, prevent changes in representation by changes in the number of directors, and will, therefore, normally be preferred.

Participation in voting for directors may be made absolute or it may be contingent, or conditional, as on passing preferred dividends for a fixed time. When both common and preferred stock are used, the voting rights of the preferred stock are usually made contingent or conditional on preferred dividends being in arrears (normally for a year or more). When that occurs the preferred shareholders become entitled to elect board members (usually a majority) until the default is cured.

So far the discussion has been limited to voting for directors and on this level it is quite clear that securities may be created without the right to vote for directors. But voting may, of course, concern other matters, and it is equally clear that a class of securities should not be created if it is barred from voting on all matters including those affecting the interests of the class. The statutes of the state of incorporation must be checked to determine the issues on which class voting is required. The issues may include certain types of charter amendments, and mergers and considerations adversely affecting the class.

On the other hand, the voting rights of particular securities may go beyond those matters as to which shareholder votes or consents are required by law. Voting rights may be conferred as to specific matters when required by the terms of the business agreement. The participation may be on the basis of class voting (requiring a certain percentage of the class) or pooling all the classes and requiring a certain percentage of the votes of all those entitled to vote on the particular issue.

[¶1611] PROVISIONS FOR REDEMPTION AND CONVERSION

Debt securities and preferred stock are used to give the investors some protection for their capital investment and some assurance of income. When the corporation has established itself, these senior securities may no longer be necessary or the capital that they represent may be had on better terms. This is what makes it desirable to make the senior securities redeemable or callable at the option of the corporation, or provision may be made for compulsory retirement. When the latter is the case, the security should provide for a sinking fund.

The law of incorporation must be checked as to permissible provisions for redemption, and their application to particular securities, i.e., debt, preferred, common.

Making senior securities convertible may be tied in with the idea of redemption. As the corporation grows and prospers, the holder of a convertible senior security may be induced to give up whatever priorities he may have as to earnings or assets, or both, in favor of a full share in the equity.

[¶1612] RIGHTS, OPTIONS, AND WARRANTS

Many corporate statutes permit rights and options to purchase shares, sometimes called "warrants." Their use may be considered but normally will be limited to later stages in the development of the business.

[¶1613] USE OF DEBT SECURITIES

Debt securities are usually issued to represent borrowed money and may take various forms, the most common being bonds, debentures, and notes. Bonds are usually secured and when secured by a mortgage may be referred to as "mortgage bonds." Those secured by a pledge of personal property may be called "collateral trust bonds." "Debentures" or "notes" are generally unsecured. Local law must be checked for provisions authorizing the holders of debt securities to vote for directors or other matters, as well as for requirements as to the consideration for their issuance. The use of debt securities in the capital structure must be with an eye to the tax consequences of "thin incorporation," discussed at ¶1606(8), and with due regard to possible nontax consequences. In case of insolvency, for example, the debt to shareholders may be subordinated to other claims, and shareholders may be held personally liable for the debts. Attention must also be focused on the effect of debt on the balance sheet. It may lead to an investigation by persons transacting business with the corporation of the relationship between the holders of the debt securities and the shareholders of the corporation. If such a relationship is discovered, the next step may be to ask for a contractual subordination of the debt. This will, of course, result in the debtholder being placed in essentially the position of a shareholder.

[¶1614] PAR OR NO-PAR STOCK?

If par or stated value shares are provided for, it will be necessary to see that the consideration for which shares may be issued under the state corporation law—usually money, property (tangible or intangible), and services—has value equal to the stated value of the shares. Otherwise, the shares are not "fully paid and nonassessable," and their issuance will be fraudulent as against the corporation, existing stockholders and creditors, and directors approving their issuance, and purchasers of the shares may be personally liable, at least to the extent of the "watering." There will usually be no dollar floor on the consideration that may be accepted for no-par shares, but there is the general requirement that the directors fix a fair value for the shares and make a determination that the corporation has received suitable consideration of that value for shares issued. Statute and case law determine for each state whether speculative patents and secrets, promoters' services, promissory notes, and obligations to render future services or to make future payments constitute suitable consideration for the issuance of shares.

To protect organizers from liability, see that the terms of the bargain between those forming the corporation do not overvalue services and assets contributed by the organizers as against third parties. The tax collector has an interest in this, too, because the value of the shares given to organizers not supported by the value of assets contributed by them may be treated as taxable compensation for services. This "watering" tax and balance sheet problem can usually be handled by getting supporting appraisals for assets or creating a debt or preferred stock leverage in the capital structure. Stamp tax considerations may also play a role in the decision to use par or no-par stock.

[¶1615] THE ARTICLES OF INCORPORATION

A corporation operates under a charter from the state, prepared by counsel for the corporation and filed and approved by the appropriate state official. Following is a checklist of points to be covered in the articles of incorporation:

❏ Corporate name.

❏ Corporate purpose—broad enough to cover all aspects of present and projected operations.

❏ Location of corporate office.

❏ Duration of corporate existence—perpetual or stated.

❏ Powers:

(a) To sue and be sued;

(b) To have a corporate seal;

(c) To purchase, take, receive, lease, acquire, own, hold, improve, use, and otherwise deal in real and personal property;

(d) To sell, convey, mortgage, pledge, lease, exchange, transfer, and dispose of property. The power to deal in property may be restricted in some jurisdictions in which property is not required to further the corporate purposes; e.g., real estate held by realty corporations, agricultural land, and the like. Local law should be checked;

(e) To sell, convey, mortgage, pledge, lease, exchange, transfer, and otherwise dispose of any part of the corporate property and assets. In some states corporate conveyances will be limited to corporate purposes;

(f) To lend money. The power to lend money may be restricted, however. In some states loans may not be made to shareholders. In other states loans may not be made to officers and directors. The authority for a corporation to lend money to its employees, officers, etc., may be important if the corporation wants to initiate a program aiding relocated employees in acquisition of homes, etc.;

(g) To deal in securities of other corporations, partnerships, and associations. Corporations may be prohibited from holding more than a certain percentage of certain types of corporations, like utilities companies or banks. In some states a corporation will be prohibited from becoming a partner or a joint venturer;

(h) To make contracts and guarantees and incur liabilities; borrow money and issue notes, bonds, and other obligations; and secure obligations by mortgage or pledge. The power to guarantee obligations may vary from state to state;

(i) To lend money, invest, and reinvest funds; take and hold real and personal property as security for the payment of funds;

(j) To conduct its business and carry on its operations in or out of the state of incorporation. Similarly, the corporate offices may be located in or out of the state of incorporation. In some states, however, the corporation must maintain some form of an office within the state of incorporation;

(k) To elect or appoint officers and agents and fix their compensation;

(l) To make and alter bylaws;

(m) To make charitable contributions. In most states there is specific statutory authorization for charitable contributions. Prior to widespread statutory enactments, there was often a question as to the corporate purpose of charitable contributions;

(n) To indemnify directors, officers, or agents. Often the power of indemnification will be coupled with a procedure spelled out in the statute, dealing with bylaw provisions in regard to indemnification;

(o) To pay pensions and establish pension plans;

(p) To cease its corporate activities and surrender its corporate franchise. Generally, state statutes provide specific machinery for the dissolution and winding up of the affairs of a corporation;

(q) To deal in its own shares. Often this power will be restricted to purchases out of earned surplus. Transactions that would render the corporation insolvent are generally prohibited. In some jurisdictions shareholders' approval will be required.

❑ Designation of Secretary of State as agent for service of process.

❑ Number of shares; how many classes of shares; par or no-par value; voting rights of shares; priority preferences of shares.

Optional items for inclusion in the articles of incorporation are:

❑ Minimum capital for commencement of business.

❑ Extension or elimination of preemptive rights.

❑ Liability of shareholders for corporate debts.

❑ Name and address of each incorporator.

❑ Number of directors on initial board.

❑ Restriction on transfer of shares.

❑ Provisions for repeal, amendment, or adoption of bylaws.

❑ Shareholders' right to fix consideration for no-par shares.

❑ Quorum requirements for shareholders' and directors' meetings.

❑ Cumulative voting requirements.

❑ Restrictions on board's powers.

❑ Classification of directors for voting control.

❑ Voting requirements for directors' meetings.

❑ Provision for executive or other (e.g., audit) committees of board.

❑ Reservations for shareholder power to elect officers.

❑ Removal of directors by shareholders.

❑ Provision for special meetings.

Frequently, it is good long-term strategy to draft the Articles of Incorporation and/or bylaws to include "shark repellent" provisions to make hostile takeovers less feasible or desirable—e.g., supermajority voting requirements; a staggered Board of Directors that makes it tougher for raiders to dominate the board.

[¶1616] THE BYLAWS

The regulation of business methods is an appropriate matter for the bylaws. Whereas the certificate of incorporation is a matter of public record, the bylaws are private and therefore not open for examination by the general public. Some look upon the bylaws as an administrative checklist for the use of officers and directors and thus include in the bylaws those matters specifically covered by state corporation law. Others follow the practice of excluding from the bylaws provisions already covered by statute and rely upon a separate memo to guide officers and directors.

Usually, bylaws are adopted by the incorporators or the shareholders at the initial meeting. Sometimes, if the certificate of incorporation or the state corporate statute so provides, the bylaws can be adopted by the directors.

Bylaws may be amended by the shareholders. In many states, bylaws can also be amended by the directors of the corporation if the bylaws adopted by the shareholders or the certificate of incorporation authorizes them to do so. In some cases, a greater than majority vote will be prescribed for amendment of the bylaws. If bylaws themselves prescribe a greater than majority vote for certain corporate actions, there should be a provision requiring an equivalent vote to remove the bylaw provision. If a bylaw provision requiring greater than majority voting can be removed or amended by simple majority vote, the control restriction would be rendered useless.

What should be included in the bylaws.

(a) Corporate office location.

(b) Time (date and hour) of shareholders' annual meeting, or procedure for determining the same.

(c) Location of the shareholders' meeting.

(d) Voting requirements—make certain to avoid conflicts between the voting requirements spelled out in the bylaws, articles of incorporation, and the corporate statute of the state of incorporation.

(e) Voting procedure.

(f) Notice requirements for shareholders' meetings.

(g) Proxy requirements. Several states also regulate the length of time for which a proxy may be valid. Proxies must also comply with the rules prescribed by the SEC if the corporation is subject to those rules.

(h) Establishment of the record date for the shareholders' meeting. The record date determines which shareholders are eligible to vote at the meeting.

(i) Authorization for the calling of special meetings of shareholders, and who will have this authority.

(j) Provision for shareholder action by shareholder consent.

(k) Quorum requirements for shareholders' meetings.

(l) The number of directors.

(m) Qualification of directors and their term of office.

(n) Cumulative voting in the election of directors. Although some states deal with this on a mandatory basis in either the articles or corporate statute, a majority of states leave this issue for inclusion in the bylaws.

(o) Procedure for filling board of director vacancies.

(p) Procedure for director removal.

(q) Time and place of directors' meetings.

(r) Notice of directors' meetings.

(s) Quorum at directors' meetings and voting requirements for director action. Provision should also be made for the approval of transactions between the corporation and a director.

(t) Compensation of directors.

(u) Authorization to delegate some board action to an executive committee. However, most states specifically proscribe certain conduct by an executive committee, so take care to check local corporation law.

(v) Indemnification of officers, directors, and other corporate employees.

(w) Identification of the corporate officers: qualifications, selection, duties, and removal. In some states the secretary and treasurer will be required to give a surety bond in an amount to be specified by the bylaws.

(x) Forms of stock to be issued, although details are usually left to the articles of incorporation, as well as provision for the transfer of stock.

(y) Determination of fiscal year and accounting practices.

[¶1617] CORPORATE BUY-SELL AGREEMENTS

Participants in a new corporate venture will usually want an agreement that will require that on the death or departure of one of them, the survivors will have the opportunity to buy out the decedent's interest. There are several kinds of buy-sell agreements:

(1) The corporation (if it cannot, then the surviving shareholders) must buy and the estate of the deceased shareholder is obligated to sell.

(2) First the corporation, then the surviving shareholders have an option to buy the stock of a deceased stockholder, and, if this option is exercised, the estate is obligated to sell.

(3) The estate of a deceased stockholder has the right to offer the stock to the survivors or to the corporation, and, if it does, either the survivors or the corporation is obligated to buy.

(4) There is no obligation either to buy or sell, but if a stockholder or his estate wants to sell, the stock must first be offered to the other stockholders or to the corporation before it can be sold to an outside party.

[¶1618] HOW TO SET THE PRICE IN A BUY-SELL AGREEMENT

There are several methods of valuing stock, a particularly controversial factor when drafting any buy-sell agreement for a closely held corporation:

(1) Fixed Price Method: This is the most common method. The stockholders set a fixed price per share in the buy-sell agreement, and leave room for revising this price, with the controlling price to be the last price stated prior to the death of the first stockholder. For example, the agreement may provide for a new price to be set annually at the close of the year. However, experience has shown that often the annual revaluation is never made. This raises the danger of an unfair depressed or inflated price being used. A possible solution is to use this method in conjunction with the appraisal method, and to provide in the contract that if no revaluation was made within 14 or more months prior to the death of a stockholder, the price of the stock will be determined by appraisal. Another way is to provide that the last agreed price is to be automatically adjusted by increases or decreases in earned surplus.

(2) Appraisal Method: Price is left open for future appraisal. The buy-sell agreement provides that value will be determined at the death of the first stockholder by a disinterested appraiser.

(3) Net Worth or Book Value Method: Valuation is based on the corporation's last balance sheet prepared prior to the death of the first stockholder, and the net worth is adjusted to the date of death. Or the company's accountants may be required to determine book value as of the date of death. Neither way is adequate, since neither reflects the true value of the business as a going concern, including the earning power of intangible assets like goodwill. The use of a stated formula, based on net worth, usually corrects this shortcoming. When this method is used the following items should be considered:

(a) Inventory. Will it be figured at cost or its real worth?

(b) Accounts Receivable. Will there be uncollectible accounts and what percentage of these does not show up in the book figures?

(c) Machinery and Equipment. Does the present book figure fairly reflect the present worth? Has it become obsolete?

(d) Buildings. Does book figure reflect current market value? Real estate is sometimes carried on books at cost and then depreciated substantially.

(e) Insurance Proceeds. If the company is to buy up the interest of the deceased associate and if there is insurance payable to the company, are the proceeds to be considered in determining book value?

(4) Straight Capitalization Method: The corporation's average net profits are capitalized at a specific rate, say 10%, and the result reflects the total value of the business including goodwill. The buy-sell agreement usually calls for averaging the net profits for the last five years immediately preceding the death of the first stockholder, after which they are capitalized at the 10% rate. The resulting total value is then divided by the number of outstanding shares to determine the value per share. Adjustment must be made to reflect the absorption of profits in the form of stockholders' salaries, or the average net profits will be distorted. The multiple at which the profits are capitalized will depend upon the nature of the business and the history of the particular corporation involved.

(5) Year's Purchase Method: This also relies on average net profits. The book value is averaged over a stated number of years, usually allowing a fair percentage return. This is then subtracted from the average net profits, and the remainder, which represents excess earnings, is multiplied by the stated number of years' purchase to arrive at the value of goodwill. This goodwill is then added to the book value to determine the total value of the business, and the corresponding value per share of stock.

(6) Combination of Methods: A combination of different valuation methods is sometimes used to overcome the shortcomings of one or the other method.

Note that in allocating the purchase price of a business to the newly acquired assets, the capitalized cost of goodwill and most other intangibles acquired after August 10, 1993, and used in a trade or business or for the production of income, are ratably amortized over a 15-year period beginning in the month of acquisition.[1]

[¶1619] PAYMENT OF PURCHASE PRICE

The agreement must specify how and when the price is to be paid. The plan must provide for the source of the funds. Life insurance on the stockholders will produce the necessary funds when they are needed. The excess of the total price over the insurance proceeds and other free cash available can be made payable on an installment basis. This obligation should be evidenced by notes and secured by the interest being purchased. Additional security can be provided in the form of mortgages on assets or additional insurance policies. Provide the right to pre-pay the obligations and for acceleration of the full obligation in the event of default of payment, bankruptcy, or sale of the business and other specified contingencies.

[¶1620] STOCK RETIREMENT OR CROSS PURCHASE?

Whether the corporation or the surviving shareholders should purchase the stock of a deceased stockholder may depend upon the following factors:

(1) Source of Funds: The stock retirement plan (i.e., purchase by the corporation) permits the use of corporate funds. The cross-purchase plan (i.e., purchase by shareholders) requires the use of funds that the stockholders have presumably taken out of the business and on which an individual income tax is payable.

(2) Enforceability: A cross-purchase agreement is clearly valid and enforceable while a stock retirement plan may not be enforceable if the corporation has or may have insufficient surplus to make the purchase, and state law requires that stock may be redeemed only out of surplus. This potential deficiency in the stock retirement plan can be met by having the agreement provide that the survivors will either purchase or contribute sufficient surplus to the corporation, in the event that the corporation is prevented from retiring the stock of a deceased stockholder by state laws requiring that such purchases be made only out of surplus. In drafting the stock retirement agreement, the corporation should first be required to increase its available surplus by reducing its required capital or by increasing its capital to reflect a value for unrealized appreciation in assets. If this is insufficient and the survivors cannot either purchase or contribute additional funds to permit the corporation to meet the surplus requirement, the decedent's legal representative can be given the right to demand that the corporation be liquidated. These supplementary steps will make the stock retirement plan sufficiently valid and enforceable.

(3) Complication in Ownership of Insurance Policies: If the plan is to be funded by insurance, the stock retirement plan requires only one policy on each stockholder and permits the corporation to have continuous ownership of that policy. In the cross-purchase plan each stockholder has to carry insurance on the lives of the others.

(4) Effect of the Alternative Minimum Tax: Where participants are subject to the Alternative Minimum Tax, the effect of this levy should be considered in choosing the form of the buy-sell agreement.

(5) Shift of Control: In the stock retirement plan, the proportionate interest of the survivors automatically remains the same when the corporation buys in the stock of a deceased shareholder.

[¶1621] HOW TO MAKE THE PURCHASE PRICE BINDING FOR ESTATE TAX PURPOSES

The price set in a mandatory buy-sell agreement is the value of the business for federal estate tax purposes if:

(1) The price is fair and reflects a normal business intent;

(2) The purchase price is fixed in the agreement; and

(3) The parties to the agreement (as well as their survivors or estates) are required to sell at the fixed price.

[¶1622] DISABILITY BUY-SELL AGREEMENTS

Perhaps even more important than the need to prepare for a shareholder's death is the need to provide for continuation of the business in the event of disability, particularly in the smaller corporation. Business owners may need two-way protection in the event of disability. First, they have to consider providing for adequate income to meet routine personal expenses, including the increased medical expenses. Second, they must protect the value of their ownership interests, which can most easily be accomplished by expanding a buy-sell agreement to cover the risk of total disability.

[¶1623] USING SPECIALIZED INSURANCE TO FUND THE BUY-SELL AGREEMENT

Three basic types of insurance policies are available to fund a buy-sell agreement:

(1) Standard Disability Income Contract: The individuals, corporation, or partnership purchases a disability income policy to protect an individual's income. The individual who is disabled beyond the elimination period receives monthly benefit payments as a wage continuation. For the individual who is still disabled at the time designated in the buy-sell agreement (e.g., after 18, 24, or 30 months), the wage continuation payments are transformed into monthly payments under the buy-sell agreement until the individual is paid the agreed purchase price of an ownership interest.

(2) A "Specialty Disability Income Contract": Evolved to meet the particular needs of buy-sell arrangements, these policies tend to be optionally renewable and tied in with the regular issue limit. Because of the higher risk of "elective dis-

ability" (a form of early retirement) than of "elective death" (suicide), most policies include a co-insurance element and will fund only from 60 to 80% of the purchase price. These policies have nonguaranteed premiums, varying definitions of disability, varying elimination periods, and varying lengths of pay-out periods (including an occasional lump-sum payment). Some companies require a trusteed agreement to assure that benefits are used only to fund the buy-sell agreement.

(3) Lump-Sum Contract: Some insurance companies have developed an even more specialized product—a "lump-sum" policy. These policies clearly set out that the intent is to purchase the ownership interest of the disabled individual once the buy-sell agreement is triggered. At the triggering point, the individual either receives a lump-sum payment for his or her business interest or opts for an installment purchase if the buy-sell agreement provides for it.

These policies contain the co-insurance element and look at disability in the context of whether the individual can still provide a valuable service to the organization. The insurance companies require the buy-sell agreement to define disability consistent with the policy definition, which is usually some variation of "completely unable to engage in his regular occupation or any other occupation in the firm he might reasonably be expected to engage in with due regard to his education, training, and experience."

Other features of lump-sum contracts include guaranteed premiums, conditional renewal, benefit reduction after age 60, conversion privilege to a noncancellable disability income policy, waiver of premium, and option to increase benefit levels.

[¶1624] CORPORATE LEGAL EXPOSURE AND LIABILITY

Most executives tend to minimize or entirely overlook the need to protect themselves and their business from loss and liability. The importance of such protection cannot be overemphasized—what good is it to operate a profitable business if the money it generates is lost through a set of unexpected circumstances for which its owners are ill-prepared? The following checklist indicates those areas that pose the greatest danger to both businesses and individual owners and should be used to review the legal posture of your business. (If the business is incorporated, an individual may be liable in his role as a corporate director or officer; this liability is discussed at ¶1501 et seq.)

❏ *Accident, Liability, and Property Damage:* What types and amounts of risk exposure exist, and what sort of insurance protection is adequate? The late 1980s saw an increasing trend toward imposition of corporate *criminal* liability for harm to employees—sometimes even resulting in jail terms for corporate officers.

❏ *Securities Law:* Especially in the mergers and acquisitions context, opportunities for insider trading, 10b-5 and proxy violations, and misuse of inside information abound. Again, fines and jail terms are real possibilities.

❏ *Antitrust Problems:* Do the corporate pricing policy, distribution and licensing agreements, sales procedures, and competitive practices in general violate federal law?

❏ *Inventions and Trade Secrets:* Are they adequately protected?

❏ *Discrimination:* Guard against discrimination in employment hiring, promotion, and firing.

❏ *Libel and Slander:* These must be guarded against, whether in the course of labor disputes, proxy contests, employee discharges, collection letters, sales letters, ordinary business letters, or disparaging a competitor's product. Be aware that statements by agents or employees may impute liability to the corporation.

❏ *Breach of Contract:* Do not induce lawsuits in hiring an employee of or taking business away from a competitor.

❏ *Product Liability:* Minimize exposure by taking the following steps:

(a) Get products pretested by an independent laboratory.

(b) Set up a quality control program.

(c) Make instructions crystal clear and display them prominently on labels.

(d) Make warranty definite—stating exactly what is being warranted and what is not. If the component parts or accessories are being warranted by others, see that these warranties are passed on.

(e) Check product advertising and promotion to see that the claims being made do not unnecessarily attract product liability lawsuits.

(f) Carry product liability insurance. A policy with proper coverage can protect from claims against defective products, mislabeled ones, products sold for improper use or under improper circumstances, negligence, and breach of implied warranty.

— ENDNOTE —

1. IRC §197.

— FOR FURTHER REFERENCE —

Start-Ups

Chittur, Krishnan S., "Resolving Close Corporation Conflict: A Fresh Approach," 10 *Harvard J. of Law and Public Policy* 129 (Winter '87).

Dible, Donald, *Business Start-Up Basics* (Prentice-Hall, 1981).

Fitzgibbon, Scott and Donald W. Glazer, "Legal Opinions on Incorporation, Good Standing, and Qualification to Do Business," 41 *Business Lawyer* 461 (February '86).

Fitzpatrick, Jon, "Determining if a Small Company Needs a Retirement Plan, and Choosing the Best Plan," 14 *Taxation for Lawyers* 76 (September-October '85).

Leffelman, Dean J., "Planning Opportunities on Incorporation," 74 *Illinois B.J.* 382 (April '87).

Lefkowitz, Alan J., "Today's Corporate Practice—Bumps and Jumps," 30 *Boston Bar J.* 4 (November-December '86).

Rands, William J., "Closely Held Businesses: Tax Advantages and Disadvantages of the Different Forms of Business Organizations," 91 *Commercial L.J.* 61 (Spring '86).

Shefsky, Lloyd E., "Counseling Little Companies with Big Ideas," 4 *Compleat Lawyer* 12 (Winter '87).

Shilling, Dana, *Business Start-Up Practice* (Prentice-Hall, 1986).

Silas, Faye A., "Risky Business: Corporate Directors Bail Out," 72 *ABA J* 24 (6/1/86).

Sullivan, J. and K. McWilliams, *Handbook of Business Litigation Tactics and Techniques* (Prentice-Hall, 1987).

Corporate Legal Exposure and Liability

Allen, Ronald J. and Cynthia M. Hazelwood, "Preserving the Confidentiality of Internal Corporate Investigations," 12 *J. of Corporation Law* 355 (Winter '87).

Androphy, Joel M., "What Corporate Counsel Need to Know About Criminal Investigations and Prosecutions," 50 *Texas Bar J.* 998 (October '87).

Bacigal, Ronald J. and Margaret I., "Criminal Prosecutions in Environmental Law," 12 *Columbia J. of Environmental Law* 291 (Spring '87).

Brickey, Katherine P., "Death in the Workplace: Corporate Liability for Criminal Homicide," 2 *Notre Dame J. of Law, Ethics, and Public Policy* 753 (Summer '87).

Lord, Miles W. "Corporate Irresponsibility: The Sin with No Sinners," 9 *Hamline L. Rev.* 53 (February '86).

Madden, M. Stuart, "Liability for Abnormally Dangerous Activities," 10 *J. Products Liability* 1 (Winter '87).

Mills, Eric Burke, "Perspectives on Corporate Crime and the Evasive Individual," 8 *Crim. Justice J.* 327 (October '86).

Rabin, Robert L., "Environmental Liability and the Tort System," 24 *Houston L. Rev.* 27 (January '87).

Vincent, E. Lawrence, "Defining Doing Business to Determine Corporate Venue," 65 *Texas L. Rev.* 153 (November '86).

Woodside, Frank C. III and Allen P. Grunes, "A Proposal to Limit a Corporation's Liability," 54 *Defense Counsel J.* 345 (July '87).

CORPORATE MERGERS, ACQUISITIONS, AND REORGANIZATIONS

[¶1701] The decision to acquire, merge, or sell a business should not be reached without careful consideration of several factors: (1) The business objectives of such a move should be evaluated; (2) the projected future state of the industry should be analyzed; and (3) a long-range (at least five-year) plan for growth should be formulated. After careful review of all the above, if the decision to acquire, merge, or sell is made, the next step is to select the company to be acquired, negotiate, and finalize the deal. In order to do this, it will be necessary to examine the tax considerations, the method of acquisition (stock or cash), existing corporate liabilities, SEC and antitrust problems, as well as any other labor or Blue Sky pitfalls.

Once the terms of the contract are agreed upon, the contract can be prepared, the necessary approvals obtained, the proper filings made, and the transaction closed. The following paragraphs highlight these important areas, and include checklists of items to be covered in any business deal.

[¶1702] MERGERS

An *acquisition* (or merger) usually involves both a willing buyer and willing seller. In this respect, it is different from a takeover or tender offer, which is usually considered an unfriendly acquisition (see ¶1735). Acquisition is an umbrella term and includes more specific terms such as merger, consolidation, asset acquisition, and stock acquisition.

[¶1703] STATUTORY MERGER

A *statutory merger* is usually regulated by the corporation laws of the states of the buyer and the seller corporations. Generally, board of director approval of both corporations is required as well as a stockholder vote to approve the merger. One corporation is merged into the other and the remaining corporation is known as the surviving corporation. The surviving corporation will own all the assets and property of both corporations and will retain the liabilities of both corporations by operation of law.

[¶1704] STATUTORY CONSOLIDATION

The *statutory consolidation* differs from the statutory merger in that there is no "surviving corporation." Instead, both merged corporations disappear and a new corporation is created. Once again, this new corporation obtains all the assets as well as the liabilities of the two now-defunct corporations.

[¶1705] ASSET ACQUISITION

In an *asset acquisition* the buyer acquires all or most of the assets and business of the seller as per a contract entered into between the buyer and the seller. This differs from the stock acquisition which is discussed below.

[¶1706] STOCK ACQUISITION

In a *stock acquisition* the buyer acquires the shares of stock from the stockholders of the seller. It differs from an asset acquisition in that the directors of the selling corporation are not consulted. Rather, the buyer goes directly to the shareholders of the corporation and offers to buy their stock. If management is opposed to the buyer's offer to purchase, you generally have a takeover bid or tender offer. Although the terms "takeover bid" and "tender offer" are used interchangeably, tender offer usually refers to an acquisition of stock or cash.

[¶1707] TARGET

A *target company* is the corporation sought to be acquired by the buyer in an unfriendly takeover offer.

[¶1708] INITIAL CONSIDERATIONS FOR THE BUYER

The decision to acquire or merge a business is not one that a buyer can enter into lightly. A great deal of planning should occur prior to the search for a company to acquire. A buyer should first undertake a self-evaluation of its own business and the development of a long-range growth policy, taking into account the following factors:

(1) Value of own business;

(2) Long-range goal;

(3) ndustry market development and competition;

(4) Value of business to be acquired.

Once this self-evaluation is completed, it will be easier to identify the type of corporation that should be acquired. In fact, the buyer may even conclude that acquisition is not the best way to remedy its own business defects and that, in fact, it may be preferable to build its company from within rather than acquire from without.

However, once the decision to acquire has been made, the next step is to determine the basic qualifications a potential target should have in order to be considered a likely candidate for acquisition. The following factors should be considered:

(1) Minimum acceptable amount of return on invested capital or earnings per share.

(2) Minimum acceptable potential growth rate for the acquired company.

(3) The sort of management that would be required; would existing management be kept on or would the acquiring company have to provide support personnel?

(4) Geographic location of the acquired company.

[¶1709] WHAT KIND OF ACQUISITION SHOULD BE CONSIDERED?

Once a company has been selected for acquisition, the process of purchasing the company begins. While a seller will normally prefer to sell stock in order to avoid the trouble, cost, and risk of liquidation and depreciation recapture, the buyer will usually want assets in order to get a high basis and to avoid the seller's liabilities, including recapture potential.

The acquisition can be either a taxable or tax-free transaction. In a taxable transaction, the entire amount of the realized gain or loss must be recognized. To qualify as a tax-free transaction, however, a specific set of statutory and judicial requirements must be met. If these requirements are met, part or all of the realized gain or loss will be unrecognized. The amount of the unrecognized gain or loss is deferred until the assets or stock involved are later sold or exchanged in a taxable transaction.

There are seven kinds of tax-free reorganizations:

(1) The statutory merger or Type "A" reorganization;

(2) The stock-for-stock or Type "B" reorganization;

(3) The stock-for-assets or Type "C" reorganization;

(4) A spin-off, split-off, or split-up;

(5) A recapitalization;

(6) A change in identity or form;

(7) A bankrupt corporation's transfer of assets to another corporation.

[¶1710] STATUTORY MERGER (TYPE "A" REORGANIZATION)

The IRC permits four kinds of Type A reorganization: mergers, consolidations, and certain variations of mergers known as *triangular* and *reverse* mergers.[1] A Type A reorganization satisfies the corporation laws of the United States, a state, or territory, or the District of Columbia. The Type A reorganization is unique in comparison to the other types of statutory reorganizations that will be discussed because state law, rather than federal law, is a vital factor is determining whether the transaction is tax-free. This advantage is not as valuable as it might first appear, since the state itself will impose its own restrictions, which may prove difficult to meet. A serious drawback to this type of transaction is the fact that the surviving corporation assumes all of the obligations of the transferor corporation by operation of law.

[¶1711] STOCK FOR STOCK (TYPE "B" REORGANIZATION)

This is described as the acquisition by one corporation, in exchange solely for all or a part of its voting stock (or part or all of the voting stock of a corporation that controls the acquiring corporation), of stock of another corporation if, immediately after the acquisition, the acquiring corporation has control of the other corporation ("regardless of whether or not it had control before"). The acquiring corporation can transfer all or part of the stock acquired to its subsidiary. "Control" means ownership of stock possessing at least 80% of the total combined voting power of all classes of stock entitled to vote and at least 80% of the total number of shares of all other classes of outstanding stock.

A unique feature of the Type "B" reorganization is that it is either fully taxable or fully nontaxable. Note that in the stock-for-stock transaction the agreement is between the *buyer* and the *shareholder* of the seller.

[¶1712] STOCK FOR ASSETS (TYPE "C" REORGANIZATION)

This is described as the acquisition by one corporation, in exchange solely for all or a part of its voting stock (or of voting stock of a corporation that controls the acquiring corporation), of substantially all the properties of another corporation. (But assumption of liabilities in connection with such acquisition or the fact that property acquired is subject to a liability is disregarded in determining whether an acquisition was solely for stock.) However, if the acquiring corporation issues anything other than its own voting stock in the exchange, the assumed liabilities are treated as cash paid by that corporation. If the assumed liabilities plus the property or securities issued in addition to voting stock exceed 20% of the value of the assets acquired, the transaction is disqualified as a C-type reorganization. And, as a general rule, the transferor corporation must distribute all its assets to shareholders (less those assets retained to meet claims) pursuant to the plan of reorganization.

In a C-type reorganization, as long as voting stock is given for property with a market value of at least 80% of the market value of all the property of the acquired corporation, the remaining consideration may be paid in money or other property (80%-20% rule).

The difficulty in successfully bringing about a C-type reorganization under the 80%-20% rule may arise in determining the amount of assumed liabilities.

The 1986 Code makes it clear that a transferor corporation will not have gain on a transfer of stock or securities to its creditors when the transferor is merged, consolidated, or liquidated in a reorganization. Nor will the §§336–337 liquidation provision apply to a liquidation under a plan of reorganization.

[¶1713] PURCHASE OF SOME STOCK AND REDEMPTION OF BALANCE

Another way to finance an acquisition is to use some of the corporation's own funds for part of the purchase price. The seller will get his money as capital gain, and there will be no unfavorable tax results to the buyer if in acquiring the initial shares he did not personally obligate himself to redeem the balance of the stock and then have the corporation take over the obligation (*Zenz v. Quinlivan*, CA-6, 213 F.2d 914, 1954). Howwever,if the buyer obligates himself to buy all the shares and has the purchased corporation provide some of the money, he will be charged with a taxable dividend (*Woodworth v. Comm.*, CA-6, 218 F.2d 719, 1955; *Wall v. U.S.*, CA-4, 164 F.2d 462, 1947).

Three other ways to finance the purchase of a new company are described in the paragraphs below.

[¶1714] RESOLUTION OF KEY TAX ISSUES

In 1990, two tax issues of mergers and acquisitions were resolved. Under Rev.Rul. 90-11, 1990-1 C.B. 10, the adoption of a poison pill plan has no tax consequences. There is no potentially taxable "income event" until the "rights" under the pill plan are no longer redeemable at the reduced price without shareholder approval. The Third Circuit's *National Starch* decision[2] denies an immediate "ordinary and necessary business expense" deduction to a target corporation for expenses (such as the fees of attorneys and investment bankers) incurred when deciding whether to accept a takeover bid. To the Third Circuit, these expenses are capital expenditures because they are of long-term benefit to the corporation; under this analysis, it is not necessary for a capitalized item to create or enhance an individual asset of the corporation.

[¶1715] TAX ATTRIBUTES

In Type A and C reorganizations, the acquiring corporation obtains both the target corporation's tax attributes and assets. However, Sections 382 and 269 of the IRC prevent the purchasing of the assets or stock of a corporation having loss carryovers primarily to acquire the corporation's tax attributes. In a similar vein, Sections 382 and 269 prevent a corporation having loss carryovers from acquiring the assets or stock of a profitable corporation for the sole purpose of permitting the loss corporation to use its carryovers.

[¶1716] BROKER'S OR FINDER'S FEE

Be sure to resolve the broker issue prior to price negotiations, since a fee or commission can influence the ultimate amount paid or received. The law varies from state to state and should be consulted if brokerage problems arise.

Lawyers for both parties should determine whether a broker or finder may have been employed by buyer or seller, which party may become legally responsible to pay him, the extent of the liability, and how it is to be divided. If the claim is not explicit, it is desirable to reduce it to a definite understanding before the contract to close the deal is signed, and the contract should represent either that there were no obligations to brokers or finders, or provide who is to pay any admitted obligations.

Many state statutes of fraud require that the broker's or finder's contract be in writing in order to be enforceable. Some states also require licensing of brokers for them to be able to receive their commissions or fees. Remember that an implied contract may exist if the broker acts with the consent of the principal, whether given in writing, orally, or by implication from the conduct of the parties. A conversation about a possible sale, and an introduction furnished by the broker to the ultimate buyer, may be enough to entitle the broker to a commission on the theory that an implied contract of employment existed between the seller and the broker. If this kind of a cloud hangs over the negotiations, try to eliminate it by a written understanding.

[¶1717] THE PURCHASE PRICE

Having decided upon the type of acquisition and the particular company, the next major task is to establish the purchase price. Buying a business is really no different from buying any other asset. The buyer wants as low a price as possible and the seller wants to maximize his gain. The only real difference in the purchase of an ongoing corporation is that there are more factors to be taken into account: for example, working capital, market conditions, price trends in the industry, patents, and goodwill. The buyer must undertake an independent investigation in order to determine the price that he is willing to pay for the company. There are several ways for a buyer to get a quick idea as to the value of a corporation under consideration.

One approach is to look at the book value of the business. Usually, however, book value is grossly understated and most sellers will not part with their corporation based on that figure. Another approach is to have an appraisal done for the value of the plant, inventories, equipment, property, and intangibles of the corporation. A third approach, when possible, is to take a look at the seller's corporation and compare it to other corporations in the same industry. The situation can be somewhat easier when you're talking about publicly held companies since their stock is traded on stock exchanges. In that case, it should be fairly simple to establish the price of a share of stock based upon an average of the trading prices.

This is frequently the method used when a buyer is interested in making a tender offer or a takeover bid.

Most authorities, however, will agree that the best approach for determining the price to pay for a corporation is by working out its projected earnings over the next five years. Then other factors can be taken into account, such as debts, capital requirements, liabilities, existing contracts, etc.

These methods are not exclusive. Each business is a separate entity, and ultimately the buyer and seller will have to work out a formula that most nearly corresponds to their own needs.

[¶1718] REPEAL OF GENERAL UTILITIES DOCTRINE

The 1986 IRC did away with one of the most hallowed rules of M & A taxation. The *General Utilities* doctrine insulated corporations from gain or loss on property distributions to stockholders when the corporation was completely liquidated. Under current law, gain or loss is recognized on nearly all nonliquidating distributions, and on most liquidating distributions where the liquidation is completed in or after 1987. However, it is generally possible to liquidate an 80% subsidiary without recognition of gain or loss.

[¶1719] BUYER'S INDEPENDENT INVESTIGATION OF SELLER

Even after the purchase price is agreed on, and the price allocated among the assets, the buyer should undertake a financial and legal investigation of the seller's business. Below are two checklists to guide the buyer during negotiations.
- ❒ Check into corporate background:
  - (a) corporate charter,
  - (b) classes of stocks,
  - (c) minority and majority ownership,
  - (d) subsidiary companies,
  - (e) legal location and principal place of business of all divisions.
- ❒ Evaluate the shares of the corporation.
- ❒ Check the financial status of the corporation:
  - (a) assets,
  - (b) inventories,
  - (c) receivables,
  - (d) bank loans,
  - (e) accounts payable.
- ❒ Check out products in which the corporation deals. (This includes the names of competitors and their ranking within the industry. Any business dealings with federal, state, or local government?)
- ❒ Analyze the corporation's sales, sales organizations, sales policies, advertising, and commercial techniques.

❏ Draw up a detailed chart of management and labor relations: e.g., number of employees by department, directors and officers of the corporation and their duties, employment contracts and benefit programs, union participation by employees.

❏ Examine property and equipment of the corporation.

[¶1720] BUYER'S LEGAL CONSIDERATIONS

The buyer has four major legal concerns:

(1) Is he assuming the seller's liabilities and obligations to its creditors?

(2) Are there any antitrust law violations?

(3) Must any special stock exchange requirements be met prior to culmination of the transaction?

(4) Are there any state Blue Sky law requirements to be met?

[¶1721] BUYER'S ASSUMPTION OF SELLER'S LIABILITIES

If a business is acquired by the acquisition of its stock, the liabilities automatically follow the business into the hands of the buyer. In this situation, the only way to protect the buyer is to require the seller to warrant that the liabilities of the corporation do not exceed those reflected in its latest financial statement and the contractual obligations specified in the purchase contract. Unfortunately, a buyer will discover that the seller is not always willing to make this representation. Therefore, this will be a matter of negotiation, and sometimes the trading power of the buyer is strong enough to get selling stockholders to agree that part of the purchase price be set aside in escrow to meet corporate liabilities or to assume such liabilities to a limited and specified extent.

When assets are purchased for cash in an arm's-length transaction, only those liabilities that are explicitly assumed should follow the buyer, unless:

(a) The buyer makes the mistake of paying the cash directly to the stockholders of the selling corporation rather than to the corporation itself. This may result in the buyer finding himself liable to undisclosed creditors of the seller.

(b) If the requirements of the state bulk sales law are not complied with, undisclosed creditors may be able to enforce their claims against the assets purchased by the buyer. This risk can be handled by requiring strict compliance, or, in the event of waiver, getting a warranty and providing for deposit or escrowing of the purchase price.

A buyer of assets for stock may find himself liable to satisfy undisclosed liabilities of the seller, even though the purchase contract specifically provides that the buyer is not assuming any of the seller's liabilities. Sometimes this result is achieved on the grounds that the assets acquired constitute a trust fund for the creditors, sometimes on the grounds that in effect the acquisition constituted a merger in which the acquirer is the continuing company and thus remains liable for all the obligations of both parties to the merger. If the state law can result in this kind of unintended assumption of liabilities, the only way the buyer can protect himself is to get an indemnification from the seller and require that enough of the purchase price be held in escrow to protect the buyer against any such unassumed liabilities.

[¶1722] ANTITRUST PROBLEMS

The seller's contracts and pricing arrangements should be studied to see whether the buyer will be inheriting any antitrust problems. Distribution contracts, the pricing of goods to large customers, and other arrangements that may be basic to the profitability of the business being acquired and to the value being placed upon it should be studied from the antitrust standpoint to determine whether there is a possibility that the value of the business may be undermined if any of these arrangements are found to be in violation of the antitrust laws. Then it is necessary to appraise the chances that the acquisition itself may be blocked as a violation of §7 of the Clayton Act. This can happen in any line of commerce or in any section of the country, if the effect of the acquisition may be to lessen competition substantially or to tend to create a monopoly.

To make an initial determination of whether there is a possible §7 violation, check the share of the market enjoyed by the buyer and seller and see whether the acquisition results in a substantial increase in the share of the market held by the buyer or makes the buyer significantly more dominant in the market. Then evaluate the impact of the acquisition in terms of whether it seeks to substantially lessen competition. Make a judgment as to whether there is likely to be any complaint from competitors, suppliers, customers, or any companies who fear the acquisition would result in the loss of an important market for their products, or that it will result in their loss of a source of supplies. There is an advance clearance procedure in the Justice Department under which, on submission of full information about the economic impact of the proposed acquisition, an informal but not necessarily binding opinion can be obtained as to whether or not the acquisition would violate §7 of the Clayton Act.

There are three other federal statutes that heavily influence the determination of whether or not corporate action is in violation of the antitrust laws.

The Sherman Act states that "every contract, combination in the form of trust or otherwise, or conspiracy, in restraint of trade or commerce . . . is declared to be illegal," and that "every person who shall monopolize, or attempt to monopolize, or . . . conspire . . . to monopolize any part of . . . commerce" is in violation of the Sherman Act. The Sherman Act has been used to prohibit price fixing, territorial distributions among competitors, and boycotts.

The Federal Trade Commission Act prohibits "unfair methods of competition in commerce, and unfair or deceptive acts or practices in commerce."

The Robinson-Patman Act (an amendment to the Clayton Act) "prohibits discriminations in prices where the probate consequences of such discriminations would be either a substantial lessening of competition or a tendency to create a monopoly or to injure competition between third parties and the person granting or receiving a discrimination."

The FTC can issue a preliminary injunction, pursuant to FTC Act Section 13(b), against a merger pending the determination of the existence of a Clayton Act Section 7 violation. In fact, the District Court can order rescission of a completed acquisition on Section 7 grounds.[3]

The Second Circuit has held[4] that Williams Act regulation of corporate takeovers overrides the Sherman Act to the extent that the shareholders of a target corporation do not have an antitrust cause of action if they allege that rival takeover bidders conspired to lower the price eventually paid to the target shareholders for their stock.

[¶1723] PRE-MERGER NOTIFICATION

The Hart-Scott-Rodino Antitrust Improvements Act of 1976 added §7A to the Clayton Act. This section requires companies that are merging to provide the government with certain information regarding the merger and to wait a prescribed amount of time prior to consummating the transaction. This time lapse enables the FTC to evaluate the possible anticompetitive effects of the merger.

Compliance with the pre-merger notification rules requires full understanding of this complex legislation and it may be advisable, in certain circumstances, to consult with specialized counsel regarding the need to file notification with the Justice Department and the FTC.

Who Must File: Both the acquiring and the acquired companies must file notification if:

(A) Either one is engaged in interstate commerce or in any activity affecting interstate commerce; and

(B) The acquiring company has $100 million in total assets or annual net sales and the acquired company has $10 million in total assets or total net sales, or vice versa; and

(C) The acquiring company would have 15% or more of the acquired company's stock, *or* the acquiring company would own more than $15 million worth of the acquired company's stock and assets, combined.

Waiting Period: Following the filing of the notification form, the acquiring and acquired companies must wait 30 days prior to consummating the transaction (15 days if it is a cash tender offer).

In *Cargill v. Monfort,* 107 S.Ct. 484 (1986), the Court held that a company may not bring a Clayton Act action against the merger of two competitors based on the allegation that the merged companies would perpetrate a "cost-price squeeze"; if such lower prices resulted, they would be deemed vigorous competition, not violative anticompetitive conduct.

[¶1724] STOCK EXCHANGE REQUIREMENTS

If the buyer or seller is listed on the stock exchange, the buyer must take care to make sure that all stock exchange requirements are met.

[¶1725] SEC REQUIREMENTS

Even though the buyer may not have to register its securities pursuant to federal law, it is not automatically exempted from state registration requirements. State law should be consulted on this point.

[¶1726] SELLER'S LEGAL CONSIDERATIONS

The seller also has several legal factors to consider when his corporation is sold or acquired:

(1) Obligation to minority shareholders.

(2) Use of inside information prior to public announcement of impending sale or merger.

(3) Demands for appraisal by minority shareholders.

[¶1727] SALE OF CONTROL AND SELLER'S OBLIGATION TO MINORITY SHAREHOLDERS

Courts have generally held that a sale of a controlling block of stock at a price above the market will not by itself subject the sellers to any liability to minority stockholders. However, where the buyers intend to loot the company and the sellers should have anticipated this possibility on the basis of the past performance of the buyers, the sellers may have incurred a liability to minority stockholders. Also, if the selling stockholders participate in a change of control, giving up their offices, resigning from the board of directors, and designating representatives of the buyers to succeed them, the courts may hold that any premium received by the sellers over and above the prevailing market price of the shares constitutes a trust fund in which minority shareholders may participate. The safest way to avoid this risk is to insist that a similar offer be made to all shareholders. If this is not practicable, then it is incumbent upon the selling shareholders to investigate carefully the reputation and the purpose of the buyers and to accept no obligation that might be deemed to constitute a sale of control and an active participation in a charge of control over and above the simple sale of their shares.

What obligation do the officers and directors who are selling their stock have to disclose the price and the transaction to minority stockholders? In some states the courts have held that insiders had an obligation to disclose all information to minority shareholders. Other states restricted the directors' fiduciary duty to the corporation and required no disclosure to other shareholders. Today, it is generally considered that Rule 10b-5 under the Securities Exchange Act of 1934 requires full disclosure to minority stockholders. In one important case under the common law, the president of a company who had a deal to sell his stock at a high figure and went out and bought up shares from other shareholders at a lower figure, so that he could profit on the difference, was obligated to turn the difference over to the shareholders whose stock he had bought up.

[1727.1]   The Board's Duties and Adoption of Defensive Measures

The business judgment rule recognizes the fact that a corporation must be managed by persons who have an intimate daily knowledge of the corporation's affairs and goals. The rule gives directors and officers wide latitude; yet they must act honestly and in the way they believe benefits the corporation and its shareholders. Furthermore, the board of directors must take steps to inform itself of the implications of the various bids that have been made, and the other options open to the company (such as seeking a "white knight," or friendly bidder); and any defensive measures taken must be rational responses to an actual threat.[5]

The so-called "Nancy Reagan defense" ("Just say no") has been accepted as long as this is a reasonable business judgment. See, for example, *Holly Farms,*[6] permitting the board to refuse to entertain an offer, and to accept the highest per-share bid made for the corporation's stock when the offer was subject to withdrawal even though a lower bidder thinks that it didn't get a fair chance. In this situation, it was held that the board was not obligated to give the lower bidder a chance to top the higher bid because the higher bid could have been withdrawn, leaving the shareholders less well off than if the higher bid were accepted immediately.

Once a board has considered the material information and decided to end the auction by accepting one of two substantially equal bids, it does not have to call for tie-breaking bids, if this carries a risk of withdrawal of the existing bids.[7]

A board is justified in maintaining and pursuing its long-range strategies (and in seeking an acquiror that fits in with its existing corporate culture, in preference to one that is discordant) even if the shareholders prefer a bid with a higher current value to the one that the board believes will maximize the long-range value of the corporation's stock.[8]

Other acceptable defensive measures include postponing the annual meeting in order to explore alternatives to a takeover bid that the board deems inadequate; in effect, lack of information sufficient to evaluate a bid is tantamount to a threat to the corporation justifying defensive measures. Another case involving the same parties approves the board's adoption of a "beneficial ownership" provision.

Another possible response (albeit drastic) to a hostile takeover threat is the "scorched earth" policy: the target makes itself less attractive by selling or otherwise divesting useful assets. However, this tactic can backfire if it gives the corporation a surplus of cash that could go straight into a raider's pocket after a takeover, and it can backfire for the directors if they are sued by angry shareholders and are found to have violated their duty of due care.

A less drastic tactic is the "crown jewel lockup" or "lockup option," under which the target agrees to sell the valuable asset to a third party in the event of a hostile takeover. The lockup is likely to be challenged by the hostile bidder. It has been held that the target's board can be protected by the business judgment rule when it grants a lockup provided that the grant takes place only after both bidders have made a full presentation to the board, and the board has had an opportunity to review both bids.[9] The *Mills* case discussed above permits a lockup only if its effect is to draw in more bidders, not to repel them; if the lockup involves "crown jewels" rather than ordinary assets, an even higher level of scrutiny is imposed. Furthermore, under *Mills*, the auction must be conducted by independent directors, not directors with a personal stake in the outcome of the transaction.

A board of directors cannot force through a union contract containing unredeemable "poison pill" provisions unless they have met their *Unocal* duty by properly informing themselves and deliberating on the pros and cons of the poison pill.[10]

Once a corporation has adopted a "shareholder rights plan" (popularly known as a "poison pill"), the question is when the board of directors can be forced to redeem the pill so that the stockholders will have the option to accept or turn down the bidder's offer for the shares. The dividing line is between fair and non-coercive offers (where the stockholders must be given a chance to consider the offer) and unfair, coercive offers (where the pill can be used to protect them).

Furthermore, once a poison pill is adopted, the board does not have free rein in amending the pill. An amendment reducing the pill "trigger" (the level of stock ownership by a bidder bringing the negative consequences of the pill into effect) from 20% to 12.5% was disapproved by the Second Circuit,[11] on the grounds that the reduction violates the New York state law that requires all shares within a class of stock to be equal. Nor can the board amend a pill plan so drastically as to constitute a new plan without getting shareholder approval, if the amended plan weakens the protection against coercive offers and self-dealing, and violates a shareholder resolution against adopting a new pill plan without shareholder approval.[12]

[¶1728] INSIDER TRADING PROBLEMS

Another problem of which the seller should be aware is the use of inside information by officers, directors, employees, or anyone else who becomes aware of the pending merger or acquisition before it is public knowledge. Of particular importance here is the application of Rule 10b-5 of the Securities Exchange Act of 1934.

Of course, this area was one of particular concern in the late 1980s (e.g., the Winans, Boesky, and "Yuppie Five" cases). Under *Chiarella v. U.S.*, 445 U.S. 222 (1980) and *Dirks v. S.E.C.*, 463 U.S. 646 (1983), the responsibility to disclose inside information is premised on a fiduciary relationship with the parties to a transaction; a "tippee" is not liable under 10b-5 unless he knows or should know that the tipper breached his fiduciary duty. However, insiders (including temporary insiders such as lawyers involved in an M & A transaction) can be liable for misappropriating corporate information for their own use. Under the Insider Trading Sanctions Act of 1984 (15 USC §78u(d)(2)), the SEC can bring an action for a civil penalty of triple the insider trader's profits.

[¶1729] SHAREHOLDER'S RIGHT OF APPRAISAL

Shareholders who dissent from a merger transaction may be entitled to have a court place a value on their stock interest, rather than agree to accept the cash value offered in the merger. However, too many demands for appraisal and payment of cash instead of stock to dissenting stockholders may put too great a financial strain on the surviving corporation. These demands can usually be presented right up to the time of the stockholders' vote on the measure, and it may be possible that appraisal demands delivered through the mail can still be effective even though received a few days subsequent to the date of stockholder approval. When the number of stockholders is limited, and the state law permits, uncertainty in this respect can be eliminated by obtaining written consent from all stockholders, so that it will be unnecessary to hold a stockholders' meeting to approve a merger. If this uncertainty cannot be avoided, the merger agreement should include a clause giving both companies the right to abandon the merger if stockholders' demands for appraisal are excessive (that is, if they exceed a specified percentage).

[¶1730] OTHER ITEMS TO BE CONSIDERED

In addition to the items previously mentioned, there are many other areas for both buyer and seller to investigate prior to binding the deal.

❏ *Transferability of Seller's Contracts:* If any contract contains a prohibition of assignment, or a requirement that the other party's consent is necessary in order to make the assignment effective, counsel for seller must make certain that the selling corporation undertakes to obtain any necessary consent.

❏ *Labor Problems:* Check to see whether union contracts contain a provision that they are binding on the buyer or whether there is a nonassignability clause. Another important question is whether the surviving corporation must bargain with the union certified as a collective bargaining agent. Courts have held that the successor employer must deal with the union during the period following the merger, usually the balance of the existing year since certification. A problem arises when the successor corporation already has a contract with another union. If the employees of the acquired corporation fall into a minority status in relationship to the employees of the combined or the survivor corporation, they may automatically be absorbed into the existing contract of the buyer's corporation. Another problem involves the consolidation of the work force and the displacement of some employees. If a union is involved the matter will probably have to be negotiated, and, in some cases, seniority will control.

☐ *Employee Benefit Plans:* How will the employee benefit plan of the seller's corporation be incorporated into the surviving corporation? Unfortunately, employee benefit plans rarely mesh satisfactorily between the surviving corporation and the absorbed corporation. The choice then is between terminating the old plan and paying out all vested amounts or freezing the old plan and holding the amounts accumulated in trust for the benefit of the employees of the absorbed company until they retire or their service is terminated.

☐ *Executive Arrangements:* The buyer will probably have to assure the management of the absorbed corporation that its services will be needed and that its rights under current executive compensation plans will be respected. This is probably an appropriate topic for inclusion in the acquisition contract. In addition, if there are stock option rights involved, these may have to be converted into stock options of the surviving corporation. If necessary, it may be advisable to have the executives of the absorbed corporation exercise their options prior to the merger.

☐ *Unemployment Insurance:* Make sure the appropriate state agency is notified of the impending merger.

☐ *Bank Loan Agreements:* Check the seller's bank loan agreements to make certain that they do not prohibit an acquisition. If such a clause is included in any loan, it may be necessary to obtain the bank's consent or a refinancing of the bank debt in order to go ahead with the merger.

☐ *Inventory Problems:* The seller should be willing to warrant that the inventory is of "merchantable" quality and adequate for the conduct of the business as previously conducted.

☐ *Accounts Receivable Problems:* Here the buyer may not wish to assume the risk that the seller's reserve for bad debts is adequate. The contract may provide for an adjustment in price to reflect any difference between the accounts receivable shown on the seller's books and the amount actually collected at the end of a specified period of time. If this is the arrangement, the seller is usually given an opportunity to take the uncollected accounts and see what he can do with them. There are usually advantages in having the accounts receivable collected by the continuing business.

☐ *Title Searches:* A real estate title search should be made early, and if there are any clouds on the title that would hurt the operation of the business, they should be brought to the buyer's attention promptly and before the purchase agreement is signed, if possible. The buyer could agree to bear the cost of such a search if the deal did not go through.

☐ *Tax Liabilities:* It's a good idea to have the seller represent the status of the company with respect to tax audits and important to have the seller assume responsibility for tax liabilities other than those represented on the balance sheet submitted.

❏ *Covenant Not to Compete:* It may be critically important to get assurance that the sellers will not compete with the business that they are selling. If there is any payment for this covenant, it will be deductible by the buyer and have the effect of converting that portion of the proceeds received by the sellers from capital gain to ordinary income. To accomplish this, it is important to specify the amount being paid for the covenant not to compete. If this result is not desired and there is a covenant not to compete in the agreement of sale, to protect the sellers from possible ordinary income it is well to provide that the covenant is incidental to the sale of the stock and has not been separately bargained or paid for.

A covenant not to compete may not be advisable if the buyer could be charged with a violation of the antitrust laws.

Courts are frequently hesitant to enforce overreaching covenants not to compete, so make certain that the geographical limits and time restraints are necessary to safeguard the buyer's business.

[¶1731] THE ACQUISITION CONTRACT

Once the contract is signed, thereby fixing the rights and obligations of both buyer and seller, neither one can unilaterally change its terms. Therefore, it is imperative that any questions about the deal be raised prior to drawing up the contract. An issue which comes to light after the contract is signed could be costly for either side.

The acquisition contract not only sets forth rights and obligations of both buyer and seller but also provides buyer with a detailed account of the seller's business. In the contract, the seller will make representations regarding the conditions of his business on a given date. It will include information regarding the finances, physical plant, and intangible properties of the seller. The contract will also set forth the transaction itself, as well as the following items: representation and warranties of buyer; assets to be acquired by buyer; purchase price; assumption of liabilities by buyer; seller's indemnification of buyer; seller's conduct of the business pending closing; conditions precedent to closing; any problems with brokerage; and other general provisions.

Once the buyer and seller have worked out the basic terms of the agreement, it is advisable to reduce this to writing, thereby binding the agreement. There are several methods available to bind the deal: option, restrictive letter, or letter of intent.

[¶1732] OPTION

Buyers usually prefer an option contract, since it gives them a specified time in which to investigate the business with the knowledge that seller can't sell prior to the expiration of the agreed-upon period. Sellers will generally favor an option if they are interested in selling the business to a particular buyer. An option contract needs consideration, which may be cash paid by the buyer for the option. An option contract usually has an acquisition contract attached.

[¶1733] RESTRICTIVE LETTER

This is similar to an option binding both seller and buyer for a fixed period of time, but it usually does not contain specific language or terms regarding the underlying acquisition.

[¶1734] LETTER OF INTENT

Usually, this is a memorandum of understanding, the acquisition being subject to the approval of the respective boards of directors; thus the letter is not legally binding.

[¶1735] USE OF A TENDER OFFER

Frequently a buyer who wants to acquire a company will find that its board of directors is unwilling to have it acquired or merged. When that occurs, a buyer might resort to the use of a tender offer made directly to the target company's shareholders. In order to make a tender offer, buyer and target must both follow the requirements set forth by the Williams Act.

The Williams Act (§§13 and 14 of the 1934 Securities Exchange Act) was designed to protect the shareholders of target corporations from some of the practices of corporate raiders by requiring more disclosure by an offeror. To some extent, §14(e) of the Williams Act parallels the disclosure requirements of §10(b) and Rule 10b-5, in that both prohibit false and misleading statements. Set forth below are the basic provisions of the Williams Act:

(A) Section 13(d)(1) requires any person who becomes the beneficial owner of 5% equity security of:

    (1) a class that is registered pursuant to §12, or

    (2) any equity security of an insurance company that would have been required to be so registered except for the exemption in §12(g)(2)(G), or

    (3) any equity security issues by a closed-end investment company registered under the Investment Company Act of 1940 within 10 days after such acquisition, to send to:

    (1) the issuer at its principal executive office (by registered or certified mail), and

    (2) each exchange where the security is traded, and

    (3) the Security and Exchange Commission,

a statement containing the following information and such additional information as the SEC may by rules and regulations require:

(1) the background, identity, residence, and citizenship of purchasers;

(2) the source and amount of the funds or other consideration used in making the purchases;

(3) the purpose of the purchases;

(4) the number of shares that are beneficially owned and the number concerning which there is a right of acquisition; and

(5) information as to any contracts, arrangements, or understandings with any person with respect to any securities of the issuer.

(B) If any material change occurs in the facts required to be set forth in the statement, an amendment to the statement must be filed.

For further specific requirements, consult the Williams Act (§§13 and 14 of the 1934 Securities Exchange Act, 15 U.S.C.A. §78m, as amended).

Also see Rule 10b-4, which forbids "short tenders" (tendering more stock than actually owned) and 10b-13, forbidding the bidder to purchase the subject security outside the tender offer.

Typically, tender offers are structured either for cash, or in a "two-tier" offer, with more favorable terms for those who tender immediately. As a result of *Schreiber v. Burlington Northern Inc.*, 105 S.Ct. 2458 (1985), it's clear that there is no remedy under §14e for allegedly improper tactics during a tender offer—as long as the tactics are fully disclosed.

Tender offers must be kept open for at least 20 business days (and at least 10 business days after a change in the consideration offered or the securities sought). The bidder must file a Tender Offer Statement (Schedule 14D-1) with the SEC, the target, other bidders, and exchanges on which the target trades. The target's shareholders must receive materials disclosing the terms of the tender offer, and any material changes. The practice of acquiring additional securities during the 10-day "window" has been criticized, but is not actually illegal.

[¶1736] LEVERAGED BUYOUTS (LBOs)

In a leveraged buyout, the acquiror borrows nearly all the consideration needed to acquire the target company—generally using the assets of the target as security. "Junk bonds" (high-risk corporate bonds) are frequently used in LBOs, and the management of the company often participates in the acquisition.

In a leveraged buyout, the board's obligation to the stockholders is to maximize the value of their shares once the decision to sell has been taken. The risk is that management's two roles—as seller and buyer of the corporation—will lead to conflict of interest. The shareholders must receive a fair deal and a fair price.

[¶1737] STATE TAKEOVER STATUTES

More than half the states have enacted some form of legislation to regulate takeovers. However, questions continue to be raised as to the constitutionality of such statutes, as well as whether or not a given statute is preempted in whole or in part of federal law.

Because jurisdictions differ significantly on these issues, local law should be checked as to the validity of an applicable statute. *Moran v. Household International Inc.,* 500 A.2d 1346 (Delaware 1985) upholds the use of the "poison pill" against threatened two-tier or partial takeovers. In 1987, in *CTS v. Dynamics Corp.* (55 LW 4478) and *Indiana v. Dynamics Corp.* (ibid), the Supreme Court upheld the Indiana law permitting shareholders to decide whether the acquiror of a substantial or majority interest can vote those shares. The law was held not to interfere unduly with interstate commerce, nor to conflict with federal securities laws or SEC rules about tender offers.

Although the Williams Act obligates offerors to disclose the source and amount of borrowed funds proposed to be used in a tender offer, such information need only be disclosed if the arrangements have already been made; would-be offerors need not wait until lending commitments have been made to initiate the tender offers: *Newmont Mining Corp. v. Pickens,* 831 F.2d 1448 (9th Cir. 1987); *IU International Corp. v. NX Acquisition Corp.,* 56 LW 1131 (4th Cir. 1988).

[¶1738]   WHAT TO DO WHEN A TENDER OFFER IS MADE

In the event an unfriendly tender offer is made, an ability to respond quickly and decisively is paramount. Morris M. Lee, Jr., a public relations consultant frequently called upon to aid target management, has suggested certain steps that should be part of a company's defensive plan:

❐ Analyze the company's true worth—the company will need this in order to argue that the offeror's price does not reflect the true worth of the stock.

❐ Guard against improper use of stockholder lists.

❐ Watch for any sudden surge in the trading of the stock.

❐ Break down the shareholder list by geographic distribution, institutional investors, etc.

❐ Establish a rapport with the largest shareholders and institutional investors.

❐ Prepare a telephone solicitation team, but remember that SEC rules prevent certain communications in telephone contacts.

❐ Set up a plan for an emergency directors' meeting.

❐ Keep up-to-date records on stock transactions by officers and directors.

❐ Prepare and address in advance shareholder mailing envelopes; know how long it will take to print a shareholder's letter.

❐ Know how long it will take to file all necessary documents with the SEC.

❐ Have skeleton 14D forms on hand.

[¶1739]   CLOSING AND POST-CLOSING STEPS

Once all the details of the merger or acquisition are agreed upon, the only steps that remain will be the closing and post-closing steps.

In order to facilitate the closing, lawyers for both buyer and seller should prepare a checklist of the items that will be exchanged upon completion of the transaction.

The buyer may also want to have some publicity regarding the acquisition. For legal reasons, as well as for commercial purposes, it may be important to inform the seller's customers and suppliers that there has been a change in ownership of the acquired corporation. Whether or not the acquisition should be emphasized depends upon the individual circumstances and, of course, the nature of the reorganization.

Finally, here is a checklist of some steps that should be taken following the closing of the acquisition:

❏ *Publicity:* Comply with the requirements of public announcement, if any, contained in the agreement. Furnish wire services with immediate accurate release. Place advertisements if required.

❏ *SEC Reports:* File Form 8-K.

❏ *Tax Returns:* Prepare tax returns for the acquired corporation for part of the fiscal year before closing.

❏ *Changeovers:* Change bank accounts, insurance policies, unemployment compensation filings, workmen's compensation filings, and similar items.

❏ *Corporate Name:* Protect the corporate name of the acquired corporation. (One way is to form a dummy corporation.)

❏ *Pending Litigation:* Effect substitutions of parties.

❏ *Registration Statements:* Check to make sure of compliance with SEC requirements including filing of post effective amendments to registration statements and prospectuses.

❏ *Withdrawal of Acquired Corporation:* See that the acquired corporation is withdrawn from states where it may be registered.

— ENDNOTES —

1. IRC §368(a)(1)(A) and Reg. Sec. 1.368-2(b)(1).

2. National Starch & Chemical Corp. v. Comm'r, 918 F.2d 426 (3d Cir. 11/13/90).

3. FTC v. Elders Grain Inc., 868 F.2d 901 (7th Cir. 1/30/89).

4. Finnegan v. Campeau, 915 F.2d 824 (2d Cir. 10/4/90).

5. Unocal v. Mesa Petroleum Co., 493 A.2d 946 (Del. Sup. 1985). See also Gilbert v. El Paso, 58 LW 2719 (Del.Sup. 5/16/90).

6. In re Holly Farms Corp. Shareholders, 58 LW 2011 (Del.Ch. 6/14/89).

7. In re RJR Nabisco Inc. Shareholders Litigation, 57 LW 2482 (Del.Ch. 1/31/89).

8. Paramount Communications Inc. v. Time Inc., 58 LW 2070 (Del.Ch. 7/14/89)(the "Time-Warner" case), aff'd 58 LW 2511 (Del. Sup 2/26/90).

9. Cottle v. Storer Communications Inc., 849 F.2d 570 (11th Cir. 7/14/88).

10. Air Line Pilots Ass'n v. UAL Corp., 717 F.Supp. 575 (N.D. Ill. 7/7/89).

11. Avon Products v. Chartwell Associates L.P., 907 F.2d 322 (2d Cir. 6/28/90).

12. In re National Intergroup Shareholder Litigation, 59 LW 2085 (Del.Ch. 7/3/90).

— FOR FURTHER REFERENCE —

Akselrad, Ira and Robert S. Bernstein, "12e Expenses Incurred in Obtaining LBO Loans Deductible?" 20 *J. Corp. Tax* 295 (Autumn '93).

Anderson, John A., "Maine's Non-Shareholder Constituency Statute," 45 *Maine L. Rev.* 153 (April '93).

Baker, Pamela, "Executive Compensation in Mergers and Acquisitions," 39 *Practical Lawyer* 75 (June '93) and 45 (July '93).

Brown, J. Robert Jr., "Discrimination, Managerial Discretion and the Corporate Contract," 26 *Wake Forest L. Rev.* 541 (Fall '91).

Comment, "The Poison Pill": A Panacea for the Hostile Corporate Takeover," 21 *John Marshall L. Rev.* 107 (Fall '87).

Garwin, Arthur, "Parent Trap: Corporate Mergers and Acquisitions Can Create Conflicts of Interest," 79 *ABA J.* 116 (September '93).

Hogan, Stephen D. and Marsha Cope Huie, "Bigness, Junk and Bust-Ups: End of the Fourth Merger Wave?" 37 *Antitrust Bulletin* 881 (Winter '92).

Hume, Evelyn C. and Ernest R. Larkins, "Takeover Expenses: National Starch and the IRS Add New Wrinkles," 174. *J. of Accountancy* 87 (August '92).

Ickowitz, Allan H. and Geoffrey D. Genz, "Courts Sift Through LBO Suits," *Nat.L.J.* 11/30/92 p. 27.

Johnson, Barret, "Tender Offer Considered an Option Under Sec. 382 Option Attribution Rule," 23 *The Tax Adviser* 463 (July '92).

Klein, Martha Sellers, "Raging Markets: Stocks and Debt Offerings Turn Bullish; M&A Faded, but Not Forgotten," 14 *Amer. Lawyer* 56 (April '92).

Lawlor, William G. and David S. Denious, "Stock-for-Stock Acquisition Transactions," 26 *Rev. of Securities & Commodities Regulation* 99 (June 9, '93).

Lowry, John P., "Poison Pills in U.S. Corporations: A Re-examination," 1992 *J. of Business Law* 314 (May '92).

Mallenbaum, Stephen J., "In Acquisitions, Revised Tax Law May Work Harsh Results," *New York Law J.* 10/12/93 p. 11.

Ordover, Janusz A. and Jonathan B. Baker, "Entry Analysis Under the 1992 Horizontal Merger Guidelines," 61 *Antitrust L.J.* 139 (Summer '92).

Pitofsky, Robert, "Merger Analysis in the '90s: The Guidelines and Beyond," 61 *Antitrust L.J.* 147 (Summer '92).

Rosen, Robert M. and Mark L. Yecies, "Consolidated Return Aspects of Acquisitions and Dispositions," 51 *Inst. on Fed'l Tax* 21 (Annual '93).

Seelig, Steven A., "Qualified Plan Distributions in Corporate Acquisitions and Mergers," 18 *J. of Pension Planning and Compliance* 53 (Summer '92).

Yadley, Gregory C. and Kent Schenkel, "Shareholder Guaranties of Corporate Debt: Considerations in Drafting and Structuring," 65 *Florida Bar J.* 39 (October '91).

CREDIT AND COLLECTIONS, DISCLOSURE, AND CONSUMER PROTECTION

[¶1801] Collecting a debt involves both legal problems (complying with the applicable disclosure statutes) and practical ones (getting the debtor to actually come through!). Effective debt collection begins at the very inception of a transaction: long forms that spell out the parties' rights and duties are usually better than short ones; they eliminate confusion and also any defense on the debtor's part that the transaction was confusing or the documents ambiguous.

Ordinary contract principles of execution generally apply to most credit transactions. Normally, the party to be charged with liability should sign the instrument. Major transactions with a corporation may have to be sanctioned by a corporate resolution or bylaw. The "ultra vires" doctrine makes it possible for a corporation to avoid a transaction entered into by a person exceeding his authority, so be sure that the signer has the power to bind the corporation. If the corporation is a small one, it may be wise to bind a major stockholder, getting the signature in an individual as well as corporate capacity. The law of suretyship is discussed at ¶4001.

Any partner can bind a partnership, because partners are generally assumed to have authority to enter into transactions and render all the partners personally liable.

In the individual and family context, parents are generally liable for "necessaries" (food, clothing, shelter, medical care) furnished to their children. Some states make each spouse liable for the other spouse's necessaries as well. But parents are no longer liable for necessaries provided to an emancipated minor. Courts in some states have held parents liable for a child's college tuition and other education expenses, based on the "necessaries" doctrine, but most courts are reluctant to do so.

Although the early 1980s were marked by a pro-business policy that some saw as limiting the protection available to consumers, Congress later passed new consumer-oriented credit legislation and some cases of interest were handed down. One of the most significant litigation issues was the extent to which 1980s DIDMCA (the bank de-control act) preempts state regulation of consumer credit issues.

A decade later, in 1992, a state-law ban on late fees imposed on credit card balances was struck down as a regulation of "interest," thus preempted by DIDMCA.[1]

[¶1802] HOW TO HANDLE COLLECTION CLAIMS

As soon as a claim is received, a numbered file should be opened and the client furnished with an acknowledgment of receipt showing the file number. The acknowledgment should also refer to any special fee arrangement that applies and should call for additional details that may be necessary to process the claim.

Debt collection is not without its legal pitfalls. In addition to liability under the Fair Debt Collection Practices Act (see below), collectors may also be sued for libel or slander, invasion of privacy, intentional or negligent infliction of mental anguish, and other civil causes of action; even criminal liability is possible in flagrant cases.

[¶1803] INFORMATION TO BE OBTAINED

Following is a checklist of questions for your client to answer before you proceed with the collection process:

☐ Name of the debtor.

☐ Address of the debtor (if a post office box, a street address also, if available).

☐ Age of the debtor, if relevant (a minor, for example).

☐ Marital status (where material).

☐ Type of debtor (partnership or corporation).

☐ Had debtor been known by any other name?

☐ Nature of claim (alimony, installment contract, goods sold and delivered, money lent, or services not received).

☐ Evidence of the claim.

☐ Other persons liable.

☐ Security involved.

☐ Nature of the liability of others (joint or several, as a guarantor or surety).

☐ Evidence of other individuals' liability.

☐ Number of bills sent by the client to the debtor and accepted without protest.

☐ Defenses, if any, to the claim.

☐ Client's evaluation of the claim.

☐ Client's estimate of the largest amount that can actually be realized (to what level will a client go to settle?).

☐ Names of witnesses and expected testimony.

☐ Valuation of business relationship and continuation.

☐ Solvency of the debtor.

☐ Did the debtor furnish any financial statement?

☐ Current credit report.

☐ Assets including real estate, bank accounts, cars, and securities of the debtor.

[¶1804] CONTACT AND SETTLEMENT

When examining the problems involved—including the amount of the claim, the relationship between the debtor and the creditor, and past efforts at collection—it is necessary to make a determination as to whether initial contact should be by personal visit, phone, or mail. Often a letter is the best approach. It should point out that the debtor will not only be liable for the amount owed, but also for the costs of legal action (including reasonable attorneys' fees).

Settlement rather than suit is ordinarily the best approach: it is both less costly and much faster for the creditor. Once settlement has been reached, an agreement should be signed in which the following factors are included:

❏ The amount initially claimed.

❏ The amount proposed for the settlement.

❏ Terms of payment.

❏ Place of payment.

❏ Grace periods (if any).

❏ Interest charges (if any; compliance with Truth-In-Lending legislation and state usury ceilings may be required).

❏ Statement of any defenses, counterclaims, or setoffs.

❏ Default clauses (in the event of nonpayment, entire amount owing becomes payable immediately).

❏ Judgment by confession (where permissible by state law).

❏ Specifics on notes or post-dated checks.

❏ Collateral (if any) for payment.

❏ Use of general release (if demanded).

❏ Means of payment (cash or certified check suggested).

[¶1805] COLLECTION BY LAWSUIT

When all other means have failed, it may be necessary to proceed by lawsuit. Even this, however, may not be an ideal situation; if there is a dispute over the debt, or the amount is very small in relation to the costs of proceeding by suit, it may be better to write off the amount.

To the extent that a choice of courts is available (generally dependent upon the jurisdictional minimums), it is often wise to choose an inferior court because of greater speed and economy of effort. Local procedural laws should be complied with, and the use of verified complaints where verified answers are required should increase the chance of settlement.

[¶1806] REMEDIES AFTER OBTAINING JUDGMENT

Once judgment has been obtained against a debtor, the number of remedies that are available to the creditor to obtain the funds vary widely from state to state. Nonetheless, there are some general rules that should be used as an operating guide. First, it is necessary to take out a judgment lien. Next, execution of the lien is necessary to enforce the judgment by reaching real or tangible personal property in a debtor's possession. Examination of the debtor is another practical tool to discover the assets that may be available for satisfaction of the judgment. Forms concerning residence, occupation, employment, salary, history, Social Security numbers, bank accounts, insurance policies, and other items are widely available.

It is sometimes also useful to examine unrelated parties who might have a knowledge of the debtor's assets. Garnishment of wages and salaries of the debtor is another possibility. For a table covering garnishment, see the Appendix.

[¶1807] SETTING ASIDE TRANSFERS

To the extent that the debtor is a business entity, the bulk sales provision of the Uniform Commercial Code (Article 6) ordinarily prevents sales that could be regarded as fraudulent. Those that are made in violation of the UCC provisions may be set aside. Under the Uniform Fraudulent Conveyance Act, it is possible to set aside a transfer made by any debtor that is either void or voidable as against the creditor, because of fraud or other reasons. In this instance, property may be levied against and sold under an execution order.

[¶1808] WHAT IS A FRAUDULENT TRANSFER?

Fraudulent conveyances involve the transfer of property that the debtor had title to when the creditor acquired the right to have the claim satisfied, and transfer was made with the aim of putting the property of the debtor beyond the creditor's reach.

In order to prove fraudulent intent, a number of statutory presumptions are made. Transfers presumed to be fraudulent include the following:

❐ Transfers that render the transferor insolvent.

❐ Transfers made without fair consideration by a person in business leaving the transferor with unreasonably small capital.

❐ Transfers made without fair consideration if the transferor intends or believes he'll incur debts beyond his ability to pay.

❐ Transfers by a partnership when insolvent if to a partner or if to a non-partner without fair consideration.

❐ Transfers made in anticipation of or pending litigation.

❐ Transfers with secret reservations of beneficial interest.

❐ Transfers that leave the transferor in possession on some fictitious ground.

[¶1809] HANDLING REMITTANCES

Upon receipt of payment of an item on which collection was sought, the client may be sent the full amount together with a bill, or the net amount after deducting the attorney's fee. Deciding which approach to use depends on the preferences of the individuals involved.

[¶1810] CHECKS MARKED "PAYMENT IN FULL"

Checks made out for less than the full amount owed that are marked "payment in full" have been termed an exquisite form of commercial torture. In general, the payee must usually regard a check drawn for less than the amount owed as an offer for accord and satisfaction. If the check is cashed, the offer is accepted. Prior to the adoption of the UCC, disclaimer of payment in full over the indorsement was ineffective—the act of cashing the check was held to have accepted the offer on the debtor's terms. UCC §1-207, however, appears to have altered the rule. Through the use of words such as "without prejudice" and "under protest," it is possible for the payee not to forfeit legal right to demand the balance of payment through the mere act of cashing the check.

[¶1811] FORWARDING OF COLLECTION ITEMS

It is clear, of course, that an attorney can have a hand in collecting items all over the country and in other countries, and is not limited to his own particular bailiwick, and this fact should be brought home to the client.

The normal way of handling out-of-town collections is by forwarding them to another attorney. Barring an established contact or a solid reference, the attorney to whom the matter is to be forwarded should be selected from one of the established law lists certified as complying with the American Bar Association standards. The publisher of the list will also have certain standards for listing that he will disclose on inquiry.

The forwarding letter to a new contact should indicate the basis of selection—law list or reference—and should discuss the fee. If, for example, you should decide to use the Commercial Law League schedule of fees, the letter should make this clear. These fees will not, of course, include the fees of the forwarding attorney who must add his own fee when he bills his client.

A number of law lists use bonded attorneys, and where this is the case you should notify the publisher of the lists as soon as you forward a matter to an attorney on his list. If you fail to do so, the bond may not be available to you if and when you need it.

The forwarding attorney can't just forget about a matter once it has been forwarded. He must check periodically with the out-of-town attorney and keep the client informed as to the status of the collection process.

[¶1812] FEES

There is, of course, no precise formula for determining fees for handling items for collection. The fee must vary with the amount collected, the nature of the item, and the nature of the services called for. Nevertheless, the schedule of rates charged by mercantile agencies may offer a worthwhile guide to the attorney in working out a fee arrangement. The schedule of the Commercial Collection

Division of Dun & Bradstreet may be considered fairly representative, and as such, useful for illustrative purposes.

[¶1813]   APPLICABILITY OF CONSUMER PROTECTION LAWS

Emerging trends in consumer credit today are governed by five basic sources of law: The Uniform Commercial Code (in effect in all states except Louisiana); The Consumer Credit Protection Act (Truth-In-Lending, 15 USC §1601 et seq. applicable to those extending credit and permitting repayment in four or more installments); state consumer protection legislation (the Uniform Consumer Credit Code and other legislation); substantive rule-making power of the Federal Trade Commission (utilizing 15 USC §57); and the due process clause of the 14th Amendment.

Among the pitfalls facing a secured creditor attempting to use Article 9 of the Uniform Commercial Code is the UCC's failure to define "default." Section 9-501(1) permits that term to be defined by the creditor in the security agreement itself. Default frequently can cause waiver or estoppel under UCC §1-103 to take effect. The use of "insecurity" clauses or acceleration clauses is an added problem.

Repossession, replevin, and self-help have been subject to new requirements in the light of *Fuentes v. Shevin* (407 US 67, 1972). Basically, *Fuentes* held that the state has the power to seize the goods of a consumer prior to final judgment in order to protect the security interests of creditors, so long as those creditors test their claim to the goods through the process of a fair prior hearing. "Due process is afforded only by the kinds of 'notice' and 'hearing' which are aimed at establishing the validity, or at least the power of the validity of the underlying claim against the alleged debtor before he can be deprived of his property . . . " (*Sniadach v. Family Finance Corp.*, 395 US 337, 1969).

The impact of *Fuentes* and *Sniadach* may have been lessened by a 1978 Supreme Court decision (*Flagg Brothers, Inc. v. Brooks,* May 15, 1978), which upheld a warehouseman's right to sell a consumer's goods in its possession to satisfy unpaid storage charges, pursuant to UCC §7-210. The Supreme Court held that no prior-to-sale hearing was required, because a state's enactment of the UCC (or any law) is not sufficient state action to trigger the application of the 14th Amendment. However, unlike the situations in *Fuentes* and *Sniadach,* the creditor in *Flagg Brothers* already had possession of the disputed goods. When the creditor is not in possession of the goods, there are three situations in which outright seizure (without an opportunity for a prior hearing) is permitted. First, when the seizure is directly necessary to secure an important governmental or general public interest (such as an attachment of property necessary to secure jurisdiction in a state court); second, when there is a special need for very prompt action; and third, when the person initiating the seizure is a government official responsible for determining, under the standards of a narrowly drawn statute, whether it was necessary and justified in the particular instance to undertake the seizure.

[¶1814] TRUTH-IN-LENDING

Truth-In-Lending (15 USC §1601 et seq.) is a basic generic term dealing with multiple types of federal consumer credit protection. Encompassing credit transactions, credit advertising, credit billing, and consumer leases, Truth-In-Lending is also supplemented by Regulation Z (12 CFR part 226) and Regulation B (12 CFR part 202), which are promulgated by the Board of Governors of the Federal Reserve System. Regulation Z covers definition and rules of construction, a listing of exempt transactions, rules for determination of finance charges, rules for determination of annual percentage rates in the granting of credit, general disclosure requirements, specific disclosure requirements on open-end credit accounts, disclosures required for credit that is not open ended, requirements for rescission of certain transactions, requirements for the statement of advertising credit terms, issuance and liability for credit card use, resolution procedures for billing errors, and consumer leasing. Regulation B covers the area of equal credit opportunity.

Truth-In-Lending covers all consumer-related installment sales that involve four or more installment payments. Truth-In-Lending disclosure must be made even if the purchase price "on time" is identical to a one-time purchase price. In this case, regulations require that the creditor state: "Cost of credit is included in the purchase price."

Disclosure of certain basic information is the keystone to Truth-In-Lending. Before extending credit, every person granting consumer credit must disclose the finance charges in dollars and cents and as an annual percentage rate (unless, of course, the transaction is exempt).

The disclosure required of credit card issuers, and available to consumers, was expanded by the Fair Credit Disclosure Act (P.L. 100-583), passed "to give consumers relevant cost information about credit and charge cards when they can shop for the best card" (i.e., before they have applied for a new card). The Fair Credit Disclosure Act requires disclosure of four key terms in mail and phone solicitations for credit card applications. (Under prior law, the disclosures were not required until the application had been made and approved, and the card issued.) The four key disclosures are the Annual Percentage Rate (APR), the annual fee for the card, the grace period extended during which payments can be made without accrual of interest, and the method used to calculate the balance on which a finance charge is assessed. Credit card issuers must also report these crucial items semiannually to the Federal Reserve Board, which can then release the information to the media for publicity (e.g., a story on which card issuers give the best deal).

The disclosures required in home equity loans were enhanced by P.L. 100-709, the Home Equity Loan Consumer Protection Act of 1988, which added 15 USC Section 1637a. For open-end consumer credit secured by the borrower's principal residence, the credit application must disclose: either a fixed APR or a method of computing a variable APR; the points or other fees that will be charged; a warning that default can lead to loss of the home; any conditions imposed on the terms offered (e.g., a limited period during which the terms will be available); the minimum periodic payments the borrower must make; and repayment options. 15 USC Section 1665b regulates advertisements for home equity loans. 15 USC Section 1647 requires that rate adjustments for home equity loans be made according to an index that is publicly available and not under the control of the creditor (e.g., the money supply; consumer or producer prices). Furthermore, the lender may not make unilateral changes in credit terms except as specifically permitted by the statute. For instance, the lender can deny a further extension of credit if the value of the home has declined significantly.

Under a 1993 Utah case, it was a violation of Sherman Act Section I for Visa USA to adopt a bylaw that prevented Sears (and other would-be issuers) from participating in the Visa joint venture and issuing Visa cards. Joint ventures are covered by the Sherman Act, and Visa had the necessary market power; Sears suffered antitrust injury; the exclusion of Sears harmed competition; and the harm outweighed any beneficial effects.[2]

[¶1815] GOVERNMENT AGENCIES REGULATING TRUTH-IN-LENDING

Compliance with the requirements imposed under Truth-In-Lending is enforced under:

(1) section 8 of the Federal Deposit Insurance Act, in the case of

    (a) national banks, by the Comptroller of the Currency;

    (b) member banks of the Federal Reserve System (other than national banks), by the board;

    (c) banks insured by the Federal Deposit Insurance Corporation (other than members of the Federal Reserve System), by the Board of Directors of the Federal Deposit Insurance Corporation.

(2) section 5(d) of the Home Owners' Loan Act of 1933, section 407 of the National Housing Act, and sections 6(i) and 17 of the Federal Home Loan Bank Act, by the Federal Home Loan Bank Board (acting directly or through the Federal Savings and Loan Insurance Corporation), in the case of any institution subject to any of those provisions.

(3) the Federal Credit Union Act, by the Administrator of the National Credit Union Administration with respect to any Federal credit union.

(4) the Federal Aviation Act of 1958, by the Department of Transportation with respect to any air carrier or foreign air carrier subject to that act.

(5) the Packers and Stockyards Act, 1921 (except as provided in section 406 of that Act), by the Secretary of Agriculture with respect to any activities subject to that Act.

(6) the Farm Credit Act of 1971, by the Farm Credit Administration with respect to any Federal land bank, Federal land bank association, Federal intermediate credit bank, or production credit association.

[¶1816] EXEMPTION OF CERTAIN STATES

States that have "substantially similar" laws regulating consumer credit transactions are eligible for exemption by the Federal Reserve Board from certain requirements of the Truth-In-Lending Act. Only to the extent that the Federal Reserve Board grants exemption do local laws prevail over specific requirements of the Truth-In-Lending Act. It should be noted that some states that have adopted the Uniform Consumer Credit Code have been granted exemption under federal Truth-In-Lending. However, not all have been granted exemption from Truth-In-Lending. It should also be noted that to the extent that any state law is more stringent in its requirements than federal Truth-In-Lending, both the federal and state laws are applicable.

[¶1817] LENDERS COVERED

Under §103 of the Truth-In-Lending Act, the only individuals required to make disclosures are those who regularly extend or arrange for the extension of credit to consumers, or regularly arrange for payments in which a finance charge is or may be required in connection with loans, sales of property, services, or otherwise. (The four-installment payment rule described above also applies, meaning that an individual who regularly extends credit in which payment can be made in three or fewer payments is not covered by Truth-In-Lending.)

[¶1818] EXEMPTIONS FROM FEDERAL TRUTH-IN-LENDING

The following transactions are exempt from the Act's provisions:

(1) Extensions of credit for business, commercial, or agricultural purposes, or to government, or to organizations.

(2) Transactions in securities or commodities accounts with a broker-dealer registered with the SEC.

(3) Credit transactions other than those in which a security interest is or will be acquired in real property, or in personal property used or expected to be used as the principal dwelling of the consumer, in which the total amount financed exceeds $25,000.

(4) Transactions involving services under public utility tariffs that are regulated by any governmental agency.

(5) Credit transactions primarily for agricultural purposes (including real property transactions) in which the amount financed exceeds $25,000.

(6) Home-fuel budget plans that call for an average monthly payment for the year's fuel bills.

(7) Federally-issued or -guaranteed student loans.

(8) Certain leases of personal property incident to leases of real property.

[¶1819] WHO IS REQUIRED TO MAKE DISCLOSURES?

Following are various categories of individuals and businesses that generally are required to make disclosures: automobile dealerships, bankers, dentists, doctors, credit unions, credit card issuers, retailers, savings and loan institutions, and even hospitals—provided they extend credit in the conventional sense or make special arrangements for payment of bills in which four or more installments are ordinarily involved, even if there is no finance charge.

[¶1820] TRUTH-IN-LENDING DISCLOSURE BY DOCTORS AND OTHER PROFESSIONALS

In a case where a patient is billed in full but unilaterally makes a partial payment that is accepted by the doctor, this does not constitute an "agreement" to accept more than four installments. Consequently, the professional is not subject to Regulation Z. Additionally, if a patient decides on his own to pay a bill in installments "or whenever he can," Truth-In-Lending does not come into play. However, if a finance charge is imposed, the transaction comes within the Act even though it is payable in fewer than four installments. If a physician agrees with the patient that all obligations may be paid in more than four installments, the obligation becomes a consumer credit transaction and Regulation Z disclosures must be made even if no finance charge is assessed.

[¶1821] NONDISCLOSURE: OVERDUE TAXES

When a state and a taxpayer enter into an agreement for payment of delinquent taxes under a plan of regular monthly installments, this is not a credit transaction covered by Truth-In-Lending because, even if interest must be paid, the debt must be voluntarily entered into in order to fall within the Act's coverage—which is not the case with delinquent taxes.

[¶1822] SPECIFIC AREAS IN WHICH DISCLOSURE IS REQUIRED

The following paragraphs discuss some of the specific areas for which federal Truth-In-Lending disclosure is required.

[¶1822.1] Commitment Fees or Standby Fees from Real Estate Developer to Lender

Such fees are to be included in the finance charge as *prepaid finance charges.*

[¶1822.2] Compensating Balance

Disclosure must be made in credit transactions that require 20% deposit balances that will be taken out of the proceeds of a separate but simultaneous loan from the identical creditor. The 20% compensating balance could be provided from either a cash fund of the debtor, proceeds of a separate loan, or withholding from the proceeds of the loan being consummated.

Observation: In order to provide the required compensating balance, sometimes a separate loan that would be subject to all the disclosure requirements of Regulation Z is granted. However, there is an exclusion provision concerning required deposit balances. The exception covers "a deposit balance or investment which was acquired or established from the proceeds of an extension of credit made for that purpose upon written request of the customer."

[¶1822.3] Note Renewals

When the original note is made, certain disclosures are required, but the original disclosures do not cover renewals. Renewals must be accompanied by full disclosure even though the interest remains unchanged and no "new" money is actually advanced.

[¶1822.4] Home Improvements

Real estate brokers who arrange financing for home improvements or remodeling as part of the sale of a house are also subject to the disclosure requirements. However, home improvement plans involving progress payments are not covered. Here the consumer pays the value of the work completed as the work progresses.

[¶1822.5] Mortgage Transactions

Those who arrange for the extension of mortgage credit, as well as those fiduciary institutions (or individuals) who actually extend financing, must make full Truth-In-Lending disclosures. Failure to do so subjects the parties to federal penalties (including attorneys' fees) and, in many instances, also subjects them to state penalties. In the paragraphs below, specific Regulation Z requirements for arranging credit, assumption of mortgages, refinancing mortgages, and issuing of second mortgages are examined.

Credit Arranger: Builders who prepare loan applications or initiate credit reports for a potential purchaser are not arrangers if they do not receive a fee for their work. If, however, the builder actually undertakes preparation of the note and mortgage or other contract documents, disclosure requirements must be met.

Assumption of Mortgages: If the purchaser of real estate will become personally liable for the debts of a primary mortgagee, Regulation Z provides that the mortgage has been assumed and the lender must give the purchaser of the real estate full and adequate disclosure. (If the mortgage lender does not participate in the assumption, no disclosure is required.)

Refinancing Mortgage: Each time a mortgage is materially altered, a new Truth-In-Lending transaction takes place, requiring additional disclosure.

Second Mortgages: Unlike first mortgages, in which the total dollar amount of the interest need not be given, full disclosure is required for all second mortgages.

Sole (Agricultural) Proprietor: Extensions of credit to a sole proprietorship for agricultural purposes are covered by Regulation Z.

Dealing with Principal Residences: The normal three-day right to rescind a transaction secured by a mortgage on the principal residence extends to three *years* if the lender fails to give the required notice of the right to rescission, according to a ruling of the Ninth Circuit.[3] In that case , a broker trying to forestall foreclosure sent the borrower documents saying that some party to be determined would extend credit; the broker eventually lent the money because no other lender was willing to do so, but failed to make the required disclosure of the right to rescind.

The Seventh Circuit ruled that the Depositary Institutions Deregulation, Management, and Control Act (DIDMCA) preempts an Illinois law that forbids interest higher than 3% on residential mortgages. Furthermore, the fee charged by the defendant bank was held to constitute points covered by DIDMCA (and not by state · usury law) rather than a prepayment fee that would not be subject to federal preemption, because the fee had to be paid whether or not the borrower prepaid the loan.[4] But although DIDMCA exempts first mortgage loans from state usury-law ceilings, it does not exempt used car loans from state usury regulation.[5]

In 1990, the Third Circuit ruled[6] that DIDMCA preempts state usury laws for all first mortgages on residential property, not just purchase money mortgages, and irrespective of the use made of the proceeds—in this case, to purchase automobiles.

[¶1822.6]   Corporate Sales of Stock

If a corporation distributes its own common stock and the purchaser may arrange to pay for it in more than four installments, the corporation cannot rely on being excluded from the definition of "creditor" simply because its primary business is other than selling stock or extending credit. Corporations are considered to be sophisticated parties fully capable of making the appropriate disclosures.

[¶1822.7] College Tuition Payment Plans

Deferred tuition payments with finance charges that may be deferred into more than four parts are covered under Truth-In-Lending. The school's comptroller should subtract the total amount of the student's other financing from the amount owed, and make disclosures on the remaining balance. However, as noted above, federally related student loans are not covered.

[¶1823] DEFINITIONS

Credit: "The right granted by a creditor to a customer to defer payment of debt . . ." The Act contemplates a voluntary agreement between a debtor and creditor that gives rise to a debt.

Consumer Credit: Credit offered or extended to a natural person for personal, family, household, or agricultural purposes and for which either a finance charge is (or may be) imposed or that, by agreement, is or may be payable in more than four installments.

Creditor: Any person or business entity that in the ordinary course of business regularly extends or arranges for the extension of credit.

If a builder takes back a purchase-money second-mortgage, that makes him a person who extends credit, and he must make disclosures. But a private party selling his own home who takes back a purchase-money mortgage is not one who extends credit under the law.

Advertisement: Any commercial message in any newspaper, magazine, or catalogue, or in a leaflet, flyer, direct-mail literature, or other printed material, or any broadcast medium such as radio, television, or even a public address system.

[¶1824] GENERAL DISCLOSURE REQUIREMENTS

Clear and conspicuous disclosure is required under indorser terms of Truth-In-Lending. All dollar amounts and percentages must be stated boldly and in numerical figures. The law also requires that annual percentage rates and finance charges be printed more conspicuously (in boldface type) than other terms. Guarantors, sureties, indorsers, and other individuals who are secondarily liable must also receive full disclosure. However, if two joint debtors (i.e., both primarily liable) are involved in a transaction, only one need be given a copy of federal disclosures.

[¶1825] CHCKLISTS OF SPECIFIC DISCLOSURE REQUIREMENTS

Federal Truth-In-Lending requires certain disclosure requirements. The Federal Reserve Board, through implementation of Regulation Z, has indicated that in connection with the sale of credit, as well as the sale of goods, certain items must be specifically listed. Checklists of these follow in the paragraphs below.

[¶1825.1] "Sale" of Credit (Extension of Credit Not in Connection with the Sale of Goods)

The following is a checklist of disclosure terms required for closed-end small loan transactions:

❒ Date of accrual of the finance charge (or date of transaction, if that is the date when accrual begins).

❒ Annual percentage rate of finance charge.

Note: If the finance charge is less than $5 and the amount financed does not exceed $75, no disclosure is required. If the total amount financed is more than $75 but the finance charge is less than $7.50, no disclosure is required.

❒ The number of scheduled payments.

❒ The dollar amount of scheduled payments.

❒ The due dates (or periods) of scheduled payments.

❒ The total amount (dollar value) of total payments.

❒ A statement of any "balloon" payment, and its amount.

❒ Means of computation of delinquency, default, or other charges resulting from late payment.

❒ Identification of any security interest retained by the creditor (UCC filings still required).

❒ Identification of the property to which the security interest attaches.

❒ Method of computation of any prepayment penalty that creditor may impose.

❒ Statement of the amount financed (the amount of credit, excluding any prepaid finance charges, that constitutes the amount of credit extended).

❒ Prepaid finance charges, if any.

❒ Amount of deposit, if any.

❒ Sum of any prepaid finance charges and deposits.

❒ Total amount of finance charge.

❒ Notes indicating rights of rescission by the consumer, if any.

[¶1825.2] Credit Sales

For all regularly occurring credit sales transactions, the following Truth-In-Lending disclosures are applicable:

❒ Date on which the finance charge begins to accrue if different from date of transaction.

❐ The finance charge expressed as an annual percentage rate, using the term "annual percentage rate."

Exception: Disclosure of finance charge as an annual percentage rate is not required if (1) the finance charge does not exceed $5 and applies to an amount financed not exceeding $75, or (2) the finance charge does not exceed $7.50 and applies to an amount financed exceeding $75.

❐ Number, amount, and due dates or periods of scheduled payments and, with certain exceptions, the sum of such payments, using the term "total of payments." This does not apply to a loan secured by a first lien or equivalent security interest on a dwelling and made to finance the purchase of that dwelling, or in the case of a sale of that house.

❐ Identification of any "balloon" payment.

❐ Amount or method of computing amount of any default, delinquency, or similar charges payable in event of late payments.

❐ Description or identification of type of security interest held or to be retained or acquired by creditor, including statements concerning after-acquired property subject to the security interest or other or future indebtedness secured by any after-acquired property where appropriate.

❐ Identification of the property to which security interest relates.

❐ Description of any prepayment penalty that may be imposed by creditor or his assignee, with an explanation of the method of computation.

❐ Provisions concerning refund of unearned finance charges in the event of prepayment.

❐ Cash price of property or service purchased, using the term "cash price."

❐ Amount of buyer's down payment, itemized as applicable, using the term "cash down payment"; for property traded in, using the term "trade in"; and the term "total down payment" for the sum of these.

❐ Difference between cash price and total down payment, using the term "unpaid balance of cash price."

❐ All charges, other than cash price, individually itemized, that are included in amount financed but that are not part of finance charge, using the term "unpaid balance."

❐ The sum of unpaid balance of cash price and all other charges that are included in amount financed but that are not part of finance charge, using the term "unpaid balance."

❐ Amounts to be deducted for prepaid finance charge or required deposit balance. "Prepaid finance charge," "required deposit balance," and "total prepaid finance charge and required deposit balance" must be used where applicable.

❐ Difference between unpaid balance and prepaid finance charge or required deposit balance or total prepaid finance charge and required deposit balance, using the term "amount financed."

❐ Total amount of finance charge, with description of each amount included, using the term "finance charge."

Note: This is not required in most sales of dwellings, nor is the next item.

❐ Sum of the cash price, all other charges included in amount financed but that are not part of finance charge, and the finance charge, using the term "deferred payment price."

❏ Notice of customer's right of rescission, if applicable.

❏ Circumstances under which the APR can change (if the transaction is variable-rate); limits on, and effect of, rate increases.

[¶1825.3] Open-End Credit Transactions

Open-end credit transactions are agreements under which a consumer may, if he desires, keep on making new purchases under the original extension of credit and add the amount of these purchases to the outstanding balance, up to an agreed ceiling (i.e., revolving charge accounts). The consumer usually has the option of prepaying or of paying in stated installments. The creditor may impose a finance charge on the balance, and it is this total finance charge that is the subject of Truth-In-Lending's main thrust.

[¶1825.4] New Accounts

Consumers seeking to open revolving credit accounts or credit card accounts from issuing authorities are entitled to certain basic information:

❏ *Conditions* under which a finance charge may be imposed, including an explanation of the time period, if any, within which any credit extended may be paid without incurring a finance charge.

❏ *Method of determining the balance* on which a finance charge may be imposed.

❏ *Method of determining the amount of the finance charge,* including the method of determining any minimum, fixed, check service, transaction, activity, or similar charge that may be imposed as a finance charge.

❏ *When one or more periodic rates* may be used to compute the finance charge, each such rate, the range of balances to which applicable, and the corresponding annual percentage rate determined by multiplying the periodic rate by the number of periods in a year.

❏ *Conditions under which any other charges* may be imposed and method by which they will be determined.

❏ *Conditions under which creditor may retain or acquire any security interest* in any property to secure payment of any credit extended on the account, and description or identification of the type of interest or interests that may be so retained or acquired.

❏ *The minimum periodic payment required.*

[¶1825.5] Periodic Billing

Creditors are required under federal Truth-In-Lending to make full disclosure of the following on each billing statement.

❏ *Outstanding balance* in the account at the beginning of the billing cycle, using the term "previous balance."

❑ *Amount and date of each extension of credit* or date such extension of credit is debited to the account during the billing cycle and, unless previously furnished, a brief identification of any goods or services purchased, or other extension of credit.

❑ *Amounts credited* to the account during the billing cycle for payments, using the term "payment," and for other credits including returns, rebates of finance charges, and adjustments, using the term "credits," and unless previously furnished, a brief identification of each item included in such other credits. Separate itemizations are permitted if they do not appear on the face of the statement. They must, however, accompany the statement and identify each charge and/or credit.

❑ *Amount of any finance charge,* using the term "finance charge," debited to the account during the billing cycle, itemized and identified to show amounts, if any, due to the application of periodic rates and the amount of any other charge included in the finance charge, such as a minimum, fixed, check service, transaction, activity, or similar charge, using appropriate descriptive terminology.

Note, however, that this does *not* require the seller to state the portions of the finance charge due to application of two or more periodic rates separately. The periodic rates that apply to the account and the applicable range of the balances must be disclosed, but no further detailed breakdown is required.

Example: If the finance charge is $1\,1/2\%$ per month for the first $500 of the balance and 1% per month for amounts exceeding $500, the total monthly charge on an outstanding balance of $600 would be $8.50, which must be stated. But the $7.50 and $1 components need not be spelled out.

❑ *Each periodic rate,* using the term "periodic rate" (or "rates"), that may be used to compute the finance charge, whether or not applied during the billing cycle, and the range of balances to which applicable.

❑ *Annual percentage rate or rates,* using the term "annual percentage rate" (or "rates"), and, if there is more than one rate, the amount of the balance to which each rate is applicable.

❑ *Balance* on which the finance charge was computed, and a statement of how that balance was determined. If the balance was determined without first deducting all credits during the billing cycle, that fact and the amount of such credits must also be disclosed.

❑ *Closing date* of billing cycle and the outstanding balance in the account on that date, using the term "new balance," accompanied by the statement of the date by which, or the period, if any, within which, payment must be made to avoid additional finance charges.

[¶1825.6] Finance Charges

Any charge that is imposed on the customer either directly or indirectly in order to obtain credit must be disclosed fully as a "finance charge." This classification includes, among others:

❑ Loan fees;
❑ Credit investigation fees;

❑ Finder's fees;
❑ Time-price differentials;
❑ Points in mortgages;
❑ Premiums for credit life or other credit insurance if required by the lender;
❑ Interest.

The following incidental charges are not deemed finance charges:

❑ Application fees charged whether or not credit is extended;
❑ Seller's points;
❑ Late payment charges and most overdraft charges;
❑ Most amounts required to be held in escrow;
❑ Taxes;
❑ License fees;
❑ Registration fees;
❑ Certain title fees;
❑ Fees fixed by law and payable to public officials;
❑ Real estate appraisal fees.

Discounts for prompt payment are deemed finance charges but do not have to be disclosed on the original contract. Inclusion on the face of the regular statement rendered is sufficient for compliance.

Finance charges must be spelled out, both in total percentages and dollars and cents, to the closest quarter of 1% for most transactions. (Finance charges involving real estate may be rounded off to the nearest 1%.)

[¶1826] CREDIT OTHER THAN OPEN-END

All required disclosures for transactions other than open-end credit agreements must be made together either (1) on the same side of the note or other instrument evidencing the obligation on the page and near the place for the customer's signature, or (2) on one side of a separate statement that identifies the transaction. The required disclosures must be made before the contractual relationship between the creditor and the customer is created, irrespective of the time of performance by either party, except in the case of orders by mail or telephone or a series of sales.

Additional disclosure is required for closed-end, adjustable-rate mortgages with a term of over one year, secured by the borrower's principal residence. Borrowers must be given the *Consumer Handbook on Adjustable Rate Mortgages* (or a comparable publication) and also supplied with detailed information on the circumstances in which the interest rate will change and how it will affect payments. (F.R. 42248, 12/24/87).

[¶1827] OPEN-END CREDIT

Required disclosures for open-end credit accounts for which a billing cycle has been established must be made on the face of the periodic statement or on its reverse side or on an attached supplementary statement. A notice must direct the buyer to see the reverse side or accompanying statement(s) for important information.

The disclosures must not be separated in any manner that might confuse or mislead the customer or obscure or detract attention from the requisite information.

[¶1828] ANNUAL PERCENTAGE RATE

The annual percentage rate is the actual true cost of the credit to a prospective customer. Actuarial tables are ordinarily used as a means of calculating this figure. To the extent that a loan is discounted, this method will show a higher rate of interest than that normally listed. For revolving charge accounts, the monthly rate is multiplied by the number of time periods used by the creditor in the course of the year. Thus, a $1\,^1/_2\%$ monthly charge on an unpaid balance has an annual percentage rate of 18%.

[¶1829] EXCEPTIONS TO DISCLOSURE REQUIREMENTS

Under the terms of Truth-In-Lending, any individual or business that regularly lends money or otherwise extends credit in which four or more installments may be used to pay back the amount (even if no actual "interest" is charged) is covered by the law. There are, however, certain specific exceptions to the disclosure requirements. These exceptions are discussed in the paragraphs that follow.

[¶1829.1] Homeowners

Second mortgages taken back as part of the purchase price are not subject to Truth-In-Lending disclosure requirements; the seller is deemed not to be a creditor for Regulation Z purposes.

[¶1829.2] Farm Loans

Loans for agricultural purposes ordinarily are involved in the extensions of credit. Because it is often difficult to estimate the annual percentage rate, repayment schedules, or finance charges on seasonal loans, the Federal Reserve Board has made it easier for lenders to comply with the law. Thus, the lender is permitted merely to state those details that are known concerning a farm loan—giving details that are accurate to the extent possible—rather than to estimate either the finance charge, the annual percentage rate, or other required information.

[¶1829.3] Periodic Statements by Mortgage Lenders

Mortgage loans are ordinarily classed as closed-end transactions, i.e., the lender doesn't have to make periodic statements. (Also, in the basic disclosure statement, the mortgage lender is not required to give the total amount financed.) If a mortgagor elects to send statements to the consumer, the disclosure of the annual percentage rate and dates by which payments must be made in order to avoid late charges must then be included.

[¶1829.4] Insurance Premiums

Direct financing of insurance premiums is an exempt transaction—even though insurance companies may levy a service charge on monthly installment payments by the insured. This opinion by the Federal Reserve Board specifically includes the situation where failure to make payments results in the cancellation of the policy. Generally, charges for property or liability insurance, as well as credit life, health, accident, or loss of income insurance written in connection with any credit transaction, must be included in the finance charge. The creditor may exclude insurance premiums from the finance charge only if: (1) insurance coverage is not required by the creditor, and (2) this fact is clearly and conspicuously disclosed in writing to the customer, and (3) any customer desiring this type of insurance coverage gives a separately signed writing (specifically dated) indicating a desire to receive the insurance after having received a written disclosure of the cost of such insurance.

[¶1829.5] Mail Order or Telephone Solicitation

Mail order and telephone solicitation based on a catalog that sets forth a deferred payment schedule (including finance charges) is specifically exempted from Truth-In-Lending disclosure requirements.

[¶1829.6] Add-on Sales

An add-on sale consists of a series of sales from the same vendor in which the deferred payment cost of the purchase price is added on to the outstanding balance contained in the consumer's account. Consumers must approve all terms in writing, and add-on sales are excluded from disclosure requirements only if the vendor takes no security interest in the property.

[¶1829.7] Student Loans

Prior to repayment, full disclosure must be made on the loan agreement. Disclosure need not be made, however, until final papers are prepared.

[¶1829.8] Purchase-Money Mortgages

When a mortgage is taken by an individual who ordinarily is not engaged in the business of extending credit, none of the Truth-In-Lending disclosure requirements is involved. If there is a first mortgage for the purchase of a home, it's ordinarily exempt from disclosure of the total dollar amount of the interest rate (although the percentage rate must always be clearly stated). The most common type of purchase-money mortgage involves two homeowners—one of whom is selling the home to the other for less cash than the actual purchase price. The balance is to be paid over a period of time by the purchaser at a specified credit rate. Ordinarily, this is not covered by federal Truth-In-Lending.

[¶1830] RIGHT OF RESCISSION

Although the Truth-In-Lending law is primarily concerned with disclosures, it does confer an important substantive right on prospective borrowers: the right to rescind a contract within three days if the collateral is a "security interest" in the borrower's home. This does not include first mortgages, purchase-money mortgages, or refinancing of transactions already secured by the borrower's residence (except for higher amounts of credit), but is aimed at situations in which an artisan's lien or mechanic's lien is retained as security. The right of rescission operates as follows:

A borrower has three days to rescind certain mortgage loans following the "date of consummation of the transaction." Under Regulation Z, that date occurs when a "contractual relationship" arises between the creditor and debtor.

A "security interest" is any interest in property that secures payment or performance of any obligation, including security interests under the Uniform Commercial Code; real property mortgages; deeds of trust; other liens whether or not recorded; mechanics', materialmen's, and artisans' liens; vendors' liens in both real and personal property; the interest of a seller in a contract for the sale of real property; any lien on property arising by operation of law; and any interest in a lease when used to secure payment or performance of an obligation.

A "residence" is any property in which the customer resides or expects to reside and includes land on which the customer resides or expects to reside.

The creditor must furnish the customer with two copies of the required notice, printed in boldface type on one side of a separate statement that identifies the transaction to which it relates.

Unless the right of rescission does not apply or the customer has waived or modified his right to rescind until the three-day period has expired, the lender may not:

❏ Disburse any money other than in escrow;
❏ Make any physical changes in customer's property;
❏ Perform any work or service for customer; or
❏ Make any deliveries to the customer's residence.

235

[¶1830.1] Timely Exercise

The right of rescission must be exercised by midnight of the third business day following consummation of the transaction or delivery of the required disclosures, whichever occurs later. Notice of rescission may be given by mail, telegram, or other writing. The creditor's notice of right to rescind can be used, if dated and signed by the customer, to rescind the transaction.

[¶1830.2] Multiple Parties

The right of rescission may be exercised by any one of the joint owners who is a party to the transaction, and the effect of rescission will apply to all the owners.

[¶1830.3] Handling Rescission from Lender's Viewpoint

Local law should be examined to ascertain whether confessions of judgment or cognovit clauses are permitted in transactions of the type governed by Truth-In-Lending. If they are still permitted in your jurisdiction, there is a strong possibility that their very inclusion in an agreement for a second mortgage or other lien on realty would trigger the borrower's exercise of the right of rescission. This would occur if the existence of such a clause results in a lien on the debtor's home without notice. The right of rescission may be sidestepped by setting up a commitment procedure with the object of creating a contract at the very outset.

[¶1830.4] Notice of Right to Rescind

In a transaction subject to rescission, a creditor shall deliver two copies of the notice of the right to rescind to each consumer entitled to rescind. The notice shall be on a separate document that identifies the transaction and shall clearly and conspicuously disclose the following:

(1) The retention or acquisition of a security interest in the consumer's principal dwelling.

(2) The consumer's right to rescind the transaction.

(3) How to exercise the right to rescind, with a form for that purpose, designating the address of the creditor's place of business.

(4) The effects of rescission.

(5) The date the rescission period expires.

[¶1830.5] Transactions to Which Right of Rescission Does Not Apply

Since the right of rescission was created primarily to avoid foreclosure on personal residences for liens not directly connected with homes, the law exempts the following transactions from the exercise of customer's right to rescind:

(a) Creation, retention, or assumption of a first lien or an equivalent security interest to finance acquisition of a dwelling in which a customer resides or expects to reside.

(b) A first lien retained or acquired by a creditor in connection with financing the initial construction of the customer's residence, or a loan committed prior to the completion of construction of the customer's residence to satisfy that construction loan and provide permanent financing.

(c) Any subordinated lien exempt from the right of rescission when originally created.

(d) Any advance for agricultural purposes made under an open-end real estate mortgage or similar lien, provided the disclosure of the right to rescind was made when the security interest was acquired by the creditor or before the first advance was made.

(e) Any transaction in which an agency of a state is a creditor.

[¶1830.6] Judgments

When a judgment is awarded by a court, the recipient is not a creditor, even if the person to whom the judgment is awarded permits satisfaction in more than four installments. Therefore, no Truth-In-Lending compliance is required,even if a charge is imposed for the deferral of the satisfaction.

[¶1830.7] Transactions by Foreign Branches of American Banks

Foreign branches of American banks do not have to comply with Truth-In-Lending requirements to Americans living or visiting abroad, unless the loan was consummated outside the United States for the express purpose of evading the requirements of Truth-In-Lending.

[¶1830.8] Medical Payments

Mere periodic payment for medical services as rendered (when there is no extension of credit) requires no disclosure. Even if services rendered outpace payments, Regulation Z is inapplicable unless more than four scheduled payments to repay the obligation are involved.

[¶1830.9] Certain Loans

Loans payable in four or fewer installments that have no finance charge are exempt under the Truth-In-Lending Act.

[¶1831] SANCTIONS IMPOSED BY TRUTH-IN-LENDING

Civil damages for failure to make proper disclosures are pegged to the finance charges in the contract and may not exceed $1,000. In some instances, damages may be doubled. Erroneous disclosure may be corrected within 15 days of discovery to avoid these sanctions.

On the criminal side, however, fines of up to $5,000 and/or jail terms up to one year may be imposed for willful failure to comply with the law.

There is a one-year statute of limitations on civil suits. Creditors must keep records of compliance open for inspection for two years from the date on which disclosures were required to be made.

Even if a debtor recovers damages against a creditor who has violated the disclosure rules, he is still liable on the principal debt. Noncompliance by the lender does not operate as forgiveness of the debt.

Creditor's Defenses to Civil Suit: The creditor has the burden of proving that a violation was not willful. This means that he must show, by a preponderance of the evidence, that his violation was unintentional and that it was the result of an "honest" error.

[¶1832] ADVERTISING OF CONSUMER CREDIT

The federal Truth-In-Lending law also applies to advertising consumer credit. "Advertising" includes all types of publications, billboards, and radio and television commercials. The law prohibits stating that the advertiser will extend certain terms to buyers unless the advertiser usually and customarily arranges such terms for its customers.

In advertising open-end credit, if one single credit term is advertised, all other credit terms must be included. For example, the retailer cannot advertise "$20 down" for a dinette set and omit the rest of the terms, which might include details such as "balance to be paid in twelve monthly installments of $20 with carrying charges of. . . ."

Moreover, for closed-end credit transactions, the total sum due after adding down payment, installments, and all service charges must be stated, because it is definitely ascertainable beforehand.

Ads that contain no specific terms are still permissible. Thus, you can make one blanket statement, "easy credit terms," without any further amplification. However, if you do state any credit term, then you must include all terms—all or nothing at all.

Advertisers of residential real estate mortgages must comply, but advertisers of purchase-money first mortgages do not have to disclose either the deferred payment price or the sum of the payments.

Exceptions: As is true of other sections of the Truth-In-Lending law, the advertising requirements do not apply to commercial or business credit, securities transactions, transactions over $25,000, credit advanced to governmental units or organizations, or certain transactions involving public utility tariffs. However, transactions with securities salespersons who are not registered with the SEC *do* come within the purview of Truth-In-Lending.

The law specifically exempts media in which credit advertising appears from any liability for circulating false or misleading credit information contained in such advertisements.

[¶1833] RESTRICTIONS ON GARNISHMENT

Title III of the Truth-In-Lending law consists of federal restrictions on garnishment of wages. The amount that can be garnisheed in any single work-week is limited to the lesser of 25% of an employee's disposable income (gross pay minus all deductions required by law) or his disposable income less 30 times the federal minimum hourly wage. The law applies to any business directly or indirectly involved in interstate commerce and thus affects virtually every employer. The law also prevents employers from firing employees merely because their wages have been garnisheed.

When there is a conflict with existing state law, the more stringent of the two prevails. Thus, in a jurisdiction where garnishment is limited to an even lower percentage of wages, the state statute will control.

Creditors' Alternatives: For those creditors who fear an upsurge of uncollectible debt as a result of limitations on garnishment, utilization of confessions of judgment or conventional wage assignments may be a more prudent course. Naturally, the credit rating of the debtor will determine the manner of assuring eventual repayment. An assignment of wages or salary is not the prudent way to deal with sales to highly paid executives or buyers who have substantial liquid or fixed assets.

[¶1834] ANTI-LOAN-SHARKING PROVISIONS

The Act makes it a federal crime to make "extortionate" loans (Title II). A loan transaction is deemed "extortionate" on its face if:

(1) It would be unenforceable at law; and

(2) The rate of interest is more than 45%; and

(3) The debtor knew, or had good reason to believe, at the time the credit was extended, that force or violence might be employed in collecting; and

(4) The debtor owes the creditor a total of more than $100.

Penalties for conviction are fines up to $10,000 and/or imprisonment for up to 20 years.

[¶1835] UNIFORM CONSUMER CREDIT CODE (U3C)

The "state rights" answer to federal Truth-In-Lending is the Uniform Consumer Credit Code, often referred to in convenient shorthand as "U3C." The U3C aims to simplify, clarify, modernize, and codify laws governing retail installment sales, consumer credit, small loans, and usury—but with the following caveat: it only covers those sales (and credit) primarily for personal, family, or household use, or for agricultural purposes. Moreover, the U3C is applicable only if the consumer credit sale involving goods or services, or the consumer lease, or the consumer loan is less than $25,000. One of the more controversial features of the U3C is the elimination of usury ceilings, subject to certain exceptions (such as 18% for ordinary consumer loans, 36% on the first $300 of the unpaid balance for consumer credit sales other than revolving charge, and other variations).

Adoption of the U3C has been considered in 46 states, but in part because Truth-In-Lending is applied in tandem with the U3C unless the Federal Reserve Board grants specific exemption, the U3C is law in only eleven states: Colorado, Idaho, Indiana, Iowa, Kansas, Maine, Oklahoma, S. Carolina, Utah, Wisconsin, Wyoming.

[¶1836] SIGNIFICANCE FOR THE PRACTITIONER

Counsel for banks, retail merchants, small loan companies, medical groups, and artisans will have to review all installment agreements and scrutinize all advertising copy to insure full compliance. The paperwork may seem astronomical at first, but there are many standard forms available.

As counsel on the other side of the fence—consumer advocate—naturally more questions about dubious practices and outright violations by lenders and sellers will arise. Remember that only the structure of the contract is covered by the federal law. Interest rates suspect as usury still are the province of local or state law. Be cognizant of consumers' civil remedies.

Other Statutory Considerations: When considering the total interest rate and all other finance charges, be certain to check local laws to guard against possible usury that would invalidate a transaction.

Also check to make sure a jurisdiction has not enacted its own version of the Uniform Consumer Credit Code or National Consumer Act that might affect the mode of making required disclosures under the federal act.

[¶1837] EQUAL CREDIT OPPORTUNITY

Discrimination against applicants in credit transactions is prohibited by the Equal Credit Opportunity Act. Under ECOA, creditors are prohibited from asking applicants certain questions or from even using what is termed "credit scoring" techniques. Under the law, creditors are prohibited from making oral or written statements in advertising or elsewhere that might have the effect of discouraging someone from applying for credit. Moreover, creditors are not permitted to use race, national origin, sex, marital status, or age for credit scoring purposes. Nor may a creditor discriminate against an applicant solely because his income derives from a public assistance program. Also, creditors may not inquire about marital status (except in community property states or where a "necessaries" doctrine is applicable). Inquiry concerning a spouse or former spouse is also prohibited conduct unless the spouse would be contractually liable (as in a jurisdiction where the husband is liable for his wife's necessaries), the applicant is relying upon a spouse's income, the spouse will be permitted to use the account, or the applicant relies on alimony or child support as the basis for repayment of the credit requested. Otherwise, a creditor may not inquire about alimony or child support payments unless the application states conspicuously that this information need not be revealed.

[¶1837.1] Action on an Application

The Equal Credit Opportunity Act requires creditors to inform applicants of the action that has been taken on a credit application within 30 days after the creditor has received the completed application. If there has been adverse action, the creditor must either (a) state the reasons in writing, or (b) notify the applicant in writing of the adverse action, and state that the applicant has a right to know why, including the identity of the person or office that the applicant may contact to learn why the adverse action was taken.

Creditors can make notification orally if they didn't receive more than 150 applications the previous year.

The Act defines "adverse action" as a denial or revocation of credit, a change in terms of an existing credit agreement, or a refusal to grant credit substantially in the same amount or on the same terms as requested in the application. Adverse action does not include a refusal to extend additional credit under an existing agreement to applicants who are delinquent, or if the additional credit would exceed a previously established limit.

[¶1837.2] Enforcement and Liability

The federal regulations that administer the other sections of Truth-In-Lending also have responsibility for enforcing Equal Credit Opportunity Compliance. (See ¶1815 for a complete listing.)

Regulation B (12 CFR part 202), promulgated by the Federal Reserve Board, comprises Regulations to enforce the Act. Under Regulation B, model application forms have been issued. However, use of these forms is not required, as long as the creditor does not request prohibited information. Also, a creditor is free to delete any information requests, or rearrange the format without modifying substance. Regulation B also makes it clear that a creditor does not have to use a written application form at all.

A creditor who violates any provisions of the Act of Regulation B may be subject to civil liability of up to $10,000 in punitive damages, plus any amount of actual damages. However, in a class action, liability may not exceed the lesser of $500,000 or 1% of the creditor's net worth, in addition to court costs and attorneys' fees.

[¶1838] CONSUMER LEASES

Regulation M is designed to insure meaningful disclosure of personal property leases undertaken by consumers. Moreover, it is designed to limit the use of "balloon payments" in consumer leasing. It has five basic parts. First is a section requiring full disclosure of all material terms to a lease before the final lease agreement is signed. Second is a limitation on the consumer's liability following the expiration or termination of a lease. The content of advertisements relating to consumer lease transactions is regulated by a third section. A fourth section permits lawsuits by consumers who have been harmed by a failure to comply with its requirements. If the lessor takes a consumer to court on a consumer leasing transaction, the lessor must pay the consumer's attorney's fees, unless the lessor can prove that excess liability resulted from unreasonable wear-and-tear or other major physical damage (Truth-In-Lending Act Section 183(a)). Finally, a fifth section is provided to indicate that new regulations do not either alter, annul, affect, or exempt any individual from complying with state law on consumer leases,except to the extent that the state law is inconsistent with federal law or regulation.

By regulation, the Federal Reserve Board may exempt from requirements of Regulation M any class of lease transactions within any state if it determines that that class of transaction is subject to requirements "substantially similar" to those of the federal Regulation. Federal law does not alter, annul, or otherwise affect state law, except to the extent of laws that are inconsistent with federal provisions.

[¶1839] PERSONAL PROPERTY LEASED FOR PERSONAL, FAMILY, OR HOUSEHOLD PURPOSES

Personal property that is leased for personal, family, or household purposes is covered under Regulation M. Leases having a total contractual obligation of more than $25,000 or extending for a period of less than four months are not covered under the Act.

[¶1840] DISCLOSURE PROVISIONS FOR CONSUMER LEASES

Mandatory disclosures must be made in writing and given to a consumer covered by the Consumer Leasing Act before the lease transaction is consummated. Federal Trade Commission rules permit imprecise amounts or other information not known when the lease is signed to be estimated, provided that the leasing party informs the consumer of that fact in the disclosure statement.

A checklist is provided in Regulation M, 12 CFR §213.2(a); 213.4(g). This indicates the basic requirements for disclosure that must be included in every consumer leasing transaction covered by the Act. The Federal Reserve Board has summarized the major required disclosures as the following:

(1) A brief description of the leased property adequate to identify it to both parties to the lease.

(2) The total amount of any payment or payments the lessee is to pay at the consummation of the lease, such as a refundable security deposit, advance payment, or the like.

(3) The number, amount, and due dates of periodic payments and their total.

(4) The total amount of taxes, fees, and other charges involved.

(5) Identification of those responsible for maintaining or servicing the leased property.

(6) How any penalty or delinquency charge will be determined, and the amount.

(7) A statement of whether the lessee has an option to purchase the property at the end of the lease term, or earlier, and at what price.

(8) A statement of the conditions under which either party to the lease may terminate it, and how any penalty or other charge will be determined.

(9) A statement that the lessee is responsible for the difference between the estimated value of the property leased and its realized value at the end of the lease or upon earlier termination, if such liability exists.

(10) A statement that in an open-end lease the lessee may obtain a professional appraisal of the property by an independent third party at the end of the lease or on earlier termination, and that this appraisal will be binding.

(11) When the lessee's liability at the end of the lease term is based on the estimated value of the property: A statement of the value of the property at the consummation of the lease, the itemized total lease obligation at the end of the lease, and the difference between them.

[¶1841] LIMITATIONS ON CONSUMER LIABILITY ON A LEASE

When a consumer's lease for personal property is either terminated or expires and the terms of the lease make the consumer responsible for making a payment to the lessor based on the estimated residual value of the property, the liability of the consumer is limited by Regulation M. Penalty charges in the amount of the actual harm caused by a delinquency, default, or early termination are recoverable; however, all penalty charges are limited by amounts that are reasonable in light of the anticipated or actual harm caused by the consumer's action. The law creates a rebuttable presumption that the lessor's estimation of the residual value of goods leased by a consumer is unreasonable if the estimated residual value exceeds three times one monthly payment. Any amount in excess of that sum can only be recovered from the consumer if the lessor undertakes legal action.

[¶1842] ADVERTISING CONSUMER LEASES

Full disclosure of all material parts of a lease transaction are required if an advertisement states the amount of any payment, the numbers of required payments, or that no down payment or any payment is required at the inception of the lease. The disclosures must include: the transaction advertised is in fact a lease; the amount of any down payments; number, amounts, due dates, or periods of scheduled payments; the total number of payments; the total amount of payments; and an explanation of any liability that a consumer may have at the end of the term of the lease. The employees or personnel of any medium in which an advertisement appears, or through which it is disseminated, have no liability under the Consumer Lease Advertising Section of the law (§184(b)).

[¶1843] FAIR CREDIT REPORTING

Federal regulation of the consumer reporting industry, under the provisions of the Fair Credit Reporting Act (15 USC §1581–1681T), is aimed at insuring that consumer reporting agencies exercise their responsibilities with fairness, impartiality, and respect for the consumer's right to privacy. The law specifically requires consumer reporting agencies to adopt reasonable procedures for providing information to credit grantors, insurers, employers, and others in a manner both fair and equitable to the consumer regarding confidentiality, accuracy, and proper use of such information. Except to the extent that they are inconsistent with or less stringent than federal law, state laws on credit reporting are valid.

Regulation of consumer reporting agencies by placing obligatory disclosure requirements on users of consumer reports is the primary purpose of fair credit reporting. Under the law, users of consumer reports must inform consumers when an adverse action (defined as a denial of credit, insurance, or employment) is made on the basis of any such report, and the user must identify the reporting agency that undertook the initial examination of the consumer.

Businesses that collect their own information are not affected by the statutory code of conduct for the consumer reporting industry, which is generally defined as credit bureaus, investigative reporting companies, and other organizations whose primary business is the gathering and reporting of information about consumers for the use of others. Additionally, information that is reported by one business to another is not considered to be a consumer report when that information relates to the company's own experience with the consumer. For example, a company could state "my records reflect that Mr. Smith was late on 8 of 12 payments," and the report would not be covered by the legislation. However, a businessman who regularly reports information that is not based on his personal knowledge has made a consumer report within the meaning of the Fair Credit Reporting Act. The Federal Trade Commission cites as an example a statement by a businessman: "I have no file on Mr. Smith, but I know that he has a poor record of payment at the bank."

Consumer reports do not necessarily have to contain derogatory information. Any information—whether good or bad, oral or in writing—that bears on a consumer's creditworthiness, credit standing, credit capacity, character, personal characteristics, mode of living, or reputation is considered a consumer report if it is either (a) used or expected to be used or (b) collected in whole or in part for the purpose of considering the consumer's eligibility for consumer credit, insurance, employment, or other related business purpose.

[¶1844] SUMMARY OF CONSUMER RIGHTS CREATED BY THE FAIR CREDIT REPORTING ACT

The Fair Credit Reporting Act (Title VII of the Truth-In-Lending Act) provides that when a consumer is rejected for credit, insurance, or employment, he must be given the name and address of the appropriate consumer reporting agency at the time of the denial. This is designed to make a consumer aware of any adverse information so that misinformation in the consumer's file may be corrected. If credit is denied based on information from a source other than the consumer reporting agency, the creditor must, at the time of such action, inform the consumer of his or her right to request the nature of the information within 60 days.

[¶1844.1] Access to Information and Credit File

Whether or not an adverse action has been taken a consumer does have the right of access to learn the nature and substance of information in the file of a consumer reporting agency. With the exception of medical information and sources of investigative information that can only be obtained through discovery procedures of a court, all information in the file is available to the consumer. The Federal Trade Commission states that "nature and substance of all information" means only that an individual need not be permitted to physically handle his file or receive a copy of the file, although the Act does not prohibit this.

[¶1844.2] Sources and Recipients of Information

Other than investigative sources, the consumer has the right to be told the sources of information for data in the file of a consumer reporting agency. The consumer also has the right to know to whom the report has been sent, in the prior two years if the report was made for employment purposes, and in the prior six months if made for any other purpose.

[¶1844.3] Reinvestigation of Disputed Entries

Consumer reporting agencies are required to reinvestigate disputed items of information and correct those found to be inaccurate. Unverified or inaccurate information must be deleted from the report of a consumer. If the dispute is not resolved, the existence of the dispute must be noted in the consumer's file and a brief, concise statement of the consumer's version of the dispute must also be included if the consumer desires.

[¶1844.4] Credit Report of Consumer Reporting Agency

General requirements under the Fair Credit Reporting Act are that agencies provide only those reports requested that bear a reasonable and legitimate business purpose, and that they maintain "reasonable procedures" to assure that report recipients are authorized to receive them. Moreover, the reporting agencies must make sure that the reports do not contain obsolete information.

[¶1844.5] Obsolete Data—Elimination

If adverse information of public record (such as lawsuits, tax liens, arrests, indictments, convictions, bankruptcies, or judgments) is reported, the agency must follow one of two procedures: it must indicate to the consumer that the information is being reported to a potential employer, or it must maintain strict procedures to verify the current status of information of public record. The general rule under the law is that information may not be reported if older than 7 years—although bankruptcy going back 10 years may be reported; suits and judgments are governed by the 7-year rule or the statute of limitations, whichever is the longer period. Such information must be excluded from consumer reports, unless the present transaction involves credit or life insurance in the amount of $50,000 or more, or employment at an annual salary of $20,000 or more.

[¶1844.6] Obtaining Information Under False Pretenses

An individual who obtains information from a consumer reporting agency under false pretenses is liable for criminal penalties, and a consumer reporting agency may be liable for providing information to someone unauthorized to receive it.

[¶1845] ENFORCEMENT OF CONSUMER REPORTING ACT

Consumers are permitted to bring civil suit for willful noncompliance with the Act; there is no ceiling on the amount of punitive damages they may receive. The consumer is also permitted to sue for negligent noncompliance in the amount of the actual damages sustained plus attorneys' fees. A two-year statute of limitations applies in civil suits under the Fair Credit Reporting Act. However, if the consumer reporting agency has willfully misrepresented information that must be disclosed under the law (and the information is material to the establishment of the liability of the consumer reporting agency), the statute of limitations does not begin to run until the discovery of the misrepresentation. Suits may be brought in any United States District Court without regard to the amount in controversy or in any other court of competent jurisdiction.

In addition to consumer enforcement, the following federal agencies have jurisdiction over Fair Credit Reporting violations, and may also issue regulations:

- ❏ Department of Agriculture;
- ❏ Civil Aeronautics Board;
- ❏ Comptroller of the Currency;
- ❏ Federal Deposit Insurance Corporation;
- ❏ Federal Home Loan Bank Board;
- ❏ Federal Reserve Board;
- ❏ Federal Trade Commission;
- ❏ Interstate Commerce Commission;
- ❏ National Credit Union Administration.

[¶1846] DEFAMATION

Suppliers of information, users of information, and consumer reporting agencies are not subject to civil action for defamation or invasion of privacy based on information disclosed to a consumer pursuant to the Act unless the information is false or furnished with malice or willful intent to injure the consumer, or there is negligent noncompliance with the Act. If the consumer learns that the information is in the files independently of disclosure by the agency, the defamation action may be brought.

[¶1847] FORMAL FTC INTERPRETATIONS UNDER FAIR CREDIT REPORTING

Following are some FTC interpretations of specific areas under the Fair Credit Reporting Act from the Code of Federal Regulations.

[¶1847.1] Credit Guides

Guides published by credit bureaus and leased on an annual basis to credit grantors that rate how a consumer pays various bills are viewed by the Federal Trade Commission as "a series of consumer reports, since they contain information which is used for the purpose of serving as a factor in establishing the consumer's eligibility for credit." The FTC believes that publication or distribution of these credit guides violates the Fair Credit Reporting Act. Its interpretation clearly pro-scribes credit guides in their present form—although it does not preclude a con-sumer reporting agency's furnishing information that is coded so that the con-sumer's identity is not disclosed, since the information is not a consumer report until decoded. The FTC suggests that using unique identification devices such as Social Security numbers, driver's license numbers, or bank account numbers would provide adequate coding.

[¶1847.2]   Protective Bulletins

Lists of consumers who have issued worthless checks or who for other rea-sons appear not to be creditworthy are frequently distributed by trade associations and other organizations. Distributions of such lists and bulletins are restricted under the Fair Credit Reporting Act.

The FTC states that restrictions against distribution of protective bulletins do not apply to those limited to a series of descriptions (usually accompanied by pho-tographs) of individuals who are being sought by law enforcement authorities. The FTC notes that these descriptions are usually accompanied by statements such as "Information as to further activities, location, or arrest of any of the following per-sons should be communicated to police authorities named in the warnings." While the FTC holds that bulletins are not consumer reports, it does state that information of this type can only be distributed "to credit grantors and others who have specif-ic legitimate business need for information" about individuals in connection with an application for credit, insurance, employment, or similar business transactions.

[¶1847.3]   Loan Exchanges

Local consumer finance companies may own and operate loan exchanges; members may be required to furnish to the exchange the full identity and loan amount of each borrower. This is covered under the Fair Credit Reporting Act.

[¶1847.4]   Reports Relating to Motor Vehicles

Reports of various state Departments of Motor Vehicles that generally reveal a consumer's entire driving record (including arrests for speeding, drunk driving, and involuntary manslaughter) are commonly used by insurance companies and others desiring information that bears on the personal characteristics of the con-sumer. Under Fair Credit Reporting, the users (i.e., insurance companies) are required to identify the Motor Vehicle Department as the source of the report if it is used as a factor in denying, cancelling, or increasing the cost of insurance. In turn, the Motor Vehicle Department is required to disclose the "nature and substance" of the consumer's motor vehicle record when requested to do so by the consumer. Moreover, reinvestigation is required if the consumer so requests.

[¶1847.5] Governmental News of Consumer Reports

Governmental agencies are entitled to receive consumer reports on credit; for insurance to be used primarily for personal, family, or household purposes; or for employment purposes; or if the government is required by law to consider a consumer's financial responsibility or status before granting a license or other particular benefit. However, if the governmental agency is not able to demonstrate its need for the consumer reports, the consumer reporting agency is not permitted to release them (*Hoke v. Retail Credit,* CA-4, 521 F.2d 1079, 1975, *cert. den.* 423 US 1087, 1976).

[¶1848] THE FAIR DEBT COLLECTION PRACTICES ACT

The Fair Debt Collection Practices Act (Truth-In-Lending §801–817) regulates creditors' collection tactics when the debtor is a consumer. Not every consumer debt is covered by the Act: the obligation to pay must arise out of a transaction in which the money, property, insurance, or services financed are primarily for personal, family, or household purposes. Therefore, a business loan would be excluded from the law's coverage.

Nor is every creditor attempting to collect a debt covered. Basically, you must be in the business of collecting debts to fall within the Act's definition of "debt collector." The Act also lists the following specific exemptions from that definition:

❒ Officers, employees, or agents of a creditor who act within the scope of employment while trying to collect a debt.

❒ Individuals acting as debt collectors for another person, if that person's business is not primarily the collection of debt.

❒ Officers or employees of the United States or any state, to the extent that the collection or attempted collection is within the scope of the performance of official duties.

❒ Individuals serving (or attempting to serve) legal process in connection with the judicial enforcement of a debt.

❒ Nonprofit organizations, acting at the request of a consumer that counsels consumers and assists them in debt liquidation.

❒ Any person attempting to collect a debt that is incidental to a fiduciary obligation or escrow arrangement.

An attorneys' fee award under the FDCPA can be made at the market rate instead of the actual cost of litigating the case, even if the attorney works for a union's prepaid legal services plan.[7] The theory is that the legal services plan and the union are separate enough entities that the award would not constitute a windfall to the union.

[¶1849] PROHIBITED CONDUCT UNDER THE FAIR DEBT COLLECTION PRACTICES ACT

The Fair Debt Collection Practices Act regulates the manner in which a debt collector may communicate with a debtor, and prohibits harassment, making misleading statements, and engaging in unfair collection practices, as defined by the Act. These subjects are treated in detail in the material that follows.

Communication with a Consumer-Debtor: A debt collector who is covered by the Fair Debt Collection Practices Act is restricted in communicating with a consumer-debtor. Absent the consumer's prior consent or express judicial permission, a debt collector may not communicate with a consumer in connection with the collection of any debt:

❏ At any unusual time or place.

❏ At any time or place that is "inconvenient" to the consumer.

❏ If the debt collector knows that the consumer is represented by an attorney and the name and address of the attorney is either available or readily ascertainable.

❏ At the debtor's place of employment (unless permitted by the employer).

❏ If the consumer gives the debt collector written notice that he refuses to pay the debt or wishes the debt collector to stop all communications, except to:

> (1) Inform the consumer that debt collection efforts are being terminated;

> (2) Notify the consumer that the debt collector or creditor may seek certain judicial remedies.

❏ Nor can a collector communicate with any third party regarding the debtor, other than the debtor's lawyer or a consumer reporting agency, unless given consent by the debtor, or a court of law.

Harassment and Abuse: Debt collectors may not resort to harassment or abusive tactics while trying to collect a debt. In addition the Act lists conduct that is absolutely prohibited:

❏ Use or threat of violence that could harm the person, property, or reputation of any individual (as opposed to the debtor alone).

❏ Use of obscene, profane, or abusive language to the debtor.

❏ Publication of a list of consumers who allegedly don't pay their debts (except to consumer reporting agencies or to persons covered by Section 603(f) or 604(3) of Truth-In-Lending).

❏ Advertising for sale any debt to coerce its payment.

❏ Making anonymous telephone calls to the debtor.

❏ Making continuous or repeated telephone calls to the debtor.

False or Misleading Statements: A debt collector may not make false or misleading representations concerning:

❏ Character, amount, or legal status of a debt.

❏ Compensation the debt collector receives.

❏ Professional status of the debt collector (such as claiming to be a lawyer).

❏ Taking legal action that is actually illegal.

❏ Crimes resulting from failure to pay a debt.

❏ Status of documents, including those purporting to be of a court or an agency of the United States, or any state.

❏ Turning accounts over to an innocent purchaser for value.

❏ Name of the debt collection agency or business.

❏ Status of legal documents received by the consumer (so as to deceive him into thinking he doesn't have to answer in court).

❏ Relations between the debt collector and a consumer reporting agency.

❏ Communicating credit information that is known to be false.

Unfair Practices: The following conduct violates the Unfair Practices Section of the Act:

❏ Collecting any money that is neither expressly authorized by the credit agreement nor otherwise permitted by law.

❏ Accepting a check postdated by more than five days, unless the debt collector gives written notice that he intends to deposit it within 3–10 days.

❏ Soliciting a postdated check with the intention of using bad check laws or creating a possibility of criminal fraud prosecution.

❏ Causing the accrual of charges to the consumer without disclosing their nature in advance (such as collect telephone calls).

❏ Threatening nonjudicial action against property in which there is no security interest, or if there is actually no intention to repossess the property, or if repossession would be illegal.

❏ Using a symbol other than the debt collector's address on an envelope used to communicate with the debtor, except that the debt collector's name may be used if it doesn't reveal the nature of its business.

— ENDNOTES —

1. Greenwood Trust Co. v. Massachusetts, 971 F.2d 818 (1st Cir. 8/6/92), cert.denied 113 S.Ct. 974.

2. SCFL ILC Inc. v. Visa USA Inc., 819 F.Supp. 956 (D.Utah 4/1/93).

3. Jackson v. Grant, 876 F.2d 764 (9th Cir. 5/31/89).

4. Currie v. Diamond Mortgage Corp., 57 LW 2374 (7th Cir. 10/19/88).

5. Smith v. Fidelity Consumer Discount Co., 898 F.2d 907 (3d Cir. 6/27/89).

6. Smith v. Fidelity Consumer Discount Co., 898 F.2d 907 (3d Cir. 1990).

7. Hollis v. Roberts, 984 F.2d 1159 (11th Cir. 3/3/93).

— FOR FURTHER REFERENCE —

Ahrens, Jane E., "Truth in Lending and Equal Credit Opportunity Commentaries: 1991 Update," 45 *Consumer Finance L.Q.* 362 (Fall '91).

Bryan W., "Extraordinary Collection Procedures," 6 *Utah Bar J.* 12 (August–September '93).

Cammarn, Scott A., "Prescreening Revisited: Is the FTC's Firm Offer of Credit Requirement Supported by the Fair Credit Reporting Act?" 45 *Consumer Finance L. Q.* 365 (Fall '91).

McCurnin, Thomas E., "Pre-Judgment Writs of Possession: Effective Claim and Delivery of Personal Property," 14 *Los Angeles Lawyer* 36 (October '91).

Tomkins, Michael C., "Interstate Consumer Credit Transactions," 47 *Consumer Finance L.Q. Report* 105 (Spring '93).

Will, Linda, "The Widening Door to Private Data: Personal Information Database Explosion." 12 *Legal Information Alert 1* (May '93).

CRIMINAL LAW AND PROCEDURE

[¶1901] For young law students, reared on a steady diet of television courtroom dramas, one of the greatest disappointments is the realization of the nature of criminal practice. No defense attorney can rely on a steady succession of martyred innocents as clients. The criminal lawyer's work consists more of plea-bargaining than of trials; and preparation for a trial consists not of finding the real murderer, but of carefully reviewing the client's arrest and detention for improprieties and the prosecution's evidence for potentially exculpatory material.

The prosecution's task is to prove the allegations against the defendant beyond a reasonable doubt; the defense's job is to demonstrate the existence of reasonable doubt.

Most criminal law involves felonies and misdemeanors. They include the two elements of *actus reus* (the guilty act) and *mens rea* (the guilty mind).

[¶1902] ELEMENTS OF OFFENSES

One of the prosecution's burdens is to charge the defendant with the appropriate offenses. Conversely, the defense can prevail by showing that one or more of the elements of the crime(s) charged has not been proven beyond a reasonable doubt. This discussion is general in nature: it is important to review your jurisdiction's criminal or penal code. For instance, if your client is charged with first degree burglary in a jurisdiction that requires that a first degree burglary be committed in the nighttime, and the accusatory instrument recites that the crime took place at noon, it will be impossible for the prosecution to make the case.

In a sharply split 1994 decision, the Supreme Court again limited the financial punishments that governments may use against drug dealers. The Court ruled 5-4 that states may not impose drug-possession "taxes" on people who have already been criminally prosecuted. The High Court struck down a Montana tax and thus cast doubt on the legality of similar laws in at least 22 other states. The majority stated that Montana's tax violated the Fifth Amendment's protection against "double jeopardy." The decision marks the first time the high court ever struck down a tax on double-jeopardy grounds.[1]

In mid-1991, the Supreme Court ruled[2] that the First Amendment is not violated by the enforcement of a law banning commercial nude dancing as public indecency even if all patrons are consenting adults.

An Ohio city ordinance created a misdemeanor of "loitering under circumstances manifesting the purpose to engage in drug-related activity"; the statute was struck down as unconstitutionally vague. No intent to sell drugs had to be shown, and merely being in a drug area or fleeing the police was criminalized.[3]

Federal penalties are imposed under 18 USC Section 924(c)(1) for "use" of a firearm in a drug-related crime. The Supreme Court decided in 1993 that this is broad enough to encompass non-weapon uses of a firearm, in a case where the defendant had traded a gun for some cocaine and the trading partner turned out to be an undercover police officer.[4]

[¶1902.1] Elements of the Crime of Murder

Although terminology varies from place to place, there are four broad categories of homicide that can be penalized as murder:

➤ "Intent to kill" murder.

➤ Homicide occurring in the context of an intent to do serious bodily injury.

➤ "Depraved heart" murder—that is, negligence or recklessness so extreme as to evidence a depraved heart.

➤ Felony murder—a death occurring in the commission of a felony. A participant in a felony can be guilty of felony murder even if the victim was a bystander; and even if he or she was killed by a police bullet rather than by direct action of the felons.

However, if there are several participants in a felony (e.g., four men engaged in burglarizing a warehouse), a defense may be available for participants other than the "triggerman"—if they did not solicit the death of the victim; were not themselves armed; had no reason to believe that a co-participant was armed or likely to kill or cause serious injury to anyone.

[¶1902.2] Elements of Manslaughter

Manslaughter is culpable homicide under circumstances not amounting to murder. Voluntary manslaughter is usually defined as an intentional homicide under circumstances that offer mitigation but not a legal excuse; for instance, under provocation that would cause a reasonable person to lose self-control, and committed before there is a chance to cool off.

Under appropriate circumstances of negligence, involuntary manslaughters may also be criminal; for instance, when a corporation creates a dangerous situation for its workers, or when an intoxicated driver kills another driver or a pedestrian.

[¶1902.3] Elements of Sex Offenses

At common law, the offense of forcible rape could only be committed by a man, and only against a woman other than his wife. The offense of statutory rape involved a male perpetrator and a female victim younger than the age of consent.

Although some criminal codes today retain those definitions, many codes have been changed, typically to penalize unconsented sexual contact committed by any person either against the will of the victim or against a person incapable of consent (e.g., under-age, mentally incapacitated, unconscious).

The severity of the contact, and its circumstances, go to the degree of the offense. Some jurisdictions criminalize marital rape, either by statute or case law; in others, it is a defense that the couple is married or married and cohabiting (in this latter group of jurisdictions, rape of a separated spouse would be criminal although rape of a cohabiting spouse would not be).

[¶1902.4] Elements of Larceny Offenses

Larceny is taking the property of another without the owner's consent. The various larceny offenses differ in the means of taking; whether or not force is involved; and the type and amount of property taken. As mentioned above, it is worthwhile for the defense attorney to scrutinize the accusatory instrument carefully; sloppy drafting errors that can redound to the benefit of the defendant are not uncommon.

[¶1902.5] Elements of Drug Offenses

The various jurisdictions criminalize the possession, possession with intent to sell, and sale of various "controlled substances." It's important to find out if the substances seized are in fact on the list of illegal substances. The test report may be exculpatory to the defendant; or the substance itself may be lost en route to the test, or after the test, leaving the prosecution without admissible evidence.

The success or failure of the defense case can turn on the amount of substance involved, so this should be scrutinized. Drug cases frequently involve "sting operations" or arrests after a police officer has purchased substances purported to be illegal drugs. The defense attorney should be alert to the possibility of an entrapment defense, and the possibility that the seizure of the alleged controlled substances was defective under Constitutional standards.

[¶1902.6] RICO

The Racketeer Influenced and Corrupt Organizations Act (RICO)[5] is a highly controversial piece of federal legislation that has given rise to a tremendous amount of litigation. Originally intended, as the name indicates, as a powerful weapon against organized crime, RICO is so broadly drafted that it permits individuals charging a wide range of economic and tort offenses against individuals and legitimate businesses to add a RICO claim to their federal complaints. The limitation "federal" is important: civil RICO claims are under exclusive jurisdiction of the federal district courts, and there is no concurrent state jurisdiction.[6]

Paradoxically, however, it has been held that the United States is not a "person" who can bring a RICO action for treble damages and an organized crime family is not a "person" that can properly be named as a RICO defendant.[7]

RICO imposes civil and criminal penalties on those who engage in a "pattern of racketeering activity" which gives courts the unenviable task of defining both "racketeering activity" and "pattern." There must be at least two "predicate acts" of racketeering activity; the pattern derives from the relationship between the acts and the threat of continuing activity.[8]

Under common-law agency principles, a corporation is vicariously liable for RICO violations committed by its agents.[9]

In the civil context, courts have been more likely to find that the alleged RICO activity did not form a pattern, because the activity was concentrated in duration and had only a single or limited goal rather than an ongoing, open-ended enterprise.[10]

It is necessary to participate in the operation or management of the enterprise to be liable under RICO, so an accounting firm cannot be RICO-liable merely because it failed to inform the Board of Directors of an audited company that a key asset should have been reported at its fair market value. (The case arose when a bankruptcy trustee attempted to make the accounting firm liable to the noteholders of a bankrupt corporation.).[11]

[¶1903] CRIMINAL LIABILITY OF PARTIES TO AN OFFENSE

Frequently, defendants are charged with participating in criminal activities in some role other than as sole culprit. In criminal law, a conspiracy is an agreement between two or more people to achieve an unlawful objective, or to use unlawful means to attain a lawful end. For example, although it is legal for an unhappily married person to obtain a divorce, it is illegal to hire a thug to frighten a spouse into consenting to an unfair settlement. Conspiracy itself is a crime, even if the crime which the conspiracy underlies is never committed. The line between conspiracy to commit a crime and attempting the crime can be an intellectually tenuous one. Even if a person requested to participate in a crime refuses to do so, the requester is guilty of solicitation to commit a crime. The Supreme Court has unanimously ruled that conspiring to commit a narcotics crime can be a violation of Federal law even if the conspiracy is never carried out.[12]

An accessory before the fact aids and abets a felony (e.g., by ordering or encouraging it)—but is not present when the felony is committed. An accessory after the fact aids in concealing a crime or in the perpetrators' escape from detection. An accomplice is actually present and participating in the crime. Some criminal codes hold accessories culpable to the same degree as principals in a crime; others require the conviction of the principals before the accessories can be convicted. However, the Model Penal Code treats accessories and accomplices on the same footing.

It is a defense if an accessory or accomplice withdraws from the criminal conspiracy. However, for this purpose, withdrawal requires more than merely ceasing to participate in the criminal transaction. The person seeking to defend by showing withdrawal must repudiate the conspiracy before the chain of events leading to a crime becomes unstoppable. Even repudiation isn't enough; the person withdrawing must take all possible steps to countermand the chain of events leading to the crime.

[¶1904] DEFENSES TO CRIMINAL CHARGES

Sometimes the defense strategy is to show that the prosecution has not met its burden of proof beyond a reasonable doubt as to the events charged and the allegedly unlawful conduct of the defendant. At other times, it is admitted that the defendant in fact performed the actions ascribed to him or her, but that there are factors amounting to a defense (that is, removing criminal culpability from these actions).

[¶1904.1] Necessity

The *necessity* defense admits that the defendant did engage in conduct that violates the literal terms of a criminal statute, but that the conduct avoided an immediate harm more serious than the harm that the criminal statute sought to prevent. For example, a person might drive under the influence of alcohol, if he were the only person who could arrive in time to prevent the explosion of a bomb.

[¶1904.2] Duress

This defense, also known as the defense of *compulsion or coercion* is applicable when an individual commits a crime when under an unlawful threat of imminent death or serious bodily injury to himself or others: for instance, when a person takes money from his or her employer's vault because his or her child has been kidnapped. However, duress will not constitute a defense to a charge of killing an innocent third party.

[¶1904.3] Entrapment

The defense of entrapment applies when an offense that would not otherwise have occurred is induced by a government agent and committed by a person not otherwise predisposed to commit the offense; e.g., when a college student is asked to buy drugs from a known or suspected drug dealer, by a purported college student who is actually an undercover police officer. However, the defense attorney must be very cautious about raising the defense of entrapment, because raising it gives the prosecution a great deal of leeway to introduce damaging (and often otherwise inadmissible) information about the defendant in order to show that he or she actually is predisposed to commit similar offenses.

[¶1904.4] Self-Defense

An individual who is not the aggressor in a violent situation is permitted to use a reasonable amount of force, given a reasonable belief that he or she is in imminent danger of unlawful bodily harm which cannot be averted without force. However, it is never considered reasonable to use deadly force (defined as force used with the intent or substantial risk of causing death or serious bodily injury to its recipient) to rebut a threat of nondeadly force.

Depending on the jurisdiction and the circumstances, there may be an obligation to retreat instead of defending oneself forcibly. However, the general rule is that retreat will not be required in a person's home or place of business.

[¶1904.5] Insanity

Insanity is a legal term related to, but by no means identical to, the psychological concept of mental illness. The prevailing test of insanity is the so-called "M'Naghten Rule": that, when the crime charged was committed, the defendant suffered from mental disease that prevented him from understanding the nature and quality of the act committed, or at least from understanding that it was wrong. Under this test, a person can be legally sane despite extremely severe mental pathology.

The Model Penal Code's formulation is different: it defines insanity as a mental disease or defect that causes the defendant to lack the substantial capacity either to understand the criminal nature of his conduct, or to conform his conduct to the requirements of the law.

The insanity defense can be used in two ways. If adjudged not competent to stand trial, the defendant will be institutionalized until he or she recovers the capacity to understand the criminal proceedings and participate in his or her own defense. If the defendant is competent to stand trial, the insanity defense can be raised at trial.

Most defenses are raised with the intention of eliminating all culpability of the defendant, in order to secure an acquittal. However, the objective when the insanity defense is raised is a special finding (usually referred to as "not guilty by reason of insanity"); the normal consequence of this finding is the institutionalization of the defendant.

Some jurisdictions permit a verdict of "guilty but mentally ill" (GBMI). If this verdict is rendered, the defendant is convicted of the charges, and is sentenced like any other convicted defendant. However, he or she will receive a psychiatric examination before sentencing; if it is determined that treatment is needed, part or all of the sentence will be served at a mental health facility rather than in a prison.

Some jurisdictions permit a defense of partial responsibility (also known as "diminished capacity," nicknamed "dim cap"), for the defendant who is mentally abnormal but not insane; for instance, one who is incapable of premeditation or deliberation. If the dim cap defense is successful, it is unlikely to result in acquittal; the usual outcome is a conviction on a lesser charge than that originally stated.

In cases in which the insanity defense will be raised, the defendant will probably be required to file notice of intent to use the defense by a specified time before the trial.

The general rule is that everyone is presumed sane; therefore, the burden of going forward on the issue of insanity belongs to the defense, which must introduce evidence creating a reasonable doubt of the defendant's sanity. The burden of persuasion (the task of convincing the jury) depends on the jurisdiction. In some, the defense must prove insanity by a preponderance of the evidence; others force the prosecution to prove sanity beyond a reasonable doubt.

Under *Ake v. Oklahoma,* 105 S.Ct. 1087 (1985), a defendant asserting an insanity defense is entitled to the appointment of psychiatric expert witness. However, *Volson v. Blackburn,* 794 F.2d 173 (5th Cir. 1986) adds the requirement that the defendant make a factual showing that insanity is an issue in the case.

[¶1904.6] Defenses and Presumptions

The normal duty of the prosecution is to meet the burden of proving each element of the offenses charged. However, certain defenses are affirmative defenses: that is, the defendant must produce at least some evidence on these issues, though not necessarily meet the burden of persuasion.

The defense of alibi is an affirmative defense, but is unlike the defenses discussed above: showing that the defendant was somewhere else at the time of the crime demonstrates that he or she is not guilty, not that he or she performed certain actions as charged but that those actions do not amount to a punishable crime because of the lack of mens rea ("evil intent"), capacity, or similar factors.

The prosecution is entitled to certain rebuttable presumptions, either at common law (for instance, the unexplained exclusive possession of stolen property creates a presumption of theft; intentional use of a deadly weapon creates a presumption of homicidal intent) or by statute (for instance, many statutes relating to the receiving of stolen property include a presumption that the accused "fence" knew the goods were stolen). Because these presumptions are rebuttable, the defense can introduce evidence to counter them.

Prosecutors did not violate a murder defendant's constitutional rights by informing the jury that was deciding whether to sentence him to death that he had been convicted of murder and sentenced to death in a previous case.[13]

[¶1905] STOPS AND ARRESTS

In a democratic society, an appropriate balance must be struck between protecting the citizens against the predation of criminals, and protecting them against police interference with legitimate activities. The police must be permitted to investigate crime and frustrate criminal activity without becoming repressive. This is a difficult task, and there is significant variation in judicial opinion (over time and from jurisdiction to jurisdiction) as to when the police have gone too far.

Under *Terry v. Ohio,* 392 U.S. 1 (1968), the police are permitted to make an investigatory stop—appropriately limited in intrusiveness and duration—based on reasonable suspicion, supported by objective facts capable of articulation (not a "hunch"), and giving rise to a reasonable belief that the individual who is detained either has committed, is in the process of committing, or is preparing to commit a criminal offense. The suspect can be detained long enough to see if the suspicions are in fact justified, and if there's probable cause to make an arrest.

The U.S. Supreme Court has held[14] that, consistent with the Fourth Amendment, federal drug agents can make an investigative stop when a nervous passenger pays cash for $2100 worth of plane tickets; does not check baggage; stays only 48 hours after a 10-hour trip to a city known as a drug source; and where the suspect traveled under a name that did not match the name under which his telephone number was listed.

There have been a number of cases relating to police stops, often in the context of drug investigations. The Supreme Court refused to impose a blanket rule against police officers "working the buses" by approaching bus passengers for questioning and asking to search their luggage during mid-trip stops.[15] Florida's Supreme Court said the procedure was unconstitutional, given that a reasonable person would not have felt free to terminate questioning and leave the bus. The U.S. Supreme Court reversed, taking the position that bus passengers don't want to leave the bus anyway, irrespective of the presence or absence of police questioning.

To the Supreme Court, police officers pursuing a group of young men (the police had no articulable suspicion) had not "seized" one of the youths at the time that he discarded some crack cocaine. Therefore, the police conduct could not be deemed an unreasonable seizure that would bar admissibility of the drug.[16] Under this analysis, there is no seizure in a situation in which a police officer seeks to apprehend a suspect who does not submit, where the police officer makes a show of authority but no force is applied.

Some courts do have a preference for establishing probable cause before the seizure. A District of Columbia court invalidated a conviction for cocaine possession, finding that a seizure occurred when there were two police confrontations within half an hour, under circumstances not constituting suspicion by the police.[17] In this reading, the confrontation escalated from a request for identification, questioning about drugs, search of bag, to body search of the defendant's companion, so that a reasonable person would not feel free to leave.

To the Fourth Circuit, a seizure clearly occurs when the police continue to question a person who emphatically refuses to answer questions and tries to walk away; the consensual stage ends with the suspect's transition from agreeing to police search of his carry-on bag to refusal to let the police search his coat.[18]

Given reasonable suspicion to stop and frisk a motorist, the New York constitution permits a search of the car (as distinct from its driver) only to the extent necessary to protect the police from immediate harm (i.e., within the radius in which a weapon could be concealed and used against the officers making the stop). Therefore, a search of a closed container inside the car, that could not be reached and used to harm the police, cannot be justified by the stop and frisk.[19]

The good-faith exception to the exclusionary rule has been held[20] to justify a warrantless stop of a truck, and seizure of evidence within that truck, where a police officer's negligent mis-transmission of vehicle registration information led the police dispatcher to state that the license plate was not registered to that truck.

It has also been held that a broken vent window made a car appear to be stolen, thus justifying a stop of the car; the police officer had more than a mere hunch that something was amiss. The combination of detention of residents of premises covered by a warrant, and a *Terry*-type search incident to arrest, justified the detention and search of a suspected World Trade Center bomber outside the building where the target apartment covered by the warrant was located.[21]

A 1993 Tenth Circuit case found that a stop was justified, and excessive force was not used, when police officers with drawn guns made a suspect and his pregnant fiancee exit his car and lie down on the ground. However, the situation was sufficiently custodial to require Miranda warnings even though the interrogation occurred during a stop rather than an arrest.[22]

[¶1906] SEARCH AND SEIZURE

Under the exclusionary rule, illegally seized evidence is inadmissible against the defendant. In many cases, most or all of the prosecution case consists of evidence seized from the defendant or the defendant's control (e.g., stolen property; drugs), so exclusion of the evidence weakens or eliminates the case against the defendant, or limits the charge that can be proven to a lesser offense.

The basic rule is that searches cannot be made, nor objects seized, without a warrant, or without compliance with a recognized exception to the warrant requirement. The Fourth Amendment protects citizens against unreasonable searches and seizures—so the first requisite of a Fourth Amendment claim is that there has been a search in the first place. For instance, observation of material in plain sight is not a search (*Coolidge v. New Hampshire,* 403 U.S. 443 (1971)).

No warrant is required for a search in a place or under circumstances that do not involve a legitimate expectation of privacy. Aerial surveillance of premises is permissible under *California v. Ciraolo,* 476 U.S. 1819 (1986) where there is no objective entitlement to privacy protection under the Fourth Amendment: the suspect's subjective desire for privacy is not relevant to the inquiry.

Another exception is that a search may be made on the consent either of the suspect, or of another person who is permitted to give access to the area to be searched. The defense attorney must be familiar with local case law on who is permitted to give consent to a search. If the suspect himself consented to the search, the defense attorney may be able to demonstrate that the consent was not freely given, and thus that the search was improper.

A search may also be made pursuant to a lawful arrest;[23] the common-sense reason behind this exception is that otherwise it would be far too easy for suspects to attack the arresting officers and escape. A search incident to an arrest may include the arrestee's person and the area within his or her immediate range. If the police have probable cause to search an automobile, they can also open and search containers inside the automobile (e.g., bags, boxes).[24] However, an arrest can't be fabricated as a pretext to perform a search.[25] The search must also be reasonably related in time and scope to the arrest. Local precedent is important here. *State v. Williams*, 42 *Crim. Law Reporter* 2301 (Fla.App. 12/16/87) permits a search of an automobile ten minutes after an arrest, although the arrestee had been handcuffed and removed to the police car and thus could not endanger the arresting officers with anything in the car. *U.S. v. Vasey*, 42 *Crim.Law Reporter* 2277 (9th Cir. 12/15/87), in contrast, invalidates a search approximately 30–45 minutes after the arrest when the arrestee was handcuffed and under police custody.

Lawful searches can be made under exigent circumstances which are those requiring action so immediate that the police cannot stop to get a warrant. If the police are in the process of obtaining a search warrant, their efforts at securing the premises when they have probable cause to believe evidence will be destroyed do not constitute a seizure.[26] In general, once the police have made a search of premises pursuant to a warrant, they may not return to make a further search without a warrant[27]—unless the exigency justifying the original search is still present.[28]

Cases involving sniffer dogs looking for drugs have become more prevalent. There must be probable cause to believe the suspect is carrying drugs before dogs can be used to sniff the suspect's person including the satchel he carries; and even with probable cause to sniff, a warrant is still required to open the satchel.[29] Warrantless dog sniffs of the outside of a warehouse are permissible; there was no reasonable expectation of privacy that the smell of marijuana would be detected; sniff evidence was used to obtain a warrant; the search pursuant to the warrant was valid.[30]

The expectation of privacy has been one of the most actively litigated areas of criminal law. Certain cases have held that no expectation of privacy can be maintained in abandoned property (such as garbage put out for collection).[31] However, it may be held that a state Constitution does provide a reasonable expectation of privacy in garbage set out for collection, asserting greater privacy protection than under the federal Constitution.[32] A defendant did not "abandon" a plastic bag that he checked in a grocery store and told the clerks to take care of for him. Therefore, the police had no justification for picking up the bag, squeezing it, then opening it to find crack.[33]

A homeless person has a reasonable expectation of privacy in a place under a bridge abutment that he considers his "home," so the Fourth Amendment is violated by a police search of a duffel bag and box kept there.[34]

Airport personnel can do warrantless "administrative searches" for guns and explosives (to preserve the safety of passengers) but this standard will not justify an agreement between airport personnel and local police under which the airport workers are given rewards if they turn over illicit cash or drugs to the police.[35]

A warrantless search can permissibly be performed on consent, which raises the question of who can give consent. *Illinois v. Rodriguez*[36] authorized a search on consent of a woman who the police believed to reside in the apartment that was searched, although she was the arrestee's former girlfriend and in fact had moved out of the apartment several weeks earlier.

An occasional overnight guest in a household who is absent when the search occurs has no legitimate expectation of privacy in the residence that would prevent a search without his consent.[37] A resident minor can give valid consent to a warrantless police entry, as long as the state can show that the minor had common authority with the absent parent to permit entry, plus clear and convincing evidence that the minor's consent to the search was voluntary.[38]

Several recent cases have involved the proper scope of search incident to arrest. It is permissible for FBI agents making an arrest for trafficking in stolen property to impound the arrestee's car, which was outside his office in the parking lot, and to open a bank bag that was in the car as part of an inventory search of the vehicle.[39] (That is, the justification of the search was the accepted concept of inventory search, not the safety of the officers; in this instance, the arrestee was not even in the car.) In a similar case, it has been held that, when state police officers impound a vehicle, they are permitted to do an inventory search but if the state's inventory search procedures are violated, any evidence so discovered is inadmissible in a federal prosecution of the owner of the impounded vehicle.[40]

A search incident to arrest and on probable cause is permissible as long as the police have the authority to make an arrest even if the purpose of the search is to discover evidence of a crime other than the crime for which the arrest is justified.[41] In exigent circumstances, a protective sweep of a house can permissibly be made, even if the suspect is arrested outside the house.[42]

The Supreme Court has permitted[43] a properly limited protective sweep of the premises subsequent to an arrest. In this case, an arrest warrant was issued for an individual suspected of committing a robbery while dressed in a red running suit. The suspect emerged from the basement and was arrested. Then the police searched the basement to see if someone else was there and found and seized a red running suit. The seizure was permitted incident to a search, which in turn was lawful because of reasonable police suspicion of the presence of someone else at the arrest scene. California permits the detention of someone reasonably suspected of connection with a business if he or she is outside the business premises when police are executing a search warrant.[44]

If the police have not an arrest warrant, but a search warrant, it does not violate the Fourth Amendment to pat down persons on the premises being searched, to see if they have weapons, even if there is no individualized suspicion of the people on the premises, and no apparent threat coming from them.[45] In this case, the officers thought the bulge in the defendant's pocket was a gun; on inspection, it proved to be a bag of crack.

Under the Supreme Court's 1993 *Dickerson* decision,[46] materials can be seized during a valid protective frisk as part of a *Terry* stop, if it is immediately apparent that the materials, though not weapons, are contraband. However, the police officer exceeded the reasonable scope of a frisk by manipulating an object in the suspect's jacket pocket before deciding that it was contraband cocaine.

A police department policy of conducting a strip and body cavity search of all persons arrested on felony charges violates the Fourth Amendment, because the indiscriminate policy is not reasonably related to the maintenance of security.[47]

The Ninth Circuit permits a warrantless body cavity search of felony arrestees where the objective is to promote prison security by searching for weapons but not where the objective is to seek evidence of a crime. In the latter case, both probable cause and either a warrant or exigent circumstances must be present.[48] A 1992 Iowa case permits pumping a suspect's stomach after he admits to having swallowed crack cocaine. The bodily invasion is valid as a search pursuant to an arrest or because of the combination of probable cause and exigent circumstances.[49] Several cases find that it is not a search, and therefore the Fourth Amendment is not implicated, if convicted sex offenders are subject to mandatory HIV testing, or if convicted felons or persons convicted of sexual or violent crimes are required to give blood samples for DNA testing, for possible use in the prosecution of other offenses.[50]

[¶1907] INTERROGATION AND SELF-INCRIMINATION

There is a deeply ingrained belief that the defendant's own admissions are the best possible evidence of guilt. In fact, the reason that the institution of judicial torture developed was that convictions were not permitted *unless* the accused confessed. Abhorrence of judicial torture is one of the inspirations for the Bill of Rights' privilege against self-incrimination; yet there is a wide range of police behavior that elicits confessions or incriminating statements, but stops short of torture. Again, the assessment of this police conduct is a difficult matter, and different courts may reach different conclusions about similar police actions.

Most criminal cases begin when the police arrest a suspect and take him or her into custody for the purpose of charging him or her with a crime. A suspect who is taken into custody or otherwise deprived of freedom in any significant way must be given the "Miranda warning" before any interrogation.[51] The import of the *Miranda* decision is that incriminating statements produced by custodial interrogation may not be used against the defendant unless he or she was first warned of the rights to counsel and to remain silent. In order to mount a *Miranda* challenge, then, there must have been both custody and interrogation. A statement overheard by a police officer on patrol, a statement made to someone other than a police officer, or a statement blurted out and not in response to police questioning, is not covered by *Miranda*.

The *Miranda* requirements apply only to custodial interrogation, so warnings are not required if the police put two suspects into a room, hoping that they will make incriminating statements. Although the suspects were in custody, the police did not interrogate them at that time.[52]

The Supreme Court has held that an undercover police officer placed in a cell with a suspect need not give a *Miranda* warning before asking a suspect if he has ever killed anyone.[53] (The suspect was arrested after he proudly replied in the affirmative.) The Court did not accept the Illinois appellate holding that *Miranda* prohibits all undercover operations reasonably likely to result in self-incrimination. It found that a warning was not required because there was no police-dominated, coercive interrogation; the suspect didn't know he was talking to a police agent.

Yet, perhaps surprisingly, the Supreme Court later deemed that a confession was coerced when it was obtained by another prisoner acting as a federal agent, who promised to protect the defendant from other inmates but only if he confessed. Admitting the confession was not harmless error, because the other evidence in the case was far from strong enough to secure a conviction.[54]

Questioning must stop when a suspect in custody invokes the Fifth Amendment right to counsel. Even if the suspect talks to his or her attorney in the interim, it is improper to restart interrogation in the absence of counsel.[55] However, a statement obtained from a suspect who has invoked the right to counsel is still admissible to impeach the defendant's trial testimony.[56]

Once a person is represented by counsel on one charge, it has been held that it is improper to question him about another crime with which he had not been charged, without notice to his attorney, and to use the resulting confession to the second crime at the sentencing hearing for the first crime (in this case, a capital crime) where he was represented by counsel.[57] But the Supreme Court later made it clear that it is permissible to interrogate a defendant who is represented by counsel for one offense, if interrogation without a lawyer present is about another offense. Asking to consult one's lawyer is deemed to be specific to each offense, unlike the general Fifth Amendment protection against compelled self-incrimination.[58] Initially, certiorari was granted on the issue of whether custodial interrogation outside the presence of counsel is permissible if the defendant asks for an attorney, but has talked to a lawyer about (and pleaded guilty to) another offense about which he was initially questioned; but certiorari was dismissed after the defendant died.[59]

An otherwise proper *Miranda* warning is not rendered improper by a police officer's statement, "We have no way of giving you a lawyer, but one will be appointed for you, if you wish, if and when you go to court": the Supreme Court has held that the *Miranda* decision merely requires the police to inform defendants of their right to counsel and that questioning will not begin until and unless the right to counsel has been waived. *Miranda* does not create an affirmative duty on the police to have attorneys available in case suspects should request them.[60]

A videotape saved the day in *California v. Jennings*:[61] although a transcript of the interrogation gave the impression that the defendant was invoking the right to remain silent, viewing of a videotape of the interrogation showed that the refusal was a refusal to talk to a particular police officer that he was afraid of, not a refusal to respond to police questioning. Therefore, his inculpatory statements were admissible.

It is neither an abuse of discretion nor a violation of the right to counsel for a court to forbid (or rather, refuse to exercise its discretion to permit) consultation between defendant and attorney during the lunch recess that broke up the defendant's cross examination. Neither is it a violation of attorney-client privilege for the judge to ask the attorney why he wanted to talk to the defendant.[62]

An accused person can be compelled to testify (for instance, against a co-defendant) only if he or she gets full transactional immunity from prosecution; use or derivative use immunity is not sufficient.[63]

Voluntarily prepared documents, whether business or personal, are not considered "testimonial," and therefore are not protected by the Fifth Amendment.[64]

[¶1907.1] Confiscation and Attorneys' Fees

Provisions of the Racketeer Influenced and Corrupt Organizations Act (RICO; 18 U.S.C. Section 3006A) and the Comprehensive Forfeiture Act of 1984 (21 U.S.C. Section 853) that are controversial permit pre-trial confiscation of the property of certain RICO defendants—including property intended to pay attorneys' fees. This has often been protested as a limitation on the defendants' right to be represented by counsel of their choice, and as extremely unfair to the attorneys. Even if the defendants are in fact guilty, and the forfeited funds represent ill-gotten gains, attorneys are the only payees who are penalized. Mercedes dealers and furriers aren't required to disgorge ill-gotten gains used to purchase luxury items.

Forfeiture issues have occupied a great deal of court time at all levels. Two 1993 Supreme Court decisions deal with Eighth Amendment implications of forfeiture. A civil in rem forfeiture of property used in drug offenses is at least partially a punishment, and therefore is subject to the Eighth Amendment ban on "excessive fines."[65] Forfeiture of the defendant's entire pornography business, including a stock of constitutionally protected materials, has been held to be punishment for his RICO crimes, not a First Amendment violation or a prior restraint of future free speech; but an in personam RICO forfeiture is a fine, therefore challengeable under the Eighth Amendment if it is perceived as excessive.[66] If a defendant makes a prima facie showing that forfeiture is grossly disproportionate to the seriousness of the crime, the Eighth Amendment requires proportionality review of the sentence, based on factors such as the seriousness of the crime, the defendant's motives and profit, and the extent of taint on the business.[67] Here, the RICO predicate offense was union-busting; the offense involved only 10% of the business assets; and the business itself was a legitimate one.

Where a civil forfeiture proceeding is based on the same facts as criminal proceeding, the defendant is entitled to an adversarial post-freeze hearing on probable cause issues if he wants to "unfreeze" some funds to hire a lawyer, but only if the government fails to show that the defendant has access to adequate unattached funds for this purpose.[68]

A corporation's activities in operating gas stations that filed false state tax returns, and its parent corporation's role in managing the stations, constitute sufficient involvement for the scheme to be an "enterprise" subject to forfeiture under RICO.[69]

Real estate owners are entitled to notice and hearing before a civil forfeiture seizure, absent exigent circumstances;[70] after all, the owners are not very likely to move the property to frustrate law enforcement. Civil in rem forfeiture cannot be taken on real property over which drugs were transported from a marina: there was not enough connection between the land and the criminal activity to justify forfeiture.[71] In contrast, money is extremely mobile, so the Second Circuit has held that the Fourth Amendment is not violated by a warrantless seizure of money being transmitted to Colombia by persons accused of drug trafficking. The speed of electronic funds transfers makes the situation extremely exigent.[72]

In a forfeiture action, lack of probable cause to believe that the property was subject to forfeiture at the time of seizure requires return of the seized property on motion by the defendant's lawyer, made under Federal Rules of Criminal Procedure 41(e)(103).

The Eastern District of New York has held[73] that the owner of property can assert a defense to forfeiture under 21 USC Section 881(a)(7) that it lacked "knowledge or consent" that drug offenses were committed on the property if the owner knew that the offenses occurred, but did not consent to their occurrence.

[¶1908] TRIAL ISSUES

Under the Sixth Amendment, the defendant is entitled to a speedy trial; failure to provide it can lead to dismissal of charges against the defendant. *Barker v. Wingo*, 407 U.S. 514 (1972) gives the tests for determining whether delay violates the Sixth Amendment right:

➤ the length of the delay;

➤ reasons for the delay;

presence or absence of prejudice to the defendant;

➤ the defendant's demand for acceleration under the speedy-trial right. Periods during which the defendant is neither in custody, under indictment, nor subject to any other restraint don't count in the calculation; neither do delays caused by appeals.

[¶1908.1] Jury Selection

The defendant is entitled to unbiased jurors, selected from a fair cross-section of the community. In *Batson v. Kentucky*,[74] the Supreme Court held that the Equal Protection clause of the 14th Amendment governs the exercise of preemptory challenges by a prosecutor in a criminal trial. The Court explained that although a defendant has "no right to a 'petit jury composed in whole or in part of persons of his own race . . . defendant does have the right to be tried by a jury whose members are selected pursuant to nondiscriminatory criteria." The Court also stated that whether the trial is criminal or civil, potential jurors, as well as litigants, have an equal protection right to jury selection procedures that are free from state-sponsored group stereotypes rooted in, and reflective of, historical prejudice.

In 1994, faced with the question whether the Equal Protection clause forbids intentional discrimination on the basis of gender, just as it prohibits discrimination on the basis of race, the Court held that gender, like race, is an unconstitutional proxy for jury competence and impartiality. Thus the Equal Protection clause prohibits the government from excluding a person from jury service on account of that person's gender.[75]

However, the prosecution is entitled to jurors who are not inherently unresponsive to its arguments. In a capital case, jurors who hold a conscientious opposition to the death penalty can be disqualified from both the guilt and the penalty phases of the case.[76]

A change of venue based on the race of the victim, but ignoring the defendant's race, is impermissible, as violating the defendant's right to fair trial and equal protection.[77]

The Supreme Court has also addressed other trial issues:

➤ A prisoner who fails to appear at the beginning of the trial cannot be tried in absentia, although trial in absentia is permissible if the prisoner flees after commencement of trial.[78]

➤ Under Federal Rules of Criminal Procedure 14 (severance for co-defendants joined under Rule 8), severance is required only if there is a serious risk that a joint trial compromises a specific trial right, or prevents the jury from reaching a reliable decision. If the co-defendants' defenses are mutually exclusive, severance is not required as a matter of law.[79]

➤ The defendant's Sixth Amendment right to effective assistance of counsel is not violated if the defendant's lawyer fails to raise a constitutional claim based on a dubious decision that was overruled.[80]

Amendments, effective 12/1/93, were made to many of the Federal Rules of Criminal Procedure, e.g., the change in Rule 26.3. The amended rule requires that, before a mistrial is ordered, the court must provide an opportunity for the prosecution and all defendants to comment, as to whether they consent or object to the mistrial, and if they have any alternatives to offer.[81]

[¶1909] EVIDENCE ISSUES

The defense is entitled to pretrial discovery. Usually, the prosecution must disclose in advance the names of the witnesses it intends to call. Under *Brady v. Maryland,* 373 U.S. 83 (1963), the defendant is entitled to disclosure of any material evidence in the prosecution's possession that is favorable to the accused. A common argument to *Brady* challenges is that the evidence once existed, but was routinely destroyed by the police or prosecution. *California v. Trombetta,* 467 U.S. 479 (1984) requires preservation of evidence that meets two tests: it possesses exculpatory value, and the defendant cannot get comparable evidence through other, reasonably available means.

However, a *Brady* violation will result in reversal of a conviction only if there is a reasonable probability that production of the evidence would have changed the outcome of the trial.[82]

A common, and dramatic, feature of criminal trials is for the prosecutor to ask a crime victim or witness if the perpetrator is in court, and to identify him or her. It is almost as common for the defense to challenge such identifications as impermissibly suggestive. *Neil v. Biggers,* 409 U.S. 198 (1973) excludes such identifications only if they are both impermissibly suggestive and lacking in reliability.

There is no constitutional right for the defendant to demand a lineup in court to lessen the suggestiveness of the identification; nor may the defendant demand to be seated away from the defense table to make the identification less likely.[83]

So-called DNA fingerprinting, which allegedly can provide a conclusive individual identification of blood, skin, saliva, and other components of the body, is one of the most dramatic recent developments in forensic medicine. DNA fingerprinting has been ruled scientifically valid and hence admissible in several jurisdictions: in the District of Vermont for federal criminal trials; in Florida, to link a defendant to body fluids found at a crime scene; in Virginia; and in New York provided, of course, that the procedures are properly performed.[84] Massachusetts required reversal of a rape conviction based on DNA evidence: the state failed to lay a foundation for the laboratory's claim that the odds were 59 million to one that the DNA print of the rapist was produced by anyone other than the defendant.[85] However, some doubt has been cast on the scientific validity of DNA testing, so future cases may see its admissibility limited or denied. In 1993, for instance, Arizona and New Mexico courts ruled that DNA evidence does not have a sufficient scientific foundation for admittance in courts of those states.[86]

If a large volume of material is made available under Federal Rules of Criminal Procedure 16, the prosecution has been held to have a duty to identify the material that it is not planning to introduce.[87] The prosecution is not entitled to discovery of which items of discoverable material the defense wants copies of; such prosecution discovery would violate work product rules and the right to effective assistance of counsel.[88]

The Grand Jury is entitled to very broad discovery, and its confidentiality must not be compromised by requiring the government to provide extensive details.[89] The Grand Jury is, however, constrained by Rule 19(c), so on motion a court can quash or modify a subpoena where compliance would be unreasonable or oppressive. The initial burden of proof is on the recipient, because the subpoena is presumed reasonable. To grant a motion to quash based on irrelevancy, the District Court must find that there is no reasonable possibility that the subpoena will uncover information relevant to the general subject of the Grand Jury investigation.

The Supreme Court has narrowed the defendant's Fourteenth Amendment challenge when the police lose or destroy evidence: *Arizona v. Youngblood* [90] holds that due process does not require the police to preserve all potentially exculpatory evidence (in this case, semen samples recovered from a child victim of a sex crime). The Fourteenth Amendment is violated only if the defendant can show official bad faith in the non-preservation of evidence.

Under a later Supreme Court case,[91] it is not required that a murder conviction be overturned merely because evidence that the defendant battered the murder victim was introduced without establishing that he had inflicted injuries on her in the past. In a child abuse case, the Supreme Court says it is permissible to introduce the children's spontaneous declarations and those made while they were receiving medical treatment (because these statements have the indicia of reliability) on a hearsay basis, at a time when the child victims are available to testify but have been excused from testifying.[92]

[¶1910] POST-TRIAL ISSUES

After a conviction, the defense may appeal on several grounds: improper admission of evidence; insufficiency of evidence; improprieties during the trial preventing a fair trial. If the appeal is successful, the outcome may be either a new trial or a reversal of the conviction. Under *Burks v. U.S.*, 437 U.S. 1 (1978), the usual result of a successful appeal for insufficient evidence is a reversal, not a new trial. However, *Duffel v. Dutton*, 785 F.2d 131 (6th Cir. 1986) holds that reversal is not required if the quantum of evidence was insufficient because the lower court improperly excluded evidence that would have made the prosecution case sufficient for a conviction.

An indigent convicted defendant is entitled to a free transcript of the trial for appellate use if the transcript is not only useful for the defense, but no other reasonably functional alternative is available: *Jeffries v. Wainwright*, 794 F.2d 1516 (11th Cir. 1986). *U.S. v. Feldman*, 788 F.2d 625 (9th Cir. 1986) holds that an indigent defendant who advances money for reasonable appellate expenses (e.g., copying) is normally entitled to reimbursement.

Federal prosecutors have 30 days to appeal a judge's order to suppress evidence, but this time period is tolled by a motion to reconsider, until such time as the motion is acted on even if the motion is based on grounds previously abandoned by the government.[93]

Federal habeas corpus relief is unavailable based on a claim that the conviction was based on a seizure in violation of the Fourth Amendment, if the defendant had a full and fair chance to litigate the claim in state court. However, the Supreme Court does not apply this rule to claims that the conviction was based on a confession obtained in violation of the *Miranda* rule.[94]

For federal habeas purposes, whether error at the state trial level was harmless depends on whether the error had a substantial and injurious effect on the verdict, not whether the error was harmless beyond a reasonable doubt. Therefore, using the defendant's silence after a *Miranda* warning to impeach him is error that is not harmless.[95]

Initially, certiorari was granted in a case dealing with whether increasing the time between prison inmates' parole hearings constitutes ex post facto punishment, but certiorari was dismissed as improvidently granted.[96]

[¶1910.1] Sentencing Guidelines

The Sentencing Guidelines for federal cases promulgated by the U.S. Sentencing Commission have been extremely controversial. The objective of the guidelines is to eliminate sentencing disparity in conceptually similar cases; yet this laudable objective conflicts with the equally laudable objective of permitting judges discretion to individualize the sentences imposed on offenders who may be quite different even if they commit the same crime.

The general validity of the Guidelines has been determined by the Supreme Court in *Mistretta v. U.S.*,[97] holding that the Guidelines are constitutional; that

Congress did not delegate excessive powers to the Commission; and that the drafting process did not violate the separation of powers doctrine by having judges serve on the Commission with non-judges. A later Supreme Court ruling finds that enhancing a sentence by two levels because of perjury at trial does not constitute an unconstitutional burden on the defendant's right to testify.[98]

Five Circuits[99] have rejected the argument that the Guidelines violate Fifth Amendment substantive and procedural due process guarantees by limiting discretion and eliminating individually tailored sentences. However, federal courts have taken widely varied approaches to the way the Guidelines have been used in practice. It has been held that (at least in non-capital cases) there is no constitutional right to individualized sentencing:[100] the policy of permitting judicial discretion in this area is just that—a policy and not a right of constitutional dimensions.

The Supreme Court addressed the sentencing Guidelines three times in 1992. It held that, if a sentencing judge was influenced by both valid and invalid factors in departing from the Guidelines, the appeals court can uphold the sentence if it would have been imposed if the invalid Guideline had not been part of the judge's decisional process.[101] It also found that there is no constitutional prohibition against giving a juvenile offender a sentence that is longer than the Guideline sentence prescribed for an adult offender convicted of the same offense,[102] and that under certain circumstances a federal court has the authority to review a prosecutor's refusal to pursue a sentence lower than the Guideline prescribes for a prisoner who has cooperated in the prosecution of other defendants. However, the review power exists only if the prosecutor's refusal was premised on improper considerations such as the defendant's race.[103]

The Supreme Court requires federal judges to warn defendants on reasonable notice of the judge's intention to impose a sentence stiffer than the Guidelines; both prosecution and defense are entitled to be heard on the departure.[104]

According to the First Circuit, defendants are entitled to timely disclosure of, and a fair opportunity to challenge, any documents used in sentencing but not covered by Federal Rules of Criminal Procedure Rule 32; e.g., letters similar to the victim impact report but not included in the pre-sentence report.[105]

U.S. v. Diaz-Villafane[106] sets up a three-part test for reviewing lower courts' departures from the sentence prescribed by the Guidelines:

➤ Plenary review of the legal sufficiency of the circumstances underlying the departure.

➤ Clear error, if the trial court made a factual determination of the existence of the factual circumstances.

➤ Reasonableness (viewed with deference) of the departure.

➤ On another sentencing issue, *Alabama v. Smith*[107] clarifies *North Carolina v. Pierce*, 395 U.S. 711 (1969), which holds that there is a presumption of vindictiveness when a defendant successfully appeals a conviction, then receives a harsher sentence after a new trial. Smith states that the presumption does not apply when the initial sentence was part of a plea bargain, and the second sentence was imposed after trial. The Supreme Court held in

1991 that imposition of a mandatory life sentence without parole for possession of more than 650 grams of cocaine does not violate the Eighth Amendment prohibition of cruel and unusual punishment.[108]

In 1993, sentencing issues occupied the courts to a significant degree. The Tenth Circuit affirmed the use of "double-counting": the use as a predicate offense of a felon's possession of a firearm both to set the offense level and increase the "criminal history" score.[109] On a related issue, certiorari was granted in a case dealing with whether the underlying felony in a felony murder case can be treated as an aggravating factor in the penalty phase, but certiorari was dismissed as improvidently granted.[110] The Third Circuit ruled that, unless the Guidelines specify to the contrary, adjustments in sentencing are cumulative, and permitted cumulative adjustments to be made for performance of a leadership role in a crime and having more than minimal influence on the planning of a crime.[111] According to the Sixth Circuit, it does not penalize a defendant's assertion of the right against self-incrimination to refuse to reduce the Guideline sentence unless the defendant accepts responsibility for other, uncharged but relevant conduct.[112]

The U.S. Sentencing Commission's Guidelines for sentencing of corporations and other organizational offenders took effect in 1991. Sentences will be more lenient if, at the time of the offense, a corporation maintained an effective program to prevent and detect illegalities. The Guidelines contain standards for corporate fines for fraud, antitrust, money laundering, tax evasion and insider trading, but not environmental offenses, which are governed by substantive environmental law.[113] According to the Seventh Circuit, defendants convicted of price fixing and mail fraud should have been sentenced under the antitrust Guidelines, not the tougher Guidelines for fraud and deceit, where the fraud was perpetrated in furtherance of price fixing and was not a separate offense.[114]

There is a constitutional right to make a collateral attack on a facially valid prior conviction, if the conviction could lead to enhanced sentencing as a career criminal.[115]

The Supreme Court ruled in 1993 that 18 USC Section 944(c)(1), which enhances the sentence for a violent crime committed with a gun from five to 20 years on a second or subsequent conviction, can be applied if the first and second convictions are obtained in the same proceeding.[116] The Court ruled in 1994 that federal defendants who face stiff minimum sentences as repeat offenders cannot ordinarily challenge the validity of earlier convictions that place them in the "career criminal" category of the Armed Career Criminal Act of 1984 (18 USC Section 924(e)).[117]

[¶1910.2] Death Penalty

Death penalty litigation is an increasing concern of the Supreme Court. The Court continued to narrow the availability of appeals in several death sentence cases, upholding the Fifth Circuit's standard for successive habeas petitions: a colorable showing of actual innocence. This test means that no reasonable person could have found the defendant deserving of a capital sentence under the applicable state law unless an error of constitutional dimensions had occurred[118]—clearly a very difficult standard to meet. The following year, *Herrera* held that newly discovered evidence of innocence will not permit federal habeas relief unless there is independent constitutional error in the state proceedings; otherwise, the due process avenue is through state clemency proceedings based on innocence, not through federal habeas litigation.[119] *Morgan*[120] permits a juror to be challenged for cause if he or she expresses an intention to vote automatically in favor of a death sentence if the defendant is convicted.

A death sentence must be overturned even if the judge has reviewed and approved the jury sentence if one of the aggravating circumstances considered by the jury was invalid.[121] A state Supreme Court's review of a death sentence based on four aggravating factors—one invalid, three valid—is inadequate if the court fails to specify whether the error was harmless.[122] An unconstitutionally vague factor (whether the crime was "especially cruel, heinous or depraved") also taints the death sentence.[123] A convicted killer's right of association is violated by treating membership in a racist gang as an aggravating factor: this membership was not relevant to the crime for which he was sentenced, and no proof was adduced as to the effect of the membership on his future dangerousness.[124] A 1993 Supreme Court ruling approves Idaho's capital punishment statute's definition of "utter disregard for human life," construed to mean "cold-blooded, pitiless slayer" as an aggravating factor.[125]

A state court has permitted the imposition of a death sentence on a defendant who entered a plea of Guilty but Mentally Ill, in light of the state's use of the M'Naghten Rule and its refusal to recognize the defense of "irresistible impulse" asserted by the defendant as the basis of his insanity defense.[126]

The first death sentence under the 1988 Anti-Drug Abuse Act (for a drug-related murder) was upheld by the Eleventh Circuit in 1993.[127]

[¶1910.3] Related Sentencing Issues

Judges are also finding creative ways of punishing defendants. When a young nonviolent offender was sentenced, the judge ordered her to write a 3,000-word essay about "Crooklyn," a film about urban family life, relating the film to her life, and explaining why she should get probation. These alternative sentencing options are the result of tight budgets and overcrowded prisons.[128]

— ENDNOTES —

1. Dept. of Revenue of Montana v. Kurth Ranch et al. No. 93-144 (6/6/94).

2. Barnes v. Glen Theatre Inc., #90-26, 111 S.Ct. 2456 (Sup.Ct. 6/21/91).

3. Akron, Ohio v. Rowland, 62 LW 2220 (Ohio Sup. 9/22/93).

4. Smith v. U.S., #91-8674, 113 S.Ct. 2050 (Sup.Ct. 6/1/93).

5. 18 USC Sections 1961-8.

6. Chivas Products Ltd. v. Owen, 864 F.2d 1280 (6th Cir. 12/28/88).

7. U.S. v. Bonanno Organization Crime Family, 879 F.2d 20 (2d Cir. 6/23/89).

8. Sedima, SPRL v. Imrex Co. Inc., 473 U.S. 479 (1985).

9. Electrical Workers, IBEW v. Sacramento Valley Chapter, Nat'l Electrical Contractors' Ass'n, 59 LW 2148 (E.D. Cal. 8/9/90).

10. Beck v. Manufacturers Hanover Trust Co., 820 F.2d 46 (2d Cir. 1987), cert. denied 484 U.S. 1005; Furman v. Cirrito, 828 F.2d 898 (2d Cir. 1987); Albany Insurance Co. v. Essex, 831 F.2d 41 (2d Cir. 1987); Creative Bath Products Inc. v. Connecticut General Life Ins., 837 F.2d 561 (2d Cir. 1988).

11. Reves v. Ernst & Young, #91-886, 113 S.Ct. 1163 (Sup.Ct. 3/3/93).

12. U.S. v. Shabani, #93-981, (11/1/94).

13. Romano v. Oklahoma, #92-9093 (Sup.Ct.6/13/94).

14. U.S. v. Sokolow, 109 S.Ct. 1581 (4/3/89).

15. Florida v. Bostick, #89-1717, 111 S.Ct. 2382 (Sup.Ct. 6/20/91).

16. California v. Hodari D., #89-1632, 111 S.Ct.1547 (Sup.Ct. 4/23/91). But see Connecticut v. Oquendo, 61 LW 2179 (Conn.Sup. 8/25/92) and Hawaii v. Quino, 61 LW 2304 (Haw.Sup. 10/28/92) imposing higher state-Constitution-based standards on permissible stops, finding that the Fourth Amendment is implicated as soon as the person stopped does not feel free to terminate an encounter with the police.

17. Guadalupe v. U.S., 585 A.2d 1348 (D.C. 1/31/91).

18. U.S. v. Wilson, 953 F.2d 116 (4th Cir. 12/19/91).

19. New York v. Torres, 58 LW 2076 (N.Y. App. 7/11/89).

20. U.S. v. DeLeon-Reyna, 930 F.2d 396 (5th Cir. 4/17/91). Be aware, however, that New Mexico v. Gutierrez, 62 LW 2370 (N.M.Sup. 10/27/93) holds that the New Mexico Constitution precludes the application of the good-faith exception within that state.

21. U.S. v. El-Gabrowny, 62 LW 2078 (S.D.N.Y. 6/23/93).

22. U.S. v. Perdue, 62 LW 2314 (10th Cir. 11/1/93).

23. (New York v. Belton, 453 U.S. 454 (1981).

24. U.S. v. Ross, 456 U.S. 798 (1982).

25. U.S. v. Smith, 802 F.2d 1119 (9th Cir. 1986).

26. Segura v. U.S., 468 U.S. 796 (1984).

27. Michigan v. Clifford, 466 U.S. 287 (1984).

28. U.S. v. Martin, 781 F.2d 671 (9th Cir. 1986).

29. Pennsylvania v. Martin, 62 LW 2063 (Pa.Sup. 6/8/93).

30. U.S. v. Lingenfelter, also 62 LW 2063 (9th Cir. 6/30/93).

31. California v. Greenwood, 486 U.S. 35 (1988); U.S. v. Hedrick, 922 F.2d 396 (7th Cir. 1/8/91) ("It is common knowledge that members of the public often sort through other people's garb•ge."); Colorado v. Hillman, 61 LW 2110 (Colo.Sup. 7/20/92); U.S. v. Scott, 975 F.2d 927 (1st Cir. 9/22/92), cert. denied 113 S.Ct. 1877 [Even if the documents were shredded before being discarded, the District Court did find a privacy expectation in shredded materials, and noted that a secretive but environmentally conscious person may refrain from burning confidential materials, preferring to shred them instead, an argument that obviously did not find favor with the Court of Appeals].

32. Pennsylvania v. Edmunds, 586 A.2d 887 (Pa.Sup. 2/4/91) and Vermont v. Oakes, 598 A.2d 118 (Vt.Sup. 7/5/91), both to the effect that the state constitution precludes any good-faith exception to the exclusionary rule. Contra, Connecticut v. DeFusco, 60 LW 2683 (Conn.App. 3/31/92).

33. U.S. v. Most, 876 F.2d 191 (D.C. Cir. 6/2/89).

34. Connecticut v. Mooney, 218 Conn. 85, 588 A.2d 145 (Conn.Sup. 3/19/91).

35. U.S. v. $124,750 U.S. Currency, 873 F.2d 1240 (9th Cir. 4/24/89).

36. 110 S.Ct. 2793 (Sup.Ct. 6/21/90).

37. Nebraska v. Cortis, 237 Neb. 97, 465 N.W.2d 132 (Neb.Sup. 1/25/91).

38. Saavedra v. Florida, 62 LW 2015 (5th Cir. 5/21/93).

39. U.S. v. Kornegay, 885 F.2d 713, cert. den. 110 S.Ct. 2179 (10th Cir. 9/25/89).

40. U.S. v. Wanless, 882 F.2d 1459 (9th Cir. 8/23/89).

41. U.S. v. Trigg, 878 F.2d 1037 (7th Cir. 7/12/89).

42. U.S. v. Hoyos, 868 F.2d 1131 (9th Cir. 3/6/89).

43. Maryland v. Buie, 110 S.Ct. 1093 (Sup.Ct. 2/28/90).

44. California v. Ingram, 62 LW 2078 (Cal.App. 7/1/93).

45. California v. Thurman, 209 Cal.App.3d 817 (Cal.App. 4/14/89).

46. Minnesota v. Dickerson, #91-2019, 113 S.Ct. 2130 (Sup.Ct. 6/7/93). But see New York v. Diaz, 81 N.Y.2d 105, 595 N.Y.S.2d 940, 612 N.E.2d 298 (4/8/93), finding that a "plain touch" perception that the bulge in the suspect's pocket consisted of crack vials did not justify a warrantless search. In this reading, there is no search if material is in "plain sight," but a search must be performed to locate material in "plain touch."

47. Kennedy v. LAPD, 901 F.2d 702 (9th Cir. 10/11/89).

48. Fuller v. MG Jewelry, 950 F.2d 1437 (9th Cir. 12/11/91).

49. Iowa v. Strong, 493 N.W.2d 834 (Ia.Sup. 12/23/92).

50. In re Juveniles A-E, 121 Wash.2d 80, 847 P.2d 455 (Wash.Sup. 3/11/93) [HIV testing]; Jones v. Murray, 962 F.2d 302 (4th Cir. 1992) [DNA testing of convicted felons]; Washington v. Olivas, 62 LW 2139 [DNA testing on conviction of sexual or violent offense].

51. Miranda v. Arizona, 86 S.Ct. 1602 (1966).

52. U.S. v. Vazquez, 857 F.2d 857 (1st Cir. 9/15/88).

53. Illinois v. Perkins, 110 S.Ct. 2394 (Sup.Ct. 6/4/90).

54. Arizona v. Fulminante, #89-839, 111 S.Ct. 1246 (Sup.Ct. 3/26/91).

55. Minnick v. Mississippi, 111 S.Ct. 486 (Sup.Ct. 12/3/90). Compare Eaton v. Virginia, 397 S.E.2d 385 (Va.Sup. 9/21/90) [police are not obligated to terminate custodial interrogation unless the suspect clearly invokes the right to counsel] with Crawford v. Delaware, 508 A.2d 571 (Del.Sup. 9/21/90) [Even an ambiguous assertion such as saying he planned to get a lawyer and asking if he should bring an attorney to the police station is enough to limit interrogation to ascertaining the suspect's intention. However, because the suspect received multiple Miranda warnings, the statements were admissible.]

56. Michigan v. Harvey, 494 U.S. 344 (Sup.Ct. 3/5/90).

57. People v. Kidd, 58 LW 2258 (Ill.Sup. 9/20/89).

58. McNeel v. Wisconsin, #90-5319, 111 S.Ct. 2204 (Sup.Ct. 6/13/91).

59. U.S. v. Green, #91-1521, cert. dismissed 61 LW 4311 (4/5/93).

60. Duckworth v. Eagan, 492 U.S. 195 (Sup.Ct. 6/26/89).

61. 44 Crim.L.Rep. 2021 (Cal.Sup. 9/19/88).

62. N.Y. v. Enrique, 165 A.D.2d 13, 566 N.Y.S.2d 201 (N.Y.A.D. 1/31/91).

63. Alaska v. Gonzalez, 61 LW 2786 (Alaska Sup. 6/4/93).

64. U.S. v. Stone, 976 F.2d 909 (4th Cir. 1992); In re Grand Jury Subpoena Duces Tecum, 62 LW 2068 (2d Cir. 7/21/93).

65. U.S. v. Saccoccia, 62 LW 2031 (D.R.I. 6/4/93).

66. Alexander v. U.S., #91-1526, 113 S.Ct. 2766 (Sup.Ct. 6/28/93).

67. U.S. v. Sarbello, 61 LW 2487 (3d Cir. 2/2/93).

68. U.S. v. All Funds on Deposit, 767 F.Supp. 36 (E.D.N.Y. 6/17/91).

69. U.S. v. Porcelli, 865 F.2d 1352 (2d Cir. 1/11/89).

70. U.S. v. James Daniel Good Real Property, #92-1180, 62 LW 4013 (Sup.Ct. 12/13/93).

71. U.S. v. Two Tracts of Real Property, 62 LW 2003 (4th Cir. 6/7/93). In contrast, U.S. v. 1990 Toyota 4 Runner, 62 LW 2344 (7th Cir. 11/16/93), does find the necessary connection between drug trafficking and an automobile driven to a meeting where drug smuggling was discussed. The automobile was forfeitable even though no drugs changed hands at the meeting.

72. U.S. v. Daccarett, 62 LW 2203 (2d Cir. 9/10/93).

73. U.S. v. Premises Known as 171-02 Liberty Avenue, 57 LW 2613 (E.D.N.Y. 4/7/89).

74. 476 U.S. 79 (1986).

75. J.E.B. v. Alabama ex rel. T.B. No. 91-1239 (4/19/94).

76. Lockhart v. McCree, 106 S.Ct. 1758 (1986).

77. Florida v. Lozano, 616 So.2d 73 (Fla.App. 3/10/93).

78. Crosby v. U.S., #91-6194, 113 S.Ct. 933 (Sup.Ct. 1/25/93).

79. Zafiro v. U.S., #91-6824, 113 S.Ct. 933 (Sup.Ct. 1/25/93).

80. Lockhart v. Fretwell, #91-1393, 113 S.Ct. 838 (Sup.Ct. 1/25/93).

81. See 61 LW 4402 (4/22/93).

82. U.S. v. Bagley, 105 S.Ct. 3375 (1985).

83. U.S. v. Domina, 784 F.2d 1361 (9th Cir. 1986).

84. U.S. v. Jacobetz, 60 LW 2470 (2d Cir. 1/9/92); Andrews v. Florida, 57 LW 2295 (Fla.App. 10/20/88); Spencer v. Virginia, 58 LW 2226 (Va.Sup. 9/22/89); Prater v. Arkansas, 60 LW 2393 (Ark. Sup. 11/11/91); Ohio v. Pierce, 61 LW 2175 (Oh.Sup. 9/2/92).

85. Massachusetts v. Curnin, 59 LW 2517 (Mass.Sup.Jud.Ct. 1/24/91); see also California v. Barney, 61 LW 2158 (Cal.App. 8/5/92) [In light of controversy and lack of scientific consensus as to reliability of DNA testing, admitting the test results was error, albeit harmless error.]

86. Arizona v. Bible, 62 LW 2140 (Ariz. Sup. 8/12/93); New Mexico v. Anderson, 61 LW 2434 (N.M.App. 12/14/92).

87. U.S. v. McDade, 61 LW 2413 (E.D. Pa. 12/11/92).

88. U.S. v. Horn, 811 F.Supp. 739 (D.N.H. 12/17/92).

89. U.S. v. R. Enterprises Inc., #89-1436, 111 S.Ct. 722 (Sup. Ct. 1/22/91).

90. 488 U.S. 51 (Sup.Ct. 11/29/88).

91. Estelle v. McGuire, #90-1074, 112 S.Ct. 475 (Sup.Ct. 12/4/91), on remand 956 F.2d 923.

92. White v. Illinois, #90-6113, 112 S.Ct. 736 (Sup.Ct. 1/15/92).

93. U.S. v. Ibarra, #90-1713, 112 S. Ct. 4 (Sup.Ct. 10/4/91).

94. Withrow v. Williams, #91-1030, 113 S.Ct. 1745 (Sup.Ct. 4/21/93). The habeas review standard derives from Stone v. Powell, 428 U.S. 465 (1976).

95. Brecht v. Abrahamson, #91-7358, 113 S.Ct. 1710 (Sup.Ct. 4/21/93).

96. Cavanaugh v. Roller, #92-1510, 113 S.Ct. 3032 (Sup.Ct. 11/29/93).

97. 488 U.S. 361 (Sup.Ct. 1/18/89).

98. U.S. v. Dunnigan, #91-1300, 113 S.Ct. 1111 (Sup.Ct. 2/23/93).

99. U.S. v. Harris, 876 F.2d 1502 (11th Cir. 7/11/89); U.S. v. Boldin, 876 F.2d 21 (4th Cir. 6/2/89); U.S. v. Seluk, 873 F.2d 15 (1st Cir. 4/27/89); U.S. v. Vizcaino, 870 F.2d 52 (2d Cir. 3/6/89); U.S. v. Brady, 890 F.2d 538 (9th Cir. 1/30/90).

100. U.S. v. Franks, 864 F.2d 992 (3d Cir. 11/7/88); U.S. v. Vizcaino, 870 F.2d 52 (2d Cir. 1989); U.S. v. White, 869 F.2d 822 (5th Cir. 1989); U.S. v. Holmes, 838 F.2d 1175 (11th Cir. 1988); U.S. v. Harris, 876 F.2d 1502 (11th Cir. 7/11/89).

101. Williams v. U.S., #90-6297, 112 S.Ct. 1112 (Sup.Ct. 3/9/92).

102. U.S. v. R.L.C., #90-1577, 112 S.Ct. 1329 (Sup.Ct. 3/24/92).

103. Wade v. U.S., #91-5771, 112 S.Ct. 1840 (Sup.Ct. 5/18/92).

104. U.S. v. Andrus, 925 F.2d 335 (9th Cir. 2/5/91).

105. U.S. v. Curran, 926 F.2d 59 (1st Cir. 2/14/91).

106. 874 F.2d 43 (1st Cir. 5/4/89).

107. #88-333, 490 U.S. 794 (Sup.Ct. 6/13/89), on remand 557 So.2d 20.

108. Harmelin v. Michigan, #89-7272, 111 S.Ct. 2680 (Sup.Ct. 6/27/91); but see Michigan v. Bullock, 61 LW 2036 (Mich.Sup. 6/16/92), finding imposition of life without parole for cocaine possession impermissible as violating the state constitution's prohibition of cruel and unusual punishment.

109. U.S. v. Alessandroni, 982 F.2d 419 (10th Cir. 12/23/92).

110. Tennesee v. Middlebrooks, #92-989, cert. dismissed 113 S.Ct. 3031, 6/28/93.

111. U.S. v. Wong, 62 LW 2130 (3d Cir. 7/30/93).

112. U.S. v. Clemons, also 62 LW 2130 (6th Cir. 7/19/93).

113. See Gregory J. Wallance, "Guidelines on Corporate Crime Emphasize Prevention Program," *Nat.L.J.* 7/1/91 p. 22.

114. U.S. v. Rubin, 62 LW 2046 (7th Cir. 6/30/93).

115. U.S. v. Vea-Gonzalez, 986 F.2d 321 (9th Cir. 2/22/93).

116. Deal v. U.S., #91-8199, 113 S.Ct. 1993 (Sup.Ct. 5/17/93).

117. Custis v. United States, #93-5209, (Sup.Ct. 5/23/94).

118. Sawyer v. Whitley, #91-6372, 112 S.Ct. 2514 (Sup.Ct. 6/22/92).

119. Herrera v. Collins, #91-7328, 113 S.Ct. 853 (Sup.Ct. 1/25/93).

120. Morgan v. Illinois, #91-5118, 112 S.Ct. 2222 (Sup.Ct. 6/22/92).

121. Espinosa v. Florida, #91-7390, 112 S.Ct. 2926 (Sup.Ct. 6/29/92).

122. Sochor v. Florida, #91-5843, 112 S.Ct. 2114 (Sup.Ct. 6/8/92).

123. Richmond v. Lewis, #91-7094, 113 S.Ct. 528 (Sup.Ct. 12/1/92).

124. Dawson v. Delaware, #90-6704, 112 S.Ct. 1093 (Sup.Ct. 3/9/92).

125. Arane v. Creech, #91-1160, 113 S.Ct. 1534 (Sup.Ct. 3/30/93), remand 989 F.2d 1574.

126. Gacy v. Welborn, 62 LW 2665 (7th Cir. 4/12/93).

127. U.S. v. Chandler, 62 LW 2083 (11th Cir. 7/19/93).

128. News item, "Judges Finding Creative Ways of Punishing," *Wall St.J.* 5/24/94 p.B1.

— FOR FURTHER REFERENCE —

Alexander, Rudolph Jr., "Slamming the Federal Courthouse Door on Inmates," 21 *J. of Criminal Justice* 103 (March-April '93).

Altschuler, Albert W., "The Failure of Sentencing Guidelines: A Plea for Less Aggregation," 58 *U. of Chicago L. Rev.* 901 (Summer '91).

Amsterdam, Anthony G., reporter, *Trial Manual 4 for the Defense of Criminal Cases* (2 volumes) (ALI/ABA, American College of Trial Lawyers; looseleaf).

Baughman, Timothy A., "Use and Misuse of Character Evidence," 29 *Trial* 26 (March '93).

Bennett, Cathy E. et. al., "How to Conduct a Meaningful and Effective Voir Dire in Criminal Cases," 46 *SMU L. Rev.* 659 (Winter '92).

Berk, Richard A., Robert Weiss and Jack Boger, "Chance and the Death Penalty," 27 *Law & Soc. Rev.* 89 (February '93).

Bernheim, David, *Defense of Narcotics Cases* (2 volumes) (Matthew Bender; looseleaf).

Bessler, John D. "Televised Executions and the Court," 45 *Fed'l Communications L.J.* 355 (August '93).

Bezak, Elizabeth Marie, "DNA Profiling Evidence: The Need for a Uniform and Workable Evidentiary Standard of Admissibility," 26 *Valparaiso U.L. Rev.* 595 (Spring '92).

Bond, James E., *Plea Bargaining and Guilty Pleas* (2d edition) (Clark Boardman; looseleaf).

Bradley, Craig M., "Reforming the Criminal Trial," 68 *Indiana L.J.* 659 (Summer '93).

Burton, E.J. and Zabihollah Rezaee, "Forensic Investigation: New Challenges for Lawyers and Accountants," 12 *Trial Advocate Q* 24 (January '93).

Capra, Daniel J., "Prisoners of Their Own Jurisprudence: Fourth and Fifth Amendment Cases in the Supreme Court," 35 *Villanova L. Rev.* 1267 (November '91).

Elledge, Christopher C., "Coram Nobis Challenges to Prior Criminal Convictions: Modern Uses of an Ancient Writ," 65 *Florida B.J.* 44 (April '91).

FitzGerald, Kerry P., "Criminal Procedure: Pretrial, Trial and Appeal," 45 *Southwestern L.J.* 1593 (Spring '92).

Guirola, Louis Jr., "Speedy Trial: The Federal Rule and Its Exceptions," 56 *Texas Bar J.* 343 (April '93).

Hamilton, Patrick, "Corporate Criminal Liability for Injuries and Death," 40 *U. of Kansas L. Rev.* 1091 (Summer '92).

Hedges, Michele M., "An Overview of Criminal Discovery for the Civil Practitioner," 54 *Texas B.J.* 600 (June '91).

Hoffman, Joseph L., "Starting from Scratch: Rethinking Federal Habeas Review of Death Penalty Cases," 20 *Florida State U.L. Rev.* 133 (Summer '92).

Husak, Douglas N., "The Serial View of Criminal Law Defenses," 3 *Crim. Law Forum* 369 (Spring '92).

Kelly, Robert Alan, "Applicability of the Rules of Evidence to the Capital Sentencing Proceeding," 60 *U. of Missouri Kansas City L. Rev.* 411 (Spring '92).

Krull, Charles R., "Eliminating Appeals from Guilty Pleas," 29 *Arizona Attorney* 34 (October '92).

Levenson, Laurie L., "Good Faith Defenses: Reshaping Strict Liability Crimes," 78 *Cornell L. Rev.* 401 (March '93).

Mandel, Roberta Goodman, "The Defense of Entrapment," 65 *Florida Bar J.* 46 (March '91).

McMahon, Katherine E., "Murder, Malice and Mental State," 78 *Mass. L. Rev.* 40 (June '93).

McKeown, Brian, "Prosecutorial Misconduct," 81 *Georgetown L.J.* 1356 (April-May '93).

Meyers, Felicia, "Proportionality in Non-Capital Cases," 14 *Whittier L. Rev.* 263 (Spring '93).

Ogletree, Charles Jr., "Arizona v. Fulminante: The Harm of Applying Harmless Error to Coerced Confessions," 105 *Harv.L. Rev.* 152 (November '91).

Parker, Jeffrey S., "The Economics of Mens Rea," 79 *Virginia L. Rev.* 741 (May '93).

Peerenboom, R.P., "Victim Harm, Retributivism, and Capital Punishment," 20 *Pepperdine L. Rev.* 27 (December '92).

Rothman, Alan J., "Creative Computing in Criminal Practice," 206 *N.Y.L.J.* 8/27/91 p. 4.

Schlueter, David, "Scientific Evidence: Good-Bye Frye," 55 *Texas Bar J.* 876 (September '92).

Skolnick, Jerome H. and Richard A. Leo, "The Ethics of Deceptive Interrogation," 11 *Criminal Justice Ethics* 3 (Winter-Spring '92).

Streib, Victor L., "Death Penalty for Battered Women," 20 *Florida State U.L. Rev.* 163 (Summer '92).

Taub, Sheila, "Competency Standard Clarified," *Nat'l L.J.* 10/18/93 p. 25.

Uphoff, Rodney J., "The Criminal Defense Lawyer: Zealous Advocate, Double Agent, or Beleaguered Dealer?" 28 *Crim.Law Bulletin* 419 (September-October '92).

Webster, Laura Gardner, "Resources and Rights Toward a New Prototype of Criminal Representation," 44 *Mercer L. Rev.* 599 (Winter '93).

DRUNK DRIVING CASES

[¶2001] Statistically speaking, drunk driving cases are the most common type of criminal cases, so they are likely to make up a large part of the caseload of the criminal lawyer. In fact, lawyers who handle very little criminal practice are likely to have to handle at least a few drunk driving cases in the course of a career, as an accommodation to clients who themselves or whose family members or business associates have been arrested for drunk driving.

But drunk driving cases are a unique blend of criminal, administrative (see below, about license revocation proceedings) and civil (tort law consequences; impact on automobile insurance) law and practice. The successful defense lawyer must keep up with changes in statutory and Constitutional law; understand the ever-changing nature of precedent in this area; and know enough about science to present a meaningful challenge to the local methods of measuring alcohol consumption and intoxification.

Several drunk driving cases[1] have held that the 2100:1 ratio of alcohol in the breath to alcohol in the blood as tested by an "intoxilyzer" breath analysis device is an average ratio, and therefore cannot be treated as a conclusive and irrebuttable presumption. These rulings are most helpful for the defense, because they require the prosecution to prove an additional, potentially very difficult element (that the ratio in the individual case of the suspect was 2100:1, or another ratio indicating a higher blood alcohol concentration). Kansas refuses to accept "horizontal gaze nystagmus" as a test of sobriety, finding that it has not met the test of general acceptance within the scientific community.[2]

Relying on *Graham v. Connor*,[3] which holds that all claims of excessive force are governed by a Fourth Amendment standard of reasonableness, not a more stringent substantive due process test, *Hammer v. Gross*[4] holds that handcuffing and holding down an unwilling suspect in order to get a blood sample does not violate the Fourth Amendment. The Ninth Circuit held that no more force was used than was necessary to get the sample.

[¶2002] IMPLIED CONSENT LAWS

The concentration of alcohol in the blood naturally declines as time elapses since it was consumed because the body metabolizes the alcohol. So the longer the elapsed time between a person's last consumption of alcohol and the taking of a breath or blood test, the lower the test result will be, and the less likely it is that the driver will be presumed intoxicated (no matter how much alcohol he or she consumed before—or even while—driving).

Although the tendency of excessive alcohol consumption is to impair judgment, it doesn't take the brilliance of an Einstein or the subtlety of a Machiavelli to realize that a delay in submitting to testing makes it hard for the prosecution to prove that the driver was intoxicated or had a BAC above the statutory level—and refusing to be tested altogether makes it almost impossible to prove this.

The criminal justice system must operate in a lawful manner, and must preserve the accused's privilege against self-incrimination. Yet the criminal justice system must also detect and penalize drunk driving. The balance is achieved in most states by the enactment of "implied consent" laws—statutes that state explicitly that driving a car at all operates as consent to a BAC test incident to an arrest made by a police officer with reasonable cause to believe the driver is intoxicated. Thus, taking the sample is conceptualized either as not being a search at all (negating any Fourth Amendment issues), or as being a search that the driver has already consented to.

Implied consent laws have practical, as well as philosophical, consequences. They impose a real dilemma on the person arrested for drunk driving. If the person refuses to submit to the test, there will be precious little prosecution evidence for the charge of drunk driving; however, the driver will immediately lose his or her driver's license, and will have to go through an administrative hearing (testing the reasonableness of the arresting officer's actions) in order to get it back. Furthermore, in some states, failure to submit to BAC testing is an offense independent of drunk driving. If the driver does submit to testing, and is found to have an impermissibly high BAC, a conviction of drunk driving is very likely; his or her license may be suspended or revoked; automobile insurance will become more expensive or unavailable except as an "assigned risk"; and the consequences will be unfavorable if the driver is involved in litigation as a result of damage to another automobile or injury to passengers or pedestrians.

Although the situation is difficult for the accused drunk driver and his or her attorney, it is not hopeless. If you have a chance to advise your client before the test (see below, on the right to counsel in drunk driving cases), your advice must be based on the risks involved in either alternative. If you enter the case at a later stage, you have several potential challenges to the implied consent procedure:

➤ The "stop" was invalid, lacking reasonable cause, and therefore the request for testing was improper.

➤ State law demands warnings to a drunk driving suspect—and your client did not receive these warnings.

➤ Your client did not "refuse" to submit to testing, as defined by state law (e.g., he was pondering his choices, not refusing to submit; he was afraid that blood testing would endanger him or her because of a clotting problem; etc.)

There is substantial conflict among jurisdictions as to whether or not the fact that a driver refused to submit to chemical testing can be introduced in the drunk driving case itself.

In 1988, the Michigan Court of Appeals struck down as unreasonable and violative of equal protection a Michigan statute that permitted prosecutors warrantless access to the results of blood tests performed when injured drivers were treated at a hospital.[5] However, in 1989, another panel of the same court overruled the decision, finding that the Fourth Amendment and the Equal Protection clause permit the extension of the implied consent concept to allow the use of blood obtained for medical treatment in a drunk driving prosecution.[6]

In 1990, Pennsylvania adopted Michigan's original position. An implied consent statute authorizing blood testing in all cases involving death or serious injury was held unconstitutional, as an authorization of unreasonable searches in cases in which there is no probable cause to believe the driver to be intoxicated.[7] Illinois joined Pennsylvania in 1992.[8]

[2002.1] License Suspension Hearings

Local practice determines license suspension procedure. Sometimes the license is confiscated on arrest (and returned if the driver prevails at an administrative hearing—a procedure upheld by *Mackey v. Montrim,* 443 U.S.1 (1979)); sometimes the license is retained until the driver loses at the hearing. At times, the hearing is automatic; at other times, the driver must request the hearing. Of course, if your jurisdiction falls into this category, you must be aware of the timing requirements for the request.

A license suspension hearing is an administrative hearing, but there is a right to counsel, to confront and cross-examine the arresting officer (it may be necessary to subpoena the officer to get him or her to appear rather than submitting an affidavit), and to get a copy of the transcript. However, direct appeal of an unfavorable judgment is not always available; review may require a writ of mandamus.

The issue at the hearing is the existence and reasonableness of a refusal to submit to testing (to be proven by a preponderance of the evidence), not actual guilt or innocence of drunk driving, so it's possible for a driver to be acquitted of drunk driving and still lose his or her license.

You should consider the license revocation hearing a very important part of the entire process arrayed against your client. If the arresting officer's testimony at trial contradicts his or her testimony at the administrative hearing, the potential for impeachment is strong.

[¶2003] CHALLENGING THE POLICE CASE

It is acknowledged that states have a grave and legitimate interest in curbing drunk driving. It has been held that a highway sobriety checkpoint program permitting the use of initial stops and the brief detention of all motorists, absent individual suspicion, set up and operated pursuant to guidelines for operation, site selection, and publicity, does not violate the Fourth Amendment.[9]

In 1993, the Michigan Supreme Court ruled that the state Constitution forbids vehicle stops without particularized suspicion.[10]

Colorado upheld stops even more restrictive than those approved by the Supreme Court (3 minutes vs. 25 seconds; the Michigan procedure detected drunk drivers in 1.4% of stops, the Colorado procedure didn't catch any). To the Colorado Supreme Court,[11] the checkpoint procedure was acceptable under a balancing test. The state's legitimate interest in preventing drunk driving, and the extent to which the checkpoints served that objective, outweighed the extent of the limited intrusion on drivers' liberty. Alabama found a Fourth Amendment violation in a roadblock to check licenses and license plates, set up near an apartment complex that had experienced problems with drunk drivers. The decision[12] found a need to safeguard the liberty interest of motorists and also found that the procedure probably wouldn't be effective to solve the apartment complex's problem.

In Texas, there is no right to consult an attorney while deciding whether or not to take a breath test; because implied consent is part of the process of getting a driver's license, a lawyer can't really counsel a client not to take the breath test.[13] Minnesota, in contrast, gives a drunk driving suspect a constitutional right to counsel before taking or refusing to take a breath test, classifying it as a "critical stage."[14] To vindicate the right, the police merely have to permit the suspect to telephone an attorney before making the decision to refuse or submit to breath testing.

Pennsylvania's Supreme Court held that the police have a duty to warn suspects of rights they do *not* have as well as the rights they have: specifically, the police gave a *Miranda* warning to a suspected drunk driver. He asked for an attorney, so the police suspended questioning but requested that he take a breath test. He refused, and his license was suspended; the suspension was invalidated because of the failure to warn him of the consequences of refusal.[15]

The Supreme Court analyzed the interface between "testimonial" information (whose collection requires a *Miranda* warning) and non-testimonial information in *Pennsylvania v. Muniz*.[16] Under this analysis, it is permissible to use videotaped evidence of the arrestee's slurred speech and lack of coordination (because this is non-testimonial in nature) but impermissible to ask the arrestee the date of his sixth birthday without a *Miranda* warning (because this is testimonial). The information volunteered by the arrestee while a police officer was reciting the breath test protocol was admissible, because it was not a response to police interrogation. Florida has ruled that asking a drunk driving arrestee to recite the alphabet violates the Fifth Amendment because it is designed to elicit an incriminating response that is distinct from the manner of speech, also requiring a *Miranda* warning.[17]

Virginia's highest court struck down the use at trial of evidence of refusal to submit to a field sobriety test, finding such use to violate the state Constitution's guarantee of freedom from compelled self-incrimination.[18]

[¶2004] Pleas and Alternatives

In addition to drunk driving, a number of other offenses may be charged, depending on the jurisdiction and the circumstances: reckless driving, vehicular assault, vehicular homicide, even manslaughter or "depraved heart" murder. It's important to examine the accusatory instrument carefully, searching for instances of improper charging (e.g., charging a person with drunk driving at a time when he or she was sleeping in a parked automobile) or potential double jeopardy problems.

At times a *nolo contendere* or guilty plea is the appropriate resolution, especially if a reduced charge can be negotiated. However, controlling drunk driving is a legislative priority, and your state's law may forbid reduction of charges as part of plea bargaining in drunk driving cases. The effect of the plea on your client's driver's license ("points," suspension, even revocation), auto insurance rates, and any civil litigation arising out of property damage and personal injuries, must also be considered.

In Colorado, a conviction of vehicular homicide can be obtained on proof of voluntary driving while intoxicated, if the driving results in death; it is not necessary for the prosecution to prove that drinking rather than excessive speed was the proximate cause of the victim's death.[19]

Especially if this is a first offense, and your client has strong ties in the community, pre-trial diversion or an Adjournment in Contemplation of Dismissal may be possible if your client completes "DWI School" (a program of alcohol education and remedial driving instruction), or enters an alcohol rehabilitation program. In the worst case, if conviction results in a sentence of incarceration, it may be possible for the sentence to be suspended, or for "jail time" to be served on weekends only so your client can keep his or her job and meet family responsibilities.

— ENDNOTES —

1. California v. McDonald, 206 Cal.App.3d 877 (Cal. App. 12/19/88) and South Dakota v. McCarty, 434 N.W.2d 67 (S.D. Sup. 12/21/88).

2. Kansas v. Witte, 51 Crim. Law Rep. 1391 (Kan. Sup. 7/10/92).

3. 109 S. Ct. 1865 (Sup. Ct. 5/15/89).

4. 884 F.2d 1200, 932 F.2d 842 (9th Cir. 9/6/89).

5. Michigan v. Perlos, 428 N.W.2d 2211 (Mich. App. 7/18/88).

6. Michigan v. England, 438 N.W.2d 908 (Mich. App. 4/4/89).

7. Pennsylvania v. Danforth, 59 LW 2031 (Pa. Super. 6/14/90); Pennsylvania v. Kohl. 61 LW 2267 (Pa-Sup. 9/16/92).

8. King v. Ryan, 61 LW 1090 (Ill. Sup. 12/4/92).

9. Michigan Dep't of State Police v. Sitz, 110 S.Ct. 2481 (Sup. Ct. 6/14/90).

10. Sitz v. Michigan Department of State Police, 62 LW 2215 (Mich. Sup. 9/14/93).

11. Colorado v. Rister, 59 LW 1394 (Colo.Sup. 12/10/90).

12. Hagood v. Town of Town Creek, 62 LW 2215 (Ala. Crim. App. 9/3/93).

13. Texas v. Forte, 759 S.W.2d 128 (Tex. Crim. App. 9/27/88).

14. Friedman v. Comm'r of Public Safety, 473 N.W.2d 828 (Minn. Sup. 6/7/91).

15. Pennsylvania v. O'Connell, 555 A.2d 873 (Pa. Sup. 3/6/89).

16. Pennsylvania v. Muniz, 110 S.Ct. 2638 (Sup. Ct. 6/18/90).

17. Allred v. Florida, 62 LW 2053 (Fla.Sup. 7/1/93).

18. Farmer v. Virginia, 390 S.E.2d 775 (Va. App. 6/6/90).

19. Colorado v. Gamer, 781 P.2d 87 (Colo. Sup. 10/23/89).

— **FOR FURTHER REFERENCE** —

Langworthy, Robert and Edward J. Latessa, "Treatment of Chronic Drunk Drivers," 21 *J. Crim. Justice* 265 (May-June '93).

Lotke, Eric, "Rethinking Refusal: Wisconsin's Implied Consent Law," 66 *Wisc. Lawyer* 26 (July '93).

Rubin, E.F., "Trying to Be Reasonable About Drunk Driving: Individualized Suspension and the Fourth Amendment," 62 *U. Cin. L. Rev.* 1105 (Winter '94).

Westfall, E.A. Penny, "The Drugged Driver: A Prosecutor's Nightmare or Challenge?" 27 *Prosecutor* 21 (July-August '93).

Wherry, E.J. Jr., "The Rush to Convict DWI Offenders: The Unintended Unconstitutional Consequences," 19 *U. Dayton L. Rev.* 429 (Winter '94).

EMPLOYER-EMPLOYEE RELATIONS

[¶2101] The relationship between employers and employees is a form of the principal-agent relationship and as such is subject to extensive legal control. There is a federal minimum wage, and maximum hour standards. Certain standards of plant safety are enforceable. Although employers are not required to provide pensions or other employee benefits, if they choose to do so they must conform to extensive regulation (especially if they choose to deduct the cost of such programs as a business expense).

[¶2102] PRIVACY AND DUE PROCESS ISSUES

The federal Employee Polygraph Protection Act of 1988,[1] limits the right of private employers to use polygraphs as a screening device for hiring, and to discipline employees and job applicants for refusing to take a polygraph test. The penalty for violation can include employment, promotion, or reinstatement of an employee disadvantaged by the violation, back pay, and a civil fine of up to $10,000 payable to the Department of Labor. However, under the Act, employers are permitted to use polygraphs on reasonable suspicion of workplace incidents that cause economic damage (e.g., theft, sabotage, industrial espionage), and as a pre-employment screening device for hiring guards, armored car drivers, and other security-related employees.

Passage of this legislation highlights one of the most important questions in current labor law: the degree to which civil rights and criminal law concepts such as privacy and due process are applicable in the workplace. These issues are especially crucial with respect to drug testing at work. Although no definitive answers have been handed down, it seems clear that drug testing (even without individualized suspicion) will be permitted for those, such as bus drivers and airline pilots, whose sobriety is necessary to protect public safety. But where only economic interests (such as workplace discipline and employee efficiency) are involved, it is more likely that employers will be required to have individualized suspicion to conduct a drug test, or else be forbidden to test.[2]

[¶2103] FEDERAL LABOR LAW

The leading federal statutes in this field are the National Labor Relations Act, as amended by the Labor-Management Relations Act of 1947 (popularly known as the Taft-Hartley Act) and the Labor-Management Reporting and Disclosure Act of 1959. Their purpose is to permit employees (who so choose) to unionize, and to control both employer behavior toward unions and unionized employees, and employee and union behavior toward the employer. If either side commits an unfair labor practice, the National Labor Relations Board (subject to court order) can issue "cease and desist" orders to terminate the undesirable practice, or affirmative orders (e.g., requiring a recalcitrant employer to recognize and bargain with a union).

The Supreme Court has decided several significant labor law cases in the 1990s. A federal court has power to restrain substantive violations of Labor-Management Relations Act Section 302 (which prohibits employers from making payments to non-qualifying union trust funds), but that power does not extend to issuing an injunction against the union trust fund to force it to be administered in compliance with the LMRA standards.[3] A state agency has the power to enforce a bidding specification that requires all contractors on agency-funded projects to abide by lawful prehire collective bargaining agreements negotiated by private parties; such a specification is not preempted by the National Labor Relations Act.[4]

There is no time limit under the Veterans' Re-Employment Rights Act: reservists are entitled to return to their civilian jobs at the same status, pay, seniority, and vacation rights no matter how long they spent in the military, and no limit of reasonableness is placed on the length of the leave.[5]

Department of Labor advisory opinion letters issued under the Fair Labor Standards Act are not a "final agency action" that can be judicially reviewed.[6]

If a state regulatory authority (e.g., casino authorities) forces a business to shut down, the business' workers are not entitled to notice under the WARN Act[7] but the closing must be absolute, and the government must assume control of the enterprise, for this exemption to apply.[8]

[¶2103.1] Unfair Labor Practices

Section 8 of the NLRA makes it an unfair labor practice to:

➤ refuse to bargain collectively (by the employer, with a properly elected union; by the union, with the employer).

➤ subject unions to domination.

➤ retaliate against employees who file charges or testify before the NLRB.

➤ discriminate against employees who do *not* wish to become union members (but see below, on union security clauses).

➤ promote featherbedding practices (require the employment of unnecessary workers).

➤ charge excessive union dues.

➤ carry out certain jurisdictional or recognition strikes or picketing.

In 1991, the Supreme Court permitted the ICC to issue an order in a railway consolidation that exempts the railroad from its collective bargaining agreements,[9] because the Interstate Commerce Act, 49 U.S.C. Sec. 11301 justifies an exemption from antitrust or any other law necessary to carry out an approved consolidation.

An employee bringing a claim under Section 301 of the Labor-Management Relations Act (LMRA) that the employer's job assignment violated the collective bargaining agreement is entitled to a jury trial; but jury trial is unavailable for the same worker's claim that the union violated its duty of fair representation by withdrawing the employee's grievance.[10]

The Supreme Court says that the Seventh Amendment gives a union member the right to a jury trial in an LMRDA Sec. 301 suit for money damages and injunction against a union that allegedly violated its own bylaws and discriminated against him in job referrals because of his criticisms of the union.[11]

The NLRB's policy is that strikers are entitled to regain their old jobs after replacement workers have been laid off, but only if the replacement workers have no reasonable expectation of being recalled, at which point the burden shifts to the employer to rebut the claim that the job is vacant or give a good reason for not rehiring the former striker. This policy has been upheld (as rational and consistent with the objectives of the NLRA) by the Seventh Circuit.[12]

In *Delta-Macon*,[13] permanent replacements of economic strikers were laid off. The employer recalled them in advance of unreinstated strikers with much greater seniority. A "Laidlaw vacancy," or "genuine job vacancy" exists, mandating the reinstatement of strikers, only if the replacement workers lack an objectively reasonable expectancy of recall. The Fifth Circuit ruled for the employer, holding that there were no Laidlaw vacancies, even though the layoffs were sweeping, of indefinite duration, and even though the replacements were not told to expect recall. In another "permanent replacement" case, the Second Circuit vacated the decision of an arbitrator who required notice to employees who honored a picket line of another union before their employer hired permanent replacements.[14] To the Second Circuit, the arbitrator's decision was improper because it did not "draw its essence" from the collective bargaining agreement; arbitrators are restricted to interpreting the collective bargaining agreement, not dispensing wide-ranging industrial justice or full-scale due process for employees.

An NLRB back pay award against a private company is a debt for Fair Debt Collection Practices Act purposes, and can be collected in any way permissible under the FDCPA including prejudgment garnishments.[15]

A "last chance" agreement provides conditional reinstatement for an employee who will not be disciplined if the employee agrees to discontinue objectionable conduct and waive certain procedural protections with respect to grievances and arbitration.

Within the United States, if undocumented aliens are discharged in a manner constituting an unfair labor practice, they are entitled to reinstatement, but can get back pay only if they can prove their legal right to work in the United States. Absent this right, they are not entitled to the job in the first place, so cannot be awarded back pay after discharge.[16]

[¶2103.2] Union Security/Compulsory Unionism

From the union's point of view, the only way the union can be powerful is if it can speak for all the employees. From the employer's point of view, compulsory unionism is a limitation on legitimate freedom to do business.

The NLRA strikes a balance between these viewpoints. It is illegal to have a "closed shop" (one where only people who are already union members can be hired) or "preferential hiring" (where the employer is obligated to hire only union members as long as the union can provide enough qualified workers for all job openings). It is legal under federal law to have a "union shop" in which all employees must be union members, and all new hires must join the union, or an "agency shop" in which employees must pay the union dues, but may refrain from union membership if they wish. Under Section 302 of the LMRA, unions are permitted automatic dues check-off (that is, dues are deducted directly from the employee's paycheck, so that the union doesn't have to wait for the member to pay his dues)—but only if the union member gives the union a written assignment, lasting not more than a year or until the union contract expires (whichever comes first).

But the NLRA doesn't apply to the activities of employers whose operations are purely intrastate; and Section 14(b) of the NLRA permits states to forbid compulsory unionism via "right to work" laws, an option chosen by several states (most of them in the South).

An employer's refusal to hire an applicant who would simultaneously work as a paid union organizer does not constitute illegal discrimination, unless it can be proved that the employer hired people who held jobs to be performed simultaneously both for the employer and for some party other than the union.[17]

The other side of the coin: the Sixth Circuit has upheld the reasonableness of a union rule that forbids members who hold supervisory positions from running for union office for two years, on the theory that a shop steward who was ambitious for promotion might be less than zealous in advocating for union members.[18]

The Supreme Court has decided that labor organizers can lawfully be denied permission to distribute leaflets in the employer's parking lot. The employer's property rights can be overriden only if the employees are so geographically isolated that the union is deprived of the opportunity to communicate with them.[19]

[¶2103.3] Controls on Strikes

The strike is the union's ultimate weapon, the threat with which it attempts to bring the employer to heel. One of the major functions of federal labor law is to guarantee the employees' rights to strike and to picket peacefully. However, like all rights, this one is subject to limits:

➤ Sabotage, violence, and threats to non-striking employees are not protected conduct.

➤ The President of the United States can order the Attorney-General to seek an 80-day injunction in the appropriate federal court, against any strike imperiling the national health or safety.

➤ Section 8(b)(4) of the NLRA forbids secondary strikes and secondary boycotts (even if peaceful). Section 303 of the LMRA permits victims of these tactics to obtain damages. A secondary strike or boycott is one called against Employer A in order to influence Employer B (for instance, if unionized plumbers refuse to install sinks made in non-unionized factories).

Although it is not a direct control on strikes, Section 109 of the Omnibus Budget Reconciliation Act of 1981 acts to discourage strikes by forbidding any member of a striker's household to receive Food Stamps.

A court that awards damages to an employer for secondary strike activity by the union also has discretion to award prejudgment interest on those damages.[20]

The Eighth Circuit held a mass-picketing statute unconstitutionally overbroad in that it prohibited more than two pickets at any time within either fifty feet of the entrance or of another picket.[21]

A union contract's "no-strike" clause should be read to prohibit sympathy strikes as well as strikes against the employer, unless either the contract as a whole or extrinsic circumstances show a different intent of the parties.[22]

A strike—even an unlawful one—is not a RICO predicate act; according to the D.C. Circuit[23] a contrary ruling would permit RICO to swallow up conventional labor law.

[¶2104] THE CERTIFICATION PROCESS

What determines whether a union is the authorized bargaining agent for the employees? The determinant is whether the union has been certified by an election conducted under the auspices of the NLRB. Once the election has been won, the union has a limited measure of security. For a one-year period, the union can negotiate a contract with the employer, knowing that no rival union can enter the picture and demand to be certified instead.

[¶2104.1] Certification Petitions

A petition for certification can be filed by an individual; a labor organization; an employee or group of employees—or even by the employer (a tack that might be taken if the employer thinks that unionization is a lesser evil than continued agitation for unionization, or who thinks that if the election is held immediately the union will be defeated).

To be valid, petitions filed by individuals or labor organizations must be accompanied by an indication of desire for representation on the part of at least 30% of the employees who would form the bargaining unit if the union were certified. The show of interest can be made via authorization cards; union membership cards or applications for union cards; receipts or record books showing payment of union dues; or petitions signed by employees.

The NLRB investigates the petition. If the employer does not object to holding an election, a "consent election" can be held. If the employer does object, and if the NLRB finds reasonable cause to believe that a question of representation exists, then a hearing is held, usually in the office of the NLRB's Regional Director for the region. In appropriate cases, the NLRB will direct that an election be held, and will supervise the election.

No petition for an election can be granted within a year of certification of a union, or of any valid election (even if the union was defeated). In general, elections will not be conducted if the employees are already covered by a valid collective bargaining agreement that is still in force. However, if the contract lasts three years or less, rival unions are permitted to file certification petitions during the period starting 90 days before the contract expires, and ending 30 days before its expiration. If the contract term is three years or more, rival unions are permitted to file a petition for certification at any time after the first three years.

[¶2104.2] The Appropriate Bargaining Unit

The purpose of the election is to certify a union if it is chosen by a majority of the workers. However, a union must be organized for an appropriate bargaining unit. Section (b) of the NLRA imposes standards for the bargaining unit. Whether a proposed bargaining unit is appropriate depends on the employees' duties, skills, and working conditions; their history of collective bargaining; and the extent of their union organization. If two or more units have been proposed, the employees' desires to belong to one or another are highly relevant.

Unions can organize according to employer, craft, plant, or any subdivision of these categories. However, plant guards can't be in the same bargaining unit as other employees (a common-sense prohibition; without it, sabotage and management spying on unions would be too tempting a tool for unscrupulous management or unions).

Professional employees can't be in a unit of nonprofessional employees, unless a majority of the professionals vote to be included. Although they may have more education, a higher salary, and higher status, professional employees can be unionized; managerial employees cannot. They have no collective bargaining rights at all, and are not even considered employees as defined by the NLRA. Confidential employees (those whose job involves access to confidential information about labor relations) can't be included in a bargaining unit with the rank and file. If a union proposes to organize a craft unit, that decision is protected: the NLRB does not have the power to decree that a different unit is appropriate.

[¶2104.3] Electioneering

It is the job of both the employer and the union to convince the employees that their best interests lie with the side doing the persuading. However, there are limits to the behavior that either side can engage in.

If the union wins the votes of a majority of those voting (not those eligible to vote), it will be certified as the bargaining representative for the unit. However, the election will not be valid unless a "representative number" of eligible employees actually votes. The level required is not set; it depends on the actual turnout, whether the employees were afforded adequate notice and opportunity to vote, and whether the employer was guilty of any unfair practices.

The election can be set aside if the employer asks the employees their views about unionization suggestively close to the time of the election, or conducts a formal pre-election poll. The employer's conduct in denying the employees a free choice can result in the election results being set aside, or even in unfair labor practices charges against the employer.

The employer has the right to assemble workers on company time for an anti-union speech, and the union is not entitled to equal time to respond as long as it is permitted to solicit the employees during their free time (e.g., lunchtime; coffee breaks). However, neither side is allowed to make speeches to massed employees on company time within 24 hours of the election.

Obviously, employers are not permitted to threaten the workers if they vote for the union; clearly, employers can present a factual statement of the disadvantages of union membership and the advantages of a non-union working environment. The difficulty is distinguishing between these two polar extremes, and categorizing an employer's actual conduct as one or the other. The election will be set aside if the employer announces benefits on election day, or explicitly promises benefits if the union loses or threatens to withhold them if the union wins. However, it *is* permissible to delay pay raises until after the election, as long as the increases will go through whatever the result of the election.

The union is allowed greater leeway; even outright insulting statements don't operate as threats to the employer. Employees are permitted to wear union buttons at work as an expression of their right of free speech; even wearing the button to the poll won't invalidate an otherwise valid election.

Just as the process of certification is initiated by a petition, a group of employees can petition to rescind the union's authority to execute a union-shop contract. An individual or a labor organization acting on behalf of the employees, or an employee or group of employees (but not an employer), can file a petition for decertification of a union.

[¶2105] PROTECTION OF EMPLOYEES AGAINST DISCRIMINATION

Federal law protects employees against employment discrimination. The federal statutes do not preempt state statutes that are *more* protective of employee rights, so the attorney is well advised to consult state statutes for additional remedies. Forty-six states have fair employment practices statutes of general applicability. (The exceptions are Alabama and Arkansas; North Carolina has a policy against employment discrimination but no statutory coverage, and Georgia forbids discrimination in government but not private-sector employment.)

Employees are protected against discrimination in all areas of the employment relationship (hiring, job duties, compensation, promotion, firing). The various statutes forbid discrimination on the grounds of race, color, religion, sex, national origin, pregnancy, and age. Retaliation against employees who exercise their rights is also forbidden, and employers are required to avoid sex discrimination in pay for jobs of equal skills, effort, and responsibility.

Because the procedures required of Title VII plaintiffs are so elaborate and time-consuming, employees may want to sue under 42 USC Section 1981 (giving all U.S. citizens the same right to make and enforce contracts as white citizens have) instead of, or in addition to, Title VII. For instance, the Eighth Circuit ruled[24] that an employee can make a Section 1981 case by proving, by a preponderance of the evidence, that race was a substantial or motivating factor in the discharge. But even under this scheme, the employer could avoid the obligation to reinstate the employee or provide back pay by showing (again by a preponderance of the evidence) that the employee would have been discharged even absent race as a motivating factor.

The Ninth Circuit treated a racially motivated refusal to promote the plaintiff from an hourly wage production job to a salaried supervisory position as a refusal to contract, and thus actionable under Section 1981.[25]

[¶2105.1] Title VII

The major federal anti-discrimination law is Title VII of the Civil Rights Act of 1964, codified at 42 U.S.C. Sec. 2000e-2000e(17). It covers the activities of labor unions and employment agencies as well as those of employers.

Five kinds of activities can constitute unlawful discrimination under Title VII:

➤ disparate treatment (overt, intentional classifications that disfavor employees or applicants on the basis of race, color, religion, sex, national origin—e.g., requiring three years' experience to promote whites, five years' experience to promote blacks).

➤ disparate impact (a facially neutral practice, not necessarily adopted in order to discriminate, which nonetheless has an unfavorable effect on a group protected by Title VII). For instance, it is not discriminatory for an airline to require that any person seeking a job as a pilot be able to fly a commercial jet; it is discriminatory to require that pilots have combat experience, because women are foreclosed from meeting this criterion.

➤ perpetuation of past discrimination.

➤ failure to make a reasonable accommodation to an employee's religious needs (e.g., allowing an employee to get someone else to "cover" for work duties on the employee's Sabbath would be a reasonable accommodation).

➤ retaliation against employees who file charges or otherwise exercise their rights.

It is not unlawful for an employer to require a "bona fide occupational qualification" (BFOQ), even if the BFOQ results in a disadvantage to a sex, religious group, or nationality. (BFOQs are never a defense to allegations of racial discrimination.)

Title VII also includes the Pregnancy Discrimination Amendment, 42 U.S.C. Sec. 2000e(k), which requires that "women affected by pregnancy, childbirth, or related medical conditions receive treatment equal to that of other employees." This is particularly significant in the context of employee benefits: the employer must provide coverage for pregnancy under its health plan if it covers comparable non-work-related conditions. Similarly, an employee who is unable to carry out certain tasks because of pregnancy, or who requires medical leave, must be treated on a parity with employees who suffer impairment or require medical leave for non-pregnancy-related, non-work-related injuries or illnesses.

Title VII prohibits many kinds of discrimination: race, sex, nationality, as well as pregnancy; it also forbids sexual harassment within the workplace.

One of the most controversial areas is the development of "fetal protection policies" by employers that keep pregnant (or potentially pregnant) women out of certain jobs that are alleged to carry a risk of miscarriage or fetal deformity. These policies are controversial because they preclude women from doing jobs that the women want, (often high-paid and with good promotion possibilities). Yet no one wants deformed children to be born; and employers certainly don't want to be sued based on prenatal injury to employees' children.

The EEOC's guidelines on fetal protection policies, adopted in 1988[26] do allow certain fetal protection policies to be adopted and carried out. The EEOC will evaluate the employer's policy to see if the job carries a substantial risk to reproduction or to fetuses; if the policy eliminates the risk; and if the job carries reproductive risks only for women, not for men. A fetal protection policy will be considered overbroad if it excludes all women of reproductive age, although all fertile women can be excluded; if the job carries a risk for only part of pregnancy, women in other stages of pregnancy cannot be excluded.

In 1991, the Supreme Court ruled that a fetal protection policy that excludes fertile women from a job entailing lead exposure is a Title VII violation, not a facially neutral policy that is potentially justified by business necessity. Not being a fertile woman cannot be considered a BFOQ, because fertility does not interfere with the ability to perform the job efficiently even if it does potentially risk adverse consequences outside the job arena. In the interim, EEOC Internal Policy Guidance[27] required the employer to make a BFOQ defense; to prove that containing the fetal hazard is reasonably necessary to normal business operations; that the exclusionary policy is reasonably necessary; and that efforts have also been made to protect the offspring of male workers. If the fetal protection policy is applied only to women, the employer must prove that the risk is only transmitted by pregnant women and that all or substantially all pregnant women are incapable of doing the job without encountering a transmission risk.

In light of the federal Pregnancy Discrimination Act and counterpart state legislation, it has been held[28] that an employee who claims that her discharge was premised on sex and pregnancy discrimination is precluded from bringing a state common-law tort action alleging abusive discharge. Instead, she must use the Title VII and related state remedies. It has also been held[29] that, because the Pregnancy Discrimination Act is part of the single consistent legislative scheme under Title VII, a disparate impact claim is cognizable under the PDA.

An employer is justified in using the efficient and economical method of hiring by word of mouth even if the result is that the workforce is 81% Korean as compared to a general population that is 3% Korean.[30]

An undocumented alien is permitted to bring a Title VII suit.[31]

Discrimination can exist within a race as well as between races: an employee can assert a cognizable Title VII claim of discrimination on the basis of "color" if the employee is a light-skinned black person charging discrimination by a dark-skinned black supervisor.[32]

Sexual and racial harassment also violate Title VII. EEOC Guidelines on sexual harassment[33] hold an employer liable for harassment within the workplace for failure to establish an explicit policy against sexual harassment and maintain an avenue for employee complaints that is reasonably available to them. The converse is that an employer will not be liable if it implements a strong anti-harassment policy and an effective complaint procedure.[34]

The EEOC issued further guidelines in 1993, using the standard of a reasonable person in similar circumstances to determine if race, sex, or other harassment violating Title VII has occurred in a workplace.[35] The employer is liable if it knew or should have known that harassment occurred, or if the harasser acts in a capacity as the employer's agent. Harassment by a co-employee subjects the employer to liability if it knew or should have known of the harassment. Similar standards are used for harassment by a non-employee (such as a restaurant patron harassing a waitress), but the employer's ability or inability to control the non-employee's behavior is relevant. Also in 1993, the Supreme Court announced a broad definition of sexual harassment in the workplace that will enable workers to win suits without having to prove that the behavior left them psychologically damaged or unable to do their jobs. In invoking the "broad rule of workplace equality" that was inherent in the federal law against job discrimination, the Court said that the law as applied to sexual harassment was violated when, for any of a variety of reasons, the environment would reasonably be perceived, and is perceived, as hostile or abusive.[36]

An employer's practice of asking female (but not male) job applicants about their plans to combine work and family has been deemed[37] to be evidence of a Title VII violation, but not to be a violation of Title VII taken by itself.

The mixed-motive case[38] holds that, once the employee proves that the prohibited factor (e.g., sex, race, nationality) played a motivating part in the employment decision, the employer can escape liability only by showing, by preponderance of the evidence, that it would have made the same decision without considering the prohibited factor.

In order to determine whether an employer corporation has enough employees to be subject to Title VII, the corporation's sole officer and her husband, who work for the corporation full-time, must be counted as employees even if they do not receive a salary for their work.[39]

As to evidence of discrimination, the Supreme Court has decided that peer-review materials prepared to determine faculty tenure have no special privileged status, and can be obtained by the EEOC on a mere showing of relevance.[40]

Generally speaking (for reasons of "deep pockets" as well as jurisdiction), the sole defendant in a Title VII case is the employer.

[¶2105.2] Civil Rights Act of 1991

By 1991, Congress had gathered enough support to pass the Civil Rights Act of 1991, P.L. 102-166. The statute makes it clear that #42 USC Sec. 1981 applies to post-hiring conduct, and to private employers as well as state actors. Under the 1991 Act, plaintiffs have the burden of persuasion, not just production, on the issue of whether a particular challenged practice caused disparate impact on the plaintiff's group. "Bottomline" figures showing gross statistical imbalances in the workforce cannot be used to prove the plaintiff's case. However, if it is impossible to break down the employer's decision-making process into separate, identifiable elements, the plaintiff is permitted to make a statistical prima facie case as to multiple employment practices operating in conjunction.

Under the 1991 Act, the terms "job-related" and "business necessity" have been added to the statute. First the employee demonstrates disparate impact (both as to imbalance and as to causation) of an employer practice. The next step is for the employer to assume the burden of persuasion and demonstrate that the practice is job-related and consistent with business necessity. The finder of fact must be able to conclude that it is more likely than not that the employer's representations are true.

In a mixed-motive case, the plaintiff can win by proving that race, sex, or other suspect classification was "a motivating factor" in the employer's conduct, even if the employer proves that it would have taken the same action even absent discrimination.

In disparate treatment cases, the 1991 Act permits the plaintiff to receive compensatory and punitive damages, not just back pay and other equitable relief, although compensatory damages are still not available under the ADEA. If damages are sought for intentional discrimination, either the plaintiff or defendant can demand a jury trial. However, damages are capped: for employers of 15-100 persons, the limit is $50,000; for 101-200 employees, $100,000; for 201-500 employees, $200,000; and $300,000 for very large companies with more than 500 employees. Prevailing plaintiffs are also permitted to recover expert witness fees.

Under the Act, the statute of limitations for a case involving an allegedly discriminatory seniority system runs from the creation of the system; the plaintiff's becoming subject to the scheme; or the plaintiff's being injured by the system, whichever is latest.

Policy guidance was issued to EEOC personnel[41] to the effect that the Act is not retroactive, and applies only to allegedly discriminatory conduct occurring on or after November 21, 1991.

[¶2105.3] The Equal Pay Act

The Equal Pay Act, or EPA (29 U.S.C. Sec. 206(d)(1)), requires employers to pay male and female employees equally for jobs involving equal skill, efforts, and responsibility (but not necessarily for jobs of "comparable worth": different jobs of similar value to the employer or to society). It is a defense under the EPA that the difference in pay is part of a seniority system; a merit system; piecework compensation; or results from factors other than the sex of the worker.

It is up to the jury, not the judge, to decide whether the employer's conduct was "willful" in order to determine whether the statute of limitations should be extended from two to three years.[42]

[¶2105.4] The Age Discrimination in Employment Act

The Age Discrimination in Employment Act, or ADEA (29 U.S.C. Sec. 621), sets a general rule that no employee who is capable of performing the job can be fired merely because of his or her age. Protection under the ADEA begins at age 40, but there are exceptions for police and firefighters. A corporation's top management can be required to retire at 70.

Employers are permitted to fire over-age employees where age is a BFOQ (where public safety requires speedy reaction times, for instance); where reasonable factors other than age are used (e.g., the employer cuts its payroll by firing the three least-productive employees in each department, regardless of age); pursuant to a bona fide seniority or benefit plan; and employers and unions are permitted to exclude applicants from an apprenticeship program based on their age.

Judicially unreviewed administrative proceedings (in this case, under the New York Human Rights Law) have no preclusive effect on federal court ADEA proceedings: the ADEA itself assumes that the federal court has jurisdiction over cases where the employer prevailed at the administrative level.[43]

If a federal employee chooses to file suit in federal court under 29 U.S.C. 633a(d) rather than using the administrative remedies specific to federal employment, the filing requirement has been held[44] satisfied by giving the EEOC notice of intent to file suit within 180 days of the occurrence of the allegedly illegal practice, not less than 30 days before actually filing suit.

Missouri's mandatory retirement at age 70 for judges has been upheld,[45] because the principle of balance of powers gives states control over management of their own internal affairs, and deterioration of capacity after age 70 occurs often enough for it to be rational to conclude that all judges must retire at 70. Appointed state judges are not "employees" under the ADEA in any event.

Massachusetts' state law requiring an annual physical examination of all state employees over 70 has also been upheld[46] as a reasonable measure to determine employees' continued fitness, and hence not an ADEA violation.

Where vesting is based on years of service rather than age, employer interference with vesting is not a per se violation of the ADEA. The same definition of willfulness (whether the employer knew or recklessly disregarded whether the conduct was prohibited by the ADEA) is applied in ADEA disparate treatment cases, whether the employer's conduct was informal or based on a formal policy. If willfulness is shown, the employee-plaintiff does not also have to show that the employer conduct was outrageous, give direct evidence of the employer's motivation, or prove that age was the predominant factor in the employment decision.[47]

An insurance agent working on a straight commission basis, and who has signed a statement that he is an independent contractor, is not an "employee" for ADEA purposes.[48]

After establishing a prima facie case, the ADEA plaintiff must present enough evidence to create a controversy over the credibility of the employer's alleged legitimate reasons for the employment action; the employee's failure to do so will result in summary judgment for the employer.[49]

An employer was granted summary judgment in a case where an employee was fired for an invalid reason (refusal to pledge complete loyalty to the CEO after a controversy resulting in several resignations from the board of directors), but there was no proof (other than speculation of non-expert witnesses) that age was a substantial factor in the employee's dismissal.[50]

If several employees have ADEA claims, the employees who failed to file timely ADEA charges with the EEOC can still participate in a suit premised on timely charges filed by other employees;[51] and if a representative ADEA action is timely filed, the statute of limitations is tolled on the claims of everyone who opts in as a plaintiff.[52]

Once individuals have fully litigated their own ADEA claims, res judicata prevents them from receiving individual relief in a subsequent EEOC action based on the same claims,[53] but the converse is not necessarily true: dismissal of an employee's suit as untimely filed is not res judicata as to an EEOC suit for injunctive relief based on the same employer conduct.[54]

The Civil Rights Act of 1991 sets the ADEA statute of limitations at 90 days from termination of the EEOC proceedings or dismissal. Also see the Age Discrimination Claims Assistance Act of 1990, P.L. 101-504, amending 29 U.S.C. 626 to extend the statute of limitations for certain claims that would be time-barred as a result of EEOC failure to process them in time.

According to the Tax Court, plaintiffs who win ADEA cases need not pay income tax on the damages they receive, but the Northern District of Florida finds the purpose of liquidated damages to be punishment and deterrence, not compensation of the victim, thus finding ADEA liquidated damages to be taxable income.[55]

In a case in which reinstatement would be dangerous to the ex-employee's health (because of the stress of harassment by a supervisor), the employee was permitted to reject reinstatement and receive front pay but not attorneys' fees.[56]

[¶2105.5] Handicap/Disability Discrimination

Title I of the Americans with Disabilities Act (P.L. 101-336, signed by the President in 1990) extends the provisions of the Rehabilitation Act to forbid employment discrimination by any employer of 25 or more employees (for the first two years the statute is in effect; 15 employees thereafter), whether or not the employer is government-funded, against a qualified disabled individual who has the capacity to perform the essential functions of the job. Furthermore, employers are required to make reasonable accommodations (such as bells instead of light signals, or vice versa; specialized computer software) to disabled employees' special needs. Disability is defined as a physical or mental impairment imposing significant limitations on major life activities. People with a history of disability, or who are perceived to be disabled, also come within the scope of the definition.

In 1991, the EEOC published both proposed and final rules under the Americans with Disabilities Act (ADA).[57] The Proposed Rule clarifies that the definition of disability does not include current drug use. Nor does it include transvestism, transsexuality, homosexuality, or bisexuality, because these are not considered impairments. The showing of undue hardship that an employer must make as a defense to a charge of failure to make reasonable accommodations as required by the ADA is defined as proof of significant difficulty or expense, considering the nature and cost of the accommodation, the employer's financial resources, its type of operation, and the effect of the accommodation on the work site.

The Final Rule maintains the proposal's case-by-case approach to reasonable accommodation and adds more detailed definitions, forbidding inquiries about an applicant's past Workers' Compensation history, explaining the effect of collective bargaining agreements, and clarifying what it means to be "substantially limited in working." It is permissible for employers to ask an applicant to describe or demonstrate how he or she can do the job with or without accommodation. The EEOC published a manual with compliance guidelines even more detailed than the Final Rule. In 1993, the EEOC and NLRB entered into a memorandum of understanding to coordinate unfair labor practice claims that are premised on allegations of ADA violations.[58]

There is limited protection against discrimination by federal contractors and recipients of federal aid, under Section 503 of the Rehabilitation Act of 1973 (29 U.S.C. Sec. 793), Section 106 of the Developmental Disabilities Assistance and Bill of Rights Act (42 U.S.C. Sec. 6005), and Section 402 of the Vietnam Era Veterans' Readjustment Assistance Act (38 U.S.C. Sec. 2012). Most of the states have provisions against handicap discrimination, even in the private sector, so the attorney should check state statute and case law to see if a would-be client has a case.

Refusing to hire a person because of his or her extreme overweight can constitute a valid handicap discrimination claim under the Rehabilitation Act,[59] but reverse discrimination claims cannot be brought under the District of Columbia anti-discrimination law by a non-handicapped individual who claims that a handicapped individual received a hiring preference.[60]

[¶2106] OTHER LIMITATIONS ON EMPLOYMENT AT WILL

Two states (Montana, South Dakota) forbid private-sector employees to be discharged without just cause. In other states, some vestige of the employment-at-will doctrine survives, usually tempered:

➤ Many statutes and cases hold that employees cannot be discharged for exercising legal rights (serving on a jury, expressing political opinions).

➤ "Whistle-blowers" (those who report wrongdoing by the employer—such as violations of anti-pollution laws) may be entitled to protection if they act in good faith.

➤ If the employer has provided an implied contract (such as a provision in the employee manual calling for due process before an employee is fired), the implied contract may be enforceable by the employees.

Although employees are entitled to get reasonable accommodations of their religious needs (e.g., being allowed to swap shifts so that no worker will have to work on a day observed by his or her religion as a holy day), the Fourth Circuit has held that there is no violation of the First Amendment guarantee of freedom of religion if a state denies unemployment compensation to a woman whose religious beliefs obligated her to quit her job and follow her husband to a new home. Even a resignation inspired by religious reasons counts as a "voluntary quit."[61]

An employer can permissibly make a unilateral change from a written policy of termination for cause only to employment-at-will, as long as the employees receive adequate notice of the change even if, at the time of hiring, the employer did not reserve the right to change the policy.[62]

An employee who alleges that his discharge was wrongfully premised on his informing the employer (accurately) that his supervisor was being investigated for embezzling from an earlier employer, and who claims that the discharge was a violation of an implied covenant of good faith and fair dealing in the employment relationship is entitled only to contract damages, not to tort damages (e.g., compensatory and punitive damages).[63] However, this ruling has been held not to bar damages for emotional distress in the rare cases in which a wrongfully discharged employee can prove intentional infliction of mental distress.[64]

This is a most volatile area, and study of current precedents is essential.

— ENDNOTES —

1. 29 USC §§2001-2009.

2. See, e.g., Transport Workers Local 234 v. Southwestern Pennsylvania Transp. Authority, 863 F.2d 1110 (3d Cir. 12/28/88) [Random drug testing of "safety sensitive" employees does not violate the Fourth Amendment, because the state has a legitimate interest in protecting public safety, drug use does imperil public safety, and the testing program contained enough safeguards to prevent abuses of discretion]; Jackson v. Liquid Carbonic Corp., 863 F.2d 111 (1st Cir. 12/1/88), cert. denied 490 U.S. 1107 [Employee's state law claim of invasion of privacy, premised on the employer's unilateral adoption of a testing program, is preempted by Section 301 of the Labor-Management Relations Act].

3. Local 144 Nursing Home Pension Fund v. Demisay, #91-610, 113 S.Ct. 2252 (Sup.Ct. 6/14/93).

4. Building & Construction Trades Council v. Association of Builders & Contractors, ##91-261, -274, 113 S.Ct. 1190 (Sup.Ct. 3/8/93).

5. King v. St. Vincent's Hospital, #90-889, 112 S.Ct. 570 (Sup.Ct. 12/16/91).

6. Taylor-Callahan-Coleman Counties v. Dole, 948 F.2d 953 (5th Cir. 12/18/91).

7. Hotel Employees and Restaurant Employees Local 54 v. Elsinore Shore Assoc's., 768 F.Supp. 1117 (D.N.J. 8/20/91).

8. Finkler v. Elsinore Shore Assoc's, 781 F.Supp.1060 (D.N.J. 1/28/92).

9. Norfolk & Western Railway v. Train Dispatchers, #89-1027, -1028, 111 S.Ct. 1156 (Sup.Ct. 3/19/91).

10. Nicely v. USX, 709 F.Supp. 646 (W.D.Pa. 3/30/89).

11. Woodell v. IBEW Local 71, #90-967, 112 S. Ct. 494 (Sup.Ct. 12/4/91), on re., and 953 F.2d 645.

12. Aqua-Chem Inc. v. NLRB, 910 F.2d 1487 (7th Cir. 8/23/90).

13. NLRB v. Delta-Macon Brick & Tile Co., 943 F.2d 567 (5th Cir. 10/4/91).

14. Harry Hoffman Printing Inc., v. Graphic Communications Int'l Union, 950 F.2d 95 (2nd Cir. 11/17/91).

15. NLRB v. EDP Medical Computer Systems Inc., 62 LW 2240 (2nd Cir. 10/8/93).

16. Del Rey Totilleria v. NLRB, 976 F.2d 1115 (9th Cir. 7/17/92).

17. H.B. Zachry Co. V. NLRB, 886 F.2d 70 (4th Cir. 9/20/89).

18. Martin v. National Ass'n of Letter Carriers, 60 LW 2773 (6th Cir. 5/27/92).

19. Lechmere v. NLRB, #90-970, 111 S.Ct. 1305 (Sup.Ct. 1/27/91), rev'd 914 F.2d 313 (1st Cir. 1990).

20. Wickman Contracting Co. v. IBEW, 955 F.2d 831 (2d Cir. 1/29/92).

21. Food and Commercial Workers v. IBP Inc., 857 F.2d 422 (8th Cir. 9/8/88).

22. Indianapolis Power & Light, 291 NLRB #145 (12/9/88).

23. Yellow Bus Lines Inc. v. Drivers, Chauffeurs & Helpers Local Union 639, 839 F.2d 782, 913 F.2d 948 (D.C. Cir. 9/4/90).

24. Edwards v. Jewish Hospital of St. Louis, 855 F.2d 1345 (8th Cir. 9/2/88).

25. Sitgraves v. Allied Signal Inc., 953 F.2d 570 (9th Cir. 1/17/92).

26. See 57 LW 2221.

27. Dated 1/24/90; see 58 LW 2461.

28. Makovi v. Sherwin-Williams Co., 58 LW 2100 (Md. App. 7/26/89).

29. Scherr v. Woodland School Community District #50, 867 F.2d 974 (7th Cir. 11/1/88).

30. EEOC v. Consolidated Service Systems, 989 F.2d 233 (7th Cir. 3/4/93).

31. EEOC v. Tortilleria "La Mejor," 758 F.Supp. 585 (E.D.Cal. 2/15/91).

32. Walker v. IRS, 57 LW 2680 (N.D. Ga. 5/11/89).

33. See 57 LW 2261.

34. Semble Steele v. Offshore Shipbuilding Inc., 867 F.2d 1311 (11th Cir. 3/15/89).

35. 29 CFR Part 609; see 62 LW 2061 (7/13/93).

36. Harris v. Forklift Systems, Inc., #92-1168, 61 LW 4004 (11/9/93).

37. Stukey v. Air Force, 809 F.Supp. 536 (S.D. Oh. 1/31/92).

38. Price Waterhouse v. Hopkins, 109 S.Ct. 1775 (Sup.Ct. 5/1/89), on remand 897 F.2d 1380 (6th Cir. 3/26/90).

39. EEOC v. Pettegrove Truck Svce. Inc., 716 F.Supp. 1430 (S.D. Fla. 5/4/89).

40. University of Pennsylvania v. EEOC, 110 S.Ct. 577 (Sup.Ct. 1/9/90).

41. See 60 LW 2418.

42. Fowler v. Land Management Groups, 978 F.2d 64 (4th Cir. 10/28/92).

43. Astoria Fed'l Savings & Loan v. Solimino, #89-1895, 111 S.Ct. 2166 (Sup.Ct. 6/10/91).

44. Stevens v. DOT, #89-1821, 111 S.Ct. 1562 (Sup.Ct. 4/24/91).

45. Gregory v. Ashcroft, #90-50, 111 S.Ct. 2395 (Sup.Ct. 6/20/91).

46. EEOC v. Massachusetts, 987 F.2d 64 (D.Mass. 4/17/92).

47. Hazen Paper Co. v. Biggins, #91-1600, 113 S.Ct. 2437 (Sup.Ct. 4/20/93).

48. Oestman v. Nat'l Farmers Union Ins. Co., 958 F.2d 303 (10th Cir. 3/3/92).

49. Bolton v. Schirmer Inc., 62 LW 2330 (W.D. Ok. 11/9/93).

50. Visser v. Packer Engineering Assocs. Inc., 924 F.2d 655 (7th Cir. 2/4/91).

51. Anderson v. Montgomery Ward & Co., 852 F.2d 1008 (7th Cir. 7/25/88).

52. Levine v. Lane Bryant, 57 LW 2336 (N.D. Ill. 11/15/88).

53. EEOC v. U.S. Steel Corp., 921 F.2d 489 (3d Cir. 12/14/90).

54. EEOC v. Harris Chernin Inc., 62 LW 2361 (7th Cir. 12/1/93).

55. Under Downey v. Comm'r, 97 TC No. 10 (7/31/91) and 62 LW 2063 (TC 6/29/93), both liquidated and nonliquidated damages received in settlement of an ADEA suit are excludable from the taxpayer's gross income; contra, Maleszewski v. U.S., 62 LW 2063 (N.D.Fla. 6/4/93).

56. Lewis v. Federal Prison Industries Inc., 953 F.2d 1277 (11th Cir. 2/18/92).

57. Prop.Regs. 2/28/91; see 59 LW 2541. Final Regs. 56 FR 35726 (7/26/91). Single copies of the EEOC manual are available without charge from the EEOC Office of Communications, 1801 L Street NW, Washington, DC 20507, (800) 669-EEOC. See 60 LW 2478.

58. 62 LW 2337 (11/16/93).

59. Cook v. Rhode Island, 62 LW 2345 (1st Cir. 11/22/93).

60. Ortner v. Paralyzed Veterans of America, 61 LW 2181 (D.C. Super. 9/11/92). Perhaps in this case being handicapped was considered a bona fide occupational qualification; the job involved working with and for paralyzed individuals.

61. Austin v. Berryman, 862 F.2d 1050, 878 F.2d 786, cert. den. 110 S.Ct. 343 (4th Cir. 6/28/89).

62. Bankey v. Storer Broadcasting Co., 882 F.2d 208 (Mich.Sup. 6/6/89).

63. Foley v. Interactive Data Corp., 765 F.2d 373 (Cal.Sup. 12/29/88).

64. Lanouette v. Ciba-Geigy Corp., 59 LW 2147 (Cal.App. 8/13/90).

— FOR FURTHER REFERENCE —

Anderson, Steven G., "Tester Standing Under Title VII: A Rose by Any Other Name," 41 *DePaul L. Rev.* 1217 (Summer '92).

Bloch, Marc J. and Scott A. Moorman, "Working to Rule and Other Alternate Job Actions," 9 *Labor Lawyer* 169 (Spring '93).

Branscomb, Melinda J., "Labor, Loyalty, and the Corporate Campaign," 73 *Boston U. L. Rev.* 291 (May '93).

Bregstein, Henry, "Secured Creditors and §15(a) of the Fair Labor Standards Act," 14 *Cardozo L. Rev.* 1965 (May '93).

Browne, Kingsley R., "Statistical Proof of Discrimination: Beyond Damned Lies," 68 *Washington L. Rev.* 477 (July '93).

Burstein, James A., "What Is Reasonable Accommodation Under the Americans With Disabilities Act?" 38 *The Practical Lawyer* 63 (July '92).

Chicoine, Jeffrey P., "The Business Necessity Defense to Unilateral Changes in Working Conditions," 8 *The Labor Lawyer* 297 (Spring '92).

Comiskey, Hope A., " 'Prompt and Effective Remedial Action?' What Must an Employer Do to Avoid Liability for 'Hostile Work Environment' Sexual Harassment?" 8 *Labor Lawyer* 181 (Spring '92).

Crow, Stephen M. and Sandra J. Hartman, "ADA Versus NLRA: Is a Showdown Imminent Over Reasonable Accommodation?" 44 *Labor Law J.* 375 (June '93).

Dooley, Cynthia J., "Wrongful Discharge: The Public Policy Exception, and Public Concern Requirement, and Employees' Private Lives," 11 *Review of Litigation* 387 (Spring '92).

Durie, Darolyn J. and Mark A. Lemley, "The Antitrust Liability of Labor Unions for Anticompetitive Litigation," 80 *California L. Rev.* 757 (May '92).

Estlund, Cynthia L., "Economic Rationality and Union Avoidance," 71 *Texas L. Rev.* 921 (April '93).

Feerick, John D., "Toward a Model Whistleblowing Law," 19 *Fordham Urban L.J.* 585 (Spring '92).

Frier, Daniel B., "Age Discrimination and the ADA," 66 *Temple L. Rev.* 173 (Spring '93).

Gordon, Philip L., "The Job Application Process After the Americans With Disabilities Act," 18 *Employee Relations L.J.* 185 (Autumn '92).

Grinstead, Kenneth, "The Arbitration of Last Chance Agreements," 48 *Arbitration J.* 71 (March '93).

Hartstein, Barry A., "An Employer's Guide to the Civil Rights Act of 1991," 8 *Corp. Counsel's Quarterly* 1 (July '92).

Hundley, Greg, "Collective Bargaining Coverage of Union Members and Nonmembers in the Public Sector," 32 *Industrial Relations* 72 (Winter '93).

Johnson, Johnnie L. Jr., "Sex Discrimination: Law Enforcement Issues for Changing Times," 19 *Ohio Northern U. L. Rev.* 673 (Summer '93).

Kolick, Joseph Jr. and Merle M. DeLancey Jr., "Can One Unilaterally Gain the Right to Make Unilateral Changes in Working Conditions?" 9 *Labor Lawyer* 137 (Spring '93).

Krugel, Charles Alan, "AIDS and the ADA: Maneuvering Through a Legal Minefield," 44 *Labor Law J.* 408 (July '93).

Moberly, Michael D., "The Recoverability of Prejudgment Interest Under the ADEA After Thurston," 8 *The Labor Lawyer* 225 (Spring '92).

Morris, Frank C. Jr., "Arbitration After Gilmer," 38 *The Practical Lawyer* 71 (June '92).

Nager, Glen D., "Affirmative Action After the Civil Rights Act of 1991," 68 *Notre Dame L. Rev.* 1057 (July '93).

Parker, George P. Jr. and Robert Shaw-Meadow, "Winning Employment Cases Through Ethical Motion Practice," 39 *Proceedings of the Institute on Labor Law Developments* 11-1 (Annual '93).

Petersen, Donald J., "Trends in Arbitrating Falsification of Employment Application Forms," 47 *Arbitration J.* 31 (September '92).

Pisorski, Thomas J., "The Growing Judicial Acceptance of Summary Judgment in Age Discrimination Cases," 18 *Employee Relations LJ.* 245 (Autumn '92).

Poor, J. Stephen, "Rights Act's Retroactivity Still Debated," *Nat. LJ.* 1/27/92 p. 20.

Ray, Douglas E., "Some Overlooked Aspects of the Strike Replacement Issue," 41 *U. of Kansas L. Rev.* 363 (Winter '93).

Scanlan, James P., "Measuring Hiring Discrimination," 44 *Labor Law J.* 387 (July '93).

Shapiro, Barry E., "The Future of Labor Relations in the Federal Sector," 43 *Labor LJ.* 508 (August '92).

Spelfogel, Evan J., "New Trends in the Arbitration of Employment Disputes," 48 *Arbitration J.* 6 (March '93).

Tien, Wendy S., "Compulsory Arbitration of ADA Claims: Disabling the Disabled," 77 *Minn. L. Rev.* 1443 (June '93).

Voos, Paula B. et al., "Reforming Labor Law to Remove Barriers to High Performance Work Organizations," 44 *Labor Law J.* 469 (August '93).

ENVIRONMENTAL LAW

[¶2201] Historically, people assumed that the air, water, and land around them could absorb their waste products. In recent times, it has become clear that nature's capacity to assimilate wastes is not infinite. Hence concern about the environment has led to a wide variety of federal laws to protect the environment; the states have played a major enforcement role; environmental litigation is very common; and landowners, developers, contractors and others who may be responsible for the enormous "response costs" of cleaning up contaminated sites are seeking legal advice. A major litigation issue, coverage of environmental liability under liability insurance policies, is discussed in ¶2515.1

The "taking" issue emerged in 1992, but the Supreme Court did not provide simple answers. According to *Lucas,*[1] a state cannot deny all (or substantially all) benefit of ownership to landowners by imposing environmental rules and then automatically deny any compensation to them. However, the Court did not set the principles for assessing the adequacy of compensation. Certiorari was granted in another case, as to whether arbitrary, capricious, or illegal denial of building permits violates the rights of property developers; but certiorari was later dismissed as improvidently granted,[2] so we don't have the Supreme Court's guidance on this issue either.

Also see P.L. 102-486, an omnibus bill to establish a national energy policy, including development of alternative fuels and vehicles to use them; consumer conservation of energy; and new standards for construction of power plants.

[¶2202] FEDERAL ENVIRONMENTAL LAWS

There are many major federal environmental protection statutes:

➤ The Clean Air Act, 42 USC Section 7404, as amended by P.L. 101-549.

➤ The Federal Water Pollution Control Act ("Clean Water Act") 33 USC Section 1365.

➤ The Comprehensive Environmental Response, Compensation and Liability Act (CERCLA; also known as "Superfund") 42 USC Section 9659. CERCLA has been amended and supplemented by SARA, the Superfund Amendments and Reauthorization Act of 1986, P.L. 99-499.

➤ An EPA ruling (granted deference by the D.C. Circuit) makes it clear that SARA's reimbursement provision applies only to cleanup orders received after Congress adopted SARA.[3]

➤ Emergency Planning and Community Right to Know Act, 42 USC Section 11046.

➤ Resource Conservation and Recovery Act (RCRA), 42 USC Section 6972. A new Subtitle J was added to RCRA by the Medical Waste Tracking Act of 1988, P.L. 100-582.

➤ Safe Drinking Water Act, 42 USC Section 300j-8.

➤ Toxic Substances Control Act, 14 USC Section 2619.

➤ Asbestos Hazard Emergency Response Act of 1986 (AHERA), P.L. 99-579 (1986).

➤ Oil Pollution Act of 1990, P.L. 101-380, imposing strict liability under federal or state law on those responsible for oil spills under federal or state law. A 5-cent-per barrel tax is imposed on oil to deal with the equivalent of "uninsured motorists": polluters who cannot be located or who cannot be subjected to liability. Transporters of oil must have plans to prevent spills, and must shift to the use of double-hulled tankers. The law also provides remedies for victims of oil spills.

These statutes call for federal and state enforcement actions, and also allow citizen suits by private plaintiffs. The citizen suit, which seeks correction of pollution and the payment of fines into the public treasury, must be distinguished from the "toxic tort" suit brought by plaintiffs seeking damages for perceived injuries caused by polluters. Toxic tort suits are often premised on traditional legal concepts such as strict liability for potentially dangerous substances allowed to escape from one's land, or for ultrahazardous activities (especially those carried out for profit). Most of the federal statutes also impose criminal penalties on violators. The Federal Facility Compliance Act of 1992, P.L. 102-386, requires all federally owned facilities to comply with federal laws respecting solid waste; the EPA has the power to issue Administrative Orders to resolve federal violations. Note, however, that states do not have the power to impose punitive fines on federal agencies that violate the state's anti-pollution laws, although states can impose sanctions, including fines, that are intended to coerce compliance rather than to punish past non-compliance.[4]

In 1991 the Department of Justice issued a 15-page statement to prosecutors, suggesting that corporations that "pollute but police themselves" should not be subjected to criminal liability. The DOJ's suggested factors in the prosecution decision include encouragement of self-policing and self-auditing and voluntary disclosure; whether a company has a good compliance record; and whether it notified the government promptly of the violation. (Note that the regular federal sentencing guidelines for corporations do not apply to environmental offenses.)

[¶2203] SCOPE OF CERCLA

CERCLA was legislated in 1980 in an attempt to provide funds and enforcement clout to clean up contaminated "waste sites" and respond to spills of dangerous substances. (The RCRA, discussed below, provides regulation of current activities involving hazardous waste; CERCLA deals with cleanups of sites where past activities occurred and resulted in contamination. However, CERCLA also requires reporting of "releases" of certain materials into the environment as they occur.)

The release (or threat of release) of any hazardous substance, pollutant, or contaminant into the air, surface water, groundwater, or soil falls under CERCLA. This is true whenever a release or threatened release causes anyone to incur response costs even if no actual contamination occurred.[5] Companies that initiate environmental cleanups, rather than wait for government action to be taken against them, can seek repayment from insurers, the Washington Supreme Court ruled in 1994.[6] The court rejected the insurers' position that such coverage takes effect only after a government agency files suit or threatens to take legal action.

The Environmental Protection Agency (EPA) publishes a list[7] of hazardous substances, intended to include anything defined as a "hazardous waste" by RCRA, anything targeted by the EPA under the Clean Air, Clean Water, or Toxic Substances Control Act. There are more than 700 substances on the list. A release is any way in which a substance can enter the environment, except for the specific exclusions found in CERCLA Section 101:

➤ Releases permitted under another federal statute, such as a release under an NPDES permit

➤ Workplace exposures (which are under the jurisdiction of OSHA)

➤ Vehicle exhaust

➤ Certain radioactive contamination already under the jurisdiction of other federal statutes

➤ Normal use of fertilizer

The EPA has published rules expanding the definition of hazardous waste and adding 25 organic chemicals (including benzene and vinyl chloride) to the scope of the RCRA. Regulatory levels were set for these chemicals.[8]

It has also been held that asbestos in a building structure does not fall within the definitions of "waste site" or "release," so response costs are not recoverable.[9]

The EPA is authorized to "respond" to the presence of forbidden substances at a site (which is why "response costs" are such a bone of contention) either through a short-term, limited "removal" or a broader "remedy." First, the EPA must enter into an agreement with the state in which the contaminated site is located. The state must furnish 10% of the cleanup costs (50% if the site is actually owned by the state) unless the responsible parties settle the case and pay for the cleanup themselves.

The Eleventh Amendment does not preclude suits against the states themselves for money damages: *Pennsylvania v. Union Gas Co.*[10] holds that CERCLA, as amended by RCRA, shows a Congressional intention to permit such suits; and that Congressional legislation under the Commerce Clause abrogates Eleventh Amendment immunity.

Because the United States has waived sovereign immunity under RCRA (and under the Clean Water Act), states can bring civil claims against the federal government as well,[11] but a later case[12] holds that sovereign immunity is not waived unless the United States government currently owns and operates the facility.

It is unclear whether there is a private right of action under CERCLA Section 107(a), the provision that makes the party responsible for arranging for the treatment or disposal of hazardous substances liable for the cost of removal.

Medical monitoring costs can be recovered under CERCLA for the limited purpose of studying the environmental impact of release of hazardous substances, but not to study the health effects of the release.[13]

CERCLA Section 107 does not provide for the award of private litigants' attorney's fees associated with bringing a cost recovery action.[14]

CERCLA Section 107(a) defines three classes of "responsible parties":

➤ Present or past "owners or operators" of the site.

➤ Those who transported waste to the site.

➤ "Generators" of the waste who arranged with the owner/operator or transporter to have the wastes either disposed of or treated. This definition includes someone who approved of previous dumping and ordered someone to "handle" a truckload of waste, because it can be inferred that he meant "dump it,"[15] but a common carrier that ships hazardous manufacturing chemicals does not "arrange with a transporter for transport or disposal" of the chemicals, and thus is not liable for response costs.[16] A pesticide manufacturer is a "generator" even though it hired a formulation facility to process pesticides, because the manufacturer arranged for and contributed to handling and disposal of the waste.[17]

The Superfund Amendments and Reauthorization Act of 1986 (SARA) imposes on the EPA a duty to select remedies that protect human health and the environment; make the maximum practicable use of permanent solutions, treatment, and resource recovery techniques; attain the "applicable, relevant and appropriate requirements" (ARARs) unless the EPA feels a waiver is acceptable; yet it must be cost-effective. The court's power to grant relief in the public interest includes authority to order a site owner to give private parties access to the site in order to clean it up.[18]

EPA has the power, under CERCLA, to disapprove the contractor that potentially responsible parties choose to do the cleanup work.[19]

If the EPA feels litigation is required to enforce CERCLA, it uses the Memorandum of Understanding (6/5/77) between EPA and the Department of Justice to have the Attorney General sue on behalf of the EPA Administrator. Either initiating or settling a suit requires approval of both the EPA Administrator and the Assistant Attorney General of the Land and Natural Resources Division, who is the Attorney General's designee in these matters.

To be adopted by the government, a consent decree must be in the public interest—that is, legal, fair, and reasonable in terms of: previous natural condition and extent of potential hazards at the site; the existence of alternatives that would also clean up the site; the technical adequacy of the proposal; and whether the consent decree serves the public interest and furthers the statutory goals. Once a consent decree is entered, it serves as a final judgment.

As originally enacted, CERCLA did not contain a statute of limitations provision. The 1986 SARA amendments stipulate that a cost recovery suit in a removal action must be brought within three years of the removal of the toxic substance. In a remedial action, the "initial action" must be brought within six years of the start of physical construction on the site. The EPA can institute further actions for follow-up costs, but all actions must be brought within three years of the end of the cleanup. CERCLA Section 309 provides that, in private tort suits alleging injury to persons or property, the state statute of limitations starts to run when the plaintiff knew or should have known that the hazardous substance, pollutant, or contaminant "caused or contributed to" the injury or damages. A CERCLA cost recovery claim is not barred by a statute of limitations that became law after the claim occurred, but before it was filed. Nor is laches a defense; CERCLA includes a list of affirmative defenses, but laches does not appear in the list.[20]

One effect of CERCLA is to make a great deal of information about waste sites and their cleanups available to the public, thus putting potential plaintiffs on notice. *Knox v. A.C.& S. Inc.*[21] holds that the commencement date is the date the plaintiff knew or should have known that a hazardous substance caused or contributed to injury but only if the injury was caused by "release" of a substance from a "facility" into the environment. In this case, involving occupational exposure to asbestos, there was no release into the environment at large, and therefore the state products liability statute of repose was not preempted.

A corporate officer's or director's personal liability under CERCLA is broader than ordinary corporate tort liability, but directors and officers are not subjected to strict liability merely for holding corporate office. The test is whether the individual's power, title, and percentage of ownership gave him or her the power to prevent or significantly abate the release of hazardous substances into the environment. Without such power, the individual will not be personally liable.[22]

An excavator that moves contaminated soil on a site can be liable for cleanup costs as an "operator" and/or "transporter";[23] but a manufacturer that gives technical advice about safe disposal of herbicide after a spill or leak cannot be held liable for "arranging for disposal."[24] As the District Court pointed out, companies should not be subjected to the risk of liability when they give safety information to others.

Toxic residue created by burning household and industrial waste in municipal incinerators must be treated as hazardous waste and not dumped in ordinary landfills.[25]

In summation, the EPA is authorized to require that a contaminated site be cleaned up by those persons responsible for contaminating it, either as owner or operator of the site, a transporter of wastes to the site, or the owner of wastes deposited at the site. Those parties responsible for the problem are jointly and severally liable.[26]

[¶2204]   THE CLEAN WATER ACT

One of the first federal anti-pollution statutes was 1972's Federal Water Pollution Control Act, which was renamed the Clean Water Act in 1977. The original goals were to improve water quality enough to protect wildlife and support recreation by 1983, and to eliminate all discharge of pollutants into water by 1985. In 1987, the Water Quality Act (P.L. 100-4) was passed to improve water quality in areas in which the national minimum discharge standards are insufficient to guarantee adequate water quality.

The Clean Water Act consists of five elements:

➤ Water quality standards

➤ A program of issuing discharge permits

➤ Industry standards for levels of effluent discharge which may not be exceeded

➤ Provisions about chemical and oil spills

➤ A program of grants and loans for construction of public water treatment facilities

In 1991, New York City was found liable for violating the Clean Water Act by chemically treating Hudson River water pumped up during droughts. The Second Circuit did not accept the defense that the fish-endangering chlorine and alum were added to the water to make it potable for human beings.[27]

States have broad authority under CWA to protect not only the quality of their water but also the quantity of water that flows in streams and rivers. Thus a state has the right to insist on the minimum water flow that is necessary to protect fish in a river.[28] Thus a state's CWA authority over a proposed hydroelectric project extends to fish-protection efforts that are broader than those necessary to protect water quality. Possible use of wetlands as a migratory bird habitat has an effect on interstate commerce, and therefore the EPA has regulatory jurisdiction over the wetlands.[29]

The National Pollutant Discharge Elimination System (NPDES)[30] obligates anyone responsible for discharging any pollutant into water to get a permit first. No permits can be issued for ocean discharges unless the issuing authority makes a determination that the discharge will not degrade the environment unreasonably.

The state of Arkansas objected to the EPA's condition in an NPDES permit that the Arkansas discharger comply with the standards of Oklahoma, where the discharged materials would end up. The Tenth Circuit ruled against the state,[31] deferring to the EPA's interpretation of the CWA: that state statutes more stringent than the federal rules can never be achieved if upstream dischargers are allowed to violate them.

Under the original CWA scheme, the EPA was the agency issuing the permits, but states were given the option to take over the process: by 1986, 37 of the states had adopted the option of issuing permits. An NPDES permit establishes "performance levels" that the discharger is expected to meet; the discharger must make a prompt report of failure to meet the standards. However, the EPA cannot subject permits to conditions that are not related to water quality, despite NEPA's mandate that the agency consider the environmental effects of its decisions.[32]

Jury trial is available in a CWA action for civil penalties.[33] Aggrieved citizens can bring suit against a discharger or against the EPA (for failing to enforce the law), pursuant to CWA Section 505. However, no citizen suit for violation of the NPDES permit system can be brought unless there is at least one continuing violation. The Supreme Court has held that the suit cannot be premised merely on past violations.[34] On remand, the Fourth Circuit required merely that a citizen plaintiff show a reasonable likelihood, determined as of the time the suit was filed, that the plaintiff will continue to commit violations; and the suit is not mooted by an absence of actual violations after the suit.[35]

The Eleventh Circuit standard is somewhat different: post-filing compliance moots a claim for injunctive relief, but does not rule out the imposition of civil penalties that were appropriate at the time the suit was filed.[36]

A suit brought by the Sierra Club alleging violations of a discharge permit was settled (without admission of liability by the defendant) under an agreement obligating the defendant to pay specified sums to environmental organizations for their efforts to preserve water quality. The federal government objected to the settlement, describing the sums to be paid as civil penalties which can go only to the U.S. Treasury. The Ninth Circuit was not persuaded by this argument.[37] To the court, the CWA does not limit the types of settlement potentially available; in any event, the payments could not constitute civil penalties because there was no admission of liability.

[¶2204.1] The Safe Drinking Water Act

The question of water quality is also addressed by this 1974 statute (as amended in 1986 and 1988). The EPA is required to set national standards for contaminants in drinking water; the EPA also instructs states on how to protect single-source aquifers. Under the amendments, lead-free materials must be used in all water systems, and water coolers must use only lead-free materials.

Nearly all the states (48 of them) have standards "no less stringent" than the federal standards, and "adequate" enforcement procedures, and therefore have applied for and been granted primary enforcement authority with regard to public water systems.

[¶2205] THE CLEAN AIR ACT

The Clean Air Act's three titles deal with stationary sources of pollution; mobile sources of pollution (e.g., vehicles); and definitions and standards for judicial review, respectively.

Section 108 of the CAA obligates the EPA to issue a list of pollutants that are emitted from numerous or diverse sources, and which can reasonably be expected to endanger public health or welfare. Section 109 requires the EPA to set a National Ambient Air Quality Standard (NAAQS) for each of these substances. All substances that endanger the public health must be placed on the list. The statute is explicit that cost and technical feasibility of eliminating the hazard cannot be considered in naming a substance or keeping it off the list.

A "PSD" area is one whose air quality is better than the national standards require; a "nonattainment area" fails to comply with the standards. In nonattainment areas, new or modified sources of pollution are required to meet additional anti-pollution requirements, based on technological feasibility.

Under CAA Section 110, each state must have a State Implementation Plan (SIP): either the state drafts an SIP that is adequate to meet the NAAQS, or the EPA imposes one. Federal district courts have jurisdiction to order the EPA administrator to decide whether or not to revise the standards for sulphur oxide emissions but the court does not have the power to order the administrator to actually revise the standards.[38]

Summary judgment was granted to the plaintiffs[39] in a CWA citizen suit challenging approvals of a major mixed-use project. The judge found that New York City was guilty of serious CWA violations because of its failure to comply with the State Implementation Plan. The city's traffic plan was inadequate, and carbon monoxide standards were not met. The court permitted the project to go forward, but threatened to enjoin all further work and fine the private and government defendants $15 million if the city failed to complete its traffic study in time for the state to meet its deadline for its revised State Implementation Plan.

The Clean Air Act Amendments of 1990[40] broaden EPA enforcement powers. Title III of the statute embodies a comprehensive plan for reducing the amount of nearly 200 toxic air pollutants emitted into the atmosphere, especially those resulting from the combustion of solid waste. Title IV adds regulatory powers to control "acid deposition." Title V creates a system of operating permits similar to the NPDES program. Title VII, dealing with enforcement, adds more criminal violations and upgrades certain existing misdemeanor violations to felonies (e.g., emission of hazardous air pollutants creating an imminent risk of death or serious injury).

[¶2206] RESOURCE CONSERVATION AND RECOVERY ACT

The RCRA, as amended by the Hazardous and Solid Waste Amendments of 1984, imposes complete control over generation, transport, and disposal of "active" waste. Under this scheme, "solid waste" is all discarded material other than household refuse[41] or industrial discharges that are otherwise subject to permit requirements. "Hazardous waste" is solid waste whose quantity, concentration, or physical, chemical, or infectious nature renders it a health risk. RCRA waives the United States' sovereign immunity as to reasonable license fees or regulatory charges that are related to state regulatory costs, but sovereign immunity has not been waived as to civil penalties for past violations.[42]

In 1991, the EPA issued the regulations on household waste landfills mandated by the 1984 RCRA amendments. The approximately 6,000 household waste landfills will have to monitor pollution of nearby air and groundwater, and on-site cleanups may be required. The costs, estimated at $300 million, will be passed along to users of the landfills.

Generators and transporters are required to handle waste properly, and to report to the EPA on what they have done. The RCRA also regulates "TSD" facilities for the treatment, storage, and disposal of waste. Under the RCRA, the EPA has broad authority to inspect operations that generate hazardous waste; an inspection pursuant to a search warrant need not be limited to the management units identified as containing hazardous waste; all units can be inspected.[43]

[¶2206.1] Medical Waste Tracking Act of 1988

P.L. 100-582, 11/1/88, added a new Subtitle J to the RCRA. It covers the states of New York, New Jersey, Connecticut, the area contiguous to the Great Lakes, and any other state or geographic region that opts into coverage. The EPA Administrator is charged with setting up a program to track the movements of medical waste from generators to disposal facilities, and EPA personnel are entitled to demand information about medical waste from any handler.

[¶2206.2] State Regulation of Solid Waste Disposal

Two state statutes were challenged on constitutional grounds in 1990. Alabama's statute (forbidding commercial facilities to treat out-of-state waste whose treatment was forbidden in the state of origin, or to treat wastes from states lacking an interstate agreement with Alabama) was struck down as violative of the Commerce Clause.[44] The court deemed the statute to be protectionist rather than protective of legitimate local concerns, and furthermore had more than the minor impact on interstate commerce that can be permitted under the Commerce Clause.

The following year, another Alabama statute survived a Commerce Clause challenge.[45] This time, the statute limited the amount of hazardous waste that could be disposed of each year at the large facilities within the state. According to the Alabama Supreme Court, the law was not preempted by any federal environmental laws. It was safe under the Commerce Clause because it applied even-handedly to both in-state and out-of-state wastes. The imposition of a higher fee on disposal of out-of-state wastes was upheld under the Commerce Clause, on the theory that protection of local health is a valid concern of the state legislature.

However, a Louisiana statute forbidding importation, storage, or disposal of hazardous waste generated in foreign countries was struck down by the Middle District of Louisiana,[46] both because it affects re-importation of foreign waste brought into another state and then transported to Louisiana, and because RCRA permits importation of hazardous waste from other countries.

Ohio tried but failed to overcome the Commerce Clause problem by imposing much higher taxes on waste brought into the state than waste originating within the state. The Southern District of Ohio struck down the statute because it was a mere revenue provision, and no compelling justification was shown for the burden placed on interstate commerce.[47]

Preliminary injunction was granted by the Fourth Circuit[48] against South Carolina's attempt to limit out-of-state waste. In the Circuit Court's analysis, the preference for disposal of in-state over out-of-state waste probably violates the Commerce Clause, and nothing in the CERCLA or RCRA allows the Commerce Clause to be violated.

The Michigan Solid Waste Management Act, making it unlawful to bring solid waste into a county (or to send solid waste into another county in Michigan) without authorization from the county plan, was sustained.[49] The Eastern District of Michigan found the benefits of the statute to the localities to outweigh the minimal burden on interstate commerce. (Shipments of waste to Michigan are merely regulated, not forbidden, so the burden is not excessive.)

The EPA approved a North Carolina statute that requires hazardous waste facilities to dilute their discharges to one part discharge to every 1,000 parts of diluent. The D.C. Circuit, in turn, upheld the EPA action as a reasonable interpretation of RCRA because it controls but does not entirely prohibit waste treatment.[50]

The Supreme Court decided that the Commerce Clause is violated by a state statute that forbids private landfill operators to accept refuse generated outside the county in which the disposal facility is located,[51] and that the EPA did not exceed its authority in deciding that the discharge of Arkansas sewage would not cause a detectable violation of the water quality standards imposed downstream in Oklahoma.[52]

The Seventh Circuit found Indiana's statute, mandating the use of special trucks to haul municipal waste, with extra fees imposed on waste generated out-of-state, an unconstitutional violation of the Commerce Clause.[53] In this reading, the provisions must be subjected to a higher level of scrutiny because of their practical effect of discouraging interstate commerce; and it was not demonstrated that the state's health and safety concerns could not be satisfied by alternatives that did not discriminate against interstate commerce. The converse is also true: a county ordinance that requires county residents to send all their waste to a county facility also violates the Commerce Clause (even if it has the legitimate purpose of making the facility economically viable) because out-of-state disposal operators must be permitted to compete for the disposal business.[54] Commerce Clause issues must be tried, and cannot be disposed of by summary judgment.[55]

A state cannot permissibly set higher fees for disposal of waste generated out-of-state. Oregon imposed a $2.50 per ton surcharge on the in-state disposal of solid waste generated in other states and an $0.85 per ton fee on the disposal of waste generated within Oregon. The Court held that Oregon's surcharge is facially invalid under the negative Commerce Clause.[56]

[¶2207] OTHER FEDERAL ENVIRONMENTAL LAWS

The first federal environmental law was the National Environmental Policy Act, 42 USC Sections 4321-4347, adopted in 1980 as P.L. 91-190. It declared that environmental protection was a national policy and that federal legislation and decisions about grants and permits must reflect concern for the environment. Title I of NEPA sets out general federal policy; Title II creates the Council on Environmental Quality, whose influential regulations can be found at 40 CFR Part 1500 et seq.

Under NEPA, all legislation and major federal actions "significantly affecting the quality of the human environment" must, as a prerequisite, have an

Environmental Impact Statement. Federal agencies must consider environmental impact throughout their processes of decision-making, although they need not prepare a final Environmental Impact Statement until they make a recommendation or report on a proposal. Under *Sierra Club v. Marsh*,[57] a NEPA plaintiff must show "irreparable harm" to get a preliminary injunction but this need not mean physical harm to the environment that cannot be repaired; harm to a litigating position is acceptable.

The National Wildlife Federation and its members were denied standing to sue the Bureau of Land Management to enjoin the reclassification of public land as open to private uses (e.g., mining). The Supreme Court held that NEPA has no private right of action (nor does the Federal Land Policy and Management Act); the plaintiff's affidavit was not specific enough as to the injury sustained to bring the claim within Section 702 of the Administrative Procedures Act.[58]

The Toxic Substances Control Act of 1986, 15 USC Section 2601-2629, gives the EPA the power to regulate all phases of chemical manufacture, processing, use and disposal. The EPA can require testing of substances such as carcinogens or teratogens that present an unreasonable risk to health or the environment (even if the substances are already in use). Manufacturers must notify the EPA 90 days before they introduce a new chemical. If the test shows a risk, the EPA must take some action: the permitted actions include mandating disclosure of the risk on the label all the way through outright prohibition of manufacturing.

A two-tier analysis is used to determine if an unreasonable risk exists: both exposure (probability of harm) and effect (severity of harm) are assessed, and a risk-benefit analysis is done. The purpose of this statute is to fill gaps in the OSHA and Consumer Product Safety Act scheme by dealing with all phases of chemical use, not just vis-à-vis occupational exposure or situations involving consumer use of the chemical. EPA's standards for hazardous solvents and dioxins were struck down by the Court of Appeals for the D.C. Circuit.[59] The court held that EPA had inadequate justification for adopting standards that were entirely technology-based, rather than standards using technology and concentration levels to screen for the need for waste treatment.

The Asbestos Hazard Emergency Response Act of 1986 (AHERA), P.L. 99-579, 20 USC Sections 4011 et seq. is Title III of the Toxic Substances Control Act. However, despite its comprehensive title, AHERA's application is limited to schools, where the EPA must inspect and set up abatement programs to control materials containing asbestos. Forty states have broader asbestos programs, usually calling for inspection of all types of buildings to see if asbestos is present and regulating those who remove and dispose of asbestos.

The EPA also regulates asbestos under several laws. The Asbestos Information Act of 1988, P.L. 100-577, streamlines discovery in cases alleging asbestos hazards in building, and entitles the EPA to information disclosure by former manufacturers of asbestos products. There are asbestos regulations under the Clean Air Act[60] dealing with asbestos emitted by manufacturers, the construction industry, and waste disposal, and under the Clean Water Act[61] for discharges of asbestos fibers into the water. Importers, manufacturers, and processors of asbestos are subject to standards under the Toxic Substances Control Act.[62]

Asbestos is listed as a hazardous substance under CERCLA,[63] although it is specifically exempted from the RCRA definition of hazardous waste, and the Occupational Safety and Health Administration (OSHA) regulates workers' on-the-job asbestos exposure.[64] The Department of Transportation regulates the shipment and handling of asbestos, mandating methods that reduce the risk of occupational exposure and release of asbestos into the air.[65]

The Emergency Planning and Community Right to Know Act, 42 USC Section 11001 (Title III of SARA) attempts to cope with the "Bhopal" situation of release of a toxic substance. Under this statute, businesses that use chemicals are required to notify state and local authorities responsible for emergency planning that the chemicals are present; notice must also be given of all planned and unplanned releases. EPA's Final Rule implementing this statute[66] permits the identity of a specific chemical to be protected as a trade secret if the substance's chemical identity has always been confidential; disclosure would cause competitive harm; the chemical's identity cannot be discovered through reverse engineering; and no other statute mandates the disclosure.

The Supreme Court held that the Federal Insecticide, Fungicide, and Rodenticide Act (FIFRA), the federal law regulating pesticidal substances (7 U.S.C. Sec. 136 et.seq.) does not preempt regulation of pesticides by local governments.[67]

— ENDNOTES —

1. Lucas v. South Carolina Coastal Comm'n, #91-453, 112 S.Ct. 2886 (Sup.Ct. 6/29/92).

2. PFZ Properties v. Rodriguez, 928 F.2d 28, cert. dismissed 112 S.Ct. 2001.

3. Wagner Seed Co. v. Bush, 946 F.2d 918 (D.C.Cir. 10/15/91).

4. D.O.E. v. Ohio, #90-1341, -1517, 112 S.Ct. 1627 (Sup.Ct. 4/21/92).

5. Dedham Water Co. v. Cumberland Farms Dairy Inc., 889 F.2d 1146 (1st Cir. 11/2/89).

6. Weyerhaeuser Co., Aetna Casualty & Surety Co. et al., Supreme Court of Washington, No. 61000-2 (1994).

7. 40 CFR Part 302.

8. See 58 LW 2521 (3/6/90).

9. Retirement Community Developers v. Merine, 713 F.Supp. 153 (D. Md. 5/18/89).

10. 491 U.S. 1 (Sup.Ct. 6/13/89).

11. Ohio v. Doe, 58 LW 2742 (6th Cir. 6/11/90).

12. Rospatch Jessco Corp. v. Chrysler Corp., 62 LW 2159 (W.D. Mich. 8/23/93).

13. Cook v. Rockwell Int'l Corp., 755 F.Supp. 1468 (D.Colo. 2/13/91).

14. Key Tronic Corp. v. U.S. et al. #93-376 (6/6/94).

15. U.S. v. Greer, 850 F.2d 1447 (11th Cir. 1988).

16. Amcast Industrial Corp. v. Detrex Corp., 62 LW 2121 (7th Cir. 8/12/93).

17. U.S. v. Aceto Agricultural Chemicals Corp., 872 F.2d 1373 (9th Cir. 4/25/89).

18. B.F. Goodrich & Co. v. Murtha, 697 F.Supp. 89 (D. Conn. 10/24/88).

19. Pollution Control Industry of America v. EPA, 58 LW 2083 (N.D. Ill. 6/26/89).

20. Velsicol Chemical Corp. v. Enenco Inc., 62 LW 2315 (6th Cir. 11/12/93).

21. 690 F.Supp. 752 (S.D. Ind. 7/8/88).

22. Michigan v. ARCO Industries Corp., 58 LW 2316 (W.D. Mich. 9/27/89).

23. Kaiser Aluminum & Chemical Corp. v. Catellus Development Corp., 976 F.2d 1338 (9th Cir. 10/8/92).

24. Jordan v. Southern Wood Piedmont Co., 805 F.Supp. 1575 (S.D. Ga. 7/14/92).

25. City of Chicago et al. v. Environmental Defense Fund et al., #92-1639 (5/2/94).

26. U.S. v. Chem-Dyne Corp. 572 F. Supp 802 (S.D. Ohio 1983).

27. Hudson River Fisherman's Ass'n v. New York City, 940 F.2d 649 (2d Cir. 6/20/91).

28. PUD No. 1 of Jefferson County et al. v. Washington Dept. of Ecology et al., #92-1911 (5/31/94).

29. Hoffman Homes Inc. v. EPA, 62 LW 2056 (7th Cir. 7/19/93).

30. Clean Water Act Section 402, 40 CFR Parts 121-125.

31. Oklahoma v. EPA, 908 F.2d 595 (10th Cir. 7/11/90).

32. Natural Resources Defense Council Inc. v. EPA, 859 F.2d 156 (D.C. Cir. 9/20/88).

33. U.S. v. Tull, 481 U.S. 412 (1987).

34. Gwaltney of Smithfield Ltd. v. Chesapeake Bay Foundation Inc., 484 U.S. 49 (1987).

35. Chesapeake Bay Foundation Inc. v. Gwaltney, 890 F.2d 690 (4th Cir. 11/30/89).

36. Atlantic States Legal Foundation Inc. v. Tyson Foods Inc., 897 F.2d 1128 (11th Cir. 4/5/90).

37. Sierra Club Inc. v. Electronic Controls Design Inc., 59 LW 2112 (9th Cir. 8/1/90).

38. Environmental Defense Fund v. Thomas, 870 F.2d 892 (2d Cir. 3/22/89).

39. Coalition Against Columbus Center v. City of New York, 769 F.Supp. 478 (S.D.N.Y. 7/10/91).

40. P.L. 101-549. See *Wall St.J.* 10/29/90 p. A7 for useful charts explaining the evolution and final terms of the statute.

41. The "household waste" exclusion protects a resource recovery factory that generates ash with hazardous properties when it burns household waste: Environmental Defense Fund v. Wheelabrator Technology Inc., 725 F.Supp. 758 (S.D.N.Y. 11/22/89).

42. Maine v. Dep't of the Navy, 973 F.2d 1007 (1st Cir. 9/1/92).

43. National-Standard Co. v. EPA, 58 LW 2114 (7th cir. 7/17/89).

44. National Solid Waste Management Association v. Alabama Dep't of Environmental Management, 924 F.2d 1001 (11th Cir. 8/8/90).

45. Hunt v. Chemical Waste Mgmt. Inc., 584 So.2d 1367 (Ala.Sup. 7/11/91).

46. Chemical Waste Mgmt. Inc. v. Templet, 770 F.Supp. 1142 (M.D.La. 7/9/91).

47. National Solid Waste Mgmt. Ass'n v. Voinovich, 763 F.Supp. 244 (S.D.Oh. 5/1/91).

48. Waste Treatment Council v. State of South Carolina, 945 F.2d 781 (4th Cir. 9/20/91).

49. Bill Kettlewell Excavating Inc. v. Michigan Dep't of Natural Resources, 732 F.Supp. 761 (E.D. Mich. 3/2/90).

50. Hazardous Waste Treatment Council v. Reilly, 938 F.2d 1390 (D.C.Cir. 7/26/91).

51. Fort Gratiot Sanitary Landfill v. Michigan Dep't of Natural Resources, #91-636, 112 S.Ct. 2019 (Sup.Ct. 6/1/92).

52. Arkansas v. Oklahoma, #90-1262, -1266, 112 S.Ct. 1046 (Sup.Ct 2/26/92), on remand 962 F.2d 996.

53. Government Suppliers Consolidating Services Inc. v. Bayh, 975 F.2d 1267 (7th Cir. 9/17/92), cert. denied 113 S.Ct. 977.

54. Waste Systems Corp. v. Martin County, 784 F.Supp. 641 (D.Minn. 2/14/92).

55. National Solid Waste Management Ass'n v. Voinovich, 959 F.2d 590 (6th Cir. 3/4/92) [Ohio statute setting higher fees for disposal of waste generated out-of-state].

56. Oregon Waste Systems v. Department of Environmental Quality of the State of Oregon, #93-70, (4/4/94).

57. 872 F.2d 497 (1st Cir. 3/31/89).

58. Lujan v. Nat'l Wildlife Federation, 110 S.Ct. 3177 (Sup.Ct. 6/27/90).

59. Hazardous Waste Treatment Council v. EPA, 869 F.2d 1526 (D.C. Cir. 9/15/89).

60. 40 CFR Part 61, Subpart M.

61. 40 CFR Part 427.

62. 40 CFR Section 263.60.

63. 40 CFR Section 302.4.

64. 29 CFR Sections 1910, 1926.58, upheld in general over constitutional challenge in Building and Construction Trades Dep't, AFL-CIO v. Sec'y of Labor, 838 F.2d 1258, (D.C. Cir. 2/2/88) but which directs OSHA to reconsider certain of its regulations, leading to a revised standard for short-term asbestos exposure being published at 53 FR 35,610 (9/14/88).

65. 49 CFR Sections 172, 173, implementing the Hazardous Materials Transportation Act of 1975, 49 USC Sections 1801 et seq.

66. See 57 LW 2080 (7/29/88).

67. Wisconsin Public Intervenor v. Mortier, #89-1905, 111 S.Ct. 2476 (Sup.Ct. 6/21/91).

— FOR FURTHER REFERENCE —

Bass, Gary D. and Alan McLean, "Enhancing the Public's Right-to-Know About Environmental Issues," 4 *Villanova Environmental L.J.* 287 (Summer '93).

Blumm, Michael C., "The Fallacies of Free Market Environmentalism," 15 *Harvard J. of Law and Public Policy* 371 (Spring '92).

Brunet, Edward, "Debunking Wholesale Private Enforcement of Environmental Rights," 15 *Harvard J. of Law and Public Policy* 311 (Spring '92).

Chen, Jim C. and Kyle E. McSlarrow, "Application of the Abnormally Dangerous Activities Doctrine to Environmental Cleanups," 47 *Business Lawyer* 1031 (May '92).

Dennis, Richard G., "Liability of Officers, Directors and Stockholders Under CERCLA," 36 *Villanova L. Rev.* 1367 (November '91).

Edley, Christopher F. Jr. and Paul C. Weiler, "Asbestos: A Multi-Billion-Dollar Crisis," 30 *Harvard J. on Legislation* 383 (Summer '93).

Elligett, Raymond T. Jr. and Charles P. Schropp, "Running for Cover: Environmental Insurance Coverage Issues," 67 *Florida Bar J.* 67 (July-August '93).

Emory, Meade et.al., "Environmental Clean-Up Costs Continue to Be an Issue for IRS," 79 *J. Tax.* 124 (August '93).

Frankel, Stuart D., "Full Disclosure: Financial Statement Disclosures Under CERCLA," 3 *Duke Environmental Law & Policy Forum* 17 (Annual '93).

French, Bruce Comly, "More Effective Citizen Participation in Environmental Decision-Making," 24 *U. of Toledo L. Rev.* 389 (Winter '93).

Gleeson, John Gerald, "Planning the Defense of the Mass Toxic Tort Case," 35 *For the Defense* 13 (June '93).

Jones, Stephen C., "Debate Rages Over Insurance Coverage," *Nat. L. J.* 2/25/92 p. 20.

Kutz, Kristy, "Who Is Going to Pay: CERCLA v. Bankruptcy," 31 *Washburn L. J.* 573 (Spring '92).

Lehner, Peter H., "Act Locally: Municipal Enforcement of Environmental Law," 12 *Stanford Environmental Law J.* 50 (Annual '93).

Lincenberg, Gary C., "Lowered Intent Requirements in Environmental Crimes Cases," 7 *Crim. Justice* 28 (Summer '92).

Lobel, Ira B., "Addressing Environmental Disputes With Labor Mediation Skills," 47 *Arbitration J.* 48 (September '92).

Merriam, Dwight H. and Jeffrey A. Benson, "Identifying and Beating a Strategic Lawsuit Against Public Participation," 3 *Duke Environmental Law & Policy Forum* 17 (Annual '93).

Mohai, Paul and Bunyan Bryant, "Environmental Injustice: Weighing Race and Class as Factors in the Distribution of Environmental Hazards," 63 *U. of Colorado L. Rev.* 921 (Fall '92).

Pelstring, Lisa, "Corporate Environmental Reporting, 10 *Environmental Forum* 43 (September-October '93).

Powell, Fiona M., "Trespass, Nuisance and the Evolution of Common Law in Modern Pollution Cases," 21 *Real Estate L.J.* 182 (Fall '92).

Racher, Peter M., "Clean Air Amendments Leave Small Businesses Up in the Air," 25 *Indiana L. Rev.* 1883 (Fall '92).

Sive, David, "Laws on Waste Hit a Constitutional Snag," *Nat. L.J.* 1/27/92 p. 18.

Sullivan, Shawn R., "Discharge of CERCLA Liability in Bankruptcy," 17 *Harvard Environmental L. Rev.* 445 (Summer '93).

Wajda, Michael J., "Determining Arranger Liability Under CERCLA," 3 *U. of Baltimore J. of Environmental Law* 114 (Winter '93).

Wall, Guy E., "Federal Oil Pollution Law and Regulatory Developments," 23 *Environmental Law Reporter* 10491 (August '93).

Ward, Catherine M., "Environmental Risk Assessment," 110 *Banking L.J.* 204 (May-June '93).

Wilkins, Timothy A., "Mootness Doctrine and the Post-Compliance Pursuit of Civil Penalties in Environmental Civil Suits," 17 *Harvard Environmental L. Rev.* 389 (Summer '93).

Zornow, David M. and Phillip D. Reed, "Guidelines Don't Fit Environmental Cases," *Nat. L.J.* 3/2/92 p. 19.

ESTATE PLANNING AND ADMINISTRATION

[¶2301] When preparing an estate plan, it is useful to take a multi-discipline approach. The planner should have a working knowledge of many fields, though he or she should not hesitate to obtain expert advise where it is needed. thus, the financial implications of every available planning technique should be examined, the legality of a particular device should be considered, and, of course, the tax consequences of each transaction must be analyzed. Finally, as the mass of tax laws and reporting requirements grows and as the complexity of the plan increases, accurate and detailed accounting systems must be employed.

The IRS has set up a test program for rendering advance rulings on estate planning matters. Rulings will not be granted on factual or actuarial matters. Advance rulings will be issued only if the taxpayer has executed a will, trust document, or deed of conveyance, or the taxpayer executes an affidavit of intent to execute such documents—in short, attorneys cannot seek advance rulings speculatively if they devise a new planning technique and want to see what its tax consequences might be. There must be an actual client using or about to use the device.

[¶2302] THE PLANNING PROCESS

The estate planning process is often thought of as solely directed at saving estate taxes at an individual's death. Ideally, however, it is a financial plan that helps attain the client's lifetime objectives and executes his dispositive scheme at death, both at minimal income and transfer costs. For information on wills see ¶4401 et seq.; for information on trusts see ¶4301 et seq.

Step 1: To prepare an effective estate plan, the planner must obtain a comprehensive breakdown of the client's assets and liabilities, and secure vital personal data about the client and his family. This information, together with a thorough knowledge of the client's personal and financial objectives, will help the planner to identify problem areas and suggest planning techniques. For example, if the client's principal asset is an interest in a closely held business, his eventual estate may experience a cash shortage when federal and state death taxes are imposed. A common solution to this problem is to prepare a buy-sell agreement funded with life insurance.

Step 2: Estimate the amount of debts and claims that will have to be paid. This estimate should include current income tax liabilities, debts, funeral and last illness expenses, and administration costs.

Step 3: After deducting from the total value of assets at death the estimate of all debts and claims, calculate the estate tax liability that will probably be due. If the individual is married, the total tax liability that will fall due at the death of both spouses should be determined. By this calculation, it can be estimated what will be left for the children if both parents should die within a relatively short period of time. If the estate tax liability is to be minimized or eliminated by the use of the unlimited marital deduction, it is necessary to determine what the liability will be when the surviving spouse passes away. The estate planner may be able to reduce or minimize the estate tax bill by combining the marital deduction with the unified estate and gift tax credit.

Step 4: Schedule the liquidation of estate liabilities. Apply cash amounts from the list of cash assets and assets convertible into cash against the schedules of debts, claims, administration costs, and estate tax liability. Then decide whether there is enough cash to meet the cash needs of the family during the administration of the estate. This comparison of cash available and liabilities will point up whether there is a surplus or deficit of liquid assets. The estate owner and the estate planner can then determine whether it is necessary to arrange for the conversion of additional assets into cash or to secure additional liquid resources such as life insurance.

Step 5: Assign the remaining assets to individuals or trusts according to the estate owner's will. This will indicate how much is available to satisfy the testamentary wishes of the estate owner and will provide a basis for his reevaluation of the disposition.

Step 6: Prepare a schedule showing the assets that will be in the hands of each beneficiary after distribution and how much annual income these assets will produce. Include the separately owned property of each beneficiary. The annual income available from these sources should be compared with the amount of annual income that the estate owner thinks should be available for the beneficiary.

Step 7: Suggest methods of reducing liabilities and administrative expenses.

Step 8: Show how assets can be increased. For example, inadequacy of liquid assets to meet cash liabilities or of net assets to produce family income may call for additional insurance or additional annual savings to complete an investment program.

Step 9: Show how income can be reorganized to increase liquidity or add to family assets.

Step 10: Make final projection of assets, liabilities, liquid assets available to meet liabilities, net assets available for distribution, and annual income produced by these assets—after considering the steps that have been recommended to increase assets, improve liquidity, and reduce estate liabilities.

Step 11: Project the increase and accumulation of estate assets until the owner's retirement age. Take annual savings, assume a conservative rate of investment return, apply a compound interest table to determine what should be accumulated at the age that the owner specifies for his own retirement. Take the cash value of insurance policies at that time and convert that into annual income. Add to this any Social Security and any retirement income or profit-sharing assets that may become available at that age. Tabulate total assets and anticipated income for the owner at retirement age. Determine whether or not additional savings or other steps are indicated to provide for the owner's retirement security.

Step 12: Review the plan whenever there are changes in the individual's financial or personal status, or in the tax law or applicable local law.

[¶2303] CHECKLIST OF DOCUMENTS NEEDED FOR ESTATE PLANNING

❑ *Birth Certificates:*
Husband
Wife
Children

❑ *Documents of Title:*
Deeds
Leases
Purchase and sale contracts

❑ *Appraisals*

❑ *Business Interests:*
Partnership agreement
Redemption agreement
Buy-Sell agreement
Disability agreement
Close corporation charters, bylaws, minute books
Balance sheets for previous five years
Profit-and-loss statements for previous five years
Federal and state income tax returns for previous five years

❑ *Employment Records:*
employment contracts
Pension benefits
Profit-sharing plan benefits

❑ *Matrimonial:*
Antenuptial agreement
Postnuptial agreement
Separation agreement
Property settlement
Divorce decree

❑ *Trust Instruments*

❑ *Wills:*
Husband
Wife
Other family members

❑ *Instruments Creating Powers of Appointment:*
Donor
Donee

❑ *Insurance Policies:*
Life insurance
General
Health

❑ *Income Tax Returns (past five years):*
Federal
State

☐ *Gift Tax Returns*
☐ *Personal Financial Statements*

[¶2304] The Unified Federal Estate and Gift Tax

The unified tax rate, which is the same for estate and gift taxes, is reproduced in the Appendix.

Starting in 1987, a decedent has been able to transfer up to $600,000 in property totally free of estate and gift taxes. Furthermore, an estate tax return does not have to be filed for any estate of $600,000 or less.

The unified estate and gift tax credit in 1987 and later years is $192,800 for decedents dying in 1987 and later years (this is equivalent to a tax-free gift and bequest threshold of $600,000).

Note: An estate can take advantage of other credits including state death taxes paid and foreign taxes paid.

[¶2305] The Unlimited Marital Deduction

An unlimited amount of property can be transferred to a spouse free of estate and gift taxes. No gift tax return is required for transfers between spouses. Under prior law, the maximum estate tax marital deduction was the greater of $250,000 or one-half of the adjusted gross estate. And gifts between spouses of more than $100,000 were subject to tax.

Although an unlimited amount of property can be transferred to a spouse free of estate and gift taxes, not all married taxpayers get this break automatically. A will should be amended if it contains a maximum deduction formula clause geared to the old tax law's marital deduction (the greater of $250,000 or one-half of the decedent's adjusted gross estate). Reason: There is a special rule for wills executed before September 12, 1981. If these wills contain a maximum marital deduction formula clause, and are not amended to reflect the unlimited deduction, the amount of property passing to the surviving spouse will be based on the old law's limited deduction. So if taxpayers want to get the benefits of the unlimited marital deduction, they will lose out unless they amend their will.

Taxpayers with maximum marital deduction formula clauses who only want to give their spouses the greater of $250,000 or one-half of their adjusted gross estates may also have to amend their wills. Reason: The tax law allows individual states to enact statutes that construe a maximum marital deduction formula clause as referring to the unlimited marital deduction. So, if taxpayers don't state exactly what the formula clauses in their wills mean, state law may construe the clause as giving everything to their surviving spouses.

Qualified terminable interest property (QTIP).

While terminable interests generally do not qualify for the marital deduction, there are a number of exceptions, the most widely used of which is the qualified terminable interest property (QTIP). The QTIP can be used to give a surviving spouse less than full ownership of estate assets while preserving a marital deduction for the estate.

There are many reasons why a testator would wish to benefit his or her spouse, yet would not want property to pass outright to the spouse. For example, the spouse might be elderly, debilitated, and unable to manage the property effectively, and in need of continuing income, so that a trust paying income for life would be more helpful than an outright bequest. Another common motivation occurs when the testator remarries, and wishes to provide long-run benefits for the adult children of the prior marriage. In this situation, a QTIP is used to benefit the second spouse for life, while passing along property to the testator's children; if the property passed outright to the spouse, he or she would be able to dispose of it without necessarily benefiting the testator's children.

Many variations are played on the simple theme of the trust paying income to the surviving spouse for life, with a remainder to another person whom the testator desires to benefit. However, careful drafting is required: if a device does not fit into the statutory, regulatory, and decisional definition of a QTIP, the marital deduction will be unavailable. In an estate too small to be taxable, this will have little practical consequence; but in a large estate, the testator's plans can be severely frustrated if much of the estate goes to pay estate taxes.

[¶2306] MAXIMUM USE OF MARITAL DEDUCTION AND UNIFIED CREDIT

Despite the unlimited marital deduction and the unified credit, estate planning is necessary for many taxpayers. Reasons: While there may be no estate tax when the decedent's property passes to the surviving spouse, there may be tax when the property goes from the surviving spouse to the children. The surviving spouse has only his or her credit to shelter the estate when it passes to the next generation. And, in many cases, that won't be enough.

For example, Client's $1 million in assets are left outright to his spouse when he dies. The spouse's will provides for everything to be left to the children. Result: Of the $1 million, $400,000 is subject to estate tax when Client's spouse dies. Reason: Spouse's unified credit shelters only $600,000 of assets. Estate tax bill: $153,000.

client's mistake was to waste his own $600,000 exemption. Combining two credits with the unlimited marital deduction shelters estates as high as $1.2 million. But knowing how to combine the tax breaks is the trick.

From the federal estate tax viewpoint, planning depends on the size of the estate.

Estates of $1.2 Million or Less

Strategy #1: Where Client owns $1 million in assets, $600,000 may be left to the spouse and $400,000 to his children. Client's estate pays no tax (what passes to his spouse is exempt and the bequest to his children is exempt because of his credit). Spouse's estate doesn't pay tax either when her property goes to the children (it is sheltered by her credit).

Strategy #2: The problem with the obvious strategy is that the surviving spouse loses the economic benefit of $400,000 after Client dies. Better approach: Client can put the $400,000 in trust for his children with his spouse having a limited right to invade trust principal and the right to payment of trust income during her lifetime. Better result: More dollar support for the surviving spouse and still no estate tax when either Client or his spouse dies.

The $600,000 passes tax-free from Client to his spouse (the marital deduction) and then to the children (her $600,000 exemption). And so does the $400,000 in Client's estate. Reason: Client's credit exempts the $400,000. And it bypasses the spouse's estate, even though she has the limited right to invade trust principal and the right to payments of trust income.

This strategy is especially well suited to older clients who have younger spouses. Chances are the spouse will survive the client by quite a few years. Where the couple are closer in age and the client survives his spouse, there may be a tax problem.

For example if client's spouse dies first, his estate will pay an estate tax (unless he remarries). His estate consists of $1 million, of which $600,000 passes tax-free to his children. The $400,000 balance is subject to tax since his marital deduction expired with his spouse. One way to mitigate this problem is with:

Strategy #3: Client and his spouse can take advantage of the unlimited gift tax marital deduction. Where feasible, the couple splits ownership of the property down the middle during their lifetimes. (There is no gift tax on transfers between spouses.) Each spouse then leaves his or her estate in trust to the children with an income interest to the other spouse. Result: No estate tax.

For example, assume that Client and his spouse are both 50 years old. Client owns property worth $1 million, but his spouse owns none. He makes a gift of one half of his assets—$500,000—to his spouse. His will provides that the other $500,000 goes to his children in trust. The spouse has the right to income, and to receive a limited amount of principal. Upon the spouse's death, the $500,000 in trust goes to the children. Client's spouse draws up a will that reads exactly the same way: If Client's spouse dies first, her $500,000 in assets go to the children in trust with an interest to client while he lives.

There is no estate tax no matter which spouse survives. The strategy also assures the surviving spouse the full use of the family wealth as long as he or she lives. If Client's spouse dies first, her $500,000 goes directly to the trust for the children. This amount is sheltered by the unified credit and passes automatically to the children when Client dies. Thus Client owns $500,000 outright (what he did not give to his spouse) and is entitled to life income from the $500,000 his spouse left in trust.

When Client dies, the $500,000 left in trust bypasses his estate and goes directly to the children. The remaining $500,000 goes directly to the children under the terms of his will—it is fully sheltered by the unified credit.

What if Client dies first? The results are exactly the same. The children ultimately get everything and no estate tax is paid.

Estates Over $1.2 Million

Strategy #4: When a client's estate exceeds $1.2 million an estate tax will have to be paid when his surviving spouse dies. It's simple arithmetic. The sum of the two $600,000 exemptions is $1.2 million. Anything over that amount is subject to tax—unless the client embarks on a program of lifetime giving.

Client can give each child $10,000 every year without paying gift tax or dipping into the unified credit. The $600,000 exemption stays intact to shelter the estate tax. Result: If enough gifts are made, a client's taxable estate will be at $1.2 million or below. If a client's spouse joins in the gift-giving, the exclusion is double—$20,000 tax-free dollars can be given to each child each year.

Strategy #5: A client's estate may exceed $1.2 million by so much that lifetime transfers can't bring his taxable estate down to the magic figure of $1.2 million. Or the client may prefer not to make lifetime gifts to his children. In either case, an estate tax will be paid. Nevertheless, there is a way to minimize the amount of the tax: The client can forego the maximum marital deduction and *balance the estates.*

Because of the graduated estate tax rates, if the client transfers enough assets to his spouse (either by gift or by will) to make her estate equal to his, the minimum possible estate tax bill is paid. the sum of the taxes on both estates is less than the tax on the total amount in one estate.

The strategy of equalizing the estates can be used to good effect even if the surviving spouse has an estate of her own. the trick is to have the surviving spouse receive only enough to balance off the two estates in roughly equal amounts. Whenever that is done—and it can be done through lifetime giving—big tax dollars can stay in the client's family.

[¶2307] VALUATION

The value of an asset for estate tax purposes is its fair market value at the date of the owner's death or the alternate valuation date. Fair market value is "that price at which the property would change hands between a willing buyer and a willing seller, neither being under any compulsion to buy or to sell and both having reasonable knowledge of all relevant facts." Property such as stock or cash usually has a readily ascertainable value, but an interest in a closely held business poses a complex and vexing valuation problem. The IRS treats the question of value as one of fact, subject to solution only in the light of all circumstances having a bearing on the issue. When a unique asset (e.g., real property, business interest, etc.) is to be valued, there is no mathematically "right" answer based on a formula or otherwise; there is only a range of possible right answers that can be supported by logical and convincing reasoning.

❑ *Listed Stocks and Bonds:* Generally the fair market value per share or bond is the mean between the highest and lowest selling prices on the valuation date. When there are no sales on the valuation date, the value may be determined by taking a weighted average of the means of prices for the days sales were made (within a reasonable time) last before and next after that date. Lacking actual sales the same process may be applied to bid and asked prices. If both sales and complete bid and asked prices are lacking, the mean of the bid and asked prices for the date either before or after the valuation date may be used. U.S. savings bonds are includible in the gross estate at their redemption value on the valuation date. Treasury bonds with a market value below par, but redeemable at par to pay estate tax, are included in the gross estate at par. Mutual fund shares are valued at the redemption price.

❑ *Real Estate:* In general, it is important to obtain experts of good standing to appraise real estate. However, an appraisal by experts is not required when the executor can arrive at a fair market value through personal knowledge or by consulting bankers or other business associates. The estate should arrive at a conservative value which will stand the test of investigation, as assessed values given in the assessment roles will not ordinarily be accepted in estate tax cases.

❑ *Life Estate, Annuity, and Remainder Interests:* The value of these types of property is their present value, except in the case of annuities under contracts issued by companies regularly engaged in their sale.

The present value of an annuity, life estate, remainder, or reversion, which is dependent upon the continuation or termination of the life of one person, is computed by the use of actuarial tables.

In any case where the value of a reversionary interest cannot be determined either on the basis of the actuarial rules or under the general rules of valuation, it is deemed to have a value of zero. A possibility that the decedent may be able to dispose of the property transferred is considered to have the same value as his right to the return of the property, assuming, of course, that the conditions on which the right is based are the same.

❑ *Cash and Bank Accounts:* Cash belonging to the decedent at the date of death is includible in the gross estate whether it is on hand or on deposit with a bank. The amount of any check written by the decedent for bona fide obligations is not includible if the checks are subsequently honored by the bank. Interest on a savings account accrued to the valuation date is includible, unless the decedent died during an interest period and under bank policy interest does not accrue until the end of the period.

❑ *Household and Personal Effects:* If the estate is relatively small, personal effects of a decedent who lived in an apartment can be assigned a minimal value. For larger estates, or if valuable items (e.g., jewelry, paintings: antique furniture, etc.) are involved, the estate practitioner has two options, (1) He may present a room-by-room itemization of the effects, describing each item and assigning a value thereto (however, items in the same room none of which exceed $100 in value, can be grouped), or (2) The estate's personal representative may submit a sworn statement setting forth the value of the decedent's effects as determined by a competent appraiser (one of recognized standing and ability).

When the estate includes items of marked artistic or intrinsic worth valued in excess of $3,000, the practitioner *must* submit an expert appraisal made under oath. The appraisal should be accompanied by a sworn statement made by the estate's personal representative as to the competency of the expert and thoroughness of the expert's appraisal.

❏ *Insurance:* The value of the proceeds of insurance on the decedent's life receivable by or for the benefit of the estate is taxable. If the proceeds are receivable by beneficiaries other than the decedent or his estate, the proceeds are includible if the decedent possessed incidents of ownership in the policy. If the insurance is on the life of an individual other than the decedent and the decedent owned the policy at the date of his death, the value is determined by the cost of a comparable contract issued by the same insurance company. If a valuation based on comparable contracts isn't readily ascertainable, the estate tax value is the interpolated terminal reserve of the policy combined with the proportionate part of the last premium paid before the date of death that covers the period between the premium due date and the date of death.

❏ *Business Interests:* If a decedent owned an interest in a business as a proprietor or partner, have all the assets of the business (including goodwill), fairly appraised as of the valuation date. Then fix the net value of the business in an amount that a willing buyer would pay to a willing seller in view of the net value of the assets of the business and its earning capacity. The value of a business interest may be fixed by a "buy and sell" agreement. To fix the value of the interest for estate tax purposes, the agreement must (1) bind the estate to sell, either by giving the survivors an option or by binding all the parties; (2) set a price which is not so grossly inadequate as to make the agreement a "mere gratuitous promise." Buy and sell agreements are often funded by insurance on the lives of the parties.

If no valid purchase agreement exists, alternative approaches must be taken to determine the estate tax value of a business interest. It is important to remember that not every approach is appropriate for every kind of business interest, and in some cases a combination of methods is advisable. The appraiser must thoroughly investigate each valuation issue, and then apply his experience, common sense, and judgment to arrive at a fair value. Particular emphasis should be placed on the income-producing ability, book value, and dividend-paying capacity of the business.

❏ *Special Use Valuation:* As a general rule, real property must be included in a decedent's gross estate at its fair market value. This value is normally based on the land's "highest and best" use. However, if the property is used for farming purposes or in some other closely held business, the fair market value of the land may greatly exceed its value to the owner's heirs, who may wish to maintain the farm or business. If the income produced by the land is insufficient to pay the additional estate tax, or no steps to increase the estate's liquidity are taken, a sale of some or all of the property may be necessary. Recognizing this hardship, Congress has given the personal representative of an estate the option to value real property that is used in a farm or other closely held business at its actual, rather than optimum, use.

[¶2308]   OTHER PLANNING TECHNIQUES

The following planning techniques can be used to (1) reduce the client's income tax burden, either through the creation of deductions or through the shifting of income to a low-bracket taxpayer; (2) "freeze" the estate so that it does not increase in value; (3) minimize the estate tax through utilization of various estate tax deductions; and (4) provide liquid assets to help meet the tax burden and other expenses incurred by the client's estate. Keep in mind that these devices can be useful for several purposes, and that none of them should be proposed unless they conform to the client's objectives.

❒ *Lifetime Trusts:* A lifetime trust can be an extremely flexible and relatively straightforward method of splitting the client's income tax bill. The various types of trusts and their functions are examined in greater detail at ¶4301 et seq.

❒ *Gift-Leasebacks:* A gift of business assets to an independent trustee, in conjunction with a leaseback of the property to the transferor, can result in considerable tax savings. The transferor can deduct his rent payments, while the trustee or trust beneficiaries pay tax on the rent income at their lower rates. However, these transactions have been challenged by the IRS.

❒ *Family Partnerships:* A partnership interest can be acquired by another member of the family either by gift or by purchase so that future income and increments of value will accrue to his benefit.

❒ *Charitable Transfers:* These can take many forms, depending on the individual donor's motives. If the charity qualifies under the IRC, the individual will be entitled to federal income, gift, and estate tax deductions.

The simplest type of charitable gift is an outright cash contribution or bequest. If the donor wishes to retain the enjoyment of the property for his life and for specified members of his family, a charitable remainder trust is a good vehicle. At the end of the designated payout period, the entire corpus of the trust must be irrevocably transferred to or for the use of a qualified charity. No deduction is allowed for the bequest of a charitable remainder unless the remainder is in a farm or personal residence, or is a trust interest in an annuity trust, unitrust, or a pooled income fund.

❒ *Salary Continuation Agreements:* An employer is committed to make continued payments to the surviving spouse of the employee. These payments, if kept in reasonable line with the value of the employee's services during his life, can shift substantial value to his spouse or children; these values will be supported by payments that the employer can deduct and the estate tax will be based on the actuarially reduced value of the future payments at the time of the employee's death.

❒ *Interest-Free Loans:* Despite restrictions on interest-free loans, they still can be a valuable estate planning tool. For example, a parent generally can lend money to his child to help pay for the child's education or to buy a home without any income tax consequences.

In essence, when a parent makes an interest-free loan to his child, he is making a taxable gift to the child equal to the amount of interest that could have been charged (computed at the going rate), but wasn't. Since the child is considered to pay this amount to the parent in the form of interest, the parent must pay an income tax on it. The child, on the other hand, comes out ahead. Reason: He does not take the gift into income, yet he may pick up a deduction for the interest he does not actually pay.

Exceptions: There is a rather generous exception to the rules on no-interest family loans. Generally speaking, there are not tax consequences to a no-interest loan if all the loans between a parent and each child come to less than $10,000 a year ($20,000 a year from two parents to each child).

❑ *Private Annuities:* Property is transferred in exchange for the promise of the transferee to make annual payments over the balance of the transferor's life. Because the property is not included in the transferor's gross estate, he pays no estate tax. Neither will the exchange of property for a private annuity give rise to a gift tax, as long as the annual income promised is set at a figure that has the same actuarial value as the present value of the transferred property.

❑ *Gifts of Life Insurance:* In general, if the owner of a policy relinquishes complete dominion and control over the policy more than three years before death, and the proceeds are not payable to the estate, the proceeds will not be subject to the unified estate tax. The estate tax saving is accomplished at the relatively minor cost of a gift tax on the value of the policy. If the gift of the policy is made when its value does not exceed the available annual exclusions, the gift tax may also be avoided.

❑ *Flower Bonds:* Certain Treasury bonds that were issued before March 4, 1971, may be purchased at a substantial discount by an individual before death, and redeemed by the estate's personal representative at par value to pay the federal estate tax. Because of the great disparity between the purchase price and redemption price, these bonds are useful in lessening the impact of the estate tax.

❑ *Marital Agreements:* Prenuptial agreements (between prospective spouses) and postnuptial contracts (for married couples) define the property rights of a husband and wife in assets acquired before and/or during marriage. These contracts are particularly useful for individuals entering into a second marriage, and for domiciliaries of community property jurisdictions.

❑ *Buy-Sell Agreements:* Buy-sell agreements are contracts that provide for the orderly transfer of an individual's business interest after death. The agreement usually binds the decedent's estate to sell and the surviving partners or shareholders to buy the business interest at a stated price. Insurance purchased on the life of the individual is normally used to fund this arrangement. If a fair price has been set for the decedent's interest, the price will be accepted by IRS as the estate tax value of the interest.

❑ *Guardianships, Conservatorships, Etc.:* Incompetency, whether due to illness, accident, or degeneration, must be anticipated by the estate planner. Depending on state law, some of the tools available to the planner are guardianships, conservatorships, durable power of attorney, and the "living will." Lifetime trusts are another useful planning alternative.

[¶2309] JOINT OWNERSHIP

Where a husband and wife have a "qualified joint interest" in property, regardless of who furnished the consideration, only one-half a spouse's qualified joint interest is included in the deceased joint tenant's gross estate. "Qualified joint interest" means interest held by the spouses as tenants by the entirety or joint tenants with the right of survivorship. Because of the unlimited marital deduction, such property passes tax free to the surviving spouse.

Income Tax Treatment of Joint Property

As a general rule, the basis of property in the hands of a beneficiary is the fair market value of the property on the date of the decedent's death or the alternate valuation date. The rule for joint property is a bit more complicated. The decedent's surviving spouse has an income tax basis that consists of two elements: (1) One-half of the original cost of the property (i.e., the surviving spouse's half), plus (2) half the fair market value of the property at the decedent's death or alternate valuation date (i.e., the half that is included in the estate).

For example, suppose Mr. and Mrs. Smith bought property as joint tenants years ago. The cost was $10,000, and the fair market value at Mr. Smith's death is $100,000. One-half of the property is included in Smith's estate, but is free of tax because of the estate tax marital deduction. Mrs. Smith's income tax basis for the property is $55,000—$5,000 (half the original cost), plus $50,000 (half the value at death). If Mrs. Smith were to sell the property for $100,000, she would have a taxable long term capital gain of $45,000.

Possible Move: If Mr. Smith were to hold the property in his name only (the change in the form of ownership can be accomplished without a gift tax), the property will be included in full in his estate. The property will still be sheltered by the unlimited estate tax marital deduction. However, when Mrs. Smith inherits it, her income tax basis will be a full $100,000 (its value for estate tax purposes). Thus, Mrs. Smith could sell the property for $100,000 and pay no federal income tax.

[¶2310] COMMUNITY PROPERTY

Community property is generally defined as property that is acquired by a husband or wife during their marriage. Nine states have laws that classify them as community property states: Arizona, California, Idaho, Louisiana, Nevada, New Mexico, Texas, Washington, and Wisconsin. Each state's individual community property law is different and must be followed. State law determines the income taxable to each spouse, the termination of the marital community, and the property interests of each spouse.

❏ *Community Income Taxation Before a Divorce:* Any income that is designated by state law as community income is taxable half to each spouse. Each spouse may claim half of the deductions and credits related to items of community property. Each spouse is entitled to claim half of the total income tax withholdings made on community income. In general, income from separate property is taxable only to the spouse who owns the property, except in Idaho, Louisiana, and Texas. IRC §66 overrides state community property laws in certain cases when the spouses are separated for the entire year. Each spouse is then taxable on his or her own income.

☐ *Rights During Life:* During life, each spouse has exclusive management and control over the separate property. In most community property jurisdictions, community assets are subject to the spouse's joint management and control. Similarly, each spouse may freely give away separate assets, but gifts of the community require mutual consent.

☐ *Rights at Death:* Each spouse has the right to make a testamentary disposition of separate property and one-half interest in the community.

☐ *Estate Taxation of Community Property:* Generally, for estate tax purposes, only one-half the value of the community property is includible in the gross estate of the spouse who dies first. But the marital deduction is allowed for such property if it passes to the surviving spouse. The estate of a resident of a community property state includes that person's interest in his or her spouse's pension benefits attributable to the employer's contributions, insofar as the non-employee spouse's interest arises under the community property laws.

☐ *Termination of Community:* Each state has its own rules for judging when the marital community has ended. A decree of divorce terminates the community in every state. Events before the divorce may also end the community for tax purposes. A decree of legal separation ends the community in some states. A separation agreement is also sufficient to terminate the pooling of income under some states' laws. The spouses are equally taxable on community income for the portion of the year until the community ends.

☐ *Community Property Rights and Divisions:* Property transfers between spouses incident to a divorce are non-taxable events. The spouse receiving the property carries over the transferring spouse's basis in the property. There are no tax consequences to the transferring spouse.

☐ *Common Law States Affected:* Property acquired while spouses live in a community property state may retain its character as community property when the spouses move to a common law state. The property may be treated as owned equally regardless of the title under the law of the common law state.

[¶2311]   Generation-Skipping Transfer Tax

A small number of very large estates will be affected by the generation-skipping transfer tax, a flat-rate tax set at the maximum gift and estate tax rate. The taxable events are certain transfers (whether direct or in trust) to beneficiaries a generation or more younger than the transferor. However, every transferor is entitled to a $1 million exemption from this tax (which rules out most estates), and pre-1990 transfers directly to grandchildren are exempt to the extent of $2 million per grandchild.

[¶2312] SELECTING THE FIDUCIARY

Unless a fiduciary is carefully selected, the most well-conceived estate plan may go awry, resulting in frustration of the client's wishes and financial loss to the client's beneficiaries. Moreover, fraud, dishonesty, or even mere mismanagement can expose the fiduciary to personal liability. Ideally, the fiduciary should be an individual or institution with a high degree of integrity, well-versed in business matters, and familiar with the client's personal and financial background. Keep in mind, however, that the fiduciary is normally allowed to seek assistance from qualified experts (e.g., attorneys, accountants, investment advisors, etc.).

Occasionally, the fiduciary nominated in the will or trust instruments is unwilling or unable to accept the position. In other cases, a fiduciary who has already been appointed may die, become disabled, or be disqualified to continue functioning. The beneficiaries may also decide that the fiduciary is simply not managing the trust or estate competently. If the will or trust instrument is silent in this respect, the parties will have to petition the appropriate court for the appointment of a successor fiduciary. This procedure can be cumbersome, time-consuming, and expensive, and can easily result in intra-family conflict. These problems can be avoided by providing for successor fiduciaries in the governing instrument or by giving a third party (e.g., a committee or even some of the beneficiaries) the power to remove a fiduciary and appoint a new one.

If the value of the trust or estate is relatively modest, the tendency is to name an individual as the fiduciary. However, as in any other area of estate planning, this rule should not be rigidly applied. Most individuals do not have the experience or time to carry out the complex, technical duties that are required of an executor or trustee, even if modest amounts are involved. On the other hand, the client may not feel comfortable with a corporate fiduciary with whom he or she has had little personal contact. Much of the uncertainty over whether to name an individual or corporate fiduciary can be resolved by selecting one of each. However, the advisability of this arrangement should be carefully examined. While the appointment of a relative, friend, or business associate can add a personal touch to the fiduciary-beneficiary relationship, a corporate fiduciary may be reluctant to share authority with another individual. Thus, this decision, too, depends on the particular case and the estate planner's judgment. Finally, remember that if an individual names his spouse as a fiduciary, adverse estate or income tax consequences may result.

[¶2313] ADMINISTERING THE ESTATE

Administering an estate can be a lengthy and complicated process, particularly as the size of the estate increases and more sophisticated planning techniques such as pourover trusts or stock redemptions are employed. Although the services of attorneys, accountants, brokers, securities analysts, and other experts may be employed, the primary responsibility for administering the estate lies with its personal representative (usually an executor or administrator). The representative must exercise reasonable care during his or her tenure; failure to do so can result in personal liability to him as fiduciary, as well as financial loss to the estate.

The important aspects of estate administration are highlighted in the paragraphs that follow. While many of these activities must be carried on simultaneously, some, of course, must precede others.

[¶2314] INITIAL STEPS

One of the first steps is to locate the decedent's will, if any exists. Even if there is reason to believe that the decedent died intestate, a diligent search is required in order to petition for letters of administration. Once the will is located, the executor named in the will (or another person qualified to do so under local law) should present the will for probate and request authorization to serve as executor or administrator. If the decedent died intestate, his or her estate is administered by a court-appointed administrator. Once letters have been issued, the personal representative will proceed to collect the decedent's assets and provide for their protection. (If it is expected to take more than a few months to procure letters, the appointment of a temporary personal representative may be necessary.)

The steps that must be taken during this phase of the administration are listed below in their approximate order of occurrence. In all cases, of course, it will be necessary to check local law and practice.

(1) Notify banks where decedent had accounts; obtain information as to date of death balance, form of ownership, etc.

(2) Arrange for the collection and custody of decedent's personal property.

(3) Check insurance coverage on all of decedent's property.

(4) Investigate all of decedent's brokerage accounts.

(5) Make a preliminary estimate of the decedent's estate to determine the form of the probate and/or administration. Obtain values as of date of death for all estate assets as soon as possible. Also obtain acquisition date and value for jointly held property.

(6) Have additional copies of the will made for beneficiaries, taxing authorities, personal representatives, etc.

(7) List contents of decedent's safe deposit box, if any, in the presence of a member of decedent's family and taxing authorities.

(8) Hold preliminary conference with family members and others named in the will for the purpose of reading the will and determining whether there will be any objections or renunciations.

(9) Hold conference with the decedent's personal representative(s) to obtain all the facts needed for the preparation of the petition for probate.

(10) Make arrangements with the post office for custody of the decedent's mail.

(11) File the will and petition for testamentary letters (or petition for administration) with probate court.

(12) Make copies of the petition available to the executor and taxing authorities, accompanied by an affidavit as to the value of the property affected by the will, and the amounts going to the beneficiaries, together with their relationships to the decedent.

(13) Obtain copies of the death certificate (as many as possible).

(14) Assist beneficiaries in the collection of life insurance proceeds, obtaining necessary IRS forms from insurance companies.

(15) Collect unpaid wages, salary, or commissions owed to the decedent.

(16) Inquire as to the exact benefits due from company pension and/or profit-sharing plans and other company programs, and from union or association benefit programs.

(17) Change automobile registration, if in the decedent's name.

(18) If decedent was a business person, check for business continuation agreements, etc.

(19) Arrange for continued collection of loans, rents, interest, dividends, royalties, etc., and attempt to collect delinquent obligations.

(20) Mail notice of hearing on petition together with order limiting time to file claims (all in accordance with local law requirements).

(21) Arrange for publication or order for hearing (in accordance with local law).

(22) File affidavit of mailing of notice of hearing (in accordance with local law requirements).

(23) Send copies of the will and preliminary estimate of estate to the appropriate heirs.

(24) Arrange for ancillary administration, if necessary.

(25) Collect all pertinent information for income tax returns.

(26)If the decedent was the sole proprietor of a business, determine if there is an outstanding obligation for employers' tax.

(27) Collect all amounts due from retirement plans, etc.

(28) File Social Security claims.

(29) File VA claims, if any.

(30) Arrange for witnesses to appear at hearing, obtaining written depositions, if necessary.

(31) Send copy of the will to surviving spouse and minor children, if not already done, and notify them as to their rights (and advise them as to tax considerations).

(32) File affidavit of mailing of notice of surviving spouse's and children's rights (as required by local law).

(33) Assemble data on all nonprobate property (joint tenancy property, life insurance, living trusts, property subject to a power in the decedent, etc.).

(34) Inquire whether the following types of transfers have been made within three years of the decedent's death: gifts of life insurance, transfers with retained life estates, transfers that take effect at death, revocable transfers, and transfers of powers of appointment. Reason: These transfers are included in the decedent's estate. As a general rule, however, the value of property transferred by the decedent before death is not included in the gross estate (IRC §2035(d)).

(35) Make inquiry as to requirements for fiduciary bond, discussing same with the named executor, and prepare application therefor, if necessary.

(36) Prepare executor's form of acceptance.

(37) Attend formal court hearing on petition for probate with witnesses and any required written testimony.

(38) File acceptance by executor.

(39) File fiduciary bond, if required.

(40) Obtain certified copies of letters testamentary.

(41) To limit appeal time, serve copy of order on petition to interested parties.

(42) Have appraisers appointed, if necessary.

(43) Executor should notify post office, banks, creditors, IRS, and others of his appointment.

(44) Documentation of all the items listed above should be obtained (originals or photocopies when appropriate). Particularly important are copies of federal gift tax returns for transfers made after 1976.

[¶2315] FIDUCIARY RESPONSIBILITY (AN OVERVIEW)

In general, the executor's duties include:

(1) The collection and conservation of the personal property of the estate. Since real property usually vests immediately in the devisees, the executor is able to sell such property only in the event that personal property is inadequate to meet claims.

(2) The payment of all valid debts, including funeral costs, fees and expenses incurred in administration, death taxes, income and other taxes owed by the decedent, etc.

(3) The distribution of remaining property in accordance with the testator's wishes.

(If a testamentary trustee is named, most of his duties are prescribed by the will; however, certain duties and restrictions may also be imposed by state law.) The trustee's duties include:

(1) Taking possession and control of the trust property.

(2) Investing and reinvesting such property prudently for the production of income.

(3) Paying all necessary taxes and other reasonable expenses of trust administration.

(4) Exercising all mandatory directions recited in the governing instrument, except those that are impossible to fulfill.

(5) Exercising any discretionary duties in good faith and within the bounds of reasonable judgment.

(6) Keeping records and rendering accounts when required to do so.

(7) Paying over income (and principal, depending on the terms of the governing instrument) to those entitled to receive it.

(8) Refraining from dealing with the trust property to his own advantage and from commingling such property with his own.

(9) Dealing impartially with the beneficiaries.

(10) Defending the trust against the claims of third parties.

(11) Refraining from delegating any of the above duties to others except to the extent permitted by the governing instrument or by local law.

[¶2316] TAX DUTIES OF FIDUCIARIES

An estate or trust is a taxable entity. The responsibility for filing returns, paying taxes, and performing other tax duties lies with the executor or trustee, as the case may be. In the case of an estate, the federal and local returns that must be prepared by the executor include the estate tax return, the estate income tax return, the decedent's final income tax return, unfiled gift tax returns, and other delinquent returns. The trustee must file the appropriate federal and local income tax returns.

[¶2317] FEDERAL ESTATE TAX RETURN (FORM 706)

The federal estate tax return (Form 706) must be filed by the executor or administrator within nine months after the date of death, unless an extension has been granted. The deadline for paying the tax is the same. Returns for deceased U.S. citizens or residents must be filed if the gross estate equals or exceeds $600,000 (minus post-1976 taxable gifts).

The return must be filed with the service center for the state or district of domicile at the time of the decedent's death. For a nonresident citizen the return must be filed with the Internal Revenue Service Center, Philadelphia, Pennsylvania 19255.

Estate tax returns generally must be filed within nine months after the decedent's date of death.[1] The Secretary of the Treasury is authorized to grant a "reasonable" extension of time for filing.[2] The maximum extension period is six months.[3] If it is impossible or impractical to timely file the return, and/or pay the tax, an extension of time to file and/or pay the tax should be requested before the time expires to avoid late filing and/or late payment penalties. Section 6601 requires interest to be paid on any portion of the tax that is not paid by the due date of the return, determined without regard to the extension period.

Election of Alternative Date

Section 2032 authorizes the executor to elect to value all property included in the gross estate at its fair market value on the alternative valuation date. Its purpose is to make sure an entire estate could not be confiscated for taxes because of a sudden substantial drop in values. The executor must make this irrevocable election on the estate tax return. The alternative valuation date election can only be made if it decreases (1) the value of the gross estate and (2) the estate tax liability (after reduction for credits).[4]

How to Compute the Taxable Estate

The taxable estate is the gross estate less certain allowable deductions. These deductions are permitted because certain expenses, like those applicable to any other taxpayer, diminish its ability to pay the applicable tax. Thus, an estate is able to deduct such expenditures as administrative and funeral expenses, casualty losses, charitable contributions, and claims against the estate.[5] The Internal Revenue Code also allows an unlimited deduction (called the marital deduction) for property passing to the decedent's spouse.[6] The taxable estate must be increased by gifts made after 1976.[7] The tax due, called the "Unified Transfer Tax," is then reduced by a tax credit of $192,800[8] and gift taxes paid after 1976 to arrive at the final tax due.

The formula for computing the taxable estate upon the death of an individual is as follows:

Gross Estate (FMV of all property owned by the decedent at the date of death or alternate valuation date)	$XXX,XXX
Less: Deduction for funeral and administrative expenses, debts of the decedent, charitable contributions, and the marital deduction for property transferred to a surviving spouse	(X,XXX)
Taxable Estate	$XXX,XXX
Plus: Taxable gifts made after 1976	XXX
Tax Base	$XXX,XXX
Times: Unified transfer tax rates(s)	XX
Unified transfer tax	$ X,XXX
Less: Tax credits (e.g. the unified tax credit of $192,800)	(XX)
Gift taxes paid after 1976	(XX)
Unified transfer tax (estate tax due)	$ XX

Example: Margo Holmes died on March 30, 1995 leaving a gross estate of $1,400,000. One half of the property was transferred to her husband. Funeral and administration expenses were $50,000, charitable contributions $10,000, and debts of the decedent were $300,000. Taxable gifts made after 1976 were $100,000 on which $4,000 in gift taxes were paid. No estate tax was due as shown by the following calculation:

Gross Estate (FMV of all property owned by the decedent at the date of death)		$1,300,000
Less: Marital deduction	$700,000	
Deduction for funeral and administrative expenses	50,000	
Charitable contributions	10,000	
Decedent's debts	290,000	1,050,000
Taxable Estate		$ 250,000
Plus: Taxable gifts made after 1976		100,000
Tax Base		**$ 350,000**
Unified transfer tax		$ 104,800*
Less: Tax creedits (e.g. the unified tax credit of $192,800)		(192,800)
Gift taxes paid after 1976		4,000
Unified transfer tax (estate tax due)		$ –0–

* $70,800 + $34,000 (34% [applicable estate tax rate] × $100,000)

[¶2318] ESTATE INCOME TAX RETURN

If the estate has $600 or more of gross income, it must file Form 1041. If there is a nonresident beneficiary, the return is required regardless of the amount of gross income. For purposes of filing, a taxable year for the estate must be selected. It need not be a calendar year and need not coincide with the date of death. It may be advantageous to use a short taxable year for the estate's initial return. Bearing in mind the tax interests of the beneficiaries, the choice of a fiscal year may help split the income and thus reduce the aggregate tax burden.

The return must be filed by the 15th day of the fourth month following the end of the tax year: it may be advisable to complete the return early in order to be able to give advance notification to the distributees of the amounts they must include in their own returns. After its second taxable year, the estate must make estimated tax payments.

[¶2319] DECEDENT'S INCOME TAX RETURN

The executor must also file the decedent's final income tax return on Form 1040 and, if necessary, delinquent returns for prior years. If death occurred between January 1 and April 15, there will generally be two returns to file, assuming the decedent was on a calendar-year basis.

The decedent's return is more difficult for the executor to compute than the estate's return. He has the information for the latter, but unless the decedent was the unusual taxpayer who kept detailed records of such things as deductions, the executor may have to make an estimate under the *Cohan* (CA-2, 39 F. 2d 540, 1930) rule.

A joint return may be filed for a married decedent for the year of death, unless the surviving spouse should remarry before the close of the tax year, or the decedent or the surviving spouse had a short tax year caused by a change of accounting period. The liability for the full tax in such cases is joint and several. If the decedent's income was less than that of the surviving spouse and the latter isn't the sole beneficiary, the executor's consent to a joint return, without limiting the estate's liability, may expose him to liability.

The surviving spouse may file a joint return if the decedent filed no return for the year and if no executor has been appointed by the time the joint or surviving spouse's return is due. If the executor qualifies within a year after the due date (including any extensions for filing), he may disaffirm the joint return by filing a separate return within the one-year period. This rule protects the estate in the event the surviving spouse files a return that is detrimental to the estate. It will be up to the executor to disaffirm unless the estate is fully indemnified.

Note: A surviving spouse may take advantage of the joint income tax rates for the two taxable years following the year of the decedent's death if he or she maintains a household that is the principal place of residence of his or her dependent child (son, stepson, daughter, or stepdaughter). The surviving spouse must furnish over half the cost of maintaining the household and be entitled to take a personal exemption deduction for the dependent under IRC §151. (See IRC §2(a)(1)).

[¶2320]　GIFT TAX RETURN FILED BY EXECUTOR

The executor should review the decedent's entire lifetime giving; a gift tax return may have been required (Form 709), even though no gift tax was payable. If there is doubt about the necessity to file, the executor probably should file anyway in order to start the statute of limitations running. The executor should always seek the surviving spouse's consent to have half the decedent's gifts attributed to him or her, so as to reduce any gift tax payable by the estate. If the spouse made the gifts during the decedent's lifetime, the personal representative must carefully weigh the consequences of attributing half to the decedent.

[¶2321]　TRUST INCOME TAX RETURN

The trustee (whether the trust is testamentary or inter vivos) must file an income tax return (Form 1041) and make quarterly estimated tax payments for any year in which the trust has any taxable income or has gross income of $600 or more. Gross income of the trust or estate is determined in the same manner as an individual's. The trust or estate reports its income and is allowed an offsetting deduction for the income distributed or required to be distributed to the beneficiary. The beneficiary, in turn, is taxable on the income required to be distributed to him or her. Post-1986, most trusts are required to be calendar-year taxpayers.

[¶2322] TAX RETURN CHART

The chart provided in the Appendix summarizes the tax duties of fiduciaries. It also briefly describes the requirements for obtaining extensions of time to file returns and to pay the tax.

[¶2323] TAX LIABILITIES OF FIDUCIARIES

The duty to discharge the tax liability may be particularly onerous. Although normally the fiduciary is responsible for paying out only the funds entrusted to him as a fiduciary, in some cases he can become personally liable for the taxes.

An executor or administrator who pays a debt due by the person or estate for whom he acts before he pays debts due to the United States becomes personally liable for these debts, to the extent they remain unpaid.

Debts due to the United States include federal taxes. Thus, whenever a personal representative makes distributions or pays other obligations, he or she runs a personal risk if the estate is unable to pay federal taxes. However, debts to the United States have no priority over prior specific and perfected liens or debts given priority by state law (such as funeral expenses, administration expenses, and, in some cases, allowances for surviving spouses). Thus, the personal representative should be able to make such payments safely.

There are two tests to determine whether a personal representative who makes payments before paying debts to the United States is personally liable:

(1) The Insolvency Test: The priority given to United States debts must be established by proving that the estate is "insolvent" or showing that it has "insufficient funds to pay all the debts due from the deceased"; and,

(2) The "Knowledge" Test: The representative must have been aware of the unpaid debt to the United States. According to Rev. Rul. 66-43 (1966-1 CB 291), the executor or administrator of an estate cannot be held personally liable unless he or she either has or should have had personal knowledge of the debt. As a general rule, the government should have no difficulty in satisfying this requirement in the case of estate taxes, since one of the executor's first duties is to estimate the amount of taxes.

In addition to his representative and personal responsibilities, the fiduciary is also subject to transferee liability like any other taxpayer [IRC §6901(h)].

[¶2324] PROTECTION FROM PERSONAL LIABILITY

Although the possibility of personal liability is a serious problem for the fiduciary, he is not without protection. For example, unpaid gift taxes are not likely to be charged against him, since the tax follows the gift and can be satisfied out of the gift property. Even if the donee has parted with the property, the fiduciary is still safe, since the gift tax then becomes a lien against the donee's other property. The fiduciary may be in some danger when the gift is in trust; because of the difficulty in reaching the beneficiaries, the Treasury may contend the trustee is to be treated as the donee.

With respect to the estate tax, the executor can ascertain the amount of estate tax due by making a written request to IRS. The latter must notify the executor of the amount within nine months of the executor's request or the filing of the Form 706 (whichever is later—but not after the end of the assessment period). If the executor pays this amount, he is entitled to a written discharge from personal liability (IRC §2204). Discharge from personal liability for decedent's gift and income taxes is also available (IRC §6905).

IRS may require the executor to furnish a bond prior to releasing him from personal liability for any amount for which an extension of time to pay has been granted.

There is also a time limit on the personal tax liability threat to the fiduciary. Any assessment against the fiduciary personally must be made not later than one year after the liability arises or not later than the expiration of the period for collection of the tax for which the liability arises, whichever is later (IRC §6901(c)(3)). This is in addition to the six-year period within which IRS is permitted to collect a validly assessed tax.

Enforcement of personal liability against the fiduciary is made by the same processes (jeopardy assessment, distraint, etc.) and is subject to the same restrictions as any other tax collection.

[¶2325] POST-MORTEM TAX PLANNING

Although the drafter of the will, the executor, and the beneficiaries can collaborate to achieve important tax savings after the testator's death, the time to think of these matters is prior to or at the time of drafting the will. However, some opportunities will remain open to the executors or present themselves for the first time after the testator's death. The tax savings available here fall into these categories:

(a) Estate tax savings by altering the testamentary dispositions;

(b) Income tax savings for the estate in administration;

(c) Income tax savings for the beneficiaries.

[¶2326] CHECKLIST OF POST-MORTEM TAX PLANNING STEPS

Here is a checklist of some post-mortem maneuvers that can be employed by executors or estate beneficiaries to achieve certain tax advantages.

❑ *Election Against the Will:* A failure to qualify for the marital deduction can be remedied by a spouse who (pursuant to local law) exercises his or her right to take against the will.

❑ *Will Contests and Family Settlements:* If a will contest or settlement results in property passing to the surviving spouse, the property qualifies for the marital deduction provided the surrender or assignment is a bona fide recognition of enforceable rights in the decedent's estate.

❑ *Renunciation or Disclaimer:* Property that passes to a surviving spouse by disclaimer qualifies for the unlimited marital deduction provided the interest itself qualifies for the deduction (IRC §2056(b)(7)). For federal tax purposes, a qualified disclaimer must meet the following requirements: (1) It is a written, irrevocable, and unqualified refusal by a person to accept an interest in property; (2) It is received by the transferor of the interest, his legal representative, or the holder of legal title to the property within nine months of (a) the day on which the transfer is made to the disclaimant or (b) the day on which the disclaimant attains age 21; (3) The disclaimant has not accepted the interest or any of its benefits; and (4) As a result of the refusal, the interest passes to a person other than the disclaimant (IRC §2518).

❑ *Electing Qualified Terminable Interest (QTIP):* As a general rule, property left to a spouse qualifies for the marital deduction only if it is a present interest. In other words, no marital deduction generally is allowed for "terminable" interests. However, at the election of the decedent's executor, a property interest passing to the decedent's spouse is eligible for the marital deduction even though it is a terminable interest if: (1) the surviving spouse receives the entire income from the property; (2) the income is payable at least annually; and (3) no person has the power to appoint the property to anyone other than the surviving spouse during the surviving spouse's life. The entire property subject to a QTIP must be included in the surviving spouse's estate even if the spouse's interest ended before death. However, the property is not included if it was transferred before the death of the spouse. In that case, the spouse's estate may recover from the remainder-man any estate taxes attributable to the remainder interest upon the death of the spouse (IRC §§2044; 2056(b)(7); 2207A).

The election to treat an otherwise terminable interest as a QTIP must be made by the executor on the estate tax return. Once made, the election is irrevocable (IRC §2056(b)(7)(B)).

❑ *Picking a Fiscal Year for the Estate:* By selecting a fiscal year that will produce a short year at the beginning of the estate administration and a short year at the end, income that will be taxed to the estate can be spread out to maximum advantage. Since an estate beneficiary must report the income during his taxable

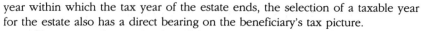

year within which the tax year of the estate ends, the selection of a taxable year for the estate also has a direct bearing on the beneficiary's tax picture.

❐ **Timing of Distribution:** If the executor has discretionary powers with respect to the distribution of estate assets, he is in a position to make substantial savings in taxes by proper timing of the distributions from the estate. In years when the estate is in a lower bracket than the beneficiaries of the estate, the executor might want to accumulate the income of the estate in order to have it taxed in its lower bracket. If the beneficiaries are in lower brackets than the estate, the executor might want to accelerate the distribution of the income of the estate in order to have it taxed as the income of the beneficiaries.

❐ **Valuation of Estate:** The valuation placed on estate assets for estate tax purposes will affect (a) the amount of the estate tax; (b) the shares of the surviving spouse and other beneficiaries; and (c) the taxable gain or loss on a subsequent sale of the assets by the estate or by the beneficiaries. The relationship of the applicable estate tax rates and the future income tax rates will point up possible tax savings here.

❐ **Deduction of Administration Expenses:** The executor must elect whether to deduct administration expenses on the estate tax return or on the estate's income tax return. They can also be split between the two returns.

❐ **Termination of Administration:** The termination of the estate closes its taxable year. While the termination cannot be unduly delayed, wherever possible the executor should avoid having more than 12 months' distributions taxed to the beneficiaries in one year. Ideally, the estate should be closed at such time as will bring the final distribution of income into another tax year of the beneficiary. On the other hand, if the final year of the estate includes excess deductions that can be claimed by the beneficiaries, it might be preferable to close the estate at a time when the beneficiaries can realize the maximum benefit from the excess deductions.

❐ **Special Use Valuation:** Real estate used by a closely held business, or farmland, can be valued for estate tax purposes 'at the value based on its actual use—not a hypothetical (and probably higher) "highest and best use." This valuation can be elected on the estate tax return.

❐ **Income in Respect of a Decedent (IRD):** Income that has been earned by the decedent during his lifetime that is received by his estate will not be taxed in the last income tax return of the decedent. Instead, it will be taxed when it is received (actually or constructively) to: (1) The decedent's estate, if it is entitled to receive IRD, or (2) The person who, due to the decedent's death, is entitled to the IRD; or (3) The person to whom IRD has been properly distributed by the estate.

Income in respect of a decedent is also included in the decedent's estate tax return, but the estate tax paid on this income can be taken by the recipient as an income tax deduction (IRC §691(c)). While most of the planning for income in respect of a decedent should be taken care of before death (via contractual provisions or will provisions), there is still much that can be done by the executor— especially if the will gives him or her discretionary powers in this regard. If the executor has the power to distribute these income rights before they are collected, they can be spread over a number of beneficiaries rather than come into the estate, which is taxed as a single taxpayer.

❏ *Sale or Exchange of Capital Assets:* Generally, when an executor sells or exchanges assets of an estate, any gain is included in the estate's gross income and any loss is deductible by the estate. The general holding period rules do not apply here: gains and losses from the sale or exchange of inherited property receive long-term treatment regardless of how long the property was held (IRC §1223(11)). Also, an amount equal to the net capital gain deduction for long-term capital gains for the tax year is a tax preference for the alternative minimum tax purposes (IRC §55).

❏ *Electing to Recognize Gain or Loss:* Although it is normal for estates to distribute items of property in kind to beneficiaries without recognizing gain or loss (e.g., heir is bequeathed a particular Degas painting; the executor transfers the painting to the heir), the 1986 Code permits an estate (or a trust) to recognize gain or loss in this situation. The property is treated as if it had been sold to the heir at its FMV as of the date of distribution. The purpose of making this election is to change the distribution deduction and beneficiary's income to the property's FMV; without the election, these amounts would be either the basis or the FMV of the property, whichever is lower. But the fiduciary can't "pick and choose"—the election must be made for all distributions during a taxable year, unless the IRS permits the election to be revoked.

❏ *Decedent's Final Income Tax Return:* If the decedent was married at the time of his death, the executor and the surviving spouse can file a joint return. This will, as a rule, bring about a lower tax than would the use of separate returns. However, local law will have to be checked if the will itself does not contain explicit authorization to the executor to join in a joint return, since the joint return may subject the estate to liability for the income tax on the surviving spouse's income.

❏ *Deferring Tax Attributable to Business Interest:* An executor may elect to defer the estate tax (but not the interest on the tax) attributable to the interest of a decedent in a closely held business for up to five years. Thereafter, the executor must pay the tax in equal installments over the succeeding ten years (IRC §6166). To qualify, the value of the decedent's interest in the closely held business included in the gross estate must exceed 35% of the adjusted gross estate. A decedent may have an interest in a closely held business by being a partner or a corporate shareholder having a 20% or more interest in the partnership or corporation. The executor must file a notice of election to pay in installments with the IRS within 60 days after notice and demand is made for payment of taxes. However, the executor can make a "protective" election even if it initially appears that the estate doesn't qualify for the extension or that no tax is due.

As a result of the election, the estate, in effect, receives a loan of the amount of the installments at a low interest rate. Thus, the executor can meet the estate tax liability without affecting the business interest, which otherwise might have to be sold or liquidated to meet the tax obligation (although the executor can dispose of up to 50% of the business without triggering acceleration of the tax).

[¶2327] Accounting Formats

There are no generally accepted forms for estate accountings. Some courts merely require statements of receipts and disbursements, especially if the estate is small. More substantial estates should have detailed statements. Although the fiduciary should check local law before submitting an accounting, a statement that separates the estate's operating and income expenses from receipts and disbursements pertaining to estate principal represents the most prudent approach. The statement should, of course, also show what assets have come into the fiduciary's hands (e.g., inventoried assets, gains on sales, income, etc.), what disbursements (expenses, payments for debts, bequests satisfied, taxes paid, etc.) have been made, and what balance remains for distribution. Each item in the statement may be supplemented by detailed schedules.

[¶2328] ESTATE ACCOUNTING

Estate accountings, whether judicially mandated or informally completed, serve several purposes. First, they provide the local court having jurisdiction over the administration of the estate with a means of overseeing and reviewing a fiduciary's activities. The court may require periodic (usually annual) accountings from the representative. When the estate is settled, a final accounting is nearly always made. However, informal accountings (not submitted to a court) are acceptable if all parties with an interest in the estate agree to such a method. A well-organized accounting and bookkeeping system also helps the fiduciary keep track of the progress of the estate. Interim accountings can alert the executor or administrator to possible cash shortages and difficulties in satisfying bequests. When a final accounting has been accepted by the local court and the estate beneficiaries, the fiduciary can be released from further liability and obligation in connection with his administration of the estate.

Finally, accountings give the beneficiaries a detailed picture of the fiduciary's activities. Thus, if they are displeased with the performance of his duties as reported in the accounting, they can raise objections in court.

— ENDNOTES —

1. IRC §6075(a).

2. IRC §6081(a).

3. IRS Form 4768 is to be used for extensions.

4. IRC §2032(c).

5. IRC §§2053, 2054.

6. IRC §2056.

7. IRC §2001(b).

8. IRC §2010(a).

— FOR FURTHER REFERENCE —

Beehler, John M., "Trust Estate Freeze Valuation Rules Under the Final Section 2702 Regulations," 70 *Taxes: The Tax Magazine* 604 (September '92).

Cahn, Charles II, "Estate Planning to Avoid Complications of Remarriage," 19 *Estate Planning* 268 (September-October 1992).

Cavaliere, Frank J. and Hez A. Aubey, "Using Trust Department Services," 39 *Practical Lawyer* 65 (June '93).

Clark, John A., "Income Tax Elections Are Principal Tools for Executors," 132 *Trusts and Estates* 26 (July '93).

Crown, Jeffrey L., "Prophylaxis for Probate Practitioners: Malpractice Protection and Malpractice Prevention," 26 *Inst. on Estate Planning* 19 (1992 annual).

Gislason, Scott H., "Split-Dollar Life Insurance: Updated Planning Techniques," 20 *Estate Planning* 201 (July-August '93).

Goldman, Foster S. and Cynthia K. Rarig, "Estate Planning for Disabled Beneficiaries," 63 *Pennsylvania Bar Ass'n Q.* 154 (July '92).

Harrison, Louis S., "Proposed Regs. Clarify Planning for GRITs, Buy-Sell Agreements," 18 *Estate Planning* 329 (November-December '91).

Hoisington, William R., "The Truth About Charitable Trusts," 45 *Tax Lawyer* 293 (Winter '92).

Jegen, Lawrence A. III, "Tax Court Held that Decedent's Devise to Charitable Organization Did Not Qualify for Charitable Deduction," 37 *Res Gestae* 72 (August '93).

Kasner, Jerry A., "To Nip It in the Bud: New Ruling Adversely Affects Charitable Planning Technique," 56 *Tax Notes* 1319 (September 7, 1992).

Katzenstein, Andrew M. and Kim Allen-Nielsen, "Keeping the Business. . . All in the Family," 10 *Compleat Lawyer* 28 (Summer '93).

Kaufman, Barton L. and Kristin D. Wheeler, "Continuing to Look a Gift Horse in the Mouth: State Death Taxes and IRC Section 6166," 47 *J. American Society of CLU/ChFC* 62 (July '93).

King, Hamlin C., "The Application of the Passive Loss Rules to the Income Taxation of Trusts and Estates," 18 *Tax Management Estates, Gifts and Trusts J.* 57 (March-April '93).

Krahmer, Johannes R., "Building Flexibility Into the Irrevocable Trust," 6 *Probate and Property* 17 (September-October '92).

Ladouceur, Raymond P., "Who Inherits the Nest? Qualified Retirement Plan Annuities in the Nonemployed Spouse's Estate," 40 *Louisiana Bar J.* 74 (June '92).

Lawler, Theresa A., "Estate and Trust Law: Legislation Governing Joint Bank Accounts," 25 *Maryland Bar J.* 51 (September-October '92).

McNair, John R., "Lifetime QTIPs Can Achieve Tax and Asset Protection Goals," 20 *Estate Planning* 290 (September-October '93).

Miedaner, Randall M., "Protecting Assets from Lawsuits and Creditors While Saving Income and Estate Taxes," 24 *Tax Adviser* 504 (August '93).

Myer, Lee, "Methods for Qualifying Plan Distributions for the Marital Deduction," 79 *J. Tax.* 30 (July '93).

Parks, John Paul, "Varied Duties Face the Successor Trustee of a Revocable Trust," 19 *Estate Planning* 203 (July-August '92).

Peithman, William A., "A Look at the Principles and Uses of Powers of Appointment," 132 *Trusts and Estates* 38 (August '93).

Radom, Carl and Michael Yuhas, "Excess Beneficiary Involvement Can Cost Trust Its Tax Status," 21 *Taxation for Lawyers* 17 (July-August '92).

Reineke, David W., "Post-Mortem Tax and Estate Planning," 9 *Cooley L. Rev.* 384 (May '92).

Stevens, Diane R., "The Closely Held Business as an Estate Asset," 35 *Res Gestae* 570 (June '92).

Stover, Thomas L., "The Will Contest Regulation and the Marital Deduction," 21 *Colo. Lawyer* 1407 (July '92).

Strauss, Benton C. and James K. Shaw, "Final Chapter 14 Regulations Refine Estate Freeze Rules," 19 *Estate Planning* 195 (July-August '92).

Street, Kimbrough, "Practical Guidelines for Selecting an Individual Trustee," 20 *Estate Planning* 268 (September-October '93).

Volkman, Ronald R., "Right of Adopted Persons to Inherit," 20 *Estate Planning* 253 (July-August '93).

Walsh, James F., "The Effect of Divorce on the Beneficiary Rights to a Nonprobate Asset," 7 *Connecticut Probate L.J.* 163 (Fall '92).

Warnken, Wayne L. and Pamela R. Champine, "Anti-Estate Freeze Rules Can Have Wide Scope," 20 *Estate Planning* 220 (July-August '93).

IMMIGRATION

[¶2401] One of the most important attributes of a sovereign nation is its ability to decide who will be admitted into the country; when and where the country's own citizens can travel; and when a person from another country can become a citizen. These concerns are especially important in the United States, because this country is so attractive to many people who wish to escape political persecution or poverty in other countries, or who see the United States as a more interesting, attractive, or economically viable place to live than their original homelands.

The basic immigration law of the United States comes from the Immigration and Nationality Act of 1952, as supplemented by the Immigration Reform and Control Act of 1986 (IRCA). This later Act added amnesty provisions (now expired) for illegal aliens and sought to make illegal immigration less attractive by penalizing employers of illegal alien workers. (There were many statutes with less dramatic impact on immigration law in the intervening years.) It has been modified by the Immigration Act of 1990.

Several federal agencies are involved in immigration. The Attorney General of the United States, with the ultimate responsibility for managing immigration, has delegated it to the Immigration and Naturalization Service (INS). The State Department, relying on a preliminary inspection of applications by the INS, determines who can get an immigrant or non-immigrant visa to enter the United States. If the alien enters the United States to take up an offer of permanent employment within the United States, the Department of Labor must certify that qualified United States citizens are not available to take the job, and that employment of the alien will not harm the compensation and working conditions of U.S. citizens holding similar jobs. (DOL does not have the power to order the employer to hire a qualified American for the job; all it can do is exclude a particular alien.)

Technically speaking, "immigration" stems from an intent to remain in the United States indefinitely or permanently; "permanent residence" is intent to reside in the United States, with or without establishing a domicile in the United States. The state of permanent residence is not necessarily incompatible with lengthy absences from the United States. It is presumed that anyone entering the United States is an immigrant (and therefore must qualify as such) unless he or she can prove to the contrary (e.g., by having a valid "B visa" for a short business (B-1) or pleasure (B-2) trip). However, visas are not required for certain visitors from the United Kingdom, Japan, Italy, the Netherlands, Sweden, Switzerland, or West Germany. These visitors can stay up to 90 days, and are not permitted to change their non-immigrant to immigrant status.[1]

A legal permanent resident of the United States can become a naturalized citizen after five years of legal permanent resident status (three years if he or she is married to a U.S. citizen) and residing in the United States for at least half this time. In other words, a person can enter the United States as a legal permanent resident rather than an immigrant (if that conforms to his or her plans, or if it is easier to be admitted as a legal permanent resident than as an immigrant), but later change plans or remain in the United States and seek citizenship.

[¶2401.1] Exclusion and Deportation

In 1992, the Eleventh Circuit ruled[2] that there is no judicial review whether under the Immigration and Nationality Act, the Refugee Act, or anything else of the procedures used to prevent Haitian boat people from entering the United States. Although certiorari was denied in that case, it was granted in another case, on the issue of returning Haitians en masse under Executive Order 12807 without consideration of their individual claims to asylum—a policy that was upheld by the Supreme Court in 1993.[3]

A Supreme Court decision of that year[4] denies political asylum to men fleeing compulsory conscription in Guatemala. The Supreme Court's analysis was that they did not experience a well-founded fear of persecution based on their political beliefs. Instead, they disapproved of the political beliefs of the government of Guatemala which did not entitle them to asylum. Another case, this time in the Seventh Circuit, found the plaintiff entitled to asylum based on his well-founded fear of religious persecution: he had converted to Christianity, and in his homeland, Iran, apostasy from Islam was a capital offense.[5] The Seventh Circuit read the test to be the reasonableness of the applicant's belief that he would be persecuted under the laws of the home state.

The purpose of the visa system is to determine which aliens are entitled to be admitted into the United States for temporary or permanent stays. The law contains 32 grounds for excluding an alien who wishes to enter the United States among which are criminal activity (such as convictions outside the United States); political grounds; violations of immigration law; "moral" grounds; and economic grounds.

"Paupers, beggars, and vagrants" cannot be admitted to the United States. However, *Zambrano v. INS*[6] grants a preliminary injunction against regulations that make an alien excludable as "likely to become a public charge" based solely on U.S. employment history and past receipt of public assistance; the District Court held that a prospective test, based on conditions likely to obtain at the time of a request for amnesty, should be used instead.

Theoretically, persons suffering from infectious diseases are not permitted to enter the United States. However, excludability for HIV ("AIDS virus") infection can be waived on grounds of family unity, humanitarian, or public interest grounds. INS Form I-693 requires all applicants for permanent U.S. residence 15 years old or older to be tested for HIV; effective May 25, 1989, HIV-positive aliens can enter the United States for up to 30 days to attend meetings, see their relatives, or get medical treatment, but they cannot be admitted as tourists.

The statute also permits exclusion of anyone who the Attorney General or any U.S. consul believes is a subversive or intends to engage in un-American activities if admitted. However, the Moynihan Amendment[7] forbade the INS to exclude applicants for permanent or temporary entry solely because of their political beliefs for one year. P.L. 100-461 extended this provision for two more years, but only for non-immigrant aliens.

Once an alien enters the United States (even illegally) he or she can no longer be excluded; if the alien's presence is deemed inappropriate, the United

States' remedy is by deportation. There are 19 legal grounds for deportability. They are similar to the grounds for exclusion, but include additional grounds based on violations of immigration law (e.g., a temporary resident who got a visa by fraud, or a temporary resident who fails to qualify for permanent residence, can be deported).

The Central District of California has found the provision permitting deportation for advocating the establishment of Communism, anarchism, or dictatorship in the United States to be extremely overbroad and in violation of the First Amendment, because the provision refers to advocacy that does not incite immediate violations of U.S. law.[8]

However, the Ninth Circuit has upheld (as consistent with its authority under the Immigration Act and not violative of the First Amendment) an INS policy of requiring applicants for naturalization to list all organizations they have ever been affiliated with, to see if any of the organizations are Communist fronts.[9]

A person threatened with deportation has more procedural rights than one facing exclusion (including a "reasonable opportunity to be present" at the deportation hearing, which precludes telephone deportation hearings even if the credibility of the alien is not an issue). The U.S. government has the burden of proof at a deportation hearing, and aliens who lose at the hearing are entitled to an automatic stay of deportation pending their petition for federal court review of the INS hearing officer's decision.

[¶2402] VISAS AND PREFERENCE CATEGORIES

In each fiscal year, 270,000 immigrants were permitted to enter the United States if they fit into one or more of the six "preference categories." Under pre-1990 law, this quota was for the entire world, and each country was assigned a portion of this quota: no country could get more than 20,000 visas in any fiscal year, regardless of its population or the reasons its citizens might have had to wish to leave. Visa applicants were "assigned" to the country in which they were born, not the country in which they lived when they applied for the visa (which worked a significant hardship on people who had fled their home country to a second or third country before attempting to emigrate to the United States).

In addition, "immediate relatives" of U.S. citizens (their spouses, minor children, and parents) and "special immigrants" were permitted to enter without limitation by the quotas. "Special immigrants" included former U.S. citizens who lost their citizenship under laws that have been declared invalid; certain employees of the U.S. government; and some members of the clergy and foreign medical graduates.

Each year, the United States sets a limit on the number of "refugees" who will be admitted to seek asylum in the United States. The test is a "well-founded fear of persecution" on account of race, religion, nationality, or membership in a particular social or political group. The Supreme Court has held[10] that the alien need not prove "clear probability" of persecution if he or she remains in the home country. This case also notes that withholding of deportation is narrower than a grant of asylum. If deportation is withheld, it merely means that the alien will not be sent back to the home country, not that he or she will be permitted to remain in the United States.

[¶2402.1]   Visas for Temporary Residence

The United States issues a confusing and heavily overlapping series of visas for individuals meeting various characteristics with various reasons for wishing to enter or remain in the United States. One of the immigration lawyer's major tasks is sorting out the different categories, and seeing which categories can be used to benefit the client.

Under the "dual intent" doctrine, it is permissible for a worker who enters the country under a visa permitting temporary residence to apply for permanent residence, as long as he or she had the proper intent at the time of each application. It is also permissible to file multiple claims (for example, "third preference" and "sixth preference," as discussed below); the INS prefers all the papers to be filed together.

The advantage of this course is that the attorney preparing several sets of papers at once can be sure to avoid inconsistent statements that would be spotted by the INS and would lead to exclusion of the alien (and perhaps to proceedings against the attorney). The disadvantage is that the INS may grant one application and not the other(s), leaving the client in limbo if there are no visas available in the category for which the application was granted. That is, applicants have two hurdles to leap: they must qualify for admission as individuals, and they must also get one of the visas available under their nation's quota, or qualify for an exemption from the quotas.

The pre-1990 visa categories for non-permanent residence are:

➤ F-1 for foreign full-time students and F-2 for their spouses and dependents; the visa lasts as long as the course of study.

➤ I for journalists, permitting multiple admissions into and departures from the . U.S.

➤ J-1 for trainees in 12 18-month exchange training programs chartered by the State Department; J-2 for their spouses and dependents.

➤ H-1 for temporary workers of "distinguished merit and ability" (such as executives and professionals on long-term temporary assignments within the U.S., lasting up to 5 years).[11]

➤ H-2 for temporary workers who do not rank as "distinguished," but whose technical or other skills are in short supply in the United States; an H-2 visa lasts up to one year. Under 20 CFR 656.10, four occupational groups have been predetermined to have skills in short supply: registered nurses and occupational therapists; scientists and artists; clergy and other religious workers; managers transferred within multi-national corporations. The Immigration Nursing Relief Act of 1989 creates a five-year pilot program of

H-1A visas for nurses. If the program succeeds and is made permanent, nurses will be permitted to remain in the United States as permanent residents with no need to qualify under the preference system. To protect the jobs of American nurses, the program is limited to foreign nurses who were working in the United States on September 1, 1989. (Under INS regulations the residency of nurses was limited to five years, with a sixth year only in extraordinary circumstances.)

➤ H-3 for trainees in a structured program of up to 18 months' duration, who are being prepared to work outside the United States once their training is complete.

➤ An H-4 visa, for spouses and dependents, lasts as long as underlying "H visa."

➤ L-1 for executives and managers transferred to the United States to work for their existing employer or for its parent, subsidiary, or affiliate company. This visa lasts for an initial three years, with a two-year renewal permitted.

➤ E-1 "treaty trader" visa, good for up to five years, for an individual who enters the United States for business purposes from a country that has a trade treaty with the United States.

➤ E-2 "treaty investor" visa is similar, for those who enter the United States to make and monitor investments.

Thus, it is clear that the immigration system greatly favors senior business men and women; and those who have a professional education (i.e., postsecondary education that is directly required to qualify for their job, not just a liberal arts degree held by a person who works in a completely unrelated field). Some temporary residence visas are available for skilled workers, but none for unskilled workers or for skilled workers whose skills are already well represented in the United States.

[¶2402.2] Permanent Residence in the United States

To become a legal permanent resident of the United States, as evidenced by the coveted "green card," an individual must apply for labor certification from the Department of Labor; file a preference petition; and make an application for permanent residence in the United States.

Under prior law, each country's quota of visas was divided according to fixed percentages:

➤ "first preference": (20% of visas) unmarried children of U.S. citizens

➤ "second preference": (26% of visas) spouses and unmarried children of U.S. permanent residents

➤ "third preference": (10% of visas) professionals and artists (e.g., actors, musicians) who have offers of permanent employment in the United States. (If they had offers of temporary employment only, they should have applied for an H-1, H-2, or L-1 visa as applicable.)

➤ "fourth preference": (10% of visas) for married children of U.S. citizens

➤ "fifth preference": (24% of visas) for brothers and sisters of U.S. citizens

➤ "sixth preference": (10% of visas) for other workers with permanent job offers in the United States

In other words, under pre-1990 law, most legal permanent immigrants to the United States (an estimated 85%) were permitted to immigrate because of their relationship to a U.S. citizen or permanent resident. (Once they become permanent residents, they are permitted to work in the U.S.) If a country had many "third preference" and "sixth preference" petitioners, but few relatives of U.S. citizens and residents, it was not permitted to transfer visas to these non-relatives; instead, they had to create a "waiting list" for third and sixth preference visas as they became available.

Non-relatives were faced with a double bind. They couldn't apply for permanent residence unless they had a permanent job offer from a company inside the U.S., but companies are often unwilling to offer a job to someone who may be denied permanent resident status. Furthermore, they were not permitted to seek U.S. residence and then look for a job. Under these circumstances, it is understandable that various types of immigration fraud (e.g., employers certifying nonexistent job offers; marriage fraud; fraudulent claims of being related to U.S. citizens) and outright illegal immigration were common.

[¶2402.3] Immigration Act of 1990

The Immigration Act of 1990 (P.L. 101-649) has had a dramatic effect on our country's immigration system. The volume of permitted immigration is greatly expanded in three major categories: visas for skilled workers, immigration to reunite families, and "diversity-based" immigration permitting immigration from countries traditionally disfavored under U.S. laws.

➤ For three years post-enactment, the total number of immigrant visas of all types granted is 700,000 per year. Then the total number of visas declines to 675,000 annually. Each country is "capped" at about 25,000 visas per year.

➤ Family-sponsored immigration levels are set at 465,000 a year for fiscal 1992-4 (including 65,000 visas for brothers and sisters of U.S. citizens; 23,400 each for married and unmarried children of U.S. citizens; in general, first priority goes to immediate rather than collateral relatives of U.S. citizens). In and after fiscal 1995, family-related immigration is permitted to increase to 480,000 individuals per year.

➤ The new law also changes the rules for the "second preference" category. Instead of 70,200 visas for spouses and unmarried children of permanent resident aliens, there is a "bifurcated" second-preference category comprising 114,200 visas plus additional visas if overall family immigration is higher than 226,000. About three-quarters of the new second preference visas must be used by spouses and minor children.

➤ The 140,000 yearly employment-based visas are grouped in five categories. "Priority workers" (40,000) are defined as individuals of extraordinary ability and/or vocational responsibility. Forty thousand more visas are available for professionals with advanced degrees and/or "exceptional ability"; 40,000 more for "other workers" (skilled workers, professionals without advanced degrees, unskilled workers but only 10,000 visas currently described as "sixth preference" are granted under this category, and DOL labor certification is required with respect to whether a surplus of citizen workers exists in the field). Ten thousand visas can go to "special immigrants" (e.g., religious workers); the last 10,000 visas are for immigrants who can invest at least $1 million and employ at least 10 U.S. workers. In addition, more H-1B "specialty occupation" non-immigrant workers are permitted (65,000 a year, not 25,000) and up to 66,000 H-2B temporary non-agricultural workers are permitted in this country each year.

➤ Starting in fiscal 1995, 55,000 visas a year will be provided under a formula designed to ease immigration from countries that have traditionally had a low rate of admission to the U.S. During the 1992-4 period, there have been 40,000 "transitional" visas a year for nationals of "adversely affected countries" who have a firm job offer within the U.S. (In practical terms, this has been most beneficial to the Irish.)

➤ Stronger provisions for keeping out criminal aliens, or deporting them if they enter the U.S., are added to the U.S. law.

The law also contains provisions dealing with the IRCA amnesty and prohibitions against discrimination by employers.

Two items of 1993 legislation provide immigration relief for special groups. P.L. 102-404 permits the Attorney General to grant permanent residence status to Chinese political refugees who have been in the United States since the Tiananmen Square massacre; P.L. 102-509 permits immigration of scientists from the former Soviet Union before they have a job lined up in the United States.

[¶2403] IMMIGRATION AND MARRIAGE

One of the simplest forms of fraud and one which the U.S. government is at pains to eliminate is the fraudulent claim of marriage to a U.S. citizen or permanent resident; or entry into a marriage with such a person that is premised only on an intent to enter the United States, not to create a legitimate marital relationship. Therefore, when the alien spouse of a U.S. citizen or legal permanent resident attains permanent resident status within two years of the marriage, this status remains conditional for two more years after the grant. Furthermore, the Immigration Marriage Fraud Amendments of 1986 require that, when an alien marries a United States citizen while deportation or exclusion proceedings are pending, the alien must reside *outside* the United States for two years before seeking "immediate relative" status. This provision has been upheld over a constitutional challenge.[12]

A ceremonial marriage entered into without valid intent to live as husband and wife in the United States is not a valid marriage, and an alien may not file a visa petition premised on marriage after a separation agreement with the U.S. citizen spouse has been entered into. However, if a marriage is not a sham at its inception, a later separation or divorce will not invalidate the alien spouse's permanent resident status. A Board of Immigration Appeals (BIA) order rescinding an alien's permanent resident status was supported by substantial and reasonable evidence that marriage to an American citizen was a sham merely to gain lawful permanent resident status.[13]

If an alien's marriage is annulled or otherwise judicially terminated less than two years after his or her entry into the United States, and the marriage was celebrated less than two years before the entry, the alien can be deported for fraud unless he or she proves that the marriage was not contracted in order to further immigration fraud. Moreover, after the deportation, the alien cannot have a subsequent petition approved under any of the six preferences. A person who knowingly enters into a "green card" fraudulent marriage can be imprisoned for up to five years, and/or fined up to $250,000; lawyers who willfully misrepresent material facts, or fail to disclose them, are also subject to prosecution.

A "green card" marriage is only voidable, not void; so an alien who enters into a later marriage without dissolving the green card marriage is guilty of bigamy, and the second "spouse" is not entitled to equitable distribution or spousal support from the alien.[14]

The "green card" itself is not a marital asset (even if acquired as a result of the marriage) and therefore cannot be valued in a divorce like a college education, business goodwill, or other marital asset.[15]

[¶2404] EXCLUSION AND DEPORTATION PROCEEDINGS

Under 8 USC Section 1226, an exclusion hearing is conducted by a special INS inquiry officer. The hearing can be closed to the public on request of the alien. The alien has the burden of proving eligibility to enter the United States; or, if the alien believes this would be impossible, he or she can voluntarily withdraw the application for admission and leave the country. Aliens are not entitled to invoke the Fourth Amendment prohibition of unreasonable searches and seizures.

An alien can get relief from a deportation order on a claim that the INS failed to comply with its own regulations; it is not necessary to prove prejudice to the particular alien.[16]

The Supreme Court has upheld Immigration and Nationality Act Section 242(a), which allows excludable aliens to be released from detention pending a determination of deportability on condition that they refrain from employment within the United States. Imposing such a condition is permissible because the Supreme Court interpreted its reach to be limited to aliens who are not authorized to work in the United States, which serves the valid purpose of promoting employment of U.S. citizens and aliens who *are* authorized to work.[17]

The Second Circuit ruled[18] that it is improper to prevent an alien from working, pending deportation or exclusion proceedings, unless the alien is subject to being placed in custody.

However, once an alien is ordered excluded from the United States and a criminal conviction leads to revocation of immigration parole, it is permissible for the United States Attorney General to detain the alien indefinitely (in the case at bar, Cuba did not want to accept the alien). According to the Fourth Circuit, the government's intention is not punitive, and there is no violation of international law or due process to impose the detention.[19]

A California District Court ruled[20] that INS' failure to require that all proceedings be interpreted in their entirety violates aliens' Fifth Amendment due process rights to be present at the hearings, examine the evidence, and confront witnesses, but the Ninth Circuit reversed[21] on the grounds that even if the INS fails to provide a complete translation, the alien can bring his or her own translator; nor is the alien denied a reasonable opportunity to be present, be assisted by counsel, give evidence, or cross-examine witnesses.

If the immigration judge rules against the alien, the alien has an automatic right of administrative appeal to the Board of Immigration Appeals (BIA); the governing rules are found in 8 CFR Sections 3.1-3.8. However, the BIA's interpretation of 8 CFR Section 3.2, re BIA reopening or reconsideration of decisions, has been struck down by the First Circuit. The BIA position was that the case of a deportable alien can't be reopened after the denial of an initial application for discretionary relief; the court found this interpretation to be arbitrary and therefore invalid.[22]

In order to exercise the right of appeal, INS Form I-290A, the Notice of Appeal, must be filed in triplicate (along with INS Form G-28, the attorney's notice of appearance), within 10 days of the date the immigration judge's decision was served (within 13 days, if the decision was served by mail). The notice must summarize the grounds for the appeal and should ask for permission to file a brief. Failure to file the notice of appeal renders the immigration judge's decision final and nonappealable. (Finality of the deportation order, for the purposes of the judicial review process, is not affected by a pending motion to reopen or reconsider the deportation.[23]) The government has the burden of proving that the alien has waived the right of appeal; the Ninth Circuit found it unacceptable to inform a group of aliens that they had a right of appeal, then assume that silence constituted a waiver of the right.[24]

If a final order of exclusion is rendered, it can be reviewed only by the District Court by way of writ of habeas corpus. There is no automatic stay of exclusion, so the alien will be forced to leave the United States unless the attorney succeeds in having a request for a stay of exclusion granted. The doctrine of exclusion of remedies, however, requires an alien who is under INS detention to seek release from the INS administrative procedure before seeking habeas corpus relief. A change in circumstances can entitle an alien subject to a final order of deportation to reopen the proceedings for a discretionary waiver of deportation.[25]

The Ninth Circuit, citing the *habeas* right to challenge deprivation of liberty, struck down the INS policy of keeping alien children in detention pending deportation proceedings if they lack an adult relative or legal guardian to assume custody. The least restrictive and therefore preferable alternative would be for the INS to release the children to a responsible adult, after an INS hearing on the issue of whether a potential custodial adult represents a threat to the alien child's well-being. However, the Supreme Court reversed the Ninth Circuit and upheld the regulations,[26] finding that it is not a violation of Fifth Amendment due process to keep the children in custody rather than releasing them to a private party preferred by the children. To the Supreme Court, the policy furthers a rational state objective of protecting the welfare of juveniles.

The deportation process begins with the filing of an Order to Show Cause for deportation, pursuant to 8 USC Section 1252(b). The alien has the option of leaving the United States voluntarily; applying for asylum; or asking for suspension of deportation (which can only be granted if the alien was in the United States for seven years; is of good moral character; and deportation would cause hardship to a spouse, parent, or child who is a U.S. citizen or lawful permanent resident).

To prevail, the alien must prove by clear, convincing, and unequivocal evidence the time, place, and manner of his or her entry into the United States. The alien has the right to post bond and take discovery of the United States. The United States has the burden of proving deportability. If the immigration judge rules that the alien is deportable, the BIA has jurisdiction to hear the appeal. The Petition for Review of a BIA decision may be made within six months, and goes to the Court of Appeals (not the District Court); the alien is entitled to automatic judicial review and an automatic stay of deportation pending the Court of Appeals decision. The right of appeal extends the voluntary departure period for the period of appellate review; the alien is entitled to the full six months, not the shorter voluntary departure period permitted by the INS.[27]

An alien who entered the United States under a temporary worker visa and later obtained permanent resident status was denied relief from an order of deportation based on the ground that the seven-year "lawful domicile" residency requirement to be eligible for discretionary relief was not satisfied.[28]

EAJA fees cannot be awarded to an alien who succeeds in defending against deportation (no matter how unjustified the government's position): the Supreme Court has identified deportation proceedings as administrative proceedings, not adversary adjudications coming within the ambit of the EAJA.[29]

[¶2405] EMPLOYER SANCTIONS

Employment of illegal immigrants carries the potential for many kinds of abuses. The employer can underpay the workers, deny them benefits, and subject them to harsh and even dangerous working conditions; competition from workers who have left a life of dire poverty depresses the wages available to U.S. citizen workers. Employers of illegal immigrants also frequently fail to withhold and pay employment taxes, depriving the treasury of needed revenue.

In response to these circumstances, IRCA added stringent employer sanctions (8 USC Section 1324a) to the immigration law. Under these provisions, it is illegal to knowingly hire or continue to employ an unauthorized alien after

November 6, 1986. For hirings after that date, the employer must use Form I-9 to verify the identity and eligibility for U.S. employment. All employees must complete and submit the form, even U.S. citizens. The employer is subject to a complex schedule of civil and criminal penalties, with escalating penalties for repeat violations.

— ENDNOTES —

1. 53 FR 24898 (6/30/88); 54 FR 27120 (6/27/89).

2. Haitian Refugee Center Inc. v. Baker, 953 F.2d 1498 (11th Cir. 2/4/92), cert. denied #91-1291, 112 S.Ct. 1245.

3. McNary v. Haitian Center Council Inc., 969 F.2d 1350 (2d Cir. 7/29/92), aff'd sub.nom. Sale v. Haitian Center Council Inc., #92-344, 113 S.Ct. 2549 (Sup.Ct. 6/21/93).

4. INS v. Elias-Zacarias, #90-1342, 112 S.Ct. 812 (Sup.Ct. 1/22/92).

5. Bastanipour v. INS, 980 F.2d 1129 (7th Cir. 12/7/92).

6. 57 LW 2117 (E.D. Cal. 8/9/88).

7. Section 901 of the Foreign Relations Authorization Act of 1987.

8. American-Arab Anti-Discrimination Committee v. Meese, 716 F.Supp. 1060 (C.D. Cal. 1/26/89).

9. Price v. INS, 941 F.2d 878 (9th Cir. 8/7/91).

10. INS v. Cardoza-Fonseca, 480 U.S. 421 (1987).

11. The "H Regulations" at 53 FR 43217 (10/26/88) give criteria such as salary over $75,000 a year, supervising at least 100 employees, and spending at least 50% of work time on professional and managerial tasks. See Stanley Mailman, "H-1 Visas for Managers," NYLJ 12/7/88 p. 3.

12. Azizi v. Thornburgh, 708 F2d 1130 (2d Cir. 7/5/90).

13. Baria v. Leno (sic) 849 F. Supp. 750 USDC Hawaii (4/29/94).

14. Kleinfield v. Veruki, 372 S.E.2d 407 (Va.App. 9/20/88).

15. Gubin v. Lodisev, 197 Mich.App. 84, 494 N.W.2d 782 (Mich.App. 2/17/93).

16. Montilla v. INS, 926 F.2d 162 (2d Cir. 2/12/91).

17. INS v. Nat'l Center for Immigrants' Rights, #90-1090, 111 S. Ct. 1412 (Sup.Ct. 12/16/91).

18. Etuk v. Slattery, 936 F.2d 1433 (2d Cir. 6/27/91).

19. Gisbert v. U.S. Attorney General, 988 F.2d 1437 (5th Cir. 4/28/93).

20. El Rescate Legal Services Inc. v. Exec. Office of Immigration Review, 727 F.Supp. 557 (C.D. Cal. 12/14/89).

21. 941 F.2d 950 (9th Cir. 8/12/91).

22. Goncalves v. INS, 62 LW 2201 (1st Cir. 9/28/93).

23. White v. INS, 62 LW 2250 (8th Cir. 10/8/93).

24. U.S. v. Lopez-Vasquez, 61 LW 2501 (9th Cir. 2/8/93).

25. Henry v. INS, 62 LW 2249 (7th Cir. 10/15/93).

26. Flores v. Meese, 942 F.2d 1352 (9th Cir. 8/9/91), rev'd sub.nom. Reno v. Flores, #91-905, 113 S.Ct. 1439 (Sup.Ct. 3/23/93).

27. Contreras-Aragon v. INS, 852 F.2d 1088 (9th Cir. 7/15/88).

28. Lloyd Aston Graham v. INS, 998 F.2d 194 (3rd Cir. 6/12/93).

29. Ardestani v. INS, #90-1141, 111 S.Ct. 2005 (Sup.Ct. 12/9/91).

— FOR FURTHER REFERENCE —

Chiao, Rebecca, "Fourth Amendment Limitations on Immigration Law Enforcement," 93 *Immigration Briefings* 1 (February '93).

Cimini, Christine N., "The United States Policy on HIV-Infected Aliens: Is Exclusion an Effective Solution?" 7 *Conn.J. of Int'l Law* 297 (June '92).

Cowen, Nancy S., "The Employer's Dilemma Under IRCA," 6 *Georgetown Immigration L.J.* 285 (June '92).

Endelman, Gary and Jeffrey Hardy, "Uncle Sam Wants You: Foreign Investments and the Immigration Act of 1990," 28 *San Diego L. Rev.* 671 (Summer '91).

Geronimides, H. Rosemary, "The H-1B Visa Category: A Tug of War," 7 *Georgetown Immigration L.J.* 367 (June '93).

Gorman, Erin Eileen, "The INS' Automatic Detention Policy for Alien Children," 7 *Georgetown Immigration L.J.* 435 (June '93).

Hassan, Dolly Z., "An Ephemeral Victory for Refugees: Temporary Protected Status Under the Immigration Act of 1990," 15 *ILSA J. of International Law* 33 . (Spring '92).

Hurley, Maureen O'Connor, "The Asylum Process: Past, Present, and Future," 26 *New England L. Rev.* 995 (Spring '92).

Irwin, Richard A., "Legal Needs and Barriers: The Case for Supporting Legal Representation of Aliens," 27 *Clearinghouse Review* 193 (July '93).

Jacob, Walter P., "Diversity Visas: Muddled Thinking and Pork Barrel Politics," 6 *Georgetown Immigration L.J.* 297 (June '92).

Johnson, Douglas Scott, "The United States' Denial of the Immigration of People with AIDS," 6 *Temple Int'l & Comparative L.J.* 145 (Spring '92).

Kozlov, Scott A., "Deportation as a Collateral Consequence of a Guilty Plea," 26 *Valparaiso U. L. Rev.* 895 (Summer '92).

Loken, Gregory A. and Lisa R. Bambino, "Harboring, Sanctuary and the Crime of Charity Under Federal Immigration Law," 28 *Harvard Civil Rights-Civil Liberties L. Rev.* 119 (Winter '93).

Marks, Stephanie, "A Practitioner's Guide to Suspension of Deportation," 93 *Immigration Briefings* 1 (June '93).

Murphy, Timothy J., "Immigration and Nationality Law for the Military Lawyer," 36 *Air Force L. Rev.* 101 (Fall '92).

Perez, Fernando III and Timothy M. Spridgeon, "Family Immigration After IMMACT '90," 66 *Florida Bar J.* 12 (May '92).

Solomon, Jay, "Priorities and Preferences: Keeping Place in the Immigrant Visa Line," 92 *Immigration Briefings* 1 (June '92).

Trucios-Haynes, Enid and Ethan Kaufman, "Training Visa Categories in the United States," 93 *Immigration Briefings* 1 (May '93).

Ware, David et al., "Immigration Law and Higher Education," 20 *J. of College and University Law* 51 (Summer '93).

Yanni, Palma R., "Business Investors: E-2 Nonimmigrants and EB-5 Immigrants," 92 *Immigration Briefings* 1 (August '92).

INSURANCE

[¶2501] Although life cannot be lived and business cannot be conducted without risk, steps can be taken to minimize risks and also to cushion their economic impact. By purchasing insurance, an individual or business makes sure that funds will be available for personal, family, or business needs in case of a breadwinner's death, interruption of business, liability judgment, or other event with negative consequences.

This discussion includes both life insurance and insurance against loss and liability.

One of the most striking trends in insurance law today is the predominance of cases involving liability insurance and environmental cleanup costs. As environmental law re-emerges as a governmental enforcement priority and as an active area of litigation, corporations and other landowners will be ordered to pay many more large judgments, so the insurer's role will be the focus of even more litigation in the future.

The Omnibus Budget Reconciliation Act of 1990 greatly expanded federal regulation of "Medi-gap" health insurance policies (policies that supplement Medicare coverage). This topic is discussed in more detail at [¶3903.2].

Also on the health care front, the Central District of California ruled that an HMO is really a "domestic insurance company," and therefore is not entitled to bankruptcy protection;[1] the Ninth Circuit held that this is a question of state law.[2]

The Supreme Court tackled insurer bankruptcy in 1993, finding that a state statute allocating priority in claims against an insurance company regulates the "business of insurance" insofar as it protects policyholders. Therefore, it is covered by the McCarran-Ferguson Act, and is not preempted by 31 U.S.C. Section 3713, which gives the United States first priority in debtors' obligations. Nevertheless, although the state statute putting policyholders first is not preempted, the claims of general creditors (including the insurers' employees) are preempted by the federal statute.[3]

Another significant trend is "insurance bad faith" litigation, premised on claims that the insurer delayed or refused to make a payment that should have been made under the policy. (The temptation to withhold payments was even greater in the early 1980s, when sky-high interest rates meant that insurers could earn a high return safely by investing unpaid claims in the money market.) If bad faith can be proved, the insurer may have to pay the entire judgment against the insured, even in excess of the policy limits, and without regard to the insured's ability to pay.[4] California has enacted a statute[5] characterizing as an illegal, unfair, or deceptive act or practice "not attempting in good faith" to settle a claim promptly once liability has become reasonably clear. The statute has survived challenges under due process, equal protection, and First Amendment commercial speech arguments.[6] However, the California Supreme Court has ruled that a defense lawyer and expert witnesses cannot be sued for conspiring with the insurance company to deny a fair settlement: the lawyer and witnesses have no duty to the insured, and therefore cannot breach this nonexistent "duty."[7]

However, an insurer was found guilty of another kind of conspiracy: the insurer offering and underwriting a group health insurance policy limited to pregnancy complications and excluding normal pregnancy was found liable for aiding and abetting the employer's discriminatory employment practice.[8]

Where an insurer has been found to have practiced fraud in the sale of a medical policy, and the court thinks the punitive damages imposed are too high and provide a windfall to the plaintiff, the court nevertheless cannot order that part of the punitive damages be paid to a charitable organization or indeed anyone except the plaintiff.[9]

The federal McCarran-Ferguson Act extends immunity from antitrust challenge to "the business of insurance." However, the FTC was permitted to bring an antitrust challenge, finding that five major title companies conspired to fix prices for title search and examination and forbidding them to use rating bureaus to set rates in New Jersey, Pennsylvania, Connecticut, Wisconsin, Arizona, or Montana. An antitrust challenge was permissible because title services do not fall under the definition of "the business of insurance."[10]

The Supreme Court later decided[11] that state officials' approval of rates does not insulate a title company from federal liability for price-fixing; states are not permitted to displace federal antitrust law. A 1993 Supreme Court decision[12] holds that, even if domestic insurers did conspire with foreign insurers to keep foreign coverage off the market unless domestic companies changed their Comprehensive General Liability provisions, the domestic insurers were nevertheless engaging in the "business of insurance" and thus protected by McCarran-Ferguson. The McCarran-Ferguson Act does not preempt a RICO action brought over alleged fraud with respect to life insurance policies.[13]

According to the Seventh Circuit, the Secretary of Housing and Urban Development's interpretation of the Fair Housing Act to prohibit racial "redlining" in property and hazard insurance is a reasonable one and thus entitled to deference.[14] The decision is limited to rate-setting based on race rather than actuarial factors; the disparate impact of risk classifications on certain racial groups was not ascertained.

A 1916 federal law, the National Bank Act Section 92, authorizing a national bank doing business in a community with a population of 5,000 or less to act as agent for any insurance company, was not repealed in 1918; the Supreme Court decided in mid-1993 that the U.S. Code statement of repeal was a scrivener's error, so the statute is still in force and banks can sell insurance.[15] The Comptroller of the Currency interpreted this statute to permit national banks, or branches of national banks, to sell insurance if the town where the bank is located has a population under 5,000, even if the bank's principal office is located in a municipality with a larger population. The D.C. Circuit upheld this interpretation in 1993.[16]

[¶2502] TYPICAL STANDARD PROVISIONS IN A LIFE INSURANCE POLICY

The life insurance policy is frequently a vital element in a plan for family security, an estate plan, a program to retire corporate stock or partnership interests, a plan to provide business continuity, an employee pension and profit-sharing plan, and other family and business arrangements. It is important for the lawyer to understand the elements of the life insurance contract, the alternatives available to the insured, the status of life insurance as property, how life insurance is taxed, and other essential elements of insurance.

The following provisions are customarily included in life insurance policies. A number of them are required by state law.

Grace Period: Generally 30 or 31 days following the premium due date, during which period the insurance company will accept payment without penalty. If death occurs during the grace period, the premium due is deducted from the proceeds paid.

Extended Term Insurance: A nonforfeiture option that provides that if premiums are not paid within the grace period, the policy will not expire. The cash surrender value, less indebtedness, is used as a single premium to purchase term insurance at the attained age of the insured for the face amount of the policy for as long a period as possible.

Reinstatement: The policyholder's right to reinstate a lapsed policy within a reasonable time by paying the unpaid premiums with interest. Satisfactory evidence of insurability is required.

Incontestability Clause: Once the policy has been in force for two years (one year in some cases), the beneficiary will receive the death proceeds without contest by the company even if misstatements were made in the original application. However, if the misstatement pertains to the insured's age, then an adjustment in the amount of the death benefit will be made.

Suicide: If death results from suicide within two years after the policy is issued (one year in some policies), the beneficiary will recover only the actual premiums advanced; after two years, the full death benefit will be paid.

Cash Value: The amount available to the owner at any given time if the policy is surrendered to the company.

Loan Values: Permanent-type insurance usually permits the owner to borrow a substantial portion of the cash value at guaranteed interest rates.

Paid-Up Insurance: The policy contains a table showing the amount of paid-up life insurance that can be taken instead of cash when the policy is surrendered. The paid-up policy also has a cash value.

Payment of Dividend and Dividend Options: Participating policies provide for payment of a dividend and describe the various dividend options, such as cash, reduced premium, paid-up additions, interest, or additional one-year term.

Ownership Clause: A provision that the policy may be owned by someone other than the insured. For example, in order to remove proceeds from the insured's estate, the insured's child or a trust may be the owner of the policy.

Beneficiary Provisions: The insured can name first, second, third, or further contingent beneficiaries and arrange payment of proceeds through settlement options. Some policies, such as group insurance, may restrict the number of beneficiaries that can be named and the variety of settlement arrangements that can be chosen.

Conversion Privilege: A provision that allows the policy owner to elect to change the policy to a different plan. Policies can generally be converted without medical examinations to higher premium plans or with a medical examination to lower premium plans. Generally, conversion to term insurance is not permitted.

Assignment: The policy outlines the procedure for making an assignment. Usually the company states that it is not bound until written notice of assignment is received, that the assignment is subject to any loan to the company, and that the company accepts no responsibility for the validity of the assignment.

[¶2503] LEGAL ASPECTS OF LIFE INSURANCE

Although a life insurance policy is a legal contract, applicable contract law has been modified by statutes in many respects. These changes protect the policyholder and cause the contract to be interpreted strictly against the insurance company in the event of a dispute between the company and an insured.

Some of the most important legal aspects of life insurance are the following:

❏ *Offer:* If the application is accompanied by payment of the first premium, an offer is deemed made by the applicant; the company generally accepts the offer by issuing a conditional receipt to insure the applicant if he meets the insurability requirements of the company. If a policy other than that applied for is issued, then the new policy becomes a counteroffer by the company. An application without the premium is merely an invitation for the company to make an offer, which it does by issuing the policy and delivering it.

❏ *Acceptance:* An offer may be accepted if the company delivers the policy or the insured pays the first premium. Unreasonable delay by the company in processing an application accompanied by the first premium is considered in most states to be a rejection of the applicant's offer; in some states, it constitutes an acceptance.

There are various forms of conditional receipts used by companies; the wording of the particular receipt determines whether the issuance of the receipt constitutes an acceptance or whether actual delivery of the policy is required.

❏ *Consideration:* The consideration given by the insurance company is the promises set forth in the contract. The consideration given by the insured is comprised of the statements made in the application and payment of the first premium.

❏ *Legal Capacity:* The insured must be of legal age and of sound mind. The usual legal age has been modified in many states for life insurance contracts.

❏ *Insurable Interest:* The applicant must have an insurable interest in the life of the insured. This has been defined as a reasonable expectation of financial benefit from the continued life of the insured, or financial loss if the insured dies. A general rule is that even though an insurable interest exists, the life of another may not be insured without his consent. Insurable interest need exist only when the policy is purchased; it need not exist when the policy becomes a claim. The insured has the right to name anyone as his beneficiary without regard to insurable interest.

Law firm partners have an insurable interest in one another's lives; the insurable interest continues even if the law firm is dissolved as a result of one partner's ill health.[17]

Lawyers who stop practicing law, whether by retirement or by changing careers, and those who transfer their affiliation, should review their professional liability insurance. The lawyer who has been in practice with a large firm for years and who retires can generally depend on the firm, if it remains in existence, to continue to maintain malpractice insurance covering acts, errors, and omissions occurring on or before the date of retirement. If the firm dissolves, its members should seriously consider buying a 'tail' on its policy. An individual who chooses to retire, go on the bench, or into academia, and who is not in a large firm should also consider buying the Extended Reporting Form Endorsement, i.e., "tail."[18]

❑ *Utmost Good Faith:* Neither "buyer beware" nor "seller beware" applies to a life insurance contract. Each party has the right to rely on the good faith of the other.

❑ *Representation:* Most states provide that in the absence of fraud, all warranties in life insurance contracts (statements in the application and medical exam) are to be interpreted as representations. The policy is voidable by the company if there is a misrepresentation of material fact, one that would have led the company to deny the insurance or charge a higher premium. However, a misrepresentation of an immaterial fact is not sufficient to cause rescission of the contract.

❑ *Concealment:* The company may rescind a contract if there has been concealment by the applicant—i.e., silence when he had a duty to speak—provided that the concealment was both material and intentional.

❑ *Creditors' Rights:* The rights of creditors of the insured (and sometimes creditors of the beneficiary) have been modified in most states to give special protection to life insurance.

❑ *Authority of Agents:* There is generally a presumption of agency if the company has supplied a person with forms, rate books, applications, etc., that make it logical for one to assume that he or she is an agent of the company. The company would be bound by acts of this person as though he or she had been given express authority to act as its agent.

The insurance agent's authority is outlined in the agent contract. Authority usually includes soliciting and taking applications for new business, arranging medical exams, and collecting the first year's premium or a partial premium. Usually excluded are the rights to make, alter, or discharge any contract; to waive any forfeiture; to waive payment in cash; to extend the time of payment for a premium; to accept payment of a past due premium; to approve evidence of good health.

In addition to the express authority granted in the agency contract, the agent is held in common law to have certain implied authority—any authority that the public may reasonably assume an agent to have. Limitations of the agent's authority are communicated to the public in application forms, conditional receipts, and in the policy. Policies contain a provision that only certain designated officers of the company have the power to make or modify the contract or extend time for paying a premium.

The knowledge of the agent is assumed to be the knowledge of the company. Thus, if the agent knows a material fact about the applicant, it is presumed that the information has been given to the company. Should the company discover the information after the policy is issued, it cannot then rescind the contract because of concealment or misrepresentation.

If an agent interprets a policy provision incorrectly to an insured, and the wording in the policy is ambiguous, the agent's interpretation is held valid.

Most states make a distinction between a broker and an agent: the broker is the agent of the insured, not the company. However, other states consider the broker the agent of the company, and some as the agent of the company only for purposes of delivering the policy and collecting the premium.

[¶2504] DIVIDEND OPTIONS

Typical dividend options available to a policyholder are as follows:

(1) Cash: The policyholder can receive his dividend in cash. The most frequent use of this option is for paid-up policies. Another situation where this option is attractive is if the insured is disabled and premiums on the policy are being waived.

(2) Reduce Premiums: The insured can apply dividends as part payment of premiums. This is used when the insured needs funds to help meet premium obligations, or if a low net expenditure for insurance is desired. It is used in minimum deposit plans when reducing coverage is desired.

(3) Accumulating at Interest: This election permits the insurance company to retain dividends on deposit and have them build up at a guaranteed rate of interest. If the company's earnings are less than the rate it guarantees, the policyholder will still be credited with the specified interest rate; should the earnings be greater he usually will receive the higher interest.

Dividend accumulations are often used when an insured policyholder wants to increase guaranteed retirement income provided under the policy's retirement options.

(4) Paid-Up Additions: Dividends are applied to buy additional paid-up insurance. The increased protection acquired via dividend additions requires no medical examination and serves as a valuable tool when poor health makes additional insurance unavailable.

(5) The "Fifth" Dividend Option: This provides for the purchase of one-year term insurance in an amount usually equal to the increase in cash value. The balance of the dividend may be left on deposit to accumulate future cash value purchases or may be applied under one of the other dividend options. This option increases the face value of the policy by the amount of the cash value. The net result is to eliminate the policy owner from becoming a co-insurer on the policy.

[¶2504.1] Investment-Oriented Life Insurance

In response to criticisms that conventional whole-life policies are not good investments, insurers now offer several types of policies aimed at combining insurance protection with enhanced investment value.

A *variable life* policy has a set death benefit, which is always at least equal to the minimum guaranteed in the contract. The death benefit can increase if the investment results of the policyholder's separate accounts justify. (That is, the policyholder takes the investment risk by directing how his or her premiums should be invested.) The policy's cash value fluctuates, and can even be reduced to zero. A variable life policy is considered a registered security, and thus may only be sold by a person licensed to sell securities, and must be accompanied by a prospectus.

A *universal life* policy guarantees the death benefit, but only for the first month of the contract; after that, a minimum interest rate is guaranteed, but the death benefit fluctuates. Another definition of universal life is that it is a flexible premium policy; the policyholder can change the death benefit and/or vary the timing and amount of premium payments. The premiums, less expense charges, go into the policy account; mortality charges are deducted, and interest credited at varying rates.

Code §7702 was enacted to limit the use of universal life insurance as a tax shelter; it should be consulted before using such policies in a financial plan.

A *single-premium* policy, as the name suggests, usually is purchased with a single, large premium (some policies permit later additions), which is large enough not only to provide life insurance but to generate significant cash value immediately.

[¶2505] LIFE INSURANCE RIDERS

There are many extras you can add to a basic life insurance policy. Some of these "riders" cost from a few cents to a few dollars per year for each $1,000 of death benefit provided in the policy; the cost of others is based on the amount of benefit provided in the rider; other valuable endorsements may be added to the policy free of charge. Whether the insured needs some of these "extras" depends on the purpose of the insurance policy—family protection, business insurance, retirement fund, etc.

[¶2505.1] Waiver of Premium

This rider provides that if the policyholder becomes totally and permanently disabled, his insurance will remain in force without any further premium payments. This waiver does not take effect until the disability has continued for a specified period, usually six months. Disabilities typically excluded from coverage are those resulting from war and those that are intentionally self-inflicted.

In addition to the waiver of premiums, if the policies are of the cash-value type—ordinary life, limited-pay life, endowment—the cash values will grow as if the insured were continuing to pay the premiums. If the need arises during the period of disability, the insured can borrow against the cash values in the policy.

For almost all types of policies and purposes, this rider is usually viewed as a necessity. In a family protection policy, it guarantees maintenance of life insurance when the insured's ability to earn enough to pay the premium is impaired. In a retirement plan, it guarantees the accumulation of the retirement fund. In a partnership agreement, it might provide part of the funds for a payout of a disabled partner.

Payor Benefit: This is a waiver of premium benefit in some juvenile policies that covers the risk of death or disability of the person responsible for paying the premiums (i.e., usually the child's father) before the policy on an insured child is fully paid or the child reaches a specified age.

[¶2505.2] Accidental Death Benefits

This rider stipulates that if the policyholder dies by "accidental death," the company will pay the beneficiary a multiple of the face amount of the policy (as much as four times in some cases).

Some typical exclusions are deaths due to war, certain kinds of flying accidents, dangerous drug use, and accidents that stem from illness or infirmity. Death generally must take place within 90 days of the accident and before the insured reaches a specified age, usually 65.

In some cases this rider can serve a useful purpose. For example, it may be used by a business to protect against the loss of key personnel. For an executive who travels extensively by airplane, it provides year-round coverage for accidental death at less cost than other airplane policies.

[¶2505.3] Accidental Death and Dismemberment

Some policies, such as group and association plans, provide additional benefits for dismemberment—loss of a limb, blindness, etc.

Some policies provide a *disability payout provision* under which the face amount of the policy is paid out in installments in the event of total disability.

[¶2505.4] Guaranteed Insurability Rider

This rider guarantees that a specified amount of insurance may be purchased by the insured on certain future "option dates" at standard rates and without evidence of insurability. The guaranteed insurability rider can be a valuable extra for a young person as it guarantees an increasing insurance program. It is also a good addition to children's life insurance policies.

[¶2505.5]　Disability Income Rider

Some life insurance policies offer a disability income rider that provides a monthly income to the insured if he or she becomes totally disabled. A typical rider provides a monthly disability income of 1% of the face amount of the policy—a $50,000 policy could provide $500 per month disability income protection; monthly payments continue until age 65; then the policy endows for its face value and all obligations under the contract cease. Thus, a person who becomes totally disabled at age 45 and who has a $50,000 life insurance policy with a 1% disability rider would receive payment of $500 a month until age 65 and then would receive $50,000 in cash. Most riders require a six-month waiting period before disability payments begin.

[¶2505.6]　Free Riders

There are a number of free riders that can be included in insurance policies:

Automatic Premium Loan Clause: This is a provision that makes a policy "lapse-proof." The company is authorized to borrow from the cash value to pay a premium if the insured fails to do so. This valuable clause may keep protection from lapsing due to an oversight or illness.

Settlement Agreement: Payment of policy proceeds under various options and different beneficiary designations can be combined in one agreement attached to the policy in order to effectuate an estate plan. For example, part of the proceeds can be paid in cash to pay off debts, estate taxes, and final expenses, with the balance being paid in the form of a monthly income to the spouse.

Retirement Options: The insured may plan to use the cash values and accumulated dividends in the policies to provide a monthly annuity at retirement either as a lifetime income, installments for a period of time, or a joint and survivor annuity.

Spendthrift Trust Clause: Some states have laws that automatically exempt proceeds of life insurance from the claims of creditors of the beneficiary. Many states also allow the insured to add a "spendthrift trust" provision to the policy to protect the proceeds. These clauses are usually worded so that proceeds are not assignable and are exempt from claims of creditors.

Common Disaster Clause: In states that did not adopt the Uniform Simultaneous Death Law, a common disaster clause might be added to the policy to achieve the same result. This clause states that if the insured and the beneficiary die in a common accident, the presumption will be that the beneficiary died first. The proceeds would then be paid to the secondary beneficiary or, in the absence of any, to the estate of the insured. This will save the cost and delay of the proceeds passing through the spouse's estate instead of going directly to the children.

Deferment Clause: This clause will defer payment of policy proceeds for a 30- or 60-day period. On the death of the insured, the proceeds are held at interest for a specified period and then paid to the primary beneficiary at the end of that period, if surviving, or else to the secondary beneficiary. This clause, like the common disaster clause, will keep proceeds out of a spouse's estate if the spouse dies shortly after the insured; proceeds will go directly to children.

[¶2506] SETTLEMENT OPTIONS

Insurance proceeds payable on the death of the insured or cash value when a policy is surrendered can, of course, be received in a lump sum, but that is not the only way. There are four other settlement options:
- ❏ The Interest Only Option.
- ❏ The Fixed Period Option.
- ❏ The Fixed Amount Option.
- ❏ The Life Income Option, which may be further subdivided as follows:
  - (a) Straight Life Income.
  - (b) Life Income with a Period Certain.
  - (c) Cash Refund Life Income.
  - (d) Refund Life Income.
  - (e) Joint and Survivor Life Income.

[¶2507] PRINCIPAL OWNERSHIP AND BENEFICIARY ARRANGEMENTS

(A) Insured purchaser and owner—executor named as beneficiary.

(B) Insured purchaser and owner—designated individual as beneficiary.

(C) Insured purchaser—another individual, corporation, or other entity as owner and beneficiary.

(D) Insured purchaser—trustee as owner and beneficiary.

(E) Person other than the insured as purchaser, owner, and beneficiary.

[¶2508] LEGAL ASPECTS OF BENEFICIARY DESIGNATIONS

The selection of a beneficiary and wording of the beneficiary designation often have important legal consequences. For example:

❏ Naming the estate of the insured as beneficiary will make policy proceeds subject to creditors of the insured; naming specific beneficiaries will protect the proceeds under state law.

❏ Naming the estate as beneficiary will make the proceeds subject to estate tax. If there is a named beneficiary, it may escape estate tax (e.g., if the spouse is the owner and beneficiary).

❏ If no beneficiary is named in the policy, or if none survives the insured, the proceeds, unless otherwise provided, are paid to the insured's estate.

❏ Failing to name a sufficient number of contingent beneficiaries may cause the proceeds to pass to unintended parties.

A "revocable" designation is one in which insured reserves the right to change the beneficiary. He may make a change without the beneficiary's permission.

[¶2508.1]   Contingent Beneficiary

In making beneficiary designations, a contingent beneficiary should be named to receive the policy proceeds in the event the first-named beneficiary is dead when the proceeds are paid. This is especially important when payment is made through long-term settlement options if a balance of installment payments or of principal may remain after the death of the primary beneficiary.

An insured might consider naming a qualified charity as a contingent beneficiary. This type of designation might save taxes, in addition to ensuring that there would be an institution which would be a worthy recipient of the benefits.

[¶2509]   LIFE INSURANCE TAXATION

Following are some of the common ways that insurance can be arranged, and the estate and gift tax consequence of each method.

(1) Insured owns the policy and names child as beneficiary: With this type of insurance setup, the insured knows the proceeds go directly to the child. Obviously, since the insured purchased the policy and retains ownership, no gift has been made. Naming the child as beneficiary is not considered a gift of the policy. Therefore, there is no gift tax due under this arrangement.

Estate tax consequences: Since the insured owns the policy, the proceeds will be included in the estate. True, most small- and medium-sized estates won't have to pay any estate taxes. But increasing financial prosperity, and inflation, could bring the insured's estate over the tax-free threshold.

Instead of retaining ownership of the policy, there may be a better course of action:

(2) Transfer of the policy to the spouse with child named as beneficiary: Upon transfer of the insurance policy to the spouse, the insured is making a gift. But the gift is tax-free due to unlimited gift tax marital deduction. This simply means that an unlimited amount of property may be transferred to the spouse without a gift tax. In fact, after transfer of the policy to the spouse, the insured can generally continue to pay premiums on the policy without worrying about gift or estate tax consequences.

Since the insured no longer owns the policy, its proceeds will not be part of his or her estate. However, there's one important exception to this rule. The tax law says that an insurance policy given away within three years of death is included in the donor's estate. So the sooner the transfer is made, the sooner the three-year period will expire.

(3) Insured owns the policy, and names spouse as beneficiary: This may be the most common of all arrangements. There won't be an estate tax on the

proceeds either, thanks to the unlimited estate tax marital deduction. Whatever is left to the spouse, including the proceeds of an insurance policy, is estate tax-free. Although technically the amount of the proceeds are included in the estate, the estate is entitled to an offsetting deduction equal to the amount that's left to the spouse.

[¶2510] PROTECTION OF LIFE INSURANCE FROM CREDITORS

These are the general rules affecting creditors' claims:

❏ *Creditors of the Insured—Cash Values:* In most states, the wording of laws exempting insurance from creditors' claims is broad enough to exempt cash values of policies from creditors of the insured. Court opinions have been divided where the statute is not clear. In some cases, where the statute uses the term "proceeds" without adding "cash values" or "avails," cases have restricted the protection to death proceeds only.

❏ *Creditors of the Insured—Death Proceeds:* Most state statutes restrict the rights of creditors of the insured in proceeds of life insurance. Some states exempt the entire proceeds; others limit it to a certain amount. Some limit the protection to proceeds payable to the insured's spouse or children; others to any dependent relative; and some to any beneficiary other than one who is himself the insured.

Proceeds paid to a trust for the benefit of a specific beneficiary normally have the same protection from creditors as if paid directly to the beneficiary.

❏ *Creditors of the Beneficiary—Cash Values:* Usually creditors of the beneficiary have no claims against cash values. The beneficiary has no vested right to cash values unless named irrevocably, and even then cannot usually cash in the policy without the insured's consent. Thus the beneficiary's creditors would have no rights without the consent of the insured.

❏ *Creditors of the Beneficiary—Death Proceeds:* Most statutes exempt proceeds from the claims of the insured's creditors only. In a few states the exemption applies to creditors of the beneficiary also.

If law does not exempt the proceeds from the beneficiary's creditors, the insured can extend this protection by adding to the settlement agreement in the policy a *spendthrift trust clause*. This states that proceeds payable to the beneficiary may not be assigned, transferred, commuted, or encumbered by the beneficiary, nor be subject to legal process, execution, garnishment, or attachment. Policy proceeds must be made payable to the beneficiary under an installment or life income option. This arrangement usually has to be set up by the insured. The spendthrift trust clause protects only the money held by the company; when the beneficiary receives a payment, the money is available to creditors.

Annuities: Creditors' rights in annuities are not usually limited by exemption laws applying to life insurance—the annuity may be reached by creditors of the annuitant. A few states give a limited exemption to annuity income.

[¶2511] INSURANCE AGAINST LOSS AND LIABILITY

Two factors that are critical in business operations and in many transactions are risk of loss and potential liabilities. Often a lawyer will be called upon to determine a client's potential loss exposure (what events could cause loss?) and loss potential (what is the maximum amount that might be lost in any single event?). Insurance coverage is the inevitable hedge against possible liabilities.

Significant questions exist as to *when* insurance coverage or liability is triggered; what events are covered "occurrences"; the respective liability when several insurance companies insure a claimant; and when insurers are liable for "bad faith" when they refuse to defend a claim or make the policy limits available for settlements or judgments.

[¶2512] LOSS EXPOSURE

This requires the identification of all possible risks that are involved in the particular business or activity in question. One way to approach the problem of loss to the insured is to study any available financial statements. The balance sheet will indicate all the assets subject to loss or damage. The profit-and-loss statement will reveal sources of income that may be shut off or interrupted. Another approach for uncovering possible liability is to analyze the property and operations of the client to determine what can happen to whom.

[¶2513] LOSS POTENTIAL

This involves an estimate of the maximum loss that may be incurred. The fact that a loss is unlikely is not usually the relevant consideration, since the purpose of insurance is to guard against the unlikely. In addition, the more likely the loss, the less is the economic justification for insurance, since the premium must be large enough to compensate for the loss and permit payment of the insurer's expenses and profit. Small losses, even though unlikely (and hence subject only to a small premium for insurance), may call for self-insurance by the client, since his own resources may be sufficient for this purpose. In brief, it is the *maximum* and *unlikely* loss that must be guarded against.

[¶2514] TYPES OF RISKS AND INSURANCE

Generally speaking, risks fall into two classes:

(1) Liability risks (the insured may be liable to others because of his own actions or those of his employees and agents).

(2) Property loss, including credit and income loss (the insured may suffer personal loss or injury due to his own actions or the actions of others).

The tables at ¶2528 list the most common types of risks for business transactions generally, for particular types of business transactions, and for the owners or lessees of real estate. The usual insurance policy to cover each risk is also indicated in the tables.

[¶2515] LIABILITY INSURANCE

Those engaged in commercial transactions are exposed to the hazard of lawsuits not only for their own negligence, but also for the negligence of their employees, agents, and other representatives. Particularly exposed are sole proprietors and partners who do not have the limited liability provided by the corporate umbrella.

The liability policy generally provides coverage only for sums which the insured becomes *legally obligated to pay resulting from a covered occurrence*. The basic policy provides no coverage against liabilities for which the insured is not obligated under negligence law, or liabilities assumed by the insured voluntarily.

Starting in the late 1980s, liability policies tended to shift from an "occurrence" basis to a "claims made" basis. That is, benefits are available if a claim is made during the time when insurance is in force—not if a liability-generating occurrence takes place in that time frame (with claims potentially made many years later). "Claims made" policies usually carry a "retroactive date" (e.g., the policy inception date); claims for incidents occurring before the retroactive date will not be covered, even if made during the coverage period.

Most liability policies are divided into two separate sections: Coverage A for bodily injury liability, and Coverage B for property damage liability. Different limits of liability may be provided for each coverage, or the policy may be written under Coverage A only.

As a result of perceived difficulties and inequities in the tort system, liability insurance has become more expensive and harder (or impossible) for many businesses and professionals to obtain. In response, Congress enacted the Risk Retention Act Amendments of 1986 (15 U.S.C. §3901—). The Amendments make it easier to buy insurance on a group basis or form "risk retention groups" (e.g., captive insurers).

A majority of the states have adopted some form of "tort reform," changing tort doctrines such as joint and several liability and collateral source, and/or limiting consequential and punitive damages and contingent fees. In return, states usually required insurers to make liability insurance more broadly available, or to roll back their rates. "Flex rating" requirements force insurers to provide statistical justification for rate changes exceeding certain percentages.

[¶2515.1] Liability Insurance and Environmental Claims

The crucial aspect of CERCLA (the "Superfund" law) for parties held responsible for hazardous waste cleanup is the virtually unlimited statutory liability. The traditional language of a standard form comprehensive general liability policy obligates the insurer to pay all "damages" that the insured person must pay. The Ninth Circuit, D.C. Circuit, Eastern District of Pennsylvania and the District of New Jersey have ruled that damages under CERCLA fall within the coverage of the comprehensive general liability policy.[19] The Ninth Circuit has held that expenses under a CERCLA consent decree are covered by the comprehensive general liability policy, and are not barred by pollution exclusions,[20] but the insurer need not pay for damage to the insured's own property where the policy contains an exclusion for property owned, rented, or occupied by the insured.[21] However, the Fourth Circuit position is that the money sought by the United States in a CERCLA suit constitutes equitable relief, *not* legal damages as covered by the comprehensive general liability policy.[22]

The Sixth Circuit has said[23] that the insurer's duty to defend is not triggered by an EPA letter telling the insured that it may be liable for CERCLA cleanup costs; the letter is not a lawsuit. According to the Eleventh Circuit, federal District Courts don't even have subject-matter jurisdiction over a declaratory judgment suit as to whether CERCLA liability is covered by a CGL policy. In this view,[24] the question is purely one of state law.

The exclusion in the comprehensive general liability policy for "property owned or occupied by or rented to insured" protected the insurer against having to pay the costs of cleaning up a site when the lessor had the pollutants and affected soil removed to prevent contamination of the groundwater. To the Eastern District of California, the contamination did not extend to anyone else's property, and thus the exclusion applied.[25]

Another environmental insurance problem arises from policy language that disclaims coverage except for "sudden and accidental" discharges, language that was included to protect the insurer against the situation in which the insured deliberately or negligently maintains a practice of dumping toxic materials, relying on the insurer to pay any cleanup costs if the insured is caught. However, the Second Circuit has held that the insurer still has a duty to defend allegations that do not "clearly negate" the possibility of a sudden and accidental discharge of toxic materials.[26] Furthermore, a New York state court has held that an undiscovered toxic discharge can be called "sudden" even if it continues over a period of years.[27]

Minnesota's Court of Appeals held that release of asbestos as a result of building deterioration was pollution, but was not sudden, so the CGL pollution exclusion applied.[28] In an asbestos personal injury pollution case, New York required the insurer to defend if the pollution exclusion clause was ambiguous as to asbestos contamination.[29]

A New Jersey court said that insurers knowingly misrepresented the intended effect of the exclusion of cleanup on gradual environmental coverage when they sought approval of policy language in 1970. Thus, the court estopped the insurers from denying coverage unless the insured intentionally discharged known pollutants.[30]

In a 1991 case, plaintiffs tried another tack: attempting to receive coverage for environmental claims under the personal-injury provisions of the policy. However, results were mixed.[31]

Under the CGL policy, for purposes of New York and Illinois law, "physical injury to tangible property" occurs when a defective component is installed in the tangible property and not when the defect subsequently causes injury.[32]

[¶2516] BASIC LIABILITY COVERAGE

In the paragraphs below, four basic types of liability coverage are explained.

❑ **Owners', Landlords', and Tenants' Liability Policy:** The basic policy insures against claims resulting from the ownership (or lease) and operation of the covered premises. Office buildings, retail stores, wholesale stores, hotels, theatres, etc., are insured under this form of policy. The policy is usually a scheduled policy; that is, it names the particular properties and risks insured against. Another type of policy, the Comprehensive General Liability Policy, offers similar coverage on a nonscheduled basis. A manufacturer or contractor can obtain parallel coverage under a Manufacturers' and Contractors' Liability Policy (M & C).

❑ **Product Liability Policy:** This covers liability arising out of the handling or use of goods or products that are manufactured, sold, handled, or distributed by the insured. The liability depends upon the existence of a defect of unsafe condition in the goods. Product liability also covers a service business or a contractor who installs equipment against claims arising from a defect in the installation or the equipment.

❑ **Contract Liability Policy:** This policy covers liability arising out of a contract or agreement. Manufacturers, distributors, retailers, and servicemen sometimes assume liability under easement agreements, railroad sidetrack agreements, purchase orders, or sales and service contracts. The contractor may enter into an agreement with his principal in which he undertakes to hold the principal harmless and indemnify him for any accidents arising out of the work being done. A lessee frequently agrees to protect his lessor from any consequences arising out of the leased property.

❑ **Owners' and Contractors' Protective Liability Policy:** This covers an owner or contractor against any liability arising out of work done by another, such as an independent contractor or a subcontractor. Both tort and contractual (including warranty) claims are covered.

A major subject of current (and foreseeable future) litigation is the status of claims relating to hazardous waste sites under Comprehensive General Liability policies.

[¶2517] SUPPLEMENTAL BENEFITS UNDER LIABILITY INSURANCE

In addition to satisfying money claims, liability insurance provides a number of valuable services and additional benefits.

(1) Defense Suits: The insurance company will defend, in the insured's name, suits brought against the insured that if successful would constitute a claim

under the policy. The policy pays all costs including investigating the claim, procuring witnesses, and legal defense.

(2) Courts Costs and Interest on Judgment: These are paid by the insurer.

(3) Premiums for Bonds: The policy also pays for bonds required in the appeal of any suit and bonds to release attachments.

(4) Reimbursement of Insured's Expenses: Reasonable expenses incurred by the insured at the company's request, other than his loss of earnings, are reimbursed. Examples of such expenses are travel, obtaining witnesses, getting affidavits, etc.

(5) Immediate Medical and Surgical First Aid: If furnished by the insured at the time of an accident, this will be paid for by the policy.

(6) Inspection Service: It is standard practice for insurance companies to inspect risks to minimize hazards.

The above benefits are payable, regardless of their amounts, *over and above* the limits of the policy.

(7) Medical Payment Coverage: This can be added to a liability policy for an additional premium. It covers all reasonable medical, surgical, funeral, etc., expenses, incurred within one year of an accident, to each person who sustains bodily injury, sickness, or disease caused by an accident regardless of whether the insured is legally liable or not. Medical payments do not usually cover the insured, any partner, tenant, or any person regularly residing on premises, or any employee of the insured or tenant.

Medical payment coverage is generally written with two limits. The first limit is the limit per person; the second is the limit payable to all persons injured in a single accident.

[¶2518] PROPERTY INSURANCE

Property insurance covers direct loss to tangible property, and usually covers loss of use of the property actually damaged. Consequential loss, such as loss of use or lessening in value of property that is not itself physically damaged, can sometimes be added for an additional premium.

There is a certain amount of overlapping among various property coverages, and it is often possible to provide coverage in several different ways. There has been a trend to combine separate coverages into one package, loosely termed "multiple-peril coverages," or to provide all-risk coverage under a "floater" policy.

In the following paragraphs, the more important types of property coverage are explained.

[¶2519] FIRE INSURANCE

This covers the perils of direct loss by fire and lightning. It also covers certain types of damage by smoke—for example, smoke damage caused by hostile fire whether involving the insured property or uninsured property, such as a neighboring building. Other types of smoke damage, caused, for instance, by a defective heating apparatus on the premises, are not covered by the basic fire policy.

☐ **Extended Coverage:** Coverage for other perils can be added by endorsement to the fire policy. The *extended coverage* endorsement insures against windstorm, hail, explosion, riot, civil commotion, aircraft, smoke, explosion, and vehicles. The *additional extended coverage* endorsement insures against collapse, explosion of steam or hot water systems, fallen trees, glass breakage, vandalism and malicious mischief, vehicles owned or operated by insured or tenant, water damage, and ice, snow, and freezing.

Some of these types of coverage may be written separately, such as the vandalism and malicious mischief endorsement. The extended coverage must be written for the same amount as the fire policy itself, and the face amount of the policy is not increased—the coverage is extended to include the added perils.

☐ **Allied Lines:** This generally is placed as an endorsement on fire insurance or may be undertaken as a separate insurance contract to cover destruction from natural disasters such as earthquakes or hail damage to growing crops, or such events as fire sprinkler leakage.

[¶2520] PHYSICAL DAMAGE TO MOTOR VEHICLES

Physical damage to autos, trucks, tractors, etc., can be insured under collision, comprehensive, fire and theft, and other policies. Type of coverage and rates will vary with the construction and use of the vehicle, the principal city in which the vehicle is garaged, and radius of miles in which the vehicle is used. Larger risks can get reductions through fleet and experience rating.

Similar physical damage coverage is available for company-owned airplanes, yachts, etc.

[¶2521] BURGLARY AND THEFT

The *open stock burglary* policy insures against loss by burglary of merchandise, furniture, fixtures, and equipment (not money, securities, records, and accounts) and damage to the premises.

The *mercantile safe burglary* policy covers loss of money, securities, and other property and other damage resulting from burglary of a safe.

The *mercantile robbery* policy covers various robbery hazards both inside and outside.

The *paymaster robbery* policy is designed for businesses where the principal danger would be robbery of payroll funds.

The *storekeeper's burglary and robbery* policy is a package policy for smaller mercantile risks.

The *office burglary and robbery* policy is a package policy for professional offices and service businesses.

The *money and securities broad form* policy is comprehensive coverage for most mercantile risks, providing coverage against virtually all risk of loss of money and securities.

[¶2522] FIDELITY BONDS

This type of bond covers an employer against the loss of any kind of property—money, securities, raw materials, merchandise, equipment, real property—resulting from dishonest actions of employees. Some bonds insure only named individuals, others cover all occupants of named positions, and others cover all employees of a firm. If the insured is a partnership, the fidelity bond will not cover actions of partners, since they are not employees. In a corporation, all officers are covered since they are employees. Directors of a corporation are excluded unless they are also officers or employees.

[¶2523] MULTIPLE PERIL COVERAGE

Multiple peril, or package, policies combine in one policy many different types of coverage. The advantage to the insured is broader coverage, elimination of overlapping coverage and claims, and lower cost. Some policies provide all-risk coverage while others insure specified perils.

Manufacturers' output policy insures merchandise and other personal property of manufacturers while the property is away from the premises of the manufacturer. It is intended for large stocks of goods in dispersed locations.

Industrial property policy covers all the personal property held by a manufacturing concern, including property of others, on its own premises, usually in diversified locations. It may also insure buildings.

Commercial property policy insures all kinds of personal property of retailers and wholesalers, including limited off-premises coverage. It is not available to businesses that can buy the "block" policy, such as jewelers or furriers.

Office contents policy covers all forms of personal property located in an office. It may be purchased by someone who owns the building, as well as by tenants. An *office package policy* is designed for the owner of an office building.

Jeweler's block policy insures a jeweler for loss or damage to goods in his possession—his own property and property of others. Other lines of business have similar types of coverage; for example, the furrier's block policy.

[¶2524] CREDIT INSURANCE

Credit insurance indemnifies a wholesaler, manufacturer, or jobber for unusual losses incurred by him through the failure of his customers to pay what is owed. This coverage is generally not available to retailers, since credit rating and information are usually lacking on their customers. Most prudent firms have a reserve for bad debts, usually the amount ascertained by experience to be the average annual loss. This may be satisfactory in a normal year, but unexpected losses, such as the bankruptcy of one large customer, might wipe out profits. This is where credit insurance comes in.

Coverage is provided under *specific* and *general policies.* Specific policies are used by businesses that have occasional, high-class accounts to whom considerable credit is extended for short terms. Coverage of these accounts is usually afforded after investigation of each specific risk by the insurance company. General policies cover the accounts of the insured described in the policy. These usually are all customers who have the credit rating required by the policy, and there is no need for investigation and approval of individual transactions.

One valuable benefit of credit insurance is the collection service offered to policyholders. Specific policies usually provide for compulsory collection of accounts due—the insured must file a claim for collection within two months after an account is due. Other types of policies provide severe penalties if claims for collection are not filed in timely fashion. A few policies make filing for collection optional with the insured.

[¶2525] SURETY BONDS

Many commercial transactions are guaranteed by suretyship—an individual, corporation, or partnership lends its name or credit to obligations of another. A typical example is a stockholder in a close corporation being co-signer of a loan to the corporation. In many types of business transactions, corporate suretyship provided by bonding companies or insurance companies is required.

❏ *Contract Bonds:* Contract bonds are required in many cases to guarantee the satisfactory completion or performance of a contract. These bonds are written for the *term of the contract* and cannot be canceled during this term. The initial premium usually covers a period of two years, and the renewal premium charged after that is based on an estimate of time needed to complete work still remaining.

❏ *Bid Bonds:* These bonds are generally required to accompany bids of contractors for public work jobs. They are sometimes required by private builders, too. The bond guarantees that the bidder, if awarded the contract, will enter into the contract and furnish the prescribed performance bond (and payment bond if required). If the bidding contractor defaults, the surety becomes liable for the difference between the bid of its principal and the next lowest bid. The bid bond may be written with a *fixed penalty* or an *open penalty.*

❏ *Performance Bonds:* The various types of performance bonds include the following:

Construction contract bond—guarantees faithful performance by the contractor for construction of a building. It may run to the lender of construction monies and may be called a *completion bond.*

Labor and material payment bond—guarantees that the contractor will pay all bills for labor and materials. This is written either as a separate policy or as part of the construction contract bond.

Maintenance bond—guarantees that work done by the contractor will be free of defective workmanship or materials. This is written either as a separate policy or as part of the construction contract bond.

Supply contract bond—guarantees a contract to supply goods or materials.

[¶2526] CONSEQUENTIAL LOSS COVERAGE

A fire or other peril may cause a financial loss other than that resulting from the direct destruction of the property. Such losses are called "consequential losses" and include those resulting from the loss of use of the property destroyed (such as interruption of business), and property loss from indirect connection with the hazard rather than from direct destruction. The main types of insurance against consequential losses are:

(1) Business interruption insurance.

(2) Contingent business interruption insurance, which covers losses resulting from the interruption not of the insured's business, but of a supplier or some other activity on which the continued conduct of the business is dependent.

(3) Extra expense insurance, which covers the cost of emergency operation.

(4) Rent insurance, which covers the loss of rents during the time when a building has become unusable because of fire or other insured peril.

(5) Delayed profits insurance, which covers loss of profits that might result from a delay in the completion of a project.

(6) Profits and commission insurance, which covers profits on finished goods when sales will be lost as a result of the destruction of goods. This is appropriate for seasonal goods, specially built machinery, etc.

(7) Leasehold insurance, which covers a tenant's financial loss if his lease is canceled.

[¶2527] HOW MUCH INSURANCE?

Probably the most difficult question that any individual considering insurance must answer from the outset is how much coverage to carry. Co-insurance and contribution clauses added to policies make the choice an important one. Owners of insurance policies that have a contribution clause and who carry insurance for less than 80% of the value of the items insured (this is the usual level) may suffer a penalty in the event of only partial loss. A co-insurance clause means that the owner is entitled to only a pro-rata share of the loss based upon the ratio of the actual amount of coverage to the required amount of coverage.

For example, a building having an insurable value of $100,000 is insured against fire under a policy bearing the 80% contribution clause. The owner should carry at least $80,000 of insurance. if he does carry $80,000, he meets the requirement of the contribution clause and any fire loss he sustains will be paid in full up to the limit of the policy.

On the other hand, if the same owner carries only $40,000 of insurance, he is carrying only half of the required amount. Under these circumstances, if he sustains a loss, he will be paid only half of the loss, up to the limit of the policy. In this example, if he sustains a loss of $1,000, he will collect only $500 and will have to contribute or absorb the other $500.

Since the contribution clause can inflict severe penalties for underinsurance, many prudent owners carry more insurance than is required by the contribution clause. For example, their policies may contain the 80% clause, yet they may carry 85% of the insurance to insurable value. This is relatively inexpensive and leaves a margin for error or for a future increase in value.

Frequently, "umbrella" policies are available at comparatively low cost to provide large amounts of additional insurance—e.g., $1 million liability coverage in a homeowner's policy.

What Amount of Liability Insurance? The limits or amounts of liability insurance to be carried are determined by the judgment of the owner. The size of a building or business is not necessarily the determining factor. Serious accidents can occur in small buildings as well as large. The extent of injuries bears no relationship whatever to the size or value of the building or to the financial responsibility of the owner. In all cases, the owner has to decide on limits that he feels will adequately cover him.

Limits are generally expressed as "$100/300" or "$100,000/300,000," each meaning the same; namely, up to $100,000 available for the payment of a claim for injuries to one person hurt in one accident and if more than one person is injured, up to $300,000 total liability, limited to $100,000 for any one person. A series of accidents is fully covered with the limits applying separately to each, and no reduction in the amount of coverage occurs by reason of payment of claims.

[¶2528] TABLES OF RISKS AND COVERAGE

The following tables summarize the various risks arising in business, the potential losses, and the available insurance coverage to protect against those risks. Unless a specific value is listed in the tables, the maximum loss would be determined by the facts in each case.

GENERAL BUSINESS RISKS

Risk	Liability to Others	Loss to Insured	Maximum Loss	Policy
Boiler or machinery explosion	Yes	Property damage (P.D.) and personal injury (P.I.)		Boiler and machinery
		Consequential damage through loss of use		Consequential damage endorsement
Tort (false arrest, libel, etc.)	Yes			Personal injury liability coverage
Tort by advertisement (defamation, etc.)	Yes			Advertiser's liability
Employee accident or disease	Yes	(Workers' compensation— or common-law liability)		Workers' compensation and employer's liability
Liability assumed by contract	Yes			Comprehensive general liability
Accident on premises	Yes			Comprehensive general liability
Accident on elevators	Yes			Comprehensive general liability
Accident due to operation of independent contractors	Yes			Comprehensive general liability
Defective or unsafe product	Yes			Product liability
Patent infringement	Yes			Patent infringement
Airplaine accidents	No	P.I.		Aviation accident

Risk	Liability to Others	Loss to Insured	Maximum Loss	Policy
Broken glass	No	P.D.	Replacement cost	Comprehensive glass
Burglary	No	Loss of inventory or equipment	Replacement cost	Mercantile open stock
Robbery (on and off premises)	No	Loss of property		Mercantile robbery
Employee fraud or dishonesty	No	Loss of property		Blanket position bond or individual fidelity bond
Damage to suppliers or purchasers	No	Loss of earnings		Contingent business interruption
Damage to business	No	Loss of earnings		Business interruption
Fire or lightning	No	P.D.		Fire
Windstorm and hail	No	P.D.		Windstorm and hail
Earthquake	No	P.D.		Earthquake
Water leakage or overflow	No	P.D.		Water damage
Loss of cargo at sea	No	Property loss	Value of cargo	Ocean marine cargo
Loss of books and records	No	Noncollection of accounts receivable	Value of accounts receivable	Accounts receivable
Loss or damage to personal property	No	P.D. or property loss		Inland transit floater
Nonpayment by customers	No	Loss of income	Loss experience	Commercial credit
Automobile accident (insured's automobile)	Yes	P.D. and P.I.		Automobile comprehensive

Risk	Liability to Others	Loss to Insured	Maximum Loss	Policy
Aircraft accident (insured's aircraft)	Yes			Aircraft liability
Decrease in corporate net worth due to its liability	No	Value of stock		Stockholder's protective insurance
Loss of securities or other instruments	No	Property loss		Lost securities bond

SOME SPECIFIC BUSINESS RISKS

Risk	Liability to Others	Loss to Insured	Maximum Loss	Policy
Banking— criminal acts and disappearance	No	Property loss	Depends on deposits	Bankers' blanket bond
Garages— accidents to person and property	Yes			Garage liability
Druggists— error in prescription	Yes			Druggists' liability
Innkeeper— loss or damage to guests' property	Yes			Inkeepers' liability
Manufacturers and contractors— accidents from operations	Yes			Manufacturers' and contractors' liability
Stockbrokers— criminal acts and disappearance	Yes			Brokers' blanket bond
Vending machines— damage or loss	No	P.D. and loss of income		Vending machine floater

Risk	Liability to Others	Loss to Insured	Maximum Loss	Policy
Warehouse-men—loss or damage to customer's property	Yes			Warehouse-men's liability
Malpractice by professionals	Yes			Professional liability

RISKS INVOLVING REAL ESTATE

Risk	Liability to Others	Loss to Insured	Maximum Loss	Policy
Damage during construction	No	P.D.	Cost of completed building	Builders' risk
Losses due to delay in construction	No	Loss of rent or use		Rent insurance
Damage to completed building	No	P.D.	Replacement cost	Fire and extended coverage
		Loss of rent or use		Rent insurance
Injuries to persons or property on premises	Yes			Landlords' protective liability
Injuries to lessees or their property	Yes			General liability
Loss of leasehold due to damage to building	No	Leasehold interest	Market value of lease minus rent	Leasehold interest

[¶2529] PROTECTING CREDITORS' INTERESTS THROUGH INSURANCE

There are a number of methods of providing insurance protection to creditors:

(1) Separate Policy for a Creditor: The creditor takes out, or is furnished with, a separate policy covering his interest. The owner may have a separate policy covering his ownership interest.

(2) Assignment of Owners' Policy: The owner assigns his policy to the creditor. Whether the consent of the insurance company is required and what the

rights of the respective parties are may depend upon the type of insurance and the jurisdiction.

(3) Loss Payable Clause: This is an endorsement on the owner's policy of a "loss payable clause" that stipulates "loss, if any, payable to _____, as his interest may appear." The effect of this varies in different jurisdictions—some put the creditor in the same position as the owner, while others give him broader rights. The creditor normally is given possession of the policy and the owner gets a certificate or memorandum of insurance.

(4) As Interest May Appear Clause: This may be found in a policy such as one covering a bailee, which covers "for the benefit of whom it may concern" or "for others as their interests may appear."

The procurement of insurance and the payment of the premiums is covered by the agreement between the debtor and creditor. The agreement should spell out the kind and amount of coverage, who is to get the coverage and keep the policy, who is to pay the premium, what happens if one party or the other fails in the duties relating to insurance or payment, and any other matters that are important in the transaction.

[¶2530] SUPPLEMENTARY BENEFITS UNDER LIABILITY INSURANCE

The federal diversity jurisdiction statute, 28 USC Section 1332(c), treats a liability insurer as a citizen of the same state as the insured in a direct suit against the insurer. The Supreme Court has construed this statute[33] to apply only to suits against insurers, not suits brought by insurers.

According to the Minnesota Court of Appeals, an insurer has a duty to defend under a homeowner's insurance policy when the insured is sued for negligent transmission of genital herpes to a sexual partner; the policy failed to specify an exclusion for sexually related tort liability.[34]

There is no duty to defend (or right to indemnification) in a products liability action where the plaintiff claims injuries from combustion products, where the policy excludes "bodily injury arising out of the discharge of smoke, vapors, soot, fumes."[35] The Internal Revenue Code's excise tax imposed on prohibited transactions by pension plans is a "penalty," and therefore is not a loss that can be covered by the employer's pension trust liability policy.[36]

The policy interpreted in *Estes v. Alaska Insurance Guaqranty Ass'n*[37] stated that the insurer had no obligation under the policy unless suit on the policy was commenced within a year after loss. However, the Alaska Supreme Court held that time limits on suits, notice of loss, proof of loss, and requirements of cooperation with the insurer are enforceable only if the insurer actually suffered prejudice of the type the clause was drafted to prevent.

— ENDNOTES —

1. In re Family Health Services Inc., 130 BR 314 (C.D. Cal. 7/8/92).

2. In re Estate of Medcare HMO, 62 LW 2025 (9th Cir. 6/30/93).

3. Department of Treasury v. Fabe, #91-1513, 113 S.Ct. 2202 (Sup.Ct. 6/11/93).

4. Frankenmuth Mutual Ins. Co. v. Keeley, 433 Mich. 525, 447 N.W.2d 691 (Mich.Sup. 10/19/89).

5. Ins. Code Section 790.03(h)(5).

6. Brandt v. State Farm Mutual Automobile Ins. Co., 693 F.Supp. 877 (E.D. Cal. 9/2/88).

7. The Doctors' Co. v. Superior Court of L.A. County, 58 LW 2078 (Cal.Sup. 7/17/89).

8. Colorado Civil Rights Comm'n v. Travellers Ins. Co., 759 P.2d 1358 (Colo.Sup. 7/18/88).

9. Smith v. States General Life Ins. Co., 60 LW 2485 (Ala.Sup. 1/17/92).

10. In re TICOR Title Ins. Co., FTC Docket #9190 (9/19/89; see 58 LW 2274).

11. F.T.C. v. Ticor Ins. Co., #91-72, 112 S.Ct. 2169 (Sup.Ct. 6/12/92).

12. Hartford Fire Ins. Co. v. California, ##91-1111, 91-1128, 113 S.Ct. 2891 (Sup.Ct. 6/28/93).

13. Thacker v. New York Life Insurance Co., 796 F.Supp. 1338 (E.D. Cal 8/14/92).

14. NAACP v. American Family Ins. Co., 978 F.2d 287 (7th Cir. 10/20/92), cert. denied 113 S.Ct. 2335.

15. U.S. National Bank of Oregon v. Independent Insurance Agents of America, ##92-484, 92-507, 113 S.Ct. 2173 (Sup.Ct. 6/7/93).

16. Independent Insurance Agents of America v. Ludwig, 62 LW 2051 (D.C. Cir. 7/16/93).

17 Herman v. Provident Mutual Life Ins. Co., 886 F.2d 529 (2d Cir. 9/29/89).

18. Commercial Law Bulletin (CLL) Volume 8, Issue 4, Jul/Aug. 1993 p. 23.

19. Aetna Casualty & Surety Co. v. Pintlar Corp., 60 LW 2351 (9th Cir. 11/7/91) [Idaho law]; Independent Petrochemical Corp. v. Aetna Casualty & Surety Co., 944 F.2d 940 (D.C.Cir. 9/13/91) [Missouri law].

20. Intel Corp. v. Hartford Accident & Indemnity Co., 952 F.2d 1551 (9th Cir. 12/24/91); New Jersey v. Signo Trading Internal Inc., #A-72 (N.J. Sup. 9/23/92). See Nat'l Law J. 10/12/92 p. 22.

21. Intel Corp. v. Hartford Accident & Indemnity Co., 952 F.2d 1551 (9th Cir. 12/24/91).

22. Cincinnati Ins. Co. v. Miliken & Co., 857 F.2d 979 (4th Cir. 9/30/88).

23. Ray Industries Inc. v. Liberty Mutual Ins. Co., 974 F.2d 754 (6th Cir. 9/10/92). Also see Park-Ohio Industries Inc. v. Home Indemnity Co. Inc., 975 F.2d 1215 (6th Cir. 9/22/92), *Nat'l Law J.* 10/12/92 p. 22.

24. Hudson Insurance Co. v. American Electric Corp., 957 F.2d 826 (11th Cir. 4/3/92), cert. denied #92-434, 61 LW 3330.

25. Western World Ins. Co. v. Dana, 765 F.Supp. 1011 (E.D.Cal. 7/20/91).

26. Avondale Industries Inc. v. Travelers Indemnity Co., 887 F.2d 1200, cert.den. 110 S.CT 2588 (2d Cir. 10/18/89).

27. State of New York v. Aetna Casualty & Surety Co., *NYLJ* 11/15/89 p. 1; A.D. 3rd Dept.

28. University of Minnesota v. Royal Insurance Co., 62 LW 2100 (Minn.App. 7/6/93).

29. Continental Casualty Co. v. Rapid-American Corp., 80 N.Y.2d 640, 593 N.Y.S.2d 966, 609 N.E.2d 506 (N.Y.App. 2/11/93).

30. Morton International Inc. v. General Accident Insurance Co. of America, 62 LW 2079 (N.J.Sup. 7/21/93).

31. Compare City of Edgerton v. Co. of Wisconsin, No. 90-CV-939 (Wis.Cir. Ct. 5/10/91) [Personal injury provisions cover cleanup costs when contaminants migrate into groundwater and impair the occupancy of surrounding properties that also have interests in the groundwaters] and NAPCO Inc. v. Fireman's Fund Ins. Co., No. 90-0993 (W.D. Pa. 5/22/91) [Under personal injury provisions, insurer has a duty to defend against allegations of environmental trespass and nuisance] with Pipefitters Welfare Educational Fund v. Westchester Fire Ins. Co., 976 F.2d 1037 (7th Cir. 1992) [There is no coverage under the personal injury provisions for private-party CERCLA response claims.].

32. Eljer Manufacturing v. Liberty Mutual Ins. Co., 972 F.2d 805 (7th Cir. 8/14/92), cert. denied 113 S.Ct. 1646; Maryland Casualty Co. v. W.R. Grace & Co., 62 LW 2178 (2d Cir. 9/3/93).

33. Northbrook National Ins. Co. v. Brewer, 110 S.Ct. 297 (Sup.Ct. 11/7/89).

34. North Star Mutual Ins. v. R.W., 431 N.W.2d 138 (Minn.App. 11/8/88).

35. Park-Ohio Industries Inc. v. Home Indemnity Co., 975 F.2d 1215 (6th Cir. 9/22/92).

36. Hofco Inc. v. Nat'l Union Fire Ins., 60 LW 2611 (Iowa Sup. 3/18/92).

37. 57 LW 2714 (Alaska Sup. 5/26/89).

— FOR FURTHER REFERENCE —

Chazan, Michael J., "Insurance Policy May Be an Ideal Asset for a Gift by the Insured," 19 *Estate Planning* 294 (September-October '92).

Davis, Victoria F., "Duking It Out With the Doctors: Litigation Between Providers and Payers," 5 *Benefits L.J.* 175 (Summer '92).

Elligett, Raymond T. Jr. and Charles P. Schropp, "Running for Cover: Environmental Insurance Coverage Issues," 67 *Florida Bar J.* 67 (July-August '93).

Ellis, Astrid E., "Insurance Coverage for Innovative Medical Treatment," 34 *For the Defense* 9 (September '92).

Genovese, Julie, "Litigation Strategies for Subrogated Parties," 65 *Wisconsin Lawyer* 22 (June '92).

Gislason, Scott, "Split-Dollar Life Insurance: Updated Planning Techniques," 20 *Estate Planning* 201 (July-August '93).

Houser, Douglas G., "Good Faith as a Matter of Law: The Insurance Company's Right to Be Wrong," 27 *Tort and Insurance L.J.* 665 (Spring '92).

Macey, Scott J., Peter A. Henricks and Thomas W. Meagher, "Installing Group Long-Term Care Insurance," 5 *Benefits L.J.* 307 (Autumn '92).

Melendez, Julia M., "The McCarran-Ferguson Act: Has It Outlived Its Intent?" 42 *Federation of Insurance and Corporate Counsel Q.* 283 (Spring '92).

Rankin, James P. and Jay M. Rector, "An Overview of the Lawyer's Role in Designing and Drafting Self-Insured Group Medical Plans," 61 *J. of the Kansas Bar Ass'n* 23 (May '92).

Saks, Howard J., "Helping a Client Who Is Charged an Extra Premium or Denied Insurance Based on Health History," 19 *Estate Planning* 316 (September-October '92).

Stone, Sandra Elizabeth, "HIV Testing and Insurance Applicants: Exploring Constitutional Alternatives to Statutory Protections," 19 *Hastings Constitutional L.Q.* 1163 (Summer '92).

Walker, James William, "Comparative Bad Faith: Its Time Has Come in Texas," 55 *Texas Bar J.* 792 (September '92).

INTELLECTUAL PROPERTY

[¶2601] The need for protection of ideas, secrets, or technological property may arise in any area of commercial practice—corporate, entertainment, or advertising—and may be associated with any number of particular transactions—employment, sale of business, manufacturing, research and distribution contracts, licensing arrangements, and international investments. Sometimes the protection is easy to achieve, especially if the idea, trade secret, or invention is patentable. Forms of expression—literary, musical, artistic, and even photographic—can be protected by copyright. Trademarks are often registered. The most difficult problem arises in connection with the protection of the "pure idea"—the concept that cannot be reduced to practice and that can have any number of modes of expression. In this section the various methods of protection afforded by federal, state, and common law are examined.

The Supreme Court ruled in the case of *Lilly v. Medtronic,*[1] dealing with patent protection for generic drugs, that it is not infringement to make reasonable use of the patented invention to comply with government testing requirements. (Another important intellectual property issue, the relationship between computers and copyright law, is discussed above in ¶1304.)

[¶2602] PATENTS

Patent law is a sophisticated field and requires the expertise of an experienced patent agent or attorney. In order to work effectively with the patent attorney, it is necessary to understand the broad procedures associated with securing a patent, as well as the related problems regarding licensing, cross-licensing, and assignments. The material provided in the following paragraph is designed to give a broad explanation of the general law.

[¶2603] AVAILABILITY OF PATENT PROTECTION

A patent grants the inventor a "statutory monopoly," the right of exclusive use for 17 years (see ¶2614). A patent can be obtained for any "new and useful process, machine, manufacture, or composition of matter, or any new and useful improvement thereof." New methods, new combinations, and new designs may be patented. However, no one can obtain a patent for a new or better idea for doing business. A so-called "plant patent" (35 U.S.C. §163) is not really issued on a plant, but on the method of asexually reproducing the plant. Today, it is not only possible to get a patent when you build a better mousetrap, but also when you build a better mouse: in 1988, the Supreme Court refused to hear a case (and thus upheld the Court of Appeals) involving the grant of a patent for a genetically engineered mouse. The advice of a patent lawyer is essential on the prospective patentability of a new development.

No patent may be granted for an invention if it was "patented or described in a printed publication in this or a foreign country, before the invention thereof by the applicant for patent" (35 U.S.C. §102(a)).

[¶2604] THE DECISION TO APPLY FOR A PATENT

A patented invention is subject to public disclosure. A new development may conceivably receive more protection if it is kept a trade secret—the probable patent protection may be so meager that it is not worth the expense, or it is considered better to rely on trade name, nondisclosure of techniques, accumulation of know-how, etc. Further, the business prospect may be worthwhile but not sufficient to justify the cost of patenting. As a general rule, if the invention is to be commercialized, patenting is advisable.

[¶2605] WHO SHOULD APPLY FOR THE PATENT?

Only the inventor should apply, the person who takes the inventive step. If there is more than one inventor, each should apply as co-owner of the patent, and each one, upon the granting of the patent, obtains an "undivided interest in the entire patent." However, the usual rules of co-ownership do not apply in the patent situation. Therefore, when one co-owner seeks to license or assign his or her rights under the patent, it is best to consult a patent attorney.

Patents issued in the name of anyone other than the true inventor or inventors are invalid if the facts are proven, except where it can be shown that a wrong party was included through error and without any deceptive intent. The employer has no right to designate an applicant who is not the true inventor. An inventor may not have multiple patents for the same invention (no "double patenting"). An inventor who later improves on an invention may apply for additional patents to cover the improvements.

Once an inventor has a patent for an invention, he or she cannot obtain a patent for the means of producing the already-patented invention.

[¶2606] PATENTING EMPLOYEE INVENTIONS

Frequently, an employee will develop an invention during the course of employment. If there is no agreement with an employee, the employer may be entitled to a "shop-right" in the employee's invention, thus claiming ownership under an implied agreement to assign. If the employee was hired to invent or in a capacity that would give rise to the exception that he or she would assign any invention to the employer, the courts will usually recognize an obligation to assign the invention to the employer. It does not matter in what capacity an employee works; if the employee patents an invention conceived and developed on the job, the employer has a "shop-right" to use the invention in the company's own business, but only if the invention was developed during working hours, on the company's time, and with its materials.

To avoid the uncertainty of proof of an implied obligation to assign and the nonexclusivity and other limitations of the shop-right, it is important to get a written agreement obligating an employee who is likely to contribute to an invention to assign it to the employer. Moreover, full protection for the employer requires more than creating an obligation to assign patent rights. It may be just as important to place the employee under obligation not to disclose secret or confidential information or knowledge obtained during employment for a period of time after termination. It may be desirable to enforce restrictions on any activity in a specified field of industry or research and development for a period of time after termination. An employee can be obligated to assign improvements to an invention made after employment, provided they relate to an invention made during employment.

[¶2607] WHEN TO APPLY FOR A PATENT

Several circumstances may trigger the need for a patent application:

(1) If the invention is described in a publication, used publicly, or placed on sale by the inventor, it is necessary for the inventor to apply for the patent within one year from the time of publication, use, or sale.

(2) If an application for a foreign patent has been filed abroad, application for a U.S. patent should be made within one year of the foreign filing.

(3) Where two or more parties are competing for a patent on the same invention, the first to file prevails in the great majority of cases. The other party has the very heavy burden of proof that he is the first inventor.

[¶2608] GUARDING AGAINST COMPETING PATENT CLAIMS

It is not uncommon for two or more applicants to lay claim to the same invention, or to challenge an existing patent on the grounds that the invention was known prior to the date of the applicant's discovery. In order to guard against this problem, one practice often used by inventors is to: (1) Write a description of the invention; (2) Execute it before a notary public; (3) Mail it to the inventor's address by registered mail; and (4) Lock it up to provide proof of date of invention, should that ever become necessary. However, this approach is of doubtful value since at best it shows only one conception. An early date of conception is of little value unless it can be shown that it was followed by diligence in adapting and perfecting the invention.

The acts that help in establishing the priority of invention are the following:

➤ Reduction to practice;

➤ Diligence in adapting and perfecting the invention;

➤ Disclosure to others;

➤ Making the first written description and the first drawing, and then only, early conception.

The date of reduction to practice is the most decisive factor bearing on the date of invention. Filing an application is constructive reduction to practice, and early filing avoids expensive proof that otherwise would be required. But if an adverse claim is based on invention before filing, it requires corroboration to establish date of invention, and disclosure of all essential details of the invention to others is important in proving not only conception but also diligence and reduction to practice. Diaries and laboratory notes are recommended as a means of recording the progress of an invention, its conception, due diligence in reducing it to practice, etc.

[¶2609] THE PATENT APPLICATION—PRELIMINARY SEARCH

In a preliminary patent search, sometimes called a patentability search, the object is to see whether there are any patents outstanding that would indicate that the proposed development is not novel and that it would therefore be a waste of money to file an application. It is also designed to turn up matters that are related and that may be of help to the patent attorney in preparing the patent application. There are other types of patent searches:

(1) Validity Search: designed to find earlier patents that would throw doubt upon the validity of a patent that has been interfering or threatens to interfere with the client's business. This is an extensive search that is usually made as a basis for a patent lawsuit contesting the validity of a patent.

(2) Infringement Search: to determine if a proposed product or improvement will infringe on the claims of an unexpired patent.

(3) Assignment Search: to determine who is the present recorded owner of a particular patent.

(4) Index Search: to determine what patents have been issued to a particular inventor or patent holder.

[¶2610] ABANDONMENT OF AN INVENTION

An inventor may not obtain a patent if "he has abandoned the invention" (35 U.S.C. §102(c)).

Abandonment may either be shown by express conduct or implied by the inventor's conduct.

An inventor who conceals an invention by not patenting it cannot claim a prior right as against a subsequent inventor who in "good faith and without knowledge" invents and applies for a patent on the same invention. The issue as to what constitutes unreasonable time so as to indicate concealment, abandonment, or delay is a question of fact to be determined on a case-by-case basis.

[¶2611] ASSIGNMENT VS. LICENSING OF PATENTS

A patent is *assigned* when all the rights to an object are granted exclusively to another party. A *license* is the grant of an exclusive right under the patent which *does not* include the right to make, the right to use, and the right to sell the object. When the full rights under a patent are confined to a particular geographic area (territorial grant), the patent has been assigned.

In deciding whether to make an assignment or merely grant a license, the following considerations should be kept in mind:

(1) Assignments should be recorded; licenses need not be.

(2) All owners of title must join in suit against an infringer but a licensee need not be joined (except in limited cases).

(3) Receipts from an assignment, although a percentage royalty, may be treated as capital gains; whereas receipts from a license are fully taxable as ordinary income. License payments may be deducted; the price paid for an assignment may be depreciated. Even when the price is not a percentage basis, these percentage payments may be deducted as depreciation of the patent.

Drafting the instrument for the assignment or license of the patent is an intricate art, best left to an experienced patent attorney.

[¶2612] MISUSE OF PATENT PRIVILEGES

The owner of a patent has the exclusive right to make, use, and sell the patented item. However, when the owner seeks to control unpatented items, sales, or otherwise unlawfully restricts the licensee by contract, he or she is misusing the patent. Such misuse can render a patent unenforceable, and misuse is frequently a defense to an owner's infringement suit.

Although a patentee may fix the price at which a licensed manufacturer may sell a patented article, he or she may *not* fix the resale price of a patented product once it is sold. The owner of a license may not combine with another patentee under a cross-license to fix prices under their respective patents. A patent owner may not compel a prospective licensee to take a license on unwanted patents in order to obtain a license under the desired patent.

Under the Patent and Trademark Act (P.L. 100-703, Title III, 11/19/88), a patentee is allowed to sell unpatented components of an invention or process without being guilty of misuse, as long as the component is a "non-staple" of the patented invention, and has no substantial non-infringing uses. Recent amendments make it clear that refusal to license a patent does not constitute misuse; and that tying a patent license or sale of a patented article to another sale or license from the same party does not constitute misuse as long as the patentee/licensor does not have market power.[2]

The Bayh-Dole Act, 35 U.S.C. Section 202(c)(7)(B), requires not-for-profit organizations (e.g, universities) that receive federal funding to share patent royalties with inventors employed by the organizations. However, the statute's purpose is to regulate the commercialization of federally funded inventions, not to benefit inventors, so there is no implied private right of action for employee-inventors seeking to collect a specified percentage of the profits.[3]

P.L. 102-560 permits states and their officers and employees to be sued in federal court for violation of patent protection (or plant variety protection). According to the Federal Circuit, this statute is supposed to put states on the same footing as other parties, and thus if the state is a patent owner, it can also be sued for a declaratory judgment of invalidity of a patent.[4]

[¶2613] REMEDIES FOR PATENT INFRINGEMENT

Preliminary injunctions are seldom obtained in patent suits because, among other reasons, if the suit fails, the party enjoined would have a case for heavy damages against the party claiming infringement. To get a preliminary injunction, it must be shown that irreparable harm would be done if the infringement continued, that the validity of the patent is clear, and that the infringement is beyond any reasonable doubt. Injunctions are almost always granted when infringement has been adjudicated, but there have been cases when an injunction was denied the victor in an infringement suit on the basis that the injury to the infringer would be greater than the benefit to the owner of the patent. Of course, the owner of the patent is entitled to an accounting of profits. In patent infringement suits, agreements with others executed in good faith before the beginning of the suit have been held to set a standard for reasonable royalty.

Patent infringement disputes can also be arbitrated under PL 97-247, 35 U.S.C. §294. The arbitrator's award is final and binding on the parties to arbitration, but has no effect on strangers to the arbitration.

In *Polaroid v. Kodak*,[5] an antitrust-oriented market analysis was applied, with the result that although Polaroid won its case it was not awarded lost profits as an element of damages in a price erosion case.

A patentee can recover lost profits (not just a reasonable royalty) in an infringement action if it competes with the infringer even if the patentee does not market the actual infringed product.[6]

The Federal Circuit routinely vacated declaratory judgments on counterclaims challenging the validity of patents if the Circuit Court affirmed the District Court that the patent had not been infringed. A 1993 Supreme Court decision disapproves this practice: the issue is not moot, in that the public has an interest in the validity of the patent. Except in rare cases, the issue should be decided.[7]

[¶2614] DURATION OF PATENT

Patents have a 17-year life (35 U.S.C. §154). Design patents can be granted for 3 $\frac{1}{2}$, 7, or 14 years, depending upon the inventor's request (35 U.S.C. §173). When the patent expires the item or process becomes public property.

The D.C. Circuit has overruled the FDA policy of treating the 180-day exclusivity period for a generic drug as running from, and being dependent upon, the institution of a suit for patent infringement.[8] The Federal Circuit has ruled that applications for extension of the term of a drug patent must be submitted to the Patent and Trademark Office within 60 days of the FDA's grant of marketing approval: the 60-day "regulatory review period" runs from marketing approval, not action by the DEA.[9]

P.L. 102-444 (1993) permits the PTO to accept late payments of patent maintenance fees.

[¶2615] TRADEMARKS AND TRADE NAMES

A trademark is usually associated with a specific product, while a trade name is representative of the business itself, its established reputation, and goodwill.

Trademarks (unlike patents and copyrights) are not exclusively within the federal domain. Federal power to regulate trademarks is based on the commerce clause and in the past a narrower view of "interstate commerce" has been adopted than in other branches of the law. For example, federal registration of trademarks has been denied hotels, restaurants, service stations, etc., even though their customers may come from across state lines and are solicited by interstate advertising. However, a recent registration of a service mark used in only one state may possibly reflect a new trend.

[¶2616] COMMON-LAW PROTECTION OF TRADEMARKS

Under common law, the true owner of a trademark used for goods and services may prevent the unauthorized use of the mark (or of a similar mark on the same or similar goods or services) by another to the confusion of the public and the owner's detriment. Thus, while the owner of a trademark operating in a common law, "no-registration" area is not completely without legal protection for the mark, it must be recognized that the absence of registration makes the establishment of ownership difficult and encourages unscrupulous competitors to try to get away with appropriating the mark. At the same time, the absence of registration makes it difficult for even well-intentioned competitors to discover the prior mark. In any case, conflicts that might have been avoided by registration are apt to flourish.

[¶2617] STATE TRADEMARK LAWS

The great diversity of the various state trademark statutes rules out detailed consideration of them in this work. However, some indication of their scope and limitations will be apparent from the following comparison with the federal law:

(1) Federal provisions are broader in terms of marks registrable than any state act;

(2) Federal law gives better relief than state law, except as to penalties;

(3) Federal registration provides notice to the entire country;

(4) Federal, but not state, registration gives the right of registration in a large number of foreign countries;

(5) Federal, but not state, registration gives the right to prevent importation of goods bearing infringing marks; and

(6) Federal registration by itself gives the right to sue in federal courts; state registration requires other elements of federal jurisdiction.

[¶2618] FEDERAL TRADEMARK ACT

The Trademark Act of 1946 (Lanham Act, 15 USC Chapter 22) defines a trademark as "any work, name, symbol, or device, or any combination thereof adopted and used by a manufacturer or merchant to identify his goods and distinguish them from those manufactured or sold by others." The Act also provides for the registration of service, certification, and collective marks.

"Service marks" are those used in the sale or advertising of services to distinguish those of one person from another.

"Certification marks" are those used on or in connection with the products or services of persons other than the owner of the mark to certify the origin or other characteristics of the goods or services. The Good Housekeeping "Seal of Approval" would be an example.

"Collective marks" are those used by a group to indicate membership in an organization.

The Trademark Law Revision Act of 1988, P.L. 100-667, enacted at 15 USC Sections 1051-1127, brings the United States into closer conformity with world trademark practice (just as implementation of the Berne Convention brings the United States into closer conformity with world copyright practice). Under the statute, trademarks can be registered in the United States based on an intention to use the trademark, before actual use has commenced. However, in order to prevent the register from being loaded up with "dead wood," the initial and renewal registration terms have been reduced from 20 to 10 years.

According to the Federal Circuit, the Lanham Act Sec. 8 requirement of filing an affidavit six years after registration to demonstrate continuing use in commerce is mandatory, and the Commissioner of Patents and Trademarks lacks authority to permit a registrant to amend its affidavit retrospectively to comply with the six-year requirement.[10]

The statute also expands Section 43 of the Lanham Act to create a cause of action for misrepresentation of the plaintiff's products and commercial activities (not just goods or services). Under prior law, "commercial defamation" was frequently held to be non-actionable. (Truthful negative statements about a competitor's product are, of course, not actionable; and, for First Amendment reasons, the scope of the new cause of action is limited to commercial advertisements and promotions rather than articles or other conventional forms of non-commercial speech.) The Third Circuit limits "any person" to a person whose commercial interests are damaged; deceived consumers cannot sue under this provision.[11]

The Supreme Court has ruled[12] that trade dress, such as a distinctive product or place of business, is protectable under trademark law even absent secondary meaning (e.g., public recognition of the source of the original use of the trade dress).

P.L. 102-542, 1993, makes it possible for a state or state officers or employees to be sued in federal court for trademark infringement.

A distinctive automobile design that has acquired secondary meaning can qualify for Lanham Act protection as trade dress, even if it is not eligible for a design patent. Therefore, it is impermissible to market fiberglass kits costing $8,500-$50,000 used to make replicas of Ferrari Daytona Spyder and Testarossa automobiles selling for $230,000-$2 million.[13]

Remedies under the new cause of action include money damages, injunction, and destruction of the violative material. The plaintiff's damages are defined as the losses it has suffered as well as the defendant's profits and costs of bringing the action. Punitive damages are not permitted,[14] and the overall damage award cannot exceed three times the plaintiff's actual damages. (This is not a treble damages provision; instead, it is a limitation on the amount of the defendant's profits that can be recouped and particularly a limit on attorneys' fees.) Under the new Section 43, competitors, potential competitors, and trade associations have standing to sue.

Even a landlord can be found contributorily liable for trademark counterfeiting on the leased premises, e.g., a flea market owner who knew or had reason to know that tenants would act tortiously[15] (but an attorney who files seizure orders that prove to be wrongful is not liable for wrongful seizure under Lanham Act Sec. 1116(d)(11)).[16]

In a trade dress case, the infringer's profits can be recovered if and only if the infringement was willful; if consumers were confused by the imitation of trade dress; and if diversion of legitimate sales unjustly enriched the trade dress imitator.[17]

Imposition of a Temporary Restraining Order freezing the defendant's assets was permitted in a case involving counterfeiting of athletic shoes,[18] the theory being that the sale of Reebok sneakers in Mexico had enough effect on commerce in the United States to support extraterritorial jurisdiction.

Section 43(c) also provides a selective cause of action for a form of trademark dilution: the use of a trademark made famous in one context, by someone other than the trademark holder, in another context, with the result that the public perception of the value of the trademark is destroyed. In other words, although it is permissible for Coca-Cola to license the manufacture of Coca-Cola clothing, it would not be permissible for a toy manufacturer to bring out a line of Coca-Cola action figures without permission.

It is to be hoped that the statute will clarify the situation that required litigation of cases before the statute's effective date, such as *Mead Data Central Inc. v. Toyota Motor Sales;*[19] *Quality Inns Int'l v.McDonald's Corp.;*[20] and *Cliffs Notes Inc. v. Bantam.*[21]

The issue in *Mead* was whether Toyota's sale of a car called "Lexus" infringed Mead's "Lexis" trademark for computerized legal research services. To the Southern District of New York, the car's name did not violate the Lanham Act (because it would take a very naive individual indeed to mix up a computer data base and a car) but it did violate New York's anti-dilution statute in that the name represented an attempt to take advantage of Mead's reputation at the forefront of legal research technology.

The Southern District ordered Toyota to compensate Mead for the diminution in the value of its trademark; to inform Lexis subscribers that there is no connection between the research service and the automobile; and to mention this in advertisements for the car. The Second Circuit reversed, stating that there was no real dilution of the trademark because the two names are not pronounced identically; because knowledge of Mead's "Lexis" trademark is more or less restricted to lawyers; and there is no blurring in the ordinary mind between the names or uses of the two products.

The alleged infringer also prevailed in *Cliffs Notes,* a case involving parodistic "Spy Notes" published by a satirical magazine in a format designed to evoke memories of the Cliffs Notes that summarize books frequently assigned in literature classes. Given the lack of strong likelihood of confusion between the original and the parody, and the First Amendment considerations, an injunction against the distribution of the "Spy Notes" was blocked.

In regard to other trademark issues, it has been held that the gray market importation of genuine merchandise does not violate the Lanham Act[22] and that Lanham Act Section 42 (which bars import of merchandise copying or simulating merchandise protected by a U.S. trademark) also bars importation of soaps and detergents from the United Kingdom, and bearing a U.S. trademark used for soaps and detergents with different characteristics even though the two companies are affiliated, and the U.S. trademark holder permitted the use of the trademark.[23] The issue here was potential consumer confusion, not infringement of the trademark owner's rights.

Where there is any difference between the trademarked product and the allegedly infringing gray good that consumers would be likely to consider relevant in making the decision to purchase, the First Circuit finds that the difference (however minor) creates a presumption of consumer confusion, giving rise to a Lanham Act claim.[24]

Unauthorized parallel importation of trademarked candy is not such extraordinarily culpable conduct as to justify an award of attorneys' fees under the Lanham Act.[25]

Once a trademark becomes incontestable (has been held for over five years), the trademark is subject to administrative cancellation by the District Court, but the court cannot cancel the trademark based on the functionality of the trademarked feature.[26]

[¶2619] FEDERAL REGISTRATION OF A TRADEMARK

The Lanham Act sets up two registers: (1) principal, and (2) supplemental. The principal register is for so-called "true" or "technical" marks—coined, arbitrary, fanciful, or suggestive marks, if otherwise qualified. A mark may not be registered on the principal register if (1) when applied to the goods of the applicant it is merely descriptive of them; (2) when applied to the goods of the applicant, it is primarily geographically descriptive or deceptively misdescriptive of them, except as indications of regional origin; or (3) it is primarily a surname, except when shown that such marks have become distinctive as applied to the applicant's goods in commerce. (Proof of continuous use for five years makes a prima facie case.)

Marks not qualified for registration on the principal register may be registered on the supplemental register, provided they (1) are capable of distinguishing the applicant's goods and (2) have been used in commerce for at least a year.

[¶2619.1] Registration in the Principal Register

Registration provides the following protection:

(1) Constructive notice of claim of ownership;

(2) Prima facie evidence of the validity of the registration, the registrant's ownership of the mark, and the registrant's exclusive right to the use of the mark, subject to any conditions and limitations that may be stated in the registration; and

(3) The right to prevent importation of goods bearing an infringing mark.

[¶2619.2] Registration in the Supplemental Register

Although registration here gives none of the above protection, it does give the registrant:

(1) The right to sue in the federal courts and statutory remedies;

(2) Possible right of registration in a foreign country whose laws require prior registration in the home country; and

(3) Protection against registration by another of the same or a confusingly similar mark in either register.

The Lanham Act requires any person opposing the registration of a trademark by the principal register to file a verified opposition (15 USC §1063). Disposition of the dispute is handled by a Trademark Trial and Appeal Board (15 USC §1067).

[¶2620]   HOW TO PRESERVE EXCLUSIVE RIGHTS IN A TRADEMARK

Rights in a trademark are first acquired through *use*—i.e., by selling the product with the mark affixed either to the product or to its container. If the mark is to be registered, it must be used in interstate commerce, so the product should be shipped to a customer in another state.

Keep a record of the first use of the trademark. The following will help substantiate the use:

➤ A copy of the invoice. The invoice must show the trademark followed by the generic description of the product.

➤ The bill of lading signed by the carrier.

➤ A letter from the buyer stating he received the product and mentioning the trademark.

This first use of the mark doesn't mean that exclusive rights have been acquired. Someone else may have been using it before; no search can guarantee that you are the first user. Therefore, don't start extensive selling and advertising campaigns until initial test sales leave you reasonably sure there's no infringement and as a result, the mark won't have to be abandoned.

After the first use, continued and proper use of the mark is necessary to establish your exclusive rights. What constitutes "proper" use? The following checklist may provide some help:

➤ Use the trademark as an adjective only to modify the *generic name* of the product, and at least once on every page. Don't separate the trademark and the generic name with another word or any punctuation.

➤ Use the mark in a distinctive way: that is, different type, italics, capitals, within quotation marks, or in some way to make it more conspicuous than the other words preceding and following it.

➤ Use of the mark must be consistent. Once adopted, the mark must be continuously used.

[¶2621]   TRADEMARK SEARCHES

In order to minimize the possibility of opposition or conflict, a trademark search may be made before applying for registration. Most searches are run in the Patent Office. Word marks are classified on an alphabetical basis. Nonword marks are classified according to a system of symbol classification. There are two main locations or collections. The first comprises subsisting and expired registrations and the second published and pending registrations. The search system is not without serious deficiencies: (1) it doesn't cover prior unregistered marks; (2) the classification system is alphabetical and not phonetic and doesn't take into account synonyms and foreign equivalents; (3) it doesn't cover applications abandoned before publication; and (4) it doesn't show current use or status of the mark.

Because of the weaknesses or deficiencies in the classification system, an effective search requires skill and imagination on the part of the searcher, takes time, and is apt to be fairly expensive. Do not be taken in by those advertising "searches" at "low, low" prices.

The Patent Office maintains records of assignments of registered marks and pending applications by which ownership of marks or of applications may be searched.

If an owner is to effectively protect his mark against dilution and be in a position to oppose published application for marks, he must maintain a continuous search of the *Official Gazette,* which is published by the Patent Office and lists registered trademarks.

Searches such as those discussed above are best done by trademark specialists. There is one type of search that the general practitioner can make and that is via the trademark section of *Shepard's United States Citations, Patents & Trademarks,* which contains a reference to every trademark litigated or mentioned in any state or federal case.

[¶2622]   APPLICATION FOR TRADEMARK REGISTRATION

An application for registration must be filed in the name of the owner of the mark. It should give details as to a variety of matters including: the date of the applicant's first use of the mark as a trademark on or in connection with goods specified in the application; the date of the first use of the mark in interstate commerce, specifying the nature of the commerce; the manner in which the mark is used in connection with the goods; and the class of merchandise according to the official classification if known to the applicant. It must also contain various averments as to ownership and right to use the mark. Further, it must be signed and verified and must include a drawing of the mark, five specimens or facsimiles, and the required filing fee. There are special rules for foreign applicants. The Patent Office will supply printed forms of applications for (1) individuals, (2) firms, or (3) corporations or associations.

The drawing must be a substantially exact representation of the mark as actually used. (If the mark is incapable of representation by drawing then the application must describe it.) Regulations cover such matters as the type of paper and ink, the size of the sheets and margins, the heading, the character of the lines, the use of linings for showing color, and how the drawings are to be shipped. The Patent Office will make drawings when possible, at the applicant's request and expense.

The five specimens should be duplicates of actually used labels, tags, containers, or displays or portions thereof if flat and not larger than the size of the drawing. If specimens can't be furnished (due to the mode of applying the mark or using it or the nature of the mark), then a photograph or other acceptable reproduction not larger than the size of the drawing may be used. If a disc recording is to be registered special regulations apply.

If on examination of the application and the accompanying papers it appears that the applicant is entitled to have his mark registered in the Principal Register, it will be published in the *Official Gazette* and will be subject to opposition by any person who believes he'll be damaged, a period of 30 days after publication being provided for filing opposition. If the Patent Office finds a conflict between two co-pending applications, it determines which applicant is entitled to register. If there's no notice of opposition and no interference, a certificate of registration will be issued in due course.

[¶2623] ASSIGNABILITY OF TRADEMARKS

Trademarks are not readily assignable, since their existence is dependent upon their connection with the business or product for which they are used. When a business using a trademark is sold or assigned, the continued use of the trademark must be for an item substantially similar to the one for which it was used by the assignor. In addition, if there is a sale of a business having a trademark registered under the Lanham Act, the assignment of such a trademark is regulated by the Act (15 USC §1060).

Trademarks or trade names representing "personal care and skill of a certain individual" are usually not assignable, for the obvious reason that the assignee cannot claim to possess the assignor's personal care and skill.

[¶2624] ABANDONMENT OF THE TRADEMARK

Failure to use a trademark or trade name may result in its abandonment under common law. Under the Lanham Act, nonuse of a registered mark for two consecutive years is prima facie abandonment (15 USC §1127).

[¶2625] SOME PRACTICAL CONSIDERATIONS IN THE SELECTION OF A TRADEMARK

Trademark registration may be a matter of law, but trademark selection is a business judgment, best left to specialists in advertising and marketing. Although registration is not obligatory, anticipate future need when making the original trademark selection and avoid adopting a mark that will be refused registration. The following checklist indicates some trademarks that can pose a problem:

➤ Name, portrait, or signature of a living person without his consent.

➤ Name, portrait, or signature of a deceased U.S. President during the life of his widow, without her consent.

➤ Flag or coat of arms of the United States, any state, municipality, or foreign nation.

➤ A mark that is merely descriptive of the goods, or deceptively misdescriptive.

➤ A mark that when applied to the goods is primarily geographically descriptive or deceptively misdescriptive of the goods.

➤ A mark that is primarily merely a surname.

➤ A mark that resembles a trademark previously registered or used by another and not abandoned, if its use is likely to cause confusion or mistake or to deceive purchasers.

➤ A mark that disparages or falsely suggests a connection with persons living or dead, institutions, beliefs, or national symbols, or brings them into disrepute, or contempt.

➤ A mark that is immoral, deceptive, or scandalous.

A mark can be registered even though it is merely descriptive, geographically descriptive, or is primarily a surname, if it has become distinctive of the registrant's goods in commerce. Five years of exclusive and continuous use prior to filing application may be accepted by the Commissioner of Patents and Trademarks as prima facie evidence that the mark has become distinctive. Marks that are unregistrable because of the other prohibitions noted above can never become registrable as distinctive.

[¶2626] CORPORATE NAME STATUTES

Trade name value may inhere in a corporate name or the name of a product. A corporate name may be protected by the creation of inactive corporations in the states in the market area. The name of a product may be protected by incorporating it in a trademark that is used and registered.

Corporate name statutes grant only limited protection. They merely insure that the name will be protected against subsequent adoption as a corporate name by another entity within the state and against granting of permission to a foreign corporation to do business in that state under that corporate name. The usual corporate name section grants no protection against use of the same name as a trade name or mark; rather, the corporation must seek its relief under the nonstatutory precedents available to it in the state law of unfair competition. Further, such statutes do not purport to protect a corporate trade name against names used by unincorporated businesses. Apart from these procedures, judicial protection of business names has developed as a part of the overall law of unfair competition.

[¶2627] FICTITIOUS NAME STATUTES

The vast majority of states have enacted a fictitious name statute in one form or another. Generally, it provides that one doing business under an assumed or fictitious name must file certain information in affidavit form in each county where business is transacted and, in addition, may require other acts on the part of the user calculated to inform the public of the actual ownership of the business. Some of these statutes apply by their terms to corporate trade names; some that do not have been construed to apply to corporations when transacting business under names other than their corporate names.

The purpose of these statutes is universally recognized to be the prevention of fraud by providing potential customers, and more particularly potential creditors, with information about those with whom they are dealing. Whether or not sanctions are enforced to a degree sufficient to compel compliance with a particular statute, it is apparent that no substantive protection is sought to be given to a name registered or certified under its terms.

[¶2628] PROTECTION OF IDEAS AND SECRETS

Protection of ideas and secrets is an integral part of commercial practice. Major problems arise in connection with ideas or accumulations of information that are not patentable but are trade secrets. The protection of an idea or secret involves not only the safeguarding of its commercial value, but also the protection of both the creator of the idea and the person to whom the idea is submitted.

Here are some initial observations regarding protection of ideas and secrets:

(1) A concept cannot be copyrighted.

(2) Copyright—statutory or common law—protects only methods of expression, the word or symbol used.

(3) Pure ideas are free for all—only when the pure idea is converted into a property right is it protected.

[¶2629] CONVERTING THE PURE IDEA INTO A PROTECTABLE INTEREST

In order for a pure idea to be a protectable property interest, two initial steps must be taken:

(1) The idea must be original or established as such. Although there are not really any truly original ideas, the idea must be established as being *different.*

(2) The idea must be reduced to concrete form. This means putting it down on paper or in some other concrete form like a model or projection. The more detail in the concrete form, the better. If it is an advertising idea, if should be

developed into a campaign. If it is an entertainment idea, it should be developed into a script.

[¶2630] UNSOLICITED IDEAS FROM OUTSIDERS

Merely listening to an idea submitted by an outsider may place the listener and his or her business under an obligation to compensate the outsider if the idea is subsequently used, even though the listener may have been developing the same idea concurrently and independently. In order to avoid possible litigation, certain precautionary measures should be taken when dealing with the ideas of persons outside the business.

In the case of inventions and technical improvements, the most satisfactory way for both the inventor and the corporation to be protected from litigation and misunderstanding is for the inventor to obtain a patent on his invention. This will clearly establish the inventor's rights and will establish a firm basis on which to negotiate with companies that may wish to use or develop the invention. But the inventor may not be able to or may not wish to patent the invention for a variety of reasons: (1) he or she may be the owner of the trade secret but not the actual inventor of it; (2) he or she may not be able to show the novelty, utility, and invention that are necessary to obtain a patent; or (3) he or she may wish to keep the invention secret.

A corporation that has invited an inventor to discuss an idea or development with the intent of purchasing it receives such a disclosure in confidence. Therefore, the corporation cannot use the idea without buying it, and if it does use it without the inventor's permission, it will be liable for the profits made from the invention.

Following are some points for a company to keep in mind when dealing with outside inventors:

➤ Prepare a form letter responding to volunteers. When an offer to disclose an idea or invention is received by the company, a properly worded letter to the suggester will help prevent liability. The courts have held that where the company makes certain stipulations or lays down certain conditions subject to which it will accept the disclosure, the inventor is then bound by these conditions.

➤ Require the person submitting the idea to sign a statement indicating that he or she agrees to stipulated conditions along these lines:

(a) In taking any suggestion or idea under consideration we assume no obligation of any kind.

(b) We will not receive any submitted material in confidence, we will not establish a confidential relationship with anyone in respect to such material, and we make no guarantee of secrecy. You agree that in consideration of our examining your idea, we may freely use and communicate it to others without any liability to you. You agree to release us from responsibility or connection with your suggestion or liability because of use of any part thereof except such liability as may arise under valid patents now or hereafter issued to you.

(c) We will not consider ideas submitted from outside the United States unless a United States patent application has been filed.

(d) If the idea you have submitted is found to be of no interest to us, we will so inform you. However, we assume no obligation to inform you of the reasons for our action.

(e) If the idea appears to be of interest to us, we may enter into negotiations to explore the possibility of acquiring rights. No obligation is assumed by the company unless or until a formal written contract has been entered into and the obligation shall be only such as is expressed in the formal written contract.

(f) It is necessary for us to retain a complete record of the matter submitted and, therefore, it must be submitted in writing. Since material may become lost or mislaid in transit between the submitter and the company or between various departments of the company, no obligation can be assumed by us for the safekeeping of submitted matter.

[¶2631] LICENSING "KNOW-HOW"

The following checklist is designed to highlight the important considerations involved in dealing with licensing "know-how."

➤ *Reduce Know-How to Tangible Form:* When know-how is being transferred or licensed, it should be reduced to tangible form. This frequently has to be accomplished by careful and sometimes exhaustive definition. The elements of know-how must be detailed, including such things as plans, calculations, design sheets, design data, manuals, drawings, processes and materials, performance and purchasing specifications, test data, operating instructions, assistance in selecting factory sites, supplying engineers and technicians for installing machinery, assistance in purchase of machinery, technical service bulletins, special assistance by engineers and other technicians, architectural assistance (factory layouts and provisions and training of key personnel).

➤ *Limitations:* If the transferor or licensor cannot or does not wish to supply know-how in a particular area of his knowledge, that fact should be spelled out.

➤ *Reciprocal Rights:* Are licensor and licensee to have reciprocal rights to all improvements during the period of the agreement, or will there be additional or cross-royalty arrangements?

➤ *Where and by Whom Will Know-How Be Used?* To what product is know-how to be applied? Is it available to licensee's subsidiaries, sublicensees, and subcontractors? Who has the obligation to insure that royalties are paid?

➤ *Exclusivity:* Is the license exclusive, or does the licensor have the right to license others? It may be desirable to restrict the right to license to organizations that by the nature of their business or their location, are not in competition with the original licensee.

➤ *Secrecy:* When the know-how involves information that is considered a trade secret, the agreement should spell out the parties' understanding with respect to procedures for maintenance of trade secret status. A procedure for placing the obligation on employees of the licensee to maintain the trade secret should also be included.

➤ *Return of Information:* Provision for termination in the agreement should call for the return of all copies of plans, drawings, and specifications delivered in connection with the license. The licensee should be under an obligation to stop using the know-how acquired under the agreement. In some cases, this may mean that activities in the field have to be stopped.

➤ *Personnel:* If personnel is provided, the agreement should clearly specify the number, the time limits within which personnel is to be made available, and who will pay the personnel during the term of the agreement, including the obligation of travel, living expenses, etc.

➤ *Minimums:* When a license of know-how is based on a sales royalty, the licensor will generally look for some form of minimum, or in the absence of a minimum license fee, it will seek an obligation on the part of the licensee to achieve a minimum level of promotion.

➤ *Duration:* Generally, technological know-how has a life of about five years; after that time it becomes obsolete. When a royalty arrangement is involved, the licensor should avoid an arrangement that can be construed as payment for a patent after the patent has expired.

➤ *Restrictive Covenants:* Know-how and trade secrets that have been licensed should be safeguarded by restrictive covenants whereby the licensee agrees not to divulge trade secrets to others or use them personally after the license expires. This restrictive covenant can also prohibit disclosure to other than indicated personnel in the licensee's organization. Generally, this type of clause is subject to enforcement through injunctions.

➤ *Know-How of Trade Secret Must Have Value:* A license that transfers know-how of little or no value together with the licensor's covenant not to compete, export, or trade in the licensee's territory is, in effect, an agreement by the licensor to keep out of the licensee's market. The licensor will be paid royalties for abiding by these terms, but such a license would probably violate the antitrust laws. For this reason, some price tag should be put on the know-how transferred, or there should at least be records to prove the value of this intangible asset.

➤ *Foreign Licenses:* If foreign manufacture and distribution are licensed to a foreign concern, it is customary to base royalties on a percentage of net sales or gross sales. They can also be based on units produced, units installed, or sale price per item. The royalty clause can further be used to keep the foreign licensee in line. For example, increased production can be stimulated by a royalty clause reducing royalties after a certain maximum production is reached. The royalty clause should be geared so that if the licensee over-steps his market, underproduces, or undersells, he must pay higher royal-ties. There should be a minimum royalty due per year to check the occa-sional foreign licensee who takes the license to prevent foreign competition in his own market.

➤ *Foreign Currency:* Difficult to draft, this clause should take account of hard or soft currency in the country involved.

➤ *Default:* Protection against nonpayment and other defaults can be covered by a clause giving the licensor the right to terminate the license, with an immediate cessation of rights as to trademarks, names, and patents when the violation occurs. When know-how has been licensed, return of all trade secrets, processes, records, etc., should be required. As a protection against default, make sure the license agreement has been drafted to satisfy all local requirements as to notarization, recording, translation, etc., so that it will be enforceable in a local court. If trademarks, patents, or copyrights are involved, local registration laws should be complied with at the outset.

[¶2632] PROTECTION OF TRADE SECRETS

"A trade secret may consist of any formula, pattern, device, or compilation of information . . . used in one's business, and which gives him an opportunity to obtain an advantage over competitors who do not know or use it" (Restatement of Torts §757, Comment b, 1939).

[¶2633] WHAT QUALIFIES AS A TRADE SECRET?

Section 757 of the Restatement of Torts says:

"The subject matter of a trade secret must be secret. Matters of public knowl-edge or of general knowledge in an industry cannot be appropriated by one as his secret. Matters which are completely disclosed by the goods which one markets cannot be his secret. Substantially, a trade secret is known only in the particular business in which it is used. It is not requisite that only the proprietor of the busi-ness know it. He may, without losing his protection, communicate it to employees involved in its use. He may likewise communicate it to others pledged to secrecy. Others may also know of it independently, as, for example, when they have dis-covered the process or formula by independent invention and are keeping it secret. Nevertheless, a substantial element of secrecy must exist, so that, except by the use of improper means, there would be difficulty in acquiring the information. An exact definition of a trade secret is not possible. Some factors to be considered in determining whether given information is one's trade secret are: (1) the extent to which the information is known outside of his business; (2) the extent to which it is known by employees and others involved in his business; (3) the extent of measures taken by him to guard the secrecy of the information; (4) the value of the information to him and to his competitors; (5) the amount of effort or money expended by him in developing the information; (6) the ease or difficulty with which the information could be properly acquired or duplicated by others."

[¶2634] TRADE SECRETS AND COVENANTS NOT TO COMPETE

As part of the written contract of employment or in a separate agreement, the employer should have employees sign an agreement not to compete with the company after they leave its employ. Key employees, such as officers, executives, supervisors, engineers, scientists, and salespersons, may be asked to sign an employment contract that incorporates the restrictions against competing after leaving the job, in an agreed area and for a specified time. Restrictions on other possible forms of competition, such as the use of trade secrets and customer lists, should also be included if applicable. Employees having less important positions may agree to such restrictions as part of their employment applications or in a separate agreement. In any case, the clause or separate agreement is usually referred to as a "covenant not to compete."

Here's a checklist for drafting a covenant that will stand up legally:

➤ Make sure the terms of the agreement are clear and unambiguous.

➤ The restrictions as to area and time should be reasonable and not greater than what is required for protection.

➤ Do not include in the restrictions an area in which the company has no business or in which the employee has never worked.

➤ If applicable, show on the face of the contract that the employee is entrusted with trade secrets, confidential information, or is in a position of close contact with customers.

➤ On the face of the contract show the relationship between the prohibited activities and their necessity for the protection of customers or trade secrets.

➤ Do not phrase the restriction in such a way as to make it an absolute prohibition against working for a competitor in any capacity, or which would force the employee to change his profession or trade in order to keep comparable employment.

[¶2635] PROTECTING CUSTOMER LISTS

Customer contacts are vital to most businesses. A valued employee will generally work directly with the customers. If the employee is hired by a competitor or sets up a competing business, it may be easy for him or her to persuade customers to switch companies.

An employee can solicit the customers of the former employer, unless the list itself is considered to be confidential information. The list is confidential if the names of the customers could have been learned by the employee only through his or her employment. This would include lists that have been assembled on the basis of past selling experience, lists combining information on customers with product purchased and price, and, generally, lists that have been accumulated as the result of much time and effort.

The term "secret list" would not include a list of firms or individuals that could be compiled from a directory or from some other source that anyone could examine. If the employee knew the customers before going to work for the original employer, there can be no accusation of learning about them only as a result of employment.

[¶2636] SCOPE OF COPYRIGHT LAW

The current copyright law, P.L.94-553 (90 Stat. 2541-2602), which has been in effect since 1978,completely revised all aspects of artistic and literary property and put many works into copyright that were not afforded protection before.

The copyright legislation is divided into eight different chapters beginning with a discussion of the subject matter and scope of copyright. Chapter 2 covers copyright ownership and transfer. Chapter 3 extends copyright duration. Chapter 4 deals with copyright notice, deposit, and registration requirements; Chapter 5, with infringement of copyright and remedial action; Chapter 6 with manufacturing requirements as well as limitations on the importation of certain copyrighted materials, and noncopyrighted materials. Chapter 7 is essentially administrative and deals with the general responsibilities and organization of the copyright offices. The final chapter creates a copyright royalty tribunal that has four essential purposes: (a) to maximize the availability of creative works to the public, (b) to afford copyright creators a fair return for their creative works and to give copyright users a fair income under existing economic conditions, (c) to help balance the interest of copyright owners and copyright users, and (d) to minimize any disruptive impact on industries and generally prevailing industry practices effectively regulated by changes in the copyright law.

Under the Berne Convention Implementation Act, P.L. 100-568 (10/31/88), the United States joins the 77 countries that are signatories to the Berne Convention of 1886. Berne implementation is extremely important to U.S. publishers who sell their books outside the United States because, to achieve full international copyright protection, they were forced to publish a book simultaneously in all of the Berne Convention countries.

An important change in practice is that a U.S. copyright in a published work can exist even without registration or display of a copyright notice. As a compromise between the Berne practice (under which registration and other formalities are not required) and earlier U.S. practice, registration remains a prerequisite to a copyright infringement action involving a work published in the United States; it is not a prerequisite if the work was published elsewhere. Inclusion of a copyright notice is not required as an element of an infringement suit (even for U.S.-source works). However, it is still useful to include a copyright notice to preclude the defense of innocent infringement. The change in practice will eliminate problems such as those involved in *Business Trends Analysts Inc. v. Freedonia Group Inc.*,[27] in which the infringement occurred before the copyright was registered, and therefore damages were limited to actual damages or the infringer's profit (including good will and market recognition reaped by the infringer, as long as these are factually quantifiable, not merely speculative).

The Berne Convention Implementation Act extends explicit copyright protection to architectural plans. It was hoped that implementation would lead to the adoption of explicit "droit morale" (moral right) provisions by the United States, to deal with situations in which a work is distorted by a purchaser, or in which the artist earns a small sum for creating a work and the buyer reaps a windfall by selling it after the artist's reputation has increased. However, Congress decided that the United States already protects creators adequately, so no new droit morale provisions were added to U.S. law. However, effective 6/1/91 certain droit morale protections were extended to works of visual art (but not works for hire) by the Visual Artists Rights Act. The artist can either claim authorship or have his or her name removed from work he or she did not create, or that has been mutilated or distorted, under the "right of attribution." The "right of integrity" permits the artist to prevent intentional distortions of original work that are prejudicial to the artist. As of 12/1/90, under the Architectural Works Protection Act, it is possible to copyright an actual building, in addition to copyrighting the building's plans.

Under the Copyright Remedy Clarification Act,[28] states, instrumentalities of states, and state officers and employees acting in their official capacity can be guilty of copyright infringement or infringement of exclusive rights in microchip mask works to the same extent as any other party, and can be subject to the same penalties.

The Copyright Renewal Act of 1992, P.L. 102-307, grants an automatic 47-year renewal of copyrights granted between 1/1/63 and 12/31/77, although it is still considered preferable for the renewal to be registered. P.L. 102-492 makes it clear that fair use can be made of an unpublished work, based on the same factors that determine whether use of a published work was fair or infringing. P.L. 102-561 amends 18 U.S.C. Sec. 2319(b) to provide felony penalties for infringement of any copyrighted work (not just a sound recording, film, or audiovisual work): up to five years' imprisonment, and/or a maximum fine of twice the gross gain or $250,000 ($500,000 if the offender is an organization), for making ten or more copies of a copyrighted work. P.L. 102-563, the Audio Home Recording Act, adds a Chapter 10 to the Copyright Act, imposing royalties on the sale and importation of Digital Audio Tape recorders and recorded media, but making it clear that DAT home taping of either digital or analog recordings will constitute fair use.

The copyright of a work made "for hire" belongs to the employer, not the employee; the vexing question of what constitutes a work for hire was addressed by the Supreme Court in 1989.[29] The test is whether the work was done by an employee or independent contractor, assessed by traditional tests such as ownership of tools, studio, hiring of assistants, availability or absence of employee benefits, and the creator's ability to set his or her own working hours. Control over the final product is *not* determinative. (This result makes sense in light of the fact that the patron or commissioner of an artwork generally indicates what subject matter and treatment will be required. A contrary result would make all artists, writers, composers, etc., employees unless they did all their work "on spec" in the hope of finding a buyer for the finished product, a more discouraging and inefficient process than doing at least a proportion of work to the specifications of those who have indicated a willingness to pay for the finished product.)

[¶2637] NEW COPYRIGHT DURATION

Works created after January 1, 1978 are given statutory copyright protection for the life of the author plus additional 50 years. (This corresponds to the time frame utilized in the Berne Convention.) On works that are done "for hire" as well as for anonymous and pseudonymous works, the new copyright term will be 75 years from the time of publication, or 100 years from creation, whichever is shorter. For those works already accorded copyright protection, the new law will retain the present term of 28 years for the date of first publication, but in the case of renewal the holding period for the second term is increased to 47 years. Copyrights in their first term must be renewed in order to receive the full 75-year maximum term permitted them by law. Copyrights in their second term between December 31, 1976 and December 31, 1977 are automatically extended up to the 75-year maximum period. Unpublished works that were in existence on the day the new copyright law went into effect are also covered. If they are not yet in the public domain, they generally will have the life plus 50 years protection. If a work has gone into public domain, there is no restoration of copyright protection available under the new law.

[¶2638] EXTENDED RENEWAL TERMS—TRANSFER OF RIGHTS

Under the original copyright legislation, when the first 28-year term of a copyright was completed, the renewal copyright reverted to the author or a specified beneficiary. Except for works that were in their first term of copyright protection on January 1, 1978, this renewal feature was dropped. Instead, the law provides that the author or certain specified heirs may terminate rights that they have transferred "at any time during a period of 5 years beginning at the end of 56 years from the date copyright was originally secured," or January 1, 1978, whichever is later.

[¶2639] NOTICE OF COPYRIGHT

The innocent omissions or errors in the placement of the notice of copyright on the published work will not immediately result in forfeiture of copyright, and can be corrected within certain time limits. However, in such cases, innocent infringement resulting from omission or error will be shielded from liability.

[¶2640] EXCLUSIVE USE OF COPYRIGHT

Generally, a copyright holder is entitled to the exclusive use of all material copyrighted. This includes permission for the owner to reproduce copyrighted works in any manner; prepare derivative works; lend, lease, rent, or transfer ownership; and perform or display them publicly—subject, however, to a number of exceptions set forth in the paragraphs below.

The Supreme Court decided *Stewart v. Abend*.[30] *Stewart* is actor James Stewart, and the case involves the Hitchcock film *Rear Window*; the issue is infringement of the Cornell Woolrich short story on which the film was based. The Ninth Circuit ruled that a derivative copyright protects only the new material in the derivative work, not the material deriving from the underlying work. Hence, an author's assignment of rights in the renewal term (this is a case stemming from a pre-1976 assignment, so a renewable term of years, not the author's life plus fifty years, is involved) is ineffective if it is made before the statutory period for renewal, and the author dies in the interim. The Ninth Circuit's conclusion was that reissuance of the Hitchcock film may infringe the copyright on the short story.

The Supreme Court affirmed, finding that, where an author dies before the copyright in a work can be renewed, an assignee has only a mere expectancy unless renewal rights are also transferred by the author's successor. The author had no successor, so the distribution of the derivative work premised on an assignment of renewal rights by Woolrich's executor constituted a violation of the copyright on the underlying short story.

Copyright registration (and not filing of a UCC-1) is the sole manner in which a security interest in the copyright of a film can be registered.[31]

Copyright Act §304(c) permits an author or author's surviving spouse to terminate a copyright assignment made "other than by will." A songwriter's widow was permitted to use this provision[32] where the songwriter assigned the copyright (and renewal right) of certain songs to his publisher, which duly renewed the copyrights. The songwriter later signed a will that purported to create a testamentary trust including the copyrights. However, because at the time of the will he had no interest in those copyrights, §304(c) was available to his widow.

[¶2641] FAIR USE

One of the most important exceptions to the exclusivity of the copyright is the principle of "fair use." Reproduction of materials for criticism, comment, news reporting, teaching (including multiple copies for classroom use), scholarship, or research is *not* infringement of copyright. In determining whether or not "fair use" is being abused, the Office of Copyright indicates that the following factors are to be considered: purpose and character of the use, the nature of the copyrighted work, the portion used in relation to the copyrighted work as a whole, and the effect of the use on the potential market for the product read.

Another aspect of derivative works fair use was examined in *Weissman v. Freeman*.[33] This held that a doctor is not entitled to list himself as a joint author of a paper prepared independently by his assistant, where the assistant did not consent to joint authorship attribution, merely because the doctor and assistant were joint authors of an earlier work of which the paper was a separately copyrightable derivative work. (In a sense, the case also involves droit morale: the right of a creator to have his or her work attributed properly, without "dilution" by attribution to other, more famous individuals.)

The Supreme Court decide[34] that a telephone book merely giving subscribers' name, town, and telephone number is not original enough to be copyrighted, and consequently a competitor's use of the directory to prepare its own directory did not constitute infringement. Creating a data base for solicitation of possible advertisers for a "yellow pages" directory by using the telephone company's Yellow Pages, but imposing geographical and other elements of selection, does not violate the telephone company copyright in its own directory. The similarities result from necessary similarities in arranging data, and do not result from copying of the telephone company's original elements of selection or classification.[35]

The Southern District of New York was unpersuaded by a copy shop's argument that it was educational fair use to prepare "anthologies" of copyrighted material and sell them for classroom use; $510,000 in damages was awarded.[36] Texaco, Inc. was not permitted to assert a fair use defense when its employees copied articles from scientific and technical journals.[37]

A vulgar rap version of a copyrighted song (a license was applied for, but refused) was entitled to protection as a fair-use parody within the meaning of the Copyright Act of 1976, 17 U.S.C. §107. Parody, like any other comment and criticism, may claim fair use. While copying the original's first line of lyrics, the second composition departed markedly from the original lyrics and produced otherwise distinctive music.[38]

Leslie Nielsen's appearance in commercials as the "Coors Light Beer Rabbit," allegedly a parody of the "Energizer Bunny," was held by the Northern District of Illinois to constitute fair use. Energizer appealed, and the case was settled pending appeal.[39]

According to the Eleventh Circuit,[40] Cable News Network's copyright of its transmission as a compilation does not prohibit copying of pre-existing material compiled, thus rendering an injunction forbidding a monitoring service to copy "any part" of CNN newscasts invalid as overbroad and in conflict with the fair use provisions and the First Amendment.

Fair use does not extend to creating an unauthorized derivative work (an abridgment) by giving detailed summaries of the plots of individual episodes of a television series, where the level of detail exceeded that needed for comment or criticism, and could impair the market for authorized primary or derivative works based on the series.[41]

There is no copyright infringement when a store (even a store with several chain outlets) uses ordinary equipment of a type found in homes to play radio music in the stores. This does not constitute a "broadcast," so charges cannot be imposed for such a "performance."[42]

[¶2642] LIBRARY REPRODUCTION

Single photocopies of certain items may be reproduced by libraries and archives for noncommercial purposes without violating the copyright law or infringing on the exclusivity otherwise mandated by law. In order to be innocent of infringement, however, the libraries or archives must open their collections to the public or to all persons doing research in a particular field. Notice of copyright on the reproduction by the library or archive is essential. Wholesale photocopying of periodicals is not permitted, though reproductions of individual articles may be.

Libraries are permitted to copy all or a substantial part of a copyrighted work that is out of print and cannot be obtained at a reasonable price. Libraries are also permitted to make multiple copies that would otherwise be impermissible, as part of an interlibrary loan process.

[¶2643] MUSIC RECORDING RIGHTS

Unauthorized duplication of sound recordings is prohibited, though no "performance right" is created under the law. Juke box operators, presently exempt from royalty payments, will be subject to an annual royalty fee (currently $50, but adjustable based on changes in the consumer price index), payable to the Register of Copyrights for distribution by the copyright royalty tribunal to the copyright owners.

[¶2644] GOVERNMENT PUBLICATIONS

Government publications may not be copyrighted. The government may, however, hold and receive copyrights transferred to it by assignment. For those wishing to compete with the government imprinting operations, note that the public printer of the United States is required to sell "to persons who may apply" additional or duplicate stereotype or electrotype plates from which government publications are printed, at a price not to exceed the cost of composition plus 10%. Because of congressional administrative action requiring all documents from the Government Printing Office to be sold at a price that is not more than 10% above actual cost, it is possible to compete with the government for the sale of their documents.

[¶2645] CABLE TELEVISION

CATV is subject to a provision in the copyright law that provides for compulsory licensing, as well as for payment of certain royalties for secondary transmission of copyrighted works. Royalties are paid to the Register of Copyrights for distribution to the copyright owners by the copyright royalty tribunal. (The copyright royalty tribunal was created for the basic purpose of determining the reasonableness of royalty rates and the distribution of statutory royalty fees.) Periodically, the holder of a copyright may be able to petition the tribunal for an adjustment in the royalty rate. Under the law, the tribunal is able to determine whether or not the applicant has a significant interest in the royalty rate in which an adjustment is requested, and if so, it is possible for an adjustment to be ordered.

[¶2646] NEW TECHNOLOGY AND COPYRIGHT

The Supreme Court has ruled that the sale of videocassette recorders to the public does *not* constitute contributory infringement (by VCR manufacturers and distributors) of film studios'/filmmakers' copyrights. Findings revealed that the average member of the public uses a VCR principally to record a program he cannot view as it is being televised and then to watch it once at a later time. This practice, known as "time shifting," enlarges the television-viewing audience. It has not been proven that the practice impairs the commercial value of the filmmakers' copyrights or has created any likelihood of future harm. Furthermore, computer-colorized prints of black-and-white films can be registered (Copyright Office Notice Docket #RM 861A, 6/22/87).

Computer programs are protectable as literary works if they embody the programmer's expression of ideas, but the ideas themselves are not copyrightable (House Report #94-1476, Senate Report #94-473). Under the 1980 amendments to 17 U.S.C. §101, a computer program is copyrightable if it's a set of statements or instructions enabling a computer to perform the operations intended by the user.

In the context of computer programs, fair use means the creation of archival copies and limited modified copies of the program. Of course, this is a particularly difficult area to police.

Data bases can be copyrighted, but only as to new material, commentary, or original systems of organizations.

The Semiconductor Chip Protection Act of 1984 provides protection for the "mask work" (pattern of materials added or removed in manufacturing a computer chip).

The issue of whether a program's "look and feel" (arrangement of computer screens; the way in which users are directed to perform operations) is copyrightable awaits final resolution.

Just as it has been held that using a VCR to "time shift" is not a public performance, it has been held that watching rented videodisks in a hotel room is not a public performance.[43] Therefore, the hotel's practice of placing videodisk players in hotel rooms, and renting disks to guests for their own entertainment, is not a violation of the copyright on the underlying film. Nevertheless, the Supreme Court held that the studios, although unsuccessful in their suit, were still making a reasonable attempt to enforce what they perceived to be their rights at a time when the state of the law was unsettled. Therefore, they were entitled to *Noerr-Pennington* immunity from the hotel's counterclaim that the suit was a cloak for an attempt at monopolization and conspiracy to restrain trade.[44]

Neither trademark, copyright, nor moral right considerations was enough to impel the grant of a preliminary injunction in *Paramount Pictures Corp. v. Video Broadcasting Systems Inc.*[45] against a distributor's practice of adding commercials to the beginning of a videocassette without the consent of the movie company holding the copyright on the film. This was not deemed to be the creation of an unauthorized derivative work.

Both these questions could be addressed by adopting a broader statutory droit morale: the "droit de suite" ("follow-on right") would give copyright proprietors a share of the aftermarket use of the copyrighted work (as well as giving authors a royalty on library borrowing of their work); moral right legislation could also deal with problems such as "colorization" against the will of the movie's screenwriter, director, producer, or other "auteur" or addition of commercials and trailers to the video version of a theatrical film.

With respect to computers, it has been held[46] that a computer program copying the Lotus 1-2-3 user interface infringes Lotus' copyright even though the protected code itself was not copied. However, the Massachusetts District Court found that certain elements of a computer program are not protectable: for instance, the use of a certain combination of keystrokes to execute an operation (given the limited number of keys available) or the use of a grid of cells to display information (part of the uncopyrightable "spreadsheet idea").

In 1992, Atari Corp. was granted a copyright on its Breakout video game, on the grounds that even a slight amount of creativity (such as was shown in the game's "simple geometric shapes and coloring") will support copyright registration.[47]

Loading copyrighted software into a computer's Random Access Memory (RAM) is a copyright infringement, because it creates a tangible, fixed (and unauthorized) copy.[48] If a software licensee allows an authorized third party to use a licensed, copyrighted computer program, the copyright holder is entitled to bring state law breach of contract claims; the issues involved are not limited to, or preempted by, federal copyright law.[49]

[¶2647] FEES

The following is a list of the charges made by the Register of Copyrights:

Registration	$10
Renewals	$6

Assignments	$10 for first 6 pp. (and only one title); $0.50 for each additional pp. or title
Searches	$10/hr
Disclosure Statement	$10 for first 6 pp. (and only one title); $1 for each additional pp. or title

Fees payable to Register of Copyrights.

Under P.L. 101-318, the fee to register a copyright has been raised from $10 to $20. The statute permits adjustment of the fee every five years in conformity to the Consumer Price Index.

[¶2648] COPYRIGHTS OWNED BY A DECEDENT

Copyrights, artistic compositions, and literary and musical properties owned by their creator are noncapital assets (IRC §1221(3)(C)).

— ENDNOTES —

1. #89-243 58 LW 4838 (Sup.Ct. 6/18/90).

2. Section 271(d).

3. Platzer v. Sloan-Kettering Inst., 983 F.2d 1086 (2d Cir. 3/2/92), cert. denied 113 S.Ct. 1648.

4. Genentech Inc. v. Eli Lilly & Co., 62 LW 2080 (Fed.Cir. 7/1/93).

5. 16 USPQ 2d 1481 (D.Mass. 1990), amended 17 USPQ 2d 1711 (D.Mass. 1991).

6. Scripto-Tokai Corp. v. Gillette, 788 F.Supp. 439 (C.D. Cal. 3/20/92).

7. Cardinal Chemical Co. v. Morton Int'l Inc., #92-114, 113 S.Ct. 1967 (Sup.Ct. 5/17/93).

8. Inwood Labs Inc. v. Young, 723 F.Supp. 1523 (D.D.C. 5/12/89).

9. Unimed Inc. v. Quigg, 888 F.2d 826 (Fed.Cir. 10/23/89).

10. In re Mother Tucker's Food Experience (Canada) Inc., 925 F.2d 1402 (Fed.Cir. 2/5/91).

11. Serbin v. Ziebart Int'l Corp., 62 LW 2368 (3d Cir. 11/30/93); Guarino v. Sun Co., 891 F.Supp. 405 (D.N.J. 4/26/93).

12. Two Pesos v. Taco Cabana, #91-971, 112 S.Ct. 2753 (Sup.Ct. 6/26/92).

13. Ferrari SPA v. Roberts, 944 F.2d 1235 (6th Cir. 9/5/91) cert. denied 112 S.Ct. 3028.

14. Nor are punitive damages available under Lanham Act Section 35 for trademark infringement: Getty Petroleum Corp. v. Bartco Petroleum Corp., 858 F.2d 103 (2d Cir. 9/2/88).

15. Hard Rock Cafe Licensing Corp. v. Concession Services Inc., 955 F.2d 1143 (7th Cir. 2/4/92).

16. Electronic Laboratory Supply Co. v. Cullen, 977 F.2d 798 (3d Cir. 10/15/92).

17. George Basch Co. v. Blue Coral Inc., 968 F.2d 1532 (2d Cir. 6/30/92), cert. denied 113 S.Ct. 510.

18. Reebok Int'l Inc. v. Marnatech Enterprises, Inc., 23 USPQ 2d 1377 (9th Cir. 7/2/92).

19. 702 F.Supp. 1031 (2d Cir. 5/18/89).

20. 695 F.Supp. 198 (D. Md. 9/16/88).

21. 886 F.2d 490 (2d Cir. 9/5/89). Also see Rogers v. Grimaldi, 875 F.2d 994 (2d Cir. 1989).

22. Yamaha Corp. of America v. ABC Int'l Traders, 703 F.Supp. 1398 (C.D. Cal. 12/23/88).

23. Lever Brothers v. U.S., 877 F.2d 101 (D.C. Cir. 6/9/89); on remand, 1992 U.S. Dist. LEXIS 7876 (D.D.C. 1992), clarified 1991 U.S. Dist. LEXIS 7805.

24. Société des Produits Nestlé S.A. v. Casa Helvetia Inc., 982 F.2d 633 (1st Cir. 12/29/92).

25. Ferrero U.S. Inc. v. Ozak Trading Co., 935 F.2d 1281 (3d Cir. 12/19/90).

26. Shakespeare Co. v. Silstar Corp. of America, 62 LW 2337 (4th Cir. 11/15/93).

27. 887 F.2d 399 (2d Cir. 10/5/89).

28. P.L. 101-553, 11/15/90, 17 U.S.C. 101 note. Also see P.L. 101-318 (7/3/90) for a revised fee schedule for copyrights and for technical amendments.

29. Marco v. Accent Publishing Co. Inc., 23 USPQ 2d 1631 (3d Cir. 1992), discussed in Charles D. Ossola, "Work-for-Hire Debate Remains Heated Over Who Is 'Author' of Art," *Nat'l Law J.* 10/12/92 p. S2.

30. Grundberg v. Upjohn Co., 140 F.R.D. 459 (D.Utah 6/14/91).

31. National Peregrine Inc. v. Capitol Federal S&L Ass'n of Denver, 116 BR 194 (C.D. Cal. 6/28/90).

32. Larry Spier Inc. v. Bourne Co., 953 F.2d 774 (2d Cir. 1/9/92).

33. 868 F.2d 1313 (2d Cir. 1989), cert. den. #89-114.

34. Feist Publishers Inc. v. Rural Telephone Service Co., #89-1909; see 111 S.Ct. 1282 (Sup.Ct. 3/27/91).

35. Bell South Advertising & Publishing Corp. v. Donnelley Information Publishing Inc., 977 F.2d 1435 (11th Cir. 9/2/93).

36. Basic Books Inc. v. Kinko's Graphics Corp., 758 F.Supp. 1522 (S.D.N.Y. 3/28/91).

37. American Geophysical Union v. Texaco Inc., 802 F.Supp. 1 (S.D.N.Y. 7/22/92). Also see Junda Woo, "Electronic Copying May Bring Lawsuits," *WSJ*

10/6/93 p. B12, discussing a $100,000 settlement in a case of computerized distribution of unauthorized copies of copyrighted newsletters.

38. Acuff Rose Music Inc. v. Campbell, 972 F.2d 1429 (6th Cir. 8/17/92), #92-1292, 113 S.Ct. 1642 (Sup.Ct. 3/7/94).

39. Eveready Battery Co. Inc. v. Adolph Coors Co., 765 F.Supp. 440 (N.D.Ill. 1991).

40. CNN v. Video Monitoring Services of America, Inc., 940 F.2d 1471 (11th Cir. 9/4/91).

41. Twin Peaks Productions Inc. v. Publications Int'l Limited, 61 LW 2794 (2d Cir. 6/7/93).

42. BMI v. Claire's Boutiques Inc., 949 F.2d 1482 (7th Cir. 12/11/91).

43. Columbia Pictures Industries Inc. v. Prof'l Real Estate Investors, 866 F.2d 278 (9th Cir. 1989).

44. Professional Real Estate Investors Inc. v. Columbia Pictures Industries Inc., #91-1043, 113 S.Ct. 1920 (Sup.Ct. 5/3/93).

45. 724 F.Supp. 808 (D. Kan. 10/11/89).

46. Lotus Software Devel. Corp. v. Paperback Software Int'l, 740 F.Supp. 37 (D. Mass. 6/28/90). Also see Apple Computer Inc. v. Microsoft Corp., 779 F.Supp. 133 (N.D. Cal. 8/7/92) ["desktop metaphor" of mini-screens and menu bars is not protectable; Microsoft products either did not infringe, or were protected by licensing agreement between Apple and Microsoft]; Lotus Development Corp. v. Borland Int'l Inc., 788 F.Supp. 78 (D.Mass. 7/31/92) [Extent of copying of non-functional, expressive elements of menu commands and command structure shows infringement of Lotus 1-2-3 spreadsheet by Borland Quattro spreadsheet].

47. See Paul M. Barrett, "Atari Corp. Wins Key Legal Victory in Copyright Case," *Wall Street J.* 11/23/92 p. B2. On video games, also see Lewis Galoob Toys Inc. v. Nintendo of America Inc., 964 F.2d 965 (9th Cir. 5/21/92) [device enhancing performance of video game, but not physically incorporating or altering the game, does not infringe game's copyright].

48. MAI Systems Corp. v. Peak Computer Inc., 991 F.2d 511 (9th Cir. 4/7/93).

49. National Car Rental System Inc. v. Computer Associates Int'l Inc., 991 F.2d 426 (8th Cir. 4/6/93).

— FOR FURTHER REFERENCE —

Bierce, William B., "New Strategies for Legal Protection of Computer Software," 26 *Law-Technology* 1 (Winter '93).

Brown, Stacy, "The Corporate Receipt Conundrum: Establishing Access in Copyright Infringement Actions," 77 *Minnesota L. Rev.* 1409 (June '93).

Cooley, Ronald B., "Overview and Statistical Study of the Law on Patent Damages," 75 *J. of the Patent and Trademark Office Society* 566 (July '93).

Farjami, Michael, "Protectable Trade Dress Without Secondary Meaning—On Second Thought," 13 *Entertainment L.J.* 381 (Winter '93).

Field, Thomas G. Jr., "Review of PTO Intramural Appeal Procedures," 33 *Idea* 117 (Winter '93).

Gerber, David A. and David Bender, "Courts Help Clear Up Legal Haze Regarding Gray Market Goods," *Nat. Law J.* 10/12/92, p. 55.

Glazier, Stephen C., "Personal Liability of Officers and Directors Regarding Patents and Copyrights," 21 *Int'l Business Lawyer* 323 (July-August '93).

Glenn, Martin and Dale M. Cendali, "Lotus Case Highlights Copyright Issues and High-Tech Problems," *Nat Law J.* 11/1/93, p. S17.

Ignatin, Gary R., "Let the Hackers Hack: Allowing the Reverse Engineering of Copyrighted Computer Programs to Achieve Compatibility," 140 *U. of Pennsylvania L. Rev.* 1999 (May '92).

Jones, Terri A., "Patenting Transgenic Animals," 17 *Vermont L. Rev.* 873 (Spring '93).

Keller, Bruce P., Alice Haemmerli and Abraham B. Hsuan, "National Laws Play a Role in International Protection," *Nat. L.J.* 12/14/92 p. 19.

Lazar, Bart A., "New Rulings Provide Ammunition in Fight Against Counterfeiters," *Nat. L.J.* 10/12/92, p. S13.

Leavitt, Richard A., "The 'Selling' of Patented Goods in Search of a Definition," 66 *Tulane L. Rev.* 1903 (June '92).

LeFevre, Karen Burke, "The Tell-Tale Heart: Determining Fair Use of Unpublished Texts," 55 *Law and Contemporary Problems* 153 (Spring '92).

Loewenson, Carl Jr. and Marta E. Nelson, "Congress Toughens Criminal Copyright Law," *N.Y.L.J.* 11/3/92 p. 1.

Losey, Ralph C., "Legal Protection of Computer Databases," 65 *Florida Bar J.* 80 (October '91).

Marchese, Christopher S., "Challenging Subject Matter Jurisdiction in Patent Infringement Suits," 61 *UMKC L. Rev.* 635 (Summer '93).

Neuner, Robert, "Trade Secret Protection for Computer Software," *N.Y.L.J.* 2/3/92 p. 3.

Ossola, Charles D., "Work-for-Hire Debate Remains Heated Over Who Is 'Author' of Art," *Nat. L.J.* 10/12/92, p. 52.

Perez, Daniel F., "Exploitation and Enforcement of Intellectual Property Rights," 10 *Computer Lawyer* 10 (August '93).

Phillips, Robyn L., "Determining if a Trade Dress Is Valid," 29 *Idaho L. Rev.* 456 (Spring '93).

Plant, David W., "Resolving Intellectual Property Disputes," *Nat L.J.* 12/29/93 p. 19.

Rubin, Harry, "Destined to Remain Grey: The Eternal Recurrence of Parallel Imports," 26 *International Lawyer* 597 (Fall '92).

Samuelson, Pamela, "Computer Programs, User Interfaces, and Section 102(b) of the Copyright Act of 1976," 55 *Law and Contemporary Problems* 311 (Spring '92).

Samuelson, Pamela and Robert J. Glushko, "Intellectual Property Rights for Digital Library and Hypertext Publishing Systems," 6 *Harvard J. of Law and Technology* 237 (Spring '93).

Schapiro, Louis A., "Copyright Law: E.C. Cases May Create Uncertainty," *Nat. L.J.* 2/24/92 p. 27.

Schwarz, Matthew H., "On Target With the Parody Defense to Copyright Infringement," 26 *Beverly Hills Bar Ass'n J.* 57 (Spring '92).

Stern, Richard H., "Copyright Infringement by Add-on Software," 24 *Intell. Prop. L. Rev.* 429 (1992 annual).

Tanenbaum, William A., "Copyright Protection Extended to Buildings," *Nat. L.J.* 2/24/92 p. 31.

Tanenbaum, William A. and William K. Wells, Jr., "Multimedia Works Require Broad Protection," *Nat. L.J.* 11/1/93 p. S11.

Yip, Philip, "Product and Process Patent Protection in Biotechnology," 17 *J. of Corporation Law* 659 (Spring '92).

Zuber, Joseph, "Do Artists Have Moral Rights?" 21 *J. of Arts Management & Law* 284 (Winter '92).

IRAs AND KEOGH PLANS

[¶2701] As discussed in Paragraph 1201 et seq., the Tax Code and ERISA have a great deal to say on the subject of what constitutes a qualified pension or profit-sharing plan; who can participate in such a plan; what benefits must be; what benefits can be provided; and the tax consequences of both contributions to the plan and the payment of benefits to retirees. However, those provisions refer to plans maintained by corporations for their employees.

There are additional mechanisms that employees can use to save for their own retirement (Individual Retirement Arrangements, comprising Individual Retirement Accounts and Individual Retirement Annuities) and that sole proprietors and partnerships can use to provide for the retirement of their owner-employees (Keogh plans). (A Keogh plan must be adopted by "an employer," so it is the partnership, rather than one or more partners, that adopts the plan—which can create problems if fewer than a majority of the partners want such a plan.)

If a Keogh plan is maintained by an unincorporated business that has common-law employees, the owner-employees must trade off the ability to provide for their own retirement against the obligation to do the same for their employees by making Keogh plan contributions for them, too. The Tax Equity and Fiscal Responsibility Act of 1982 more or less equalizes the treatment of Keogh plans and corporate plans. Therefore, the attorney creating a Keogh plan must be familiar with the qualified-plan rules for such matters as participation, vesting, funding, and contributions.

[¶2702] INDIVIDUAL RETIREMENT ARRANGEMENTS

Since 1981, anyone earning $2,000 or more in compensation has been permitted to make annual contributions of up to $2,000 to an Individual Retirement Arrangement (IRA). (Alimony is defined as compensation for this purpose.) A married couple, both of whom earn compensation over $2,000, is permitted contributions of up to $4,000; a married couple with only one earner is allowed to use the "spousal IRA" provisions to make contributions of up to $2,250 a year. The additional $250 spousal IRA deduction is available either if the spouse has no compensation for the year or an election is made to treat the low-income spouse as having no compensation. There is a 6% excise tax on contributions made in excess of the permitted amount.

The contribution can be made up to the due date of the return (but not up to the date of any extension obtained for filing the return). It's even permitted for the taxpayer to file his or her return, claiming any applicable IRA deduction, and *then* make the contribution (although an amended return must be filed if April 15 comes and goes without a contribution being made). Taxpayers who make contributions during the January 1–April 15 period must be careful to inform the IRA trustee whether the contribution is being made for the prior year (and thus reflected on the tax return to be filed on or before April 15) or for the current year (reflected on the tax return filed the following April 15).

[¶2702.1] Deductibility of IRA Contributions

The Tax Code of 1986 limits the deductibility of IRA contributions made by persons who are active participants in qualified plans (or, if it's a joint return, who are married to active participants). An active participant is one who is covered by (though not necessarily vested in) an employer-sponsored plan such as a qualified pension, profit-sharing, stock bonus, or annuity plan; a tax-sheltered annuity plan; a government agency's pension plan; or a Simplified Employee Pension (SEP) plan. Contributions made by self-employed persons, or employees who are not active plan participants, remain fully deductible.

For active participants, the deduction is phased out based on adjusted gross income over $25,000 (for single persons) or $40,000 (for married couples filing jointly). The "threshold amount" for married persons filing separate returns is $0. The deductible amount is calculated by subtracting the threshold amount from AGI to find "excess AGI"; the deduction equals the IRA contribution times ($10,000—excess AGI)/$10,000. There is a minimum permitted deduction of $200, where the formula yields a result between $0 and $200.

[¶2702.2] Rollovers

An individual who receives a distribution from a qualified plan (including a Keogh plan), but does not wish to have the money available (or to pay tax on it) can place the distribution in "cold storage," and defer taxation, by rolling over the contribution into an IRA, and leaving it there until distribution is permitted under the IRA rules (see ¶2702.3, below). An IRA can also be used as a "conduit" for tax-free transfers of funds from one qualified plan to another qualified plan. IRA owners can also use rollovers to transfer assets from one type of IRA to another (e.g., a transfer from bank Certificates of Deposit to an equity mutual fund).

[¶2702.3] IRA Distributions and Taxation

The advantage of an IRA (even if no tax deduction is available for the contribution) is that no current tax is charged on the account's appreciation in value. Taxation is deferred until the taxpayer withdraws funds from the IRA.

Before the Tax Code of 1986, all IRA contributions were made with before-tax funds, so all withdrawals were currently taxable (although income averaging might be available to blunt the effect of very large withdrawals on a single year's income). Current tax law includes both deductible and nondeductible contributions; in future years (unless Congress once again changes its mind), taxpayers will have to allocate IRA withdrawals between amounts deriving from previously untaxed and already-taxed sources, with the latter being tax-free.

The Congressional purpose behind the IRA rules is to permit taxpayers to fund retirement. This purpose is construed narrowly. Taxpayers must pay income tax on any amount withdrawn before age 59 1/2 (except in case of disability)—and must also pay a 10% excise tax on the withdrawals.

However, the purpose is the creation of retirement funds, not estate planning. So there is also a 50% excise tax on withdrawals that do not meet the minimum standards of the Tax Code. That is, IRA owners must begin withdrawals no later than age 70 1/2, and must either withdraw the entire amount in a lump sum at that time, or schedule withdrawals over a period of time lasting no longer than the joint lifetimes of the account owner and beneficiary.

[¶2703] Simplified Employee Pension (SEP) Plans

Small business owners may want to motivate employees by establishing a retirement plan (not to mention saving money for their own retirement)—yet may be reluctant to undergo the difficulties and transaction costs of setting up and maintaining a qualified plan. The SEP was added to the tax law to deal with this situation.

A SEP functions similarly to a defined-contribution pension plan. However, the SEP rules (unlike the Keogh rules) require the employer to make plan contributions for certain part-time and seasonal employees. The maximum deduction is $30,000 or 15% of income, and this amount is excludible from the employee's taxable income.

A SEP is considered a qualified plan, so the limitations on deductibility of the employee's IRA contribution applies.

If the employer has 25 or fewer employees, and if at least half of them so elect, amounts up to $7,000 (this amount will be indexed for changes in the cost of living) can either be contributed to the employee's SEP account or paid directly to the employee in cash. Amounts that are deferred will not be treated as taxable income for the year in which they were placed in the SEP account.

[¶2704] Keogh Plans

Keogh, or H.R.10, plans permit sole proprietors and partnerships to create retirement plans. Keogh plans entered the tax law under the Self-Employed Individuals Tax Retirement Act of 1962 (PL 87—792). Originally, they were subject to a set of rules significantly different from the rules applied to the qualified plans of corporations; however, in 1982 TEFRA more or less placed Keogh plans on the same footing (in terms of employee eligibility for plan participation, vesting, contributions, and other aspects of plan funding and administration) as corporate plans.

[¶2704.1] Eligibility for Keogh Plans

A self-employed person, or a partnership, is permitted to create a Keogh plan; however, to be qualified, the plan must cover both owner-employees and common-law employees who meet the participation tests of the Internal Revenue Code. For this purpose, the definition of "self-employed" includes those who are subject to FICA self-employment tax, plus ministers, agent-drivers (such as those who sell bakery products), traveling salespersons (but not fulltime insurance salespersons), and homeworkers.

An individual seeking to establish a Keogh plan must perform personal services for the business, not merely contribute to its financial well-being—which excludes limited partners and retired partners from Keogh plan participation.

By and large, Keogh plans are free of Department of Labor regulation under ERISA, though they are very much subject to the provisions of the Internal Revenue Code. For instance, ERISA's requirement that plans maintain termination insurance is relaxed for "individual account plans" (there is a partial exemption for plans consisting in part of individual accounts), covering only those owning a 10% or greater interest in the business, or established by a professional service employer where there are 25 or fewer active participants.

[¶2704.2] Types of Keogh Plans

A Keogh plan can be set up either as a pension or as a profit-sharing plan: the distinction is whether funding depends on the presence or absence of profits (making it a profit-sharing plan) or each participant's compensation (making it a pension plan). Or, the plan can base contributions for the owner-employee on his or her income (making it a profit-sharing plan as to him or her) and on the common-law employees' compensation (making it a pension plan as to them). Keogh pension plans, in turn, can take either defined benefit or defined contribution form.

In order to be a qualified plan, a Keogh plan must be in writing; communicated to the employees; operate exclusively for the benefit of employees and their beneficiaries (a test that can be met if the plan covers only a self-employed person who has no common-law employees); must not discriminate in favor of highly compensated employees; and (except for some profit-sharing plans) must provide a joint and survivor annuity and qualified preretirement survivor annuity to participants.

ERISA's minimum funding standards do not apply to profit-sharing Keogh plans; there is a partial exemption for hybrid profit-sharing/pension plans. Nor do the funding standards apply if the plan is exclusively funded by the purchase of certain insurance contracts.

Defined-benefit Keogh plans are required to fully fund their current service costs (the cost of benefits that employees are now earning); to amortize their unfunded accrued liabilities over a 30-year period (40 years in the plan was adopted before the effective date of ERISA); and to amortize gains and losses of pre-1988 plan years over a 15-year period.

Defined-contribution Keogh plans must make contributions according to the plan formula.

Failure to meet the minimum funding standards (if they apply) leads to the imposition of a 10% initial excise tax (under Code Section 4971). This tax is annual and cumulative; a 100% excise tax is imposed if a funding deficiency is not corrected within a specified time.

[¶2704.3] Keogh Plan Contributions

The major methods of funding Keogh plans are creating a trust; buying contracts (usually annuity contracts) from an insurance company; or establishing a special custodial account with a bank or credit union.

The maximum permitted contribution and benefit levels for a Keogh plan are the same as those for corporate qualified plans under Code Section 415; the employer's limit on deductions is found in Code Section 404.

The maximum annual addition for a defined-contribution pension or profit-sharing plan is the smaller of 25% of the participant's compensation or $30,000. If the only plan is a profit-sharing plan, the maximum that the employer can deduct is 15% of the employee's compensation. Furthermore, a self-employed individual's own earned income, for the purpose of his or her own Keogh contributions, is reduced by the amount of those contributions—so the maximum that he or she can contribute for his or her own benefit is 20% of earned income.

The maximum annual benefit from a defined-benefit Keogh plan is the smaller of $90,000 a year (adjusted for inflation) or 100% of the average of the employee's three highest-paid consecutive years. But only $200,000 of an owner-employee's compensation can be taken into account. The defined benefit must be reduced actuarially (or increased actuarially) if a defined-benefit Keogh plan participant retires before or after the normal Social Security retirement age.

The Internal Revenue Code contains further, even more complex rules about the aggregate limits when an employer maintains more than one Keogh plan.

Code Section 4972 imposes an annual, nondeductible excise tax on the employer's contributions in excess of the limits; the excise tax is imposed until the employer eliminates the excess contribution.

[¶2704.4] Keogh Reporting Requirements

The filing requirements depend on the number of participants in the plan. Since 1986, single-participant plans (those covering only a sole proprietor with no common-law employees and his or her spouse, or only partners in a partnership, or partners and spouses) must file the short-form 5500EZ. Plans with multiple participants, but fewer than 100, file Form 5500-C for the initial plan year and the plan's final year; in other years, Form 5500-R is due. The long-form 5500 is required for plans with 100 or more participants. Filings are due on or before the last day of the seventh month after a plan's year ends; failure to file required reports, or incomplete filing, carries a penalty of $25 a day, up to a maximum of $15,000 a year.

[¶2704.5] Distribution and Taxation of Keogh Benefits

The distribution of benefits from Keogh plans is treated under rules similar to those governing the qualified plans of corporations. Distributions made to a 5% owner of the business who is under $59\,^1/_2$ (unless he or she is disabled) are premature, and subject to a 10% additional income tax.

However, all participants' entire interest must be distributed no later than the calendar year after the year in which they reach $70\,^1/_2$. (For 5% owners, the distribution must begin by April 1 of that year.) The distribution can be made in a lump sum, or in the form of an annuity.

If a Keogh participant dies while payments are being made, the remaining portion of his or her interest in the plan must be distributed at least as fast as before death; the beneficiary can accelerate payments. If the participant dies before payments begin, the entire interest must be distributed in five years, or over the lifetime of the participant's beneficiary; or if the benefits start, no later than the time the beneficiary would have reached age $70\,^1/_2$ and last no longer than the beneficiary's lifetime.

Code Section 4974 imposes a nondeductible 50% excise tax on the difference between Keogh (or, for that matter, IRA) distributions actually made and the minimum required contributions. However, there is also an excise tax (at a 15% rate, this time, reduced by any 10% excise on premature withdrawals) on excess distributions: distributions greater than $150,000 (or $112,500 indexed for inflation, whichever is greater). The tax on excessive distributions does not apply to distributions after the death of a participant; distributions under a Qualified Domestic Relations Order; amounts traceable to rollovers; and amounts traceable to after-tax employee contributions.

When Keogh plans make payments in annuity form, the taxpayer is permitted to receive a portion of each payment tax-free: the portion attributable to the employee's own contributions.

Taxpayers who reach the age of 50 before January 1, 1986 get a one-time election to save taxes on lump sums received from Keogh plans. They can either use a 5-year income averaging (using the tax rates current at the time the lump sum is received), or use 10-year averaging and 1986 tax rates. Younger taxpayers can't use 10-year averaging, but are permitted to use 5-year income averaging for lump sums received from Keogh plans after they reach $59\,^1/_2$.

— For Further Reference —

Baker, Pamela, "Nondeductible IRAs and New Break-Even Points," 4 *J. of Taxation of Investments* 359 (Summer '87).

Bearden, Frank C., "Estate Planning with the IRA Rollover," 41 *J. of the American Society of CLU and ChFC* 60 (September '87).

Bierman, Jacquin D., "Brokerage Fees Paid by Qualified Plans and IRAs Not Separately Deductible," 66 *J. of Taxation* 182 (March '87).

Deppe, E. DeVon, "Advising Clients About IRA Distributions," 65 *Taxes* 402 (December '86).

Hagerty, George E. and Kristin T. Westfall, "Allowable Contribution to a Defined Contribution Keogh Plan Clarified by New Law," 15 *Taxation for Lawyers* 248 (January–February '87).

Langstraat, Craig J., "The Individual Retirement Account: Retirement Help for the Masses, or Another Tax Break for the Wealthy?" 60 *St. John's L. Rev.* 437 (Spring '86).

Sollee, William L., "IRA Rules: What Is Active Participation?" 65 *J. of Taxation* 402 (December '86).

Yoder, Loes J., "A Comparative Study of the State Income Tax Treatment of IRAs," 5 *J. of State Taxation* 329 (Winter '87).

LANDLORD AND TENANT

[¶2801] A lease can be defined as a contract between the owner of the land (the landlord or lessor) and a tenant (lessee) in which the lessee agrees to pay a stipulated sum (rent) for the use and enjoyment of the property for a specified period of time. Besides determining the legal rights and duties of the parties, the lease also serves as a basis for assessing the tax treatment of each of the parties.

Each party to a lease will naturally try to shape the various lease provisions to achieve maximum legal as well as tax advantages from the relationship. The wording of the lease is all-important, since it can determine upon whom the tax burden will fall, when the tax will be imposed, whether or not certain deductions will be allowed, which party will be entitled to these deductions, when the deductions may be claimed, and so on. To summarize these points and to provide a quick reference, the table on the following pages will tell at a glance the tax consequences of payments, deposits, improvements, and alterations for all parties to the lease.

[¶2802] COMMERCIAL TAX CONSEQUENCES TO LANDLORD AND TENANT OF PAYMENTS, DEPOSITS, IMPROVEMENTS, AND ALTERATIONS

Item	Effect on Landlord	Effect on Tenant
Tenant's Security Deposit	No immediate tax effect on either landlord or tenant if the deposit is properly restricted. If forfeited, the security deposit is treated for tax purposes the same as a payment of the obligation for which it is forfeited would have been treated.	
Tenant's Payment to Renew	Rental income to landlord.	Cost of renewal amortizable over life of lease.
Payment by Tenant to Modify	Rental income to landlord.	Cost of modifying lease amortizable over life of lease.
Payment of Broker's Commission by Tenant	None	Amount amortizable by tenant over life of lease. In case of premature cancellation of lease, amount not recovered is deductible in year of cancellation.

Item	Effect on Landlord	Effect on Tenant
Payment of Broker's Commission by Landlord	Amount amortizable by landlord over life of lease. If lease prematurely canceled, amount not recovered is deductible in year of cancellation.	None.
Payment of Bonus by Tenant to Landlord for Lease.	Taxable when received by landlord as additional rental income.	Amortizable by tenant over life of lease.
Advanced Payment of Rent by Tenant	Rental income to landlord.	Amortizable by tenant over life of lease.
Payment by Landlord to Cancel	Capitalized or amortized over the useful life of the replacement building substituted on the site.	Amount is treated as capital gain when received.
Payment by Tenant to Cancel	Additional rental income to landlord.	Deductible as rent by tenant in year paid.
Payment of Taxes, Interest; Insurance, and Operating Costs by Tenant	Additional rental income to landlord.	Deductible as rent by tenant.
Payment of Debt Against Property by Tenant	Additional rental income to landlord.	Deductible as rent by tenant when paid.
Alteration of Premises by Landlord for Tenant	Landlord can take depreciation deductions for improvements. Cost is amortizable by landlord over life of lease if improvements are suitable only for tenant.	None.
Installation of Trade Fixtures by Tenant	None.	Tenant may take depreciation deductions if useful life exceeds a year; otherwise currently deductible.
Permanent Improvements by Tenant Not Intended as Rent	Not income to landlord when improvements are made or when lease terminates.	Tenant may take depreciation deductions over useful life (or ACRS or MACRS recovery period) of improvements or over life of lease, whichever is shorter.

Item	Effect on Landlord	Effect on Tenant
Restoration of Premises by by Tenant at End of Lease	Landlord can deduct depreciation improvements to leasehold unless lessee is required to replace improvement.	Cost is deductible by tenant when restoration is made.

[¶2803] NEGOTIATING AND DRAFTING LEASES

At the negotiating stages the lessor and the lessee will each normally try to slant the lease so that the various provisions will yield the maximum economic and tax advantages to each party. The reconciliation of the two possibly conflicting viewpoints shows the necessity for proper planning and drafting at the earliest stages of any lease arrangement.

These problems are less likely to arise in a short-term lease, involving a residence, an apartment, or the average retail store, than in a long-term lease involving substantial business properties. In the former case, standard forms are generally used, and the tax effects are usually accepted by the parties without further negotiation. While this may be the common practice, it should not be inferred that the short-term lease does not present various points of contact with the tax laws.

In long-term leases, the tax advantages that are obtainable by either the lessor or the lessee may not only be substantial—they may, in fact, be the motivating force behind the whole transaction. This is especially true when the lessee is required to erect new buildings on the property or to make substantial improvements or alterations to the property. Since the lessor and the lessee usually have equal bargaining power in the long-term situation, the final lease is ordinarily preceded by extensive negotiations at both the economic and the tax levels. The number of detailed provisions in the lease will ordinarily reflect this bargaining process.

[¶2803.1] Construction of Lease

It is the objective of every person who prepares a lease to use language that will convey the intention of the parties as clearly and exactly as possible. The nature of a lease—the complex nature of the property rights and obligations it covers, the many different situations and contingencies it must anticipate—makes it inevitable under certain conditions that outside construction of its provisions will be required. If the courts are called upon to settle disputes between the parties as to the meaning of a lease, the instrument will generally be construed against the person who drew it, usually the lessor. Before executing a lease, both parties should understand not only the terms of the instrument, but also the legal and tax effect of those terms.

Construction of a lease may also be necessary in tax proceedings before IRS and the courts. The intent of the parties may have been clear to them, but for tax purposes intent is evidenced to some degree by the provisions of the written agreement. The written agreement is therefore a most important document. The following paragraphs highlight the significant points to be kept in mind when negotiating and drafting leases.

[¶ 2803.2]   Worksheet for Negotiating and Drafting a Lease

(A) Nature and Duration
(1) Number of years lease will run.
(2) Is lease a net lease? (Give details.)
(3) Give details of duties undertaken by lessor.
(4) State when the lessee is entitled to take possession of the premises.

(B) Renewal and Purchase Options
(1) Will there be an option to renew the lease?
(2) How many options to renew will there be? Under what conditions can the landlord deny renewal or remove the tenant?
(3) What does it take to exercise the option to renew? (Give details.)
(4) What is the term of each option to renew in years?
(5) State the rent for each option term.
(6) Will the rent decrease on successive options in response to the fact that the lessor has liquidated the mortgage loan over the original lease term?
(7) Will the lessee get an option to purchase building and land?
(8) When is the option to purchase to be exercised? (Give date.)
(9) State method of exercising option to purchase.
(10) What price does the option to purchase call for?

(C) Holding Over
(1) If the lessee holds over, will there be a month-to-month tenancy?

(D) Rent
(1) What is the gross annual rent?
(2) When and how is the rent payable? (State details.)
(3) State the gross annual rental per square foot of usable space.
(4) If a month-to-month tenancy is created by the lessee's holding over, what will the rental be during such tenancy?

(E) Grace Period
(1) What is the number of days of grace, if any, during which a default may be cured?
(2) Grace period for default in payment of rent.
(3) Grace period for other breach of lease.
(4) Will the lease carry a confession of judgment clause? (Such a clause may be unenforceable in a residential lease.)

(F) Measure of Damages and Attorney's Fees
(1) Will the lease set forth a measure of damages for particular breaches of lease terms?

438

(2) On a breach by the lessee, will the measure of lessor's damages be the deficiency in rental that the lessor realizes by renting to another lessee? How about liquidated damages?

(3) Is the lessee obligated to pay the lessor's attorney's fees incurred in enforcing the lease? Are there any qualifications or limitations on lessor's right to recover attorney's fees; e.g., must fees be reasonable, arise out of court action, be approved by court? Must lessor prevail in court action to recover attorney's fees? Will the lease provide that the party that wins the court action is entitled to attorney's fees? Such provisions may be limited or barred in residential leases.

(G) Subletting and Assignment

(1) Will the lessee be entitled to sublet the premises?

(2) Will the lessee be entitled to assign the lease?

(3) Will the lessor's written consent be required for a subletting of the premises or an assignment of the lease by lessee?

(4) Will the lessor agree not to withhold consent unreasonably?

(5) Will the lessee be given the right to sublet without lessor's consent provided the sublessee is responsible and has a specified credit rating?

(6) Will the lessee be given the right to assign to a subsidiary without lessor's consent?

(7) What is the legal effect of the lease on a merger of lessor or lessee?

(8) In a residential lease, is the landlord obliged to consent? What status does a tenant's sublessee, assignee, cohabitant or roommate acquire?

(H) Lessee's Status Under Existing Lease

(1) How much longer does the lessee's term under the present lease have to run?

(2) Does the lessee have the right to assign or sublet under the terms of the present lease?

(3) If the present lease requires the lessor's consent to an assignment or subletting by lessee, will consent be forthcoming?

(4) Will the prospective lessor assume lessee's liability under the present lease? (Give details.)

(I) Responsibility for Taxes, Charges, and Expenses

(1) Who is responsible for real estate taxes?

(2) If lessee is to pay all the real estate taxes, what were the taxes on the property for the past five years?

(3) Were these taxes on vacant land or on improved property?

(4) What is the trend in real estate taxes in the area?

(5) If the lessee is to pay any increase in taxes over the base year, what is the base tax payable to lessor?

(6) Will there be a maximum annual increase payable by the lessee?

(7) What is the annual increase payable by the lessee stated as a percent of the base tax?

(8) Who is to pay utility charges?

(9) Who is to pay maintenance and service charges (snow removal, painting, cleaning, refuse disposal, janitorial, etc.)? (Give details.)

(10) If lessee is to pay for these items, will he or she have the right to contract for them directly rather than purchase them from the lessor?

(11) Will the lessor pay the normal utility service connection expenses?

(12) Is the lessee to make all ordinary and necessary repairs to the building, roadways, etc.?

(13) Is the lessee to perform all the usual maintenance?

(14) Who is to be responsible for extraordinary repairs?

(15) Who is to be responsible for structural repairs and alterations?

(16) Who is responsible for making the premises suitable for computers and other electronic devices?

(17) What are the landlord's and tenant's responsibility for physical security of the premises?

(J) Title, Zoning, and Other Restrictions on Use of Land

(1) Does the lessor have simple title to the land?

(2) What is the legal description of the land?

(3) Will the lessee receive copies of all covenants and restrictions of record that regulate the use of the property?

(4) Will lessee have to cross the land of other property owners or use private roadways to get to public streets or highways? Are there recorded easements entitling lessee to use such land or roadway for ingress and egress? Will lessee be furnished with copies of those easements?

(5) Are there utility easements to serve the property? Will lessee be furnished with copies of those recorded easements?

(6) What are the zoning regulations applicable to the building?

(7) Is the contemplated use permissible?

(8) Is lessee to be provided with a copy of the local zoning ordinance and a plat of survey?

(9) In an apartment building, is it a legal 2- or 3-family house, or a legal multiple dwelling?

(K) Building and Construction

(1) If the building is constructed for the lessee, will lessor obtain and deliver to lessee a certificate of occupancy or certificate of compliance showing that the building conforms to all laws, ordinances, building codes, etc.?

(2) In the case of an existing building, will lessor agree to warrant that he or she has conformed to all the laws, etc., and that he or she will fully reimburse lessee for the cost of necessary repairs or alterations after the lease commences to correct code violations that existed before lessee took possession?

(3) Has lessee considered retaining the services of a local attorney to check these matters if answers to (1) and (2) are "No"?

(4) Will a building be constructed on vacant land by lessor or lessee?

(5) Have plans and specifications been prepared?

(6) Who is the architect retained by the lessor to prepare the plans and specifications?

(7) Will the plans and specifications be made part of the lease as an exhibit?

(8) Is the lessor to pay the architect's fees?

(9) In the event that final plans and specifications are not ready when the lease is signed, will the final plans and specifications be subject to review and approval by lessee?

(10) If only the preliminary plans will be attached to the lease, what limitations will there be on lessee's right to withhold approval of final plans and specifications?

(11) What is the cut-off for delivery to lessee of a complete set of final plans and specifications?

(12) When is constructions to begin?

(13) When is construction to be completed?

(14) Will there be liquidated damages payable by lessor if construction is not completed by the date specified and lessee is forced to vacate space in his or her former building?

(15) Will lessee be entitled to terminate the lease because of a delay in completing building beyond agreed period? What is effect of act of God, strikes, etc.?

(16) In the case of an existing building, has lessee inspected the building?

(17) What is the condition of existing building?

(18) Will lessee have the right to inspect the building before execution of the lease and before taking actual possession?

(19) What is the actual size of the building and its usable floor area?

(20) Can the building be enlarged? Additional stories? A wing or addition? Is adequate land available? Does zoning ordinance permit expansion or addition? Set-back and side-yard lines preventing additions?

(21) Location of the building?

(22) Type of construction?

(23) Age of building?

(24) Condition of equipment in building?

(25) Will lessor warrant equipment to be in good operating condition at the beginning of the lease term?

(26) Is lessee to have the benefit of equipment warranties?

(27) Will lessor make alterations and improvements to make building suitable for lessee's use? What improvements will be made? At whose expense? Name and address of architect who will prepare plans and specifications? Will these plans be subject to lessee's prior approval? When will the work start? When will the work be completed?

(28) Will dock and loading facilities be available and accessible to large trucks?

(29) Will rail transportation service to the building be available?

(30) Will truck transportation service to building be available and adequate?

(31) Will there be ample room to maneuver, load, and park trucks?

(32) Will there be ample parking for employees who will drive to work?

(33) Is public transportation available for employees who do not drive to work?

(L) Liability, Insurance, Coverage, and Subrogation

(1) Will lessee carry public liability insurance for both lessor and lessee?

(2) What are the policy limits to be carried? For personal injury? For property damage? For workers' compensation?

(3) Will lessor agree to accept lessee's liability insurance company and the policy form it issues?

(4) Will lessee carry fire and extended insurance for both lessor and lessee?

(5) What is the amount of insurance to be carried?

(6) Will lessor agree to accept lessee's fire insurance company and the policy form it issues in the state where the building is located?

(7) Will lessor and lessee waive claims against the other party for damage to property?

(8) Will waiver be only to the extent property is covered by fire insurance policies?

(9) Will each party agree to notify its fire insurance carrier of this provision?

(10) Will each party agree to have fire insurance policies endorsed to prevent invalidation of coverage because of such mutual waivers?

(11) Will lessor be excused from all liability for injuries to persons or property arising out of the use of the property?

(12) Will lessor be excused from injuries resulting from lessor's own negligence in making structural repairs, alterations, etc.?

(13) Will lessee excuse lessor from injuries caused by latent defects existing in the building when turned over to the lessee?

(M) Destruction or Condemnation of Premises

(1) Will lessor have responsibility to rebuild if building is a total loss by fire or other casualty?

(2) Will parties agree that fire insurance proceeds will be made available for such rebuilding?

(3) Will lessor have a reasonable time after the fire to decide whether to rebuild?

(4) Will lessor have the right to elect not to rebuild only if a year or two is left to the lease term when the fire occurred?

(5) Will lessor agree to notify lessee of his decision on whether or not he elects to rebuild within that time?

(6) Will lessor agree to abatement of rent from date of the fire until the premises are rebuilt and are again ready for occupancy?

(7) Define what constitutes "total destruction."

(8) If the lessor is required or elects to rebuild, will lease continue in effect during rebuilding? Will rent abate during rebuilding? When is rebuilding work to begin? Will lessor agree to undertake the work promptly after taking possession and to prosecute the work with due diligence? When

will the rebuilding work be completed? Will lessee have the right to approve lessor's architect who will supervise the rebuilding? If insurance proceeds are insufficient to cover the entire cost of rebuilding, will the lessor put up the difference?

(9) If lessor elects not to rebuild, will the lease terminate as of the date of the fire or other casualty? Will the rent abate as of that date? Will lessee have right then to elect to rebuild, using the fire insurance proceeds to do so? Will the lessee give the lessor notice of his election within a specified time?

(10) Who will be responsible for rebuilding if building is partially destroyed or damaged by fire or other casualty?

(11) Will lessor agree to abatement of portion of the rent from the date of fire until the premises are rebuilt and again ready for occupancy?

(12) What is the formula for measuring what portion of the rent is to abate?

(13) Define what constitutes partial destruction.

(14) When is the rebuilding work to begin?

(15) Will the party responsible for rebuilding agree to undertake the work promptly after being able to take possession of the damaged portion and to prosecute the work with due diligence?

(16) When is the rebuilding work to be finished?

(17) If lessor selects the architect who is to supervise the rebuilding, will the lessee have a right to approve the choice?

(18) What is the standard of quality of the rebuilding?

(19) Should insurance proceeds be insufficient to cover the entire cost of the rebuilding, will the lessor or lessee put up the difference? What is the maximum limit on the amount to be put up?

(20) If insurance proceeds go to the lessor's mortgagee to pay off part of the outstanding mortgage debt, will the lessor agree to replace the proceeds thus diverted?

(21) Will lessee surrender his share of a condemnation award if all or part of the land and building are taken for public purposes?

(22) If only part of the property is taken, will lessee be entitled to terminate the lease if remaining portion is insufficient for lessee's needs?

(23) Will rent abate from the date that lessee has to surrender possession, rather than date title to the property passes to the public body?

(24) To what extent will rent be abated on a partial taking?

(25) How will this be determined? Set up a formula?

[¶2804]   RENTAL PAYMENTS

Commercial rent is ordinarily treated as income by the lessor and is deductible by the lessee. The most important question about it normally is the amount to be paid. There are a number of ways to fix rent, as described in the following paragraphs.

[¶2804.1] Flat Rental

This calls for a uniform rate throughout the term and is most common in short-term office leases. Its drawback for the landlord is that it fails to protect him against increases in taxes and operating expenses.

[¶2804.2] Step-Up Lease

This arrangement provides for a gradually increasing amount of rent, stepped up at specified intervals. It may be used to compensate the landlord for increased expenses, but it is most commonly used as an inducement for a tenant who is starting in business and initially can only afford a small rental.

[¶2804.3] Expense-Participating Lease or Escalator Lease

Long-term office leases usually are of this type. Under it, the tenant pays a basic fixed rent plus a specified portion of the real estate taxes, insurance, and repairs other than structural ones. The expense-participating lease requires the tenant to pay an immediate share of these costs, while under an escalator lease the tenant pays only his proportionate share of any increases in costs during the lease term.

[¶2804.4] Net Lease

Under this type of lease, the tenant agrees to pay, in addition to the fixed rental, *all* other costs, expenses, and obligations connected with the property, including such expenses and charges as real estate taxes and assessments, insurance, maintenance and repairs, heat, water, etc. In short, the idea behind a net lease is that the rent paid to the landlord is a net rent that comes to him free and clear of any offsets or deductions.

[¶2804.5] Cost-of-Living Lease

Here, the tenant's rental obligation is increased or decreased at specified intervals depending on the fluctuation of the dollar according to price indices or other agreed-upon measures of the economy.

[¶2804.6] Re-evaluation Lease

This calls for an appraisal of the property and a fixing of the rent as a percentage of the appraised value at specified intervals. The new rental value may be fixed on the basis of the value of the land and building, or on the rental value of the premises occupied by the tenant. The latter method may result in a higher figure because the appraisers may take into consideration the business success of the tenant.

[¶2804.7] Specifying When Payments Are to Be Made

In addition to the amount of rent, the lease should set forth the method of payment. Many leases state the rental obligation in terms of a yearly figure and in theory the landlord may require it to be paid one year in advance, even though monthly payments are customary. Sometimes, when the tenant's income is seasonal, monthly payments may be of unequal amounts.

The date for the initial rental payment should be set forth specifically. The tenant will want the lease to postpone the payment of rent if occupancy is unavailable at the agreed-on date. If the landlord has granted rent concessions, the lease should indicate the months that are to be rent-free. Part of the concession may come at the beginning of the lease and the remainder at the end.

[¶2805] PERCENTAGE RENTALS

In leases of commercial space for terms of three years or more, percentage rental arrangements are commonplace. Figuring the rent on a minimum rental basis plus a percentage of sales above an established minimum permits the owner to cope with inflation and also share in the success of the enterprise. The tenant benefits in that he pays only the minimum rent unless his sales rise above a specified figure, and then he pays the agreed percentage of the excess. The minimum and percentage rental must be acceptable to both sides. A method must be established for measuring the lessee's sales on which the percentage rental will be based so that it is as simple and foolproof as possible and lessens the chance for future disputes.

There are at least four possible types of percentage rentals:

(1) Fixed minimum rent with a percentage of gross sales added to the minimum.

(2) Fixed minimum rent with additional rent based on percentage of gross sales being payable only after the applicable percentage applying to the gross has earned the minimum.

(3) Percentage lease with no minimum.

(4) Minimum rent plus the percentage with a maximum rent that the percentage may produce.

[¶2805.1] Some Important Bases to Touch in Providing for a Percentage Rental

❏ *Definition of Gross Sales:* What is included in "gross sales" should be clearly covered. Generally, gross sales should be defined to include all sales made from or at the demised premises, whether for cash or credit, deductions being allowed for refunds for returned merchandise.

❏ *Methods of Payment:* The lessee may be required to report gross sales, in writing, to the lessor at specified times and to pay sums due within an agreed time thereafter.

Where dealing with a seasonal business, the lessee may insist on a provision whereby percentage rentals are paid monthly, but if the total percentage rentals paid over a 12-month period are greater than the specified percentage of the total volume of business for that period, the lessee is entitled to a refund or a credit for the excess. Another method is to provide for percentage rentals to be paid after the expiration of each lease year or to fix payment periods that include anticipated periods of seasonal variations in business volume, thereby eliminating the need for making adjustments. Of course, if the minimum rental is set at a figure that allows for slack months, the lessor should be entitled to look to the high-volume months to make up the difference.

❏ *Records of Gross Sales:* The lessee should be required to maintain, and the lessor should be entitled to audit, books and records in which all transactions on which percentages may become due are entered. If any deficiency is found, the lessor should be entitled to immediate payment. Provisions for payment of expenses of audits should also be included.

❏ *Diligent Operation of the Business:* The lessor may want to covenant that the lessee will devote his full time to the business. If the tenant has other outlets, he may be required to give assurance that he won't try to divert business to them. A provision under which the lessee agrees that he will not compete with the business opened on the leased premises in any way within a specified radius may be desired. Also, provisions should require the lessee (1) to be open for business during those business hours that are customary for its particular type of business, (2) to maintain a staff of personnel adequate to assure the maximum in gross sales, and (3) to have sufficient stock for sale as compared with similar enterprises.

❏ *Tax Participation:* The lessee may be required to pay, in addition to the stipulated rental, increases in taxes or assessments over and above the taxes and assessments for a specified year. A provision whereby the excess taxes paid by the lessee are credited against the total percentage rentals due may be included.

❏ *Lessor's Option to Terminate:* When the minimum rental fixed in a long-term lease is lower than what is normal for a similar business in a similar location or when the volume of business done is expected to increase substantially, a provision may be included that if gross sales do not reach a specified figure within a specified time, the lessor is entitled to terminate the lease, or the lessee may elect to increase the minimum rent to a sum that the lessor would receive if a stated amount of gross sales had been achieved, thereby keeping the lease in full force and effect.

❏ *No Partnership Created:* Because he or she is sharing profits, the landlord may be construed to be a partner of the tenant unless a contrary intention is clearly spelled out in the lease.

[¶2806] Security Deposits and Advance Rents

For protection against a tenant's abandonment, nonpayment of rent, or default, the landlord will use one of the following security devices:

Security Deposits: The tenant is required to deposit security or rents with the landlord. Frequently, a lease will provide that if the tenant abandons the property or is evicted for a default in rent, the landlord may re-let the premises and collect damages out of the security deposit. For tax purposes, a security deposit is not the landlord's property. It remains the tenant's property, with the landlord holding it in trust. Of course, the security deposit will become income if and when appropriated by the landlord because of default, abandonment, etc. If the lease is residential, state or local law may limit the size of security deposits and/or require the landlord to keep them in an interest-paying account for the tenant's benefit.

If security deposit treatment is desired, the lease should not contain provisions that apply the security deposit to the last month's rent. If the lease contains an option to purchase and the lessee makes a security deposit, the following rules apply: if the deposit is to be applied to the purchase price if the option is exercised, and is otherwise returnable, the payment is considered a security deposit. But if the lessor is not obligated to refund the money if the lessee fails to exercise the purchase option, the money is considered advance rent and is taxable on payment.

Advance Rent: The tenant is required to pay a bonus for obtaining a lease and the landlord is entitled to this money whether or not the tenant fulfills any obligations under the lease. For the landlord, advance rent, whether or not it is to be eventually returned to the tenant, is treated as income when received. The tenant who pays a landlord rent in advance, commissions, or other expenses for acquiring a lease must capitalize such sums and write them off over the term of the lease (Reg. §1.162-1(a)).

[¶2807] Terms of the Lease

The tenant's willingness to sign a long-term lease will depend in part on his or her privilege to increase or decrease the amount of space to be paid for. Therefore, the space and time provisions of the lease should be treated as interrelated obligations.

Usually, basic terms of a lease are 5, 10, 15, 21, or more years. New buildings usually require terms of 10 or more years. The landlord normally wants as long a lease as he can get. His ability to obtain financing depends, among other things, on the stability of his rent roll. The tenants may prefer a shorter term, on the theory that as newer buildings are put up, their bargaining position will become stronger. However, a tenant who expects to make expensive alterations will want a term that's sufficiently long enough to amortize them. An especially powerful tenant may demand an "equity kicker" as an incentive to lease large amounts of space.

A tenant who is in a position to demand it will want a renewal option at the same or at a slightly higher rental. At the very least, however, the landlord will demand that the renewal rental cover any increase in real estate taxes and operating costs. For this purpose, an escalator clause may be used.

[¶2807.1] Cancellation and Additional Space Options

Two common problems for tenants who sign long-term leases are what happens if expected growth fails to occur, and what happens if growth is far greater than anticipated? Both of these can be solved by options, if the landlord will grant them. Under a cancellation option, the tenant has the right at designated periods and upon adequate notice to drop a specified amount of space. Usually a penalty will be payable to the landlord. The additional space option works in a similar manner: at designated periods, the tenant is given the right to lease additional space at a fixed rental.

The landlord should not overlook the benefits of these types of options. With a cancellation option, he may be able to fill up the building more quickly and with a fewer number of tenants, which simplifies his financing and book-keeping. In many cases, normal growth in white-collar workers will insure that cancellation options are not used. The additional space option is even more beneficial to the landlord. According to some experts, 80% of the tenants who leave well-maintained office buildings do so because they can't obtain additional space in the building. In some cases, a landlord will go so far as to make short-term leases for space adjoining that of the major tenants so that space will be available when and if required by them.

[¶2808] SUBLETTING SPACE

A provision giving the tenant the right to sublease space (or requiring the landlord to have reasonable cause for refusing consent) will not only protect the tenant against unexpected developments but is one way to solve the problems of changing space requirements. If the tenant believes he will need less space in the future, a sublease clause can be substituted for a cancellation option. If more space will be needed, the tenant can lease it immediately and sublet it during the interval when it isn't required. Sometimes, the landlord himself will agree to be the subtenant; then he has the responsibility of finding someone to occupy the space.

Apart from local variations, there are two basic types of sublease clauses. One is a standard clause contained in the printed form of many commercial leases. This states that the tenant may sublease with the written consent of the landlord. The other modified version of this clause adds that the landlord will not unreasonably withhold his consent.

In leases where the standard form is used, there are few alternatives open to the tenant if the landlord is unwilling to give his consent. Consequently, a tenant signing such a lease should be prepared to remain at the location for the full term; in the event he does wish to move, the landlord is in a position to demand a substantial consideration even though he may already have another tenant ready to move in.

[¶2808.1] When Is a Landlord's Refusal Reasonable?

Even when the modified clause prohibits an unreasonable withholding of consent, the landlord may refuse to approve a sublease for a number of reasons that could not be anticipated at the time the original lease was executed.

A landlord refusing consent, of course, risks the possibility that the tenant will begin a court action to determine if such actions are actually reasonable. Or, as an alternative, the tenant may proceed to make the sublease with the prospective subtenant even without the landlord's consent. The lease should contain a stipulation that no brokerage commission will be payable until the necessary consent has been obtained. The present tenant could then draft a letter to the landlord giving a detailed description of the new tenant's business, reliability, and background, pointing out that the new tenant meets all reasonable requirements relative to leasing space in the building, and requesting the landlord's consent. The tenant could take the position that a refusal under these circumstances would be unjustifiable, capricious, a violation of the original leasing agreement, and would render the original lease null and void.

The next move, in this event, is up to the landlord. Should the decision be to continue to withhold consent, the tenant will probably stop paying rent, which leaves the landlord in a position in which he must go to court to collect. Should the next resort be to legal action, the tenant can file a counter-suit for the landlord's failing to approve the sublease. Of course, the tenant also takes the risk that the court will find the refusal reasonable, in which case full back rent must be paid out and the tenant has lost any opportunity to negotiate a lease termination.

[¶2808.2] The Difference Between Subletting and Assigning

The difference between subletting and assigning depends on how much the tenant is giving away: if the tenant transfers the remainder of the term created by the lease, there is an assignment. On the other hand, the transfer is a sublease if the tenant retains part of his interest in the lease (no matter how small it might be). An assignee becomes liable to the original landlord for rent under the lease. The subtenant is liable only to his sublandlord (the original tenant), who remains liable to his landlord.

[¶2808.3] The Back-to-Back Lease

In some cities, the competition for tenants will force the landlord to offer to take over the unexpired term of an existing lease in order to rent space. If such a concession has been offered, the landlord's obligations should be spelled out in the new lease. If the landlord already has found a subtenant for the old space, the lease should specify any obligation on his part if the subtenant defaults on the sub-lease.

Parties who enter into such a "back-to-back" lease should be aware of the problems involved. One is that the landlord under the existing lease will very often have no incentive to make alterations when there is already a signed lease for the space. So this will deter a prospective new subtenant. Sometimes the tenant may be persuaded to make a contribution towards alterations of its present space to conform to the requirements of its prospective subtenant. If not, the landlord must make a careful analysis of the space to show a prospective subtenant that a move would require little or no alteration.

Another problem presented by "back-to-back" leasing is the reluctance of prospective subtenants to negotiate for space occupied by a tenant who has not signed a lease for other quarters in another building. It is not uncommon to find both the sublandlord and the subtenant in agreement and ready to execute a sub-lease only to discover that the new space for the proposed sublandlord has already been leased to someone else during the time that the sublandlord was seeking to obtain a subtenant.

Try to avoid this situation by keeping the owner of the new building informed of what is going on. The full leasing negotiations can be simultaneously planned and executed. There can also be a simultaneous closing arranged, involving the two tenants and the owners of both the new and the old buildings.

[¶2809] ALTERATIONS

The alteration clause is very important and should cover a number of points. If the landlord is to make alterations for the tenant, the nature and extent of such alterations should be spelled out in detail and quality specifications should be included when relevant. The obligation to pay rent should be conditioned on these alterations, so that the tenant need not move in until they are made.

Alterations made by the tenant are usually subject to the landlord's consent. Potential disputes can be reduced if a list of approved alterations is included in the lease. Denial of consent for future alterations should require reasonable cause for the lessor's objections. In addition, the lessor may agree that certain minor types of alterations can be made at any time without consent.

Finally, the lease should provide for disposition of any fixtures attached or affixed to the premises by the tenant. The standard lease provides that all alterations shall be the property of the lessor unless he or she elects otherwise; in that case, the tenant is responsible for removing them (and restoring the space to its original condition). The tenant may seek to modify this clause to provide (a) that the tenant may remove specified fixtures upon vacating, or (b) that the tenant need not remove specified alterations upon vacating, because of the expense involved.

[¶2810] IMPROVEMENTS

Leased property is almost always improved property or property that will be improved during the term of the lease. An important factor in measuring the value of the lease and in negotiating rent and other terms is who will make the improvements and who will be entitled to take the depreciation for them. In the following paragraphs the tax and economic consequences of improvements made by either the landlord or tenant will be examined.

[¶2810.1] Improvements Made by the Landlord

Improvements made by the owner of leased property are capital expenditures and as such are depreciable over the ACRS or MACRS recovery period without regard to the lease terms.

In exchange for the costs incurred to improve the property, the landlord will normally demand a higher rent. In effect, at the expense of laying out the cash for the improvements (or the cost of financing them), the landlord will receive (1) an annual depreciation deduction measured by the ACRS or MACRS recovery period and (2) a higher rent, which is taxable as ordinary income. Depending on the circumstances, the net additional rent income may or may not offset the net cost of the improvements.

On the other side, the tenant, by paying the additional higher rent, (1) is saving cash that might be better used in business and (2) has a fixed annual rental deduction instead of an amortization deduction that (if there is a renewal option) may have to be spread over the renewal period as well as the initial term of the lease.

[¶2810.2] Improvements Made by the Tenant

Improvements made by the tenant are not included in the landlord's taxable income if they are not rent (IRC §109), nor is the landlord's basis affected. In other words, the landlord realizes no income either when the improvement is made or at the termination of the lease (§109). In effect, when the tenant makes the improvements, the landlord anticipates an increase in the value of the property at no personal cost, in lieu of receiving a higher rent and an additional depreciation deduction.

The tenant, on the other hand, may depreciate the improvements over (a) the ACRS or MACRS recovery period, or (b) the term of the lease, whichever is shorter. Regs. §1.162-11(b), 1.167(a)-(4), and 1.178 explain the effect of renewal on the term of a lease. In addition, the tenant pays a lower rental than if the landlord did the work even though the cash or financing for the initial expenditures must be provided.

If, in return for the tenant's improvements, the landlord reduces the rent, the fair market value of the improvements will be treated as rental income to the landlord (Reg. §1.109-1(a)). The amount added to the landlord's income then becomes the basis with regard to the improvements, and is recoverable via depreciation. For the tenant, the cost of the improvements is deductible as rent (as it corresponds to the landlord's income). Whether improvements made by the tenant will be deemed rent depends on the intent of the parties as seen from the terms of the lease and the surrounding circumstances.

[¶2810.3] Summary of Consequences of Improvements

The following table summarizes the advantages and disadvantages—from both the landlord's and tenant's points of view—of improvements made by either of them:

Improvements by Landlord

From landlord's point of view:

(1) Higher rental obtainable.
(2) Landlord bears cost of construction.
(3) Rental taxable at ordinary income rates.
(4) Landlord may deduct for depreciation. Basis may be increased. Possible recapture of excess depreciation.

From tenant's point of view:

(1) Tenant pays more rent.
(2) No cost of construction.

Improvements by Tenant

From landlord's point of view:

(1) Lower rental obtainable.
(2) No cost of construction.
(3) Increase in value recognized only on disposition of property, and usually treated as capital gain.
(4) No deduction for depreciation.

From tenant's point of view:

(1) Tenant pays less rent.
(2) Tenant bears cost of construction, but is entitled to depreciation deductions or amortization. Possible recapture on disposition.

[¶2811] REPAIRS

Repairs are an area in which tenants may take on unexpectedly burdensome obligations. Naturally, the tenant should be responsible for personal neglect, as well as that of any employees, so there must should be adequate insurance. But the repair clause in most standard leases goes beyond this and makes the tenant responsible for damage from the air-conditioning unit or system (without distinguishing whether the air-conditioning was the landlord's or the tenant's), short circuits, flow or leakage of water, steam gas, sewer gas, sewerage or odors, frost, bursting or leaking of pipes or plumbing works or gas, or from any other cause of any kind or nature whatsoever due to carelessness, neglect, etc. This is fine where the tenant is in possession of the entire building, but the tenant may well consider the clause too broad when he or she merely occupies a part of a building that is under the landlord's control. The tenant may want a clause that provides that the only obligation to make repairs is if damage is the result of tenant misuse of the property and that all other repairs are the landlord's responsibility.

[¶2812] LEASE SUBORDINATION

Ordinarily, a subordination clause will provide a blanket subordination of the lease to any future underlying mortgage or any future underlying lease. This may be all right if the future mortgage is placed with a lending institution. But a private individual may toss out all of the tenants if he or she forecloses. Therefore, a tenant might try to have a clause provide that the lease will be subordinated only if the holder of any future lease or mortgage agrees that the lease will not be terminated or otherwise affected by an enforcement of such mortgage or lease as long as the tenant is not in default. A tenant who can't get this type of clause might try to limit subordination to mortgages placed with lending institutions. Before signing the lease, the tenant should try to get a nondisturbance agreement from the holder of any existing mortgages or underlying leases.

[¶2813] DESTRUCTION OR CONDEMNATION OF PREMISES

If the premises are completely destroyed, the landlord has the option of rebuilding, but, in the usual standard lease form, may notify the tenant, within 90 days of the casualty, of a decision not to rebuild. At this point the lease will come to an end. But the tenant is given no option to cancel a lease even though the remaining period may be short and it would be more practical to permanently relocate elsewhere. Nor does the clause usually spell out the tenant's rent obligation adequately during the period between the destruction of the premises and its restoration.

Several things can be done to improve this clause from the tenant's point of view. For one thing, the tenant can provide that the landlord's insurance policies cover all possible causes of destruction so that the landlord can and will look to insurance in the event of such a disaster. The tenant will want no distinction to be made regarding whose neglect may have caused the destruction. In the event of a total destruction of the premises, the tenant will want an option to cancel the lease if the destruction occurs during the last few years of the term. The tenant may also try to keep the period during which the landlord has the option to cancel relatively short, about 30 days rather than the usual 90.

As far as condemnation is concerned, the landlord will ordinarily want to include a clause entitling him or her to the full condemnation award. A tenant who plans to make substantial improvements and who is in a strong bargaining position may be able to modify this in order to obtain some reimbursement for investment. Otherwise, a tenant can only try to ascertain if there is any risk of condemnation during the term of the lease.

[¶2814] SOME LEGAL ELEMENTS OF THE LANDLORD-TENANT RELATIONSHIP

As defined earlier, a lease is a contract, and the parties to it may insert any provisions they want (with a few exceptions) to govern their relationship. In some instances a tenant will occupy property without entering into a formal agreement with the landlord. Sometimes a comprehensive lease may leave certain matters to be governed by common law or statutory rules. While such rules may differ in detail from one jurisdiction to the next, there is a general similarity in the legal principles involved. Some of the more important points are discussed in the following paragraphs.

[¶2814.1] Types of Tenancies

The landlord-tenant relationship exists by virtue of either a formal written lease or a periodic tenancy. The basic difference between the two is that when a written lease exists it is deemed to be the complete agreement between the parties, and the rights and obligations of the parties are governed by this instrument. If there is no formal lease and a periodic tenancy exists, the rights and obligations of the parties are governed by the jurisdiction's rules of law.

What follows is a brief discussion of the various types of tenancies that exist in the absence of a formal written lease.

Periodic Tenancy: This type of tenancy is created when the tenant occupies the property without any agreement as to term. There is deemed to be a tenancy for a period measured by the rental payments. Therefore, unless an intent to the contrary is expressed, a periodic tenancy or a tenancy from year to year exists if a yearly rent is paid, even if such rent is paid in quarterly or monthly installments. When the rent is not an annual rent but is for a shorter term, such as the common situation where monthly rent is paid, a month-to-month tenancy is said to exist. When a lease is of unspecified duration and rent is payable monthly, the tenancy is from month to month even if the tenant remains in possession of the premises and pays rent for more than a year.

A periodic tenancy continues until the party who wishes to terminate the tenancy serves a proper notice of termination on the other party. In order for such notice to be proper it must be served at the proper time under state law and must state the proper termination date. (A periodic tenancy may not be discontinued nor may the rent be increased at any time except at the end of the term.) Thus, where a month-to-month tenancy commences on, say, January 15, the notice of termination must state that the tenancy is to terminate on the 14th day of the desired month.

Tenancy at Will: This type of tenancy, which is for an indefinite term, may be terminated by either party to the transaction. The courts do not favor this form of tenancy and will, where possible, construe the lease in question as being a periodic tenancy. Unlike a periodic tenancy, which may be terminated only by giving proper notice, a tenancy at will may be terminated by the death of either the landlord or the tenant.

Tenancy at Sufferance: This type of tenancy is created when a tenant who has rightfully possessed the premises continues to possess the property after the expiration or termination of the lease. The tenant at sufferance may be ousted by the landlord at any time without notice. The death of a tenant at sufferance terminates the relationship.

[¶2814.2] Holding Over

It is agreed, either expressly or impliedly, in all leases that at the end of the term the tenant will deliver possession of the premises back to the landlord. Therefore, a tenant who continues to remain in possession of leased premises after the lease term, without the landlord's consent, is a wrongdoer. (It should be noted that the holdover tenant who is considered a wrongdoer is not immediately treated as a trespasser.) In states that have not changed the common-law rule by statute, a holdover tenant may be held by the landlord for a further term. This is true even if the tenant holds over just for a day. Of course, the landlord, rather than holding the tenant to an additional term, may evict him or her. Once the landlord elects how to treat the tenant (i.e., eviction or holdover), that decision is binding. It should be noted that a tenant has no reciprocal right to hold the landlord.

As can be seen, the holdover rule is harsh. Courts will often not apply it if they find that the tenant was unable to move for compelling reasons or if the landlord impliedly consented to the holding over. For example, if the parties are actively negotiating a new lease when the old lease expires, the tenant will usually be considered as a month-to-month tenant. In addition, the parties may agree in the original lease that holding over will not convert the tenancy into a year-to-year one.

[¶2814.3] Eviction

Technically interpreted, an eviction may be defined as the disturbance of a tenant's possession, or expulsion so that the tenant is deprived of enjoyment of the demised premises, in whole or in part, by reason of the landlord's title, entry, or act. An eviction can be either actual or constructive. An *actual* eviction is deemed to occur when the landlord's acts deprive the tenant of some right to the premises to which the tenant is entitled. If the landlord's acts merely interfere with the tenant's beneficial enjoyment of the premises, the eviction is *constructive*. It is not to be inferred from this that all landlord interferences with tenants' possession or enjoyment constitute constructive evictions. To qualify as a constructive eviction the landlord's interference must be intentional and so substantial as to deprive the tenant of enjoyment of the premises and the tenant must in turn, as a result of such interference, abandon possession of the premises within a reasonable time. Whether the landlord's acts constitute a constructive eviction is usually a question of fact.

[¶2814.4] Possession

Leases are frequently silent about the landlord's duty to deliver actual (as opposed to legal) possession of the property at the commencement of the term. In such cases, the states are divided as to whether the landlord or the new tenant has the duty of evicting a holdover tenant.

[¶2814.5] Implied Covenants in a Lease

Most courts in this country agree that when an agreement to lease real estate employs the terms "demise," "let," or "grant", the landlord impliedly covenants possession of good title to make the lease and enter into the landlord-tenant relationship.

Also, as agreed to by most courts, a covenant of quiet enjoyment is implied in a valid lease. The purpose of this covenant is to protect the tenant from people who claim to have title that is better than the landlord's. Thus, in the usual situation, the covenant of quiet enjoyment protects the tenant's status under the lease when ownership of the property is transferred.

[¶2814.6] Repairs

Frequently, a lease will specify which party has the duty to repair the premises but will not indicate what the other party may do if the duty is breached. In most jurisdictions, if the landlord breaches a duty to repair, the tenant has several alternatives: make the repairs and deduct the cost from the rent; pay the rent and sue the landlord for the decrease in rental value; or pay a lesser rental due to the decreased value of the premises. If the tenant is injured by the landlord's failure to repair, there is a split as to whether the landlord is liable for the injuries. The states that hold no liability do so on the theory that the tenant had the duty to make the repairs and then seek to recover the cost from the landlord.

If a defective condition exists in an area over which the landlord does not retain control, the landlord's duty to repair (if it exists) depends on prior notice of the defective condition. Since this is invariably a matter of dispute between the parties, such notice should always be in writing.

[¶2815] Lease-Closing Checklist

In order to avoid any unanticipated problems at the last minute, use the lease-closing checklist that follows. Geared to the landlord's attorney, it is not exhaustive but may serve as a basic guide.

☐ *Lease:* Be sure to bring enough copies of the lease, fully prepared and ready to be signed.

☐ *Signatures:* Be sure all necessary signatories are present.

☐ *Bill of Sale:* If personal property is being sold when the property is leased, the lessee will want a bill of sale for items conveyed.

☐ *Property Data:* It's a good idea to bring appropriate maps, surveys, and diagrams to the closing, as they may contain information that will be useful to the tenant.

☐ *Additional Data:* Just in case any questions might arise at the closing, bring the following items: title abstracts, certificates and guarantees, certificates of occupancy and inspection, and mortgage data.

☐ *Notary*

☐ *Costs:* Tax receipts, assessments, as well as bills for water, fuel, utilities, and other expenses that may be apportioned when the premises are leased, should be brought along.

☐ *Maintenance Contracts*

☐ *Insurance Policies*

☐ *Forms for Consenting to Alterations and Repairs*

☐ *Leasing Material:* Bring subordinate leases as well as necessary information about security deposits.

☐ *Receipts:* To avoid embarrassment or disagreements, be sure to bring receipts for documents and money delivered to you, the attorney, or the tenant.

❑ **Miscellaneous:** Before the closing, it may be desirable to write a reminder letter to the prospective tenant to bring necessary documents such as power of attorney or other authorizations. Also remind the prospective tenant to bring cash or a check for rent, security, or adjustments.

[¶2816] SPECIAL ASPECTS OF THE RESIDENTIAL LEASE

Because of the importance of a family's home, and because of the imbalance of power between the residential landlord and tenant, the residential landlord-tenant relationship is a heavily regulated one. In most communities, landlords are obligated by the "warranty of habitability" to offer premises that are fit for habitation (e.g., are heated when necessary, have hot water, have functioning mechanical systems). Certain communities impose regulation on the amount of rent that may be charged, and the circumstances under which renewal leases must be offered to tenants (and, in some cases, family members who lived with tenants who have moved away or died).

If the tenant fails to meet any obligations, the landlord's remedy is to seek eviction (for nonpayment, failure to honor the lease relation, or as a holdover). If the landlord fails to meet any obligations, the tenant's remedy (depending on jurisdiction, the facts of the case and the tenant's own inclinations) may include having repairs performed and deducting their cost from the rent; withholding rent and raising the landlord's nonperformance as a defense in the eventual eviction action; joining or organizing a "rent strike" of other tenants; or petitioning that the building be placed under court supervision or receivership so that it can be managed properly.

Frequently, owners of residential buildings will seek the conversion of rental units to cooperative or condominium ownership and management. See ¶1401 et seq. for a discussion of this process.

— FOR FURTHER REFERENCE —

Armstrong, George M. Jr. and John C. LaMaster, "Retaliatory Eviction as Abuse of Rights," 47 *Louisiana L. Rev.* 1 (September '86).

Chase, Edward and E. Hunter Taylor, "Landlord and Tenant: A Study in Property and Contract," 30 *Villanova L. Rev.* 571 (June '85).

Halper, Emanuel B., "Can You Find a Fair Lease?" 14 *Real Estate L.J.* 99 (Fall '85).

Kratovil, Robert, "Unconscionability: Real Property Lawyers Confront a New Problem," 21 *John Marshal L.J.* 1 (Fall '87).

Krieger, Walter W., "Housing Code Violations and Tenant Remedies," 19 *Indiana L. Rev.* 299 (Winter '86).

Payne, John M., "Rent Control and the Low-Income Tenant," 14 *Real Estate L.J.* 156 (Fall '85).

Reskin, Lauren Rubenstein, "Commercial Landlords Must Be Reasonable," 72 *ABA J.* 90 (April '86).

Rose, Alan D., "The Landlord's Obligation to Act Reasonably in Consenting to an Assignment," 30 *Boston Bar J.* 28 (July–August '86).

Stauffer, Robert R., "Tenant Blacklisting: Tenant Screening Services and the Right to Privacy," 21 *Harvard J. on Legislation* 239 (Winter '87).

Tun, Harry, "Implied Warranty of Habitability," 29 *Howard L.J.* 103 (Winter '86).

Weiss, James L., "Landlord and Liability," 59 *Tulane L. Rev.* 701 (January '85).

MATRIMONIAL MATTERS

[¶2901] Matrimonial matters include premarital planning as well as separation and divorce proceedings. Protection of property rights of individuals prior to marriage, upon separation, and at the time of dissolution are important considerations for any lawyer. Antenuptial agreements, alimony, child support, custody and visitation, and the tax consequences of these matters, are among the elements that must be carefully examined for each prospective client.

The perennial problems of family law include deciding what constitutes marital property; dividing the property at divorce; determining when alimony or maintenance payments to an ex-spouse should be modified or discontinued; and determining who should care for, and who should pay for, the couple's children. During the following paragraphs, the most characteristic themes are an attempt to broaden the definition of marital assets, and cases involving interrelations between pension and bankruptcy law and the law of divorce and child support.

The High Court has taken the position that diversity jurisdiction is appropriate in a tort suit brought by one spouse against another spouse who resides in another state. In this reading, the "domestic relations" exception is limited to actions involving divorce, alimony, or child custody decrees.[1] Another kind of federal court—the bankruptcy court—has been permitted to lift the automatic bankruptcy stay in order to permit continuation of a state divorce action or equitable distribution of the couple's property.[2]

P.L. 102-537 requires credit bureaus to include child support arrears of $1,000 or more, as reported by state child support agencies, in credit reports. This statute also makes it a federal crime to fail willfully to pay past-due support for a child who lives in another state. The federal court can make compliance with a child support order a condition of probation in any federal case, whether or not related to child support. OBRA '93 (P.L. 103-66) adds a new Section 609 to ERISA, making employer group health plans recognize "qualified medical child support orders" (similar to Qualified Domestic Relations Orders) issued by divorce courts. States must enact and enforce laws dealing with the child support orders, so that Medicaid rolls will not be burdened by children whose non-custodial parents fail to provide for their medical care.

The American Academy of Matrimonial Lawyers has promulgated a statement, "Bounds of Advocacy," to give ethical guidance to matrimonial lawyers.[3] Some principles from this document:

➤ It may be impossible to represent a client adequately in a matrimonial matter without also considering the best interests of other family members, especially children.

➤ It may be necessary to consult another lawyer or an accountant if consultation is required on matters such as bankruptcy, taxes, or estate planning.

➤ It may be ethically incumbent on a matrimonial attorney to recommend that a client seek psychological or psychiatric counseling.

➤ Matrimonial attorneys should be knowledgeable about Alternative Dispute Resolution, but should serve as arbitrators or mediators only if competent to do so.

➤ The attorney should never advise a client to hide assets, and has a duty to dissuade clients from prolonging litigation. Lawyers must advise their clients against making bad-faith custody claims; the lawyer has a duty to withdraw rather than pursue spurious claims (e.g., fabricated allegations of sexual abuse).

The document advises against joint representation even if the divorcing spouses don't want separate lawyers, and advises against sexual relationships with clients *or opposing counsel.*

[¶2902] ANTENUPTIAL AGREEMENTS

Prospective spouses may use an antenuptial agreement to define their property rights in property already existing or to be acquired during the marriage. By such an agreement, which may also be executed with a third party (e.g., parents), the property rights that would otherwise arise upon the marriage by operation of law are often substantially altered. Assuming that the parties have contractual capacity, antenuptial agreements are per se valid in all states. However, some states will not uphold an antenuptial ban on alimony in the case of an eventual divorce, on the grounds that such agreements are against public policy in that they encourage divorce. Note that since 1981, transfers of property between spouses (i.e., while the parties are married) generally are not subject to income or gift taxes. However, tax problems can arise where the transfer is made *before* the parties are married or after they are divorced.

In Michigan, a fair antenuptial agreement that is procured in a lawful manner is effective to govern property distribution on divorce, as well as the death of a spouse.[4]

However, some courts[5] take the position that an antenuptial agreement cannot be used to waive rights in the spouse's pension plan, or the right to receive a joint and survivor annuity when the spouse retires.

[¶2903] NONTAX CONSIDERATIONS

In order to be enforceable, an antenuptial agreement must comply with local law concerning consideration, disclosure of husband's assets, adequacy of the provision for the wife, undue influence, and other matters. In the majority of states, the Statute of Frauds requires that the agreement be in writing. In some states, the agreements must be executed in accordance with strict statutory requirements or else risk being declared void. The requirements pertaining to disclosure are particularly stringent, in light of the intimate nature of the relationship between the prospective spouses. The duty to disclose encompasses advising the relinquishing spouse of the nature, extent, and value of the released interest. Fraud, deceit, misrepresentation, or concealment by either party, or the exercise of duress or undue influence, may void the agreement.

[¶2904] ESTATE TAX CONSEQUENCES

The typical antenuptial agreement involves a payment by one spouse in exchange for relinquishment by the other of dower, curtesy, or other survivorship rights in the transferor's property. Since an individual's lifetime transfers may be includible in his or her gross estate under IRC §2036—2038 and §2041, except in the case of bona fide sales or an adequate and full consideration in money or money's worth, the following basic principles should be kept in mind:

❏ Inclusion under IRC §2036 can be avoided if the decedent retains no life interest in the transferred property;

❏ In order to escape IRC §2037, the transfer must take effect before death and the transferor must not retain a reversionary interest;

❏ To avoid taxation under IRC §2038, the transfer must not be subject to revocation or amendment;

❏ Section 2041 of the IRC will not apply as long as the transferor has no general power of appointment over the transferred property.

However, if a transfer that would be subject to estate tax under one of these IRC sections is made in consideration of the release of support rights, instead of marital rights, there is no tax liability to the extent of the value of the support rights.

These considerations would come into play if the parties are not married at the time of the transferor spouse's death. As mentioned earlier, if the parties are married at the time of the transferor spouse's death, the transferred property generally will qualify for the unlimited estate tax marital deduction under Section 2056(a). Result: no estate tax consequences.

[¶2905] GIFT TAX CONSEQUENCES

A transfer under an antenuptial agreement in exchange for the relinquishment of marital rights is treated as a taxable gift. If the transfer is in consideration for the release of support rights, instead of marital rights, there is no gift to the extent of the value of the support rights (*Rev. Rul. 68-379*, 1968-2 CB, 414).

The courts have held that an unconditional promise to make a series of payments constitutes a taxable gift of the entire amount when the promise binding upon the promisor is made and not when the property is actually transferred. The timing of the antenuptial agreement can give rise to important tax savings. If the agreement is treated as being executed *prior* to marriage, only the $10,000 annual exclusion is available. But if the "transfer" does not take place until *after* the marriage, the gift would qualify for the unlimited gift tax marital deduction under IRC §2523.

[¶2906] CLAIMS AGAINST THE ESTATE

Under pre-1984 law, a claim against the payor spouse's estate was deductible under IRC §2053 if it was supported by an adequate and full consideration in money or money's worth. Claims by a former spouse against the estate based on the surrender of *marital* or *property* rights did not meet the consideration test and were not deductible. On the other hand, a claim by a former spouse based on the release of marital or property rights based on a *court decree,* where the court had the power to determine the marital or property rights of the spouse, was deductible. In addition, transfers under an antenuptial agreement made in consideration of the release of *support* rights would be deductible.

The 1984 Tax Law expanded the rules for allowing claims against the payor spouse's estate to be estate-tax deductible. Transfers made as a result of claims based on a court decree or in consideration for the release of support rights continue to be deductible. In addition, if property is transferred to a former spouse pursuant to an agreement entered into not more than two years prior to a divorce, it will be deductible. (Note: This change will probably have more of an impact on parties who enter into agreements *after* marriage or in contemplation of a divorce than on those entering into antenuptial agreements. Reason: It is less likely that an antenuptial agreement will qualify under the two-years-before-divorce rule.)

[¶2907] INCOME TAX CONSEQUENCES

Section 2516 of the IRC specifies circumstances in which property settlements in connection with a divorce are automatically exempted from being treated as gifts. Thus, for qualifying transfers it is not necessary to deliberate whether the transferee furnished consideration in money or money's worth. For Section 2516 to be applicable, the spouses must adopt a written agreement concerning their marital and property rights and the divorce must occur during a three-year period beginning one year before the agreement is made.

No gift arises from any transfer made in accordance with such agreement if property is transferred (1) to either spouse in settlement of marital or property rights or (2) to provide reasonable support for the children while they are minors.

If property is transferred in trust, the gain is recognized to the transferor to the extent that the liabilities assumed by the trust exceed the transferor's basis.[6]

[¶2907.1] Liability for Tax on a Joint Return

Married taxpayers who file joint tax returns are jointly and individually liable for any tax, interest, or penalty applicable to the return.[7] Therefore, one spouse may be liable for the full amount of the tax liability even if all of the income was earned by the other spouse.

However, under the "innocent spouse" rule, an innocent spouse may be relieved of the entire tax, including interest and penalties and other amounts, if (1) a substantial tax understatement is attributable to "grossly erroneous items" of one spouse, including claims for deductions and credits for which there is no basis in fact or in law; (2) the other spouse can establish that at the signing of the personal tax return, he or she did not know, nor have reason to know, that there was a substantial understatement; and (3) taking into account all of the facts of circumstances, it would be inequitable to hold the other spouse liable for the deficiency in tax for such taxable year attributable to such substantial understatement. Generally, a "substantial understatement" is one that exceeds $500.[8] Congress regards the "innocent spouse" rule as an important adjunct to the privilege of filing joint returns.[9] Under this rule, an innocent spouse had reason to know of the omission of income of a salesman spouse due to his lavish expenditures and extensive efforts in the pursuit of sales.[10]

[¶2907.2] The Recapture Trap

Paid correctly, alimony is deductible to the person who pays it and taxable income to the person who gets it. Federal law, not a state court determination of the nature of the payments, determines whether a payment does or does not qualify as deductible "alimony."[11]

Mere characterization of an arrangement as alimony will not make the payments deductible. Payments that evidently were intended as a property settlement to permit the divorcing husband to retain the farm he inherited did not qualify for tax treatment as alimony.[12] A taxpayer-wife has been permitted[13] to deduct the amount she refunded to her ex-husband after a modification of the decree; the amount can be construed as repayment of an overpayment of alimony.

To qualify as alimony, the payments must be in cash, they must end when the recipient dies and they can't be disguised child-support payments, among other rules.

But under some circumstances, the IRS may force a spouse who paid otherwise deductible alimony in the first three years after divorcing to pay tax on a portion of it in a later year. In general, "recapture rules" trigger tax on annual payments greater than about $15,000 in the first three years after a divorce if the size of payments decreases significantly during that three-year period.[14] The recapture rules are designed to prevent couples from front-loading alimony payments in the first years after a divorce.[15]

[¶2907.3] The Dependency Exemption

The parent with custody of a child for the greater part of the year is entitled to the deduction unless he or she waives the right to the deduction *in writing*. The custodial parent who elects to release the exemption to the noncustodial parent should use Form 8332, Release of Claim to Exemption for Child of Divorced or Separated Parent or a similar statement. The written waiver may cover one or more years, or can be a permanent waiver. Note, however, agreements executed before January 1, 1985 which grant the noncustodial spouse the deduction will be enforced provided he or she provides at least $600 per year support for the child.

If a child lives in one parent's household the entire year, the custodial parent can (if otherwise qualified) benefit from head of household tax status—even if the child is claimed as a dependent by the other parent. Also note that medical expenses for the children paid by a parent are deductible by that parent. It doesn't matter that the other parent gets the dependency exemption or has custody of the children. Each parent can deduct the medical expenses he or she pays.

[¶2907.4] Alimony Trusts

A trust, the income of which is taxable to the grantor husband, will be taxable to the wife if the income is payable to her under a written separation or divorce agreement.[16]

Any income that must be used to support the grantor's children shall continue to be taxed to the grantor husband.

[¶2908] TERMINATION OF THE MARRIAGE

In most states, the ways of ending or suspending a marriage are: divorce, annulment, judicial separation, separation agreement, absence (presumption of death), and, of course, death.

Just as the state legislatures have power to regulate the creation of marriages, they also have the power to enact statutes prescribing the grounds for ending them. Accordingly, the grounds for termination of the marital relationship vary extensively from state to state.

As a general rule, an annulment differs from a divorce in that an annulment proceeding is brought to have a marriage declared void from its inception, whereas a divorce arises from causes after the marriage. In many states, separation for a specified period of time is grounds for divorce.

[¶2909] ADULTERY

In most states, either spouse is given the right to an absolute divorce for the adultery of the other. The two essential elements of adultery are:
(1) Voluntary intercourse, and
(2) Guilty intent.

To prove adultery, both direct and circumstantial evidence, if competent, are generally admissible.

Adultery need not be continuing to constitute sufficient ground for a divorce decree—proof of a single act of adultery will be sufficient. Where adultery is relied upon as grounds for a judicial separation, it may be necessary to prove that the adultery is so open and notorious as to be cruel and inhuman.

Although there are few prosecutions, adultery is a crime in most states.

Nearly all the states have abolished the cause of action for "criminal conversation" (roughly speaking, a suit for damages occasioned by a third party's seduction of the plaintiff's spouse); Mississippi and Kentucky waited until 1992 to do so.[17] A 1993 Oklahoma case rejects a married couple's tort action premised on a minister's sexual relationship with the wife during marriage counseling. The minister himself could not be sued for seduction or alienation of affections, so the church had no tort liability.[18]

[¶2910] BIGAMY

When one spouse has a prior spouse living, the second marriage will be void and not merely voidable. In most states, bigamy constitutes grounds for annulment; in a few states, it also constitutes grounds for a divorce. In states where bigamy is the basis of both a divorce and annulment action, the party bringing the action will have the option for annulment or for divorce.

Before deciding whether or not to bring an action for annulment or divorce, local law should be checked; in some jurisdictions, alimony can only be awarded in a divorce action.

Because a bigamous marriage is void and not merely voidable, the parties may treat the marriage as a nullity without bringing formal proceedings. However, in many jurisdictions, the parties seek an annulment in order to have a decree rendered awarding alimony, child custody, and child support.

[¶2911] AGE

Each state imposes statutory age requirements for the issuance of marriage licenses. A marriage involving a spouse who has not reached the legal age for marriage, either with or without consent, is voidable rather than void in most jurisdictions. An action to have the marriage annulled may be maintained by the spouse who had reached the legal age for marriage, the guardian of the infant, or the infant's "next best friend." Annulment for non-age will not be available if the spouse who had not reached the legal age at the time of the marriage freely cohabited after reaching the legal age. The non-age of the one spouse will not be available as grounds for an action of annulment to the spouse who was of legal age at the time of marriage.

[¶2912] CRIME

In many jurisdictions, a criminal conviction and imprisonment may constitute grounds for divorce or the termination of the marital relationship. In some states, if either spouse is sentenced to life imprisonment, the marriage is absolutely and automatically dissolved without the need for legal process. The statutory provisions establishing grounds for divorce often include "infamous crimes," "crimes involving moral turpitude," or a felony.

Some states provide that a divorce may be granted even if the crime was committed before the marriage as long as the sentence was imposed after the marriage.

Although some state laws differ, the subsequent pardon of a convict should not destroy the right to a divorce declared by statute to arise on conviction and sentence.

[¶2913] CRUELTY

In most states, cruelty constitutes grounds for a divorce or separation. Cruelty is not limited as a rule to physical violence or effects of physical violence but may include mental cruelty. Whether the misconduct constitutes cruelty for divorce purposes is determined by its effect on the person complaining about the acts. The important consideration is the health and safety of the suffering spouse; the motives of the offender are immaterial. What may be cruel behavior toward one person may not be cruel toward another.

The following specific acts of cruelty have been held sufficient grounds for divorce:

❏ Physical violence, even a single act if sufficient to endanger life. However, a divorce will not necessarily be granted for an isolated instance of less serious physical violence.

❏ Threat of physical violence.

❏ Habitual intemperance coupled with other acts that make it dangerous for the other spouse to continue in the marital relation. Addiction to narcotic drugs, together with other misconduct, may constitute cruelty.

❏ Deliberate use of intemperate language with an intent to injure the other spouse.

❏ False and unfounded accusations of adultery, especially when made against the wife or a false and unfounded accusation that the wife is a prostitute.

❏ Refusal of one spouse to speak to the other for an extended period of time.

❏ Cruel treatment of a child in the presence of the wife.

❏ Adultery may constitute legal cruelty.

❏ Continuation of sexual relations after a spouse knows that he or she is afflicted with venereal disease and communication of the disease to the other.

[¶2913.1] Interspousal Torts

A divorcing spouse can sue the other for negligent or intentional infliction of emotional distress, whether or not physical injury occurred;[19] Florida abrogates interspousal immunity in cases (e.g., where one spouse attacked the other with a machete) where the traditional policy objectives of preserving the family and discouraging collusive suits are not applicable.[20] New Mexico does not absolutely bar claims of intentional infliction of emotional distress in divorce cases, but the existence of a marriage is still relevant in tort cases; truly outrageous spousal conduct is a prerequisite to the action.[21]

A surprisingly large number of cases involving interspousal phone tapping have been litigated. The majority rule seems to be[22] that the spouse whose communications are monitored is entitled to damages.

[¶2914] DESERTION AND ABANDONMENT

In most states, desertion or abandonment for a statutory period of time—ranging from six months to five years—will be grounds for divorce. To establish desertion or abandonment, the plaintiff must establish an intent on the part of the other spouse to abandon or desert. There must be no justification for the desertion and it must be against the will and without the consent of the plaintiff. Leaving home to serve in the armed forces, to seek employment in a foreign city, to visit a health resort, etc., will not constitute desertion or abandonment. Similarly, separation pursuant to a valid separation agreement will not constitute desertion or abandonment. However, as noted below, where the parties separate pursuant to an agreement, the agreement should be made at or after the time of separation (see ¶2919).

Constructive abandonment will be a defense to an action for desertion or abandonment. If the defendant was justified in abandoning the plaintiff (e.g., for extreme cruelty), he or she will have a complete defense to the plaintiff's action for abandonment. The doctrine of constructive abandonment is only applied in extreme circumstances.

Many states have enacted so-called Enoch Arden laws that permit the spouse to apply for a dissolution of the marriage if the other spouse has been absent for a statutorily defined period and he or she is believed to be dead. Generally, it is necessary to show the circumstances under which the missing spouse disappeared and that diligent efforts were made to locate the spouse. But if the absent spouse disappeared under circumstances that indicate that he or she would not attempt to contact the other spouse and that efforts to locate would be pointless, these rules will not be applied. If the spouse remarries after a dissolution of the earlier marriage because of the absence of the first spouse and the initial spouse reappears, the validity of the second marriage will not be affected.

One spouse's complete refusal to have marital sexual relations may be legally equivalent to desertion or abandonment (and may also constitute mental cruelty, or provide evidence of irreconcilable differences as required by a no-fault statute).

[¶2915] DRUNKENNESS

Habitual intoxication constitutes a statutory ground for divorce in most jurisdictions. A single instance of overindulgence or a tendency to overindulge on occasion will not constitute sufficient intoxication to be grounds for divorce. A statutory cause of action for divorce requires a fixed and almost irresistible habit of drinking alcoholic beverages with considerable frequency so as to produce intoxication. The spouse must have developed the habit after marriage. In some states, the statute requires that the habit must have continued for a period of one to two years.

[¶2916] FRAUD

Marriages induced by fraud are not absolutely void but merely voidable at the suit of the injured party for annulment during his or her lifetime. In a few jurisdictions, fraud is also recognized as a ground for divorce. To be a ground for divorce, fraud must relate to a matter essential to the validity of the marriage itself.

Marriage is essentially a contract and the rules relating to an ordinary contract will be applicable. Fraud that goes to the essence of the contract will constitute grounds for setting aside the contract. In the following situations, fraud has been sufficient to constitute grounds for annulment:

❑ Misrepresentation as to, or concealment of, prior marital status.

❑ Misrepresentation as to intention to subsequently go through a religious ceremony.

❑ Secret intent not to cohabit or have children.

❑ Concealment of a venereal disease or other serious health impairment.

❑ Concealment of a pregnancy at the time of marriage when the husband is not the father.

❑ False representations as to citizenship.

[¶2917] INSANITY

The usual remedy for dissolution of a marriage where one of the parties was insane at the time of the ceremony is by a proceeding for annulment. The majority of states permit divorce on the ground of insanity or incurable insanity.

If the insanity existed at the time of the marriage, the sane spouse, in order to maintain an action for annulment, must establish that he or she did not know of the condition at the time of the marriage. If an action for annulment because of insanity at the time of the marriage is maintained by the insane spouse after regaining sanity, it is generally necessary to establish that the parties did not cohabit after the insane spouse regained sanity.

Where a spouse has been incurably insane for a statutory period of time (varying from 2 to 10 years), the statutes of several states specify a procedure whereby the marriage may be annulled. If the plaintiff is the husband, the court may require the husband to make provision for the support of his insane wife.

[¶2918]　No-Fault Divorce

The majority of states now have no-fault divorce. In some states the action is based on a separation of the parties for a statutorily prescribed period (usually 12 to 18 consecutive months). In other states, parties may need to allege and show an irretrievable breakdown of the marriage or irreconcilable differences.

Depending on state law (especially if the parties are childless), a summary no-fault divorce may be available more or less by agreement, with few legal formalities.

Furthermore, no-fault laws eliminate the traditional defenses to divorce actions (e.g., wrongdoing by both spouses; condonation of marital misconduct).

[¶2919]　Separation Agreement

Generally, a separation agreement will be enforceable where the parties are about to be separated when the agreement is made or the parties have previously separated. If the parties separate without an agreement, one party may be found to have abandoned or deserted the other. The parties must also comply with the statutory requirements as to the manner of execution. For example, most states require that the agreement be in writing. In some jurisdictions, the parties must execute a separation agreement if they want a no-fault divorce.

The separation agreement is an agreement between the parties that they will live separate and apart from one another. It generally will also make provisions for the disposition of joint property and support rights; waiver and release of all future rights as spouse in each other's property; surrender of rights of inheritance, homestead, and dower in each other's estate; and the execution of documents needed to implement the agreement.

If it appears that the benefits under the contract are conditioned on one party obtaining a divorce or the terms of the agreement encourage divorce, the agreement may be attacked as violative of the public policy against divorce (see *Pryor v. Pryor*, 88 Ark. 302; *Miller v. Miller*, 284 Pa. 414).

In some jurisdictions, a valid contract for support is binding on the divorce court. In others, the agreement is merely evidential and the divorce court is not controlled by it. A divorce court has the power to incorporate the agreement in the divorce decree or base the decree on its provisions.

The most delicate portion of the separation agreement often involves the question of child custody. Numerous factors including the age, health, schooling, and sex of the child will be important in determining which parent is to have custody. Similarly, the ability and the relative willingness of each parent to care for the child will be important. There is an increasing tendency on the part of the courts to award custody to the more qualified parent, regardless of sex.

The separation agreement should also deal with the question of insurance. The agreement will often provide that one spouse should keep the insurance in effect and appoint the other spouse or children as irrevocable beneficiaries.

The distinction between *merger* of the separation agreement into the court's decree, and *survival* of the agreement, is an important one. If the separation agreement merges, its provisions can be enforced by contempt proceedings—but the court retains the power to modify the agreement at either party's insistence. If the separation agreement survives, it can only be modified by mutual consent, but the contempt power is unavailable. Whether the agreement merges or survives, the court system retains continuing jurisdiction over issues affecting the best interests of children.

[¶2920] PROCEDURAL REQUIREMENTS FOR DIVORCE ACTIONS

When bringing an action for divorce, the plaintiff must first select the proper court. A court has no power to grant a divorce without state statutory or constitutional authority. A second essential element of the court's divorce power is jurisdiction over the marriage status—that is, one of the spouses must have domicile in the state.

In personam jurisdiction is generally not a prerequisite to a valid matrimonial decree, although it is necessary for a valid support order, alimony decree or order, or any other decree or order having the effect of an alimony decree.

[¶2921] PROCESS AND APPEARANCE

In many states, there is a special procedure for service of a summons in a matrimonial action. In some states, substituted service may not be available. In other states, notation of the nature of the action must be indicated on the summons if a summons is served without the complaint. Stricter rules concerning the process server's proof of service may be applicable. The process server may be required to prove how he or she identified the defendant.

In divorce actions, as in any other action, the court will not have jurisdiction to grant a divorce unless service of process has been made in accordance with both the state and U.S. Constitutional requirements.

[¶2922] RESIDENCE REQUIREMENTS

Courts are generally less liberal in taking jurisdiction in matrimonial cases than in other civil actions. In most states, there is a statutory requirement that a person maintaining a matrimonial action be a resident of the state for a specified period of time prior to commencing the action. The residence requirement will often vary depending on factors such as the state's public policy toward matrimonial actions, whether the cause of action accrued in the state, whether the parties were married in the state, whether the parties are both residents of the state, and the nature of the action.

The residence requirements generally cannot be waived by consent between the parties.

Given the wide availability of no-fault divorce, and the comparative uniformity of state provisions dealing with marital property, incentives to seek an out-of-state divorce are few, and ordinarily the divorce will be sought in a state that is a bona fide permanent residence of one or both spouses.

[¶2923] PREPARATION, SETTLEMENT NEGOTIATION, AND TRIAL

Getting full command of the facts, preparing a comprehensive memorandum of law, and obtaining complete information about the financial situation are basic to successful negotiation, settlement, and trial.

This information-gathering process has three primary aims:

(1) Establishment of the acts or the facts that constitute the basis for separation and divorce.

(2) Development of financial factors that are the basis for alimony and settlement of property.

(3) Development of the factors that govern custody and visitation arrangements.

Because of the increasingly liberal divorce statutes, the divorce decree may be a near certainty. The real questions to be resolved will involve the financial and custody arrangements. It is essential to get all the information about family finances, standards of living, insurance policies, real estate, gifts, how living expenses were met, how support was provided, etc. As to children, a case history should be developed as to attitude, responsibility, and interest taken by each parent; medical and psychiatric histories; persons who might testify as to the best interests of the children and the relationship of possible witnesses to the parents; etc.

[¶2924] RECOGNITION OF FOREIGN DECREES

When a court with jurisdiction grants a divorce that is valid within that state, it is regarded as valid in every other jurisdiction.

The Full Faith and Credit clause of the United States Constitution requires that the courts of one state give full faith and credit to the judgments and decrees of the courts in another state. However, full faith and credit are not afforded a decree if the court rendering the decree did not have jurisdiction over the parties to the action; i.e., if neither party had a domicile within the divorce state or the defendant did not receive proper service of process and did not appear in the action.

Similarly, a court need not give any greater credit to a decree of a court rendered in another jurisdiction than the court rendering the decree would have given. For example, a New York court will look beyond the decree to determine if fraud was committed on an Alabama court in rendering an Alabama divorce if the Alabama court would look beyond the decree for that purpose. However, when a foreign decree has been rendered based on jurisdiction over the parties to the action, the courts in another state, even though it is the domicile of one of the parties to the action, cannot refuse to give the decree full faith and credit.

Foreign divorce decrees are governed by the rules of international comity rather than the stricter rules of full faith and credit dictated by the United States Constitution. However, as a matter of comity, foreign courts will generally recognize a decree of another country, provided it was based on a proper jurisdictional predicate.

The Uniform Reciprocal Enforcement of Support Act, and various federal laws dealing with child support enforcement, should be consulted in this connection.

[¶2925] ALIMONY

The court with jurisdiction over the divorce action may order one spouse to make a series of continuing payments to the other spouse, as a substitute for support during the marriage. Such payments may be called "alimony," "maintenance," "spousal support," or other names dictated by local practice, and should be distinguished from the equitable distribution or community property division of marital property.

To render a decree including alimony, the court must have in personam jurisdiction of the defendant against whom the decree is to be entered. If the court's jurisdiction is limited to in rem jurisdiction over the marital res because of constructive service on a nonresident defendant, the court will be limited to subjecting the local property of the nonresident defendant to the effect of the alimony decree, provided the property was attached prior to the decree.

Alimony may be permanent or temporary. After jurisdiction over the parties has been obtained, temporary alimony ("alimony pendente lite" or "suit money") may be awarded in the court's sound discretion, to provide support for the needy spouse while the action is pending.

Permanent alimony is generally awarded as part of the divorce decree when all parties are before the court. If the parties entered into a separation agreement prior to the divorce, the agreement may be merged into the decree. Upon being merged into the decree, the agreement will become an integral part of the decree and can be enforced as an alimony decree. The agreement will not be binding on the court; the court may alter, increase, or decrease the provisions of the agreement. If the court has altered a separation agreement, it is the altered amount and not the original amount that is entitled to the special enforcement procedures of the equity court.

State law may limit the duration of permanent alimony, or may deny permanent alimony (permitting only short-term rehabilitative alimony) unless the recipient spouse is incapable of self-support.

[¶2926] FACTORS INFLUENCING ALIMONY AWARD

In the absence of an agreement to incorporate a prior separation agreement into the divorce decree, the court will set alimony in its sound discretion. Factors used by courts in setting alimony may include:

(1) Conduct of the parties (which party is the guilty party).

(2) Financial condition of the parties.

(3) Anticipated earning capacity.

(4) Social standing of the parties.

(Note: Many states have laws setting out various factors upon which alimony awards can be based.)

In most cases, alimony will continue until the death of either spouse or the remarriage of the recipient. When a separation agreement is involved, this rule may be modified by the specific agreement of the parties. The cases are in conflict as to whether the remarriage of the recipient terminates the right to receive alimony when the second marriage is subsequently declared void or voidable.

A decree of permanent alimony may be modified by the court rendering it upon application of either party. Generally, an alimony decree will be modified when there is a showing of need or substantial alteration in financial conditions. The decree will also be modified upon a showing that the payor spouse concealed his or her assets when the decree was originally entered.

In a few states, the courts have held that they may modify a divorce decree rendered in another state involving a domiciliary where they have jurisdiction over the parties (see *Worthley v. Worthley,* 44 Cal. 2d 465). However, the majority rule is still that a divorce decree must be modified by the court entering it.

Various approaches have been taken to the common situation in which an ex-spouse receiving alimony or maintenance enters into a cohabitation relationship. Usually, the relationship (even if it is quasi-marital) will not lead to an automatic decrease or termination of the payments; it will merely be considered as one factor in the recipient ex-spouse's financial situation. The payor ex-spouse will not be relieved of obligations unless the cohabitant makes significant financial contributions to the recipient ex-spouse.[23]

Pensions have a peculiar amphibian status in matrimonial litigation; the pension can be considered both as a source of income (or future income) and as a lump-sum asset susceptible to current or future division. Most states treat cost-of-living increases that will be granted in the future on one spouse's pension as marital property, to the extent that the right to get the increases was earned during the marriage.[24] Michigan has held[25] that pension payments in current pay status can be considered in determining the pension beneficiary's ability to pay alimony even if the retirement benefits are not taken into account in the property division. In Wisconsin, if pension benefits are divided equally on divorce, it is not permissible to limit the non-employee spouse's share of the benefits to a life estate whether the life in question is that of the employee or the non-employee spouse.[26]

A New York ex-wife was held to be entitled to the entire death benefit payable to her husband under his pension account, because the separation agreement incorporated into the divorce decree assigned this sum to her. This result was reached even though the account's beneficiary designation called for division of the account between the ex-wife and the woman the employee was married to at the time of his death.[27]

Under a 1993 Wisconsin case, the support obligation can be reduced when a non-custodial parent leaves a full-time job to return to graduate school, if the additional education is reasonably in pursuance of career objectives;[28] a California case of the same vintage uses a stage hand's earning capacity rather than actual income to compute the support obligation when he switched from stage to lower-paid TV work.[29] However, the California court used a reasonable schedule, not the double shifts routinely worked during the marriage, to calculate support.

[¶2927] COMMUNITY PROPERTY

The community property system in the United States is in effect in Arizona, California, Idaho, Louisiana, New Mexico, Nevada, Texas, Washington, and Wisconsin.

The premise underlying this system is that all earnings, and accumulations from earnings, after marriage belong to the husband and wife together as community property. State practice varies as to treatment of income earned on separate property during the marriage. This is in contrast to the rest of the United States where each spouse's earnings remain his or her separate property unless these monies or assets are put into joint ownership.

Bank deposits that derive from a husband's Social Security benefits received during the marriage are his separate property unless he transmutes them into community property;[30] the Idaho court's rationale is that, although pension benefits received during marriage are community property, the anti-alienation provisions of the Social Security Act reflect a legislative intent that the benefits be separate property.

[¶2928] EQUITABLE DISTRIBUTION OF PROPERTY

No-fault divorce laws in the common-law (non-community property) states provide for equitable distribution upon divorce of all property acquired by the husband and wife during the marriage. This applies to both real and personal property.

Property owned by the husband or the wife prior to the marriage remains his or her separate property and is not subject to equitable distribution. The burden of establishing this immunity is on the spouse who asserts it.

In arriving at a distribution which is "equitable," courts have considered the following factors: (1) respective age, background, and earning abilities of parties, (2) duration of the marriage, (3) standard of living of the parties during the marriage, (4) what money or property each brought into the marriage, (5) present income of the parties, (6) property acquired during marriage by either or both parties, (7) source of acquisition, (8) current value and income-producing capacity of property, (9) debts and liabilities of parties to marriage, (10) probability of continuing present employment at present earnings or better in future, (11) effect of distribution of assets on ability to pay alimony and support, and (12) gifts from one spouse to other during marriage.

The threshold question is what constitutes marital property that is potentially amenable to equitable distribution. One of the most controversial "assets" is goodwill in one spouse's professional practice. The majority view is that if the goodwill is marketable, has ascertainable value, and was developed during the marriage, it is a marital asset subject to distribution.[31] But other states (such as Wisconsin)[32] take the position that normal goodwill developed in a professional practice is not a distributable asset because it is inherently non-marketable.

Even where the goodwill is divisible, a covenant not to compete is not included in the value of the goodwill of a dental practice.[33]

Where a divorcing spouse is not party to a buy-sell agreement with respect to a professional corporation, several courts take the position that the valuation in the buy-sell agreement will not control a property division on divorce. Under the theory, the agreement is just one factor, and national valuation surveys can properly be considered,[34] but there is a split in authority.[35]

A closely held business is less personal in nature than a professional practice, so most people would be comfortable with the idea of treating the goodwill of the business as a divisible marital asset.[36]

A New York court has held that a master's degree, earned based on study during the marriage, is marital property (because it has a discernible monetary value in the form of enhanced income opportunities), but a teaching certificate (reflecting premarital education and training) is not.[37]

Iowa and Michigan have taken similar positions on advanced degrees (Michigan even takes this position on degrees earned during the marriage where the student's employer paid the tuition[38]) but Colorado, Massachusetts, Ohio, Wisconsin and Vermont[39] use the degree as a factor in setting the non-degreed spouse's alimony but do not treat the degree as an asset. *Riaz*[40] deals with the related issue of post-graduate professional certification. In this case, the divorcing wife had already earned an M.D. degree before the marriage, and obtained advanced certification as a neurologist during the marriage. The certification was held not to be marital property, because the divorcing husband had not undergone financial sacrifice or lost career opportunities so that the wife could earn the certification.

A "green card" permitting lawful residence in the United States is not a marital asset and cannot be valued like a degree, even though it is acquired as a result of the marriage.[41]

Although the general principle of property distribution is "equal is equitable," some states[42] do not apply a presumption of equal distribution if the marriage lasted only a short time and did not create a true economic unit. Instead, they prefer to return the spouses to the pre-marital status quo. Fault can be treated as a factor in the property division even in a state where a no-fault divorce can be granted.[43]

If there is an unrelated lawsuit for money damages pending at the time of the divorce, involving income and assets lost during the marriage, the chose in action can become part of the marital estate;[44] and the majority rule is that a personal injury award received by one spouse during the marriage is marital property subject to equitable distribution.[45]

Courts have applied a partnership theory of marriage to justify equal division of the yearly payouts of lottery jackpots won during marriage on tickets purchased with marital funds,[46] but a jackpot won on a lottery ticket purchased by one spouse after separation is entirely the property of the purchaser spouse (even if the jackpot was awarded before the divorce was final).[47]

[¶2928.1] Attorneys' Fees

Despite achieving an excellent settlement (about $1.6 million) for a divorce client, a South Carolina attorney's fee was reduced from the $150,000 allegedly agreed to by the client after entry of the decree, to $51,000 set by the court based on reported hours worked.[48]

More recently, it has been held that an attorney violated state conduct rules by adding an enhancement to the hourly fee because the client received so much alimony; this was deemed to be a forbidden contingent fee.[49] A contingent fee was permitted in post-divorce matters such as support enforcement, provided that the attorney first seeks a fee award under the state's substantive divorce law; this award offsets the subsequent contingent fee.[50]

In North Carolina, a contingent fee is permissible if the work is limited to representation in property division, but not if divorce, alimony, or child support are involved; nor is the attorney permitted to claim that the entire fee is earned for the property division, with the other work done gratuitously.[51]

A divorce lawyer's acceptance of sexual services from a client in lieu of cash payment, although unethical, is not the type of injury to the client's "business or property" that will support a RICO claim.[52]

California has compelled an ex-husband to pay an attorney's fee award to the legal services organization that represented his destitute wife in a support action, on a pro bono basis, on the grounds that the organization was not responsible for the ex-wife's impoverished condition.[53] However, the same state has ruled[54] that an indigent person who faces a jail term because of delinquency in child support payments is entitled to a court-appointed attorney, at public expense, for the contempt proceeding arising out of noncompliance with the support order.

A California divorce court properly ordered the wife to pay her husband's attorneys' fees because of the outrageous conduct of the wife's attorney at trial, as a party sanction; the court said that the wife should look to her own attorney for reimbursement if the attorney was not acting on the wife's instructions to misbehave.[55]

Despite the general prohibition on contingent fees in matrimonial cases, Iowa permitted a contingent fee in a case brought to void a divorce judgment for intrinsic fraud, with the objective of getting a statutory share in the deceased ex-husband's estate. A contingent fee was deemed permissible because the case was limited to economic rather than domestic relations issues, and the deceased ex-husband could not suffer personal harm no matter how the case turned out.[56]

[¶2929] PAYMENTS FOR SUPPORT OF MINOR CHILDREN

One important trend is for ever-stricter enforcement of child support obligations, and an ever-increasing group of weapons that states can use to recoup public assistance funds that were used to support the children of non-paying parents. Title IV-D of the Social Security Act forces the states to enact child support mechanisms (e.g., seizure of tax refunds). However, there is no private right of action under 42 USC Section 1983 *against* a state by an AFDC recipient who alleges that the state did not do an adequate job of locating her children's father and getting him to pay child support.[57]

An SSI check, unlike Social Security disability payments, cannot be garnisheed to meet child support obligations, because the disability payment is linked to past earnings and is supposed to benefit dependents as well as the disabled person, but SSI benefits are public assistance rendered to an individual.[58]

The presumptive applicability of the child support guidelines can be rebutted by a high-income non-custodial parent's showing that the formula would give the children a much higher standard of living than they enjoyed before the divorce. Nevertheless, children are entitled to share in any post-divorce enhancement of a parent's income, as long as this can be done without distributing the *assets* acquired by the non-custodial parent after the divorce.[59]

The child support obligation generally ends at the death of the obligor (perhaps the ultimate change in circumstances). Nevertheless, the West Virginia Supreme Court has held that the trial court's broad equitable powers to promote the best interests of the child can extend to the imposition of a lien on a deceased parent's estate to enforce court-ordered child support.[60] As this case points out, under the Uniform Marriage and Divorce Act, the child support obligation survives the obligor unless there is an agreement to the contrary.

There is a split in authority as to whether trial courts have the power to award the dependency deduction to the non-custodial (and presumably higher-bracket) parent and to compel the custodial parent to execute a waiver of the deduction.[61]

New Jersey's Laws 1990 Chapter 53 allows child support (as well as alimony and maintenance) to be paid by credit card or Electronic Funds Transfer to the family court probation service.

[¶2930] ENFORCEMENT OF ALIMONY DECREES

A decree for permanent alimony may be enforced in the same manner as any debt. However, in most states, the equity court can enforce an alimony decree through contempt proceedings. In most states a spouse may be committed for contempt of court after notice and a demand for payment. Alimony does not constitute a debt within the meaning of the constitutional prohibition of imprisonment for debt.

Although bankruptcy does not bar the receiving spouse's claims for alimony, the payor will not be required to stay in jail if he establishes a bona fide inability to pay (see *Bradshaw v. Bradshaw,* 133 S.W. 2d 617).

Sequestration is a means whereby the alimony-receiving spouse may obtain security for future payments of alimony or a fund from which defaulted payments of alimony may be collected. When the remedy of sequestration is relied upon, the court may cause the payor's personal property and the rents and profits of his real property to be sequestered and may appoint a receiver for them. In most jurisdictions, enforcement through sequestration will be available for either a domestic or foreign divorce decree.

[¶2931] UNIFORM RECIPROCAL ENFORCEMENT OF SUPPORT ACT

All states have adopted a version of the Uniform Reciprocal Enforcement of Support Act. Where this Act is in force, it provides the legal means for reciprocal interstate enforcement of child support obligations when the child and the defaulting supporting parent do not live in the same state.

The Federal Child Support Enforcement Amendments of 1984 (P.L. 98-378) require each state to have child support guidelines *and* effective enforcement measures, such as wage withholding, interception of state tax refunds, and the like. The guidelines must be objective and quantitative in nature. There are four theoretical approaches which may be taken in the guidelines: (1) equalizing the spouses' standards of living; (2) sharing the costs of child-rearing; (3) sharing income; (4) sharing both costs and income (e.g., Delaware's Melson Formula).

[¶2932] CHILD CUSTODY

When confronted with the question of child custody, the welfare of the child is the paramount consideration before the court. Although a divorce decree may fix the custody of the child, the court, at any time, may alter or amend the custodial provisions. Courts may renew the issue of child custody upon a writ of habeas corpus. Although courts often favor the mother when custody is at issue, they will not hesitate to give custody to the spouse who, in the opinion of the court, will be best for the child. If the child is sufficiently mature, the court will generally inquire as to the wishes of the child, although they will be far from conclusive. When the circumstances of the case require it, the court may grant custody to a grandparent, relative, or other third party to the action. Although they will generally be recognized, contracts between spouses as to the custody of children will not be controlling on the court if the welfare of the child dictates otherwise.

When custody is awarded to one parent, visitation rights will generally be awarded to the other parent. However, the court may limit the right to visit the child to a particular time and place or make the right conditional upon notice, etc.

Upon the death of the spouse having custody of the child, it is generally held that the right to custody will revert to the surviving spouse. However, the surviving spouse will not be entitled to custody if he or she cannot provide a suitable home.

The court rendering the divorce decree and determining the issue of custody retains jurisdiction to modify or alter the decree as to divorce at any time when it is in the best interests of the child. However, the doctrine of *res judicata* applies to that part of the divorce decree that grants custody, and the court cannot reexamine the facts formerly adjudicated and make a different order upon them. There must be a substantial change of circumstances to justify a substantial change in the custody order. When necessary to achieve the purposes of public policy—the best interests of the infant—the custody order may be modified because of facts existing at the time of the original order, although not brought out in court at that time.

Provision should also be made for visitation rights. If the parties enter into a separation agreement, they will generally make some arrangement whereby the children will spend part of their vacations, holidays, and weekends with the other parent. When there is a determination, however, that one parent is not a fit parent, the visitation rights may be highly restricted.

The remarriage of either spouse will not automatically affect the custody of children by the former marriage. However, upon remarriage, the argument is often made that the remarried spouse now has a home for the child to replace the one broken by the divorce.

The fact that a parent was the primary caregiving parent during the marriage is a factor in a custody determination, but there is no presumption that the child's best interests require custody in the primary caregiver.[62]

Maryland recently joined several other states by taking the position that only one state at a time can modify custody under the Uniform Child Custody Jurisdiction Act, with the result that Colorado would not be able to modify a Maryland judgment even though the child in question lives in Colorado, because the child has a "significant connection" with Maryland, the father's residence.[63]

A federal court does not have jurisdiction over a dispute between parents, each of whom has a custody judgment from the home state; the Parental Kidnapping Prevention Act (PKPA) does not create a federal private right of action premised on the mere possibility that a parent might kidnap a child incident to a custody dispute.[64]

Custody cases tend to be variations on the theme of the "best interests of the child": so that New Jersey recently held[65] that a custodial parent wishing to move the child to another state must show that the proposed relocation is sought in good faith and will not hamper the relationship with the non-custodial parent. The test is no longer the real advantage of the move to the custodial parent, but the child's best interests.

A recent Vermont case[66] holds that, in a custody modification action, a father seeking to prevent the custodial mother from moving out of state must prove that the relocation would harm the best interests of the children and therefore that custody should be transferred to the father. New Mexico analyzed the issue differently,[67] finding an unconstitutional infringement of the right to travel in imposing the burden of proof as to the child's best interests in the move on the parent with joint custody and primary physical custody. Under this analysis, each parent has the burden of showing the superiority of his or her proposed custody arrangement.

Similarly, the standard of proof for a change from joint custody to sole custody of one parent is the necessity of terminating joint custody in order to promote the best interests of the child. First, joint custody is dissolved; then the court determines which parent is better qualified for sole custody.[68]

New York has ruled that, in custody determinations, a "working mother's" employment must be treated on a parity with a "working father's" employment.[69]

A California statute[70] permits courts hearing custody cases to impose sanctions of up to $1,000 plus attorneys' fees to penalize false accusations of child abuse or neglect.

[¶ 2932.1] Surrogate Motherhood

Recent decisions on opposite coasts refuse to give the support of the court system to surrogacy, albeit with different legal theories. The California case[71] says that a gestational surrogate impregnated with another woman's egg and the sperm of that woman's husband is not a natural parent and has no legal relationship with the child she gestated: the married couple are the child's legal as well as social parents.

In the New York case,[72] the Family Court refused even to hear a filiation petition brought by a surrogate mother and her husband, pursuant to a surrogacy agreement, in order to have the man with whose sperm the baby was conceived named on the birth certificate as the baby's father. The court found the entire arrangement contrary to the state prohibition of baby-selling.

In a case arising before Michigan's statute criminalizing surrogacy, the Sixth Circuit ruled that everyone involved in a surrogate parenting contract enters into a special relationship with the intended legal parents of the child to be born. Thus, there is an affirmative duty to avoid all foreseeable risks of harm, which creates a duty to test the surrogate father and the husband of the surrogate for the CMV virus that led to serious birth defects in the baby.[73]

When a Tennessee couple's marriage was intact, they created seven frozen embryos using the husband's sperm and wife's ova. After divorce, she wanted to give the embryos to a childless couple; he refused. The state Supreme Court assigned the primary right to decide to the "parents," but to the court in cases of disagreement. The court deemed the ex-husband's right not to procreate to out-weigh the ex-wife's interest in making the donation, and hence the clinic was ordered to dispose of the embryos instead of giving them to the childless couple.[74]

A decedent was held to have a quasi-property interest in the sperm he deposited with a sperm bank. He could validly dispose of the sperm by will (he bequeathed it to his girlfriend), and the probate court could not assert a public policy interest to grant his children's petition, under the will contest, that the sperm samples be destroyed.[75]

Three recent cases permit joint adoption by a lesbian couple of a child conceived by artificial insemination by one partner.[76] Ordinarily, adoption will sever the parental rights of the biological parent, but there is a "stepparent" exception under which a parent can retain parental rights to be shared with a marital partner; the three cases extend this provision to an adoption by a female couple.

[¶2933]   UNIFORM CHILD CUSTODY JURISDICTION ACT

Nearly all states have now enacted the Uniform Child Custody Jurisdiction Act. Where it is in force, the Act restricts a court's power to modify custody decrees rendered in other states. Even physical presence of the child and the contesting parent in the state is not, in itself, sufficient to confer jurisdiction on the state for the purpose of modifying the initial custody decree issued by a court in another state. An exception to this rule can be made in the case of a genuine emergency. The Act does not require reciprocity, and can take effect immediately in each state when the Act is adopted.

[¶2934]   SUPPORT AGREEMENTS BETWEEN UNMARRIED COHABITANTS

Unmarried cohabitants who agree to live together as husband and wife may further agree that, in the event of separation, they will divide the property acquired by either of them during the cohabitation. Some courts will only enforce these agreements if they find that there was an express contract (i.e., in writing) to this effect. Other courts will enforce even *oral* agreements if the parties' conduct demonstrates an *implied contract*. The courts can use principles of constructive trust, resulting trust, or quantum merit to enforce the expectations of the parties.

On the other hand, a number of states have *refused* to enforce cohabitation agreements, express or implied. Generally, these courts refuse to enforce these agreements on policy grounds—they don't want to condone this lifestyle. But overall, the trend seems to be in favor of enforcing these agreements, especially with the growing number of couples living together without getting married.

To safeguard enforceability, a cohabitation agreement should spell out consideration other than the "meretricious" relationship—e.g., domestic services; capital contributions to, or work in, a co-owned business.

— ENDNOTES —

1. Hohenberg v. Hohenberg, 18 Fam. Law Rep. 1480 (Bank.-W.D. Tenn. 7/10/92) [divorce action]; Robbins v. Robbins, 964 F.2d 342 (4th Cir. 5/19/92) [equitable distribution].

2. Ankenbrandt v. Richards, #91-367, 112 S.Ct. 2206 (6/15/92). Also see Lanna v. Maul, 979 F.2d 627 (8th Cir. 11/9/92), reaching a similar result for a child's suit against his father's estate for proceeds of the life insurance policy that the father was obligated to maintain for the child's benefit under a divorce settlement. The Eighth Circuit interpreted this suit as a third-party-beneficiary contract action, not a domestic relations matter.

3. See 17 *Family Law Reporter* 1543 (9/24/91).

4. Rinvelt v. Rinvelt, 18 *Fam. Law Rep.* 1028 (Mich.App. 10/28/91).

5. Nellis v. Boeing Co., 18 *Fam. Law Rep.* 1374 (D.Kan. 5/8/92); Hurwitz v. Sher, 982 F.2d 778 (2d Cir. 12/28/92), cert. denied 113 S.Ct. 2345.

6. IRC Sec. 1041.

7. IRC §6013(d)(3); Reg. §1.6013-4(b).

8. IRC §6013(e)(3).

9. Sonneborn v. IRS, 57 TC 373, pgs. 381-383 (1971).

10. Vesco v. IRS, Para. 79,374 P-H Memo. TC (1979).

11. East v. Comm'r, TC Memo 1989-658 (12/18/89).

12. Steen v. Comm'r, 923 F.2d 621 (8th Cir. 1/15/91).

13. Feldman v. Comm'r, TC Memo 1991-153 (4/4/91).

14. IRC Sec. 71(f).

15. See Deborah Lohse, "Your Money Matters: Weekend Report, For a Less-Taxing Divorce, Avoid These Pitfalls," *Wall Street J.* 7/8/94 p. C1.

16. IRC Sec. 682.

17. Hoye v. Hoye, 18 *Fam. Law Rep.* 1188 (Ky.Sup. 2/13/92); Saunders v. Alford, 18 *Fam. Law Rep.* 1592 (Miss.Sup. 10/8/92).

18. Bladen v. First Presbyterian Church, 62 LW 2131 (Okla.Sup. 7/20/93).

19. Massey v. Massey, 807 S.W.2d 391 (Tex.App. 3/7/91).

20. Waite v. Waite, 17 *Fam. Law Rep.* 1392 (Fla.App. 5/28/91).

21. Hakkila v. Hakkila, 811 P.2d 575 (N.M.App. 6/5/91).

22. Heggy v. Heggy, 17 *Fam. Law Rep.* 1595 (10th Cir. 10/2/91) [upholds award of $215,000 as a civil remedy under Title III of 18 U.S.C. 2510-2521, a federal anti-crime bill with wiretapping provisions]; Thompson v. Dulaney, 18 *Fam. Law Rep.* 1460 (10th Cir. 7/22/92); Standiford v. Standiford, 18 *Fam. Law Rep.* 1107 (Md.App. 11/17/92) [$12,500 damages awarded under Maryland's Wiretapping and Electronic Surveillance Act]; California v. Otto, 277 *Cal. Rep.* 596 (App. 1991).

23. See, e.g., In re Tower, 55 Wash.App. 697, 780 P.2d 863 (Wash.App. 10/16/89); Tapia v. Tapia, 15 *Fam. Law Rep.* 1417 (Cal.App. 6/16/89).

24. Moore v. Moore, 553 A.2d 20 (N.J. Sup. 2/15/89).

25. Stoltman v. Stoltman, 429 N.W.2d 220 (Mich.App. 8/16/88).

26. Mausing v. Mausing, 429 N.W.2d 768 (Wisc.App. 10/7/88).

27. Kaplan v. Kaplan, 18 *Fam. Law Rep.* 1498 (N.Y.App.Div. 7/20/92).

28. Kelly v. Hougham, 62 LW 2116 (Wis.App. 7/29/93).

29. Simpson v. Simpson, 4 Cal.4th 225, 14 Cal.Rptr. 2d 411, 841 P.2d 931 (Cal.Sup. 12/17/92).

30. Bowlden v. Bowlden, 58 LW 2259 (Ida.App. 10/3/89).

31. Eslami v. Eslami, 218 Conn. 801, 591 A.2d 411 (Ct.Sup. 5/21/91). Goodwill is distinct from professional reputation and is a distributable marital asset (Thompson v. Thompson, 576 So.2d 267 (Fla.Sup. 1/10/91)). A doctor who is a salaried employee of a medical group, lacking an ownership interest, has no goodwill that can be treated as marital property: Sonek v. Sonek, 412 S.E.2d 917 (N.C.App. 2/4/92).

32. Hollander v. Hollander, 18 *Fam. Law Rep.* 1027 (Md.App. 11/1/91) distinguishes between goodwill in a law practice (nondivisible) and goodwill in a dental practice (divisible but only if it is a solo, not a group, practice). In Utah, the discounted value of the accounts receivable of a solo dental practice is a marital asset, but goodwill is not until and unless the dentist sells the practice: Sorensen v. Sorensen, 18 *Fam. Law Rep.* 1311 (Utah Sup. 3/30/92).

33. Johnston v. Johnston, 15 *Fam. Law Rep.* 1499 (Mo.App. 8/8/89).

34. In re Keyser, 18 *Fam. Law Rep.* 1029 (Colo.App. 10/24/91); Bosserman v. Bosserman, 384 S.E.2d 104 (Va.App. 1989); Bettinger v. Bettinger, 396 S.E.2d 709 (W.Va.Sup. 1990); In re Huff, 18 *Fam. Law Rep.* 1455 (Colo.Sup. 7/20/92).

35. Compare the above with Stern v. Stern, 331 A.2d 257 (N.J.Sup. 1975), Hertz v. Hertz, 657 P.2d 1169 (N.M.Sup. 1983).

36. See, e.g., Ullom v. Ullom, 15 *Fam. Law Rep.* 1396 (Pa.Super. 5/26/89).

37. McGowan v. McGowan, *NYLJ* 1/12/89 p.21 (A.D. 2d Dept.).

38. Lewis v. Lewis, 448 N.W.2d 735 (Mich.App. 11/6/89).

39. Downs v. Downs, 574 A.2d 156 (Vt.Sup. 4/6/90), summarizing the decisions of other states.

40. Riaz v. Riaz, 789 S.W.2d 224 (Mo.App. 5/9/90).

41. Gubin v. Lodisev, 197 Mich.App. 84, 494 N.W.2d 782 (Mich.App. 2/17/93).

42. E.g., Alaska: Rose v. Rose, 755 P.2d 1121 (Ala.Sup. 6/10/88), referring to the similar Oregon approach.

43. Sparks v. Sparks, 18 *Fam. Law Rep.* 14213 (Mich.Sup. 6/30/92).

44. Hanify v. Hanify, 403 Mass. 184 (8/8/88).

45. Powell v. Powell, 547 A.2d 973 (Kan.App. 12/22/88).

46. Ullah v. Ullah, 555 N.Y.S.2d 834 (5/21/90). Also see Gerrits v. Gerrits, 482 N.W.2d 134 (Wis.App. 2/27/92) [divorced lottery winner may have to increase his support payments to ex-wife, but only if the support payments before the lottery win were below the standard of living prevailing during the marriage]; Giha v. Giha, 18 *Fam. Law. Rep.* 1383 (R.I.Sup. 6/4/92) [winning ticket purchased after trial of divorce case was completed, but before entry of final decree, was marital property because marriage continues until entry of decree].

47. Alston v. Alston, 62 LW 2099 (Md.App. 7/23/93).

48. Nicoles v. U.S., 19 *Fam. Law Rep.* 1004 (W.D. Pa. 10/20/92).

49. Oklahoma ex.rel. Oklahoma Bar Ass'n v. Fagin, 18 *Fam. Law Rep.* 1443 (Ok.Sup. 7/14/92).

50. Fletcher (Watson) v. Fletcher, 18 *Fam. Law Rep.* 1299 (Ill.App. 4/15/92).

51. Ronald Williams, P.A. v. Garrison, 411 S.E.2d 633 (N.C.App. 1/7/92).

52. Doe v. Roe, 958 F.2d 763 (7th Cir. 3/9/92).

53. Hayes v. Ward, 4 Cal.Rptr.2d 365 (Cal.App. 2/10/92).

54. Santa Clara County v. Sup.Ct., 18 *Fam. Law Rep.* 1190 (Cal.App. 1/29/92).

55. Daniels v. Daniels, 62 LW 2323 (Cal.App. 10/27/93).

56. Iowa State Bar Comm. on Prof'l Ethics v. McCullough, 468 N.W.2d 458 (La.Sup. 4/17/91).

57. Wehunt v. Ledbetter, 875 F.2d 1558 (11th Cir. 6/27/89), cert. denied 494 U.S. 1027.

58. Tennessee DSS ex.rel. Young v. Young, 802 S.W.2d 594 (Tenn.Sup. 12/31/90).

59. Ford v. Ford, 18 *Fam. Law Rep.* 1015 (Del.Sup. 10/17/91).

60. Scott v. Estate of Wagoner, 400 S.E.2d 556 (W. Va.Sup. 1/17/91).

61. YES: Ford v. Ford, 18 *Fam. Law Rep.* 1108 (Fla.App. 12/11/91); Monterey v. Cornejo, 238 *Cal.Rptr.* 405, 812 P.2d 586 (Cal.Sup. 7/18/91); NO: Blanchard v. Blanchard, 401 S.E.2d 714 (Ga.Sup. 3/15/91).

62. In re Kovacs, 62 LW 2079 (Wash.Sup. 7/8/93).

63. Harris v. Melnick, 552 A.2d 38 (Md.App. 1/19/89).

64. Esser v. Roach, 62 LW 2131 (E.D.Va. 8/3/93).

65. Holder v. Polanski, 544 A.2d 852 (N.J. Sup. 8/9/88).

66. Lane v. Schenck, 18 *Fam. Law Rep.* 1388 (Vt.Sup. 5/22/92).

67. Jaramillo v. Jaramillo, 18 *Fam. Law Rep.* 1115 (N.M.Sup. 12/24/91).

68. Herrell v. Herrell, 424 N.W.2d 403 (Wis. Sup. 6/15/88).

69. Linda R. v. Richard E., 17 *Fam. Law Rep.* 1006 (N.Y.A.D. 10/1/90).

70. Laws 1990 Chapter 297.

71. Anna J. v. Mark C., 17 *Fam. Law Rep.* 1598 (Cal. App. 10/8/91).

72. Anonymous v. Anonymous, *N.Y.L.J.* 10/10/91 (Fam.Ct. Bronx Cou.).

73. Stiver v. Parker, 61 LW 2166 (6th Cir. 9/15/92).

74. Davis v. Davis, 18 *Fam. Law Rep.* 1359 (Tenn. Sup. 6/1/92). Note that the court did not attribute a right to life to the embryos that would favor donation over disposal.

75. Hecht v. L.A. County Superior Court, 62 LW 2007 (Cal. App. 6/17/93).

76. Adoption of Tammy, 416 Mass. 205 (Sup.Jud.Ct. 9/10/93); In re Adoption of BLVB and ELVB, 62 LW 2063 (Vt.Sup. 6/18/93); In re Adoption by JMB, 62 LW 2387 (N.J. Super. 11/9/93).

— FOR FURTHER REFERENCE —

Ain, Sanford K. and Faith D. Dornbrand, "Taxation Issues Affecting the Older Divorce Client," 16 *Family Adviser* 34 (Summer '93).

Baggett, Courtney R., "Sexual Orientation: Should It Affect Child Custody Rulings?" 16 *Law and Psychology Review* 189 (Spring '92).

Bebensee, Paula K., "In the Best Interests of Children and Adoptive Parents: The Need for Disclosure," 78 *Iowa L. Rev.* 397 (January '93).

Bierman, Jacquin D. and Steven L. Severin, "No Bad Debt for Make-Up of Unpaid Child Support," 79 *J. Tax.* 159 (September '93).

Blumberg, Grace Ganz, "Identifying and Valuing Goodwill at Divorce," 56 *Law & Contemporary Problems* 217 (Spring '93).

Burden, Deanne S., "Divorce in the Golden Years," 16 *Family Advocate* 28 (Summer '93).

Crouch, Richard E., "Use, Abuse and Misuse of the UCCJA and PKPA," 6 *American J. of Family L.* 147 (Fall '92).

Dilbeck, Harold R., "The Effect of Loan Principal Payments on Determination of Income for Support," 6 *Am. J. of Family L.* 105 (Summer '92).

Erickson, Nancy S., "Obtaining Adequate Support for Children: Preventing Downward Deviations from the Presumptive Guidelines Amount," 26 *Clearinghouse Review* 530 (September '92).

Fazio, Anthony M., "The Use of Medical Records in Child Custody Cases," 40 *Louisiana Bar J.* 178 (August '92).

Feigenbaum, Matthew S., "Minors, Medical Treatment and Interspousal Disagreement," 41 *DePaul L. Rev.* 841 (Spring '92).

Headley, Richard A., "S Election Issues for Community Property Shareholders," 24 *Tax Adviser* 499 (August '93).

Hoffman, Michael J.R. and Kenneth N. Orbach, "Assignment of Income and Divorce," 23 *The Tax Adviser* 601 (September '92).

Jenny, Carol and Thomas Roesler, "Medical Evaluation of Children in Custody Disputes," 7 *Am.J. of Family Law* 111 (Fall '93).

Lazarus, Lauren C., "Should Fault Be a Significant Consideration in Property Division?" 66 *Florida Bar J.* 76 (October '92).

Maiman, Richard et.al., "Gender and Specialization in the Practice of Divorce Law," 44 *Maine L. Rev.* 39 (1992).

Mirman, Joel J., "Father Knows Best? Male Parent Issues in Custody Cases," 29 *Trial* 16 (June '93).

Morgan, Laura W. and Brett R. Turner, "Attacking and Defending Antenuptial Agreements: A 1993 Update," 5 *Divorce Litigation* 129 (July '93).

Natoli, Susan L., "Chapter 14 and Divorce Issues," 24 *Tax Adviser* 502 (August '93).

Pope, Ralph A., "Evaluating Pension Benefits in Divorce," 176 *J. of Accountancy* 62 (August '93).

Post, Libby, "The Question of Family: Lesbians and Gay Men Reflecting a Redefined Society," 19 *Fordham Urban L.J.* 747 (Spring '92).

Shoop, Julie Gannon, "Court Cites Privacy Rights in Embryo Decisions," 28 *Trial* 16 (September '92).

Turner, Brett R., "Deciding Who Decides: A Critical Review of the Law of Jurisdiction in Child Custody Cases," 4 *Divorce Litigation*–153 (August '92).

Weiss, Terri J., "The Enforceability of Marital Agreements: Maintenance and Property Distribution Clauses," 7 *Am.J. of Family Law* 151 (Fall '93).

MORTGAGES AND FORECLOSURE

[¶3001] Mortgages are the most traditional way of financing real estate. Ordinarily the arrangement is as follows: in response to a request or application, a lender advances money to a borrower. This is evidenced by a bond or note. To protect his or her interest, the lender requires the borrower to put up or mortgage his or her property. Thus a mortgage is an instrument by which the owner (mortgagor) offers property as security to a lender (mortgagee). In this country there are two legal theories on how mortgages operate. Under the title theory (the minority view), the mortgagee holds title to the property and permits the mortgagor to possess the property. Once the mortgagor settles the debt with the mortgagee, title revests in him or her. The *lien theory* is the prevailing view among the states today. It provides that the mortgagee merely has a lien on the property as security for the loan made. In the event of default, the mortgagor can retain possession. Under either theory the premise is the same: the lender's interest is created to protect an interest in the money loaned. In addition to providing the property as security for the loan, the borrower may also be personally liable for the obligation. This liability is evidenced by the borrower's note. If on foreclosure a balance is still outstanding, the lender may obtain a deficiency judgment, which is enforceable against any of the borrower's assets.

Mortgages are classified in terms of *time* or *priority*. In time, mortgages are either short-term (usually one year) or long-term (over five years). By priority, mortgages are either senior or primary (first mortgages) or junior or secondary (second, third, or fourth mortgages). The priority of a mortgage is determined by its date of recordation. Therefore, if one mortgage is senior to another it was recorded first; it takes priority over all mortgages that were recorded after it. Even if a junior mortgage involves more money than a senior mortgage, it is lower in priority, which means that if the senior mortgage is foreclosed, the junior mortgagee will receive nothing until the senior mortgage is satisfied.

Local practice may call for the use of a deed of trust rather than a mortgage. Under a deed of trust, the mortgagor conveys the property to a trustee, in trust for the mortgagee, until the debt is satisfied and the property reconveyed to the mortgagor. In case of default, there is no foreclosure: the trustee exercises its power of sale.

[¶3002] CONSTRUCTION FINANCING

The most important use of the short-term mortgage is to provide financing for construction of new buildings, or the improvement of existing structures. Some lenders are restricted by law from making these loans, and others do not do so from choice. The furthest these lenders will go is to issue a commitment for a "permanent" mortgage when the building is completed (known as a "take-out" commitment). There are two reasons why construction loans involve extra risk: first, possible delays in construction, or unanticipated costs, can result in failure of the project. Second, changes in the real estate or economic picture can make it impossible to obtain a profitable rent roll.

Short-term construction loans are made by commercial banks, some savings institutions, and private mortgage companies and investors who are attracted by the high return. The loans usually run for 12 to 18 months, although shorter periods can be arranged. The usual procedure for obtaining a construction loan is for the owner to approach the prospective lender with full details about the projected improvements and his or her own financial position. If the lender agrees to make the loan, it will issue a letter of commitment, which may or may not be legally binding on it, and this will be followed by a formal building loan contract and mortgage. Since it is the intention of both lender and borrower that the building loan will be paid off immediately upon completion of the improvements, there is often an agreement or understanding with the lender who will provide the permanent financing at that time. The result has aptly been termed a financing web in which each party is dependent on the ability and willingness of the others to live up to their commitments. Since the lenders are providing the bulk of the funds for a fixed interest return while the owner keeps the profits, if any, it is understandable that the former impose strict requirements for their loans and subject the property to continuous inspections. In the following paragraphs, which discuss the construction financing procedure in detail, emphasis is on the role of the property owner and his attorney and the extent to which they may be able to vary the relatively fixed requirements of the large institutional lenders that do much of the construction financing in this country.

[¶3003] OBTAINING THE COMMITMENT

The following steps describe the procedure to obtain a construction loan from a large commercial bank in New York City.

(1) Application to Lender: The prospective borrower submits all information about the property and preliminary plans and specifications for the improvements. Included should be the name of the architect, whose experience can be an important factor, and that of the general contractor (assuming the owner will not act as his own contractor) whose credit will be checked along with that of the owner. The borrower should already have ascertained that the particular lender is interested in the type of loan being sought (e.g., fee or leasehold mortgage, specialty loan, assignment of rents) since lenders vary their loans from time to time in order to keep a balanced portfolio and to seek out areas of highest interest return.

(2) Appraisal by Lender: The lender will first obtain a desk opinion (D.O.) from its appraisal division to see if its minimum loan requirements are met. This involves a study of the plans and specifications, a survey or plat plan, zoning requirements, and the economic potential of the proposed building. If this opinion is satisfactory, a physical inspection of the site is made, the title is searched, a formal appraisal (usually using the income capitalization approach) is prepared, and the credit rating of the owner and contractor is checked. The lender will also

want to know where the balance of the construction funds will come from and any arrangements that have been made for permanent financing when the building is completed.

(3) Out-of-State Loans: If the borrower and the lender are citizens of different states, the lender will normally want to satisfy itself about several important legal matters. One is whether the lender will be "doing business" in the foreign state if it makes the loan or if it later resorts to the foreign court to foreclose its loan. If the lender must qualify to do business in the state, it will want to know what is involved. Sometimes, this problem is avoided by having a local lender participate in the loan and carry on the proceedings in its name. The lender will also inquire about the redemption period in the event of foreclosure; this may be several years, during which the lender will be unable to dispose of the property. Mechanic's liens vary from state to state, and the lender will want to know if its loan will be subordinate to them. Finally, the lender will want to know about local property taxes and the likelihood of future increases.

(4) Terms of the Loan: The borrower will normally state in the application the amount of the loan requested and the interest rate he or she is willing to pay. When the lender comes to fixing the amount of the loan, it will make it a percentage of the value of the improved property. For example, 70% of the value of an apartment or office building may be loaned, or 50% of the value of a motel or other specialized type of business. In addition, the lender may limit the construction loan to 90% of the "take-out" (the commitment for the permanent mortgage loan). The interest rate will be that prevailing for the type of loan involved: typically, a floating rate several points above prime. In addition, the lender will charge a "processing fee," which in reality is a discount. The discount varies with the term of the loan and the amount of risk. For example, a $1,000,000 loan may be made at 18% interest plus a $10,000 processing fee. Half the processing fee may be due at the time the letter of commitment is issued and will be nonrefundable if the loan does not go through. The other half will be paid at the closing of the loan. The 18% interest will be payable only on funds actually advanced to the owner (although sometimes there is a provision for stand-by interest, payable even though no money is actually loaned). All these factors make the actual interest rate different from the stated rate.

(5) Commitment Letter: If the loan negotiations are concluded satisfactorily, the lender will issue a letter of commitment, which constitutes an approval of the loan application. The letter sets forth the details of the loan as well as the conditions that must be satisfied before the loan closing (final plans and specifications, bonds, etc.). It is unclear whether the commitment letter is legally binding on the lender. Most jurisdictions do not permit the borrower to sue for specific performance of the commitment, but in some states special damages may be recovered if they can be shown.

(6) Closing the Loan: The final step in the procedure is the loan closing, at which time the mortgage, bond, if any, and other documents are executed.

The lender then will advance funds to the owner in accordance with their agreement.

[¶3004] CHECKLIST FOR CONTENTS OF A COMMITMENT LETTER

The commitment letter for the construction or interim loan will usually cover the following basic points:

❑ Amount and Terms of Loan (details of terms, including interest rate and method of computing it, amount of loan, etc.).

❑ Service Charge or Loan Fee.

❑ Status of Lien (mortgage or trust deed shall be first lien).

❑ Secondary Financing (no secondary financing permitted).

❑ Loan Documents (execution and recording of documents such as promissory note, mortgage, or trust deed, construction loan agreement, assignment of rents, borrower's receipt, tenant's acceptance statement, estoppel certificate, personal guarantees if any, and agreements creating security interests in personal property if appropriate).

❑ Title (title insurance or other evidence of title).

❑ Construction Contract (copy executed by all the parties, submitted before opening the loan, along with copy of building permit).

❑ Survey (obligation of lender conditioned on receipt of survey).

❑ Building and Zoning Requirements (lender's obligation contingent on improvements conforming to zoning and building requirements).

❑ Permanent Mortgage Commitment (borrower to comply with permanent mortgage commitment).

❑ Leases (assignment of leases, if any).

❑ Insurance (fire and extended coverage with standard mortgage clause, liability, business interruption, rent loss, workers' compensation, completion bonds, with lender named as co-obligee, etc.).

❑ Completion of Improvements (substantial conformity with plans and specifications on which appraisal was based; part of loan balance withheld pending final completion).

❑ Opening of Loan (conditions precedent—such as, for example, that loan balance be deposited with lender in cash or mechanic's lien waivers).

❑ Progress Payments (percentage of completion and number, payment to general contractor on presentation of lien waivers or directly to subcontractors, architect's certificates).

❑ Time for Acceptance (limitation of time for acceptance of commitment and payment of commitment fee).

❑ Accuracy of Application (lender's obligation conditioned on accuracy of information contained in loan application and supplementary documents).

❑ Expiration Date (date when commitment expires).

[¶3005] CHECKLIST OF BORROWER'S IMPORTANT CONSIDERATIONS IN REVIEWING A MORTGAGE COMMITMENT

The following checklist gives a rundown on the important provisions of a commitment for a permanent mortgage, along with suggested accommodations and modifications a borrower might request of the lender under particular circumstances:

❏ *Obligation to Take Loan:* The commitment or acceptance by the borrower will obligate the borrower to take the loan unless it is a standby commitment, in which case provisions obligating the borrower to take the loan and for damages on the borrower's failure to close are not appropriate.

❏ *Evidence of Indebtedness and Security:* The commitment will set forth the amount and terms of the loan and the mortgage note or extension agreement. Since the loan will probably be made on the strength of the security (the property), the borrower might be able to get a provision in the note and mortgage limiting the borrower's liability to its interest in the property.

❏ *Mortgage Lien:* The commitment will provide that the mortgage will be a first lien on a good and marketable title in fee simple. The borrower might want to add language making the coverage subject to covenants, agreements, restrictions, and easements of right-of-way for utilities that are not to be violated by the buildings constructed unless the borrower has a title search, in which case exceptions should be approved in advance.

❏ *Security Interest:* In addition, the loan may be secured by a security interest duly perfected under the UCC, covering fixtures, equipment, articles of personal property, etc. The borrower should make sure that the security interest covers only property owned by the borrower.

❏ *Prepayment Privilege:* The borrower will want to avoid, if possible, specified prepayment dates and stiff penalties.

❏ *Title and Marketability of Title:* Where the commitment is conditioned on approval by the lender's attorneys as to all matters concerning title and marketability of title, the borrower should make explicit the identity of the title company or companies that will be used and whether the lender, if several are to be used, will accept reinsurance or will insist on coinsurance of title.

❏ *Certificate of Occupancy:* The borrower will try to get approval by the lender's attorneys to close the loan without a certificate of occupancy on a showing that the property has been built in accordance with the building and zoning code and can be legally occupied.

❏ *Appraisal:* The commitment will be conditioned on receipt by the lender of a satisfactory appraisal. The borrower should get a refund of the deposit and a termination of all liability if the appraisal proves unsatisfactory.

❏ *Construction Lender:* The commitment will be conditioned on the execution of a buy-sell agreement with the construction or interim lender. The buyer will want to obtain notification as to whether the interim or construction lender is acceptable to the permanent lender if the permanent lender will take by assignment only.

❏ *Leases and Tenancies:* The commitment will be conditioned on the approval of leases and tenancies. The borrower will want the lender to agree to enter into nondisturbance agreements with tenants whose leases are superior, especially with major tenants who can be expected to insist on nondisturbance agreements.

❏ *Condemnation:* The borrower will want the lender to agree to use condemnation and casualty awards for restoration purposes. Frequently, a lender will want the right to apply the award to the reduction of the balance of the loan still due. The tenant, of course, will want the award to be applied to restoration work.

❏ *Possession of Premises by Tenants:* The borrower should try to include a provision that the tenants' acceptance of the premises and commencement of rent payments are sufficient rather than that the tenants must be in physical possession of the demised premises and open for business (if this type of provision is applicable).

❏ *Substitution of Tenants:* The borrower should negotiate for the right to substitute tenants for any of the tenants that appear in the commitment as long as the substituted tenants are of equal credit standing.

❏ *Modifications, Prepayments, or Termination of Leases:* The commitment may be conditioned on giving the lender control as to modifications, prepayment, or termination of leases, and on the assignment to the lender as additional security of the landlord's interest in the affected lease. The borrower should get a copy of the instrument used by the lender to safeguard the rights covered by this provision of the commitment.

❏ *Deposit:* The commitment may require a deposit of cash by the borrower on acceptance of the commitment. The borrower might try to substitute a letter of credit or a certificate of deposit for a refundable commitment fee in cash. If the borrower's note and mortgage or a letter of credit is substituted for cash, the borrower's costs can be further reduced.

❏ *Real Estate Taxes:* A requirement that the mortgage or extension agreement include a provision for deposits with the mortgagee of estimated real estate taxes should be modified to reflect net leases and the lender's approval of net leases.

❏ *Overages:* Overage provisions should be carefully checked to see whether they include fees collected by the landlord-borrower for services rendered to the tenant. If overages are figured on the rent of each rentable unit, the borrower may be hurt, since he gets no offset for units whose rent was decreased or units that are vacant. Ask for copies of the mortgage instruments.

❏ *Insurance:* The commitment will be conditioned on the delivery to the lender of satisfactory fire insurance policies appropriately endorsed to show the lender's interest as mortgagee. If a borrower has a single major tenant that is a self-insurer, this should be stated in the commitment.

❏ *Fees and Disbursements:* The borrower will be required to pay disbursements and fees. If the lender's attorney gets a title commission, the cost to the borrower may be higher. Disbursements incurred by the lender's attorney to a local attorney should be checked.

❏ *Participations:* If the commitment provides for participations, the borrower should see whether participants will create additional counsel fees.

[¶3006] CHECKLIST FOR BUILDING LOAN AGREEMENT AND MORTGAGE

The building loan agreement (or the letter of commitment when no formal agreement has been made) substantially sets forth the obligation of the lender to make the loan, and of the owner to construct the improvements described therein. The loan is not made at one time, but portions or advances are given when the building reaches each stage of construction specified in the payment schedule. A typical schedule for a large office building might have 12 stages, the final one being full completion of the building, including the issuance of a certificate of occupancy. Other significant provisions of the agreement are as follows:

[¶3007] REPRESENTATIONS BY THE BORROWER

(1) Corporate Existence: A corporation eliminates the possibility that outside creditors will be able to proceed against the particular property. The borrower will have to represent that the corporation is in valid existence and that all necessary resolutions of the directors and shareholders have been passed.

(2) Capital Stock of the Corporation: Since the lender will want to know the true identity of the borrower, the names of all shareholders will have to be submitted. In addition, the corporation and its shareholders may be asked to covenant that no stock will be transferred or issued so that the present shareholders will own less than 51%. The construction lender, more than the permanent lender, looks to the experience and integrity of the building owner, since failure to complete the building on time may endanger the loan.

(3) No Violations or Damage: The borrower must represent that no violations exist and that the property has suffered no damage at the time of the loan. This too is important because it might affect the completion date.

(4) Building Leases: The construction lender is vitally interested in leases that the builder makes with tenants because the permanent mortgage, the proceeds of which will pay off the construction loan, is conditioned upon satisfactory leases in terms of both quality and amount of rent. The borrower will have to submit copies of any leases already entered into. Sometimes, a "step-up" loan will be made; i.e., the amount of the loan may be increased as new tenants are signed up.

(5) Construction Plans and Specifications: The lender will want to see completed plans for the improvements and the agreement with the general contractor, unless the borrower intends to act as his own contractor. The lender may want to make a separate agreement with the general contractor and the architect so that, in the event of a default by the borrower, they will work for the lender under the same agreements they have with the borrower. If permitted by state law,

the lender may also want the borrower to obtain waivers (in favor of the lender) by the general contractor and major subcontractors of their rights under the lien law.

(6) Performance or Completion Bonds: The borrower-contractor may be required to post a bond for the purpose of insuring completion of the building by a specified date.

(7) Permanent Financing: Representations about permanent financing are discussed at ¶3010.

[¶3008] COVENANTS BY THE BORROWER

(1) Completion of the Improvements: The borrower normally must agree to a definite completion date and agree to proceed with "all reasonable dispatch." Since the failure to comply with either of these stipulations usually constitutes a default and accelerates the entire loan, the borrower should make provision for contingencies, such as weather, labor disputes, fire, etc.

(2) Approval of Lender to Change in Plan: The lender wants the right to approve changes because any substantial modifications may terminate the obligation of the permanent lender.

(3) Inspection of Premises; Financial Statements: The lender will reserve the right to inspect the premises during construction and prior to making any advances. Similarly, it will require the borrower to submit financial statements periodically so that any financial difficulties may be anticipated.

[¶3009] RELATIONSHIP BETWEEN THE CONSTRUCTION LOAN AND THE PERMANENT MORTGAGE

Construction financing is short-term when the source of repayment is clearly understood to be the permanent mortgage that will be placed on the completed building. Construction loans can be classified into four types, depending on their relationship to the permanent financing.

(1) Open-End: In an open-end loan, the borrower has no commitment for permanent financing. The construction lender thus assumes a risk that no mortgage can be obtained when the building is completed. This risk normally is assumed only when the real estate market is very strong or when the borrower has an outstanding reputation.

(2) Take-Out: This is the most common type of construction financing. At the time the construction loan is closed, the borrower already has a commitment for a permanent mortgage. The construction lender thus has an assured source of repayment, *provided* the borrower meets the conditions of the permanent loan commitment. See below.

A variation of the "take-out" commitment is the "standby" commitment. This involves an agreement by a lender to make a permanent mortgage loan in a specified amount within a specified period, when called upon by the borrower. The amount of the mortgage loan is substantially below its face amount (that is, the lender will get the mortgage loan at a discount), and the borrower must pay a standby fee, usually 1% or more. The standby commitment is generally used when mortgage money is tight. At such times, interest rates are high and lenders usually demand a discount to make a permanent mortgage loan. In effect, the builder is gambling that the mortgage money picture will change by the time the project is completed, and that full financing will then be available at a lower rate of interest.

Buy-sell agreements are frequently used in connection with the "take-out" form of construction loan. The agreement essentially provides that the permanent lender will, when the building is completed, buy the construction loan or advance the necessary funds so that the borrower can pay it off. The advantage of the agreement for the construction lender is that he can enforce the agreement against the permanent lender, something he cannot do when there is only a "take-out" commitment in favor of the borrower. The agreement, however, does contain the same conditions as the commitment; e.g., completion by a given date, satisfactory leases, etc.

In a *two-party* buy-sell agreement, the parties are the construction lender and the permanent lender. Since this doesn't bind the borrower, he might conceivably find a lender willing to make a permanent mortgage under more favorable terms and abandon the original commitment. To prevent this, a *three-party* buy-sell agreement is sometimes used, in which the borrower also is a party and is obliged to accept the permanent loan.

(3) Combination Loan: Sometimes the construction lender will also provide the permanent financing, combining the two loans into one. The advantage of this procedure for the builder is that he makes all his financing arrangements at one place and at one time, thus eliminating extra commissions, service charges, and fees. The lender benefits in several possible ways: (1) It assures itself of getting the permanent loan, which is the source of most of its profit. (2) By inspecting the building during construction, it can see that the plans and specifications are properly followed. (3) It can charge a slightly higher overall rate because of the extra risk involved in the construction part of the loan.

The other side of the picture, for the builder, is that by waiting until completion of the building, he may be able to get a 20% larger loan at an interest rate $1/4$ to $1/2$ point lower. There are several reasons for this. First, more lenders make permanent loans than construction loans. Second, there is considerably less risk in lending on a completed building. Finally, the builder himself is frequently under less pressure in arranging the permanent financing and so he can shop around more.

(4) Guarantee of Payment: This very unusual type of loan is conditioned upon the borrower's guarantee that the loan will be repaid upon completion of the building. Very few builders are in a position to give such a guarantee, and if they were, there would normally be no need for the loan in the first place. Sometimes, the builder may be able to obtain the guarantee of a third party.

[¶3010] PERMANENT FINANCING

The long-term mortgage loan is the key feature distinguishing real estate from all other forms of investment. In no other area will a lender agree to lend 60% to 75% or more of the value of the security for terms of up to 30 years. Real estate will support such loans because of its *stability* and *long-term growth potential*. These features in turn derive from the limited and fixed supply of land that must support a constantly growing population.

Actually, the long-term mortgage reflects the same underlying division of interest in real estate as does the long-term lease. Both divide the long-term investor seeking a fixed return from the short- or medium-term operator who seeks a higher but more speculative return. The lender who extends a 20-year mortgage on a building (and who probably will be willing to refinance it at the end of that period, assuming it has been well maintained) can be compared to the owner who extends a 20-year net lease with renewal options. Looking at it from the other side, the borrower-owner can be compared to the net lessee. Both may have invested approximately the same amount of "equity" money (the former to buy the building, and the latter to buy the leasehold) and both anticipate an operating income that will represent a high return on their leveraged investment. If the building loses money, each is prepared to abandon his interest to the long-term investor who has provided the major financing. (This assumes, as is usually the case, nonrecourse loans when neither the operator-owner nor the net lessee is personally liable for his obligations.)

The major sources of long-term mortgage money are insurance companies, pension funds, savings and loan associations, mutual savings banks, and commercial banks.

[¶3011] CHECKLIST FOR LONG-TERM MORTGAGES

The procedure for obtaining permanent financing is similar to that for construction financing. The borrower applies to the lender, submitting all pertinent data and asking for a loan of a stated amount, term, and interest. If the lender agrees to make the loan, a letter of commitment will be issued. In the case of an existing structure, the closing of the loan will follow shortly thereafter. When new construction is involved, the formal closing will be postponed until the building is completed and only at that time, and provided the conditions set forth in the commitment are met, will the mortgage be signed and the money paid. Many states have statutory forms of mortgages that may be used if the parties wish; their value is that the meaning of many phrases and clauses is spelled out in the statute. Institutional lenders usually have their own forms that they will require to be used; these, naturally, will tend to favor the lenders' position.

The following is a brief description of the important provisions of the long-term mortgage:

❏ *Amount:* The amount of the loan is most often determined as a percentage of the value of the property at the time of the loan. Thus many institutional lenders are limited to a ratio of 66 $^2/_3$% or 75%. The lender will make its own careful appraisal of the property to determine its value. Frequently, however, the value of the completed building is substantially higher than the cost of the vacant land plus construction. This is most often true when value is computed by the income capitalization method (i.e., by capitalizing the rental income provided by the existing leases).

❏ *Interest Rate:* This is determined by current money market rates. Normally, a portion of each repayment by the borrower represents interest to date and the remainder is amortization.

❏ *Amortization:* Long-term loans may be classified into several groups, depending on the extent that they are repaid prior to maturity:

(1) The Standing Mortgage or Straight Loan: This risky and increasingly rare mortgage would be available only under special conditions. It is a loan for a definite term of years, payable in full at maturity. Throughout the term of the loan, the borrower pays only the interest on the loan; he makes no payments in reduction of the mortgage principal. When the loan matures, the borrower must either (a) pay the loan in full, (b) ask the lender to extend the loan for another term, (c) refinance the loan for another term with another lender, or (d) have the lender carry the loan as an open or past-due debt.

(2) The Partially Amortized Mortgage or Balloon Mortgage: Today, partial amortization is common for income-producing properties but such loans are being made for home mortgages as well. The borrower's periodic payments will not completely liquidate the mortgage loan at maturity. Instead, a substantial amount called the "balloon" will remain unpaid. The lender is willing to agree to the balloon because the loan is based primarily on the property itself, rather than on the credit of the borrower.

(3) The Fully Amortized or Self-Liquidating Mortgage: Here the periodic payments made by the borrower during the term of the loan result in the mortgage being paid in full at maturity. Virtually all home mortgage loans are self-liquidating. This means that homeowners are constantly increasing the equity in their homes, though not at a constant rate, since most of their payments go for interest in the early years. (Some of the new adjustable loans are balloons—see below.) Commercial loans on shopping centers, motels, and other specialty properties are ordinarily fully amortized, since the lender is looking to the credit of the borrower as his primary security and is not counting on the property to retain or increase in value. Monthly payment tables are contained in the Appendix.

(4) The Home Mortgage with Variable Payments or Interest Rates: Lenders now offer several substitutes for the long-term, fixed-rate home mortgage. The majority of homebuyers prefer the standard loan, but three variations of it have become accepted. Except where noted, these new mortgages are paid off like a long-term loan; however, the interest rate or the amount of the monthly payment changes:

a. *The adjustable rate mortgage (ARM)* usually carries a below-market interest rate for the first year. Periodically, the interest is raised or lowered according to a financial market index. The borrower's monthly payment, however, is not always adjusted as frequently. As a result, most or even all of the monthly payment may wind up going for interest during a stretch of inflation (this drawback is called "negative amortization"—unless the "( )" on rate increases mandated by federal law on all residential mortgages prevents this.). There is no standard "adjustable" mortgage because lenders have been granted great leeway in the frequency with which they can refigure the interest rate. Some of these loans can be "balloon" mortgages, payable in full after three to five years. The term "adjustable" is not always used; "floating" and "flexible" are popular substitutes.

b. *The graduated payment mortgage* (also called the GPM) has unusually low monthly payments in the early years; gradually the payments increase to stabilize at an amount much higher than what a borrower would pay on a standard mortgage for the same amount at the same interest rate.

c. *The growing equity mortgage* (or GEM) is initially offered at a below-market interest rate; the rate remains throughout the loan but the monthly payment increases systematically. The increase in a GEM, however, is always treated as a periodic prepayment of *principal*. Result: a 30-year GEM is paid off in 12 to 15 years, saving the homebuyer tens of thousands of dollars in interest costs.

(5) *The Combination Loan and the Variable Amortization Loan:* This commercial loan combines a period of straight lending with a period of amortization. The smaller the proportion of the loan to the value of the property, the longer the period of straight lending that will be allowed. Sometimes the first few years will be without amortization. This gives the borrower a chance to develop the property and build up income; consequently, it is used mostly for new properties. On the other hand, the lender may want amortization to begin at once so that the amount at risk is reduced; once it reaches a certain proportion of the value of the property, the lender will permit it to be carried as a straight loan. These same objectives can be achieved by the use of variable amortization as well. If the parties estimate that the income from the property will be highest in the first few years, higher amortization during that period will be borne most easily by the borrower. Alternatively, the amortization can be tied to a varying rate of depreciation.

(6) *Participation loan:* The lender requires "equity kickers"—equity or participation in the cash flow from a project—as a further incentive to lend.

❒ ***Covenant of Repayment:*** In most long-term loans on real estate, the lender regards the property as his primary security. With respect to the personal obligation of the borrower, three alternatives exist:

(1) Personal liability: The lender may insist that the borrower assume personal liability, either by a covenant to pay included in the mortgage or by a separate instrument. In the latter event, a corporate borrower should seek to use a note instead of a bond, since this eliminates the cost of revenue stamps. This may not be possible when the lender, by law, is limited to loans on *bonds.*

(2) Use of nominee or dummy: The lender may be willing to waive personal liability but a statute may require it. In that case, a nominee without assets may act for the borrower and later convey the property to him subject to the mortgage. Local law must be checked, however, to see if the assumption of liability by the nominee (who is the borrower's agent) is imputed to his principal.

(3) No personal liability: When the lender agrees to waive any personal liability and the borrower's cash investment in the property is small, the borrower in effect has a long-term option.

❏ *Security:* The mortgage lien covers all of the real estate described therein, including *fixtures;* i.e., personal property affixed to the realty. The lender may want the mortgage to include a lien on personal property. Since the definition of a fixture varies from jurisdiction to jurisdiction, the lender may list all items of personal property in order to eliminate any question about coverage. Sometimes the security clause will apply to after-acquired property as well. Strictly speaking, this is merely a covenant to give a mortgage at the time the property is acquired. Many lenders will require additional mortgage instruments to be executed at that time. The lender must be sure to record the mortgage both as a *real estate* mortgage and as a *chattel* mortgage in order to preserve his rights.

❏ *Prepayment:* This is a vital clause for the borrower. In its absence, he or she may not be able to pay off the mortgage even though the property is condemned or destroyed. Or, as is more often the case, refinancing may seem very attractive at a time when interest rates have declined. The lender frequently will agree to prepayment after a minimum period (e.g., five years) and at a reasonable penalty.

❏ *Demolition of Improvements:* In the usual printed mortgage, any demolition of existing improvements will continue a default, since it impairs the lender's security. If the borrower is contemplating demolition, appropriate provision should be made. The lender's agreement will be conditioned on the borrower's obligation to install new improvements.

❏ *Insurance Proceeds:* The lender, of course, will require the borrower to maintain fire and other insurance on the property for the lender's benefit. If the mortgage is silent, the lender may apply the insurance proceeds to payment of part of the mortgage debt instead of for restoration of the property. In that case, the borrower will have to arrange new financing, and if he can't prepay the outstanding mortgage, this may be impossible. The borrower should seek to require the lender to use the proceeds for restoration or, if that is not possible, obtain the right to prepay the remaining loan.

❏ *Condemnation Awards:* In the case of a partial condemnation, the problems are similar to those with insurance proceeds. The lender in this case is much less likely to agree to use the proceeds to restore the property, since its security has been reduced by the condemnation.

❏ ***Prohibition Against Junior Liens:*** The lender may not want the property encumbered by a second mortgage since this increases the risk of a default followed by a foreclosure by the junior mortgagee, to the possible detriment of the primary mortgagee. A possible compromise is for the borrower to agree that any junior lien will be made subordinate to the existing leases; in this way, a foreclosure cannot terminate the leases, which constitute the real security for the primary lender.

❏ ***Encumbrances:*** The lender will normally require that there be no encumbrances on the property ahead of the first mortgage, such as mechanic's liens. In addition, this may be a statutory requirement for institutional lenders. In the case of *leases,* however, the situation may be different. Since, as we noted above, the leases are the true security for the loan, the lender wants to be sure that they will not terminate if the first mortgage is foreclosed. The mortgage must make provision for this in light of local law. There are two situations:

(1) Foreclosure terminates all subordinate liens: If the jurisdiction requires the mortgagee to join all subordinate liens (and terminate them) in a foreclosure action, the mortgagee can make existing leases *superior* to the mortgage lien. If the lender is prohibited from doing this by statute, it may execute a nondisturbance agreement, in which it agrees not to terminate the lease as long as the rent is paid. A nondisturbance agreement may be so broad as to be the equivalent of making the first mortgage a subordinate lien.

(2) Foreclosure terminates subordinate liens at lender's option: When the lender may join only such tenants as he or she wishes in the foreclosure action, it need make no provision in the mortgage. However, certain of the *tenants* may be in a position to demand nondisturbance agreements from the lender in order to protect themselves.

❏ ***Assignment of Leases:*** The lender may fear that if the borrower is heading toward a default, he may cancel or amend certain leases in favor of the tenants in exchange for cash payments. An "anti-milking" provision may require the borrower to assign all leases to the lender to protect against this contingency. Since this amounts to a future assignment, it may be deemed fraudulent and void in some jurisdictions. As an alternative, the lender may require that no lease be amended or canceled without its consent.

[¶3012] LEASEHOLD FINANCING

Leasehold financing is a special form of secondary financing in which the builder or investor enters into a lease with the property owner and then gets a mortgage on the leasehold. The mortgagee gets a secondary lien, even if the mortgage is a first mortgage, because the lessor's interest takes priority over it. (Note, however, that the lessor can voluntarily subordinate his fee to the leasehold mortgage.) A leasehold mortgage is distinguished from a fee mortgage in that the security for a leasehold mortgage is a defeasible estate (the lease).

Subordination: As indicated above, the owner (lessor) of the property may or may not subordinate interest in the property to the interest of the leasehold mortgagee. If the lessor's interest is subordinated, the leasehold mortgagee is in almost the same position as if he or she were the mortgagee of the fee. Because complications can arise under a subordination agreement, some lenders require a mortgage on the fee along with the leasehold mortgage. Owners, however, are often averse to this arrangement, and some won't consent to a subordination agreement. Besides putting owned land in jeopardy, subordination also restricts the owner's power to borrow in the future. To overcome the owner-lessor's hesitation, the following points can be raised:

(1) If the owner subordinates or mortgages his or her interest, the lessee can get a larger or better loan, which means he or she can pay a higher rental.

(2) Subordination allows the lessee to put up a more expensive building, which is to the lessor's benefit.

(3) An owner who erected the building would have to mortgage the property anyway, so in terms of risk and credit the owner is no worse off with subordination.

[¶3012.1] Sources of Leasehold Mortgage Financing

Life insurance companies are the prime lending source for leasehold financing. They are extremely flexible both as to the type of properties and the geographic distribution of their loans. Other lenders include national commercial banks and federal savings and loan associations, and in some states the state counterparts of these institutions, as well as mutual savings banks.

[¶3013] WHEN LEASEHOLD FINANCING IS USED

When investing in income-producing property, it's important to consider at the outset whether a long-term ground lease (subject to a leasehold mortgage) is better under the circumstances than acquiring outright ownership (subject to a long-term mortgage). With a lease, the existing owner in effect provides part of the financing, since, as a lessor, he or she retains an interest in the property. The lessee has to raise only the funds necessary to buy the leasehold (or construct the improvements) and then pay the yearly rent. Whether this will work out depends on the prospective seller's evaluation of the property as a good long-term investment for the money the seller could have obtained from the sale, and on the prospective buyer's willingness to settle for a long-term lease. If the lease is entered into, the buyer gets the tax benefit of deducting rent payments and, in effect, puts the land on a tax-deductible basis. (If he or she buys, payments of mortgage principal would not be deductible—only the interest payments would be deductible.)

Careful analysis is necessary before deciding that a lease (plus a leasehold mortgage) is the best approach under a particular set of circumstances. If minimum capital is available for the investment, maximum financing is available via the lease plus leasehold mortgage rather than via a fee mortgage. However, analysis might reveal that less capital is, in fact, needed or that it is possible to raise the same amount through a fee mortgage plus an unsecured loan for the balance. (Such an unsecured loan would depend on the personal credit of the builder or investor.)

Sometimes property can only be obtained by way of a lease. For example, prime land in cities may be held by owners who never intended to sell. In addition, both the investor and the owner can obtain certain tax benefits by a lease that they could not obtain by a sale. For example, an owner may find it advantageous to lease his property, if real estate has appreciated to a point that the tax payable on a sale (even at capital gain rates) would be prohibitive.

[¶3014] LEASEHOLD MORTGAGE CHECKLIST

❏ *Amount:* The loan will be a percentage of the value of the improved property. Because of the somewhat greater risk in a leasehold mortgage, the ratio is frequently lower than that in a fee mortgage. The value of the property is computed in the same manner as for the fee mortgage, except that the ground rental is an additional item of expense. Put another way, the value of a leasehold is its economic rent (the rent income received from the sublessees) minus the contract rent (the ground rental). This value is the security for the loan.

❏ *Term and Interest:* Because of the higher risk, interest rates are somewhat higher on leasehold mortgages. The term of the loan will not exceed the term of the lease, and normally must be fully amortized within that period. If renewal terms have been included in measuring the term of the lease, the lender may require the borrower to exercise the renewal option at once or within the first few years of the loan. In the case of an institutional lender, the governing statute may prohibit leasehold mortgages for longer than the initial term (regardless of renewal terms). The statute also may require that the initial term be for at least a certain period of years.

❏ *Subordination of the Fee:* The lender, as well as the borrower, will benefit if the landowner agrees to join in the leasehold mortgage and make the land additional security for the loan. (However, the landowner will not assume personal liability for the loan.) The lender benefits because in the event of foreclosure, it may proceed against both land and improvements. This may justify a higher loan than otherwise, benefiting not only the borrower but also the landowner since this will permit a more extensive improvement, creating more income to the lessee and more security for the rent obligation (and perhaps more rent if the lease relates the ground rent to the lessee's income). On the other hand, subordination prevents the landowner from mortgaging the fee and reduces its value, since there is a risk that it can be foreclosed. A borrower who contemplates refinancing the leasehold mortgage in the future should try to get the subordination agreement to apply to such future financing. The landowner is not likely to agree, however, unless he or she shares in the refinancing proceeds.

❏ *Violation of Lease as Default:* Since the mortgagee must be sure it can act for the lessee in case of a default under the lease, the mortgage will provide that a lease default also constitutes a default under the mortgage.

❏ *Insurance Proceeds:* In a fee mortgage, the lender often refuses to agree to apply insurance proceeds to restoration. In a leasehold situation, however, the lessor will not permit this, since it might mean the property would be left unimproved and no income would be available to pay the ground rent. The lender will want to retain the proceeds and pay them out directly to the contractors working on the property. The application of any excess proceeds is a matter for negotiation. The lender will want to use it to reduce the mortgage while the borrower-lessee will want to keep it.

[¶3015] CHECKLIST FOR LEASE UNDERLYING LEASEHOLD MORTGAGE

The underlying lease ordinarily will have been signed at the time the lessee seeks leasehold financing. However, the lessee should be prepared for requests by the lender to modify the lease as a condition to the loan. Whether or not the landowner will agree depends on the relative bargaining positions of the parties.

❏ *Term of Lease; Renewal Options:* The greater the time "cushion" is, the greater the assurance that the mortgagee will be able to recover its loan in the event financial difficulty requires an extension of the loan or foreclosure. In the event of a takeover, the lender will want the right to exercise any renewal options.

❏ *Subordination of Lease:* The lease should not be made subject to any existing or future mortgage on the fee since this would place two claims ahead of the leasehold mortgage (the lessor's rent claim and the rights of the fee mortgagee). The lender will want any fee mortgage to be subordinate not only to the lease, but to the leasehold mortgage as well. The lender will also want to be sure that the lease is not subordinate to any restriction of record on the fee, such as a reverter or possibility of forfeiture.

❏ *Assignment:* Any restriction on the lessee's right to assign or sublet may make the lease unsalable by the mortgagee after a foreclosure. The lessor may be willing to extend this right to the mortgagee in the event it takes over the lease after a default on the mortgage.

❏ *Default:* Here, the leasehold mortgagee, interested in assuring that there is no automatic default provision, will want the protection for a period of time sufficient for the lessee to cure any default. In addition, the mortgagee will want to make sure there is no provision for default on the filing of a petition in bankruptcy or a reorganization. If the lessor won't agree to this, the lender will want an agreement that the lender can have a new lease on the same terms as the old one. Similarly, if the lessee abandons the lease, or any other noncurable default occurs, the lender will want the right to a new lease. The lender must have control over any contingency, curable or otherwise, that might terminate the lease, which is its only security for the loan.

❏ *Notice of Default:* The mortgagee will want any notices to be served on both the lessee and the mortgagee, with ample time to both to cure the default. The mortgagee will want a longer time for itself, since it will be unable to act until the period for action by the lessee (specified in the mortgage) has expired. The mortgagee will also want a right to enter the premises for the purpose of curing a default of the covenant to repair.

❑ *Covenant to Rebuild or Restore:* If the lease requires the lessee to rebuild the improvements in the event they are damaged or destroyed, the mortgagee will want to insure that the lessee has adequate time to complete the work and that the mortgagee can protect itself if the lessee fails to act.

❑ *Insurance Proceeds:* The lender will want to see that the lease requires the lessee to carry all necessary insurance. In addition, it will object to a provision giving the insurance proceeds to the lessor instead of requiring their use to restore the premises. If this occurred, it would eliminate the lender's security. From the lender's point of view, the best provision is one assigning the insurance proceeds to it for use in restoring the property.

❑ *Condemnation Awards:* The mortgagee's primary concern is to see that the mortgage is reduced to the extent that the leasehold's income-producing capacity is reduced. There are three situations:

(a) *Full taking:* If the entire property is condemned, the lessee's share should at least be equal to the mortgage debt. Since the lessee will normally want his or her share to be equal to the cost of the improvements, the lender will be protected. Apportioning the award between the lessee and the lessor on the basis of value may involve a risk to the lender in the event land values rise rapidly.

(b) *Partial taking:* If the lease provides that a partial taking will terminate the lease, the lessee's share of the award should be sufficient to pay the mortgage debt. If a partial taking will abate the rent, the lessor will probably want as much of the award as represents the capitalization of the lost rent. The remainder should go to restoration of the premises and any excess to reducing the mortgage debt. In the absence of any lease provision, a partial taking at common law did not abate the rent; in this event, the lender would probably have wanted the entire condemnation award to reduce the mortgage.

(c) *Damage without taking:* This might arise through loss of access, etc. The problem is the same as in the case of a partial taking, except that restoration of the premises is not a factor.

❑ *Mortgagee's Obligations:* The mortgagee will want to make sure that if it takes over the property, neither it nor any subsequent owner will be liable under any covenants of the lease except during periods of actual ownership. Certain "title-theory" states make the mortgagee liable on the lessee's covenants, even though the mortgagee is not in possession. In addition, the lease sometimes seeks to make subsequent leases liable for the obligations of their predecessors. This may affect marketability of the lease.

❑ *Option to Purchase:* If the lessee has an option to buy, the lender will want the mortgage debt to be an encumbrance on it as well as on the lease.

❑ *Transfer of Subleases:* The lessor will normally insert a provision in the lease (and in each sublease) that if the lessee defaults and the main lease terminates, the subleases will continue as a direct lease between the owner and the subtenants. The mortgagee, who anticipates taking over the lease if the lessee defaults, will want the owner to agree to assign to it (as the new lessee) its interest in the subleases.

❐ *Modification of Lease:* To protect itself, the mortgagee will want the lease to provide that it may not be amended or modified without its consent.

❐ *Estoppel Certificate:* The lease should require the lessor to provide an estoppel certificate, at the time of the mortgage closing, stating the date to which the rent has been paid, that no default exists under the lease, and that the lease has not been modified.

[¶3016] FORECLOSURE OF REAL ESTATE AND OTHER COLLATERAL FOR DEFAULTED LOANS

The foreclosure of real estate and chattel mortgages and similar security interests in personal property is largely statutory and subject to local variances. Hence, it will always be necessary to check specific statutory provisions. Nevertheless, the Uniform Commercial Code marks out a common pattern for the foreclosure of security interests in personal property, and a common pattern is also discernible in the case of real estate mortgages, although there is no "uniform" law as such in this area.

[¶3017] FORECLOSING AND REDEEMING A REAL ESTATE MORTGAGE

The attorney in general practice will on occasion be faced with the problem of representing either the mortgagor or the mortgagee in a foreclosure proceeding. Financial institutions in many cases are reluctant to foreclose because legal expenses, loss of interest, and commissions often exceed 20% of the value of the property. This frequently will exceed the property owner's equity and thus result in loss to the lending institution. So the attorney representing a client faced with foreclosure should always first attempt to obtain a period of forbearance by the lender or an extension agreement that will reduce monthly payments without scaling down the total debt. To make an extension stick, it must normally be supported by consideration. If no satisfactory agreement can be reached, however, the following points should be borne in mind.

[¶3018] NOTICE REQUIREMENTS

Many mortgage instruments prevent the lender from commencing foreclosure proceedings until notice of the default has been given to the property owner who has had a chance to cure the default within a specified period. Usually this will be 30 days, although in certain circumstances it may be more.

[¶3019] THE FORECLOSURE PROCESS

A mortgage may be in form an absolute conveyance of property that will become void upon the mortgagor's compliance with stated conditions (payment of the debt and compliance with other conditions such as payment of taxes, etc.). Some authorities say a breach of any condition by the mortgagor immediately vests absolute title in the mortgagee. Others minimize or deny that a mortgage operates as a conveyance and regard it as a security or lien for the performance of an obligation. In fact, all jurisdictions require the mortgagee *either* to initiate a judicial proceeding *or* to make a public sale of the property. The purpose of these requirements is to give the mortgagor an opportunity to redeem his interest or to insure that, if the value of the property exceeds the mortgage debt, the excess will be returned to the mortgagor. There are four variations of the foreclosure process followed in the various American jurisdictions.

[¶3020] STRICT FORECLOSURE

This method requires the mortgagee to maintain an action for foreclosure. Once a decree of foreclosure is issued by the court, the mortgagor has a relatively short period of time (up to six months) in which to regain or redeem the property by payment of the mortgage debt plus litigation expenses incurred by the mortgagee. If the mortgagor fails to pay within the redemption period, the court will then confirm title in the mortgagee, without any requirement of a public sale.

[¶3021] JUDICIAL FORECLOSURE FOLLOWED BY SALE

This is the most commonly used method of foreclosure. It varies from strict foreclosure in that, after the redemption period has expired, a public sale of the property is required. In theory, this will result in the mortgagor receiving the difference between the value of the property and the mortgage debt. However, since these sales often take place during depressed markets or because the property has undesirable features, the mortgagee is often the only bidder. In some states, a redemption period also follows the sale. This further reduces the probability that the property's true value will be realized. To insure an adequate price, the court, which has the power not to confirm a sale, may set an *upset price;* i.e., the lowest acceptable bid. Once the sale is made, the title so acquired relates back to the original recording of title and wipes out all claims of the mortgagor and all those obtaining interests.

[¶3022] NONJUDICIAL FORECLOSURE FOLLOWED BY SALE

Although barred in some states, a frequently used method of foreclosing is by the exercise of a power of sale that is given to the mortgagee in the mortgage instrument (usually a deed of trust). The power of sale clause authorizing this method will spell out what constitutes defaults that permit the power to sell as well as the manner in which the sale will be advertised, where it is to be held, and when the deed is to be given. This eliminates any need for a judicial proceeding, which, in addition to being time-consuming, is expensive. The sale must be a public one, preceded by proper public notice and advertisement. There may or may not be a period of redemption following the sale.

[¶3023] JUDICIAL FORECLOSURE BY ENTRY AND POSSESSION

In several New England states, the mortgagee obtains a decree of foreclosure after a judicial proceeding, and after the redemption period may enter and take possession of the property. A period of redemption also follows the repossession. This method may be used without a judicial proceeding provided repossession can be made without force. In effect, this type of proceeding is similar to strict foreclosure.

[¶3024] REDEMPTION

Even after a default in the payment of a mortgage obligation, the mortgagor is given a chance to pay his or her debt and cure the default. This is known as equitable redemption, and this right continues until the property is sold under a foreclosure judgment or decree. Some states provide a statutory right of redemption whereby the mortgagor may redeem the property after the sale (the statutory redemption period will vary from state to state but it's usually one year). This gives the mortgagor a last chance to redeem property, and if he or she fails to redeem the property it is deeded to the purchaser who receives such title as the mortgagor had at the time the mortgage was made.

[¶3025] DEEDS IN LIEU OF FORECLOSURE

If foreclosure seems imminent and the mortgagor has no hopes of redeeming the property or realizing an excess on foreclosure, the parties should consider a voluntary conveyance to the mortgagee to avoid the expense and delay of a judicial proceeding. The consideration for the transfer of the property is the cancellation of the mortgage debt.

[¶3026]　PERSONAL JUDGMENT FOR DEFICIENCY

If the proceeds from the sale of the property following the foreclosure are insufficient to satisfy the mortgage debt, the mortgagee in most states may obtain a personal judgment against the mortgagor for the deficiency. As a practical matter, this is not often done since the mortgagor presumably is without assets. However, if the mortgagor is a business concern that remains in operation, a deficiency judgment may well be sought. As a result of the experience of the 1930s, when foreclosed properties were often bid in far below their value, many states now give the mortgagor a defense of "fair market value" in a proceeding for a deficiency judgment. The effect of this is to limit the judgment to the difference between the unpaid mortgage debt and the fair market value of the property. The bid price at the foreclosure sale is irrelevant. Since these laws have never been tested in a period of severe recession, it is impossible to say how well they would protect mortgagors under such circumstances.

[¶3027]　ADDITIONS TO MORTGAGE INDEBTEDNESS

The mortgagee is entitled to add to the unpaid debt the expenses of foreclosure as well as taxes and other obligations of the property that are paid by the mortgagee. Generally, the mortgage instrument will provide for interest to be paid even after default and this will usually be allowed by the court. Attorneys' fees will be allowed if provided for in the instrument; otherwise, they may not. However, any specified amount must be reasonable. Similarly, insurance premiums on the property may be added to the unpaid debt in some jurisdictions provided the mortgage instrument so provides.

[¶3028]　TAX DEDUCTIBILITY OF MORTGAGE INTEREST

Qualified Residence Interest. Subject to certain limitations, certain individuals may deduct *qualified residence interest.* In order to be qualified residence interest the interest payment must be for either (1) acquisition indebtedness or (2) home equity indebtedness with respect to a qualified residence of the taxpayer.[1] In all cases the debt must be secured by the residence.[2] A qualified residence may consist of the taxpayer's principal residence and a second residence.

Acquisition indebtedness is any debt which is secured by the residence and is incurred in acquiring, constructing, or substantially improving the qualified residence. Subject to certain limits, home equity indebtedness is any indebtedness (other than acquisition indebtedness) that is secured by a qualified residence of the taxpayer. The proceeds of the loan may be used for any purpose (including purchasing or improving a qualified residence), as long as the loan is secured by the taxpayer's qualified residence.

Qualified acquisition indebtedness is limited to $1,000,000 ($500,000 for a married individual filing a separate return).[3] Qualified acquisition indebtedness incurred prior to October 13, 1987 (pre-October 13, 1987 indebtedness) is not subject to any limitation.[4] However, the aggregate amount of pre-October 13, 1987 indebtedness reduces the $1,000,000 limitation on the indebtedness incurred after October 13, 1987.

Home equity indebtedness is limited to the lesser of:

➤ the FMV of the qualified residence in excess of the acquisition indebtedness with respect to that residence, or

➤ $100,000 ($50,000 for a married individual filing a separate return)

The $1,000,000 limit on acquisition indebtedness and the $100,000 limit on home equity indebtedness are two separate limits. The maximum amount of indebtedness upon which a taxpayer may deduct qualified residence interest is generally limited to $1,100,000 if an individual has $100,000 or more equity in the property.

— ENDNOTES —

1. IRC Sec. 163(h)(3)(A).

2. IRC Sec. 163(h)(3)(B).

3. IRC Sec. 163(h)(3)(B)(ii).

4. IRC Sec. 163(h)(3)(D).

— FOR FURTHER REFERENCE —

Mortgage Financing for Real Estate

Alexander, Frank S., "Mortgage Prepayment: The Trial of Common Sense," 72 *Cornell L. Rev.* 288 (January '87).

Bradner, JoAnne, "The Secondary Mortgage Market and State Regulation of Real Estate Financing," 36 *Emory L.J.* 971 (Summer '87).

Braxton, Kerry E., "Due-on-Sale Clauses and Their Effect Upon Alienation," 11 *Thurgood Marshall L. Rev.* 415 (Spring '86).

Eckman, Richard P. and Andrew T. Semmelman, "A Look at Home Equity Loans," 41 *Business Lawyer* 1079 (May '86).

Fiore, Nicholas J., "IRS Sets Procedures for Allocating Points over Loan Life," 18 *Tax Adviser* 354 (May '87).

Jacobs, John E., "Everything the Home Owner's Counsel Wanted to Know About Adjustable Rate Mortgages," 65 *Michigan B.J.* 156 (February '86).

Kiefer, Matthew J., "Participating Mortgages: The Risk for Lenders," 14 *Real Estate L.J.* 218 (Winter '86).

Mattis, Taylor, "Joint Tenancy: Notice of Severance; Mortgage and Survivorship," 7 *Northern Ill. U.L. Rev.* 41 (Winter '87).

Nelson, Grant S. and Dale A. Whitman, *Real Estate Finance Law (2d edition)* (West, 1985).

Sharkey, Eileen M. and George R. Guerin, "Cashing in on Mortgage Rates," 72 *ABA J.* 94 (6/1/86).

Foreclosure

Berger, Lawrence, "Solving the Problem of Abusive Mortgage Foreclosure Sales," 66 *Nebraska L. Rev.* 373 (Spring '87).

Burford, Robert, "Can Mortgage Foreclosure Sales Really Be Fraudulent Conveyances?" 22 *Houston L. Rev.* 1221 (October '85).

Holmes, Robert A., "Deeds in Lieu of Foreclosure," 15 *Colo. Lawyer* 394 (March '86).

Logan, Michael A., "Power of Sale Foreclosure: What Process Is Due?" 36 *Alabama L. Rev.* 1083 (Summer '85).

Mertens, Cynthia, "California's Foreclosure Statutes: Some Proposals for Reform," 26 *Santa Clara L. Rev.* 533 (Summer-Fall '86).

Mitnick, Daniel W., "Foreclosures and Bankruptcy: The Mortgagee-Mortgagor Relationship," 2 *Bankruptcy Developments J.* 317 (Summer '85).

Page, Michael, "Use of Receivers in Real Estate Foreclosures," 16 *Colorado Lawyer* 988 (June '87).

Preble, Laurence G. and David W. Cartwright, "Clogging the Equity of Redemption," 1 *Probate and Property* 6 (November—December '87).

Shepard, James I., "Foreclosure, Forfeiture, and Abandonment of Real Property," 8 *J. of Agricultural Taxation and Law* 132 (Summer '86).

Strassberg, Jonathan E., "Priorities and Statutory Construction," 7 *Cardozo L. Rev.* 585 (Winter '86).

[¶3101] A partnership is an association of two or more individuals who carry on a business for profit as co-owners. Joint tenancies, tenancies by the entirety, joint property, common property, tenancies in common, or part ownership do not of themselves establish a partnership relationship—even if the co-owners share profits made by the use of the property. While the sharing of gross receipts does not of itself establish a partnership, the receipt by any person of a share of profits of a business is prima facie evidence that the individual is a partner in the business—unless the profits were installment payments to a creditor, wages to an employee, annuities to a surviving spouse or representative of a deceased partner, interest to a lender, or consideration to a seller of business goodwill. Properties brought into the partnership or subsequently acquired by purchase for the partnership account are partnership property.

Every partner is an agent of the partnership for the purpose of its business, and the act of every partner when undertaking and carrying on the usual business of the partnership will bind the partnership unless the partner acting has no authority and the person with whom the partner is dealing has knowledge that the partner has no authority. If an act by a partner is apparently not for the purpose of carrying on the business of the partnership in the usual way, the act does not bind that partnership unless all of the other partners authorize it. Under certain circumstances, some actions require approval of all the partners; it is not possible for a single partner without their consent to dispose of partnership goodwill, to undertake any act that would make it impossible to carry out the order of business of the partnership, to confess a judgment, to submit a partnership claim, to arbitrate, or, under certain circumstances, to pay partnership debts by assigning partnership property in trust for creditors.

When a partner is acting in the ordinary course of business or with the authority of his co-partners, any loss or injury caused to an individual who is not a partner creates a liability to the entire partnership. If the loss results from a partner's tort or breach of trust, all partners are jointly and severally liable. On the other hand, a partner is only jointly liable for the contractual obligations of his firm. Additionally, when an individual represents that a partnership exists and credit is given on the faith of the representation, a partnership by estoppel may be created. Individuals who enter a partnership are liable for all obligations of the partnership, even those arising prior to their admission as partners. Liability, however, may be satisfied only out of partnership property.

[¶3102] PARTNERSHIPS VS. CORPORATIONS

Partnerships and corporations are the two most common methods of more than one individual doing business. Corporations are independent legal entities; partnerships are not. In the paragraphs below, the advantages of the partnership over the corporation, as well as the disadvantages, are explored.

[¶3103] ADVANTAGES OF A PARTNERSHIP OVER A CORPORATION

Basic advantages of a partnership over a corporation include avoidance of additional income tax (the double taxation on original corporate income and on dividends). In some respects operating a partnership is simpler than operating a corporation. There are no formal annual meeting requirements such as those mandated for corporations and it is not subject to as many other formal reporting requirements. Under subchapter K of the Internal Revenue Code, which governs the taxation of partnerships, a partnership is not directly subject to Federal income tax and merely files Form 1065, which is an informational return only. Profits and losses, as reported on the partnership tax return, flow through to each individual partner and are reported on his or her personal tax return, whether or not actually distributed. Thus it acts as a "conduit" for partnership profits and losses. Partnerships can utilize various qualified pension and profit-sharing plans.

Example: The partnership of M, N, and P reports a net income of $30,000 for the tax year 1995. If profits and losses are shared equally, each partner will report $10,000 on his or her personal tax return.

In the area of passive activities operated as limited partnerships, or so called *"tax shelters,"* for taxable years beginning in 1994, partners are permitted to offset net passive losses from rental real estate activities in which they *materially* participate against income from all other sources.[1] Previously, passive losses could only offset passive gains and were therefore of limited deductibility.

A taxpayer is eligible for this relief in the taxable year of the rental real estate loss if:

(1) The taxpayer's services performed in real property trades or businesses in which he or she materially participates are (a) over half of the personal services performed by the taxpayer and (b) more than 750 hours.

(2) The taxpayer materially participates in the rental real estate activities generating the net loss that he or she wants to deduct. A taxpayer can elect to treat all of his or her interests in rental real estate as one activity to meet the material participation test.

Many rental real estate activities are not considered real estate businesses, and are therefore subject to the passive loss rules. However, if an individual taxpayer meets certain requirements, up to $25,000 of annual losses from these passive real estate activities may still offset a taxpayer's other income. In order to meet this exception, the individual must *actively* participate in the activity,[2] and own at least 10% of the value of the activity for the entire year.

Passive loss limitations do not apply to partnerships, but to the partners themselves.

Other advantages include:

➤ Freedom from certain statutory regulations.

➤ Freedom from miscellaneous taxes including the corporate franchise tax.

➤ Simplicity in organization.

➤ Availability of a "veto" power by each partner over partnership decisions.

[¶3104] DISADVANTAGES OF A PARTNERSHIP

Following are the disadvantages of using a partnership for purposes of doing business:

➤ Each partner is the agent for the other, capable of making decisions binding all other partners.

➤ Personal liability of each partner for all obligations of business (partners do have a right of contribution from other partners to mitigate damages).

➤ Dissolution of partnership upon death.

➤ Unlimited personal liability (avoidable by use of a limited partnership).

[¶3105] RIGHTS AND DUTIES OF PARTNERS

Every partner, at all times, is permitted to have access to the books of the partnership. Subject to agreement between the partners, books are to be kept at the principal place of business. Partners must account to the partnership for any benefit they derive and for profits derived without the consent of the other partners. The individual acts as a trustee (thus prohibiting the personal use of the funds and profits). Any partner has the right to a formal accounting of partnership affairs if he is wrongfully excluded from partnership business or under other circumstances where it is deemed necessary.

[¶3106] DISSOLUTION

Dissolution of a partnership may be accomplished in several ways. Two of these relate to the partnership agreement itself, others to events frequently beyond the control of the partnership.

A partnership for a definite term dissolves at the conclusion of that term. If no definite term is specified, a partnership at will is created, and any partner may express a desire to terminate the partnership—at which time the partnership is dissolved and "winding up" begins. Similarly, a partnership may be dissolved without violating the agreement by the express will of all the partners who have not assigned their interests. If the partnership permits expulsion of a partner pursuant to agreement between the other partners, the partnership is also dissolved. Other events that may cause a dissolution are the death of any partner, bankruptcy of any partner or of the partnership itself, or an event that makes it unlawful for the partnership business to be carried on (or for the members to carry it on in a partnership). In all instances, the partnership is dissolved, but business may continue through the conclusion of the winding-up process. When a partner has been declared mentally incompetent in any judicial proceeding, or becomes incapable of performing part of the partnership contract, or is guilty of prejudicial conduct in the carrying on of business, or is in such consistent breach of the partnership agreement as to make it reasonably impractical to continue the partnership business, a court must decree dissolution on application of any partner. The same holds true if the partnership business can only be carried on at a loss.

[¶3107] RULES FOR DISTRIBUTION OF PARTNERSHIP ASSETS

Once a partnership has been dissolved and the winding-up process concluded, the assets of the partnership are distributed in this order: Partnership property and then the contributions of partners necessary for the payment of liabilities. Partnership liabilities are satisfied in the following order of priority: (1) Creditors other than partners, (2) Loans from partners (other than capital and profits), (3) Capital contributions of partners, (4) Profits of partners.

[¶3108] CHECKLIST FOR ORGANIZING A PARTNERSHIP

The following paragraphs comprise a 20-item checklist that should be used in the organization of any partnership. The Uniform Partnership Act (and the Uniform Limited Partnership Act) have been adopted by most states. Rules and limitations differ slightly from state to state, but are for the most part quite similar.

[¶3108.1] Name

Any name may be used for a partnership unless specifically prohibited by law. Use of a name deceptively similar to that of another business may lead to litigation. Many states have a statutory requirement that partnership names be registered with the Secretary of State, county clerk, or other appropriate filing officer. If individuals' names are used in the partnership name, consideration should be given to whether the name will be continued after the death of a partner and whether this is permitted under local law. The use of the name itself will not make the individual property of the deceased partner liable for any debts contracted by the partnership.

[¶3108.2] Business Activity

A careful statement of the nature of the business is necessary to define the scope of the partnership so that no partner becomes involved in a business against his wishes.

[¶3108.3] Licensing

If the nature of the business is one that might require licensing, etc., state and federal regulatory statutes should be checked. When a license or permit is required, it is wise to provide that the partnership agreement will not become effective until the license or permit is procured.

[¶3108.4] Term

A definite term of years for the continuation of the partnership business may be agreed upon or the partnership may continue at will. However, any partner may terminate a relationship with the partnership even though it be in contravention of the partnership agreement. This may give rise to a suit for damages by the remaining partners, but the partnership nevertheless is dissolved. The partnership agreement may contain a provision for liquidated damages for a partner's premature withdrawal. However, to be enforceable, it must be compensatory in nature rather than punitive. When the agreement specifies a fixed term, the parties may continue the business beyond that term as a partnership at will. However, it is advisable that they either extend the term of the partnership or enter into a new partnership agreement.

[¶3108.5] Partnership Contributions

Careful distinction should be drawn between contributions to the partnership capital and other types of financial relationships (such as loans) between the partners and the partnership. Contributions to partnership capital may consist of cash, property, or services. When property is contributed, consideration should be given to the statutory right of the partners to reconcile the tax bases and accounting values of the contributed property. These adjustments may be necessary to prevent distortions in the partnership income shares.

[¶3108.6] Loans and Leases with the Partnership

A partner may, in an individual capacity, lend or rent property to the partnership and receive interest or rent. Since the money loaned or the property leased is not part of the partnership capital, it will not be available in the first instance for the satisfaction of partnership debts.

[¶3108.7] Interest on Partnership Capital

Generally, the partnership will not pay interest on its capital. If interest is to be paid, the agreement should so state. In businesses that require a large amount of liquid capital to meet regulatory requirements, the parties may feel that payment of interest should be made, particularly when the capital contributions of various partners differ and the distributions of profits do not reflect each partner's capital contributions. Interest paid by the partnership is deductible for income tax purposes.

[¶3108.8] Salary

Ordinarily, a partner is compensated for services and for contributions of capital by a share of the profits. Unless provided for in the partnership agreement, a partner will not be entitled to salary or other compensation for services except in the case of a partner winding up the business of a partnership. However, if a partner does receive a salary, this expense is deductible by the partnership.

[¶3108.9] Sharing Profits and Losses

The essential element in the partnership is the sharing of profits between the partners. While losses are ordinarily shared also, this is not always the case (as when the partner who contributes services only may be relieved from any liability from losses). When both profits and losses are shared, they are usually shared in the same ratio (that is, a partner who is entitled to 10% of the profits is liable for 10% of the losses). However, profits and losses may or may not be shared equally between the partners. (For example, a partner putting up 50% of the capital may be entitled to receive 75% of the profit.) Sometimes, different distribution ratios will apply to different kinds of income (e.g., operating income and capital gains). All of these matters must be spelled out in the partnership agreement. One solution to the problem of unequal financial contributions is to create equal capital accounts and treat additional funds as loans. For tax purposes, a partner's loss is limited to the adjusted basis of the partnership interest (before reduction for the current year's loss), and by the "at-risk" rules of Code §465.

[¶3108.10] Right to Withdraw Capital

If the right to withdraw funds from the partnership is limited, this should be spelled out in the partnership agreement. If a substantial amount of money is to be accumulated in the partnership, the partners should be permitted to take out sufficient money to meet their income tax obligations.

[¶3108.11] Payments to Retired or Deceased Partner

When payments are made to a partner who retires, or to the estate or heir of a deceased partner, the money paid may represent the withdrawing partner's capital interest, the pro rata interest in unrealized receivables and fees, his or her share of the potential gain or loss on partnership inventory, or mutual insurance among the partners.

[¶3108.12] Management

In the absence of an agreement to the contrary, all partners have equal rights in the management and conduct of the partnership business. It is, therefore, necessary to have the agreement clearly state each partner's rights and duties. The extent to which the partners are authorized as between themselves to commit and bind the partnership should be clearly spelled out in the agreement. When a partner assigns an interest in the partnership, the assignee during the continuance of the partnership will not have the right to interfere in the management or administration of the partnership business or affairs unless the partnership agreement provides otherwise.

[¶3108.13] Books and Records

Local law frequently requires that books and records must be kept at the principal place of business of the partnership and every partner shall at all times have access to and may inspect and copy them.

[¶3108.14] Death or Withdrawal of a Partner

Provision can be made in the agreement for the continuation of the business after the death or withdrawal of a partner, bearing in mind that such a provision may, along with other corporate attributes, give the partnership the tax status of a corporation. In the absence of such a provision, the partnership will be required to wind up its affairs.

[¶3108.15] Partnership Property

Unless a contrary intention appears, all property acquired with partnership funds will be partnership property.

[¶3108.16] Accounting by Partners

The agreement should require all partners to give to the partnership full information on matters affecting the partnership.

See Code §§6221–6233 for determination of treatment of partnership items at the partnership level for partnerships of over 10 partners (or of any size with one or more corporate partners). The IRS will not determine the treatment of such items in separate proceedings with partners for large partnerships, or for small partnerships electing "single audit" treatment.

[¶3108.17] Indemnification of Partner

Without any provision in the agreement, the partnership may be required to indemnify each partner for payments made and personal liabilities reasonably incurred in the ordinary and necessary fulfillment of the partnership business.

[¶3108.18] Family Partnerships

Partnership interests can be given to family members and in that way income can be spread over a number of low-bracket taxpayers. But keep in mind that this can be done only when capital is a substantial income-producing factor in the partnership. And the donor-partner must get fair compensation before the balance of the partnership profits is distributed among the remaining partners.

The usefulness of family partnerships as an income-splitting device was greatly limited by the Tax Code of 1986, which imposed a "kiddie tax" on certain unearned income of children under 14 (see ¶4227). By decreasing the number of tax brackets and the differences between brackets, TC '86 made income-splitting less useful in reducing tax liability.

If a trust is a partner, the trustee should have broad powers and be able to act independently as a partner.

[¶3108.19] Partnership Treated as a Corporation

In some cases, a partnership will be treated as a corporation despite the wishes of the partners. This will come about when the partnership has more corporate characteristics than noncorporate characteristics under the federal regulations. The four elements that point to a corporation are continuity, centralized management, limited liability, and free transferability of interest. If a partnership has three or more of these elements, it may become subject to a double tax on its income (a corporate tax plus a personal tax on each partner.[3]) This risk is especially severe for publicly traded Master Limited Partnerships.

[¶3108.20] Limited Partnerships

A limited partnership is one step closer to a corporation than is a general partnership because it includes partners who, like shareholders in a corporation, invest capital, have limited liability, and do not share in the management of partnership affairs. The partnership agreement may provide that the limited partner share in profits or be paid a specific amount of income whether or not there are partnership profits. In organizing a limited partnership, it is important that the limited partner be given no rights or powers over partnership affairs that may cause him or her to be treated as a general partner.

Losses and credits that are attributable to limited partnership interests are generally treated as arising from a passive activity and are therefore subject to certain limitations (see [¶3103] above).

— ENDNOTES —

1. Temp. Reg. Sec. 1.469-5T(a).

2. IRC Sec. 469(i)(1).

3. IRC Reg. Sec. 301.7701-2(a)(3).

— **FOR FURTHER REFERENCE** —

ALI/ABA, *Partnerships: Resource Materials* (7th edition, 1987).

Charyx, William R., "Selected Problems Involving Service Partners," 13 *J. of Real Estate Taxation* 273 (Spring '86).

Close, Michael A. and Dan A. Kusnetz, "The Final Section 704(b) Regulations," 40 *Tax Lawyer* 307 (Winter '87).

Cuff, Terence F., "Drafting Partnership Allocations," 9 *Los Angeles Lawyer* 36 (November '86).

Cullen, Jeffrey P., "S Corporations vs. Partnerships," 40 *J. of American Society of CLU* 62 (May '86).

Gobbi, Mark, "Section 9.1 of the U.P.A.: Expectations and Partnership Liability," 8 *Whittier L. Rev.* 801 (Summer '86).

Goldstein, Jeremy E. and John Goode, "Entity and Aggregate Theories of Partnership: The Need for Clarification," 1 *Probate and Property* 14 (November–December '87).

Kaster, Lewis R. and Jeffrey K. Cymbler, "The Impact of a General Partner's Bankruptcy Upon the Remaining Partners," 21 *Real Property, Probate & Trust J.* 539 (Fall '86).

Laveson, Avi O., "The Partnership Basis Election Analyzed," 14 *Estate Planning* 138 (May–June '87).

McGuire, John A., "Adjustments to Basis of Partnership Property," 14 *Journal of Real Estate Taxation* 275 (Spring '87).

McNamara, David J., "Rights of a Deceased Partner's Estate in Partnership Assets," 24 *J. Family Law* 673 (June '86).

Volz, Marlin M., C. Christopher Trainer, and Debbie F. Reiss, *The Drafting of Partnership Agreements* (ALI/ABA, 1986).

PERSONAL INJURY AND NO-FAULT

[¶3201] As long as human beings have been living together, there have been personal injuries—whether the result of an intentional blow or an accidental collision between two ox-carts. As technology becomes more complex, the risks become greater, and previously unthinkable situations (such as substances that were considered safe at the time they were installed, but are later found to cause harm; drugs that produce birth defects) must be dealt with by the legal system.

The legal system has many responses to personal injury. Perhaps the first one that comes to mind is the tort system: those who believe they are injured sue those whom they believe to be responsible for their injuries. However, this simple two-party interaction is made immensely more complicated by the widespread use of liability insurance. The major factor often becomes the extent of the defendant's insurance coverage, rather than the actual causation of the harm.

Many observers believe that our legal system is caught up in a "tort crisis" or "litigation crisis," in which there is a tendency for large awards to be made in favor of innocent persons who have suffered severe harm—even if the defendant or defendant's insurer is merely a "deep pocket," not a tortfeasor.

Insurance is also important to the redress of personal injuries in other ways. Liability insurance is "third-party" coverage, payable when the insured is found liable for harming another. Many cases never enter the court system, because the injured person has already recovered elements of loss such as compensation for property damage and medical expenses on a "first-party" basis: from his, her, or its own insurer. The effect of "no-fault" statutes dealing with automobile accidents is to shift coverage from third-party to first-party principles.

Furthermore, although the tort system is based on the idea of finding and apportioning fault, there are circumstances in which society has deemed it appropriate to bypass the litigation process and award payments to injured persons regardless of fault (for instance, in the Workers' Compensation system). Or, the litigation system may still be involved, but liability may be imposed even without fault (for instance, in certain products liability cases).

The present focus is on products liability, especially these vital areas such as the liability of manufacturers of birth control devices, tampons, drugs used in pregnancy, the anesthetic Versed, tranquilizer Halcion and silicone gel-filled breast implants, and vaccines. The legal issues include traditional tort issues as well as the extent to which state-law actions are preempted by federal legislation.

The Supreme Court made a rare foray into tort law in a case involving an allegedly libelous statement of opinion.[1] The High Court ruled that there is no plenary constitutional privilege for opinions, and the distinction between fact and opinion is one of law, not of fact. The high court made another excursion into tort law in *Masson*,[2] ruling that when a public figure alleges libel, actual malice can be inferred from evidence that quotes attributed to the figure are materially different from what he or she said. The First Amendment does not protect fabricated quotations even if they are a "rational interpretation" of actual statements made by the public-figure plaintiff.

In 1992, the Supreme Court decided a tobacco liability case that turned in large part on the issue of preemption, discussed in greater detail below. The ruling in *Cipollone*[3] permitted claims against tobacco manufacturers, alleging concealment of health risks of smoking, but found that state tort claims based on inadequacy of warning labels are preempted by the federal law mandating those labels.

A 1993 case looks at admissibility of scientific analysis, finding that evidence need not be generally accepted within the scientific community to be admissible; it's the job of the trial judge to let in only expert testimony that is relevant and adequately supported by scientific research.[4]

[¶3201.1] Personal Injury Damages

The main elements of damages in personal injury tort cases are:

➤ Medical expenses reasonably incurred by the injured party.

➤ The injured party's lost wages or loss of earning capacity.

➤ Physical and mental pain and suffering.

➤ Other specifically identifiable harm, such as the expenses of traveling to seek medical attention.

At the time of trial, the plaintiff must be able to prove the extent of damages suffered up to the time of trial, and must present evidence to make a reasonable estimate of future economic loss, medical expenses, and pain and suffering. This calculation involves estimating the plaintiff's life expectancy as well as the amounts to be expended. Generally, the award for future damages will then be reduced to present value to account for the amount of investment income the plaintiff can earn from the damages. Many courts will also take inflation into account, perhaps by increasing the award to make up for the ravages of inflation, or by changing the discount rate used to reduce the sum to present value.

Theoretically punitive damages are reserved for situations in which the defendant's conduct has been extreme or outrageous, but sometimes the award is focused more on the factor of deterring similar conduct by others than on punishing the defendant, who may not even have acted with wrongful intent.

The availability of punitive damages depends both on the judge and jury. The judge determines whether, on the evidence presented, punitive damages can be awarded at all. If this determination is in the affirmative, the jury must decide whether or not to award them and in what amount. In the none-too-unlikely case that the defendant believes a punitive damages award to be excessive, the award can be reviewed either by a motion for new trial or by taking an appeal. However, the plaintiff does not have the right to challenge the punitive damages award for inadequacy.

Where two or more defendants act in concert to cause harm to the plaintiff, they are jointly and severally liable, and the plaintiff can sue either or both, but cannot collect a total recovery in excess of damages. In general, defendants paying a judgment are entitled to contribution from the co-defendants in an amount proportionate to their share of fault.

[¶3201.2] Intervening Force of Nature

According to the Restatement of Torts 2d Section 451, a defendant can be freed from liability because of the intervening operation of a force of nature if the natural phenomenon (say, a flood that washes away the plaintiff's car after a collision with the defendant's car) is a "but-for" cause of the harm; if the operation of the force of nature is extraordinary; and if the resultant harm is different in kind from the harm whose risk rendered the defendant's conduct negligent.

[¶3202] INTENTIONAL TORTS

There are three bases for imposing liability for personal injury: intentional torts; negligent torts; and strict liability (liability without fault). This discussion centers on intentional torts causing physical injury; the legal system also recognizes intentional torts causing nonphysical injury (e.g., slander and libel that cause injury to reputation; the tort of interference with contractual relations).

A defendant who is guilty of an intentional tort (at least one involving conscious wrongdoing) is liable for all the damages caused by the tortious conduct, even if they were not intended by the tortfeasor, or even foreseeable.

[¶3202.1] Battery; Assault

The tort of battery consists of offensive touching—that is, touching in a way that offends a reasonable sense of dignity, performed by one who intends to cause harmful or offensive conduct. Thus, this tort involves wrongs of the type criminalized as assault and sexual battery. Battery can be committed even without what is normally thought of as physical violence: for example, certain instances of job-related sexual harassment involve the tort of battery as well.

A tortfeasor who performs an act intended to cause physical injury to one person will be liable in battery to anyone who is actually struck as a result of the act.

The tort of assault, unlike the crime of assault, consists not of actual touching, but of placing the victim in apprehension of imminent unwelcome contact. The criminal counterpart of the tort concept of assault would be menacing.

[¶3202.2] False Imprisonment

The tort of false imprisonment occurs when the defendant intentionally confines the plaintiff, who is aware of his confinement. (That is, this tort cannot be committed against an unconscious person, with the exception, however, that if actual harm results, the plaintiff can collect damages even if he or she lacked knowledge of the confinement at the time.) Suits for false imprisonment arise most often in the context of accusations of shoplifting; the main issue is the reasonableness of the conduct of the store detective or other person or organization detaining the accused shoplifter.

[¶3202.3] Intentional Inflictions of Mental Distress (or Anguish)

This tort consists of extreme or outrageous conduct that intentionally or recklessly causes severe emotional distress. The tortfeasor's conduct must be exceptionally subject to censure; the degree of upset experienced by the potential plaintiff is not determinative. The tortfeasor is liable to a member of the intended victim's immediate family who is present at the time of the conduct, and who suffers severe emotional distress. The tortfeasor is also liable to anyone else who is present when the conduct is committed, and who suffers bodily sequelae of mental distress (e.g., a heart attack).

[¶3203] NEGLIGENCE

The general rule is that a defendant is liable for negligence if the defendant breaches a duty (usually the duty of reasonable care), and if this breach is both the factual and the legal (proximate) cause of the harm to the plaintiff or plaintiffs. A "but-for" rule is applied to determine cause in fact: unless the harm would not have occurred but for the defendant's conduct, the defendant's conduct is not a cause in fact of the harm.

Violation of a statute (e.g., the speed limit; a law against dumping toxic waste) is sometimes treated as negligence per se, provided that the injured person is within the class of people intended to be protected, and the harm that ensues is of the type the statute is designed to avoid. Certain states (including California and Michigan) permit a presumption of negligence from a violation of statute.

The defendant's duty is to behave as a reasonable individual in the same situation would behave. Thus, the plaintiff is usually permitted to introduce evidence of customary safety precautions that are taken by those similarly situated to the defendant, and to show that the defendant's failure to observe the custom caused the injury. As to the converse, the defendant is not always relieved of liability by following industry custom; if the entire industry is unreasonably careless, then liability will attach.

[¶3203.1] Res Ipsa Loquitur

Res ipsa loquitur ("the thing speaks for itself") is an inference that can be drawn for the plaintiff's benefit in appropriate instances. The Restatement of Torts 2d Section 328D says that the inference is available if:

➤ The event ordinarily does not happen absent negligence (the classic law school example is the package of chewing tobacco also containing a human toe).

➤ The evidence eliminates the possibility of negligence on the part of the plaintiff and third persons (e.g., the alleged negligence concerns goods sold in a sealed package).

➤ The negligence alleged falls within the scope of the defendant's duty to the plaintiff.

In situations where different conclusions may reasonably be reached as to these points, it is for the jury to decide whether or not to apply res ipsa loquitur.

[¶3203.2] Effect of the Plaintiff's Negligence

Not infrequently, an incident involves two parties, both negligent, rather than an entirely innocent plaintiff victimized by an entirely culpable defendant. In fact, it's common for the defendant to have counter-claims against the plaintiff.

Originally, any contributory negligence on the plaintiff's part (defined as failure to exercise ordinary care to protect one's own safety, whether or not the plaintiff was also negligent in the sense of failing to exercise ordinary care to protect the safety of others) would entirely bar recovery. (Similarly, any marital misconduct on the part of a divorce plaintiff once precluded a divorce being granted to either "guilty" party.) The rule was applied only in negligence cases, not intentional tort cases.

However, the harshness of this rule was mitigated by exceptions such as the "last clear chance" rule. This rule obligated a defendant to use ordinary care to protect a plaintiff who could no longer protect himself. That is, the plaintiff's contributory negligence would no longer serve as a defense if the defendant became or continued to be negligent after the plaintiff was helpless. A variation of this rule was the "discovered peril" rule, which functioned similarly but only came into play if the defendant became aware of the plaintiff's peril.

There was a trend away from the contributory negligence standard, and most of the states have eliminated the rule in favor of a pure or modified comparative negligence rule. Under a pure comparative negligence rule, a negligent plaintiff can recover, but the amount of the recovery is reduced proportionate to his, her, or its negligence. Under a modified comparative negligence rule, the plaintiff is permitted to sue only if the defendant's degree of fault is greater than the plaintiff's; if suit is permitted, once again the recovery is reduced to account for the plaintiff's own negligence.

Colorado no longer imputes a driver's contributory negligence to a car owner and passenger who sues a third party (e.g., the other driver) for negligence.[5]

A New Jersey jury is permitted to consider a plaintiff's failure to wear a seat belt (and to reduce the plaintiff's damages) if the failure increases the severity of the plaintiff's injury even if this form of comparative negligence occurred before the effective date of the state's seat belt law, which made failure to wear a belt negligence per se. This is in contrast to some states which refuse to allow evidence about seat-belt use, on the theory that drivers and passengers are not obligated to anticipate the negligence of other drivers. Wisconsin has always treated non-use of the seat belt as comparative negligence; New York and Florida consider it a possible breach of the duty to mitigate damages.[6]

[¶3203.3] Medical Malpractice

Certainly one of the most newsworthy varieties of negligence action is the medical malpractice case—perhaps because of the almost godlike reverence we accord to doctors (and our corresponding willingness to demand huge damages if these deities fail to meet our expectations).

Medical malpractice is not defined as failure of the doctor to provide a positive medical outcome; it is the failure to meet the standard of good medical practice, usually as found in "the same or similar" localities (the "locality rule"). Specialists will be held to the standard of care of their specialty.

The law of implied consent bridges both medical malpractice and battery. Every competent person has the right to decide what will be done to his or her body, so failing to warn patients appropriately of the risks of medical treatment and carrying out treatment without informed consent can be both malpractice and a tortious unpermitted touching.

Responding to protests by doctors and liability insurers, many jurisdictions have passed "tort reform" bills dealing with medical malpractice cases. States have imposed "caps" on noneconomic damages (e.g., pain and suffering) that can be recovered in medical malpractice actions. Some states do not permit a medical malpractice complaint to state the amount of damages sought, because sometimes extensive publicity is given to complaints demanding high damages, even if the case is eventually settled for small damages, or even decided in favor of the defendant doctor.

Some of the reform statutes eliminate the use of res ipsa loquitur in medical malpractice cases: the plaintiff must prove actual negligence. The standard of care may be restricted to the locality, not extended throughout the nation (a nationwide standard makes it easier to recover against a "provincial" doctor who is not aware of new developments). The statute may apply the statute of limitations in an absolute fashion, regardless of when the plaintiff discovered or could have discovered the malpractice. The informed consent claim may be limited or discouraged. Although tort cases in general follow the "collateral source" rule (funds received from sources collateral to the tort action, such as health insurance, do not reduce the recovery), tort reform medical malpractice statutes may abolish the collateral source rule to prevent double recovery.

In fact, some statutes limit or eliminate the medical malpractice plaintiff's right to conventional litigation, by requiring the case to be submitted (either first or in lieu of litigation) to a malpractice arbitration panel. Depending on the state statute, the panel may have to rule that the claim is justified before the plaintiff can proceed to litigation, or the panel may be the sole forum for determination of the claim.

[¶3203.4] Other Tort Reform Statutes

Growing numbers of states (but not Congress, despite a great deal of lobbying and the introduction of many bills) have passed tort reform bills. Many states have modified their rules as to joint and several liability; the new laws limit any one tortfeasor's share of damages to his, her, or its actual fault in the matter. Even these statutes have exceptions (e.g., pollution liability; medical malpractice).

Numerous states imposed "caps" on damages for pain and suffering and other non-economic matters. The cap could be a dollar amount, such as $350,000 to $875,000, or a variable amount proportioned to the plaintiff's life expectancy. As discussed below in connection with "no-fault," some of the "cap" statutes have exceptions, so that a very seriously injured plaintiff can recover despite the limitations under the cap.

Other states set limits or abolished punitive damages; eight states placed limitations on attorney's contingent fees; some of them subjected attorneys to sanctions for frivolous or vexatious litigation.

See ¶3406 for developments with respect to punitive damages. Maryland's $350,000 cap on personal injury damages was upheld[7] over constitutional challenges premised on the right to a jury trial. The Washington Supreme Court reached the opposite conclusion about a statute that limited the non-economic damages in personal injury and wrongful death cases.[8] The court held that the cap interfered with jury discretion and therefore violated the state Constitution's guarantee of the right to a jury trial.

The District Court of New Jersey has held that multiple punitive damage awards imposed in a mass-tort asbestos products liability case for the same conduct by the manufacturer violate the due process clause of the Fourteenth Amendment;[9] later, the Third Circuit ruled in another case that multiple punitive damages are constitutionally permissible (although the court did lower the award, finding that the District Court failed to give adequate consideration of the effect of the multiple punitive damage awards).[10] However, New Jersey's statute on punitive damages in product liability cases has been upheld over a due process challenge.[11] The statute (which contains detailed standards for jury charges in such cases) does not impose a ceiling on punitive damages and does not require plaintiffs to establish a relationship between compensatory and punitive damages.

In contrast, Georgia's Tort Reform Act has been struck down by lower courts on constitutional grounds.[12] The objectionable provision did not limit the amount of punitive damages per se, but permitted only a single award of punitive damages in any case regardless of the number of claims asserted. It also mandated forfeiture of 75% of the punitive damage award to the state treasury. The statute was struck down as vague, arbitrary, and unreasonable. Payments to the state treasury were deemed to violate the Constitution's Excessive Fines clause, and also to discriminate against plaintiffs whose claims involved punitive damages. Yet a 1993 Georgia Supreme Court case[13] upholds the statute, finding that the state exercised a proper purpose in espousing punitive damages to harm the malefactor, not to benefit the tort victim.

Idaho's products liability statute of repose, which ends with the passage of the product's "useful safe life" (rebuttably presumed to be ten years) has been upheld over claims of a violation of due process and the state Constitution's guarantees of "open courts."[14]

[¶3204] No-Fault

The hundreds of thousands of automobile accidents a year range from minor fender-benders to tragic multi-car collisions causing several deaths and atrocious injuries. It seems reasonable to treat these cases differently depending on the type and severity of damages asserted.

Automobile accidents also differ greatly in the conduct and liability of the drivers involved. Sometimes both were grossly negligent; sometimes both exercised due care, and the accident was caused by a slippery highway, a patch of ice, or a malfunctioning car.

The sheer volume of automobile accidents is burdensome to the court system. There's certainly no shortage of other litigation business to be handled! At the same time, insurance companies have a well-defined system for assessing, handling, and (sometimes) paying claims.

All these forces combined to motivate states to adopt some degree of no-fault system for automobile injury claims. The common feature of these plans is their stress on "first-party" coverage: that is, instead of finding a tortfeasor to blame and recovering from him (or, in the real world, from his liability insurer), the no-fault system requires drivers to carry first-party coverage for their own injuries, and injuries of their passengers and pedestrians. Thus, recovery depends on proving that injuries occurred, not on allocating blame to someone else.

Although they differ in details, no-fault laws have certain similarities:

➤ Tort suits arising out of automobile accidents are either precluded or limited to suits in connection with claims above a specified minimum amount of injuries.

➤ Property damage is usually not covered by the no-fault system; instead, it is relegated to first-party coverage (e.g., collision insurance) purchased from a driver's own insurance company.

➤ The focus is on compensation of economic losses (e.g., medical bills; lost time at work), not pain and suffering, so pain and suffering damages are either precluded altogether or limited to cases defined as "serious" by the no-fault statute.

➤ About one-third of the states have "add-on" no-fault statutes. That is, drivers can buy no-fault benefit insurance, but do not have to prove they have done so to register their cars. Injured persons can collect no-fault benefits and also bring a tort suit; however, amounts collected through litigation are subject to subrogation by the insurer that issued the no-fault policy.

[¶3205] PRODUCTS LIABILITY

Injury (and property damage) can be caused by defective products in several ways. The individual example of the product can be poorly manufactured (the archetypal "car made on a Monday"). The design of the product itself can create danger (a chain saw with an improperly secured blade that flies off when the motor is running). A reasonably safe product can be rendered unsafe because the manufacturer fails to supply adequate warnings about its risks and safe use. The danger can also be caused by the buyer's own misuse of the product: removing safety features to make the product more convenient to operate, for instance.

In many instances, the manufacturer (and others in the chain of distribution) will be held strictly liable for personal injury and property damage caused by abnormally dangerous activities (such as blasting) or defective products. That is, liability is strict, based on the risk of harm rather than on any negligence or fault of the manufacturer. If a "middleman" such as a distributor or wholesaler is sued (or, more commonly, joined as one of a number of co-defendants), it will not be able to escape liability based on its status, but will probably have an indemnity claim against the manufacturer.

Under Restatement of Torts 2d Section 402A, any seller is liable for the sale of "any product in a defective condition unreasonably dangerous to the user or consumer or to his property," as long as the seller is engaged in the business of selling such products, and as long as the product reaches the user or consumer without a substantial change from the condition in which it was sold (i.e., "souping up" a product can relieve the seller of liability). Privity of contract is not required; it is no defense for a manufacturer who is sued to claim that it had no contractual relationship with the buyer. Products must be safe for their intended use; they must also be safe for foreseeable results (although cars are not designed to crash, collisions are foreseeable, and cars must be designed to cope with that eventuality), and even sometimes for foreseeable misuses (manufacturers must be aware of the tendency to remove safety devices to speed up operation of machinery).

Finally, some products are considered "unavoidably unsafe"; as defined by the famous Comment K to Section 402A of the Restatement Second of Torts, they cannot be made safe for their intended use within the present state of knowledge. If these products (e.g., potent drugs with dangerous side effects) are sold with the proper warnings, they are deemed neither defective nor unreasonably dangerous, so the manufacturer is not liable for any harm so caused. However, a drug manufacturer can be liable if it is negligent in failing to discover the dangers of its products (e.g., if it fails to test the drugs adequately before sale) or if it is negligent in failing to warn of known dangers.

Thus, although the usual rationale is that the doctor is the "learned intermediary" who warns patients about potential drug side-effects, birth control pills and some other drugs that have given rise to extensive litigation are dispensed with "Patient Package Inserts" that convey additional warnings.

Because injury may not manifest itself for many years, it can be difficult for the injured person to remember or ascertain the manufacturer of the drug, giving rise to serious statute of limitations and joinder problems. Some courts have attempted to cope with these problems by imposing "enterprise liability" or "market-share liability," permitting the defendant to sue all manufacturers of the relevant drug and either forcing the manufacturers to exculpate themselves, or subjecting them to liability based on their share of the market for the drug at the relevant time.

Contrary to the practice of some states, it has been held that Delaware does not impose on the successor a continuing duty to warn of the dangers of a product manufactured by a predecessor corporation.[15]

Nor does Maryland impose liability on a successor corporation that acquires the assets of a predecessor corporation in a situation where strict liability is not imposed.[16]

According to the District of Maryland, an IUD manufacturer did not have enough contacts with that state to be sued there merely because it was alleged to have tested a defective IUD there, or to have filed a false report with the FDA from Maryland.[17]

In a case in which pain-reliever capsules were tampered with after leaving the manufacturer, leading to the death of the plaintiff's decedent, the Southern District of New York held[18] that the manufacturer was not liable. Although the packaging was evidently not "tamper-proof," it did have three tamper-resistant features, so the design was not defective; nor can packaging the medication in capsule form, which is easier to tamper with than tablet or caplet form, be deemed a design defect that would justify imposition of strict liability.

Although many plaintiffs have brought suits claiming that Bendectin (a drug used to control nausea in pregnancy) causes birth defects, they have had little success: e.g., In re *Bendectin Litigation*[19] affirming a defense jury verdict in 1,100 cases; the Sixth Circuit believed that the plaintiffs failed to prove that the drug caused the birth defects complained of. In some cases, the plaintiffs prevailed with the jury but not with the judge: the Fifth and D.C. Circuits have permitted the judge to disregard the testimony of the plaintiffs' expert witnesses and grant judgment *non obstante veredicto* if there is a substantial body of epidemiologic evidence that is uniform in holding that Bendectin does not cause birth defects.[20]

Another product used in pregnancy—diethylstilbestrol, or DES—creates especially difficult evidentiary problems, because it was frequently prescribed as a generic drug, and it is impossible to determine who manufactured the drug actually taken by the plaintiff's mother and allegedly causing the plaintiff's birth defects. New York permits market share liability: i.e., the plaintiff sues all manufacturers, who can then be held liable based on their share of the market. *Hymowitz v. Eli Lilly & Co.*[21] permits the decision to be made based on the national market. It also upholds New York's toxic tort revival statute (which granted an additional year for pursuing certain time-barred DES cases) over due process and equal protection challenges. However, the revival statute does not prevent the use of New York's "borrowing statute" to import a shorter statute of limitations from a relevant foreign state. A New York lower court also permitted a strict-liability action to be brought by an infant plaintiff who sustained injury as a result of the mother's exposure to DES taken by the plaintiff's grandmother, but New York's highest court subsequently reversed the lower court's decision.[22] Ohio refused to countenance an action by a "DES grandson," because such persons were neither exposed to the drug directly nor as fetuses, although the dissent called DES grandsons foreseeable plaintiffs to whom a duty is owed.[23] Illinois has rejected the use of market-share theory in a DES negligence or strict liability case in which the actual manufacturer of the drug cannot be identified.[24]

The District Court for the District of Massachusetts refused to apply market-share theory in a case alleging injuries caused by lead paint, finding that it was not clear that the plaintiffs had indeed suffered injuries from any manufacturer's lead paint.[25]

New Jersey refused to apply the concept of market-share liability to cases involving DPT (diphtheria-pertussis-tetanus; pertussis is whooping cough) vaccine.[26] New Jersey's Supreme Court refused to apply the concept for two reasons: first, on public policy grounds (the state does not want to discourage manufacturers from providing useful vaccines), and second, because those claiming injury due to vaccines can use the federal National Childhood Vaccine Injury Act[27] to gain administrative redress without the necessity of proving causation, negligence, or defect.

The Fifth Circuit notes that this statute does not preempt all state remedies; in fact, it makes state recovery easier in some cases. The court held that state-law claims involving design defects and failure to warn and claiming that DPT vaccine is an unreasonably dangerous product are not preempted by the National Childhood Vaccine Injury Act or by other federal laws such as the Food, Drug and Cosmetics Act and the Public Health Service Act.[28]

The National Traffic and Motor Vehicle Safety Act does not preempt a state-law claim that a car's airbag is defectively designed;[29] in contrast, the 1978 Airline Deregulation Act does preempt an airplane passenger's state tort claim for injuries caused by the unsafe condition of the plane, because the claim relates to the "services" provided by the air carrier.[30]

The subject of preemption can be studied by reading *Cipollone with Mortier*,[31] which rules that the Federal Insecticide, Fungicide, and Rodenticide Act (FIFRA) does not fully preempt the entire subject of regulation of pesticides. The lesson of *Cipollone* is that a federal law preempts state regulation only if Congress intended that preemption occur.

A Florida federal court ruled that the duty to warn begins when a reasonable person would want to be informed of risk. Therefore, the duty of a manufacturer of blood products to warn hemophiliacs of the risk of AIDS was applicable in 1982 when the manufacturer should have known of the medical authority as to risk. It is improper for a manufacturer to wait for consensus within the medical profession before warning consumers.[32] An AIDS negligence action against a blood bank is governed by the three-year personal injury statute of limitations, not the medical malpractice statute of limitations (one year post-discovery); the blood bank merely supplies a product, and is not a health care provider.[33]

A manufacturer of baby oil has been held liable, to the extent of $2.5 million, for failure to warn of the danger of cardiac arrest, brain damage, and other hazards consequent upon aspiration of baby oil when babies swallow the oil despite its intended use for external application only.[34]

Even if warnings are inadequate, a corporation is not liable if the plaintiff fails to heed the warnings that were given, and if following the actual instructions would have averted the injury. In such circumstances, causality is absent and thus the manufacturer is not to blame for the harm.[35]

If the label on an OTC drug meets state and federal requirements, the manufacturer is not liable for failure to warn in languages other than English.[36]

The duty to warn is not limited to commercial situations: for instance, laboratory researchers are entitled to be warned by the laboratory of the possible ineffectiveness of a vaccine to protect them against aerosol exposure to rabies virus.[37]

Tampons are federally regulated as "Class II medical devices" under the Medical Device Amendments to the Food, Drug, and Cosmetic Act.[38] Although the District of Minnesota has ruled that the federal law and regulations preempt state law failure-to-warn claims,[39] and that permitting state juries to award damages would contravene the Congressional intent of a single nationwide scheme of regulation, the Fifth Circuit takes the position that the federal regulation does not preempt state tort claims involving the design, composition, or construction of tampons.[40]

The Southern District of New York has ruled that a $1.5 million jury award was not excessive for a breast implant user who suffered infection, implant rupture and silicone leakage. She may require a second mastectomy; the displaced silicone makes mammograms unreadable.[41]

It has been held that gun manufacturers cannot be held liable under negligence, strict liability, or "social utility" theories for injuries inflicted by gun buyers, even if the plaintiffs claim that the product is not socially valuable and therefore should be judged by a stricter standard.[42] A suit by police officers against a gun manufacturer, alleging permanent hearing loss suffered from the noise level at gun proficiency classes was reinstated[43] on the theory that there may be a duty to warn, and that the plaintiffs should be allowed to present a case that strict liability should be imposed because the risk of hearing loss was not generally known. There may also be a negligence claim if the manufacturers are held to have a duty to provide instructions for use if guns are to be made reasonably safe.

Manufacturers are not strictly liable for failure to make a cigarette lighter childproof (after all, children are not supposed to use the product at all) but can still be liable in negligence for creating an unreasonable risk of foreseeable harm to foreseeable users, who do include children.[44]

[¶3205.1]   Warranty Aspects of Products Liability

The products liability cause of action is a hybrid between tort actions for strict liability and warranty actions (which are contractual in nature). A common approach is for courts to analyze claims of economic damage resulting from defective products under contract principles, and personal injury products liability claims under tort principles.

This hybrid nature creates difficulties as to the statute of limitations (and when it starts to run—whether from the sale of the defective product, the injury caused by the product defect, or the discovery of the injury, which can be many years later) and the potential defendants.

Privity of contract is, as the name suggests, a concept of contract law. Thus, consideration of privity is important in the warranty context. Section 2-318 of the Uniform Commercial Code gives states three alternative treatments of the privity issues. Under alternative A, warranty liability extends to the buyer, natural persons in his or her household, and some guests. Alternative B makes the warrantor liable to the buyer plus any natural person expected to use or be affected by the goods. However, this alternative relates to personal injuries only, not property damage. Alternative C, the broadest, makes the warrantor liable for any form of harm caused by the product, to any user.

Note that express warranties can be disclaimed, but that strict tort liability cannot be.

[¶3205.2]   Statute of Limitations Problems

If a claim is for personal injuries and is based entirely on tort doctrines, the tort statute of limitations governs. Generally speaking, the claim accrues and the statute of limitations begins to run at the time of the injury, not the time the product was sold. Depending on the jurisdiction and the circumstances, accrual of the claim may be delayed until the injury is either perceived by the plaintiff or perceptible.

However, the statute of limitations in warranty claims is often computed from the sale of the product, so many otherwise meritorious claims are foreclosed because the injury is not discovered until the warranty statute of limitation has run.

In addition to the statute of limitations, the state may impose a "statute of repose" to protect professionals such as doctors and architects against "long-tail" claims. Under a statute of repose, a claim must be brought within a defined (albeit long) time after the sale of the product or rendering of the services: 10, 12, or 25 years, for example.

Missouri's statute of limitations for negligence and strict liability asbestos claims has been held to begin when the damage is "capable of ascertainment," not when the asbestos-containing material is purchased. The Western District of Missouri court saw this as a fair compromise between a "discovery" test that favors the plaintiff unduly and a "wrongful act" test that makes it too easy for the defendant to escape liability.[45]

A later Pennsylvania case, taking the position that asbestos exposure can cause several diseases to the same exposed individual, starts the discovery statute of limitations running from the plaintiff's lung cancer diagnosis, not the earlier diagnosis of pleural placques caused by asbestos exposure.[46]

The Second Circuit weighed in to the debate, finding that, for liability insurance purposes, asbestos-related property damage is a one-time event that occurs at the installation of the asbestos-containing material, not at the time when the insured discovers that asbestos is present and hazardous.[47]

[¶3206] THE WRONGFUL DEATH ACTION

An additional series of problems is imposed on the case when a person injured by the actions of another dies of those injuries. The case for personal injuries thus becomes one for wrongful death. It's important to distinguish between two types of wrongful death case. One of them is merely a continuation of the tort action the deceased would have brought, with the estate or executor substituted as a plaintiff. Thus, the deceased is entitled to compensation for pre-death medical costs and conscious pain and suffering.

The second type of action is brought by the widow or widower, surviving child, or parents of the deceased, and involves elements such as loss of support (because the deceased is no longer able to earn) and loss of consortium. Local practice differs greatly as to who can bring such actions and what elements of damages will be recognized. Frequently, a perverse set of incentives is imposed: if a tortfeasor injures someone (especially a young person with substantial earning capacity), the tortfeasor can expect to be assessed heavy damages. However, if the victim is killed outright, leaving no survivors, or if the tortfeasor also kills the victim's spouse and/or children, the damages can be minimal.

Punitive damages are usually not permitted in wrongful death cases. The "survival action" (the continuation of the victim's action) is a claim of the victim's estate and is subject to the debts of the estate. The pure "wrongful death" action brought by the survivors is not subject to estate debts.

The National Traffic and Motor Vehicle Safety Act has been held to preempt state law; therefore, a wrongful death action cannot be brought against a car manufacturer premised on the absence of airbags in the decedent's car, because federal law permits cars to be sold without airbags.[48] State common-law claims premised on a manufacturer's failure to install airbags or automatic seat belts have been held preempted by this federal law but this is not the case for claims of failure to install protective netting on car windows,[49] which are not preempted.

In New Jersey, no cause of action for the wrongful death of a stillborn infant can be maintained against the doctor who managed (or mismanaged) the delivery; however, the parents have a common-law cause of action for emotional distress occasioned by the stillbirth.[50]

— ENDNOTES —

1. Milkovich v. Lorain Journal, 110 S.Ct. 2695 (Sup.Ct. 6/21/90).

2. Masson v. *New Yorker Magazine,* #89-1799, 111 S.Ct. 2149 (Sup.Ct. 6/20/91). The Ninth Circuit required *The New Yorker* magazine to join writer Janet Malcolm as a co-defendant: Masson v. The New Yorker, #87-2665. See Gail Diane Cox, "Kozinski Gets Second Crack in *Masson,*" *Nat.L.J.* 4/20/92 p. 18.

3. Cipollone v. Liggett Group Inc., #90-1038, 112 S.Ct. 2608 (Sup.Ct. 6/24/92). Ironically, although the Supreme Court sent the case back to the District Court for retrial, the plaintiffs dropped the case, possibly because of the dif-

ficulty and cost of further litigation. See Charles Strum, "Major Lawsuit on Smoking Is Dropped," *New York Times* 11/6/92 p.B1; Junda Woo, "Anti-Cigarette Suit Withdrawn in New Jersey," *Wall Street J.* 11/6/92 p. A3.

4. Daubert v. Merrell Dow Pharmaceuticals Inc., #92-102, 113 S.Ct. 2786 (Sup.Ct. 6/28/93). Also see Conde v. Velsicol Chemical Corp., 816 F.Supp. 453 (S.D. Ohio 12/28/92), dismissing personal injury claims against the manufacturers of a termite-killing chemical. The plaintiffs' expert witnesses were not heard, because the court found that the scientific consensus is that there is no causal connection between the plaintiffs' level of exposure to the chemical and the injuries alleged in the complaint.

5. Watson v. Regional Transp. Dist., 762 P.2d 133 (Colo.Sup. 9/12/88).

6. Waterson v. GM, 544 A.2d 357 (N.J. Sup. 7/27/88).

7. Franklin v. Mazda Motor Corp., 704 F.Supp. 1325 (D. Md. 2/2/89).

8. Sofie v. Fibreboard Co., 57 LW 2655 (Wash.Sup. 4/27/89).

9. Juzwin v. Amtorg Trading Corp., 705 F.Supp. 1053 (D. N.J. 3/9/89).

10. Dunn v. HOVIC, 62 LW 2075 (3d Cir. 7/27/93).

11. Germanio v. Goodyear Tire & Rubber Co., 732 F.Supp. 1297 (D.N.J. 3/26/90).

12. McBride v. General Motors Corp., 737 F.Supp. 1563 (M.D. Ga. 4/10/90); Moseley v. General Motors Corp., 61 LW 2564 (Ga. 2/26/93).

13. Mack Trucks Inc. v. Conkle, 62 LW 2349 (Ga.Sup. 11/22/93).

14. Olsen v. J.A. Freeman Co., 58 LW 2672 (Ida. Sup. 5/7/90).

15. Elmer v. Tenneco Resins Inc., 698 F.Supp. 535 (D.Del. 11/1/88).

16. Nissen Corp. v. Miller, 323 Md. 613, 594 A.2d 564 (Md.App. 8/17/91). But see Davis v. Celotex Corp., 61 LW 2112 (W.Va.Sup. 7/21/92) [Company that merges with a manufacturer of a known unsafe product such as asbestos, and continues to manufacture the same substance in the same manner, can be held liable for punitive damages against the predecessor corporation].

17. Nichols v. G.D. Searle & Co., 783 F.Supp. 233 (D.Md. 1/22/92).

18. Elsroth v. Johnson & Johnson, 700 F.Supp. 151 (S.D.N.Y. 11/15/88).

19. 857 F.2d 290 (6th Cir. 6/30/88).

20. Richardson v. Richardson-Merrell Inc., 857 F.2d 823 (D.C. Cir. 1988); Brock v. Merrell Dow Pharmaceuticals Inc., 874 F.2d 307 (5th Cir. 6/6/89).

21. 73 NY2d 487 (N.Y. App. 4/4/89). New York has jurisdiction over DES manufacturers based on this nationwide market share liability theory, even if they never sold their products in the state: Ashley v. Abbott Laboratories Inc., 60 LW 2700 (E.D.N.Y. 4/13/92). Furthermore, plaintiffs are entitled to jury trial on the issue of market share: In re DES Market Share Litigation, 60 LW 2644 (N.Y.App. 3/31/92).

22. Enright v. Eli Lilly & Co., 155 A.D.2d 64, 553 N.Y.S.2d 494 (N.Y.Sup. 3/22/90), rev'd 77 N.Y.2d 377, 568 N.Y.S.2d 550, 570 N.E.2d 198 (2/19/91).

23. Grover v. Eli Lilly & Co., 61 LW 2048 (Ohio Sup. 6/10/92).

24. Smith v. Eli Lilly & Co., 59 LW 2051 (Ill.Sup. 7/3/90).

25. Santiago v. Sherwin-Williams Co., 782 F.Supp. 186 (D.Mass. 1/13/92).

26. Shackil v. Lederle Laboratories, 561 A.2d 511 (N.J. 7/31/89).

27. 42 USC Section 300aa-1 et seq. (1986).

28. Hurley v. Lederle Laboratories, 851 F.2d 1536 (5th Cir. 8/17/88); Semble Abbot v. American Cyanamid, 844 F.2d 1108 (4th Cir. 1988).

29. Perry v. Mercedes-Benz of North America Inc., 957 F.2d 1257 (5th Cir. 4/10/92).

30. Hodges v. Delta Airlines Inc., 62 LW 2233 (5th Cir. 10/14/93).

31. Wisconsin Public Intervenor v. Mortier, #89-1905, 111 S.Ct. 2476 (Sup.Ct. 6/21/91). See Sheila L. Birnbaum and Gary E. Crawford, "How Cipollone Affects Other Industries," *Nat. Law J.* 8/24/92 p. 20.

32. Moore v. Armour Pharmaceutical Co., 59 LW 2212 (M.D. Fla. 8/28/90). In the same court, the first failure-to-warn jury verdict ($2 million) was upheld to the parents of a hemophiliac who died of AIDS: Walls v. Armour Pharmaceutical Corp., 61 LW 2499 (M.D.Fla. 1/22/93).

33. Doe v. American National Red Cross, 62 LW 2016 (Wis.Sup. 6/3/93).

34. Ayers v. Johnson & Johnson, 117 Wash.2d 747, 818 P.2d 1337 (1991). See Stuart A. Schlesinger, "Warnings Commensurate with Risks," *N.Y.L.J.* 4/30/92 p. 3 col. 3.

35. General Motors Corp. v. Saenz, 62 LW 2384 (Tex.Sup. 11/24/93).

36. Ramirez v. Plough Inc., 62 LW 2383 (Cal.Sup. 12/9/93), rev'd 61 LW 2278 (Cal.App. 10/7/92).

37. Andrulonis v. U.S., 924 F.2d 1210 (2d Cir. 1991).

38. 21 USC Section 360k; Regulations at 21 CFR Section 801.1(b).

39. Lindquist v. Tambrands Inc., 721 F.Supp. 1058 (D. Minn. 9/21/89).

40. Moore v. Kimberly-Clark Corp., 867 F.2d 243 (5th Cir. 3/8/89).

41. Livshits v. Natural Y Surgical Specialties, #87 Civ 2403 (WK) (S.D.N.Y. 11/27/91).

42. Delahanty v. Hinckley, 900 F.2d 368 (D.C. Cir. 10/11/89).

43. Snyder v. Philadelphia, 58 LW 2259 (Pa. Comm. 10/2/89).

44. Griggs v. BIC Corp., 981 F.2d 1429 (3d Cir. 12/31/92).

45. Columbia Public School Dist. v. U.S. Gypsum Co., 57 LW 2748 (W.D. Mo. 5/1/89).

46. Marinari v. Asbestos Corp. Ltd., 61 LW 2144 (Pa. Super. 7/20/92).

47. Maryland Casualty Co. v. W.R. Grace & Co., 62 LW 2178 (2d Cir. 9/3/93).

48. Taylor v. General Motors, 875 F.2d 816 (11th Cir. 6/14/89).

49. Pokorny v. Ford Motor Co., 902 F.2d 1116 (3d Cir. 4/30/90).

50. Giardina v. Bennett, 57 LW 2127 (N.J. Sup. 8/10/88).

— FOR FURTHER REFERENCE —

Bernstein, Anita, "A Model of Products Liability Reform," 27 *Valparaiso U.L. Rev.* 637 (Summer '93).

Bernstein, Paul, "Breast Implant Litigation: Setting a Technology Standard," 29 *Trial* 95 (July '93).

Bieger, Daniel R., "The Pre-Existing Condition in a Personal Injury Claim: Weakness or Weapon?" 16 *Trial Diplomacy J.* 189 (September-October '93).

Bower, Mark R., "Discovery of Plaintiff's Medical Information in DES Litigation," 22 *Trial Lawyers Q.* 28 (Summer '92).

Bowman, William J. and Patrick F. Hofer, "The Fallacy of Personal Injury Liability Insurance Coverage for Environmental Claims," 12 *Virginia Environmental L.J.* 393 (Spring '93).

Dombroff, Mark A., editor, *Personal Injury Defense Techniques* (3 volumes) (Matthew Bender; looseleaf).

Eisenberg, Theodore and James A. Henderson Jr., "Inside the Quiet Revolution in Products Liability," 39 *UCLA L. Rev.* 731 (April '92).

Fisk, Margaret Cronin, "The Reform Juggernaut Slows Down," *Nat. Law J.* 11/9/92 p. 1.

Gilles, Stephen G., "Negligence, Strict Liability, and the Cheapest Cost-Avoider," 78 *Virginia L. Rev.* 1291 (September '92).

Habert, Tricia E., "Day in the Life and Surveillance Videos," 97 *Dickinson L. Rev.* 305 (Winter '93).

Henderson, James Jr. and Aaron D. Twerski, "A Proposed Revision of §402A of the Restatement (Second) of Torts," 77 *Cornell L. Rev.* 1512 (September '92).

Ireland, Thomas R., "The Meaning of Hedonic Damages in Tort Litigation," 6 *J. of Forensic Economics* 99 (Spring-Summer '93).

Nelson, Susan Richard, "Federal Preemption of State Tort Claims," 22 *Trial Lawyers Q.* 11 (Summer '92).

Orbach, Kenneth N., "Exclusion of Punitive Damages Under §104(a)(2)," 24 *Tax Adviser* 570 (September '93).

Ortego, Joseph J., John H. Kardisch and Kevin McElroy, "Circuit Courts Split on FIFRA," *Nat. Law J.* 11/2/92 p. 21.

Owen, Ronald D., "Carpal Tunnel Syndrome: A Products Liability Perspective," 14 *J. of Products Liability* 41 (Winter '92).

Pollard, Michael and Robert E. Blevans, "Spousal Torts: Protecting the Victim," 16 *Los Angeles Lawyer* 13 (June '93).

Raby, William I., "Can Personal Injury Lawyers Pay the Expenses of Litigation?" 59 *Tax Notes* 1659 (6/21/93).

Reske, Henry J., "Asbestos Makers Lose Big Trial," 78 *ABA J.* 18 (October '92).

Smoger, Gerson H., "Using Experts Wisely in Toxic Tort Cases," 29 *Trial* 30 (September '93).

REAL ESTATE TRANSACTIONS

[¶3301] The essential elements in the sale and purchase of real estate come together in the contract of sale. To be enforceable, this instrument is required by law to be in writing and signed by the parties to the transaction. Because the contract of sale will control the transaction and will prescribe much of what will follow between the parties, it is vitally important that this instrument be well thought out and explicit with regard to the exact terms of the transaction. The contract must be complete: all the terms of the sale must be settled with none left to be determined by future negotiations. For example, it was held that failure to specify when a purchase-money mortgage fell due made a contract unenforceable.

The contract will specify the kind of title that the seller is to deliver and will prevent the seller from turning around and selling the property to another party while the purchaser is awaiting the title report. The contract will also prevent the purchaser from changing his or her mind and backing out as long as the seller can deliver the kind of title promised.

In the paragraphs that follow, some of the key terms mentioned in a contract of sale are discussed.

[¶3302] MARKETABLE TITLE

The kind of title that a seller must deliver will depend on the terms and provisions of the contract of sale. If the contract is silent, the seller must deliver marketable title, free from encumbrances. If the contract requires the seller to deliver title "free from all defects or encumbrances," the buyer may be able to reject title if there is even a trivial encroachment or a beneficial easement. Usually the seller lists in the contract the encumbrances that exist and the buyer agrees to take title subject to these encumbrances (e.g., building restrictions, existing mortgages, etc.). If the contract is subject to general language such as "conditions and restrictions of records, easements, existing tenancies, any state of facts which an accurate survey may show," etc., the seller can probably succeed in delivering.

One practical way for the seller and buyer to make definite the kind of title they are talking about is to check the examination of title made at the time the seller acquired the property, and if the restrictions that then existed are satisfactory to the buyer, the seller should commit to deliver a title subject only to the limitations existing when the property was acquired. Another way is for the contract to require the seller to deliver a marketable title and a policy of title insurance. This permits the buyer to walk out on a contract if the title is not marketable or if the title insurance is not forthcoming. If the contract merely requires the seller to furnish title insurance, then the buyer is required to take a title even if it is technically unmarketable as long as a title company will issue insurance, which it will sometimes do on the basis that there is little business risk in a technical defect that may render the title less than fully marketable.

What renders title unmarketable? Liens, adverse possession, easements, and outstanding mineral rights are examples. As a general rule, zoning ordinances do not serve to render title unmarketable, but a seller's misrepresentation that the property is zoned for the buyer's intended use may raise the ordinance to the status of encumbrance.

In order to avoid delay caused by clearing a defective title, the buyer may want to fix a time for delivery of the deed and have the contract provide that time is of the essence. If the seller does not have good title at the time fixed for delivering the deed, the buyer can relieve himself of the obligations of the contract.

The buyer should insist that the contract specify the kind of evidence of good title that the seller will be required to produce: e.g., title insurance, abstracts, certificate of title, etc. Evidence of title should show the condition of the title as of the date on which the deed is delivered rather than the date of contract. The contract should give the seller a reasonable time to furnish the buyer with evidence of title, the buyer a reasonable time to examine such evidence and point out any defects, then a further reasonable time for the seller to eliminate or cure any such defects and a further time within which the buyer can decide to accept or reject a title still carrying a defect that the seller has been unable to cure.

[¶3303] DEPOSITS

When the buyer makes a deposit or a down payment on the contract, that money applies as part payment of the purchase price if he conforms; if he defaults it can be retained by the seller. This should be specifically covered by the contract. The seller, for self-protection, should require a large enough deposit to cover the broker's commission, expense of title search, and compensation for loss of time and loss of opportunity to sell elsewhere if the buyer should default. If the seller can't deliver clear title, then the buyer is entitled to take back the deposit.

State law may require that the deposit be placed in escrow and maintained there until the sale is consummated (or the contract of sale ceases to be operative).

[¶3304] MORTGAGES

If the buyer is to take the property subject to an existing mortgage, the contract should so state. It should specify whether the buyer is assuming an existing mortgage or merely taking subject to the mortgage. If the buyer is giving a purchase-money mortgage as part of the payment, the contract should spell out the interest rates, maturity, amortization payments, form of the mortgage, etc.

A homebuyer's chances at assuming a mortgage were drastically decreased in 1982 when a lender's right to enforce the due-on-sale clause was confirmed by the Depository Institutions Act and by a U.S. Supreme Court decision. However, loans backed by the Federal Housing Administration and by the Veterans Administration remain assumable at their original interest rate.

[¶3305] CONTINGENCIES AND LOSS

The buyer's obligation may be made subject to contingencies such as an ability to obtain a mortgage or sell a present home at a minimum price or higher, the ability to get a zoning variance, etc. It is important that the contract spell out the kind of mortgage, the kind of variance, who has the responsibility for getting the mortgage or variance, the time within which the contingency is to be satisfied, when the deal is to be terminated if the contingency has not been satisfied by that time, etc. Specify who is to carry the risk of loss for damage and buyer's right to cancel or receive compensation.

[¶3306] SURVEY

If the buyer wants the seller to provide a survey at the seller's cost, this should be stated in the contract. The time for delivery of the survey should also be specified. The contract should require the survey to be satisfactory to the buyer's lawyer and a time should be fixed for the buyer to raise objections based on the survey.

The survey should be verified with local ordinances, private covenants and restrictions, party wall agreements, and setback requirements.

Protecting the Buyer When Survey Not Available: The risk of violations, encumbrances, and restrictions can be put on the seller by inserting these provisions in the contract.

(1) Subject to local zoning and setback ordinances that are not violated by the present structure.

(2) Subject to the state of facts an accurate survey will show, provided they do not render the title unmarketable.

(3) Subject to covenants and restrictions of record not rendering title unmarketable or revertible.

A seller will normally refuse to warrant that the property may be used in ways other than that currently used. A buyer in a strong bargaining position, however, may be able to obtain such a warranty with respect to a use specified in the contract.

[¶3307] OUTSTANDING LEASES AND LEASE PROVISIONS

The purchaser who is buying income-producing property as an investment, will want an attorney to examine the leases and check the rentals in those leases against the rental information that has been furnished by the seller. The attorney will also want to look for provisions of leases that include any unusual clauses, particularly those that concern the landlord's obligations to make repairs and the tenants' rights to cancel or renew. Clauses that concern damage or destruction to the premises, either by casualty or fire or taking through eminent domain, will require intensive scrutiny.

[¶3308] LIMITATIONS AS TO USE

The purchaser's attorney will examine the types of restrictions—area restrictions, and use restrictions imposed on the property either by government regulation or by private covenant. In order to protect the client, the buyer's attorney may require a provision that the purchaser will not have to buy the property if its intended use is prohibited by such restrictions. The seller of the property usually will not object to this type of a provision unless market conditions are in his or her favor and tying up the property during the contract period could unfavorably affect the value of the property. A possible compromise for both parties might be the requirement that the purchaser must acquire the necessary knowledge about existing regulations and covenants within a certain period of time after the contract of sale has been entered into. Typically, this type of provision will give the purchaser an option to terminate the contract during the specified period of time if there is any prohibition on the particular use for which the property is intended.

[¶3309] ZONING

The seller will ordinarily provide a warranty that existing structures on the property are not in violation of any zoning regulations and ordinances. If the purchaser plans to change the existing use of the property, this warranty is not enough. The same considerations will also apply to a purchaser who is acquiring vacant land on which a building devoted to a particular use is to be erected. Here the purchaser will insist on a repetition by the seller that the purchaser's contemplated use of the land will not violate zoning regulations and ordinances. The seller, of course, may not be willing to offer such assurances. The ultimate disposition of this problem depends on the parties' bargaining position.

Land-use regulators must pay landowners when they grant public access to provide property, and the grant must be tied directly to a proper governmental purpose.

[¶3310] PERFORMANCE TIME

The seller may want to receive the proceeds of the sale of the property on a particular day in order to either enter into a new venture or discharge an obligation. Therefore, making time for performance under the contract is *of the essence*. Under a "time of the essence" arrangement, the seller's obligation to convey the property to the purchaser will be relieved by the purchaser's failure to meet the payments on the specific day. In addition, the seller may have a suit for damages against the purchaser. The purchaser's attorney may insist that if time is of the essence it should be so for both parties. The seller will have a good argument against this type of arrangement since the purchaser's only requirement generally is to pay cash on the day of title closing, but the seller has numerous obligations to clear up the property before conveying it to the purchaser. As a possible compromise, the parties may agree that time for performance is of the essence for both parties, but that the purchaser will notify the seller in writing a specified number of days before the date set for the closing of title of all obligations to the seller's title. This provision allows the seller to clear up those objections.

[¶3311] PURCHASE-MONEY MORTGAGE

Sellers often take back a purchase-money second mortgage as part of their purchase price for the property. Here, the seller will want to be assured that the purchaser will not milk the property by collecting rents for a certain number of months and then default on the mortgages. The solution is to prepare a timetable that integrates principal and interest payments on the purchase-money mortgage with the purchaser's other obligations (including water charges, taxes, and interest and principal on the first mortgage). Such a timetable assures that the purchaser is obligated to make payments for these different items in different months. This means that the seller can quickly determine whether or not the purchaser has defaulted in any obligations.

Another provision that the seller will want is one protecting against a default in the payment of principal or interest on the purchase-money mortgage, or on the payment of principal on any other mortgage or on the payment of taxes, water rates, or assessments. This provision gives the seller the option and the right to accelerate all of the principal amount of the purchase-money mortgage on default of any one of the above-named obligations by the purchaser.

[¶3312] PERSONAL PROPERTY

A purchaser who acquires a building ordinarily expects to acquire title to the property within that building (as, for example, gas ranges and refrigerators in an apartment house). But gas ranges and refrigerators are usually considered to be personal property and will not be included in the sale of the real estate unless there is an express provision covering them. It is, therefore, very important for the contract to specify all of the personal property included in the sale. The best practice is to require a bill of sale from the seller covering personal property free of all liens and encumbrances.

[¶3313] PRE-CONTRACT CHECKLISTS

Prior to executing the contract of sale for a particular property (here, a house), there are a number of matters that the attorneys for the buyer and seller will want to see to.

Seller's Checklist: The following are concerns of the seller that should be taken care of before going to contract:

❐ ***Broker:*** If a broker is responsible for bringing about the sale, the seller's attorney should prepare a written brokerage agreement. The attorney should contact the broker and confirm the amount of his or her commission. If a binder has been given, the seller or her attorney should obtain a copy of such written binder. Be sure that the broker is present at the execution of the contract to sign the brokerage agreement.

❐ ***Payment:*** The purchase price must be set and the method of payment established. Will the buyer assume the seller's mortgage? Will the seller offer a purchase-money mortgage? If the buyer does not assume the present mortgage on the property it must be satisfied or else the property will be transferred subject to the lien.

❐ ***Personal Property:*** The seller's attorney should itemize any and all personal property that is to be transferred with title.

❐ ***Date:*** The seller should have a rough idea of the date on which title is to pass.

❐ ***Documents:*** The seller should furnish the following documents to the attorney in preparation for the closing:

    (a) Deed;

    (b) Survey;

    (c) Title insurance policy;

    (d) Tax receipts;

    (e) Certificate of occupancy;

    (f) A copy of the present mortgage; and

    (g) Homeowner's insurance policy.

Buyer's Checklist: The following are concerns of the purchaser that should be taken care of before going to contract:

❐ ***Price:*** The buyer's attorney should check with the seller's attorney to confirm the price, as well as the terms of sale. If the buyer is taking subject to or assumes the seller's mortgage, it should be determined if the mortgage is in fact transferable.

❐ ***Binder:*** If the buyer has given the seller a binder, he or she should obtain a copy of the agreement under which the money was given. The buyer should either have the money returned or a credit should be awarded against the contract price.

❐ ***Inspection:*** Because most contracts provide that the home is to be transferred "as is," it's a good idea to see to it that the seller makes any necessary repairs prior to contract or that the contract lists any repairs to be made by the seller. Therefore, the purchaser should have the house and the equipment inspected by a qualified engineer before going to contract. The buyer should also arrange to have the property inspected for termite infestation. Copies of all reports should be received before the contract is executed.

❏ **Form of Ownership:** How are the purchasers going to take title? As tenants in common, joint tenants, or tenants by the entirety?

❏ **Moving:** What does the buyer intend to do about living accommodations? Must he or she sell a home? When? If the buyer currently has a lease, will it be necessary to breach it?

[¶3314] CHECKLIST OF PRACTICAL NEGOTIATING AND DRAFTING CONSIDERATIONS

Although in every jurisdiction there is a standard form of contract of sale incorporating many provisions to which there is rarely any disagreement, there are always areas about which the parties feel free to bargain and different provisions used under different circumstances. In addition, each party will want the contract to contain certain protective clauses that will cover unexpected contingencies. The following checklist points out important considerations to be borne in mind by the attorneys for both parties.

The normal practice is for the seller's attorney to draft the contract, with his or her client's interests in mind. Included in the following checklist are special considerations of the buyer to which the attorney may want to pay particular attention.

❏ **Form of Contract:** The contract may be a straight bilateral agreement between the buyer and the seller, in offer and acceptance form (in which the seller accepts the offer with all its attendant conditions), or a deposit receipt prepared by a broker containing the conditions of the sale. In some states, the papers and the down payment are held by a third party escrow agent. Regardless of the form of the contract, however, the following considerations should be carefully noted:

❏ **Date of Execution of the Contract.**

❏ **Names and Addresses of the Parties:** The full names and addresses of parties to the contract should appear in the appropriate places. It's good practice to have all of the parties present when the contract is executed.

Buyer's Considerations: Be sure the named seller is competent, is the sole owner, or if there are co-owners, has the authority to enter into the contract and pass good title.

If the seller is an individual, the buyer should ascertain if his or her spouse died within the past few years. In some states, any unpaid tax on the decedent's estate becomes a lien on the property in which he or she has an interest, and this lien will carry over to a later buyer. There is, however, no problem with regard to the federal estate tax, which does not remain a lien on property sold for a fair consideration.

If the seller has a living spouse, determine if there are any dower or other rights in the property. If so, both must sign the contract or it will not be effective.

If the seller is a corporation or a fiduciary, be sure that such representative is acting within the scope of authority. The buyer should ask for and examine corporate resolutions authorizing the sale or a certificate of letters testamentary or administration.

❑ *Description of the Property:* Usually, the description used in the prior deed is satisfactory, but a later survey or title company report should be used if there have been any changes. If the seller has any rights in the street in front of the property, those rights should be included. The same applies for riparian (water) rights.

❑ *Buyer's Consideration:* The description of the property should be read and compared with the survey of the property. The description must comply with the survey.

❑ *Purchase Price:* The contract should state the entire purchase price, including any and all mortgages. The price should then be broken down into various components.

❑ *Down Payment:* Ordinarily 10% of the purchase price.

Buyer's Consideration: A problem may arise as to whether the down payment should be held in escrow by the seller's attorney between the contract execution and title closing dates. The buyer should insist that the money be held in escrow if the contract is conditional on the buyer obtaining financing. Even if the contract is not conditional, it's a good idea to have the down payment held in escrow pending the title report showing that the seller has good title and can convey marketable title. If the seller doesn't own the property he is selling (e.g., he may have only a contract to buy it), the buyer should insist on an escrow arrangement. Similarly, if the seller is moving to another state before the closing, the buyer may want the protection of an escrow.

❑ *Mortgage:* Most contracts of sale are conditioned on the purchaser obtaining mortgage financing (included as a "subject to" clause). The conditional contract will recite that the buyer, within a specified period of time, must obtain a commitment from a lender for a first mortgage in a stated amount and for a specified term. An interest rate may also be indicated. If, after using best efforts to obtain financing, the buyer is not successful, the contract should provide the right to cancel on written notice to the seller.

A buyer who is to take title subject to or assuming the seller's existing mortgage should get a copy of that mortgage which should spell out in detail all pertinent information.

If the seller is to take back, as part of the purchase price, a purchase-money mortgage, a copy of the proposed mortgage should be attached to the contract. Otherwise, the contract should indicate such matters as: the amount and how it will be amortized, the due date, the interest rate and how it is payable, the right to prepay in whole or in part, the type of mortgage form to be used, subordination to any existing or future mortgage, and who shall draw the bond and mortgage (ordinarily the seller's attorney is responsible for doing this for an additional fee).

❑ *Balance of Purchase Price:* The balance of the purchase price should be made due and payable at the time of closing. Seller's attorney should request that payment be made by certified check.

Buyer's Consideration: It's a good idea to have this and any other certified checks made out to the buyer and then have the buyer endorse to the seller. This avoids problems in redepositing the checks should the deal fall through.

❑ **Mortgage Satisfaction:** When the seller's present mortgage is to be satisfied at the closing, the contract should so state. The seller's attorney should write to the mortgage holder requesting a statement of the balance due, as well as any additional charges associated with satisfaction of the mortgage. This letter must be presented to the other parties at the closing.

❑ **"Subject to" Clause:** This is one of the most important clauses in the contract and should be considered carefully by the buyer in particular, since a loosely drawn clause may require taking the property even though it cannot be used in the anticipated manner. This clause lists the conditions and circumstances to which the property may be subject, without rendering the contract void:

❑ **Zoning and Building Ordinances:** The buyer will, at the least, want the following to be added to the above clause: "provided the same are not violated by existing structures." In other words, the buyer wants to be sure the property at present doesn't violate the law. The buyer may also ask that this provision be extended to contemplated structures. The seller, however, is likely to say that this is a risk to be assumed by the buyer since it relates to future events.

❑ **Private Covenants and Restrictions:** These will be contained in prior deeds and possibly in a master declaration recorded at the time the original tract was platted. The first thing the buyer should do is inquire if the seller knows of any restrictions. If possible, the original documents containing the covenants, restrictions, and easements should be examined (a prior title report may have them). If they are not available, add the following: "provided the same are not violated by the existing structure or the present use of the premises, and provided the same may not result in forfeiture." A purchaser in a strong bargaining position may also be able to add the clause "provided the same are not violated by (specified) future structures or uses." In addition, the buyer must modify the exception as stated or else may find that the property can only be used in a very limited number of ways. One modification is to add "provided they do not make title unmarketable." The seller may object to this since, in some states, almost any minor restriction may make the title unmarketable. A compromise would be to substitute "provided they do not prohibit existing (or contemplated) structures and uses."

The buyer should refuse to take subject to any restrictions that, if violated, would cause a forfeiture of the property to a prior owner, since this is an unreasonable risk to assume.

❑ **State of Facts Shown by Survey:** If, at the time the contract is executed, the buyer does not have a current survey, a clause providing that the sale is subject to the state of facts shown by a survey should not be accepted by the buyer. Such a clause is acceptable only if it goes on to say "provided they do not make title unmarketable."

❑ **Any Violations of Municipal Ordinances That Have Been Noted Against the Property:** This would require the buyer to take the property regardless of the number or nature of violations noted against it. Unless the buyer is taking dilapidated property "as is," he should insist either that the seller cure any such violations or that the contract be canceled if they are not cured at the date of closing. The seller may be willing to cure the violations provided the expense doesn't exceed a stated figure.

❑ *Assessments That May Be Levied Against the Property:* The problem here is that the purchase price may reflect improvements (e.g., sewers) that have already been installed but not yet paid for. The buyer will thus be paying twice unless this clause is modified.

❑ *Termite Infestation and Damage:* Usually a provision is included that gives the seller the option to remedy any such condition or cancel the contract. Some termite clauses permit the buyer the final option of accepting the property with the existing condition.

❑ *Violations of Law:* Violations of law do not ordinarily affect marketability of title. Therefore, the buyer is responsible (civilly, criminally, and financially) for removing any violations unless the contract provides for removal by the seller. The seller will want to limit his liability to violations "noted" of record.

Buyer's Consideration: The purchaser will want the seller's obligation to survive delivery of the deed or provide for escrow of part of the purchase price as security for removal. The buyer will also want the contract to indicate that the seller is to provide him with the following at the closing: a certificate of occupancy; plumbing, heating, and electrical inspection certificates; and permits necessary for use and occupancy of the premises.

❑ *Adjustments:* Depending upon the property and the circumstances surrounding the sale, various costs associated with the property will be apportioned between the seller and the buyer at the date of closing:

❑ *Rents:* If there is a tenant on the premises, rent paid to the date of closing will be apportioned between the parties.

❑ *Interest:* If the sale is subject to an existing mortgage, interest on the mortgage should be apportioned.

❑ *Insurance:* Because not all policies can be transferred, the seller's policy should be checked.

Buyer's Consideration: When the buyer is asked to take over a policy, the attorney should insist on examining the policy at the closing.

❑ *Taxes:* The seller's attorney should bring all tax bills to the closing. The tax calendar should be ascertained and the amounts paid or due should be apportioned.

Buyer's Consideration: The buyer should demand proof that all back taxes have been paid because arrears may become a lien on the property.

❑ *Fuel:* If oil is used for heating the home, the seller should have the supplier prepare a letter for the closing, stating how much oil is in the tank and the oil cost per gallon. The buyer will be required to pay this amount.

❑ *Deed:* The contract should specify the type and form of deed the seller is to give. Local custom is usually controlling.

❑ *Title Insurance:* In some areas the buyer's attorney or some other attorney will conduct a title search and prepare an abstract of title. However, in the great majority of cases the purchaser or his attorney will engage a title company to search and insure the title. Ordinarily a lender will require the buyer to obtain title insurance.

❏ *Lien:* The down payment creates a vendee's lien in favor of the buyer. The contract should expressly extend this lien to include amounts expended for the title examination and the survey. If the seller is unable to convey title for reasons other than personal acts, liability will be limited to the down payment, the title examination fee, and the cost of the survey.

Buyer's Consideration: The buyer should try to extend this liability to include the attorney's fees as well.

❏ *Risk of Loss:* In the absence of an express provision on risk of loss, different rules may apply, depending on the jurisdiction: (1) Risk of loss may be on the purchaser as soon as the contract is signed (majority rule); (2) Risk may be on the seller prior to closing (minority rule); or (3) The Uniform Vendor and Purchaser Risk Act, which makes possession decisive, may be controlling. Risks should be spelled out (e.g., fire, windstorm, etc.)

❏ *Broker:* If a broker brought about the sale, the contract should state this fact, the broker's name, and that the seller is to pay the commission.

❏ *Personal Property:* The contract should specify all personal property and fixtures that pass with title to the real estate, as well as those items that are to be excluded.

❏ *"As Is" Clause:* The seller's attorney may wish to extend the coverage of the "as is" clause beyond the building to include the personal property.

Buyer's Consideration: The buyer will want to limit this by having the seller state in the contract, "Plumbing, heating, electrical utilities, and appliances shall be in good working order at the time title passes." When buying a new home, specify that all warranties will survive delivery of the deed. The seller is to deliver all such warranties to the purchaser at the closing.

❏ *Time and Date of Closing:* The contract will state where the closing is to occur. Closings usually take place at the seller's attorney's office or, if the buyer gets a mortgage, at the lender's office or the office of the lender's attorney. The contract will set a date at which the title will pass. In the absence of a clause making time of the essence, either party is entitled to a reasonable adjournment if one becomes necessary. This may prove embarrassing when, for example, the buyer is selling his or her old house and is planning to take possession of the new one on the same day. A time of the essence clause puts the burden on the seller, in this instance, to complete the transaction on time.

If the problem is that the seller may not be able to move out in time, the buyer may be willing to let him stay on for a designated period. This can be on a daily basis or without charge until a certain date, after which a per diem penalty is payable, backed up by an escrow clause.

[¶3315] CLOSING THE TITLE

Closing the title occurs when the transaction is consummated, the deed and final evidence of good title are delivered, the money is paid, the mortgages are executed, and charges against the property are adjusted between the parties.

Depending on local practice, the entire closing may be handled by the title company (also known as the escrow company—see ¶3321) or by the lawyers for buyer and seller, with the buyer and seller physically present at the closing. If the seller is not present, it is good practice to make contact so you are sure he or she is still alive and competent.

The buyer should get the deed; a title report or policy or other evidence of good title; a bill of sale for any personal property passing with the real estate; a receipt for the purchase price paid; a survey of the property; insurance policies or assignments thereof; a statement from the mortgagee of the amount due on any existing mortgage; release and satisfaction of any mortgage or other lien paid off but not yet recorded; leases and assignments thereof; a letter by the seller notifying tenants to pay future rents to the buyer; a letter by the seller advising the managing agent of the sale and the termination of his or her authority; a statement by the seller as to rents paid and due; receipts for taxes, water, gas, electricity, special assessments, assessment of any service contracts, and building maintenance guarantees; the seller's affidavit of title security deposits and tenants' consent to transfer if required; Social Security and payroll data on building employees; and keys to the building.

The seller receives the balance of the purchase price including any purchase-money mortgage and notes, and will want evidence of fire insurance protection if there is a continuing mortgage interest.

[¶3316]   TITLE CLOSING CHECKLISTS

If the preliminary work has been handled properly, the physical act of closing the title can be accomplished quickly. In order for this to occur, however, all the necessary documents (deeds, bills of sale, mortgages, bonds, etc.) must be ready and checked in advance. The actual formal closing then consists of an exchange of documents and checks. The following checklists will help the parties in preparing for a smooth closing.

[¶3317]   SELLER'S CONSIDERATIONS

(1) Verifying title—the seller's attorney will want to check title and remove any possible objections. The following considerations should be covered:

(a) Make certain that title evidence has been brought up to date and is in the form agreed upon in the contract. Resolve position as to exceptions and encumbrances (that is, whether or not material; if survey is required by contract, check same). Have building plans and specifications available.

(b) Is title insurance in the agreed amount and form?

(c) Does deed conform to contract requirements? (Marital status of seller, acknowledgement, legal description, tax stamps.) The deed should specify that the conveyance is subject to exceptions, liens, encumbrances, restrictions, and reservations provided for in the contract. Otherwise, seller will be warranting a better title than he or she has.

(d) Title affidavits to cover period between title evidence and the closing.

(e) Affidavits to clear up objections revealed by abstract and covering mechanics' liens.

(f) Obtain proper waivers, contractors' statements, and architect's certificate for new construction.

(g) Obtain bill of sale covering any personal property included.

(2) Amount of unpaid taxes, liens, assessments, water, sewerage charges, etc., on the property should be ascertained.

(3) Get statement of amount due on existing mortgages, showing unpaid principal and interest, rate of interest, and date of maturity.

(4) Produce the following:

(a) Policies of insurance to be transferred.

(b) Schedule of rents.

(c) Deed from predecessor.

(d) Power of attorney.

(5) Deed.

(a) Include full names and addresses of seller and purchaser.

(b) Description of property (same as in contract of sale unless there has been a new survey).

(c) Covenants and warranties provided for in the contract of sale.

(d) Special clauses in contract of sale.

(e) Recital of exceptions, restrictions, easements, etc., provided in contract of sale.

(f) Description of mortgages, both the mortgages that the purchaser is taking subject to and that the purchaser is assuming. Also include a recital of purchase-money mortgage if there is one.

(6) Additional papers.

(a) Satisfaction, release, or discharge of liens.

(b) Purchase-money bond and mortgage.

(c) Bill of sale of personal property included in the sale.

(d) Letter of introduction to tenants.

(e) Satisfaction of judgments.

(f) Authorization of sale by corporation (if owner is corporation).

(7) Prepare statement showing apportionment of:

(a) Taxes.

(b) Electric, gas, and water charges.

(c) Rents—as adjusted, for prepaid and accrued rent.

(d) Salaries.

(e) Services—exterminator, burglary alarm systems.

(8) Have the deed signed, sealed, and executed by the parties necessary to convey good title. Acknowledgements of signatures required. Affix appropriate revenue stamps and prepare proper closing statement and then record purchase-money mortgages.

[¶3318] PURCHASER'S CONSIDERATIONS

(1) Get affidavit of title.

(2) Obtain letter of introduction to tenants. Find out if a real estate transfer tax is due. If the property is a co-op apartment, find out if approval of the board is required for the sale, and if a "flip tax" is payable.

(3) Check violations of building regulations, any dwelling laws, health and fire agencies. Determine whether there is a certificate of occupancy outstanding.

(4) Look for chattel mortgages or conditional sales contracts on personal property if the latter is included in the sale.

(5) Examine mortgages and satisfactions of record.

(6) Look at existing leases.

(7) Check town, city, village, and school taxes, water and sewerage rates, and assessments.

(8) If corporations are involved make sure that state franchise taxes have been paid.

(9) See that the premises comply with zoning rules and restrictive covenants.

(10) Find out who is in possession, and whether they are entitled to be.

(11) Are there licenses and permits for signs on the street?

(12) Have state and federal transfer and estate taxes been paid?

(13) Inspect the premises.

(14) Check the age and competency of the seller.

(15) Look at insurance policies and assignments of service contracts.

(16) Contiguity clause if more than one lot is involved.

(17) Final matters—acknowledgement of seller's signature; title company report; power of attorney recorded, if any; revenue stamps on deed and bond.

(18) Record deed, have endorsements on transfer of ownership on insurance policies, and prepare closing statement.

(19) How must the balance be paid? If the contract of sale calls for a certified check, tender of a personal or cashier's check constitutes noncompliance.

[¶3319] AFTER THE CLOSING

The buyer should record the deed and any releases obtained at the closing. The seller should record any purchase-money mortgage. The seller should notify the managing agent and employees that he or she is no longer responsible for their compensation. The buyer should arrange for necessary services; get the consent of the insurance company to assignment of policies; get any new insurance necessary; have water, gas, electric, and tax bills changed to the buyer's name.

[¶3320] THE CLOSING STATEMENT

The contract of sale should provide for the adjustment of costs and income. Rents up to the time of closing are credited to the seller and costs are charged against him. Any costs paid beyond the closing date are credited to the seller.

Customary items to seller's credit are: (1) Unexpired portion of current real estate taxes paid by seller; (2) Unearned insurance premiums; (3) Unexpired portion of service contracts paid in advance; (4) Unexpired portion of water tax; (5) Fuel on hand; (6) Supplies; (7) Delinquent rents.

Customary items to buyer's credit are: (1) Initial deposit or payment; (2) Current balance on existing mortgages; (3) Unpaid taxes for prior years and pro rata portion of taxes for current year; (4) Special assessments due and unpaid; (5) Amounts due for electricity, gas, and water based on meter readings; (6) Accrued wages; (7) Prepaid rents; (8) Tenants' cash security deposits.

The seller pays for revenue stamps, if any, on the deed and the buyer pays for recording unless the contract provides otherwise.

[¶3321] ESCROW CLOSING

In some areas, sales are closed in escrow. An escrow is "the deposit by the vendor of his deed with a third party to be delivered to the purchaser upon payment of the purchase price." That third party is the escrowee. Escrows provide a mechanism to insure safety and convenience in carrying out the provisions of previously executed real estate sales contracts. In some cases, however, there is no written contract; the escrow agreement is the sole contract between the parties.

Most of the matters mentioned in the checklist for real estate closings are applicable when the deal is closed through an escrowee. The mechanical details of the closing, however, are turned over to the escrowee.

Among the many advantages of escrows are the following: the escrowee assumes responsibility for the many ministerial tasks involved in a closing; the danger of title defects arising in the gap between the effective date of title evidence and the date of the deed is avoided; and the possibility that the deal may fail is decreased.

[¶3322] CONTENTS OF ESCROW AGREEMENT

(1) Documents to be deposited by seller, such as deed, insurance policies, separate assignments of insurance policies, leases, assignments of leases, abstract or other evidence of title, tax bills, canceled mortgage notes, notice to tenants to pay rent to buyer, and service contracts.

(2) Deposits to be made by buyer, such as purchase price and purchase-money mortgage, if any.

(3) When deed is to be recorded, whether immediately or after buyer's check clears or after seller furnishes evidence of good title at date of contract.

(4) Objections to which buyer agrees to take subject.

(5) Type of evidence of title to be furnished.

(6) Time allowed seller to clear defects in title.

(7) How and when purchase price is to be disbursed, with directions as to when items are to be prorated or apportioned, if escrow holder is to do the pro-rating.

(8) Directions to deliver deed, leases, insurance policies, assignments of policy, and service contracts to buyer when title is clear.

(9) Return of deposits to the respective parties if title cannot be cleared.

(10) Reconveyance by buyer to seller if deed to buyer has been recorded immediately on signing of escrow agreement and examination of title thereafter discloses seller's title was defective and incurable.

(11) Payment of escrow, title and recording charges, broker's commission, and attorneys' fees.

[¶3323] CONSUMER PROTECTION IN REAL ESTATE TRANSACTIONS

In addition to Truth-in-Lending provisions that apply to consumer real estate transactions, another federal law regulates this area—the Real Estate Settlement Procedures Act of 1974 (RESPA). This law was passed on the basis of Congress' finding that significant reforms in the real estate settlement process were needed to insure that homeowners are provided with greater and more timely information on its nature and costs. Under this law, lenders are required to disclose to buyers and sellers the various costs of settlement.

[¶3324] COVERAGE OF RESPA

RESPA covers all first mortgages on one- to- four-family residential proper-ties made by federally insured or regulated lenders (federally related mortgages).

Specifically exempted from coverage are the following:

☐ A loan to cover the purchase or transfer of more than 25 acres;

☐ A home improvement loan, loan to refinance, or other loan whose pro-ceeds are not used to acquire title to property;

☐ A loan to finance the purchase or transfer of a vacant lot, if net proceeds of the loan are used for the construction of a one- to four-family residential struc-ture or for the purchase of a mobile home to be placed on the lot;

☐ An assumption, novation, or sale or transfer subject to a pre-existing loan, except the use of or conversion of a construction loan to a permanent mortgage loan to finance purchase by the first user;

❑ A construction loan, except if it is intended to be used as or converted to a permanent loan to finance purchase by the first user;

❑ A permanent loan whose proceeds will be used to finance the construction of a one- to four-family structure, when the lot is already owned by the borrower or borrowers; or

❑ A loan to finance the purchase of a property when the primary purpose of the purchase is resale.

❑ Execution of land sale contracts.

[¶3325] DEFINITION OF FEDERALLY RELATED MORTGAGE

The HUD regulations define "federally related mortgage" as a loan that is not made to finance an exempt transaction (see above) and that meets all four of the following requirements:

(1) The proceeds of the loan are used in whole or in part to finance the purchase by the borrower, or other transfer of title, of the mortgaged property;

(2) The loan is secured by a first lien or other first security interest covering real estate, including a fee simple, life estate, remainder interest, ground lease, or other long-term household estate

    (a) That has a structure designed principally for the occupancy of from one to four families, or

    (b) That has a mobile home, or

    (c) Upon which a structure designed principally for the occupancy of from one to four families is to be constructed using proceeds of the loan, or

    (d) Upon which there will be placed a mobile home to be purchased using proceeds of the loan, or

    (e) That has a one- to four-family residential condominium unit (or the first lien covering a cooperative unit);

(3) The mortgaged property is located in a state; and

(4) The loan

    (a) Is made by a lender meeting certain specified requirements, or

    (b) Is made in whole or in part, or insured, guaranteed, supplemented, or assisted in any way, by the Secretary of HUD or any other officer or agency of the federal government, or

    (c) Is made in connection with a housing or urban development program administered by the Secretary or other agency of the federal government, or

    (d) Is intended to be sold by the originating lender to the Federal National Mortgage Association (FNMA), the Government National Mortgage Association (GNMA), or the Federal Home Loan Mortgage Corporation (FHLMC), or to a financial institution that intends to sell the mortgage to FHLMC.

[¶3326] INFORMATION BOOKLETS

Lenders covered by RESPA are required to mail a copy of *Settlement Costs, a HUD Guide* to every loan applicant within three days after a loan application is received. This booklet provides loan applicants with detailed information about the entire settlement process and includes explanations of the various settlement services and costs. For adjustable-rate mortgages lasting more than one year, Regulation Z also requires creditors to give borrowers either the official *Consumer Handbook on Adjustable-Rate Mortgages,* or a comparable publication.

[¶3327] GOOD-FAITH ESTIMATES

Within three days after receiving a loan application, the lender must provide the applicant with good-faith estimates of settlement costs.

The HUD regulations state that such estimates "must bear a reasonable relationship to the charge a borrower is likely to be required to pay at settlement, and must be based upon experience in the locality or area in which the mortgaged property is located."

If the lender requires the borrower to use a particular attorney, title company, or insurance company and to pay for all or part of such services, these costs must be included in the estimates and must state whether or not the attorney or company has a business relationship with the lender.

[¶3328] SETTLEMENT STATEMENT

Under one of RESPA's provisions, the person conducting the closing in every qualified "federally related mortgage loan" transaction must complete the Uniform Settlement Statement (HUD Form 1). This is done by itemizing all charges to be paid by the borrower and seller, except those charges that the lender does not impose on them or charges that the parties agree to pay "outside of closing." The person conducting the settlement must deliver the completed settlement statement to the borrower and seller at or before the closing. If the borrower requests, the person conducting the settlement must allow the borrower to inspect the completed settlement statement during the business day that immediately precedes the closing date.

If the borrower or her agent doesn't attend the closing or a formal closing meeting is not required, the transaction is exempt from the above requirement; however, the lender must deliver a completed settlement statement to the borrower as soon as practicable after the closing.

The borrower may waive any right to have the completed settlement statement delivered no later than at the closing. The waiver must be made in writing at or before settlement. Even if the borrower exercises this right of waiver, the lender must still deliver the completed statement to the seller and borrower as soon as possible after the closing.

The Uniform Settlement Statement is not used in two situations: (1) If there are no settlement fees charged to the buyer (because the seller has assumed all settlement-related expenses), or (2) The total amount the borrower must pay at settlement is determined by a fixed amount and the borrower is informed of this fixed amount at the time of loan application. In the latter case, the lender is required to provide the borrower, within three business days of application, with an itemized list of services rendered.

The lender must provide the borrower with a Truth-In-Lending statement at the time that the loan is consummated. This statement must disclose the annual percentage rate or affective interest rate that the borrower will have to pay on the mortgage loan. Although the lender is not required to give the Truth-In-Lending statement to the applicant when he gives him the information booklet and good-faith estimate of costs, the borrower may request this information when he makes his application.

The lender or the person who conducts the settlement may not charge either the borrower or the seller a fee for preparing the settlement statement.

[¶3329] PROHIBITION AGAINST KICKBACKS AND UNEARNED FEES

Section 8 of RESPA prohibits kickbacks and the splitting of unearned fees, stating: "(a) No person shall give and no person shall accept any fee, kickback, or thing of value pursuant to any agreement or understanding, oral or otherwise, that business incident to or part of a real estate settlement service involving a federally related mortgage loan shall be referred to any person."

"(b) No person shall give and no person shall accept any portion, split, or percentage of any charge made or received for the rendering of a real estate settlement service in connection with a transaction involving a federally related mortgage loan other than for services actually performed."

The Amendments specifically exempt from §8 "payments pursuant to cooperative brokerage and referral arrangements or agreements between real estate agents and brokers."

[¶3330] TITLE INSURANCE

A seller of real estate that will be financed by a federally related mortgage is prohibited from directly or indirectly conditioning a sale on the buyer's purchase of title insurance from a particular company. A seller who violates this provision of the Act is liable to the buyer for a sum of money that is equal to three times all the charges imposed for such title insurance.

[¶3331]　LIMITATION ON ESCROW ACCOUNTS

Lenders are restricted in the amount of advance deposits they can require buyers to place in escrow accounts for the purpose of insuring payment of real estate taxes and insurance. Under the Act, lenders may require borrowers to place in escrow no more than the amounts due and payable at the time of settlement, plus one-twelfth of the estimated total amount that will be due during the first year after the closing.

[¶3332]　RESPA's RELATION TO STATE LAW

RESPA does not exempt lenders from complying with any state law (i.e., does not preempt any state law) on settlement practices. However, if any state law is inconsistent with the Act (as determined by the Secretary of HUD), then the Act overrides the state law, but only to the extent of the state law's inconsistency. If a state law is inconsistent, but offers consumers greater protection than the Act, then the state law takes precedence over the Act.

[¶3333]　REAL PROPERTY TAX DEDUCTION

When a taxpayer feels that real property has been assessed too high, local law affords him an opportunity to petition for a reduction of the assessment. Such a proceeding is usually initiated by making a formal protest with an application for correction to the taxing authority itself. Only after such an application is denied, either in whole or in part, may a proceeding for judicial review of the assessment be initiated. When tax officials turn down the property owner's protest, this action is usually subject to review by a court in an appeals proceeding. This is a proceeding whereby the tax officials are called upon to produce their records and to certify them to the court so that the court may determine whether the officials have proceeded according to the principles of law that they are required to follow in the performance of their assessing duties.

[¶3334]　GROUNDS FOR CHALLENGING ASSESSMENTS

Local tax authorities usually have forms of application to be used in asking for an assessment review. If this application of protest is rejected, the next step is to initiate a proceeding in the appropriate court to review the final assessment. The grounds upon which an assessment may be reduced are usually: (1) overvaluation, (2) inequality, and (3) illegality.

[¶3335] OVERVALUATION

This can be established by showing that the assessment of real property has been set at a sum that is higher than the full and fair market value of the property.

[¶3336] INEQUALITY

This somewhat overlaps with overvaluation and can be established by showing that the assessment was made at a higher proportionate valuation than the assessment of other real estate of a like character in the same area. To obtain relief it is usually necessary to show that the assessment is out of proportion as compared with valuations in the municipality generally. To prove inequality it is necessary to examine a considerable number of parcels of real estate for the purpose of comparing the market values of these properties with their assessed valuation and ascertaining the ratio of assessed value to market value in each instance. A case of inequality exists if such a study shows that the ratio of assessed values to market values generally is substantially lower than the ratio between the assessed value and the market value of the property in question.

[¶3337] ILLEGALITY

This exists when the assessment has been levied in an irregular manner or on a basis erroneous in law or in fact other than an error in the evaluation itself. An example of an illegal assessment is the inclusion on the tax rolls of an assessment of a parcel of real estate that is legally exempt from taxation.

[¶3338] PREPARING THE CHALLENGE

Here are some steps that can be taken to prepare a challenge:

(1) Assessor's Report: First, carefully examine the assessor's report for the property. If it is predicated on some factual error such as an incorrect description of the property, an incorrect statement of its actual income or expense, or any other matter that concerns the property itself, submit proof of the correct facts.

(2) Cost: Compare the actual cost of the property with its assessed valuation. If the purchase price is substantially below the assessed valuation that's being challenged, and the date of purchase is not too remote from the assessment date, this information will be relevant, provided it can be proven that this property was purchased in an arm's-length transaction.

(3) Operation: Dig out and study the records of income received from the property and the expenses of operation over several years before the tax date. The earning capacity of income-producing property is the most significant single factor in determining its market value for purposes of seeking tax assessment reduction.

(4) Similar Properties: Make a comparison of sales prices and assessed valuations and of market value and assessed valuations for other comparable properties in the area. This kind of comparison may have already been made by others, so it may be possible to obtain a great deal of information without having to go to the trouble and expense of getting appraisals on a large number of properties.

(5) Experts: The testimony of expert witnesses is usually the most important part of a court case to reduce taxes. Consider using the testimony of a building expert as well as a real estate expert. While the real estate expert will testify about the market value of the property, the building expert can go beyond this and testify about the building's sound structural value or its reproduction cost.

[¶3339] REVIEW PROCEDURE

The course of a proceeding to review a real property assessment usually runs in the following way after the attorney is employed. The appraiser is hired to select a number of sample properties anywhere in the assessing jurisdiction whose ratios of assessed valuation he or she believes to be substantially lower than that of the client. The attorney for the assessing jurisdiction likewise selects samples whose assessed valuation ratios will tend to support what he or she contends to be the prevailing ratio. If the opposing attorneys cannot agree on which of these are to be placed in evidence (and such agreement is hardly likely) they submit both lists to the court, which proceeds to choose from such lists an agreed-upon number of samples. The appraisers for both sides evaluate and analyze these sample properties before the court, and are examined and cross-examined as to their respective appraisals of these samples. The court then makes a finding of the true value of each, compares it with assessed valuation, computes all the ratios, averages them, and accepts the result as the prevailing ratio for this particular proceeding. (This finding does not bind any other litigant in any other proceeding, nor may it be used in the litigant's own case over objection.)

Finally, the court listens to both appraisers give their opinions of the full, fair market value of the petitioner's own property, arrives at a decision, applies the "prevailing ratio" just found, and thus determines what the assessed valuation of the subject property should have been.

Of course, this is how the practice works in general. The specific procedure in a particular case will vary depending on whether the state constitution does or does not call for uniformity in real estate taxation, provisions of state real property and tax laws with respect to establishing ratios and providing for equalization rates, and establishing procedural rules for the review of real property tax burdens. For example, in New York, the state establishes equalization rights to be used for the distribution of state aid to localities and for other purposes and by legislative enactment that may be offered in evidence by a party to a certiorari proceeding.

— **FOR FURTHER REFERENCE** —

Real Estate Transactions

Barasch, Clarence S., "Negotiating Real Estate Brokerage Agreements," 8 *Real Estate Law J.* 240 (Winter '80).

Bernstein, Joel A., "A Primer on Computer Real Estate Conveyancing," 1 *Probate and Property* 48 (November–December '87).

Comment, "Real Property and Real Estate Transactions," 37 *Syracuse L. Rev.* 641 (Summer '86).

Friedman, Milton R., *Contracts and Conveyances of Real Property (4th edition)* (Practising Law Institute; 1984 with 1988 supplement).

Hoffman, Fredric A. and Leigh M. Rosenthal, "Investing in Real Estate: Additional Changes Made by the Tax Reform Act of 1986," 61 *Florida Bar J.* 39 (March '87).

Levine, Howard J. and Peter A. Glicklich, "Tax-Free Real Estate Transactions," 14 *J. of Real Estate Taxation* 333 (Summer '87).

Levine, Mark Lee, *Real Estate Transactions* (West, 1987).

Levinton, Howard, "Ownership of Real Estate Limited Partnership Interests at Death," 11 *Tax Management Estates, Gifts, and Trusts J.* 48 (3/13/86).

Lewis, Daniel B., "Creative Financing Techniques in Commercial Real Estate," 72 *ABA J.* 60 (February '86).

Subotnick, Dan, "Easing the Pain of Modern Home Economics," 30 *Tax Notes* 267 (1/20/86).

Taddeo, Frank, *Representing the Residential Real Estate Client* (Prentice Hall, 1987).

Real Estate Transactions: Consumer Protection

Ardaugh, John R., "Mandatory Disclosure: The Key to Residential Real Estate Brokers' Conflicting Obligations," 19 *John Marshall L. Rev.* 201 (Fall '85).

Knowles, Stuart, "Real Estate Broker's Liability for Failure to Disclose," 17 *Pacific LJ.* 327 (October '85).

Kratovil, Robert, "Unconscionability: Real Estate Lawyers Confront a New Problem," 21 *John Marshall L. Rev.* 1 (1987).

McConnell, Rose, "Protecting the Real Estate Consumer," 65 *Nebraska L. Rev.* 188 (Winter '86).

Morris, Aaron Paul, "Vendors of Real Estate: When Does Liability for Dangerous Conditions End?" 17 *Southwestern U. L. Rev.* 23 (1987).

Note, "Legal Profession: Real Estate Brokers and the Practice of Law," 35 *Arkansas L. Rev.* 384 (Spring '82).

Real Property Tax Relief

Bloom, Robert T., "Tax Valuation of Condominiums and Cooperatives," 11 *Real Estate Law Journal* 240 (Winter '83).

Goldstein, M. Robert and Michael J., "Transition Assessments—A Taxing Dialogue," 193 *New York Law J.* 1 (1/16/85).

Gustafson, Earl B., "Challenging Unequal Property Tax Assessments in Minnesota," 13 *William Mitchell L. Rev.* 461 (Summer '87).

Hogan, Howard T. and Richard P. DeBragga, "Proving Inequality in Property Tax Assessment," 59 *New York State Bar J.* 44 (December '87).

Koeppel, Adolph and Saul R. Fenchel, "Challenging Ad Valorem Real Property Assessments in Florida," 3 *J. of State Taxation* 113 (Summer '84).

Kraft, Melvin D., "Arbitration of Real Estate Valuation Disputes," 42 *Arbitration J.* 15 (September '87).

Low, Andrew W., "Appealing Property Tax Assessments," 15 *Colorado Lawyer* #798 (May '86).

Morris, Eugene J. and William D. Siegel, "Proof of Inequality: A Shifting Sea of Sand," 59 *New York State Bar J.* 26 (November '86).

Rohan, Patrick J., *Real Estate Tax Appeals* (3 volumes) (Matthew Bender, loose-leaf).

REMEDIES AND DEFENSES

[¶3401] The rights and liabilities of a client are inevitably the most immediate concern of any lawyer. Enforcement, protection, and assertion of those rights and remedies are the nuts and bolts of an everyday law practice. When a party has a claim, it is necessary to determine what remedy or remedies may be available. In the paragraphs that follow, a number of different remedies and defenses are examined at length.

[¶3402] GENERAL REMEDIES

Distinctions between actions at law and suits in equity have gone by the wayside. Nonetheless, it is important to distinguish between the two types of relief sought because legal remedies afford a right to a jury trial. Claims for legal relief fall under four main headings:
(1) Enforcement of money obligations;
(2) Breach of contract damages;
(3) Tort damages;
(4) Recovery of property (real or personal).
Each of these is part of the law of restitution.

[¶3403] RESTITUTION

Perhaps the single most pervasive idea in the law of restitution is to prevent unjust enrichment. A number of different remedies, two of the most important being quasi-contract and constructive trusts, are used to achieve this end. At common law, enforcement of a debt (general assumpsit) was the action utilized to provide for the payment of money. Special assumpsit, on the other hand, was originally developed as an action to enforce a simple contract. The theory behind this is that whenever there is a contractual debt, a promise to pay the debt would be implied as a matter of law.

The most common types of debt are for goods sold and delivered (quantum valebant) or for work and labor done (quantum meruit), a quasi-contract action. The main benefit of a quasi-contract as a remedy is the important privilege of attachment. The most common form of state law provides for attachment "in an action upon a contract, express or implied." In seeking a particular remedy, the attorney should carefully frame his cause of action, anticipating the probable defense. It is useful to consult local statutes of limitations, since under certain circumstances, counterclaim or setoff is available even though a statute of limitations that would support an independent action has expired. This is a means of equity that the law provides—a remedy that usually is not permitted to be used to achieve positive recovery, but can be used to the extent of the amount claimed.

Restitution will be denied in certain circumstances, e.g., where there has been a change in the parties' circumstances rendering restitution unjust, or where restitution is sought from a bona fide purchaser for value.

Rescission is a contract remedy used when it is possible to return the parties to their condition before the contract was made. Rescission can be granted if the contract was illegal, obtained by fraud, or if both parties entertained a mutual mistake about the contract. The rescission remedy can be elected by the parties themselves (by their agreement to rescind the contract) or through the court system.

[¶3404] ENFORCEMENT OF MONEY OBLIGATIONS

In an action to enforce a money obligation, the aim is to recover judgment for the plaintiff plus interest, costs, and disbursements. Essentially, there are four basic classes of actions:

(1) Contract debts;
(2) Judgment debts;
(3) Statutory penalties (such as antitrust);
(4) Unjust enrichment.

These are explained in the paragraphs below.

[¶3404.1] Contract Debt

In actions for contract debt, the plaintiff must show: (a) promise to pay money (promise may be implied from conduct, as by retention of goods for which defendant has been billed); (b) consideration for the promise, except when statutory provision eliminates the requirement; (c) performance or happening of conditions, if any, of payment; and (d) nonpayment.

[¶3404.2] Judgment Debt

A new judgment for a money debt may be called for when execution of the prior judgment is in jeopardy by reason of the statute of limitations or when property subject to execution is not within the reach of the prior judgment. The plaintiff must show: (a) judgment, and (b) nonpayment.

[¶3404.3] Statutory Penalty

These are actions based on a statutory obligation to pay money. The plaintiff must show: (a) violation of statute by the defendant either by act of commission or omission, (b) resulting injury, and (c) nonpayment.

[¶3404.4] Unjust Enrichment

This is a type of indebtedness, not created by contract, based on the receipt by the defendant of a benefit he may not in fairness retain. The plaintiff must show: (a) receipt by the defendant from the plaintiff of benefits amounting to unjust enrichment, and (b) nonpayment.

[¶3405] DAMAGES FOR BREACH OF CONTRACT

Contracts are nothing more than promises that something will or will not happen. In the event that there is a breach of that promise, the plaintiff must show: (1) an express promise (a writing may be required if the statute of frauds so provides), (2) consideration for the promise, (3) performance or nonperformance of the promise, and (4) the resulting damage.

Where damages for breach of contract would be difficult to ascertain, the parties can stipulate to an amount of "liquidated damages"—i.e., a sum that will be accepted as damages in case of breach. Liquidated damages clauses are usually upheld by courts unless the stipulated amount is grossly unjust and/or operates as a penalty.

[¶3406] TORT DAMAGES

Protection of person and property against unauthorized invasion or damage characterizes tort. In most instances, a plaintiff must show actual damages, although nominal damages may be obtained in other instances. In certain instances, there may be an action in either tort or contract.

Under certain circumstances, a plaintiff may seek to waive the tort and sue on the underlying contractual obligation that may be implied as a matter of law. This is phrased in terms of quasi-contract and, while the damages for tort may be quite nominal, those for quasi-contract can often be substantial. The careful attorney will phrase the pleadings in such a manner as to allow for the best possible course of action for affirmative recovery. In any case, under the laws of most states, pleadings today are liberally construed; thus, it may be possible, even after the proof has been entered into the record, to make a motion to modify the pleadings to conform to the proof.

Especially where the defendant has a "deep pocket," juries may award multimillion-dollar punitive damages—a possibility which alters trial strategy by making settlement more attractive—even in cases where liability is far from certain. Punitive (also known as exemplary) damages are never automatic; they depend on conduct by the defendant so outrageous that the defendant must be "made an example of." The usual rule is that punitive damages cannot exist in isolation: the plaintiff must also recover compensatory damages.

The "collateral source" rule says that a defendant's liability for damages is not reduced by benefits the plaintiff receives from sources other than the defendant (such as the plaintiff's own insurance company). Although there is a policy against double recovery for the plaintiff, the policy against windfalls for the defendant tortfeasor is stronger.

In cases of intentional discrimination, compensatory damages are available under the Rehabilitation Act (here, discrimination against an HIV-positive individual).[1] However, ERISA Sec. 502(a), which allows recovery of benefits due and equitable relief, does not permit award of any extracontractual damages whether compensatory or punitive.[2]

Prejudgment interest can be awarded in a civil rights action under 42 U.S.C. Sec. 1983,[3] or under Labor Management Relations Act Sec. 303(b) (the civil remedy for secondary strike activity carried out by a union).[4]

The Civil Rights Act of 1991 imposes caps on the damages recoverable in an employment discrimination action; the caps are applied as an aggregate that can be recovered against the employer and any and all individual defendants (i.e., the presence of individual defendants does not increase the overall potential damages).[5]

Equal protection bars the admission of evidence of collateral-source benefits if, but only if, the *ad damnum* clause of the plaintiff's complaint asks for more than $150,000 in damages; according to the Kansas Supreme Court, there is no way to determine if $150,000 is an appropriate dividing line or not.[6]

[¶3407] PUNITIVE DAMAGES

In a series of developments, potential defendants were disappointed when the Supreme Court ruled that in the most extreme case of unbridled jury discretion, a state's punitive damage provisions may violate the due process clause but states can also mandate acceptable procedures for imposing punitive damages, even if the damages are large as measured in comparison with the compensatory damages.[7]

The Supreme Court has also found that due process is not violated by the imposition of $10 million in punitive damages in a common-law slander of title action where the compensatory damages were only $19,000.[8]

A California plaintiff seeking punitive damages has the burden of proof as to the defendant's financial condition; the court must determine that the award is not disproportionate to the defendant's ability to pay.[9] A later New Jersey case makes the defendant's financial condition relevant in all punitive damage awards, because the award must reflect the defendant's profits from misconduct, but also the punishment the defendant receives from other sources.[10]

A West Virginia case[11] makes many interesting points. It permits punitive damages to be commensurate to potential harm, even if the actual harm was lesser in extent. The reprehensibility of the defendant's conduct is an issue; the punitive damages should exceed the profits obtained from the wrongful conduct, but the financial position of the defendant must also be taken into account.

In a 42 U.S.C. Sec. 1983 civil rights suit brought in Colorado, the Colorado state-law requirement that a person seeking civil punitive damages must prove the claim beyond a reasonable doubt will be applied.[12]

A significant question that has received extensive attention recently is which causes of action will support an award of punitive damages. Punitive damages were not available in a securities case in which the standard arbitration agreement was governed by the law of New York where punitive damages are not available in arbitration cases. It was held that the Federal Arbitration Act did not preempt the choice-of-law clause sufficiently to permit a punitive damage award.[13] In contrast, a later Eighth Circuit case does permit an award of punitive damages in a case arbitrated under American Arbitration Association rules even where arbitration punitive damages are not recognized under state law.[14]

The Civil Rights Act of 1991 (see ¶2105.2) permits awards of punitive damages in appropriate circumstances. The Northern District of California has ruled[15] that, in a case of sex and race discrimination, proof by preponderance of evidence of intentional violation of Title VII will constitute the "reckless indifference" that will support a CRA 1991 Section 102(b)(1) punitive damage award. However, the Eastern District of Louisiana did not find a defendant's conduct callous or malicious enough to award punitive or emotional distress damages under CRA 1991.[16] The Tax Court has held that punitive damages awarded in a personal injury case are not taxable income; in this analysis, all tort damages are excludable.[17]

[¶3408] RECOVERY OF PROPERTY

Individuals in possession of real or personal property, whose rights in the property are violated, may seek a judgment for damages. An individual not in possession, but who has an immediate right of possession, may seek one of three common law actions or their statutory equivalents: Ejectment, forcible entry and detainer, and replevin. These are described below.

[¶3409] EJECTMENT

To recover real property, an action in the nature of an ejectment or recovery of real property may be instituted. To succeed, it must be shown (1) that the plaintiff has an interest in the property and a right to immediate possession or control, (2) a withholding or denial of possession by the defendant, and (3) the nature and extent of damages.

In an action for ejectment, it is important to recognize that the operation of law will sometimes be slow, especially in a residential landlord-tenant situation. Under most circumstances, a tenant will be able to successfully remain in possession for a period of six months following the attempted ejectment. (Of course, the laws of each state vary as to this time period.) Landlord-tenant courts and other judicial authorities that handle this type of law are increasingly tenant-oriented in remedial action.

In dealing with the purchase of realty in which a tenant is involved, it is the wise attorney who insists on a clause that premises are to be delivered vacant at closing of title. Otherwise, the purchaser may end up with a new home and tenants whom it is impossible to eject for at least several months or longer.

[¶3410] Forcible Entry and Detainer

When an individual is forcibly removed from land, an action may be brought to restore possession. To recover, the plaintiff must show that (1) there was prior peaceable possession, (2) the defendant forcibly entered the land and dispossessed the plaintiff, and (3) that there was a forcible detention of property by the defendant.

[¶3411] Replevin

Recovery of personal property is most commonly known as replevin, but may also be referred to by the older name of detinue, or as a claim and delivery. To recover, the plaintiff must show (1) an interest in the property and a right to both immediate possession and control, (2) wrongful detention by the defendant, and (3) to the extent suffered, any loss resulting in damages.

In terms of secured transactions, it is useful to note that under §9-503 of the Uniform Commercial Code, a secured party has the right to take possession of the debtor's collateral on default. In taking possession, the UCC states that the secured party may proceed without judicial process, if it can be done without breach of the peace.

[¶3412] Equitable Relief

The main types of equitable relief fall within one of these classes:
(1) Injunctions;
(2) Specific performance of contracts;
(3) Recovery of property by equitable means;
(4) Enforcement of money obligations by equitable means; and
(5) Protection against future and multiple claims.
These are explained in more detail in the paragraphs below.

[¶3412.1] Injunctions

Injunctions are an extraordinary remedy used by a court to prevent an occurrence of irreparable harm. The individual seeking the injunction must demonstrate not only that the potential for harm exists, but that other means of judicial process that proceed more slowly are not more appropriate. Courts use injunctions sparingly and cautiously. Under the laws of many states, preliminary injunctions or temporary restraining orders may be granted without notice, provided it appears that irreparable injury will result in the absence of such an order.

[¶3412.2] Specific Performance

A party may be compelled judicially to do what a contract requires (but the individual refuses to do) in an action for specific performance. The plaintiff must prove (1) the making of a promise, (2) performance of all obligations on the part of the plaintiff, including performance of all conditions precedent, (3) breach of a promise or contract by the defendant, (4) facts showing the inadequacy of any legal remedy—for example, money damages are not an actual substitute for land or unique items (e.g., works of art).

If the contract includes a liquidated damages provision, specific performance can be granted if the sum specified as liquidated damages is merely meant as security for performance of the obligations under the contract. However, specific performance won't be granted if the clause itself specifies that liquidated damages are the "sole" or "only" remedy.

[¶3412.3] Equitable Recovery (Restitution)

When legal means are inadequate or impractical, the plaintiff may be able to use equity as a way of achieving restitution. This concept covers the principles of equitable accounting, constructive trusts, equitable liens, mistakes as to basic assumption, mistakes as to the existence of a contract, mistakes as to property ownership, mistakes in gift transactions, and mistakes of law.

[¶3412.4] Enforcement of Money Obligations by Equitable Means

Money obligations may be enforced by equitable means in these situations: (1) the plaintiff's interest is one that historically was protected only in equity; e.g., right to trust proceeds, right to alimony, or support payments; (2) when the money obligation is secured and enforcement of the security is sought; (3) accounting; (4) as incident to a suit for other relief that is by itself within the jurisdiction of equity; (5) when a person wrongfully takes the money of another individual, places it with his own money in an account, and subsequently makes withdrawals from the mingled funds (equitable lien devolves on the part that remains). When embezzlement occurs, a constructive trust is imposed upon the proceeds—if they advance in value, the beneficiary of this increase is not the embezzler, but the party from whom the funds were embezzled. This basic principle of restitution, called tracing, is to prevent the unjust enrichment of any individual.

[¶3412.5] Protection Against Future (or Multiple) Claims

Equity may be utilized to prevent multiple suits or future actions or to aid in either the prosecution or defense of anticipated suits. The most common types of equitable relief sought are interpretations of a will or other instrument, cancellation or interpretation of a writing, quieting title to land, removing clouds on title, declaratory judgments, and interpleader suits.

[¶3413] PARTITION

An action for partition is a request for a division of property among co-owners. It may be undertaken either voluntarily by contract or through judicial division. Jointly held property, as well as property held by tenants in common, is generally subject to an action in partition.

When parties take title to property as tenants by the entirety, there is no basis for an action for partition. The purpose of a tenancy by the entirety is to protect and sustain the family unit to which partition is inimical. In the event that a judgment debtor is married, the creditor is entitled to control that portion of the tenancy by the entirety that the judgment debtor owns (a one-half undivided interest), but is unable to effect partition. In the event the judgment debtor dies prior to his or her spouse, the creditor's holding of that portion is, of course, extinguished.

[¶3414] REFORMATION

Contracts that do not accurately express the intention of the parties may be subject to reformation. Reformation may sometimes be ineffective because of the parol evidence rule. It is useful to note, however, that a court of equity may grant reformation based upon mistakes.

[¶3415] CANCELLATION OF CONTRACTS OR OBLIGATIONS

The destruction or cancellation of the document embodying a contract will discharge a contractual duty that arises under a formal unilateral contract where done with the intent to discharge the duty. Surrender of the document to the party subject to the duty or someone on his or her behalf will have a similar effect.

[¶3416] DECLARATORY JUDGMENTS

Declaratory judgments are recognized under both federal and state law. Federal law requires that there be an actual controversy. On both the federal and state levels, courts retain considerable discretion in granting this remedy. The Uniform Declaratory Judgment Act, adopted by the vast majority of the states, covers many different areas, some of which are explored below.

(1) **Scope:** Courts have the power to declare rights, status, and other relations (even if no further relief is claimed). The declaration may be positive or negative and has the effect of a final judgment or decree.

(2) **Power to Construe:** Determination of a question of construction or validity of an instrument, ordinance, statute, contract, or other legal relation of an individual interested in any written instrument is permissible under the Uniform Act.

(3) **Before Breach:** Contracts may be construed either before or after a breach has occurred.

(4) **Executors:** Declarations of rights or relationships in ascertaining creditors, heirs, or others, or in directing an executor, trustee, or administrator to undertake (or to abstain from undertaking) a particular transaction in a fiduciary capacity, or determination of any facet of will construction is permissible by declaratory judgment.

[¶3417] MANDAMUS

Mandamus is the single most powerful writ available to require performance of a ministerial government duty or function. It is always issued in the sound discretion of the court and will not lie in doubtful cases. In many states, mandamus proceedings have been formally abolished by statute, and replaced by other procedural devices.

[¶3418] QUO WARRANTO

Quo warranto is generally invoked to test the right or title to office, remedy the usurpation or abuse of franchises, test primary nominations, and test the right to judicial office. In many states the availability of quo warranto is governed by statutes that have spelled out the cases in which the remedy will lie.

[¶3419] TAXPAYERS' ACTIONS

Proceedings against municipal corporations, counties, towns, and villages are often lodged by taxpayers. Generally speaking, the interest of a taxpayer in a federal treasury is insufficient to maintain a taxpayer's action against the federal government.

In *Walz v. Tax Commission* (397 US 664, 1970), the Supreme Court held that the de minimis effects on taxpayers do not give them the standing to challenge certain tax exemptions given to religious institutions.

[¶3420] ATTACHMENT

Attachment is a proceeding under which the plaintiff acquires control of the defendant's property before determination of any of the issues involved in a lawsuit. Attachment may serve to compel a defendant's appearance before the court or to furnish security for a debt.

Attachment is an area of the law in which serious constitutional questions have been raised. Normally, any debt or property against which a money judgment may be enforced is subject to attachment. Ordinarily, a sheriff or comparable official is used to levy prior to final judgment.

The Supreme Court found a Connecticut statute authorizing pre-judgment attachment of real property invalid on due process grounds.[18] The statute allowed attachment pursuant to an ex parte showing by the plaintiff that there was probable cause to sustain the plaintiff's claim, but with no showing of extraordinary or exigent circumstances mandating or even justifying attachment before notice and hearing.

The Tenth Circuit used a similar due process analysis to invalidate a New Mexico statute requiring debtors to be given notice of "exemption in lieu of homestead" and "other exemptions," but no further description, in post-judgment executions.[19] The bare mention of exemptions was insufficient to inform debtors of their property rights.

[¶3421] WRIT OF ASSISTANCE

The writ of assistance is utilized in carrying out equity decrees in much the same manner as the execution is utilized in carrying out an action at law. Essentially, this writ is a mandatory injunction used to bring about a change in the possession of real property.

[¶3422] CERTIORARI

Certiorari is available in many jurisdictions to review the findings of a lower tribunal or an administrative agency. The availability of certiorari varies from state to state. In some states its availability is governed exclusively by statute. Unless otherwise provided by statute, the court may in its discretion determine whether certiorari will be granted. Essentially, certiorari represents the review of a judicial determination. However, the nature of the action rather than the body taking the action will usually determine whether certiorari is available.

[¶3423] COMMON DEFENSES

The paragraphs below provide basic information concerning various legal defenses.

[¶3424] ACCORD AND SATISFACTION

Accord and satisfaction is a means of discharging a contract or settling a contract or tort claim by substituting for the contract or claim an agreement for its satisfaction and then performing in accordance with the agreement. It bars the original claim. Generally, to have this effect, the agreement must be fully executed. But the parties themselves may, by clear language, make the agreement itself and not its performance operate as satisfaction of the original claim.

[¶3425] ACT OF GOD

This may be used as a defense to action in contract or in tort. The defendant must show that: (a) the act or event complained of was the result of an act of God; (b) the defendant was not responsible and negligence did not contribute to it in any way.

[¶3426] ADVERSE POSSESSION

The defendant must show that his or her possession was actual and not constructive, under a claim of right, hostile, open and notorious, exclusive and continuous for the period of time required by law.

[¶3427] ANOTHER ACTION PENDING

The defendant must show that there is pending and undisposed of another action in another court by the same plaintiff against the same defendant based on the same cause of action and involving the same parties.

[¶3428] ARBITRATION AND AWARD

An award made under a valid arbitration decision ordinarily operates to discharge the claim submitted to arbitration. It, therefore, operates as a ban to resubmission of the same claim to a second arbitration or to litigation of the claim before a court of law. The party relying on this defense must show: (a) an agreement on the part of the plaintiff to submit a claim to arbitration; (b) submission of the claim to arbitration as agreed; and (c) making of the award, and notice of publication, if required for enforcement.

[¶3429] ASSUMPTION OF RISK

In negligence cases, it is a recognized principle that one who voluntarily assumes the risk of injury from a known danger can't recover. Under some rules of procedure, assumption of risk is regarded as an affirmative defense that must be specially pleaded, but under others it may be proved under a general denial. While often closely associated with contributory negligence, it is distinguishable. (In fact, in a number of states, the assumption of risk defense has been abolished in favor of contributory or comparative negligence defenses.) Assumption of risk, for example, may bar recovery even though the plaintiff may have acted with what might be considered due care. Usually this defense is invoked in cases involving a contractual relationship between a plaintiff and a defendant. The defendant must show: (a) an unreasonable risk in the situation or thing causing the injury; and (b) knowledge of the risk by the plaintiff at the time.

[¶3430] BREACH OF CONDITION SUBSEQUENT

Breach of a condition subsequent operates to destroy vested estates and contract rights. Because of their effect, they are not favored and will be found to exist only where the language creating them is very clear. In any case, if found to exist, the condition subsequent will be strictly construed.

[¶3431] CAPACITY OR RIGHT OF PARTY TO SUE OR BE SUED

This defense may be raised in the following situations:

(1) The plaintiff is a foreign corporation doing business within the state without having been qualified to do so, suing on a business transaction arising within the state;

(2) The plaintiff is not the real party in interest;

(3) The plaintiff is not sui juris;

(4) Other necessary parties are not joined;

(5) The defendant is a foreign corporation, is not qualified to do business within the state, and does not do business within the state, and the cause of action alleged did not arise within the state;

(6) The defendant is without capacity to be sued (as by reason of infancy).

[¶3432] CONTRIBUTORY AND COMPARATIVE NEGLIGENCE

Contributory negligence is recognized as a defense in one of the following two ways, varying with the jurisdiction in which it is asserted.

In jurisdictions which continue to follow the traditional common law rule, contributory negligence of the plaintiff operates as a complete bar to recovery.

In other jurisdictions, plaintiff's contributory negligence does not operate as a complete bar to recovery. Many states have enacted comparative negligence laws which provide for damages to be divided in proportion to the fault of the parties (e.g., if plaintiff's damages are $10,000, but it is determined that plaintiff was 20% contributorily negligent in occasioning that damage, plaintiff's recovery will be only $8,000). It is essential to consult local law on this subject and to be sure to frame pleadings as they are required in the relevant jurisdiction. For example, if it is a condition precedent to jurisdiction that the plaintiff not be contributorily negligent, this must be explicitly pleaded in the complaint.

[¶3433] DISCHARGE IN BANKRUPTCY

The defendant must show: (a) details as to filing of petition by or against him or her, adjudication of bankruptcy, and granting of discharge; (b) that the plaintiff's claim was due and owing at the time of the bankruptcy proceedings and was included in the schedules filed or was omitted for specified reasons.

[¶3434] DURESS

The defendant must show that execution of the instrument relied on by the plaintiff was induced by fear of violence or imprisonment or the result of other wrongful pressure.

[¶3435] ELECTION OF REMEDIES

The defendant must show that the plaintiff had two existing alternative remedial rights, inconsistent and not reconcilable with each other based on the state of facts alleged in the present action, and that the plaintiff prior to the commencement of the present action elected to pursue the alternative remedy.

At the pleading stage, it is possible to plead inconsistently, provided that prior to trial or at trial an election of remedies is made.

[¶3436] ESTOPPEL

The defendant must show conduct or acts, words, or silence on the part of the plaintiff amounting to representation or concealment of material facts, with knowledge or imputed knowledge thereof, and that such representation, silence, or concealment was relied on by the defendant to his damage or detriment.

[¶3437] EXTENSION OF TIME FOR PAYMENT

The defendant must show written agreement based on valuable consideration extending the time of payment until a certain date and that by reason of the extension the amount claimed is not due and payable.

[¶3438] FAILURE OR WANT OF CONSIDERATION

Whenever consideration is required, want or failure of consideration is a defense. If consideration is required but need not be alleged, want or failure is an affirmative defense. Check state statutes making consideration unnecessary for written promises or creating presumption of consideration when a promise is in writing.

[¶3439] FRAUD

Some courts distinguish between fraud in the making (the person didn't know what he was signing) and fraud in the inducement (she knew what she was signing but was induced to sign by fraudulent misrepresentations), and make the former a negative defense and the latter an affirmative defense requiring a special plea. The defendant must show false representation by the plaintiff, with knowledge of falsity made with intent to defraud the defendant, and that it was relied on by the defendant to his damage.

[¶3440] LACHES

The defendant must show a claim for equitable relief has been unreasonably delayed, and that hardship or injustice to the defendant will result from its enforcement.

[¶3441] LICENSE

In actions for damages based on intentional wrong to the plaintiff, a showing that the plaintiff consented to the wrong will usually bar relief. In actions for assault and battery and false imprisonment, the plaintiff must generally show absence of consent, but in actions for intentional damage to property, real or personal, license is an affirmative defense.

[¶3442] PAYMENT

Payment is normally utilized as an affirmative defense. The most common approach is to utilize it in an answer to a complaint. Ordinarily, a requisite element is that proof of payment be shown.

[¶3443] PRIVILEGE

Conduct that, under ordinary circumstances, will subject the actor to liability may, under particular circumstances, not subject him to liability; that is, the conduct may be privileged. Examples: (a) self-defense; (b) defense of a third person; (c) public necessity, as where property is destroyed to prevent spread of fire; (d) protection or defense of property; (e) parental discipline; (f) seizure under legal process; and (g) privilege to abate nuisance.

[¶3444] RELEASE

A release may take the form of a declaration that a particular claim or cause of action has been discharged or the form of an agreement not to sue. In either form, if it is in writing and supported by consideration, or local law dispenses with the requirement of consideration, it may be pleaded as a defense.

[¶3445] RES JUDICATA

This defense is based on two concepts: (a) merger (claim is merged in judgment recovered by the plaintiff) and (b) bar (in prior action on the same claim the plaintiff failed to obtain a favorable judgment). If prior judgment is not on the merits, but is based on a procedural defect, it will not have the effect of res judicata.

[¶3446] COLLATERAL ESTOPPEL

Whereas res judicata is based on prior litigation of the same cause of action, collateral estoppel is based on prior litigation of a particular issue which was the subject of controversy in a prior cause of action. For example, if an issue involved in a current action was settled by judgment of a court in a prior action, the plaintiff is estopped from relitigating the same issue; this is so even though the cause of action in the current matter is different from the prior action and the plaintiff cannot recover in the current action unless the issue is resolved in his favor.

[¶3447] STATUTE OF FRAUDS

Specified transactions are unenforceable unless evidenced by a writing signed by the party to be charged. Transactions within statute: (a) special promise to answer for debt or default of another (contracts of suretyship and guarantee); (b) contracts for sale of interests in real property; (c) contracts for sale of goods of more than a certain value (under the Uniform Commercial Code, the common sum is $500); (d) contracts not to be performed within a year; (e) contracts to lease real property for more than a year; (f) contracts to bequeath property; (g) contracts to establish a trust; (h) conveyance or assignment of a trust in personal property; (i) promise to pay debt discharged in bankruptcy; and (j) contracts made in consideration of marriage.

[¶3448] STATUTE OF LIMITATIONS

Generally, failure of the plaintiff to bring an action within the time limited by statute is an affirmative defense. Sometimes the plaintiff must show, as a condition of relief, that action is brought within the time limit. There are general and special statutes, and the defense must make sure it isn't relying on a general statute when a special statute applies.

[¶3449] ULTRA VIRES

The application of the defense of ultra vires has been significantly limited under modern statutes and decisional law. In jurisdictions where it is still a viable defense, the defendant corporation must show that the transaction on which the action is based was beyond its express or implied powers. Local law should be consulted because there are jurisdictions which have abolished it as a common law defense.

[¶3450] UNCLEAN HANDS

In an equitable action, the defendant can show that the plaintiff is guilty of some improper conduct in the same transaction, such that the court will deny its assistance to the plaintiff.

[¶3451] USURY

Local law must be checked as to legal rates of interest, effect of usury (collection of excessive interest barred, collection of all interest, forfeiture of principal), and whether or not a corporation may plead it as a defense.

[¶3452] WAIVER

The defendant must show that prior to the action, the plaintiff voluntarily relinquished the interest asserted in action and that the defendant relied on the relinquishment.

[¶3453] WANT OF JURISDICTION

Want of jurisdiction of the person of the defendant must be properly pleaded (almost universally, a *special* appearance is called for) and will be waived by a general appearance. Want of jurisdiction of the subject matter may be raised at any time either by the defendant or by the court on its own motion.

— ENDNOTES —

1. Tanberg v. Weld County Sheriff, 60 LW 2591 (D.Colo. 3/18/92).
2. Harsch v. Eisenberg, 956 F.2d 651 (7th Cir. 2/10/92).
3. Golden State Transit Corp. v. Los Angeles, 773 F.Supp. 204 (C.D.Cal. 8/23/91).
4. Wickham Contracting Co. v. IBEW, 955 F.2d 831 (2d Cir. 1/29/92).
5. EEOC v. AIC Security Investigations Ltd., 61 LW 2770 (N.D. Ill. 6/7/93).
6. Thompson v. KFB Insurance Co., 232 Kan. 1010, 850 P.2d 773 (Kan.Sup. 4/16/93).
7. Pacific Mutual Life Ins. v. Haslip, #89-1279, 111 S.Ct. 1032 (3/4/92).

8. TXO Production Corp. v. Alliance Resources Corp., #92-479, 113 S.Ct. 2711 (Sup.Ct. 6/25/93).

9. Adams v. Murakami, 813 P.2d 1348 (Cal.Sup. 8/15/91).

10. Herman v. Sunshine Chemical Specialties, Inc. 62 LW 2112 (N.J. Sup. 7/28/93).

11. Fleming Landfill Inc. v. Garnes, 60 LW 2417 (W.Va.App. 12/5/91), *cert. denied* 111 S.Ct. 2881.

12. Boulder Valley School Dist. v. Price, 805 P.2d 1085 (Colo.Supp. 1/28/91).

13. Thomson McKinnon Securities Inc. v. Cucchiella, 61 LW 2033 (Mass.App. 6/22/92).

14. Lee v. Chica, 62 LW 2421 (8th Cir. 1/12/93).

15. Stender v. Lucky Stores Inc., 780 F.Supp. 1302 (N.D. Cal. 4/28/92).

16. Koppman v. South Central Bell Co., 61 LW 2063 (E.D.La. 6/16/92).

17. Ernest Horton, 100 T.C. No. 8 (2/9/93). But *interest* on damages received in a wrongful death case is taxable income: Rosemary Kovacs, 100 T.C. No. 10 (2/24/93).

18. Connecticut v. Doehr, #90-143, 111 S.Ct. 2105 (Sup.Ct. 6/6/91).

19. Aacen v. San Juan Cou. Sheriff's Dep't, 944 F.2d 691 (10th Cir. 9/5/91).

— FOR FURTHER REFERENCE —

Cooper, Alan, "Due Process KO's 2 Awards of Punitives," *Nat. Law J.* 10/28/91 p. 3.

Friend, Charles E., editor, *Actions and Remedies* (6 volumes) (Callaghan & Co., looseleaf).

Goodman, Jane et al., "Money, Sex, and Death: Gender Bias in Wrongful Death Damage Awards," 25 *Law & Soc. Rev.* 263 (May '91).

Koslow, Jon, "Estimating Aggregate Damages in Class-Action Litigation Under Rule 10b-5 for Purposes of Settlement," 59 *Fordham L. Rev.* 811 (April '91).

Loftus, Elizabeth F. and Laura A. Rosenwald, "Damage Control: How to Reduce Guess Work and Bias in Jury Awards," 15 *Trial Diplomacy J.* 183 (July–August '92).

Paray, Paul E., "Freedom of Contract Under the UCC: The Ability of Software Vendors to Exclude Recovery of Consequential Damages," 25 *Uniform Commercial Code L.J.* 133 (Fall '92).

Riley, Stephen T. and Jaiann B. Machell, "The Economics of Hedonic Damages," 1 *Nevada Lawyer* 24 (September '93).

Robinson, Glen O. and Kenneth S. Abraham, "Collective Justice in Tort Law," 78 *Virginia L. Rev.* 1481 (October '92).

Roddewig, Richard J. and Christopher Duerksen, "Measuring Damages in Takings Cases: The Next Frontier," 15 *Zoning and Planning Law Report* 49 (July–August '92).

Rundlett, Ellsworth T. III, "Negotiating a Small Personal Injury Claim: Fifteen Points to Remember," 27 *Trial* 55 (October '91).

Schwartz, Victor E. and Mark A. Behrens, "Haslip May Alter Tort-Claim Strategies," *Nat. Law J* 2/17/92 p. 23.

Waldman, Michael, "Damage Control: A Defendant's Approach to the Damage and Penalty Provisions of the Civil False Claims Act," 21 *Public Contract L.J.* 131 (Winter '92).

SALES AND PURCHASES

[¶3501] Adoption of the Uniform Commercial Code in 49 states, the District of Columbia, and the Virgin Islands (Louisiana has not adopted the entire Code) has served to integrate on a national level buying and selling practices of not only merchants but also consumers. The underlying purpose of the Uniform Commercial Code is to simplify, clarify, and modernize the law governing commercial transactions; to permit a continued expansion of commercial practices through usage, custom, and agreement of the parties; and to make the law uniform among the various states. The effect of any provision in the UCC may be varied by agreement of the parties (unless otherwise provided by the Code). Obligations that are reasonably undertaken in good faith may not be disclaimed by agreement although the parties may agree by what standards the performance of all obligations may be measured if the standards are not unreasonable (UCC §1-102(3)).

[¶3502] HISTORY

Article II of the Uniform Commercial Code, which governs sales, is a complete modernization and revision of what was formerly the Uniform Sales Act, which was written in 1906 and had been adopted by 36 states and the District of Columbia. Coverage in the UCC is far more extensive than the old sales act and was specifically designed to include various bodies of case law that had been developed under the Uniform Sales Act, as well as outside its scope. Article II is arranged in terms of a contract for sale and the various steps of its performance. Legal consequences are stated in a manner that flows directly from the contract. When property or title passes, or was to pass, is no longer a determining factor. Thus, the written instrument is of paramount importance to a commercial transaction (and, in fact, is required to enforce a contract that is valued at more than $500 or one that, by its terms, cannot be performed within one year).

In 1987, the Permanent Editorial Board for the UCC presented a Final Draft of proposed UCC Article 2A, to deal with personal property leasing. (Leases intended as security are covered by Article 9.) Several state legislatures (e.g., California, Connecticut, New Hampshire) considered it even before its official adoption as part of the UCC.

[¶3503] OTHER UCC SECTIONS RELATING TO SALES

Sales transactions relating to commercial paper are discussed beginning at ¶1101, investment securities at ¶3701, and secured transactions at ¶3601.

[¶3504] FORMATION OF A CONTRACT

Contracts for the sale of goods for a price of $500 or more are not enforceable unless some writing between the parties indicates that a contract for sale has been made. The UCC provides that even if a contract omits or incorrectly states a term agreed upon, or material terms are omitted (or imprecisely stated), the contract may be enforced. The price, time, place of payment or delivery, general quantity of goods, or even particular warranties all may be omitted. (To the extent that the quantity of goods is incorrectly stated, a sales contract is only enforceable to the extent of the quantity shown on the writing.) The only requirements are that the writing be a contract for the sale of goods, that it be signed by the party to be charged, and that it specify a quantity. Even a pencil writing on a scratch pad may bind the parties to be charged (UCC §2-201).

[¶3505] WRITTEN CONFIRMATION BETWEEN MERCHANTS

Oral contracts between merchants upon which a written confirmation is subsequently made are binding between parties if the party receiving the written confirmation fails to object to its contents within 10 days after receipt (UCC §2-201(2)).

[¶3506] THE WRITTEN CONTRACT

Written contracts under the Uniform Commercial Code have a paramount priority and may not be contradicted by evidence of prior agreement or contemporaneous oral conversations that alter the terms of the written agreement (the parol evidence rule). However, the written contract may either be explained or supplemented by evidence of consistent additional terms, or by any course of usual dealing or usage of trade. Even the inclusion of a "merger clause" (stating that this writing contains the entire agreement between the parties) does not bar the use of additional "usual" terms (UCC §2-202).

[¶3507] THE OFFER

When a merchant makes a firm offer to buy or sell goods in a signed agreement, and no term for either purchase or sale is provided, it is assumed under the Code that the offer will remain open for a reasonable time which in no event will exceed three months (UCC §2-205). An offer by a merchant is construed as inviting acceptance in any manner and in any medium reasonable under the circumstances, modifying the older rule that required acceptance to be made in the manner of the offer (e.g., a mailed offer requiring a mailed acceptance) (UCC §2-206). Firm offers no longer require consideration in order to bind the parties. Instead, they must merely be characterized as offers and expressed in signed writing by the party to be charged.

[¶3508] MODIFICATION TO A CONTRACT

Acceptance or written confirmation of a contract, even if additional or different terms are agreed to, operates as an acceptance of the contract. Additional terms are construed as proposals to the addition of the contract and, between merchants, all such additions become part of the contract unless: the addition constitutes a material alteration, the offer expressly prohibits the use of additional terms, or notice of objection to the additional terms is received within a reasonable time. This so-called "battle of the forms" found in UCC §2-207 substantively changes prior law, which generally required an acceptance of the offer exactly as it stood.

[¶3509] HOW TO LIMIT ALTERATION OF WRITTEN PURCHASE AND SALES AGREEMENTS

Between merchants, written purchase and sales agreements are necessary in order to prevent the use of unwanted conditions to a transaction, to disclaim warranties, and to control the risk of loss. To the extent that a seller wants no contract formed other than by the terms of sale, a clause in conspicuous type limiting the acceptance of the exact terms of the offer is required (UCC §2-207(2)(a)).

[¶3510] WRITTEN CONTRACT REQUIREMENTS

The statute of frauds requires a contract to be in writing for the sale of goods for the *price* of $500 or more (UCC §2-201(1)). However, part performance would take a contract out of the statute of frauds to the extent of the part performance (UCC §1-103).

In cases where goods are to be specially manufactured and are not ordinarily resalable in the normal course of the seller's business, an oral agreement will be binding if the seller has made a substantial beginning on or a commitment to acquire the goods called for in an agreement (UCC §2-201(3)).

To meet the requirements of the statute of frauds, the agreement generally must be signed by the party against whom it is to be enforced. However, the Uniform Commercial Code provides for the enforcement of a letter of confirmation in transactions between merchants if the person receiving the letter has reason to know of its contents. A person receiving a letter of confirmation may object within 10 days, and avoid its effect (UCC §2-201(2)).

Contracts for the sale of personal property (not the sale of goods or securities, or pursuant to security agreements) are subject to a different statute of frauds limitation. They're not enforceable by way of action, or defense beyond $5,000, unless there is some writing to indicate that a contract for sale has been made between the parties at a definite or stated price. The subject matter must be reasonably identified, and the party against whom enforcement is sought must have signed the document (UCC §1-206).

[¶3511] WARRANTIES: THE UCC STANDARD

Under the UCC, warranty by description and warranty by sample are express warranties and they may not be avoided by any disclaimer that is not consistent with the warranty itself. This means that any disclaimer must be explicit and should immediately follow the language of description.

The implied warranty of "merchantability" and "fitness" can be avoided only by a disclaimer that is written conspicuously and expressed in specific language. All implied warranties are excluded by expressions like "as is," "with all faults," or other language that in common understanding calls the buyer's attention to the exclusion and makes plain that there are no implied warranties.

Note that by making claims on a label or container, the seller undertakes that his goods will conform to the claims.

For a table of UCC warranty rules, see ¶3529.

[¶3512] FEDERAL WARRANTY STANDARDS

Notwithstanding UCC express and implied warranty provisions, the federal government has entered the field with the Magnuson-Moss Act (88 Stat. 2183, 15 USC §2301-2312, Supp. V. 1975). During debate in Congress on this warranty protection bill, it was described as "one of the most important pieces of consumer protection legislation . . . since the Federal Trade Commission Act itself was passed in 1914." The Act creates an entirely new body of federal law with respect to consumer warranties. However, the legislation does not displace pertinent provisions of the Uniform Commercial Code, state requirements that relate to labeling, or disclosure with respect to written warranties or performance not applicable to written warranties complying with the Magnuson-Moss legislation. Magnuson-Moss neither invalidates nor restricts any right or remedy of a consumer under state law or any other federal law, nor does it affect or impose liability on any person for personal injury or supersede any provision of state law regarding consequential damages for injury to the person, or other injury.

The Magnuson-Moss Act applies to consumer products which cost $15 or more. While the Act *does not require* that such products (or their components) be warranted by the manufacturer, it does impose specific duties upon manufacturers who have chosen to offer written warranties on consumer products.

[¶3513] DISCLOSURE REQUIREMENTS UNDER MAGNUSON-MOSS

For products costing more than $15, the following information must be included if a written warranty is supplied to the consumer.

❒ Who is entitled to the protection.

❒ Identification of the parts covered by the warranty.

❒ Indication of what will be done to correct defects or failures (including which items or services will be paid for by the warrantor and which expenses must be borne by the consumer).

❒ The date that the warranty becomes effective (unless it is the date of purchase).

❒ Steps the consumer must follow to obtain performance under the warranty (including a statement of the name of the warrantor, the mailing address, name and address of a department responsible for warranty obligations, or a telephone number that the consumer may use without charge to obtain information).

Separate warranty requirements cover the sale of used cars.

[¶3514] COVERAGE AND DEFINITIONS UNDER MAGNUSON-MOSS

Magnuson-Moss applies only to "consumer products," which means any tangible personal property normally used for personal, family, or household purposes (including any property that is intended to be attached or installed in any real property). Products purchased solely for commercial or industrial use are excluded.

[¶3515] PRESERVATION OF CONSUMER CLAIMS AND DEFENSES

As a means of giving consumers recourse when the goods that they purchase prove unsatisfactory, the Federal Trade Commission has promulgated rules to preserve certain consumer claims and defenses (16 CFR Part 433). The aim of the Federal Trade Commission's regulations is to insure that a seller fulfills all warranty obligations to the consumer by declaring it an unfair and deceptive practice for a seller in the course of financing a consumer purchase of goods to employ procedures (generally known as a "holder-in-due-course defense") that would make the consumer's duty to pay independent of the seller's duty to fulfill contractual obligations.

In the course of public proceedings, the FTC documented numerous cases in which consumer purchase transactions were financed in such a way that the consumer was legally obligated to make full payment to the creditor despite a breach of warranty, misrepresentation, or even fraud on the part of the seller. Previously, a seller was able to execute a credit contract with a buyer containing a promissory note that was subsequently assigned to a credit company—which took free of any claim or defense that the buyer might have had against the seller (such as breach of warranty). If local statutes prohibited the use of these promissory devices, some sellers inserted a "waiver of defense" in installment sale agreements. The FTC rules are designed to prevent widespread abuses of credit terms and preserve a consumer's legally sufficient claims and defenses so that they may be asserted to either defeat or diminish the right of a creditor to be paid whenever a seller who arranges financing for a buyer fails to keep his or her side of the bargain. The basic mechanism for accomplishing this is the requirement that a clause be placed in all consumer credit contracts that states, "Any holder of this consumer credit contract is subject to all claims and defenses which the debtor could assert against the seller of goods or services obtained . . ." (text varies according to circumstances, see 16 CFR Part 433.2, 1978).

[¶3516] WARRANTIES (UCC vs. MAGNUSON-MOSS)

It is important to distinguish between commercial obligations and those involving consumer transactions. The Magnuson-Moss Act, described at ¶3512 is applicable to all consumer goods costing $15 or more for which a written warranty is supplied by the seller. Under the Act, the seller is not required to give a written warranty,but if the seller so elects in a consumer transaction, certain requirements must be met, including a prohibition against disclaimer. For commercial transactions, the UCC governs, not Magnuson-Moss.

[¶3517] DESCRIPTION OF GOODS

Specifications, samples, models, or general descriptive language may be used as a means of describing the subject matter of a sales contract. To the extent that sample and technical specifications conflict, the latter prevails (UCC §2-317(a)). To the extent that a general description differs from a sample, the sample prevails for warranties either expressed or implied (UCC §2-317(b)). If a buyer relies on the seller's skill and judgment in either selecting or furnishing the goods (even if the seller did not know of this reliance, but had reason to know of its possibility), a warranty has been created (UCC §2-315). (See table at ¶3529).

Note that for consumer sales, the Magnuson-Moss Act requires that certain aspects of warranty be designated. The sellers of consumer products with written warranties are required to display the warranty conspicuously or to maintain a binder or series of binders in each department in which a consumer product with a written warranty is offered for sale or for inspection by consumers (16 CFR Part 702.3, 1976). Magnuson-Moss permits the disclaimer of consequential damages under a full warranty only if the exclusion on limitations appears conspicuously on the face of the warranty. It does not permit exclusion of consequential damages if state or other federal law does not so permit.

[¶3518] PRICE

It is possible for a contract of sale to be concluded without a price being specified. If this occurs, the price of the goods purchased will be a reasonable price at the time of the delivery (UCC §2-305(1)).

Below in checklist form are some of the more popular methods for determining price:

☐ **Cost Plus:** The plus factor here is overhead and profit, and any agreement should spell out precisely what is to be included in the cost factor.

☐ **Market Price:** Normally relates to the selling price on some organized mercantile or other exchange that is directly ascertainable.

☐ **Price in a Trade Journal:** If the journal ceases publication, the price is the reasonable price at the time of delivery.

☐ **Government-Related Price:** Used in time of price control or other regulatory schemes.

☐ **Price by Leading Suppliers:** Industry leaders' prices are used as a means of pegging the contract price. (It is important to avoid violation of antitrust trade regulations statutes.)

☐ **Price by Appraisal:** An expert in the field sets the price. Unless otherwise agreed, if this method fails, the price will be a reasonable price at the time of delivery.

☐ **Price to Be Agreed Upon:** Ordinarily, this means a fair market price. Should the parties fail to agree, UCC §2-305 requires a reasonable price unless the agreement indicates that the parties did not intend the contract to be made if there was no agreement on price.

☐ **Price Set by Seller:** UCC §2-305(2) requires that the seller use "good faith" in setting prices under this standard.

☐ **Escalator Clauses:** Use of standard price indices published by the U.S. Department of Labor, the Department of Commerce, or other recognized entities reflecting overall economic trends, including price rises, such as the Consumer Price Index or Wholesale Price Index.

☐ **Gold or Foreign Currency Clauses:** An agreement that payment be made in gold, foreign currency, or their dollar equivalents involves some risk that the price of gold or the exchange rate of a "stable" foreign currency is related more to speculation that cannot be anticipated than to actual economic conditions.

[¶3519] DELIVERY

In the absence of a specific agreement between the parties, the place of delivery will be the locale of the goods where they were identified to the agreement at the time the agreement was made. Where the goods were not identified to the agreement at the time the agreement was made, the place of delivery will be the seller's place of business, or if he has no place of business, his home, unless otherwise agreed (UCC §2-208).

Delivery terms are often spelled out in terms of standard commercial abbreviations. The following checklist of obligations arising from the use of these terms is based upon the definitions contained in the Uniform Commercial Code.

FOB (Place of Shipment): Unless otherwise agreed, the seller must ship the goods and bear the expense of putting the goods in the hands of the shipper. The seller must notify the buyer of the shipment and obtain and deliver necessary documents of title so as to enable the buyer to obtain possession. The buyer must reasonably give the seller proper shipping instructions (UCC §2-504 and 2-319).

FOB (Place of Destination): Unless otherwise agreed, the seller must at his own expense transport the goods to the place of destination, give the buyer reasonable notification to enable him to take delivery, tender delivery at a reasonable time, and keep the goods available for a reasonable time to permit the buyer to take possession (UCC §2-319 and 2-503).

FOB (Car or Other Vehicle): In addition to putting the goods in the possession of the carrier the seller must load them on board the truck, car, or other vehicle used by the carrier (UCC §2-319).

FOB (Vessel): The seller must place the goods on board the vessel designated by the buyer and furnish a proper form bill of lading in an appropriate case (UCC §2-319).

FAS (Vessel): The seller must, at his own expense, deliver the goods alongside the vessel designated by the buyer or on the dock designated in the manner usual in the particular port, and obtain a receipt in exchange for which the carrier is obligated to issue a bill of lading (UCC §2-319).

CIF: The price stated includes the cost of goods, insurance, and freight to the named destination. The seller is obligated to load the goods, obtain a receipt showing that the freight has been paid or provided for, obtain a negotiable bill of lading, insure the goods for the account of the buyer, and forward all necessary documents to the buyer with commercial promptness (UCC §2-320).

If delivery is to be made to the buyer, the buyer must furnish facilities reasonably suited for accepting delivery (UCC §2-503).

When goods are in a warehouse or otherwise in possession of a bailee and the agreement calls for delivery to the buyer without moving the goods, the seller must render a negotiable document of title or procure acknowledgment by the bailee or warehouseman of the buyer's right to possession of the goods. Unless the buyer objects, a nonnegotiable document of title or a written direction to the warehouseman or bailee to deliver is sufficient tender of delivery. When the bailee receives notice of the buyer's rights in the goods, those rights are fixed as to the bailee and all third persons. The risk of loss of the goods will not pass to the buyer until the buyer has had a reasonable time to present the document or direction to the warehouseman or bailee to deliver. If delivery is tendered in the form of a nonnegotiable document of title, the liability for the failure of the warehouseman to honor the document of title remains upon the seller until the buyer has had reasonable opportunity to present the document. Failure of the bailee to honor the document of title defeats the tender.

C & F or CF: These terms are equivalent to CIF, except that the price includes only the cost of goods plus freight to the named destination; insurance is not included. Otherwise, the terms impose the same duties on buyer and seller as under the CIF designation (UCC §2-320).

[¶3520] BUYER'S RIGHT OF INSPECTION

Upon tender of delivery or identification of goods, the UCC provides that a buyer has the right to inspect goods that are being purchased (UCC §2-513). If the contract requires payment prior to inspection, the nonconformity of the goods does not excuse the buyer unless the nonconformity appears without inspection (UCC §2-512). However, an agreement to pay against documents may be construed as waiving the buyer's right to inspection. When the parties have agreed to a C.O.D. delivery, the buyer is presumed to have waived any right of inspection prior to payment (UCC §2-513).

The right of inspection afforded by the UCC includes the right to inspect goods in any reasonable manner. Inspection may include testing, if the nature of the goods cannot be adequately determined without testing. If the testing by the buyer is unreasonable, such as when the buyer uses an extraordinary quantity of the goods in testing or performs needless tests, the testing itself may be construed as an acceptance. The cost of testing and inspecting will be borne by the buyer except if the goods fail to conform to the agreement. In that case, the UCC provides that the buyer may recover the reasonable cost of inspection and testing from the seller (UCC §2-513).

[¶3521] TIME OF DELIVERY

Using the standard of commercial reasonableness, the UCC provides that if the agreement is silent as to the time of delivery, it shall take place within a reasonable time (UCC §2-309). Even contract language calling for immediate delivery is construed as being reasonably thereafter. A "time is of the essence" clause (bargained for in the agreement) means what it says—a delayed delivery may be unacceptable and cause a breach of contract.

Late delivery will be excused if caused by the occurrence of a contingency, the nonoccurrence of which was a basic assumption on which the agreement was made, or the seller's compliance in good faith within the applicable governmental regulations whether or not the regulation later proves invalid (UCC §2-615). The UCC also provides that the seller's delay in delivery will be excused if performance is suspended due to the buyer's repudiation or the buyer's failure to cooperate as required in the agreement (UCC §2-311 and 2-611).

[¶3522] OPTIONS AS TO PERFORMANCE

If one party to an agreement has the right to specify the terms of performance, the UCC provides that if the specifications are made in good faith and within the limits of commercial standards of reasonableness, they will be upheld (UCC §2-311, Official Comment 1). When the agreement calls for the buyer to receive an assortment of goods, the buyer is permitted to determine the assortment, unless otherwise provided by the parties.

[¶3523] Right to Return

The buyer has the right to return goods if they fail to conform to the agreement. However, the agreement may specifically provide for the right to return goods. If the buyer has the right to return goods that he is purchasing for his own use, the contract is considered a sale on approval. If the buyer is purchasing the goods for resale, the contract is characterized as a sale or return (UCC §2-326). In a sale on approval, the obligation of return and the risk of loss are on the seller; in a sale or return, the obligation of return is on the buyer unless otherwise agreed (UCC §2-326 and §2-327). A "consignment" or "on memorandum" sale is characterized by the UCC as a sale or return.

[¶3524] Passage of Title

The importance of title in commercial transactions has been substantially reduced through promulgation of the Uniform Commercial Code. However, for purposes of delivery and other requirements, it is necessary to understand the applicability of certain rules set forth in the paragraphs below.

[¶3524.1 Seller Controls Performance

Title passes to the buyer when the seller has completed performance with regard to delivery of the goods to the buyer (UCC §2-401(2)).

For example, if the contract calls for delivery FOB cars at the seller's warehouse, title passes when the goods are placed on the cars at the seller's warehouse.

[¶3524.2] Seller to Ship

When the agreement requires the seller to send the goods to the buyer but does not require delivery at the place of destination, title to the goods passes to the buyer at the time and place of shipment (UCC §2-401(2)(a)).

For example, if the agreement calls for delivery FOB New York and the goods are to be shipped to San Francisco, title passes to the buyer when the goods are shipped from New York.

[¶3524.3] Seller to Deliver

If an agreement requires the seller to deliver the goods to the buyer at the place of destination, title to the goods passes to the buyer on delivery (UCC §2-401(2)(b)).

For example, if the agreement calls for delivery by the seller at the buyer's place of business, title passes when the goods are delivered.

[¶3524.4] Delivery Without Moving Goods—Document of Title

If delivery is to be made without moving the goods and the seller is required to deliver a document of title, title passes at the time and place where the document of title is delivered (UCC §2-401(e)(a)).

For example, if goods in a warehouse are sold with the understanding that delivery will be made by the delivery of a warehouse receipt by which the buyer may take possession of the goods, title passes on the delivery of the warehouse receipt by the seller to the buyer.

[¶3524.5] Delivery Without Moving Goods—No Document of Title

If delivery is to be made without moving the goods and the goods have been identified to the agreement at the time of making the agreement and no document of title is to be delivered, title to the goods passes to the buyer at the time of making the agreement (UCC §2-401(3)(b)).

For example, if the buyer agrees to purchase an identified machine located in the seller's yard, the title passes at the time of making the agreement, if nothing else remains to be done.

[¶3524.6] Withdrawal of Acceptance

If the buyer refuses to accept the goods or withdraws acceptance of the goods, title revests in the seller by operation of law (UCC §2-401(4)).

[¶3524.7] Sale on Approval

When goods are sold primarily for the use of the buyer rather than for resale, with the understanding that they may be returned, and the agreement is characterized as one of sale on approval, title passes to the buyer upon his or her approval (UCC §2-326 and §2-327).

For example, if the agreement calls for sale of a machine that the buyer will use in a manufacturing process, he or she may be given a reasonable time for trial. If there is approval after a reasonable trial, title passes upon approval or decision to keep it. Similarly, if there is no disapproval or rejection of the goods before the end of the prescribed trial period, title passes at the termination of that period.

[¶3525] RISK OF LOSS

Risk of loss is no longer part of the question of title: the UCC's major innovation in this area is the separation of these two principles. As a general rule, the Code's position on risk of loss is that the party that is best equipped to bear the loss (or the party who should be expected to bear it) will bear it. The following paragraphs set forth the rules derived from the UCC for determining risk of loss where the parties have not provided such items in the contract.

[¶3525.1] Goods to Be Delivered to Carrier

If the seller is required to deliver the goods to a carrier, the risk of loss shifts to the buyer when the seller duly delivers the goods to the carrier (UCC §2-509).

[¶3525.2] FOB—Place of Shipment

When goods are sold FOB place of shipment, the risk of loss shifts to the buyer when the goods are placed in the hands of the shipper (UCC §2-319).

[¶3525.3] FOB—Destination

For goods sold FOB place of destination, the risk of loss shifts to the buyer at the time and place of delivery or the time and place where tender of delivery is made to the buyer (UCC §2-319).

[¶3525.4] Seller to Deliver

If the seller must deliver the goods to the destination, the risk of loss shifts to the buyer when the delivery is tendered to the buyer to enable taking possession (UCC §2-509).

[¶3525.5] Sale or Return

If the goods are sold to the buyer for resale, rather than for the buyer's use, with the understanding that they may be returned, the risk of loss during the return is on the buyer (UCC §2-327).

[¶3525.6] Sale on Approval

If the goods are sold to a buyer primarily for his or her own use, rather than resale, and the agreement calls for a "sale on approval," the risk of loss shifts to the buyer when the buyer accepts the goods. If the goods are not accepted, the return is at the seller's risk (UCC §2-327).

[¶3525.7] Goods Fail to Conform

When goods delivered fail to conform to the requirements of the agreement, the risk of loss remains on the seller until the nonconformity is cured or the non-conforming goods are accepted by the buyer (UCC §2-510).

[¶3525.8] Buyer Revokes Acceptance

If the buyer initially accepts the goods but subsequently (and justifiably) revokes his acceptance, the buyer may treat the risk of loss as having rested on the seller to the extent of any deficiency in his or her insurance coverage (UCC §2-510).

[¶3525.9] Repudiation

If the buyer repudiates the agreement before title to the goods passes over, the seller may treat the risk of loss as having rested on the buyer for a commercially reasonable time. However, the buyer's liability is limited to the extent of any deficiency in the seller's effective insurance coverage (UCC §2-510).

[¶3525.10] Delivery of Goods at Buyer's Place of Business—Merchant Seller

If a merchant seller is to deliver the goods at the seller's place of business or the present location of the goods, the risk of loss passes to the buyer upon his or her receipt of the goods (UCC §2-509).

[¶3525.11] Delivery of Goods at Buyer's Place of Business—Non-Merchant Seller

If a non-merchant seller is to deliver the goods at the seller's place of business or at the present location of the goods to a non-merchant buyer, the risk of loss passes to the buyer ˙n tender of delivery (UCC §2-509).

[¶3525.12] Casualty to Identified Goods

When goods identified to the agreement are destroyed (without fault of the buyer or the seller) prior to the time the risk of loss would normally have shifted to the buyer, the risk of loss is on the seller. However, he may avoid the agreement if the destruction of the goods is total. If the destruction of the goods is partial, the buyer has the option of accepting the goods with a proper price concession or permitting the seller to void the agreement (UCC §2-613).

[¶3525.13] Nonconforming Goods

When the goods or their tender fail to conform to the agreement to an extent that the buyer would be entitled to reject the tender of delivery, the risk of loss remains on the seller until he or she has cured the defect, or the buyer has accepted (UCC §2-510(1)).

[¶3525.14] Revocation of Acceptance—Insurance Coverage

The buyer who rightly revokes a prior acceptance may, to the extent of any deficiency in effective insurance coverage, run the risk of loss as having been on the seller from the beginning (UCC §2-510(2)).

[¶3525.15] Repudiation—Insurance Coverage

When the buyer repudiates an agreement as to goods that conform to the agreement, the seller may treat the risk of loss as resting on the buyer to the extent of any deficiency in effective insurance coverage (UCC §2-510(3)).

[¶3525.16] Loss Caused by Third Party—Prior to Identification

If a loss is caused by a third party prior to the identification of the goods to the agreement, the seller may maintain an action against the third party (UCC §2-722).

[¶3525.17] Loss Caused by Third Party—After Identification

If a loss is caused by a third party after identification of the goods to the agreement, the seller and the buyer both may maintain an action against the third party. Regardless of who sues, any award goes to the one who bore the risk of loss at the time of loss (UCC §2-722(b)).

[¶3525.18] Intention of Parties

Whenever possible, courts will look to the intention of the parties to determine the risk of loss. For example, a manufacturer borrowed a gluing machine under circumstances showing that he intended to buy a larger machine. A court found an agreement to return the machine in the same condition and imposed the risk of loss on the borrower.

[¶3525.19] Usage of Trade

If it is the custom or usage of trade for an owner to assume the responsibility for insuring work in progress against risk of loss by fire, in the absence of inconsistent terms in the agreement of the parties, the owner bears the risk of loss.

[¶3525.20] Bailee Goods and Possession

Relinquishment of dominion and control so as to constitute delivery to a bailee for storage, as authorized by the buyer, is the ingredient normally required to shift risk of loss from the seller to the buyer.

[¶3526] Excused Performance

When goods are destroyed prior to the time the risk of loss shifts from the seller to the buyer, the agreement will be voided if they were identified to the agreement prior to their destruction and the destruction was without the fault of either party. If goods identified to the agreement when made are so deteriorated that they no longer conform to the requirements of the agreement or have been partially destroyed without the fault of either party, the buyer has the option of treating the contract as voided or accepting the goods with allowance for the deterioration or destruction (UCC §2-613).

The seller will be excused from performance if performance becomes commercially impracticable due to the occurrence of a contingency, the non-occurrence of which was a basic assumption on which the agreement was founded (UCC §2-615). Similarly, the seller's performance will be excused if his performance is rendered impracticable by compliance in good faith with any foreign or domestic governmental regulations.

When the inability to perform applies to only part of the seller's productive capacity, the UCC imposes an obligation on the seller to divide any remaining productive capacity among his or her customers. The seller must seasonably notify customers of their quota of his or her reduced capacity. Upon receipt of the seller's notification, if the prospective deficiency substantially impairs the value of the contract, the buyer has the option of terminating the agreement or accepting the quantity which the seller proposes to provide (UCC §2-616). The seller may include regular customers in the allocation of production whether or not there is a binding contractual obligation to supply them.

Deposits, Prepayments, and Liquidated Damages: The seller is entitled to keep the buyer's deposit if the buyer refuses to accept the goods or otherwise breaches the agreement, provided the deposit does not exceed either 20% of the buyer's obligation or $500 (whichever is smaller), unless the buyer has received a benefit or the seller has incurred damages. In such a case, the amount of the deposit that the seller may keep is increased to reflect the benefit or the damages. The UCC recognizes liquidated damages provided they are limited to an amount that is reasonable in light of the anticipated or actual harm caused by the breach. When an agreement calls for liquidated damages, the seller may keep the deposit if it does not exceed the liquidated damages (UCC §2-718).

[¶3527] MODIFICATION

The UCC provides that any modification of an agreement must be in writing if the statute of frauds requires that the agreement as modified be in writing. The parties may, however, agree that any modifications of a written agreement must be in writing even though the statute of frauds does not require it (UCC §2-209).

In transactions involving merchants, a provision requiring written modifications must be separately signed by the party receiving the form if that provision appears in a form supplied by the other party.

[¶3528] ASSIGNMENT

Sellers may delegate their obligation to perform unless the buyer has a substantial interest in having the original seller perform (or control the performance). Assignment, unless specifically prohibited by the terms of agreement, is permissible, although delegation will not relieve the seller of any duty to perform, or prevent liability for breach on failure to perform (UCC §2-210).

All rights of the seller or the buyer arising out of an agreement governed by the UCC may be assigned unless: the assignment would materially change the duty of the other party; materially increase the burden of risk imposed upon the other party by the contract; or materially impair the chance of the other party obtaining return performance. The right to assign may be restricted by the parties in their agreement. It is essential to note that the Magnuson-Moss Act gives consumers a right of redress against assignees of their consumer credit contracts—thus, the so-called "holder-in-due-course" defense is not available to the innocent purchaser for the value of a consumer's debt, which is sometimes repudiated when a consumer is dissatisfied with the merchantability of the product (¶3515).

[¶3529] WARRANTY

The following table summarizes the UCC warranty rules:

WARRANTIES UNDER THE UNIFORM COMMERCIAL CODE

	Warranty	*Method of Exclusion*
Warranty of Title	Seller warrants that good title is conveyed and that title will be free of any security interest or lien of which the buyer is unaware (UCC §2-312). The warranty of title may be breached by disturbance of quiet possession.	Excluded only by specific language indicating that if the seller does not claim title in himself or that he is selling only the title or rights that he has.
Warranty Against Infringement	A merchant warrants that goods that he sells are free of infringement. A buyer, if he has provided detailed specifications, agrees to hold the seller harmless against infringement (UCC §2-312).	May be excluded by agreement.
Warranty of Merchant-ability	A merchant warrants that goods will be merchantable (UCC §2-314). To be merchantable, goods must: (a) Pass without objection in the trade under the contract description. (b) Be fit for the ordinary purposes for which such goods are used. (c) Run with an even kind of quality and quantity. (d) Be adequately packaged and labeled as required by the agreement. (e) Conform to promises or statements on the label.	Excluded only by language expressly mentioning merchantability. In a written contract, the exclusion must be conspicuous (UCC §2-316).
Course of Dealing; Usage of Trade	Course of dealing or usage of trade may give rise to an implied warranty based on a particular course of dealing or usage of trade (UCC §2-314).	May be excluded or modified by agreement.

	Warranty	Method of Exclusion
Service of Food	The service of food in a restaurant implies a warranty that goods will be merchantable and fit for consumption.	
Fit for Particular Purpose	If a merchant has reason to know any particular purpose for which goods are required and the buyer is relying on the seller's judgment or skill, he warrants that the goods are fit for that purpose (UCC §2-315).	May be excluded by conspicuous language excluding implied warranties, such as "There are no warranties which extend beyond the description on the face hereof" (UCC §2-316).
Sale by Description	If goods are sold by a description that becomes part of the basis of the transaction, there is an express warranty that they will conform to the description. The description need not be words but may be technical specifications, blueprints, etc. (UCC §2-313).	Language excluding warranties and descriptive language are to be construed as consistent with each other whenever reasonable (UCC §2-316). General language of disclaimer will not disclaim the warranties of description if the disclaimer is inconsistent with the description.
Sale by Sample	A sample or model, if part of the basis of the agreement, will create an express warranty that the goods delivered will conform to the sample. Exact or technical specifications displace a sample if there is a conflict. A sample from existing bulk displaces inconsistent general language of description (UCC §2-317).	General language of disclaimer will not disclaim the warranties that arise from a sale by sample, if the disclaimer is inconsistent with the sample.
Express Warranty by Affirmation of Fact or Promise	Any affirmation of fact or promise made by the seller to the buyer that relates to the goods and becomes part of the basis of the bargain becomes an express warranty. Mere statement of opinion as salesman's talk does not (UCC §2-313). It is not necessary that specific language of guarantee or warranty be used to create an express warranty.	Express warranties may be excluded or limited by agreement.

	Warranty	Method of Exclusion
Warranty to Third Parties of Consumer Goods	UCC §2-318 Alternative A extends warranty coverage to a buyer, his family, and reasonably foreseeable users who are household members or guests who sustain personal injuries. Alternative B provides coverage for personal injuries sustained by any reasonably foreseeable user. Alternative C expands Alternative B to include property damage. Refer to state law for the applicable provision.	A seller may not exclude or limit the operation of this section (UCC §2-318).
When There is No Warranty	If the agreement uses language "as is" or "with all faults" or other language that calls to the buyer's attention the exclusion of warranties, no warranty arises. If the seller examines the goods or is given an opportunity to examine the goods and refuses, no warranty will arise as to defects that the examination revealed or should have revealed (UCC §2-316).	

[¶3530] WARRANTY AND PRIVITY

Under certain circumstances, consumer goods purchased by an individual carry a warranty that extends to consumers other than the purchaser—frequently, members of the consumer's household or those who might reasonably be expected to come in contact with the goods, such as a repairman or guest. In some jurisdictions, there is still a requirement of privity of contract. In this situation, a relationship between the injured party claiming under the breach of warranty and the seller must be shown. It is important to consult local law to determine the applicable status in this regard, including the most current judicial decisions.

[¶3531] SELLER'S REMEDIES

Just as the buyer has various means of assuring performance, the seller also requires various means of dealing with prospective purchasers under a variety of circumstances. The seller's remedies under the UCC are spelled out in the following paragraphs.

[¶3531.1] Buyer's Insolvency

When the seller learns of the buyer's insolvency, the seller may:

(1) Stop delivery unless the goods have been received by the buyer, acknowledgment has been made by a warehouseman to the buyer, the goods have been reshipped by the carrier (which constitutes an acknowledgment to the buyer that the carrier holds the goods for the buyer), or the carrier has notified the buyer, in which case he was holding the goods as a warehouseman for the buyer rather than as a carrier.

The seller must notify the carrier with reasonable diligence in time to enable a stop to the shipment. If a negotiable document of title is involved, it should be presented to the carrier with the order to stop shipment (UCC §2-705).

(2) Withhold delivery if the goods have not been shipped and wait for the buyer to prepay, even though the contract called for shipment on credit (UCC §2-702).

(3) Reclaim the goods if they were received while the buyer was insolvent, provided notice is given within 10 days. The 10-day limitation does not apply if the buyer has falsely represented solvency to the seller within three months of delivery (UCC §2-705).

See also the discussion of bankruptcy beginning at ¶701.

[¶3531.2] Buyer's Repudiation of Agreement

When the buyer repudiates the agreement, the seller may:

(1) Withhold delivery.

(2) Stop delivery if the goods have not been delivered to the buyer, provided the shipment meets the quantity requirements spelled out in the UCC; i.e., carload, truckload, ship, etc.

(3) Identify and sell conforming goods as well as recover damages for the difference between the resale price and the contract price.

(4) Recover damages for repudiation. When there is an established market price, the damages are the difference between the market price and the contract-

price at the time and place for the tentative delivery together with incidental damages but less any expenses saved as a result of the buyer's breach (UCC §2-708(1)). Incidental damages include commercially reasonable charges, expenses, or commissions incurred in stopping shipment; commercially reasonable charges, expenses, or commissions incurred in transportation or care of goods after breach; commercially reasonable charges, expenses, or commissions incurred in resale or return of goods; other commercially reasonable charges, expenses, or commissions resulting from the breach. If there is no established market at a place specified for tender, the market price at another locale is substituted, although adjustment is made for transportation differentials. When the damages computed by the difference between contract price and market price are inadequate (i.e., fail to put the seller in as good a position as he or she would have been had the buyer not repudiated), the UCC permits the seller to recover the profit that would have been made from full performance (§2-710 and 2-708(2)).

Cancellation after the buyer's repudiation does not extinguish the seller's right to proceed against the buyer for damages (UCC §2-106 and §2-703).

If the contract is repudiated after acceptance by the buyer, the seller may maintain an action for the price. An action for the price may also be maintained when the seller has been unable to resell goods identified to the agreement at a reasonable price or the circumstances indicate that efforts to resell would be fruitless. A seller who maintains an action for the price must remain prepared to deliver the goods. However, if an opportunity arises to sell the goods, he or she may do so and deduct the resale price from any claim (UCC §2-709).

A resale must be made in good faith and in a commercially reasonable manner, under the terms outlined in the main text (UCC §2-706).

(5) Suspend performance and await withdrawal of the repudiation for a commercially reasonable time and demand adequate assurance of performance.

The seller must suspend performance if he or she has not finished the goods and the completion of the goods or the completion of performance would result in a material increase in damages.

[¶3531.3] Buyer's Failure to Cooperate

When the buyer fails to cooperate as required by the agreement (i.e., fails to specify assortment or give needed instruction, etc.), a seller may follow any of these three courses:

(1) Delay performance without incurring any liability for breach by reason of late delivery.

(2) Proceed to perform in a commercially reasonable manner.

(3) Treat the failure to cooperate as a breach of the agreement (UCC §2-610).

[¶3531.4] Buyer's Refusal to Accept Conforming Goods

If the buyer refuses to accept conforming goods or wrongfully withdraws acceptance of conforming goods, the seller may resell the goods and recover damages. Damages constitute the difference between the contract price and the resale price less any expenses saved as a result of the breach, but including any costs incurred in reselling (UCC §§2-703 and §2-706).

[¶3531.5] Resale

The UCC authorizes, as an element of resale costs, reasonable commission charges and transportation charges plus other incidental damages (UCC §2-701).

When goods are resold, the UCC rules for resale must be followed. However, resale need not be by public sale.

A private sale is justifiable depending on the circumstances, except that the buyer must be notified of the sale. The seller must use reasonable efforts to get the highest possible price for the goods.

For goods resold at auction, the sale must be held at the usual place or market for selling such goods if one is available. The goods must also be available for inspection prior to or at the sale (UCC §2-706).

[¶3531.6] Damages

Generally speaking, damages are measured by the difference between market price (at the time and place specified for delivery) and the contract price, provided such damages are adequate to put the seller in as good a position as he or she would have been had the buyer accepted the goods (instead of wrongfully rejecting conforming goods or wrongfully withdrawing acceptance of conforming goods). In that case, the seller is entitled to at least the profits that would have been made if the buyer had accepted the goods and fully performed the agreement.

The seller may also bring an action for the price for goods that are not readily resalable or may cancel the contract (UCC §2-708).

[¶3532] BUYER'S REMEDIES

Purchasers coping with insolvent sellers, repudiation of contracts, and nonconforming goods also have remedies under the Uniform Commercial Code. These are explored in the paragraphs below.

[¶3532.1] Seller's Insolvency

When the buyer learns that the seller is insolvent, he or she may:

(1) Demand adequate assurance of performance if there are reasonable grounds for feeling insecure about the seller's ability to perform.

If the seller fails to give adequate assurance of performance, the buyer may cancel;cancellation will not relieve the seller of the obligations under the contract.

(2) Recover deposits and prepayments by making provision to obtain the goods elsewhere and recover the difference between the cost of covering and the contract price from the seller.

The buyer also is entitled to recover reasonable expenses from the seller (UCC §§2-609 and 2-711).

[¶3532.2] Seller's Repudiation

If the seller repudiates the agreement, the buyer may:

(1) Cancel and thereby be relieved of any obligation to perform. Cancellation will not relieve the seller of any obligation under the agreement.

The buyer may also recover damages in the amount of the difference between the contract price and the market price (determined at the time the buyer learned of the breach). He or she may cover by making other provision to obtain the goods.

The buyer is entitled to recover from the seller the loss incurred by covering, including reasonable commissions and expenses incurred in covering.

(2) Obtain specific performance if the agreement involves unique goods.

(3) Recover the goods if they were identified to the agreement prior to the seller's repudiation if, after reasonable effort, the buyer is unable to effect cover or the circumstances reasonably indicate that an attempt to effect cover would be useless (UCC §§2-610 and 2-711—2-713).

[¶3532.3] Goods That Fail to Conform

If goods fail to conform to written terms of the agreement, a buyer has three basic alternatives:rejection of performance, acceptance of performance, or cancellation. These three remedies are explored in the paragraphs below.

[¶3532.4] Rejection of Performance

In the case of an installment contract, the buyer's rights to reject the entire contract, due to nonconformity of one or more installments, are limited to instances where the nonconformity substantially impairs the value of the whole contract (UCC §2-612).

When the buyer elects to reject the goods, the rejection must be made within a reasonable time after delivery and the buyer must reasonably notify the seller of rejection. If the goods are in the buyer's physical possession when rejected, the buyer has an obligation to hold them with reasonable care at the seller's disposition to permit the seller to recover the goods.

A buyer who is a merchant normally dealing in goods of the kind called for in the contract may have a duty to follow reasonable instructions (regarding their care) from a seller who has no agent or place of business in the buyer's locale (UCC §2-608).

[¶3532.5] Acceptance of Performance

Acceptance does not extinguish other available remedies unless the buyer fails to notify the seller of the nonconformity within a reasonable time.

If the buyer accepts nonconforming goods he or she cannot return them because of the nonconformity if the buyer knows of the nonconformity at the time of acceptance or should have discovered it by reasonable inspection (UCC §2-607).

[¶3532.6] Cancellation of Performance

After refusing to accept nonconforming goods, without extinguishing rights to cover or recover damages from the seller (UCC §2-106), a buyer may cancel or may also cover by making other provision to obtain the goods (see ¶332.2).

A buyer who does not cover may be entitled to recover the difference between the market price and the contract price plus incidental and consequential damages.

Incidental damages might include any of the following: expenses reasonably incurred in inspecting the nonconforming goods; expenses reasonably incurred in the receipt of nonconforming goods; expenses reasonably incurred in transporting the nonconforming goods; loss resulting from general or particular requirements and needs of which the seller had reason to know at the time of entering into the agreement and that could not have been prevented by cover (UCC §2-715).

— **FOR FURTHER REFERENCE** —

Anderson, Roy Ryden, "Market-Based Damages for Buyers Under the Uniform Commercial Code," 6 *Rev. of Litigation* 1 (Winter '87).

Casey, Robert M., "An Economic View of the UCC Seller's Damage Measures and the Identification of the Lost-Volume Seller," 49 *Albany L. Rev.* 889 (Summer '85).

Hawkland, William D., "Sales Contract Terms Under the UCC," 17 *Uniform Commercial Code L.J.* 195 (Winter '85).

Hillinger, Ingrid Michelsen, "The Article 2 Merchant Rules," 73 *Georgetown L.J.* 1141 (April '85).

Kullby, Roy S. and Stephen K. Smith, "Jury Instructions in Sales Litigation," 33 *Practical Lawyer* 31 (July '87).

Lavers, Richard M., "Contracts for the International Sale of Goods," 60 *Wisconsin Bar Bulletin* 11 (November '87).

Meanor, Frank G., "Commercial Law: Application of the UCC Statute of Frauds to Hybrid Contracts for both Goods and Services," 16 *Creighton L. Rev.* 926 (Fall '83).

Robertson, R.J. Jr., "Rights and Obligations of Buyers with Respect to Goods in Their Possession After Rightful Rejection of Justifiable Revocation of Acceptance," 60 *Indiana L.J.* 663 (Fall '85).

Squillante, Alphonse M., "Uniform Commercial Code Bibliography," 91 *Commercial L.J.* 290 (Summer '86).

SECURED TRANSACTIONS

[¶3601] Under the Uniform Commercial Code (Article 9, Secured Transactions), a security interest includes pledges, conditional sales contracts, liens, chattel mortgages, trust receipts, and all other security devices used to secure a monetary obligation with personal property.

Throughout secured transactions, the keystone is who will have priority. It is sometimes said that the acid test is whether the secured creditor's claim will stand up against a federal tax lien. (See ¶4101 et seq. for an additional discussion on federal tax liens.) In addition, at the time a secured transaction is contemplated, the following risks should be taken into account: destruction of the goods, loss of value, expense of litigation to collect in default.

From a purely legal standpoint, the greatest security is the creditor's actual possession of the collateral, as is the case in a pledge. This eliminates the risk that the debtor will wrongfully deal with the property or that creditors of the debtor will be able to claim an interest by reason of the debtor's apparently unencumbered ownership. But practical business necessities in most instances demand that the security be left in the possession of the debtor and that he be permitted to use it or try to sell it.

There are presently two versions of UCC Article 9, the 1962 version and the 1972 version. Missouri and Vermont are the only states maintaining the 1962 version of Article 9. Louisiana, the long-time holdout, adopted portions of the UCC—but not Article 2 or Article 9—in 1974 and 1978. The other states follow the 1972 version of Article 9.

[¶3602] DEFINITIONS (SECURED TRANSACTIONS)

Among the important terms that frequently recur in the area of secured transactions are the following:

❏ *Account:* A right to payment for goods or services rendered.

❏ *Account Debtor:* An individual obligated on a contract right, general intangible, chattel paper, or account.

❏ *Chattel Paper:* Evidence of a monetary obligation and security interest in specific goods.

❏ *Consumer Goods:* Those used or bought primarily for personal, family, or household purposes.

❏ *Contract Right:* A right to payment on an unperformed contract.

❏ *Equipment:* Goods used or bought primarily for use in business (including farming and professions), or if the goods do not fit under the definitions of consumer goods, farm products, or inventory.

❏ *Farm Products:* Crops, livestock, or unmanufactured products of crops or livestock (such as eggs, maple syrup, or wool-clips) that are used or produced in farming operations, if they are in the possession of a farmer-debtor (for example, one who engages in raising, fattening, grazing, or other farming operations).

❏ **General Intangibles:** Personal property (including choses in action) other than goods, contract rights, negotiable instruments, or accounts.

❏ **Inventory:** Goods held for the purpose of sale, lease, or to be furnished under service contracts, or for work in progress for eventual use in business (i.e., raw materials).

❏ **Purchase-Money Security Interest:** An interest taken or retained by the seller of collateral to secure a portion or all of the purchase price of the collateral; or held by a financing agency when it has advanced money to the seller in exchange for an assignment of the chattel paper of the transaction; or when the financing agency or an individual has made an advance to the buyer for the purpose of purchasing the collateral.

[¶3603] MAXIMUM PROTECTION UNDER THE UCC

In secured transactions, there are three critical goals that must be achieved to afford maximum protection. The aim is to be sure that the security interest:
(1) Attaches,
(2) Is perfected, and
(3) Has priority over conflicting interests.

[¶3604] HOW A SECURITY INTEREST ATTACHES

A security interest, *attaches* when there is an agreement between the parties that will attach, value (including the satisfaction of a preexisting debt) has been given, the debtor has acquired rights in the collateral, and the agreement has been put in writing (UCC §9-203).

[¶3605] PERFECTION

Perfection of a security interest, required under the UCC in order to have a recorded priority, may be accomplished by one of two means. A creditor either takes possession of the collateral or files a financing statement in a required place—either at a centrally located office within the state or in an individual county, depending on the jurisdiction. Certain security interests are automatically perfected under the UCC; principal among those interests is a purchase-money security interest in consumer goods other than motor vehicles requiring registration (UCC §§9-113, 9-203, and 9-302).

[¶3606] STEP-BY-STEP PROCEDURE TO OBTAIN MAXIMUM PROTECTION

Following are four basic rules that should be followed in order to protect a seller against improperly filing and perfecting a security interest:

(1) Do not make any advance unless all of the requirements below for creating a perfected and enforceable security interest have previously been met or are thereby met. In addition, before the advance is made, be satisfied that the debtor's rights in the collateral are adequate.

(2) If the security interest is to be perfected by possession, at the time that the advance is made, the creditor or the creditor's bailee should have actual possession of the collateral. There should be no other currently existing security interest in the collateral, including any that had been perfected through filing.

(3) If the security interest is to be perfected by filing, the lender should be satisfied (a) that at the time the advance is made the collateral is not held by or for another secured party; (b) that at the time the advance is made there is no other perfected security interest in existence; and, equally important, (c) that at the time of the secured party's filing there is on record no financing statement with an earlier filing date that mentions any "type" of collateral into which the collateral could fit. If, for example, an earlier financing statement on file mentioned "machinery" or "equipment" or the like, a security interest created later (even under an agreement not yet contemplated) could be perfected through the earlier filing, and under the UCC's "first-to-file" rule would take priority over the earlier perfected interest.

(4) Regardless of the method of perfection, the lender must be satisfied that at the time of the advance there is no federal tax lien or other statutory lien (whether for taxes or other purposes) on the debtor's property that might come ahead of his security interest.

(5) Make sure that a correct filing is made in all the required places. This is especially important in multi-state transactions (UCC §9-103). State-to-state variations are especially dramatic with respect to filing; check the relevant state(s)' version of 9-403.

[¶3607] CHECKLIST FOR SECURITY AGREEMENTS

Every security agreement should be signed by the debtor and should contain the following basic information:
- ❏ What is the collateral?
- ❏ Does the debtor own the collateral free of any other security interests?
- ❏ Is the collateral in the debtor's possession at the present time?
- ❏ Are there prior liens on other assets of the debtor?
- ❏ Is there notice of a federal tax lien against the debtor?

❒ If a corporation is involved, have proper resolutions been passed to make the agreement enforceable and effective?

❒ Is after-acquired collateral contemplated?

❒ How are the goods characterized under Article 9:

    (1) Goods—farm products, farm equipment, inventory, or consumer goods.

    (2) Documents of title, stocks, bonds, notes, chattel paper.

    (3) Accounts or general intangibles.

    (4) Are the goods likely to become fixtures (of attached real estate)?

    (5) Should proceeds be identified at the outset?

    (6) Is a purchase-money security interest involved?

❒ Language sufficient to embody a "security agreement" (UCC §9-203).

❒ Potential claims of debtor's spouse or ex-spouse on the collateral.

❒ Check with the loan note for conflicts; make sure the loan note satisfies any applicable Truth-in-Lending requirements.

[¶3608] IDENTIFICATION OF COLLATERAL

Express identification of collateral that is the subject of a secured transaction is prescribed by UCC §9-110, which merely requires information that could "reasonably identify what is described." Ordinarily, for specific machinery, the manufacturer's name and machine's serial number should be included.

[¶3609] HOW TO MAKE THE SEARCH AND THE ADVANCE

Search the UCC filing records and any applicable pre-UCC chattel security record in order to supplement the debtor's representations. The search, of course, should not be limited to present security interests, but must include present filings under which any future security interests could be perfected. Although filing the financing statement may be done at the same time that a search is conducted, the date that the financing statement is filed does not control all priorities if, between that date and the date value is given, a conflicting lien is obtained by legal proceedings or a federal tax lien is filed. Since the actual date of perfection of each security interest may control priorities between them, the debtor could wrongfully create a possessory lien between the time of filing and the time value is given.

Searching the file is not a perfect check; conceivably a filing could have been made in another district or state where the goods were then located. No legal record would disclose that the equipment was stolen goods, or was subject to a possessory security interest, or was the property of a lessor. Here the secured party must rely on credit investigation, checking the location of the property, a bill of sale or the like, rather than legal records.

A commitment to make an advance constitutes value just as well as the actual making of the advance. Any commitment obviously should be made subject to the condition that the debtor's claims to the collateral are satisfactory at the time the advance is actually made.

[¶3610] Effectiveness of a Secured Interest

The effectiveness of a secured interest will vary with the degree of priority it is deemed to have. Prompt filing is therefore advisable as priority is generally ranked on a "first-to-file" basis. For example, a *prior unsecured possessory interest* will not prevail (even if it is later secured) over an *earlier secured interest* (UCC §9-301 *et seq.*).

[¶3611] After-Acquired Property

Generally, after-acquired property clauses are valid under the UCC (UCC §9-204); that is, the underlying obligation and/or future advances can be secured by goods acquired by the debtor after the security agreement is signed.

[¶3612] Inapplicability of After-Acquired Property Clauses

An after-acquired property clause may not be used in a security agreement concerning consumer goods unless the debtor gets rights to them within 10 days after the secured party gives value (UCC §9-204); or unless the consumer goods qualify as "accessions" under §9-314 (that is, they are installed or affixed to other consumer goods).

[¶3613] The Floating Lien

Floating liens are secured transactions on a shifting stock of goods or inventory. The collateral is in constant flux, undergoing quantitative and qualitative changes, but the lien holder nonetheless retains the security interest. It is no longer necessary to resort to field warehousing in connection with inventory financing, although the lender may still wish to police the collateral as an additional protection device. Even though the UCC permits floating liens, there is no guarantee that the secured creditor will have priority over all liens subsequently attaching or perfected in the same collateral. It may be subordinate to purchase-money interests or federal tax liens.

[¶3614] Future Advances

The UCC makes it clear that you can have a valid security interest in collateral to secure amounts to be advanced in the future, whether or not the advances are to be made pursuant to prior commitment (§9-204(3)).

[¶3615] Purchase-Money Interests

Purchase-money security interests have important preferential rights under the Uniform Commercial Code. In some instances (consumer goods, for example) a security interest may be perfected without filing (§9-302(1)); when filing is required, a grace period of 10 days is allowed against creditors and transferees in bulk (§9-301(2)); and the purchase-money interest may take priority over conflicting security interests under an after-acquired property clause (§9-312(3), (4)).

To get the preferred status, it is not necessary that the secured party be the seller of the collateral; it is enough that he or she gives value to enable the debtor to acquire rights in or the use of the collateral if such value is in fact used for either purpose (UCC §9-107(b)). The best way for a lender to be protected is to pay the seller directly.

[¶3616] Priorities Under the UCC

Special rules under UCC Article 9 affect creditors' priorities. These are covered in the subparagraphs below. Even for states that have adopted the amended Article 9 (1972 revision), some substantive law areas have changed. Therefore, local law should be consulted.

[¶3616.1] Goods Covered by Documents

While goods are in the possession of the issuer of a negotiable document covering the goods, a security interest in the goods is perfected by perfecting a security interest in the document (UCC §9-304(2)).

[¶3616.2] Proceeds

The secured party has a security interest in identifiable proceeds of collateral. But an interest in proceeds becomes unperfected 10 days after receipt by the debtor unless the filed financing statement also covers proceeds or the secured party gets possession within a 10-day period. In the event of the debtor's insolvency, the secured party's interest in the proceeds may extend under some conditions to cash and bank accounts of the debtor without regard to whether or not the funds are identifiable as cash proceeds of the collateral (UCC §9-306(2)-(4)).

[¶3616.3] Repossessions

Goods that were subject to a security interest and then sold are resubjected to the prior security interest if they are returned to the seller. This interest is superior to the security interest of the assignee of the account created by the sale. However, a transferee of the chattel paper created by the sale may have a superior security interest (UCC §9-306(5) and §9-308).

[¶3616.4] Buyers of Goods Protected

Generally, a buyer in the ordinary course of business takes free of the security interest even if it is perfected and he or she knows about it. In the case of consumer goods a bona fide purchaser for value who has no knowledge of the security interest, buying for personal, family, or household use, takes free of an *unfiled* security interest (UCC §9-307).

[¶3616.5] Purchaser of Chattel Paper or Nonnegotiable Instruments

A purchaser (including holder of security interest (§1-201(32),(33)) who gives new value and takes possession in the ordinary course of business and without knowledge has priority over prior security interest perfected by filing or temporary perfection without filing. The purchaser also has priority over a security interest in chattel paper that is claimed merely as proceeds of inventory, even though he or she knows of prior interest (UCC §9-308).

[¶3616.6] Purchasers of Instruments and Documents

A holder in due course of a negotiable instrument, a holder to whom a negotiable document of title has been duly negotiated, or a bona fide purchaser of a security takes priority over an earlier security interest even though it was perfected (UCC §9-309). An Article 9 filing does not constitute notice of the security interest to the holders or purchasers.

[¶3616.7] Liens by Operation of Law

Common law or statutory liens for services or materials have priority, unless a statute provides otherwise (UCC §9-310).

[¶3616.8] Crops

A party who gives new value within three months before planting, in order to enable the debtor to produce the crops, has priority over an earlier security interest in the crops that secures an obligation that is due more than six months before planting (UCC §9-312(2)).

[¶3616.9] Purchase-Money Security Interests

A purchase-money security interest has priority over a conflicting security interest in collateral other than inventory, if it's perfected within 10 days after the debtor receives the collateral. If the collateral is inventory, it has priority over a conflicting security interest if it's filed and notice to other known or filed security interests is given before the debtor receives the collateral (UCC §9-312(3), (4)). Also, UCC §9-301(2) provides that if a purchase-money security interest is filed within 10 days after the debtor takes possession of the collateral, it takes priority over the rights of a transferee in bulk or of a lien creditor arising between the time the security interest attaches and is filed.

[¶3616.10] Fixtures

A security interest *attaching to goods before they become fixtures* is superior to all prior claims in the real estate and also to all subsequent claims in the real estate, if it is filed before the later claims arise. A security interest in goods *attaching after they become fixtures* is superior only to subsequent interests in the real estate if filed before the later claims arise, or to prior claimants who have consented in writing to the security interest in the goods as fixtures (UCC §9-313). Both types of security interest, those attaching before and those attaching after the goods become fixtures, are subject to the interest of a prior construction mortgage of record (UCC §9-313(6)), if the goods became fixtures before construction was completed.

[¶3616.11] Goods Attached to Other Goods—Accessions

A security interest in goods attaching before the goods become accessions is superior to prior claims in the goods to which they are attached and is also superior to subsequent claims in the whole goods, if it is filed before the later claims arise. If the security interest attaches after the goods have become accessions, it is superior only to subsequent interests in the whole if it is filed before the subsequent interests arise. Both types of interest in accessions are subject to the subsequent advances contracted for under a prior perfected security interest (UCC §9-314).

[¶3616.12] Commingled or Processed Goods

A perfected interest in goods that become part of a product or mass continues in the product or mass if (a) the goods lose their identity in processing, or (b) the financing statement covers the product. When more than one interest attaches to the mass or product, they rank equally in proportion to their cost contribution to the mass (UCC §9-315).

[¶3616.13] Unperfected Security Interests vs. Various Third Parties

An unperfected security interest is subordinate to the rights of:

(a) Persons entitled to priority under the special rules discussed above or the general rules of priority in UCC §9-312;

(b) A person who becomes a lien creditor before the security interest is perfected;

(c) In the case of goods, instruments, documents, and chattel paper, a person who is not a secured party and who is a transferee in bulk or other buyer not in the ordinary course of business to the extent that he or she gives value and *receives* delivery of the collateral without knowledge of the security interest and before it is perfected;

(d) In the case of accounts and general intangibles, a person who is not a secured party and who is a transferee to the extent that he or she gives value without knowledge of the security interest and before it is perfected.

These rules are subject to the rule that if the secured party files with respect to a purchase-money interest within 10 days after the collateral comes into possession of the debtor, he or she takes priority over the rights of a transferee in bulk or of a lien creditor arising between the time the purchase-money interest attached and was perfected (UCC §9-301).

[¶3617] Special Rules for Special Types of Collateral

While most of the provisions of Article 9 apply regardless of the type of collateral involved, some sections state special rules for particular types of collateral. The Official Comments following §9-102 set forth a complete index of these special rules for various types of collateral, more specifically, accounts, chattel paper, documents and instruments, general intangibles, goods, consumer goods, equipment, farm products, and inventory.

[¶3618] Insurance for Creditors

Insurance for creditors is sometimes deemed essential in a secured transaction, particularly when field warehousing is undertaken or when the creditor has possession of the debtor's goods. (See ¶2511 et seq. for additional information.)

[¶3619] Default

When a debtor defaults under a security agreement, the proceedings are governed by Part 5 of Article 9 (UCC §9-501 et seq.). Under the UCC, the secured party may reduce a claim to judgment, foreclose, or enforce the security interest by any available judicial procedure. Unless otherwise agreed between the parties, a secured party has the right to take possession of the collateral when the debtor defaults. This may be done *without* judicial process if it can be accomplished without a breach of the peace. Alternatively, the second party is permitted to render equipment unusable in the event of default (UCC §9-503).

Following default, a secured party may sell, lease, or otherwise dispose of collateral. Proceeds must then be applied in the following order: to reasonable expenses for the retaking, holding, and selling of the collateral (plus reasonable attorney's fees—usually no more than 20%); satisfaction of the indebtedness secured by the security interest; satisfaction of indebtedness secured by any subordinate security agreement (junior debtors). Under all circumstances, the secured party must account to the debtor for any surplus above the amount that the agreement secures. The debtor is liable for any deficiency. (If the underlying secured transaction is the sale of a contract right or chattel paper or other "paper" sale, the debtor is not entitled to any surplus—and is not liable for any deficiency, unless the security agreement expressly provides for it (UCC §9-504).

Disposition of collateral may be done publicly or privately. Commercial reasonableness and notice to the debtor are the key ingredients (§9-504(3)). Notice to the debtor is required unless a perishable commodity is involved or there is a recognized market on which it may be sold. This is designed to protect the debtor from a secured party's selling a particular item at an unusually low price and then holding the debtor liable for the difference. Purchasers of items sold by a secured party take free and clear of all rights and interests that the debtor may have had—even if the secured party fails to comply with the requirements of the UCC or any judicial proceedings (UCC §9-504).

[¶3620] CONSTITUTIONAL PROBLEMS

Some very serious constitutional problems have resulted in the area of secured transactions as they relate to consumer-debtors. Principally, they relate to the ability of a secured creditor to seize collateral of the debtor without notice upon default, or when the secured creditor feels "insecure." This particular area of the law is in a state of flux, and the practitioner is well advised not only to consult local law, but also to keep abreast of pronouncements from the Supreme Court. To the extent possible, it is inevitably wiser for the practitioner to make use of judicial remedy than to exercise self-help. At least in the case of an individual, it is clear that consumers have rights beyond those spelled out in Article 9 of the UCC. (See ¶3501 et seq. for additional discussion of consumers' rights.) Courts tend to look with a somewhat less critical eye on seeming violations of the rights of corporate debtors. In all instances, however, caution should be exercised to avoid any course under which fundamental fairness (or due process) might be deemed by a court to be lacking—unless there is a danger of a sudden dissipation of the original asset for which the secured party holds the agreement.

— FOR FURTHER REFERENCE —

Bahrick, Thomas L., "Security Interests in Intellectual Property." 15 *AIPLA Quarterly J.* 30 (Winter '87).

Burns, Maryellen, "UCC, Public Filing, and Personal Property Leases," 22 *Wake Forest L. Rev.* 425 (Fall '87).

Carlson, David Gray, "Rationality, Accident, and Priority Under Article 9 of the Uniform Commercial Code," 71 *Minn.L. Rev.* 207 (December '86).

Chobot, John C., "Purchase Money Security Interests: Preference Pitfalls Under the Bankruptcy Code," 20 *U.C.C. LJ.* 81 (Summer '87).

Clark, Barkley, *The Law of Secured Transactions* (Warren, Gorham & Lamont; 1980 with 1988 supplement).

Cornman, Jack T., "When Is a Debtor in Possession Under UCC 9-312(4)?" 19 *Arizona State LJ.* 261 (Spring '87).

Holmes, E. and P. Shedd, *Practical Guide to the Law of Secured Lending,* Prentice-Hall, 1986.

Rason, Paul B., "A Critical Look at Secured Transactions Under Revised UCC Article 8," 14 *Florida State U.L. Rev.* 859 (Winter '87).

White, James J., "Dancing on the Edge of Article 9," 91 *Commercial LJ.* 385 (Winter '86).

Whitford, William C., "The Appropriate Role of Security Interests in Consumer Transactions," 7 *Cardozo L. Rev.* 959 (Summer '86).

Wilcox, Gregory C. and Frank B. Harty, "The Relative Priority of a Landlord's Lien and Article 9 Security Interest," 35 *Drake L. Rev.* 27 (Winter '86).

SECURITIES: THEIR OWNERSHIP AND TRANSFER

[¶3701] Article 8 of the Uniform Commercial Code governs the registration, negotiability and transfer of securities. Unlike a corporation code, it doesn't spell out general rules defining property rights that accrue to security holders. And, unlike a Blue Sky law, it doesn't set out specific requirements for disclosing to the public the nature of the property interest that is the security. Rather, Article 8 sets out rules relating to the transfer of the rights that constitute a security and the rights and obligations of issuers and purchasers of securities as against each other and of purchasers among themselves. Where Article 8 has been adopted (the District of Columbia and all states except Louisiana), it supplants both the Uniform Stock Transfer Act and the Uniform Negotiable Instruments Act.

In 1977, the American Law Institute and the National Conference of Commissioners on Uniform State Laws approved a comprehensive set of rule changes to Article 8. These 1977 changes were incorporated into the Uniform Commercial Code-1978 Official Text with Comments. The Article 8 changes essentially set out rules governing the rights, duties, and obligations of the issuers of, and persons dealing with, "uncertificated investment securities" (basically, a security not represented by an instrument and that is always registered).

Definition: As used in Article 8 and defined in §8-102, a "security" is an instrument that:

(1) Is issued in bearer or registered form;

(2) Is a type commonly dealt in on securities exchanges or markets, or commonly recognized in any area in which it is issued, or dealt in as a medium for investment;

(3) Is either one of a class or series, or by its terms is divisible into a class or series of instruments; and

(4) Evidences a share, participation, or other interest in property or in an enterprise, or evidences an obligation of the issuer.

As noted above, the 1977 amendments to Article 8 essentially add rules for dealing with uncertificated securities. Therefore, §8-102 under the 1977 changes distinguishes between *certificated* securities and *uncertificated* securities.

Section §8-102 states that an "uncertificated security" is a share, participation, or other interest in property of or an enterprise of the issuer or *is* an obligation of the issuer which:

(1) Is not represented by an instrument and the transfer of which is registered upon books maintained for that purpose by or on behalf of the issuer; and

(2) Is of a type commonly dealt in upon securities exchanges or markets; and

(3) Is either one of a class or series or by its terms is divisible into a class or series of shares, participations, interests, or obligations.

An uncertificated security is distinguished from a certificated security in two respects. First, an uncertificated security is not represented by an instrument and is always registered (§8-102(b)(i)). Second, the definition of uncertificated security does not include the phrase "or commonly recognized in any area in which it is issued or dealt in as a medium for investment." Because there is no requirement for representation by an instrument, it was thought that a great many interests that might be regarded as media for investment would be classified as securities under the umbrella of the omitted phrase. For example, since interests such as bank checking and saving accounts are commonly recognized as media for investment, it might be argued that they are securities as a result of the omitted language.

However, the Official Comments make it clear that these interests are not securities since they are not "commonly traded." On the other hand, stock of a closely held corporation is intended to be covered by this section; although such stock is not actually traded upon securities exchanges, it is "of a type" commonly traded on those markets (§8-102(b)(ii)).

Article 8 is exclusive in its application to the extent that an instrument that falls within the "security" definition of §8-102 is to be governed solely by Article 8, even though it may also come within the scope of Article 3.

Initial Transaction Statements: Article 8 discusses the use of so-called *initial transaction statements* (ITS), which are instruments used in connection with uncertificated securities. The ITS has a similar function as the security instrument itself; that is, it serves as prima facie evidence of the holder's rights. However, it is much more limited than a security.

The ITS is a signed statement sent by the issuer of an uncertificated security to the transferee, pledgee, or owner upon the registration of transfer, pledge, or release of the security. Like a certificated security, an ITS acts as an estoppel against the issuer. However, unlike a certificated security, an ITS only protects *the addressee,* and deals only with the time of the ITS's issuance. Therefore, other parties, especially as subsequent purchasers, have to be careful. They can't justifiably rely on what an ITS does or does not contain. (See "Transfer of Uncertificated Securities" below for more details.)

Statute of Frauds: UCC §8-319 is the Statute of Frauds for the transfer of securities. It provides that a contract for the sale of securities is not enforceable by way of action or defense unless:

(a) There is some writing signed by the party against whom enforcement is sought, or by his authorized agent or broker, sufficient to indicate that a contract has been made for sale of a stated quantity of described securities at a defined or stated price; or

(b) Delivery of the security has been accepted or payment has been made, but the contract is enforceable under this provision only to the extent of such delivery or payment; or

(c) Within a reasonable time a writing in confirmation of the sale or purchase and sufficient against the sender in paragraph (a) has been received by the party against whom enforcement is sought and who has failed to send written objection to its contents within 10 days after its receipt; or

(d) The party against whom enforcement is sought admits in a pleading, testimony, or otherwise in court that a contract was made for sale of a stated quantity of described securities at a defined or stated price.

Section §8-319 extends the coverage of the Statute of Frauds to contracts for the sale of uncertificated as well as certificated securities. Under §8-319(b), a contract for the sale of securities is not enforceable by way of action or defense unless:

"Delivery of a certificated security or transfer instruction has been accepted, or transfer of an uncertificated security has been registered and the transferee has failed to send written objection to the issuer within ten days after receipt of the initial transaction statement conforming such registration or that payment has been made. . . ." In any case, the contract is enforceable only to the extent of such delivery, registration, or payment.

Transfer of Uncertificated Securities: This section of Article 8 (UCC §8-408) requires the issuer of uncertificated securities to send certain statements to the new registered owner of securities: transaction statements (analogous to debit and credit advices) and periodic statements (analogous to bank statements). Transaction statements must be sent within two days after the relevant registration; periodic statements must be sent at least once a year.

Among other requirements, the statements must be in writing and must be signed by, or on behalf of, the issuer. All statements sent by the issuer pursuant to UCC SS8-408 must bear the following cautionary notice:

"This statement is merely a record of the rights of the addressee as of the time of its issuance. Delivery of this statement, of itself, confers no rights on the recipient. This statement is neither a negotiable instrument nor a security" (UCC §8-408:9).

[¶3702] Delivery Requirement for Completion of Transfer

A transfer is not effective between the parties until delivery takes place. When seller and buyer deal with each other directly, fulfilling the requirement of delivery is simple enough: the seller hands the certificate to the buyer. When dealing with a listed stock through a broker on a national or regional exchange, there might be a time lag of several days between the purchase and the purchaser's actual possession of the stock. Under the Uniform Stock Transfer Act (and the Negotiable Instruments Law in the case of bonds) transfer of possession of stock to the purchaser was the only method of delivery contemplated. However, the Uniform Commercial Code broadens the concept of delivery to conform to present-day conditions under which most stock transfers take place through brokers on organized exchanges. UCC §8-313 provides that delivery to the purchaser occurs when the purchaser's broker gets possession of a security specially endorsed to or issued in the name of the purchaser, or the broker *sends* him or her confirmation of the purchase, or makes a book entry or otherwise identifies a specific security in possession as belonging to the purchaser.

Section 8-313 identifies the time when both certificated and uncertificated securities are transferred to purchasers. In addition, the section is the result of the recognition that many security transactions are conducted through financial intermediaries, other than brokers. Therefore, banks, clearing corporations, and "any other person which, in the ordinary course of business, maintains security accounts for its customers . . ." are covered by this section.

[¶3703] ISSUER'S DEFENSES AND RESPONSIBILITIES

The Article 8 definition of "issuer" is set forth at UCC §8-201.

An issuer may set forth the terms of the security on its face and may also incorporate additional terms by reference to "another instrument, indenture or document or to a constitution, statute, ordinance, rule, regulation, order or the like to the extent that the terms so referred to do not conflict with the stated terms" (§8-202(1). These terms apply even as against a purchaser for value and without notice.

This section also covers uncertificated securities. As a result, the terms noted or referred to in the initial transaction statement sent to the purchaser of an uncertificated security will constitute constructive notice to persons who deal with the securities.

Section 8-202(3) notes that an issuer may always assert the lack of genuineness of a security as a complete defense, even as against a purchaser for value and without notice. This section similarly gives alleged senders of an initial transaction statement the same defense of lack of genuineness. However, this is qualified somewhat by §8-205, which states that an *unauthorized* signature placed on an initial transaction statement or security prior to or in the course of issue is ineffective, except in favor of a purchaser for value and without notice of the lack of authority, if the signing has been done by (a) an authenticating trustee, registrar, transfer agent, or other person entrusted by the issuer with the signing of the security or of similar securities or their immediate preparation for signing, or (b) an employee of the issuer or of any of the foregoing entrusted with responsible handling of the security.

Section 8-202(4) makes it clear that "all other defenses of the issuer including nondelivery and conditional delivery of the security are ineffective against a purchaser for value who has taken without notice of the particular defense." (This section applies to both certificated and uncertificated securities.)

Alteration of Securities: Section 8-206 provides that any holder may enforce the original terms of an altered security. In addition, when a security contains the signatures necessary to its issue or transfer but is incomplete in any other respect, any person may complete it by filling in the blanks as authorized, and even though the blanks are incorrectly filled in, the security as completed is enforceable by a purchaser for value who took without notice of its incorrectness. (These rules also apply to the completion or alteration of initial transaction statements.)

[¶3704] PURCHASER FOR VALUE

Defenses of the issuer and those not available as against a "purchaser for value and without notice" are examined in the preceding paragraph. Article 8 defines "bona fide purchaser" in UCC §8-302 as a purchaser for value in good faith and without notice of any adverse claim who takes delivery of a security in bearer form, or of one in registered form issued to him, or endorsed to him, or in blank. A similar rule applies to purchases of uncertificated securities. Note that the relevant time for testing the knowledge or constructive knowledge of a purchaser is the time of delivery in the case of a certificated security and the time of registration in the case of an uncertificated security.

[¶3705] RECORDING TRANSFERS

The stock book, usually open to reasonable inspection by shareholders (and sometimes others), shows record ownership. Corporations are authorized by statute to rely on record ownership in determining to whom notices are to be sent, who may vote, receive dividends, etc. For these purposes a reasonable record date may be fixed, or the books may be closed to transfers. Bylaws may contain provisions regulating the transfer of stock. The recording of transfers, cancellation of the surrender certificates, and the issuance of new certificates in the name of the transferee may be carried out by an independent agent, e.g., the transfer agent, or by a department or employee of the corporation.

[¶3706] LIABILITY FOR RECORDING TRANSFERS

The Uniform Commercial Code, §8-401 through 8-406, spells out the specific requirements in the registering, transferring, pledging, or releasing of stock transfers and the duties and liabilities arising therefrom. The UCC follows the "well-settled rules found in the case law as to duty to register and as to liability for improper registration of an unauthorized signature, or where the indorsement is not that of an appropriate person." In other areas, the potential liability for the issuer has been "substantially reduced."

Section 8-401 indicates that the issuer has a duty to record a transfer, provided that certain preconditions have been met:

(1) Appropriate indorsement (§8-308)

(2) Reasonable assurance as to genuineness of indorsements (§8-402);

(3) Compliance with applicable law regarding collection of taxes;

(4) Transfer made to bona fide purchaser, or transfer is otherwise rightful;

(5) Discharge of any duty to check into adverse claims (§8-403).

Section 8-401 also states that an issuer has the same duty to register the transfer, pledge, or release of uncertificated securities on the same terms and with the same conditions as would have to be done with certificated securities.

It should be noted that §8-401 is not absolute, in that the issuer can waive certain conditions, such as the assurances in (2) above, or the proof that the tax laws have been met.

If the issuer is presented with a security for transfer and registration, it may have a limited duty to inquire into adverse claims if it has received a written stop transfer" notice from the owner of a lost or stolen security prior to a request for transfer, or if the issuer had any other reason to believe there were adverse claims.

Section 8-404 states the basic exonerative policy regarding an issuer's transfer of a security when there was no duty to inquire into adverse claims and when the security was properly indorsed. (This section also contains an analogous remedy for issuers of uncertificated securities.) The Official Comment to this Section notes that the rightful owner of a wrongfully transferred security has the right to receive a new certificate, "except where an overissue would result [§8-104] and a similar security is not available for purchase."

[¶3707] CHECKLIST FOR STOCK TRANSFER REQUIREMENTS

In addition to indorsement, delivery, and guarantee of signature, the requirements are these:

Registered Owner	Endorsement	Tax Waivers	Special Requirements
Individual(s)	Owner(s)	None	None
Individual	Agent or Attorney	None	Certified copy of power
Joint tenants	Surviving joint tenant	Usually from state of domicile of deceased— sometimes from state of incorporation. Affidavit of domicile may be called for.	Certified copy of death certificate of deceased joint tenant
Decendent	Executor or administrator	Usually from state of domicile of deceased— sometimes from state of incorporation. Affidavit of domicile may be called for.	Copy of letters testamentary or of administration certified within 60 days
Custodian for minor	Custodian	None	None
Minor or ward	Guardian	None	Copy of letters of guardianship certified within 60 days

Registered Owner	Endorsement	Tax Waivers	Special Requirements
Trustee, executor, administrator, or guardian	Registered owner	None	None
Corporation	Officer acting for corporation	None	Certified copy of resolutions or bylaws creating officer's authority for the transaction
Deceased or resigned trustee	Endorsement by successor trustee	None	Certified copy of trust instrument showing succession

[¶3708] NOTICE OF RESTRICTIONS ON TRANSFER

If the corporation or the transfer agent is notified that there is an adverse claim to stock affected by a proposed transfer or a restriction on transfer, the immunity from liability afforded by statutory enactments is withdrawn. This situation may exist in these circumstances:

(1) Corporations frequently file, and are sometimes required by the SEC to file, with the transfer agent a "stop transfer" notice if the shares have not been registered and if the transfer might require such registration—usually shares held by control stockholders. Such a "stop transfer" order usually requires that transfer may be made only with the submission of an opinion, usually by corporate or other designated counsel, that registration would not be required to make a particular transfer legal.

(2) Restrictions on transfer may be noted on the certificate; i.e., as is commonly done under an agreement for the restriction of transfers entered into by control stockholders.

(3) By formal written communications from a claimant of the shares that identify him and the registered owner and the issue of which the security (certificated or uncertificated) is a part (see UCC §8-402(1)(a)).

(4) The corporation or the transfer agent has demanded and received, in support of application for registration and for some purpose other than checking the endorsements, copies of the will, trust agreement, or other controlling instrument that indicates that the proposed transfer would not be proper.

[¶3709] LOST, STOLEN, OR DESTROYED STOCK CERTIFICATES

If stock certificates are lost, stolen, or destroyed and the corporation replaces them with new certificates, it might incur a liability if the original certificates later appear in the hands of a bona fide purchaser. Corporate bylaws frequently provide for replacement conditioned upon the posting of an adequate bond to indemnify the corporation. The Uniform Stock Transfer Act provides for court procedure to compel replacement of a lost or destroyed certificate upon the posting of an adequate bond. Under UCC §8-405, the issuer is required to replace the lost certificate on the posting of a bond by the owner of the lost certificate, provided that the owner also satisfies any other requirements of the issuer.

If an owner of a security fails to inform the issuer in a timely and reasonable manner that the security has been lost, stolen, or destroyed, and the issuer subsequently registers a transfer of the security before such notification, the owner will not be able to sue the issuer for registering the security transfer, nor will the owner be able to sue for a replacement of the transferred security (§8-405(1)).

Once again, as in other UCC sections, the bona fide purchaser of the " original" security is protected even after the issuance of a new security, and the owner of the replacement security may have to return it to the issuer (§8-405(3)).

SECURITIES REGULATION

[¶3801] In the search for profit, Americans have developed a large and often bewildering variety of investment vehicles. Not all of these seekers are trying to turn an honest profit; others are making a sincere but misguided effort. In order to protect investors against fraud, and to give them a reasonable chance to assess the risk of potential investments, federal laws regulate the issue and sale of securities and the activities of investment advisers.

Securities law is important for attorneys advising corporate clients. Corporate clients can raise impressive amounts of money by selling their stock or other securities; however, they must either conform with the federal registration process (or any applicable state law) or qualify for one of the many exemptions from the registration requirement. Once the securities are issued, the corporation may have to report to the SEC on a regular basis.

In recent years, securities regulation has been a topic of absorbing legal and practical interest. Other issues of interest are discussed at ¶1704 (Corporate Mergers, Acquisitions, and Reorganizations). A great deal of attention has been given to the question of when arbitration of securities claims is permissible, when compulsory; this major issue is discussed in ¶407 (Arbitration).

The securities market constantly generates new forms of trading, and new instruments to be traded. The Eleventh Circuit has held that the trading of Treasury bond ("T-bond") futures is governed by federal commodities regulation, not the Securities Acts of 1933 and 1934.[1] 1993's P.L. 102-546 puts the Board of Governors of the Federal Reserve Board in charge of general oversight of the margin levels of stock index futures. This statute also forbids brokers to deal in a commodity both for customers and for themselves, unless the commodity market has an effective electronic audit trail.

The SEC already allows "multiple trading" (i.e., listing on more than one exchange) of over-the-counter and non-equity securities; multiple market trading of standardized options is also permissible.

Congress has enacted three major securities statutes: the Securities Enforcement Remedies and Penny Stock Reform Act (P.L. 101-249); the Market Reform Act (P.L. 101-432); and the Securities Acts Amendments (P.L. 101-550). P.L. 101-249 strengthens the SEC's enforcement powers and adds new SEC remedies:

➤ Cease and desist orders against securities violations

➤ Disgorgement and civil money penalties[2]

➤ Ability to petition federal courts for civil money penalties over and above disgorgement, or for injunctions forbidding individuals guilty of fraud offenses to serve as officers or directors of reporting companies

This Act adds a new statutory definition of "penny stock," and expands penny stock disclosure and SEC authority to bar individuals from the market based on their improper conduct. The SEC is directed to facilitate the creation of an automated quotation system for penny stocks and to study the self-regulatory organizations that regulate penny stocks. These associations are ordered to develop a toll-free customer complaint telephone line.

P.L. 101-249 amends the Exchange Act to give the SEC more power to prevent market crashes, by giving the SEC broader emergency powers and more tools to combat market volatility.

P.L. 101-550 extends the SEC's power to fight international securities fraud and work with other governments for this purpose. The Act also improves mutual fund shareholders' access to information and speeds up delivery of proxy materials to promote informed voting. Procedures for issuing debt securities under the Trust Indenture Act are simplified, but the SEC's enforcement power is broadened.

There are also rules for disclosure of the compensation of the CEO and four top executives of the corporation, especially with respect to stock options and stock appreciation rights. Broker-dealers are obligated to provide additional disclosure to their customers in penny-stock transactions.

[¶3801.1]   Securities Litigation and Settlement

The SIPC (federal agency responsible for reimbursing defrauded or otherwise disadvantaged stockholders) cannot use RICO to recoup the money it pays out to the customers of failed brokerage firms that were alleged to have engaged in a fraudulent conspiracy to manipulate securities markets.[3]

Section 6 of the '34 Act, which requires exchanges to register with the SEC, cannot be used to imply a private right of action by an investor against exchange members who break the exchange's rules, or against the exchange itself for failing to enforce its own rules.[4]

It is not clear whether Section 17(a) of the '33 Act (a general antifraud provision) gives investors a private right of action, or whether this section can only be enforced by the government. The Western District of New York has ruled that there is a private right of action;[5] the Fourth Circuit has ruled that there is no private right of action under Section 17(a) in churning cases,[6] nor is there a private right of action among securities fraud defendants under Section 12(2) of the '33 Act for indemnity or contribution.[7]

The Seventh Circuit also denied a private right of action for indemnification among securities fraud defendants, on the theory that Section 10(b) of the '34 Act and Rule 10b-5 do not grant the right explicitly, nor does federal common law imply it.[8]

The Seventh Circuit later relaxed its position somewhat,[9] finding an implied private right of action under 10b-5, but requiring proof of "loss causation"; that is, that the value of the investment would not have declined if the facts had been as they were represented by the defendants. Under this analysis, it is insufficient for a plaintiff to allege that, absent misrepresentation, he would not have invested and hence would not have lost money.

The Eighth Circuit also refused to imply a private right of action among 10(b) and 10b-5 defendants.[10] The Ninth Circuit permitted settling defendants to bring a suit for contribution against persons who were involved in securities violations but were not sued by the plaintiff; i.e., the settlement agreement was held not to bar a suit against those who were non-parties to the litigation.

The Supreme Court decided that federal courts can properly imply a right to contribution as a matter of federal law.[11] The result was that the insurers could get contributions from partners, attorneys, and accountants involved in the stock offering.

The Supreme Court has ruled that a Rule 10b-5 plaintiff must bring suit within three years of the occurrence of the fraud or one year of the discovery, regardless of the forum state's statute of limitations.[12] Thus, the same statute of limitation is applied for implied 10(b) claims and '34 Act Section 9 and 18 claims for misleading filing and willful manipulation of securities prices, and for '34 Act Section 14(a) claims.[13] It has been held that this rule does not apply to SEC civil enforcement actions which do not have a statute of limitations (although the court has discretion to grant equitable relief to the defendant if the violations are extremely remote in time)[14] or claims under state securities law.[15]

The purchaser of a call option is entitled to use a fraud on the market theory based on misrepresentations made by the issuer of the underlying stock.[16]

Insider trading claims can be brought under Rule 10b-5 only if the plaintiff traded contemporaneously with the insider; this must be plead with particularity under Federal Rules of Civil Procedure 9(b).[17]

In a 10(b) action, the defendant can introduce evidence of the plaintiff's recklessness prior to the sale in ignoring certain facts about an acquired corporation: at least in the Seventh Circuit, a plaintiff's "recklessly remiss" conduct acts to offset intentional deception on the part of the defendant.[18]

The SEC does not have to prove reliance to get an injunction against future violations of Section 10(b) or Rule 10b-5.[19]

According to the Ninth Circuit, a corporate employee who uses material non-public information about the employer corporation's intention to acquire another company to trade in the target company's stock can be guilty of 10(b) and 10b-5 violations.[20]

Under the "misappropriation theory," even an outsider who is not a fiduciary has a common-law duty to protect confidential information, and the duty extends even after termination of employment. Thus, a fired bank employee who kept his ID card and used it to get confidential information about tender offers and LBOs, then traded on the information, was guilty of 10(b) and 10b-5 violations.[21]

Each count of a 10(b) indictment must be based on a separate purchase or sale, and must specify at least one false statement of material fact in connection with that purchase or sale. The unit is the individual misrepresentation, and not the individual use of the mails.[22]

A divorcing spouse who was awarded one-quarter of the amount her husband received from sale of his company did not have standing to assert 10(b) violations arising out of the sale. She had no standing under the antifraud provisions because she was neither buyer nor seller of shares in either company that was party to the merger.[23]

A Supreme Court decision[24] requires a court hearing a derivative suit under the Investment Company Act to apply the law of the state of incorporation as to whether a demand must be made even if it is futile. The theory is that this is a substantive question of standing to sue, and that states recognizing a futility objection choose to shift control of the litigation from the board of directors to the shareholders.

[¶3802] THE SECURITIES ACT OF 1933

The Securities Act of 1933 (often referred to as "The '33 Act" to distinguish it from the Securities Exchange Act of 1934) is codified in 15 U.S.C. §77a-77aa. Although there is extensive case law on the definition of "security" under the '33 Act, the safest course is to assume that any form of investment offered to the public *is* a security within the ambit of the '33 Act (except for bonds: they're covered by the Trust Indentures Act).

The general rule is that, whenever securities are issued (that is, created and sold to the public), they must be registered unless the issuer meets the tests of one of the exemptions from the registration requirement. Registration implies two things: disclosure of a great deal of information about the securities and their issuer to the SEC, and disclosure of somewhat less information, in the form of a prospectus, to potential buyers.

The '33 Act also provides remedies for investors who are injured by violations of the Act's provisions. (The '33 Act's remedies are available only to purchasers; there are remedies under the '34 Act for sellers as well.) The '33 Act also contains general provisions against fraud, penalizing material omissions, and misrepresentations in connection with the sale of securities.

The Supreme Court has ruled on what constitutes a "security," and has identified the main test as the investment nature of the device.[25] A note is not necessarily a security, but is presumed to be one because of the "family resemblance" between notes and other securities, unless the note falls into one of the four classes specifically identified as non-securities by the Supreme Court.

Stock certificates tendered in a merger that wipes out the corporate existence cease to be securities. Therefore, a tendering stockholder is not a person acquiring such securities, and a '33 Act Section 11 action (misstatement or material omission in a registration statement) is no longer available.[26]

Readers will no doubt be relieved to know that attorneys who merely render legal services to sellers of securities are not themselves liable under Section 12(1) of the '33 Act to defrauded buyers of the securities.[27]

[¶3802.1] Underwriting and the Process of Registration

The issuer of the securities begins by selecting an underwriter or underwriters to aid in distributing the securities. The issuer and managing underwriters collect the information needed for the registration statement; the registration statement is prepared, with due attention to the detailed Instructions provided on each SEC registration form, and to the General Rules and Regulations of the SEC. The SEC has also issued Securities Act Industry Guides for certain industries (e.g., utility companies; bank holding companies) which should be consulted by the attorney.

The statutory filing requirements appear in Sections 6 and 7 of the '33 Act; the SEC's Regulation C (17 CFR Section 230.400-.494) gives the procedural requirements for disclosure, and the actual substantive disclosures to be made appear in Regulation S-K (17 CFR Section 229.10-.802). Most initial public offerings (IPOs) use the SEC's "long form," Form S-1; companies with a history of issuing securities may qualify for use of a shorter, more summary form.

Three copies of the complete registration statement, including the exhibits and all the required relevant papers and documents, must be filed with the SEC. An additional 10 staff copies must be furnished, but these need not contain all the exhibits.

Theoretically, the registration statement is effective twenty days after the filing. However, it's almost impossible for a statement to go through without an amendment: even if the SEC doesn't require any, it's unusual for the registration statement to contain the final price of the securities and the underwriters' compensation, which are usually determined only a few days before the proposed date of the offering.

A registration statement will be effective twenty days after the last amendment. However, the issuer won't want to wait twenty days after the price is set for the statement to become effective: intervening market forces could make the price so determined extremely unfavorable to the issuer. In recognition of this, the SEC's Rule 461 permits issuers to request "acceleration," to have the registration statement effective on a date chosen by the issuer without waiting the twenty days.

The SEC has the power to accelerate effectiveness, but also to delay it; the Commission can impose a "stop order" postponing the effective date until the stop order is removed.

The underwriters act as "wholesalers," purchasing securities from the issuer, the "manufacturer," and distributing them to buyers (institutions, brokerage firms, members of the public). There are two types of underwriting arrangements in common use. In a "firm commitment" underwriting, the underwriter purchases the securities outright from the issuer. In a "best efforts" arrangement, which might be conceptualized as similar to a consignment, the underwriter agrees to use its best efforts to sell the securities, but is not legally obligated to purchase them from the issuer if there is insufficient investor interest.

The usual process is for securities to be registered, and then distributed immediately. For a company's initial public offering, this is the only route. However, for a more "experienced" issuer, one who qualifies for use of a "short-form" registration statement on Forms S-2 or S-3 instead of S-1, "shelf registration" under the SEC's Rule 415 (17 CFR Section 230.415) is an option. That is, the issuer can register an offering of securities at one time, and either distribute them over a period of time (not in a single "burst" of underwriting activity), or register them at one time and distribute them at a later time.

[¶3802.2] Timing and Prospectus Requirements

Why is the effective date so important? Remember, it is illegal to sell securities without either an effective registration or a valid exemption. Section 5 of the '33 Act (15 U.S.C. §77e) creates three time periods in the registration process:

➤ the pre-filing period, during which time no offers to buy or sell can be made (§5(c)).

➤ the waiting period, starting when the registration statement is filed with the SEC, ending with the effective date. During this time, offers can be made, provided that a prospectus in proper form is delivered (§5(b)); no delivery of securities for sale can be made until the registration statement is in effect (§5(a)(2)).

➤ the post-effective period (from the effective date until the initial distribution of the issue is completed). Offers can be made; securities can be sold and delivered, again if the prospectus is provided in the proper form.

[¶3803] EXEMPTIONS FROM REGISTRATION

It is a truism that every business operated in corporate form issues stock. It would clearly be impossible for a corner grocery store to spend hundreds of thousands of dollars to register its securities merely in order to sell a few shares of stock. Even if this massive burden were imposed on every corporate enterprise, the SEC would be unable to handle the huge volume of registrations generated by hopeful new businesses (most of which will shortly disappear).

As a matter of policy, corporations are encouraged to use the securities market as a way to raise new capital for expansion and innovation. As a matter of policy, the registration process exists to compel disclosure to the investing public and to the SEC. These two policies are harmonized by exempting many issues and issuers from registration—provided that the issuer is careful to conform to SEC rules. Exemption can be granted based on characteristics of the securities themselves; on characteristics of the issue or issuer; or because the securities are marketed in a way that does not expose naive investors to a risk of purchasing securities without adequate disclosure. There are overlaps among these categories, and the choice of which category to fit a particular exemption into is somewhat arbitrary.

[¶3803.1] Exemptions Based on the Nature of the Securities

Under §3(a)(3) of the '33 Act (15 U.S.C. §77c(a)(3)), registration is not required (but the anti-fraud rules are in effect) for issue of short-term commercial paper; that is, paper with a term under nine months—what you might call a pregnant pause.

Under §3(a)(8), an exemption is available for the sale of insurance policies and annuities contracts if the seller is subject to state insurance or banking regulation.

[¶3803.2] Exemptions Based on the Nature of the Sale Transaction

The purpose of the '33 Act is to regulate the activities of issuers and underwriters, so §4(4) of the Act exempts transactions that do not involve an issuer, underwriter, or dealer. This exemption frees most securities transactions from registration: the vast "secondary" market, in which investors buy and sell shares through brokers, on exchanges or over-the-counter, is exempt under this provision.

Similarly, nonpublic offerings by an issuer are exempt under Section 4(2), because the purpose of protecting the public is not involved. In a typical §4(2) private placement, all the offerees are either institutional investors or sophisticated private individuals. Of course, advertisements to the public are forbidden, but a brokerage firm handling a private placement is permitted to communicate to those among its customers who have the requisite degree of sophistication.

The range of the federal laws extends only to interstate commerce, so that a purely intrastate offering (where the issuer and all offerees and purchasers are residents of the same state) is exempt from registration under §3(a)(11). However, this exemption can be tricky: it is lost entirely (not proportionately) if any of the offerees or purchasers of the securities reside outside the state. The unwary issuer can easily assemble a group, all of whom work in the same city, but who live in several neighboring states.

The range of the federal laws stops at the U.S. border: the SEC has no jurisdiction over securities sold outside the United States, to foreign nationals, as long as care is taken to ensure that the securities are not re-sold to Americans.

The SEC has sought modifications to Rule 144A that would facilitate institutional investors' trading in unregistered securities.[28] The theory is that the sophistication and market power of institutional investors mean that they can make trading decisions without paternalistic protection. A later Rule 144A release (No. 33-6862) creates a safe harbor for resale of restricted securities that are neither exchange-listed nor NASDAQ-quoted, if the purchaser is a qualified institution and specified disclosure requirements are met.

[¶3803.3] Exemptions Based on the Insurer and Terms of Issue

These are often known as "small offering" exemptions, although in fact the SEC possesses—and exercises—the power to exempt a fairly large offering (up to $5 million) which can be made under certain of these exemptions. Under §3(b) of the '33 Act, the SEC can exempt issues of $5 million or under. Under §4(6), issues of up to $5 million can be sold to accredited investors, on two conditions: that there be no public advertising of, or solicitation for, the offering, and that the issuer must file a notice with the SEC advising that it relies on this exemption.

Remember, the purpose of the securities laws is to give investors the information they need to make informed investment choices. If the investors already have other sources of such information, SEC protection is not needed. So an accredited investor is one who, based on "such factors as financial sophistication, net worth, knowledge, and experience in financial matters, or amount of assets under management," can look out for him-, her-, or itself (many accredited investors are institutions).

Regulation A, found at 17 CFR §230.251–264 is the most widely used exemption under §3(b). The exemption is available for up to $1.5 million in securities as integrated: that is, the issuer is permitted a total of $1.5 million per year in issues exempted under any provision of §3(b).

Compliance with Regulation A is sometimes termed "mini-registration," because the issuer must comply with disclosure requirements, and must provide offerees and purchasers with an "offering circular" which is similar to a prospectus. Rule 255 outlines the disclosure requirements: four copies of Form 1-A must be submitted to the appropriate SEC Regional Office.

Although Reg. A securities may lawfully be sold without registration, they are *not* registered. Therefore, if the issuer is in a state with a Blue Sky law calling for registration of such securities, and permitting "registration by coordination" (see below), Reg. A may not be the optimal exemption. Reg. A is not available to "bad boys": if either the corporation or an officer, director, or major stockholder has ever been found culpable for disclosure violations, another exemption must be used, or the securities must be registered.

There are three exemptions available as part of Regulation D:

➤ Rule 504 exempts small offerings (up to $1 million a year, if at least $500,000 is registered under the applicable state Blue Sky law) of small issuers (those that are neither investment companies nor "reporting companies" under the '34 Act—see below). No general advertising or solicitation is permitted for Rule 504 securities, unless these activities take place entirely in a state whose Blue Sky laws call for delivery of a disclosure document before a sale (and, of course, if the disclosure document is delivered as required). Rule 504 securities are not registered, and therefore cannot be re-sold unless they are eventually registered, or unless the seller qualifies for an exemption. Furthermore, the issuer must find out whether the buyers have the requisite "investment intent" or whether they plan to re-sell the securities in a manner violative of the securities laws. (If the offering is limited to the state of registration, and the disclosure document is provided, the resale restrictions do not apply.) As a result of SEC Release 33-6758 (March 3, 1988), the size of the Rule 504 exemption was extended from the prior $500,000 to $1 million. Through this Release, Rule 504 offerings are permitted in states that do not register securities, or that register securities but do not require disclosure documents. However, sales in non-qualifying states may not exceed $500,000.

➤ Rule 505 exempts offerings of up to $5 million per year. The offering can be made to any number of accredited investors, and not more than 35 "other purchasers." A corporation counts as a single purchaser; however, so does each client of an investment adviser or broker. So this exemption cannot be used to distribute securities widely among a broker's clients. Note that what counts is the number of offerees, not the number of purchasers: the issuer does not have the option of hunting up another group of purchasers if the original offerees are not interested in the securities.

➤ Rule 506 permits the offering *and sale* of securities—in any amount—to a group of not more than 35 investors qualified by "knowledge and experience in financial matters." The qualifications can be provided either by the investors themselves, or by their purchaser representatives. The issuer is responsible for checking the credentials of all purchasers (though not necessarily of all offerees). Accredited investors aren't counted toward the magic number of 35. If all the offerees are accredited investors, the issuer can even dispense with providing a disclosure document in a Rule 506 offering.

Rule 501 defines "accredited investor" to include institutional investors; private business development companies; tax-exempt organizations with more than $5 million in assets; corporations and partnerships (other than those formed specifically to acquire the securities) with assets over $5 million; trusts with assets over $5 million and a sophisticated adviser; and entities wholly owned by accredited investors.

Natural persons can be accredited investors. The issuer's officers, directors, and general partners fall into this category. So do people whose net worth (or net worth with their spouses) exceeds $1 million, or people who earned at least $200,000 a year in the past two years (or at least $300,000 a year with his or her spouse), and can be expected to continue a similar income level.

[¶3804] STATE SECURITIES REGULATION

State "Blue Sky" laws pre-date 1933: they began as a way to check the—let's say, extremely *creative* methods developed by the securities promoters of the late 19th century.

State securities regulation covers many areas. The states regulate the issue of securities, and may require a registration process even for securities that are exempt from federal registration. However, "Blue Skying" an issue is usually a lot less complex (and less expensive) than federal registration.

Although federal registration focuses entirely on disclosure (the SEC does not "approve" securities in the sense that registration is a judgment about the soundness of the company issuing the securities), some states do have "merit regulation": state securities regulators can deny approval of an issue if they believe the issuer or issue is financially unsound. Other states follow the federal model and limit the registration process to disclosure; in fact, most states permit "registration by coordination," in which federal registration of an issue also operates as state registration. About three-quarters of the states have adopted the Uniform Securities

Act, which permits registration by coordination; by qualification (full-scale disclosure); or by notification (a simplified procedure for established corporations that have already issued securities to the public).

The states also license broker-dealers in securities. Most of the states also regulate the activities of investment advisers; the exceptions are Alabama, Arizona, Colorado, Georgia, Iowa, Maine, Maryland, Massachusetts, North Carolina, Wyoming, and the District of Columbia. There are also state-law remedies for investors injured by the conduct of issuers or brokers. Depending on the state and the facts of the case, rescission may be available at the buyer's option if the Blue Sky laws are violated. An issuer may also be able to purge itself of state securities violations by offering to rescind all purchases of an issue. The offer must be made to all purchasers, with adequate disclosure of the nature of the violations involved.

[¶3805] THE SECURITIES EXCHANGE ACT

The Securities Exchange Act of 1934, in contrast to the '33 Act, deals with what happens to securities after they have been released onto the market. Large companies (those with more than 500 shareholders of record and total assets over $5 million) and companies whose securities are listed on an exchange must "report" under Section 13 of the '34 Act (becoming "reporting companies"), by providing regular quarterly (Form 10-Q) and annual reports (Form 10-K) to the SEC, and by disclosing (on Form 8-K) certain material transactions and events (e.g., acquiring or divesting major assets; change in auditor).

The '34 Act also places limitations on the behavior of a reporting company's directors, officers, and 10% shareholders. Under §16 of the '34 Act, these individuals are not allowed any short sales of the corporation's stock; they must also file reports with the SEC disclosing their holdings and transactions in the issuer's securities. Under §16(b) of the '34 Act, the issuer itself, or any shareholder suing on the issuer's behalf, can force the insider to disgorge "short-swing" profits earned by buying and then selling (or selling and then buying) the issuer's stock without a six-month holding period. These "short-swing" profits are recoverable even if the insider did not make use of inside information; however, SEC's Rule 16b-3 exempts many transactions involving employee benefit plans from the short-swing rule.

The Insider Trading Sanctions Act of 1984 (15 U.S.C. §78u(d)(2)(A)) imposes a civil penalty, payable to the U.S. Treasury, of up to three times the gains unlawfully earned through insider trading. Administrative sanctions are also available against anyone who causes or induces a failure to submit a report required by the '34 Act or the Williams Act (governing mergers and acquisitions).

Section 13(d) and 13(g) of the '34 Act require any individual who is beneficial owner of 5% or more of a reporting company's securities to file a statement with the SEC disclosing the amount of these holdings.

An important function of the Exchange Act is to penalize securities fraud and manipulation, and provide a remedy for those injured. Section 9 forbids manipulative practices in trading the securities of reporting companies listed on a national exchange; the victim's damages include recovery of the difference between the security's actual value and the price as affected by manipulation, plus costs and attorney's fees. Section 10(b) forbids any deception or omission of material fact in securities transactions, even if the issuer is not a reporting company and its shares are not listed on an exchange. This section prohibits "any manipulative or deceptive device or contrivance in contravention of such rules and regulations as the commission may prescribe as necessary or appropriate in the public interest or for the protection of investors."

The SEC has acted on this invitation, and numerous SEC anti-fraud rules have been promulgated pursuant to the '34 Act, either under the Section 10(b) prohibition of use of the means and instrumentalities of interstate commerce to carry out manipulative or deceptive practices, or the Section 15(c) prohibition of manipulative, deceptive, or fraudulent acts or practices by broker-dealers:

➤ Rule 10b-1 forbids market manipulation, even if the securities are exempt from registration.

➤ 10b-2 forbids persons (except broker-dealers) participating in securities distribution to solicit purchases on an exchange to facilitate the transaction.

➤ 10b-3 forbids broker-dealers to use manipulative or deceptive acts and practices with regard to municipal securities or securities not listed on an exchange.

➤ 10b-4 forbids "short tenders" (tendering stock that one does not own); short tenders on stock on which one has an option are permitted.

➤ The famous Rule 10b-5 forbids material misstatements and omissions. 10b-8 forbids manipulative and deceptive devices in rights offerings.

➤ 10b-17 requires announcements of events such as dividends and stock splits either to be made pursuant to exchange rules, or to be disclosed to NASD at least ten days before the record date.

➤ Rule 15c1-2 also forbids fraud and misrepresentation.

➤ 15c2-5 requires broker-dealers who control or are controlled by an issuer to disclose the relationship before entering into a customer's transaction; under 15c1-6, they must disclose their extent of participation or interest in a distribution.

➤ 15c1-8 forbids sales "at the market" unless the broker-dealer has a reasonable belief that a market exists.

➤ 15c1-9 requires disclosure of the underlying assumptions whenever pro forma financial statements are disseminated.

➤ 15c2-3 forbids broker-dealers to hypothecate their customers' securities; it also places limits on commingling of securities held for customers.

➤ Under 15c2-7, fictitious market quotations are forbidden; the identity of the broker-dealer placing each quote must be disclosed.

Section 18(a) imposes liability on anyone responsible for material misstatements or omissions in any document filed with the SEC under the '34 Act (that is, continuing disclosure from reporting companies, not registration statements). There is a private right of action for investors who read and rely on such documents. Liability extends to officers and directors of the reporting company—unless they acted in good faith and without knowledge that their statements were false and misleading.

Under Exchange Act Section 14(a), a knowingly false statement of reasons, opinions or beliefs published in a proxy statement can be actionable, but mere proof of disbelief or undisclosed belief or motivation cannot be a source of liability absent proof that the statement also expressly or impliedly stated something false or misleading about the subject matter. A shareholder whose vote is not required to authorize a transaction does not have an implied private right of action under 14(a), because such a shareholder is unable to show causation of damages.

The Third Circuit has applied this latter rule about minority shareholders to preclude 10b-5 damages for minority shareholders who allege misrepresentations in connection with a freeze-out merger.[29]

The concept of insider trading was the subject of further legislation, the Insider Trading and Securities Fraud Enforcement Act of 1988, P.L. 100-704 (10/21/88). Interestingly, there is still no statutory definition of "insider trading."

The statute amends Section 21(d) of the '34 Act to impose a penalty on those "controlling persons" (e.g., the employers of individuals who engage in illegal insider trading) who knew of the violations, or who recklessly disregarded the likelihood of insider trading and failed to take the necessary steps to prevent it. The statute adds a new Section 15(f) of the '34 Act (with a counterpart provision in new Section 204A of the Investment Advisers Act) obligating the maintenance of written policies to prevent the misuse of material nonpublic information. The criminal penalties under Section 32 of the '34 Act are strengthened, and a bounty program has been created to reward SEC informants.

Furthermore, "contemporaneous traders" (those who trade at the same time as the insiders, but without access to the material information) are granted a private right of action under a newly added Section 20A of the '34 Act. The new legislation is especially useful because it has been held that no Rule 10b-5 action is available to shareholders who claim that their investments declined in value because of the corporation's activities or the activities of its insiders,[30] because 10b-5 actions are available only to those who have suffered damages as a direct result of fraudulent conduct by the defendant.

On August 15, 1988, the SEC adopted a temporary Rule 10b-21 (no expiration date was set) defining the practice of selling a stock short before a public offering, then covering the short sale with stock from the offering, as unfair and deceptive.

On December 2, 1988, the SEC also published for comment significant changes in the rules and disclosure forms dealing with short-swing profits,[31] in the form of Proposed Rules 16a-1, 16a-3, 16a-4, and 16b-6. Under the short-swing rules, a person's status as an "officer" depends on job duties and access to inside information (whether or not the prosecution can prove actual use of inside information), not on the job title. Therefore, a corporate vice president would not be treated as an officer if he did not have a seat on the board of directors; the board did not communicate to him any information not available to the general public; and if he had no access to the corporation's financial and operational plans.[32]

The Supreme Court has stated that a plaintiff in a Section 16(b) action to recover short-swing profits is not deprived of standing by a merger that gives the plaintiff shareholder stock in the issuer's new corporate parent.[33]

The SEC's Exchange Act Rule 15c2-6 (announced in Release No. 34-27160) imposes additional sales practice requirements on broker-dealers who recommend "penny" stocks to individuals who are not their regular customers. For this purpose, a "penny stock" is a low-price (under $5 a share) over-the-counter stock that is not NASDAQ-listed and whose issuer has net tangible assets under $2 million. The broker-dealer is obligated to approve the purchaser's account in advance for the securities, based on an assessment of the suitability of the investment, and must get written approval of the transactions. There are exemptions under the new rule for transactions by accredited investors or established customers of the broker-dealer; transactions initiated by the customer, not recommended by the broker-dealer; and transactions in securities in which the broker-dealer is not a market-maker, and from which the broker-dealer derives less than 5% of its sales revenue.

The Second Circuit has upheld the SEC's authority to promulgate Exchange Act Rule 14e-3(a) (trading on material non-public information about a tender offer)[34] although the rule dispenses with the element of common-law fraud in breach of fiduciary duty. The Second Circuit interpreted the rule as a disclosure provision, requiring traders to disclose or abstain, whether or not the trader has a pre-existing fiduciary duty to keep the information confidential. However, in this case, the Second Circuit found that the tippee could not be liable because the tipper did not have a duty to his family to refrain from disclosing a pending tender offer.

The SEC itself has ruled[35] that the SEC's authority under Exchange Act Section 15(c)(4) to order general future compliance does not extend to administrative proceedings brought before the 1990 amendments that were the first explicit authorization for orders of general future compliance.

An attorney representing a securities fraud defendant is not liable on '34 Act or common-law fraud grounds with respect to misrepresentation or failure to disclose information that was independently available to the purchasing plaintiff.[36]

Winning securities fraud plaintiffs can recover their "actual damages," defined as the "market-adjusted" value of their fraud-induced losses; the market adjusted value, in turn, is the amount by which their securities fail to keep pace with the market; their recovery is not limited to out-of-pocket losses.[37] However, they may have to wait forever to actually collect: a federal tax lien applied to a securities law violator's ill-gotten gains before he entered into a consent agreement calling for disgorgement takes precedence over the fraud victims' rights under the consent agreement.[38]

Bondholders were unsuccessful in a 10b-5 action in which they claimed that the issuer failed to disclose its status as a potential takeover target when the notes were issued. The Southern District of New York ruled[39] that the omission was not material because, despite widespread rumors, the probability of an actual acquisition was very low at the time of the issue of the notes. In any event, the bondholders were aware of the rumors, so disclosure by the corporation would not have increased the total mix of information available to investors. However, in a later case, the Second Circuit reinstated a fraud action based on literally true statements about holders' rights to tender debentures; it was alleged that, in practice, the statements were misleading because the right to tender was in fact valueless.[40] The Second Circuit, in another takeover-related case[41] found that the Williams Act supersedes the Sherman Act, ruling out antitrust claims regarding joint tender offers by rival bidders for a takeover target.

[¶3805.1] Regulation of Broker-Dealers

Under §15(a) of the Exchange Act, securities broker-dealers must register with the SEC unless their activities are purely intrastate (which is true of many broker-dealers) and do not involve any facility of a national securities exchange (which is not true of many broker-dealers). Section 15(b)(7) permits the SEC to impose standards on broker-dealers' operational and financial competence. Rule 15c1-7 forbids "churning" (recommendations that clients buy and sell securities, motivated by a desire for increased commissions rather than a belief that the transactions will be beneficial to the client) of discretionary accounts. Rule 10b-6 forces broker-dealers to give customers adequate disclosure of the cost of securities transactions in which credit is extended ("margin" transactions). Although there is no explicit private remedy provision, courts tend to imply a private remedy for misleading disclosures in the margin context.

Naturally, brokers are in no position to guarantee that all their recommendations will be profitable for their clients (and a look at the broker's experience investing his or her own money will confirm this). However, the federal securities laws are interpreted under a "shingle theory": the broker, by "hanging out a shingle," holds him- or herself out as an expert either in investments in general or in a particular issuer's security. Therefore, the broker will be held to a high standard of care in making representations and investment recommendations; the recommendation is an implied representation of possession of enough information to form an opinion about the merits of the security.

Broker-dealers belong to self-regulatory organizations (SROs); the SROs have their own rules about "suitability" and "know-your-customer," imposing a burden on brokers to refrain from recommending investments that are unsuitable for a particular client.

Angry clients who want to storm the courts to sue their brokers must first read the fine print of their brokerage agreements. These agreements typically contain arbitration clauses. *Shearson-American Express v. McMahon,* 107 S.Ct. 2332 (1987) compels enforcement of the arbitration clause when the client asserts a claim under Section 10b of the '34 Act. This decision builds on *Dean Witter Reynolds Inc. v. Byrd,* 470 U.S. 213 (1985), which compels arbitration of pendent state-law claims against a broker (e.g., claims under the remedies provision of a state's Blue Sky Laws)—even if such arbitration leads to bifurcated proceedings in more than one forum.

[¶3805.2] Regulation of the Proxy Process

The securities laws are an uneasy balance between an ideal of corporate democracy and shareholder suffrage, and the realities that most of a corporation's stockholders are entirely without knowledge of, or interest in, the day-to-day decisions of the corporation's management and directors. When an issuer or any other party solicits proxies for a vote on the election of directors or other major corporate decisions, the provisions of the Exchange Act must be followed. Furthermore, under Rule 14a-8, stockholders have a limited power to include their own proposals in the proxy materials under the appropriate circumstances.

All holders of the issuer's securities must get an annual report every year, conforming to Rule 14a-3. False and misleading statements in proxy statements are forbidden by Rule 14a-9. Rule 14a-5 and Schedule 14A specify the form and content of proxy statements.

Dissident shareholders lost in a proxy solicitation case: they claimed that management, in seeking proxies for its own slate of candidates, was guilty of material misstatement or omission when it released a short version of a report about the company's prospects, based on optimistic projections. The Western District of Michigan held that the "total mix" of information available to stockholders was not altered by failure to disclose the underlying assumptions behind the management's projections; the proxy materials included other, more conservative, projections. Nor did omission of historical data from the short-form report alter the "total mix," because stockholders had free access to past annual reports.[42]

The Ninth Circuit has held[43] that even a stockholder who knows that certain statements in a proxy statement are false and misleading (and therefore does not rely on them) has standing to bring a direct suit under Exchange Act Section 14(a), and that the suit can be filed either before or after the vote for which the proxy is sought.

ERISA does not impose a fiduciary duty on the trustee of an employee benefit plan to provide a list of plan participants' names, addresses, and shareholdings on request from the union president who wants the information to solicit votes in the election for the board of directors.[44]

[¶3805.3] Williams Act Disclosure (Tender Offers)

13D filings are not required by parties with purely ministerial responsibilities, so a nominee (in this case, an attorney) who must have directions from a third party to vote or dispose of stock is not a "beneficial owner" required to make 13D filings.[45]

An arbitrageur's Williams Act reporting obligation is triggered by a formed intent to gain control of a target, but mere consideration of undertaking a proxy contest as a possible tactic does not require a filing. A decision must be made to attempt to acquire the corporation.[46]

A would-be acquiror filed a Schedule 13D to disclose its purchases of the target company's stock, but failed to disclose that most of the funds for the purchase were borrowed from a particular bank. The D.C. District Court ruled[47] that the non-disclosure was a material omission that would support a Section 10(b) claim, on the grounds that the Section 13(d) requirement that such information be disclosed is strong evidence of Section 10(b) materiality. Information about source of funds is material because a reasonable shareholder, assessing the likelihood of a consummation of the proposed takeover, would want to know about the loan terms as well as the fact of the loan.

Stockholders do not have derivative claims under either Section 13(d) or Section 10(b) if they claim that a raider was obligated to disclose his plans to "greenmail" the company in which the stockholders held shares. To prevail on a claim based on a false or misleading Schedule 13D, the plaintiff must use Exchange Act Section 18(a), which requires proof of reliance on the information in the schedule when buying or selling a security whose price was affected by the misstatement. In the greenmail non-disclosure situation, the derivative plaintiff cannot prove that the greenmailed corporation relied on the Schedule 13D in deciding to buy back the stock.[48]

Disgorgement is an appropriate remedy under Section 13(d) of the Williams Act; even though the statute does not explicitly state this, the D.C. Circuit has held it[49] to be a reasonable exercise of the court's inherent equitable powers. Therefore, disgorgement of $2.7 million in greenmail profits, calculated from the date filing was first required to the date of the actual Williams Act filing, was ordered.

Investors who constituted a "group" for Section 13(d) purposes, but none of whom owned more than 10% of the securities purchased by the group, did not constitute a "group" subject to the Section 16(b) short-swing liability rules, because no individual owned more than 10% of the target company's common stock, and therefore could not derive "benefits" from the short-swing sale of the common stock.[50]

In the early days of hostile takeovers, bidders were permitted to place additional pressure on target shareholders by making discriminatory tender offers that were more favorable to the earliest tenderers. However, the "all-holders" rule now requires all holders of the target securities to be given equal access to the tender offer. But even if a tender offer violated the all-holders rule by excluding ESOP shares, the target corporation does not have standing to sue under the "all-holders" rule; only the stockholders have this right.[51]

Another SEC rule this time, the "one share-one vote" rule, placing stringent limits on discrepancies in voting power of different shares, was struck down by the D.C. Circuit.[52] The court's rationale was that Exchange Act Section 19 gives the SEC power to regulate corporate voting *procedures,* but the allocation of voting power is a matter of internal corporate governance that must be determined by the corporations themselves.

[¶3806]   THE INVESTMENT COMPANIES ACT OF 1940

This statute (15 U.S.C. §80a-1-80a-54) exists to protect investors who entrust investment companies (e.g., mutual funds) with their funds in order to obtain diversification and expert management. All non-exempt investment companies must register with the SEC (using Form N-8A). The Investment Companies Act also includes disclosure and reporting requirements as well as protections: all sales literature must be filed with the SEC within 10 days of issuance; fees paid to the investment company's own investment advisers must be disclosed; protects investors against conflicts of interest on the part of investment companies; and supplements the anti-fraud and private remedies provisions of the '33 and '34 Acts. One powerful sanction is that the contracts of non-registered, non-exempt investment companies are unenforceable.

Broker-dealers, banks, insurance companies, savings and loan institutions, and small loan companies are exempt from the Act's coverage (they're already regulated); so are pension plans and not-for-profit voting trusts.

Companies subject to the Act are divided into three groups: companies that issue face-amount certificates; unit investment trusts; and management companies (the most common category, and the one that includes mutual funds). Management companies, in turn, are classified as open-end or closed-end, diversified or non-diversified.

[¶3807]   INVESTMENT ADVISERS ACT OF 1940

The potential for abuse of the investing public by those who are paid to provide advice is enormous and obvious. A measure of protection is provided by the Investment Advisers Act (15 U.S.C. §§ 80b-1 et seq.)

"Investment advisers" are required to register with the SEC on Form ADV, provide periodic disclosure to the SEC (ADV-5 reports), give much of this information to prospective and actual clients, and maintain their records for periodic SEC inspection. Investment advisers are forbidden to collect their compensation directly in the form of contingent fees (that is, to receive a percentage of the benefits their clients derive from their advice), though they can receive indirect contingent fees by charging a percentage of the value of the client's portfolio at a particular time—increased value would mean higher fees.

"Investment adviser" is very much a term of art. Theoretically, it is any individual who receives compensation for advising others "as to the value of securities or as to the advisability of investing in, purchasing, or selling securities." However, a number of professional groups are excluded from this definition: advisers who work solely for insurance companies (who, presumably, can protect themselves); banks (already regulated); lawyers, accountants, engineers, and teachers rendering incidental advice to their clients; broker-dealers providing incidental advisory service; and bona fide news media including financial publications of general circulation.

The question of investment newsletters is a difficult one. The protection of the public must be balanced against the First Amendment. The Supreme Court finally determined the balance in *Lowe v. SEC,* 472 U.S. 181 (1985), ruling that an investment newsletter that renders impersonal investment advice (that is, not related to the specific needs of individual clients) is not an investment adviser.

Certain investment advisers are exempt from the registration requirement, but not from the anti-fraud provisions of the Investment Advisers Act: "local advisers," all of whose clients are from the state of the adviser's principal place of business; advisers with up to 15 clients, as long as they do not hold themselves out to the public or to investment companies as investment advisers.

Must a "financial planner" (or a member of another profession providing financial planning services) register as an investment adviser? Only if the planner provides personal advice recommending the purchase or sale of specific securities (e.g., "buy 5,000 shares of Amalgamated Consolidations preferred," not "allocate 10% of your portfolio to preferred stock of manufacturing corporations"). However, there is an increasing trend toward state regulation of financial planners.

— ENDNOTES —

1. Messer v. E.F. Hutton Co., 847 F.2d 673 (11th Cir. 6/16/88).

2. An SEC disgorgement order is not a "debt" falling under the Fair Debt Collection Practices Act, thus is not subject to state-law FDCPA exemptions such as the homestead. The disgorgement order can be enforced via contempt proceedings: SEC v. Huffman, 996 F.2d 800 (5th Cir. 8/2/93); SEC v. AMX, Int'l Inc., 62 LW 2335 (5th Cir. 8/2/93).

3. Holmes v. SIPC, #90-727, 112 S.Ct. 1311 (Sup. Ct. 3/24/92), on remand 964 F.2d 924.

4. Spicer v. Chicago Board of Options Exchange Inc., 977 F.2d 255 (7th Cir. 9/24/92).

5. Kitto v. Thrash Oil & Gas Co., 57 LW 2644 (W.D.N.Y. 3/24/89).

6. .Newcome v. Esrey, 862 F.2d 1099 (4th Cir. 12/16/88).

7. Baker, Watts & Co. v. Miles & Stockbridge, 876 F.2d 1101 (4th Cir. 6/7/89).

8. King v. Gibbs, 876 F.2d 1275 (7th Cir. 6/1/89).

9. Bastian v. Petren Resources Corp., 892 F.2d 680 (7th Cir. 1/9/90).

10. Greenwood v. Touche Ross & Co., 60 LW 2646 (8th Cir. 3/30/92).

11. Musick, Peeler & Garrett v. Employers Insurance of Wausau, Inc., #92-34, 113 S.Ct. 2085 (Sup. Ct. 6/1/93).

12. Lampf Pleva Lipkind Prupis & Petigrow v. Gilbertson, 111 S.Ct. 2773 (6/20/91). Congress succeeded in passing anti-Lampf legislation (P.L. 102-242, Sec.476, 12/19/91), but the Northern District of California found the law unconstitutional: see Amy Stevens, "Judge Voids Law on Securities-Fraud Suits," *Wall St.J.* 3/4/92 p. B8.

13. Westinghouse Electric Corp. v. Franklin, 993 F.2d 349 (3d Cir. 5/19/93).

14. SEC v. Rind, 991 F.2d 1486 (9th Cir. 4/19/93).

15. Geisenberger v. John Hancock Distrib's Inc., 774 F.Supp. 1045 (S.D. Miss. 1991).

16. Deutschman v. Beneficial Corp., 59 LW 2224 (D.Del. 9/21/90), 841 F.2d 502, *cert. denied* 490 U.S. 1114.

17. Neubronner v. Milken, 62 LW 2226 (9th Cir. 10/4/93).

18. Elco Industries Inc. v. Hogg, 713 F.Supp. 1215 (N.D. Ill. 5/16/89).

19. SEC v. Rana Research Inc., 62 LW 2304 (9th Cir. 11/3/93).

20. SEC v. Clark 915 F.2d 439 (9th Cir. 9/24/90).

21. SEC v. Cherif, 933 F.2d 403 (7th Cir. 4/29/91), *cert. denied* 112 S.Ct. 966.

22. U.S. v. Langford, 946 F.2d 798 (11th Cir. 11/5/91).

23. Davidson v. Belcor Inc., 933 F.2d 603 (7th Cir. 6/5/91).

24. Kamen v. Kemper Financial Services Inc., #90-516, 111 S.Ct. 1711 (5/20/91).

25. Reves v. Ernest & Young, 110 S.Ct. 945 (Sup.Ct. 2/21/90).

26. Versyss Inc. v. Coopers & Lybrand, 982 F.2d 653 (1st Cir. 12/30/92).

27. Moore v. Kayport Package Express Inc., 885 F.2d 531 (9th Cir. 9/6/89).

28. Release No. 33-6086.

29. Scattergood v. Perelman, 945 F.2d 618 (3d Cir. 9/23/91).

30. Vetzner v. Northwest Industries, FSLR #94,715 (N.D. Ill. 5/12/89).

31. Release No. 26333.

32. CRA Realty Corp. v. Crotty, 878 F.2d 562 (2d Cir. 6/14/89).

33. Gollust v. Mendell, #90-659, 111 S.Ct. 2173 (Sup.Ct. 6/10/91).

34. U.S. v. Chestman, 947 F.2d 551 (2d Cir. 1/7/91), *cert. denied* 112 S.Ct. 1759; SEC v. Peters, 978 F.2d 1162 (10th Cir. 10/26/92).

35. In re kern, SEC Admin. Proc. File #3-6869 (6/21/91); see 60 LW 2029.

36. Royal American Managers Inc. v. IRC Holding Corp., 885 F.2d 1011 (2d Cir. 9/1/89).

37. Medical Associates of Hamburg PC v. Advest Inc., 58 LW 2056 (W.D.N.Y. 7/5/89).

38. SEC v. Levine, 881 F.2d 1165 (2d Cir. 8/2/89).

39. Hartford Fire Ins. Co. v. Federated Dep't Stores, 723 F.Supp. 976 (S.D.N.Y. 10/13/89).

40. McMahan v. Wherehouse Entertainment Inc., 900 F.2d 576 (2d Cir. 4/10/90).

41. Finnegan v. Campeau Corp., 915 F.2d 824 (2d Cir. 10/4/90).

42. Alizac Partners v. Rospatch Corp., 712 F.Supp. 599 (WD Mich. 5/4/89).

43. Stahl v. Gibraltar Financial Co., 967 F.2d 335 (9th Cir. 6/23/92).

44. Acosta v. Pacific Enterprises, 950 F.2d 611 (9th Cir. 12/11/91).

45. Calvary Holdings Inc. v. Chandler, 948 F.2d 59 (1st Cir. 10/30/91).

46. SEC v. Amster & Co., 762 F.Supp. 604 (S.D.N.Y. 5/20/91).

47. SEC v. Levy, 706 F.Supp. 61 (D.D.C. 2/2/89).

48. Kamerman v. Steinberg, 891 F.2d 424 (2d Cir. 12/6/89).

49. SEC v. First City Financial Corp., 890 F.2d 1215 (D.C. Cir. 12/1/89).

50. Rothenberg v. Jacobs, 57 LW 2660 (S.D.N.Y. 1/11/89).

51. Polaroid Corp. v. Disney, 862 F.2d 987 (3d Cir. 11/23/88).

52. Business Roundtable v. SEC, 905 F.2d 406 (D.C. Cir. 6/12/90).

— FOR FURTHER REFERENCE —

Branson, Douglas M., "Collateral Participant Liability Under State Security Laws," 19 *Pepperdine L. Rev.* 1027 (April '92).

Conard, Alfred F., "Control, Responsibility and Abdication: A Dilemma of Securities Regulation," 17 *J. of Corporate Law* 539 (Spring '92).

Dawes, Paul H. and Mark W. Smith, "The Demand Requirement and the Special Litigation Committee in Derivative Actions," 26 *Rev. of Securities and Commodities Reg.* 77 (5/12/93).

Doherty, Mary T., "Aiding and Abetting Securities Fraud," 25 *Indiana L. Rev.* 829 (Summer '92).

Johnson, Lyman, "Securities Fraud and the Mirage of Repose," 1992 *Wisc. L. Rev.* 607.

Kaslow, Jon, "Estimating Aggregate Damages in Class-Action Litigation Under Rule 10b-5 for Purposes of Settlement," 59 *Fordham L. Rev.* 811 (April '91).

Kelly, Eileen P., Eugene L. Donahue and Lawrence S. Clark, "Legal and Ethical Perspectives on the Use of Arbitration in the Securities Industry," 25 *Creighton L. Rev.* 1311 (June '92).

Kenny, Michael P. and Theresa D. Thebaut, "Defending 'Bet the Company' Cases: Pretrial Defenses in Securities Fraud Class Actions," 29 *Georgia State B.J.* 206 (May '93).

Kidd, Ronald F., "Insider Trading: The Misappropriation Theory Versus an Access to Information Perspective," 18 *Del. J. of Corporate Law* 101 (Winter '93).

Letsou, Peter V., "Shareholder Voice and the Market for Corporate Control," 70 *Washington U.L.Q.* 755 (Fall '92).

Levine, Lance, "Compliance with GAAP and GAAS: Its Proper Use as an Accountant's Defense in a Rule 10b-5 Suit," 1993 *Columbia Business L. Rev.* 109 (Winter '93).

Olson, John M., "The Fiduciary Duties of Insurgent Boards," 47 *Business Lawyer* 1011 (May '92).

Pengia, R. Rene, "Insider Trading, Debt Securities, and Rule 10b-5," 67 *N.Y.U. L. Rev.* 1354 (December '92).

Prendergast, James D., "Replacing Judicial Discretion With Federal Securities Laws," 25 *Review of Securities & Commodities Regulation* 81 (4/8/92).

Sabino, Anthony Michael, "The New Uniform Statute of Limitations for Federal Securities Fraud Actions," 19 *Pepperdine L. Rev.* 485 (January '92).

Starr, Judith R., "Jurisdiction Under Federal Securities Law to Recover Ill-Gotten Gains From Third Parties," 20 *Securities Regulation L.J.* 313 (Fall '92).

Steinberg, Marc I., "Attorney Liability Under the Securities Laws," 45 *Southwestern L.J.* 711 (Fall '91).

Steinberg, Marc I., "Securities Malpractice Exposure: Client Representation—Certain Problematic Solutions," 20 *Securities Regulation L.J.* 199 (Summer '92).

Steinberg, Marc I. and Daryl L. Lansdale Jr., "Standing Under Section 16(b) of the Securities Exchange Act," 21 *Securities Regulation L.J.* 178 (Summer '93).

Stewart, C. Evan, "Securities Fraud Bar Considers the Demise of Equitable Tolling," *Nat. Law J.* 9/9/91 p. S14.

Troy, Richard H., "Proxy Solicitation Rules Hold Surprises," *Nat. Law J.* 10/13/92 p. 7.

White, David L., "Outside Directors Under the Federal Securities Laws: Fraudulent Actors or Innocent Victims?" 21 *Securities Regulation L.J.* 297 (Fall '93).

SOCIAL SECURITY, MEDICARE, AND MEDICAID

[¶3901] The Social Security Act (42 U.S.C. §401 et seq.) is a long, complex, confusing, oft-amended statute that governs three very important social programs: the OASDI (Old Age, Survivors, and Disability Insurance) system; Medicare (a non-means-tested program providing medical care for those over 65); and Medicaid (a joint federal-state program providing medical care for the indigent and medically indigent, regardless of age). The Social Security Act also governs the SSI (Supplemental Security Income) income-supplementation program for the indigent elderly and disabled.

[¶3902] OASDI RETIREMENT BENEFITS

Its solvency always in doubt, always rescued at the last minute, the OASDI system lurches on. The system is supported by Federal Insurance Contribution Act (FICA) taxes paid by employers, employees, and the self-employed. (Part of the FICA tax is applied toward the funding of the Medicare system, discussed below.)

The OASDI system centers around the concept of the "fully insured" worker: broadly, one who has worked at a job covered by the Social Security system for at least forty calendar quarters, or at least one quarter in every year since 1950, earning at least $470 per quarter. (The amount required for a quarter of coverage changes annually, but is always minimal.) A "fully insured" worker is eligible to receive retirement benefits starting at age 62; a disabled worker may be able to receive disability benefits under the OASDI system.

Furthermore, an insured worker's spouse, surviving spouse, ex-spouse, or surviving ex-spouse, children, and/or parents may be eligible to receive benefits based on the earnings record of the insured worker. If these people are insured workers themselves, they will be eligible to receive either benefits based on their own earnings record, or on the insured worker's earnings record, whichever is higher (but not both); and there is a "family maximum" on benefits received by all members of a family under a single insured worker's earnings record.

A 1993 Fifth Circuit case involves a remarried widow who was separated from her second husband. When she applied for Social Security benefits, she signed a form stating that she had not remarried although she never divorced the second husband, and eventually they reconciled. The Social Security Administration was entitled to recoupment of about $25,000 in incorrectly paid benefits, and she was not entitled to a waiver of recoupment. She could not be said to be "without fault" for signing a form without reading it. Nor could she get a jury trial, because the Secretary's cause of action was based on the equitable remedy of restitution.[1]

[¶3902.1] Timing of Retirement Benefits

A fully insured worker who retires from his or her job is entitled to receive OASDI retirement benefits in the first month he or she meets all three of these conditions:

➤ He or she is over 62.

➤ He or she is fully insured.

➤ He or she has filed an application for retirement benefits.

Note that, unlike Medicare, the application is based on retired status as well as age. It *is* possible for an individual to retire, collect retirement benefits, and then return to work.

If an individual retires and then decides to go back to work, his or her Social Security benefits will get trimmed. Those individuals under 65 lose $1 of Social Security benefits for every $2 of earned income above $8,160. For those between 65 and 69, the reduction is $1 of benefits for every $3 of earned income above $11,280.

[¶3902.2] Derivative Benefits

In addition to benefits payable to an insured worker paid on his or her own earnings record, the OASDI system contains derivative benefits, payable to other individuals because of their relationship to an insured worker, and measured as a percentage of the insured worker's PIA. The total benefits payable to a family (including the insured worker's benefits) are limited to a total of 150% of the first bend point; 272% of PIA from the first to the second bend point; 134% of PIA from the second to third bend point; and 175% of PIA in excess of the third bend point.

Derivative benefits can be paid to an insured worker's husband or wife if the spouse:

➤ Is over 62; or is younger and responsible for the care of the insured worker's minor child.

➤ Is not entitled to a higher benefit based on his or her own earnings record.

Benefits are payable to the divorced ex-spouse of an insured worker if:

➤ The ex-spouse is 62 or over.

➤ The marriage to the insured worker lasted at least ten years.

➤ The ex-spouse is not entitled to a higher benefit based on his or her own earnings.

➤ The ex-spouse is not married at the time of the application (although a marriage that ended before the application for benefits will not bar receipt of benefits).

The basic benefit for a spouse or ex-spouse is half of the insured worker's PIA; however, the spouse's or ex-spouse's benefit is reduced if the maximum family benefit amount has been reached; if the worker retires before normal retirement age (the spouse's benefit is *not* increased if the insured worker continues working past normal retirement age); or if the insured worker has post-retirement earnings requiring a cut in his or her Social Security benefits.

If an insured worker dies, his or her survivors are entitled to a lump-sum Social Security death benefit. Monthly benefits are also payable to surviving spouse and/or ex-spouse (it's possible for more than one survivor of a deceased worker to receive spousal benefits). Spousal benefits are payable if:

➤ The marriage lasted at least nine months before the insured worker's death (this requirement is relaxed if the death was accidental; it is intended to bar marriages in name only, entered into for the sole purpose of collecting survivor's benefits) or produced a child.

➤ The surviving spouse or ex-spouse is over 60; over 50 and disabled; or cares for the insured worker's minor child.

➤ Is not entitled to a higher benefit on his or her own earnings record.

➤ Has not remarried. However, protests that this requirement forced elderly widows and widowers either to "live in sin" or to forfeit critically needed benefits led to an amendment: remarriage does not affect the benefit eligibility of widows and widowers over 62 or disabled widows or widowers over 54.

The basic survivor's benefit equals the deceased insured worker's full PIA. However, if the worker's benefit was reduced because of early retirement, the surviving spouse and/or ex-spouse is entitled to either the benefit the insured worker was receiving or $82\frac{1}{2}\%$ of his or her PIA, whichever is larger.

If an insured worker is survived by a minor child (a term defined to include other dependents, such as stepchildren and grandchildren), the child is entitled to collect a survivor's benefit, provided that the child is an unmarried minor, or a disabled person who became disabled before the age of 22.

[¶3902.3] Social Security Disability Benefits

The Supreme Court ruled that the Secretary of the Department of Health and Human Services (the federal agency that administers the Social Security program) is entitled to take an immediate appeal when a District Court order invalidates HHS regulations about the scope of the inquiries that HHS can make in ruling on an application for benefits paid to disabled widows.[2]

The "current condition" of a claimant must be considered at a benefits termination hearing; according to the Sixth Circuit,[3] this means the condition at the time of the termination hearing, *not* the time when the decision to terminate benefits was made.

Rules have been promulgated for evaluation of pain and other symptoms.[4] According to the Ninth Circuit, in a disability case involving subjective pain, the claimant must produce medical evidence of underlying impairment reasonably likely to cause pain, but is not obligated to produce objective medical evidence of the severity of the pain.[5]

HHS interpreted 42 U.S.C. 422(c) to forbid payment of disability benefits in a case where a trial work period began more than five, but less than 12 months after an injury, and before disability benefits were awarded. However, the Tenth Circuit struck down this interpretation as unreasonable.[6] To the Court of Appeals, a trial work period should be permitted whenever a disability has lasted five months and is expected to last 12 months.

If disability benefits are denied, and the Appeals Council denies review of the denial, a federal court cannot reverse the ALJ decision based on evidence that was first submitted to the Appeals Council (and was not before the ALJ)—unless the Council's failure to consider the evidence constituted an error of law.[7]

[¶3903] MEDICARE

The Medicare program (enacted by Title XVIII of the Social Security Act), divided into Parts A and B, provides substantial payments for health care costs of senior citizens (persons over 65). Part A provides coverage for inpatient hospital treatment, and skilled nursing care and home care when they are sequels to hospitalization. Part B provides coverage for outpatient visits to doctors, certain diagnostic procedures, and certain drugs and medical supplies (not, however, routine self-administered prescription drugs).

To qualify for Medicare, a person need only be over 65. No means test is involved. Those receiving Social Security or Railroad Retirement benefits (whether based on their own or someone else's earnings record) are automatically enrolled in Medicare Part A. An application is required for those who want Medicare but not retirement benefits (for instance, a person who continues to be employed past age 65). Medicare is only a secondary payor for persons covered by employer-paid health insurance plans: that is, the older employee must look to the employer plan for payment of covered expenses before filing a Medicare claim.

Persons over 65 who are not otherwise eligible can buy Medicare Part A coverage for a monthly premium. However, this is not a popular option: most people are covered by the Social Security system, and those who are not are unlikely to be able to afford more than $2,000 a year for health insurance.

Participation in Part B of Medicare, however, is optional, and coverage must be purchased. The amount paid is deducted from the Social Security checks of Medicare participants who receive Social Security benefits, billed (usually quarterly) to others.

The "Medicare tax" of 1.45 percent, instead of being limited to the FICA wage base of $60,600 for 1994, ($61,200 for 1995), continues to apply to all wages above this amount (Revenue Reconciliation Act of 1993 (part of OBRA '93, P.L. 103-66).

The Act also expands the reach of the "Medicare Secondary Payor" provisions that shift part of the cost of health care for the elderly to employers and private insurers.

Health care providers who receive reimbursement from Medicare (or Medicaid) must have written policies and procedures to deal with "Living Wills" and other advance directives expressing a person's wishes with regard to life support technology. All adult patients must be advised of their rights under state law (including the right to refuse treatment and to make advance directives).

At the end of 1991, a Final Rule was issued on the Resource-Based Relative Value Scale system of reimbursement for physicians under Medicare Plan B.[8] The reimbursement system will be phased in over a five-year period. Payments for care and cognitive services are enhanced, but fees based on procedures performed are reduced from previously prevailing Medicare levels. The final schedule of fees is 132% higher than the proposed fee schedule, but even so, doctors were greatly displeased and threatened to restrict treatment on Medicare patients.

Although hospitals that receive federal funding are subject to penalties for "dumping" (refusing to admit, or improperly transferring, patients who are not in stable condition), the penalties can only be assessed by the Medicare system; there is no private right of action against a doctor who "dumps" a patient from the hospital.[9]

"Dual eligibles" are persons who qualify for both Medicare and Medicaid (i.e., they are over 65 or disabled, and also indigent or incapable of paying their medical bills).

[¶3903.1] Medicare Coverage

Part A provides inpatient services—that is, services to those occupying a bed for the receipt of inpatient hospital services (bed and board, in a semiprivate room unless the patient's condition requires a private room, or unless no semiprivate or ward accommodations are available; services of medical and nursing personnel within the hospital; drugs and supplies provided during the hospital stay; and physical, speech, and occupational therapy if they are reasonable, necessary, and part of a doctor's written treatment plan).

Payment for Medicare hospitalization has been revolutionized by the Medicare Catastrophic Coverage Act of 1988 (P.L. 100—360). Under prior law, Medicare patients were required to pay an initial deductible before Medicare began to pay for hospital costs. Then, for the first 60 days of hospitalization, Medicare would assume the rest. For days 61–90 of a hospital stay, patients were required to pay a "coinsurance" amount. Medicare coverage was limited to 90 days per "spell of illness" (a technical term, which can be defined simplistically as a separate episode of illness), but beneficiaries were entitled to up to 60 "lifetime reserve days." Patients had to pay twice the normal coinsurance amount during these days; once they were used up (i.e., if a spell of illness extended past 150 days), they could not be re-used in another spell of illness.

The effect of MCCA is to eliminate the "spell of illness" concept. Beneficiaries pay only one deductible per year (not per spell of illness). Inpatient hospital services are now covered for an unlimited number of days, as long as medically required. Nor must patients pay coinsurance amounts for inpatient hospitalization.

However, this expanded coverage comes at a price. All Medicare beneficiaries with income tax liability over $150 must pay a supplemental Medicare premium in the form of an income tax surcharge. (Conventional Medicare premiums will also be raised to finance the broader benefits.) The supplemental premium rate is expressed as a dollar figure per $150 of tax liability, up to a maximum amount.

Part A is not limited to inpatient hospital services. Benefits are also available for up to 150 days of "skilled nursing facility" (SNF) services per year (up from 100 days before the Catastrophic Coverage Act), with a coinsurance requirement (but no deductible) for the first eight days of coverage only. The coinsurance amount equals 20% of the national average cost of SNF care. However, Part A nursing home services are for recuperation from acute illness, not for the custodial care required by many frail elderly persons.

Medicare Part A also covers home health services (e.g., skilled nursing; assistance from a home health aide; physical, speech, and occupational therapy) provided by and through a home health agency participating in the Medicare program. A physician must certify that the Medicare beneficiary is confined to home by his or her medical condition, and requires part-time or intermittent skilled nursing care.

Medicare Part B covers outpatient medical visits, certain diagnostic tests, and certain home health care services. As of January 1, 1991, Part B also covers most prescription drugs. Part B pays 100% of the reasonable cost of covered home health services, certain diagnostic tests, and X-rays and pathology services for hospital inpatients.

There is an annual Part B deductible of $75. Physicians who "accept assignment" under Part B agree to be paid directly by Medicare, and to accept Medicare's definition of the "reasonable charge for a covered service" as their entire fee for the medical visit or other treatment. Otherwise, the patient pays the physician directly, and applies for Medicare reimbursement, which will be limited to 80% of the Medicare-defined reasonable charge. The patient is responsible for paying the other 20%, and for any amount the physician charges in excess of the reasonable charge as defined by Medicare.

Another effect of the Medicare Catastrophic Coverage Act is to limit senior citizens' out-of-pocket expenses. The senior citizen pays the annual deductible, a deductible for the first three pints of blood received, and the 20% coinsurance. However, once the out-of-pocket limit is reached, Medicare will pay 100% of Part B expenses up to the level of "reasonable charges" for each service. The senior citizen still has to pay any amount billed in excess of the reasonable charges.

Although Part A is administered directly by the Health Care Finance Administration of the Social Security Administration, Part B is administered by "carriers," also called "intermediaries": private insurance companies selected by the Department of Health and Human Services. The carriers set the payment rates, pay claims, and field complaints from beneficiaries and health care providers.

[¶3903.2] "Medi-Gap" Insurance

Although the Catastrophic Coverage Act provides coverage more extensive than that under prior law, Medicare beneficiaries are still responsible for deductibles, coinsurance, the Part B out-of-pocket amount, and Part B fees over and above the official reasonable charges. Private insurers sell policies (nicknamed "Medi-Gap" policies) to cover such amounts. The urgency of purchasing such policies is somewhat diminished by the Catastrophic Coverage Act, but they still retain some usefulness.

Medi-Gap policies span a wide range, from excellent, comprehensive, and reasonably priced insurance products to overpriced rip-offs providing minimal benefits at maximum cost. State statutes control terms such as" disclosure" and "loss ratios" (percentage of premiums collected that must be disbursed in paying benefits). The Catastrophic Coverage Act mandates that the National Association of Insurance Commissioners update its standards for Medi-Gap policies to deal with the new legislation. Many state statutes adopt the NAIC standards for state regulatory purposes; in other states, advise your clients that selecting a policy lacking the NAIC seal of approval is a poor financial planning move.

OBRA '90 (P.L. 101-508, Sections 4351-4361) significantly tightened federal regulation of "Medi-Gap" insurance policies. Insurers are subject to civil penalties if they issue and sell Medi-Gap policies that fail to meet the new standards. Policies win be highly standardized, because the National Association of Insurance Commissioners is mandated to identify a core of basic benefit provisions. Insurers must offer stripped-down policies limited to core benefits—and only ten "benefit package" options can be offered by any or all insurers.

Medi-Gap policies must be guaranteed renewable; that is, the insurer can stop offering a policy altogether, but cannot refuse renewal based on a person's health status, or for reasons other than nonpayment of premium or misrepresentation on the application.

Insurers are no longer permitted to sell duplicative Medi-Gap policies to persons who already own policies, or to sell any Medi-Gap policies to Medicaid-eligible individuals.

[¶3904] MEDICAID

Despite the extensions of coverage under the Catastrophic Coverage Act, at least one very important area remains uncovered by Medicare: custodial care for chronically ill elderly persons needing assistance with the activities of daily living. Nursing home care usually costs over $20,000 a year and can cost more than $60,000 a year.

Medicare won't pay these bills. Some private insurers do offer long-term care insurance, but these products are new, untested, and not yet a solution for today's senior citizens, although they may be for those requiring chronic care in the next decade or so.

For most chronically ill elderly persons, there are a few choices, all unpalatable. They can struggle along, doing without needed care. They can devote all their income, and the hard-earned resources of a lifetime, to the cost of medical care. In many cases, even this isn't enough, and a person or couple becomes destitute and qualifies for Medicaid, the means-tested ("Welfare") program for the indigent. To qualify for Medicaid, the recipient must devote virtually all income (except for a minimal monthly personal needs allowance) to medical care, and must be virtually devoid of non-exempt resources.

The Medicare Catastrophic Coverage Act contains extensive Medicaid provisions, but they are so badly drafted that there is a great deal of uncertainty about their reach and meaning. Federal litigation will be necessary to interpret these highly ambiguous provisions, and Congressional action is not unlikely.

The most recent development was the passage of OBRA '93, P.L. 103-66. OBRA '93 attempts to reduce the cost of Medicaid by reducing the number of people who apply, and by increasing the power of states to seek estate recovery after the death of a Medicaid beneficiary.

Before OBRA '93, the look-back period for Medicaid applications (the period of time during which transfers by an applicant or applicant's spouse would be scrutinized) was 30 months. Coincidentally, the longest penalty period that could be imposed if the applicant made uncompensated transfers of assets during the look-back period was also 30 months. OBRA '93 extended the look-back period to 36 months for most transfers (and to 60 months for certain transfers involving irrevocable trusts), and removed the penalty cap, with the result that a large transfer of assets can give rise to a delay of so many months that a Medicaid application becomes unfeasible.

Prior law restricted states' power of estate recovery to placing a lien on the Medicaid recipient's homestead. There were several restrictions on when the lien could be placed and when it could be enforced: if a spouse, minor, or disabled child lived in the home, enforcement would be delayed or prevented. OBRA '93 requires that states seek estate recovery from the estates of Medicaid beneficiaries who obtained institutional level services (nursing home care and home care under certain programs), and allows estate recovery in the case of other types of Medicaid home care. Furthermore, estate recovery is possible against the beneficiary's interest in all types of real and personal property, not just the homestead; and recoveries are permissible whether or not the asset is part of the probate estate.

New York's "census" requirement, forcing nursing homes that join the Medicaid program to admit a percentage of Medicaid patients has been upheld as a reasonable exercise of statutory policy to protect Medicaid recipients from discrimination in nursing home entrance.[10]

A Medicaid regulation (42 CFR 456.653(a)(3), implementing 42 U.S.C. Section 1396b(g)(4)(b)) penalizes states that fail to inspect all Medicaid nursing homes within the state. The penalty is a reduction in federal Medicaid funding. A penalty is not imposed either if a state has exercised good faith and due diligence in its inspections, or if it would have inspected 100% of all nursing homes except for failings of a purely technical nature. Good faith and due diligence mean that some facilities were not inspected because of events beyond the state's control, which it could not reasonably have anticipated.

The Ninth Circuit has permitted the Medicaid system to treat child support paid, and income tax withheld, as income that remains available to a person receiving Medicaid benefits for institutional care. That means that, although the Medicaid beneficiary does not receive these amounts in cash, they still affect his eligibility for Medicaid and also affect the amount of his income that he must "spend down" on medical care as a condition of receiving Medicaid benefits.[11]

[¶3904.1] Medicaid Coverage

Medicaid (Title XIX of the Social Security Act) is both a federal and a state program. The federal government provides much of the funding, and sets minimum standards for state Medicaid programs. The states are permitted to provide for extensive services, to larger groups of people, on terms more favorable to the applicant, but may not fall below federal requirements. Thus, consulting state law is essential in dealing with any Medicaid problem or planning situation.

Federal law requires states to provide Medicaid coverage to the "categorically needy"; that is, those who fall into certain categories. Those who receive Aid to Families with Dependent Children or Supplemental Security Income (SSI) are eligible for Medicaid because they fall into these categories.

"Optionally categorically needy" people (who can be covered or not, at the state's option) include those who would be eligible for SSI, except for the fact that they live in institutions (e.g., nursing homes) and those who are institutionalized and whose income is less than three times the level of SSI payments.

"Medically needy" people are those who are not indigent by normal standards, but whose income and resources are too small to pay their medical bills. Once again, it's up to the states to decide whether to cover the medically needy or restrict coverage to the categorically needy or categorically and optionally categorically needy. Medically needy individuals must be allowed to "spend down"— to use their excess income to pay medical bills, then apply for Medicaid. (Some states allow Medicaid applicants to spend down their excess resources also.) Medicaid coverage for pregnant women with incomes below the poverty level, and their infants, is required.

The Catastrophic Coverage Act requires states to pay Medicare premiums, deductibles, and coinsurance for senior citizens with below-poverty-level incomes, on a phased-in basis beginning in 1989 over five years.

[¶3904.2] Income and Resource Limitations

Federal law imposes a complex, technical system of limitations on the states' power to set income and resource limitations. Medicaid eligibility depends on all earned and unearned income, and all resources unless specifically exempt from consideration. Because it is a welfare program, income and resource limitations are quite low (only a few hundred dollars in monthly income, and an amount of resources under $5,000, are permitted). State standards must be based on family size, and must be reasonable.

Federal law requires certain assets to be treated as exempt: the applicant's home (although it may be possible for a lien to be placed on the home after the applicant's death, if no surviving spouse, minor child, or disabled child lives there); household goods; an automobile; a burial plot; burial insurance. This requirement makes it inadvisable for your elderly clients to sell their homes and move to rented accommodations.

Although this strategy may seem desirable to save trouble and take advantage of the exclusion from income of up to $125,000 in home-sale profits received by a senior citizen, it is undesirable if either spouse may ever need nursing home care. A substantial exempt resource, which can be passed on to the spouse, is converted into cash, which can either preclude Medicaid eligibility or delay it until the excess income has been "spent down."

Each spouse's income and resources can be "deemed" available to the other spouse who requires nursing-home care or otherwise needs Medicaid benefits. The degree to which deeming is carried out in a particular state, and whether the state's policy complies with federal rules, are complex technical matters; the practitioner must keep up with current local caselaw and administrative rulemaking.

However, once a couple is separated by the institutionalization of one spouse, "deeming" is limited, and stops either six months or one month after the separation. Once the deeming stops, only actual contributions by the community spouse are considered in determining the institutionalized spouse's income and resources.

Deeming harms the ill elderly in two ways. First, it makes it difficult to obtain Medicaid. Second, if the deemed amounts are used to pay for the sick spouse's medical care, the community spouse may not have enough to live on.

[¶3904.3] Availability and Asset Transfers

The most obvious response to an asset limitation is to transfer assets (e.g., to the spouse; to the Medicaid applicant's children) in order to reduce the applicant's assets to acceptable levels. This response is so obvious that Congress and the states have riposted by legislating about gratuitous or not fully compensated asset transfers within a certain period of time (usually thirty months) of a Medicaid application. The general rule is that transfers will be disregarded, and the applicant treated as if he or she still had the resources available; and Medicaid will be denied until the applicant has spent at least the equivalent of the transferred amounts on medical care. There is a rebuttable presumption that transfers were made specifically to qualify for benefits; the presumption can be rebutted by showing other purposes (e.g., helping a family member in need). Transfers before the statutory period will not be taken into account.

A more subtle response to qualifications based on assets "available to" the applicant (that is, resources that he or she can turn into cash and use to pay medical bills) is the creation of trusts tied up in various ways to prevent the trust assets' characterization as available to the trust beneficiary and potential Medicaid applicant. However, the Comprehensive Omnibus Budget Reconciliation Act of 1985 defines the principal of a "Medicaid qualifying trust" as available to the applicant. A Medicaid qualifying trust is one established by the applicant or spouse, giving the trustee discretion to distribute income and/or principal to a group including the applicant. However, states do have the power to waive the application of this rule if it causes "undue hardship"—as it is bound to do in many cases.

The Catastrophic Coverage Act has adopted a new "snapshot rule" as of September 30, 1989. If a person is already institutionalized and applies for Medicaid, at a time when he or she has a spouse in a community, the state must take a "snapshot" of the couple's non-exempt resources at the time of the application. The resources must then be divided in half and half assigned to each spouse; the community spouse must be allowed to retain assets of at least $12,000 (regardless of whose name title to the assets was held in). States are allowed to protect even more resources for the community spouse—up to $60,000. If the community spouse can prevail in court or at a Medicaid fair hearing, he or she can retain assets in addition to the $60,000.

The transfer rules under the Catastrophic Coverage Act are so confusing that no definite statement can be made at this time as to what they say or how you should advise your clients.

[¶3905] SUPPLEMENTAL SECURITY INCOME (SSI)

Supplemental Security Income is a federal welfare program providing small income payments to extremely poor elderly (over 65), blind, or disabled persons. The states have the option of providing payments to supplement SSI; all of them have adopted this option to a greater or lesser degree.

The federal SSI rules, found at 42 U.S.C. §1381 et. seq., are significant and worth studying—not only because they provide income for some poverty-stricken individuals, but because a great deal of SSI methodology has been adopted in, or adapted by, the Medicaid program. Therefore, a secure understanding of Medicaid law and practice requires a thorough grounding in the SSI rules.

Under P.L. 102-265, the SSI benefits of a blind person who has a plan for achieving self-support will not be treated as income in determining food stamp eligibility.

To claim SSI benefits based on an alcoholism disability, the claimant must prove inability to perform the previous occupation, not just that he or she has been diagnosed as an alcoholic.[12]

An SSI check cannot be garnisheed to meet child support obligations, because SSI checks are public assistance to individuals, rather than earnings-linked payments intended to benefit an entire family.[13]

— ENDNOTES —

1. Austin v. Shalala, 994 F.2d 1170 (5th Cir. 7/13/93).

2. Sullivan v. Finklestein, 110 S.Ct 2658 (Sup.Ct. 6/18/90).

3. Difford v. Sec'y of HHS, 910 F.2d 1316 (6th Cir. 8/10/90).

4. 56 FR 57928 (11/14/91), affecting 20 CFR 404-1529(a) [OASDI] and 416.929(a) [SSI].

5. Bumell v. Sullivan, 947 F.2d 321 (9th Cir. 10/1/91).

6 Walker v. Sec'y of HHS, 943 F.2d 1257 (10th Cir. 9/5/91).

7. Eads v. Secretary of HHS, 983 F-2d 815 (7th Cir. 1/11/93).

8. 56 FR 59502 (11/15/91).

9. Baber v. Hospital Corp. of America, 977 F.2d 872 (4th Cir. 10/7/92).

10. New York State Health Facilities Ass'n v. Axelrod, 77 N.Y.2d 340, 568 N.Y.S.2d 385, 564 N.E.2d 1051 (N.Y. App. 2/19/91).

11. Peura v. Mala, 977 F.2d 484 (9th Cir. 10/9/92).

12. Clem v. Sullivan, 894 F.2d 328 (9th Cir. 1/22/90).

13. Tennessee Dep't of Social Svce. *ex.rel* Young v. Young, 802 S.W.2d 594 (Tenn.Sup. 12/31/90).

— FOR FURTHER REFERENCE —

Brewer, Bess M., "Risky Business: Five Years of Navigating the Medicare Part B Appeals Process," 26 *Clearinghouse Review* 537 (September '92).

Chiplin, Alfred J. Jr., "The Medicare Limiting Charge: An Issue of Implementation and Enforcement," 26 *Clearinghouse Review* 167 (May–June '92).

Christensen, Sandra, "Tbe Subsidy Provided Under Medicare to Current Enrollees," 17 *J. of Health Politics, Policy & Law* 255 (Summer '92).

Feldstein, Martin S. and Andrew Samwick, "Social Security Rules and Marginal Tax Rates," 45 *National Tax J.* 1 (March '92).

Goldhammer, Alan K., "Evidentiary Considerations in Disability Adjudication—A Judge's Perspective," 44 *Administrative L. Rev.* 445 (Spring '92).

Hollen, Charles R., "The Unintended Evolution of Medicare Fraud and Abuse," 35 *Trauma* 45 (August '92).

Kennedy, Lenna, "Children Receiving SSI Payments," 56 *Social Security Bulletin* 77 (Summer '93).

Kochhar, Satya, "Denial of SSI Because of Excess Resources," 55 *Social Security Bulletin* 52 (Summer '92).

Kruse, Clifton B. Jr., "Trusts That May Prove Useful in Medicaid Planning," 131 *Trusts and Estates* 22 (July '92).

Leonesio, Michael V., "Social Security and Older Workers," 56 *Social Security Bulletin* 47 (Summer '93).

Mehlman, Maxwell J. and Karen A. Visocan, "Medicare and Medicaid: Are They Just Health Care Systems?" 29 *Houston L. Rev.* 835 (Winter '92).

Scott, Charles G., "Disabled SSI Recipients Who Work," *55 Social Security Bulletin* 26 (Spring '92).

Sproghe, Hans and Carl A. Brooks, "Understanding Social Security Retirement Benefits," 174 *J. of Accountancy* 53 (August '92).

Zelenski, Ethel, "Social Security: Navigating the Appeals Process," 16 *Family Advocate* 46 (Summer '93).

SURETIES, GUARANTORS, AND INDEMNIFICATION

[¶4001] Business people use various devices to assure that obligations owed to them will be fulfilled. One common method of protection is the use of a surety or guarantor. The law governing sureties and guarantors is somewhat specialized. Basically, it deals with the relationship of three individuals:

(1) The *obligee:* the person to be protected (the creditor);

(2) The *principal obligor:* the buyer, borrower, or contractor;

(3) The *surety or guarantor:* the person supplying the protection.

[¶4002] USE OF THE SURETY OR GUARANTOR

Sureties and guarantors are used most frequently when the obligee demands security because of the obligor's weak financial position. They can be used to secure an installment sale, for example, even though the seller retains a security interest in the property sold. Similarly, they may be used to back up a secured loan.

There are certain areas in which the functions of the surety and guarantor have special uses. One important area is in dealing with a newly formed corporation with thin capitalization. In such cases the stockholders will ordinarily be called on to act as sureties or guarantors for the corporation. In so doing they will aid both the creditor and the corporation. The creditor gets the personal liability of the stockholders; the corporation benefits to the degree that the stockholders, realizing their personal liability, will be less disposed to weaken the corporation's financial condition by making large withdrawals.

Sureties and guarantors are frequently required in building and construction contracts in order to guarantee performance. As a matter of fact, statutes may require the posting of surety bonds, especially when public contracts and, in some instances, private contracts are involved. Such surety contracts take on the appearance of insurance contracts, and some states do look on them as such.

A third area of general use will involve the guarantee of a loan for a close relative who is starting a new venture. In addition, businesses that have successfully operated for a while but have begun to falter may also be called on to furnish a surety or guarantor.

[¶4003] DISTINCTION BETWEEN SURETY AND GUARANTOR

Although some people tend to use the terms "surety" and "guarantor" interchangeably, there are some legal distinctions.

Both sureties and guarantors perform essentially the same commercial function. Both lend their names and credit standing to the principal obligor and agree to make good any shortcomings in the performance of his or her obligations to the obligee. But, according to many courts, there are differences:

❑ A surety is a co-promissor with the principal obligor and is equally liable with him on the obligation.

❑ A guarantor is a collateral promissor whose liability arises only after all attempts to make the principal obligor perform have failed.

On this basis, the guarantor must receive notice of the principal obligor's default before there can be any obligation on his or her part. However, the differences begin to break down when some of the same courts pronouncing these distinctions talk about sureties being guarantors of payment—a true guarantor, they say, is merely a guarantor of collection.

Other courts use the terms "surety" and "guarantor" interchangeably; the Uniform Commercial Code says the term "surety" includes "guarantor" (UCC §1-201(40)).

In view of these problems, some states spell out specifically the obligation or liability of the third party to the deal. Generally, for a third party to guarantee payment, it will not be enough to have him or her simply sign the instrument or contract to be guaranteed as a guarantor; the third party will have to endorse "payment guaranteed." On the other hand, someone who is asked to give a guarantee who only wants to give a guarantee of *collection* will have to spell that out—"collection guaranteed." This is important when dealing with an "instrument" within the reach of the Commercial Paper Article of the UCC, which says that use of words of guarantee, without more, operates to guarantee payment (UCC §316(3)).

[¶4004] CAPACITY OF A PARTNERSHIP TO BECOME A SURETY OR GUARANTOR

Sureties and guarantors must have legal capacity to enter into a contract relationship. However, a problem may arise when a partnership acts as a surety or guarantor. Ordinarily, a partner has no implied authority to enter into a contract of surety or guarantee in the firm name. Sometimes the required authority may be implied from the common course of business of the firm or from a previous course of dealing with the partnership. If the partner or partners do not have the express or implied authority to bind the firm, the obligee may only get the *individual* obligations of those purporting to act for the firm.

[¶4005] CAPACITY OF A CORPORATION TO BECOME A SURETY OR GUARANTOR

A corporation's capacity to act as an uncompensated surety or guarantor is severely limited, as the following rules point out.

The first rule is that a corporation cannot become a surety or guarantor *solely* for the principal obligor's benefit, unless it is given such power by its charter or statute—as when it is in the business of being a surety. Within this prohibition are guarantees of loans to directors, officers, or stockholders. So far as the rule operates to protect stockholders, it can be circumvented by getting the consent of all of the stockholders. However, creditors of the corporation may claim that the obligation assumed was beyond the corporation's authority. Usually, such a claim would be made only in situations when the corporation is not meeting its obligations to its creditors and shouldn't present a grave problem if the corporation has a good credit rating.

The second rule to bear in mind is that a corporation does not need *express* power to act as a surety or guarantor but has *implied* power to do so when such action will "directly" promote its business purpose. What kind of activity promotes business purpose? The following acts have been held to directly benefit the corporate business purpose:

(1) Guaranteeing a customer's loan when there is a potential benefit from increased sales.

(2) Protecting the corporation's own interest by guaranteeing a loan to a subsidiary.

(3) Guaranteeing a debt of one of the corporation's own debtors in order to keep him going and so increase its chances of being paid.

In order to rely on the corporation's obligation, a corporate resolution that directly relates the guarantee to the promotion of a business purpose must be passed. If a resolution cannot be legitimately formulated in these terms, two courses of action are then available: (1) unanimous stockholder consent; or (2) a guarantee by the stockholders or directors or some of them as individuals.

[¶4006] Selecting a Surety or Guarantor

When dealing with a paid surety (one who is in the business of being a surety), ordinarily there will be no need to worry about the surety being able to make good on the principal's obligations. Since paid sureties are subject to state regulation, this gives some assurance of their financial condition. As for private sureties and guarantors, their obligation is no better than their financial standing.

To rely on a nonprofessional guarantor or surety to back up the principal's obligation, run a credit check through an established agency and get character references and financial statements. The relationship of the surety or guarantor to the principal obligor is often an important consideration. The chances are that a surety acting for his or her son, for example, will be more apt to fulfill an obligation than if a stranger is involved.

[¶4007] THE SURETY OR GUARANTEE AGREEMENT—WRITING REQUIREMENT

The surety or guarantor's contract should be put in writing. Since these contracts are generally regarded as contracts to answer for the debt or default of another, they must be in writing in accordance with the Statute of Frauds. In addition, a written agreement helps avoid disputes as to the rights and obligations of the parties. What finally goes into the contract will depend on the skill and judgment of the parties and their relative bargaining position.

[¶4008] CHECKLIST FOR DRAFTING THE AGREEMENT

Here is a checklist for drafting a suretyship or guarantee agreement.
- The obligation(s) secured—present, past, future.
- The nature of the guarantee or the suretyship.
  (1) Primary or secondary, payment or collection.
  (2) Conditions of liability.
  (3) Amount of liability.
      (a) Costs and expenses.
      (b) Attorney's fee.
      (c) Interest.
      (d) Limitation of liability to a specified maximum.
      (e) When there are two or more guarantors or sureties.
  (4) Duration of liability.
      (a) Revocation—when and how agreement can be revoked.
      (b) Effect of death, insolvency, etc., of co-sureties or co-guarantors.
  (5) Exceptions to liability—e.g., acts of God as excusing performance.
  (6) Persons protected and persons bound by the agreement.
- Notice to the guarantor or surety.
  (1) Principal's default.
  (2) Creation or amount of indebtedness.
  (3) Alterations or changes in contract.
  (4) Claims or liens against principal.
- The effect of alterations or changes in the principal's obligation.
  (1) Generally.
  (2) Compromise or settlement with principal debtor.
  (3) Time extensions to principal debtor.
- Indemnification of the surety or the guarantor.
- Subrogation to the rights of the principal or obligee.

❏ Waivers—necessity of having these in writing.

As stated above, these are the main points to watch for. Special situations may call for special provisions not suggested in this list.

[¶4009] THE CONTINUING AND RESTRICTED GUARANTEE

A guarantee need not be restricted to a specific transaction. It can be a continuing one, contemplating future uses or a series of transactions.

The continuing guarantee can be a very dangerous and expensive instrument from the guarantor's point of view. Therefore, it is wise to set forth in detail the conditions of the guarantee. The most important thing is to limit the amount guaranteed, the period over which it will be effective, and the type of transaction for which it can be used. If this is not done, the guarantor may be guaranteeing some of the principal obligor's personal obligations.

[¶4010] PRINCIPAL OBLIGOR'S SIGNATURE

Whether the principial obligor's signature must appear on the contract of the surety or guarantor is an issue that has given the courts considerable difficulty. While there are numerous decisions to the effect that the signature is not necessary, it is advisable to obtain the signature. In the rare instance when the principal is not to know that the obligation is being guaranteed, check applicable state law before entering into the contract.

[¶4011] ACCEPTANCE, APPROVAL, AND FILING

A contract of suretyship, like any other contract, requires acceptance. When the obligation runs to a governmental body or agency, certain persons or officers will usually be entrusted with the duty of accepting and approving the bond or contract, and there may be special provisions for filing or recording the instrument after its approval.

[¶4012] THE PRINCIPLE OF INDEMNITY

A surety or guarantor who has paid the principal obligor's debt *or* performed his or her contract has a right to be reimbursed—indemnified—by the principal for the amount paid. There is no right of indemnity until the surety or guarantor has paid out money. Therefore, if a compromise and settlement with the obligee for less than the full amount owing has been worked out, the surety or guarantor can enforce a right to indemnity only up to the compromised amount. A right of indemnity does not have to be spelled out in the contract; it will be implied. Nevertheless, it is best to put it in writing, specifying just how far indemnification goes (court costs, counsel fees, etc.) and how the surety or guarantor is to prove a payment before his or her right to indemnification accrues.

[¶4013] UNDERSTANDING THE CONCEPT OF EXONERATION

If the principal obligor's debt or performance becomes due, and the obligee fails to take action, statutes in many states allow the surety to bring a suit and compel the creditor (obligee) to sue the obligor and thus collect the debt. Some states even allow the surety to sue the principal to compel payment. In other words, the surety need not pay the obligee and then try to get reimbursed from the principal obligor; he or she can take the initiative in forcing the obligor to pay.

In the case of co-guarantors, one guarantor may sue the other guarantors to compel payment of their share of the guarantee to the creditor, instead of paying the full amount due and then seeking contribution from the co-guarantors (see ¶4015). Use of exoneration will prevent the co-guarantor from having to pay more than this share of the guarantee, and will safeguard the creditor's rights. However, if the legal process of compelling such exoneration will be lengthy, many courts may be hesitant to require the creditor to wait so long for payment, and may require the guarantor to seek contribution from the other guarantors.

[¶4014] SURROGATION

The surety or guarantor can "step into" the obligee's shoes after she has paid the obligation. She is entitled to all the remedies that the obligee had against the principal and she can also have any collateral securities that the obligor pledged with the obligee. When the right of subrogation is coupled with indemnity, the surety may, in certain instances, acquire the preferred status of the obligee and thus be more likely to receive reimbursement. For example, suppose a person becomes a surety on a government contract and the principal obligor fails to perform. After the surety pays or performs for the government, she will be subrogated to the rights of the principal obligor and will then have the government's preferred status over other creditors.

[¶4015] CONTRIBUTION

The issue of contribution only arises when there are two or more sureties or guarantors. Contribution means that a surety who pays the obligee can compel the other sureties to pay their shares in order to make all the shares equal. The only requisite for this right is that all concerned be sureties for the same principal and the same obligation. They may, however, be bound on separate instruments and they may not have ever been aware of one another.

[¶4016] DISCHARGE OF THE SURETY OR GUARANTOR

Some actions may automatically discharge the surety or guarantor's obligations, unless prior consent was obtained or subsequent approval by the surety or guarantor was given. Listed below are some of the main causes of automatic discharge:

(1) Material alteration of the principal obligor's contract.

(2) Extension of time for payment of the principal debt.

(3) Failure of obligee to comply with request or notice to sue the principal obligor where a statute gives the surety or guarantor that right.

(4) Release or loss of the security.

(5) Payment or performance by the principal obligor.

(6) Release or discharge of the principal obligor.

(7) Change of principals or obligees.

The following paragraph discusses some of the related problems regarding such a discharge.

[¶4017] ADDITIONAL COMPLICATIONS IN THE DISCHARGE OF THE SURETY OR GUARANTOR

A material alteration, even though it may be to the advantage of the principal, may cause a discharge in some states. Usually, a compensated surety will be less likely to be discharged than an unpaid one. The compensated surety will usually have to prove damages before release from the obligation.

Mere failure to pursue the principal when the debt falls due does not operate as an extension. The extension has to be the result of a positive act. Most states have an exception to the rule of discharge by extension: there is no discharge if the obligee, in granting an extension, reserves rights against the surety.

Release of the security held by the obligee will operate to release the surety *to the extent that the remaining security is not enough to cover the debt.* Similarly, negligence on the part of the obligee in dealing with the security in his or her hands, resulting in its loss, may release the surety. Failure to perfect or to record the security interest can also result in discharge. (See ¶3601 et seq. for perfecting and recording a security interest.)

A surety may be discharged in some states if the Statute of Limitations runs out on the principal debt. In other states this won't work a discharge. An obligee should avoid being put in a position where the rule can be applied against him or her—go after the principal obligor as soon as he or she is in default.

Bankruptcy of the principal obligor, although it results in personal discharge, won't discharge the surety. The surety in this situation can only claim reimbursement from the bankrupt's estate.

Changes in the personnel of a partnership, even though the partnership keeps the same name, can result in discharge. But a mere change in name of the principal obligor, whether a partnership or a corporation, will not have that effect.

[¶4018] ANTICIPATE AND PREVENT AUTOMATIC DISCHARGE

Try to anticipate the various causes for discharge when structuring the surety or guarantor relationship. Where necessary, insert in the agreement any limitations that give the surety or guarantor the protection he demands. If the requisite consent is not obtained initially, try to get it before anything occurs that can result in discharge. Consent to an extension of time, for example, may not be too hard to obtain if the surety can also see personal benefits. If the consent is obtained, be sure to get it in writing.

In addition to "discharge" of the surety, there are other points for the obligee to remember in holding the surety or guarantor to his or her contract. Although these things may not operate to "discharge," the effect will be the same. Included in this category are some matters already discussed, such as the capacity or authority of the surety or guarantor, and the necessity of a written agreement to hold someone responsible for the debt of another. Certain defects in the principal obligor's contract may discharge the surety's obligation, such as lack of consideration, illegality, usury, or impossibility of performance. The defect must be one that *voids* the contract, not one that makes it *voidable*. For example, if a principal has not reached the age required to enter into a legally binding contract, this fact will ordinarily operate to make his or her contract *voidable* and will not automatically relieve the surety of an obligation.

[¶4019] PROTECTING THE SURETY'S INTEREST IN OBLIGOR'S COLLATERAL

Sureties often require some type of security from the principal obligor. Usually it will be quite obvious that the security interest granted, if it's to be good against third persons, will have to be perfected in one of the ways discussed in the chapter on secured transactions (see ¶3601). But sometimes this won't be so obvious. For example, the surety on a contractor's bond demands and gets an assignment of the payments that become due under the contract in order to secure her rights against the principal. The surety will have to follow UCC procedures to perfect her interest and make it stand up against other creditors of the principal obligor or others claiming an interest in the payments through her.

If the assignment of payments under a contract covers payments due at the time of the assignment, a somewhat different approach may be required. A surety who requires tangible or intangible security from the obligor for self-protection must be alert to the possibility that there is a security interest that is not perfected against third persons unless positive steps are taken to this end.

[¶4020] SURETIES AND GUARANTORS ON COMMERCIAL PAPER

Accommodation parties on commercial paper, whether their names appear as makers, drawers, acceptors, or endorsers, are, in effect, sureties or guarantors, despite the lack of a separate contract or use of the term "surety" or "guarantor."

[¶4021] LIABILITY UNDER THE UCC

Under UCC §3415(2), an accommodation party incurs contract liability on the instrument *in the capacity in which he or she signs*. Therefore, a person who signs a note as a maker will have the liability of a maker; a person who signs as an endorser will have the liability of an endorser. Payment by the accommodating party to the holder creates a cause of action in favor of the accommodating party based on the accommodated party's implied obligation to indemnify the accommodating party. Accommodation endorsers should include a waiver of suretyship defenses if that is the parties' intent. These various liabilities are discussed in detail beginning at ¶1101. It is sufficient to point out that the obligee will be in a better position if the accommodation party can be induced to sign as maker. As maker, that person's liability will be primary and not conditioned on presentment of the note, as might be the case if he or she signs as endorser.

Under the UCC, the liability of an accommodation party will run to a holder for value, even though the holder knows of the accommodation nature. Under UCC §3415(2), this is true only if the holder takes the instrument before it is due. And under this section of the UCC, liability is imposed on an accommodation endorser even though the endorsement takes place after delivery to the holder.

Under the UCC, as against anyone taking the paper with knowledge of the accommodation character, or a holder who is not a holder in due course, the accommodation party can set up any of the defenses that an ordinary surety might set up to relieve herself of liability. For example, she can avoid liability by showing an extension of time for payment made without her consent, and without an effective reservation of rights against her (see UCC §3-606). She will also be discharged by a release of collateral. If the accommodation party consents to any action that might discharge her, she will not be discharged. Therefore, consent in advance to certain actions, such as extension of time, is commonly incorporated in the instrument over the accommodation party's signature. If such consent is not obtained in advance, it can be given afterwards, and it will be binding even without consideration.

Normally, a holder in due course without actual notice of the accommodation need not be concerned about the defense of the accommodation party. However, an endorsement that is not in the chain of title—the irregular or anomalous endorsement—will be notice of the accommodation character (UCC §3-415(4)). Here's an example of such an endorsement: a note payable to Able or his order and made by Baker is endorsed by Charlie (the accommodation party) before Baker negotiates the note to a holder in due course.

The UCC makes it clear that both paid and gratuitous sureties may be accommodation parties.

[¶4022] UCC DISTINCTION BETWEEN GUARANTEEING PAYMENT AND COLLECTION

One who guarantees payment says in effect that he or she will pay the instrument when it becomes due, regardless of whether the holder has tried to collect from the party primarily liable. The guarantor of payment waives presentment and any necessary notice of dishonor and protest and any demand the holder has against the maker or drawer. In short, that person becomes a co-maker or co-drawer, jointly and separately liable.

On the other hand, one who guarantees collection says in effect that if the instrument is not paid when it becomes due, he or she will pay it, *if and only if* the holder first proceeds against the maker, drawer, or acceptor by suit and execution or shows that such action would be useless. A guarantor of collection also waives presentment and any necessary notice of dishonor or protest.

UCC §3-416 codifies these different meanings in accordance with commercial understanding and the accepted meaning of these terms under prior law.

When using these forms of guarantee consider:

(1) Limitation on the amount of the guarantee. It doesn't necessarily have to be for the full amount of the instrument.

(2) Consent to extension of time for payment or release of collateral.

(3) Payment of collection expenses, including attorneys' fees.

[¶4023] INDEMNITY AND HOLD HARMLESS AGREEMENTS

A business that can reduce its "cost of doing business" risks or shift these risks to others will be able to reduce costs and thus improve its competitive position. Indemnity and hold harmless agreements can be used to accomplish this.

Indemnity and hold harmless agreements are closely related. Whatever fine-spun distinctions there may be, the two forms of agreement can, for the most part, be considered identical, the terms used interchangeably, and refer to the parties in both types of agreements as indemnitor and indemnitee. These agreements may be used to:

(1) Assume the legal liability of others.

(2) Create an entirely new liability for the indemnitor.

(3) Create a contractual liability for the indemnitor in cases in which he or she is already liable in tort for the same risk.

Examples of these different uses appear in the following paragraphs. In connection with (3) above, there is the question of why anyone would want to add contractual liability to tort liability. Let's say a business person buys a heating system for a plant and the seller agrees to install it. The seller will be liable in any case for negligence in installing it, but the buyer is in a better position with not only the seller's tort liability (negligence) but also the contractual liability to hold the buyer harmless as well. There are a number of reasons for this, but the main ones are:

(1) In a contract action, all the buyer will have to prove is the contract and the damages. The buyer won't have to show negligence on the part of the seller and won't have to worry about the defenses of contributory negligence or assumption of risk.

(2) The measure of damages can be spelled out in a contract action.

(3) The time to sue is usually longer for contract actions than for tort actions.

The indemnification of corporate directors, officers, and other employees is discussed in ¶1526 et seq.

[¶4024] LEGALITY OF A HOLD HARMLESS AGREEMENT

An indemnity agreement will not offer the indemnitee positive protection against any wrongful or illegal acts if they are willful, grossly negligent, or contrary to strong public policy. The Restatement of Contracts §572 states that a bargain to indemnify another against the consequences of committing a tortious act is illegal, unless the performance of the tortious act is only an undesired possibility in the performance of the bargain and the bargain does not tend to induce the act. This leaves the door open for indemnification against acts of ordinary negligence and, in this respect, is in line with the law in most states. However, check state law.

Bear in mind that even though *contractual liability insurance* may be used to insure the hold harmless agreement as discussed at ¶4027, the insurance cannot be any better than the agreement; if the agreement is void, the insurance will be useless.

[¶4025] CHECKLIST OF USE OF HOLD HARMLESS AGREEMENTS IN COMMERCIAL TRANSACTIONS

Indemnity or hold harmless agreements may be useful in the following situations:

❑ Protection of retailer or wholesaler against product liability suits.

❒ Protection of purchaser against claims, losses, or expenses growing out of delivery, installation, or use of equipment or merchandise.

❒ Protection of lessor of equipment against claims, losses, or expenses growing out of lessee's use of the equipment or failure to insure against liability or loss of the property leased.

❒ Protection of a secured creditor against failure of a debtor to insure his or her collateral.

❒ Protection of a guarantor.

❒ Protection of the endorser of commercial paper.

[¶4026] THE INDEMNITOR AS AN INSURER

A hold harmless agreement, in effect, puts the indemnitor in the insurance business. But the usual indemnitor is not in the same class as a seasoned insurance carrier. Therefore, a hold harmless agreement will not be as good for the indemnitee as an insurance policy.

(1) If the hold harmless agreement is merely against loss, the indemnitee must pay the loss before seeking reimbursement from the insurer.

(2) The defense clause in an insurance policy is usually more favorable to the insured than a similar clause in a hold harmless agreement is likely to be.

(3) Insurance carriers are likely to do a better job than the usual indemnitor in investigating and defending claims and suits.

(4) The financial worth of an insurance carrier and ability to make good on its obligation to the policyholder is apt to be better than that of the usual indemnitor.

[¶4027] INSURING THE HOLD HARMLESS AGREEMENT

Many indemnitees will not be satisfied with a simple hold harmless agreement; they will want it backed up by insurance. The indemnitor may also want to insure the hold harmless agreement since he or she probably lacks the ability to spread the risk assumed.

A special form of insurance known as *contractual liability insurance* can be used. This coverage is usually obtained by way of a special endorsement on the indemnitor's liability policy. (The usual liability policy won't cover assumed or contractual liability without a special endorsement because the standard form of exclusion in almost all forms of liability policies reads: "This policy does not apply to liability assumed by the insured under any contract or agreement.")

Contractual liability coverage will not automatically cover all contracts that the insured has undertaken or may undertake during the policy period. It will be tailored to the insured's particular situation and will cover only specific contracts or types of contracts, and will be subject to the exclusions set out therein. The policy limits, in respect to amount, will normally be the same as those used in manufacturers' and contractors' liability policies. Rates will normally be fixed after submission of the specific contracts or types of contracts for rating.

[¶4028] ADDITIONAL INSURANCE COVERAGE MAY BE REQUIRED

The standard contractual liability endorsement has a number of exclusions (some of which may be deleted for an additional premium), such as:

❏ Liability for any warranty of goods or products. Products liability coverage is needed for this.

❏ Damages awarded in arbitration proceedings in which the insurer is not permitted to participate. Therefore, when drafting a hold harmless agreement that provides for arbitration, make sure that the insurer is permitted to participate.

❏ Any obligation for which the insured may be held liable by a third-party beneficiary of a contract.

❏ Defects in maps, plans, designs, or specifications of the insured.

❏ War damages.

❏ Dram shop. Many states impose absolute liability on those selling or giving drinks to one already drunk for the damage the drunken person may do.

❏ Worker's compensation, unemployment compensation, or disability benefits laws. However, contractual claims brought by an employee are not excluded.

❏ Property owned, occupied, rented, or in the care, custody, or control of the indemnitor insured. If the hold harmless agreement includes claims for these types of property by the indemnitor insured, the purchaser should obtain property damage insurance.

❏ Goods, products, or work completed out of which the accident arises. This is the same exclusion found in products liability insurance and is used in contractual liability insurance for the same reason—to bar covering the insured's own business risk of replacing defective products or work out of which the accident arises.

❏ Water damage.

❏ Nuclear energy. This hazard is covered by the nuclear energy pools.

[¶4029] CHECKLIST FOR DRAFTING HOLD HARMLESS AGREEMENTS

Here are some main points to be covered in negotiating and drafting a hold harmless agreement:

❏ Names and addresses of indemnitors and indemnitees.

❏ Consideration for the agreement; if it is part of a sale or of a lease, a separate statement of consideration will not be necessary.

❏ Scope of the indemnity:

(1) Is the indemnity to be against *liability* or against *loss?* If against liability, the indemnitee's legal rights arise as soon as the liability becomes fixed. If against loss, the rights arise only after the indemnitee has made payment or suffered an actual loss.

(2) Does it cover the costs and expenses of investigating or defending against liability or loss, including attorneys' fees?

(3) Does it obligate the indemnitor to investigate and defend claims against the indemnitee?

(4) Is the indemnity agreement in limited, intermediate, or broad form? The limited form gives indemnification where the indemnitor is guilty of active negligence and the indemnitee's negligence, if any, is at most passive. The intermediate form indemnifies even though the indemnitee may be guilty of active negligence. The broad form gives third parties rights against the indemnitor irrespective of his, her or anyone else's fault. These forms correspond to the classes used for normal rating purposes when contractual liability insurance coverage is to be used. Insurance rates will vary considerably, depending on which form is adopted.

(5) Is interest to be included? If the parties intend indemnification for damages and interest, interest should be expressly mentioned because there have been decisions excluding interest unless it is expressly included.

(6) Maximum amount of liability of the indemnitor.

❏ Duration of the indemnity.

❏ Notice to the indemnitor.

(1) When necessary.

(2) Time, mode of service.

(3) Contents.

❏ Rule of strict construction against the indemnitee. Bear in mind that courts often manage to cut the heart out of indemnity agreements by adopting a rule of strict construction against the indemnitee—especially in the case of agreements in intermediate or broad form. If indemnification against the indemnitee's own acts of negligence is intended, say so expressly.

❏ Compromise of claims by the indemnitee.

❏ Evidence of liability or loss.

❏ Security for the performance of the indemnitor's obligations under the agreement:

(1) Insurance.

(2) Bond.

(3) Deposit.

[¶4030] TAX ASPECTS OF GUARANTEES AND INDEMNIFICATIONS

The different and not wholly consistent tax treatment given bad debts and losses under the tax law gives rise to the need for precision in the drafting of guarantee, surety, and indemnity agreements. If the deal goes sour, the party ultimately making good may have (1) the status of a creditor of the defaulting obligor (as in the case of a guarantor) and suffer a bad debt if collection is not possible, or (2) the legal status of an independent obligor (as in the case of an indemnitor) and simply be considered to have suffered a loss.

[¶4031]   BAD DEBTS VS. LOSSES

The tax treatment of bad debts and losses as allowable deductions from taxable income revolves around four variables: Transactions by (1) individuals or (2) corporations that are (3) business or (4) nonbusiness. Corporations are generally deemed to be business entities, so their bad debts or losses are fully deductible. An individual is allowed a full deduction in a business transaction whether the obligation arises by way of bad debt or loss. Thus, in the case of corporations and individuals becoming obligated in *business* transactions, the distinction need not be so sharply drawn for tax purposes, unless the business nature of the transaction is itself in question. However, IRC §166(d) provides an individual with a limited deduction, equivalent to a short-term capital loss, for a nonbusiness bad debt when the obligation becomes totally worthless, but allows no deduction at all for a loss sustained in a transaction not entered into for profit.

Note that IRC §166(d)(1)(B) provides that in the case of a taxpayer other than a corporation, if any nonbusiness debt becomes worthless within the taxable year, the loss resulting therefrom shall be considered a loss from the sale or exchange, during the taxable year, of a capital asset *held for not more than one year.* Nonbusiness bad debt is defined at IRC §166(d)(2).

[¶4032]   BUSINESS VS. NONBUSINESS BAD DEBTS

The development of judicial distinctions between transactions deemed to be business and those deemed nonbusiness has resulted in a confusing case law. The distinction between business bad debt and nonbusiness bad debt rests on whether the debt was incurred in connection with the trade or business of the taxpayer (covering debts becoming worthless after the taxpayer has gone out of business) or incurred in the taxpayer's business. If it was, it is business bad debt.

Of course, the IRC also provides for nonbusiness casualty losses at §165(c), subject to a floor of 10% of AGI.

[¶4033]   STOCKHOLDER AS GUARANTOR OF CORPORATE DEBT

A stockholder's guarantee of the corporation's obligation is considered to be a nonbusiness transaction. If the stockholder is an individual and she has to make good, she is entitled to a short-term capital loss on a nonbusiness bad debt (*Putnam,* 352 US 82, 1952). It is clear that this is the tax treatment even if the corporation is insolvent at the time of payment and it could be argued that a claim to reimbursement by subrogation to creditor's rights is worthless. Ordinary loss treatment is available to an officer or employee who had to make loans to hold onto a job (*Generes,* 405 US 93, 1972).

[¶4034] PARENT CORPORATION AS GUARANTOR OF SUBSIDIARY'S EXPENSES AND DIVIDENDS

Generally a parent corporation must capitalize payments made to pay a subsidiary's business expenses and dividends (when called upon to honor its guarantee) by adding the same to its basis for the stock of the subsidiary, unless a direct benefit to the parent can be shown—for example, when the subsidiary performs vital services for the parent. A bona fide loan by a parent to its subsidiary might be better, since at best a full business bad debt deduction could be taken and at worst it would be treated as a capital expenditure.

[¶4035] PAYMENTS UNDER CERTAIN GUARANTEE AGREEMENTS NOT DEDUCTIBLE

Bad debt deductions are not allowed in the following situations:

(1) When the guarantee is given as a part of the purchase price of a capital asset, as distinguished from guaranteeing a loan, the guarantor's payment to the creditor is treated as a capital expenditure when the debtor doesn't pay up.

(2) If a corporate guarantor pays off obligations of its stockholders, such payments are considered as dividends and are not deductible.

(3) Guarantee of the obligation of family member. This is closely scrutinized to determine whether there is a valid business purpose before the business bad debt deduction is allowed. If the guarantor never expected repayment from the debtor-relative, the transaction might be considered a gift.

(4) If debtor is not liable to guarantor at law or, at the time of making the guarantee, there was no reasonable expectation of repayment. Before the guarantor can get a bad debt deduction she must be able to show that (1) originally she had reason to expect repayment and (2) after he honors his guarantee, the debtor's obligation to her is worthless.

[¶4036] TIMING OF LOSS BY CASH-BASIS TAXPAYER

To a large extent, given business justification, a cash basis guarantor or indemnitor can choose the year in which a loss will occur, since the loss is sustained only when (1) the guarantor's claim against the original debtor is worthless due to the latter's insolvency, and (2) the guarantor actually makes out of pocket cash disbursements in satisfaction of liability under the guarantee. If the guarantor gives the creditor a new note covering his or her liability under the guarantee, such a note does not constitute a cash disbursement until payments are made on it. But the deduction can be lost if the guarantor does not exercise legal rights—e.g., the statute of limitations.

[¶4037] TIMING OF LOSS BY ACCRUAL-BASIS TAXPAYER

An accrual-basis taxpayer who is an indemnitor may be able to deduct an indemnity loss in advance of the actual payment, but if she is a guarantor, she will have to wait until the year of payment, since the debt between the guarantor and the debtor doesn't arise until then (which becomes bad if the debtor can't pay off the guarantor).

[¶4038] CAPITAL LOSS BY INDEMNITOR

Payment made under an indemnity agreement will be treated as a capital loss if the indemnity was given as a part of the consideration for the sale of a capital asset.

— FOR FURTHER REFERENCE —

Barker, Ronald K., "Third Party Tort Claimants and the Contract Bond Surety," 5 *Construction Lawyer* 7 (Spring '84).

Edwards, Carolyn, "Impairment of Collateral Under Section 3-606 of the UCC," 12 *U. of Dayton L. Rev.* 509 (Spring '87).

Harrell, Thomas A., "Security Devices," 47 *Louisiana L. Rev.* 453 (November '86).

Leibowitz, Ephraim K., "Insider Preferences," 193 *New York L.J.* 1 (5/16/85).

McDonnell, Julian B., "Problems with Notes: Accrual, Acceleration, and Suretyship," 18 *Uniform Commercial Code Law J.* 40 (Summer '85).

Murray, Jerome and Michael Maillet, "Extra-Contractual Remedies and Punitive Damages in First Party Insurance Claims," 53 *Insurance Counsel J.* 251 (April '86).

Opperman, Leonard, "Pitfalls and Opportunities in Representing Guarantors," 30 *Res Gestae* 189 (October '86).

Petrie, Gregory S., "The Surety Bond: Insurance for the Construction Project," 13 *Barrister* 35 (Winter '86).

Pope, Thomas R. and Kevin A. Duvall, "Shareholder Guarantee of S Corporation Debt," 65 *Taxes* 330 (May '87).

Sterling, Harry M. and Jonathan A. Margolies, "Avoidance of Guarantees as Fraudulent Conveyances," 16 *Colorado Lawyer* 239 (February '87).

TAX ENFORCEMENT

[¶4101] Tax disputes are seldom simple matters. Knowledge of IRS procedures is the basic ingredient for success. The person unfamiliar with the way IRS operates may use improper tactics or contact the wrong person in the course of the dispute, and IRS may end up with more than its due. The paragraphs below form a basic guide to successful negotiation of a tax dispute.

In the absence of negotiation, or where negotiation fails, tax liens may be imposed, as discussed starting at ¶4119.

In a case affecting the individual income tax, the Supreme Court decided *Cheek v. U.S.*[1] on the issue of "willfulness." Mr. Cheek, a tax protestor, did not file tax returns; his litigating position was that non-filing was not "willful" because he believed that enforcement of the tax laws violated the Constitution. The Court held that a good-faith misunderstanding or belief that one is not breaking the law whether or not the belief is reasonable is sufficient to negate willfulness. However, the Court also held that it was proper to instruct the jury not to consider his claim of unconstitutionality of the tax laws, because he had options of paying the tax and filing for a refund (raising the unconstitutionality argument at that point) or going to the Tax Court.

A bankruptcy trustee is considered to be the fiduciary of a trust, and thus the IRS can look to the trustee, and not the actual debtor, for filing of returns and payment of any federal taxes due on the sale of the debtor's property.[2] And if the debtor wrongfully transfers money to the government in this case, by using company money to pay personal income taxes, sovereign immunity will prevent the trustee from suing the federal government to recoup the money for the bankruptcy estate.[3]

A 1992 case permits taxpayers to challenge an IRS summons even after complying with a District Court order enforcing the summons, on the grounds that the taxpayer could get meaningful relief if the IRS returned the disputed information (here, tape recordings) and thus the issue was not moot.[4]

Another case holds that a federal tax lien filed before the taxpayer acquires the real estate subject to the lien is entitled to priority over a judgment lien filed by a private creditor on the same party before the federal tax lien.[5]

Although many cases have been decided on the scope and procedures of IRS tax enforcement, perhaps the most significant development has been the enactment of the "Omnibus Taxpayer Bill of Rights" as Sections 6227-6235 of the Tax and Miscellaneous Revenue Act of 1988 (TAMRA; H.R. 4333). The Taxpayer Bill of Rights obligates the Secretary of the Treasury to prepare a statement that sets out, in plain English, both IRS duties and taxpayer rights during an audit; appeal procedures; procedures for seeking refunds and stating complaints; and an explanation of IRS enforcement tactics such as assessment, jeopardy assessment, levy, and liens. The statement must then be distributed by the Treasury to all taxpayers contacted "with respect to the determination or collection of any tax" except for routine mailing of tax forms.

At a taxpayer interview (other than an interview that is part of a criminal investigation of a taxpayer, or an IRS internal investigation) the IRS must inform the taxpayer in advance if the interview will be recorded; and the taxpayer can get a transcript or copy of the recording on payment of the cost of duplication or transcription. Taxpayers can also make an advance request and bring their own recording equipment. Before or at the initial interview, the taxpayer is entitled to an explanation of the audit or collection process (and the taxpayer's rights) from an IRS officer or employee. Even after the taxpayer has begun to answer questions, the IRS must suspend the interview whenever the taxpayer states that he or she wants to consult a lawyer, CPA, enrolled agent, enrolled actuary, or other authorized representative. Any authorized representative who holds the taxpayer's power of attorney can represent the taxpayer at the IRS interview; the IRS cannot demand that the taxpayer be present in person.

All notices of deficiency or tax due must describe the basis for the IRS action, and identify the tax due, interest, additional amounts, additions to tax, and possible penalties under the notice (although failure to do so will not invalidate an otherwise valid notice).

A perennial staple newspaper story, run every April whenever there are a few extra column inches to fill, involves calling up various IRS offices with questions, then reporting gleefully that the callers got many different and usually wrong answers. Taxpayers who take the precaution of getting their answers from the IRS in writing gain protection under the Taxpayers' Bill of Rights; the Treasury must abate any penalty or addition to tax assessed on a taxpayer who reasonably relied on written IRS advice given in response to a written query, providing adequate and accurate information, from the taxpayer. However, it will be more difficult for taxpayers to get written responses in the form of letter rulings. Except in "extraordinary circumstances," the IRS will not issue a private letter ruling with respect to an issue that is "clearly and adequately addressed by published authority." Thus, an applicant for a private letter ruling must state that the issue is not determined by the Tax Code or Regulations, a Supreme Court decision, a Revenue Ruling, or Revenue Procedure.[6] This Revenue Procedure is applied only for requests made after February 4, 1990.[7] Also see Rev. Proc. 93-23, 1993-19 IRB 6, explaining the new user fees for letter rulings and determination letters.

Taxpayers can apply for "taxpayer assistance orders" (e.g., for release of property subject to a levy; suspension of collection actions) whenever tax enforcement measures would cause "significant hardship." The order will, however, suspend running of any statute of limitations. Whenever it would facilitate tax collection, the Treasury must sign written agreements under which taxpayers can make installment payments; but the agreement can be suspended if it is discovered that the taxpayer provided inadequate or inaccurate information to motivate the agreement, if tax collection is in jeopardy, or if the taxpayer's financial condition changes significantly.

As a result of the Taxpayer Bill of Rights, a new office of Assistant Commissioner for Taxpayer Services has been created, to administer services to inform and counsel taxpayers. The IRS must now issue all temporary regulations in the form of proposed regulations; and temporary regulations must not be kept in effect for more than three years. Furthermore, the impact of all proposed regulations on small business must be reviewed, and the Administrator of the Small Business Administration must be permitted to comment on the proposal.

The IRS can no longer impose production quotas or goals on its employees, and cannot use tax enforcement results to rate employees.

Even after the Taxpayer Bill of Rights, a taxpayer's rights vis-a-vis the IRS are not exactly those of a suspect vis-a-vis the criminal justice system. In general, Code Section 6103 does impose a duty of confidentiality on the IRS, but a taxpayer's return can be inspected by any authorized person. Therefore, the Seventh Circuit held[8] that the IRS was permitted to inform tax shelter investors that the shelter promoter was being audited and to ask for copies of the investors' personal returns for the years in question. The IRS was not required to keep the audit confidential, because it would not be helpful to the investors merely to inform them that their returns were affected, but not how and why. Furthermore, even if the IRS violates a taxpayer's Constitutional rights, for instance by tricking a taxpayer into making self-incriminatory statements at a time when it was evident that criminal proceedings were justified, the exclusionary rule will not be applied in a *civil* enforcement proceeding.[9]

In contrast, a later case[10] holds that the Right to Financial Privacy Act bars a bank whose president suspects a customer of tax evasion from voluntarily sending customer records to the IRS without notice to the customer. Confidential taxpayer information can be divulged by the IRS to a state tax enforcement authority; the state's written request under an "agreement on coordination" acts as a blanket request for this information.[11] But if tax returns are wrongfully disclosed in some context other than the determination or collection of taxes, the plaintiff's ability to recover attorneys' fees from the federal government is governed by the Equal Access to Justice Act, not Code Section 7430.[12]

[¶4101.1] Bankruptcy and Tax Enforcement

Where a bankrupt officer of a bankrupt corporation is a "responsible person" for nonpayment of payroll taxes, but the corporation eventually makes the payments, the corporation's payments cannot be credited against the officer's personal liability in Chapter 11 (although this could be done in a Chapter 7 reorganization).[13] However, it is permissible for a bankruptcy court to order the IRS to allocate the payment of taxes under a Chapter 11 plan first to trust fund taxes, with the result that the corporate officer's liability as "responsible person" can be discharged.[14] Priority will be given in a Chapter 11 case to the Code Sec. 4980 excise tax imposed on reversions of funds from a qualified plan to the employer, because this is treated as an excise tax rather than a penalty.[15]

A bankruptcy judge does not have discretion to reduce penalties imposed by the IRS; however, if there is good cause shown for noncompliance, the judge can waive the penalty in its entirety for a particular tax year.[16]

[¶4102]　PROCESSING OF RETURNS

When a tax return is filed, usually with a regional service center, it is first checked by IRS for form, execution, and mathematical accuracy. Math errors are corrected, and a notice of the error is sent to the taxpayer. Payment of any additional tax resulting from a math error is then demanded, or a refund of any overpayment is made.

Tax returns are classified for examination at the regional service center. Individual income tax returns with potentially unallowable items may be turned over to the Examination Division at the service center for correction by correspondence with the taxpayer. Otherwise, returns selected for their highest potential are turned over to the district Examination Divisions. Those most in need of review are selected for office or field examination by a Revenue Agent.

Taxpayers who intend to file electronically must apply for permission, using Form 8633 (Application to Participate in the Electronic Filing Program).[17] Even returns with a balance due can be filed electronically, through the use of Form 9282, the Electronic Payment Voucher. The IRS can refuse to grant permission, e.g., to a taxpayer with one or more convictions for moral turpitude offenses, or one who has failed to file timely personal or business returns.

A taxpayer charged with failure to file a return has the right to file a joint return even after receiving a notice of deficiency and challenging it in Tax Court, despite the IRS' preparation of a "substitute return" reflecting the higher rates for married persons filing separate returns.[18]

The IRS is not barred from issuing a deficiency notice based on a fraud discovered after a Tax Court adjudication of the original deficiency notice issued for that year.[19]

A deficiency notice is proper if it is mailed to the taxpayer's attorney, and the taxpayer gets actual notice in the form of an exact copy of the notice;[20] but a notice mailed to a married taxpayer's last known address, but not to his wife's, is invalid as to the wife.[21]

Current Regulations deal with substantial understatement of income tax; negligence or disregard of rules and regulations; and substantial misstatement of valuation. Issues not addressed by these Regs. and left to further rulemaking include substantial overstatement of pension liabilities and substantial understatement of valuation for estate or gift tax purposes. Under these final Regs., the IRS will not consider the lateness of a return in determining whether accuracy-related penalties should be imposed; and whether a misstatement is substantial will be determined on a case-by-case basis, without aggregation.

IR 93-25 (3/3/93) and IR 93-26 (3/4/93) give the rules for the new Form 9465 (Installment Agreement Request), under which a taxpayer unable to fully settle a tax liability can propose an amount of monthly installment payments to satisfy the obligation. It is not necessary to provide financial data with the form, and the taxpayer is not required to exhaust other payment possibilities before proposing an installment plan. The IRS will respond within 30 days, and has the option of rejecting a plan that provides for insufficient payments. Interest and late-payment penalties continue to apply if an installment agreement is in place, but no tax lien will be filed if the taxpayer keeps up with the scheduled payments.

IR 93-37 (4/7/93) announces that the IRS will accept a Form 4868 (automatic extension of time to file) that is not accompanied by payment in full as long as the tax liability is properly estimated on the form.

[¶ 4102.1] Preparer Penalties

An "income tax return preparer" is any person who prepares for compensation, or who employs one or more persons to prepare for compensation, any return of tax or claim for refund of tax.

Some of the penalties which apply to tax return preparers, including attorneys, are:

(1) Understating a taxpayer's tax liability when the understatement was due to unrealistic positions—$250 penalty for each return or claim that shows such understatement.[22]

(2) Willful understatement or intentional or reckless conduct—$1,000 penalty for any return or claim, less any penalty paid under (1) above.[23]

(3) Preparer not signing a return or claim—$50 penalty for each return or claim not signed. The maximum penalty imposed on any person with respect to documents filed during any calendar year shall not exceed $25,000.[24]

(4) Negotiating or indorsing a federal income tax check issued to a taxpayer—$500 penalty for each check.[25]

(5) Except as otherwise provided by law, disclosure of information furnished to a preparer in connection with the preparation of federal tax returns is subject to a civil penalty of $250 for each such disclosure up to a maximum that shall not exceed $10,000 in a calendar year.[26]

(6) A $500 penalty can be imposed upon any taxpayer who files a frivolous return.[27] An appellate court held that an attorney and client can be jointly and severally liable for damages. The attorney had represented other taxpayers in similar cases and was thus put on notice that his appeal lacked merit.[28]

Under Code Sec. 6701, there is no statute of limitations regarding penalties for aiding and abetting understatement of tax liability.[29] This is an anti-fraud provision which can be enforced at any time. The preparer is not entitled to claim protection under the general federal five-year statute of limitations for civil penalties (28 U.S.C. Section 2562). Each quarterly filing can be construed as a "taxable period" giving rise to a penalty. There is no restriction limiting penalties to one per year. A tax shelter promoter who participated in the filing of an S corporation's returns and disclosures to stockholders that understated corporate income can be assessed a separate penalty for each return prepared, not merely a single penalty for the S corporation's return; the S corporation didn't have a tax liability to understate.[30]

The government has the burden of proof, using a preponderance of evidence standard, as to the preparer's liability. If a preparer's understatements are related, the taxpayer for whom the return was prepared can be penalized for the original year, but not for carryover year returns reflecting the error.[31]

The innocent spouse of a taxpayer who commits tax malfeasance is entitled to innocent spouse relief even if malfeasance is committed on a supporting document incorporated into a return rather than the return itself.[32]

An estate was obligated to pay additions to tax, because reliance on a lawyer's advice was not deemed to be reasonable cause for the failure to file and pay the taxes.[33] In this reading, the estate should have made a prompt filing with the best available information, instead of waiting for complete data, and should have paid as soon as the IRS denied the second application for an extension of time to file. The repeat denial proved that the lawyer was incorrect in asserting that the IRS would grant any extensions necessary for preparation of a "complete" return.

In an issue relating to attorneys, the IRS has announced that attorneys failing to file Form 8300 (reporting cash transactions in excess of $10,000), or filing forms that omit clients' names, will be subject to the Code Section 6721 penalty for "intentional disregard" of Code requirements. The penalty is the greater of $25,000 or the amount of cash in the transaction (but not to exceed $100,000).

[¶4103] DEALING WITH THE REVENUE AGENT

Original examination of a selected tax return falls to the examining officers in the Examination Division of each IRS district office, otherwise known as Revenue Agents. The Revenue Agent may examine a taxpayer's books, papers, records, or memoranda relating to items that should be included in the return. If, during the course of an examination, the Agent determines that there is a deficiency, the taxpayer may agree to pay the additional tax, which ends the dispute at that point. The Agent will require the signing of a formal settlement agreement.

Of course, the first opportunity to settle the controversy is with the Revenue Agent. In dealing with the Revenue Agent, the taxpayer should remember that the Agent is trying to discharge a duty to the government and still dispose of the matter the best way possible. The most satisfactory results come from a climate within which the taxpayer and the Agent engage in a mutual endeavor to determine the proper tax liability.

[¶4103.1] Limited Authority of Revenue Agent

The Revenue Agent is the principal fact-finder of IRS. He has the authority to determine what the facts are and apply them to the legal position taken by IRS. A Revenue Agent, however, does not have discretion to dispose of an issue if:

(1) IRS has taken a position contrary to the Tax Court. He must follow the position taken by the IRS.

(2) Regulations and rulings are available. He must follow these rules.

(3) The law on the subject is not clear.

Since the Revenue Agent has no authority to settle these issues, it's better not to argue with him or her. No purpose is served. The best course for the taxpayer is to inform the Agent that he or she will not agree and give the Agent as much information on the issues as is pertinent.

[¶4103.2]   Advantages of Settlement with the Revenue Agent

The advantages of a taxpayer's settling on the Revenue Agent's level are:

❏ Requirement to show less evidence to establish a claim.

❏ Avoiding the possibility of having other issues raised by other more experienced IRS agents.

❏ Avoiding the expense and anxiety of further proceedings.

[¶4104]   OFFICE EXAMINATION PROCEDURE

There are two general types of audit, commonly called "office examinations" and "field examinations." An office examination may be conducted either through correspondence with the taxpayer or through an in-person interview at the district offices.

[¶4104.1]   Adjustments by Examination Division at Regional Service Center

If a return is identified as containing a potentially unallowable item, it may be handled by the Examination Division of the Regional Service Center where the return was filed. Audits conducted from service centers involve correspondence only. If the taxpayer does not agree to proposed adjustments, then the regular IRS appeal procedures outlined in the following paragraphs will apply. If an interview becomes necessary, the case will be transferred to the IRS district office.

[¶4104.2]   Examinations at the District Office

Individual income tax returns and some business returns are generally examined at district offices using the office examination technique which is primarily by interview of the taxpayer. Examinations conducted by a district office are conducted by correspondence only when appropriate because of the nature of the questionable items on a return and the convenience and nature of the taxpayer.

If a return is subjected to an office examination by correspondence, the taxpayer will be asked to explain or send supporting evidence by mail. In an interview examination, the taxpayer is directed to go to the district office for an interview and to take certain records that will support the questionable items on his return.

During an interview examination, the taxpayer has the right to point out to the Agent any amounts included in the return that are not taxable, or any deductions that were not claimed. If it develops that a field examination is necessary, the Revenue Agent may conduct one.

[¶4104.3] Statute of Limitations Questions

Collection of defaulted student loans from tax refunds (under 26 USC Section 6402(d)) is permissible even after the six-year statute of limitations has run on suits for "money damages" brought by the United States government (28 USC Section 2415(a)).[34]

A taxpayer's execution of an open-ended waiver of the statute of limitations for assessment of tax deficiencies (Form 872-A) is only terminated if the taxpayer files a Form 872-T giving the IRS 90 days to assess the deficiency; the 872-A is not terminated by the IRS' sending a deficiency notice that is defective in form[35] or by sending the deficiency notice to the wrong address for the taxpayer.[36]

The three-year statute of limitation on assessment of taxes does not apply to assessment of *penalties* for sale of abusive tax shelters, because the penalties are not imposed on any particular tax return or tax year. Therefore, the only time limit imposed on IRS enforcement is one of laches.[37]

The limitations period for filing a tax refund claim under Code Sec. 6511(a) is subject to equitable tolling, e.g., during a period of time when the taxpayer is mentally incapacitated.[38]

If an individual taxpayer has a deficiency solely due to an investment in a Subchapter S corporation, the statute of limitations for assessment of the deficiency begins with the date of filing of the individual return, not the Sub S information return.[39]

[¶4105] FIELD EXAMINATION PROCEDURE

Certain returns are examined by field examination, which involves inspection of the taxpayer's books and records on the taxpayer's premises. If a return is subjected to a field examination, the Agent will check the entire return and will examine all pertinent books, papers, records, and memoranda dealing with anything that is required to be included.

If a return presents an engineering or appraisal problem, such as depreciation or depletion deductions, gains or losses from the sale of property, or abandonment losses, it may also be examined by an engineer agent. The engineer agent will make a separate report.

[¶4106] CONCLUDING THE OFFICE OR FIELD EXAMINATION

When the Revenue Agent concludes the examination of a return, the taxpayer will be asked to agree with the findings. If there is no agreement, the taxpayer has a right of appeal. These rights are discussed in the following paragraphs.

The taxpayer who agrees to the Agent's proposed changes will be asked to sign Form 870 and will also be asked to pay the additional tax plus any interest or penalties at this time.

[¶4107] TECHNICAL ADVICE

During the examination of a return, the district office may request technical advice from the National Office. Technical advice is usually made available if the disputed issue is either extremely complex or the disposition of similar cases has not been uniform among the district offices.

A taxpayer has the right to review the facts and issues presented to the National Office. The taxpayer who disagrees with the district office's presentation can submit his or her own statement of facts.

[¶4107.1] Taxpayer's Request for Technical Advice

Taxpayers themselves can initiate the request for technical advice. IRS must make public its private letter rulings. Since a response to a request for technical advice is considered a ruling, it should be pointed out that information contained in a request *may* be made public. This may not be in a taxpayer's best interest, since confidential information may be revealed despite the law's requirement that private rulings be "sanitized" before release.

[¶4108] APPEALS OFFICE CONFERENCE

Failure to reach agreement with the Revenue Agent moves the tax dispute on to the next stage—the Appeals Office conference. The Appeals Office is a type of appellate tribunal within IRS. It is not a division of the district director's office; the district director has no jurisdiction over this department. The Appeals Office settlement authority is derived from the Regional Commissioners.

[¶4109] CONFERENCE PROCEDURES FOR OFFICE EXAMINATIONS

Conference procedures for office examinations are explained in the paragraphs that follow.

[¶4109.1] Correspondence Examination

In a correspondence office examination, the taxpayer is notified of the Agent's proposed findings by form letter. She can sign an agreement if she accepts the Agent's findings. If she disagrees, the form letter also instructs her on the course of appeal available to her.

If she disagrees with the Agent following a correspondence office examination, she is granted an Appeals Office conference on request. There is no need to submit a formal written protest.

[¶4109.2] Interview Examination

If the taxpayer disagrees with the Agent following an office interview examination, he is granted an immediate conference if possible, and if he so requests. If he does request an immediate conference, the examination report is mailed to him along with instructions for appeal. He will be granted a conference upon request, and he does not have to file a protest.

Note, however, that business returns examined in an office examination are handled in the same manner as returns examined in a field examination.

[¶4109.3] Closing Agreements

The taxpayer and the IRS can enter into a closing agreement, making a final disposition of tax liability for a period, or tax treatment of an item or items. Closing agreements can only be reopened or modified for fraud, malfeasance, or material misrepresentation. Otherwise, they are final and binding on both parties.

[¶4109.4] Offer in Compromise

Reg. §601.203(b) permits the IRS to compromise virtually all civil and criminal tax cases, including interest and penalties. The taxpayer's offer is submitted on Form 656; if the premise of the offer is the taxpayer's inability to pay, Form 433 must be submitted to document the taxpayer's financial condition. The offer and acceptance must be made in writing, not orally: *Boulez v. Comm'r*, 810 F.2d 209 (D.C. Cir. 1987), cert. den. 56 LW 3266.

[¶4110] CONFERENCE PROCEDURE FOR FIELD EXAMINATIONS

Following a field examination of a return, a complete examination report is prepared that fully explains all proposed adjustments. This report and the overall case file are submitted to a District Review Staff for review. After the review, the taxpayer receives a copy of the examination report along with a 30-day letter outlining choices of action.

If the proposed adjustment does not exceed $2,500, a conference is granted upon request without the taxpayer having to file a protest.

If more than $2,500 is involved, a conference is granted only after the filing of a written protest, setting forth the facts, law, and the arguments on which the taxpayer relies.

[¶4111] Authority of Appeals Office

The Appeals Office has broad authority to settle cases. It can evaluate and settle cases on the basis of IRS's and the taxpayer's respective strength and weakness and the risk of litigation. Issues of law and mixed issues of law and fact can be settled at this level. A settlement by the Appeals Office is considered by IRS to be a final disposition of the case.

[¶4112] Appeal in the Courts

If settlement is not reached in the Appeals Office, or the conference is waived, IRS then issues a statutory notice of deficiency setting forth its claim for additional tax. This notice is called the "90-day letter."

In 1992, P.L. 102-572 changed the name of the U.S. Claims Court to the U.S. Court of Federal Claims.

It is permissible (and not an instance of double jeopardy) for federal prosecutors to bring separate charges for distinct, significant, affirmative acts of tax evasion committed within a single year.[40]

If the taxpayer applies for litigation costs under Code Section 7430, the position taken by the IRS in the deficiency notice, not the Service's position in response to the taxpayer's Tax Court petition, will be considered in determining the "reasonableness" of the government's position.[41] This is true whether or not IRS Counsel is involved in issuing the notice.

A CPA who convinced a jury that he was not subject to preparer penalties under Code Section 6694(a) nevertheless was not entitled to an EAJA fee, where the government introduced enough evidence to show substantial justification for its position.[42]

To be entitled to attorney's fees, the taxpayer must establish separately at the administrative and the judicial stages that the IRS position was unjustified. However, once this is done, the taxpayer can recover a reasonable fee of any size; the $75/hour lodestar does not act as a limit. However, the fee will not be enhanced based on the attorney's tax expertise.[43]

[¶4112.1] Taxpayer's Alternatives After Receiving "90-Day Letter"

(1) Pay the tax and close the matter.

(2) Pay the tax demanded and file a suit for refund in the district court or in the United States Court of Federal Claims.

(3) File a petition for redetermination in the Tax Court.

[¶4113] THE REFUND ROUTE

Refund claims and demands for return of overpayments can be made via amended tax return (e.g., 1040X, 1120X).

The taxpayer who takes this route has two courts in which to bring his suit: The United States District Court in the district where the tax was paid or the United States Claims Court. Before a taxpayer is allowed to bring suit in one of these courts, he or she must pay the *entire* tax that is due (including interest and penalties). In these Courts a taxpayer can only sue for refund of taxes paid.

The way to proceed is to first pay the tax and then file a claim for refund with IRS. Upon its rejection by IRS, or the expiration of six months, suit for refund is filed.

The taxpayer who takes this route cannot later bring suit in the Tax Court. In the first place, the 90-day period in all likelihood would have expired. Secondly, since the tax due is paid, there is no deficiency over which the Tax Court could take jurisdiction.

Taxpayers may not file petitions in the Tax Court and then pay the tax and sue for refund. Once the Tax Court has acquired jurisdiction it will not let go— even upon stipulation of counsel.

[¶4114] SUIT FOR REFUND IN THE DISTRICT COURT

Suit in the district court is brought against the IRS District Director (personally) who collected the tax, or the United States Government. In either event, a jury trial is available. The availability of a jury is the major advantage of bringing the suit in the district court. Decisions in this court are appealable to the United States Circuit Court of Appeals.

[¶4115] SUIT FOR REFUND IN THE CLAIMS COURT

The Claims Court is a trial court. A decision by this Court is appealable to the Court of Appeals for the Federal Circuit.

[¶4116] BURDEN OF PROOF

In either the district court or Court of Claims, the burden of proof is on the taxpayer to establish entitlement to the refund. But this is the same as in the Tax Court, except that in Tax Court proof that the deficiency is wrong is required.

[¶4117] TAX COURT ROUTE

The Tax Court's jurisdiction is invoked only after IRS has issued its "90-day letter," and the taxpayer has filed a *timely* petition to have its case heard. This petition must be filed within 90 days or the Tax Court will not get jurisdiction. There can be no extensions of time to file a petition.

One of the major advantages in filing a petition in the Tax Court is that the taxpayer can have the deficiency determined without paying any part of the tax that is due. Some taxpayers, after filing a petition, do pay the tax, but this is only to stop the running of interest. It is not necessary. In fact, if the tax is paid before the mailing of a statutory notice of deficiency, the Tax Court would not have jurisdiction over the dispute.

If the taxpayer goes to the Tax Court after receiving a notice of deficiency, the taxpayer is precluded from obtaining a credit or refund, and from suing in any other court with regard to the tax year in question—except for amounts determined by a final decision of the Tax Court; amounts collected after expiration of the limitations period; and overpayments attributable to partnership items.

Decisions by the Tax Court are appealable to the United States Circuit Courts of Appeal. The circuit where a taxpayer files a return is normally the place where an appeal will be taken. The Circuit Courts of Appeal have exclusive jurisdiction over decisions by the Tax Court and the district courts.

If the suit is settled in the taxpayer's favor, the taxpayer's motion for litigation costs is timely if filed within 30 days after the court's decision, incorporating the settlement agreement, is filed.[44]

If taxpayers agree to be bound by the Tax Court's ruling in a representative lead case (a tax shelter case, in the case at bar), and if they fail to appeal the adverse decisions against them after the Tax Court makes its ruling, the Tax Court will not have jurisdiction to vacate the judgments against the taxpayers after the lead cases are reversed on appeal.[45]

In a June 5, 1990 Press Release, the Tax Court announced a complete republication of the Tax Court Rules of Practice and Procedure. The revision includes 14 new rules as well as amendments to 103 existing rules. Much of the impetus for the change comes from the need to conform to the Taxpayer Bill of Rights. Also note new Rule 124, which permits parties to submit to voluntary binding arbitration to resolve any factual issue in dispute.

It is permissible for the IRS to use information obtained pursuant to an administrative summons in a Tax Court case, even if the information was obtained after the petition was filed and was not discoverable in Tax Court.[46] Because prepetition IRS summonses are outside the Tax Court's jurisdiction, the Tax Court cannot prevent their issuance; and the Tax Court will prevent the use of information obtained under such summonses only if the IRS issued the summons without having some sufficient reason unrelated to the pending case.

[¶4118] TAX COURT SMALL CLAIMS PROCEDURE

The Tax Court has a small claims division that handles cases involving tax deficiencies or overpayments that do not exceed $10,000. Both income and estate tax deficiencies are handled here. The decisions in these cases are based upon a brief summary opinion instead of formal findings of fact, and are not precedent for future cases. The procedure is optional with the taxpayer.

In addition to not serving as precedent for other cases, decisions rendered under the "small tax case" rules are final. Taxpayers electing this procedure give up any right to appeal the dispute to the Circuit Courts of Appeal.

[¶4119] TAX LIENS

Federal tax liens may accrue against any person who neglects or refuses to pay taxes. They apply to both real and personal property belonging to a taxpayer who is liable for the tax (IRC §6321). Liens in favor of the federal government arise at the time the assessment is made by IRS and continue until the lien is satisfied or expires through lapse of time. Priority over a federal tax lien accrues to any purchaser, the holder of a mechanic's lien, a judgment lien creditor, or the holder of a security interest who has established priority under the Uniform Commercial Code or other pertinent statutory device prior to the filing by IRS. The lien is enforced under Code §7403.

Even if notice of a lien imposed by IRS has been filed, it is ineffective with respect to a security interest that came into existence *after* filing of the tax lien by reason of a disbursement made prior to the 46th day after the date of filing. This exemption applies only to property covered by terms of a written agreement entered into prior to the filing of a tax lien that local law protects against judgment liens arising out of an unsecured obligation (IRC §6323(d)).

Final regulations have been published for administrative appeal of erroneously filed notices of tax lien, TD 8347, which provides four grounds for appeal:

➤ The tax liability was satisfied before the lien was filed;

➤ The assessment of the underlying liability violates the Bankruptcy Code; or

➤ It violates the Section 6213 deficiency procedure;

➤ The statutory period for collection of the underlying liability expired before the IRS filed the notice of lien.

Under TD 8347, the taxpayer who seeks to appeal must do so in writing, addressed to the Chief of Special Procedures Functions in the Office of District Director in the district where the notice of lien was filed. When it is subsequently determined that an IRS assessment was excessive but not entirely invalid, the taxpayer is entitled to abatement of the assessment but not to release of the lien securing the original assessment.[47]

Amended Regulations have been proposed under Section 301.6332-3 (GL-172-89), under which a delinquent taxpayer's bank account can be frozen (up to the amount of the tax levy) for 21 days. The taxpayer has this three-week period to notify the IRS of errors in the levy. When the 21 days expire, the bank must surrender the levied amount (plus interest) to the IRS, unless the District Director either releases the levy or asks for a continued holding period.

A deficiency notice sent by certified mail to the taxpayer's former address was invalid, and the levy therefore enjoined[48] although the notice was forwarded to his last known address (but not picked up there). The injunction was granted because an IRS levy has exceedingly serious consequences amounting to irreparable injury. In this case, the IRS knew the taxpayer's new address and in fact had mailed a refund check there.

People who are in trouble for not paying their taxes are, of course, likely to have other debts; so the interaction between tax liens and other enforcement mechanisms is a perpetual source of litigation. Cases hold that a federal tax lien always defeats a bank's right of setoff against the funds in the taxpayer's bank account, no matter when the administrative levy was filed[49] but that a state's "buying in" of seized property at a tax sale will not extinguish the state's tax lien, which retains its priority over a junior federal tax lien even if the state failed to provide notice to the IRS under Code Section 7425.[50]

The IRS can't assert a tax lien on property bought in by a delinquent taxpayer where title was in the name of the taxpayer's wife, who transferred it to the couple's children, retaining a life estate. Applicable state law did not recognize a resulting trust arising out of interspousal transactions, and the delinquent taxpayer had no interest in the property.[51] But the divorce court's continuing jurisdiction over marital property does not invalidate an existing tax lien on one spouse's interest in marital property.[52]

A federal tax lien has priority over a bank's security in a bankrupt taxpayer's accounts receivable.[53] The Tenth Circuit said that the loan was made to permit the borrower to perform its preexisting contracts in the ordinary course of business. Credit was not advanced to purchase new collateral, so the bank could not claim to have a purchase-money security interest under UCC Section 9-107 that would take priority over a federal tax lien.

[¶4120] PLACE OF FILING FEDERAL TAX LIENS

The federal government may establish priority for federal tax lien purposes by filing (in the case of real property) in an office within the state, county, or other governmental subdivision designated by local law in which the property subject to the lien is situated (IRC §6323(f)(1)(A)).

[¶4121] LIENS AGAINST STOCKS AND SECURITIES

Any bond, debenture, note, or certificate of other indebtedness issued either by a corporation or a political subdivision of a government, interest coupons, shares of stock, warrants, negotiable instruments, or money may not be subject to a federal lien priority if the purchaser had no actual knowledge or notice of the existence of the lien, and if the holder of the security interest in those items also had no bona fide actual knowledge or notice of existence of the lien (IRC §6323(b)(1)).

[¶4122] AUTOMOBILES AND FEDERAL TAX LIEN PRIORITY

A federal tax lien with respect to a motor vehicle (provided the auto is registered under the laws of any state or foreign country) is ineffective provided there was a bona fide purchase for value without notice or knowledge of the existence of the lien, and after the purchaser does obtain knowledge or notice of the lien there is no relinquishment of possession of the motor vehicle to the original seller or agent of the seller.

[¶4123] "CASUAL SALES" AND FEDERAL TAX LIENS

Household goods, personal effects, or other tangible personal property purchased in a casual sale for less than $250 that are not intended for resale are taken free of any federal tax lien, provided the purchaser has no actual knowledge of the existence of the lien (§6323(b)(2)(4)).

[¶4124] MECHANICS' LIENS ON REAL PROPERTY

Personal residences containing not more than four dwelling units on which a mechanic's lien has been levied are subject to federal tax lien priorities if the mechanic's lien for work performed is more than $1,000. If the contract with the owner amounts to less than $1,000, the workman has a lien priority over the federal government (§6323(b)(7)).

[¶4125] ATTORNEYS' LIENS

An attorney is entitled to a lien priority to the extent of reasonable compensation for obtaining a judgment or procuring a settlement (IRC §6323(b)(8)).

[¶4126] REPAIRMEN'S LIENS

Tangible personal property that has been repaired or improved and is in the continuing possession of the repairman from the time the repair or improvement was initiated is subject to priority over a federal tax lien (IRC §6323(b)(5)).

[¶4127] CERTAIN LOANS

Passbook loans (provided the bank keeps the passbook in its possession until the loan is paid) and insurance policy loans also have priority over a federal tax lien (IRC §6323(d)(9)-(10)). A requisite element of this rule is that neither the insurance company nor the savings institution has actual notice or knowledge of the existence of the lien.

[¶4128] COMMERCIAL FINANCING AGREEMENTS

Loans to a taxpayer secured by commercial financing acquired in the ordinary course of trade or business (resulting in the creation of commercial paper) are not subject to a federal tax lien on the resulting security interest, provided there is a written agreement entered into prior to the filing of the tax lien that constitutes a commercial transaction financing agreement, or a real property construction or improvement financing agreement, or a disbursement agreement, provided that the underlying agreement under local law would be protected against a judgment lien arising out of an unsecured obligation (IRC §6323(c)).

[¶4129] EXTENSION OF PRIORITY FOR INTEREST AND OTHER EXPENSES

If the federal tax lien is not valid against other nongovernmental lien creditors or holders of securities interests, the priorities also extend to six years to the extent that under local law any of the items would have the same priority as the lien or security interest to which it relates. These include:

➤ Interest or carrying charges on the secured obligation;

➤ Reasonable charges and expenses of an indentured trustee holding the security interest;

➤ Reasonable expenses (including reasonable compensation for attorneys) incurred in the collection or enforcement of the secured obligation;

➤ Reasonable cost for insurance, preservation, or repair of the property to which the lien relates;

➤ Reasonable insurance costs;

➤ Amounts paid to satisfy any lien on the property to which the lien or security interest relates (§6323(e)).

— Endnotes —

1. #89-658, 111 S.Ct. 604 (1/8/91). Also see Domanus v. U.S., 961 F.2d 1323 (7th Cir. 4/22/92) [To impose civil liability for willful failure to pay taxes, the government must prove voluntary, conscious and intentional conduct; the criminal standard of intentional violation of a known legal duty does not apply].

2. Holywell v. Smith, #90-1361, -1484, 112 S.Ct. 1021 (Sup.Ct. 2/25/92).

3. U.S. v. Nordic Village, #90-1629, 112 S.Ct. 1011 (Sup.Ct. 2/25/92), on remand 963 F.2d 118.

4. Church of Scientology of California v. U.S., #91-946, 113 S.Ct. 447 (Sup.Ct. 11/16/92). The IRS apparently had some hostility toward Scientology: Smith v. Brady, 972 F.2d 573 (9th Cir. 8/17/92) involves taxpayers who sued for violation of their constitutional rights after getting a letter from the IRS calling their religion, the Church of Scientology, a "sham." The IRS admitted its error, and the case was settled out of court; the taxpayers were denied an attorneys' fee award because the Code, rather than the Equal Access to Justice Act, governed the availability of fees, and the taxpayers failed to exhaust their administrative remedies as required by the Code.

5. U.S. v. McDermott, #91-1229, 113 S.Ct. 1526 (Sup.Ct. 3/24/93).

6. Rev.Proc. 89-34, 1989-20 IRB 145.

7. Announcement 89-105, 1989-35 IRB 145.

8. Solargistic Corp. v. U.S., 921 F.2d 729 (7th Cir. 1/11/91).

9. Jones v. Comm'r, 97 TC No. 2 (7/3/91).

10. Neece v. IRS, 922 F.2d 573 (10th Cir. 12/19/90).

11. Smith v. U.S., 964 F.2d 630 (7th Cir. 5/15/92), *cert. denied* 113 S.Ct. 1015.

12. McLarty v. U.S., 62 LW 2227 (9th Cir. 10/1/93).

13. U.S. v. Pepperman, 976 F.2d 123 (3d Cir. 9/3/92).

14. IRS v. Creditors' Committee (In re Deer Park Inc.), 62 LW 2375 (9th Cir. 12/6/93).

15. U.S. v. Unsecured Creditors' Committee of C-T of Virginia, Inc., 977 F.2d 137 (4th Cir. 10/2/92).

16. U.S. v. Sanford, 979 F.2d 1511 (11th Cir. 1992); see Neal Lipschitz, "Tax Briefs," *Nat. Law J.* 2/1/93 p. 5.

17. See IRS *Handbook for Electronic Filers of Individual Income Tax Returns* (Publication 1345) revised each tax year.

18. Phillips v. Comm'r, 851 F.2d 1492 (D.C. Cir. 7/22/88).

19. Zackim v. Comm'r, 887 F.2d 455 (3d Cir. 10/13/89).

20. McKay v. Comm'r, 886 F.2d 1237 (9th Cir. 10/6/89).

21. I.P. Monge, 93 TC No. 4 (1989).

22. IRC Sec. 6694(a).

23. IRC Sec. 6694(b).

24. IRC Sec. 6695.

25. IRC Sec. 6695(f).

26. IRC Sec. 6713(a)(1),(2).

27. IRC Sec. 6702.

28. D. Kalgaard, (CA-9) 85-2 USTC ¶9513, aff'g TC, 48 TCM 106, Dec. 41,246(M).

29. Mullikan v. U.S., 952 F.2d 920 (6th Cir. 12/30/91); Capozzi v. U.S., 980 F.2d 872 (2d Cir. 12/8/92).

30. Mitchell v. U.S., 977 F.2d 1318 (9th Cir. 10/9/92).

31. Mattingly v. U.S., 924 F.2d 785 (8th Cir. 2/1/91).

32. Friedman v. Comm'r, 97 TC No. 42 (11/26/91).

33. Hopping v. U.S., CCH Fed'l Estate & Gift Tax Rep. #60,098 (S.D. Ind. 3/30/92). Also see In re American Biomaterials Corp., 954 F.2d 919 (3d Cir. 1/23/92) [to escape penalty for failure to pay, corporation must prove it has a reasonable cause for the failure, and that it was not neglectful. Corporations are not automatically liable for failures; here, it was due to embezzlement, which is not within the scope of employment of the perpetrator].

34. Thomas v. Bennett, 856 F.2d 1165 (8th Cir. 9/15/88).

35. Hubbard v. Comm'r, 872 F.2d 183 (6th Cir. 4/12/89).

36. Holof v. Comm'r, 872 F.2d 50 (3d Cir. 4/12/89).

37. Sage v. U.S., 908 F.2d 18 (5th Cir. 8/13/90); Capozzi v. U.S., 61 LW 2386 (2d Cir. 12/8/92).

38. Scott v. U.S., 795 F.Supp. 1028 (D.Haw. 6/4/92).

39. Fehlhaber v. Comm'r, 954 F.2d 653 (11th Cir. 2/24/92); Green v. Comm'r, 963 F.2d 783 (5th Cir. 6/22/92), cert. denied 113 S.Ct. 1251.

40. U.S. v. Pollen, 978 F.2d 78 (3d Cir. 10/13/92).

41. Weiss v. Comm'r, 850 F.2d 111 (2d Cir. 6/27/88).

42. Wilfong v. U.S., 991 F.2d 359 (7th Cir. 4/8/93).

43. Huffman v. Comm'r, 978 F.2d 1139 (9th Cir. 1992).

44. Comer v. Comm'r, 856 F.2d 775 (6th Cir. 9/9/88).

45. Abatti v. Comm'r, 859 F.2d 115 (9th Cir. 10/25/88).

46. Mary Kay Ash, 96 TC No. 16 (3/11/91).

47. Burns v. U.S., 764 F.2d 722 (9th Cir. 8/31/92).

48. Gibson v. U.S., 68 AFTR2d 91-5102 (C.D. Cal. 4/4/91).

49. U.S. v. Cache Valley Bank, 866 F.2d 1242 (10th Cir. 1/27/89).

50. U.S. v. Colorado, 872 F.2d 338 (10th Cir. 4/7/89).

51. Pate v. U.S., 68 AFTR2d 91-5922 (10th Cir. 11/20/91).

52. Nicoles v. U.S., 19 Family Law Rep. 1004 (W.D. Pa. 10/20/92).

53. First Interstate Bank of Utah v. IRS, 930 F.2d 1521 (10th Cir. 4/25/91).

— For Further Reference —

Blumenthal, Marsha and Joel Slemrod, "The Compliance Cost of U.S. Individual Tax System," 45 *National Tax J.* 185 (July '92).

Dooher, Patrick G., "Recovering Attorneys' Fees and Other Costs Incurred in Tax Controversies: Recent Developments," 33 *Tax Management Memorandum* 197 (6/29/92).

Feldman, Stephen M., "The ABCs of a Tax Controversy," 71 *Michigan Bar J.* 646 (July '92).

Furay, Catherine J., "Dischargeability of Taxes in Bankruptcy," 66 *Wisconsin Lawyer* 14 (June '93).

Jochner, Michele M., "When the Taxman Cometh: Challenging an IRS Summons," 80 *Illinois Bar J.* 360 (July '92).

Johnson, Barret, "Tender Offer Considered an Option Under Sec. 382 Option Attribution Rule," 23 *Tax Adviser* 463 (July '92).

Lore, Martin M. and L. Paige Marvel, "When Will IRS Remedies Be Exhausted?" 77 *J. of Taxation* 58 (July '92).

McLachlan, C. Ian, "Spousal Liability and Federal Income Taxes," 10 *J. of the American Academy of Matrimonial Lawyers* 65 (Summer '93).

Press, Martin L., "Offers in Compromise as to Collectability of Taxes: The New Government Policy," 66 *Florida Bar J.* 60 (July–August '92).

Ritholz, Jules, "More Liberal View of Willful in Civil Tax Cases," 77 *J. of Taxation* 107 (August '92).

Rocen, Donald T., "Federal Tax Procedures in Bankruptcy Proceedings," 51 *Inst. on Federal Taxation* 24-1 (Annual '93).

Roginski, Charles J., "Effect of Chapter 11 on State and Local Taxes," 11 *J. of State Taxation* 53 (Summer '92).

Sterrett, Samuel B., "Tax Court Tactics," 6 *Practical Tax Lawyer* 71 (Summer '92).

Wadhwa, Darshan L., "The 100% Penalty," 23 *Tax Adviser* 608 (September '92).

Zeidner, Rita L., "New Collection Methods Emphasize the Carrot Instead of the Stick," 56 *Tax Notes* 259 (7/20/92).

TAX PLANNING

[¶4201] Tax planning usually has some combination of the following objectives:

(1) To reduce unnecessary costs and increase net profit.

(2) To increase the amount of cash at work in the business.

(3) To secure business and competitive advantages through the desire of customers, suppliers, investors, and employees to minimize their own tax liability.

The main routes by which taxes can be saved are these:

(1) Stabilizing income to keep out of peak brackets.

(2) Spreading income over a long period of time to avoid peak rates and defer tax.

(3) Accelerating or postponing income and expenses as indicated by the tax rates, (as high as 39.6% for individuals and 35% for corporations plus the tax on tax-preference income).

(4) Dividing income among a number of taxpayers; i.e., spreading income among the members of a family partnership or the beneficiaries of a family trust.

(5) Making optimum use of remaining Tax Code provisions dealing with capital gains.

(6) Utilizing the exemptions and deductions allowed under the law; for example, the depletion allowance or tax-exempt bonds.

(7) Selecting a form of business appropriate for withdrawing income; for example, using a limited partnership, a proprietorship, or S corporation to carry a venture through the period when anticipated losses can be charged against highly taxed personal income.

(8) Utilizing specific elections in the law; i.e., accounting elections, choices as to method of depreciation, etc.

(9) Creating business relationships between taxable entities that will make the most effective total use of applicable tax rates, earning power, actual and potential losses, depreciable assets (e.g., mergers, sale-leasebacks, other arm's-length contractual relationships).

(10) Avoiding application of the Alternative Minimum Tax (AMT).

[¶4202] TAX CONSIDERATIONS IN SETTING UP A BUSINESS

The form a business takes can make a world of difference in arriving at the bottom line for tax purposes, since the tax law treats various forms of business differently, recognizing some as separate entities and others as extensions of their owners. Under the tax law, there are three main forms of business—the sole proprietorship, the corporation, and the partnership. In addition, the tax law also recognizes some hybrids.

[¶4202.1]   General Considerations in Choosing Form

Different forms of business will be indicated at different times. The business owner and his or her advisor must determine what form should be adopted by studying the total economic situation surrounding the business. This includes the sources of outside income for each party involved in the business, the family composition, and tax status of each party.

The determination will be based on the following considerations:

❏ The form that provides the individual owners with the most after-tax business profits.

❏ Possibilities of greater tax savings by further subdividing corporations and partnerships into other entities.

❏ The tax cost of changing from one form to another form.

[¶4202.2]   Particular Factors That Influence Choice of Business Form

Apart from the general considerations, the particular aspects of the business venture play a large part in choosing the optimum vehicle for carrying on a business. Here are some examples of how particular circumstances influence the decision.

❏ *Is the Business Risky?* If the business venture is a risky one, a form of doing business should be adopted that allows the investors the maximum protection in the event the investment turns sour. For example, IRC §1244 stock allows a more favorable ordinary loss deduction ($50,000 for a single taxpayer, $100,000 for joint filers) if a corporate venture fails.

❏ *What Is the Spread Between Tax Rates?* When the business is one in which both personal services and capital are material income-producing factors, the corporate form may offer some tax shelter, at least temporarily, to the owners if there is a spread between their effective individual tax rates and that of the corporation.

❏ *Will Interest Deductions Be Lost?* When substantial sums of money have to be borrowed to acquire or carry an investment-type asset, the use of the corporate form avoids the limitation on the deduction for investment interest. If the corporate form is unsuitable for other reasons, the owners should consider converting the investment property to avoid the limitation. This can be done, for example, by turning a passive investment, such as land, into income-producing property.

❏ *Can Income Be Split Within the Family?* Taxes may be reduced by the use of family partnerships or family controlled corporations. Family members in lower tax brackets could receive some of the business income—subject to the passive income and "kiddie tax" rules.

❏ *Will There Be Passive Income?* When the business will produce substantial passive income, the corporate form carries with it the danger of the imposition of the personal holding company penalty tax. If the corporate form is desirable for other reasons, increasing operating income or the number of shareholders may work to avoid the penalty.

❑ *Will There Be Start-Up Losses?* If it's anticipated that the business will incur operating losses during the initial years of operation, a form of business that allows the offset of business losses against the owner's other income should be used.

❑ *Will the Business Incur Debt?* Partnerships and S corporations both allow a passthrough of losses to the owners, but only to the extent of their bases. If losses may be higher than the owners' capital contributions and loans to the business, the use of a partnership may be called for since the basis of a partner in the partnership includes the debts of the partnership, while the basis of S corporation stock does not include corporate debts.

❑ *Can the Business Be Divided?* Taxes may be reduced if the operations of a business are divided into different taxable entities. For example, using a partnership to operate the business and a corporation to own and hold the real estate that houses the business may produce some tax shelter for the owners.

[¶4203] Tax Features of Sole Proprietorship

The uncomplicated tax treatment of the sole proprietorship is one of the reasons behind the popularity of this form of business. Basically, the entire profits of the proprietorship are taxed to the individual owner as income in the year earned. The owner computes the business profits on Schedule C of Form 1040 by reporting the gross income of the business and deducting all business expenses. The net figure is then added to other income on the personal tax return.

The sole proprietorship qualifies for no special deductions and must meet the same rules of deductibility that any other business must meet. So in terms of income and deductions, there is nothing special about it.

The sole proprietorship is unique, however, in one particular situation. That is when the proprietor sells the business. Since the business is not recognized as a separate entity under the tax law, the proprietor is not allowed to engage in the fiction that he or she has sold a single asset—the business—but rather is considered to have sold all the individual assets of the business and must allocate the purchase price to all the individual assets carried on the books, including goodwill. This means that the proprietor must recognize ordinary income on some of the assets, rather than report the whole gain as capital gain, which could be done if he or she sold all the stock in an incorporated business.

The obvious advantage of a sole proprietorship is that the business pays no tax at all; the income is taxed only to the proprietor. So unless the business produces a very large income, it is less costly for the owner to personally pick up the one tax, rather than pay two smaller taxes.

[¶4204] Tax Features of Partnership Operation

The tax treatment of the partnership lies somewhere between that of the sole proprietorship and that of the corporation. Like the corporation, the partnership is considered a separate entity—rather, the earnings are taxed directly to the partners, whether distributed or not.

The partnership, however, is required to file a tax return, Form 1065, although it is merely an information return. The net income for the year shown on this return is deemed to be distributed to the partners ratably on the last day of the partnership year, and each partner must pick up a distributive share on a personal income tax return. Each partner's share is normally computed in accordance with the partnership agreement.

A key difference between a corporation and a partnership is that losses to the partnership are passed directly through to the partners. This passthrough is not unlimited, but it can provide potential tax shelter. For this reason, many risky ventures are set up as partnerships, rather than some other form of business. Since joint ventures, syndicates, groups, or pools are taxed as partnerships, these forms are also used in such cases. However, the "passive activity" rules limit the use of these forms for tax shelter.

Under the tax law, and regardless of any state law to the contrary, a partnership is terminated only when no further business is carried on by any of the partners or there is a sale or exchange of 50% or more of the total interest in partnership capital and profits within 12 months. The partnership tax year closes on termination; it also closes as to a partner on sale, exchange, or liquidation of the partner's entire interest. This allows the partnership to continue as a tax entity when one of the members dies or resigns, which would be a technical termination under the laws of many states. There are, however, special rules for mergers or divisions of partnerships.

Unlike the sole proprietorship, the partner's interest in her firm is nominally considered a capital asset. Thus, she will generally realize capital gain on the sale of it, or, if the partnership is liquidated and properly distributed in kind to her, she will recognize no gain or loss until she disposes of the property. However, to the extent that the assets include "unrealized receivables" and "substantially appreciated inventory," the partner may realize ordinary income. These two categories also include IRC §1245 and §1250 recapture property.

The IRS will determine the treatment of partnership items in a single administrative proceeding at the partnership level, *not* in separate proceedings with the partner. The partnership must designate a partner to handle tax matters. In general, partners must treat items consistently with their treatment on the partnership return. Partnerships consisting of ten or fewer natural persons (or their estates) can opt out of these rules.

[¶4204.1]   Checklist of Tax Advantages of Doing Business as a Partnership

Here are the basic tax advantages to be derived from doing business as a partnership:

❏ Earnings of a partnership are only subject to one tax. In a corporation, there is a double tax on profits when they are distributed as dividends.

❏ The tax rate on the individual partners may be less than the corporate tax rates (but this difference is trivial post-1986).

❐ Partners are not taxed on exempt interest income or nontaxable amounts, like insurance proceeds, received from the firm—while dividends received from a corporation are taxable even if they are out of income that was not taxable to the corporation.

❐ Partnership losses (subject to the "at-risk" limitation of IRC §465 and the passive-activities rules) can reduce a partner's other personal ordinary income. This may also result in a carryover that can reduce a partner's future taxes, or a carryback that will result in a return of a prior year's taxes.

❐ If capital gains are realized by the firm, the partners only have to pay one capital gain tax. Stockholders of a corporation realizing capital gain cannot ordinarily get this treatment. However, partnerships cannot claim net operating losses (although partners can).

❐ A decision can be made as to how to divide profits among the partners.

❐ Earnings already taxed increase the cost basis to the partner of his interest in his company. This is not true of the stockholder.

❐ The owner of a corporate business who is also employed by the corporation may have to draw a salary in loss years to justify its reasonableness in other years. Thus, the owner will have taxable income even though the business doesn't show a profit; not so in a partnership since distributions can be geared to the partnership's annual income.

❐ Capital losses of a partnership reduce capital gains of individual partners. This is not true for corporate shareholders.

❐ Note that a partnership is precluded from using the cash method of accounting if any partner is a C Corporation.

[¶4205] THE FAMILY PARTNERSHIP

Under the Tax Code, the family partnership has become less useful as a planning device because tax rates are lower and there are fewer brackets (i.e., income shifting is less worthwhile). Furthermore, if the donee of a family partnership is 14 or younger, the "kiddie tax" rules will generally operate to tax his or her unearned income in excess of $1,300 at the parents' highest rate.

[¶4206] TAX FEATURES OF CORPORATIONS

The tax treatment of corporations, in contrast to that of proprietorships and partnerships, is exceedingly complex. The main tax feature of the corporation is that it is treated as a separate entity under the tax law and pays tax at rates graduated up to 35%, and may be subject to a 20% Alternative Minimum Tax, depending on how much income it makes. In addition, the corporation is not permitted to deduct dividends it pays to its shareholders, and they, in turn, must report the dividends as income. So, in most cases, unless S corporation status is elected, corporate earnings are taxed twice before they bring any benefit to the shareholder—once as corporate income and again as dividends.

Corporate deductions are also different from individual deductions and are generally more favorable. To the extent they are available, they also can provide potential tax shelter.

Finally, corporate ownership presents capital gain opportunities. Earnings accumulated in the corporation can be realized as capital gain by selling the stock. There are countless variations of this technique, involving not only sales, but liquidations, redemptions, reorganizations, and any number of other stock arrangements. The point is simply that since the stock is a capital asset whose value will depend on the earnings of the corporation, it presents many capital gain opportunities.

All these facts, plus the deduction for corporate salaries paid to shareholders, explain why the corporation can be a form of business with important tax advantages. Of course, there are many other advantages as well. These are summarized in the checklist below.

[¶4206.1] Checklist of Tax Advantages of the Corporate Form

The following is a list of the main tax advantages that can result from operating a business in corporate form. Some may not apply in a particular case, but all can potentially result in tax savings.

❏ The corporate form may be used as a tax shelter. However, this result is questionable, especially for personal service corporations, which pay a flat rate of 35%.

❏ Corporations in foreign trade or in other ventures can get special tax exemptions.

❏ Members of a family may be stockholders without many of the burdens and restrictions of family partnerships.

❏ Death benefits of up to $5,000 can be paid tax free to the beneficiaries of an employee.

❏ Incorporating avoids questions of the right to deduct losses. Individuals can deduct only casualty losses or losses incurred in a trade or business or in transactions entered into for profit (IRC §165(c)). Corporations are not so restricted. Losses are assumed to be incident to the business of the corporation.

❏ Deferred compensation and stock retirement plans can be utilized to achieve the financial planning purposes of the owner and the owner's family, and the employees.

❏ Only 30% (sometimes less) of dividend income is taxed to the corporation—100% is taxed to the partner or sole proprietor.

❏ The corporate form may facilitate saving income and estate taxes by gifts to children or to a family foundation.

❏ A new corporation is a new taxpayer. There may be a substantial advantage in choosing new tax elections.

❏ A corporation may be able to carry insurance on the lives of owner-executives at a reduced annual tax cost and then, without any further income tax burden, realize the proceeds and make them available to pay estate taxes. Working stockholders are eligible for $50,000 of tax-free group insurance coverage.

❏ Corporation stockholders can often control the dividend process. Therefore, unlike partners or sole proprietors, they usually can dictate the year in which they will receive income, and can select the most favorable one. Control of dividends by corporate holders permits averaging of stockholders' income over a long period.

❏ Stockholders have a capital gain when the corporation is liquidated. This is not always so with partnerships. Stockholders may be able to liquidate in a year when they have losses to offset the gain from liquidation.

❏ A special provision allows withdrawal of accumulated corporate profits in an amount equal to death taxes and expenses on death of an owner-stockholder through a partial stock redemption.

❏ A corporation is allowed to accumulate earnings, free from penalty, for purposes of redeeming stock to pay death taxes of one or more of the owners.

❏ A corporation is also allowed, under certain circumstances, to accumulate earnings to redeem the stock held by a private foundation.

❏ Corporate owners are not likely to have ordinary income when their interest is sold and the business has substantially appreciated inventory. Non-corporate business property gives rise to full tax on the appreciation if the owner sells his or her interest or dies or retires.

❏ The working owners get the benefit of tax-free medical and hospital insurance, and the corporation is entitled to deduct its cost.

❏ The working owners may also receive tax-free salary continuation payments made on account of disability.

❏ Another incidental benefit concerns meals and lodging. Working stockholders may exclude from income the value of any meals or lodging furnished by the corporation for its convenience.

[¶4207] TAX FEATURES OF S CORPORATIONS

The corporate form of doing business offers many advantages—for example, to limit personal liability. But in return, the incorporated taxpayer pays a big price—a double tax on business earnings. Profits are taxed once at the corporate level and again when they are distributed to the shareholders as dividends. Congress provided a way for closely held businesses to avoid the double tax when it enacted Subchapter S of the Internal Revenue Code. Subchapter S allows small corporations (in number of shareholders alone; it can be a multi-million dollar business) to elect the best of both worlds.

If the corporation qualifies, the shareholders can get (1) the benefits of the corporate setup (2) without a double tax. A corporation electing Sub S treatment is taxed basically like a partnership. There is no tax at the corporate level; profits and losses are passed directly through to the shareholders.

[¶4207.1] Rules for Electing Corporations

Electing corporations are simply called S corporations. Income, deductions, and credits retain their tax character when passed through to shareholders; loss carryovers are permitted; revocation of the election to be taxed as an S corporation is made easier. Here's an overview of the rules for S Corporations:

[¶4207.2] Eligibility Rules

An S corporation election can be made by a domestic corporation if all of the following criteria are met. The corporation must have: (1) no more than 35 shareholders, but a husband and wife are treated as one shareholder for this purpose; (2) only individuals, estates, and certain types of trusts as shareholders; (3) no nonresident alien shareholders; (4) not be a member of an affiliated group of corporations; and (5) only one class of stock. However, differences in stock voting rights will not create separate classes of stock [§1361]. And a straight debt instrument (e.g., a corporate bond) is not treated as a second class of stock even if it would be classified as stock under general tax principles. Payment of the debt instrument may not be contingent on the profits or discretion of the corporation. The bond cannot be convertible into stock, and it must be held by a person eligible to hold Sub S stock [§1361(c)(5)].

A "Qualified Subchapter S Trust" can become an S Corporation shareholder if the individual trust beneficiary (or legal representative) makes an irrevocable election to be treated as the owner of the part of the trust comprising the S Corporation stock.

[¶4207.3] Election Requirements

A corporation can elect S corporation status during the first 75 days of a tax year by filing Form 2553 with the IRS Service Center where the corporation files its Form 1120S. The election is retroactive to the beginning of that year and continues in effect until revoked or terminated. However, for the election to be effective in the year it's made, the corporation and its shareholders must have been eligible during the entire tax year in which the election is made. *All* persons who held stock in the corporation at any time during the period of the year prior to the election must consent to the election [§1362(a)].

Result: If the eligibility requirements are not met during the entire pre-election period, or the consent of all shareholders who dispose of their stock during the pre-election period is not secured, the election is not effective until the following year.

[¶4207.4] Shareholder Tax

S corporations are not subject to corporate income tax (except for tax on capital gains in some situations). Instead, the S corporation shareholders pay tax on their pro-rata share of the corporation's distributed and undistributed income. Most S corporation income, deduction and credit items are passed through pro rata and entered on the shareholder's returns. What's left—the corporate equivalent of partnership taxable income—is taxed to the shareholder at the end of the year, whether or not any cash distributions are made during the year. The shareholder's taxable portion of the income is based on his or her percentage of stock owner-ship and the amount of time the shares were owned during the year.

Capital gains and losses, charitable contributions, tax-exempt interest, for-eign tax credits, investment credits, Section 1231 gains and losses, depletion allowances, foreign income and loss and other items pass separately to the share-holders. The items retain their individual characteristics on the shareholders' returns [§1366(a)]. For example, tax-exempt interest paid to the corporation is also tax-exempt to the shareholder.

Corporate losses: The shareholder's pro rata share of losses is limited to the sum of the shareholder's tax basis in the S corporation's stock, plus the basis of any corporate indebtedness to the shareholder.

Losses in excess of a shareholder's adjusted basis can be carried forward to any year in which the shareholder has enough basis in stock or debt to enable the loss to be passed through [§1366(d)(2)].

The shareholder's tax basis for S corporation stock is increased when the corporation has income (either taxable or non-taxable) and decreased by losses and expenses. The basis is adjusted before the distribution rules are applied.

Example: Mr. Smith paid $10,000 for his stock in XYZ Inc., an S corporation, so his unadjusted tax basis is $10,000. His share of XYZ's "taxable" income for the year is $2,000. His basis is therefore increased to $12,000 (and later reduced if any cash distributions are made).

[¶4207.5] Distribution Rules

The tax treatment of distributions from an S corporation is similar to current *partnership* rules. How a shareholder is taxed depends on whether or not the S corporation has accumulated earnings from its years as a Sub S corporation before 1983 or as a regular corporation.

A distribution by an S corporation without accumulated earnings and prof-its is tax-free to the extent of the shareholder's tax basis in his stock. (The distrib-ution reduces the shareholder's basis in the corporation's stock.) Distributions in excess of the stock's basis generally result in capital gains.

A distribution by a Sub S corporation *with* accumulated earnings and prof-its is tax-free to the extent of the corporation's "accumulated adjustment account" (the amount of undistributed income for years after 1982 while an S corporation). Excess distributions are then taxed as dividends up to the amount of accumulated earnings and profits less previously taxed undistributed income. Any additional distributions will be a tax-free return of capital (to the extent of the shareholder's stock basis), and then capital gain (to the extent of the excess over basis).

On consent of all stockholders who receive a distribution during the year, the S Corporation can elect to treat distributions as dividends.

[¶4207.6] Choice of Tax Year Limited

The tax year of an S corporation has to be a calendar year, unless it can establish a business purpose for a non-calendar tax year [§1378].

Existing S corporations on non-calendar tax years generally must comply with this rule. But an existing S corporation will be permitted to retain its non-calendar year if at least 50% of the stock in the corporation is owned by the same persons who owned such stock on December 31, 1982. (For this purpose, transfers of shares to family members or by reason of the shareholder's death will not be considered changes in ownership.)

[¶4207.7] Passive Investment Income

Where the S corporation's Subchapter C earnings and profits and passive investment income are higher than 25% of gross receipts, the S corporation will be taxed at the highest corporate rate on its taxable income or "excess net passive income"—whichever is smaller. The rules for computing excess net passive income, too complex to summarize here, are found in Code §1362(d)(3)(D).

[¶4207.8] Fringe Benefits

An S corporation receives a deduction only for the cost of providing benefits to employees who are not stockholders, or who hold 2% or less of the corporation's stock.

[¶4207.9] Built-in Gains

A corporation changing status from C corporation to S corporation after 1986 is taxable on any "built-in gain" recognized when it disposes of an asset in the ten years following the S corporation election. The tax, payable at the corporation's highest rate or alternative corporate rate, is assessed on the excess of the fair market value of the corporation's assets over its adjusted bases at the time of the election, minus gain recognized on the distribution of the asset. The Revenue Act of 1987 also requires recapture of gain built in when a C corporation using the LIFO method converts to S corporation status: Code §1363(d).

[¶4208] How to Create a Tax-Free Transfer to a Corporation

A gain or loss realized by transfer of assets that have appreciated in value will not result in a taxable event if the following three requirements are met:

(1) The person or persons making the transfer to the corporation must together control the corporation immediately after the exchange.

(2) Each of the transferors must receive back solely stock of such corporation.

(3) The corporation does not assume any liabilities of a particular transferor or acquire property from a particular transferor subject to a liability if the purpose is to avoid a Federal income tax on the exchange.

The utilization of IRC §351 results in the following tax consequences:

(1) No gain or loss is recognized by the transferor(s) after the exchange is consummated.

(2) The corporation succeeds to the transferor's adjusted basis for the property received by it.

(3) The transferor's basis for the stock or securities received is the same as the adjusted basis for the property transferred.

Example: Malone owns a special machine with a cost basis of $2,000 and a fair market value of $20,000. Grant owns land with a cost basis of $40,000 and a fair market value of $20,000. They both transfer their property to a newly organized corporation in exchange for equal shares of stock. Under §351, Malone's $18,000 gain and Grant's $20,000 loss are *not* recognized.

[¶4209] Partial Capital Gain Exclusion for Small Business Stock

Under OBRA '93, a noncorporate taxpayer who holds for more than five years qualified small business stock issued after August 10, 1993, can exclude 50 percent of any gain on the investor's sale or exchange of the stock. The amount of gain eligible for the exclusion is limited to the greater of (1) 10 times the taxpayer's basis in the stock or (2) $10 million of gain from stock in that corporation. That exclusion is on a shareholder-by-shareholder basis.

The rules establishing what constitutes qualified small business stock for purposes of this rule are the following:

(1) The stock must be acquired by the taxpayer at original issuance after August 10, 1993. Thus, stock acquired by purchase from a prior stockholder is not eligible for the exclusion.

(2) The corporation must be a C corporation that uses at least 80 percent of its gross assets in the active conduct of a qualified trade or business.

(3) A qualified trade or business is any trade or business other than personal service type businesses, such as health, law, or engineering.

(4) As of the date of issuance of the stock, the corporation's gross assets cannot exceed $50 million.

[¶4210] SPECIAL CORPORATE TAX TRAPS

There are two possible penalty taxes that can be imposed upon a corporation. Tax planning for the incorporated business must be aimed at avoiding them. The penalty taxes are assessed for unreasonable accumulations of corporate income, and for the use of the corporation as a personal holding company. These penalty taxes are discussed in the following paragraphs.

[¶4210.1] Unreasonable Accumulations

When a corporation accumulates earnings and profits in excess of $250,000 ($150,000 in the case of personal service corporations), it runs the risk of a penalty tax under IRC §531–537. The penalty applies to corporations formed or availed of for purposes of avoiding taxes by accumulating earnings instead of distributing them as dividends (IRC §532).

The tax is imposed on the current year's "accumulated taxable income" at the rate of $27\,^1/_2\%$ on the first $100,000 and $38\,^1/_2\%$ on any excess. This tax, like the personal holding company penalty surtax, is in addition to the regular corporate tax (IRC §532).

If the accumulation exceeds $250,000, the penalty tax can still be avoided by showing "reasonably anticipated needs of the business" as the purpose for the accumulation (IRC §537). It is not necessary to show that earnings and profits must be reinvested in the business immediately. It is enough to show that future needs of the business will require that these earnings and profits be plowed back (IRC §535(c)), but these future needs must be more than just vague or uncertain plans or ideas.

[¶4210.2] Personal Holding Companies

A 35% flat tax is imposed on income retained by personal service corporations. Because this is higher than the maximum personal rate, the formation of new personal service corporations is likely to be slowed down. (There are still certain practical and tax advantages to operating in corporate form, so the personal service corporation form is unlikely to disappear.) Under Code §541, there is a penalty tax of 38.5% (over and above normal income tax) on the undistributed income (roughly equivalent to after-tax income minus dividends) of a personal holding company. A corporation is a personal holding company if more than 50% of its stock is owned by five or fewer individuals, and at least 60% of its adjusted ordinary gross income comes from §543 sources such as royalties, film rentals, and amounts received by the corporation for an individual's personal services.

Also note that §469(d)(2) applies the passive-loss rules to closely held C corporations and personal service corporations; that a personal service corporation must have a calendar year (§441(i)(1)); and that a personal service corporation may be permitted to use the cash method, under appropriate circumstances, even if it is a C corporation (§448).

[¶4210.3] The Requirement of Showing a Profit Motive

When starting a business, the taxpayer must be able to show that the business has a genuine *profit motive* behind its activity. The IRS is usually suspicious of loss deductions from hobby-like activities. This does not mean that you must make a profit or even expect to make a profit in the near future. Many legitimate businesses often incur losses over long periods of time, especially in the startup phase. The taxpayer simply must conduct the activity in a business-like manner, meaning accurate and complete business records. An activity is presumed to have a profit motive, (as opposed to a hobby) if profits result in any three of five consecutive tax years ending with the tax year in question, unless the IRS proves otherwise §183(d).

Observation: If the IRS challenges the business status of your sideline activity, you can file IRS Form 5213, *Election to Postpone Determination as to Whether the Presumption that Activity Engaged In Is For Profit.* This delays the determination of the activity's business status until after the taxpayer has been in business five years. It also gives the taxpayer extra time to qualify the activity as a business. In the meantime, the taxpayer can claim business deductions.

If the activity fails to qualify as a business at the end of five years, the taxpayer will owe back taxes and penalties.

[¶4211] LIMITED LIABILITY COMPANIES

When forming or reorganizing a company or venture, the choice of what form of organization to use has expanded in recent years to include limited liability companies (LLCs). An LLC has the advantages of a partnership's flow-through tax treatment, a corporation's limited liability, and an owner's control of management.[1]

An LLC resembles a partnership, but it is a legal entity distinct from its members. A business wishing to exist in the form of an LLC must meet the partnership requirements of the Internal Revenue Code, as well as file documents (e.g., Articles of Organization) with its respective state and meet the state's requirements for organization. LLC statutes presently vary from state to state.

The LLC form of organization may be more desirable than other business forms for various reasons, such as:

Limited liability: members of LLCs are not liable for the organization's debts, obligations, or liabilities; they are generally liable only to the extent of their capital contribution to the LLC.

Tax purposes: LLCs are taxed as partnerships, rather than as corporations. This means, among other things, a single level of Federal income tax and much greater tax flexibility.

Management flexibility: unlike S corporations, there are no limitations on the number and type of owners, and unlike limited partnerships, all members may manage the corporation without losing liability protection.

The IRS has issued a private letter ruling approving the conversion of a limited partnership to an LLC without the partnership being considered terminated, thus resulting in the recognition of gain or loss.[2]

LLCs are still not recognized in a limited number of states so members in these states may still have personal liability.

[¶4212] Cushioning Personal and Business Losses

The following checklist shows how the impact of a loss can be softened considerably through careful tax planning.

❐ Operating losses can be deducted against the investor's outside income by using a partnership or an S corporation, subject to passive-activities rules.

❐ Investment loss on stock can be deducted against ordinary income by issuing the stock under IRC §1244. Investors in small business corporations can get up to $50,000 in ordinary deductions ($100,000 on a joint return) per year for loss on common stock that is considered to be small business stock (§1244). This rule applies whether the loss was incurred on sale of the stock or on its becoming worthless. It can only be used by the original purchaser of the stock. Only $1,000,000 in small-business corporate stock qualifies for this special treatment.

[¶4213] Accounting Methods and Taxable Years

Having set up the business, consideration (from a tax viewpoint) is then focused on the accounting year and methods. While many of the accounting aspects of the business will naturally be the concern of the accountant, the lawyer has to be aware of the tax consequences of the selection of an accounting period and method in order to help the client with proper preparation.

Tax accounting in many respects differs from conventional business accounting. In other cases, it is the same, but elections of available choices must be made.

A good deal of tax planning may go into the choice of an accounting year. As for accounting method, in addition to the usual choice between a cash and accrual method (when that choice is available), special methods must be considered for special situations—i.e., deferring income on installment sales, treatment of long-term construction contracts.

Choice of methods also arises on valuing inventories—generally between the First-In-First-Out (FIFO) and the Last-In-First-Out (LIFO) methods.

Advance IRS permission is not required to use LIFO, but Form 970 must be filed in the year of adoption. When LIFO is used for tax purposes, it must also be used for reporting purposes—making the reported results less favorable; tax savings should be weighed against loss of stockholder and investor confidence.

For post-1986 years, Code §474 provides a simplified dollar-value LIFO method which may be elected by businesses with average gross receipts of under $5 million.

[¶4214] Cash Method of Accounting

The cash receipts and disbursements method is used largely by individuals whose income is derived principally from salaries and wages; by retail merchants, shopkeepers, and professional men; and also by many large business enterprises in the service, financial, and real estate fields, when merchandise inventories are not a material income-producing factor.

[¶4214.1] Basic Principles of Cash Method

Under this method, a taxpayer has income to the extent of cash or property actually or "constructively" (see below) received during the tax year; it makes no difference how much the taxpayer actually earned during the year—it is the amount received that is important under this method.

If payment is made in the form of property, there is income to the extent of the fair market value of the property. For example, if stock is given for services, income to the extent of its fair market value is received.

[¶4214.2] Deductions Under Cash Method

Generally, deductions will be allowed in the year paid, even though they are incurred or relate to another year. Prepayment of supplies that are to be delivered the following year is deductible in the year of payment.

If the prepayment results in the acquisition of a "capital asset," the deduction must be prorated over the related years. Thus, for example, commissions, legal fees, and other expenses incurred in negotiating a long-term lease or mortgage loan must be spread over the term of the lease or loan. In addition, prepaid interest must be spread over the term of the loan.

[¶4214.3] "Constructive Receipt"

Under this doctrine, a taxpayer is taxed on income even before it is actually received, if it is available for the asking. The most common examples are: matured interest coupons on bonds that have not been cashed, declared dividends unqualifiedly subject to the stockholder's demand, and interest credited on savings bank deposits although not withdrawn.

[¶4214.4] Who May Use the Cash Method?

It *may* be used by any taxpayer who does not use inventories to determine income or who does not keep books of account. Stockpiling of items used in a business can be construed to be an inventory. *Wilkinson-Bean, Inc.* (TC Memo

1969–79) involved a funeral director who kept a substantial supply of caskets because his supplier was far from his place of business. The Tax Court forced the funeral director to use the accrual method because it found that the income (about 14% of the gross income) from the sale of caskets was a significant income factor requiring the use of an inventory.

[¶4214.5] Advantages of the Cash Method

❏ Taxes are not paid until the income is received.

❏ Receipts and disbursements for each year can be controlled so as to avoid higher tax rates on income piled up in a single year.

❏ Complicated records or books of account need not be maintained. In most cases, a checkbook or simple cashbook showing receipts and disbursements will suffice. There is no need for accruals.

Post-1986, there are limits on the use of the cash method. However, qualified personal services corporations and small businesses averaging under $5 million in yearly gross receipts may still be able to use this method.

[¶4214.6] Disadvantages of the Cash Method

❏ The chief defect of the cash method is that it does not truly reflect annual net income. It produces "peaks" and "valleys."

❏ Income may pile up in a single year despite meticulous efforts to regulate income and outgo. For example, advance payments of rents, salaries, royalties, interest, etc.

❏ If the business is liquidated or sold, income may be "bunched" into one year and deductions forever lost. *Example:* When a cash-basis corporation liquidated and transferred its accounts receivable to its stockholders, the court held that the accounts receivable were taxable to the corporation as income realized prior to dissolution. The best way to avoid this tax trap is to continue the corporation in existence for a reasonable period until the outstanding accounts receivable are collected and the debts paid off. In any event, prepay all deductible items before dissolution.

[¶4215] ACCRUAL METHOD OF ACCOUNTING

This method is used by businesses with numerous and complex transactions because it is a more scientific and accurate method for determining true income for any given period of time. It is used in practically all manufacturing, wholesale, or retail businesses, and service establishments when the production, purchase, or sale of merchandise is an "income-producing" factor.

After 1986, C corporations, tax shelters, and partnerships with C corporation partners *must* use the accrual method, except as explained above.

[¶4215.1] Basic Principles of Accrual Method

The accrual of income depends on the right to receive it, rather than actual receipt. There are three basic rules as to when the right to receive income becomes fixed and accruable: (1) The taxpayer must have a valid, unconditional, and enforceable right to receive the income within the taxable year; (2) the amount due must be determinable or susceptible of reasonable estimate; (3) there must be a reasonable expectancy that the amount due will be paid and collected in due course.

The same rules apply to the deduction of expenses on the accrual basis. When all the events have occurred within the taxable year that fix the amount and the fact of the taxpayer's liability, such expenses are properly accruable and deductible for tax purposes, even though paid in a subsequent year. However, for expenses accruing after July 18, 1984, expenses must generally meet an additional requirement to be deductible: "economic performance" must have occurred. For example, if an expense is owed another person for the performance of services, the expense is deductible only when the services are performed.

The accrual method may be used by any taxpayer who maintains records or books of account; it must be used by a taxpayer who uses inventories to determine income.

[¶4215.2] Accrued Expenses to Related Taxpayers

In the past, an accrual-basis taxpayer had to pay such accrued interest or expense within $2\frac{1}{2}$ months after the close of the accrual year or else the deduction was permanently lost. Those rules were changed by TRA '84.

[¶4215.3] Adjustment of Accrued Liabilities

If the amount actually paid turns out to be more or less than the amount of expense accrued and deducted, it becomes necessary to reflect the difference in the tax return for the year of accrual or the year of payment.

When a dispute as to liability has been settled or finally adjudicated, you can deduct the amount determined to be due in the year of final determination, but you have to make the deduction in the year of actual payment if that occurs before the contest is settled.

[¶4216] HYBRID ACCOUNTING

The Internal Revenue Code permits hybrid accounting when it is approved by the Regulations (see Reg. §1.446-1) as clearly reflecting income (§446(c)(4)). A hybrid method of accounting combines the principles of several recognized accounting methods. For example, many small retail stores use a combination of the cash and accrual methods. By this system, they are permitted to report gross income (gross receipts less cost of goods sold) on the accrual basis and deduct selling and administration expenses on the cash basis. This combination of accounting methods simply removes the bother of accruing small expenses and can be of substantial benefit in small business operations.

[¶4217] INSTALLMENT SALES

If you're to be paid in installments, you're taxed pro rata as proceeds are received. The installment sale is available only to a person who sells real property, or a person who makes a casual sale of personal property (other than merchandise).

For a sale of real property or a casual sale of personal property to qualify, there's one basic requirement: the seller must receive at least one payment after the tax year in which the sale took place.

Under the installment sale method, gross profit is allocated as payments are made. The installment sale method requires at least one payment in a tax year other than the year of sale; it is not available for sales made at a loss, or to sales of depreciable property between related parties. The method is applied automatically to casual sales of real property and non-inventory personal property, unless the seller opts out. The Revenue Act of 1987 forbids dealers in any kind of property to use the installment sales method for sales after 12/31/87. But dealers in timeshares and residential lots can make limited use of the method. Code §453(1)(2)).

[¶4218] DEFERRED PAYMENT SALES

If the seller elects *not* to report gain on the installment method, then an installment sale is treated as a deferred-payment sale. The entire gain is reported in the year of sale, even if the installment obligations are payable over a period of years.

[¶4219] LONG-TERM CONTRACTS

Taxpayers engaged in heavy construction work meet special accounting problems. Usually building, installation, and construction projects require a considerable length of time to complete. Frequently, unforeseen difficulties are encountered before the contract is complete—for example, there may be price changes in materials used; losses and increased expenses due to strikes, weather conditions and work stoppages; penalties for delay; and unexpected difficulties in laying foundations.

These conditions make it impossible for a construction contractor, no matter how careful the estimate, to tell with any certainty whether a particular contract will produce a profit or sustain a loss until it is completed.

Because of these problems, contractors are permitted to use two special methods of reporting their income from long-term contracts: the percentage of completion method and the completed contract method (Reg. §1.451-3). Code §460 added special rules for contracts entered into after 2/28/86.

[¶4220] WHEN SHOULD THE TAX YEAR START?

Picking the right taxable year for a business pays off in substantial tax savings as well as in other ways. The initial choice of an accounting period is generally within the control of the taxpayer and does not require the permission of IRS. However, many taxpayers forfeit this right of choice by giving the matter haphazard, last-minute consideration, with the result that they are forced to adopt an annual accounting period ill-suited to their business needs.

To be sure, it is possible to change your accounting period if the wrong one was selected in the first instance. However, that's not always easy to accomplish, because IRS's permission must be obtained (see Form 1128, *Application for Change in Accounting Period*) and it won't be granted unless there is a valid business reason for making the change.

Four Possible Choices: The law requires that taxable income be computed on the basis of the taxpayer's taxable year. Generally, the taxable year covers a 12-month period. In certain exceptional instances, it may be a "short period" of less than 12 months. It may never be more than a full 12-month period, except in the case of a 52–53 week year.

Under the Internal Revenue Code (IRC §441), only four types of taxable years are recognized. They are (Reg. §1.441-1):

(1) Calendar Year: A 12-month period ending on Dec. 31 (§441(d)).

(2) Fiscal Year: A 12-month period ending on the last day of any month other than December (§441(e)).

(3) 52–53 Week Year: A fiscal year, varying from 52 to 53 weeks in duration, which always ends on the same day of the week, which—

      (a) occurs for the last time in a calendar month, or

      (b) falls nearest the end of a calendar month (§441(f), Reg. §1.441-2).

(4) Short Period: A period of less than 12 months (allowed only in certain special situations such as initial return, final return, and change in accounting period (§443(a)).

In general, partnerships, S Corporations, and personal service corporations must either use the tax years of their owners, or establish a business purpose for the choice—so they will probably be calendar-year taxpayers. (Code §444 lets such entities retain fiscal years they adopted prior to the 1986 Code. However, if they do so, they must accelerate payment of income tax via "required payments" defined by Code §7519.) Furthermore, personal service corporations with fiscal years must meet Code §280H's minimum distribution requirements, or their deduction for payments to employee-owners will be limited.

[¶4220.1] Factors Determining Choice of Accounting Period

The conditions for each type of annual accounting period may be summarized as follows:

Taxable Year	*Conditions*
(1) Calendar Year *must* be used by a taxpayer, if . . .	(a) he keeps no books, (b) he has no annual account period, or (c) he has an accounting period (other than a calendar year) that does not qualify as a fiscal year.
(2) Fiscal Year *may* be used by a taxpayer, if . . .	(a) he keeps books, (b) he has definitely established such fiscal year as his accounting period before the close of his first fiscal year, and (c) his books are kept in accordance with such fiscal year.
(3) 52–53 Week Taxable Year *may* be used by a taxpayer, if . . .	(a) he keeps books, (b) he regularly computes his income on a 52–53 week basis, and (c) his books are kept on such 52–53 week basis.

[¶4221] NATURAL BUSINESS YEAR

You won't find the term "natural business year" in the tax law. However, IRS looks upon it with favor and will often grant permission to a taxpayer to change an established accounting period to conform with the natural business year.

What is the natural business year? It is an annual cycle of 12 consecutive months (or 52 to 53 weeks) that ends when the business activities of the enterprise are at their lowest point. At this point of the annual cycle, sales and production activities are at their lowest level, inventories and accounts receivable are at a minimum, and the cash or liquid position of the enterprise is at its highest level.

[¶4222] PLANT AND EQUIPMENT

Once the business is ready to operate, a major expenditure will involve its plant and equipment. Tax considerations can have a decided influence on the methods of acquisition and maintenance of the property. Many of these factors will, of course, be taken into account by the lawyer in planning with the client the setting up of the business. In projecting capital needs, for example, the availability of tax credits and deductions can play a major role.

Many choices are available as to how necessary plant and equipment is acquired, maintained, and charged off. First, plant and equipment can be leased or purchased. If owned, it can be converted into working cash by a sale-leaseback.

Qualifying business property can be "expensed" (deducted in a single year) to the extent of $17,500 per year.[3]

Beginning in 1987, the Code substitutes the MACRS (Modified Accelerated Cost Recovery System) for ACRS for most tangible depreciable personal property placed in service in 1987 and later. (Property already in service on 1/1/87 will continue to be depreciated under the rules originally applicable.) MACRS, as defined in §168, sets up an 8-class system, with recovery periods ranging from 3 to 31.5 years.

Intangibles such as goodwill, licenses, patents, and covenants not to compete are amortizable over a period of 15 years beginning with the month of acquisition.[4]

[¶4223] TAKING MONEY OUT OF THE CORPORATION

As early as the time a new corporation is set up, consider the tax cost of taking profits out of the business and getting them into the hands of the stockholders. Projecting ahead is an important tax planning requirement in determining the pros and cons of different business forms for a particular client.

Once the corporation is in operation, the owners can take money out as compensation to the extent of the reasonable value of the services they render to a corporation.

The owners may come out better in the long run if they accumulate earnings in the corporation and cash in by selling or redeeming stock or by selling or liquidating the entire business. There are, however, restrictions and penalties for accumulating earnings and failing to distribute the earnings of a personal holding company.

When money has been accumulated in the corporation, it may be withdrawn as capital gain by sales of stock, by liquidation, partial or complete, or by redemption of stock. At all times, however, the collapsible corporation rules must be kept in mind. Planners should also note that Code §162 has been amended to deny a corporation a deduction for its expenses in connection with redemption of its stock.

[¶4224] PLANNING FOR CAPITAL TRANSACTIONS

Excess losses can be deducted to the extent of $3,000 ($1,500 for married taxpayers filing separately), and carried forward indefinitely if they exceed that limit.

[¶4225] INVESTMENT PLANNING

Many investments are particularly appealing because of the "tax shelter" or other tax advantage they may offer, subject to the possible effect of the "at risk rule" (IRC §465), the "passive activities" rule (§469), and the alternative minimum tax (IRC §55).

Some factors that give tax shelter to an investment are:

(1) The yield of tax-free income—e.g., tax-exempt bonds. Note that "private activity" bonds are *not* tax-exempt even if issued by a governmental entity. Furthermore, all taxpayers (not just those receiving taxable Social Security benefits) must now report tax-exempt interest so the IRS can monitor compliance.

(2) A deduction from income that has no relationship to actual costs—e.g., the percentage depletion deduction allowed against income from oil, gas, and minerals.

(3) A return of capital tax-free while investment yield is maintained and money value of the property may be maintained—e.g., income buildings, the cost of which is returned tax-free via depreciation allowance, while inflation and deductible repairs may maintain—and even enhance—the value of the property.

(4) An assured buildup in value that can be realized tax-free—e.g., life insurance proceeds.

(5) Definite buildup in value that cannot be taxed until realized and on which a substantial part of the realization can be indefinitely postponed—e.g., building up a cattle herd in which value is enhanced by both growth and propagation.

(6) Investments with a high degree of security against loss and also a potential of sizable capital gain—e.g., convertible bonds.

(7) Investment yields having special protection—e.g., dividends received by a corporation.

Taxpayers (except some C corporations) must determine whether investment activities are "active" or "passive." Passive losses and credits can be used only to offset passive (roughly speaking, tax shelter) income only—*not* earned income or portfolio income. The rules are phased in over five years for interests held prior to the passage of the new Code.

In general rental activities are considered passive activities. However, for tax years beginning after December 31, 1993, passive loss rules no longer apply to certain taxpayers that are involved in real property trades or businesses. Instead they are treated as active businesses. Under the new law, this means that the taxpayer may be able to deduct up to $25,000 of the loss from the activity from nonpassive income.[5] This "special allowance" is an exception to the general rule disallowing losses in excess of income from passive activities.

Note that this $25,000 deduction is available to individuals with AGI up to $100,000. Between $100,001 and $150,000 of AGI, the $25,000 deduction is reduced on a "two-for-one basis" so that the loss is completely eliminated when AGI reaches $150,000.

[¶4226] INVESTMENTS IN REAL ESTATE

From the tax and financial standpoint, real estate is a highly flexible and versatile type of asset. Here are 19 tax features that can be used to bring about profitable real estate deals.

(1) Real estate can be purchased or rented, sold or leased, with different tax results. A piece of real estate can be divided into different types of fees, leasehold and mortgage investments, each tailored to the tax position of its owner.

(2) When sold at a loss, the loss may be fully deductible.

(3) When sold at a profit all or part of the gain may be qualified for favorable capital gain treatment.

(4) When leased, the cost of occupancy can be charged off fully.

(5) A properly arranged security deposit isn't taxed until the end of the lease.

(6) When owned, much of the cost of the investment can be recovered tax-free by depreciation deductions. This reduces the size of the investment and steps up the yield that a real estate investment can show.

(7) Ownership can be financed in a way that gives the owner depreciation charges on the mortgagee's investment, increasing equity with tax-free funds.

(8) The cost of land can be made tax deductible by a sale, followed by a leaseback for a long period. The investment in the building is recovered tax-free through depreciation charges.

(9) The owner of real estate may be able to get his or her property improved tax-free by having a tenant make the improvements.

(10) The owner can elect to deduct or capitalize interest and taxes paid to carry unimproved property.

(11) The owner of real estate can sometimes build up the value of his or her holdings by tax-deductible repair expenditures.

(12) The ownership of real estate can be held in whatever entity—partnership, corporation, trust, or personal ownership—will best protect the income from tax. The tax savings can be applied to build up equity and future capital gain by improving the property and paying off mortgages.

(13) Tax on the sale of real estate may be postponed by electing the installment method of sale, or by using option agreements, executory contracts, conditional contracts, and leases with purchase options.

(14) Even after an installment sale, the gain can be taxed earlier, if that should prove to be desirable, by disposing of the installment obligations.

(15) On the sale of real estate, there are methods of getting cash in advance, yet deferring the taxability of gain.

(16) Real estate held for investment can be built up in value and traded tax-free for other real estate to be held for investment.

(17) Leases can be canceled for money that is taxed as capital gain.

(18) Condemnation awards can be received without tax if reinvested in real estate.

(19) A residence can be sold with no or reduced tax if the proceeds are used to buy or build a new residence—or without reinvestment when sold by an individual over 55.

The Code provisions dealing with REITs (e.g., §856) with provisions create a new pass-through entity called a REMIC (Real Estate Mortgage Investment Conduit). The REMIC provisions (Code §860D) define the REMIC as a fixed mortgage pool owned by investors with multiple classes of interests.

Nondealers who sell real property used in trade or business for more than $150,000 (which, these days, means most sellers) must pay interest on certain tax deferrals produced by installment sales: see Code §453A.

[¶4227] SHIFTING INCOME IN THE FAMILY

Part of the answer to the problem of accumulating funds for education, retirement, etc., lies in shifting income into lower brackets—a difficult tactic. Here's a list of some methods that might be used:

❑ *Shifting income to relatives*—The "kiddie tax" concept subjects the "net unearned income" of a child under 14 to taxation at the parents' marginal rate. The rule thus makes the transfer of income property less attractive; however, the rule applies regardless of the source of the child's assets. Earned income is taxed at the child's rate. Net unearned income is defined as unearned income minus $600 (the child's standard deduction) and also minus either $600 or the deductions allocable to production of the unearned income, whichever is greater.

❑ *Passing up the income-splitting device normally used by the husband and wife*—letting each make a separate return—and letting each pay his or her own medical expenses or charitable contributions. The law limits the deduction for those items to percentage computations. Sometimes it is possible to gain considerably by having the husband and wife pay their own costs, or those of their direct dependents.

❑ *Moving property and its income to lower-bracket members of the family*—here you figure the graduated tax of a child, or a parent, against the taxpayer's. Then try to find the gift tax cost of what income-producing property can be given to them. In the end, there may be a lower tax in the assignments.

❑ *Managing investments*—shifting income within the family so one member fairly charges the other for the right to use the property—this involves deductions charged the high-bracket taxpayer, and income assumed by the lower-bracket child, parent, or dependent.

❑ *Incorporating family-owned property*—or family-owned business in order to get the advantages of stepped-up costs for assets (paying capital gain tax) and many other advantages that come with the incorporation of the family business. The corporation can be a tax shelter, but see that business policy and the character of investments afford protection from the penalty tax aimed at a tight dividend policy and the use of incorporated pocketbooks.

❑ *Splitting a family business into a partnership*—or subdividing existing partnerships to get further income splitting can keep family business income in lower brackets. Limited partnerships can also be useful planning instruments. Great care must be exercised in drawing partnership agreements because they have so serious an impact on the tax result.

❑ *Planning new ventures, new investments, new undertakings—so that the members of the family ratably take their share of income and losses—* for example, it is possible (without any gift tax) to take a couple of members of the family into a new business, and they might gain without additional tax cost.

❑ *Buying property through estates by entirety, or joint tenancies or tenancies in common*—each of these setups has its distinct tax pros and cons to consider with members of the family.

❑ *Setting up family insurance in the most advantageous manner—* the net protection available may vary widely as ownership and premium-paying responsibility falls on the insured, members of his or her family, a trust, a corporation.

❑ *Setting up interfamily annuities in which one member of a family transfers something for income from another*—these might produce considerable savings without gift taxes.

❑ *Setting up family foundations* in which family income and capital can be conserved for educational, charitable, scientific, and religious work.

❑ *Careful nursing of interfamily deals for interest, pay, rent, or anything else they may have between them*—penalty for sloppiness is usually loss of the deduction for the loss. Be sure to watch the ritual here if the tax saving is to be made.

❑ *Making sure that alimony or separation payments allot the tax between the couple fairly*—the lawyer making these arrangements has a great deal to study if the goal is to seek the full deduction for the paying spouse.

❑ *Taking advantage of the child care credit*—a single parent, or a two-earner couple, can claim a credit of up to $2,400 (for one dependent) or $4,800 (for more than one) for expenses undertaken to provide care for a child or other dependent in order to permit the parent(s) to work. Low-income workers in this situation may also be entitled to the §32 Earned Income Credit.

— ENDNOTES —

1. Rev. Rul. 88-76, 1988-2 CB 360.
2. Letter Ruling 9010027, 12-7-89, CCH IRS LETTER RULING REPORTS.
3. IRC Sec. 179.
4. IRC Sec. 197.
5. Temp. Reg. Sec.1.469-1T(e)(3)(viii), Example (10).

— FOR FURTHER REFERENCE —

Ain, Sanford K. and Faith D. Dornbrand, "Taxation Issues Affecting the Older Divorce Client," 16 *Family Advisor* 34 (Summer '93).

Akselrad, Ira and Robert S. Bernstein, "Are Expenses Incurred in Obtaining LBO Loans Deductible?" 20 *J. Corporate Tax* 295 (Autumn '93).

Blumberg, Grace Ganz, "Identifying and Valuing Goodwill at Divorce," 56 *Law and Contemporary Problems* 217 (Spring '93).

Chazan, Michael J., "Insurance Policy May Be an Ideal Asset for a Gift by the Insured," 19 *Estate Planning* 294 (September–October '92).

Eule, Norman L. and Michael B. Richman, "Refinancing a Home Mortgage May Have Adverse Tax Costs," 21 *Taxation for Lawyers* 100 (September–October '92).

Fiore, Nicholas, "The New Tax Law: Individual Highlights," 176 *J. of Accountancy* 38 (September '93).

Friedrich, Craig W., "Tax Consequences Taken into Account in Determining Whether to Allow Bankruptcy Trustee to Abandon Property," 20 *J. of Real Estate Taxation* 94 (Fall '92).

Geier, Deborah A., "Form, Substance and Section 1041," 60 *Tax Notes* 519 (7/26/93).

Headley, Richard A., "S Election Issues for Community Property Shareholders," 24 *Tax Adviser* 499 (August '93).

Hereth, Russell H. and John C. Talbott, "Deductibility of Expenses Under the Business/Hobby Rules," 24 *Tax Adviser* 566 (September '93).

Hoffman, Michael J.R. and Kenneth N. Orbach, "Assignment of Income and Divorce," 23 *The Tax Adviser* 601 (September '92).

Knight, Ray A. and Lee G. Knight, "Tax Treatment of Takeover Costs," 9 *Akron Tax J.* 1 (Spring '92).

Kritzberg, Joan H., "Considerations for Real Estate Investors Planning Tax-Free Exchanges," 20 *Colorado Lawyer* 2085 (October '91).

Lubin, Mark L., "Two Approaches Can Avoid Tax Problems for Affiliates Sharing Employees," 79 *J. Tax.* 150 (September '93).

McCoy, Jerry J., "Tax Planning: Beyond the Charitable Remainder Trust," 132 *Trusts and Estates* 24 (August '93).

Mulroney, Michael, "A Primer on Return Filing and Compliance for Foreign Transactions and Persons," 6 *Practical Tax Lawyer* 57 (Summer '92).

Parker, James O., "Fine-Tuning the Use of the Bracket Run," 130 *Trusts and Estates* 8 (November '91).

Schmudde, David, "Should Your Married Clients File Joint Returns?" 6 *Practical Tax Lawyer* 43 (Summer '92).

Sellner, Mark A., "Record Retention Under Rev.Proc. 91-59: A Checklist Approach," 45 *Tax Executive* 217 (May–June '93).

Teitell, Conrad, "Contribution or Business Expense Deduction," 132 *Trusts and Estates* 58 (July '93).

Thomas, William R., "Tax Deductibility of Legal Fees," 7 *CBA Record* 14 (April '93).

Toolson, Richard B. and Thomas R. Nunamaker, "Computation of the Corporate Marginal Tax Rate," 69 *Taxes* 625 (October '91).

Yasukochi, David K., "Nonqualified Stock Options and the Research Credit," 23 *Tax Adviser* 440 (July '92).

TRUSTS

[¶4301] When a trust is created, a fiduciary relationship arises between the trustee and beneficiaries. The trustee, who holds legal title to the trust property, must manage the assets prudently for the benefit of those named by the creator (settlor) of the trust. Trusts are created during the lifetime of the settlor (inter vivos trusts) or by will (testamentary trusts).

A trust is created when a settlor delivers trust property to a trustee, who is directed to manage the assets for the benefit of beneficiaries named by the settlor. The settlor must have intended to create the trust and may not form the trust for an unlawful purpose. Both settlor and trustee must be legally competent (i.e., of sound mind). Failure to designate the trustee will not invalidate the trust.

The trustee is deemed to have mere legal title to the property, while the beneficiaries hold the equitable interest in the trust assets. To be valid, the trust must also consist of property that is conveyable by the settlor. No formalities need be observed when the trust is created; however, a writing evidencing its creation may be necessary if an interest in real property is involved.

[¶4302] HOW TRUSTS ARE USED

There are three broad reasons for the creation of a lifetime trust:

(1) To transfer the property beyond the control of the grantor to save estate taxes,

(2) To shift investment income produced by the trust property to the tax return of the trust or that of the trust beneficiaries. These purposes require an irrevocable trust,

(3) To transfer property to a trust for management during the life of the grantor and, if the grantor doesn't revoke the trust before death, to have the trustee either continue to manage the property or make the testamentary distribution spelled out in the trust instrument. This is a revocable trust.

Apart from the tax savings, the practical purposes of a trust are to:

(1) Place the property beyond the reach of an inexperienced and possibly improvident member of the family or one who might be able to exercise an unfavorable influence over the beneficiary if the property were given to the beneficiary outright.

(2) Place the management of the trust property in the hands of an experienced and reliable trustee who can be given broad powers to manage the property to its best advantage, or whose investment activities can be restricted, controlled, and directed by the trust instrument.

(3) Create the authority and the capacity to apply the income and corpus of the trust to the problems of the beneficiaries as they develop in the future. This can be done through discretionary powers to distribute, giving the beneficiary limited rights for withdrawal, or creating powers of appointment over the corpus of

the trust in persons who will be in a position to watch and understand the needs and problems of the family in the future.

(4) Obtain privacy and save probate expenses at the death of the grantor who would, in the absence of the trust, own the property, and through whose estate it would have to pass.

[¶4303] TYPES OF TRUSTS

The following types of trusts are commonly employed:

(1) Revocable Trusts: Usually the settlor reserves the right to amend the trust terms, vary the amount of income to be paid out, alter the beneficiaries, change trustees, or affect the disposition of the remainder interest.

(2) Pourover Trusts: Most states permit a testator to "pour over"the residuary estate into a pre-existing inter vivos trust. It's most useful as a receptacle for benefits from a qualified employee benefit plan or insurance proceeds.

(3) Life Insurance Trusts: These trusts, whether testamentary or inter vivos, are funded by the proceeds of insurance on the settlor's life.

(4) Totten Trusts: This familiar transaction results when a settlor deposits her own funds into a bank in her own name, in trust for another. These trusts are revocable but become irrevocable at death, unless state law permits alteration of the trust in the settlor's will.

(5) Land Trusts: The land trust is basically a passive trust that consists of real estate. Often used as financing devices, land trusts permit convenient disposition of the beneficiaries' interests in the trust, without affecting title to the underlying property.

(6) Accumulation Trusts: Trusts that are directed to accumulate income are permissible for certain purposes; they cannot violate the rules against accumulations in the various states. The planner must also consult the "throwback" rules of Code §665–667.

(7) Charitable Trusts: Trusts established for charitable purposes are governed by special tax rules.

(8) Resulting Trusts: If a settlor fails to fully provide for the disposition of the trust assets, there arises a resulting trust in his or her favor.

(9) Constructive Trusts: These are not actually trusts, but are equitable devices used by the courts to rectify some sort of injustice. Thus, one who has wronged another will usually be deemed the constructive trustee of property for the benefit of the injured party. The "trust" serves as a mere conduit for passage of the property to the wronged party.

(10) Alimony Trusts: Trusts may be established to provide for the support of a separated or divorced spouse. They add a measure of security for the payee-spouse since trust assets cannot be attacked or withdrawn by the payor-spouse.

(11) Spendthrift Trusts: A settlor can provide that the beneficiary be unable to pledge or assign interest for the benefit of creditors. This provision is designed to protect the beneficiary from his or her own weakness or financial inabilities, while providing a steady income flow from the trust. The trust income may be sub-

ject to the payment of debts and expenses under state law, but the corpus is normally protected by the spendthrift clause. Note that not all states recognize the validity of spendthrift clauses, and those that do often place restrictions on them. The IRC also limits the use of spendthrift trusts to qualify for Medicaid benefits.

(12) Charitable Remainder Trusts: Code §664 permits a charitable contribution donation for trusts in which the remainderman is a charity and the beneficiary(ies) is(are) noncharitable—e.g., members of the grantor's family. Such a trust can be either an annuity trust or a unitrust. A similar concept, the pooled income fund, is defined in Code §642.

[¶4304] TAXATION OF TRUSTS

The creation of a trust may result in the application of several taxes—mincome, estate, and gift. Some trusts are also affected by the generation-skipping tax.

[¶4305] INCOME TAXATION OF TRUSTS

A trust is a separate taxpaying entity. Under the IRC, the trust and its beneficiaries share the income tax burden on trust income. In general, income that is actually distributed or required to be distributed by the trust is taxable to its beneficiaries (this is the "conduit" concept). Under this approach, the distributed income has the same character in the hands of the beneficiary as it has to the trust. Income that is retained and accumulated by the trust is taxable to the trust and is subject to an income tax at a rate between 15% and 39.6%.

The creation of a trust by lifetime transfer can save income taxes and accelerate the accumulation of capital in three basic ways, all of which can be combined with each other.

(1) Annual income tax savings can be achieved by the transfer of income-producing property to a trust in which the income is taxed either to the trust or to the trust beneficiary. This step will transfer income from the high tax brackets of the settlor to the lower bracket of a trust or beneficiary. Under IRC §677, income is taxed to the grantor if he or she retains any interest or power; §666 and §667 deal with the taxation of distributions of accumulated income.

(2) A trust arrangement may utilize the additional exemptions of the trust or the beneficiary to provide tax-free income.

(3) Income tax savings can be achieved by the so-called sprinkling trust, which gives the trustee discretion to distribute trust income among beneficiaries in varying proportions from year to year, depending on their needs (e.g., one beneficiary may become handicapped or ill; one may be less financially successful than another). Trust income can be kept out of the higher income tax brackets by giving it to the beneficiaries in lower income brackets, who presumably need it more.

A "simple" trust is required to distribute all of its income currently, and is not drafted to permit charitable contributions by the trust itself. All other trusts are classified as "complex trusts." Trusts are permitted a deduction for amounts distributed to beneficiaries, up to the limit of "distributable net income" (DNI) as defined by §643.

The usefulness of trusts in estate tax planning is governed by the following tax precepts:

(1) The usefulness of inter vivos (lifetime) irrevocable trusts is limited by the unified tax rate and unified credit system. Creation of an inter vivos irrevocable trust is a gift subject to the gift tax. This tax consequence must be considered before a determination can be made as to whether such an irrevocable trust should be created as a part of the client's estate plan.

(2) The unified tax rate and unified credit system do not affect the considerations for creation of a revocable inter vivos trust, since such revocable trusts are not transfers subject to gift tax and have always been subject to federal estate tax at death.

Also affecting all trusts, whether inter vivos (revocable or irrevocable) or testamentary (established in decedent's will to become effective at his or her death), are the rules governing income taxation of distributions from trusts of accumulated income. These rules should be taken into consideration in determining whether the trust should provide for the accumulation of income.

(3) For most transfers made after 3/1/86, the grantor will be taxed on trust income if the corpus will revert to the grantor or spouse (e.g., the value of the reversionary interest is at least 5% of the value of a portion of the trust) (Code §673).

(4) Code §677(b) makes the grantor taxable on income that is, or could be given to, or accumulated for the grantor or spouse. The grantor is also taxable on income used to pay insurance premiums on his, her or the spouse's life (unless the policy has irrevocably designated a charitable beneficiary). Income used to satisfy the grantor's support obligations—e.g., to a child but *not* to a spouse—is also taxable to the grantor.

(5) Under §678, anyone who has the power to demand trust income or corpus may be taxable on trust income unless the power is renounced within a reasonable amount of time, or unless its exercise requires the cooperation of someone else (e.g., the trustee).

[¶4306] ESTATE AND GIFT TAXATION OF TRUSTS

Since the estate and gift tax laws have been consolidated into a unified system, the mere creation of an irrevocable trust does not serve to reduce the settlor's eventual estate. However, if these trusts are funded with amounts not in excess of the $10,000 annual gift tax exclusion, an estate tax saving may be realized. Any appreciation of these assets will also escape tax on the settlor's death. Otherwise gratuitous transfers to irrevocable trusts will incur gift tax if the value of the property transferred exceeds the settlor's available exclusion and credits.

Where an irrevocable inter vivos trust gave each of the decedent's minor grandchildren the right to withdraw up to $10,000 within 15 days of the settlor's contribution to the trust, the grandchildren had present interests of the type qualifying for the gift tax annual exclusion, because the potential recipients never agreed not to exercise the withdrawal right, and the trustees could not prevent them from doing so.[1]

In the *Jalkut* case,[2] the decedent was the trustee and sole permissible recipient of the income and principal of a revocable trust; gifts of trust property he made within three years of his death were not included in his estate, because he was deemed to have made the gifts in his individual capacity. However, once the trust was amended to add co-trustees for the situation in which Mr. Jalkut became incapacitated and unable to act, gift transfers made by the co-trustees during his incapacity were included in his estate, because they were not treated as withdrawals by the decedent, but rather relinquishments of the power to revoke the trust, exercised through the co-trustees.

A "family trust" was included in the estate of a decedent beneficiary/co-trustee at the Tax Court level, because he had a general power of appointment over the trust principal at the time of his death. A bank served as co-trustee but did not have a substantial adverse interest. The decedent suffered from Alzheimer's disease and was placed under guardianship, but was not removed as trustee. The terms of the trust allowed him to distribute principal to himself for his "continued comfort, support, maintenance or education." At first glance, this might appear to be a power limited by an ascertainable standard and therefore not constituting a general power of appointment, but Florida state law refers to ascertainable standards limited only to health, education, support, and maintenance. Under the Tax Court's interpretation, adding the word "comfort" entirely defeated the drafter's intention. However, the Tenth Circuit reversed, making the common-sense decision that a requirement of supporting the beneficiary in continued comfort is an ascertainable standard.[3]

Under Reg. Section 25.25034(b)(1), a trust subject to a "substantial restriction" is a taxable gift, yet is includable in the estate of the grantor where trust funds could only be used for the minor beneficiary's education or for the care of the minor in case of death or disability of the minor's parents. This standard gives the trustee less discretion than a guardian would have under applicable state (Illinois) law, and therefore the trust was subject to a "substantial restriction."[4]

Life insurance trusts can create significant planning opportunities, even if the creator of the trust is insured under policies placed into the trust, and even if the insured is the purchaser of the policies—as long as he or she has no incidents of ownership in the policies within three years of death.[5]

In addition to tax consequences, the creation of trusts, receipt of income from trusts, invasion of trust principal or the trustee's power to invade may all have Medicaid consequences. Trust transactions of one spouse are likely to affect the Medicaid eligibility of the other spouse. As discussed at [¶3904], the Omnibus Budget Reconciliation Act of 1993 (P.L. 103-66) amends the Medicaid treatment of trusts. Notably, certain transactions involving irrevocable trusts create a Medicaid penalty period of five years, versus 36 months for other financial transactions. Furthermore, after the death of a Medicaid applicant who was a trust beneficiary, the trust is likely to be subject to recoupment claims made by the state that paid Medicaid benefits.

[¶4306.1] Reserving Power to Alter, Amend, Revoke, or Terminate

The value of any property transferred by the decedent during life is included in his or her estate if at the time of death the decedent had the power to make a substantial change in the beneficial enjoyment of the property transferred, or gave up such a power within three years of death. It does not matter whether the power can be exercised by the grantor alone, or with a beneficiary, even if the beneficiary's interest is substantial and adverse [IRC §2038; Reg. §20.2038-1].

[¶4306.2] Transfers Taking Effect at Death

Property interests transferred by a decedent during life (except a bona fide sale for adequate consideration) generally must be included in the decedent's gross estate if: (1) the decedent has a reversionary interest in the transferred property which, immediately before death, was worth more than 5% of the value of the property; and (2) possession or enjoyment of the transferred interest could be obtained only by the transferee surviving the decedent (IRC §2037; Reg. §20.2037-1).

A reversionary interest includes the possibility that the transferred property may return to the decedent or his or her estate or may be subject to his or her power of disposition. (Note that it does not include reservation of a life estate, or the possible return of, or power or disposition over, income alone from the property.)

A transfer that takes effect at death is not taxable unless the transferee's possession or enjoyment of the property is dependent on surviving the decedent. Thus, if immediately before the transferor's death, the possession or enjoyment by the transferee depends on surviving the transferor or some alternative event, such as the expiration of a term of years or the exercise of a power of appointment, the property generally is not included in the gross estate.

[¶4307] GENERATION-SKIPPING TRUSTS

Generally, a generation-skipping trust is any trust or trust-like transfer with two or more generations of beneficiaries belonging to generations which are younger than the grantor's generation. Typically, the beneficiaries of such trusts are the children of the settlor, with the settlor's grandchildren holding the remainder interest. The purpose of the generation-skipping trust is to skip the estate tax on one or more generations of beneficiaries.

The generation-skipping rules need not concern most drafters, because every person is entitled to an exemption of $1 million; the person (or the person's executor) can allocate this exemption to any of the person's transferred property. Furthermore, a married couple can elect to "gift-split" the transfers, so a couple is entitled to a GST (generation-skipping transfer tax) exemption of $2 million. Under Code §2652(a)(3), an estate is entitled to disregard a QTIP election, where part of the $1 million exclusion would otherwise be unused and wasted.

The tax on generation-skipping transfers is computed with reference to a flat rate equal to the product of the maximum estate tax rate (55%) and the inclusion ratio with respect to the transfer.

[¶4308] INVASION OF TRUST PRINCIPAL

Trusts usually allow the beneficiary or trustee to invade trust principal in order to meet emergencies. If the invasion power is governed by an "ascertainable" standard (e.g., support or maintenance of the beneficiary), the trustee can be compelled to make distributions from principal to satisfy the beneficiary's needs. If no power of invasion is specified in the trust, the courts can step in to authorize principal payments. Typical arrangements, along with their estate tax implications, are outlined below.

(1) Beneficiary has an unlimited right to withdraw all or any part of the trust corpus—The entire trust corpus would be included in the beneficiary's gross estate (IRC §2041(a)(2)).

(2) Beneficiary has a noncumulative right to withdraw up to 5% of the trust corpus or $5,000 annually, whichever is greater—This right will cause the inclusion in the beneficiary's estate of only the amount of the unexercised withdrawal privilege in the year of the beneficiary's death (IRC §2041(b)(2)).

(3) Beneficiary has a right to withdraw such sums from trust corpus in his own discretion for health, support, and maintenance—No part of the trust corpus would be included in the beneficiary's gross estate solely due to this provision (IRC §2041(b)(1)(A)).

(4) Beneficiary is to receive a fixed amount of principal each year, these payments to cease upon the beneficiary's death—No part of the trust corpus would be included in the beneficiary's gross estate solely due to this provision.

(5) Beneficiary has no right of withdrawal, but trustee has the power to make payments of principal to the beneficiary for the beneficiary's support and maintenance, or for any reason—No part of the trust corpus should be included in the beneficiary's gross estate solely due to this provision. (*Note:* If a provision is made authorizing the trustee to invade principal for the income beneficiary's support and maintenance, sometimes a question arises as to whether the trustee should take the beneficiary's independent income and/or capital into account. It is wise to make a clear-cut provision covering this in the governing instrument so as to avoid a costly construction suit later on.)

[¶4309] TERMINATION OF THE TRUST

The disposition of trust assets remaining after the trust has been terminated may be specified in the trust instrument or by giving someone a lifetime or testamentary power of appointment over the assets.

If the power given is a *general power of appointment* so that the trust principal may be appointed to anybody at all including the holder, creditors, estate or creditors of the estate, the principal will be included in the holder's gross estate whether or not the power is in fact exercised. (A beneficiary's absolute power to invade trust corpus for him- or herself is the equivalent of a general power of appointment exercisable during lifetime.) A general power can be limited so that it can only be exercised by will.

If the right to appoint principal is limited to a certain class of beneficiaries—e.g., children, etc.,—then a *limited* or a *special power of appointment* results. Thus, if a power is given to a spouse as beneficiary to dispose of the trust corpus at his or her death only among the couple's issue, the trust corpus will not be included in the gross estate.

[¶4310] TRUST ADMINISTRATION

All jurisdictions impose certain duties on trustees. In general, these include fairness to all trust beneficiaries, restrictions on the types of investments that may be made, standards pertaining to the management of trust assets, and prohibitions against self-dealing. Most of the provisions may, however, be overridden by the settlor in the trust instruments. A grantor should seriously consider specifically exempting the trustee from these restrictions, as they often serve more as a hindrance than as a safeguard.

(1) Powers and Duties: Trustees must exercise reasonable care and skill when handling trust assets. For example, they may invest in various kinds of enterprises (check local law), insure and repair trust property, and engage professional advice. They are usually required to make periodic accountings and to keep trust property separate from personal assets.

(2) Liabilities: A trustee who violates fiduciary duties may be surcharged and made personally liable for any harm incurred by the beneficiaries. Many states prohibit clauses in trust instruments that excuse a trustee for breaching these duties. Trustees may also be personally liable in trust or contracts with third parties; however, then they may be entitled to indemnification by the trust (again depending on local law).

(3) Investments: Trustees may invest in those assets that a reasonable, prudent person would consider. While some estates restrict investments to "legals" (e.g., traded stocks), other jurisdictions merely apply the prudence standard.

(4) Allocation of Principal and Income: Proper application of the fairness standard requires trustees to allocate trust receipts and disbursements equitably between principal and income. Trustees must balance the interests of income beneficiaries (who would prefer investments in high-yield securities) and remaindermen (who would prefer growth property). Unless provided to the contrary in the trust instrument, statutory rules of allocation (e.g., the Uniform Principal and Income Act) govern. For example, interests and rates are allocated to income under the Uniform Act, while capital gains are attributed to principal.

(5) Tax Compliance: Trusts (and estates) make estimated tax payments (Form 1041-ES Estimated Income Tax for Fiduciaries), and also brings them within the ambit of the Alternative Minimum Tax.

— ENDNOTES —

1. Estate of Cristofani, 97 TC No. 5 (7/29/91).

2. Estate of Jalkut, 96 TC No. 27 (4/29/91), acq. Federal Estate and Gift Tax Reporter (FEGT)(CCH) ¶12,342.

3. Estate of Vissering, 96 TC No. 33 (5/23/91), *rev'd* 990 F.2d 578 (10th Cir. 4/6/93).

4. Illinois Nat'l Bank of Springfield, Exec'r v. U.S., FEGT ¶60,063 (C.D.M. 1/22/91).

5. Estate of Richins, TC Memo 1991-23 (1/22/91); Estate of Perry, FEGT ¶60,064 (5th Cir. 3/22/91).

— FOR FURTHER REFERENCE —

Averill, Lawrence H. Jr., William Tucker Dean, and Nancy Shurtz, "Significant Probate and Trust Literature," 22 *Real Property, Probate, and Trust J.* 479 (Summer '87).

Bogert, George T., *Trusts (Practitioner's Edition) (6th edition)* (West, 1987).

Christensen, Burke A., "Keeping the Benefits of Irrevocable Life Insurance Trusts," 125 *Trusts & Estates* 57 (April '86).

Comment, "Significant Probate and Trust Literature," 21 *Real Property, Probate, and Trust J.* 339 (Summer '86).

Comment, "Statutory Procedures for the Combination or Division of Trusts," 21 *Real Property, Probate and Trust J.* 561 (Fall '86).

Hirschson, Linda B., "The Income Tax Treatment of Multiple Trusts," 10 *Rev. of Taxation of Individuals* 97 (Winter '86).

Loftis, Robert O. Jr., "Problems in the Use of Trusts for Funding Private Annuities," 23 *Cal. Western L. Rev.* 1 (Fall '86).

Mortland, Jean A., "Trustees' Duty to Diversify and Manage Assets Properly," 13 *Estate Planning* 379 (November–December '86).

Quattlebaum, Owen J., "Choosing the Right Assets," 126 *Trusts and Estates* 40 (May '87).

Sederbaum, Arthur D., "Use of Trusts in Estate Planning," Estate Planning Institute 877 (Annual '85).

WILLS

[¶4401] Before actually drafting a will, it is essential to take the client through the estate planning process. The following sections provide some guides to the procedure and mechanical steps in completing a will. (See ¶4301 for a discussion of trusts.)

[¶4402] WILL CHECKLIST

There is an infinite variety of detail that should be considered and discussed preliminary to the preparation of a will. Much of this detail comes out of the testator's own experience, an appraisal of property, heirs, and the testator's aspirations for them. There are some technical matters to be considered so that the testator can discuss them properly with the estate planner.

The following checklist is designed to stimulate the estate owner's thinking prior to the preliminary conversation with an estate planner, and to help the planner make sure all the necessary information has been obtained.

❒ *Funeral Arrangements, Upkeep of Cemetery Plot, etc.:* Instructions can be spelled out in the will. However, burial instructions in a will are useless if the provisions of the will remain secret until some date after death and after burial has already taken place. The matter can be left to the discretion of the family, or a special letter may be left addressed to the executor or to the family to acquaint them with the testator's wishes.

❒ *Personal Belongings:* If the disposition of clothing, jewelry, furniture, etc., is not provided for, such articles (unless state law provides otherwise) will go into the residue of the estate and possibly impose upon the executor the obligation to sell them. Tangible personal property should always be disposed of by separate will provisions, because under IRC §662, all amounts distributed to a beneficiary for the taxable year are included in the gross income of the beneficiary to the extent of the distributable net income of the estate. Under IRC §663, any amount that, under the terms of the will, is distributed as a gift of specific property all at once or in not more than three installments is excluded from the operation of IRC §662. Thus, if the tangible personal property is separately disposed of in the will and is distributed to the legatee all at once, its distribution will have no income tax consequences. However, if disposed of as part of the residue, its distribution might be taxable as income to the legatee. It may be wise to specify in the will the individuals who are to receive the most valuable personal possessions and leave the balance to someone in whom the testator has confidence, with instructions to divide them among those close to the testator.

❒ *Cash Bequests:* When a specific amount of money is left to an individual or to a charity, the executor is required to pay that amount in full before he makes any distribution to the beneficiaries who are to share the balance of the estate. If the estate should be smaller than expected, such a cash bequest could result in unintentionally making inadequate provision for other beneficiaries.

Guard against this contingency by providing that cash bequests be paid only if the total estate exceeds a specified minimum, or make bequests to individuals and charities in fractions or percentages of the estate, rather than in fixed dollar amounts.

❑ *Real Estate:* Is solely owned real estate to be: (1) left outright, (2) left in trust (possibly a residence trust where a spouse has the rights to the house), (3) sold and the proceeds distributed, or (4) left to one beneficiary who has the right to use it for life with ownership going to the testator's children on his or her death? Under the law of some states, the testator's spouse may have dower or curtesy rights in the real estate. Indicate if mortgages are exonerated or the property passes subject to mortgage.

❑ *Income Interests:* The testator may want to assure a regular income for parents, dependent relatives, or others. This can be done through a trust established by will or by directing the executors to buy annuities for named beneficiaries. In the event that a trust is established, the testator can specify the individual to whom the trust property will go after it has produced the required income for a specified period of time.

❑ *The Remainder:* Decide who is to share in the bulk of the estate. Then divide the balance, after specific bequests, in fractions or percentages. By being overly exact in allocating particular assets to certain beneficiaries, or in specifying interest in dollar amounts, the testator can frustrate personal objectives in the event of important changes in the size or value of the estate. But if the bulk of the estate is divided into fractions of a share, the testator won't be in the position of having to revise the will repeatedly because of changes in asset values. Be sure the will names alternate or contingent beneficiaries who are to receive the share of any beneficiary who does not survive the testator.

❑ *Protection of Interests of Minor Beneficiaries:* It is usually necessary to have a guardian appointed by the court to manage the child's property until majority. The guardian must furnish bond, make periodic accountings, and secure court approval on many of the actions he or she will have to take (unless the testator provides otherwise in the will). Guardianship is both burdensome and expensive. The will can simplify this matter by directing that the property be turned over to a trust to be held for the benefit of minors until majority. The trustee can be authorized to use the trust property to provide maintenance, support, and education for the minor.

❑ *Trust Property:* Subject to local law, the testator can determine whether the income of trust property is to be distributed or accumulated in order to build up future value. The testator can also determine how much of the income is to be distributed and how much of it is to go to each beneficiary, or authorize the trustee to distribute some of the trust principal if income is insufficient to maintain the beneficiaries' living standards or meet emergencies.

❑ *Selection of Executor and Trustee:* An executor and possibly a trustee must be designated to handle the settlement and management of the estate. This responsibility must be accepted; the details of settling an estate must be handled.

The testator's property must be managed until it is turned over to the beneficiaries. These are tasks that call for a high degree of skill and experience. The choice of an executor and trustee may determine whether the testator's plans for family and property succeed or fail.

❑ *Joint and Mutual Wills:* This is where two related individuals, generally husband and wife, combine two wills on one piece of paper because the provisions are reciprocal. Although perfectly legal, the practice is a bad one and should be avoided. It creates two important practical problems. First the survivor may not be free to change her will. It is possible for a testator to bind herself by contract to a fixed, dispositive scheme that can be enforced against her estate after death, even though she later changes her will. Where two wills are combined in one document, the question may arise after the death of the spouse first to die whether the joint document was actually a contract which the survivor isn't free to alter. Second, a joint will raises a practical problem. Although it is only one piece of paper, it represents the separate will of each spouse. Therefore, a joint will must be probated twice, on the death of each spouse.

❑ *Other Points to Consider:* Whether or not the testator has a will, changes in the law and new developments in his or her affairs may have made testamentary plans obsolete. For example,

(1) Does the will take full advantage of the marital deduction?

(2) Are insurance arrangements integrated with the will?

(3) Are inheritance taxes to be paid by each beneficiary or by the estate?

(4) Should the executor have authority to carry on the business or should he or she be directed to dispose of it?

(5) Have safeguards been established to minimize the possibility that the testator's property will be taxed twice—once upon the death of the testator, and again upon the death of the spouse?

(6) Has provision been made for the possibility that the testator and spouse may die under such circumstances that it is impossible to determine who died first?

(7) Does the executor have the right to borrow money, pledge estate assets, and renew existing obligations?

(8) Should the executor have the power to retain real estate or sell, mortgage, or lease it?

(9) Should the executor have the right to retain assets owned by the testator at the time of death, whether or not they constitute a legal investment for trust and estate funds?

(10) Does the trustee have broad discretion in the investment and reinvestment of trust funds? Should the trustee receive any specific instructions?

(11) Have income provisions for trust beneficiaries been protected against inflation?

(12) Does the trustee have the right to make special provision for beneficiaries in the event of emergencies?

(13) Will there be enough liquid funds to meet estate tax obligations and other cash requirements that will confront the executor and trustee?

(14) Has the future distribution of the estate been studied with a view to minimizing the tax drain on the income it will produce?

(15) Does the executor have the right to file a joint income tax return with the surviving spouse?

[¶4403]　WILL PROVISIONS CHECKLIST

Set out below is a checklist of will provisions, in approximately the order in which they might appear in wills.

❏ *Basic Introduction Identifying Testator*

❏ *Declaration of Domicile:* Of governing law, of place and probate of property covered by this will (where other property is disposed of by another will)

❏ *Revocation of Prior Wills and Codicils*

❏ *Declaration of Marital Status:* Possible preliminary naming of spouse and living children, together with birthdates, and obligations arising from divorce or prenuptial agreement

❏ *Disposition of Body:* Better handled by supplementary instructions to members of immediate family.

❏ *Funeral Directions:* Same as Disposition of Body

❏ *Cemetery, Masses, Monument, etc.*

❏ *Payment of Debts:* Long-term debts, funeral expenses, discharge, charge to general estate or specific property

❏ *Separate Distribution of Personalty:* Avoiding income to beneficiaries under IRC §662, personal and household effects, disputes, insurance

❏ *Legacies:* General, specific, demonstrative

❏ *Percentage Limitation:* General legacy, residue

❏ *Charitable Bequest:* Statutory limitation, tax exemption, ability to take, contingent on size of estate

❏ *Ademption*

❏ *Abatement*

❏ *Lapse*

❏ *Advancements*

❏ *Release of Indebtedness*

❏ *Family Support During Administration:* Provision

❏ *Real Estate:* Encumbrances

❏ *Life Estate:* Residence, waste, sale, maintenance costs

❏ *Residence Left in Trust*

❏ *Surviving Spouse's Rights:* Election against will, antenuptial agreement (reference to in will), abandonment

❏ *Marital Deduction Bequest:* Formula (pecuniary or fractional), non-formula

❏ *Residue*

❏ *Children:* Adopted, afterborn, step-children

❏ *Class Gifts:* Per capital, per stirpes

❏ *Foreign Beneficiaries*

❏ *Infants, Incompetents:* Guardianship, power in trust

❐ **Trusts:** Pourover, spendthrift, sprinkling, marital deduction, power of appointment, discretionary, accumulation, perpetuities, invasion of corpus for or by beneficiary, persons to receive principal, declaration of purpose (e.g., charitable)

❐ **Power of Appointment in Testator:** Separate provision exercising or refraining to exercise (otherwise will may operate or may not operate, depending on applicable state law, as an exercise of power)

❐ **Appointment of Fiduciaries:** Successors and alternates, bond, compensation, foreign fiduciaries, delegation among fiduciaries, resignation of fiduciary, appointment of substitute, exoneration, replacement

❐ **Annuities:** Trust or purchase of policy, assignment

❐ **Insurance Policies:** Owned by testator, payable to estate, marital deduction

❐ **Common Disaster:** Simultaneous death, survival for certain period of time (e.g., 30 days), etc.

❐ **Taxes:** Provisions for, apportionment, allocation, nontestamentary property, compromise, authority to file joint returns, elections

❐ **Business Interest:** Partnership, close corporation, proprietorship, lifetime agreements, employee interests

❐ **Administrative Powers of Fiduciaries:** Investments, sales and exchanges, borrowing, voting

❐ **Disinheritance:** Right of election

❐ **Clauses to Avoid Litigation**

❐ **Execution:** Subscription at end, sign or initial each page, attestation clause for witnesses, residence of witnesses

[¶4404] PREREQUISITES FOR VALID WILLS

A number of conditions must be satisfied before a document can be judicially accepted as a decedent's last will and testament.

❐ **Testamentary Capacity:** An individual of sound mind is considered competent to dispose of his or her property by will. As a corollary rule, minors are not deemed capable of making wills; the age requirement varies from state to state.

Therefore, if the testator understands what he or she is doing, generally knows the nature and extent of property owned, knows who the next of kin are, and understands the provisions of the will, he or she is deemed capable of making and executing a will.

❐ **Intent to Make a Will:** The intent to make a will, manifested by a positive act (such as the naming of an executor), is also required.

❐ **Knowledge:** An understanding of the contents of one's will is another prerequisite.

❐ **Formal Requirements:** A will must comply with several statutory rules. In general, a will must be in writing and signed by the testator before several witnesses. Some jurisdictions require an individual to communicate to the witness that the document being signed is, in fact, his or her will. Attestation—that is, an affirmation by a witness that the will has been signed in accordance with statutory requirements—may also be required in some states.

❑ *Revocation:* A will may be revoked wholly or partially by operation of law; e.g., the death of a spouse, subsequent birth of a child, or by an act performed by the testator (or another at the testator's direction). The basic requirement here is that the testator must intend to revoke the will. This can be accomplished by physical destruction or impliedly by the terms of a later will.

❑ *Special Wills:* Contracts to make wills are generally recognized. They do not have to comply with statutory provisions pertaining to wills but do, of course, have to be valid contracts.

Holographic wills (wills written entirely in an individual's own handwriting or combined with pre-printed forms) and nuncupative wills (oral wills) are valid in certain circumstances. Local law must be checked to determine the validity of such wills.

❑ *Other Elements:* In addition to the conditions above, a will cannot be probated if it has been procured through undue influence, fraud, or mistake.

[¶4405] EXECUTION AND MAINTENANCE OF A WILL

The execution of a will should take place under the supervision of an attorney who is fully familiar with the requirements for the execution of wills. Only in exceptional cases should a will be executed without the presence of an attorney.

Strict observance of the statutory formalities governing the execution of wills is a must. To avoid invalidity or litigation, the attorney drafting the will must assume that the will may be offered for probate anywhere. In general, the validity of a will is judged by the law of the situs as to immovables (i.e., real property) and the law of the decedent's domicile at death as to movables (i.e., personal property). Every attorney should establish the exact procedure that will satisfy the laws of all states and follow it. (Some states, however, allow a decedent to direct in the will the law that governs the disposition of his or her property.)

[¶4406] CHECKLIST FOR EXECUTING A WILL

The first step is to carefully check the statutory requirements of state law, as in the following checklist:

❑ The will should be declared in an instrument in writing.

❑ The testator should sign it; if he or she can't do so, another person should sign for the testator in his or her presence and at his or her request.

❑ This signature of either the testator or the person who signs for the testator must follow the text of the will immediately, without leaving any intervening space.

❑ At least three witnesses should attest the testator's signature.

❑ None of the witnesses should be a beneficiary or person with a financial interest in the estate.

❑ The testator should expressly:

(a) Declare the instrument to be his or her will; and

(b) Ask the attesting witnesses to witness "the execution of his or her will."

❑ All the witnesses to the testator's signature should either:

(a) See her sign; or

(b) Hear her say that she acknowledges as her own a signature that is already on the instrument and that is pointed out to them and actually seen by all of them.

If she can't write her signature, all of the witnesses should observe that:

(1) The testator expressly requests the person who signs for her to sign; and

(2) The person requested does sign in the presence of the testator.

❑ Each witness should sign his name and write his address in the testator's presence.

❑ All of the witnesses, the testator, and (if that is the case) the one who signs for the testator, should be present simultaneously throughout the entire process of execution. (Even if not required in some states, it is good practice to have witnesses and testator present throughout and see each other sign the will.)

❑ The will should be dated by fully and correctly stating the place and the day, month, and year it was executed.

❑ The typical attestation clause recites the formalities of execution in some detail. If none of the witnesses is available at the time of probate, the clause can be used to show that statutory requirements were observed. It is not required by most states, but is used by most will drafters.

The procedure of execution should follow precisely the statements that appear in the attestation clause. So where the clause recites ". . . this attestation clause having first been read aloud," the clause should be read out loud so all those present can hear what has been said.

❑ Only the original of the will should be subscribed by the testator and the witnesses. Where copies are signed, loss or inability to account for any one of the signed copies in the possession of or accessible to the testator may result in a presumption of revocation of the original. Far fewer problems arise if only the original is signed and then kept in a safe place.

❑ The original will should be placed in a safe place as soon as possible after execution. For convenience, the safe deposit box of either the drafter or the named executor would be suitable. It should *not* be stored in the testator's safe deposit box. Reason: If the testator's box is used, a court order to open the box must be obtained after the testator's death in most states before the will can be obtained. Also, if the original is in the possession of the testator, failure to produce it at the time of probate will bring into play the presumption of revocation by destruction by the testator.

❑ Prior wills are, normally, revoked by later ones by specific language to that effect. But where nothing is said about prior wills, a will of prior date would be effective to dispose of property not covered by the later will. Also, where the testator has property in a number of states and foreign countries, it is not at all uncommon to have an "American Will," "French Will," etc., each disposing of property within the stated countries or places. In these instances, all pertinent wills would be probatable and should be treated as if they were the original and kept in the same place.

In other cases, a later will may be invalid for a number of reasons such as lack of testamentary capacity. In such cases, a prior last will, executed during a time when the testator did have testamentary capacity, may be probatable.

[¶4407] WITNESSES

Although most states require only two witnesses, it is good practice to have three whenever possible. The will is then qualified for probate (at least as to the number of witnesses) in every state. Even though only two witnesses prove necessary, having a choice makes it easier to obtain two at probate.

Since the witnesses may be considered the most qualified persons to testify as to the testamentary capacity of the testator, if there are apt to be any questions on this score they should be persons who know the testator well, can give favorable testimony, and are likely to be available when needed. The drafter should be a witness unless he or she is named as a beneficiary, since this person is perhaps the best qualified to testify as to the testamentary capacity of the testator.

The testator who wishes a beneficiary to be a witness should be informed that should such beneficiary be necessary as a witness to probate the will, he or she may lose any bequest (at least to the extent it exceeds the intestate share).

In many jurisdictions, a will can be made "self-proving" (removing the need for witness' testimony at the probate proceeding) by attaching an affidavit made by the witnesses as to the matters they would testify to (the testator's identity, that he or she signed a document identified as a will; in some jurisdictions, that the witness believes the testator to be of sound mind). If a self-proving affidavit is used, the drafter must make sure that the testator and witnesses sign *both* the will and the affidavit, in the appropriate places—extensive litigation has arisen from the situation in which only one is signed.

[¶4408] MAINTAINING THE WILL

To ensure that the will is kept intact and no pages or provisions are substituted, the following procedures are suggested:

(1) When a will is being typed, make it an invariable practice to use the same typewriter throughout. This may facilitate detection of forgery by typewriter.

(2) Avoid erasures (never allow corrections of figures or names). Use uniform margins at top, bottom, and sides of each page, leaving as little room as possible for additional words to be filled in. Some drafters make it a practice to rule out all blank spaces at the end of sentences, etc.

(3) Tie the pages together with a ribbon and seal the ribbon on the last page, next to the testator's signature. Staples, brass fasteners, and the like may be removed and replaced without detection and don't give much protection.

(4) Have the testator sign or initial each page in the margin and refer to this fact in the attestation clause. A signature is harder to imitate than initials and so gives better protection.

(5) Have witnesses sign in the space provided and, in addition, initial each page in the margin underneath the testator's signature for initials.

— FOR FURTHER REFERENCE —

Buckley, William R., "Videotaped Wills: More than a Testator's Curtain Call," 126 *Trusts and Estates* 48 (October '87).

Burke, Thomas M., "Plain Language Estate Plan for Dick and Jane," 59 *New York State Bar J.* 38 (January '87).

Dubovich, Debra Lynch, "The Blockbuster Will," 21 *Valparaiso U. L. Rev.* 719 (Spring '87).

Jegen, Lawrence A. III, "Drafting Wills and Trust Appointments," 29 *Res Gestae* 355 (January '86).

Johnson, Rodney J., "Why You Need a Will: A Pamphlet Which Will Explain the Need to a Layman," 12 *Virginia Bar Ass'n J.* 16 (Winter '86).

Keydel, Frederick R., "Are Simple Wills Really Right for Your Clients?" 66 *Michigan Bar J.* 1030 (October '87).

Laurino, Louis D., "Avoiding Will Construction Problems," 11 *ALI-ABA Course Materials J.* 83 (April '87).

Mann, Bruce H., "Self-Proving Affidavits and Formalism in Will Adjudication," 63 *Washington U. L. Q.* 39 (Spring '85).

Mohan, Robert P., "The Will as the Blueprint of the Estate Plan," 39 *Journal of the American Society of CLU* 62 (January '85).

Pierson, Donald R. II, "Steps a Practitioner Can Take to Facilitate the Planning and Probate of a Client's Estate," 14 *Estate Planning* 88 (March–April '87).

Shayne, Neil T., "The Pre-Will Letter," 9 *Trial Diplomacy J.* 3 (Winter '86).

Shilling, Dana, *Will Drafting* (Prentice-Hall, 1986).

Shumaker, Roger L., "Drafting Wills and Trust Agreements: A Systems Approach," 14 *Probate and Property* 16 (Fall '85).

Wilsey, George F., "Testamentary Capacity and Undue Influence," 61 *Florida B.J.* 13 (May '87).

DIRECTORY OF THE UNITED STATES GOVERNMENT—
GOVERNMENT AGENCIES

Legislative Branch

The Senate	The Capitol Washington, DC 20510	202-224-3121
The House of Representatives	The Capitol Washington, DC 20515	202-224-3121
General Accounting Office	441 G St. NW Washington, DC 20548	202-512-3000
Government Printing Office	North Capitol & H Streets NW Washington, DC 20401	202-512-0000
Library of Congress	101 Independence Ave. SE Washington, DC 20540	202-707-5000
Office of Technology Assessment, U.S. Congress	600 Pennsylvania Ave. SE Washington, DC 20510-8025	202-224-8713 (Personnel Locator) 202-224-9241 (Congressional & Public Affairs) 202-228-6204 (Press) 202-224-8996 (Publications) 202-228-6098 (Fax)
Congressional Budget Office	Second & D Streets SW Washington, DC 20515	202-226-2621
Copyright Royalty Tribunal	1825 Connecticut Ave. NW Washington, DC 20009	202-606-4400

Judicial Branch

The Supreme Court of the United States	United States Supreme Court Building 1 First St. NE Washington, DC 20543	202-479-3000

743

Judicial Branch *(cont'd)*

Administrative Office of the United States Courts	Washington, DC 20544	202-273-1900 (Bankruptcy Div.) 202-273-2100 (Budget Div.) 202-273-1530 (Court Administration Div. 202-273-1670 (Defender Services Div.) 202-273-1100 (General Counsel) 202-273-1270 (Human Resources Div.) 202-273-1140 (Judicial Conference Secretariat) 202-273-1120 ((Legislative & Public Affairs Office) 202-273-1830 (Magistrate Judges Div.) 202-273-1600 ('?robation & Pretrial Services Div.) 202-273-2240 (Statistics Div.)
Federal Judicial Center	Thurgood Marshall Federal Judiciary Bldg. One Columbus Circle NE Washington, DC 20002	202-273-4165 (Personnel Locator) 202-273-4153 (Publications)
United States Sentencing Commission	Suite 2-500 South Lobby One Columbus Circle NE Washington, DC 20002-8002	202-273-4500

Executive Branch

The White House Office	1600 Pennsylvania Ave. NW Washington, DC 20500	202-456-1111
Office of Management and Budget	Executive Office Building Washington, DC 20503	202-395-3080
Council of Economic Advisers	Old Executive Office Building Washington, DC 20500	202-395-5084
National Security Council	Old Executive Office Building Washington, DC 20506	202-456-7430
Office of the United States Trade Representative	600 Seventeenth St. NW Washington, DC 20506	202-395-3230
Council on Environmental Quality	722 Jackson Place NW Washington, DC 20503	202-395-5750

Executive Branch *(cont'd)*

Office of Science and Technology Policy	Old Executive Office Building Washington, DC 20500	202-395-7347 202-395-3719 (fax)
Office of National Drug Control Policy	Executive Office of the President Washington, DC 20500	202-467-9800
National Critical Materials Council	810 Seventh St. NW Washington, DC 20241	202-501-3737
Office of Administration	725 Seventeenth St. NW Washington, DC 20503	202-395-6963
Office of the Vice President of the United States	Old Executive Office Building Washington, DC 20501	202-456-2326

Executive Departments

Department of Agriculture	Fourteenth St. & Independence Ave. SW Washington, DC 20250	202-447-2791
Department of Commerce	Fourteenth St. between Constitution Ave & E St. NW Washington, DC 20230	202-482-2000
Department of Defense	Office of the Secretary The Pentagon Washington, DC 20301-1155	703-545-6700
Department of Education	400 Maryland Ave. SW Washington, DC 20202	202-708-5366
Department of Energy	1000 Independence Ave. SW Washington, DC 20585	202-586-5000
Department of Health and Human Services	200 Independence Ave. SW Washington, DC 20201	202-619-0257
Department of Housing and Urban Development	451 Seventh St. SW Washington, DC 20410	202-708-1422
Department of the Interior	1849 C St. NW Washington, DC 20240	202-208-3171
Department of Justice	Constitution Ave. & Tenth St. NW Washington, DC 20530	202-514-2000 (Locator) 202-514-4019 (TDD)
Department of Labor	200 Constitution Ave. NW Washington, DC 20210	202-219-6411

Executive Departments *(cont'd)*

Department of State	2201 C St. NW Washington, DC 20520	202-647-4000
Department of Transportation	400 Seventh St. SW Washington, DC 20590	202-366-4000
Department of the Treasury:	1500 Pennsylvania Ave., NW Washington, DC 20220	202-622-2000
United States Customs Service	1301 Constitution Ave. NW Washington, DC 20229	202-927-2095
Internal Revenue Service	1111 Constitution Ave. NW Washington, DC 20224	202-566-5000
United States Secret Service	1800 G St. NW Washington, DC 20223	202-435-5708
Department of Veterans Affairs	810 Vermont Ave. NW Washington, DC 20420	202-233-2300

DIRECTORY OF THE UNITED STATES GOVERNMENT—INDEPENDENT ESTABLISHMENTS AND GOVERNMENT CORPORATIONS

ACTION	1100 Vermont Ave. NW Washington, DC 20525	202-606-5108
Administrative Conference of the United States	Suite 500 2120 L St. NW Washington, DC 20037-1568	202-254-7020
African Development Foundation	1400 I St. NW Washington, DC 20005	202-673-3916
Central Intelligence Agency	Washington, DC	703-482-1100
Commission on Civil Rights	624 9th St. NW Washington, DC 20425	202-376-8177
Commission on National and Community Service	Suite 542 529 14th St. NW Washington, DC 20045	202-724-0600
Commodity Futures Trading Commission	2033 K St. NW Washington, DC 20581	202-254-6387
Consumer Product Safety Commission	East West Towers 4340 East West Highway Bethesda, MD 20814	301-504-0580
Defense Nuclear Facilities Safety Board	Suite 700 625 Indiana Ave. NW Washington, DC 20004	202-208-6400
Environmental Protection Agency	401 M St. SW Washington, DC 20460	202-260-2090
Equal Employment Opportunity Commission	1801 L St. NW Washington, DC 20507	202-663-4900 202-663-4494 (TDD)
Export-Import Bank of the U.S.	811 Vermont Ave. NW Washington, DC 20571	202-566-8990
Farm Credit Administration	1501 Farm Credit Drive McLean, VA 22102-5090	703-883-4000
Federal Communications Commission	1919 M St. NW Washington, DC 20554	202-632-7000 202-632-6999 (TDD)
Federal Deposit Insurance Corp.	550 Seventeenth St. NW Washington, DC 20429	202-393-8400
Federal Election Commission	999 E St. NW Washington, DC 20463	202-219-3420 800-424-9530 (toll-free)

Federal Emergency Management Agency	500 C St. SW Washington, DC 20472	202-646-4600
Federal Housing Finance Board	1777 F St. NW Washington, DC 20006	202-408-2500
Federal Labor Relations Authority	607 Fourteenth St. NW Washington, DC 20424-0001	202-482-6560
Federal Maritime Commission	800 North Capitol St. NW Washington, DC 20573-0001	202-523-5707
Federal Mediation and Conciliation Service	2100 K St. NW Washington, DC 20427	202-653-5290
Federal Mine Safety and Health Review Commission	1730 K St. NW Washington, DC 20006	202-653-5625
Federal Reserve System	Twentieth St. & Constitution Ave. NW Washington, DC 20551	202-452-3000
Federal Retirement Thrift Investment Board	1250 H St. NW Washington, DC 20005	202-942-1600
Federal Trade Commission	Pennsylvania Ave. at Sixth St. NW Washington, DC 20580	202-326-2222
General Services Administration	General Services Bldg. Eighteenth & F Streets NW Washington, DC 20405	202-708-5082
Interstate Commerce Commission	Twelfth St. & Constitution Ave. Ave. NW Washington, DC 20423	202-927-7119
Merit Systems Protection Board	1120 Vermont Ave. NW Washington, DC 20419	202-653-7124
National Aeronautics and Space Administration	300 E St. SW Washington, DC 20546	202-358-1000
National Archives and Records Administration	Seventh St. & Pennsylvania Ave. NW Washington, DC 20408	202-501-5400
National Capital Planning Commission	Suite 301, 801 Pennsylvania Ave. NW Washington, DC 20576	202-724-0174
National Credit Union Administration	1776 G St. NW Washington, DC 20456	202-682-9600

National Endowment for the Arts	1100 Pennsylvania Ave. NW Washington, DC 20506	202-682-5400
National Endowment for the Humanities	1100 Pennsylvania Ave. NW Washington, DC 20506	202-606-8438
National Labor Relations Board	1099 Fourteenth St. NW Washington, DC 20570	202-273-1000 (Central Locator) 202-273-4300 (TDD)
National Mediation Board	Suite 250 East, 1301 K St. NW Washington, DC 20572	202-523-5920
National Railroad Passenger Corporation (AMTRAK)	60 Massachusetts Ave. NE Washington, DC 20002	202-906-3000
National Science Foundation	1800 G St. NW Washington, DC 20550	202-357-5000
National Transportation Safety Board	490 L'Enfant Plaza SW Washington, DC 20594	202-382-6600
Nuclear Regulatory Commission	Washington, DC 20555	301-492-7000
Occupational Safety and Health Review Commission	1120 Twentieth St. NW Washington, DC 20036-3419	202-606-5100
Office of Government Ethics	Suite 500, 1201 New York Ave. NW Washington, DC 20005-3917	202-523-5757
Office of Personnel Management	1900 E St. NW Washington, DC 20415-0001	202-606-1800
Office of Special Counsel	Suite 300, 1730 M St. NW Washington, DC 20036-4505	202-653-7188 (Locator) 1-800-872-9855 (toll-free)
Panama Canal Commission	Suite 1050, 1825 I St. NW Washington, DC 20006	202-634-6441
Peace Corps	1900 K St. NW Washington, DC 20526	202-606-3886 (Locator) 1-800-424-8580 (toll-free) 202-606-3108 (fax)
Pension Benefit Guaranty Corporation	2020 K St. NW Washington, DC 20006	202-778-8800
Postal Rate Commission	1333 H St. NW Washington, DC 20268-0001	202-789-6800
Railroad Retirement Board	844 North Rush St. Chicago, IL 60611-2092	312-751-4776

Resolution Trust Corporation	801 Seventeenth St. NW Washington, DC 20434	202-416-6900
Securities and Exchange Commission	450 Fifth St. NW Washington, DC 20549	202-272-3100
Selective Service System	National Headquarters Washington, DC 20435	202-724-0820
Small Business Administration	409 Third St. SW Washington, DC 20416	202-205-6600 (Personnel Locator) 800-U-ASK-SBA (toll-free Answer Desk) 202-205-7151 (Fraud-waste)
Tennessee Valley Authority	Room 300, 412 First St. SE Washington, DC 20444-2003	202-479-4412
Thrift Depositor Protection Oversight Board	Suite 600, 1777 F St. NW Washington, DC 20232	202-786-9661
Trade and Development Agency	Room 309, State Annex 16 Washington, DC 20523-1602	703-875-4357
United States Information Agency	301 Fourth St. SW Washington, DC 20547	202-619-4700
United States International Development Cooperation Agency	320 Twenty-First St. NW Washington, DC 20523-0001	202-647-1850
United States International Trade Commission	500 E St. SW Washington, DC 20436	202-205-2000
United States Postal Service	475 L'Enfant Plaza SW Washington, DC 20260-0010	202-268-2000

FILING OF INCORPORATION PAPERS

In most jurisdictions, the charter and related papers must be filed with the secretary of state or other state officer. Except for two states, as indicated in the footnotes, this state officer is also empowered to receive service of process against a corporation chartered in the state. Here is a list of the appropriate state officers.

State	Filing
Alabama	Secretary of State Montgomery, AL 36100
Alaska	Commissioner of Commerce Juneau, AK 99811
Arizona	Corporation Commission Phoenix, AZ 85000
Arkansas	Secretary of State Little Rock, AR 72200
California	Secretary of State Sacramento, CA 95801
Colorado	Secretary of State Denver, CO 80203
Connecticut	Secretary of State Hartford, CT 06115
Delaware	Director, Division of Corporations Department of State Dover, DE 19901
District of Columbia	Dept. of Consumer and Regulatory Affairs Washington, D.C. 20001
Florida	Secretary of State Tallahassee, FL 32301
Georgia	Secretary of State Atlanta, GA 30334
Hawaii	Corporations and Securities Administrator Honolulu, HI 96813
Idaho*	Secretary of State Boise, ID 83720
Illinois	Secretary of State Springfield, IL 62700
Indiana	Secretary of State Indianapolis, IN 46204
Iowa	Secretary of State Des Moines, IA 50300

State	Filing
Kansas	Secretary of State Topeka, KS 66612
Kentucky	Secretary of State Frankfort, KY 40601
Louisiana	Secretary of State Baton Rouge, LA 70804
Maine	Secretary of State Augusta, ME 04333
Maryland	State Dept. of Assessments and Taxation Baltimore, MD 21201
Massachusetts	Secretary of the Commonwealth Boston, MA 02202
Michigan	Department of Commerce Corporation Division P.O. Drawer C Lansing, MI 48904
Minnesota	Secretary of State St. Paul, MN 55100
Mississippi	Secretary of State Jackson, MS 39200
Missouri	Secretary of State Jefferson City, MO 65101
Montana	Secretary of State Helena, MT 59620
Nebraska	Secretary of State Lincoln, NE 68500
Nevada	Secretary of State Carson City, NV 89701
New Hampshire	Secretary of State Concord, NH 03300
New Jersey	Secretary of State Trenton, NJ 08600
New Mexico	State Corporation Commission Santa Fe, NM 87501
New York	Secretary of State Albany, NY 12200
North Carolina	Secretary of State Raleigh, NC 27600

State	Filing
North Dakota	Secretary of State Bismarck, ND 58501
Ohio	Secretary of State Columbus, OH 43215
Oklahoma	Secretary of State Oklahoma City, OK 73100
Oregon	Corporation Commissioner Salem, OR 97301
Pennsylvania**	Department of State Harrisburg, PA 17101
Rhode Island	Secretary of State Providence, RI 02903
South Carolina	Secretary of State Columbia, SC 29200
South Dakota	Secretary of State Pierre, SD 57501
Tennessee	Secretary of State Nashville, TN 37219
Texas	Secretary of State Austin, TX 78701
Utah	Secretary of State Salt Lake City, UT 84114
Vermont	Secretary of State Montpelier, VT 05601
Virginia	State Corporation Commission Richmond, VA 23219
Washington	Secretary of State Olympia, WA 98504
West Virginia	Secretary of State Charleston, WV 25300
Wisconsin	Secretary of State Madison, WI 53700
Wyoming	Secretary of State Cheyenne, WY 82001

* Service of process is made upon the county auditor.
** Service of process is made upon the Secretary of the Commonwealth.

ANNUAL CORPORATE TAXES AND FEES

The table below shows the annual costs, taxes, and fees incident to operation of a corporation in the various states. These taxes and fees are subject to frequent change, so applicable state laws should be checked for any "last minute" changes.

Alabama

Franchise Tax: $10 on each $1,000 of capital stock paid in and subject to call. Minimum—$50.

Income Tax: 5% on the entire net income. Certain deductions are allowed.

Alaska

Income Tax: Under $10,000, 1% of taxable income; $10,000-$20,000, $100 plus 2% of taxable income over $10,000; $20,000-$30,000, $300 plus 3% over $20,000; $30,000-$40,000, $600 plus 4% over $30,000; $40,000-$50,000, $1,000 plus 5% over $40,000; $50,000-$60,000, $1,500 plus 6% over $50,000; $60,000-$70,000, $2,100 plus 7% over $60,000; $70,000-$80,000, $2,800 plus 8% over $70,000; $80,000-$90,000, $3,600 plus 9% over $80,000; $90,000 or more, $4,500 plus 9.4% over $90,000.

Arizona

Net Income Tax: 9.3% of taxable income: minimum—$50.

Annual Report Fee: $45.

Arkansas

Franchise Tax: 0.27% on proportion of capital stock outstanding preceding December 31, which is employed in Arkansas. Minimum—$50, maximum—$1,075,000.

Income Tax: First $3,000 of net income or part thereof—1%; next $3,000—2%; next $5.000—3%; next $14,000—5%; next $75,000—6%; on all net income over $100,000—6.5%.

California

Franchise Income Tax: 9.3% of net income. Minimum—$800.

Colorado

Franchise Tax: $25 biennial fee plus 25% surcharge as determined by secretary of state.

Income Tax: 5% of net income derived from property located in Colorado and business transacted in Colorado, or $1/2$ of 1% of gross receipts of Colorado sales if selling is only Colorado activity.

Connecticut

Franchise Income Tax: For tax years before 1/1/95—11.5% of net income allocable to the state; 1/1/95 to 12/31/96—11.25%; 1/1/97 to 12/31/97—11%; 1/1/98 to 12/31/98—10.5%; 1/1/99 and beyond—10%.

Minimum tax: $250.

Delaware

Franchise Tax: Based on authorized shares—up to 3,000 shares—$30; over 3,000 shares up to 5,000 shares—$50; over 5,000 shares up to 10,000 shares—$90; over 10,000 shares—$90 plus $50 for each 10,000 shares, or fraction thereof in excess of 10,000 shares.

Income Tax: 8.7% of taxable income from business and property within Delaware.

District of Columbia

Franchise Tax: 10% + 2.5% surtax on taxable income derived from District of Columbia sources.

Minimum tax: $100.

Annual Report Fee: $100.

Florida

Income Tax: 5.5% of net taxable income. Based on adjusted federal income. With adjustments, allocable to Florida law.

Annual Report Filing Fee: $61.25.

Georgia

Franchise Tax: Based on net worth including capital stock. Paid in surplus and earned surplus:

Net worth over	But not over	Tax
$ 0	$ 10,000	$ 10
10,000	25,000	20
25,000	40,000	40
40,000	60,000	60
60,000	80,000	75
80,000	100,000	100
100,000	150,000	125
150,000	200,000	150
200,000	300,000	200
300,000	500,000	250
500,000	750,000	300
750,000	1,000,000	500

Net worth over	But not over	Tax
$ 1,000,000	$ 2,000,000	$ 750
2,000,000	4,000,000	1,000
4,000,000	6,000,000	1,250
6,000,000	8,000,000	1,500
8,000,000	10,000,000	1,750
10,000,000	12,000,000	2,000
12,000,000	14,000,000	2,500
14,000,000	16,000,000	3,000
16,000,000	18,000,000	3,500
18,000,000	20,000,000	4,000
20,000,000	22,000,000	4,500
22,000,000		5,000

Income Tax: 6% of net income from property owned and/or business done in Georgia. Adjustments may be made under Georgia law.

Hawaii

Annual Exhibit Fee: $15.

Income Tax: 4.4% on first $25,000 net taxable income; 5.4% on taxable income between $25,000 and $100,000; 6.4% on taxable income over $100,000. Capital gain taxed at rate of 4% is entitled to alternative tax treatment under IRC.

Excise Tax: Rates depend on class of business engaged in; highest rate is 4% and lowest is 3/4%. The tax is measured by the application of rates against values, gross proceeds of sales, or gross income.

Idaho

Franchise Tax: 8% of income derived from exercising corporate franchise in Idaho.

Illinois

Annual Report Fee: $15.

Income Tax: 4.8% of corporation's net income for taxable years based upon the corporation's federal taxable income allocated and apportioned to Illinois.

Franchise Tax: 0.1% (0.15% in first year) of proportion of stated capital and paid-in surplus represented by property and business in Illinois. Computation of tax is made from following formula:

$$\text{Total stated capital and paid-in surplus} \times \frac{\text{Illinois property} + \text{Illinois gross receipts}}{\text{Total property} + \text{Total gross receipts}} \times 0.1\%$$

Indiana

Annual Report Fee: $15.

Income Tax: 3.4% of adjusted gross income.

Supplemental Net Income Tax: 4.5%.

Iowa

Annual Filing Fee: $30.

Income Tax: 6% on first $25,000 or part thereof; 8% for $25,000 to $100,000; 10% for $100,000 to $250,000; 12% for $250,000 and above.

Kansas

Annual Franchise Tax: $1 per $1,000 of shareholders' equity attributable to Kansas. Minimum: $20; Maximum: $2,500. Paid when filing annual report.

Income Tax: Based upon doing business in or deriving income from within Kansas at rate of 4% on Kansas taxable income. A surtax of 3.35% is added on Kansas taxable income over $50,000.

Kentucky

License Tax: $2.10 on each $1,000 based on fair value of the capital employed in business within the state. Minimum: $30.

Income Tax: Tax levied on "taxable net income"; first $25,000—4%; 2nd $25,000—5%; next $50,000—6%; next $150,000—7%; over $250,000—8.25%.

Annual Report Fee: $15.

Louisiana

Income Tax: 4% on 1st $25,000 net income; 5% on 2nd $25,000; 6% next $50,000; 7% next $100,000; 8% over $200,000. Graduated rate.

Franchise Tax: Basis for computation is determined by taking arithmetical average of (1) ratio that net sales in Louisiana and other revenue attributable to Louisiana bears to total net sales in regular course of business and other revenue, and (2) ratio of value of property in Louisiana to value of all property. All shares taken at book value. Rate: $1.50 per $1,000 on first $300,000, $3 per $1,000 thereafter. Minimum: $10.

Maine

Annual Filing Fee: $60.

Income Tax: 3.5% on 1st $25,000; 7.93% next $50,000: 8.33%, $75,000-$250,000; 8.93% over $250,000.

Maryland

Annual Report Fee: $100 (in lieu of franchise tax).

Income Tax: 7% of portion of net income allocable to state.

Massachusetts

Excise Tax: 8.3% of net income attributable to Mass., plus $7 per $1,000 of taxable tangible property. Minimum tax: $400.

Annual Report Filing Fee: $85.

Michigan

Single Business Tax: 2.35% of "adjusted tax base" (federal taxable income allocable to Michigan less deductions and exemptions) of every person with business activity in state allocated or apportioned to state.

Annual Report Filing Fee: $15.

Minnesota

Income Tax: 6% on 1st $25,000 based on net income earned in or allocable to activities in Minnesota less allowable deductions: 12% on balance.

Mississippi

Income Tax: 3% on first $5,000 of net income, 4% on next $5,000, and 5% on income over $10,000.

Annual Report Fee: $25.

Franchise Tax: $2.50 per $1,000 or fraction of capital used, invested, or employed in Mississippi. Minimum: $25.

Missouri

Annual Registration Fee: $40.

Income Tax: 6.25% of net income allocable to Missouri.

Franchise Tax: $1/_{20}$ of 1% of par value of outstanding stock and surplus, or portion thereof employed in state.

Montana

Annual Report Fee: $5.

License Tax: 6.75% for first $500,000 of net income received from all sources within or allocable to Montana, 7.25% for net income in excess of $500,000. Minimum tax: $100.

Nebraska

Occupational Tax: Based on the amount of paid-up capital stock according to statutory rate table, with annual fees ranging from $43 (for up to $20,000 paid-up capital stock) to $12,150 (for 100 million or more paid-up capital stock).

Income Tax: Income or franchise tax applies to taxable income of corporations derived from sources within state; 5.58% on 1st $50,000; 7.81% over $50,000. 15% surtax on taxable income over $200,000.

Nevada

Annual Report Fee: $85.

New Hampshire

Business Profits: Imposed on taxable business profits, at a rate of 7% (after 7/1/94).

Franchise Tax: Every domestic corporation must pay annually at time of making its annual return a fee equal to amount paid upon filing its original record of organization, plus an amount equal to any additional payments for increases in authorized capital. If authorized capital is reduced, annual fee is amount required for original fee of a corporation capitalized at reduced amount. Minimum: $100; maximum: $2,000.
Annual Report Fee: $100.

New Jersey

Annual Report Fee: $20.

Franchise Tax: 9% based on net income and net worth. Minimum tax: $50 in 1994, $100 in 1995, $150 in 1996, $200 in 1997.

New Mexico

Franchise Tax: $50 a year.

Net Income Tax: Imposed on the corporation's entire net income or portion thereof from business done or property located in the state. Rates: Up to $500,000—4.8%; $500,000 to $1 million—$24,000 plus 6.4% of excess over $500,000; over $1 million—$56,000 plus 7.6% of excess over $1 million.

Annual Report Fee: $25.

New York

Franchise Tax: The larger of: (1) 9% of entire net income allocated to New York; (2) 3.5% of apportioned income; (3) 1.78 mills on each dollar of allocated business and investment capital; or (4) payroll tax base of $325 for gross payroll of $1 million or less, $425 for payroll up to $6.25 million, $1,500 for payroll of $6.25 million or more. In addition there is a tax of $9/10$ of a mill on each dollar of allocated subsidiary capital.

North Carolina

Income Tax: 7.75% of net income allocable to North Carolina, plus surtax of 2% in 1993 and 1% in 1994.
Franchise Tax: $1.50 for each $1,000 of proportion of total issued and outstanding capital stock, surplus and undivided profits allocable to business in North Carolina; $35 minimum.

North Dakota

Income Tax: Based on net income attributable to sources within the state at the following rates: First $3,000—3%; over $3,000, up to $8,000—4.5%; over $8,000, up to $20,000—6%; $20,001 to $30,000—7.5%; $30,001 to $50,000—9%; over $50,000—10.5%.

Annual Report Fee: $25.

Ohio

Franchise Tax: 5.1% on 1st $50,000 plus 8.9% over $50,000. Min. $50.

Oklahoma

Franchise Tax: $1.25 for each $1,000 or fraction thereof of the corporate capital used, invested, or employed in Oklahoma. Minimum fee: $10; maximum fee: $20,000.

Income Tax: 6% based on income derived from property owned and business transacted in the state, less applicable credits.

Oregon

License Fee: Corporation must pay annual $30 license tax.

Corporate Excise Tax: Business corporations doing business in state must pay excise tax on net income—6.6%. Minimum tax is $10.

Pennsylvania

Capital Stock Tax: 12.75 mills per dollar of taxable portion of the actual value of the whole capital stock or $300, whichever is greater.

Corporate Net Income Tax: 12.25% of net income allocated to Pennsylvania.

Rhode Island

Franchise Tax: $2.50 per $10,000 or part thereof of authorized capital stock.

Business Corporation Tax: 9% of net income. Minimum of $250. 11% surtax through end of 1996.

South Carolina

License Tax: $15 plus one mill on each dollar paid to the corporation on account of capital stock and paid in surplus. Minimum fee: $25.

Income Tax: 5% of net income for corporations whose entire business is transacted or conducted in the state, or for net income allocable to state.

South Dakota

Annual Report Filing Fee: $10.

Tennessee

Annual Report Fee: $20.

Excise Tax: Based on net earnings arising from business done in the state at the rate of 6%.

Franchise Tax: Based on worth of capital invested in the state—25 cents per $100 or major fraction thereof.

Texas

Franchise Tax: 0.25% of net taxable capital plus 4.5% of net capital earned surplus.

Utah

Franchise Tax: 5% based on income attributable to the state. Minimum: $100.
Annual Report Fee: $15.

Vermont

Income Tax: 5.5% on Vermont net income of $10,000 or less; 6.6% for $10,001-$25,000; 7.7% for $25,001-$250,000; 8.25% over $250,000. Minimum: $150.

Virginia

Income Tax: 6% based on net income attributable to business within the state.

Registration Fee: Up to 5,000 shares of capital stock issued: $50; over 5,000 shares: $50 plus $15 per additional 5,000 shares, but not more than $850.

Washington

Franchise Tax: $175 first year and $50 each later year.

West Virginia

License Tax: Based on authorized capital stock. If the authorized capital stock is $5,000 or less-$20; over $5,000 to $10,000—$30; over $10,000 to $25,000—$40; over $25,000 to $50,000—$50; over $50,000 to $75,000—$80; over $75,000 to $100,000—$100; over $100,000 to $125,000—$110; over $125,000 to $150,000—$120; over $150,000 to $175,000—$140; over $175,000 to $200,000-$150; over $200,000 to $1 million—$180 plus 20 cents on each $1,000 or fraction thereof over $200,000; over $1 million to $15 million—$340 plus 15 cents on each fraction thereof over $1 million; over $15 million—$2,500.

Corporate Net Income Tax: 9% of corporation's taxable income derived from activity in state.

Wisconsin

Annual Report Fee: $25.

Income Tax: 7.9% of net income.

Wyoming

License Tax: Based on value of capital, property, and assets in state. If the value is $50,000 or less—$25; over $50,000 up to $100,000—$50; over $100,000 up to $500,000—$100; over $500,000 up to $1 million—$200; over $1 million—$200 per $1 million or fraction thereof. Maximum tax: $50,000.

REGIONAL OFFICES OF THE AMERICAN ARBITRATION ASSOCATION

ATLANTA, GA 30345-3203
1975 Century Blvd. NE, Suite 1
Phone: 404-325-0101
Fax: 404-325-8034

BOSTON, MA 02110-1703
133 Federal Street
Phone: 617-451-6600
Fax: 617-451-0763

CHARLOTTE, NC 28202-2431
428 East Fourth St., Suite 300
Phone: 704-347-0200
Fax: 704-347-2804

CHICAGO, IL 60601-7601
225 N. Michigan Ave., Suite 2527
Phone: 312-616-6560
Fax: 312-819-0404

CINCINNATI, OH 45202-2973
441 Vine St., Suite 3308
Phone: 513-241-8434
Fax: 513-241-8437

CLEVELAND, OH 44130-3490
17900 Jefferson Rd., Suite 101
Phone: 216-891-4741
Fax: 216-891-4740

DALLAS, TX 75240-6620
13455 Noel Rd., Suite 1440
Phone: 214-702-8222
Fax: 214-490-9008

DENVER, CO 80264-2101
1660 Lincoln St., Suite 2150
Phone: 303-831-0823
Fax: 303-832-3626

GARDEN CITY, NY 11530-2004
666 Old Country Rd., Suite 603
Phone: 516-222-1660
Fax: 516-745-6447

HARTFORD, CT 06108-3240
111 Founders Place, 17th Floor
Phone: 203-289-3993
Fax: 203-282-0459

HONOLULU, HI 96813-4714
810 Richards St., Suite 641
Phone: 808-531-0541
Fax: 808-533-2306

HOUSTON, TX 77002-6708
1001 Fannin St., Suite 1005
Phone: 713-739-1302
Fax: 713-739-1702

KANSAS CITY, MO 64106-2110
1001 Walnut St., Suite 903
Phone: 816-221-6401
Fax: 816-471-5264

LAS VEGAS, NV 89102-8719
4425 Spring Mountain Rd., Suite 310
Phone: 702-364-8009
Fax: 702-364-8084

LOS ANGELES, CA 90010-1108
3055 Wilshire Blvd., 7th Fl.
Phone: 213-383-6516
Fax: 213-386-2251

MIAMI, FL 33131-2808
799 Brickell Plaza, Suite 600
Phone: 305-358-7777
Fax: 305-358-4931

MINNEAPOLIS, MN 55402-1092
514 Nicollet Mall, Suite 670
Phone: 612-332-6545
Fax: 612-342-2334

NEW ORLEANS, LA 70130-6101
650 Poydras St., Suite 1535
Phone: 504-522-8781
Fax: 504-561-8041

NEW YORK, NY 10020-1203
140 West 51st St., 9th Floor
Phone: 212-484-4095
Fax: 212-307-4387

ORLANDO, FL 32801-2742
201 East Pine St., Suite 800
Phone: 407-648-1185
Fax: 407-649-8668

PHILADELPHIA, PA 19102-4106
230 South Broad St.
Phone: 215-732-5260
Fax: 215-732-5002

PHOENIX, AZ 85012-2365
333 E. Osborn Rd., Suite 310
Phone: 602-234-0950
Fax: 602-230-2151

PITTSBURGH, PA 15222-1207
Four Gateway Center, Rm. 419
Phone: 412-261-3617
Fax: 412-261-6055

St. LOUIS, MO 63101-1614
One Mercantile Center, Suite 2512
Phone: 314-621-7175
Fax: 314-621-3730

SALT LAKE CITY, UT 84111-3834
645 S. 200 East, Suite 203
Phone: 801-531-9748
Fax: 801-531-0660 (Bar Assn.)

SAN DIEGO, CA 92101-4586
600 B St., Suite 1450
Phone: 619-239-3051
Fax: 619-239-3807

SAN FRANCISCO, CA 94104-1113
417 Montgomery St., 5th Floor
Phone: 415-981-3901
Fax: 415-781-8426

SEATTLE, WA 98101-2511
1325 Fourth Ave., Suite 1414
Phone: 206-622-6435
Fax: 206-343-5679

SOMERSET, NJ 08873-4120
265 Davidson Ave., Suite 140
Phone: 908-560-9560
Fax: 908-560-8850

SOUTHFIELD, MI 48076-3728
One Towne Square, Suite 1600
Phone: 810-352-5500
Fax: 810-352-3147

SYRACUSE, NY 13202-1376
205 South Salina St.
Phone: 315-472-5483
Fax: 315-472-0966

WASHINGTON, DC 20036-4104
1150 Connecticut Ave. NW, 6th Floor
Phone: 202-296-8510
Fax: 202-572-9574

WHITE PLAINS, NY 10603-1916
399 Knollwood Rd., Suite 116
Phone: 914-945-1119
Fax: 914-946-2661

MODERN ARBITRATION STATUTES IN THE UNITED STATES †

(Unless otherwise noted, references are to the state's statutory compilation)

United States Arbitration Act, 9 U.S.C. §1 et seq.

Alabama	§6-6-1 et seq.*
Alaska	§09.43.010 et seq.* (4)
Arizona	§12-1501* (4)
Arkansas	§16-108-201 et seq.* (2, 4, 7)
California	Civ. Proc. §1280 et seq.
Colorado	§13-22-201 et seq.*
Connecticut	§52-408 et seq.
Delaware	T10 §5701 et seq.* (4)
District of Columbia	§16-4301 et seq.*
Florida	§682.01 et seq.
Georgia	§9-9-1 et seq.
Hawaii	§658-1 et seq.
Idaho	§7-901 et seq.* (4)
Illinois	Ch. 710 Act 5 (Smith Hurd)*
Indiana	§34-4-2-1 et seq.* (3, 5, 6)
Iowa	§679A-1 et seq.
Kansas	§5-401 et seq.* (2, 4, 7)
Kentucky	§417.045 et seq.*
Louisiana	§9:4201 et seq.* (4)
Maine	T14 §5927 et seq.* (8)
Maryland	Cts. & Jud. Proc. §3-201 et seq.* (4)
Massachusetts	Ch. 251 §1 et seq.* (4)
Michigan	§600.5001 et seq.
Minnesota	§572.08 et seq.*
Mississippi	11-15-101 et seq.
Missouri	§435.350 et seq.* (2)
Montana	§27-5-111*
Nevada	§38.015 et seq.*
New Hampshire	§542:1 et seq.
New Jersey	§2A:24-1 et seq.
New Mexico	§44-7-1
New York	Civ. Prac. §7501 et seq.
North Carolina	§1-567.1 et seq.* (4)
North Dakota	§32-29.2-01 et seq.*
Ohio	§2711.01 et seq.
Oklahoma	T 15 §801 et seq.* (2, 4)
Oregon	§36.300 et seq.
Pennsylvania	T 42 §7301 et seq.*

Rhode Island	§10-3-1 et seq.
South Carolina	§15-48-10 et seq.* (2, 4, 7, 9)
South Dakota	§21-25A-1 et seq.* (2)
Tennessee	§29-5-301 et seq.*
Texas	Civ. Stat. Art. 224 et seq.* (1, 2, 4)
Utah	§78-31a-1 et seq.*
Vermont	T 12 §5651 et seq.*
Virginia	§8.01-577 et seq.
Washington	§7.04.010 et seq.
Wisconsin	§788.01 et seq.
Wyoming	§1-36-101 et seq.

---

† Modern arbitration statutes are those enforcing agreements to arbitrate existing controversies and any arising in the future. West Virginia's arbitration statute (§55-10-1) applies to existing controversies only.

* Referred to as Uniform Arbitration Act. Numbers following the asterisk indicate statutory exclusions as to: (1) construction, (2) insurance, (3) leases, (4) labor contracts, (5) loans, (6) sales, (7) torts, (8) uninsured motorists, (9) doctors, lawyers.

CORPORATE INDEMNIFICATION STATUTES

(Unless otherwise noted, references are to the state's statutory compilation)

Alabama	§10-2B-8.50 et seq.
Alaska	§10.06.490
Arizona	§10-856
Arkansas	§4-26-814
California	Corp. Code §317
Colorado	§7-109-101 et seq.
Connecticut	§33-320a
Delaware	T 8 §145
District of Columbia	D.C. Code §29-304
Florida	§607.0850
Georgia	§14-2-851 et seq.
Hawaii	§415-48.5
Idaho	§30-1-5
Illinois	Ch. 805, Act 5 (Smith Hurd)
Indiana	§23-1-37-1 et seq.
Iowa	§490.850 et seq.
Kansas	§17-6305
Kentucky	§271B.8-500 et seq.
Louisiana	§12:83
Maine	T 13A §719
Maryland	Corp. & Assoc. §2-418
Massachusetts	Ch. 156B §67
Michigan	§450.1561
Minnesota	§302A.521
Mississippi	§79-4-8.50 et seq.
Missouri	§351.355
Montana	§35-1-451 et seq.
Nebraska	§21-2004
Nevada	§78.751
New Hampshire	§293-A:5
New Jersey	§14A:3-5
New Mexico	§53-11-4.1
New York	Bus. Corp. §721 et seq.
North Carolina	§55-8-50 et seq.
North Dakota	§10-19.1-91
Ohio	§1701.13(E)
Oklahoma	T 18 §1031
Oregon	§60.387 et seq.
Pennsylvania	T 15 §1741 et seq.

Rhode Island	§7-1.1-4.1
South Carolina	§33-8-500 et seq.
South Dakota	§47-2-58.2
Tennessee	§48-18-501 et seq.
Texas	Bus. Corp. Act Art. 2.02
Utah	§16-10a-901 et seq.
Vermont	T 11 §1852(15)
Virginia	§13.1-696 et seq.
Washington	§23B.08.570
West Virginia	§31-1-9
Wisconsin	§180.05
Wyoming	§17-16-850 et seq.

STATE BLUE SKY LAWS

(Unless otherwise noted, references are to the state's statutory compilation)

Alabama	§8-6-1 et seq.
Alaska	§45.55.010 et seq.
Arizona	§44-1801 et seq.
Arkansas	§23-42-101 et seq.
California	Corp. Code §25,000 et seq.
Colorado	§11-51-101 et seq.
Connecticut	§36-470 et seq.
Delaware	T 6 §7301 et seq.
District of Columbia	§2-2601 et seq.
Florida	§517.011 et seq.
Georgia	§10-5-1 et seq.
Hawaii	§485-1 et seq.
Idaho	§30.1401 et seq.
Illinois	Ch. 815 Act 5 (Smith Hurd)
Indiana	§23-2-1-1 et seq.
Iowa	§502.101 et seq.
Kansas	§17-1252 et seq.
Kentucky	§292.310 et seq.
Louisiana	§51:701 et seq.
Maine	T 32 §10101 et seq.
Maryland	Corp. & Assn. §11-101 et seq.
Massachusetts	Ch. 110A §101 et seq.
Michigan	§451.501 et seq.
Minnesota	§80A.01 et seq.
Mississippi	§75-71-101 et seq.
Missouri	§409.101 et seq.
Montana	§30-10-101 et seq.
Nebraska	§8-1101 et seq.
Nevada	§90.211 et seq.
New Hampshire	§421-B:1 et seq.
New Jersey	§49:3-47 et seq.
New Mexico	§58-13B-1 et seq.
New York	Gen. Bus. Law §352 et seq.
North Carolina	§78A-1 et seq.
North Dakota	§10-04-01 et seq.
Ohio	§1707.01 et seq.
Oklahoma	T 71 §1 et seq.
Oregon	§59.005 et seq.
Pennsylvania	T 70 §1-101 et seq.

Rhode Island	§71-11-101 et seq.
South Carolina	§35-1-10 et seq.
South Dakota	§47-31A101 et seq.
Tennessee	§48-2-101 et seq.
Texas	Civ. Stat. Art.581-1 et seq.
Utah	§61-1-1 et seq.
Vermont	T 9 §4201 et seq.
Virginia	§13.1-501 et seq.
Washington	§21.20.005 et seq.
West Virginia	§32-1-101 et seq.
Wisconsin	§551.01 et seq.
Wyoming	§17-4-101 et seq.

WHEN MINORS ARE COMPETENT TO CONTRACT

State	Age	State	Age
Alabama	19 (1) (12)	Montana	18
Alaska	18 (8)	Nebraska	19 (2)
Arizona	18	Nevada	18
Arkansas	18 (5)	New Hampshire	18
California	18 (2) (6)	New Jersey	18 (15)
Colorado	18	New Mexico	18 (2) (5) (6)
Connecticut	18 (1)	New York	18 (2) (12)
Delaware	18	North Carolina	18 (2)
District of Columbia	18	North Dakota	18 (10)
Florida	18 (2)	Ohio	18
Georgia	18 (2) (11)	Oklahoma	18 (5)
Hawaii	18 (2)	Oregon	18 (5)
Idaho	18 (2) (12)	Pennyslvania	18
Illinois	18 (5)	Rhode Island	18
Indiana	18 (13)	South Carolina	18
Iowa	18 (2)	South Dakota	18
Kansas	18 (5) (11)	Tennessee	18 (5)
Kentucky	18	Texas	18 (5)
Louisiana	18 (5) (9)	Utah	18 (2) (13)
Maine	18	Vermont	18
Maryland	18	Virginia	18
Massachusetts	18 (12)	Washington	18
Michigan	18 (2) (5) (10) (13)	West Virginia	21
Minnesota	18	Wisconsin	18
Mississippi	21 (3) (5) (14)	Wyoming	19
Missouri	18		

(1) All married persons, widows and widowers over 18.
(2) By marriage.
(3) Married persons 18 and over.
(4) Married person has limited rights if spouse is of age.
(5) Court may authorize minors to transact business.
(6) Active duty in the military or living apart from parent or guardian with consent or is managing own financial affairs.
(7) Minors engaged in business with consent from parent or guardian.
(8) Insurance payments up to $3,000.
(9) Parents may declare emancipation of minor at age 15.
(10) Active duty in the military or parental conduct or document indicating release of parental rights.
(11) Married persons 16 and over.
(12) 15 and over for insurance.
(13) 16 and over for insurance.
(14) Everyone 18 or older can contract, sue, or be sued.
(15) 17 and over for sale of property.

STATE GUIDE TO INTEREST RATES

State	Maximum Legal Rate	Maximum Contract Rate	Maximum Judgment Rate	Penalty for Usury	Corporation's Defense of Usury
Alabama	6%	8% or discount + 1% or prime + 2% + surcharge	12%	Forfeit all interest.	No defense over $2,000.
Alaska	10.5%	10.5%; no limit for contracts over $25,000	10.5% or rate in contract.	Borrower recovers double interest paid; lender forfeits all interest.	No provision.
Arizona	10%	Any rate agreed to in writing in the contract.	10% or as set out in contract.	Forfeit all interest; borrower recovers interest payments applied them against principal.	No provision.
Arkansas	6%	10.5%	10% or rate in contract, whichever is higher.	Contract void; borrower can recover twice the paid interest.	No provision.
California	7%	10-10.5%	10%	Forfeit all interest; borrower recovers triple interest within 1 year, violation is felony.	Can defend.
Colorado	8%	As set out in contract, not to exceed 45%.	8% or contract rate.	No provision.	No provision.
Connecticut	8%	12%	10%	Forfeiture of paid and unpaid interest and principal. Violation is a misdemeanor.	No provision.

State	Maximum Legal Rate	Maximum Contract Rate	Maximum Judgment Rate	Penalty for Usury	Corporation's Defense of Usury
Delaware	11.5% + surcharge.	10.5% + surcharge: no limit on secured demand notes over $5,000 or non-mortgage loans over $100,000.	12% or contract rate.	Borrower recovers excess paid; greater of $500 or three times excess paid after maturity.	No defense.
District of Columbia	6%	24% or as set out in contract; no limit on loans over $1,000.	70% of interest rate set by the Secretary of the Treasury for underpayment and overpayment of tax to the IRS.	Forfeit all interest. Borrower recovers interest or applies it against principal.	No defense.
Florida	12%	18%; 25% over $500,000.	Lesser of 12% or rate agreed on.	Borrower recovers twice the interest paid.	No provision.
Georgia	7%	16% where principal amount is $3,000 or less. Above $3,000, any rate agreed upon.	12%	Forfeit all interest; borrower may set off excess interest paid against principal.	No provision.
Hawaii	10%	1% a month.	10%	Recover only principal less interest paid.	No defense on loan over $750,000.
Idaho	12¢ for each hundred a year.	Any amount agreed upon by parties.	18¢ on each hundred a year.	Interest is forfeited; borrower recovers triple interest.	No provision.
Illinois	$5 for each $100 a year.	9%. No limit on residential loans or secured notes over $5,000.	9%	Borrower recovers double interest.	No provision.

State	Maximum Legal Rate	Maximum Contract Rate	Maximum Judgment Rate	Penalty for Usury	Corporation's Defense of Usury
Indiana	8%	15-21%, depending on the balance.	12%	Greater of the service charge or ten times the excessive charge.	No provision.
Iowa	5¢ for each hundred year.	10.75%; no limit on real estate loans or personal credit over $25,000.	10% per year or up to contract rate.	Forfeit all interest, plus 8¢ per $100 of principal unpaid at time of judgment; additional 8¢ per $100 to school fund.	No defense.
Kansas	10%	11.28%; 11.72% on mortgages.	9.5%	Excessive interest is forfeited.	No defense.
Kentucky	8%	9.5% on loans up to $15,000; 6.5% on bank or trust company loans up to $15,000; no limit otherwise.	12%	Forfeit interest; debtor can recover twice interest paid.	No defense unless principal asset is one- or two-family house.
Louisiana	12%	12%	Prime + 1% (but not less than 7% or more than 14%).	Forfeit all interest.	No defense.
Maine	6%	No maximum, if in writing.	8% or contract note; 15% after date of judgment.	No provision.	No provision.

773

State	Maximum Legal Rate	Maximum Contract Rate	Maximum Judgment Rate	Penalty for Usury	Corporation's Defense of Usury
Maryland	6%	8%; no limit on business loans over $15,000 (over $75,000 if secured by a mortgage) or mortgage loans.	10% or contract rate.	Forfeit greater of 3 times excess interest and charges or $500.	No defense.
Massachusetts	$6 a year for each $100.	No maximum stated.	12% or contract rate.	Criminal penalties.	No provision.
Michigan	$5 a year for each 100.	7%; no limit on business loans made by banks, insurance carriers, manufacturers' finance subsidiaries; 15% on business loans made by other entities; 11% on mortgage loans.	12%	Forfeit all interest and charges, plus attorney's fee and court cost. It's criminal usury to charge interest over 25% a year.	No defense. Can agree in writing to any rate of interest.
Minnesota	$6 a year for each $100.	$8 a year per hundred. (no limit on loans of $100,000 or more); 10% on bank or savings bank loans and business loans.	Minimum of 8%; rate based on secondary market yield on U.S. Treasury bills with one-year maturities.	Contract void, borrower gets back all interest paid but one-half goes to school fund.	No defense.
Mississippi	8%	10.5%; 11.5% for corporations.	8%, or rate in contract.	Forfeit all interest.	Defense subject to corporate rate.

State	Maximum Legal Rate	Maximum Contract Rate	Maximum Judgment Rate	Penalty for Usury	Corporation's Defense of Usury
Missouri	9%	11.8%; no limit for business loans over $5,000 or secured note over $5,000.	9% or rate in contract.	Borrower recovers double interest paid; lender pays lawsuit costs.	No defense.
Montana	10%	6% over prime rate of major New York banks as published in *Wall Street Journal* dated 3 business days prior to execution of agreement.	10%	Double interest charged.	No provision.
Nebraska	6%	16%; no limit over $25,000	Treasury Bill rate + 1%.	Forfeit all interest; lender pays costs.	No provision.
Nevada	Prime + 2%	Any rate agreed to by parties.	Prime + 2%.	No provision.	No provision.
New Hampshire	10%	No limit.	10%	No provision.	No provision.
New Jersey	$6 per $100.	16%; or 17% or mortgages of 1-6 family units; no limit on loans over $50,000.	Forfeit all interest and costs.	Forfeit all interest and costs.	No defense.
New Mexico	15%	Any rate agreed to in writing by the parties.	15% or contract rate.	Forfeit all interest; borrower recovers double interest paid.	No defense.

State	Maximum Legal Rate	Maximum Contract Rate	Maximum Judgment Rate	Penalty for Usury	Corporation's Defense of Usury
New York	16%	No limit on business loans over $25,000, any loans over $2.5 million; the discount rate + 5% on commercial paper (90 day).	9%	Contract void. Exception: savings banks and savings and loan assns. which forfeit all interest.	No defense unless (1) the corporation asserts a defense of criminal usury, or (2) corporation's principal asset is 1- or 2-family house and corporation was formed or control of it acquired within 6 mos. before loan and mortgage.
North Carolina	8%	16%. No limit on loans over $25,000 or first mortgages.	8%	Forfeit all interest; borrower recovers double interest.	No defense.
North Dakota	6%	5½% above the average rate for interest on 6-month U.S. Treasury bills in effect 6 months prior to the transaction, but not less than 7%.	12% or rate in contract up to maximum contract rate.	Forfeit all interest plus 25% of principal; borrower recovers double interest paid plus 25% of principal or set off double interest against principal debt. Also criminal penalty.	No provision.
Ohio	10%	8%. Mortgages: 8.5%. No limit on loans over $100,000 or business loans.	10% or contract rate.	Apply excess interest paid against principal.	No defense.

State	Maximum Legal Rate	Maximum Contract Rate	Maximum Judgment Rate	Penalty for Usury	Corporation's Defense of Usury
Oklahoma	6%	No limit if not subject to U3C.	Treasury Bill rate + 4%.	Greater of finance charge or ten times the excessive charge.	No defense.
Oregon	9%	Any rate agreed to by parties; 10.5% + surcharge on certain loans over $50,000.	9%, or rate in contract.	Forfeit entire interest.	No provision.
Pennsylvania	6% up to $50,000.	Mortgages, 11.25%; bank loans, 10.5%; no limit over $50,000.	6%	Forfeit excess over lawful rate; borrower recovers 3 times excess.	No defense.
Rhode Island	$12 for each $100 a year unless a different rate is expressly stipulated.	21% or 9% over the treasury bill index on U.S. treasury bills with a maturity of 1 year or less (whichever is greater).	12%	Contract void; borrower recovers all payments.	No provision.
South Carolina	6%	Repealed. See state UCCC (¶326).	14%	Forfeit all interest; borrower recovers double interest paid.	No provision.
South Dakota	15%	No limit.	12%	Repealed by SL 1982. ch 341, §8.	No provision.
Tennessee	10%	12.43%; home mortgage 12.64%.	10%	Excess interest can be recovered.	Can plead.

777

State	Maximum Legal Rate	Maximum Contract Rate	Maximum Judgment Rate	Penalty for Usury	Corporation's Defense of Usury
Texas	6%	Formula rates published by consumer credit commissioner (18-24%).	If based on contract, the contract rate, up to 18%; otherwise, set by commissioner between 10-20%.	Forfeit three times amount of interest charged; however amount forfeited shall not be less than $2,000 or 20% of principal.	Subject to corporate rate of 1½% a month on amounts of $5,000 or more.
Utah	10%	No limit if not subject to U3C.	12% or rate in contract.	Repealed. See Utah ¶.619 UCCC ¶12.619.	No provision.
Vermont *(continued)*	12%	For single payment loans by Tit. 8 lenders and federal S&Ls, 18%; for retail installment contracts, 18% of first $500, 15% of balance; for open-end credit, 1½% per month on first $500, 1¼% per month on balance; for loans secured by motor vehicles, aircraft and farm equipment, 18% per year; for install- ment loans not other- wise covered, 24% on first $1,000, 12% on balance, or 18% on total balance, whichever is higher.	No provision.	Lender forfeits all interest and half of principal; borrower recovers excess paid plus interest, costs, and attorney's fees; willful violation $500 fine, 6 mos. jail, or both.	No provision.

State	Maximum Legal Rate	Maximum Contract Rate	Maximum Judgment Rate	Penalty for Usury	Corporation's Defense of Usury
Virginia	8%	12% (6.5% for state banks); no limit on first mortgage loans.	8% or contract rate.	Borrower can recover twice interest paid.	No defense.
Washington (continued)	12%	Greater of 12% or 4% above the equivalent coupon issue yield (pub. by FRB of San Francisco) of the average bill rate for 26-week treasury bills at 1st bill market auction of preceding calendar month.	Greater of 12% or T-bill rate + 4%.	Forfeit all interest: borrower may apply double interest paid against principal; or can collect costs and reasonable attorney's fees.	No defense.
West Virginia	10.25%	18% for most transactions.	$10 upon $100 per year.	Forfeit all interest: borrower can recover greater of $100 or 4 times interest charged.	No defense.
Wisconsin	$5 for each $100 a year.	No limit.	12%	No statutory penalty.	No provision.
Wyoming	7%	See UCCC limits.	10% or rate in contract.	The greater of the finance charge or ten times the excessive charge.	No provision.

779

JUDGMENT NOTES AND ATTORNEYS' FEES

Following is a chart designed to give basic information concerning confessions of judgment, judgment notes, and attorneys' fees provisions with pertinent limitations. The material appears courtesy of Prentice-Hall, Inc., Installment Sales (looseleaf service).

ALABAMA (Code of 1975). *Judgment notes:* No statutory provision. *Confessions of judgment:* Invalid, if made before suit. *Attorneys' fees:* Forbidden unless consumer debt exceeds $300; for bigger debts, can provide for reasonable fees to nonsalaried lawyer; limit, 15%.

ALASKA (Statutes). *Judgement notes:* No statutory provision. *Confessions of judgment:* Valid, if made by debtor in person, or by debtor's attorney-in-fact under power of attorney. *Attorneys' fees:* Retail installment contract may provide for reasonable fees to nonsalaried attorney.

ARIZONA (Revised Statutes). *Judgment notes:* No statutory provision. *Confessions of judgment:* Valid only if executed after note matures; cannot be made in connection with small loan. *Attorneys' fees:* Retail installment contracts or retail charge account agreements may provide for reasonable fees to nonsalaried attorneys.

ARKANSAS (Statutes). *Judgment notes:* No statutory provision. *Confessions of judgment:* Valid if personally made by debtor in court. *Attorneys' fees:* Enforceable, if don't exceed 10% of principal and accrued interest.

CALIFORNIA (Calif. Codes). *Judgement notes:* No statutory provision. *Confessions of judgment:* Valid, if taken for money due or to become due, or to secure contingent liability, and signed by debtor's attorney. But prohibited in time sales contract; also, in contracts of industrial loan company or property broker or small loan licensee. *Attorneys' fees:* May be awarded to prevailing party in any action on time sales contract or installment contract, or on motor vehicle time sales contract.

COLORADO (Revised Statutes, 1973). *Judgment notes:* No statutory provision. *Confessions of judgment:* Void in consumer credit transactions. *Attorneys' fees:* Not over 15% or as directed by court.

CONNECTICUT (General Statutes). *Judgment notes:* No statutory provision. *Confessions of judgment:* May be offered by plaintiff before trial in pending action. Not permitted in time sales contract or installment loan contract, or in small loan contracts. *Attorneys' fees:* Valid in note or other evidence of indebtedness, but court may modify amount. Also valid in installment contract or installment loan contract, if not more than 15% of balance due.

DELAWARE (Code Anno.). *Judgment notes:* Valid. *Confessions of judgment:* Permitted, if made by warrant of attorney. *Attorneys' fees:* In action on note, contract, or other written instrument, court may award reasonable fees (up to 5% of amount awarded for principal and interest), if instrument provides for payment of such fees.

FLORIDA (Statutes, 1981). *Judgment notes:* No statutory provision. *Confessions of judgment:* Void if executed before or without an action; not permitted in small loan contracts. *Attorneys' fees:* Valid in time sales contracts of motor vehicles, or of other goods. *Note:* Courts have decided there is no confession of judgment or other handling under the judgment rate situation without appropriate service of process and proof of damages.

GEORGIA (Code). *Judgment notes:* No statutory provision. *Confessions of judgment:* Permitted only in suit; invalid in small loan contracts. *Attorneys' fees:* Provision valid up to 15% of principal and interest due. If no provision, then can collect 15% of first $500 due and 10% in excess of that. Debtor must also be given 10 days notice before suit to pay balance.

HAWAII (Revised Statutes). *Judgment notes:* No statutory provision. *Confessions of judgment:* Not enforceable. Not permitted in small loan contracts. *Attorneys' fees:* Court will award in actions on notes or contracts, if fees specified therein or in separate agreement; but not more than 25%.

IDAHO (Code). *Judgment notes:* No statutory provision. *Confessions of judgment:* In general, not permitted. Void in consumer credit transactions. Not permitted in small loan contracts. *Attorneys' fees:* Reasonable.

ILLINOIS (Revised Statutes). *Judgment notes:* Void only in consumer transactions. *Confessions of judgment:* Valid in small loan contracts. *Attorneys' fees:* Enforceable in time sales contracts, if fee reasonable.

INDIANA (Burns Statutes, Anno.). *Judgment notes:* Void. *Confessions of judgment:* Void. Use of same or judgment note is misdemeanor. Void in consumer credit transactions. *Attorneys' fees:* Reasonable.

IOWA (Code, 1962). *Judgment notes:* No statutory provision. *Confessions of judgment:* Valid, if for money due or to become due, or to secure against contingent liability. Void in consumer credit transactions unless executed after default. *Attorneys' fees:* If note or contract provides for payment of fees, court will award reasonable fees.

KANSAS (General Statutes, 1949). *Judgment notes:* No statutory provision. *Confessions of judgment:* Void in consumer credit transactions. *Attorneys' fees:* Unenforceable in consumer credit transactions; void in any note, bill of exchange, bond or mortgage.

KENTUCKY (Revised Statutes). *Judgment notes:* No statutory provision. *Confessions of judgment:* Void. May not be included in motor vehicle time sales contracts, or in small loan contracts. *Attorneys' fees:* Permitted for nonsalaried attorney in motor vehicle time sales contracts, but can't exceed 15% of balance due.

LOUISIANA (Revised Statutes). *Judgment notes:* No statutory provision. *Confessions of judgment:* No statutory provision. *Attorneys' fees:* Permitted in motor vehicle time sales contract, if not more than 25% of balance due, with $15 minimum.

MAINE (Revised Statutes). *Judgment notes:* No statutory provision. *Confessions of judgment:* Prohibited in home repair agreement, and in consumer credit transactions. *Attorneys' fees:* Prohibited in consumer credit sale, lease, or supervised loan; in any other consumer credit transaction up to 15% of unpaid debt.

MARYLAND (Code Anno., 1975-76 Supp.). *Judgment notes:* No statutory provision. *Confessions of judgment:* Prohibited in all time sales contracts; also, in small loan contracts. *Attorneys' fees:* Permitted to nonsalaried attorney in time sales contracts, up to 15% of balance due, and in retail credit accounts, if reasonable.

MASSACHUSETTS (Anno. Laws). *Judgment notes:* Prohibited. *Confessions of judgment:* Inclusion in note or contract void. Prohibited in time sales contracts of goods and motor vehicles. *Attorneys' fees:* No statutory provision.

MICHIGAN (Statutes, Anno.). *Judgment notes:* No statutory provision. *Confessions of judgment:* Valid, if made in separate instrument. Prohibited in time sales contracts or retail charge agreements; also, in small loan contracts. *Attorneys' fees:* Permitted in home repair installment contract, but not to exceed 20% of balance due. Also permitted in retail charge agreements, if fee reasonable.

MINNESOTA Statutes, 1980). *Judgment notes:* No statutory provision. *Confessions of judgment:* Valid, if made in separate verified statement. Prohibited in consumer credit transactions. *Attorneys' fees:* Enforceable in motor vehicle time sales contracts up to 15% of balance due.

MISSISSIPPI (Code, 1972). *Judgment notes:* Void. *Confessions of judgment:* Void, including small loan contracts. *Attorneys' fees:* Enforceable for nonsalaried attorney in motor vehicle time sales contracts, up to 15% of balance due.

MISSOURI (Revised Statutes). *Judgment notes:* No statutory provision. *Confessions of judgment:* Valid, if taken for money due or to become due, or as security against contingent liability, and made in separate verified statements. *Attorneys' fees:* Enforceable for nonsalaried attorney in time sales contracts of goods, up to 15% of balance due; also, on same conditions, in motor vehicle time sales contracts.

MONTANA (Code 1981). *Judgment notes:* Void, if in contract or in separate writing executed as part of same transaction. *Confessions of judgment:* Valid, without action. *Attorneys' fees:* Enforceable in time sales contracts up to 15% of balance due.

NEBRASKA (Revised Statutes). *Judgment notes:* No statutory provision. *Confessions of judgment:* May be made by debtor in person, with creditor's consent. Not valid in small loan contracts. *Attorneys' fees:* Court may grant reasonable fees in action for balance due on purchase of necessaries, up to $1,000, and debtor failed to pay after 90-days' notice.

NEVADA (Revised Statutes). *Judgment notes:* No statutory provision. *Confessions of judgment:* Valid, if for sums due or to become due, or to secure contingent liability. *Attorneys' fees:* Provision for reasonable fee in time sales contract valid.

NEW HAMPSHIRE (Revised Statutes). *Judgment notes:* No statutory provision. *Confessions of judgment:* Prohibited in motor vehicle time sales contracts; also prohibited in small loan contracts. *Attorneys' fees:* Provision for reasonable fee in motor vehicle time sales contracts valid; not r~cognized as permissible delinquency charge under small loan laws.

NEW JERSEY (Revised Statutes, 1937). *Judgment notes:* Not permitted. *Confessions of judgment:* Invalid in time sales contracts, or in separate instrument relating thereto; also invalid in home repair contracts and small loan contracts. *Attorneys' fees:* Enforceable in time sales contracts, and retail charge accounts if not more than 20% of first $500 and 10% of excess; also, in home repair contracts, if "reasonable." If state credit union reduces loan to judgment or gives to attorney for collection after default, it may collect attorneys' fees not to exceed 20% (minimum fee $10). Case law holds 20% fee for federal credit unions was reasonable (*Alcoa Edgewater No. FCU v. Carroll*, 210 A.2d 68, 1965).

NEW MEXICO (Statutes, Anno., 1978). *Judgment notes:* Void. *Confessions of judgment:* Void, if made before cause of action accrues on negotiable instrument or contract to pay money. Not permitted in time sales contracts or retail charge agreements. *Attorneys' fees:* Provisions for reasonable fees permitted in time sales contracts, retail charge agreements, or small loan agreements.

NEW YORK (Consolidated Laws). *Judgment notes:* No statutory provision. *Confessions of judgment:* May be made on debtor's affidavit; but judgment void if entered on affidavit made before debtor's default on installment purchases up to $1,500 of goods for nonbusiness or noncommercial use. Prohibited in time sales contracts, including motor vehicles; revolving credit agreements; small loan contracts. *Attorneys' fees:* Valid up to 20% of balance due on revolving credit agreements; up to 15% of balance due on motor vehicle time sales contracts; void on retail installment contracts. Credit unions may collect reasonable fees actually spent for necessary court process after debtor's default.

NORTH CAROLINA (General Statutes). *Judgment notes:* No statutory provision. *Confessions of judgment:* Enforceable, if made by signed, verified statement for money due or to become due, or to secure against a contingent liability. Prohibited in small loan contracts. *Attorneys' fees:* Enforceable up to 15% of outstanding balance.

NORTH DAKOTA (Century Code, Anno.). *Judgment notes:* No statutory provision. *Confessions of judgment:* Enforceable, if entered on debtor's signed, verified statement for a specific sum. Invalid in time sales contracts; also, small loan contracts. *Attorneys' fees:* Void as against public policy in notes and other evidences of debt.

OHIO (Revised Code). *Judgment notes:* Recognized. *Confessions of judgment:* Invalid if made in connection with consumer loans or consumer transactions, unless there is a conspicuous warning. *Attorneys' fees:* Not permitted in time sales contracts.

OKLAHOMA (Statutes, 1961). *Judgment notes:* No statutory provision. *Confessions of judgment:* Enforceable, if entered under warrant of attorney acknowledged by debtor, and if debtor first files affidavit as to the facts. Void in consumer credit transactions. *Attorneys' fees:* Reasonable if amount financed exceeds $1,000, and the credit service charge exceeds 10% per year.

OREGON (Revised Statutes). *Judgment notes:* No statutory provision. *Confessions of judgment:* Unenforceable in motor vehicle time sales contracts; invalid as to small loan contracts. *Attorneys' fees:* May provide for reasonable fees to nonsalaried attorney in time sales contracts of goods and revolving charge accounts; also, in motor vehicle time sales contracts. Prevailing party in suit on contract gets reasonable fee.

PENNSYLVANIA (Purdon's Statutes). *Judgment notes:* Recognized. *Confessions of judgment:* Valid. *Attorneys' fees:* Permitted in consumer financing. Fees up to 20% of balance due permitted in home improvement contracts. Credit unions may collect fees to public officals and reasonable fees of attorneys and outside collection agencies; but total of such fees can't exceed 20% of outstanding loan balance.

782

RHODE ISLAND (General Laws, 1956). *Judgment notes:* No statutory provision. *Confessions of judgment:* Prohibited in small loan contract. *Attorneys' fees:* Reasonable attorney's fees allowed.

SOUTH CAROLINA (Code, 1976). *Judgment notes:* No statutory provision. *Confessions of judgment:* Enforceable, if made by verified statement. Prohibited in small loan contracts. *Attorneys' fees:* In consumer credit sale, up to 15% of unpaid debt to nonsalaried attorney. May provide in small loan contracts for reasonable fee to be fixed by court. Reasonable fees permitted in motor vehicle time sales contracts.

SOUTH DAKOTA (Laws). *Judgment notes:* No statutory provision. *Confessions of judgment:* Valid, if made by verified statement. *Attorneys' fees:* Void as against public policy.

TENNESSEE (Code Anno.) *Judgment notes:* Invalid. *Confessions of judgment:* Invalid, if made before action started. *Attorneys' fees:* No statutory provision.

TEXAS (Vernon's Statutes). *Judgment notes:* Invalid. *Confessions of judgment:* Invalid, if made before action started. Prohibited in small loan contracts and retail installment contracts. *Attorneys' fees:* Assessed by the court in regulated loans and institutional loans. Reasonable fees awarded to nonsalaried attorneys in retail installment contracts and motor vehicle time sales contracts.

UTAH (Code Anno., 1953). *Judgment notes:* Not recognized. *Confessions of judgment:* Valid, if made on debtor's verified statement for money due or to become due or to secure contingent liability. Prohibited in consumer credit transactions. *Attorneys' fees:* Reasonable fee for loan contract.

VERMONT (Statutes, Anno.). *Judgment notes:* No statutory provision. *Confessions of judgment:* Valid, if made by debtor in writing, with creditor's consent; void in consumer contracts. Prohibited in small loan contracts. *Attorneys' fees:* Enforceable as to time sales contracts of goods and revolving charge accounts.

VIRGINIA (Code of 1950). *Judgment notes:* Valid; but warranty of attorney in note must name attorney and court in which judgment may be confessed. *Confessions of judgment:* May be entered in clerk's office at any time, but debtor has 21 days after notice of entry in which to move to have judgment set aside. Prohibited in small loan contracts. *Attorneys' fees:* No statutory provision.

WASHINGTON (Revised Code). *Judgment notes:* No statutory provision. *Confessions of judgment:* May be made on debtor's verified statement. Prohibited in small loan contracts. *Attorneys' fees:* May provide for reasonable fee in time sales contracts or revolving charge accounts.

WEST VIRGINIA (Code of 1961, Anno.). *Judgment notes:* No statutory provision. *Confessions of judgment:* May be made in action. Prohibited in small loan contracts. *Attorneys' fees:* No statutory provision.

WISCONSIN (Statutes, 1979-80). *Judgment notes:* Void and unenforceable. *Confessions of judgment:* Void and unenforceable. Prohibited in consumer credit transactions. *Attorneys' fees:* Enforceable under case law.

WYOMING (Statutes, 1977). *Judgment notes:* Valid. *Confessions of judgment:* May be made by debtor in open court, with creditor's consent; but attorney confessing judgment must show warrant of attorney. Void in consumer credit transactions. *Attorneys' fees:* Reasonable.

GARNISHMENT GUIDE

Below is a chart of state garnishment laws that summarizes the limitations imposed in each jurisdiction on wages subject to garnishment. Specific types of wage earners (such as heads of households) sometimes have different garnishment rates than other individuals, and these are noted in the chart. The figures in brackets following each state name refer to the footnotes following the chart, which indicate the penaltties that may result from failure to follow the state practice correctly.

Federal restrictions: Federal law exempts an employee's earnings during a workweek equal to 30 times the federal minimum wage or 75% of an employee's "disposable earnings," whichever is greater. "Disposable earnings" means earnings minus all deductions required by law. Union dues, initiation fees, employees' share of health and welfare premiums, and repayment of credit union loans aren't considered deductions required by law in determining "disposable income," but amounts withheld for unemployment and worker's compensation insurance pursuant to state law are considered such deductions.

Earning exemptions don't apply, however, to any court order for support of any person, court order of bankruptcy (under Chapter 13 of the Bankruptcy Act), or any debt due for state and federal taxes. These deductions do not lower the amount of disposable income. However, they are considered garnishments. Result: They count towards the 25% of disposable income that's available to other creditors. Therefore, when garnishment for taxes, support or under a bankruptcy order equals or exceeds the 25% figure, no deduction can be made to satisfy a second garnishment.

Law also prohibits an employer from firing an employee by reason of the fact his wages have been garnished for *any one indebtedness* (i.e., a single debt regardless of number of garnishment proceedings brought to collect it). Penalty for willful violation: up to $1,000 fine or one year's imprisonment, or both.

Alimony and child support: 60% of the disposable earnings of someone who isn't already supporting a spouse or child can be garnisheed for support; 65% if the employee's payments are more than 12 weeks in arrears. But if the employee supports another spouse or child, no more than 50% of disposable earnings can be garnisheed for support, or 55% if the payments are more than 12 weeks in arrears.

Federal taxes: The first $75 on a weekly basis of wages and salary is exempt from levy for U.S. taxes. There's an additional exemption of $25 per dependent per week if the employee furnished more than half the support during the payroll period and the person is the spouse or dependent of the employee. The exemption doesn't apply for a minor child who is receiving support from the employee under a court order. If the payroll period is other than a week, an equivalent amount will be exempt from levy over a period of time as if on a weekly basis.

If federal and state laws do not agree, law that provides for lesser garnishment or greater restriction on firing will control.

The U.S. Secretary of Labor, acting through the Wage Hour Division, will enforce federal garnishment provisions.

The chart and related materials originally appeared in Prentice-Hall, Inc., Installment Sales (looseleaf service).

ALABAMA (Code). [2] [5] *Laborers and resident employees:* 75% of wages is exempt. Up to 40% of parent's disposable earnings may be garnished for support of minor child. "Disposable earnings" includes compensation for personal services remaining after deduction of amounts required by law.

Judgments on consumer credit sale, lease, or loan: Greater of 80% of disposable weekly earnings or 50 times federal hourly minimum wage in effect when payable is exempt; disposable earnings doesn't include periodic payments pursuant to pension, retirement, or disability program. No garnishment can be made before judgment.

ALASKA (Statutes). [2] Debtor is entitled to exemption from garnishment of $192.50 for weekly net earnings ($302.50 if debtor's earnings alone support his or her household). Divide wages of employee paid semi-monthly by 2.16 to get weekly earnings; for employees paid monthly divide by 4.3. Doesn't apply to child support orders, unpaid earnings up to one month's compensation for personal services of an employee, or state and local taxes.

Employer must pay into court all nonexempt earnings subject to garnishment. Garnishments are effective when served on employer. Exemptions aren't applicable in claims for child support, unpaid earnings up to one month's compensation for personal services to employee, or state and local taxes.

Discharge: Employee can't be discharged for garnishment for any one indebtedness.

ARIZONA (Revised Statutes). [3] [5] [8] Lesser of 25% of disposable income or 30 times the federal minimum hourly wage in effect when payable is exempt. This exemption doesn't apply to court support orders; in this case only 50% of disposable income is exempt; nor does it apply to any bankruptcy orders or debts for state or federal taxes where there is no exemption.

Earnings of a minor child aren't subject to garnishment for parent's debt if the debt wasn't for the special benefit of the child.

ARKANSAS (Statutes). [2] *Laborers and mechanics:* Wages for 60 days are exempt if employee files affidavit with court stating that 60 days' wages together with other personal property he owns doesn't exceed state constitutional limitation ($200 for single resident not head of family, $500 for married resident or head of family). First $25 of "net wages" of all mechanics and laborers absolutely exempt without need for filing schedule of exemptions. "Net wages" means gross wages less following deductions actually withheld: Ark. income tax, fed. income tax, Social Security, group retirement, group hospitalization insurance premiums, and group life insurance premiums.

Employees of railroads have exemption of $200 before judgment by creditor.

Child support: Court order for child support can require employer to deduct from earnings amount necessary to comply with order.

CALIFORNIA (Deering's Calif. Codes) [2] Maximum amount subject to garnishment can't exceed lesser of (a) 25% of weekly disposable income, or (b) amount by which disposable earnings for week exceeds 30 times federal minimum hourly wage in effect when payable. Exemptions: all earnings necessary for the support of employee or his family *unless* (1) debt is incurred for personal services rendered for the employer; (2) debt is incurred by employee or his or her family for necessaries; (3) withholding order is for support; or (4) withholding order is for state taxes. If withholding order is for support, 50% of employee's earnings plus amounts withheld for court-ordered child support payments. The 50% share of a monthly pension payment awarded to a divorced spouse under California's community property law is considered the divorced spouse's separate property and not a part of ex-mate's disposable earnings. Therefore, withholding 55% of the remaining pension allotment does not violate federal garnishment restrictions.

Retirement plans: All amounts held, controlled, or in process of distribution under a public or private retirement plan are exempt from garnishment. However, when they become payable to a person, they are exempt only to the extent determined by the court if they are sought to be applied to a judgment for support. If the amounts are payable periodically, they are subject to wage assignment for support or any other applicable enforcement procedure, up to 50% of disposable earnings.

Priorities: Employer must comply in order service is made. If more than one order is served on same day, the order based on the earlier judgment is to be honored. If judgments are entered on the same day, employer may choose which to honor. Withholding for support takes priority over other earnings withholding orders. However, wage assignment for support of a minor child will not be affected and employer could withhold earnings under both an earnings withholding order and court-ordered child support payment.

Employer may be required to attend court and be examined [Civ. Pro. Code §491.010].

Discharge: Employer can't be discharged because garnishment has been threatened or because wages have been subjected to garnishment for one judgment or for any one indebtedness.

COLORADO (Revised Statutes, 1973). [2] [5] Maximum amount subject to garnishment is the lesser of 25% of weekly disposable earnings or amount by which weekly earnings exceed 30 times federal minimum hourly wage in effect when payable. Maximum amount subject to garnishment for support can't exceed 50% of weekly disposable earnings where employee is supporting a child or spouse (in addition to child or spouse covered in garnishment order); 60% if employee isn't supporting other spouse or dependent; if there are arrearages in support payments of over 12 weeks, additional 5% can be garnished [§13-54-104].

No garnishment can be made before judgment.

Priorities: Employer can withhold claims that it would have had if not garnisheed.

Discharge: Employee can't be discharged or refused employment because garnishment has been attempted or because his wages have been garnisheed.

Judgment, on consumer credit sale, lease, or loan: Lesser of 25% of disposable weekly earnings or excess over 30 times federal minimum hourly wage is maximum subject to garnishment.

CONNECTICUT (General Statutes). [2] [5] Greater of: 75% of disposable income or 40 times the federal minimum wage in effect when payable, is exempt.

Support: The first $100 or 50% of disposable income (whichever is greater) is exempt if the obligor must also support another spouse and/or children; the first 40% is exempt if he or she is not. An additional 5% is subject to garnishment if the support order is 12 or more weeks in default. *Special exemption:* Police officers, teachers, and Board of Education members are all immune from property attachments if a judgment is obtained based on their conduct in those capacities.

Priorities: Only one money judgment execution at a time can be satisfied. They're satisfied in the order they're presented to employer. Execution on wages for support of wife or minor child (children) takes priority over other executions and two or more can be levied at the same time provided total levy leaves the statutory minimum of disposable earnings a week. Voluntary wage deduction authorization for payment of amounts due for support in public welfare and other cases has same priority as execution on wages for support. (Voluntary wage execution will not be allowed unless prior order of support has been filed in circuit court. No voluntary wage deduction authorization will be effective less than 14 days from date of signing of authorization.)

Discharge: Employer can't discipline, suspend, or discharge employee because his wages have been garnished, unless more than 7 garnishments in calendar year. Employer who violates provision is liable to employee for all wages and employment benefits lost by employee from time of unlawful discipline, suspension, or discharge to time of reinstatement.

DELAWARE (Code Anno.) [5] 85% of wages is exempt for all residents; *but* if debt is for a fine or costs, or state taxes, limit doesn't apply; no wage garnishment for 60 days of default on contract or installment payments.

Support: Court may attach employee's wages if, after notice to employee and a hearing, it finds a support order has been violated. Attachment applies without regard to the exemptions and limitations provided for other garnishments, up to the federal limits; up to 50% of unemployment compensation can be attached. A voluntary assignment of wages may be accepted in lieu of attachment. Employer will deduct specified amount from net wages for the duration of employment or until otherwise ordered. Failure to comply or discharge of employee because of attachment will result in penalty of $1000 or up to 90 days' imprisonment for first offense, $5000 or up to 1 year's imprisonment for subsequent offenses. When an employee defending against a support order fails to notify the family court within 5 days after a change of address, the employee can be held in contempt of court and have wages attached.

Priorities: Only one attachment may be made per month; support attachments have priority over everything except federal tax liens.

Discharge: It is unlawful for employer to dismiss employee for garnishment.

DISTRICT OF COLUMBIA (Code, 1973). [2] Greater of: (1) 75% of disposable weekly wages or (2) 30 times federal minimum hourly wage in effect when payable, is exempt. (Doesn't apply to judgments for support; instead, 50% of employee's gross wages is exempt.) Wages of D.C. employees are subject to garnishment for child support, maintenance, or alimony. Employer can't withhold more than 10% of employee's gross wages until total amount paid employee for all pay periods in month exceeds $200; can't withhold more than 20% of wages over $200 until total amount paid employee equals $500.

Wages of nonresident (if major portion earned outside D.C.) are exempt to same extent provided by laws of state of his residence. Exemption applies only to contracts or transactions entered into outside D.C.

$200 of earnings (other than wages), insurance, annuities, or pension or retirement payments for 2 months preceding issuance of garnishment is exempt if person is resident or earns major portion of his livelihood in D.C. and is principal supporter of family before service of garnishment papers. If husband and wife live together, their total earnings determine exemption; $60 of earnings (other than wages), insurance, etc., for 2 months before service of garnishment papers is exempt if person doesn't support family.

No garnishment can be made before judgment.

Priorities: Only one attachment is satisfied at a time in order of priority of delivery to marshal. However, judgment for support may take priority (in discretion of court).

Discharge: Employee can't be discharged for garnishment or for attempted garnishment. The employer can collect a $2 fee for each support withholding.

FLORIDA (Statutes). [4] [17] [24] [25] *Head of family residing in Fla.* All wages are exempt.

Earnings of any person or public officer, state or county (whether head of family residing in Fla. or not), are subject to garnishment to enforce Florida court order for alimony, suit money, or support. Court, in its discretion, determines amount to be garnished. Court may issue continuing writ of garnishment for periodic payment of child support, alimony, or both.

Support: A court can order continuing garnishment to enforce existing alimony or support order or judgment, in an amount up to 65% of disposable income (if payments must be made to a central depository). Income deductions can also be made if the parent is two or more child support payments delinquent, and the child receives public assistance. Employers can collect a $1 fee for costs of withholding income.

GEORGIA (Code Anno.). [3] [5] [8] Greater of 75% of disposable weekly earnings or 30 times federal minimum wage, in effect when payable is exempt. All post-1985 support orders contain a provision that default of a month's support or more can be enforced by garnishment. Maximum subject to garnishment for alimony or support is 50% of disposable weekly earnings. $2,500 of wages due deceased employee of railroad company or other corporation is exempt. Wages due employee after he's been ordered involuntarily hospitalized for mental illness are exempt. Salaries of employees and officers of the state and its political subdivisions are subject to garnishment, except where liability for the garnishment is incurred as a result of responding to an emergency while engaged in the scope of their employment. Under these circumstances, the garnishment summons is served upon the appropriate person of the political entity for which the official or employee works.

Default judgment against employer for failure to answer can be modified on motion to the greater of $50 or $50 plus 100% of amount due employee, less exemption, from time of service to last day timely answer could be made.

Discharge: Employee can't be discharged for garnishment for any one indebtedness.

HAWAII (Revised Statutes). [5] Following wages are exempt from garnishment: 95% of first $100 per month, 90% of next $100, and 80% of all sums over $200; all compensation for personal

787

services that were rendered during a 31-day period before the date of the garnishment proceedings.

Wages subject to garnishment are those earnings remaining after the deduction of any amounts required by law to be withheld.

Employee can withhold (liquidated) claims that he would have had if he hadn't been garnished.

Priorities: Garnishments are paid in order of service of process on employer. If 2 or more are served at same time, order of issuance from court determines priority. In general, child support takes first priority.

Discharge: Employer can't suspend or discharge employee because he was summoned as garnishee in action where employee is debtor or because employee filed petition to pay debts under wage earner plan of Bankruptcy Act; can't refuse to hire or take other disciplinary action because of child support orders.

IDAHO (Code). [4] [5] Greater of 75% of disposable earnings or 30 times federal minimum hourly wage, in effect when payable, is exempt. Doesn't apply to support orders, bankruptcy orders, debt for state or federal tax.

Support: Maximum earnings subject to garnishment: 50% of disposable earnings if supporting a dependent child or spouse other than the spouse or child covered by the support order (55% if there are arrearages over 12 weeks); 60% if not supporting other spouse or dependent child (65% if there are arrearages over 12 weeks).

Married woman's wages are exempt from execution for husband's debt.

Child support: 50% of disposable earnings *or* earnings minus the sum of current support plus amounts ordered to be paid toward arrears.

Priorities: Support (especially child support) is entitled to priority; two or more withholding orders, nonexempt earnings are apportioned among creditors to pay current support, then arrears.

Discharge: Discharge premised on consumer credit garnishment is forbidden; so is disciplinary action or employment discrimination based on withholding for child support.

Judgments on consumer credit sale, lease, or loan: Lesser of 25% of disposable earnings or excess over 40 times federal minimum hourly wage, in effect when payable, is maximum subject to garnishment. No prejudgment garnishment permitted. Employee can't be discharged for garnishment; employee discharged in violation of provision has 60 days to bring civil action to recover lost wages and for order requiring reinstatement.

ILLINOIS (Anno. Statutes). [2] [22] Lesser of: 15% of gross maximum wages, salary, commissions and bonuses paid for the week or the amount by which disposable earnings for the week exceed 40 times the federal minimum hourly wage in effect when paid. No payroll deductions required by law to be withheld may be taken from the nonexempt amount.

Employer is entitled to fee consisting of the greater of $8 or 2% of amount paid pursuant to deduction order or series or orders on the same debt; $4 or actual processing cost for support orders.

Support: Court must order withholding in amount ordered for support, plus up to an additional 20% for arrears.

Priorities: First summons served has priority over subsequent garnishments, which are effective until paid or until end of payroll period immediately prior to 56 days after service in the order in which they are served. Employer can withhold claims it would have had if it hadn't been garnished. *Note:* Claims for the support of a spouse or dependent children have priority over all other claims for garnishment of property or other liens obtained on an employee's wages.

INDIANA (Statutes Anno.). [4] [18]. Wages can't be garnished if employee and creditor are nonresidents and, employer is doing business in Indiana. In other situations, lesser of 25% of disposable earnings or 30 times the federal minimum wage.

Support: Maximum earnings subject to garnishment is: 50% (55% if there are arrearages over 12 weeks) of disposable earnings if supporting a dependent child or spouse other than the spouse or child covered by support order; 60% (65% if there are arrearages over 12 weeks) if not supporting other spouse or dependent child.

Judgments on consumer credit sale, lease, or loan: Maximum subject to garnishment is 25% of disposable weekly earnings in excess of 30 times federal minimum wage in effect when payable. Doesn't apply to court orders for support of any person or decrees awarding alimony or attorney's fees. No prejudgment garnishment permitted. Employees can't be discharged for such garnishment; employees discharged in violation of provision have 6 months to bring civil action to recover lost wages and for order requiring reinstatement.

Employer can deduct a fee of greater of $12 or 3% of total required to be garnisheed. If employer chooses to impose fee, fee is collectible $1/2$ from debtor and $1/2$ from creditor and can be collected only once for each garnishment order or series of orders from same judgment debt. Deductions for a collection of fee do not increase judgment debt for which fee is collected.

Priorities: Court-ordered assignment for child support has priority over all other assignments, garnishments, and attachments (except taxes).

IOWA (Code). [2] [5] [19] Greater of 75% of disposable earnings or 30 times federal minimum hourly wage, in effect when payable, in judgment on consumer credit sale, lease, or loan, is exempt. Consumer can get a higher exemption on proof of hardship. Maximum amount that can be garnisheed in one calendar year is $250 for each creditor (except under decrees for support of minors).

However, if a head of household's expected earnings for the year are at least $12,000 but less than $16,000—the maximum is $400; if at least $16,000 but less than $24,000—the maximum is $800; if at least $24,000 but less than $35,000—$1,500; if at least $35,000 but less than $50,000—$2,000; if $50,000 or more—10% of expected earnings.

Exemptions don't apply to judgments for (1) alimony or (2) support of minors.

Wages earned outside Iowa by nonresident, payable outside state, are exempt from garnishment where creditor is nonresident and cause of action arose outside state.

Priorities: Delinquent child support has priority over other garnishments and attachments. Exemptions don't apply to orders of bankruptcy court.

Discharge: Employee can't be discharged for garnishment.

Judgment on consumer credit sale, lease, or loan: Lesser of 25% of disposable earnings for week or excess over 40 times federal hourly wage in effect when payable; no pre-judgment garnishments are permitted; employee can't be discharged for garnishment arising from consumer credit transaction.

KANSAS (Statutes Anno.) [2] [5] [13] Greater of 75% of disposable weekly earnings or 30 times federal minimum hourly wage. Doesn't apply to court order for support, order of bankruptcy court, or debt for state or federal tax. Limitation on garnishment for support of any person is 50% of an individual's disposable earnings *unless person seeking the garnishment specifies a greater amount to be withheld;* then maximum disposable earnings in a workweek subject to garnishment can't exceed: (1) 60% (65% if there are arrearages over 12 weeks), or (2) 50% if worker is supporting a spouse or dependent child other than the ones in the court order (55% if there are arrearages over 12 weeks). Those grounds must be clearly stated on order of garnishment.

Order effective against nonexempt portion of earnings for entire normal pay period in which order is served.

Wages earned and payable outside state are exempt where cause of action arose outside state unless debtor is personally served with garnishment.

If employee has been out of work for more than 2 weeks because of sickness (or sickness of family member), evidenced by his affidavit, all wages are exempt until 2 months after recovery.

Wages can't be garnisheed by collector or collecting agency.

No prejudgment garnishment orders can be issued against wages. *Exceptions:* Prejudgment garnishment allowed for support payments granted in divorce proceedings.

Discharge: Employee can't be discharged for garnishment or subjected to disciplinary action because of a withholding order.

KENTUCKY (Revised Statutes). [3] [5] Greater of 75% of disposable earnings or 30 times federal minimum hourly wage in effect when payable is exempt. Doesn't apply to support orders, bankruptcy court orders, debt for state or federal tax.

Where wages are earned and payable outside of state, that state's law concerning exemptions applies to Kentucky garnishment *unless* employee was personally served in Kentucky or was Kentucky resident when debt or cause of action arose.

Prejudgment garnishments can be obtained by making demand on defendant in writing, advising him of grounds of suit and his right to hearing.

Support: (administrative child support orders) 50% of disposable income, up to federal limits; (court-ordered) federal limits.

Priorities: Orders have priority according to date of service on employer. Court-ordered or administrative assignment for support of minor child has priority.

Discharge: No discharge for garnishment for any one indebtedness; no adverse action for a withholding order.

LOUISIANA (Revised Statutes). [2] [14] 75% of disposable earnings for any week, but exemption can't be less than 30 times the federal minimum hourly wage in effect at time earnings are payable; 50% of disposable earnings is exempt for purposes of paying current or past due support obligation or for payment of support obligation for a spouse or former spouse receiving support enforcement services from the Dept. of Health & Human Resources.

Exemption doesn't apply to court-ordered support payments for parents by children or grandchildren.

Wages earned and payable outside state are exempt where cause of action arose outside of state.

Priorities: Debt between employer and employee is treated as prior garnishment. However, garnishment or mandatory assignment of person's wages for child's support always takes priority over all garnishment orders.

Discharge: Employee can't be discharged or denied employment because of a single garnishment; employee's remedy includes award for reinstatement and backpay. (Discharge for 3 unrelated garnishments in 2 years is permitted.)

MAINE (Revised Statutes). [2] Greater of 75% of disposable earnings or 30 times federal minimum hourly wage prescribed by 206(a)(1) of Title 29 U.S.C. is exempt. Exempt amounts do not apply to support orders, bankruptcy orders, debt for federal or state taxes, and consumer credit transactions. If garnishment order is issued without notice (because employee failed to make payments under earlier order), exemption can't be less than $100 a week.

Wages of minor children and wife aren't subject to garnishment for parent's or husband's debt.

Support: Maximum amount subject to garnishment for support orders will not exceed 50% of disposable income if person owing support is supporting another spouse or dependent child; 60% if person not supporting another spouse or child. Additional 5% subject to garnishment for support if there are arrearages over 12 weeks.

Discharge: Employee can't be discharged because earnings have been subject to garnishment orders, or subjected to adverse employment action because of support orders.

Judgments on consumer credit sale, lease, or loan: Greater of 75% of disposable weekly earnings or 40 times federal minimum hourly wage in effect when payable is exempt; no prejudgment garnishments are permitted; employee can't be discharged for garnishment arising from consumer credit transaction.

MARYLAND (Code). [2][9] Greater of $120 times number of weeks wages due at date of attachment, when earned, or 75% of such wages due, is exempt. *Caroline, Worcester, Kent, and Queen Anne's Counties:* Greater of 75% of wages due or 30 times federal minimum hourly wage in effect when payable is exempt. $50 plus $15 for each withholding exemption claimed by employee is exempt per week.

Court can order lien on earnings of defendant in paternity suit. Nonsupport court orders will be lien on notification by Probation Dept.

Priorities: Only one attachment is satisfied at a time in order of priority of service. Withholding orders for support take priority over other liens.

Discharge: Employee can't be discharged for garnishment on any one indebtedness in calendar year; violations are misdemeanors punishable by fines of up to $1,000 and/or a year's imprisonment.

MASSACHUSETTS (General Laws). [4] $125 a week of wages due is exempt. $100 a week of pensions payable to employee is exempt. Exemptions do not apply to court-ordered family support obligations including action for trustee process to enforce support order; federal provisions apply instead.

Wages due for personal services of defendant's (employee's) wife or minor child are exempt. Seaman's wages can't be garnisheed (subject to attachment by trustee process), but fisherman's can.

Support: Dept. of Public Welfare—in order to locate and establish liability of any person legally obligated to pay spousal or child support—can ask an employer to provide information concerning that person's wages and dates paid, last known address, social security number, and available health or medical insurance benefits. Inquiries can be made only once every 4 months. Employees must give full written responses for the period beginning 4 months before date of request. Complying employers aren't liable in any suit brought by an employee because of their compliance. Any employer that fails to comply or willfully gives false information can be fined $100 for each violation.

Priorities: Employer can withhold (liquidated) claims that he would have had if he hadn't been garnisheed (summoned as trustee). Valid wage assignment held as security for a debt has priority over garnishment (trustee process).

MICHIGAN (Statutes Anno.). [3][5] Federal exemptions apply: maximum subject to garnishment is lesser of 25% of disposable wages or 30 times federal minimum wage in effect.

Support: Order of income withholding for support may be applied to any wages, commissions, or other income from employer and to any payment from profit-sharing plan, pension plan, insurance, annuity, social security, unemployment compensation, supplemental unemployment benefits and workers' compensation. Order is binding 7 days after service on employer. Compliance discharges employer's liability to employee for income affected. Court may find employer in contempt for failure to comply. Employer must notify court if payments to employee terminate. Employer may deduct additional 50¢ for each payment under a withholding order. Withholding order may not be used as basis of discharge, discipline, or penalty. Employer who penalizes employee because of withholding order is guilty of misdemeanor, subject to fine of not more than $500, and will be required to make full restitution, including reinstatement and back pay.

Discharge: No employer can use garnishment as sole cause of discharge.

MINNESOTA (Statutes). [2] [5] Greater of 75% of disposable earnings for a pay period or an amount of such wages equal to 40 times the federal minimum hourly wage in effect when payable, times the number of work weeks in such pay period, is exempt. Orders for support of spouse or minor child are not subject to statutory limitations. If the employee was on relief or in a state correctional institution, all wages for 6 months after return to work, and after all public assistance has ended, are exempt. Such exemption can be applied only once every 3 years. Exempt disposable earnings are exempt for 20 days after deposit in any financial institution; and for 60 days after deposit if the employee was on relief or an inmate in a correctional institution prior to employment. Assignment, sale, or transfer of any earned or unearned wages is invalid if made after service of a garnishment exemption notice and within 10 days before receipt of the first garnishment or execution on the debt.

Earnings of minor child can't be garnisheed for debt of parent unless debt was for special benefit of minor.

If amount garnisheed is less than $10, it will not be withheld. Employer is relieved of liability after the expiration of 270 days in a prejudgment summons, or 180 days in summons served after garnishment.

Priorities: Garnishments are paid in order of service of garnishee papers on employer. More than one garnishment can be paid at a time limited to total nonexempt disposable earnings.

Discharge: Employee can't be discharged for garnishment, or wage withholding for support purposes. Employee has 90 days from discharge to bring civil action for twice wages lost due to violation and for reinstatement order.

Support: If court orders deductions from employee's pay for support of child supported in whole or part by public agency, employee must notify employer, who must withhold money according to order and remit quarterly to Commissioner of Public Welfare, Attn.: Accounting Dept., Administrative Services.

State taxes: Commissioner of Revenue can require withholding from wages of employee delinquent in state taxes. Employer must withhold subject to garnishment exemptions and continue to withhold each pay period until total amount is paid. State claim has priority over any subsequent garnishments or wage assignments. Employer can't discharge employee because of filing for delinquent taxes.

MISSISSIPPI (Code). [2][5] Wages are exempt for 30 days from date employer received writ of garnishment. After 30 days, lesser of 25% of disposable weekly earnings or amount by which disposable weekly earnings exceed 30 times the federal minimum hourly wage if subject to garnishment. Limitations don't apply to court orders for support and debts due for any state tax. Employer indebted to an employee for wages or other compensation during first 30 days after service of writ of garnishment must pay over to employee all indebtedness and thereafter retain that nonexempt percentage of disposable earnings for a period of time necessary to accumulate amount due the court as shown on writ. Unless otherwise authorized by the court, employer must keep all sums collected and make only one payment when total due on writ has accumulated. At least one payment per year must be made of amount withheld during the previous year. If employment is terminated for any reason, employer must, within 15 days, report to the court and pay all sums withheld [§11-35-23].

Support: Maximum earnings subject to garnishment is: 50% (55% if there are arrearages over 12 weeks) of disposable weekly earnings if employee is supporting a spouse or dependent (other than spouse or child for whom support order was issued); 60% (65% if there are arrearages over 12 weeks) if employee isn't supporting a spouse or dependent child.

Proceeds of any trust created by employer as part of pension plan, disability or death benefit plan, or any trust created under retirement plan that is exempt from federal income tax aren't subject to garnishment.

Priorities: Employer complies first with garnishment first served; if more than one received on same day, writ with smallest amount is satisfied first. Garnishment issued under order for child support gets first priority even if others are in effect or pending. Conflicting or later garnishments must be returned to the issuing court with a statement that a previous garnishment is in effect; statement will hold a garnishment until prior ones are satisfied, then collection is immediately begun of writ with next priority.

MISSOURI (Revised Statutes). [4][5] Greater of (a) 75% of disposable weekly earnings; (b) 30 times federal minimum hourly wage in effect when payable; or (c) if resident head of family, 90% of disposable earnings is exempt. Doesn't apply to support orders, orders of bankruptcy court, or for debt due for state or federal taxes. (This includes garnishment to collect attorney's fees granted to wife in matrimonial action).

Where wages are earned and payable outside of state, employee is exempt from garnishment *unless* personally served.

Support: Dir. of the Div. of Family Services can issue garnishment order in an amount not to exceed federal wage garnishment limitations when support payments under state plan are in arrears. It has priority over all later executions or garnishments. Where there are multiple orders exceeding the statutory limits, current support is satisfied first in the order the orders were served, then delinquencies in the order served. Any employer that willfully refuses to comply with an order is liable for amount that should have been withheld. Compliance relieves employer of any liability for wrongful withholding.

Discharge: Employee can't be fired for garnishment for any one indebtedness, or suffer job adverse action because of support withholding.

MONTANA (Code Anno.). [2][5] Greater of (a) 75% of disposable weekly earnings; (b) 30 times federal minimum hourly wage in effect when payable.

Child support: Substituted percentages of disposable earnings: 60% if debtor is not supporting another spouse or child, 50% if he is—plus an additional 5% if arrears greater than 12 weeks. Garnishment is set at a level that will clear the arrears within 2 years; *or* 25% of disposable income, but not more than the federal limits.

All earnings for preceding 30 days are exempt in actions for $10 or less.

Order for deduction from wages of delinquent court-ordered child support has priority over any assignment of wages, voluntary deductions, or other court-ordered garnishment.

Priorities: Executed in order received by the sheriff.

Discharge: Employee can't be discharged for garnishment served on employer or subject to adverse job action for support order.

NEBRASKA (Revised Statutes). [2][5] Lesser of (a) 25% of weekly disposable earnings (including pension or retirement program payments); (b) excess of 30 times federal minimum hourly wage in effect when payable; or (c) 15% of disposable earnings if employee head of household, is subject to garnishment. Doesn't apply to support orders of any person, orders of bankruptcy court, or for debt due for state or federal taxes.

No prejudgment action for garnishment may be filed in small claims court.

Discharge: Employees can't be discharged for garnishment for any one indebtedness.

Child support: Court order for child support can require employer to withhold fixed amount or percentage from employee's nonexempt disposable earnings to reduce arrears or to pay child support payments and any attorney's fees. (Nonexempt disposable earnings are excess for each workweek of 30 times federal minimum hourly wage in effect when payable.) Employer can deduct a court-fixed amount up to $5 a month for costs. Employee can't be dismissed or penalized for any orders. Orders to withhold have priority over any other garnishment or wage assignment, unless otherwise ordered by court.

NEVADA (Revised Statutes). [2][5][8] Lesser of 25% of disposable weekly earnings or excess over 30 times federal minimum hourly wage in effect when payable is subject to garnishment. Exemption doesn't apply to any court orders in bankruptcy, for support or debt due for state or federal taxes.

Employer can offset amounts due him from employee *and* creditor.

Creditor must pay employer $5 fee at time of service of the writ of garnishment.

Child support: Exempt amounts range from 45–65% of disposable earnings, depending on whether there are arrears, and whether the obligor is supporting others. An additional 10% of current support can be ordered to pay off arrears.

NEW HAMPSHIRE (Revised Statutes). [2][5] All wages earned by employee after service of garnishment papers on employer are exempt.

All wages earned before service of garnishment papers are exempt, unless judgment on debt was issued by N.H. court. In such cases, exemption for each week is 50 times federal minimum wage as set by the federal Wage-Hour Law.

Earnings of wife and minor children of employee are exempt.

$50 a week of wages earned by employee before service of garnishment papers is exempt if main action is based on small loan contract.

All wages of married woman are exempt if action is based on small loan contract to which her husband is, or was at any time, obligor.

Exemptions don't apply in action for taxes by Tax Collector.

Child support: 50% of disposable earnings of responsible parent is exempt from garnishment for court order for child support. Order remains in effect until entire support debt is paid. Employee can't be discharged for support lien served on employer.

NEW JERSEY (Statutes Anno.). [1] (If employee earns $48 or more a week, 10% of his wages may be garnisheed, if he earns less than $48, no garnishment. If employee earns more than $7,500 a year, a Court may increase percentage to be garnisheed. Wages of nonresident employee can't be attached by nonresident creditor or his assigns.

Support: Every court order for alimony, maintenance, or child support must include a notice stating that order can be enforced by an income execution. The person owed support or the county agency administering the Federal Social Security Act on that person's behalf can apply to the county probation office for an income execution after the employee fails to make a payment equivalent to 14 days' support. Income executions for support have priority over all other executions and are binding on employer 1 week after service. Employer can deduct $1 for each payment from the employee's remaining salary. The employer can't discharge or discipline an employee because of an income execution.

Employer can retain as compensation 5% of amount deducted pursuant to garnishment.

Priorities: Only one execution can be satisfied at a time in order in which they are served on employer. *Exceptions:* Support orders for child or wife have priority over other executions; withholdings for support made by the probation department have priority over other withholdings.

NEW MEXICO (Statutes, Anno.). [2][5] Either 75% of disposable earnings each pay period or 40 times federal minimum hourly wage each week, whichever is greater, is exempt.

Child support: 50% of disposable earnings for any pay period is exempt from garnishment for child support. Court may order wage deductions if payments are delinquent 60 days or more. Maximum of 50% of disposable earnings may be taken under both garnishment and wage deduction procedure. Employee may be charged up to $1 for each pay period in which deduction is made.

Priorities: Liens will be satisfied in order in which they are served on employer.

Support: Enforcement Act withholding takes priority over all other legal process.

NEW YORK (Consolidated Laws). [2][5][7] *Income execution:* 90% of earnings for personal services rendered within 60 days before, and any time after, income execution is exempt, *but* employees may be garnisheed to the extent of 10% of his wages only when they're receiving or will receive more than $85 a week. Only cash wages may be used in determining whether wages are subject to execution.

Earnings of actual or potential recipients of public assistance are exempt.

Garnishment proceeding, court not of record: 10% of earnings can be garnisheed by court order if judgment has been recovered in a court not of record against an employee whose income is (1) $30 or more a week if he resides or works in a city of 250,000 or more, or (2) $25 a week in any other case. Only one garnishment can be satisfied at a time. If 2 or more are issued simultaneously, they are satisfied in the order they are served on the employer.

Child support: 35-50% of disposable income is exempt (depending on the presence or absence of arrears and other dependents); if the support deduction is less than 25% of disposable income, deductions can be made to satisfy the other orders until the 25% limit is reached.

Priorities: Garnishments are paid in the order in which the executions were delivered to an officer authorized to levy in the county, town, or city in which the employee resides or, if the employee's a nonresident, the county, town, or city in which he's employed. Assignment or court order for support of minor child and/or spouse takes priority over other assignment or garnishment of wages, etc., except as to deductions made mandatory by law. Support income executions precede all other assignments, levies, and process.

Discharge: No employee may be laid off or discharged because one or more executions have been served against his wages; employee has 90 days from discharge to bring civil action for damages for wages lost (not to exceed lost wages for 6 weeks); court may order reinstatement. Not more than 10% of the damages recovered in such action may be subjected to claims, attachments, or executions.

NORTH CAROLINA (General Statutes). [2] *Head of family:* All earnings for 60 days before service of garnishment papers are exempt if necessary for support of employee's family.

Garnishment is limited to 10% of salary or wages paid in any one month in state tax collection proceedings; to 10% of wages in any one pay period in municipal and county property tax collection proceeding. Wages due officials or employees of N.C., its agencies, instrumentalities, and political subdivisions are subject to garnishment for delinquent taxes.

Priorities: Priority in the order attachments were levied.

Child support: Independent garnishment proceeding is available for enforcement of child support obligations; 40% of responsible parent's disposable earnings is subject to garnishment for court-ordered child support. Total withholding can reach 45-50% for multiple child support withholding orders. Child support enforcement agency may garnishee unemployment benefits due responsible parent to satisfy child support obligation. Withholding for current support takes precedence over past-due support. If two families are entitled to support orders, they divide the withheld amounts pro rata according to the amount of the orders. Child support orders cannot be used as a premise for subjecting the obligor to adverse employment action.

NORTH DAKOTA (Century Code, Anno.). [4][8][16] Greater of 75% of disposable weekly earnings or 40 times federal minimum hourly wage in effect when payable is exempt. Doesn't apply to court orders for support of any person or of bankruptcy court or for debt for state or federal taxes. Maximum amount subject to garnishment for support can't exceed 50% of weekly disposable earnings if employee is supporting spouse or minor child in addition to spouse or child in garnishment order; 60% if employee isn't supporting other spouse or child. Another 5% can be garnisheed if there are arrearages in support payments of over 12 weeks. The maximum child support withholding order is 50% of disposable income.

Judge may order all of employee's earnings for personal services within 60 days of order exempted if affidavit shows they're necessary for support of employee's family.

Discharge: Employer may not discharge an employee because earnings have been subjected to garnishment—or a child support income withholding order.

Termination: Garnishee summons lapses and garnishee discharged of any liability after 180 days from service of summons unless otherwise ordered by court or agreed to in writing by debtor and creditor.

OHIO (Revised Code). [2][12] Greater of the following owed employee for services rendered within 30 days before attachment, process, judgment, or order is exempt: (1) 75% of disposable earnings owed, or (2) 30 times current federal minimum hourly wage in effect at time earnings are payable if paid weekly; 60 times if paid bi-weekly; 65 times if paid semi-monthly; 130 times if paid monthly. There must be at least 30 days between garnishments. Earnings can't be garnished for a debt that's the subject of debt scheduling agreement between employee and consumer credit counseling service (unless any payment under agreement is more than 45 days overdue or agreement is terminated).

Support orders have priority over all other garnishments and no part of wages is exempt from them (up to Federal limits). They are paid in order received. Employer may deduct up to 1% (but not over $2) as service charge.

Judgments for taxes, except for real estate, aren't entitled to exemptions.

Resident and nonresident can apply to court in jurisdiction of place of employment for appointment of trustee to avoid garnishment of nonexempt earnings.

Wages may be garnisheed only through an action in garnishment of personal earnings after a judgment is obtained by a creditor. If there are several orders of garnishment against the same employee, they must be served in order received by the levying officer. The employer must pay the earnings included in the garnishment order to the court ordering payment. Compliance discharges the employer from liability for wrongful withholding.

Discharge: Employee can't be discharged solely for attachment for no more than one action in garnishment in any 12-month period, or subjected to adverse action because of a support order.

OKLAHOMA (Statutes). [2][3][5] *Residents:* 75% of all wages for services performed within last 90 days is exempt except for certain collections of child support.

Employee can request for hearing to have portion of wages for services performed exempted from garnishment by reason of undue hardship if necessary for support of family, but not if judgment is for child support or maintenance.

Exemptions don't apply to nonresidents, or to debtor in the act of removing his family from the state or who has absconded, taking with him his family.

Wages of any clerk, mechanic, laborer, or servant aren't entitled to exemption.

Prejudgment garnishment: Prejudgment garnishment of wages can be made for support payments provided in a divorce proceeding interlocutory order; 75% of earnings for personal services earned during last 90 days are exempt *except* for child support obligations.

Child support: Exemption of 35-50% of disposable earnings (level calibrated on presence or absence of dependents, arrears). Support income assignments have priority over garnishments, but support income assignments and garnishments are equal in priority. Current support has priority over arrears.

Priorities: Priorities may be determined by court order.

Judgments on consumer credit sale, lease, or loan: Lesser of 25% of disposable earnings or excess over 30 times federal minimum hourly wage in effect when payable is maximum subject to garnishment. Employee's wages can't be garnisheed before judgment in an action. Employee can't be discharged unless employer garnisheed for 1 or more judgments on more than 2 occasions in 1 year.

OREGON (Revised Statutes). [3][4][5] Greater of 75% of disposable weekly earnings or 40 times federal minimum hourly wage is exempt. Doesn't apply to support orders (including awards of attorneys' fees or costs), bankruptcy orders, debt for state or federal tax. Protection of law can't be waived. Limitations don't apply to wage assignments for child support. Withholding as requested by the obligor, or on delinquent support payments, is at least 25% of disposable earnings or the amount of support, whichever is greater.

Any legal process served must indicate whether it is subject to garnishment restrictions.

Discharge: No employer can discharge any person for garnishment.

PENNSYLVANIA (Statutes, Anno.). [2][26] All wages are exempt.

Exceptions: Wages are subject to garnishment for 4 weeks' board and lodging.

Husband's wages can be garnisheed to pay support for wife and children. Under Civil Procedural Support Law, wages may be attached to enforce support ordered by court; employer is authorized to deduct 2% of amount paid under order from employee's wages for clerical work and expense of complying.

On tax collector's written notice and demand, employer must deduct from employee's wages, commissions, or earnings then owing (or that become due within 60 days thereafter), or from any unpaid commissioners or earnings in his possession (or that come into his possession within 60 days thereafter), a sum sufficient to pay employee's or his wife's delinquent *per capita, poll, occupation, occupational privilege, local earned income taxes,* and costs, and must pay this sum to tax collector within 60 days after receipt of notice. No more than 10% of wages, commissions, or earnings of delinquent taxpayer or husband can be deducted at one time. Employer may keep up to 2% of money collected for extra bookkeeping expenses.

RHODE ISLAND (General Laws). [2] $50 a week of earnings is exempt; all earnings of wife and minor child of employee are exempt; all wages of seamen are exempt. If employee was on relief, all his wages for one year are exempt. Garnishment for future wages is valid.

Priorities: Priority in order attachments were procured. Support has priority over all other garnishments.

SOUTH CAROLINA (Code of Laws). All earnings for personal services are exempt.

Judgments on consumer credit sale, lease, or loan: Creditor can't attach unpaid earnings of debtor by garnishment or like proceedings. Employee can't be discharged because of such garnishment.

Support: Court-ordered support withholding has the highest priority of any legal process against wages.

SOUTH DAKOTA (Compiled Laws, Anno.). [2][5] All earnings for personal services performed within 60 days before garnishment order are exempt if necessary for the use of a family supported wholly or partly by employee's labor.

Payments for foster care of children under programs of the division of child welfare of the department of public welfare aren't subject to garnishment, except for necessaries furnished for the subsistence and maintenance of such children.

Support: Secretary of social services may issue order to withhold and deliver up to 50% of earnings due a parent in arrears of any support payment, if support order has been issued by the secretary or by a court. Order to withhold and deliver is continuing and binding until further order and has priority over any other subsequent execution or garnishment. Employer may not discharge or refuse to hire because of such order. Person refusing to comply is liable for 100% of debt plus interest.

Garnishment of earnings is prohibited before final judgment. ("Earnings" include periodic payments under pension or retirement programs.)

TENNESSEE (Code, Anno.). [2][5][23] Lesser of 25% of disposable earnings for the week, or excess over 30 times the federal minimum hourly wage in effect when earnings payable is subject to garnishment. Additional $2.50 a week for each dependent child under 16 is exempt. Judgment is a lien on wages due at time of service of execution and on subsequent earnings until judgment is satisfied or until expiration of payroll period immediately prior to 3 calendar months after service, whichever is first.

Exemptions don't apply if judgment against employee is for alimony or child support; maximum support order is 50% of income less FICA and withholding taxes. Employers who handle support income assignments can charge up to 5% of salary or $5 per month as a transaction charge.

Above exemptions don't apply to taxes; or to fines and costs for voting out of district or ward where voter lives, carrying deadly or concealed weapons, or giving away or selling intoxicating liquors on election days.

Where wages are earned and payable outside of state, employee is exempt from garnishment *unless* served with process.

Priorities: Support income assignments have the highest priority (except legally mandated deductions). Among multiple support assignments, current support takes precedence over arrears.

TEXAS (West's Texas Statutes and Codes).

All current wages are exempt from garnishment, other than wage assignments for the enforcement of support orders. Only 50% of the obligor's disposable earnings are subject to withholding for support. A withholding order or writ has higher priority than any other legal process affecting the same wages. An employer may not premise adverse job action on the existence of a support order or writ, but may charge a monthly $5 administrative fee for performing the withholding.

UTAH (Code Anno.). [2][5][21] Employer can withhold claims that he would have had if he weren't garnisheed.

Discharge: Employee can't be discharged for garnishment for any one indebtedness; discharged or subjected to adverse employment action because of an income withholding notice or order (whether for child support or in connection with a civil action).

Judgments on consumer credit sale, lease, or loan: Greater of 75% of disposable weekly earnings or 30 times federal minimum hourly wage in effect when payable is exempt. No prejudgment garnishment is permitted.

Child support: Maximum disposable earnings for any work pay period that can be garnisheed to enforce judgment arising out of failure to support dependent children can't exceed federal limits.

VERMONT (Statutes, Anno.). [2][5] Greater of 75% of weekly disposable earnings or 30 times the federal minimum hourly wage is exempt. If debt arose from consumer credit transaction, the greater of 85% of weekly disposable earnings or 40 times the federal minimum hourly wages is exempt. Court can order a greater amount of earnings be exempt if employee's expenses for maintenance of self and dependents exceed exempt amounts.

No garnishment against wages can be made before final judgments.

Wages due minor child can't be garnisheed in action against parent; wages due married woman can't be garnisheed in action against husband.

Wages earned outside state by nonresident employee of a corporation are exempt if employee's state of residence also exempts them.

Employer can withhold claims (based on express or implied contract) that he would have had if he hadn't been garnisheed.

Weekly disposable earnings due in excess of 30 times federal minimum hourly wage in effect when payable are subject to a lien for delinquent poll tax or old age assistance tax at rate of $4 a week, regardless of any assignment of earnings.

Discharge: No employee can be discharged for garnishment. If employee is discharged within 60 days of employer's receipt of garnishment order, there is a rebuttable presumption that employee was discharged for garnishment. Employees discharged for garnishment can sue for reinstatement, back wages, and damages. Failure to withhold and deliver non-exempt earnings may make employer liable for such amounts plus costs.

VIRGINIA (Code). [1][5][6][11] Greater of 75% of disposable weekly earnings or 30 times federal minimum hourly wage in effect when payable is exempt unless otherwise specified on summons or ordered by court. Doesn't apply to court-ordered support, bankruptcy order, or debt for state or federal taxes. Limitations on garnishment for support of any person: (1) 60% of disposable earnings for a workweek (65% if arrearages of over 12 weeks); or (2) 50% of disposable earnings if supporting a spouse or dependent child other than person provided for in garnishment order (55% if arrearages of over 12 weeks). (Exemption doesn't extend to collection of local taxes.) "Earnings" includes periodic payments under pension or retirement program.

Every householder or head of a family residing in the state, in addition to the above exemption, is entitled to a $5,000 exemption. Veterans with a service-related disability of 40% or more also get another $2,000 exemption.

Wages of minors are exempt from garnishment for debts of parents.

Child support obligations recoverable through garnishment may include interest payable on arrearages. Deductions required to be made under an order for child support will be made at regular intervals consistent with the pay period of the person owing child support unless the person and employer expressly agree to a different interval for deduction; in a single monetary amount or the 50% maximum, whichever is less, beginning with the person's next regular pay period following service of the order on the employer.

Employers can collect $5 fee for each deduction made for employee's support debt. Employers with over 10,000 employees can collect a fee of up to $10 for their expenses in processing each garnishment summons.

Discharge: Employee can't be discharged for garnishment for any one indebtedness or for a support debt; employer can be fined up to $1,000 for the latter violation.

Note: Garnishments issued under the law of Virginia are exempt from federal restrictions on amounts that can be garnisheed because the state law has been found "substantially similar" to the federal.

WASHINGTON (Revised Code). [3][5] Greater of 30 times state minimum hourly wage or 75% of disposable weekly earnings is exempt. Deductions as contributions toward pension or retirement plan established pursuant to collective bargaining agreement aren't part of disposable earnings. Exemption doesn't apply to garnishment for child support if (a) based on judgment, court order, or order issued by Dept. of Social and Health Services, (b) amount doesn't exceed 2 months support payments, and (c) writ contains specific statutory language. Continuing lien on wages can be obtained.

"Earnings" includes periodic payments received pursuant to a pension or retirement program.

Priorities: Support orders have first priority over support wage assignments and garnishments; garnishments for continuing liens have priority over subsequent wage assignments or garnishment liens.

Discharge: Employer can't discharge employee unless employer is garnisheed on 3 or more separate indebtednesses, served within 12 consecutive months, or take adverse action against an employee who has assigned earnings to pay a support debt.

WEST VIRGINIA (Code, Anno.). [2][5][20] Greater of 80% of earnings in a week or 30 times federal minimum wage in effect is exempt; weekly wages payable to employee must exceed 30 times federal minimum hourly wage in effect.

Support: 35-50% of disposable income is exempt (depending on the number of persons supported and the presence or absence of arrears of 12 weeks or more). The employer is entitled to a 50¢ fee whenever withholding is made.

Priorities: Only one garnishment is satisfied at a time. However, where 2 or more have been served and first garnishment has been satisfied, non-exempt wages remaining are applied toward satisfaction of junior garnishments in order of their priority. Garnishment has priority over assignment filed subsequent to notice of garnishment.

Judgments on consumer credit sale or loan: Greater of 80% of disposable weekly earnings or 30 times federal minimum hourly wage in effect when payable is exempt. No prejudgment garnishment is permitted. Employee can't be discharged because of such garnishment.

WISCONSIN (Statutes). [2][5][15] *Worker with no dependents:* Basic exemption—60% of income of employee for each 30-day period before service of process in proceeding to collect debt. Exemption cannot be less than $75 nor more than $100. Employee can elect to have exemption computed on 90-day basis.

Worker with dependents: Basic exemption—On income of employee for each 30-day period before service of process in proceeding to collect debt, $120 plus $20 for each dependent. However, total exemption cannot exceed 75% of total income. Employee can elect to have exemption computed on 90-day basis.

"Income" means gross receipts less federal and state withholding and Social Security taxes. A person's interest in any employee benefit plan, retirement, pension, disability, death benefit, stock bonus, or profit-sharing plan is not subject to garnishment.

Subsistence allowance: When earnings are subjected to garnishment, employer pays, on date earnings are payable, subsistence allowance to employee of greater of 75% of disposable weekly earnings or 30 times federal minimum hourly wage. Doesn't apply to support orders, bankruptcy orders, debt for state or federal tax, or orders in voluntary proceedings by wage earners. Garnishment action against earnings can't be started before judgment.

"Earnings" include periodic payments received pursuant to a pension or retirement program.

No garnishment action can be brought to recover the price or value of spirituous, malt, ardent or intoxicating liquors sold at retail.

Priorities: Garnishment has priority over assignment by public employee filed with employer subsequent to service of the garnishee summons.

Discharge: Employer can't discharge employee because his earnings have been garnisheed for any one indebtedness. Willful violation may result in fine of up to $1,000 and/or imprisonment for up to one year.

Judgments on consumer credit transactions: Exemption is the greater of (1) 75% of disposable earnings, or (2) $15 per week per dependent (other than employee) claimed for federal income tax withholding purposes, plus 40 times federal minimum hourly wage in effect when payable. Employee can't be discharged for such garnishment; violations result in recovery of back wages and reinstatement if employee files action within 90 days.

WYOMING (Statutes). [1][5] 30 times the federal minimum hourly wage, or 75% of weekly disposable earnings—whichever is greater.

Child support: 75% of disposable income is exempt (the employer can charge a $2 fee per withholding); only 70% of disposable income is exempt if arrears are 12 weeks or more.

Priorities: Income withholding orders for child support have the highest priority as to any income. Given more than one writ of garnishment, the first served has priority.

Discharge: Forbidden for consumer credit garnishment; adverse job action for child support income withholding orders forbidden.

Footnotes

[1] Employer who doesn't follow garnishment procedure may be subject to civil action by employee's creditor.

[2] Employer who doesn't follow garnishment procedure may be liable for all or part of claim that creditor has against employee.

[3] Employer who doesn't follow garnishment procedure may be subject to contempt proceedings; in *Mich.*, may be committed to jail.

[4] If employer doesn't follow garnishment procedure, judgment may be taken against it.

[5] Salaries of employees of state and/or its subdivisions may be subject to garnishment. In *Tenn.*, includes members of General Assembly.

[6] Employer is governed by return date of summons but after service of knowledge of issuance of summons, employer can only pay employee exempt wages (*Va*).

[7] $85 a week floor on garnishable earnings applies to all income executions in effect on or after 9/1/70 even if previously filed; applies to gross income (*N.Y.*).

[8] Based on decision in *Sniadach* case, laws in following states allowing prejudgment garnishments were ruled invalid: *Ariz.; Nev.; N.Dak.*

[9] Under both state and federal law, exemption applies to employee's disposable earnings or net take-home pay after all lawful deductions or withholdings. (*Md.*).

[10] Reserved.

[11] State exempt from federal wage garnishment restrictions: *Va.*, U. S. Labor Dept. retains enforcement responsibility for discharge provisions.

[12] One-garnishment-a-month provision stands.

[13] When a person is employed out of state by employer doing "substantial" business in state, particularly when employer has resident agent in state, garnishment for unpaid state income tax can

be used and taxpayer needn't be personally served with any papers. The exemption applies to court-ordered alimony payments, but after a hearing, court can order that exemption does not apply unless there's a garnishment for child support for the same pay period and it has taken wages in excess of the exemption. (*Kans.*).

[14] State law on garnishment applies to teachers. (*La.*).

[15] *Judgment on consumer credit transactions:* When pay period is one calendar week or less, amount of wages exempt under provision exempting $15 per week per dependent plus 40 times federal minimum hourly wage is determined on calendar-week basis regardless of number of hours worked; when pay period is multiple of whole calendar weeks, exemption is weekly rate under exemption formula times number of calendar weeks in such pay period; when pay period is greater than one calendar week and not a multiple of whole calendar weeks, exemption is sum of exemption for each calendar week plus 1/7th of weekly rate of each additional day in pay period. (*Wis.*).

[16] N. Dak. Code violates federal restrictions by allowing employer to pay entire amount of employee's paycheck to sheriff or clerk of court. Employee could be deprived of all accrued earnings pending court determination (*N. Dak.*).

[17] Federal maximum amount of earnings allowed to be garnished pre-empts Fla. garnishment provision. Pre-emption doesn't invalidate entire Fla. garnishment statute (*Fla.*).

[18] Debtor who satisfied resident-householder garnishment exemption requirements and whose indebtedness comes from breach of contract will have protection of either this or the consumer credit exemption, whichever results in lesser amount of garnished income (*Ind.*).

[19] $250 maximum amount of earnings that can be garnisheed includes any costs of garnishment proceedings (*Iowa*).

[20] For purposes of judgments on *consumer credit sale or lease*, to determine number of weeks in pay period, month equals 4 1/3 weeks; half month 2 1/6 weeks (*W. Va.*).

[21] Judgment for delinquent taxes obtained under garnishment procedures is subject to the 25% Utah ceiling (*Utah*).

[22] Municipal corporation isn't exempt from garnishment provisions (*Ill.*).

[23] Costs of all garnishments are to be deducted from funds paid into court and not from funds exempt from garnishment (*Tenn.*).

[24] Florida's garnishment was found to be constitutional by Fifth Circuit even though it permitted post-judgment garnishment of wages without prior notice of or an opportunity for a hearing.

[25] Prejudgment garnishment procedure providing for no notice to debtor, and under which writ of garnishment may be issued on unsworn testimony of creditor or his attorney, violates due process (*Fla.*).

[26] Wages earned in Pa. may be attached for judgment entered in another state for debt incurred in that state (*Pa.*).

FEDERAL ESTATE AND GIFT TAX RATES

The uniform rate table, which is to be used to calculate both estate and gift taxes for gifts made and decedents dying after 1983 and before 1993, is as follows:

If the amount with respect to which the tentative tax to be computed is:	The tentative tax is:
Not over $10,000	18 percent of such amount.
Over $10,000 but not over $20,000	$1,800, plus 20 percent of the excess of such amount over $10,000.
Over $20,000 but not over $40,000	$3,800, plus 22 percent of the excess of such amount over $20,000.
Over $40,000 but not over $60,000	$8,200, plus 24 percent of the excess of such amount over $40,000.
Over $60,000 but not over $80,000	$13,000, plus 26 percent of the excess of such amount over $60,000.
Over $80,000 but not over $100,000	$18,200, plus 28 percent of the excess of such amount over $80,000.
Over $100,000 but not over $150,000	$23,800, plus 30 percent of the excess of such amount over $100,000.
Over $150,000 but not over $250,000	$38,800, plus 32 percent of the excess of such amount over $150,000.
Over $250,000 but not over $500,000	$70,800, plus 34 percent of the excess of such amount over $250,000.
Over $500,000 but not over $750,000	$155,800, plus 37 percent of the excess of such amount over $500,000.
Over $750,000 but not over $1,000,000	$248,300, plus 39 percent of the excess of such amount over $750,000.
Over $1,000,000 but not over $1,250,000	$345,800, plus 41 percent of the excess of such amount over $1,000,000.
Over $1,250,000 but not over $1,500,000	$448,300, plus 43 percent of the excess of such amount over $1,250,000.
Over $1,500,000 but not over $2,000,000	$555,800, plus 45 percent of the excess of such amount over $1,500,000.
Over $2,000,000 but not over $2,500,000	$780,800, plus 49 percent of the excess of such amount over $2,000,000.
Over $2,500,000 but not over $3,000,000	$1,025,800, plus 53 percent of the excess of such amount over $2,500,000.
Over $3,000,000	$1,290,800, plus 55 percent of the excess of such amount over $3,000,000.

For deaths and transfers in the period 1/1/88-12/31/92, the benefit of the graduated rates is phased out for transfers over $10 million. A 5% surcharge is imposed on transfers between $10 million and $21,040,000, so that the 55% rate becomes the rate of taxation. Post-1992 transfers are subject to adjustments up to $18,340,000, after which the tax rate is 50%.

STATE GIFT TAXES

Alabama	No gift tax.
Alaska	No gift tax.
Arizona	No gift tax.
Arkansas	No gift tax.
California	No gift tax.
Colorado	No gift tax.
Connecticut	No gift tax.
Delaware	*Exemptions:* None. *Annual exclusion:* $10,000 and payments for qualified tuition and medical expenses. *Range of rates:* 1% to 6%.
District of Columbia	No gift tax.
Florida	No gift tax.
Georgia	No gift tax.
Hawaii	No gift tax.
Idaho	No gift tax.
Illinois	No gift tax.
Indiana	No gift tax.
Iowa	No gift tax.
Kansas	No gift tax.
Kentucky	No gift tax.
Louisiana	*Exemptions:* No personal. Specific lifetime—$30,000. *Annual exclusion:* $10,000. *Range of rates:* 2% to 3%.
Maine	No gift tax.
Maryland	No gift tax.
Massachusetts	No gift tax.
Michigan	No gift tax.
Minnesota	No gift tax.
Mississippi	No gift tax.
Missouri	No gift tax.
Montana	No gift tax.
Nebraska	No gift tax.
Nevada	No gift tax.
New Hampshire	No gift tax.
New Jersey	No gift tax.
New Mexico	No gift tax.

New York	*Exemptions:* Gifts to spouse. *Annual exclusion:* $10,000 and payments for qualified tuition and medical expenses. *Range of rates:* 2% to 21%.
North Carolina	*Exemptions:* Class A—lineal issue, lineal ancestors, spouse, adopted child or stepchild, $100,000; Class B—siblings or their descendants, uncles or aunts, by blood of the donor, no exemption; Class C—all others, no exemption. *Annual exclusion:* $10,000 per donee and payments for qualified tuition and medical expenses. *Range of rates:* Class A—1% to 12%; Class B—4% to 16%; Class C—8% to 17%.
North Dakota	No gift tax.
Ohio	No gift tax.
Oklahoma	No gift tax.
Oregon	No gift tax.
Pennsylvania	No gift tax.
Rhode Island	No gift tax.
South Carolina	Former gift tax repealed as to gifts post-12/31/91.
South Dakota	No gift tax.
Tennessee	*Exemptions:* Class A—spouse, children, lineal ancestor, lineal descendant, or legally adopted person, sibling, stepchild, daughter in-law, son-in law, $10,000 annually. *Annual exclusion:* Class A—$3,000 per donee; Class B—$3,000 per donee. Payments for qualified tuition and medical expenses. *Range of rates:* Class A—5.5% to 9.5%; Class B—6.5% to 16%.
Texas	No gift tax.
Utah	No gift tax.
Vermont	No gift tax.
Virginia	No gift tax.
Washington	No gift tax.
West Virginia	No gift tax.
Wisconsin	*Exemptions:* Transfers to spouse—completely exempt; Class A—lineal issue, lineal ancestor, or a mutually acknowledged child including his or her spouse and issue, $50,000; Class B—siblings or a descendant, no exemption; Class C—aunt or uncle or a descendant, no exemption; Class D—all others, no exemption. *Annual exclusion:* $10,000. *Range of rates:* Class A—2.5% to 12.5%; Class B—5% to 25%; Class C—7.5% to 30%; Class D—10% to 30%. Respealed eff. 1/1/92.
Wyoming	No gift tax.

STATE DEATH TAXES

The following chart provides a capsule description of each state's statutory scheme. Where the type of tax is listed as "credit estate tax," the tax levied is the maximum federal credit for state death taxes allowed under Code §2011. Where the tax is an inheritance tax, the exemptions and tax rates listed are the maximum and minimum amounts. Where both an inheritance or estate tax and a credit estate tax is listed, the credit estate tax is payable only if the tax under the basic state death tax is less than the maximum federal credit. "Payment due" indicates the time after death when the state tax is due (unless an extension is granted and payable without penalty). "Assessed on" indicates whether the tax is payable from the residuary estate or is paid proportionately by the beneficiaries (unless the will provides otherwise).

Caution: Local law should always be checked for recent changes enacted by state legislatures.

Alabama

Type: Credit estate tax
Payment due: 9 months
Assessed on: Residuary estate

Alaska

Type: Credit estate tax
Payment due: 15 months
Assessed on: Pro rata

Arizona

Type: Credit estate tax
Payment due: On or before date of federal estate tax return; may be paid in installments if the federal tax is so paid.
Assessed on: Residuary estate

Arkansas

Type: Credit estate tax
Payment due: 9 months
Assessed on: Pro rata

California

Type: Credit estate tax
Payment due: 9 months
Assessed on: Pro rata

Colorado

Type: Credit estate tax
Payment due: On or before date of filing of federal estate tax return
Assessed on: Pro rata

Connecticut

Type: Inheritance tax and credit estate tax
Exemptions:
    Class AA: Spouse: $300,000 (death before 7/1/88)
    Class A: Parent, child, grandparent: $50,000
    Class B: Sibling: $6,000
    Class C: Others: $1,000
Rates:
    Class A: 3-8%
    Class B: 4-10%
    Class C: 8-14% (10% and 30% surcharges are applicable)

Payment due: 9 months

Assessed on: Pro rata

For deaths after 7/1/88, no tax on net taxable estate passing to surviving spouse.

Delaware

Type: Inheritance tax and credit estate tax

Exemptions:

Class A: Spouse: $70,000

Class B: Child, parent, grandparent, child's spouse, lineal descendant: $25,000

Class C: Sibling: $5,000

Class D: Others: $1,000

Rates:

Class A: 2%-4%

Class B: 2%-6%

Class C: 5%-10%

Class D: 10%-16%

Payment due:

Inheritance tax: 9 months

Estate tax: 9 months

Assessed on: Pro rata

District of Columbia

Type: Credit estate tax

Payment due: 10 months

Assessed on: Pro rata

Florida

Type: Credit estate tax

Payment due: When federal estate tax due (including extensions)

Assessed on: Residuary estate

Georgia

Type: Credit estate tax

Payment due: On or before date of filing of the duplicate federal estate tax return.

Assessed on: Residuary estate

Hawaii

Type: Credit estate tax

Payment due: On or before date of filing of federal estate tax return.

Assessed on: Pro rata

Idaho

Type: Credit estate tax

Payment due: 9 months

Assessed on: Pro rata

Illinois

Type: Credit estate tax

Payment due: At the time for filing federal estate tax return. May be paid in installments if federal tax is.

Assessed on: Residuary estate (pro rata) between probate and non-probate estate.

Indiana

Type: Inheritance tax and credit estate tax

Exemptions:

Class A: Surviving spouse: all transfers exempt. Lineal ancestor or descendant. Child under 21: $10,000

Parent and child over 20: $5,000

Other lineal ancestors or descendants: $2,000

Class B: Siblings and their descendants, child's spouse: $500

Class C: Others (exc. surviving spouse): $100

Rates:

Class A: 1%-10%

Class B: 7%-15%

Class C: 10%-20%

Payment due: 18 months; 5% discount for payment within 1 year of death.

Assessed on: Pro rata

Iowa

Type: Inheritance tax and credit estate tax

Exemptions:

Class 1: Spouse: completely exempt

Child: $50,000

Parent, other lineal descendant: $15,000

Class 2: Sibling, child's spouse: none
Class 3: Others: none
Class 4: Societies, institutions, or associations organized under law, for charitable, educational, or religious purposes: none
Class 5: Firm, or corporation for profit: none

Rates:
Class 1: 1%-8%
Class 2: 5%-10%
Class 3: 10%-15%
Class 4: Flat 10%
Class 5: Flat 15%

Payment due:
Inheritance tax: 9 months
Estate tax: 12 months

Assessed on: Pro rata

Kansas

Type: Inheritance tax and credit estate tax
Exemptions:
Transfers to spouse: Completely exempt
Class A: Lineal descendants and ancestors, spouse of child: $30,000
Class B: Sibling: $5,000
Class C: Others: none (unless the share is less than $200, in which case the entire amount is exempt)

Rates:
Class A: Lineal descendants and ancestors, child's spouse: 1%-5%
Class B: 3%-12.5%
Class C: 10%-15%

Payment due: 9 months
Assessed on: Pro rata

Kentucky

Type: Inheritance tax and credit estate tax
Exemptions:
Class A: Spouse: total inheritable interest
Minor child: $20,000
Parent, grandchild: $5,000
Class B: Sibling, aunt, uncle, niece, nephew, daughter-in-law, son-in-law: $1,000
Class C: Others: $500

Rates:
Class A: 2%-10%
Class B: 4%-16%
Class C: 6%-16%

Payment due: 9 months
Assessed on: Pro rata

Louisiana

Type: Inheritance tax and credit estate tax
Exemptions:
Class A: Spouse, direct descendants and ascendants: 1987-1992: $25,000. After 1992, all inheritance of surviving spouse is exempt.
Class B: Sibling: $1,000
Class C: Others: $500

Rates:
Class A: 2%-3%
Class B: 5%-7%
Class C: 5%-10%

Payment due: 9 months
Assessed on: Pro rata

Maine

Type: Credit estate tax
Payment due: 12 months
Assessed on: Pro rata

Maryland

Type: Inheritance tax and credit estate tax
Exemptions:
Class A: Spouse, parent, children, lineal descendant: None, unless $150 or less, then entirely exempt
Surviving spouse: $2,000 allowance exempt from tax
Unmarried child (under age 18): $1,000 allowance exempt from tax
Class B: Others: None, unless $150 or less, then entirely exempt

Rates:
Class A: Flat 1%
Class B: Flat 10%

There is a 1% rate on amounts up to $2,000 in joint savings accounts passing to the spouse of the lineal descendant. There is no tax on joint tenancy amounts passing to the decedent's spouse.

Payment due: Within 30 days after the time of the accounting for its distribution

Assessed on: Pro rata

Massachusetts

Type: Estate tax and credit estate tax

Exemptions: $300,000 in 1993, $400,000 in 1994, $500,000 in 1995, $600,000 in 1996. Thereafter the estate tax is equal to the credit allowed for state death taxes under federal estate tax law.

Rates: 5%-16% (before 1997)

Payment due: 9 months

Assessed on: Pro rata

Michigan

Type: Credit estate tax

Payment due: 9 months

Assessed on: Pro rata

Minnesota

Type: Estate tax and credit estate tax

Payment due: 9 months

Assessed on: Pro rata

Mississippi

Type: Estate tax

Exemptions: Specific exemption: $600,000

Rates: 1%-16%

Payment due: 9 months

Assessed on: Residuary estate

Missouri

Type: Credit estate tax

Payment due: 9 months

Assessed on: Pro rata

Montana

Type: Inheritance tax and credit estate tax

Exemptions:
   Class A: Spouse, child or lineal descendant: all property exempt
   Class B: Lineal ancestor: $7,000
   Class C: Siblings and their descendants, child's spouse: $1,000
   Class D: Aunt, uncle, first cousin: None
   Class E: Others: None

Rates:
   Class B: 2%-8%
   Class C: 4%-16%
   Class D: 6%-24%
   Class E: 8%-32%

Payment due: 18 months

Assessed on: Pro rata

Nebraska

Type: Inheritance tax and credit estate tax

Exemptions:
   Transfers to spouse: Completely exempt
   Class I: Parent, child, sibling, lineal descendant, child's, sibling's and lineal descendant's spouse: $10,000
   Class II: Uncle, aunt, niece, nephew and their spouses: $2,000
   Class III: Others: $500

Rates:
   Class I: Flat 1%
   Class II: 6%-9%
   Class III: 6%-18%

Payment due: 12 months

Assessed on: Pro rata

Nevada

No state death tax.

New Hampshire

Type: Inheritance tax and credit estate tax

Exemptions: No tax on spouse, lineal ascendants and descendants, and their spouses.

Rates: Flat 18%

Payment due: 12 months
Assessed on: Pro rata

New Jersey

Type: Inheritance tax and credit estate tax
Exemptions: Transfers to spouse:completely exempt
Class A (parent, grandparent, child or issue of child): $15,000
Class C (sibling, spouse of child): none
Class D (all other non-charitable beneficiaries): none
Rates:
Class A: 2%-16%
Class C: 11%-16%
Class D: 15%-16%
Payment due: 8 months
Assessed on: Pro rata

New Mexico

Type: Credit estate tax
Payment due: On or before date of filing of federal estate tax return
Assessed on: Pro rata

New York

Type: Estate tax and credit estate tax
Credits: If tax is $2,750 or less: full amount of tax. If tax is between $2,750 and $5,000: difference between tax and $5,500. If tax is more than $5,000: $500. Other credits: see statute.
Rates: 2%-21%
Payment due: 6 months
Assessed on: Pro rata

North Carolina

Type: Inheritance tax and credit estate tax
Credits:
Class A: Spouse: Transfers to tax-exempt Lineal ancestors or descendants: $26,150
Class B: Siblings and their descendants, aunt, uncle: none
Class C: Others: none

Rates:
Class A: 1%-12%
Class B: 4%-16%
Class C: 8%-17%
Payment due: 9 months
Assessed on: Pro rata

North Dakota

Type: Credit estate tax
Payment due: 15 months
Assessed on: Pro rata

Ohio

Type: Estate tax and credit estate tax
Rates: 2%-7%
Payment due: 9 months
Assessed on: Pro rata

Oklahoma

Type: Estate tax and credit estate tax
Exemptions:
Class 1: Parent, child, and lineal descendant: aggregate of $175,000 (there is a complete exemption for spouse except for calculating credit estate tax)
Class 2: Others: none, but estate less than $100 is exempt
Rates:
Class 1: 0.5%-10%
Class 2: 1%-15%
Payment due: 9 months
Assessed on: Residuary estate

Oregon

Type: Inheritance tax and credit estate tax
Payment due: 9 months
Assessed on: Pro rata

Pennsylvania

Type: Inheritance tax and credit estate tax

Exemptions:
    Class A: Spouse, parents, grandparents, child, lineal descendants, spouse of child: none (except, there is a $2,000 family exemption).
    Class B: Others: none

Rates:
    Class A: Flat 6%
    Class B: Flat 15%

Payment due:
    Inheritance tax: 9 months
    Estate tax: 18 months

Assessed on: Pro rata

Rhode Island

Type: Estate tax and credit estate tax
Payment due: 10 months
Assessed on: Pro rata

South Carolina

Type: Estate tax and credit estate tax
Exemptions: $320,000
Rates: 6%-8%
Payment due: 9 months
Assessed on: Pro rata

South Dakota

Type: Inheritance tax and credit estate tax
Exemptions:
    Class 1: Spouse: all exempt lineal issue: $30,000
    Class 2: Lineal ancestor: $3,000
    Class 3: Siblings and their descendants, child's spouse: $500
    Class 4: Aunt, uncle: $200
    Class 5: Others: $100
    Class 6: Sibling who was continuously engaged in business or farming with decedent for minimum of 10 years: $500

Rates:
    Class 1: 3.75%-7.5%
    Class 2: 3%-15%
    Class 3: 4%-20%
    Class 4: 5%-25%
    Class 5: 6%-30%
    Class 6: 3%-15%

Payment due: 12 months
Assessed on: Pro rata

Tennessee

Type: Inheritance tax and credit estate tax
Exemptions: $600,000 against the net estate
Payment due: 9 months
Assessed on: Pro rata

Texas

Type: Credit estate tax
Payment due: 9 months
Assessed on: Pro rata

Utah

Type: Credit estate tax
Payment due: On or before the date the federal estate tax return is due
Assessed on: Pro rata

Vermont

Type: Credit estate tax
Payment due: 15 months
Assessed on: Pro rata

Virginia

Type: Credit estate tax
Payment due: On or before the date the federal estate tax return is due
Assessed on: Pro rata

Washington

Type: Credit estate tax
Payment due: On or before the date the federal estate tax return is due
Assessed on: Pro rata

West Virginia

Type: Inheritance tax and credit estate tax

Exemptions:
  Class A: Spouse: $30,000
  Children and their descendants, parent: $10,000
  Grandchild: $5,000
  Class B: Sibling: none (but if decedent dies unmarried, $10,000 exemption)
  Class C: Persons further removed than sibling: none
  Class D: Others: none
  If share is less than $200, no tax

Rates:
  Class A: 3%-13%
  Class B: 4%-18%
  Class C: 7%-25%
  Class D: 10%-30%

Payment due: 11months

Assessed on: Pro rata

Wisconsin

Type: Inheritance tax and credit estate tax
Exemptions: Spouse: All exempt

Class A: Lineal issue, child's spouse: $10,000
Class B: Siblings and their descendants: $1,000
Class C: Aunt, uncle, and their descendants: $1,000
Class D: Others: $500

Rates:
  Class A: 2.5%-12.5%
  Class B: 5%-25%
  Class C: 7.5%-30%
  Class D: 10%-30%
  Maximum inheritance tax limited to 20% of property transferred

Payment due: 12 months

Assessed on: Pro rata

Wyoming

Type: Credit estate tax
Payment due: At time federal estate tax return is to be filed
Assessed on: Pro rata

FEDERAL ESTATE AND GIFT TAX RETURNS—FILING DATES, REQUIREMENTS

Type of Tax	Taxable Event	Person Liable	Due Date of Return and Tax	Threshold Amount	Requirements for Extension of Time to Pay Tax	Period of Extension
A. Income	(1) Income earned by decedent	Executor or administrator, and/or surviving spouse if joint return is filed	April 15 for calendar year taxpayers (Form 1040)	Gross income $6,400-$12,300 (for 1995) depending on age, marital status, and whether joint return	None, for automatic filing extension	Up to 4 months
					Undue hardship, for further extension	Up to 6 months
	(2) Income earned by estate	Executor or administrator	15th day of 4th month following close of fiscal year (Form 1041)	Gross income in taxable year over $600 OR $0 if any beneficiary is a nonresident alien	Undue hardship OR Tax may be paid in 4 equal, quarterly installments, beginning with due date of tax	Up to 6 months

FEDERAL ESTATE AND GIFT TAX RETURNS—FILING DATES, REQUIREMENTS

Type of Tax	Taxable Event	Person Liable	Due Date of Return and Tax	Threshold Amount	Requirements for Extension of Time to Pay Tax	Period of Extension
B. Estate	(3) Death of U.S. citizen or resident	Executor or administrator	9 months after date of death (Form 706)	Gross estate over $600,000 (for date of death after 1986)	Reasonable cause OR Future interest included in estate OR Closely held interest represents over 35% of adjusted gross estate	Up to 6 months (or longer for special extensions)
	(4) Death of nonresident alien	Executor or administrator	9 months after date of death (Form 706NA)	Gross estate of U.S. property over $60,000	Reasonable cause	Up to 12 months
C. Gift	(5) Lifetime transfer to donee other than spouse or qualified charities	Donor	April 15 for gifts made during preceding year (Form 709)	$10,000 per donee ($20,000 for split gifts)	Undue hardship	Up to 6 months

FEDERAL ESTATE AND GIFT TAX RETURNS—FILING DATES, REQUIREMENTS

Type of Tax	Taxable Event	Person Liable	Due Date of Return and Tax	Threshold Amount	Requirements for Extension of Time to Pay Tax	Period of Extension
D. Generation-skipping	(6) Generation-skipping transfers	Trustee in case of taxable termination; distributees in case of taxable distribution	90th day after close of taxable year of trust if transfer occurred before death of deemed transferor	Same as (5)	Undue hardship	Up to 6 months (longer if taxpayer is abroad)
			90th day after last day estate tax return is due (including extensions) for estate of deemed transferor who has died on or before transfer OR, if later, 9 months after date of transfer	Same as (3)	Reasonable cause	Up to 12 months or 10 years

COMPUTATION OF MAXIMUM CREDIT FOR STATE DEATH TAXES

Adjusted taxable estate* more than—	But not more than—	Maximum Credit on amount in col. (A)	Rate of credit on excess of amt. in col. (A)
(A)	(B)	(C)	(D)
$ 40,000	$ 90,000	$	0.8%
90,000	140,000	400	1.6%
140,000	240,000	1,200	2.4%
240,000	440,000	3,600	3.2%
440,000	640,000	10,000	4.0%
640,000	840,000	18,000	4.8%
840,000	1,040,000	27,600	5.6%
1,040,000	1,540,000	38,800	6.4%
1,540,000	2,040,000	70,800	7.2%
2,040,000	2,540,000	106,800	8.0%
2,540,000	3,040,000	146,800	8.8%
3,040,000	3,540,000	190,800	9.6%
3,540,000	4,040,000	238,800	10.4%
4,040,000	5,040,000	290,800	11.2%
5,040,000	6,040,000	402,800	12.0%
6,040,000	7,040,000	522,800	12.8%
7,040,000	8,040,000	650,800	13.6%
8,040,000	9,040,000	786,800	14.4%
9,040,000	10,040,000	930,800	15.2%
10,040,000		1,082,800	16.0%

*Adjusted taxable estate means taxable estate reduced by $60,000.

EXECUTORS' COMMISSIONS

Most states have a statutory schedule of fees for executors. Some merely call for reasonable fees, the reasonableness to be determined by the courts. In a number of states, fees for testamentary trusts are the same as those allowed to executors. Some states provide for a distinct statutory fee for trusts, others provide for reasonable fees to be determined by the court, more often than not based in large measure on trust receipts—with 5% annually being a fairly reasonable national average. In the case of both executors and testamentary trustees, additional reasonable fees may be charged for extraordinary services (these states are denoted by an asterisk).

The basis on which commissions are calculated also varies among the states. While many allow the fiduciary a percentage of all probate property, others exclude the value of unsold real property.

Alabama*

Not more than 2 1/2% of receipts and disbursements. Additional $2\,^1/_2$% allowed if land is sold for division (but limited to $100 unless otherwise specified in the will).

Alaska

Reasonable compensation allowed.

Arizona

Reasonable compensation allowed.

Arkansas

First $1,000—not more than 10%
Next $1,000 to $5,000—5%
Above $5,000—3%
Additional compensation allowed for substantial duties pertaining to real property.

California*

First $15,000—4%
Next $85,000—3%
Next $900,000—2%
Next $9,000,000—1%
Next $15,000,000—1/2%
Above $25,000,000—reasonable amount determined by court.

Colorado

Reasonable compensation allowed.

Connecticut

Reasonable compensation allowed.

Delaware

Reasonable compensation allowed (usually 10% of estate).

District of Columbia

Reasonable compensation allowed.

Florida

Reasonable compensation allowed.

Georgia*

Flat $2\,^1/_2$%.

Hawaii

First $15,000—4%
Next $85,000—3%
Next $900,000—2%
Next $2,000,000—1 1/2%
Above $3,000,000—1%
Additional fees allowed for estate's income are 7% of first $5,000 and 5% above $5,000.

Idaho

Reasonable compensation allowed.

Illinois

Reasonable compensation allowed.

Indiana

Reasonable compensation allowed.

Iowa

First $1,000—6%
Next $4,000—4%
All above $5,000—2%

Kansas

Reasonable compensation allowed.

Kentucky*

Not more than 5% of income and 5% of personal estate.

Louisiana

Fee is $2\frac{1}{2}$% of the inventory of the estate; it may be increased by the court upon showing that the usual commission is inadequate.

Maine

Reasonable compensation allowed.

Maryland

For personal property:
First $20,000—up to 10%
Above $20,000—$2,000 plus 4% of excess over $20,000
For real property, up to 10% if sold.

Massachusetts

Reasonable compensation allowed.

Michigan

First $5,000—5%
Next $20,000—4%
Next $50,000—3%
Above $75,000—2%

Minnesota

Reasonable compensation allowed.

Mississippi

Not less than 1% nor more than 7% on amount of estate administered.

Missouri

First $5,000—5%
Next $20,000—4%
Next $75,000—3%
Next $300,000—2 3/4%
Next $600,000—2 1/2%
All above $1,000,000—2%

Montana

First $40,000—3%
Above $40,000—2%

Nebraska

Reasonable compensation allowed.

Nevada

First $15,000—4%
Next $85,000—3%
Above $100,000—2%

New Hampshire

No statutory provisions, but probate court allows for reasonable compensation when executor's claim is presented.

New Jersey

On income, 6%. On corpus not exceeding $200,000, 5%. On excess over $200,000, a percentage at the discretion of the court, not exceeding 5%.

New Mexico

Reasonable compensation allowed.

New York

First $25,000—4%
Next $125,000—3 1/2%
Next $150,000—3%
Above $300,000—2%

North Carolina

Not more than 5% of receipts and disbursements. If the gross value of the estate is $2,000 or less, the commission is at the discretion of the clerk of the Superior Court.

North Dakota

Reasonable compensation allowed.

Ohio

First $100,000—4%
Next $300,000—3%
Above $400,000—2%

1% additional for unsold real property and nonprobate property subject to state estate tax.

Oklahoma

First $1,000—5%
Next $4,000—4%
Above $5,000—2 1/2%

Oregon

First $1,000—7%
Next $9,000—4%

Next $40,000—3%
Above $50,000—2%

1% additional for nonprobate property (excluding insurance) that is subject to estate tax.

Pennsylvania

Reasonable compensation allowed (usually 5% for small estates and 3% for large estates).

Rhode Island

Reasonable compensation allowed.

South Carolina*

Not more than 5% of appraised value of personal property plus sales proceeds of real property plus estate income.

South Dakota

First $1,000—5%
Next $4,000—4%
All above $5,000—2 1/2%

Tennessee

Reasonable compensation allowed.

Texas

Not more than 5% of the value of the administered estate. If compensation is unreasonably low, the court may allow reasonable compensation.

Utah

Reasonable compensation allowed.

Vermont*

Reasonable compensation allowed.

Virginia

Reasonable compensation allowed.

Washington

Reasonable compensation allowed.

West Virginia

Reasonable compensation allowed.

Wisconsin*

2% of estate.

Wyoming*

First $1,000—10%

Next $4,000—5%

Next $15,000—3%

Above $20,000—2%

The general rule is that there is nothing to prevent the testator from specifying the executor's commissions in the will, or even directing that there shall be no commissions. Then it is up to the executor to accept or refuse appointment.

REVOCATION OF WILLS

by Marriage, Divorce, or Birth of Child

All states recognize that wills are revocable. Revocation may occur by operation of law, by some physical act performed upon the will with intent to revoke, or expressly or impliedly by a subsequent instrument meeting the statutory requirements. The tables that follow outline the grounds that may cause revocation by operation of law: marriage, divorce, or birth of a child. Hence, they serve as a working guide to the situations in which a will should be revised to avoid revocation or modification.

EFFECT OF MARRIAGE

Alabama

No effect.

Alaska

Modifies will to give intestate share.

Arizona

Modifies will to give intestate share.

Arkansas

No effect.

California

The will is revoked as to the spouse, unless provision has been made for the spouse by marriage contract.

Colorado

Modifies will to give intestate share.

Connecticut

Completely revokes will.

Delaware

Modifies will to give intestate share.

District of Columbia

No effect.

Florida

Modifies will to give intestate share.

Georgia

Completely revokes will.

Hawaii

Modifies will to give intestate share.

Idaho

Modifies will to give intestate share.

Illinois

No effect.

Indiana

No effect.

Iowa

No effect.

819

EFFECT OF MARRIAGE
(cont'd)

Kansas

No effect, except it is revoked if the testator marries and has a child after he/she made the will.

Kentucky

Completely revokes will.

Louisiana

No effect.

Maine

Modifies will to give intestate share.

Maryland

No effect unless marriage is followed by birth of a child after will was made; then the will is revoked.

Massachusetts

Completely revokes will.

Michigan

Modifies will to give intestate share.

Minnesota

No effect.

Mississippi

No effect.

Missouri

Modifies will to give intestate share.

Montana

Modifies will to give intestate share.

Nebraska

Modifies will to give intestate share.

Nevada

Will is revoked only as to the spouse.

New Hampshire

May modify will.

New Jersey

Modifies will to give intestate share.

New Mexico

Modifies will to give interstate share.

New York

Modifies will to give intestate share.

North Carolina

No effect, except surviving spouse may dissent from will as though will were made subsequent to marriage.

North Dakota

Modifies will to give intestate share.

Ohio

Will made by unmarried person isn't revoked by marriage.

820

EFFECT OF MARRIAGE
(cont'd)

Oklahoma

No effect, except if the testator marries and has a child after his/her will was executed. It is then revoked.

Oregon

Will is completely revoked.

Pennsylvania

Modifies will to give intestate share.

Puerto Rico

No effect.

Rhode Island

Will is completely revoked.

South Carolina

No effect.

South Dakota

Revokes will completely.

Tennessee

No effect. except if will is made before both marriage and birth of child.

Texas

No effect.

Utah

Modifies will to give intestate share.

Vermont

No effect.

Virginia

Modifies will to give intestate share.

Washington

Completely revokes will.

West Virgina

Completely revokes will.

Wisconsin

Completely revokes will, unless will is in contemplation of marriage or there is a valid antenuptial contract.

Wyoming

No effect.

EFFECT OF DIVORCE

Alabama

Revokes part of will making provision for spouse.

Alaska

Revokes part of will making provision for spouse.

Arizona

Revokes part of will making provision for spouse.

Arkansas

Revokes part of will making provision for spouse.

California

No effect.

Colorado

Revokes part of will making provision for spouse.

Connecticut

Completely revoked unless the ex-spouse was not a beneficiary.

Delaware

Revokes part of will making provision for spouse.

District of Columbia

No effect except the common-law rule that a divorce with property settlement may revoke husband's will by implication of law.

Florida

Revokes part of will making provision for spouse.

Georgia

Will is completely revoked.

Hawaii

Revokes part of will making provision for spouse.

Idaho

Revokes part of will making provision for spouse.

Illinois

Revokes part of will making provision for spouse.

Indiana

Revokes part of will making provision for spouse.

Iowa

Revokes part of will making provision for spouse.

Kansas

Revokes part of will making provision for spouse.

Kentucky

Revokes entire will.

EFFECT OF DIVORCE
(cont'd)

Louisiana

No effect.

Maine

Revokes part of will making provision for spouse.

Maryland

Revokes part of will making provision for spouse.

Massachusetts

Revokes part of will making provision for spouse.

Michigan

Revokes part of will making provision for spouse.

Minnesota

Revokes part of will making provision for spouse.

Mississippi

No effect.

Missouri

Revokes part of will making provision for spouse.

Montana

Revokes part of will making provision for spouse.

Nebraska

Revokes part of will making provision for spouse.

Nevada

Revokes part of will making provision for spouse.

New Hampshire

No effect.

New Jersey

Revokes part of will making provision for spouse.

New Mexico

Revokes part of will making provision for spouse.

New York

Revokes part of will making provision for spouse.

North Carolina

Revokes part of will making provision for spouse.

North Dakota

Revokes part of will making provision for spouse.

Ohio

Revokes part of will making provision for spouse—also revokes dispositions for spouse in certain trusts. Separation agreement has the same effect.

EFFECT OF DIVORCE
(cont'd)

Oklahoma

Revokes part of will making provision for spouse.

Oregon

Revokes part of will making provision for spouse.

Pennsylvania

Revokes part of will making provision for spouse.

Rhode Island

Revokes part of will making provision for spouse—unless will was made in contemplation of divorce.

South Carolina

Revokes part of will making provision for spouse.

South Dakota

No effect.

Tennessee

Revokes part of will making provision for spouse.

Texas

Revokes part of will making provision for spouse.

Utah

Revokes part of will making provision for spouse.

Vermont

No effect.

Virginia

Revokes part of will making provision for spouse.

Washington

Revokes part of will making provision for spouse.

West Virginia

Revokes entire will.

Wisconsin

Revokes part of will making provision for spouse.

Wyoming

Revokes part of will making provision for spouse.

EFFECT OF BIRTH OF A CHILD

Alabama

Partially revokes will to give child intestate share.

Alaska

Modifies will to give child intestate share.

Arizona

Modifies will to give child intestate share.

Arkansas

Modifies will to give child intestate share.

California

Modifies will to give child intestate share.

Colorado

Modifies will to give child intestate share.

Connecticut

Completely revokes will.

Delaware

Modifies will to give child intestate share.

District of Columbia

No provision.

Florida

Modifies will to give child intestate share.

Georgia

Will is completely revoked.

Hawaii

Modifies will to give child intestate share.

Idaho

Modifies will to give child intestate share.

Illinois

Modifies will to give child intestate share.

Indiana

Modifies will to give child intestate share.

Iowa

Modifies will to give child intestate share.

Kansas

No effect, except will is revoked if testator marries and has a child after he or she makes the will.

Kentucky

Modifies will to give child intestate share.

Louisiana

Completely revokes will.

Maine

Modifies will to give child intestate share.

Maryland

Modifies will to give child intestate share.

Massachusetts

Modifies will to give child intestate share.

Michigan

Modifies will to give child intestate share.

Minnesota

Modifies will to give child intestate share.

EFFECT OF BIRTH OF A CHILD
(cont'd)

Mississippi

Modifies will to give child intestate share.

Missouri

Modifies will to give child intestate share.

Montana

Modifies will to give child intestate share.

Nebraska

Modifies will to give child intestate share.

Nevada

Modifies will to give child intestate share.

New Hampshire

Modifies will to give child intestate share.

New Jersey

Modifies will to give child intestate share.

New Mexico

Modifies will to give child intestate share.

New York

Modifies will to give child intestate share.

North Carolina

Modifies will to give child intestate share.

North Dakota

Modifies will to give child intestate share.

Ohio

Modifies will to give child intestate share.

Oklahoma

Modifies will to give child intestate share.

Oregon

Modifies will to give child intestate share.

Pennsylvania

Modifies will to give child intestate share.

Rhode Island

Modifies will to give child intestate share.

South Carolina

Modifies will to give child intestate share.

South Dakota

Modifies will to give child intestate share.

Tennessee

Will is revoked by marriage and birth of a child.

Texas

Modifies will to give child intestate share.

Utah

Modifies will to give child intestate share.

Vermont

Modifies will to give child intestate share.

EFFECT OF BIRTH OF A CHILD
(cont'd)

Virginia

Modifies will to give child intestate share.

Washington

Modifies will to give child intestate share.

West Virginia

Modifies will to give child intestate share.

Wisconsin

Modifies will to give child intestate share.

Wyoming

Modifies will to give child intestate share.

SIMPLE INTEREST TABLE

Example of use of this table:
Find amount of $500 in 8 years at 9% simple interest.
From table for 8 years at 9% for $1:. 1.72
Value in 8 years for $500 (500 × 1.72): $860

Number of Years	5%	6%	7%	8%	9%	10%	11%	12%
1	1.05	1.06	1.07	1.08	1.09	1.10	1.11	1.12
2	1.10	1.12	1.14	1.16	1.18	1.20	1.22	1.24
3	1.15	1.18	1.21	1.24	1.27	1.30	1.33	1.36
4	1.20	1.24	1.28	1.32	1.36	1.40	1.44	1.48
5	1.25	1.30	1.35	1.40	1.45	1.50	1.55	1.60
6	1.30	1.36	1.42	1.48	1.54	1.60	1.66	1.72
7	1.35	1.42	1.49	1.56	1.63	1.70	1.77	1.84
8	1.40	1.48	1.56	1.64	1.72	1.80	1.88	1.96
9	1.45	1.54	1.63	1.72	1.81	1.90	1.99	2.08
10	1.50	1.60	1.70	1.80	1.90	2.00	2.10	2.20
11	1.55	1.66	1.77	1.88	1.99	2.10	2.21	2.32
12	1.60	1.72	1.84	1.96	2.08	2.20	2.32	2.44
13	1.65	1.78	1.91	2.04	2.17	2.30	2.43	2.56
14	1.70	1.84	1.98	2.12	2.26	2.40	2.54	2.68
15	1.75	1.90	2.05	2.20	2.35	2.50	2.65	2.80
16	1.80	1.96	2.12	2.28	2.44	2.60	2.76	2.92
17	1.85	2.02	2.19	2.36	2.53	2.70	2.87	3.04
18	1.90	2.08	2.26	2.44	2.62	2.80	2.98	3.16
19	1.95	2.14	2.33	2.52	2.71	2.90	3.09	3.28
20	2.00	2.20	2.40	2.60	2.80	3.00	3.20	3.40
21	2.05	2.26	2.47	2.68	2.89	3.10	3.31	3.52
22	2.10	2.32	2.54	2.76	2.98	3.20	3.42	3.64
23	2.15	2.38	2.61	2.84	3.07	3.30	3.53	3.76
24	2.20	2.44	2.68	2.92	3.16	3.40	3.64	3.88
25	2.25	2.50	2.75	3.00	3.25	3.50	3.75	4.00
26	2.30	2.56	2.82	3.08	3.34	3.60	3.86	4.12
27	2.35	2.62	2.89	3.16	3.43	3.70	3.97	4.24
28	2.40	2.68	2.96	3.24	3.52	3.80	4.08	4.36
29	2.45	2.74	3.03	3.32	3.61	3.90	4.19	4.48
30	2.50	2.80	3.10	3.40	3.70	4.00	4.30	4.60
31	2.55	2.86	3.17	3.48	3.79	4.10	4.41	4.72
32	2.60	2.92	3.24	3.56	3.88	4.20	4.52	4.84
33	2.65	2.98	3.31	3.64	3.97	4.30	4.63	4.96
34	2.70	3.04	3.38	3.72	4.06	4.40	4.74	5.08
35	2.75	3.10	3.45	3.80	4.15	4.50	4.85	5.20
36	2.80	3.16	3.52	3.88	4.24	4.60	4.96	5.32
37	2.85	3.22	3.59	3.96	4.33	4.70	5.07	5.44
38	2.90	3.28	3.66	4.04	4.42	4.80	5.18	5.56
39	2.95	3.34	3.73	4.12	4.51	4.90	5.29	5.68
40	3.00	3.40	3.80	4.20	4.60	5.00	5.40	5.80

COMPOUND INTEREST TABLE

Example of use of this table:
Find how much $1,000 in bank now will grow to in 14 years at 9% simple interest.
From table for 14 years at 9%:. 3.3417
Value in 14 years for $1,000: $3,341.70

Number of Years	5%	6%	7%	8%	9%	10%	11%	12%
1	1.0500	1.0600	1.0700	1.0800	1.0900	1.1000	1.1100	1.1200
2	1.1025	1.1236	1.1449	1.1664	1.1881	1.2100	1.2321	1.2544
3	1.1576	1.1910	1.2250	1.2597	1.2950	1.3310	1.3576	1.4049
4	1.2155	1.2625	1.3107	1.3604	1.4115	1.4647	1.5180	1.5735
5	1.2763	1.3382	1.4025	1.4693	1.5386	1.6105	1.6350	1.7623
6	1.3401	1.4185	1.5007	1.5868	1.6771	1.7715	1.8704	1.9738
7	1.4071	1.5036	1.6057	1.7138	1.8230	1.9487	2.0761	2.2106
8	1.4775	1.5938	1.7181	1.8509	1.9925	2.1435	2.3045	2.4759
9	1.5513	1.6895	1.8384	1.9990	2.1718	2.3579	2.5580	2.7730
10	1.6289	1.7908	1.9671	2.1589	2.3673	2.5937	2.8394	3.1058
11	1.7103	1.8983	2.1048	2.3316	2.5804	2.8531	3.1517	3.4785
12	1.7959	2.0122	2.2521	2.5181	2.8126	3.1384	3.4984	3.8959
13	1.8856	2.1329	2.4098	2.7196	3.0658	3.4522	3.8832	4.3634
14	1.9799	2.2609	2.5785	2.9371	3.3417	3.7974	4.3104	4.8871
15	2.0789	2.3966	2.7590	3.1721	3.6424	4.1772	4.7845	5.4735
16	2.1829	2.5404	2.9521	3.4259	3.9703	4.5949	5.3108	6.1303
17	2.2920	2.6928	3.1588	3.7000	4.3276	5.0544	5.8950	6.8660
18	2.8543	2.8543	3.3799	3.9960	4.7171	5.5599	6.5435	7.6899
19	2.5270	3.0256	3.6165	4.3157	5.1416	6.1159	7.2633	8.6127
20	2.6533	3.2071	3.8696	4.6609	5.6044	6.7274	8.0623	9.6462
21	2.7860	3.3996	4.1405	5.0338	6.1088	7.4002	8.9491	10.8038
22	2.9253	3.6035	4.4304	5.4365	6.6586	8.1402	9.9335	12.1003
23	3.0715	3.8197	4.7405	5.8714	7.2578	8.9543	11.0262	13.5523
24	3.2251	4.0489	5.0723	6.3411	7.9110	9.8497	12.2391	15.1786
25	3.3864	4.2919	5.4274	6.8484	8.6230	10.8347	13.5854	17.0000
26	3.5557	4.5494	5.8073	7.3963	9.3991	11.9181	15.0793	19.0400
27	3.7335	4.8223	6.2138	7.9880	10.2450	13.1099	16.7386	21.3248
28	3.9201	5.1117	6.6488	8.6271	11.1671	14.4209	18.5799	23.8838
29	4.1161	5.4184	7.1142	9.3172	12.1721	15.8630	20.6236	26.7499
30	4.3219	5.7435	7.6122	10.5582	13.2676	17.4494	22.8922	29.9599
31	4.5380	6.0881	8.1451	10.8676	14.4617	19.1943	25.4104	33.5551
32	4.7649	6.4534	8.7152	11.7370	15.7633	21.1137	28.2055	37.5817
33	5.0032	6.8406	9.3253	12.6760	17.1820	23.2251	31.3082	42.0915
34	5.2533	7.2510	9.9781	13.6901	18.7284	25.5476	34.7521	47.1425
35	5.5160	7.6861	10.6765	14.7853	20.4139	28.1024	38.5748	52.7996
36	5.7918	8.1473	11.4239	15.9681	22.2512	30.9128	42.8180	59.1355
37	6.0814	8.6361	12.2236	17.2456	24.2538	34.0039	47.5280	66.2318
38	6.3855	9.1543	13.0792	18.6252	26.4366	37.4048	52.7561	74.1796
39	6.7048	9.7035	13.9948	20.1152	28.8159	41.1447	58.5593	83.0812
40	7.0400	10.2857	14.9744	21.7245	31.4094	45.2592	65.0008	93.0509

How Much $1 a Year Will Equal

Example: If you put $1,000 in an IRA at the end of each year, and the account earned 8% interest, how much would your money grow to after 20 years?

Answer: $45,761.90 (factor for 20 years, 45.7619 times $1,000).

If you put $1,000 in at the beginning of each year, take the dollar amount found after applying the factor, and multiply it by 1 plus the interest rate: $45,761.90 × 1.08 = $49,422.85.

Number of Years	5%	6%	7%	8%	9%	10%	11%	12%
1	1.0000	1.0000	1.0000	1.0000	1.0000	1.0000	1.0000	1.0000
2	2.0500	2.0600	2.0700	2.0800	2.0900	2.1000	2.1100	2.1200
3	3.1525	3.1836	3.2149	3.2464	3.2781	3.3100	3.3421	3.3744
4	4.3101	4.3746	4.4399	4.5061	4.5731	4.6410	4.7097	4.7793
5	5.5256	5.6370	5.7507	5.8666	5.9847	6.1051	6.2278	6.3528
6	6.8019	6.9753	7.1532	7.3359	7.5233	7.7156	7.9128	8.1151
7	8.1420	8.3938	8.6540	8.9228	9.2004	9.4871	9.7832	10.0890
8	9.5491	9.8974	10.2598	10.6366	11.0284	11.4358	11.8594	12.2996
9	11.0265	11.4913	11.9779	12.4875	13.0210	13.5794	14.1639	14.7756
10	12.5778	13.1807	13.8164	14.4865	15.1929	15.9374	16.7220	17.5487
11	14.2067	14.9716	15.7835	16.6454	17.5602	18.5311	19.5614	20.6545
12	15.9171	16.8699	17.8884	18.9771	20.1407	21.3842	22.7131	24.1331
13	17.7129	18.8821	20.1406	21.4952	22.9533	24.5227	26.2116	28.0291
14	19.5986	21.0150	22.5504	24.2149	26.0191	27.9749	30.0949	32.3926
15	21.5785	23.2759	25.1290	27.1521	29.3609	31.7724	34.4053	37.2797
16	23.6574	25.6725	27.8880	30.3242	33.0033	35.9497	39.1899	42.7532
17	25.8403	28.2128	30.8402	33.7502	36.9737	40.5447	44.5008	48.8836
18	28.1323	30.9056	33.9990	37.4502	41.3013	45.5991	50.3959	55.7497
19	30.5390	33.7599	37.3789	41.4462	46.0184	51.1590	56.9394	63.4396
20	33.0659	36.7855	40.9954	45.7619	51.1601	57.2749	64.2028	72.0524
21	35.7192	39.9927	44.8651	50.4229	56.7645	64.0024	72.2651	81.6987
22	38.5052	43.3922	49.0057	55.4567	62.8733	71.4027	81.2143	92.5025
23	41.4304	46.9958	53.4361	60.8932	69.5319	79.5430	91.1478	104.6028
24	44.5019	50.8155	58.1766	66.7647	76.7898	88.4973	102.1741	118.1552
25	47.7270	54.8645	63.2490	73.1059	84.7008	98.3470	114.4133	133.3338
26	51.1134	59.1653	68.6764	79.9544	93.3239	109.1817	127.9987	150.3339
27	54.6691	63.7057	74.4838	87.3507	102.7231	121.0999	143.0786	169.3740
28	58.4025	68.5281	80.6976	95.3388	112.9682	134.2099	159.8172	190.6988
29	62.3227	73.6397	87.3465	103.9659	124.1353	148.6309	178.3971	214.5827
30	66.4388	79.0581	94.4607	113.2832	136.3075	164.4940	199.0208	241.3326
31	70.7607	84.8016	102.0730	123.3458	149.5752	181.9434	221.9131	271.2926
32	75.2988	90.8897	110.2181	134.2135	164.0369	201.1377	247.3236	304.8477
33	80.0637	97.3431	118.9334	145.9506	179.8003	222.2515	275.5292	342.4294
34	85.0669	104.1837	128.2587	158.6266	196.9823	245.4766	306.8374	384.5209
35	90.3203	111.4347	138.2368	172.3168	215.7107	271.0243	341.5895	431.6634
36	95.8363	119.1208	148.9134	187.1021	236.1247	299.1268	380.1644	484.4631
37	101.6281	127.2681	160.3374	203.0703	258.3759	330.0394	422.9824	543.5986
38	107.7095	135.9042	172.5610	220.3159	282.6297	364.0434	470.5105	609.8305
39	114.0950	145.0584	185.6402	238.9412	309.0664	401.4477	523.2667	684.0101
40	120.7997	154.7619	199.6351	259.0565	337.8824	442.5925	581.8260	767.0914

DOLLAR BUYING POWER

Example of use of this table:

If I put $1,000 in the bank, how much can I take out each year for 5 years to use up the entire sum if the interest rate is 6%?

From the table at 5 years 0.2374

For $1,000 (1,000 × 0.2374). $237.40

Note: This does not necessarily represent the annuity payable under an annuity or insurance contract.

Number of Years	5%	6%	7%	8%	9%	10%	11%	12%
1	1.0500	1.0600	1.0700	1.0800	1.0900	1.1000	1.1100	1.1200
2	0.5378	0.5454	0.5501	0.5608	0.5685	0.5762	0.5839	0.5917
3	0.3672	0.3741	0.3811	0.3880	0.3950	0.4021	0.4092	0.4163
4	0.2820	0.2886	0.2952	0.3019	0.3087	0.3155	0.3223	0.3292
5	0.2310	0.2374	0.2439	0.2505	0.2571	0.2638	0.2706	0.2774
6	0.1970	0.2034	0.2098	0.2163	0.2229	0.2296	0.2364	0.2432
7	0.1728	0.1791	0.1856	0.1921	0.1987	0.2054	0.2122	0.2191
8	0.1547	0.1610	0.1675	0.1740	0.1807	0.1874	0.1943	0.2013
9	0.1407	0.1470	0.1535	0.1601	0.1668	0.1736	0.1806	0.1877
10	0.1295	0.1359	0.1424	0.1490	0.1558	0.1627	0.1698	0.1770
11	0.1204	0.1268	0.1334	0.1401	0.1469	0.1540	0.1611	0.1684
12	0.1128	0.1193	0.1259	0.1327	0.1396	0.1468	0.1540	0.1614
13	0.1065	0.1129	0.1197	0.1265	0.1330	0.1408	0.1481	0.1557
14	0.1010	0.1076	0.1143	0.1213	0.1284	0.1357	0.1432	0.1509
15	0.0963	0.1029	0.1098	0.1168	0.1241	0.1315	0.1391	0.1468
16	0.0923	0.0989	0.1059	0.1129	0.1203	0.1278	0.1355	0.1434
17	0.0887	0.0954	0.1024	0.1096	0.1170	0.1247	0.1325	0.1405
18	0.0855	0.0924	0.0994	0.1067	0.1142	0.1219	0.1298	0.1379
19	0.0827	0.0896	0.0968	0.1041	0.1117	0.1195	0.1276	0.1358
20	0.0802	0.0872	0.0944	0.1019	0.1095	0.1175	0.1256	0.1339
21	0.0780	0.0850	0.0923	0.0998	0.1076	0.1156	0.1238	0.1322
22	0.0760	0.0837	0.0904	0.0980	0.1059	0.1140	0.1223	0.1308
23	0.0741	0.0813	0.0887	0.0964	0.1044	0.1126	0.1211	0.1296
24	0.0725	0.0797	0.0872	0.0949	0.1030	0.1113	0.1198	0.1285
25	0.0710	0.0782	0.0858	0.0937	0.1018	0.1102	0.1187	0.1275
26	0.0696	0.0769	0.0846	0.0925	0.1007	0.1092	0.1178	0.1266
27	0.0683	0.0757	0.0834	0.0914	0.0998	0.1083	0.1170	0.1259
28	0.0671	0.0746	0.0824	0.0905	0.0989	0.1074	0.1163	0.1252
29	0.0660	0.0736	0.0814	0.0896	0.0980	0.1067	0.1156	0.1247
30	0.0651	0.0726	0.0806	0.0888	0.0973	0.1061	0.1150	0.1241
31	0.0641	0.0718	0.0798	0.0881	0.0967	0.1055	0.1146	0.1237
32	0.0633	0.0710	0.0791	0.0875	0.0961	0.1050	0.1140	0.1233
33	0.0625	0.0703	0.0784	0.0869	0.0956	0.1045	0.1136	0.1229
34	0.0618	0.0696	0.0778	0.0863	0.0951	0.1041	0.1133	0.1226
35	0.0611	0.0686	0.0772	0.0858	0.0946	0.1037	0.1129	0.1223
36	0.0604	0.0684	0.0767	0.0853	0.0942	0.1033	0.1126	0.1221
37	0.0598	0.0679	0.0762	0.0849	0.0939	0.1030	0.1124	0.1218
38	0.0593	0.0674	0.0758	0.0845	0.0935	0.1027	0.1121	0.1216
39	0.0588	0.0669	0.0754	0.0842	0.0932	0.1025	0.1119	0.1215
40	0.0583	0.0665	0.0750	0.0839	0.0930	0.1023	0.1117	0.1213

PRESENT WORTH OF A SINGLE FUTURE PAYMENT*

Example of use of this table:

Find out how much must be invested now to equal $10,000 in 12 years at 7% interest rate.

From table for 12 years at 7%:. 0.4440

Invest now for $10,000 ($10,000 × 0.4440): $4,440

Number of Years	5%	6%	7%	8%	9%	10%	11%	12%
1	0.9524	.9434	.9346	.9259	.9174	.9091	.9009	.8929
2	.9070	.8900	.8734	.8573	.8417	.8264	.8116	.7972
3	.8638	.8396	.8163	.7938	.7722	.7513	.7312	.7118
4	.8227	.7921	.7629	.7350	.7084	.6830	.6587	.6355
5	.7835	.7473	.7130	.6806	.6499	.6209	.5935	.5674
6	.7462	.7050	.6663	.6302	.5963	.5645	.5346	.5066
7	.7107	.6651	.6227	.5835	.5470	.5132	.4816	.4523
8	.6768	.6274	.5820	.5403	.5019	.4665	.4339	.4039
9	.6446	.5919	.5439	.5002	.4604	.4241	.3909	.3606
10	.6139	.5584	.5083	.4632	.4224	.3855	.3522	.3220
11	.5847	.5268	.4751	.4289	.3875	.3505	.3173	.2875
12	.5568	.4970	.4440	.3971	.3555	.3186	.2858	.2567
13	.5303	.4688	.4150	.3677	.3262	.2897	.2575	.2292
14	.5051	.4423	.3878	.3405	.2992	.2633	.2320	.2046
15	.4810	.4173	.3624	.3152	.2745	.2394	.2090	.1827
16	.4581	.3936	.3387	.2919	.2519	.2176	.1883	.1631
17	.4363	.3714	.3166	.2703	.2311	.1978	.1696	.1456
18	.4155	.3503	.2959	.2502	.2120	.1799	.1528	.1300
19	.3957	.3305	.2765	.2317	.1945	.1635	.1377	.1161
20	.3769	.3118	.2584	.2145	.1784	.1486	.1240	.1037
21	.3589	.2942	.2415	.1987	.1637	.1351	.1117	.0925
22	.3418	.2775	.2257	.1839	.1502	.1228	.1007	.0826
23	.3256	.2618	.2109	.1703	.1378	.1117	.0907	.0738
24	.3101	.2470	.1971	.1577	.1264	.1015	.0817	.0659
25	.2953	.2330	.1842	.1460	.1160	.0923	.0736	.0588
26	.2812	.2198	.1722	.1352	.1064	.0839	.0663	.0525
27	.2678	.2074	.1609	.1252	.0976	.0763	.0597	.0469
28	.2551	.1956	.1504	.1159	.0895	.0693	.0538	.0419
29	.2429	.1846	.1406	.1073	.0822	.0630	.0485	.0374
30	.2314	.1741	.1314	.0994	.0754	.0573	.0437	.0334
31	.2204	.1643	.1228	.0920	.0691	.0521	.0394	.0298
32	.2099	.1550	.1147	.0852	.0634	.0474	.0354	.0266
33	.1999	.1462	.1072	.0789	.0582	.0431	.0319	.0238
34	.1904	.1379	.1002	.0730	.0534	.0391	.0288	.0212
35	.1813	.1301	.0937	.0676	.0490	.0356	.0259	.0189
36	.1727	.1227	.0875	.0626	.0449	.0323	.0234	.0169
37	.1644	.1158	.0818	.0580	.0412	.0294	.0210	.0151
38	.1566	.1092	.0765	.0537	.0378	.0267	.0189	.0135
39	.1491	.1031	.0715	.0497	.0347	.0243	.0171	.0120
40	.1420	.0972	.0668	.0460	.0318	.0221	.0154	.0107

* This is a single deposit today which, with interest, will amount to 1 in a given time; or, the present or discounted value of 1 due at a given future time.

UNIFORM ONE-YEAR TERM PREMIUM IN PENSION AND PROFIT-SHARING COVERAGE AND SPLIT-DOLLAR PLANS

When current life insurance protection is given to an employee as part of the employer contribution for retirement or other form of insurance in a pension or profit-sharing plan, the cost of the so-called "pure insurance" factor of the coverage is taxable to the employee at the time of the employer's contribution. When an employee works out a split-dollar arrangement with his employer, the difference between what the employee contributes towards each year's premium and the one-year cost of the declining life insurance protection to which he is entitled from year to year is included in his gross income. The following Government table gives an acceptable-to-the-Government cost of one-year term insurance for these purposes:

Age	Cost per $1,000 of protection	Age	Cost per $1,000 of protection	Age	Cost per $1,000 of protection
15	$1.27	37	$3.63	60	$20.73
16	1.38	38	3.87	61	22.53
17	1.48	39	4.14	62	24.50
18	1.52			63	26.63
19	1.56	40	4.42	64	28.98
		41	4.73		
20	1.61	42	5.07	65	31.51
21	1.67	43	5.44	66	34.28
22	1.73	44	5.85	67	37.31
23	1.79			68	40.59
24	1.86	45	6.30	69	44.17
		46	6.78		
25	1.93	47	7.32	70	48.06
26	2.02	48	7.89	71	52.29
27	2.11	49	8.53	72	56.89
28	2.20			73	61.89
29	2.31	50	9.22	74	67.33
		51	9.97		
30	2.43	52	10.79	75	73.23
31	2.57	53	11.69	76	79.63
32	2.70	54	12.67	77	86.57
33	2.86			78	94.09
34	3.02	55	13.74	79	102.23
		56	14.91		
35	3.21	57	16.18	80	111.04
36	3.41	58	17.56	81	120.57
		59	19.08		

FAMILY INCOME RIDER

The family income rider provides a monthly income in the event of the death of the insured during the period selected. The period begins when the policy becomes effective. If, for example, the period selected is 20 years and the insured dies after the policy has been in effect 10 years, the beneficiary will receive payments for 10 years under the family income rider. After the 10-year period ends, the face amount of the policy will be paid. Each agreement may be written for any amount of monthly income from $10 to $50 for each $1,000 face amount of basic policy. This plan was designed primarily to provide (a) income during the school period, (b) a life income to the surviving spouse, and (c) funds to pay off a mortgage.

Tax Aspects of Family Income Rider: Regs. §1.101-3 and 1.101-4 say that a portion of each monthly payment under a family income rider represents interest on the proceeds of the basic policy retained by the insurance company until the end of the term period. To that extent, a surviving spouse is taxed each year on such interest. The monthly yield per $1,000 face amount depends upon the rate of interest guaranteed under the policy.

The balance of each payment under the family income rider is attributable to both principal and interest payable in installments from the term rider. To the extent that such installment payment reflects interest, it is taxable. But the surviving spouse is entitled to exclude from gross income an amount up to $1,000 a year. The commuted value of the family income rider is income tax free as death proceeds.

As an example of how IRS taxes a surviving spouse as beneficiary of a policy with a family income rider, let's assume the insured (a married man) held a $100,000 ordinary life policy with a $1,000-a-month, 20-year rider. Suppose he died at the end of the seventeenth year, so that there are 36 monthly payments to be made to his widow under the family income rider. At the time of his death, the commuted value of the $36,000 total payments ($1,000 x 36) is $28,409.

Assuming an interest rate of 2¼%, here's how to figure the amount of each $1,000 monthly payment includible in the widow's gross income:

First: Compute the annual interest on the $100,000 basic policy which is retained by the insurance company for the duration of payments under the rider ($1,000 x 2¼% = $2,250). When reduced to 12 monthly installments with the necessary adjustments for monthly payments, this comes to $185. Thus, the widow will include in her gross income the $185 monthly payments under Code §101(c).

Second: Divide the commuted value of the family income rider by the number of monthly payments, $28,409 ÷ 36 = $789.14. So the $789.14 which represents distribution of principal under the rider is excluded under Code §101(d).

Third: The balance of each monthly installment, $25.86 ($1,000 minus $789.14 minus $185 = $25.86), represents interest on the proceeds of the family income rider. Since the sum of $25.86 is being distributed to the widow along with the principal, it qualifies for the annual exclusion. And since the annual total is less than $1,000 ($25.86 x 12 = $310.32), the entire amount is tax free.

Fourth: At the end of the monthly payments under the family income rider, the $100,000 proceeds of the basic ordinary life policy will then go to the widow tax free under Code §101(a).

SETTLEMENT OPTIONS

Optional modes of settlement provide that the whole or part of the net proceeds of a policy payable at death, or at maturity as an endowment, or of the cash value of a policy in force may be retained by the company for periodic disbursement in a number of ways.

To ascertain insurance requirements for income needs, it is necessary to determine what the settlement options will do in the way of income.

The following tables give the income payable, either for a specified number of years or for life under various insurance policy settlement options. The tables show how long various amounts of insurance will provide stipulated amounts of monthly income at various rates of interest and how much monthly life income will be available for periods certain for males and females. The tables are very conservative. Most insurance companies currently pay benefits computed at higher interest than the guaranteed rates.

Proceeds at Interest

The table on page 716 shows the monthly interest payable, at various guaranteed interest rates, when the proceeds are left with the insurance company to draw interest.

Interest Rate	Monthly per $1,000 Proceeds
2% guaranteed	$1.65
2½% guaranteed	2.06
3% guaranteed	2.46

Settlement Options (*continued*)

	Proceeds Payable in Equal Monthly Payments for Fixed Period of Years								
	When 3% Is Guaranteed			When 2½% Is Guaranteed			When 2% Is Guaranteed		
No. of Years Payable	Payments per $1,000 Proceeds	Proceeds Required for Payments of		Payments per $1,000 Proceeds	Proceeds Required for Payments of		Payments per $1,000 Proceeds	Proceeds Required for Payments of	
		$25	$100		$25	$100		$25	$100
1	$84.47	$ 296	$ 1,184	$84.28	$ 297	$ 1,187	$84.09	$ 298	$ 1,190
2	42.86	584	2,334	42.66	587	2,345	42.46	589	2,356
3	28.99	863	3,450	28.79	869	3,474	28.59	875	3,498
4	22.06	1,134	4,534	21.86	1,144	4,575	21.65	1,155	4,619
5	17.91	1,396	5,584	17.70	1,413	5,650	17.49	1,430	5,718
6	15.14	1,652	6,606	14.93	1,675	6,698	14.72	1,699	6,794
7	13.16	1,900	7,599	12.95	1,931	7,723	12.74	1,963	7,850
8	11.68	2,141	8,562	11.47	2,180	8,719	11.25	2,223	8,889
9	10.53	2,375	9,497	10.32	2,423	9,690	10.10	2,476	9,901
10	9.61	2,602	10,406	9.39	2,663	10,650	9.18	2,724	10,894
11	8.86	2,822	11,287	8.64	2,894	11,575	8.42	2,970	11,877
12	8.24	3,034	12,136	8.02	3,118	12,469	7.80	3,206	12,821
13	7.71	3,243	12,971	7.49	3,338	13,352	7.26	3,444	13,775
14	7.26	3,444	13,775	7.03	3,557	14,225	6.81	3,672	14,685
15	6.87	3,640	14,557	6.64	3,766	15,061	6.42	3,895	15,577
16	6.53	3,829	15,314	6.30	3,969	15,874	6.07	4,119	16,475
17	6.23	4,013	16,052	6.00	4,167	16,667	5.77	4,333	17,332
18	5.96	4,195	16,779	5.73	4,364	17,453	5.50	4,546	18,182
19	5.73	4,364	17,453	5.49	4,554	18,215	5.26	4,753	19,012
20	5.51	4,538	18,149	5.27	4,744	18,976	5.04	4,961	19,842
21	5.32	4,700	18,797	5.08	4,922	19,686	4.85	5,155	20,619
22	5.15	4,855	19,416	4.90	5,103	20,409	4.67	5,354	21,414
23	4.99	5,011	20,041	4.74	5,275	21,098	4.51	5,544	22,173
24	4.84	5,166	20,662	4.60	5,435	21,740	4.36	5,734	22,936
25	4.71	5,308	21,232	4.46	5,606	22,422	4.22	5,925	23,697
26	4.59	5,447	21,787	4.34	5,761	23,042	4.10	6,098	24,391
27	4.47	5,583	22,372	4.22	5,925	23,697	3.98	6,282	25,126
28	4.37	5,721	22,884	4.12	6,068	24,272	3.87	6,460	25,840
29	4.27	5,855	23,420	4.03	6,219	24,876	3.77	6,632	26,526
30	4.18	5,981	23,924	3.93	6,362	25,446	3.68	6,794	27,174

How Long Insurance Proceeds Will Last if Paid Out Monthly Until Principal and Interest Are Exhausted

% of proceeds Paid each year or	Dollars per Month per $1,000 of proceeds	Fund Will Last - When Guaranteed Rate of Interest Is:					
		2%		2-1/2%		3%	
		Yrs.	Mos.	Yrs.	Mos.	Yrs.	Mos.
5.0%	$ 4.17	25	5	27	6	30	2
5.4	4.50	23	0	24	8	26	9
5.5	4.58	22	6	24	1	26	0
6.0	5.00	20	2	21	5	22	11
6.5	5.42	18	3	19	3	20	5
6.6	5.50	17	11	18	11	20	0
7.0	5.83	16	9	17	7	18	6
7.2	6.00	16	2	16	11	17	10
7.5	6.25	15	5	16	1	16	11
7.8	6.50	14	9	15	4	16	1
8.0	6.67	14	4	14	11	15	7
3.4	7.00	13	6	14	0	14	7
8.5	7.08	13	4	13	10	14	5
9.0	7.50	12	6	12	11	13	5
9.5	7.92	11	9	12	2	12	7
10.0	8.33	11	1	11	5	11	10
10.2	8.50	10	10	11	2	11	6
10.5	8.75	10	6	10	10	11	2
10.8	9.00	10	2	10	6	10	9
11.0	9.17	10	0	10	3	10	6
11.4	9.50	9	7	9	10	10	1
12.0	10.00	9	1	9	3	9	6
12.5	10.42	8	8	8	10	9	1
13.0	10.83	8	4	8	6	8	8
13.5	11.25	8	0	8	2	8	4
14.0	11.67	7	8	7	10	8	0
15.0	12.50	7	1	7	3	7	5
16.0	13.33	6	7	6	9	6	10
17.0	14.17	6	2	6	4	6	5
18.0	15.00	5	10	5	11	6	0
19.0	15.83	5	6	5	7	5	8
20.0	16.67	5	3	5	3	5	4
21.0	17.50	4	11	5	0	5	1
22.0	18.33	4	9	4	9	4	10
23.0	19.17	4	6	4	7	4	7
24.0	20.00	4	4	4	4	4	5
25.0	20.83	4	1	4	2	4	3

SELF-LIQUIDATING MORTGAGES—MONTHLY PAYMENTS

The following tables are useful planning tools that are to be used for quickly determining the constant monthly payments, annual interest, annual amortization payments, and remaining balance for mortgages at various interest rates, at different payout terms. In all cases the amounts shown are for $1,000 mortgages. Therefore, if you want to know the monthly payments on a $35,000 mortgage at 8¹/2% interest to be liquidated over 25 years, take the following steps:

(1) Turn to the table titled 25-YEAR TERM and locate the chart of 8¹/2% interest, which shows a monthly payment of $8.05.

(2) Since $8.05 is the monthly payment on a $1,000 mortgage, multiply this by your mortgage amount to determine what your constant monthly payment will be (35 x $8.05 = $281.75).

5-YEAR TERM

Year	4% interest - $18.42 monthly payment			4-1/2% interest - $18.65 monthly payment			5% interest - $18.88 monthly payment		
	Interest	Amort.	Balance	Interest	Amort.	Balance	Interest	Amort.	Balance
1	38.63	184.41	815.59	41.26	182.54	817.46	45.91	180.65	819.35
2	29.14	191.90	623.69	32.88	190.92	626.54	36.64	189.92	629.43
3	21.31	199.73	423.96	24.11	199.69	426.85	26.92	199.64	429.79
4	13.19	207.85	216.11	14.94	208.86	217.99	16.74	209.82	219.97
5	4.67	216.11	0	5.34	217.99	0	5.99	219.97	0

Year	5-1/4% interest - $18.99 monthly payment			5-1/2% interest - $19.11 monthly payment			5-3/4% interest - $19.22 monthly payment		
	Interest	Amort.	Balance	Interest	Amort.	Balance	Interest	Amort.	Balance
1	48.23	179.65	820.35	50.53	178.79	821.21	52.85	177.79	822.21
2	38.55	189.33	631.02	40.44	188.88	632.33	42.37	188.27	633.94
3	28.37	199.51	431.51	29.79	199.53	432.80	31.26	199.38	434.56
4	17.65	210.23	221.28	18.58	210.74	222.06	19.47	211.17	223.39
5	6.33	221.28	0	6.63	222.06	0	7.00	223.39	0

Year	6% interest - $19.34 monthly payment			6-1/4% interest - $19.45 monthly payment			6-1/2% interest - $19.57 monthly payment		
	Interest	Amort.	Balance	Interest	Amort.	Balance	Interest	Amort.	Balance
1	55.19	176.89	823.11	57.51	175.89	824.11	59.85	174.99	825.01
2	44.29	187.79	635.32	46.18	187.22	636.89	48.13	186.71	638.30
3	32.70	199.38	435.94	34.16	199.24	437.65	35.63	199.21	439.09
4	20.39	211.68	224.26	21.35	212.05	225.60	22.30	212.54	226.55
5	7.33	224.26	0	7.72	225.60	0	8.04	226.55	0

Year	6-3/4% interest - $19.69 monthly payment			7% interest - $19.81 monthly payment			7-1/4% interest - $19.92 monthly payment		
	Interest	Amort.	Balance	Interest	Amort.	Balance	Interest	Amort.	Balance
1	62.30	174.08	825.92	64.51	173.21	826.79	66.85	172.19	827.81
2	50.07	186.21	639.71	52.01	185.71	641.08	53.95	185.09	642.72
3	37.10	199.18	440.53	38.57	199.15	441.93	40.06	198.98	443.74
4	23.23	213.05	227.48	24.18	213.54	228.39	25.17	213.87	229.87
5	8.41	227.48	0	8.75	228.39	0	9.13	229.87	0

Year	7-1/2% interest - $20.04 monthly payment			7-3/4% interest - $20.16 monthly payment			8% interest - $20.28 monthly payment		
	Interest	Amort.	Balance	Interest	Amort.	Balance	Interest	Amort.	Balance
1	69.18	171.30	828.70	71.54	170.38	829.62	73.87	169.49	830.51
2	55.89	184.59	644.11	57.83	184.09	645.53	59.81	183.55	646.96
3	41.58	198.90	445.21	43.08	198.84	446.69	44.56	198.80	448.16
4	26.12	214.36	230.85	27.08	214.84	231.85	28.06	215.30	232.86
5	9.45	230.85	0	9.85	231.85	0	10.21	232.86	0

Year	9% interest - $20.76 monthly payment			10% interest - $21.25 monthly payment		
	Interest	Amort.	Balance	Interest	Amort.	Balance
1	83.27	165.85	834.15	92.71	162.29	837.71
2	67.72	181.40	652.75	75.70	179.30	658.41
3	50.40	198.42	454.33	56.91	198.09	460.32
4	32.10	217.02	237.31	36.20	218.80	241.52
5	11.71	237.31	0	13.25	241.52	0

838

10-YEAR TERM

	4% interest - $10.13 monthly payment			4-1/2% interest - $10.37 monthly payment			5% interest - $10.61 monthly payment		
Year	Interest	Amort.	Balance	Interest	Amort.	Balance	Interest	Amort.	Balance
1	38.49	83.07	916.93	43.34	81.10	918.90	48.21	79.11	920.89
2	35.11	86.45	830.48	39.62	84.82	834.08	44.16	83.16	837.73
3	31.56	90.00	740.48	35.72	88.72	745.36	39.90	87.42	750.31
4	27.92	93.64	646.84	31.65	92.79	652.57	35.44	91.88	658.43
5	24.11	97.45	549.39	27.41	97.03	555.54	30.72	96.60	561.83
6	20.13	101.43	447.96	22.92	101.52	454.02	25.79	101.53	460.30
7	16.00	105.56	342.40	18.26	106.18	347.84	20.60	106.72	353.58
8	11.70	109.86	232.54	13.37	111.07	236.77	15.13	112.19	241.39
9	7.23	114.33	118.21	8.29	116.15	120.62	9.41	117.91	123.48
10	2.54	118.21	0	2.94	120.62	0	3.35	123.48	0

	5-1/4% interest - $10.73 monthly payment			5-1/2% interest - $10.86 monthly payment			5-3/4% interest - $10.98 monthly payment		
Year	Interest	Amort.	Balance	Interest	Amort.	Balance	Interest	Amort.	Balance
1	50.64	78.12	921.88	53.08	77.24	922.76	55.50	76.26	923.74
2	46.43	82.33	839.55	48.72	81.60	841.16	51.01	80.75	842.99
3	42.01	86.75	752.80	44.11	86.21	754.95	46.24	85.52	757.47
4	37.35	91.41	661.39	39.24	91.08	663.87	41.19	90.57	666.90
5	32.43	96.33	565.06	34.11	96.21	567.66	35.85	95.91	570.99
6	27.25	101.51	463.55	28.68	101.64	466.02	30.20	101.56	469.43
7	21.79	106.97	356.58	22.96	107.36	358.66	24.20	107.56	361.87
8	16.04	112.72	243.86	16.89	113.43	245.23	17.83	113.93	247.94
9	9.98	118.78	125.08	10.49	119.83	125.40	11.12	120.64	127.30
10	3.58	125.08	0	3.71	125.40	0	3.98	127.30	0

	6% interest - $11.11 monthly payment			6-1/4% interest - $11.23 monthly payment			6-1/2% interest - $11.36 monthly payment		
Year	Interest	Amort.	Balance	Interest	Amort.	Balance	Interest	Amort.	Balance
1	57.96	75.36	924.64	60.40	74.36	925.64	59.83	73.49	926.51
2	53.31	80.01	844.63	55.60	79.16	846.48	57.90	78.42	848.09
3	48.35	84.97	759.66	50.53	84.23	762.25	52.66	83.66	764.43
4	43.13	90.19	669.47	45.09	89.67	672.58	47.04	89.28	675.15
5	37.56	95.76	573.71	39.33	95.43	577.15	41.09	95.23	579.92
6	31.67	101.65	472.06	33.20	101.56	475.59	34.71	101.61	478.31
7	25.38	107.94	364.11	26.67	108.09	367.50	27.88	108.44	369.87
8	18.73	114.59	249.52	19.73	115.03	252.47	20.63	115.69	254.18
9	11.68	121.64	127.88	12.31	122.45	130.02	12.91	123.41	130.77
10	4.14	127.88	0	4.44	130.02	0	4.63	130.77	0

	6-3/4% interest - $11.49 monthly payment			7% interest - $11.62 monthly payment			7-1/4% interest - $11.75 monthly payment		
Year	Interest	Amort.	Balance	Interest	Amort.	Balance	Interest	Amort.	Balance
1	65.29	72.59	927.41	67.73	71.71	928.29	70.18	70.82	929.18
2	60.23	77.65	849.76	62.55	76.89	851.40	64.86	76.14	853.04
3	54.81	83.07	766.69	57.01	82.44	768.97	59.14	81.86	771.18
4	49.04	88.84	677.85	51.02	88.41	680.55	53.02	87.98	683.20
5	42.85	95.03	582.82	44.64	94.80	585.75	45.43	94.57	588.63
6	36.23	101.65	481.17	37.79	101.65	484.10	39.36	101.64	486.99
7	29.17	108.71	372.46	30.42	109.02	375.08	31.73	109.27	377.72
8	21.59	116.29	256.17	22.55	116.89	258.19	23.50	117.50	260.22
9	13.50	124.38	131.79	14.12	125.32	132.87	14.71	126.29	133.93
10	4.82	131.79	0	5.06	132.87	0	5.27	133.93	0

	7-1/2% interest - $11.88 monthly payment			7-3/4% interest - $12.01 monthly payment			8% interest - $12.14 monthly payment		
Year	Interest	Amort.	Balance	Interest	Amort.	Balance	Interest	Amort.	Balance
1	72.60	69.93	930.07	75.08	69.04	930.96	77.54	68.14	931.86
2	67.19	75.37	854.70	69.54	74.58	856.38	71.87	73.81	858.05
3	61.35	81.21	773.49	63.55	80.57	775.81	65.74	79.94	778.11
4	55.04	87.52	685.97	57.07	87.05	688.76	59.12	86.56	691.55
5	48.26	94.30	591.67	50.09	94.03	594.73	51.94	93.74	597.81
6	40.94	101.62	490.05	42.53	101.59	493.14	44.17	101.51	496.30
7	33.04	109.52	380.53	34.38	109.74	383.40	35.73	109.95	386.35
8	24.54	118.02	262.51	25.56	118.56	264.84	26.61	119.07	267.28
9	15.38	127.18	135.33	16.05	128.07	136.77	16.72	128.96	138.32
10	5.51	135.33	0	5.75	136.77	0	6.02	138.32	0

10-YEAR TERM (continued)

	8-1/2% interest - $12.40 monthly payment			8-3/4% interest - $12.53 monthly payment			9% interest - $12.67 monthly payment		
Year	Interest	Amort.	Balance	Interest	Amort.	Balance	Interest	Amort.	Balance
1	82.46	66.34	933.66	84.91	65.45	934.55	87.36	64.68	935.32
2	76.59	72.21	861.45	78.95	71.41	863.14	81.31	70.73	864.59
3	70.21	78.59	782.86	72.45	77.91	785.23	74.65	77.39	787.20
4	63.27	85.53	697.32	65.35	85.01	700.22	67.40	84.64	702.56
5	55.71	93.09	604.23	57.61	92.75	607.47	59.46	92.58	609.98
6	47.48	101.32	502.91	49.16	101.20	506.27	50.78	101.26	508.72
7	38.52	110.28	392.63	39.94	110.42	395.85	41.30	110.74	397.98
8	28.78	120.02	272.61	29.89	120.47	275.38	30.90	121.14	276.84
9	18.17	130.63	141.98	18.92	131.44	143.94	19.56	132.48	144.36
10	6.63	142.17	0.18	6.94	143.42	0.52	7.10	144.36	0

	9-1/4% interest - $12.80 monthly payment			9-1/2% interest - $12.94 monthly payment			9-3/4% interest - $13.08 monthly payment		
Year	Interest	Amort.	Balance	Interest	Amort.	Balance	Interest	Amort.	Balance
1	89.84	63.76	936.23	92.31	62.97	937.03	94.76	62.20	937.80
2	83.68	69.92	866.32	86.06	69.22	867.81	88.42	68.54	869.26
3	76.93	76.67	789.65	79.19	76.09	791.71	81.43	75.53	793.74
4	69.53	84.07	705.51	71.64	83.64	708.07	73.73	83.23	710.51
5	61.42	92.18	613.40	63.34	91.94	616.13	65.25	91.71	618.79
6	52.52	101.08	512.33	54.21	101.07	515.06	55.89	101.07	517.73
7	42.77	110.83	401.50	44.18	111.10	403.97	45.59	111.37	406.36
8	32.07	121.53	279.97	33.16	122.12	281.85	34.23	122.73	283.63
9	20.34	133.26	146.72	21.04	134.24	147.61	21.72	135.24	148.38
10	7.48	146.12	0.60	7.72	147.56	0.05	7.93	149.03	0.64

	10% interest - $13.22 monthly payment			10-1/4% interest - $13.35 monthly payment			10-1/2% interest - $13.49 monthly payment		
Year	Interest	Amort.	Balance	Interest	Amort.	Balance	Interest	Amort.	Balance
1	97.23	61.41	938.59	99.71	60.49	939.51	102.18	59.70	940.30
2	90.81	67.83	870.76	93.21	66.99	872.51	95.61	66.27	874.03
3	83.72	74.92	795.84	86.01	74.19	798.32	88.30	73.58	800.45
4	75.86	82.78	713.06	78.04	82.16	716.16	80.19	81.69	718.77
5	67.19	91.45	621.61	69.21	90.99	625.17	71.19	90.69	628.08
6	57.62	101.02	520.59	59.44	100.76	524.41	61.20	100.68	527.40
7	47.03	111.61	408.98	48.61	111.59	412.82	50.10	111.78	415.62
8	35.35	123.29	285.69	36.62	123.58	289.24	37.79	124.09	291.53
9	22.44	136.20	149.49	23.34	136.86	152.38	24.11	137.77	153.76
10	8.17	149.49	0	8.64	151.56	0.82	8.93	152.95	0.81

	10-3/4% interest - $13.63 monthly payment			11% interest - $13.77 monthly payment			11-1/4% interest - $13.92 monthly payment		
Year	Interest	Amort.	Balance	Interest	Amort.	Balance	Interest	Amort.	Balance
1	104.65	58.91	941.09	107.12	58.12	941.88	109.59	57.45	942.55
2	98.00	65.56	875.53	100.39	64.85	877.03	102.79	64.25	878.30
3	90.59	72.97	802.56	92.89	72.35	804.68	95.18	71.86	806.44
4	82.35	81.21	721.35	84.52	80.72	723.96	86.66	80.38	726.06
5	73.18	90.38	630.96	75.18	90.06	633.90	77.14	89.90	636.16
6	62.79	100.59	530.37	64.76	100.48	533.42	66.49	100.55	535.60
7	51.61	111.95	418.42	53.13	112.11	421.32	54.57	112.47	423.14
8	38.96	124.60	293.82	40.16	125.08	296.24	41.25	125.79	297.35
9	24.89	138.67	155.15	25.69	139.55	156.69	26.34	140.70	156.65
10	9.23	154.33	0.82	9.54	155.70	1.00	9.68	157.36	0.70

	11-1/2% interest - $14.06 monthly payment			11-3/4% interest - $14.20 monthly payment			12% interest - $14.35 monthly payment		
Year	Interest	Amort.	Balance	Interest	Amort.	Balance	Interest	Amort.	Balance
1	112.07	56.65	943.35	114.55	55.85	944.15	117.03	55.17	944.83
2	105.20	63.52	879.83	107.63	62.77	881.38	110.03	62.17	882.65
3	97.50	71.22	808.61	99.84	70.56	810.82	102.15	70.05	812.60
4	88.86	79.86	728.75	91.09	79.31	731.51	93.26	78.94	733.66
5	79.18	89.54	639.21	81.25	89.15	642.37	83.25	88.95	644.71
6	68.33	100.39	538.82	70.20	100.20	542.16	71.97	100.23	544.49
7	56.15	112.57	426.25	57.77	112.63	429.53	59.26	112.94	431.55
8	42.50	126.22	300.03	43.80	126.60	302.93	44.94	127.26	304.29
9	27.20	141.52	158.51	28.10	142.30	160.63	28.80	143.40	160.90
10	10.04	158.68	-0.15	10.45	159.95	0.67	10.62	161.58	-0.67

10-YEAR TERM (Continued)

12-1/4% interest - $14.49 monthly payment   12-1/2% interest - $14.64 monthly payment

Year	Interest	Amort.	Balance	Accrued Interest	Interest	Amort.	Balance	Accrued Interest
1	119.51	54.37	945.63	119.51	121.99	53.69	946.31	121.99
2	112.47	61.41	884.22	131.98	114.88	60.80	885.52	236.88
3	104.51	69.37	814.85	336.49	106.83	68.85	816.67	343.71
4	95.52	78.36	736.49	432.01	97.72	77.96	738.71	441.43
5	85.36	88.52	647.97	517.37	87.39	88.29	650.42	528.82
6	73.89	99.99	547.97	591.25	75.70	99.98	550.45	604.53
7	60.92	112.96	435.02	652.18	62.47	113.21	437.23	666.99
8	46.28	127.60	307.42	698.46	47.47	128.21	309.03	714.47
9	29.74	144.14	163.28	738.20	30.50	145.18	163.84	744.96
10	11.06	162.82	.46	739.26	11.27	164.41	-.56	756.24

12-3/4% interest - $14.78 monthly payment   13% interest - $14.93 monthly payment

Year	Interest	Amort.	Balance	Accrued Interest	Interest	Amort.	Balance	Accrued Interest
1	124.48	52.88	947.12	124.48	126.96	52.20	947.80	126.96
2	117.33	60.03	887.09	241.81	119.75	59.40	888.40	246.72
3	109.21	68.15	818.94	351.02	111.56	67.60	820.80	358.28
4	100.00	77.36	741.58	451.02	102.23	76.93	743.86	460.50
5	89.54	87.82	653.76	540.56	91.61	87.55	656.31	552.11
6	77.66	99.70	554.06	618.22	79.52	99.64	556.67	631.63
7	64.18	113.18	440.88	682.40	65.77	113.39	443.28	697.40
8	48.88	128.48	312.40	731.28	50.12	129.04	314.24	747.52
9	31.50	145.86	166.54	762.78	32.31	146.85	167.39	779.83
10	11.78	165.58	.96	774.56	12.03	167.13	.26	791.86

13-1/4% interest - $15.08 monthly payment   13-1/2% interest - $15.23 monthly payment

Year	Interest	Amort.	Balance	Accrued Interest	Interest	Amort.	Balance	Accrued Interest
1	129.45	51.51	948.49	129.45	131.93	50.83	949.17	131.93
2	122.19	58.77	889.72	251.64	124.63	58.13	891.04	256.56
3	113.91	67.05	822.67	365.55	116.28	66.48	824.56	372.84
4	104.47	76.49	746.18	470.02	106.72	76.04	748.52	479.56
5	93.70	87.26	658.91	563.71	95.80	86.96	661.56	575.36
6	81.40	99.56	559.36	645.12	83.31	99.45	562.11	658.67
7	67.38	113.58	445.78	712.50	69.02	113.74	448.36	727.68
8	51.38	129.58	316.20	763.88	52.68	130.08	318.28	780.36
9	33.13	147.83	168.37	797.01	33.99	148.77	169.50	814.34
10	12.31	166.65	-.27	809.33	12.61	170.15	-.65	826.95

13-3/4% interest - $15.38 monthly payment   14% interest - $15.53 monthly payment

Year	Interest	Amort.	Balance	Accrued Interest	Interest	Amort.	Balance	Accrued Interest
1	134.42	50.14	949.86	134.42	136.91	49.45	950.55	136.91
2	127.07	57.49	892.37	261.49	129.52	56.84	893.71	266.43
3	118.65	65.91	826.46	380.14	121.03	65.33	828.38	387.46
4	108.99	75.57	750.89	489.13	111.28	75.08	753.30	498.74
5	97.92	86.64	664.26	587.06	100.06	86.30	667.00	598.80
6	85.23	99.33	564.93	672.29	87.18	99.18	567.81	685.97
7	70.68	113.88	451.04	742.96	72.36	114.00	453.82	758.34
8	53.99	130.57	320.48	796.96	55.34	131.02	322.80	813.68
9	34.86	149.70	170.78	831.82	35.77	150.59	172.21	849.45
10	12.93	171.63	-.85	844.75	13.28	173.08	-.87	862.73

15-YEAR TERM

	4% interest - $7.40 monthly payment			4-1/2% interest - $7.65 monthly payment			5% interest - $7.91 monthly payment		
Year	Interest	Amort.	Balance	Interest	Amort.	Balance	Interest	Amort.	Balance
1	39.10	49.70	950.30	44.04	47.76	952.24	48.96	45.96	954.04
2	37.06	51.74	898.56	41.83	49.97	902.27	46.62	48.30	905.74
3	34.99	53.81	844.75	39.53	52.27	850.00	44.13	50.79	854.95
4	32.77	56.03	788.72	37.12	54.68	795.32	41.54	53.38	801.57
5	30.49	58.31	730.41	34.62	57.18	738.14	38.80	56.12	745.45
6	28.10	60.70	669.71	31.99	59.81	678.33	35.94	58.98	686.47
7	25.65	63.15	606.56	29.26	62.54	615.79	32.92	62.00	624.47
8	23.07	65.73	540.83	26.39	65.41	550.38	29.74	65.18	559.29
9	20.38	68.42	472.41	23.36	68.44	481.94	26.41	68.50	490.79
10	17.63	71.17	401.24	20.22	71.58	410.36	22.91	72.01	418.78
11	14.71	74.09	327.15	16.94	74.86	335.50	19.22	75.70	343.08
12	11.69	77.11	250.04	13.49	78.31	257.19	15.35	79.57	263.51
13	8.54	80.26	169.78	9.89	81.91	175.28	11.28	83.64	179.87
14	5.27	83.53	86.25	6.14	85.66	89.62	7.02	87.90	91.97
15	1.86	86.25	0	2.20	89.62	0	2.50	91.97	0

	5-1/4% interest - $8.04 monthly payment			5-1/2% interest - $8.18 monthly payment			5-3/4% interest - $8.31 monthly payment		
Year	Interest	Amort.	Balance	Interest	Amort.	Balance	Interest	Amort.	Balance
1	51.42	45.06	954.94	53.90	44.26	955.74	56.36	43.36	956.64
2	49.00	47.48	907.46	51.39	46.77	908.97	53.81	45.91	910.73
3	46.46	50.02	857.44	48.77	49.39	859.58	51.10	48.62	862.11
4	43.76	52.72	804.72	45.96	52.20	807.38	48.24	51.48	810.63
5	40.92	55.56	749.16	43.03	55.13	752.25	45.19	54.53	756.10
6	37.94	58.54	690.62	39.92	58.24	694.01	41.97	57.75	698.35
7	34.79	61.69	628.93	36.63	61.53	632.48	38.56	61.16	637.19
8	31.47	65.01	563.92	33.17	64.99	567.49	34.95	64.77	572.42
9	27.96	68.52	495.40	29.20	68.66	498.83	31.13	68.59	503.83
10	24.30	72.18	423.22	25.62	72.54	426.29	26.97	72.65	431.18
11	20.41	76.07	347.15	21.53	76.63	349.66	22.80	76.92	354.26
12	16.32	80.16	266.99	17.20	80.96	268.70	18.25	81.47	272.79
13	12.01	84.47	182.52	12.65	85.51	183.19	13.43	86.29	186.50
14	7.48	89.00	93.52	7.84	90.32	92.87	8.34	91.38	95.12
15	2.66	93.52	0	2.73	92.87	0	2.94	95.12	0

	6% interest - $8.44 monthly payment			6-1/4% interest - $8.58 monthly payment			6-1/2% interest - $8.72 monthly payment		
Year	Interest	Amort.	Balance	Interest	Amort.	Balance	Interest	Amort.	Balance
1	58.85	42.43	957.57	61.33	41.63	958.37	63.79	40.85	959.15
2	56.23	45.05	912.52	58.65	44.31	914.06	61.08	43.56	915.59
3	53.40	47.88	864.64	55.80	47.16	866.90	58.15	46.49	869.10
4	50.49	50.79	813.85	52.76	50.20	816.70	55.03	49.61	819.49
5	47.37	53.91	759.94	49.53	53.43	763.27	51.72	52.92	766.57
6	44.04	57.24	702.70	46.08	56.88	706.39	48.16	56.48	710.09
7	40.50	60.78	641.92	42.43	60.53	645.86	44.39	60.25	649.84
8	36.75	64.53	577.39	38.54	64.42	581.44	40.34	64.30	585.54
9	32.78	68.50	508.89	34.38	68.58	512.86	36.04	68.60	516.94
10	28.58	72.72	436.17	29.99	72.97	439.89	31.46	73.18	443.76
11	24.07	77.21	358.96	25.30	77.66	362.23	26.55	78.09	365.67
12	19.29	81.99	276.97	20.30	82.66	279.57	21.31	83.33	282.34
13	14.24	87.04	189.93	14.99	87.97	191.60	15.72	88.92	193.42
14	8.89	92.39	97.54	9.35	93.61	97.99	9.79	94.85	98.57
15	3.19	97.54	0	3.29	97.99	0	3.41	98.57	0

15-YEAR TERM (continued)

6-3/4% interest - $8.85 monthly payment

Year	Interest	Amort.	Balance
1	66.29	39.91	960.09
2	63.48	42.72	917.37
3	60.54	45.66	871.71
4	57.35	48.85	822.86
5	53.93	52.27	770.59
6	50.30	55.90	714.69
7	46.41	59.79	654.90
8	42.28	63.92	590.98
9	37.80	68.40	522.58
10	33.04	73.16	449.42
11	27.94	78.26	371.16
12	22.51	83.69	287.47
13	16.68	89.52	197.95
14	10.42	95.78	102.17
15	3.76	102.17	0

7% interest - $8.99 monthly payment

Year	Interest	Amort.	Balance
1	68.74	39.14	960.86
2	65.94	41.94	918.92
3	62.90	44.98	873.94
4	59.65	48.23	825.71
5	56.16	51.72	773.99
6	52.42	55.46	718.53
7	48.39	59.49	659.04
8	44.10	63.78	595.26
9	39.56	68.32	526.89
10	34.55	73.33	453.56
11	29.26	78.62	374.94
12	23.59	84.39	290.65
13	17.48	90.40	200.25
14	10.96	96.92	103.33
15	3.94	103.33	0

7-1/4% interest - $9.13 monthly payment

Year	Interest	Amort.	Balance
1	71.25	38.31	961.69
2	68.38	41.18	920.51
3	65.29	44.27	876.24
4	61.96	47.58	828.66
5	58.39	51.17	777.49
6	54.55	55.01	722.48
7	50.45	59.11	663.37
8	46.02	63.54	599.83
9	41.25	68.31	531.52
10	36.13	73.43	458.09
11	30.60	78.96	379.13
12	24.71	84.85	294.28
13	18.33	91.23	203.05
14	11.52	98.04	105.01
15	4.16	105.01	0

7-1/2% interest - $9.28 monthly payment

Year	Interest	Amort.	Balance
1	73.73	37.63	962.37
2	70.77	40.59	921.78
3	67.64	43.72	878.06
4	64.25	47.11	830.95
5	60.59	50.77	780.18
6	56.66	54.70	725.48
7	52.38	58.98	666.50
8	47.83	63.53	602.97
9	42.89	68.47	534.50
10	37.59	73.77	460.73
11	31.87	79.49	381.24
12	25.68	85.68	295.56
13	19.04	92.32	203.24
14	11.88	99.48	103.76
15	4.15	103.76	0

7-3/4% interest - $9.42 monthly payment

Year	Interest	Amort.	Balance
1	76.20	36.84	963.16
2	73.26	39.78	923.38
3	70.05	42.99	880.39
4	66.59	46.45	833.94
5	62.89	50.15	783.79
6	58.84	54.20	729.59
7	54.49	58.55	671.04
8	49.78	63.26	607.78
9	44.71	68.33	539.45
10	39.23	73.81	465.64
11	33.29	79.75	385.89
12	26.89	86.15	299.74
13	19.98	93.06	206.68
14	12.49	100.55	106.13
15	4.41	106.13	0

8% interest - $9.56 monthly payment

Year	Interest	Amort.	Balance
1	78.72	36.00	964.00
2	75.71	39.01	924.99
3	72.48	42.24	882.75
4	68.98	45.74	837.01
5	65.17	49.55	787.46
6	61.02	53.70	733.76
7	56.60	58.12	675.64
8	51.77	62.95	612.69
9	46.55	68.17	544.52
10	40.89	73.83	470.69
11	34.78	79.94	390.75
12	28.15	86.57	304.18
13	20.96	93.76	210.42
14	13.16	101.56	108.86
15	4.76	108.86	0

8-1/4% interest - $9.70 monthly payment

Year	Interest	Amort.	Balance
1	81.19	35.22	964.79
2	78.18	38.23	926.56
3	74.90	41.51	885.06
4	71.34	45.07	840.00
5	67.48	48.93	791.07
6	63.29	53.12	737.96
7	58.74	57.67	680.29
8	53.80	62.61	617.68
9	48.43	67.98	549.71
10	42.61	73.80	475.91
11	36.28	80.13	395.79
12	29.42	86.99	308.80
13	21.96	94.45	214.36
14	13.87	102.54	111.82
15	5.08	111.33	0.50

8-1/2% interest - $9.85 monthly payment

Year	Interest	Amort.	Balance
1	83.68	34.53	965.48
2	80.63	37.58	927.90
3	77.31	40.90	887.01
4	73.69	44.52	842.49
5	69.76	48.45	794.05
6	65.48	52.73	741.32
7	60.82	57.39	683.93
8	55.74	62.47	621.47
9	50.22	67.99	553.48
10	44.21	74.00	479.49
11	37.67	80.54	398.96
12	30.55	87.66	311.30
13	22.81	95.40	215.90
14	14.37	103.84	112.07
15	5.20	113.01	0.94

8-3/4% interest - $9.99 monthly payment

Year	Interest	Amort.	Balance
1	86.17	33.72	966.29
2	83.10	36.79	929.51
3	79.75	40.14	889.38
4	76.10	43.79	845.59
5	72.11	47.78	797.82
6	67.76	52.13	745.69
7	63.01	56.88	688.81
8	57.83	62.06	626.75
9	52.17	67.72	559.04
10	46.00	73.89	485.15
11	39.27	80.62	404.54
12	31.93	87.96	316.59
13	23.92	95.97	220.62
14	15.18	104.71	115.91
15	5.65	114.25	1.66

15-YEAR TERM (continued)

9% interest - $10.15 monthly payment

Year	Interest	Amort.	Balance
1	88.66	33.14	966.86
2	85.55	36.25	930.61
3	82.14	39.66	890.95
4	78.43	43.37	847.58
5	74.34	47.46	800.12
6	69.92	51.88	748.24
7	65.03	56.77	691.97
8	59.72	62.08	629.39
9	53.90	67.90	561.49
10	47.53	74.27	487.22
11	40.57	81.23	405.99
12	32.92	88.88	317.11
13	24.59	97.21	219.90
14	15.50	106.30	113.60
15	5.51	113.60	0

9-1/4% interest - $10.29 monthly payment

Year	Interest	Amort.	Balance
1	91.16	32.33	967.68
2	88.04	35.45	932.23
3	84.62	38.87	893.36
4	80.86	42.63	850.74
5	76.75	46.74	804.00
6	72.24	51.25	752.76
7	67.29	56.20	696.56
8	61.87	61.62	634.94
9	55.92	67.57	567.38
10	49.40	74.09	493.29
11	42.25	81.24	412.06
12	34.41	89.08	322.98
13	25.81	97.68	225.30
14	16.38	107.11	118.19
15	6.04	117.45	0.75

9-1/2% interest - $10.44 monthly payment

Year	Interest	Amort.	Balance
1	93.65	31.64	968.37
2	90.51	34.78	933.60
3	87.06	38.23	895.37
4	83.27	42.02	853.35
5	79.10	46.19	807.17
6	74.51	50.78	756.39
7	69.47	55.82	700.58
8	63.93	61.36	639.23
9	57.85	67.44	571.79
10	51.15	74.14	497.66
11	43.79	81.50	416.17
12	35.71	89.58	326.59
13	26.82	98.47	228.12
14	17.04	108.25	119.88
15	6.30	118.99	0.89

9-3/4% interest - $10.59 monthly payment

Year	Interest	Amort.	Balance
1	96.15	30.94	969.07
2	92.99	34.10	934.97
3	89.51	37.58	897.40
4	85.68	41.41	856.00
5	81.46	45.63	810.38
6	76.81	50.28	760.10
7	71.68	55.41	704.70
8	66.03	61.06	643.65
9	59.81	67.28	576.37
10	52.95	74.14	502.23
11	45.38	81.71	420.53
12	37.05	90.04	330.50
13	27.87	99.22	231.28
14	17.75	109.34	121.95
15	6.61	120.48	1.47

10% interest - $10.75 monthly payment

Year	Interest	Amort.	Balance
1	98.62	30.38	969.62
2	95.46	33.54	936.08
3	91.95	37.05	899.03
4	88.06	40.94	858.09
5	83.78	45.22	812.87
6	79.04	49.96	762.91
7	73.81	55.19	707.72
8	68.03	60.97	646.75
9	61.64	67.36	579.39
10	54.30	74.40	504.99
11	46.79	82.21	422.78
12	38.18	90.82	331.96
13	28.70	100.30	231.66
14	18.20	110.80	120.86
15	6.57	120.86	0

10-1/4% interest - $10.90 monthly payment

Year	Interest	Amort.	Balance
1	101.14	29.67	970.34
2	97.95	32.86	937.48
3	94.42	36.39	901.09
4	90.51	40.30	860.80
5	86.18	44.63	816.17
6	81.38	49.43	766.75
7	76.07	54.74	712.02
8	70.19	60.62	651.40
9	63.68	67.13	584.28
10	56.46	74.35	509.93
11	48.48	82.33	427.61
12	39.63	91.18	336.43
13	29.83	100.98	235.46
14	18.98	111.83	123.64
15	6.97	123.84	.20

10-1/2% interest - $11.05 monthly payment

Year	Interest	Amort.	Balance
1	103.64	28.97	971.04
2	100.44	32.17	938.88
3	96.90	35.71	903.17
4	92.97	39.64	863.53
5	88.60	44.01	819.53
6	83.75	48.86	770.67
7	78.36	54.25	716.43
8	72.39	60.22	656.21
9	65.75	66.86	589.35
10	58.38	74.23	515.13
11	50.20	82.41	432.73
12	41.12	91.49	341.24
13	31.04	101.57	239.68
14	19.85	112.76	126.92
15	7.42	125.19	1.74

10-3/4% interest - $11.21 monthly payment

Year	Interest	Amort.	Balance
1	106.13	28.40	971.61
2	102.93	31.60	940.01
3	99.36	35.17	904.85
4	95.38	39.15	865.71
5	90.96	43.57	822.14
6	86.04	48.49	773.66
7	80.57	53.96	719.70
8	74.47	60.06	659.65
9	67.69	66.84	592.81
10	60.14	74.39	518.42
11	51.73	82.80	435.63
12	42.38	92.15	343.49
13	31.97	102.56	240.94
14	20.39	114.14	126.80
15	7.50	127.03	0.23

11% interest - $11.37 monthly payment

Year	Interest	Amort.	Balance
1	108.63	27.82	972.19
2	105.41	31.04	941.16
3	101.82	34.63	906.53
4	97.81	38.64	867.90
5	93.34	43.11	824.80
6	88.36	48.09	776.71
7	82.79	53.66	723.06
8	76.58	59.87	663.19
9	69.66	66.79	596.40
10	61.93	74.52	521.89
11	53.30	83.15	438.74
12	43.68	92.77	345.98
13	32.95	103.50	242.48
14	20.97	115.48	127.01
15	7.61	128.84	1.83

15-YEAR TERM (continued)

Year	11-1/4% interest - $11.52 monthly payment			11-1/2% interest - $11.68 monthly payment			11-3/4% interest - $11.84 monthly payment		
	Interest	Amort.	Balance	Interest	Amort.	Balance	Interest	Amort.	Balance
1	111.14	27.11	972.90	113.64	26.53	973.48	116.14	25.95	974.06
2	107.92	30.33	942.57	110.42	29.75	943.73	112.92	29.17	944.89
3	104.33	33.92	908.66	106.81	33.36	910.38	109.30	32.79	912.11
4	100.31	37.94	870.73	102.77	37.40	872.98	105.23	36.86	875.26
5	95.82	42.43	828.30	98.23	41.94	831.05	100.66	41.43	833.83
6	90.79	47.46	780.85	93.15	47.02	784.03	95.53	46.56	787.27
7	85.17	53.08	727.77	87.45	52.72	731.31	89.75	52.34	734.94
8	78.88	59.37	668.40	81.05	59.12	672.20	83.26	58.83	676.11
9	71.85	66.40	602.00	73.89	66.28	605.92	75.96	66.13	609.99
10	63.98	74.27	527.74	65.85	74.32	531.60	67.76	74.33	535.67
11	55.18	83.07	444.67	56.84	83.33	448.28	58.54	83.55	452.12
12	45.34	92.91	351.76	46.73	93.44	354.84	48.18	93.91	358.21
13	34.33	103.92	247.84	35.40	104.77	250.08	36.53	105.56	252.66
14	22.01	116.24	131.61	22.70	117.47	132.62	23.44	118.65	134.01
15	8.24	130.01	1.61	8.46	131.71	0.91	8.72	133.37	0.65

	12% interest - $12.00 monthly payment		
Year	Interest	Amort.	Balance
1	118.64	25.37	974.64
2	115.42	28.59	946.06
3	111.80	32.21	913.85
4	107.71	36.30	877.56
5	103.11	40.90	836.67
6	97.92	46.09	790.59
7	92.08	51.93	738.66
8	85.49	58.52	680.15
9	78.07	65.94	614.22
10	69.71	74.30	539.93
11	60.29	83.72	456.21
12	49.67	94.34	361.88
13	37.71	106.30	255.59
14	24.23	119.78	135.81
15	9.04	134.97	0.84

845

15-YEAR TERM (Continued)

12-1/4% interest - $12.16 monthly payment

Year	Interest	Amort.	Balance	Accrued Interest
1	121.14	24.78	975.22	121.14
2	117.93	27.97	947.23	239.07
3	114.30	31.62	915.61	353.37
4	110.20	35.72	879.89	463.57
5	105.57	40.35	839.54	569.14
6	100.34	45.58	793.96	669.48
7	94.43	51.49	742.47	763.91
8	87.76	58.16	684.31	851.67
9	80.22	65.70	618.61	931.89
10	71.70	74.22	544.39	1003.59
11	62.08	83.84	460.56	1065.68
12	51.22	94.70	365.85	1116.89
13	38.94	106.98	258.88	1155.84
14	25.08	120.84	138.03	1180.91
15	9.41	136.51	1.53	1190.33

12-1/2% interest - $12.33 monthly payment

Year	Interest	Amort.	Balance	Accrued Interest
1	123.64	24.32	975.68	123.64
2	120.42	27.54	948.13	244.05
3	116.77	31.19	916.95	360.83
4	112.64	35.32	881.63	473.47
5	107.96	40.00	841.63	581.43
6	102.67	45.29	796.33	684.09
7	96.67	51.29	745.04	780.76
8	89.88	58.08	686.96	870.64
9	82.19	65.77	621.19	952.83
10	73.48	74.48	546.71	1026.31
11	63.61	84.35	462.36	1089.92
12	52.45	95.51	366.85	1142.37
13	39.80	108.16	258.68	1182.16
14	25.48	122.48	136.20	1207.64
15	9.26	138.70	-2.50	1216.90

12-3/4% interest - $12.49 monthly payment

Year	Interest	Amort.	Balance	Accrued Interest
1	126.14	23.74	976.26	126.14
2	122.94	26.94	949.32	249.08
3	119.29	30.59	918.73	368.37
4	115.16	34.72	884.01	483.53
5	110.46	39.42	844.59	593.99
6	105.13	44.75	799.84	699.12
7	99.08	50.80	749.04	798.20
8	92.21	57.67	691.36	890.40
9	84.41	65.47	625.89	974.81
10	75.56	74.32	551.57	1050.37
11	65.51	84.37	467.20	1115.88
12	54.10	95.78	371.42	1169.98
13	41.15	108.73	262.69	1211.13
14	26.44	123.44	139.25	1237.57
15	9.75	140.13	-.87	1247.33

13% interest - $12.65 monthly payment

Year	Interest	Amort.	Balance	Accrued Interest
1	128.65	23.15	976.85	128.65
2	125.46	26.34	950.51	254.11
3	121.82	29.98	920.53	375.93
4	117.68	34.12	886.42	493.62
5	112.97	38.83	847.59	606.59
6	107.62	44.18	803.41	714.21
7	101.52	50.28	753.12	815.72
8	94.58	57.22	695.90	910.30
9	86.68	65.12	630.78	996.98
10	77.69	74.11	556.67	1074.67
11	67.46	84.34	472.32	1142.12
12	55.82	95.98	376.34	1197.94
13	42.57	109.23	267.11	1240.51
14	27.49	124.31	142.80	1268.00
15	10.33	141.47	1.33	1278.33

13-1/4% interest - $12.82 monthly payment

Year	Interest	Amort.	Balance	Accrued Interest
1	131.16	22.68	977.32	131.16
2	127.96	25.88	951.44	259.12
3	124.31	29.53	921.91	383.43
4	120.16	33.68	888.23	503.59
5	115.41	38.43	849.80	619.00
6	110.00	43.84	805.96	729.00
7	103.82	50.02	755.94	832.82
8	96.78	57.06	698.88	929.60
9	88.74	65.10	633.78	1018.34
10	79.57	74.27	559.52	1097.92
11	69.11	84.73	474.79	1167.03
12	57.18	96.66	378.13	1224.21
13	43.55	110.28	267.85	1267.77
14	28.03	125.81	142.04	1295.80
15	10.31	143.53	-1.48	1306.12

13-1/2% interest - $12.98 monthly payment

Year	Interest	Amort.	Balance	Accrued Interest
1	133.67	22.09	977.91	133.67
2	130.49	25.27	952.64	264.16
3	126.86	28.90	923.74	391.02
4	122.71	33.05	890.69	513.73
5	117.96	37.80	852.89	631.69
6	112.53	43.23	809.66	744.22
7	106.32	49.44	760.22	850.54
8	99.22	56.54	703.67	949.75
9	91.09	64.67	639.01	1040.85
10	81.80	73.96	565.05	1122.65
11	71.17	85.49	480.46	1193.82
12	59.02	96.74	383.72	1252.84
13	45.12	110.64	273.08	1297.96
14	29.23	126.53	146.55	1327.19
15	11.05	144.71	1.84	1338.24

846

15-YEAR TERM (Continued)

	13-3/4 interest - $13.15 monthly payment				14% interest - $13.32 monthly payment			
Year	Interest	Amort.	Balance	Accrued Interest	Interest	Amort.	Balance	Accrued Interest
1	136.17	21.63	978.37	136.17	138.68	21.16	978.84	138.68
2	133.00	24.80	953.57	269.17	135.52	24.32	954.51	274.19
3	129.37	28.43	925.14	398.54	131.88	27.96	926.55	406.07
4	125.20	32.60	892.54	523.74	127.71	32.13	894.42	533.78
5	120.43	37.37	855.17	644.27	122.91	36.93	857.49	656.69
6	114.95	42.85	812.32	759.12	117.39	42.45	815.04	774.08
7	108.68	49.12	763.20	867.80	111.05	48.79	766.26	885.14
8	101.48	56.32	706.88	969.28	103.77	56.07	710.19	988.91
9	93.23	64.57	642.30	1062.50	95.39	64.45	645.74	1084.30
10	83.77	74.03	568.27	1146.27	85.77	74.07	571.67	1170.07
11	72.92	84.88	483.39	1219.19	74.71	85.13	486.54	1244.78
12	60.48	97.32	386.08	1279.68	62.00	97.84	388.70	1306.78
13	46.23	111.57	274.50	1325.90	47.38	112.46	276.24	1354.16
14	29.88	127.92	146.58	1355.78	30.59	129.25	146.99	1384.75
15	11.14	146.66	-.08	1366.92	11.29	148.55	-1.57	1396.03

20-YEAR TERM

Year	4% interest - $6.06 monthly payment Interest	Amort.	Balance	4-1/2% interest - $6.33 monthly payment Interest	Amort.	Balance	5% interest - $6.60 monthly payment Interest	Amort.	Balance
1	39.49	33.32	966.68	44.34	31.62	968.38	49.33	29.87	970.13
2	38.03	34.69	931.99	42.90	33.06	935.32	47.79	31.41	938.72
3	36.66	36.06	895.93	41.38	34.58	900.74	46.19	33.01	905.71
4	35.15	37.57	858.36	39.80	36.16	864.58	44.50	34.70	871.01
5	33.62	39.10	819.26	38.12	37.84	826.74	42.71	36.49	834.52
6	32.04	40.68	778.58	36.40	39.56	787.18	40.83	38.37	796.15
7	30.38	42.34	736.24	34.58	41.38	745.80	38.90	40.30	755.85
8	28.64	44.08	692.16	32.68	43.28	702.52	36.84	42.36	713.49
9	26.85	45.87	646.29	30.68	45.28	657.24	34.66	44.54	668.95
10	24.99	47.73	598.56	28.61	47.35	609.89	32.39	46.81	622.14
11	23.05	49.67	548.89	26.44	49.52	560.37	29.99	49.21	572.93
12	21.01	51.71	497.18	24.16	51.80	508.57	27.47	51.73	521.20
13	18.90	53.82	443.36	21.78	54.18	454.39	24.80	54.40	466.80
14	16.72	56.00	387.36	19.29	56.67	397.72	22.09	57.11	409.69
15	14.43	58.29	329.07	16.70	59.26	338.46	19.13	60.07	349.62
16	12.06	60.66	268.41	13.95	62.01	276.45	16.05	66.39	286.47
17	9.59	63.13	205.28	11.14	64.82	211.63	12.81	66.39	220.08
18	7.01	65.71	139.57	8.13	67.83	143.80	9.42	69.78	150.30
19	4.36	68.36	71.21	5.02	70.94	72.86	5.85	73.35	76.95
20	1.56	71.21	0	1.76	72.86	0	2.10	76.95	0

Year	5-1/4% interest - $6.74 monthly payment Interest	Amort.	Balance	5-1/2% interest - $6.88 monthly payment Interest	Amort.	Balance	5-3/4% interest - $7.03 monthly payment Interest	Amort.	Balance
1	51.79	29.09	970.91	54.29	28.27	971.73	56.78	27.58	972.42
2	50.25	30.63	940.28	52.69	29.87	941.86	55.16	29.20	943.22
3	48.60	32.28	908.00	51.02	31.54	910.32	53.43	30.93	912.29
4	46.86	34.02	873.98	49.23	33.33	876.99	51.60	32.76	879.53
5	45.02	35.86	838.12	47.36	35.20	841.79	49.66	34.70	844.83
6	43.11	37.77	800.35	45.37	37.19	804.60	47.93	36.43	808.10
7	41.07	39.81	760.54	43.26	39.30	765.30	45.45	38.91	769.19
8	38.94	41.94	718.60	41.06	41.50	723.80	43.16	41.20	727.99
9	36.67	44.21	674.39	38.70	43.86	679.94	40.72	43.64	684.35
10	34.29	46.59	627.80	36.25	46.31	633.63	38.14	46.22	638.13
11	31.78	49.10	578.70	33.63	48.93	584.70	35.41	48.95	589.18
12	29.14	51.74	526.96	30.84	51.72	532.98	32.51	51.85	537.33
13	26.40	54.48	472.48	27.96	54.60	478.38	29.46	54.90	482.43
14	23.45	57.43	415.05	24.86	57.70	420.68	26.21	58.15	424.28
15	20.34	60.54	354.51	21.62	60.94	359.74	22.80	61.56	362.72
16	17.10	63.78	290.73	18.16	64.40	295.34	19.16	65.20	297.52
17	13.66	67.22	223.51	14.56	68.00	227.34	15.30	69.06	228.46
18	10.04	70.84	152.67	10.71	71.85	155.49	11.20	73.16	155.30
19	6.22	74.66	78.01	6.65	75.91	79.58	6.90	77.46	77.84
20	2.22	78.01	0	2.34	79.58	0	2.33	77.84	0

848

20-YEAR TERM (continued)

	6% interest - $7.17 monthly payment			6-1/4% interest - $7.31 monthly payment			6-1/2% interest - $7.46 monthly payment		
Year	Interest	Amort.	Balance	Interest	Amort.	Balance	Interest	Amort.	Balance
1	59.28	26.76	973.24	61.77	25.95	974.05	64.25	25.27	974.73
2	57.62	28.42	944.82	60.09	27.63	946.42	62.58	26.94	947.78
3	55.86	30.18	914.64	58.31	29.41	917.01	60.75	28.77	919.01
4	54.01	32.03	882.61	56.44	31.28	885.73	58.83	30.69	888.32
5	52.03	34.01	848.60	54.42	33.30	852.43	56.76	32.76	855.56
6	49.92	36.12	812.48	52.25	35.47	816.96	54.57	34.95	820.61
7	47.72	38.32	774.16	50.00	37.72	779.24	52.25	37.27	783.34
8	45.32	40.72	733.44	47.58	40.14	739.10	49.76	39.76	743.58
9	42.83	43.21	690.23	44.97	42.75	696.35	47.09	42.43	701.15
10	40.16	45.88	644.35	42.25	45.47	650.88	44.26	45.26	655.89
11	37.33	48.71	595.64	39.30	48.42	602.46	41.21	48.31	607.58
12	34.34	51.70	543.94	36.19	51.53	550.93	37.99	51.53	556.05
13	31.14	54.90	489.04	32.90	54.82	496.11	34.52	55.00	501.05
14	27.77	58.27	430.77	29.35	58.37	437.74	30.82	58.70	442.35
15	24.16	61.88	368.89	25.58	62.14	375.60	26.91	62.61	379.74
16	20.35	65.69	303.20	21.62	66.10	309.50	22.74	66.78	312.96
17	16.30	69.74	233.46	17.33	70.39	239.11	18.25	71.27	241.69
18	12.01	74.03	159.43	12.82	74.90	164.21	13.47	76.05	165.64
19	7.44	78.60	80.83	8.03	79.69	84.52	8.39	81.13	84.51
20	2.54	80.83	0	2.88	84.52	0	2.95	84.51	0

	6-3/4% interest - $7.61 monthly payment			7% interest - $7.76 monthly payment			7-1/4% interest - $7.91 monthly payment		
Year	Interest	Amort.	Balance	Interest	Amort.	Balance	Interest	Amort.	Balance
1	66.75	24.57	975.43	69.24	23.88	976.12	71.74	23.18	976.82
2	65.03	26.29	949.14	67.52	25.60	950.52	70.01	24.91	951.91
3	63.20	28.12	921.02	65.67	27.45	923.07	68.13	26.79	925.12
4	61.25	30.07	890.95	63.68	29.44	893.63	66.13	28.79	896.33
5	59.16	32.16	858.79	61.54	31.58	862.05	63.96	30.96	865.37
6	56.92	34.40	824.39	59.28	33.84	828.21	61.65	33.27	832.10
7	54.52	36.80	787.59	56.83	36.29	791.92	59.16	35.76	796.34
8	51.97	39.35	748.24	54.19	38.93	752.99	56.47	38.45	757.89
9	49.20	42.12	706.12	51.37	41.75	711.24	53.61	41.31	716.58
10	46.28	45.04	661.08	48.38	44.74	666.50	50.50	44.42	672.16
11	43.15	48.17	612.91	45.12	48.00	618.50	47.17	47.75	624.41
12	39.81	51.51	561.40	41.67	51.45	567.05	43.59	51.33	573.08
13	36.20	55.12	506.28	37.95	55.17	511.88	39.74	55.18	517.90
14	32.36	58.96	447.32	33.97	59.15	452.73	35.58	59.34	458.56
15	28.26	63.06	384.26	29.68	63.44	389.29	31.16	63.76	394.80
16	23.87	67.45	316.81	25.10	68.02	321.27	26.37	68.55	326.25
17	19.18	72.14	244.67	20.19	72.93	248.34	21.25	73.67	252.58
18	14.15	77.17	167.50	14.90	78.22	170.12	15.72	79.20	173.38
19	8.80	82.52	84.98	9.25	83.87	86.25	9.79	85.13	88.25
20	3.05	84.98	0	3.19	86.25	0	3.40	88.25	0

849

20-YEAR TERM (continued)

Year	7-1/2% interest - $8.06 monthly payment			7-3/4% interest - $8.21 monthly payment			8% interest - $8.37 monthly payment		
	Interest	Amort.	Balance	Interest	Amort.	Balance	Interest	Amort.	Balance
1	74.24	22.48	977.52	76.74	21.78	978.22	79.24	21.20	978.80
2	72.49	24.23	953.29	75.00	23.52	954.70	77.47	22.97	955.83
3	70.63	26.09	927.20	73.10	25.42	929.28	75.58	24.86	930.97
4	68.58	28.14	899.06	71.05	27.47	901.81	73.49	26.95	904.02
5	66.40	30.32	868.74	68.84	29.68	872.13	71.29	29.15	874.87
6	64.04	32.68	836.06	66.47	32.05	840.08	68.85	31.59	843.28
7	61.51	35.21	800.85	63.89	34.63	805.45	66.21	34.23	809.05
8	58.81	37.91	762.94	61.09	37.43	768.02	63.37	37.07	771.98
9	55.83	40.89	722.05	58.11	40.41	727.61	60.32	40.12	731.86
10	52.66	44.06	677.99	54.86	43.66	683.95	56.99	43.45	688.41
11	49.25	47.47	630.52	51.35	47.17	636.78	53.36	47.08	641.33
12	45.56	51.16	579.36	47.56	50.96	585.82	49.46	50.98	590.35
13	41.58	55.14	524.22	43.49	55.03	530.79	45.26	55.18	535.17
14	37.32	59.40	464.82	39.05	59.47	471.32	40.67	59.77	475.40
15	32.69	64.03	400.79	34.28	64.24	407.08	35.67	64.77	410.63
16	27.73	68.99	331.80	29.12	69.40	337.68	30.31	70.13	340.50
17	22.37	74.35	257.45	23.52	75.00	262.68	24.51	75.93	264.57
18	16.61	80.11	177.34	17.53	80.99	181.69	18.20	82.24	182.33
19	10.37	86.35	90.99	11.01	87.51	94.18	11.33	89.11	93.22
20	3.67	90.99	0	3.99	94.18	0	3.97	93.22	0

Year	8-1/4% interest - $8.52 monthly payment			8-1/2% interest - $8.68 monthly payment			8-3/4% interest - $8.84 monthly payment		
	Interest	Amort.	Balance	Interest	Amort.	Balance	Interest	Amort.	Balance
1	81.74	20.51	979.50	84.24	19.93	980.08	86.74	19.35	980.66
2	79.98	22.27	957.24	82.48	21.69	958.40	84.98	21.11	959.56
3	78.08	24.17	933.07	80.56	23.61	934.79	83.06	23.03	936.53
4	76.01	26.24	906.83	78.48	25.69	909.10	80.96	25.13	911.40
5	73.76	28.49	878.34	76.21	27.96	881.15	78.67	27.42	883.99
6	71.32	30.93	847.42	73.73	30.44	850.71	76.17	29.92	854.07
7	68.67	33.58	813.84	71.04	33.13	817.59	73.45	32.64	821.44
8	65.79	36.46	777.38	68.12	36.05	781.55	70.47	35.62	785.83
9	62.66	39.59	737.80	64.93	39.24	742.31	67.23	38.86	746.97
10	59.27	42.98	694.83	61.46	42.71	699.61	63.69	42.40	704.58
11	55.59	46.66	648.17	57.69	46.48	653.13	59.83	46.26	658.32
12	51.59	50.66	597.52	53.58	50.59	602.55	55.62	50.47	607.85
13	47.25	55.00	542.52	49.11	55.06	547.49	51.02	55.07	552.79
14	42.54	59.71	482.82	44.24	59.93	487.57	46.00	60.09	492.70
15	37.42	64.83	417.99	38.95	65.22	422.35	40.53	65.56	427.15
16	31.87	70.38	347.62	33.18	70.99	351.37	34.56	71.53	355.62
17	25.84	76.41	271.21	26.91	77.26	274.11	28.04	78.05	277.57
18	19.29	82.96	188.25	20.08	84.09	190.02	20.93	85.16	192.42
19	12.18	90.07	98.19	12.65	91.52	98.51	13.17	92.92	99.51
20	4.46	97.79	.40	4.56	99.61	1.10	4.71	101.38	1.87

20-YEAR TERM (continued)

	9% interest - $9.00 monthly payment			9-1/4% interest - $9.16 monthly payment			9-1/2% interest - $9.32 monthly payment		
Year	Interest	Amort.	Balance	Interest	Amort.	Balance	Interest	Amort.	Balance
1	89.24	18.76	981.24	91.75	18.16	981.83	94.25	17.60	982.41
2	87.47	20.53	960.71	89.99	19.94	961.89	92.51	19.34	963.07
3	85.56	22.44	938.27	88.07	21.86	940.04	90.59	21.26	941.81
4	83.45	24.55	913.72	85.96	23.97	916.07	88.48	23.37	918.45
5	81.14	26.86	886.86	83.65	26.28	889.79	86.16	25.69	892.76
6	78.64	29.36	857.50	81.11	28.82	860.98	83.61	28.24	864.52
7	75.83	32.17	825.33	78.33	31.60	829.38	80.81	31.04	833.48
8	72.85	35.15	790.18	75.28	34.65	794.73	77.73	34.12	799.36
9	69.56	38.44	751.74	71.93	38.00	756.74	74.34	37.51	761.86
10	65.96	42.04	709.70	68.27	41.66	715.08	70.62	41.23	720.63
11	62.01	45.99	663.71	64.25	45.68	669.40	66.52	45.33	675.31
12	57.70	50.30	613.41	59.84	50.09	619.31	62.03	49.82	625.49
13	52.97	55.03	558.38	55.00	54.93	564.39	57.08	54.77	570.73
14	47.80	60.20	498.18	49.70	60.23	504.16	51.65	60.20	510.53
15	42.19	65.81	432.37	43.89	66.04	438.13	45.67	66.18	444.36
16	35.99	72.01	360.36	37.51	72.42	365.71	39.11	72.74	371.62
17	29.20	78.80	281.56	30.52	79.41	286.31	31.89	79.96	291.66
18	21.86	86.14	195.42	22.86	87.07	199.24	23.95	87.90	203.76
19	13.76	94.24	101.18	14.45	95.48	103.77	15.23	96.62	107.15
20	4.93	101.18	0	5.24	104.69	0.91	5.64	106.21	0.94

	9-3/4% interest - $9.49 monthly payment			10% interest - $9.66 monthly payment			10-1/4% interest - $9.82 monthly payment		
Year	Interest	Amort.	Balance	Interest	Amort.	Balance	Interest	Amort.	Balance
1	96.75	17.14	982.87	99.25	16.67	983.33	101.76	16.09	983.92
2	95.01	18.88	963.99	97.49	18.43	964.90	100.04	17.81	966.11
3	93.08	20.81	943.19	95.59	20.33	944.57	98.12	19.73	946.39
4	90.96	22.93	920.26	93.44	22.48	922.09	96.00	21.85	924.55
5	88.62	25.27	895.00	91.09	24.83	897.26	93.66	24.19	900.36
6	86.04	27.85	867.16	88.51	27.41	869.85	91.06	26.79	873.57
7	83.21	30.68	836.48	85.62	30.30	839.55	88.18	29.67	843.90
8	80.08	33.81	802.67	82.45	33.47	806.08	84.99	32.86	811.05
9	76.63	37.26	765.42	78.94	36.98	769.10	81.46	36.39	774.66
10	72.83	41.06	724.36	75.08	40.84	728.26	77.55	40.30	734.36
11	68.64	45.25	679.12	70.81	45.11	683.15	73.22	44.63	689.74
12	64.03	49.86	629.26	66.07	49.85	633.30	68.42	49.43	640.31
13	58.95	54.94	574.32	60.86	55.06	578.24	63.11	54.74	585.58
14	53.34	60.55	513.78	55.11	60.81	517.43	57.23	60.62	524.97
15	47.17	66.72	447.07	48.71	67.21	450.22	50.72	67.13	457.84
16	40.37	73.52	373.55	41.68	74.24	375.98	43.51	74.34	383.50
17	32.87	81.02	292.53	33.90	82.02	293.96	35.52	82.33	301.18
18	24.61	89.28	203.25	25.32	90.60	203.36	26.67	91.18	210.00
19	15.50	98.39	104.87	15.83	100.09	103.27	16.87	100.98	109.03
20	5.47	108.42	3.55	5.35	103.27	0	6.02	111.83	2.79

	10-1/2% interest - $9.98 monthly payment			10-3/4% interest - $10.15 monthly payment			11% interest - $10.32 monthly payment		
Year	Interest	Amort.	Balance	Interest	Amort.	Balance	Interest	Amort.	Balance
1	104.27	15.50	984.51	106.78	15.03	984.98	109.29	14.56	985.45
2	102.57	17.20	967.31	105.08	16.73	968.26	107.60	16.25	969.20
3	100.67	19.10	948.22	103.19	18.62	949.64	105.72	18.13	951.08
4	98.57	21.20	927.02	101.09	20.72	928.93	103.62	20.23	930.86
5	96.23	23.54	903.49	98.75	23.06	905.87	101.28	22.57	908.29
6	93.64	26.13	877.36	96.15	25.66	880.21	98.67	25.18	883.12
7	90.76	29.01	848.35	93.25	28.56	851.66	95.76	28.09	855.04
8	87.56	32.21	816.15	90.02	31.79	819.87	92.51	31.34	823.70
9	84.01	35.76	780.40	86.43	35.38	784.50	88.88	34.97	788.74
10	80.07	39.70	740.70	82.44	39.37	745.13	84.84	39.01	749.73

20-YEAR TERM (continued)

	10-1/2% interest - $9.98 monthly payment (cont.)			10-3/4% interest - $10.15 monthly payment (cont.)			11% interest - $10.32 monthly payment (cont.)		
Year	Interest	Amort.	Balance	Interest	Amort.	Balance	Interest	Amort.	Balance
11	75.70	44.07	696.64	77.99	43.82	701.32	80.32	43.53	706.21
12	70.84	48.93	647.71	73.04	48.77	652.55	75.29	48.56	657.66
13	65.45	54.32	593.40	67.53	54.28	598.28	69.67	54.18	603.48
14	59.46	60.31	533.09	61.40	60.41	537.87	63.40	60.45	543.04
15	52.82	66.95	466.15	54.58	67.23	470.65	56.41	67.44	475.60
16	45.44	74.33	391.82	46.98	74.83	395.82	48.60	75.25	400.35
17	37.25	82.52	309.31	38.53	83.28	312.55	39.89	83.96	316.40
18	28.16	91.61	217.70	29.13	92.68	219.87	30.18	93.67	222.74
19	18.06	101.71	116.00	18.66	103.15	116.72	19.34	104.51	118.23
20	6.85	112.92	3.08	7.01	114.80	1.92	7.25	116.60	1.64

	11-1/4% interest - $10.49 monthly payment			11-1/2% interest - $10.66 monthly payment			11-3/4% interest - $10.84 monthly payment		
Year	Interest	Amort.	Balance	Interest	Amort.	Balance	Interest	Amort.	Balance
1	111.79	14.10	985.91	114.30	13.63	986.38	116.80	13.29	986.72
2	110.12	15.77	970.15	112.65	15.28	971.11	115.16	14.93	971.80
3	108.26	17.63	952.52	110.80	17.13	953.98	113.31	16.78	955.02
4	106.17	19.72	932.80	108.72	19.21	934.77	111.22	18.87	936.16
5	103.83	22.06	910.75	106.39	21.54	913.24	108.89	21.20	914.96
6	101.22	24.67	886.08	103.78	24.15	889.10	106.26	23.83	891.13
7	98.29	27.60	858.49	100.85	27.08	862.03	103.30	26.79	864.34
8	95.03	30.86	827.63	97.57	30.36	831.67	99.98	30.11	834.24
9	91.37	34.52	793.12	93.89	34.04	797.64	96.24	33.85	800.40
10	87.28	38.61	754.51	89.76	38.17	759.47	92.05	38.04	762.36
11	82.71	43.18	711.33	85.14	42.79	716.68	87.33	42.76	719.60
12	77.59	48.30	663.04	79.95	47.98	668.71	82.02	48.07	671.54
13	71.87	54.02	609.02	74.13	53.80	614.91	76.06	54.03	617.51
14	65.47	60.42	548.60	67.61	60.32	554.59	69.36	60.73	556.79
15	58.31	67.58	481.03	60.29	67.64	486.96	61.83	68.26	488.53
16	50.30	75.59	405.44	52.09	75.84	411.12	53.36	76.73	411.81
17	41.35	84.54	320.90	42.89	85.04	326.09	43.85	86.24	325.57
18	31.33	94.56	226.35	32.58	95.35	230.75	33.15	96.94	228.64
19	20.13	105.76	120.59	21.02	106.91	123.85	21.13	108.96	119.68
20	7.59	118.30	2.30	8.06	119.87	3.98	7.61	122.48	2.80

	12% interest - $11.01 monthly payment		
Year	Interest	Amort.	Balance
1	119.32	12.81	987.20
2	117.69	14.44	972.76
3	115.86	16.27	956.50
4	113.80	18.33	938.17
5	111.47	20.66	917.52
6	108.85	23.28	894.25
7	105.90	26.23	868.03
8	102.58	29.55	838.48
9	98.83	33.30	805.18
10	94.61	37.52	767.67
11	89.85	42.28	725.39
12	84.49	47.64	677.75
13	78.45	53.68	624.07
14	71.64	60.49	563.59
15	63.97	68.16	495.43
16	55.32	76.81	418.63
17	45.58	86.55	332.08
18	34.61	97.52	234.57
19	22.24	109.89	124.68
20	8.30	123.83	.86

20-YEAR TERM (Continued)

12-1/4% interest - $11.19 monthly payment

Year	Interest	Amort.	Balance	Accrued Interest
1	121.82	12.46	987.54	121.82
2	120.20	14.08	973.46	242.02
3	118.37	15.91	957.55	360.39
4	116.31	17.97	939.58	476.70
5	113.98	20.30	919.29	590.69
6	111.35	22.93	896.36	702.04
7	108.38	25.90	870.46	810.42
8	105.03	29.25	841.21	915.45
9	101.23	33.05	808.16	1016.68
10	96.95	37.33	770.83	1113.63
11	92.11	42.17	726.67	1205.75
12	86.65	47.63	681.03	1292.39
13	80.47	53.81	627.22	1372.86
14	73.50	60.78	566.44	1446.36
15	65.62	68.66	497.78	1511.98
16	56.72	77.56	420.22	1568.70
17	46.67	87.61	332.60	1615.36
18	35.31	98.97	233.63	1650.67
19	22.48	111.80	121.84	1673.16
20	7.99	126.29	-4.45	1681.15

12-1/2% interest - $11.36 monthly payment

Year	Interest	Amort.	Balance	Accrued Interest
1	124.33	11.99	988.01	124.33
2	122.74	13.58	974.43	247.07
3	120.94	15.38	959.05	368.01
4	118.91	17.41	941.64	486.92
5	116.60	19.72	921.92	603.52
6	113.99	22.33	899.59	717.51
7	111.03	25.29	874.30	828.54
8	107.68	28.64	845.66	936.22
9	103.89	32.43	813.23	1040.11
10	99.60	36.72	776.51	1139.71
11	94.73	41.59	734.93	1234.45
12	89.23	47.09	687.83	1323.67
13	82.99	53.33	634.51	1406.67
14	75.93	60.39	574.12	1482.60
15	67.93	68.39	505.73	1550.53
16	58.88	77.44	428.29	1609.41
17	48.63	87.69	340.60	1658.04
18	37.01	99.31	241.29	1695.05
19	23.86	112.46	128.84	1718.92
20	8.97	127.35	1.49	1727.89

12-3/4% interest - $11.54 monthly payment

Year	Interest	Amort.	Balance	Accrued Interest
1	126.84	11.64	988.36	126.84
2	125.26	13.22	975.14	252.10
3	123.47	15.01	960.13	375.57
4	121.44	17.04	943.09	497.01
5	119.14	19.34	923.75	616.15
6	116.52	21.96	901.80	732.68
7	113.56	24.92	876.87	846.23
8	110.19	28.29	848.58	956.42
9	106.36	32.12	816.46	1062.78
10	102.02	36.46	779.99	1164.79
11	97.09	41.39	738.60	1261.88
12	91.49	46.99	691.61	1353.37
13	85.13	53.35	638.26	1438.50
14	77.92	60.56	577.70	1516.42
15	69.73	68.75	508.95	1586.15
16	60.44	78.04	430.91	1646.59
17	49.88	88.60	342.31	1696.47
18	37.90	100.58	241.73	1734.37
19	24.30	114.18	127.55	1758.67
20	8.86	129.62	-2.06	1767.54

13% interest - $11.72 monthly payment

Year	Interest	Amort.	Balance	Accrued Interest
1	129.34	11.30	988.70	129.34
2	127.78	12.86	975.85	257.13
3	126.01	14.63	961.21	383.13
4	123.99	16.65	944.56	507.12
5	121.69	18.95	925.61	628.81
6	119.07	21.57	904.05	747.89
7	116.10	24.54	879.51	863.99
8	112.71	27.93	851.58	976.70
9	108.86	31.78	819.79	1085.55
10	104.47	36.17	783.62	1190.02
11	99.48	41.16	742.46	1289.50
12	93.79	46.85	695.61	1383.29
13	87.33	53.31	642.30	1470.62
14	79.97	60.67	581.62	1550.58
15	71.59	69.05	512.58	1622.18
16	62.06	78.58	434.00	1684.24
17	51.22	89.42	344.57	1735.45
18	38.87	101.77	242.81	1774.33
19	24.83	115.81	126.99	1799.15
20	8.84	131.80	-4.81	1807.99

853

20-YEAR TERM (Continued)

13-1/4% interest - $11.89
monthly payment

Year	Interest	Amort.	Balance	Accrued Interest
1	131.86	10.82	989.18	131.86
2	130.33	12.35	976.83	262.19
3	128.60	14.08	962.75	390.79
4	126.61	16.07	946.68	517.40
5	124.35	18.33	928.35	641.75
6	121.77	20.91	907.43	763.51
7	118.82	23.86	883.57	882.33
8	115.46	27.22	856.35	997.79
9	111.63	31.05	825.30	1109.42
10	107.25	35.43	789.87	1216.67
11	102.26	40.42	749.45	1318.93
12	96.57	46.11	703.34	1415.50
13	90.07	52.61	650.74	1505.58
14	82.66	60.02	590.72	1588.24
15	74.21	68.47	522.25	1662.45
16	64.57	78.11	444.14	1727.02
17	53.57	89.11	355.03	1780.59
18	41.01	101.67	253.36	1821.60
19	26.69	115.99	137.37	1848.29
20	10.36	132.32	5.05	1858.65

13-1/2% interest - $12.07
monthly payment

Interest	Amort.	Balance	Accrued Interest
134.37	10.47	989.53	134.37
132.86	11.98	977.55	267.23
131.14	13.70	963.85	398.37
129.17	15.67	948.19	527.55
126.92	17.92	930.27	654.47
124.35	20.49	909.78	778.82
121.41	23.43	886.35	900.23
118.04	26.80	859.54	1018.26
114.19	30.65	828.89	1132.45
109.76	35.06	793.84	1242.24
104.75	40.09	753.74	1346.98
98.99	45.85	707.89	1445.97
92.40	52.44	655.45	1538.37
84.86	59.98	595.47	1623.23
76.25	68.59	526.88	1699.48
66.39	78.45	448.44	1765.88
55.12	89.72	358.72	1821.00
42.23	102.61	256.11	1863.23
27.49	117.35	138.76	1890.72
10.63	134.21	4.55	1901.35

13-3/4% interest - $12.25
monthly payment

Year	Interest	Amort.	Balance	Accrued Interest
1	136.88	10.12	999.88	136.88
2	135.39	11.61	978.27	272.27
3	133.69	13.31	964.97	405.97
4	131.75	15.25	949.71	537.71
5	129.51	17.49	932.22	667.22
6	126.95	20.05	912.17	794.17
7	124.01	22.99	889.18	918.18
8	120.64	26.36	862.82	1038.82
9	116.78	30.22	832.61	1155.61
10	112.35	34.65	797.96	1267.96
11	107.28	39.72	758.24	1375.24
12	101.46	45.54	712.70	1476.70
13	94.79	52.21	660.48	1571.48
14	87.14	59.86	600.62	1658.61
15	78.37	68.63	531.98	1736.98
16	68.31	78.69	453.30	1805.30
17	56.78	90.22	363.08	1862.08
18	43.57	103.43	259.64	1905.64
19	28.41	118.59	141.06	1934.06
20	11.04	135.96	5.09	1945.09

14% interest - $12.44
monthly payment

Interest	Amort.	Balance	Accrued Interest
139.38	9.90	990.10	139.38
137.90	11.38	978.72	277.28
136.20	13.08	965.65	413.49
134.25	15.03	950.62	547.74
132.01	17.27	933.34	679.74
129.43	19.85	913.49	809.17
126.46	22.82	890.67	935.63
123.05	26.23	864.44	1058.68
119.14	30.14	834.30	1177.82
114.63	34.65	799.65	1292.45
109.46	39.82	759.83	1401.91
103.51	45.77	714.07	1505.43
96.68	52.60	661.47	1602.11
88.82	60.46	601.01	1690.93
79.79	69.49	531.53	1770.73
69.42	79.86	451.66	1840.14
57.49	91.79	359.87	1897.63
43.78	105.50	254.38	1941.42
28.03	121.25	133.12	1969.44
9.92	139.36	-6.24	1979.36

854

25-YEAR TERM

	4% interest - $5.28 monthly payment			4-1/2% interest - $5.56 monthly payment			5% interest - $5.85 monthly payment		
Year	Interest	Amort.	Balance	Interest	Amort.	Balance	Interest	Amort.	Balance
1	39.56	23.80	976.20	44.54	22.18	977.82	49.54	20.66	979.34
2	38.60	24.76	951.44	43.54	23.18	954.64	48.48	21.72	957.62
3	37.57	25.79	925.65	42.44	24.28	930.36	47.36	22.84	934.78
4	36.55	26.81	898.84	41.35	25.37	904.99	46.19	24.01	910.77
5	35.45	27.91	870.93	40.18	26.54	878.45	44.98	25.22	885.55
6	34.31	29.05	841.88	38.97	27.75	850.70	43.67	26.53	859.02
7	33.13	30.23	811.65	37.70	29.02	821.68	42.30	27.90	831.12
8	31.89	31.47	780.18	36.34	30.38	791.30	40.87	29.33	801.79
9	30.61	32.75	747.43	34.98	31.74	759.56	39.39	30.81	770.98
10	29.28	34.08	713.35	33.53	33.19	726.37	37.81	32.39	738.59
11	27.91	35.45	677.90	31.96	34.76	691.61	36.16	34.04	704.55
12	26.45	36.91	640.99	30.38	36.34	655.27	34.41	35.79	668.76
13	24.94	38.42	602.57	28.71	38.01	617.26	32.59	37.61	631.15
14	23.38	39.98	562.59	26.96	39.76	577.50	30.66	39.54	591.61
15	21.75	41.61	520.98	25.14	41.58	535.92	28.65	41.55	550.06
16	20.05	43.31	477.67	23.22	43.50	492.42	26.52	43.68	506.38
17	18.29	45.07	432.60	21.23	45.49	446.93	24.27	45.93	460.45
18	16.46	46.90	385.70	19.14	47.58	399.35	21.93	48.27	412.18
19	14.54	48.82	336.88	16.97	49.75	349.60	19.46	50.74	361.44
20	12.55	50.81	286.07	14.66	52.06	297.54	16.86	53.34	308.10
21	10.49	52.87	233.20	12.28	54.44	243.10	14.15	56.05	252.05
22	8.32	55.04	178.16	9.77	56.95	186.15	11.57	58.63	193.12
23	6.10	57.26	120.90	7.15	59.57	126.58	8.24	61.96	131.16
24	3.73	59.63	61.27	4.44	62.28	64.30	5.07	65.13	66.03
25	1.31	61.27	0	1.56	64.30	0	1.75	66.03	0

	5-1/4% interest - $6.00 monthly payment			5-1/2% interest - $6.15 monthly payment			5-3/4% interest - $6.30 monthly payment		
Year	Interest	Amort.	Balance	Interest	Amort.	Balance	Interest	Amort.	Balance
1	52.03	19.97	980.03	54.51	19.29	980.71	57.02	18.58	981.42
2	50.96	21.04	958.99	53.44	20.36	960.35	55.90	19.70	961.72
3	49.82	22.18	936.81	52.27	21.53	938.82	54.77	20.83	940.89
4	48.63	23.37	913.44	51.07	22.73	916.09	53.52	22.08	918.82
5	47.38	24.62	888.82	49.79	24.01	892.08	52.23	23.37	895.44
6	46.01	25.99	862.83	48.42	25.38	866.70	50.82	24.78	870.66
7	44.70	27.30	835.53	46.98	26.82	839.88	49.39	26.21	844.45
8	43.16	28.84	806.69	45.50	28.30	811.58	47.83	27.77	816.68
9	41.63	30.37	776.32	43.88	29.92	781.66	46.18	29.42	787.26
10	40.00	32.00	744.32	42.20	31.60	750.06	44.48	31.12	756.14
11	38.27	33.73	710.59	40.42	33.38	716.68	42.61	32.99	723.15
12	36.47	35.53	675.06	38.55	35.25	681.43	40.67	34.93	688.22
13	34.55	37.45	637.61	36.55	37.25	644.18	38.62	36.98	651.24
14	32.54	39.46	598.15	34.44	39.36	604.82	36.41	39.18	612.06
15	30.42	41.58	556.57	32.22	41.58	563.24	34.11	41.49	570.57
16	28.16	43.84	512.73	29.90	43.90	519.34	31.65	43.95	526.62
17	25.82	46.18	466.55	27.41	46.39	472.95	29.07	46.53	480.09
18	23.34	48.66	417.89	24.79	49.01	423.94	26.27	49.33	430.76
19	20.71	51.29	366.60	22.04	51.76	372.18	23.41	52.19	378.57
20	17.98	54.02	312.58	19.12	54.68	317.50	20.33	55.27	323.30
21	15.06	56.94	255.64	16.01	57.79	259.71	17.05	58.55	264.75
22	11.99	60.01	195.63	12.76	61.04	198.67	13.61	61.99	202.76
23	8.76	63.24	132.39	9.32	64.48	134.19	9.94	65.66	137.10
24	5.36	66.64	65.75	5.70	68.10	66.09	6.07	69.53	67.57
25	1.78	65.75	0	1.83	66.09	0	1.97	67.57	0

855

25-YEAR TERM (continued)

	6% interest - $6.45 monthly payment			6-1/4% interest - $6.60 monthly payment			6-1/2% interest - $6.76 monthly payment		
Year	Interest	Amort.	Balance	Interest	Amort.	Balance	Interest	Amort.	Balance
1	59.52	17.88	982.12	62.01	17.19	982.81	64.50	16.62	983.38
2	58.41	18.99	963.13	60.91	18.29	964.52	63.41	17.71	965.67
3	57.24	20.16	942.97	59.73	19.47	945.05	62.21	18.91	946.76
4	55.99	21.41	921.56	58.48	20.72	924.33	60.95	20.17	926.59
5	54.66	22.74	898.82	57.17	22.03	902.30	59.58	21.54	905.05
6	53.23	24.17	874.65	55.73	23.47	878.83	58.14	22.98	882.07
7	51.78	25.62	849.03	54.22	24.98	853.85	56.62	24.50	857.57
8	50.20	27.20	821.83	52.61	26.59	827.26	54.97	26.15	831.42
9	48.53	28.87	792.96	50.89	28.31	798.95	53.23	27.89	803.53
10	46.74	30.66	762.30	49.09	30.11	768.84	51.37	29.75	773.78
11	44.84	32.56	729.74	47.14	32.06	736.78	49.34	31.78	742.00
12	42.84	34.56	695.18	45.08	34.12	702.66	47.22	33.90	708.10
13	40.72	36.68	658.50	42.88	36.32	666.34	44.98	36.14	671.96
14	38.44	38.96	619.54	40.54	38.66	627.68	42.54	38.58	633.38
15	36.05	41.35	578.19	38.06	41.14	586.54	39.95	41.17	592.21
16	33.50	43.90	534.29	35.42	43.78	542.76	37.21	43.91	548.30
17	30.80	46.60	487.69	32.64	46.56	496.20	34.26	46.86	501.44
18	27.93	49.47	438.22	29.60	49.60	446.60	31.12	50.00	451.44
19	24.87	52.53	385.69	26.40	52.80	393.80	27.17	53.34	398.10
20	21.62	55.78	329.91	23.03	56.17	337.63	24.19	56.93	341.17
21	18.18	59.22	270.69	19.41	59.79	277.84	20.40	60.72	280.45
22	14.53	62.87	207.82	15.56	63.64	214.20	16.32	64.80	215.65
23	10.64	66.76	141.06	11.46	67.74	146.46	12.00	69.12	146.53
24	6.53	70.87	70.19	7.10	72.10	74.36	7.34	73.78	72.75
25	2.17	70.19	0	2.48	74.36	0	2.40	72.75	0

	6-3/4% interest - $6.91 monthly payment			7% interest - $7.07 monthly payment			7-1/4% interest - $7.23 monthly payment		
Year	Interest	Amort.	Balance	Interest	Amort.	Balance	Interest	Amort.	Balance
1	67.02	15.90	984.10	69.51	15.33	984.67	72.02	14.74	985.26
2	65.92	17.00	967.10	68.40	16.44	968.23	70.91	15.85	969.41
3	64.72	18.20	948.90	67.20	17.64	950.59	69.72	17.04	952.37
4	63.45	19.47	929.43	65.94	18.90	931.69	68.44	18.32	934.05
5	62.10	20.82	908.61	64.62	20.22	911.47	67.01	19.75	914.30
6	60.66	22.26	886.35	63.12	21.72	889.75	65.58	21.18	893.12
7	59.09	23.83	862.52	61.55	23.29	866.46	64.01	22.75	870.37
8	57.44	25.48	837.04	59.85	24.99	841.47	62.30	24.46	845.91
9	55.68	27.24	809.80	58.06	26.78	814.69	60.47	26.29	819.62
10	53.77	29.15	780.65	56.12	28.72	785.97	58.49	28.27	791.35
11	51.74	31.18	749.47	54.05	30.79	755.18	56.39	30.37	760.98
12	49.57	33.35	716.12	51.81	33.03	722.15	54.10	32.66	728.32
13	47.24	35.68	680.44	49.44	35.40	686.75	51.66	35.10	693.22
14	44.78	38.14	642.30	46.87	37.97	648.78	49.02	37.74	655.48
15	42.10	40.82	601.48	44.14	40.70	608.08	46.20	40.56	614.92
16	39.24	43.68	557.80	41.20	43.64	564.44	43.15	43.61	571.31
17	36.22	46.70	511.10	38.03	46.81	517.63	39.89	46.87	524.44
18	32.98	49.94	461.16	34.65	50.19	467.44	36.35	50.41	474.03
19	29.51	53.41	407.75	31.02	53.82	413.62	32.59	54.17	419.86
20	25.79	57.13	350.62	27.12	57.72	355.90	28.53	58.23	361.63
21	21.79	61.13	289.49	22.99	61.85	294.05	24.15	62.61	299.02
22	17.56	65.36	224.13	18.48	66.36	227.69	19.47	67.29	231.73
23	12.99	69.93	154.20	13.67	71.17	156.52	14.43	72.33	159.40
24	8.11	74.81	79.39	8.52	76.32	80.20	8.98	77.78	81.62
25	2.92	79.39	0	3.01	80.20	0	3.17	81.62	0

25-YEAR TERM (continued)

Year	7-1/2% interest - $7.39 monthly payment			7-3/4% interest - $7.56 monthly payment			8% interest - $7.72 monthly payment		
	Interest	Amort.	Balance	Interest	Amort.	Balance	Interest	Amort.	Balance
1	74.52	14.16	985.84	77.02	13.70	986.30	79.53	13.11	986.89
2	73.42	15.26	970.58	75.92	14.80	971.50	78.43	14.21	972.68
3	72.23	16.45	954.13	74.72	16.00	955.50	77.26	15.38	957.30
4	70.96	17.72	936.41	73.45	17.27	938.23	75.99	16.65	940.65
5	69.54	19.14	917.27	72.06	18.66	919.57	74.58	18.06	922.59
6	68.11	20.57	896.70	70.57	20.15	899.42	73.10	19.54	903.05
7	66.48	22.20	874.50	68.95	21.77	877.65	71.49	21.15	881.90
8	64.77	23.91	850.59	67.19	23.53	854.12	69.72	22.92	858.98
9	62.92	25.76	824.83	65.30	25.42	828.70	67.83	24.81	834.17
10	60.93	27.75	797.08	63.28	27.44	801.26	65.76	26.88	807.29
11	58.78	29.90	767.18	61.05	29.67	771.59	63.52	29.12	778.17
12	56.44	32.24	734.94	58.67	32.05	739.54	61.11	31.53	746.64
13	53.94	34.74	700.20	56.10	34.62	704.92	58.50	34.14	712.50
14	51.23	37.45	662.75	53.29	37.43	667.49	55.67	36.97	675.53
15	48.33	40.35	622.40	50.31	40.41	627.08	52.59	40.05	635.48
16	45.21	43.47	578.98	47.06	43.66	583.42	49.26	43.38	592.10
17	41.83	46.85	532.08	43.57	47.15	536.27	45.68	46.96	545.14
18	38.20	50.48	481.60	39.77	50.95	485.32	41.76	50.88	494.26
19	34.28	54.40	427.20	35.69	55.03	430.29	37.57	55.07	439.19
20	30.05	58.63	368.57	31.26	59.46	370.83	32.98	59.66	379.53
21	25.51	63.17	305.40	26.51	64.21	306.62	28.03	64.61	314.92
22	20.59	68.09	237.31	21.33	69.39	237.23	22.65	69.99	244.93
23	15.30	73.38	163.93	15.72	75.00	162.23	16.85	75.79	169.14
24	9.59	79.09	84.84	9.74	80.98	81.25	10.53	82.11	87.03
25	3.47	84.84	0	3.22	81.25	0	3.74	87.03	0

Year	8-1/4% interest - $7.88 monthly payment			8-1/2% interest - $8.05 monthly payment			8-3/4% interest - $8.22 monthly payment		
	Interest	Amort.	Balance	Interest	Amort.	Balance	Interest	Amort.	Balance
1	82.04	12.53	987.48	84.54	12.07	987.94	87.05	11.60	988.41
2	80.96	13.61	973.88	83.48	13.13	974.81	85.99	12.66	975.75
3	79.80	14.77	959.11	82.32	14.29	960.52	84.84	13.81	961.95
4	78.53	16.04	943.08	81.05	15.56	944.97	83.58	15.07	946.88
5	77.16	17.41	925.68	79.68	16.93	928.04	82.21	16.44	930.44
6	75.87	18.90	906.78	78.18	18.43	909.62	80.71	17.94	912.51
7	74.05	20.52	886.27	76.55	20.06	889.57	79.08	19.57	892.94
8	72.29	22.28	863.99	74.78	21.83	867.74	77.29	21.36	871.59
9	70.38	24.19	839.81	72.85	23.76	843.99	75.35	23.30	848.29
10	68.31	26.26	813.56	70.75	25.86	818.14	73.23	25.42	822.88
11	66.06	28.51	785.05	68.47	28.14	790.00	70.91	27.74	795.14
12	63.62	30.95	754.11	65.98	30.63	759.37	68.39	30.26	764.88
13	60.97	33.60	720.51	63.27	33.34	726.04	65.63	33.02	731.87
14	58.09	36.48	684.03	60.33	36.28	689.76	62.62	36.03	695.84
15	54.96	39.61	644.43	57.12	39.49	650.28	59.34	39.31	656.54
16	51.57	43.00	601.43	53.63	42.98	607.30	55.76	42.89	613.65
17	47.88	46.69	554.75	49.83	46.78	560.53	51.85	46.80	566.86
18	43.88	50.69	504.07	45.70	50.91	509.62	47.59	51.06	515.80
19	39.54	55.03	449.05	41.20	55.41	454.21	42.94	55.71	460.09
20	34.83	59.74	389.31	36.30	60.31	393.91	37.86	60.79	399.31
21	29.71	64.86	324.45	30.97	65.64	328.27	32.33	66.32	332.99
22	24.15	70.42	254.03	25.17	71.44	256.83	26.29	72.36	260.64
23	18.11	76.46	177.58	18.85	77.76	179.08	19.69	78.96	181.68
24	11.56	83.01	94.58	11.98	84.63	94.45	12.50	86.15	95.54
25	4.45	90.12	4.46	4.50	92.11	2.35	4.65	94.00	1.55

25-YEAR TERM (continued)

	9% interest - $8.40 monthly payment			9-1/4% interest - $8.56 monthly payment			9-1/2% interest - $8.74 monthly payment		
Year	Interest	Amort.	Balance	Interest	Amort.	Balance	Interest	Amort.	Balance
1	89.54	11.26	988.74	92.06	10.67	989.34	94.56	10.33	989.68
2	88.49	12.31	976.43	91.03	11.70	977.65	93.54	11.35	978.34
3	87.34	13.46	962.97	89.90	12.83	964.82	92.41	12.48	965.86
4	86.07	14.73	948.24	88.66	14.07	950.76	91.17	13.72	952.15
5	84.66	16.14	932.10	87.31	15.42	935.35	89.81	15.08	937.08
6	83.18	17.62	914.48	85.82	16.91	918.44	88.32	16.57	920.52
7	81.52	19.28	895.20	84.19	18.54	899.90	86.67	18.22	902.31
8	79.72	21.08	874.12	82.40	20.33	879.58	84.87	20.02	882.29
9	77.73	23.07	851.05	80.44	22.29	857.29	82.88	22.01	860.28
10	75.58	25.22	825.83	78.28	24.45	832.85	80.70	24.19	836.10
11	74.10	27.60	798.23	75.93	26.80	806.05	78.30	26.59	809.51
12	70.62	30.18	768.05	73.34	29.39	776.66	75.66	29.23	780.28
13	67.79	33.01	735.04	70.50	32.23	744.44	72.76	32.13	748.15
14	64.69	36.11	698.93	67.39	35.34	709.10	69.57	35.32	712.83
15	61.29	39.51	659.42	63.98	38.75	670.36	66.06	38.83	674.01
16	57.60	43.20	616.22	60.24	42.49	627.88	62.21	42.68	631.33
17	53.56	47.24	568.98	56.14	46.59	581.29	57.97	46.92	584.42
18	49.12	51.68	517.30	51.64	51.09	530.21	53.32	51.57	532.85
19	44.27	56.53	460.77	46.71	56.02	474.20	48.20	56.69	476.17
20	38.96	61.84	398.93	41.31	61.42	412.78	42.57	62.32	413.85
21	33.17	67.63	331.30	35.38	67.35	345.44	36.39	68.50	345.36
22	26.81	73.99	257.31	28.88	73.85	271.59	29.59	75.30	270.07
23	19.86	80.94	176.37	21.75	80.98	190.62	22.12	82.77	187.30
24	12.27	88.53	87.84	13.94	88.79	101.83	13.90	90.99	96.32
25	3.96	87.84	0	5.36	97.37	4.47	4.87	100.02	3.69

	9-3/4% interest - $8.91 monthly payment			10% interest - $9.09 monthly payment			10-1/4% interest - $9.26 monthly payment		
Year	Interest	Amort.	Balance	Interest	Amort.	Balance	Interest	Amort.	Balance
1	97.07	9.86	990.15	99.56	9.52	990.48	102.09	9.04	990.97
2	96.07	10.86	979.30	98.57	10.51	979.97	101.12	10.01	980.96
3	94.96	11.97	967.33	97.48	11.60	968.37	100.04	11.09	969.88
4	93.74	13.19	954.15	96.25	12.83	955.54	98.85	12.28	957.60
5	92.40	14.53	939.62	94.93	14.15	941.39	97.53	13.60	944.01
6	90.91	16.02	923.61	93.44	15.64	925.75	96.07	15.06	928.96
7	89.28	17.65	905.96	91.78	17.30	908.45	94.45	16.68	912.29
8	87.48	19.45	886.52	90.01	19.07	889.38	92.66	18.47	893.82
9	85.50	21.43	865.09	87.99	21.09	868.29	90.68	20.45	873.38
10	83.31	23.62	841.48	85.78	23.30	844.99	88.48	22.65	850.73
11	80.91	26.02	815.47	83.33	25.75	819.24	86.05	25.08	825.66
12	78.25	28.68	786.79	80.63	28.45	790.79	83.35	27.78	797.88
13	75.33	31.60	755.20	77.68	31.40	759.39	80.37	30.76	767.13
14	72.11	34.82	720.38	74.39	34.69	724.70	77.06	34.07	733.07
15	68.56	38.37	682.01	70.74	38.34	686.36	73.40	37.73	695.35
16	64.64	42.29	639.73	66.74	42.34	644.02	69.35	41.78	653.57
17	60.33	46.60	593.14	62.29	46.79	597.23	64.86	46.27	607.31
18	55.58	51.35	541.80	57.39	51.69	545.54	59.89	51.24	556.08
19	50.35	56.58	485.22	51.96	57.12	488.42	54.39	56.74	499.34
20	44.58	62.35	422.87	46.01	63.07	425.35	48.29	62.84	436.50
21	38.22	68.71	354.16	39.37	69.71	355.64	41.54	69.59	366.92
22	31.21	75.72	278.45	32.09	76.99	278.65	34.06	77.07	289.85
23	23.49	83.44	195.02	24.06	85.02	193.63	25.78	85.35	204.50
24	14.98	91.95	103.07	15.13	93.95	99.68	16.61	94.52	109.99
25	5.61	101.32	1.75	5.29	99.68	0	6.45	104.68	5.31

858

25-YEAR TERM (continued)

Year	10-1/2% interest - $9.44 monthly payment			10-3/4% interest - $9.62 monthly payment			11% interest - $9.80 monthly payment		
	Interest	Amort.	Balance	Interest	Amort.	Balance	Interest	Amort.	Balance
1	104.59	8.70	991.31	107.10	8.35	991.66	109.61	8.00	992.01
2	103.64	9.65	981.67	106.16	9.29	982.38	108.68	8.93	983.09
3	102.57	10.72	970.96	105.11	10.34	972.04	107.65	9.96	973.14
4	101.39	11.90	959.06	103.94	11.51	960.54	106.50	11.11	962.03
5	100.08	13.21	945.86	102.64	12.81	947.74	105.22	12.39	949.64
6	98.63	14.66	931.20	101.20	14.25	933.49	103.78	13.83	935.82
7	97.01	16.28	914.93	99.59	15.86	917.64	102.18	15.43	920.40
8	95.22	18.07	896.87	97.80	17.65	899.99	100.40	17.21	903.19
9	93.23	20.06	876.81	95.80	19.65	880.35	98.41	19.20	883.99
10	91.02	22.27	854.54	93.59	21.86	858.49	96.19	21.42	862.57
11	88.56	24.73	829.82	91.12	24.33	834.16	93.71	23.90	838.67
12	85.84	27.45	802.38	88.37	27.08	807.08	90.94	26.67	812.01
13	82.82	30.47	771.91	85.31	30.14	776.95	87.86	29.75	782.26
14	79.46	33.83	738.08	81.91	33.54	743.41	84.41	33.20	749.07
15	75.73	37.56	700.52	78.12	37.33	706.08	80.57	37.04	712.03
16	71.59	41.70	658.83	73.90	41.55	664.54	76.29	41.32	670.72
17	67.00	46.29	612.54	69.21	46.24	618.30	71.50	46.11	624.62
18	61.89	51.40	561.15	63.99	51.46	566.84	66.17	51.44	573.18
19	56.23	57.06	504.10	58.17	57.28	509.57	60.22	57.39	515.79
20	49.94	63.35	440.76	51.70	63.75	445.82	53.58	64.03	451.77
21	42.96	70.33	370.44	44.50	70.95	374.88	46.17	71.44	380.33
22	35.21	78.08	292.36	36.49	78.96	295.93	37.90	79.71	300.63
23	26.61	86.68	205.69	27.57	87.88	208.05	28.68	88.93	211.70
24	17.06	96.23	109.46	17.64	97.81	110.25	18.39	99.22	112.49
25	6.45	106.84	2.63	6.60	108.85	1.40	6.91	110.70	1.79

Year	11-1/4% interest - $9.98 monthly payment			11-1/2% interest - $10.16 monthly payment			11-3/4% interest - $10.35 monthly payment		
	Interest	Amort.	Balance	Interest	Amort.	Balance	Interest	Amort.	Balance
1	112.12	7.65	992.36	114.63	7.30	992.71	117.13	7.08	992.93
2	111.21	8.56	983.81	113.74	8.19	984.53	116.25	7.96	984.98
3	110.20	9.57	974.24	112.75	9.18	975.35	115.27	8.94	976.05
4	109.07	10.70	963.54	111.64	10.29	965.07	114.16	10.05	966.00
5	107.80	11.97	951.58	110.39	11.54	953.53	112.91	11.30	954.71
6	106.38	13.39	938.19	108.99	12.94	940.60	111.51	12.70	942.02
7	104.79	14.98	923.22	107.43	14.50	926.10	109.94	14.27	927.75
8	103.02	16.75	906.48	105.67	16.26	909.85	108.17	16.04	911.72
9	101.04	18.73	887.75	103.70	18.23	891.62	106.18	18.03	893.69
10	98.82	20.95	866.80	101.49	20.44	871.18	103.95	20.26	873.44
11	96.34	23.43	843.37	99.01	22.92	848.26	101.43	22.78	850.66
12	93.56	26.21	817.17	96.23	25.70	822.56	98.61	25.60	825.07
13	90.45	29.32	787.86	93.11	28.82	793.75	95.43	28.78	796.29
14	86.98	32.79	755.07	89.62	32.31	761.44	91.86	32.35	763.95
15	83.10	36.67	718.41	85.70	36.23	725.21	87.85	36.36	727.60
16	78.75	41.02	677.39	81.31	40.62	684.60	83.34	40.87	686.74
17	73.89	45.88	631.52	76.38	45.55	639.05	78.27	45.94	640.81
18	68.46	51.31	580.22	70.86	51.07	587.99	72.58	51.63	589.18
19	62.38	57.39	522.83	64.67	57.26	530.73	66.17	58.04	531.15
20	55.58	64.19	458.65	57.72	64.21	466.53	58.96	65.23	465.92
21	47.98	71.79	386.86	49.94	71.99	394.54	50.88	73.33	392.60
22	39.47	80.30	306.56	41.21	80.72	313.83	41.79	82.42	310.19
23	29.96	89.81	216.75	31.42	90.51	223.33	31.57	92.64	217.55
24	19.31	100.46	116.30	20.45	101.48	121.85	20.08	104.13	113.42
25	7.41	112.36	3.95	8.14	113.79	8.07	7.16	117.05	3.62

25-YEAR TERM (continued)

12% interest - $10.35
monthly payment

Year	Interest	Amort.	Balance
1	119.64	6.73	993.28
2	118.79	7.58	985.71
3	117.83	8.54	977.17
4	116.75	9.62	967.56
5	115.53	10.84	956.72
6	114.15	12.22	944.51
7	112.60	13.77	930.75
8	110.86	15.51	915.24
9	108.89	17.48	897.77
10	106.68	19.69	878.08
11	104.18	22.19	855.90
12	101.37	25.00	830.90
13	98.20	28.17	802.73
14	94.62	31.75	770.99
15	90.60	35.77	735.23
16	86.06	40.31	694.93
17	80.95	45.42	649.51
18	75.19	51.18	598.34
19	68.70	57.67	540.68
20	61.39	64.98	475.70
21	53.15	73.22	402.48
22	43.86	82.51	319.9?
23	33.40	92.97	227.01
24	21.61	104.76	122.26
25	8.32	118.05	4.22

25-YEAR TERM (Continued)

12-1/4% interest - $10.72 monthly payment / 12-1/2% interest - $10.90 monthly payment

Year	Interest	Amort.	Balance	Accrued Interest	Interest	Amort.	Balance	Accrued Interest
1	122.14	6.50	993.50	122.14	124.66	6.14	993.86	124.66
2	121.30	7.34	986.16	243.44	123.84	6.96	986.90	248.50
3	120.35	8.29	977.87	363.79	122.92	7.88	979.02	371.42
4	119.28	9.36	968.51	483.07	121.88	8.92	970.10	493.30
5	118.06	10.58	957.93	601.13	120.70	10.10	959.99	613.99
6	116.69	11.95	945.98	717.82	119.36	11.44	948.55	733.35
7	115.14	13.50	932.48	832.96	117.84	12.96	935.59	851.19
8	113.39	15.25	917.24	946.36	116.13	14.67	920.92	967.32
9	111.42	17.22	900.01	1057.77	114.18	16.62	904.31	1081.51
10	109.18	19.46	880.55	1166.95	111.98	18.82	885.49	1193.49
11	106.66	21.98	858.57	1273.61	109.49	21.31	864.18	1302.98
12	103.81	24.83	833.75	1377.43	106.67	24.13	840.06	1409.66
13	100.59	28.05	805.70	1478.02	103.48	27.32	812.73	1513.13
14	96.96	31.68	774.02	1574.98	99.86	30.94	781.79	1612.99
15	92.85	35.79	738.23	1667.83	95.76	35.04	746.75	1708.75
16	88.21	40.43	697.81	1756.05	91.12	39.68	707.08	1799.88
17	82.97	45.67	652.14	1839.02	85.87	44.93	662.14	1885.74
18	77.05	51.59	600.55	1916.07	79.92	50.86	611.26	1965.66
19	70.37	58.27	542.28	1986.44	73.18	57.62	553.64	2038.84
20	62.81	65.83	476.46	2049.26	65.55	65.25	488.39	2104.39
21	54.28	74.36	402.10	2103.54	56.91	73.89	414.51	2161.31
22	44.64	84.00	318.10	2148.18	47.13	83.67	330.83	2208.43
23	33.76	94.88	223.22	2181.94	36.05	94.75	236.08	2244.48
24	21.46	107.18	116.04	2203.40	23.50	107.30	128.78	2267.98
25	7.57	121.07	-5.03	2210.97	9.29	121.51	7.27	2277.27

12-3/4% interest - $11.09 monthly payment / 13% interest - $11.28 monthly payment

Year	Interest	Amort.	Balance	Accrued Interest	Interest	Amort.	Balance	Accrued Interest
1	127.16	5.92	994.08	127.16	129.67	5.69	994.31	129.67
2	126.36	6.72	987.36	253.52	128.88	6.48	987.83	258.55
3	125.45	7.63	979.74	378.98	127.99	7.37	980.46	386.54
4	124.42	8.66	971.08	503.40	126.97	8.39	972.07	513.51
5	123.25	9.83	961.25	626.65	125.81	9.55	962.53	639.33
6	121.92	11.16	950.09	748.57	124.50	10.86	951.66	763.82
7	120.41	12.67	937.43	868.99	123.00	12.36	939.30	886.82
8	118.70	14.38	923.05	987.69	121.29	14.07	925.23	1008.11
9	116.76	16.32	906.72	1104.44	119.35	16.01	909.22	1127.46
10	114.55	18.53	888.19	1218.99	117.14	18.22	891.00	1244.60
11	112.04	21.04	867.16	1331.04	114.62	20.74	870.26	1359.22
12	109.20	23.88	843.28	1440.24	111.76	23.60	846.66	1470.98
13	105.97	27.11	816.17	1546.21	108.50	26.86	819.80	1579.48
14	102.30	30.78	785.39	1648.51	104.80	30.56	789.24	1684.28
15	98.14	34.94	750.45	1746.65	100.58	34.78	754.46	1784.86
16	93.42	39.66	710.73	1840.07	95.78	39.58	714.87	1880.63
17	88.05	45.03	665.76	1928.12	90.31	45.05	669.82	1970.94
18	81.97	51.11	614.65	2010.09	84.09	51.27	618.56	2055.04
19	75.05	58.03	556.63	2085.15	77.02	58.34	560.21	2132.05
20	67.21	65.87	490.75	2152.35	68.96	66.40	493.82	2201.02
21	58.30	74.78	415.98	2210.66	59.80	75.56	418.26	2260.82
22	48.19	84.89	331.09	2258.85	49.37	85.99	332.27	2310.19
23	36.71	96.37	234.72	2295.56	37.50	97.86	234.41	2347.69
24	23.68	109.40	125.32	2319.24	23.99	111.37	123.04	2317.68
25	8.89	124.19	1.12	2328.12	8.62	126.74	-3.70	2380.30

25-YEAR TERM (Continued)

13-1/4% interest - $11.47 monthly payment / 13-1/2% interest - $11.66 monthly payment

Year	Interest	Amort.	Balance	Accrued Interest	Interest	Amort.	Balance	Accrued Interest
1	132.18	5.46	994.54	132.18	134.68	5.24	994.76	134.68
2	131.41	6.23	988.30	263.58	133.93	5.99	988.78	268.62
3	130.53	7.11	981.19	394.11	133.07	6.85	981.93	401.69
4	129.53	8.11	973.08	523.64	132.09	7.83	974.09	533.77
5	128.39	9.26	963.82	651.02	130.96	8.96	965.14	664.74
6	127.08	10.56	953.26	779.10	129.67	10.25	954.89	794.41
7	125.59	12.05	941.22	904.70	128.20	11.72	943.17	922.61
8	123.90	13.74	927.47	1028.59	126.52	13.40	929.77	1049.13
9	121.96	15.68	911.79	1150.55	124.59	15.33	914.45	1173.73
10	119.75	17.89	893.90	1270.30	122.39	17.53	896.92	1296.12
11	117.23	20.41	873.50	1387.54	119.87	20.05	876.87	1415.99
12	114.36	23.28	850.21	1501.89	116.99	22.93	853.95	1532.99
13	111.08	25.56	823.65	1612.97	113.70	26.22	827.73	1646.69
14	107.34	30.30	793.35	1720.31	109.93	29.99	797.74	1756.62
15	103.07	34.57	758.78	1823.38	105.62	34.30	763.44	1862.24
16	98.20	39.44	719.34	1921.58	100.70	39.22	724.22	1962.94
17	92.65	44.99	674.35	2014.23	95.06	44.86	679.36	2058.00
18	86.31	51.33	623.01	2100.53	88.62	51.30	628.05	2146.61
19	79.08	58.56	564.45	2179.61	81.24	58.68	569.38	2227.86
20	70.83	66.81	497.64	2250.44	72.81	67.11	502.27	2300.67
21	61.42	76.22	421.42	2311.86	63.17	76.75	425.53	2363.85
22	50.68	86.96	334.46	2362.54	52.15	87.77	337.75	2415.99
23	38.43	99.21	235.25	2400.97	39.54	100.38	237.37	2455.53
24	24.46	113.18	122.08	2425.44	25.11	114.81	122.56	2480.64
25	8.52	129.12	-7.04	2433.96	8.62	131.30	-8.74	2489.26

13-3/4% interest - $11.85 monthly payment / 14% interest - $12.04 monthly payment

Year	Interest	Amort.	Balance	Accrued Interest	Interest	Amort.	Balance	Accrued Interest
1	137.19	5.01	994.99	137.19	139.70	4.78	995.22	139.70
2	136.46	5.74	989.25	273.65	138.99	5.49	989.73	278.69
3	135.62	6.58	982.67	409.27	138.17	6.31	983.42	416.86
4	134.65	7.55	975.12	543.92	137.22	7.26	976.16	554.08
5	133.55	8.65	966.47	677.47	136.14	8.34	987.82	690.22
6	132.28	9.92	956.55	809.75	134.90	9.56	958.24	825.12
7	130.83	11.37	945.17	940.57	133.46	11.02	947.22	958.58
8	129.16	13.04	932.13	1069.73	131.82	12.66	934.56	1090.40
9	127.25	14.95	917.18	1196.98	129.93	14.55	920.01	1220.33
10	125.06	17.14	900.04	1322.04	127.75	16.73	903.28	1348.08
11	122.55	19.65	880.39	1440.59	125.26	19.22	884.06	1473.34
12	119.67	22.53	857.86	1564.26	122.39	22.09	861.96	1595.72
13	116.37	25.83	832.03	1680.63	119.09	25.39	836.57	1714.81
14	112.58	29.62	802.41	1793.21	115.29	29.19	807.38	1830.10
15	108.24	33.96	768.46	1901.46	110.94	33.54	773.84	1941.04
16	103.27	38.93	729.53	2004.73	105.93	38.55	735.29	2046.97
17	97.57	44.63	684.89	2101.29	100.17	44.31	690.97	2147.13
18	91.03	51.17	633.72	2193.32	93.55	50.93	640.04	2240.68
19	83.53	58.67	575.05	2276.85	85.94	58.54	581.51	2326.63
20	74.93	67.27	507.78	2351.78	77.20	67.28	514.23	2403.83
21	65.08	77.12	430.66	2416.86	67.16	77.32	436.91	2470.99
22	53.78	88.42	342.25	2475.65	55.61	88.87	348.03	2526.59
23	40.83	101.37	240.87	2511.47	42.34	102.14	245.89	2568.93
24	25.98	116.22	124.65	2537.45	27.08	117.40	128.49	2596.01
25	8.95	133.25	-8.60	2546.40	9.55	134.93	-6.44	2605.56

30-YEAR TERM

Year	4% interest - $4.77 monthly payment			4-1/4% interest - $4.92 monthly payment			4-1/2% interest - $5.07 monthly payment		
	Interest	Amort.	Balance	Interest	Amort.	Balance	Interest	Amort.	Balance
1	39.69	17.56	982.45	42.18	16.87	983.14	44.67	16.18	983.83
2	38.97	18.28	964.17	41.45	17.60	965.54	43.93	16.92	966.92
3	38.23	19.02	945.15	40.69	18.36	947.18	43.15	17.70	949.23
4	37.45	19.80	925.36	39.89	19.16	928.03	42.34	18.51	930.73
5	36.64	20.61	904.76	39.06	19.99	908.04	41.49	19.36	911.37
6	35.80	21.45	883.32	38.19	20.86	887.19	40.60	20.25	891.13
7	34.93	22.32	861.00	37.29	21.76	865.44	39.67	21.18	869.96
8	34.02	23.23	837.78	36.35	22.70	842.74	38.70	22.15	847.81
9	33.08	24.17	813.61	35.36	23.69	819.06	37.68	23.17	824.65
10	32.09	25.16	788.46	34.34	24.71	794.35	36.62	24.23	800.42
11	31.07	26.18	762.28	33.27	25.78	768.57	35.51	25.34	775.08
12	30.00	27.25	735.03	32.15	26.90	741.67	34.34	26.51	748.58
13	28.89	28.36	706.68	30.98	28.07	713.61	33.12	27.73	720.86
14	27.73	29.52	677.17	29.77	29.28	684.33	31.85	29.00	691.86
15	26.53	30.72	646.45	28.50	30.55	653.79	30.52	30.33	661.54
16	25.28	31.97	614.49	27.17	31.88	621.92	29.13	31.72	629.82
17	23.98	33.27	581.23	25.79	33.26	588.67	27.67	33.18	596.64
18	22.62	34.63	546.60	24.35	34.70	553.97	26.14	34.71	561.94
19	21.21	36.04	510.57	22.85	36.20	517.78	24.55	36.30	525.64
20	19.75	37.50	473.07	21.28	37.77	480.01	22.88	37.97	487.68
21	18.22	39.03	434.04	19.64	39.41	440.61	21.14	39.71	447.97
22	16.63	40.62	393.43	17.94	41.11	399.50	19.31	41.54	406.44
23	14.97	42.28	351.15	16.15	42.90	356.61	17.41	43.44	363.00
24	13.25	44.00	307.16	14.30	44.75	311.86	15.41	45.44	317.57
25	11.46	45.79	261.37	12.36	46.69	265.17	13.32	47.53	270.05
26	9.59	47.66	213.72	10.33	48.72	216.46	11.14	49.71	220.34
27	7.65	49.60	164.13	8.22	50.83	165.64	8.86	51.99	168.35
28	5.63	51.62	112.51	6.02	53.03	112.61	6.47	54.38	113.98
29	3.53	53.72	58.79	3.72	55.33	57.29	3.97	56.88	57.10
30	1.34	55.91	2.89	1.32	57.73	.43	1.36	59.49	2.38

Year	4-3/4% interest - $5.22 monthly payment			5% interest - $5.37 monthly payment			5-1/4% interest - $5.52 monthly payment		
	Interest	Amort.	Balance	Interest	Amort.	Balance	Interest	Amort.	Balance
1	47.17	15.48	984.53	49.67	14.78	985.23	52.17	14.08	985.93
2	46.42	16.23	968.31	48.91	15.54	969.70	51.41	14.84	971.10
3	45.63	17.02	951.29	48.12	16.33	953.37	50.61	15.64	955.47
4	44.81	17.84	933.45	47.28	17.17	936.21	49.77	16.48	939.00
5	43.94	18.71	914.75	46.41	18.04	918.17	48.89	17.36	921.64
6	43.03	19.62	895.14	45.48	18.97	899.21	47.95	18.30	903.35
7	42.08	20.57	874.57	44.51	19.94	879.28	46.97	19.28	884.08
8	41.08	21.57	853.01	43.49	20.96	858.32	45.93	20.32	863.76
9	40.03	22.62	830.40	42.42	22.03	836.30	44.84	21.41	842.36
10	38.94	23.71	806.69	41.29	23.16	813.15	43.69	22.56	819.81
11	37.79	24.86	781.83	40.11	24.34	788.81	42.48	23.77	796.04
12	36.58	26.07	755.76	38.86	25.59	763.23	41.20	25.05	771.00
13	35.31	27.34	728.43	37.56	26.89	736.34	39.85	26.40	744.60
14	33.99	28.66	699.77	36.18	28.27	708.08	38.43	27.82	716.79
15	32.60	30.05	669.72	34.73	29.72	678.37	36.94	29.31	687.49
16	31.14	31.51	638.22	33.21	31.24	647.14	35.36	30.89	656.60
17	29.61	33.04	605.18	31.62	32.83	614.31	33.70	32.55	624.06
18	28.00	34.65	570.54	29.94	34.51	579.80	31.95	34.30	589.76
19	26.32	36.33	534.21	28.17	36.28	543.52	30.11	36.14	553.62
20	24.56	38.09	496.12	26.32	38.13	505.39	28.16	38.09	515.54
21	22.71	39.94	456.19	24.36	40.09	465.31	26.11	40.14	475.41
22	20.77	41.88	414.31	22.31	42.14	423.18	23.96	42.29	433.12
23	18.74	43.91	370.41	20.16	44.29	378.90	21.68	44.57	388.56
24	16.61	46.04	324.37	17.89	46.56	332.34	19.28	46.97	341.60
25	14.37	48.28	276.09	15.51	48.94	283.41	16.76	49.49	292.11
26	12.03	50.62	225.47	13.01	51.44	231.97	14.10	52.15	239.97
27	9.57	53.08	172.40	10.38	54.07	177.90	11.29	54.96	185.01
28	6.99	55.66	116.74	7.61	56.84	121.06	8.34	57.91	127.11
29	4.29	58.36	58.39	4.70	59.75	61.32	5.22	61.03	66.08
30	1.46	61.19	2.80	1.64	62.81	1.48	1.94	64.31	1.78

30-YEAR TERM (continued)

	5-1/2% interest - $5.68 monthly payment			5-3/4% interest - $5.84 monthly payment			6% interest - $6.00 monthly payment		
Year	Interest	Amort.	Balance	Interest	Amort.	Balance	Interest	Amort.	Balance
1	54.67	13.50	986.51	57.17	12.92	987.09	59.67	12.34	987.67
2	53.91	14.26	972.25	56.41	13.68	973.41	58.91	13.10	974.57
3	53.10	15.07	957.19	55.60	14.49	958.92	58.10	13.91	960.67
4	52.25	15.92	941.28	54.74	15.35	943.58	57.24	14.77	945.91
5	51.36	16.81	924.47	53.84	16.25	927.33	56.33	15.68	930.23
6	50.41	17.76	906.71	52.88	17.21	910.12	55.37	16.64	913.60
7	49.41	18.76	887.95	51.86	18.23	891.90	54.34	17.67	895.93
8	48.35	19.82	868.13	50.79	19.30	872.60	53.25	18.76	877.18
9	47.23	20.94	847.19	49.65	20.44	852.16	52.09	19.92	857.27
10	46.05	22.12	825.08	48.44	21.65	830.52	50.87	21.14	836.13
11	44.80	23.37	801.71	47.16	22.93	807.59	49.56	22.45	813.68
12	43.48	24.69	777.03	45.81	24.28	783.32	48.18	23.83	789.85
13	42.09	26.08	750.96	44.37	25.72	757.61	46.71	25.30	764.56
14	40.62	27.55	723.41	42.86	27.23	730.38	45.15	26.86	737.70
15	39.07	29.10	694.31	41.25	28.84	701.54	43.49	28.52	709.19
16	37.42	30.75	663.57	39.55	30.54	671.00	41.73	30.28	678.91
17	35.6ъ	32.48	631.10	37.74	32.35	638.66	39.87	32.14	646.77
18	33.86	34.31	596.79	35.83	34.26	604.41	37.88	34.13	612.65
19	31.92	36.25	560.55	33.81	36.28	568.14	35.78	36.23	576.43
20	29.88	38.29	522.27	31.67	38.42	529.72	33.54	38.47	537.96
21	27.72	40.45	481.82	29.40	40.69	489.04	31.17	40.84	497.13
22	25.44	42.73	439.10	27.00	43.09	445.96	28.65	43.36	453.78
23	23.03	45.14	393.96	24.46	45.63	400.33	25.98	46.03	407.75
24	20.48	47.69	346.28	21.76	48.33	352.01	23.14	48.87	358.89
25	17.79	50.38	295.90	18.91	51.18	300.84	20.13	51.88	307.01
26	14.95	53.22	242.69	15.89	54.20	246.64	16.93	55.08	251.93
27	11.95	56.22	186.47	12.69	57.40	189.24	13.53	58.48	193.46
28	8.78	59.39	127.09	9.30	60.79	128.46	9.92	62.09	131.38
29	5.43	62.74	64.35	5.71	64.38	64.09	6.09	65.92	65.47
30	1.89	66.28	1.92	1.91	68.18	4.09	2.03	69.98	4.51

	6-1/4% interest - $6.16 monthly payment			6-1/2% interest - $6.32 monthly payment			6-3/4% interest - $6.49 monthly payment		
Year	Interest	Amort.	Balance	Interest	Amort.	Balance	Interest	Amort.	Balance
1	62.17	11.76	988.25	64.68	11.17	988.84	67.18	10.71	989.30
2	61.42	12.51	975.74	63.93	11.92	976.92	66.43	11.46	977.85
3	60.61	13.32	962.43	63.13	12.72	964.20	65.63	12.26	965.59
4	59.76	14.17	948.26	62.28	13.57	950.64	64.78	13.11	952.49
5	58.84	15.09	933.18	61.37	14.48	936.16	63.87	14.02	938.48
6	57.87	16.06	917.13	60.40	15.45	920.72	62.89	15.00	923.48
7	56.84	17.09	900.04	59.37	16.48	904.24	61.85	16.04	907.45
8	55.74	18.19	881.86	58.26	17.59	886.66	60.73	17.16	890.30
9	54.57	19.36	862.51	57.09	18.76	867.90	59.54	18.35	871.95
10	53.33	20.60	841.91	55.83	20.02	847.88	58.26	19.63	852.33
11	52.00	21.93	819.99	54.49	21.36	826.52	56.90	20.99	831.34
12	50.59	23.34	796.66	53.06	22.79	803.74	55.43	22.46	808.89
13	49.09	24.84	771.83	51.53	24.32	779.42	53.87	24.02	784.87
14	47.50	26.43	745.40	49.90	25.95	753.48	52.20	25.69	759.19
15	45.80	28.13	717.27	48.17	27.68	725.80	50.41	27.48	731.71
16	43.99	29.94	687.33	46.31	29.54	696.27	48.50	29.39	702.32
17	42.06	31.87	655.46	44.33	31.52	664.76	46.45	31.44	670.89
18	40.01	33.92	621.55	42.22	33.63	631.14	44.26	33.63	637.27
19	37.83	36.10	585.45	39.97	35.88	595.27	41.92	35.97	601.30
20	35.51	38.42	547.04	37.57	38.28	556.99	39.42	38.47	562.84
21	33.04	40.89	506.15	35.01	40.84	516.15	36.74	41.15	521.69
22	30.41	43.52	462.63	32.27	43.58	472.58	33.87	44.02	477.68
23	27.61	46.32	416.31	29.35	46.50	426.09	30.81	47.08	430.60
24	24.63	49.30	367.01	26.24	49.61	376.48	27.53	50.36	380.25
25	21.46	52.47	314.54	22.92	52.93	323.56	24.03	53.86	326.39
26	18.08	55.85	258.70	19.37	56.48	267.08	20.28	57.61	268.78
27	14.49	59.44	199.27	15.59	60.26	206.83	16.26	61.63	207.16
28	10.67	63.26	136.01	11.56	64.29	142.54	11.97	65.92	141.25
29	6.60	67.33	68.68	7.25	68.60	73.95	7.38	70.51	70.75
30	2.27	71.66	2.98	2.66	73.19	.76	2.48	75.41	4.66

30-YEAR TERM (continued)

Year	7% interest - $6.65 monthly payment			7-1/4% interest - $6.82 monthly payment			7-1/2% interest - $6.99 monthly payment		
	Interest	Amort.	Balance	Interest	Amort.	Balance	Interest	Amort.	Balance
1	69.68	10.13	989.88	72.19	9.66	990.35	74.69	9.20	990.81
2	68.95	10.86	979.03	71.46	10.39	979.97	73.98	9.91	980.91
3	68.17	11.64	967.40	70.69	11.16	968.81	73.21	10.68	970.23
4	67.33	12.48	954.92	69.85	12.00	956.81	72.38	11.51	958.73
5	66.43	13.38	941.54	68.95	12.90	943.92	71.49	12.40	946.33
6	65.46	14.35	927.19	67.98	13.87	930.06	70.53	13.36	932.98
7	64.42	15.39	911.81	66.95	14.90	915.16	69.49	14.40	918.58
8	63.31	16.50	895.31	65.83	16.02	899.14	68.37	15.52	903.07
9	62.12	17.69	877.62	64.63	17.22	881.93	67.17	16.72	886.35
10	60.84	18.97	858.65	63.34	18.51	863.42	65.87	18.02	868.34
11	59.47	20.34	838.31	61.95	19.90	843.52	64.47	19.42	848.92
12	58.00	21.81	816.50	60.46	21.39	822.14	62.96	20.93	828.00
13	56.42	23.39	793.12	58.86	22.99	799.15	61.34	22.55	805.46
14	54.73	25.08	768.04	57.13	24.72	774.43	59.59	24.30	781.16
15	52.92	26.89	741.15	55.28	26.57	747.87	57.70	26.19	754.98
16	50.97	28.84	712.32	53.29	28.56	719.31	55.67	28.22	726.77
17	48.89	30.92	681.40	51.15	30.70	688.62	53.48	30.41	696.36
18	46.65	33.16	648.25	48.85	33.00	655.62	51.12	32.77	663.60
19	44.26	35.55	612.70	46.37	35.48	620.15	48.58	35.31	628.29
20	41.69	38.12	574.58	43.71	38.14	582.02	45.84	38.05	590.24
21	36.93	40.88	533.71	40.86	40.99	541.03	42.88	41.01	549.24
22	35.98	43.83	489.88	37.78	44.07	496.97	39.70	44.19	505.06
23	32.81	47.00	442.88	34.48	47.37	449.60	36.27	47.62	457.44
24	29.41	50.40	392.48	30.93	50.92	398.69	32.57	51.32	406.13
25	25.77	54.04	338.45	27.11	54.74	343.96	28.59	55.30	350.83
26	21.86	57.95	280.50	23.01	58.84	285.13	24.30	59.59	291.24
27	17.67	62.14	218.37	18.60	63.25	221.88	19.67	64.22	227.03
28	13.18	66.63	151.74	13.86	67.99	153.90	14.69	69.20	157.83
29	8.36	71.45	80.30	8.77	73.08	80.82	9.31	74.58	83.26
30	3.20	76.61	3.70	3.29	78.56	2.26	3.52	80.37	2.90

Year	7-3/4% interest - $7.16 monthly payment			8% interest - $7.34 monthly payment			8-1/4% interest - $7.51 monthly payment		
	Interest	Amort.	Balance	Interest	Amort.	Balance	Interest	Amort.	Balance
1	77.20	8.73	991.28	79.70	8.39	991.62	82.21	7.92	992.09
2	76.50	9.43	981.85	79.01	9.08	982.54	81.53	8.60	983.50
3	75.74	10.19	971.67	78.25	9.84	972.71	80.80	9.33	974.17
4	74.92	11.01	960.67	77.44	10.65	962.06	80.00	10.13	964.04
5	74.04	11.89	948.78	76.55	11.54	950.53	79.13	11.00	953.04
6	73.09	12.84	935.94	75.60	12.49	938.04	78.19	11.94	941.10
7	72.05	13.88	922.07	74.56	13.53	924.52	77.16	12.97	928.14
8	70.94	14.99	907.09	73.44	14.65	909.87	76.05	14.08	914.07
9	69.74	16.19	890.90	72.22	15.87	894.00	74.85	15.28	898.79
10	68.44	17.49	873.41	70.90	17.19	876.82	73.54	16.59	882.20
11	67.03	18.90	854.52	69.48	18.61	858.21	72.12	18.01	864.19
12	65.52	20.41	834.11	67.93	20.16	838.06	70.57	19.56	844.64
13	63.88	22.05	812.06	66.26	21.83	816.24	68.90	21.23	823.41
14	62.11	23.82	788.24	64.45	23.64	792.60	67.08	23.05	800.36
15	60.19	25.74	762.51	62.49	25.60	767.01	65.10	25.03	775.34
16	58.13	27.80	734.71	60.36	27.73	739.28	62.96	27.17	748.17
17	55.89	30.04	704.68	58.06	30.03	709.26	60.63	29.50	718.68
18	53.48	32.45	672.23	55.57	32.52	676.75	58.10	32.03	686.65
19	50.87	35.06	637.18	52.87	35.22	641.53	55.36	34.77	651.89
20	48.06	37.87	599.32	49.95	38.14	603.40	52.38	37.75	614.14
21	45.02	40.91	558.41	46.78	41.31	562.10	49.14	40.99	573.16
22	41.73	44.20	514.22	43.36	44.73	517.37	45.63	44.50	528.67
23	38.18	47.75	466.48	39.64	48.45	468.93	41.82	48.31	480.36
24	34.35	51.58	414.90	35.62	52.47	416.46	37.68	52.45	427.92
25	30.21	55.72	359.19	31.27	56.82	359.65	33.19	56.94	370.98
26	25.73	60.20	299.00	26.55	61.54	298.11	28.31	61.82	309.16
27	20.90	65.03	233.97	21.45	66.64	231.48	23.01	67.12	242.05
28	15.68	70.25	163.72	15.91	72.18	159.30	17.26	72.87	169.18
29	10.03	75.90	87.83	9.92	78.17	81.14	11.02	79.11	90.07
30	3.94	81.99	5.85	3.44	84.65	-3.50	4.24	85.89	4.19

30-YEAR TERM (continued)

Year	8-1/2% interest - $7.69 monthly payment			8-3/4% interest - $7.87 monthly payment			9% interest - $8.05 monthly payment		
	Interest	Amort.	Balance	Interest	Amort.	Balance	Interest	Amort.	Balance
1	84.71	7.58	992.43	87.22	7.23	992.78	89.73	6.88	993.13
2	84.05	8.24	984.20	86.56	7.89	984.90	89.08	7.53	985.60
3	83.32	8.97	975.23	85.84	8.61	976.29	88.37	8.2•	977.37
4	82.52	9.77	965.47	85.06	9.39	966.91	87.60	9.01	968.37
5	81.66	10.63	954.84	84.20	10.25	956.67	86.76	9.85	958.52
6	80.72	11.57	943.28	83.27	11.18	945.50	85.83	10.78	947.75
7	79.70	12.59	930.70	82.25	12.20	933.31	84.82	11.79	935.97
8	78.59	13.70	917.00	81.14	13.31	920.01	83.72	12.89	923.08
9	77.38	14.91	902.09	79.93	14.52	905.49	82.51	14.10	908.99
10	76.06	16.23	885.87	78.61	15.84	889.66	81.19	15.42	893.57
11	74.63	17.66	868.21	77.17	17.28	872.38	79.74	16.87	876.71
12	73.06	19.23	848.99	75.59	18.86	853.53	78.16	18.45	858.26
13	71.37	20.92	828.07	73.88	20.57	832.96	76.43	20.18	838.09
14	69.52	22.77	805.30	72.00	22.45	810.52	74.54	22.07	816.02
15	67.50	24.79	780.52	69.96	24.49	786.03	72.47	24.14	791.88
16	65.31	26.98	753.55	67.73	26.72	759.31	70.20	26.41	765.48
17	62.93	29.36	724.20	65.29	29.16	730.16	67.73	28.88	736.60
18	60.34	31.95	692.25	62.64	31.81	698.36	65.02	31.59	705.01
19	57.51	34.78	657.47	59.74	34.71	663.65	62.05	34.56	670.46
20	54.44	37.85	619.63	56.58	37.87	625.79	58.81	37.80	632.67
21	51.09	41.20	578.43	53.13	41.32	584.47	55.27	41.34	591.33
22	47.45	44.84	533.60	49.37	45.08	539.39	51.39	45.22	546.11
23	43.49	48.80	484.80	45.26	49.19	490.21	47.15	49.46	496.66
24	39.18	53.11	431.69	40.78	53.67	436.54	42.51	54.10	442.56
25	34.48	57.81	373.89	35.89	58.56	377.99	37.43	59.18	383.39
26	29.37	62.92	310.98	30.56	63.89	314.10	31.88	64.73	318.67
27	23.81	68.48	242.50	24.74	69.71	244.39	25.81	70.80	247.87
28	17.76	74.53	167.98	18.39	76.06	168.33	19.17	77.44	170.44
29	11.17	81.12	86.86	11.46	82.99	85.34	11.91	84.70	85.74
30	4.00	88.29	1.42	3.90	90.55	5.20	3.96	92.65	6.90

Year	9-1/4% interest - $8.23 monthly payment			9-1/2% interest - $8.41 monthly payment			9-3/4% interest - $8.59 monthly payment		
	Interest	Amort.	Balance	Interest	Amort.	Balance	Interest	Amort.	Balance
1	92.23	6.54	993.47	94.74	6.19	993.82	97.25	5.84	994.17
2	91.60	7.17	986.31	94.13	6.80	987.02	96.65	6.44	987.74
3	90.91	7.86	978.46	93.45	7.48	979.55	96.00	7.09	980.65
4	90.15	8.62	969.84	92.71	8.22	971.33	95.28	7.81	972.84
5	89.32	9.45	960.40	91.89	9.04	962.30	94.48	8.61	964.23
6	88.41	10.36	950.04	91.00	9.93	952.38	93.60	9.49	954.75
7	87.41	11.36	938.69	90.01	10.92	941.47	92.63	10.46	944.30
8	86.31	12.46	926.24	88.93	12.00	929.47	91.57	11.52	932.78
9	85.11	13.66	912.59	87.74	13.19	916.29	90.39	12.70	920.09
10	83.79	14.98	897.62	86.43	14.50	901.79	89.10	13.99	906.10
11	82.35	16.42	881.20	84.99	15.94	885.86	87.67	15.42	890.69
12	80.77	18.00	863.20	83.41	17.52	868.35	86.10	16.99	873.71
13	79.03	19.74	843.46	81.67	19.26	849.09	84.37	18.72	854.99
14	77.12	21.65	821.82	79.76	21.17	827.93	82.46	20.63	834.37
15	75.03	23.74	798.09	77.66	23.27	804.67	80.36	22.73	811.64
16	72.74	26.03	772.07	75.35	25.58	779.10	78.04	25.05	786.60
17	70.23	28.54	743.53	72.82	28.11	750.99	75.49	27.60	759.00
18	67.48	31.29	712.25	70.03	30.90	720.09	72.67	30.42	728.58
19	64.46	34.31	677.94	66.96	33.97	686.13	69.57	33.52	695.07
20	61.15	37.62	640.32	63.59	37.34	648.79	66.15	36.94	658.14
21	57.51	41.26	599.07	59.88	41.05	607.75	62.39	40.70	617.44
22	53.53	45.24	553.83	55.81	45.12	562.63	58.24	44.85	572.59
23	49.17	49.60	504.24	51.33	49.60	513.04	53.66	49.43	523.16
24	44.38	54.39	449.85	46.41	54.52	458.52	48.62	54.47	468.70
25	39.13	59.64	390.21	41.00	59.93	398.60	43.07	60.02	408.68
26	33.37	65.40	324.82	35.05	65.88	332.73	36.95	66.14	342.55
27	27.06	71.71	253.12	28.51	72.42	260.32	30.20	72.89	269.66
28	20.14	78.63	174.49	21.33	79.60	180.72	22.77	80.32	189.35
29	12.55	86.22	88.28	13.43	87.50	93.22	14.58	88.51	100.84
30	4.23	94.54	6.26	4.74	96.19	2.96	5.55	97.54	3.31

866

30-YEAR TERM (continued)

Year	10% interest - $8.78 monthly payment			10-1/4% interest - $8.96 monthly payment			10-1/2% interest - $9.15 monthly payment		
	Interest	Amort.	Balance	Interest	Amort.	Balance	Interest	Amort.	Balance
1	99.75	5.62	994.39	102.26	5.27	994.74	104.77	5.04	994.97
2	99.16	6.21	988.19	101.70	5.83	988.91	104.21	5.60	989.37
3	98.52	6.85	981.34	101.07	6.46	982.46	103.60	6.21	983.16
4	97.80	7.57	973.78	100.38	7.15	975.31	102.91	6.90	976.27
5	97.01	8.36	965.42	99.61	7.92	967.40	102.15	7.66	968.62
6	96.13	9.24	956.18	98.76	8.77	958.63	101.31	8.50	960.12
7	95.16	10.21	945.98	97.82	9.71	948.92	100.37	9.44	950.69
8	94.10	11.27	934.71	96.77	10.76	938.17	99.33	10.48	940.21
9	92.92	12.45	922.26	95.62	11.91	926.26	98.18	11.63	928.59
10	91.61	13.76	908.51	94.34	13.19	913.07	96.90	12.91	915.68
11	90.17	15.20	893.31	92.92	14.61	898.47	95.47	14.34	901.35
12	88.58	16.79	876.53	91.35	16.18	882.30	93.89	15.92	885.44
13	86.82	18.55	857.99	89.61	17.92	864.39	92.14	17.67	867.77
14	84.88	20.49	837.50	87.69	19.84	844.55	90.19	19.62	848.16
15	82.74	22.63	814.87	85.56	21.97	822.58	88.03	21.78	826.39
16	80.37	25.00	789.88	83.20	24.33	798.26	85.63	24.18	802.22
17	77.75	27.62	762.26	80.58	26.95	771.31	82.97	26.84	775.39
18	74.86	30.51	731.75	77.69	29.84	741.48	80.01	29.80	745.60
19	71.66	33.71	698.05	74.48	33.05	708.43	76.73	33.08	712.52
20	68.13	37.24	660.82	70.93	36.60	671.84	73.09	36.72	675.80
21	64.24	41.13	619.69	67.00	40.53	631.31	69.04	40.77	635.04
22	59.93	45.44	574.25	62.64	44.89	586.43	64.55	45.26	589.78
23	55.17	50.20	524.06	57.82	49.71	536.73	59.56	50.25	539.53
24	49.91	55.46	468.61	52.48	55.05	481.69	54.02	55.79	483.75
25	44.11	61.26	407.35	46.57	60.96	420.73	47.87	61.94	421.82
26	37.69	67.68	339.68	40.02	67.51	353.22	41.05	68.76	353.06
27	30.61	74.76	264.92	32.76	74.77	278.46	33.47	76.34	276.73
28	22.78	82.59	182.34	24.73	82.80	195.66	25.06	84.75	191.98
29	14.13	91.24	91.11	15.83	91.70	103.97	15.72	94.09	97.90
30	4.58	100.79	9.68	5.98	101.55	2.42	5.35	104.46	6.56

Year	10-3/4% interest - $9.33 monthly payment			11% interest - $9.52 monthly payment			11-1/4% interest - $9.71 monthly payment		
	Interest	Amort.	Balance	Interest	Amort.	Balance	Interest	Amort.	Balance
1	107.28	4.69	995.32	109.78	4.47	995.54	112.29	4.24	995.77
2	106.75	5.22	990.10	109.27	4.98	990.57	111.79	4.74	991.04
3	106.16	5.81	984.30	108.69	5.56	985.02	111.23	5.30	985.74
4	105.50	6.47	977.84	108.05	6.20	978.82	110.60	5.93	979.81
5	104.77	7.20	970.65	107.33	6.92	971.91	109.90	6.63	973.19
6	103.96	8.01	962.64	106.53	7.72	964.20	109.11	7.42	965.78
7	103.06	8.91	953.74	105.64	8.61	955.59	108.24	8.29	957.49
8	102.05	9.92	943.82	104.65	9.60	945.99	107.25	9.28	948.22
9	100.93	11.04	932.79	103.53	10.72	935.28	106.15	10.38	937.85
10	99.69	12.28	920.51	102.29	11.96	923.33	104.93	11.60	926.25
11	98.30	13.67	906.85	100.91	13.34	910.00	103.55	12.98	913.27
12	96.76	15.21	891.64	99.37	14.88	895.12	102.01	14.52	898.76
13	95.04	16.93	874.71	97.37	16.60	878.53	100.30	16.23	882.53
14	93.13	18.84	855.87	95.73	18.52	860.01	98.37	18.16	864.38
15	91.00	20.97	834.90	93.58	20.67	839.35	96.22	20.31	844.08
16	88.63	23.34	811.57	91.19	23.06	816.30	93.82	22.71	821.37
17	85.99	25.98	785.60	88.53	25.72	790.58	91.13	25.40	795.97
18	83.06	28.91	756.69	85.55	28.70	761.88	88.12	28.41	767.56
19	79.79	32.18	724.52	82.23	32.02	729.87	84.75	31.78	735.79
20	76.16	35.81	688.71	78.52	35.73	694.15	80.98	35.55	700.24
21	72.12	39.85	648.87	74.39	39.86	654.29	76.77	39.76	660.49
22	67.61	44.36	604.52	69.78	44.47	609.83	72.06	44.47	616.03
23	62.60	49.37	555.16	64.63	49.62	560.21	66.80	49.73	566.30
24	57.03	54.94	500.22	58.89	55.36	504.86	60.90	55.63	510.68
25	50.82	61.15	439.08	52.49	61.76	443.10	54.31	62.22	448.47
26	43.92	68.05	371.03	45.34	68.91	374.20	46.94	69.59	378.89
27	36.23	75.74	295.30	37.37	76.88	297.32	38.70	77.83	301.06
28	27.68	84.29	211.01	28.47	85.78	211.55	29.48 ·	87.05	214.01
29	18.15	93.82	117.20	18.55	95.70	115.85	19.16	97.37	116.65
30	7.56	104.41	12.79	7.47	106.78	9.07	7.63	108.90	7.75

30-YEAR TERM (continued)

	11-1/2% interest - $9.90 monthly payment			11-3/4% interest - $10.09 monthly payment			12% interest - $10.29 monthly payment		
Year	Interest	Amort.	Balance	Interest	Amort.	Balance	Interest	Amort.	Balance
1	114.80	4.01	996.00	117.31	3.78	996.23	119.81	3.68	996.33
2	114.31	4.50	991.51	116.84	4.25	991.98	119.34	4.15	992.18
3	113.77	5.04	986.47	116.31	4.78	987.20	118.82	4.67	987.51
4	113.16	5.65	980.82	115.72	5.37	981.84	118.22	5.27	982.25
5	112.47	6.34	974.49	115.05	6.04	975.80	117.56	5.93	976.32
6	111.70	7.11	967.39	114.30	6.79	969.02	116.80	6.69	969.64
7	110.84	7.97	959.42	113.46	7.63	961.40	115.96	7.53	962.11
8	109.88	8.93	950.50	112.52	8.57	952.83	115.00	8.49	953.63
9	108.79	10.02	940.48	111.45	9.64	943.20	113.93	9.56	944.07
10	107.58	11.23	929.26	110.26	10.83	932.38	112.71	10.78	933.29
11	106.22	12.59	916.68	108.92	12.17	920.21	111.35	12.14	921.16
12	104.69	14.12	902.56	107.41	13.68	906.53	109.81	13.68	907.48
13	102.98	15.83	886.74	105.71	15.38	891.16	108.07	15.42	892.06
14	101.06	17.75	869.00	103.80	17.29	873.88	106.12	17.37	874.70
15	98.91	19.90	849.11	101.66	19.43	854.45	103.91	19.58	855.13
16	96.50	22.31	826.80	99.25	21.84	832.62	101.43	22.06	833.07
17	93.80	25.01	801.79	96.54	24.55	808.08	98.64	24.85	808.23
18	90.76	28.05	773.75	93.50	27.59	780.49	95.48	28.01	780.23
19	87.36	31.45	742.31	90.08	31.01	749.48	91.93	31.56	748.67
20	83.55	35.26	707.06	86.23	34.86	714.63	87.93	35.56	713.12
21	79.28	39.53	667.53	81.91	39.18	675.45	83.42	40.07	673.06
22	74.48	44.33	623.20	77.05	44.04	631.42	78.34	45.15	627.92
23	69.11	49.70	573.51	71.59	49.50	581.92	72.62	50.87	577.05
24	63.08	55.73	517.78	65.45	55.64	526.28	66.17	57.32	519.73
25	56.32	62.49	455.30	58.55	62.54	463.74	58.90	64.59	455.14
26	48.75	70.06	385.24	50.79	70.30	393.44	50.70	72.79	382.36
27	40.25	78.56	306.69	42.07	79.02	314.42	41.47	82.02	300.35
28	30.73	88.08	218.61	32.27	88.82	225.61	31.07	92.42	207.94
29	20.05	98.76	119.86	21.25	99.84	125.77	19.35	104.14	103.80
30	8.07	110.74	9.12	8.87	112.22	13.55	6.15	117.34	-13.53

	12-1/4% interest - $10.47 monthly payment				12-1/2% interest - $10.67 monthly payment			
Year	Interest	Amort.	Balance	Accrued Interest	Interest	Amort.	Balance	Accrued Interest
1	122.21	3.43	996.57	122.21	124.82	3.22	996.78	124.82
2	121.77	3.87	992.70	243.98	124.39	3.65	993.13	249.21
3	121.27	4.37	986.33	365.25	123.91	4.13	989.00	373.12
4	120.70	4.94	983.39	485.95	123.36	4.68	984.33	496.49
5	120.06	5.58	977.81	606.01	122.74	5.30	979.03	619.23
6	119.34	6.30	971.50	725.34	122.04	6.00	973.03	741.27
7	118.52	7.12	964.39	843.87	121.25	6.79	966.24	862.52
8	117.60	8.04	956.35	961.47	120.35	7.69	958.55	982.87
9	116.56	9.08	947.26	1078.02	119.33	8.71	949.84	1102.20
10	115.38	10.26	937.01	1193.41	118.18	9.86	939.98	1220.38
11	114.05	11.59	925.42	1307.46	116.87	11.17	928.81	1337.25
12	112.55	13.09	912.33	1420.01	115.39	12.65	916.17	1452.65
13	110.86	14.78	897.55	1530.87	113.72	14.32	901.85	1566.37
14	108.94	16.70	880.86	1639.82	111.82	16.22	885.63	1678.19
15	106.78	18.86	862.00	1746.60	109.68	18.36	867.26	1787.86
16	104.34	21.30	840.70	1850.94	107.24	20.80	846.47	1895.11
17	101.58	24.06	816.64	1952.52	104.49	23.55	822.92	1999.60
18	98.47	27.17	789.47	1050.99	101.37	26.67	796.25	2100.97
19	94.95	30.69	758.77	2145.93	97.84	30.20	766.05	2198.81
20	90.97	34.67	724.11	2236.91	93.84	34.20	731.85	2292.65
21	86.48	39.16	684.95	2323.39	89.31	38.73	693.12	2381.96
22	81.41	44.23	640.72	2404.80	84.18	43.86	649.26	2466.14
23	75.68	49.96	590.76	2480.48	78.38	49.66	599.60	2544.52
24	69.21	56.43	534.34	2549.70	71.80	56.24	543.36	2616.32
25	61.91	63.73	470.60	2611.60	64.35	63.69	479.67	2680.67
26	53.65	71.99	398.61	2665.25	55.92	72.12	407.55	2736.59
27	44.33	81.31	317.30	2709.58	46.37	81.67	325.88	2782.96
28	33.80	91.84	225.46	2743.38	35.56	92.48	233.40	2818.52
29	21.90	103.74	121.73	2765.29	23.31	104.73	128.67	2841.83
30	8.47	117.17	4.56	2773.76	9.44	118.60	10.07	2851.27

30-YEAR TERM (Continued)

12-3/4% interest - $10.87 monthly payment   13% interest - $11.06 monthly payment

Year	Interest	Amort.	Balance	Accrued Interest	Interest	Amort.	Balance	Accrued Interest
1	127.32	3.12	996.88	127.32	129.83	2.89	997.11	129.83
2	126.90	3.54	993.34	254.22	129.43	3.29	993.83	259.27
3	126.42	40.2	989.32	380.64	128.98	3.74	990.08	388.24
4	125.88	4.56	984.76	506.52	128.46	4.26	985.83	516.71
5	125.26	5.18	979.58	631.78	127.88	4.84	980.98	644.58
6	124.56	5.88	973.71	756.35	127.21	5.51	975.47	771.79
7	123.77	6.67	967.03	880.11	126.45	6.27	969.20	898.24
8	122.86	7.58	959.46	1002.96	125.58	7.14	962.06	1023.82
9	121.84	8.60	950.85	1124.81	124.59	8.13	953.93	1148.41
10	120.68	9.76	941.09	1245.49	123.47	9.25	944.68	1271.88
11	119.36	11.08	930.01	1364.85	122.20	10.52	934.16	1394.08
12	117.86	12.58	917.43	1482.71	120.74	11.98	922.19	1514.83
13	116.16	14.28	903.14	1598.86	119.09	13.63	908.56	1633.92
14	114.22	16.22	886.93	1713.09	117.21	15.51	893.05	1751.13
15	112.03	18.41	868.52	1825.12	115.07	17.65	875.40	1866.20
16	109.54	20.90	847.62	1934.66	112.63	20.09	855.31	1978.83
17	106.72	23.72	823.90	2041.38	109.86	22.86	832.45	2088.69
18	103.51	26.93	796.97	2144.89	106.70	26.02	806.43	2195.39
19	99.87	30.57	766.39	2244.75	103.11	29.61	♦6.83	2298.51
20	95.73	34.71	731.69	2340.49	99.03	33.69	743.13	2397.53
21	91.04	39.40	692.29	2431.53	94.38	38.34	704.79	2491.91
22	85.71	44.73	647.56	2517.24	89.08	43.64	661.15	2580.99
23	79.66	50.78	596.79	2596.91	83.06	49.66	611.49	2664.05
24	72.80	57.64	539.15	2669.71	76.20	56.52	554.98	2740.26
25	65.00	65.44	473.71	2734.71	68.40	64.32	490.66	2808.66
26	56.16	74.28	399.43	2790.87	59.53	73.19	417.47	2868.19
27	46.11	84.33	315.10	2836.98	49.42	83.30	334.17	2917.61
28	34.71	95.73	219.37	2871.69	37.93	94.79	239.37	2955.53
29	21.76	108.68	110.69	2893.45	24.84	107.88	131.50	2980.38
30	7.07	123.37	-12.68	2900.52	9.95	122.77	8.73	2990.33

13-1/4% interest - $11.26 monthly payment   13-1/2% interest - $11.45 monthly payment

Year	Interest	Amort.	Balance	Accrued Interest	Interest	Amort.	Balance	Accrued Interest
1	132.33	2.79	997.21	132.33	134.85	2.55	997.45	134.85
2	131.94	3.18	994.04	264.28	134.48	2.92	994.52	269.32
3	131.50	3.62	990.41	395.77	134.06	3.34	991.18	403.38
4	130.98	4.14	986.28	526.76	133.58	3.82	987.36	536.96
5	130.40	4.72	981.56	657.16	133.03	4.37	982.99	669.99
6	129.74	5.38	976.18	786.90	132.40	5.00	978.00	802.40
7	128.98	6.14	970.04	915.88	131.68	5.72	972.28	934.08
8	128.11	7.01	963.03	1043.99	130.86	6.54	965.74	1064.94
9	127.13	7.99	955.04	1171.12	129.92	7.48	958.27	1194.87
10	126.00	9.12	945.92	1297.12	128.85	8.55	949.72	1323.72
11	124.72	10.40	935.52	1421.84	127.62	9.78	939.94	1451.34
12	123.25	11.87	923.65	1545.09	126.22	11.18	928.75	1577.55
13	121.58	13.54	910.11	1666.67	124.61	12.79	915.96	1702.16
14	119.67	15.45	894.67	1786.35	122.77	14.63	901.34	1824.94
15	117.50	17.62	877.04	1903.84	120.67	16.73	884.61	1945.61
16	115.02	20.10	856.94	2018.86	118.27	19.13	865.47	2063.87
17	112.18	22.94	834.00	2131.04	115.52	21.88	843.59	2179.39
18	108.95	26.17	807.84	2240.00	112.37	25.03	818.56	2291.76
19	105.27	29.85	777.99	2345.27	108.78	28.62	789.94	2400.54
20	101.06	34.06	743.93	2446.33	104.67	32.73	757.21	2505.21
21	96.27	38.85	705.08	2542.60	99.96	37.44	719.77	2605.17
22	90.80	44.32	660.76	2633.40	94.58	42.82	676.95	2699.75
23	84.55	50.57	610.19	2717.95	88.43	48.97	627.99	2788.19
24	77.43	57.69	552.50	2795.38	81.40	56.00	571.98	2869.58
25	69.30	65.82	486.68	2864.68	73.35	64.05	507.93	2942.93
26	60.03	75.09	411.60	2924.72	64.15	73.25	434.68	3007.08
27	49.46	85.66	325.93	2974.17	53.62	83.78	350.91	3060.71
28	37.39	97.73	228.21	3011.57	41.59	95.81	255.09	3102.29
29	23.63	111.49	116.71	3035.19	27.82	109.58	145.51	3130.11
30	7.92	127.20	-10.48	3043.12	12.08	125.32	20.19	3142.19

30-YEAR TERM (Continued)

13-3/4% interest - $11.65 monthly payment   14% interest - $11.85 monthly payment

Year	Interest	Amort.	Balance	Accrued Interest	Interest	Amort.	Balance	Accrued Interest
1	137.35	2.45	997.55	137.35	139.85	2.35	997.65	139.85
2	136.99	2.81	994.74	274.34	139.50	2.70	994.96	279.36
3	136.58	3.22	991.52	410.92	139.10	3.10	991.86	418.46
4	136.11	3.69	987.83	547.03	138.64	3.56	988.29	557.09
5	135.57	4.23	983.59	682.59	138.10	4.10	984.20	695.20
6	134.95	4.85	978.74	817.54	137.49	4.71	979.49	832.69
7	134.23	5.57	973.17	951.77	136.79	5.41	974.08	969.48
8	133.42	6.38	966.79	1085.19	135.98	6.22	967.86	1105.46
9	132.48	7.32	959.47	1217.67	135.05	7.15	960.72	1240.52
10	131.41	8.39	951.08	1349.08	133.99	8.21	952.50	1374.50
11	130.18	9.62	942.47	1479.27	132.76	9.44	943.06	1507.26
12	128.77	11.03	930.44	1608.04	131.35	10.85	932.21	1638.61
13	127.16	12.64	917.80	1735.20	129.73	12.47	919.74	1768.34
14	125.31	14.49	903.31	1860.51	127.87	14.33	905.41	1896.21
15	123.18	16.61	886.69	1983.69	125.73	16.47	888.94	2021.94
16	120.75	19.05	867.64	2104.44	123.27	18.93	870.01	2145.21
17	117.96	21.84	845.80	2222.40	120.44	21.76	848.25	2265.65
18	114.76	25.04	820.76	2337.16	117.19	25.01	823.24	2382.84
19	111.09	28.71	792.05	2448.25	113.45	28.75	794.49	2496.29
20	106.88	32.92	759.13	2555.13	109.16	33.04	761.45	2605.45
21	102.06	37.74	721.39	2657.19	104.23	37.97	723.48	2709.68
22	96.53	43.27	678.12	2753.72	98.56	43.64	679.84	2808.24
23	90.19	49.61	628.51	2843.91	92.04	50.16	629.68	2900.28
24	82.92	56.88	571.64	2926.84	84.55	57.65	572.03	2984.83
25	74.59	65.21	506.43	3001.43	75.94	66.26	505.77	3060.77
26	65.04	74.76	431.67	3006.47	66.04	76.16	429.61	3126.81
27	54.09	85.71	345.95	3120.55	54.67	87.53	342.08	3181.48
28	42.53	98.27	247.68	3162.08	41.60	100.60	241.48	3223.08
29	27.13	112.67	135.01	3189.21	26.57	115.63	125.85	3249.65
30	10.62	129.18	5.84	3199.84	9.31	132.89	-7.04	3258.96

INDEX

Drunk driving *(cont'd)*
    check points, S1905
    implied consent laws, 2002
    license suspension hearing, 2002.1
    pleas in, 2004, S1906
Durable power of attorney. S2212.1
Duress defense 3434, 1904.2
Duty of care, corporate directors/
    officers 1507
Duty of loyalty, corporate directors/
    officers 1508

E

Ejectment 3409
Electioneering, unions. 2104.3
Emergency Planning and Community
    Right to Know Act S2056
    insurance issues, S2315.1
    lender liability, S2052
    Medical Waste Tracking Act of 1988,
        2055.1
    National Environmental Policy Act,
        S2056
    Oil Pollution Act of 1990, S2051
    Resources Conservation and Recovery
        Act, S2055
    Safe Drinking Water Act, S2053.1
    solid waste, S2055.2
    statute of limitations issues, S2053
    taking, S2050
    Toxic Substances Control Act, S2056
Employee stock ownership plan
    (ESOP) 1208
Employer-employee relations S2001
    age discrimination, S2004.3, 2105.4
    anti-discrimination laws, 2105
    arbitration, S401.2
    Civil Rights Act of 1991, S2001.1,
        2105.2
    compulsory unionism, S2002.2
    discrimination protection, S2004
    due process issues, 2102
    employment-at-will doctrine, 2106,
        S2005
    Equal Pay Act, S2004.2, 2105.3
    federal labor law, 2103
    fetal protection policies, S2004.1, 2105.1
    handicaps, S2004.4
    pregnancy discrimination, 2105.1
    privacy issues, 2102

    sexual harassment, 2105.1
    strikes, S2002.3
    Title VII, S2004.1, 2105.1
    unfair labor practices, S2002.1
Employer sanctions, immigration. . . S2254
Employment-at-will doctrine. . 2106, S2005
Enoch Arden laws. 2914
Entrapment defense 1904.3
Environmental claims, and liability
    insurance 2515.1
Environmental law
    accounting issues, S2053
    Asbestos Hazard Emergency Response
        Act, 2207, S2056
    Asbestos Information Act, 2207, S2056
    and bankruptcy, S719, S720, S2052
    Clean Air Act, 2205, S2054
    Clean Water Act, 2204, S2053
    commerce clause, S2055.2
    Comprehensive Environmental
        Response, Compensation and
        Liability Act (CERCLA), 2203, S2052
    Medical Waste Tracking Act of 1988,
        2206.1
    National Environmental Policy Act, 2207
    Resource Conservation and Recovery
        Act, 2206
    Safe Drinking Water Act, 2204.1
    solid waste disposal, 2206.2
    Toxic Substances Control Act of 1986,
        2207
Environmental Protection Agency
    (EPA) 2203
Equal Access to Justice Act 501
Equal Credit Opportunity Act . . 1837-1838
Equal Pay Act S2004.2, 2105.3
Equitable distribution S2730, S2730.1
Equitable relief 3412
ERISA 502, 707
Escalator lease 2804.3
Escrow
    federally related mortgage, 3325
    real estate, 3321, 3322
    Real Estate Settlement Procedures Act
        of 1974, 3323-3332
Estate planning
    administration of estate, 2313
    community property, 2310
    documents needed, 2302
    estate accounting, 2327, 2328
    fiduciary responsibility, 2315

P